GUY FAWKES.

LONDON LABOUR

AND THE LONDON POOR

BY

HENRY MAYHEW

WITH A NEW INTRODUCTION BY

JOHN D. ROSENBERG

Professor of English, Columbia University

IN FOUR VOLUMES

VOLUME III

The London Street-Folk (concluded)

DOVER PUBLICATIONS, INC.

NEW YORK

Published in Canada by General Publishing Company, Ltd.,
30 Lesmill Road, Don Mills, Toronto, Ontario.

Published in the United Kingdom by Constable and Company, Ltd.,
10 Orange Street, London WC 2.

This Dover edition, first published in 1968, is an unabridged
republication of the work as published by Griffin, Bohn, and Company in 1861–1862, to which has been added a new Introduction by
John D. Rosenberg.

Standard Book Number: 486-21936-4
Library of Congress Catalog Card Number: 68-19549

MANUFACTURED IN THE UNITED STATES OF AMERICA

DOVER PUBLICATIONS, INC.
180 VARICK STREET
NEW YORK, N. Y. 10014

LONDON LABOUR

AND THE

LONDON POOR;

A

CYCLOPÆDIA OF THE CONDITION AND EARNINGS

OF

THOSE THAT *WILL* WORK,
THOSE THAT *CANNOT* WORK, AND
THOSE THAT *WILL NOT* WORK.

BY

HENRY MAYHEW.

THE LONDON STREET-FOLK;

COMPRISING,

STREET SELLERS.	STREET PERFORMERS.
STREET BUYERS.	STREET ARTIZANS.
STREET FINDERS.	STREET LABOURERS.

WITH NUMEROUS ILLUSTRATIONS FROM PHOTOGRAPHS.

VOLUME III.

LONDON:
GRIFFIN, BOHN, AND COMPANY,
STATIONERS' HALL COURT.
1861.

CONTENTS

OF

VOLUME III.

~~~~~~~~~~~~~~~~~~~~~~~~~

THE STREET-FOLK.

LIST OF ILLUSTRATIONS

LONDON LABOUR

AND

THE LONDON POOR.

THE DESTROYERS OF VERMIN.

THE RAT-KILLER.

IN " the Brill," or rather in Brill-place, Somers'-town, there is a variety of courts branching out into Chapel-street, and in one of the most angular and obscure of these is to be found a perfect nest of rat-catchers—not altogether professional rat-catchers, but for the most part sporting mechanics and coster-mongers. The court is not easily to be found, being inhabited by men not so well known in the immediate neighbourhood as perhaps a mile or two away, and only to be discovered by the aid and direction of the little girl at the neighbouring cat's-meat shop.

My first experience of this court was the usual disturbance at the entrance. I found one end or branch of it filled with a mob of eager listeners, principally women, all attracted to a particular house by the sounds of quarrelling. One man gave it as his opinion that the dis-turbers must have earned too much money yesterday; and a woman, speaking to another who had just come out, lifting up both her hands and laughing, said, " Here they are—*at it* again ! "

The rat-killer whom we were in search of was out at his stall in Chapel-street when we called, but his wife soon fetched him. He was a strong, sturdy-looking man, rather above the middle height, with light hair, ending in sandy whiskers, reaching under his chin, sharp deep-set eyes, a tight-skinned nose that looked as if the cuticle had been stretched to its utmost on its bridge. He was dressed in the ordinary corduroy costermonger habit, having, in addi-tion, a dark blue Guernsey drawn over his waistcoat.

The man's first anxiety was to show us that rats were not his only diversion; and in con-sequence he took us into the yard of the house, where in a shed lay a bull-dog, a bull-bitch, and a litter of pups just a week old. They did not belong to him, but he said he did a good deal in the way of curing dogs when he could get 'em.

On a shelf in this shed were two large dishes, the one containing mussels without the shells, and the other eels ; these are the com-modities in which he deals at present, so that he is properly what one would call a "pickled-eel seller."

We found his room on the first-floor clean and tidy, of a good size, containing two bed-steads and a large sea-chest, besides an old-fashioned, rickety, mahogany table, while in a far corner of the room, perhaps waiting for the cold weather and the winter's fire, was an arm-chair. Behind the door hung a couple of dog-leads, made of strong leather, and ornamented with brass. Against one side of the wall were two framed engravings of animals, and a sort of chart of animated nature, while over the mantel-shelf was a variety of most character-istic articles. Among these appeared a model of a bull-dog's head, cut out of sandstone, and painted in imitation of nature—a most mar-vellous piece of ugliness. " He was the best dog I ever see," said the host, " and when I parted with him for a ten-pound note, a man as worked in the New Road took and made this model—he was a real beauty, was that dog. The man as carved that there, didn't have no difficulty in holdin' him still, becos he was very good at that sort o' thing ; and when he'd looked at anything he couldn't be off doin' it."

There were also a great many common prints about the walls, " a penny each, frame and all," amongst which were four dogs—all ratting—a game cock, two Robinson Crusoes, and three scripture subjects.

There was, besides, a photograph of another favourite dog which he'd " had give him."

The man apologised for the bareness of the room, but said, " You see, master, my brother went over to 'Merica contracting for a railway under Peto's, and they sends to me about a year ago, telling me to get together as many likely fellows as I could (about a dozen), and take them over as excavators; and when I was ready, to go to Peto's and get what money I wanted. But when I'd got the men, sold off all my sticks, and went for the money, they told me my brother had got plenty, and that if he wanted me he ought to be ashamed of hisself not to send some over hisself; so I just got together these few things again, and I ain't heard of nothing at all about it since."

After I had satisfied him that I was not a collector of dog-tax, trying to find out how many animals he kept, he gave me what he evidently thought was "a treat"—a peep at his bull-dog, which he fetched from upstairs, and let it jump about the room with a most unpleasant liberty, informing me the while how he had given five pound for him, and that one of the first pups he got by a bull he had got five pounds for, and that cleared him. "That Punch" (the bull-dog's name), he said, "is as quiet as a lamb—wouldn't hurt nobody; I frequently takes him through the streets without a lead. Sartainly he killed a cat the t'other afternoon, but he couldn't help that, 'cause the cat flew at him; though he took it as quietly as a man would a woman in a passion, and only went at her just to save his eyes. But you couldn't easy get him off, master, when he once got a holt. He was a good one for rats, and, he believed, the stanchest and tricksiest dog in London."

When he had taken the brute upstairs, for which I was not a little thankful, the man made the following statement:—

"I a'n't a Londoner. I've travelled all about the country. I'm a native of Iver, in Buckinghamshire. I've been three year here at these lodgings, and five year in London altogether up to last September.

"Before I come to London I was nothink, sir—a labouring man, an eshkewator. I come to London the same as the rest, to do anythink I could. I was at work at the eshkewations at King's Cross Station. I work as hard as any man in London, I think.

"When the station was finished, I, having a large family, thought I'd do the best I could, so I went to be foreman at the Caledonian Sawmills. I stopped there a twelvemonth; but one day I went for a load and a-half of lime, and where you fetches a load and a-half of lime they always gives you fourpence. So as I was having a pint of beer out of it, my master come by and saw me drinking, and give me the sack. Then he wanted me to ax his pardon, and I might stop; but I told him I wouldn't beg no one's pardon for drinking a pint of beer as was give me. So I left there.

"Ever since the Great Western was begun, my family has been distributed all over the country, wherever there was a railway making. My brothers were contractors for Peto, and I generally worked for my brothers; but they've gone to America, and taken a contract for a railway at St. John's, New Brunswick, British North America. I can do anything in the eshkewating way—I don't care what it is.

"After I left the Caledonian Sawmills I went to Billingsgate, and bought anythink I could see a chance of gettin' a shilling out on, or to'ards keeping my family.

"All my lifetime I've been a-dealing a little in rats; but it was not till I come to London that I turned my mind fully to that sort of thing. My father always had a great notion of the same. We all like the sport. When any on us was in the country, and the farmers wanted us to, we'd do it. If anybody heerd tell of my being an activish chap like, in that sort of way, they'd get me to come for a day or so.

"If anybody has a place that's eaten up with rats, I goes and gets some ferruts, and takes a dog, if I've got one, and manages to kill 'em. Sometimes I keep my own ferruts, but mostly I borrows them. This young man that's with me, he'll sometimes have an order to go fifty or sixty mile into the country, and then he buys his ferruts, or gets them the best way he can. They charges a good sum for the loan of 'em—sometimes as much as you get for the job.

"You can buy ferruts at Leadenhall-market for 5s. or 7s.—it all depends; you can't get them all at one price, some of 'em is real cowards to what others is; some won't even kill a rat. The way we tries 'em is, we puts 'em down anywhere, in a room maybe, with a rat, and if they smell about and won't go up to it, why they won't do; 'cause you see, sometimes the ferrut has to go up a hole, and at the end there may be a dozen or sixteen rats, and if he hasn't got the heart to tackle one on 'em, why he ain't worth a farden.

"I have kept ferruts for four or five months at a time, but they're nasty stinking things. I've had them get loose; but, bless you, they do no harm, they're as hinnocent as cats; they won't hurt nothink; you can play with them like a kitten. Some puts things down to ketch rats—sorts of pison, which is their secret—but I don't. I relies upon my dogs and ferruts, and nothink else.

"I went to destroy a few rats up at Russell-square; there was a shore come right along, and a few holes—they was swarmed with 'em there—and didn't know how it was; but the cleverest men in the world couldn't ketch many there, 'cause you see, master, they run down the hole into the shore, and no dog could get through a rat-hole.

"I couldn't get my living, though, at that business. If any gentleman comes to me and says he wants a dog cured, or a few rats destroyed, I does it.

"In the country they give you fourpence a rat, and you can kill sometimes as many in a farmyard as you can in London. The most I ever got for destroying rats was four bob, and then I filled up the brickwork and made the holes good, and there was no more come.

"I calls myself a coster; some calls theirselves general dealers, but I doesn't. I goes to market, and if one thing don't suit, why I buys another.

"I don't know whether you've heerd of it, master, or not, but I'm the man as they say kills rats—that's to say, I kills 'em like a dog. I'm almost ashamed to mention it, and I shall never do it any more, but I've killed rats for a wager often. You see it's only been done like for a lark; we've bin all together daring one another, and trying to do something as nobody else could. I remember the first time I did it for a wager, it was up at ——, where they've got a pit. There was a bull-dog a killing rats, so I says,

"'Oh, that's a duffin' dog; any dog coud kill quicker than him. I'd kill again him myself.'

"Well, then they chaffed me, and I warn't goin' to be done; so I says,

"'I'll kill again that dog for a sov'rin.'

"The sov'rin was staked. I went down to kill eight rats again the dog, and I beat him. I killed 'em like a dog, with my teeth. I went down hands and knees and bit 'em. I've done it three times for a sov'rin, and I've won each time. I feels very much ashamed of it, though.

"On the hind part of my neck, as you may see, sir, there's a scar; that's where I was bit by one; the rat twisted hisself round and held on like a vice. It was very bad, sir, for a long time; it festered, and broke out once or twice, but it's all right now."

RATS.

"THE rat, though small, weak, and contemptible in its appearance, possesses properties that render it a more formidable enemy to mankind, and more injurious to the interests of society, than even those animals that are endued with the greatest strength and the most rapacious dispositions. To the one we can oppose united powers and superior arts; with regard to the other, experience has convinced us that no art can counteract the effects of its amazing fecundity, and that force is ineffectually directed against an animal possessed of such variety of means to elude it.

"There are two kinds of rats known in this country,—the black rat, which was formerly universal here, but is now very rarely seen, having been almost extirpated by the large brown kind, which is generally distinguished by the name of the *Norway rat.*

"This formidable invader is now universally diffused through the whole country, from whence every method has been tried in vain to exterminate it. This species is about nine inches long, of a light-brown colour, mixed with tawny and ash; the throat and belly are of a dirty white, inclining to grey; its feet are naked, and of a pale flesh-colour; the tail is as long as the body, covered with minute dusky scales, thinly interspersed with short hairs. In summer it frequents the banks of rivers, ponds, and ditches, where it lives on frogs, fishes, and small animals. But its rapacity is not entirely confined to these. It destroys rabbits, poultry, young pigeons, &c. It infests the granary, the barn, and the storehouse; does infinite mischief among corn and fruit of all kinds; and not content with satisfying its hunger, frequently carries off large quantities to its hiding-place. It is a bold and fierce little animal, and when closely pursued, will turn and fasten on its assailant. Its bite is keen, and the wound it inflicts is painful and difficult to heal, owing to the form of its teeth, which are long, sharp, and of an irregular shape.

"The rat is amazingly prolific, usually producing from twelve to eighteen young ones at one time. Their numbers would soon increase beyond all power of restraint, were it not for an insatiable appetite, that impels them to destroy and devour each other. The weaker always fall a prey to the stronger; and a large male rat, which usually lives by itself, is dreaded by those of its own species as their most formidable enemy.

"It is a singular fact in the history of those animals, that the skins of such of them as have been devoured in their holes have frequently been found curiously turned inside out, every part being completely inverted, even to the ends of the toes. How the operation is performed it would be difficult to ascertain; but it appears to be effected in some peculiar mode of eating out the contents.

"Besides the numbers that perish in these unnatural conflicts, they have many fierce and inveterate enemies, that take every occasion to destroy them. Mankind have contrived various methods of exterminating these bold intruders. For this purpose traps are often found ineffectual, such being the sagacity of the animals, that when any are drawn into the snare, the others by such means learn to avoid the dangerous allurement, notwithstanding the utmost caution may have been used to conceal the design. The surest method of killing them is by poison. Nux vomica ground and mixed with oatmeal, with a small proportion of oil of rhodium and musk, have been found from experience to be very effectual.

"The water-rat is somewhat smaller than the Norway rat; its head larger and its nose thicker; its eyes are small; its ears short; scarcely appearing through the hair; its teeth are large, strong, and yellow; the hair on its body thicker and longer than that of the common rat, and chiefly of a dark brown colour mixed with red; the belly is grey; the tail five inches long, covered with short black hairs, and the tip with white.

" The water-rat generally frequents the sides of rivers, ponds, and ditches, where it burrows and forms its nest. It feeds on frogs, small fish and spawn, swims and dives remarkably fast, and can continue a long time under water."*

In Mr. Charles Fothergill's *Essay on the Philosophy, Study, and Use of Natural History* (1813), we find some reflections which remind us of Ray and Derham. We shall extract a few paragraphs which relate to the subject in hand.

" Nothing can afford a finer illustration of the beautiful order and simplicity of the laws which govern the creation, than the certainty, precision, and regularity with which the natural checks in the superabundant increase of each tribe of animals are managed ; and every family is subject to the operation of checks peculiar to the species—whatever it may be— and established by a wise law of the Most High, to counteract the fatal effects that might arise from an ever-active populative principle. It is by the admirable disposition of these checks, the contemplation of which is alone sufficient to astonish the loftiest and most comprehensive soul of man, that the whole system of animal life, in all its various forms, is kept in due strength and equilibrium.

" This subject is worthy of the naturalist's most serious consideration."

" This great law," Mr. F. proceeds, " pervades and affects the whole animal creation, and so active, unwearied, and rapid is the principle of increase over the means of subsistence amongst the inferior animals, that it is evident whole genera of carnivorous beings amongst beasts, birds, fish, reptiles, and insects, have been created for the *express purpose* (?) of suppressing the redundancy of others, and restraining their numbers within proper limits.

" But even the natural checks are insufficient to restrain the effects of a too-rapid populative principle in some animals, which have, therefore, certain destructive propensities given to them by the Creator, that operate powerfully upon themselves and their offspring, as may be particularly observed in the natural history of the *rabbit*, but which is still more evidently and strikingly displayed in the life and economy of the *rat*.

" It has been calculated by Mr. Pennant, and there can be no doubt of the truth of the statement, that the astonishing number of 1,274,840 may be produced from a single pair of rabbits in the short space of four years, as these animals in their wild state breed seven times in a-year, and generally produce eight young ones each time. They are capable of procreation at the age of five or six months, and the doe carries her burthen no more than thirty days.

" But the principle of increase is much more powerful, active, and effective in the common grey rat than in any other animal of equal size. This destructive animal is continually under the *furor* of animal love. The female carries her young for one month only ; and she seldom or never produces a less number than twelve, but sometimes as many as eighteen at a litter—the medium number may be taken for an average — and the period of gestation, though of such short continuance, is confined to no particular season of the year.

" The embraces of the male are admitted immediately after the birth of the vindictive progeny; and it is a fact which I have ascertained beyond any doubt, that the female suckles her young ones almost to the very moment when another litter is dropping into the world as their successors.

" A celebrated Yorkshire rat-catcher whom I have occasionally employed, one day killed a large female rat, that was in the act of suckling twelve young ones, which had attained a very considerable growth; nevertheless, upon opening her swollen body, he found thirteen quick young, that were within a few days of their birth. Supposing, therefore, that the rat produces ten litters in the course of a year, and that no check on their increase should operate destructively for the space of four years, a number not far short of 3,000,000 might be produced from a single pair in that time !

" Now, the consequence of such an active and productive principle of increase, if suffered continually to operate without check, would soon be fatally obvious. We have heard of fertile plains devastated, and large towns undermined, in Spain, by rabbits; and even that a military force from Rome was once requested of the great Augustus to suppress the astonishing numbers of the same animal overrunning the island of Majorca and Minorca. This circumstance is recorded by Pliny.

" If, therefore, rats were suffered to multiply without the restraint of the most powerful and positive natural checks, not only would fertile plains and rich cities be undermined and destroyed, but the whole surface of the earth in a very few years would be rendered a barren and hideous waste, covered with myriads of famished grey rats, against which man himself would contend in vain. But the same Almighty Being who perceived a necessity for their existence, has also restricted their numbers within proper bounds, by creating to them many very powerful enemies, and still more effectually by establishing a propensity in themselves, the gratification of which has continually the effect of lessening their numbers, even more than any of their foreign enemies.

" The male rat has an insatiable thirst for the blood of his own offspring; the female, being aware of this passion, hides her young in such secret places as she supposes likely to escape notice or discovery, till her progeny are old enough to venture forth and stand upon

* Bewick's *History of Quadrupeds*, 1790, 354 *et seq.*

their own energies; but, notwithstanding this precaution, the male rat frequently discovers them, and destroys as many as he can; nor is the defence of the mother any very effectual protection, since she herself sometimes falls a victim to her temerity and her maternal tenderness.

" Besides this propensity to the destruction of their own offspring, when other food fails them, rats hunt down and prey upon each other with the most ferocious and desperate avidity, inasmuch as it not unfrequently happens, in a colony of these destructive animals, that a single male of more than ordinary powers, after having overcome and devoured all competitors with the exception of a few females, reigns the sole bloody and much-dreaded tyrant over a considerable territory, dwelling by himself in some solitary hole, and never appearing abroad without spreading terror and dismay even amongst the females whose embraces he seeks. In this relentless and bloody character may be found one of the most powerful and positive of the checks which operate to the repression of this species within proper bounds; a character which attaches, in a greater or less degree, to the whole *Mus* genus, and in which we may readily perceive the cause of the extirpation of the old black rats of England, *Mus rathus;* for the large grey rats, having superior bodily powers united to the same carnivorous propensities, would easily conquer and destroy their black opponents wherever they could be found, and whenever they met to dispute the title of possession or of sovereignty."

When the young rats begin to issue from their holes, the mother watches, defends, and even fights with the cats, in order to save them. A large rat is more mischievous than a young cat, and nearly as strong: the rat uses her fore-teeth, and the cat makes most use of her claws; so that the latter requires both to be vigorous and accustomed to fight, in order to destroy her adversary.

The weasel, though smaller, is a much more dangerous and formidable enemy to the rat, because it can follow it into its retreat. Its strength being nearly equal to that of the rat, the combat often continues for a long time, but the method of using their arms by the opponents is very different. The rat wounds only by repeated strokes with his fore-teeth, which are better formed for gnawing than biting; and, being situated at the extremity of the lever or jaw, they have not much force. But the weasel bites cruelly with the whole jaw, and, instead of letting go its hold, sucks the blood from the wounded part, so that the rat is always killed.

A NIGHT AT RAT-KILLING.

CONSIDERING the immense number of rats which form an article of commerce with many of the lower orders, whose business it is to keep them for the purpose of rat matches, I thought it necessary, for the full elucidation of my subject, to visit the well-known public-house in London, where, on a certain night in the week, a pit is built up, and regular rat-killing matches take place, and where those who have sporting dogs, and are anxious to test their qualities, can, after such matches are finished, purchase half a dozen or a dozen rats for them to practise upon, and judge for themselves of their dogs' " performances."

To quote the words printed on the proprietor's card, " he is always at his old house at home, as usual, to discuss the FANCY generally."

I arrived at about eight o'clock at the tavern where the performances were to take place. I was too early, but there was plenty to occupy my leisure in looking at the curious scene around me, and taking notes of the habits and conversation of the customers who were flocking in.

The front of the long bar was crowded with men of every grade of society, all smoking, drinking, and talking about dogs. Many of them had brought with them their " fancy" animals, so that a kind of " canine exhibition" was going on; some carried under their arm small bull-dogs, whose flat pink noses rubbed against my arm as I passed; others had Skye-terriers, curled up like balls of hair, and sleeping like children, as they were nursed by their owners. The only animals that seemed awake, and under continual excitement, were the little brown English terriers, who, despite the neat black leathern collars by which they were held, struggled to get loose, as if they smelt the rats in the room above, and were impatient to begin the fray.

There is a business-like look about this tavern which at once lets you into the character of the person who owns it. The drinking seems to have been a secondary notion in its formation, for it is a low-roofed room without any of those adornments which are now generally considered so necessary to render a public-house attractive. The tubs where the spirits are kept are blistered with the heat of the gas, and so dirty that the once brilliant gilt hoops are now quite black.

Sleeping on an old hall-chair lay an enormous white bulldog, " a great beauty," as I was informed, with a head as round and smooth as a clenched boxing-glove, and seemingly too large for the body. Its forehead appeared to protrude in a manner significant of water on the brain, and almost overhung the short nose, through which the animal breathed heavily. When this dog, which was the admiration of all beholders, rose up, its legs were as bowed as a tailor's, leaving a peculiar pear-shaped opening between them, which, I was informed, was one of its points of beauty. It was a white dog, with a sore look, from its being peculiarly pink round the eyes, nose, and indeed at all the edges of its body.

On the other side of the fire-place was a white bull-terrier dog, with a black patch over the eye, which gave him rather a disreputable look. This animal was watching the movements of the customers in front, and occasionally, when the entrance-door was swung back, would give a growl of inquiry as to what the fresh-comer wanted. The proprietor was kind enough to inform me, as he patted this animal's ribs, which showed like the hoops on a butter-firkin, that he considered there had been a "little of the greyhound in some of his back generations."

About the walls were hung clusters of black leather collars, adorned with brass rings and clasps, and pre-eminent was a silver dog-collar, which, from the conversation of those about me, I learnt was to be the prize in a rat-match to be "killed for" in a fortnight's time.

As the visitors poured in, they, at the request of the proprietor "not to block up the bar," took their seats in the parlour, and, accompanied by a waiter, who kept shouting, "Give your orders, gentlemen," I entered the room.

I found that, like the bar, no pains had been taken to render the room attractive to the customers, for, with the exception of the sporting pictures hung against the dingy paper, it was devoid of all adornment. Over the fire-place were square glazed boxes, in which were the stuffed forms of dogs famous in their day. Pre-eminent among the prints was that representing the "Wonder" Tiny, "five pounds and a half in weight," as he appeared killing 200 rats. This engraving had a singular look, from its having been printed upon a silk handkerchief. Tiny had been a great favourite with the proprietor, and used to wear a lady's bracelet as a collar.

Among the stuffed heads was one of a white bull-dog, with tremendous glass eyes sticking out, as if it had died of strangulation. The proprietor's son was kind enough to explain to me the qualities that had once belonged to this favourite. "They've spoilt her in stuffing, sir," he said; "made her so short in the head; but she was the wonder of her day. There wasn't a dog in England as would come nigh her. There's her daughter," he added, pointing to another head, something like that of a seal, "but she wasn't reckoned half as handsome as her mother, though she was very much admired in her time.

"That there is a dog," he continued, pointing to one represented with a rat in its mouth, "it was as good as any in England, though it's so small. I've seen her kill a dozen rats almost as big as herself, though they killed her at last; for sewer-rats are dreadful for giving dogs canker in the mouth, and she wore herself out with continually killing them, though we always rinsed her mouth out well with peppermint and water while she were at work. When rats bite they are pisonous, and

an ulcer is formed, which we are obleeged to lance; that's what killed her."

The company assembled in "the parlour" consisted of sporting men, or those who, from curiosity, had come to witness what a rat-match was like. Seated at the same table, talking together, were those dressed in the costermonger's suit of corduroy, soldiers with their uniforms carelessly unbuttoned, coachmen in their livery, and tradesmen who had slipped on their evening frock-coats, and run out from the shop to see the sport.

The dogs belonging to the company were standing on the different tables, or tied to the legs of the forms, or sleeping in their owners' arms, and were in turn minutely criticised — their limbs being stretched out as if they were being felt for fractures, and their mouths looked into, as if a dentist were examining their teeth. Nearly all the little animals were marked with scars from bites. "Pity to bring him up to rat-killing," said one, who had been admiring a fierce-looking bull-terrier, although he did not mention at the same time what line in life the little animal ought to pursue.

At another table one man was declaring that his pet animal was the exact image of the celebrated rat-killing dog "Billy," at the same time pointing to the picture against the wall of that famous animal, "as he performed his wonderful feat of killing 500 rats in five minutes and a half."

There were amongst the visitors some French gentlemen, who had evidently witnessed nothing of the kind before; and whilst they endeavoured to drink their hot gin and water, they made their interpreter translate to them the contents of a large placard hung upon a hatpeg, and headed —

"EVERY MAN HAS HIS FANCY.

RATTING SPORTS IN REALITY."

About nine o'clock the proprietor took the chair in the parlour, at the same time giving the order to "shut up the shutters in the room above, and light up the pit." This announcement seemed to rouse the spirits of the impatient assembly, and even the dogs tied to the legs of the tables ran out to the length of their leathern thongs, and their tails curled like eels, as if they understood the meaning of the words.

"Why, that's the little champion," said the proprietor, patting a dog with thighs like a grasshopper, and whose mouth opened back to its ears. "Well, it is a beauty! I wish I could gammon you to take a 'fiver' for it." Then looking round the room, he added, "Well, gents, I'm glad to see you look so comfortable."

The performances of the evening were somewhat hurried on by the entering of a young gentleman, whom the waiters called "Cap'an."

"Now, Jem, when is this match coming off?" the Captain asked impatiently; and despite the assurance that they were getting ready, he threatened to leave the place if kept waiting much longer. This young officer seemed to be a great "fancier" of dogs, for he made the round of the room, handling each animal in its turn, feeling and squeezing its feet, and scrutinising its eyes and limbs with such minuteness, that the French gentlemen were forced to inquire who he was.

There was no announcement that the room above was ready, though everybody seemed to understand it; for all rose at once, and mounting the broad wooden staircase, which led to what was once the "drawing-room," dropped their shillings into the hand of the proprietor, and entered the rat-killing apartment.

"The pit," as it is called, consists of a small circus, some six feet in diameter. It is about as large as a centre flower-bed, and is fitted with a high wooden rim that reaches to elbow height. Over it the branches of a gas lamp are arranged, which light up the white painted floor, and every part of the little arena. On one side of the room is a recess, which the proprietor calls his "private box," and this apartment the Captain and his friend soon took possession of, whilst the audience generally clambered upon the tables and forms, or hung over the sides of the pit itself.

All the little dogs which the visitors had brought up with them were now squalling and barking, and struggling in their masters' arms, as if they were thoroughly acquainted with the uses of the pit; and when a rusty wire cage of rats, filled with the dark moving mass, was brought forward, the noise of the dogs was so great that the proprietor was obliged to shout out—"Now, you that have dogs *do* make 'em shut up."

The Captain was the first to jump into the pit. A man wanted to sell him a bull-terrier, spotted like a fancy rabbit, and a dozen of rats was the consequent order.

The Captain preferred pulling the rats out of the cage himself, laying hold of them by their tails and jerking them into the arena. He was cautioned by one of the men not to let them bite him, for "believe me," were the words, "you'll never forget, Cap'an; these 'ere are none of the cleanest."

Whilst the rats were being counted out, some of those that had been taken from the cage ran about the painted floor and climbed up the young officer's legs, making him shake them off and exclaim, "Get out, you varmint!" whilst others of the ugly little animals sat upon their hind legs, cleaning their faces with their paws.

When the dog in question was brought forth and shown the dozen rats, he grew excited, and stretched himself in his owner's arms, whilst all the other animals joined in a full chorus of whining.

"Chuck him in," said the Captain, and over went the dog; and in a second the rats were running round the circus, or trying to hide themselves between the small openings in the boards round the pit.

Although the proprietor of the dog endeavoured to speak up for it, by declaring "it was a good 'un, and a very pretty performer," still it was evidently not worth much in a rat-killing sense; and if it had not been for his "second," who beat the sides of the pit with his hand, and shouted "Hi! hi! at 'em!" in a most bewildering manner, we doubt if the terrier would not have preferred leaving the rats to themselves, to enjoy their lives. Some of the rats, when the dog advanced towards them, sprang up in his face, making him draw back with astonishment. Others, as he bit them, curled round in his mouth and fastened on his nose, so that he had to carry them as a cat does its kittens. It also required many shouts of "Drop it—dead 'un," before he would leave those he had killed.

We cannot say whether the dog was eventually bought; but from its owner's exclaiming, in a kind of apologetic tone, "Why, he never saw a rat before in all his life," we fancy no dealings took place.

The Captain seemed anxious to see as much sport as he could, for he frequently asked those who carried dogs in their arms whether "his little 'un would kill," and appeared sorry when such answers were given as—"My dog's mouth's a little out of order, Cap'an," or "I've only tried him at very small 'uns."

One little dog was put in the pit to amuse himself with the dead bodies. He seized hold of one almost as big as himself, shook it furiously till the head thumped the floor like a drumstick, making those around shout with laughter, and causing one man to exclaim, "He's a good 'un at shaking heads and tails, ain't he?"

Preparations now began for the grand match of the evening, in which fifty rats were to be killed. The "dead 'uns" were gathered up by their tails and flung into the corner. The floor was swept, and a big flat basket produced, like those in which chickens are brought to market, and under whose iron wire top could be seen small mounds of closely packed rats. This match seemed to be between the proprietor and his son, and the stake to be gained was only a bottle of lemonade, of which the father stipulated he should have first drink.

It was strange to observe the daring manner in which the lad introduced his hand into the rat cage, sometimes keeping it there for more than a minute at a time, as he fumbled about and stirred up with his fingers the living mass, picking out, as he had been requested, "only the big 'uns."

When the fifty animals had been flung into the pit, they gathered themselves together into a mound which reached one-third up the sides, and which reminded one of the heap of hair-sweepings in a barber's shop after a heavy day's cutting. These were all sewer and water-ditch rats, and the smell that rose from them was like that from a hot drain.

The Captain amused himself by flicking at them with his pocket handkerchief, and offering them the lighted end of his cigar, which the little creatures tamely snuffed at, and drew back from, as they singed their noses.

It was also a favourite amusement to blow on the mound of rats, for they seemed to dislike the cold wind, which sent them fluttering about like so many feathers; indeed, whilst the match was going on, whenever the little animals collected together, and formed a barricade as it were to the dog, the cry of " Blow on 'em! blow on 'em!" was given by the spectators, and the dog's second puffed at them as if extinguishing a fire, when they would dart off like so many sparks.

The company was kept waiting so long for the match to begin that the impatient Captain again threatened to leave the house, and was only quieted by the proprietor's reply of " My dear friend, be easy, the boy's on the stairs with the dog;" and true enough we shortly heard a wheezing and a screaming in the passage without, as if some strong-winded animal were being strangled, and presently a boy entered, carrying in his arms a bull-terrier in a perfect fit of excitement, foaming at the mouth and stretching its neck forward, so that the collar which held it back seemed to be cutting its throat in two.

The animal was nearly mad with rage— scratching and struggling to get loose. " Lay hold a little closer up to the head or he'll turn round and nip yer," said the proprietor to his son.

Whilst the gasping dog was fastened up in a corner to writhe its impatience away, the landlord made inquiries for a stop-watch, and also for an umpire to decide, as he added, " whether the rats were dead or alive when they're ' killed,' as Paddy says."

When all the arrangements had been made the " second" and the dog jumped into the pit, and after " letting him see 'em a bit," the terrier was let loose.

The moment the dog was " free," he became quiet in a most business-like manner, and rushed at the rats, burying his nose in the mound till he brought out one in his mouth. In a short time a dozen rats with wetted necks were lying bleeding on the floor, and the white paint of the pit became grained with blood.

In a little time the terrier had a rat hanging to his nose, which, despite his tossing, still held on. He dashed up against the sides, leaving a patch of blood as if a strawberry had been smashed there.

" He doesn't squeal, that's one good thing," said one of the lookers-on.

As the rats fell on their sides after a bite they were collected together in the centre, where they lay quivering in their death-gasps!

" Hi, Butcher! hi, Butcher!" shouted the second, " good dog! bur-r-r-r-r-h!" and he beat the sides of the pit like a drum till the dog flew about with new life.

" Dead 'un! drop it!" he cried, when the terrier " nosed" a rat kicking on its side, as it slowly expired of its broken neck.

" Time!" said the proprietor, when four of the eight minutes had expired, and the dog was caught up and held panting, his neck stretched out like a serpent's, staring intently at the rats which still kept crawling about.

The poor little wretches in this brief interval, as if forgetting their danger, again commenced cleaning themselves, some nibbling the ends of their tails, others hopping about, going now to the legs of the lad in the pit, and sniffing at his trousers, or, strange to say, advancing, smelling, to within a few paces of their enemy the dog.

The dog lost the match, and the proprietor, we presume, honourably paid the bottle of lemonade to his son. But he was evidently displeased with the dog's behaviour, for he said, " He won't do for me—he's not one of my sort! Here, Jim, tell Mr. G. he may have him if he likes; I won't give him house room."

A plentiful shower of halfpence was thrown into the pit as a reward for the second who had backed the dog.

A slight pause now took place in the proceedings, during which the landlord requested that the gentlemen " would give their minds up to drinking; you know the love I have for you," he added jocularly, " and that I don't care for any of you;" whilst the waiter accompanied the invitation with a cry of " Give your orders, gentlemen," and the lad with the rats asked if " any other gentleman would like any rats."

Several other dogs were tried, and amongst them one who, from the size of his stomach, had evidently been accustomed to large dinners, and looked upon rat-killing as a sport and not as a business. The appearance of this fat animal was greeted with remarks such as " Why don't you feed your dog?" and " You shouldn't give him more than five meals a-day."

Another impatient bull-terrier was thrown into the midst of a dozen rats. He did his duty so well, that the admiration of the spectators was focussed upon him.

" Ah," said one, " he'd do better at a hundred than twelve;" whilst another observed, " Rat-killing's his game, I can see;" while the landlord himself said, " He's a very pretty creetur', and I'd back him to kill against anybody's dog at eight and a half or nine."

The Captain was so startled with this terrier's " cleverness," that he vowed that if she could kill fifteen in a minute " he'd give a hundred guineas for her."

It was nearly twelve o'clock before the evening's performance concluded. Several of the

RATTING—"THE GRAHAM ARMS," GRAHAM STREET.

[*From a Photograph.*]

JACK BLACK, HER MAJESTY'S RATCATCHER.

[From a Photograph.]

spectators tried their dogs upon two or three rats, either the biggest or the smallest that could be found: and many offers as to what " he wanted for the dog," and many inquiries as to " who was its father," were made before the company broke up.

At last the landlord, finding that no " gentleman would like a few rats," and that his exhortations to " give their minds up to drinking" produced no further effect upon the company, spoke the epilogue of the rat tragedies in these words;—

" Gentlemen, I give a very handsome solid silver collar to be killed for next Tuesday. Open to all the world, only they must be novice dogs, or at least such as is not considered *phee*nomenons. We shall have plenty of sport, gentlemen, and there will be loads of rat-killing. I hope to see all my kind friends, not forgetting your dogs, likewise; and may they be like the Irishman all over, who had good trouble to catch and kill 'em, and took good care they didn't come to life again. Gentlemen, there is a good parlour down-stairs, where we meets for harmony and entertainment."

JIMMY SHAW.

THE proprietor of one of the largest sporting public-houses in London, who is celebrated for the rat-matches which come off weekly at his establishment, was kind enough to favour me with a few details as to the quality of those animals which are destroyed in his pit. His statement was certainly one of the most curious that I have listened to, and it was given to me with a readiness and a courtesy of manner such as I have not often met with during my researches. The landlord himself is known in pugilistic circles as one of the most skilful boxers among what is termed the " light weights."

His statement is curious, as a proof of the large trade which is carried on in these animals, for it would seem that the men who make a business of catching rats are not always employed as " exterminators," for they make a good living as " purveyors" for supplying the demands of the sporting portion of London.

" The poor people," said the sporting landlord, " who supply me with rats, are what you may call barn-door labouring poor, for they are the most ignorant people I ever come near. Really you would not believe people could live in such ignorance. Talk about Latin and Greek, sir, why English is Latin to them—in fact, I have a difficulty to understand them myself. When the harvest is got in, they go hunting the hedges and ditches for rats. Once the farmers had to pay 2*d.* a-head for all rats caught on their grounds, and they nailed them up against the wall. But now that the rat-ketchers can get 3*d.* each by bringing the vermin up to town, the farmers don't pay

them anything for what they ketch, but merely give them permission to hunt them in their stacks and barns, so that they no longer get their 2*d.* in the country, though they get their 3*d.* in town.

" I have some twenty families depending upon me. From Clavering, in Essex, I suppose I have hundreds of thousands of rats sent to me in wire cages fitted into baskets. From Enfield I have a great. quantity, but the ketchers don't get them all there, but travel round the country for scores of miles, for you see 3*d.* a-head is money; besides, there are some liberal farmers who will still give them a halfpenny a-head into the bargain. Enfield is a kind of head-quarters for rat-ketchers.

" It's dangerous work, though, for you see there is a wonderful deal of difference in the specie of rats. The bite of sewer or water-ditch rats is very bad. The water and ditch rat lives on filth, but your barn-rat is a plump fellow, and he lives on the best of everything. He's well off. There's as much difference between the barn and sewer-rats as between a brewer's horse and a costermonger's. Sewer-rats are very bad for dogs, their coats is poisonous.

" Some of the rats that are brought to me are caught in the warehouses in the City. Wherever there is anything in the shape of provisions, there you are sure to find Mr. Rat an intruder. The ketchers are paid for ketching them in the warehouses, and then they are sold to me as well, so the men must make a good thing of it. Many of the more courageous kind of warehousemen will take a pleasure in hunting the rats themselves.

" I should think I buy in the course of the year, on the average, from 300 to 700 rats a-week." (Taking 500 as the weekly average, this gives a yearly purchase of 26,000 live rats.) " That's what I kill taking all the year round, you see. Some first-class chaps will come here in the day-time, and they'll try their dogs. They'll say, 'Jimmy, give the dog 100.' After he's polished them off they'll say, perhaps, 'Hang it, give him another 100.' Bless you!" he added, in a kind of whisper, " I've had noble ladies and titled ladies come here to see the sport—on the quiet, you know. When my wife was here they would come regular, but now she's away they don't come so often.

" The largest quantity of rats I've bought from one man was five guineas' worth, or thirty-five dozen at 3*d.* a-head, and that's a load for a horse. This man comes up from Clavering in a kind of cart, with a horse that's a regular phenomena, for it ain't like a beast nor nothing. I pays him a good deal of money at times, and I'm sure I can't tell what he does with it; but they *do* tell me that he deals in old iron, and goes buying it up, though he don't seem to have much of a head-piece for that sort of fancy neither.

" During the harvest-time the rats run scarcer you see, and the ketcher turns up rat-ketching for harvest work. After the harvest rats gets plentiful again.

"I've had as many as 2000 rats in this very house at one time. They'll consume a sack of barley-meal a week, and the brutes, if you don't give 'em good stuff, they'll eat one another, hang 'em!

"I'm the oldest canine fancier in London, and I'm the first that started ratting; in fact, I know I'm the oldest caterer in rat-killing in the metropolis. I began as a lad, and I had many noble friends, and was as good a man then as I am now. In fact, when I was seventeen or eighteen years of age I was just like what my boy is now. I used at that time to be a great public charakter, and had many liberal friends —very liberal friends. I used to give them rat sports, and I have kept to it ever since. My boy can handle rats now just as I used to then.

"Have I been bit by them? Aye, hundreds of times. Now, some people will say, 'Rub yourself over with caraway and stuff, and then rats won't bite you.' But I give you my word and honour it's all nonsense, sir.

"As I said, I was the first in London to give rat sports, and I've kept to it ever since. Bless you, there's nothing that a rat won't bite through. I've seen my lads standing in the pit with the rats running about them, and if they haven't taken the precaution to tie their trousers round with a bit of string at the bottom, they'd have as many as five or six rats run up their trouser-legs. They'll deliberately take off their clothes and pick them out from their shirts, and bosoms, and breeches. Some people is amused, and others is horror-struck. People have asked them whether they ain't rubbed? They'll say 'Yes,' but that's as a lark; 'cos, sometimes when my boy has been taking the rats out of the cage, and somebody has taken his attention off, talking to him, he has had a bite, and will turn to me with his finger bleeding, and say, 'Yes, I'm rubbed, ain't I, father? look here!'

"A rat's bite is very singular, it's a three-cornered one, like a leech's, only deeper, of course, and it will bleed for ever such a time. My boys have sometimes had their fingers go dreadfully bad from rat-bites, so that they turn all black and putrid like—aye, as black as the horse-hair covering to my sofa. People have said to me, 'You ought to send the lad to the hospital, and have his finger took off;' but I've always left it to the lads, and they've said, 'Oh, don't mind it, father; it'll get all right by and by.' And so it has.

"The best thing I ever found for a rat-bite was the thick bottoms of porter casks put on as a poultice. The only thing you can do is to poultice, and these porter bottoms is so powerful and draws so, that they'll actually take thorns out of horses' hoofs and feet after steeplechasing.

"In handling rats, it's nothing more in the world but nerve that does it. I should faint now if a rat was to run up my breeches, but I have known the time when I've been kivered with 'em.

"I generally throw my dead rats away now; but two or three years since my boys took the idea of skinning them into their heads, and they did about 300 of them, and their skins was very promising. The boys was, after all, obliged to give them away to a furrier, for my wife didn't like the notion, and I said, 'Throw them away;' but the idea strikes me to be something, and one that is lost sight of, for the skins are warm and handsome-looking—a beautiful grey.

"There's nothing turns so quickly as dead rats, so I am obleeged to have my dustmen come round every Wednesday morning; and regularly enough they call too, for they know where there is a bob and a pot. I generally prefers using the authorised dustmen, though the others come sometimes—the flying dustmen they call 'em—and if they're first, they has the job.

"It strikes me, though, that to throw away so many valuable skins is a good thing lost sight of.

"The rats want a deal of watching, and a deal of sorting. Now you can't put a sewer and a barn-rat together, it's like putting a Roosshian and a Turk under the same roof.

"I can tell a barn-rat from a ship-rat or a sewer-rat in a minute, and I have to look over my stock when they come in, or they'd fight to the death. There's six or seven different kinds of rats, and if we don't sort 'em they tear one another to pieces. I think when I have a number of rats in the house, that I am a lucky man if I don't find a dozen dead when I go up to them in the morning; and when I tell you that at times—when I've wanted to make up my number for a match—I've given 21s. for twenty rats, you may think I lose something that way every year. Rats, even now, is occasionally 6s. a-dozen; but that, I think, is most inconsistent.

"If I had my will, I wouldn't allow sewer ratting, for the rats in the shores eats up a great quantity of sewer filth and rubbish, and is another specie of scavenger in their own way."

After finishing his statement, the landlord showed me some very curious specimens of tame rats—some piebald, and others quite white, with pink eyes, which he kept in cages in his sitting-room. He took them out from their cages, and handled them without the least fear, and even handled them rather rudely, as he showed me the peculiarities of their colours; yet the little tame creatures did not once attempt to bite him. Indeed, they appeared to have lost the notion of regaining their liberty, and when near their cages struggled to return to their nests.

In one of these boxes a black and a white rat were confined together, and the proprietor, pointing to them, remarked, "I hope they'll breed, for though white rats is very scarce, only occurring in fact by a freak of nature, I fancy I shall be able, with time and trouble, to breed 'em myself. The old English rat is a small jet-black rat; but the first white rat as I heard of come out of a burial-ground. At one time I bred rats very largely, but now I leaves that fancy to my boys, for I've as much as I can do continuing to serve my worthy patrons."

JACK BLACK.

As I wished to obtain the best information about rat and vermin destroying, I thought I could not do better now than apply to that eminent authority "the Queen's ratcatcher," and accordingly I sought an interview with Mr. "Jack" Black, whose hand-bills are headed — " V.R. Rat and mole destroyer to Her Majesty."

I had already had a statement from the royal bug-destroyer relative to the habits and means of exterminating those offensive vermin, and I was desirous of pairing it with an account of the personal experience of the Queen of England's ratcatcher.

In the sporting world, and among his regular customers, the Queen's ratcatcher is better known by the name of Jack Black. He enjoys the reputation of being the most fearless handler of rats of any man living, playing with them—as one man expressed it to me—" as if they were so many blind kittens."

The first time I ever saw Mr. Black was in the streets of London, at the corner of Hart-street, where he was exhibiting the rapid effects of his rat poison, by placing some of it in the mouth of a living animal. He had a cart then with rats painted on the panels, and at the tailboard, where he stood lecturing, he had a kind of stage rigged up, on which were cages filled with rats, and pills, and poison packages. Here I saw him dip his hand into this cage of rats and take out as many as he could hold, a feat which generally caused an "oh!" of wonder to escape from the crowd, especially when they observed that his hands were un-bitten. Women more particularly shuddered when they beheld him place some half-dozen of the dusty-looking brutes within his shirt next his skin; and men swore the animals had been tamed, as he let them run up his arms like squirrels, and the people gathered round beheld them sitting on his shoulders cleaning their faces with their front-paws, or rising up on their hind legs like little kangaroos, and sniffing about his ears and cheeks.

But those who knew Mr. Black better, were well aware that the animals he took up in his hand were as wild as any of the rats in the sewers of London, and that the only mystery in the exhibition was that of a man having courage enough to undertake the work.

I afterwards visited Jack Black at his house in Battersea. I had some difficulty in dis-covering his country residence, and was indebted to a group of children gathered round and staring at the bird-cage in the window of his cottage for his address. Their exclamations of delight at a grey parrot climbing with his beak and claws about the zinc wires of his cage, and the hopping of the little linnets there, in the square boxes scarcely bigger than a brick, made me glance up at the door to discover who the bird-fancier was; when painted on a bit of zinc—just large enough to fit the shaft of a tax cart—I saw the words, "J. Black, Rat De-stroyer to Her Majesty," surmounted by the royal initials, V.R., together with the painting of a white rat.

Mr. Black was out "sparrer ketching," as his wife informed me, for he had an order for three dozen, "which was to be shot in a match" at some tea-gardens close by.

When I called again Mr. Black had re-turned, and I found him kneeling before a big, rusty iron-wire cage, as large as a sea-chest, and transferring the sparrows from his bird-catching apparatus to the more roomy prison.

He transacted a little business before I spoke to him, for the boys about the door were ask-ing, " Can I have one for a penny, master?"

There is evidently a great art in handling birds; for when Mr. Black held one, he took hold of it by the wings and tail, so that the little creature seemed to be sitting upright and had not a feather rumpled, while it stretched out its neck and looked around it; the boys, on the contrary, first made them flutter their feathers as rough as a hair ball, and then half smothered them between their two hands, by holding them as if they wished to keep them hot.

I was soon at home with Mr. Black. He was a very different man from what I had ex-pected to meet, for there was an expression of kindliness in his countenance, a quality which does not exactly agree with one's preconceived notions of ratcatchers. His face had a strange appearance, from his rough, uncombed hair, be-ing nearly grey, and his eyebrows and whiskers black, so that he looked as if he wore powder.

Mr. Black informed me that the big iron-wire cage, in which the sparrows were flutter-ing about, had been constructed by him for rats, and that it held over a thousand when full—for rats are packed like cups, he said, one over the other. " But," he added, " business is bad. for rats, and it makes a splendid havery; be-sides, sparrers is the rats of birds, sir, for if you look at 'em in a cage they always huddles up in a corner like rats in a pit, and they are a'most vermin in colour and habits, and eats anything."

The ratcatcher's parlour was more like a shop than a family apartment. In a box, with iron bars before it, like a rabbit-hutch, was a white ferret, twisting its long thin body with a snake-like motion up and down the length of its prison, as restlessly as if it were a miniature polar bear.

When Mr. Black called "Polly" to the ferret, it came to the bars and fixed its pink eyes on him. A child lying on the floor poked its fingers into the cage, but Polly only smelt at them, and, finding them not good to eat, went away.

Mr. Black stuffs animals and birds, and also catches fish for vivaria. Against the walls were the furred and feathered remains of departed favourites, each in its glazed box and appropriate attitude. There was a famous polecat—"a first-rater at rats" we were informed. Here a ferret "that never was equalled." This canary "had earned pounds." That linnet "was the wonder of its day." The enormous pot-bellied carp, with the miniature rushes painted at the back of its case, was caught in the Regent's Park waters.

"In another part of the room hung fishing-lines, and a badger's skin, and lead-bobs and curious eel-hooks—the latter as big as the curls on the temples of a Spanish dancer, and from here Mr. Black took down a transparent-looking fish, like a slip of parchment, and told me that it was a fresh-water smelt, and that he caught it in the Thames—"the first he ever heard of." Then he showed me a beetle suspended to a piece of thread, like a big spider to its web, and this he informed me was the Thames beetle, "which either live by land or water."

"You ketch 'em," continued Mr. Black, "when they are swimming on their backs, which is their nature, and when they turns over you finds 'em beautifully crossed and marked."

Round the room were hung paper bags, like those in which housewives keep their sweet herbs. "All of them there, sir, contain cured fish for eating," Mr. Black explained to me.

"I'm called down here the Battersea otter," he went on, "for I can go out at four in the morning, and come home by eight with a barrowful of freshwater fish. Nobody knows how I do it, because I never takes no nets or lines with me. I assure them I ketch 'em with my hands, which I do, but they only laughs increderlous like. I knows the fishes' harnts, and watches the tides. I sells fresh fish—perch, roach, dace, gudgeon, and such-like, and even small jack, at threepence a pound, or what they'll fetch; and I've caught near the Wandsworth 'Black Sea,' as we calls it, half a hundred weight sometimes, and I never took less than my handkerchey full."

I was inclined—like the inhabitants of Battersea—to be incredulous of the rat-catcher's hand-fishing, until, under a promise of secrecy, he confided his process to me, and then not only was I perfectly convinced of its truth, but startled that so simple a method had never before been taken advantage of.

Later in the day Mr. Black became very communicative. We sat chatting together in his sanded bird shop, and he told me all his misfortunes, and how bad luck had pressed upon him, and driven him out of London.

"I was fool enough to take a public-house in Regent-street, sir," he said. "My daughter used to dress as the 'Ratketcher's Daughter,' and serve behind the bar, and that did pretty well for a time; but it was a brewer's house, and they ruined me."

The costume of the "ratketcher's daughter" was shown to me by her mother. It was a red velvet bodice, embroidered with silver lace.

"With a muslin skirt, and her hair down her back, she looked wery genteel," added the parent.

Mr. Black's chief complaint was that he could not "make an appearance," for his "uniform"—a beautiful green coat and red waistcoat—were pledged."

Whilst giving me his statement, Mr. Black, in proof of his assertions of the biting powers of rats, drew my attention to the leathern breeches he wore, "as were given him twelve years ago by Captain B——."

These were pierced in some places with the teeth of the animals, and in others were scratched and fringed like the washleather of a street knife-seller.

His hands, too, and even his face, had scars upon them from bites.

Mr. Black informed me that he had given up tobacco "since a haccident he met with from a pipe. I was smoking a pipe," he said, "and a friend of mine by chance jobbed it into my mouth, and it went right through to the back of my palate, and I nearly died."

Here his wife added, "There's a hole there to this day you could put your thumb into; you never saw such a mouth."

Mr. Black informed me in secret that he had often, "unbeknown to his wife," tasted what cooked rats were like, and he asserted that they were as moist as rabbits, and quite as nice.

"If they are shewer-rats," he continued, "just chase them for two or three days before you kill them, and they are as good as barn-rats, I give you my word, sir."

Mr. Black's statement was as follows:—

"I should think I've been at ratting a'most for five-and-thirty year; indeed, I may say from my childhood, for I've kept at it a'most all my life. I've been dead near three times from bites—as near as a toucher. I once had the teeth of a rat break in my finger, which was dreadful bad, and swole, and putrified, so that I had to have the broken bits pulled out with tweezers. When the bite is a bad one, it festers and forms a hard core in the ulcer, which is very painful, and throbs very much indeed; and after that core comes away, unless you cleans 'em out well, the sores, even after they seemed to be healed, break out over and over again, and never cure perfectly. This core is as big as a boiled fish's eye, and as hard as a stone. I generally cuts the bite out clean with a lancet, and squeege the humour well from it, and that's the only way to cure it thorough—as you see my hands is all covered with scars from bites.

"The worst bite I ever had was at the Manor House, Hornsey, kept by Mr. Burnell. One day when I was there, he had some rats get loose, and he asked me to ketch 'em for him, as they was wanted for a match that was coming on that afternoon. I had picked up a lot—indeed, I had one in each hand, and another again my knee, when I happened to come to a sheaf of straw, which I turned over, and there was a rat there. I couldn't lay hold on him 'cause my hands was full, and as I stooped down he ran up the sleeve of my coat, and bit me on the muscle of the arm. I shall never forget it. It turned me all of a sudden, and made me feel numb. In less than half-an-hour I was took so bad I was obleeged to be sent home, and I had to get some one to drive my cart for me. It was terrible to see the blood that came from me—I bled awful. Burnell seeing me go so queer, says, 'Here, Jack, take some brandy, you look so awful bad.' The arm swole, and went as heavy as a ton weight pretty well, so that I couldn't even lift it, and so painful I couldn't bear my wife to ferment it. I was kept in bed for two months through that bite at Burnell's. I was so weak I couldn't stand, and I was dreadful feverish—all warmth like. I knew I was going to die, 'cause I remember the doctor coming and opening my eyes, to see if I was still alive.

"I've been bitten nearly everywhere, even where I can't name to you, sir, and right through my thumb nail too, which, as you see, always has a split in it, though it's years since I was wounded. I suffered as much from that bite on my thumb as anything. It went right up to my ear. I felt the pain in both places at once—a regular twinge, like touching the nerve of a tooth. The thumb went black, and I was told I ought to have it off; but I knew a young chap at the Middlesex Hospital who wasn't out of his time, and he said, ' No, I wouldn't, Jack;' and no more I did; and he used to strap it up for me. But the worst of it was, I had a job at Camden Town one after-noon after he had dressed the wound, and I got another bite lower down on the same thumb, and that flung me down on my bed, and there I stopped, I should think, six weeks.

"I was bit bad, too, in Edwards-street, Hampstead-road; and that time I was sick near three months, and close upon dying. Whether it was the poison of the bite, or the medicine the doctor give me, I can't say; but the flesh seemed to swell up like a bladder—regular blowed like. After all, I think I cured myself by cheating the doctor, as they calls it; for instead of taking the medicine, I used to go to Mr.——'s house in Albany-street (the pub-lican), and he'd say, 'What'll yer have, Jack?'

and I used to take a glass of stout, and that seemed to give me strength to overcome the pison of the bite, for I began to pick up as soon as I left off doctor's stuff.

"When a rat's bite touches the bone, it makes you faint in a minute, and it bleeds dreadful—ah, most terrible—just as if you had been stuck with a penknife. You couldn't believe the quantity of blood that come away, sir.

"The first rats I caught was when I was about nine years of age. I ketched them at Mr. Strickland's, a large cow-keeper, in Little Albany-street, Regent's-park. At that time it was all fields and meaders in them parts, and I recollect there was a big orchard on one side of the sheds. I was only doing it for a game, and there was lots of ladies and gents looking on, and wondering at seeing me taking the rats out from under a heap of old bricks and wood, where they had collected theirselves. I had a little dog—a little red 'un it was, who was well known through the fancy—and I wanted the rats for to test my dog with, I being a lad what was fond of the sport.

"I wasn't afraid to handle rats even then; it seemed to come nat'ral to me. I very soon had some in my pocket, and some in my hands, carrying them away as fast as I could, and putting them into my wire cage. You see, the rats began to run as soon as we shifted them bricks, and I had to scramble for them. Many of them bit me, and, to tell you the truth, I didn't know the bites were so many, or I dare say I shouldn't have been so ven-turesome as I was.

"After that I bought some ferruts—four of them—of a man of the name of Butler, what was in the rat-ketching line, and afterwards went out to Jamaicer, to kill rats there. I was getting on to ten years of age then, and I was, I think, the first that regularly began hunting rats to sterminate them; for all those before me used to do it with drugs, and perhaps never handled rats in their lives.

"With my ferruts I at first used to go out hunting rats round by the ponds in Regent's-park, and the ditches, and in the cow-sheds roundabout. People never paid me for ketch-ing, though, maybe, if they was very much infested, they might give me a trifle; but I used to make my money by selling the rats to gents as was fond of sport, and wanted them for their little dogs.

"I kept to this till I was thirteen or four-teen year of age, always using the ferruts; and I bred from them, too,—indeed, I've still got the ' strain' (breed) of them same ferruts by me now. I've sold them ferruts about everywhere; to Jim Burn I've sold some of the strain; and to Mr. Anderson, the pro-vision-merchant; and to a man that went to Ireland. Indeed, that strain of ferruts has gone nearly all over the world.

"I never lost a ferrut out ratting. I always let them loose, and put a bell on mine—arranged in a peculiar manner, which is a secret—and I then puts him into the main run of the rats, and lets him go to work. But they must be ferruts that's well trained for working dwellings, or you'll lose them as safe as death. I've had 'em go away two houses off, and come back to me. My ferruts is very tame, and so well trained, that I'd put them into a house and guarantee that they'd come back to me. In Grosvenor-street I was clearing once, and the ferruts went next door, and nearly cleared the house—which is the Honourable Mrs. F——'s—before they came back to me.

" Ferruts are very dangerous to handle if not well trained. They are very savage, and will attack a man or a child as well as a rat. It was well known at Mr. Hamilton's at Hampstead—it's years ago this is—there was a ferrut that got loose what killed a child, and was found sucking it. The bite of 'em is very dangerous—not so pisonous as a rat's—but very painful; and when the little things is hungry they'll attack anythink. I've seen two of them kill a cat, and then they'll suck the blood till they fills theirselves, after which they'll fall off like leeches.

" The weasel and the stoat are, I think, more dangerous than the ferrut in their bite. I had a stoat once, which I caught when out ratting at Hampstead for Mr. Cunningham, the butcher, and it bit one of my dogs—Black Bess by name, the truest bitch in the world, sir—in the mouth, and she died three days arterwards at the Ball at Kilburn. I was along with Captain K——, who'd come out to see the sport, and whilst we were at dinner, and the poor bitch lying under my chair, my boy says, says he, ' Father, Black Bess is dying;' and had scarce spoke the speech when she was dead. It was all through the bite of that stoat, for I opened the wound in the lip, and it was all swole, and dreadful ulcerated, and all down the throat it was inflamed most shocking, and so was the lungs quite red and fiery. She was hot with work when she got the bite, and perhaps that made her take the pison quicker.

" To give you a proof, sir, of the savage nature of the ferruts, I was one night at Jimmy Shaw's, where there was a match to come off with rats, which the ferrut was to kill; and young Bob Shaw (Jim's son) was holding the ferrut up to his mouth and giving it spittle, when the animal seized him by the lip, and bit it right through, and hung on as tight as a vice, which shows the spitefulness of the ferrut, and how it will attack the human frame. Young Shaw still held the ferrut in his hand whilst it was fastened to his lip, and he was saying, ' Oh, oh !' in pain. You see, I think Jim kept it very hard to make it kill the rats better. There was some noblemen there, and also Mr. George, of Kensal New-town, was there, which is one of the

largest dog-fanciers we have. To make the ferrut leave go of young Shaw, they bit its feet and tail, and it wouldn't, 'cos—as I could have told 'em—it only made it bite all the more. At last Mr. George, says he to me, ' For God's sake, Jack, take the ferret off.' I didn't like to intrude myself upon the company before, not being in my own place, and I didn't know how Jimmy would take it. Everybody in the room was at a standstill, quite horrerfied, and Jimmy himself was in a dreadful way for his boy. I went up, and quietly forced my thumb into his mouth and loosed him, and he killed a dozen rats after that. They all said, ' Bravo, Jack, you are a plucked one ; ' and the little chap said, ' Well, Jack, I didn't like to holla, but it was dreadful painful.' His lip swole up directly as big as a nigger's, and the company made a collection for the lad of some dozen shillings. This shows that, although a ferrut will kill a rat, yet, like the rat, it is always wicious, and will attack the human frame.

" When I was about fifteen, sir, I turned to bird-fancying. I was very fond of the sombre linnet. I was very successful in raising them, and sold them for a deal of money. I've got the strain of them by me now. I've ris them from some I purchased from a person in the Coal-yard, Drury-lane. I give him 2l. for one of the periwinkle strain, but afterwards I heard of a person with, as I thought, a better strain—Lawson of Holloway—and I went and give him 30s. for a bird. I then ris them. I used to go and ketch the nestlings off the common, and ris them under the old trained birds.

" Originally linnets was taught to sing by a bird-organ—principally among the weavers, years ago,—but I used to make the old birds teach the young ones. I used to molt them off in the dark, by kivering the cages up, and then they'd learn from hearing the old ones singing, and would take the song. If any did not sing perfectly I used to sell 'em as cast-offs.

" The linnet's is a beautiful song. There are four-and-twenty changes in a linnet's song. It's one of the beautifullest song-birds we've got. It sings ' toys,' as we call them ; that is, it makes sounds which we distinguish in the fancy as the ' tollock eeke eeke quake le wheet; single eke eke quake wheets, or eek eek quake chowls ; eege pipe chowl : laugh; eege poy chowls ; rattle ; pipe ; fear; pugh and poy.'

" This seems like Greek to you, sir, but it's the tunes we use in the fancy. What we terms ' fear' is a sound like fear, as if they was frightened; ' laugh ' is a kind of shake, nearly the same as the ' rattle.'

" I know the sounds of all the English birds, and what they say. I could tell you about the nightingale, the black cap, hedge warbler, garden warbler, petty chat, red start—a beautiful song-bird—the willow wren—little warblers they are—linnets, or any of them, for I have got their sounds in my ear and my mouth."

As if to prove this, he drew from a side-pocket a couple of tin bird-whistles, which were attached by a string to a button-hole. He instantly began to imitate the different birds, commencing with their call, and then explaining how, when answered to in such a way, they gave another note, and how, if still responded to, they uttered a different sound.

In fact, he gave me the whole of the conversation he usually carried on with the different kinds of birds, each one being as it were in a different language. He also showed me how he allured them to him, when they were in the air singing in the distance, and he did this by giving their entire song. His cheeks and throat seemed to be in constant motion as he filled the room with his loud imitations of the lark, and so closely did he resemble the notes of the bird, that it was no longer any wonder how the little things could be deceived.

In the same manner he illustrated the songs of the nightingale, and so many birds, that I did not recognise the names of some of them. He knew all their habits as well as notes, and repeated to me the peculiar chirp they make on rising from the ground, as well as the sound by which he distinguishes that it is " uneasy with curiosity," or that it has settled on a tree. Indeed, he appeared to be acquainted with all the chirps which distinguished any action in the bird up to the point when, as he told me, it " circles about, and then falls like a stone to the ground with its pitch."

" The nightingale," he continued, " is a beautiful song-bird. They're plucky birds, too, and they hear a call and answer to anybody; and when taken in April they're plucked enough to sing as soon as put in a cage. I can ketch a nightingale in less than five minutes; as soon as he calls, I calls to him with my mouth, and he'll answer me (both by night or day), either from a spinny (a little copse), a dell, or a wood, wherever he may be. I make my scrapes, (that is, clear away the dirt), set my traps, and catch 'em almost before I've tried my luck. I've ketched sometimes thirty in a day, for although people have got a notion that nightingales is scarce, still those who can distinguish their song in the daytime know that they are plentiful enough — almost like the lark. You see persons fancy that them nightingales as sings at night is the only ones living, but it's wrong, for many on them only sings in the day.

" You see it was when I was about eighteen, I was beginning to get such a judge about birds, sir. I sold to a butcher, of the name of Jackson, the first young un that I made money out of — for two pounds it was — and I've sold loads of 'em since for thirty shillings or two pounds each, and I've got the strain by me now. I've also got by me now the bird that won the match at Mr. Lock-wood's in Drury-lane, and won the return match at my own place in High-street, Mara-bun. It was in the presence of all the fancy. He's moulted pied (pie-bald) since, and gone a little white on the head and the back. We only sang for two pounds a side — it wasn't a great deal of money. In our matches we sing by both gas and daylight. He was a master-baker I sang against, but I forget his name. They do call him 'Holy Face," but that's a nick-name, because he's very much pock-marked. I wouldn't sell that bird at all for anythink; I've been offered ten pounds for it. Captain K—— put ten sovereigns down on the counter for him, and I wouldn't pick 'em up, for I've sold lots of his strain for a pound each.

" When I found I was a master of the birds, then I turned to my rat business again. I had a little rat dog — a black tan terrier of the name of Billy — which was the greatest stock dog in London of that day. He is the father of the greatest portion of the small black tan dogs in London now, which Mr. Isaac, the bird-fancier in Princes-street, purchased one of the strain for six or seven pounds; which Jimmy Massey afterwards purchased another of the strain, for a monkey, a bottle of wine, and three pounds. That was the rummest bargain I ever made.

" I've ris and trained monkeys by shoals. Some of mine is about now in shows exhibiting; one in particular — Jimmy.

" One of the strain of this little black tan dog would draw a badger twelve or fourteen lbs. to his six lbs., which was done for a wager, 'cos it was thought the badger had his teeth drawn, but he hadn't, as was proved by his biting Mr. P—— from Birmingham, for he took a piece clean out of his trousers, which was pretty good proof, and astonished them all in the room.

" I've been offered a sovereign a-pound for some of my little terriers, but it wouldn't pay me at that price, for they weren't heavier than two or three pounds. I once sold one of the dogs, of this same strain, for fourteen pounds, to the Austrian Ambassador. Mrs. H—— the banker's lady, wished to get my strain of terriers, and she give me five pounds for the use of him; in fact, my terrier dog was known to all the London fancy. As rat-killing dogs, there's no equal to that strain of black tan terriers.

" It's fifteen year ago since I first worked for Goverment. I found that the parks was much infested with rats, which had under-minded the bridges and gnawed the drains, and I made application to Mr. Westley, who was superintendent of the park, and he spoke of it, and then it was wrote to me that I was to fulfil the siterwation, and I was to have six pounds a-year. But after that it was altered, and I was to have so much a-head, which is threepence. After that, Newton, what was a warmint destroyer to her Majesty, dying, I wrote in to the Board of Hordnance, when they appointed me to each station in London—that was, to Regentsey-park-barracks, to the Knightsbridge and Portland-barracks, and to all the other barracks in the metropolis. I've got the letter now by me, in which they says ' they is proud to appint me.'

" I've taken thirty-two rats out of one hole in the islands in Regentsey-park, and found in it fish, birds, and loads of eggs—duck-eggs, and every kind.

" It must be fourteen year since I first went about the streets exhibiting with rats. I began with a cart and a'most a donkey; for it was a pony scarce bigger; but I've had three or four big horses since that, and ask anybody, and they'll tell you I'm noted for my cattle. I thought that by having a kind of costume, and the rats painted on the cart, and going round the country, I should get my name about, and get myself knowed; and so I did, for folks 'ud come to me, so that sometimes I've had four jobs of a-day, from people seeing my cart. I found I was quite the master of the rat, and could do pretty well what I liked with him; so I used to go round Finchley, Highgate, and all the sububs, and show myself, and how I handled the warmint.

" I used to wear a costume of white leather breeches, and a green coat and scarlet waist-kit, and a goold band round my hat, and a belt across my shoulder. I used to make a first-rate appearance, such as was becoming the uniform of the Queen's rat-ketcher.

" Lor' bless you! I've travell'd all over London, and I'll kill rats again anybody. I'm open to all the world for any sum, from one pound to fifty. I used to have my belts painted at first by Mr. Bailey, the animal painter—with four white rats; but the idea come into my head that I'd cast the rats in metal, just to make more appearance for the belt, to come out in the world. I was nights and days at it, and it give me a deal of bother. I could manage it no how; but by my own ingenuity and persewerance I succeeded. A man axed me a pound a-piece for casting the rats—that would ha' been four pound. I was very certain that my belt, being a handsome one, would help my business tremenjous in the sale of my composition. So I took a mould from a dead rat in plaster, and then I got some of my wife's sarsepans, and, by G—, I casted 'em with some of my own pewter-pots."

The wife, who was standing by, here exclaimed—

" Oh, my poor sarsepans! I remember 'em. There was scarce one left to cook our wittels with."

" Thousands of moulders," continued Jack Black, " used to come to see me do the casting of the rats, and they kept saying, ' You'll never do it, Jack.' The great difficulty, you see, was casting the heye—which is a black bead—into the metal.

" When the belt was done, I had a great success; for, bless you, I couldn't go a yard without a crowd after me.

" When I was out with the cart selling my composition, my usual method was this. I used to put a board across the top, and form a kind of counter. I always took with me a iron-wire cage—so big a one, that Mr. Barnet, a Jew, laid a wager that he could get into it, and he did. I used to form this cage at one end of the cart, and sell my composition at the other. There were rats painted round the cart—that was the only show I had about the wehicle. I used to take out the rats, and put them outside the cage; and used to begin the show by putting rats inside my shirt next my buzzum, or in my coat and breeches pockets, or on my shoulder —in fact, all about me, anywhere. The people would stand to see me take up rats without being bit. I never said much, but I used to handle the rats in every possible manner, letting 'em run up my arm, and stroking their backs and playing with 'em. Most of the people used to fancy they had been tamed on purpose, until they'd see me take fresh ones from the cage, and play with them in the same manner. I all this time kept on selling my composition, which my man Joe used to offer about; and whenever a packet was sold, I always tested its wirtues by killing a rat with it afore the people's own eyes.

" I once went to Tottenham to sell my composition, and to exhibit with my rats afore the country people. Some countrymen, which said they were rat-ketchers, came up to me whilst I was playing with some rats, and said —' Ugh, you're not a rat-ketcher; that's not the way to do it.' They were startled at seeing me selling the pison at such a rate, for the shilling packets was going uncommon well, sir. I said, ' No, I ain't a rat-ketcher, and don't know nothink about it. You come up and show me how to do it.' One of them come up on the cart, and put his hand in the cage, and curous enough he got three bites directly, and afore he could take his hands out they was nearly bit to ribands. My man Joe, says he, ' I tell you, if we ain't rat-ketchers, who is? We are the regular rat-ketchers; my master kills 'em, and then I eats 'em'—and he takes up a live one and puts its head into his mouth, and I puts my hand in the cage and pulls out six or seven in a cluster, and holds 'em up in the air, without even a bite. The countrymen bust out laughing; and they said, ' Well, you're the best we ever see.' I sold near 4*l.* worth of composition that day.

" Another day, when I'd been out flying pigeons as well—carriers, which I fancies to— I drove the cart, after selling the composition, to the King's Arms, Hanwell, and there was a feller there—a tailor by trade—what had turned rat-ketcher. He had got with him some fifty or sixty rats—the miserablest mangey brutes you ever seed in a tub—taking 'em up to London to sell. I, hearing of it, was determined to have a lark, so I goes up and takes out ten of them rats, and puts them inside my shirt, next my buzzum, and then I walks into the parlour and sits down, and begins drinking my ale as right as if nothink had happened. I scarce had seated myself, when the landlord —who was in the lay—says, ' I know a man who'll ketch rats quicker than anybody in the world.' This put the tailor chap up, so he offers to bet half-a-gallon of ale he would, and I takes him. He goes to the tub and brings out a very large rat, and walks with it into the room to show to the company. ' Well,' says I to the man, ' why I, who ain't a rat-ketcher, I've got a bigger one here,' and I pulls one out from my buzzum. ' And here's another, and another, and another,' says I, till I had placed the whole ten on the table. ' That's the way I ketch 'em,' says I,—' they comes of their own accord to me.' He tried to handle the warmints, but the poor fellow was bit, and his hands was soon bleeding fur'ously, and I without a mark. A gentleman as knowed me said, ' This must be the Queen's rat-ketcher, and that spilt the fun. The poor fellow seemed regular done up, and said, ' I shall give up rat-ketching, you've beat me! Here I've been travelling with rats all my life, and I never see such a thing afore.'

" When I've been in a mind for travelling I've never sold less than ten shillings' worth of my composition, and I've many a time sold five pounds' worth. Ten shillings' worth was the least I ever sold. During my younger career, if I'd had a backer, I might, one week with another, have made my clear three pounds a-week, after paying all my expenses and feeding my horse and all.

" I challenge my composition, and sell the art of rat-destroying, against any chemical rat-destroyer in the world, for any sum—I don't care what it is. Let anybody, either a medical or druggist manufacturer of composition, come and test with rats again me, and they'll pretty soon find it out. People pay for composition instead of employing the Queen's rat-ketcher, what kills the warmint and lays down his composition for nothink into the bargain likewise.

" I also destroy black beedles with a composition which I always keep with me again it's wanted. I often have to destroy the beedles in wine-cellars, which gnaw the paper off the bottles, such as is round the champagne and French wine bottles. I've killed lots of beedles too for bakers. I've also sterminated some thousands of beedles for linen-drapers and pork-sassage shops. There's two kinds of beedles, the hard-shell and the soft-shell beedle. The hard-shell one is the worst, and that will gnaw cork, paper, and anythink woollen. The soft-shell'd one will gnaw bread or food, and it also lays its eggs in the food, which is dreadful nasty.

" There's the house ant too, which there is some thousands of people as never saw—I sterminate them as well. There's a Mrs. B. at the William the Fourth public-house, Hampstead; she couldn't lay her child's clothes down without getting 'em full of ants. They've got a sting something in feel like a horse-fly's, and is more annoying than dangerous. It's cockroaches that are found in houses. They're dreadful nasty things, and will bite, and they are equal to the Spanish flies for blistering. I've tried all insects on my flesh to see how they bite me. Cockroaches will undermine similar to the ant, and loosen the bricks the same as the cricket. It's astonishing how so small an insect as them will scrape away such a quantity of mortar as they do—which thing infests grates, floorings, and such-like.

" The beedle is a most 'strordinary thing, which will puzzle most people to sterminate, for they lays sitch a lot of eggs as I would never guarantee to do away with beedles—only to keep them clear; for if you kills the old ones the eggs will rewive, and young ones come out of the wainskitting and sitch-like, and then your employers will say, ' Why you were paid for sterminating, and yet here they are.'

" One night in August— the night of a very heavy storm, which, maybe, you may remember, sir—I was sent for by a medical gent as lived opposite the Load of Hay, Hampstead, whose two children had been attacked by rats while they was sleeping in their little cots. I traced the blood, which had left lines from their tails, through the openings in the lath and plaster, which I follered to where my ferruts come out of, and they must have come up from the bottom of the house to the attics. The rats gnawed the hands and feet of the little children. The lady heard them crying, and got out of her bed and called to the servant to know what the child was making such a noise for, when they struck a light, and then they see the rats running away to the holes; their little night-gownds was kivered with blood, as if their throats had been cut. I asked the lady to give me one of the night-gownds to keep as a cur'osity, for I considered it a *phee-nomenon*, and she give it to me, but I never was so vexed in all my life as when I was told the next day that a maid had washed it. I went down the next morning and sterminated them rats. I found they was of the specie of rat which we term the blood-rat, which is a dreadful spiteful feller—a snake-headed rat, and infests the dwellings. There may have been some dozens of 'em altogether, but it's so long ago I a'most forget how many I took in that house. The gent behaved uncommon handsome, and said, ' Mr. Black, I can never pay you for this;' and ever arterwards, when I used to pass by that there house, the little dears when they see me used to call out to their mamma, ' O, here's Mr. Ratty, ma !' They were very pretty little fine children— uncommon handsome, to be sure.

" I once went to Mr. Hollins's, in Edward-street Regent's-park—a cow-keeper he was— where he was so infested that the cows could not lay down or eat their food, for the rats used to go into the manger, and fight at 'em. Mr. Hollins said to me, 'Black, what shall I give you to get rid of them rats?' and I said to him, says I, 'Well, Mr. Hollins, you're a poor man, and I leave it to you.' (He's got awful rich since then.) I went to work, and I actually took out 300 rats from one hole in the wall, which I had to carry them in my mouth and hands, and under my arms, and in my buzzum and pockets, to take them to the cage. I was bit dreadful by them, and suffered greatly by the bites; but nothink to lay up for, though very painful to the hands. To pervent the rats from getting out of the hole, I had to stop it up by putting my breast again it, and then they was jumping up again me and gnawing at my waistkit. I should think I sterminated 500 from them premises. Ah! I did wonders round there, and everybody was talking of my feats.

"I'll tell you about another cow-keeper's, which Mr. Hollins was so gratified with my skill what I had done, that he pays me handsome and generous, and gives me a recommendation to Mrs. Brown's, of Camden-town, and there I sterminated above 700 rats; and I was a-near being killed, for I was stooping down under the manger, when a cow heerd the rats squeak, and she butts at me and sends me up again the bull. The bull was very savage, and I fainted; but I was picked up and washed, and then I come to.

"Whilst doing that job at Mrs. Brown's I had to lie down on the ground, and push my naked arm into the hole till I could reach the rats as I'd driven up in the corner, and then pull them out with my hand. I was dreadful bit, for I was obleeged to handle them anyhow; my flesh was cut to ribands and dreadful lacerated.

"There was a man Mrs. Brown had got of the name of John, and he wouldn't believe about the rats, and half thought I brought 'em with me. So I showed him how to ketch rats.

"You see rats have always got a main run, and from it go the branch runs on each side like on a herring-bone, and at the end of the branch runs is the bolt-holes, for coming in and out at. I instantly stopped up all the bolt-holes and worked the rats down to the end of the main run, then I broke up the branch runs and stopped the rats getting back, and then, when I'd got 'em all together at the end of the main run, I put my arm down and lifted them up. I have had at times to put half my body into a hole and thrust down my arm just like getting rabbits out of their burrers.

"Sometimes I have to go myself into the holes, for the rats make such big ones, there's plenty of room. There was a Mrs. Perry in Albany-street, that kept an oil and coke shop —she were infested with rats dreadful. Three of her shop-boys had been sent away on suspicion of stealing fat, instead of which it was the rats, for between the walls and the vault I found a hundred and a half of fat stowed away. The rats was very savage, and I should think there was 200 of them. I made a good bit of money by that job, for Mrs. Perry give the fat to me.

"I have had some good finds at times, rat-hunting. I found under one floor in a gent's house a great quantity of table napkins and silver spoons and forks, which the rats had carried away for the grease on 'em — shoes and boots gnawed to pieces, shifts, aprons, gownds, pieces of silk, and I don't know what not. Sarvants had been discharged accused of stealing them there things. Of course I had to give them up; but there they was.

"I was once induced to go to a mews in Tavistock-place, near Russell-square, which was reg'lar infested by rats. They had sent to a man before, and he couldn't do nothink with 'em, but I soon sterminated them. The rats there had worried a pair of beautiful chestnut horses, by gnawing away their hoofs and nearly driving them mad, which I saw myself, and there was all their teeth-marks, for I could scarcely believe it myself till I see it. I found them near a cart-load of common bricks, under the floor, and near the partition of the stable, which, when the men pulled the wood-work down, the coachman, says he, 'Well, rat-ketcher, if you'd been employed years ago a deal more corn would have gone into the horses.'

"This coachman give me a recommendato to a muffin-maker in Hanway-yard, and I went there and killed the rats. But a most sing'lar thing took place there; my ferret got away and run through into a house in Oxford-street kept by a linen-draper, for the young men come to say that the rat-ketcher's ferret was in their shop, and had bit one of their lady customers. I worked the ferrut through three times to make sure of this; and each time my little dog told me it was true. You see a well-trained dog will watch and stand and point to the ferrut working under ground just as a pinter does to game; and although he's above ground, yet he'll track the ferret through the runs underneath by the smell. If the ferrut is lost — which I tell by the dog being uneasy —I say to the dog, 'Hi, lost;' and then he instantly goes on scent, and smells about in every direction, and I follers him, till he stands exactly over the spot where it may be, and then I have either to rise a stone or lift a board to get him out.

"I've ratted for years for Mr. Hodges, of Hodges and Lowman's, in Regent-street; and he once said to me, that he was infested dreadful with rats at the house, which he took for the children, at Hampstead; so I went there, and witnessed, certainly, the most cur'ous circumstance, which puzzles me to this day. I had to lay on my belly half in the hole and pull out the rats; and, on looking at them, as I brings them up, I am astonished to find that nearly every one of them is blind, and has a speck in the eye. I was never so much astonished in my life, for they was as a wall-eyed dog might be. I supposed it to be from lightning (I couldn't account for it no other ways), for at that time there was very heavy lightning and floods up there, which maybe you might remember, sir. They was chiefly of the blood-rat specie — small snake-headed rats, with a big, fine tail. They was very savage with me, and I had them run all over me before I ketched them.

"Rats are everywhere about London, both in rich and poor places. I've ketched rats in 44 Portland-place, at a clergyman's house there. There was 200 and odd. They had underminded the oven so, that they could neither bile nor bake; they had under-pinioned the stables, and let every stone down throughout the premises, pretty well. I had to crawl under a big leaden cistern which the rats had under-pinioned, and I expected it would come down upon me every minute. I had one little ferrut kill thirty-two rats under one stone, and I lifted the dead ones up in the presence of the cook and the butler. He didn't behave well to me — the gent didn't — for I had to go to my lawyer's afore I could get paid, and after the use of my skill; and I had to tell the lawyer I'd pawn my bed to stick to him and get my earnings; but, after all, I had to take one-third less than my bill. This, thinks I, isn't the right thing for Portland-place.

"Rats will eat each other like rabbits, which I've watched them, and seen them turn the dead one's skins out like pusses, and eat the flesh off beautiful clean. I've got cages of iron-wire, which I made myself, which will hold 1000 rats at a time, and I've had these cages piled up with rats, solid like. No one would ever believe it; to look at a quantity of rats, and see how they will fight and tear one another about, — it's astonishing, so it is! I never found any rats smothered, by putting them in a cage so full; but if you don't feed them every day, they'll fight and eat one another — they will, like cannibals.

"I general contracts with my customers, by the year, or month, or job. There's some gents I've worked for these fifteen years — sitch as Mr. Robson, the coach-builder, Mivart's Hotel, Shoulbreds', Mr. Lloyds, the large tobacconist, the Commercial Life Assurance, Lord Duncannon's, and I can't recollect how many more. My terms is from one guinea to five pounds per annum, according to the premises. Besides this, I have all the rats that I ketch, and they sell for threepence each. But I've done my work too well, and wherever I went I've cleared the rats right out, and so my customers have fell off. I have got the best testimonials of any man in London, and I could get a hatful more to-morrer. Ask anybody I've worked for, and they'll tell you about Jack Black.

"One night I had two hundred rats in a cage, placed in my sitting-room, and a gent's dog happened to get at the cage, and undid the door, snuffing about, and let 'em all loose. Directly I come in I knew they was loose by the smell. I had to go on my knees and stomach under the beds and sofas, and all over the house, and before twelve o'clock that night I had got 'em all back again into the cage, and sold them after for a match. I was so fearful they'd get gnawing the children, having sterminated them in a house where children had been gnawed.

"I've turned my attention to everything connected with animals. I've got the best composition for curing the mange in a horse or a dog, which has reg'lar astonished medical gents. I've also been bit by a mad dog — a black retriever dog, that died raving mad in a cellar afterwards. The only thing I did was, I washed the wound with salt and water, and used a turpentine poultice."

Mrs. Black here interposed, exclaiming, —

"O dear me! the salt and water he's had to his flesh, it ought to be as hard as iron. I've seen him put lumps of salt into his wounds."

Mr. Black then continued:—

"I never had any uneasiness from that bite of a mad dog; indeed, I never troubled myself about it, or even thought of it.

"I've caught some other things besides rats in my time. One night, I saw a little South African cat going along the New-road. I thought it was a cur'ous specie of rat, and chased it, and brought it home with me; but it proved to belong to Mr. Herring's menagerie in the New-road, so I let him have it back again.

"Another time I met with two racoons, which I found could handle me just as well as I could handle a rat, for they did bite and scratch awful. I put 'em in the cart, and brought them home in a basket. I never found out to whom *they* belonged. I got them in Ratcliffe-highway, and no doubt some sailors had brought them over, and got drunk, and let 'em loose. I tried them at killing rats, but they weren't no good at that.

"I've learnt a monkey to kill rats, but he wouldn't do much, and only give them a good shaking when they bit him. After I found the racoons no good, I trained a badger to kill rats, and he was superior to any dog, but very difficult in training to get him to kill, though they'll kill rabbits fast enough, or any other kind of game, for they're rare poachers are badgers. I used to call her Polly. She killed in my own pit, for I used to obleege my friends that wouldn't believe it possible with the sight. She won several matches — the largest was in a hundred match.

"I also sterminate moles for her Majesty, and the Woods and Forests, and I've sterminated some hundreds for different farmers in the country. It's a cur'ous thing, but a mole will kill a rat and eat it afterwards, and two moles will fight wonderful. They've got a mouth exactly like a shark, and teeth like saws; ah, a wonderful saw mouth. They're a very sharp-biting little animal, and very painful. A rat is frightened of one, and don't like fighting them at all.

"I've bred the finest collection of pied rats which has ever been knowed in the world. I had above eleven hundred of them—all wariegated rats, and of a different specie and colour, and all of them in the first instance bred from the Norwegian and the white rat, and afterwards crossed with other specie.

"I have ris some of the largest tailed rats ever seen. I've sent them to all parts of the globe, and near every town in England. When I sold 'em off, three hundred of them went to France. I ketched the first white rat I had at Hampstead; and the black ones at Messrs. Hodges and Lowman's, in Regent-street, and them I bred in. I have 'em fawn and white, black and white, brown and white, red and white, blue-black and white, black-white and red.

"People come from all parts of London to see them rats, and I supplied near all the 'happy families' with them. Burke, who had the 'happy family' showing about London, has had hundreds from me. They got very tame, and you could do anythink with them. I've sold many to ladies for keeping in squirrel cages. Years ago I sold 'em for five and ten shillings a-piece, but towards the end of my breeding them, I let 'em go for two-and-six. At a shop in Leicester-square, where Cantello's hatching-eggs machine was, I sold a sow and six young ones for ten shillings, which formerly I have had five pounds for, being so docile, like a sow sucking her pigs."

THE SEWERMAN.

HE is a broad-shouldered, strongly-built man, with a stoop in his shoulders, and a rather dull cast of features; from living so much in the "shores" (sewers), his eyes have assumed a *peering* kind of look, that is quite rat-like in its furtiveness.

He answered our questions with great good humour, but in short monosyllabic terms, peculiar to men who have little communion with their fellows.

The "parlour" in which the man lives was literally swarming with children when we paid him a visit (they were not all "belonging" to him). Nor was it quite pleasant to find that the smell of the tea, which had just been made, was overpowered by the odour of the rats which he keeps in the same room.

The week's wash was hanging across the apartment, and gave rather a slovenly aspect to the room, not otherwise peculiar for its untidyness; against the wall were pasted some children's "characters," which his second son, who is at the coal-shed, has a taste for, and which, as the "shoreman" observed, "is better than sweet-stuff for him, at all events."

A little terrier was jumping playfully about the room, a much more acceptable companion than the bull-dog whose acquaintance we had been invited to make (in the same court) by the "rat-killer."

The furniture and appointments of the "parlour" were extremely humble—not to say meagre in their character. After some trouble in getting sufficiently lucid answers, the following was the result:—

"There are not so many rats about as there used to be—not a five-hundredth part so many. I've seen long ago twenty or thirty in a row near where the slaughter-houses are, and that like. I ketch them all down the shores. I run after them and pick them up with my hand, and I take my lantern with me.

"I have caught rats these six or seven years. When the money got to be lowered, I took to ketching on them. One time I used to take a dog with me, when I worked down St. John's-wood way.

"They fetches all prices, does rats; some I get threepence a-piece for, some twopence, some twopence-halfpenny—'cordin' who has 'em.

"I works on the shores, and our time to leave off is four. I comes home and gets my tea, and if there's sale for them, why I goes out and ketches a few rats. When I goes out I can ketch a dozen; but, years ago, I could ketch two or three dozen without going so far, and that shows there's not so many now about.

"I finds some difficulty in ketching on them. If they gets into the drain you can't get 'em. Where the drains lay low to the shore it's most difficult, but where the drain is about two feet and a-half from the shore you gets a better chance.

"Three or four dozen I used to ketch, but I haven't ketched any this last two or three weeks. In this hot weather people don't like to be in a room where 'killing' is going on; but in the winter time a man will have his pint of beer and see a little sport that way. Three or four year ago I did ketch a good many; there was a sale for 'em. I could go and ketch two dozen in three hours, and that sooner than I can do a dozen now. It's varmint as wants to be destroyed.

"Rats'll turn round when they finds theirselves beat, and sometimes fly at your hand. Sometimes I've got bit—not very badly, though. To tell the truth, I don't like it. When they grip, they do holt so tight before they'll let go.

"I've been a shoreman these fifteen or sixteen year, ever since this flushing commenced. I was put on by the Commissioners in Hatting Garding; but the Commissioners is all done away with since Government took to it. I'm employed by the parish now. Every parish has to do its own flushing.

"We cleanses away all the soil what's down

below, and keeps the shore as sweet as what we possibly can.

"Before I took to this life I was what they call a navvy; I used to help to *make* the shores, and before that, I was in the country at farmers' work.

"Ketching them rats ain't all profit, 'cause you have to keep 'em and feed 'em. I've some here, if I was to get sixpence a-piece for, why it wouldn't pay me for their feed. I give them barley generally, and bits of bread.

"There's a many about now ketchin' who does nothink else, and who goes down in the shores when they have no business there at all. They does well by rats when they've good call for 'em. They can go down two or three times a-day, and ketch a dozen and a half a time; but they can't do much now, there's no killing going on. They takes 'em to beer-shops, and sells 'em to the landlords, who gets their own price for 'em if there's a pit.

"Time ago you couldn't get a rat under sixpence. But the tax on dogs has done away wonderful with rat-killing. London would swarm with rats if they hadn't been ketched as they has been. I can go along shores and only see one or two now, sometimes see none. Times ago I've drove away twenty or thirty afore me. Round Newport-market I've seen a hundred together, and now I go round there and perhaps won't ketch one.

"As for poisonin' 'em under buildings, that's wrong; they're sure to lay there and rot, and then they smells so. No, pisoning a'n't no good, specially where there's many on 'em.

"I've sold Jack Black a good many. He don't ketch so many as he gets killed. He's what they call rat-ketcher to her Majesty.

"When I goes rat-ketching, I generally takes a bag with me; a trap is too much to lug about.

"Some parts of the shores I can find my way about better than I can up above. I could get in nigh here and come out at High Park; only the worst of it is, you're always on the stoop. I never heerd talk of anybody losing theirselves in the shores, but a stranger might.

"There's some what we calls 'gully-hunters' as goes about with a sieve, and near the gratings find perhaps a few ha'pence. Years ago we used to find a little now and then, but we may go about now and not find twopence in a week. I don't think any shoreman ever finds much. But years ago, in the city, perhaps a robbery might be committed, and then they might be afraid of being found out, and chuck the things down the drains.

"I come from Oxfordshire, about four miles from Henley-'pon-Thames. I haven't got now quite so many clods to tramp over, nor so many hills to climb.

"I gets two shillings a-dozen if I sells the rats to a dealer, but if I takes 'em to the pit myself I gets three shillings. Rats has come down lately. There's more pits, and they kills 'em cheaper; they used to kill 'em at six shillings a-dozen.

"I've got five children. These here are not all belonging to me. Their mother's gone out a-nussing, and my wife's got to mind 'em.

"My oldest son is sixteen. He's off for a sailor. I had him on me for two years doin' nothink. He couldn't get a place, and towards the last he didn't care about it. He *would* go to sea; so he went to the Marine School, and now he's in the East Ingy Sarvice. My second is at a coal-shed. He gets three shillings a-week; but, Lord, what's that? He eats more than that, let alone clothes, and he wears out such a lot of shoe-leather. There's a good deal of wear and tear, I can tell yer, in carrying out coals and such-like."

THE PENNY MOUSE-TRAP MAKER.

THIS man lived in a small cottage at the back of Bethnal Green-road, and the little railed space in front of the humble dwelling was littered with sundry evidences of the inmate's ingenuity. Here was a mechanical carriage the crippled father had made to drive himself along, and a large thaumatrope, or disc of painted figures, that seemed to move while revolving rapidly before the eye; and this, I afterwards learnt, the ingenious cripple had made, as a street exhibition, for a poor man, whom he was anxious to put in the way of doing something for himself.

The principal apartment in the little two-roomed house was blocked up with carpenters' benches, and long planks were resting against the wall, while the walls themselves were partly covered with tools and patterns of the craft pursued; and in one corner there were heaps of the penny mouse-traps and penny money-boxes, that formed the main articles of manufacture.

In a little room adjoining this, and about the size of a hen-house, I found the cripple himself in bed, but still sitting up with a small desk-like bench before him, and engaged in the act of cutting and arranging the wires for the little wooden traps in which he dealt. And as I sat by his bedside he told me the following story:—

"I am," he said, "a white-wood toy-maker, in a small way; that is, I make a variety of cheap articles,—nothing beyond a penny,—in sawed and planed pine-wood. I manufacture penny and halfpenny money-boxes, penny and halfpenny toy bellows, penny carts, penny garden-rollers, penny and halfpenny dolls' tables and washhand-stands, chiefly for baby-houses; penny dressers, with drawers, for the same purpose; penny wheelbarrows and bedsteads; penny crossbows; and the mouse-trap that I am about now. I make all the things I have named for warehouses—for what are called the cheap Birmingham and Sheffield houses. I am paid the same price for whatever I make, with the exception of the mouse-trap. For the principal part of the penny articles that I make I get 7s. for twelve dozen, that is 7d. a-dozen; and for the halfpenny articles I get 3s. 6d., at the rate of 3½d. a-dozen. For the penny mouse-traps, however, I am paid only 1l. for thirty-six dozen, and that's a shilling less than I get for the same quantity of the other shilling articles; whilst for the penny boxes I'm paid only at the rate of a halfpenny each.

"You will please to look at that, sir," he said, handing me his account-book with one of his employers for the last year; "you will see there that what I am saying is perfectly correct, for there is the price put to every article; and it is but right that you should have proof that what I'm a-telling you is the truth. I took of one master, for penny mouse-traps alone, you perceive, 36l. 10s. from January to December, 1849; but that is not all gain, you'll understand. Out of that I have to pay above one half for material. I think, altogether, my receipts of the different masters I worked for last year came to about 120l.—I can't lay my hands on the bills just now.— Yes, it's about 120l. I know, for our income,— that is, my clear gains is about 1l. to 1l. 5s. every week. So, calculating more than one half what I take to go for the expense for material, that will bring it to just about to what I state. To earn the 25s. a-week, you'll understand, there are four of us engaged,—myself, my wife, my daughter, and son. My daughter is eighteen, and my son eleven : that is my boy, sir; he's reading the *Family Friend* just now. It's a little work I take in for my girl, for her future benefit. My girl is as fond of reading as I am, and always was. My boy goes to school every evening, and twice on a Sunday. I am willing that they should find as much pleasure from reading as I have in my illness. I found books often lull my pain. Yes, I have, indeed, for many hours. For nine months I couldn't handle a tool; and my only comfort was the love of my family, and my books. I can't afford them now, for I have no wish to incur any extraneous expense, while the weight of the labour lies on my family more than it does on myself. Over and over again, when I have been in acute pain with my thigh, a scientific book, or a work on history, or a volume of travels, would carry my thoughts far away, and I should be happy in all my misery—hardly conscious that I had a trouble, a care, or a pang to vex me. I always had love of solid works. For an hour's light reading, I have often turned to a work of imagination, such as Milton's *Paradise Lost*, and Shakspeare's Plays; but I prefer science to poetry. I think every working man ought to be acquainted with general science. If he is a mechanic—let his station be ever so simple,—he will be sure to find the

benefit of it. It gives a man a greater insight into the world and creation, and it makes his labour a pleasure and a pride to him, when he can work with his head as well as his hands. I think I have made, altogether, about one hundred and six gross of mouse-traps for the master whose account I have given you, and as many more for other employers, in the course of the last year. I calculate that I made more than thirty thousand mouse-traps from January to December, 1849. There are three or four other people in London making penny mouse-traps, besides myself. I reckon they may make among them near upon half as many as I do ; and that would give about forty-five or fifty thousand penny mouse-traps made in London in the course of the year. I myself brought out the penny mouse-trap in its improved shape, and with the improved lever spring. I have no calculations as to the number of mice in the country, or how soon we should have caught them if we go on at this rate; but I think my traps have to do with that. They are bought more for toys than for use, though they are good for mice as well as children; and though we have so many dozen mouse-traps about the house, I can assure you we are more troubled with mice here than most people. The four of us here can make twenty-four dozen traps in the day, but that is all we can get through comfortable. For eighteen dozen we get about 10s. at the warehouse, and out of that I reckon our clear gains are near upon 4s., or a little less than 1s. a head. Take one with the other, we can earn about a penny an hour; and if it wasn't for me having been a tailor originally, and applying some of my old tools to the business, we shouldn't get on so quick as we do. With my shears I can cut twenty-four wires at a time, and with my thimble I thread the wires through the holes in the sides. I make the springs, cut the wires, and put them in the traps. My daughter planes the wood and gauges out the sides and bottom, bores the wire-holes and makes the door as well. My wife nails the frames ready for wiring, and my son fixes the wires in their places when I have entered them; then the wife springs them, after which the daughter puts in the doors and so completes them. I can't form an idea as to how many penny and halfpenny money-boxes I made last year. I might have made, altogether, eight thousand, or five thousand halfpenny and three thousand penny ones. I was originally brought up to the tailoring business, but my master failed, and my sight kept growing weaker every year; so, as I found a good deal of trouble in getting employment at my own trade, I thought I would take to the bird-cage making—I had been doing a little at it before, as a pastime. I was fond of birds, and fonder still of mechanics, so I was always practising my hands at some craft or other in my over-time. I used to make dissected maps and puzzles, and so, when standing for employment, I managed to get through the slack of the year. I think it is solely due to my taste for mechanics and my love of reading scientific books that I am able to live so comfortably as I do in my affliction. After I took to bird-cage making, I found the employment at it so casual that I could not support my family at it. This led my mind to toy making, for I found that cheap toys were articles of more general sale. Then I got my children and my wife to help me, and we managed to get along somehow, for you see they were learning the business, and I myself was not in much of a condition to teach them, being almost as inexperienced at the trade as they were; and, besides that, we were continually changing the description of toy that we manufactured, so we had no time to perfect ourselves. One day we were all at work at garden-rollers; the next, perhaps, we should be upon little carts; then, may-be, we should have to go to dolls' tables or wheel-barrows: so that, with the continual changing the description of toy that we manufactured from one thing to another, we had a great difficulty in getting practised in anything. While we were all learning you may imagine that, not being so quick then as we are now, we found a great difficulty in making a living at the penny-toy business: often we had merely dry bread for breakfast, tea, and supper, but we ate it with a light heart, for I knew repining wouldn't mend it, and I always taught myself and those about me to bear our trials with fortitude. At last I got to work regularly at the mouse-traps, and having less changing we learnt to turn them out of hand quicker, and to make more money at the business : that was about four years ago, and then I was laid up with a strumous abscess in the thigh. This caused necrosis, or decay of the thigh-bone, to take place, and it was necessary that I should be confined to my bed until such time as a new thigh-bone was formed, and the old decayed one had sloughed away. Before I lay up I stood at the bench until I was ready to drop, for I had no one who could plane the boards for me; and what could I do? If I didn't keep up, I thought we should all starve. The pain was dreadful, and the anxiety of mind I suffered for my wife and children made it a thousand times worse. I couldn't bear the idea of going to the workhouse, and I kept on my feet until I couldn't stand no longer. My daughter was only sixteen then, and I saw no means of escape. It was at that time my office to prepare the boards for my family, and without that they could do nothing. Well, sir, I saw utter ruin and starvation before us. The doctor told me it would take four years before a new bone would be formed, and that I must lay up all the while. What was to become of us all in the mean time I could not tell. Then it was that my daughter, seeing the pain I suffered both in body and mind, came to me, and told me not to grieve, for that she would do all the heavy work for me, and

plane up the boards and cut out the work as I had done; but I thought it impossible for her to get through such hard work, even for my sake. I knew she could do almost any-thing that she set her mind to, but I little dreamt that she would be able to compass that. However, with the instinct of her affection—I can't call it anything else (for she learnt at once what it had taken me months to acquire), she planed and shaped the boards as well as I myself could have done after years of practice. The first board she did was as cleanly done as she can do it now, and when you think of the difficulties she had to overcome, what a mere child she was, and that she had never handled a plane before, how she had the grain of the wood to find out, to learn the right handling of her tools, and a many little niceties of touch that workmen only can understand, it does seem to me as if some superior Power had inspired her to aid me. I have often heard of birds building their nests of the most beautiful structure, without ever having seen one built before, and my daughter's handiwork seemed to me exactly like that. It was a thing not learnt by practice, but done in an instant, without teaching or experience of any kind. She is the best creature I ever knew or ever heard tell of on earth—at least, so she has been to me all her life; aye, without a single exception. If it hadn't been for her devotion I must have gone to the workhouse, and perhaps never been able to have got away from it, and had my children brought up as paupers. Where she got the strength to do it is as much a mystery to me as how she did it. Though she was but a mere child, so to speak, she did the work of a grown man, and I assure you the labour of working at the bench all day is heavy, even for the strongest workman, and my girl is not over-strong now; indeed she was always delicate from a baby: nevertheless she went through the labour, and would stand to the bench the whole of the day, and with such cheerful good humour too that I cannot but see the hand of the Almighty in it all. I never knew her to complain of fatigue, or ever go to her work without a smile on her face. Her only anxiety was to get done, and to afford me every comfort in my affliction that she could. For three years and two months now have I been confined to my bed, and for two years and a half of that time I have not left it, even to breathe the fresh open air. Almost all that period I have been suffering intense and continued pain from the formation of abscesses in my thigh previous to the slough-ing away of the decayed bones. I have taken out of the sores at least two hundred pieces, some as small as needles and some not less than an inch and a half long, which required to be pulled out with tweezers from the wound. Often, when I was getting a bit better and able to go about in the cart you see there outside, with the gravel in it—(I made that on this bed here, so as to be able to move about on it ; the two front wheels I made myself, and the two back were old ones that I repaired here. I made the whole of the body, and my daughter planed up the boards for me)—well, often when I could just get along in that, have I gone about with a large piece of decayed bone projecting through my thigh, in hopes that the jolting would force it through the wound. The pain before the bone came away was often intense, especially when it had to work its way through the thick of the muscle. Night after night have I laid awake here. I didn't wish, of course, to distress the minds of my family any more than I could help. It would not have been fair; so I bore all with patience, and since I have been here I have got through a great deal of work in my little way. In bed, as I sit with my little bench, I do my share of eight dozen of these penny traps a-day. Last August I made a 'thaumatrope' for a young man that I had known since a lad of twelve years of age; he got off work and couldn't find anything to turn his hand to, so I advised him to get up an exhibition: anything was better than starving. He had a wife and two children, and I can't bear to see any one want, let alone the young ones; and so, cripple as I was, I set to work here in my bed and made him a large set of magic circles. I painted all the figures myself in this place, though I had never handled a brush before, and that has kept him in bread up to this time. I did it to cause him to exert himself, but now he has got a situation, and is doing middling to what he has been: there's one thing though, a little money, with care, will go farther than a great deal without it. I shall never be able to get about as I used, for you see the knee is set stiff and the thigh-bone is arched with the hip, so that the one leg is three inches shorter than the other. The bone broke spontaneously, like a bit of rotten wood, the other day, while I was rubbing my hand down my thigh, and in growing together again it got out of straight. I am just able to stir about now with a crutch and stick. I can sometimes treat myself to a walk about the house and yard, but that is not often, and last Saturday night I *did* make a struggle to get out in the Bethnal Green-road, and there, as I was coming along, my stick tripped against a stone and I fell. If it hadn't been for my crutch throwing me forward, I might have fallen on my new bone and broken it again. But as it was, the crutch threw me forward and saved me. My doctor tells me my new bone would bear a blow, but I shouldn't like to try after all I have gone through. I shall not be about again till I get my carriage done, and that I intend to construct so as to drive it with one hand, by means of a new ratchet lever motion."

The daughter of the toy-maker, with whom I spoke afterwards, and who was rather "good-looking," in the literal sense of the word, than beautiful, said that she could not describe how it was that she had learnt to plane and gauge the boards. It seemed to come to her all of a sudden—quite natural-like, she told me; though, she added, it was most likely her affection for her poor father that made her take to it so quick. "I felt it deeply" she said, "to see him take to his bed, and knew that I alone could save him from the workhouse. No! I never felt tired over the work," she continued, in answer to my questions, "because I know that it is to make him comfortable."

I should add, that I was first taken to this man by the surgeon who attended him during his long suffering, and that gentleman not only fully corroborated all I heard from his ingenious and heroic patient, but spoke in the highest possible terms of both father and daughter.

FLIES.

THESE winged tormentors are not, like most of our apterous enemies, calculated to excite disgust and nausea when we see or speak of them; nor do they usually steal upon us during the silent hours of repose (though the gnat or mosquito must be here excepted), but are many of them very beautiful, and boldly make their attack upon us in open day, when we are best able to defend ourselves.

The active fly, so frequently an unbidden guest at your table (Mouffet, 56), whose delicate palate selects your choicest viands, at one time extending his proboscis to the margin of a drop of wine, and then gaily flying to take a more solid repast from a pear or a peach— now gambolling with his comrades in the air, now gracefully carrying his furled wings with his taper feet—was but the other day a disgusting grub, without wings, without legs, without eyes, wallowing, well pleased, in the midst of a mass of excrement.

"The common house-fly," says Kirby, "is with us sufficiently annoying at the close of summer, so as to have led the celebrated Italian Ugo Foscolo, when residing here, to call it one of the 'three miseries of life.'" But we know nothing of it as a tormentor, compared with the inhabitants of southern Europe, "I met," says Arthur Young, in his interesting *Travels through France*, between Pradelles and Thurytz, "mulberries and flies at the same time. By the term *flies*, I mean those myriads of them which form the most disagreeable circumstances of the southern climates. They are the first torments in Spain, Italy, and the olive district of France; it is not that they bite, sting, or hurt, but they buzz, teaze, and worry; your mouth, eyes, ears, and nose are full of them: they swarm on every eatable—fruit, sugar, everything is attacked by them in such myriads, that if they are not incessantly driven away by a person who has nothing else to do, to eat a meal is impossible. They are, however, caught on prepared paper, and other contrivances, with so much ease and in such quantities, that were it not for negligence they could not abound in such incredible quantities. If I farmed in these countries, I should manure four or five acres every year with dead flies. I have been much surprised that the learned Mr. Harmer should think it odd to find, by writers who treated of southern climates, that driving away flies was of importance. Had he been with me in Spain and in Languedoc in July and August, he would have been very far from thinking there was anything odd in it."—(*Young's Travels in France*, i. 298.)

It is a remarkable, and, as yet, unexplained fact, that if nets of thread or string, with meshes a full inch square, be stretched over the open windows of a room in summer or autumn, when flies are the greatest nuisance, not a single one will venture to enter from without; so that by this simple plan, a house may be kept free from these pests, while the adjoining ones which have not had nets applied to their windows will swarm with them. In order, however, that the protection should be efficient, it is necessary that the rooms to which it is applied should have the light enter by *one side* only; for in those which have a thorough light, the flies, strange to say, pass through the meshes without scruple.

For a fuller account of these singular facts, the reader is referred to a paper by W. Spence, in *Trans. Ent. Soc.* vol. i. p. 1, and also to one in the same work by the Rev. E. Stanley, late Lord Bishop of Norwich, who, having made some of the experiments suggested by Mr. Spence, found that by extending over the outside of his windows nets of a very fine pack-thread, with meshes one inch and a quarter to the square, so fine and comparatively invisible that there was no apparent diminution either of light or the distant view, he was enabled for the remainder of the summer and autumn to enjoy the fresh air with open windows, without the annoyance he had previously experienced from the intrusion of flies—often so troublesome that he was obliged on the hottest days to forego the luxury of admitting the air by even partially raising the sashes.

"But no sooner," he observes, "had I set my nets than I was relieved from my disagreeable visitors. I could perceive and hear them hovering on the other side of my barriers; but though they now and then settled on the meshes, I do not recollect a single instance of one venturing to cross the boundary."

"The number of house-flies," he adds, "might be greatly lessened in large towns, if the stable-dung in which their larvæ are chiefly supposed to feed were kept in pits closed by trap-doors, so that the females could not deposit their eggs in it. At Venice, where no horses are kept, it is said there are no house-flies; a statement which I regret not having heard before being there, that I might have inquired as to its truth."—(*Kirby and Spence's Entom.* i. 102, 3.)

This short account of flies would be incomplete without a description of their mode of proceeding when they regale themselves upon a piece of loaf-sugar, and an account of the apparatus with which the Creator has furnished them in order to enable them to walk on bodies possessing smooth surfaces, and in any position.

"It is a remark* which will be found to hold good, both in animals and vegetables, that no important motion or feeling can take place without the presence of moisture. In man, the part of the eye which is the seat of vision is always bedewed with moisture; the skin is softened with a delicate oil; the sensitive part of the ear is filled with a liquid; but moisture is still more abundant in our organs of taste and smell than in any of the other senses. In the case of taste, moisture is supplied to our mouth and tongue from several reservoirs (*glands*) in their neighbourhood, whence pipes are laid and run to the mouth. The whole surface, indeed, of the mouth and tongue, as well as the other internal parts of our body, give out more or less moisture; but besides this, the mouth, as we have just mentioned, has a number of fountains expressly for its own use. The largest of these fountains lies as far off as the ear on each side, and is formed of a great number of round, soft bodies, about the size of garden-peas, from each of which a pipe goes out, and all of these uniting together, form a common channel on each side. This runs across the cheek, nearly in a line with the lap of the ear and the corner of the mouth, and enters the mouth opposite to the second or third of the double teeth (*molares*) by a hole, into which a hog's bristle can be introduced. There are, besides, several other pairs of fountains, in different parts adjacent, for a similar purpose.

"We have been thus particular in our description, in order to illustrate an analogous structure in insects, for they also seem to be furnished with salivary fountains for moistening their organs of taste. One of the circumstances that first awakened our curiosity with regard to insects, was the manner in which a fly contrives to suck up through its narrow sucker (*haustellum*) a bit of dry lump-sugar; for the small crystals are not only unfitted to pass, from their angularity, but adhere too firmly together to be separated by any force the insect can exert. Eager to solve the difficulty, for there could be no doubt of the fly's sucking the dry sugar, we watched its proceedings with no little attention; but it was not till we fell upon the device of placing some sugar on the outside of a window, while we looked through a magnifying-glass on the inside, that we had the satisfaction of repeatedly witnessing a fly let fall a drop of fluid upon the sugar, in order to melt it, and thereby render it fit to be sucked up; on precisely the same principle that we moisten with saliva, in the process of mastication, a mouthful of dry

* "Insect Miscellanies," p. 86.

bread, to fit it for being swallowed—the action of the jaws, by a beautiful contrivance of Providence, preparing the moisture along the channels at the time it is most wanted. Readers who may be disposed to think the circumstance of the fly thus moistening a bit of sugar fanciful, may readily verify the fact themselves in the way we have described. At the time when we made this little experiment, we were not aware that several naturalists of high authority had actually discovered by dissection the vessels which supply the saliva in more than one species of insect."

"In the case of their drinking fluids, like water, saliva is not wanted; and it may be remarked, when we drink cold water it actually astringes and shuts up the openings of the salivary pipes. Hence it is that drinking does not quench thirst when the saliva is rendered viscid and scanty by heat, by fatigue, or by the use of stimulant food and liquor; and sometimes a draught of cold water, by carrying off all the saliva from the mouth, and at the same time astringing the orifices of the ducts, may actually produce thirst. Ices produce this effect on many persons. It is, no doubt, in consequence of their laborious exertions, as well as of the hot nature of their acid fluids producing similar effects, that ants are so fond of water. We have seen one quaff a drop of dew almost as large as its whole body; and when we present those in our glass formicaries with water, they seem quite insatiable in drinking it."[*]

Rennie, in his *Insect Miscellanies*, after describing the pedestrian contrivances with which various insects are furnished, says,[†]—"The most perfect contrivance of this kind, however, occurs in the domestic fly (*Musca domestica*), and its congeners, as well as in several other insects. Few can have failed to remark that flies walk with the utmost ease along the ceiling of a room, and no less so upon a perpendicular looking-glass; and though this were turned downwards, the flies would not fall off, but could maintain their position undisturbed wtth their backs hanging downwards. The conjectures devised by naturalists to account for this singular circumstance, previous to the ascertaining of the actual facts, are not a little amusing. 'Some suppose,' says the Abbé de la Pluche, 'that when the fly marches over any polished body, on which neither its claws nor its points can fasten, it sometimes compresses her sponge and causes it to evacuate a fluid, which fixes it in such a manner as prevents its falling without diminishing the facility of its progress; but it is much more probable that the sponges correspond with the fleshy balls which accompany the claws of dogs and cats, and that they enable the fly to proceed with a softer pace, and contribute to the preservation of the claws, whose pointed extremities would

soon be impaired without this prevention.' (*Spect. de la Nat.* vol. i. p. 116.) 'Its ability to walk on glass,' says S. Shaw, 'proceeds partly from some little ruggedness thereon, but chiefly from a tarnish, or dirty, smoky substance, adhering to the surface; so that, though the sharp points on the sponges cannot penetrate the surface of the glass, it may easily catch hold of the tarnish.' (*Nature Displ.* vol. iii. p. 98, Lond. 1823.) But," adds Rennie, "it is singular that none of these fanciers ever took the trouble to ascertain the existence of either a gluten squeezed out by the fly, or of the smoky tarnish on glass. Even the shrewd Réaumur could not give a satisfactory explanation of the circumstance."

"The earliest correct notion on this curious subject was entertained by Derham, who, in mentioning the provision made for insects that hang on smooth surfaces, says, 'I might here name divers flies and other insects who, besides their sharp-hooked nails, have also skinny palms to their feet, to enable them to stick to glass and other smooth bodies by means of the pressure of the atmosphere—after the manner as I have seen boys carry heavy stones with only a wet piece of leather clapped on the top of the stone.' (*Physico-Theology*, vol. ii. p. 194, note *b*, 11th edit.) The justly-celebrated Mr. White, of Selborne, apparently without the aid of microscopical investigation, adopted Derham's opinion, adding the interesting illustration, that in the decline of the year, when the flies crowd to windows and become sluggish and torpid, they are scarcely able to lift their legs, which seem glued to the glass, where many actually stick till they die; whereas they are, during warm weather, so brisk and alert, that they easily overcome the pressure of the atmosphere."—(*Nat. Hist. of Selborne*, vol. ii. p. 274.)

"This singular mechanism, however," continues Rennie, "is not peculiar to flies, for some animals a hundred times as large can walk upon glass by the same means." St. Pierre mentions "a very small lizard, about a finger's length, which climbs along the walls, and even along glass, in pursuit of flies and other insects" (*Voyage to the Isle of France*, p. 73); and Sir Joseph Banks noticed another lizard, named the Gecke (*Lacerta Gecha*, LINN.), which could walk against gravity, and which made him desirous of having the subject thoroughly investigated. On mentioning it to Sir Everard Home, he and Mr. Bauer commenced a series of researches, by which they proved incontrovertibly, that in climbing upon glass, and walking along the ceilings with the back downwards, a vacuum is produced by a particular apparatus in the feet, sufficient to cause atmospheric pressure upon their exterior surface.

"The apparatus in the feet of the fly consists of two or three membranous suckers, connected with the last joint of the foot by a narrow neck, of a funnel-shape, immediately

---

[*] "Insect Miscellanies," p. 38.   [†] Ibid. p. 368.

under the base of each jaw, and movable in all directions. These suckers are convex above and hollow below, the edges being margined with minute serratures, and the hollow portion covered with down. In order to produce the vacuum and the pressure, these membranes are separated and expanded, and when the fly is about to lift its foot, it brings them together, and folds them up, as it were, between the two claws. By means of a common microscope, these interesting movements may be observed when a fly is confined in a wine-glass." (*Phil. Trans. for* 1816, p. 325.)

"It must have attracted the attention of the most incurious to see, during the summer, swarms of flies crowding about the droppings of cattle, so as almost to conceal the nuisance, and presenting instead a display of their shining corslets and twinkling wings. The object of all this busy bustle is to deposit their eggs where their progeny may find abundant food; and the final cause is obviously both to remove the nuisance, and to provide abundant food for birds and other animals which prey upon flies or their larvæ.

"The same remarks apply with no less force to the 'blow-flies,' which deposit their eggs, and in some cases their young, upon carcases. The common house-fly (the female of which generally lays 144 eggs) belongs to the first division, the natural food of its larvæ being horse-dung; consequently, it is always most abundant in houses in the vicinity of stables, cucumber-beds, &c., to which, when its numbers become annoying, attention should be primarily directed, rather than having recourse to fly-waters."—(RENNIE's *Insect Miscellany*, p. 265.)

Besides the *common* house-fly, and the other genera of the dipterous order of insects, there is another not unfrequent intruding visitor of the fly kind which we must not omit to mention, commonly known as the *blue-bottle* (*Musca vomitoria*, LINN.). The disgust with which these insects are generally viewed will perhaps be diminished when our readers are informed that they are destined to perform a very important part in the economy of nature. Amongst a number of the insect tribe whose office it is to remove nuisances the most disgusting to the eye, and the most offensive to the smell, the varieties of the blue-bottle fly belong to the most useful.

"When the dead carcases of animals begin to grow putrid, every one knows what dreadful miasmata exhale from them, and taint the air we breathe. But no sooner does life depart from the body of any creature—at least from any which, from its size, is likely to become a nuisance—than myriads of different sorts of insects attack it, and in various ways. First come the *histers*, and pierce the skin. Next follow the *flesh-flies*, covering it with millions of eggs, whence in a day or two proceed innumerable devourers. An idea of the despatch made by these gourmands may be gained from the combined consideration of their numbers, voracity, and rapid development. The larvæ of many flesh-flies, as Redi ascertained, will in twenty-four hours devour so much food, and gnaw so quickly, as to increase their weight two hundred-fold! In five days after being hatched they arrive at their full growth and size, which is a remarkable instance of the care of Providence in fitting them for the part they are destined to act; for if a longer time was required for their growth, their food would not be a fit aliment for them, or they would be too long in removing the nuisance it is given them to dissipate. Thus we see there was some ground for Linnæus's assertion, under *Musca vomitoria*, that three of these flies will devour a dead horse as quickly as would a lion."—(KIRBY and SPENCE, i.)

The following extraordinary fact, given by Kirby and Spence, concerning the voracity of the larvæ of the blow-fly, or blue-bottle (*Musca vomitoria*), is worth while appending :—

"On Thursday, June 25th, died at Asbornby, Lincolnshire, John Page, a pauper belonging to Silk-Willoughby, under circumstances truly singular. He being of a restless disposition, and not choosing to stay in the parish workhouse, was in the habit of strolling about the neighbouring villages, subsisting on the pittance obtained from door to door. The support he usually received from the benevolent was bread and meat; and after satisfying the cravings of nature, it was his custom to deposit the surplus provision, particularly the meat, between his shirt and skin. Having a considerable portion of this provision in store, so deposited, he was taken rather unwell, and laid himself down in a field in the parish of Stredington; when, from the heat of the season at that time, the meat speedily became putrid, and was of course struck by the flies. These not only proceeded to devour the inanimate pieces of flesh, but also literally to prey upon the living substance; and when the wretched man was accidentally found by some of the inhabitants, he was so eaten by the maggots, that his death seemed inevitable. After clearing away, as well as they were able, these shocking vermin, those who found Page conveyed him to Asbornby, and a surgeon was immediately procured, who declared that his body was in such a state that dressing it must be little short of instantaneous death; and, in fact, the man did survive the operation but for a few hours. When first found, and again when examined by the surgeon, he presented a sight loathsome in the extreme. White maggots of enormous size were crawling in and upon his body, which they had most shockingly mangled, and the removal of the external ones served only to render the sight more horrid." Kirby adds, "In passing through this parish last spring, I inquired of the mail-coachman whether he had heard this story; and he said the fact was well known."

One species of fly infests our houses

(*Stomoxys calcitrans*), which so nearly resembles the common house-fly (*Musca domestica*), that the difference is not easily detected except by an entomologist; indeed the resemblance is so close as to have led to the vulgar error that the common house-fly occasionally indulges itself by a feast upon our blood, after it has fed to satiety upon the delicacies which it picks from our tables. It is even a greater torment than the horse-fly.

"This little pest," says Kirby, referring to the *Stomoxys*, "I speak feelingly, incessantly interrupts our studies and comfort in showery weather, making us even stamp like the cattle by its attacks on our legs, and if we drive it away ever so often, returning again and again to the charge." In Canada they are infinitely worse. "I have sat down to write," says Lambert, (who, though he calls it the house-fly, is evidently speaking of the Stomoxys), "and have been obliged to throw away my pen in consequence of their irritating bite, which has obliged me every moment to raise my hand to my eyes, nose, mouth, and ears, in constant succession. When I could no longer write, I began to read, and was always obliged to keep one hand constantly on the move towards my head. Sometimes, in the course of a few minutes, I would take half-a-dozen of my tormentors from my lips, between which I caught them just as they perched."—(*Travels.* &c. i. 126.)

But of all the insect-tormentors of man, none are so loudly and universally complained of as the species of the genus *Culex*, L., whether known by the name of gnats or mosquitos. It has been generally supposed by naturalists that the mosquitos of America belong to the Linnæan genus *Culex;* but Humboldt asserts that the term *mosquito*, signifying *a little fly*, is applied there to a *Senicilium*, LATR. (*Senicilia*, MEIG.), and that the *Culices*, which are equally numerous and annoying, are called *Zancudoes*, which means *long-legs*. The former, he says, are what the French call *Moustiques*, and the latter *Maringouins*. (*Personal Narrative*, E.T., v. 93.)

Humboldt's remark, however, refers only to South America. Mr. Westwood informs us that *Mosquito* is certainly applied to a species of *Culex* in the United States, the inhabitants giving the name of *black*-fly to a small *Senicilium*. Pliny, after Aristotle, distinguishes well between *Hymenoptera* and *Diptera*, when he says the former have their sting in the *tail*, and the latter in the *mouth;* and that to the one this instrument is given as the instrument of vengeance, and to the other of avidity.

But the instrument of avidity in the genus of which I am speaking is even more terrible than that of vengeance in most insects that are armed with it. It instils into its wound a poison (as appears from the consequent inflammation and tumour), the principal use of which is to render the blood more fluid and fitter for suction. This weapon, which is more complex than the sting of hymenopterous insects, consisting of five pieces besides the exterior sheath — some of which seem simply lancets, while others are barbed like the spiculæ of a bee's sting — is at once calculated for piercing the flesh and forming a syphon adapted to imbibe the blood. There are several species of this genus whose bite is severe; but none is to be compared to the common gnat (*Culex pipiens*, L.), if, as has been generally affirmed, it be synonymous with the mosquito, though, in all probability, several species are confounded under both names.

In this country they are justly regarded as no trifling evil; for they follow us to all our haunts, intrude into our most secret retirements, assail us in the city and in the country, in our houses and in our fields, in the sun and in the shade; nay, they pursue us to our pillows, and keep us awake by the ceaseless hum of their rapid wings (which, according to the Baron C. de Latour, are vibrated 3000 times per minute), and their incessant endeavours to fix themselves upon our face, or some uncovered part of our body; whilst, if in spite of them we fall asleep, they awaken us by the acute pain which attends the insertion of their oral stings, attacking with most avidity the softer sex, and trying their temper by disfiguring their beauty.

In Marshland in Norfolk, the inhabitants are said to be so annoyed by the gnats, that the better sort of them, as in many hot climates, have recourse to a gauze covering for their beds to keep them off during the night.

"CATCH-'EM-ALIVE" SELLERS.

I DISCOVERED a colony of "catch'-em-alive" boys residing in Pheasant-court, Gray's-inn-lane.

From the pleasing title given to this alley, one might almost be led to imagine it was a very delightful spot, though it is only necessary to look down the little bricken archway that marks its entrance, and see the houses—dirty as the sides of a dust-bin, and with patched counterpanes and yellow sheets hanging from the windows — to feel assured that it is one of the most squalid of the many wretched courts that branch out from Gray's-inn-lane.

I found the lads playing at "pitch and toss" in the middle of the paved yard. They were all willing enough to give me their statements; indeed, the only difficulty I had was in making my choice among the youths.

"Please, sir, I've been at it longer than him," cried one with teeth ribbed like celery.

"Please, sir, he ain't been out this year with the papers," said another, who was hiding a handful of buttons behind his back.

"He's been at shoe-blacking, sir; I'm the only reg'lar fly-boy," shouted a third, eating a piece of bread as dirty as London snow.

A big lad with a dirty face, and hair like

hemp, was the first of the " catch-'em-alive" boys who gave me his account of the trade. He was a swarthy-featured boy, with a broad nose like a negro's, and on his temple was a big half-healed scar, which he accounted for by saying that " he had been runned over" by a cab, though, judging from the blackness of one eye, it seemed to have been the result of some street-fight. He said :—

" I'm an Irish boy, and near turned sixteen, and I've been silling fly-papers for between eight and nine year. I must have begun to sill them when they first come out. Another boy first tould me of them, and he'd been silling them about three weeks before me. He used to buy them of a party as lives in a back-room near Drury-lane, what buys paper and makes the catch 'em alive himself. When they first came out they used to charge sixpence a-dozen for 'em, but now they've got 'em to twopence ha'penny. When I first took to silling 'em, there was a tidy lot of boys at the business, but not so many as now, for all the boys seem at it. In our court alone I should think there was above twenty boys silling the things.

" At first, when there was a good time, we used to buy three or four gross together, but now we don't do more than half a gross. As we go along the streets we call out different cries. Some of us says, ' Fly-papers, fly-papers, ketch 'em all alive.' Others make a kind of song of it, singing out, ' Fly-paper, ketch 'em all alive, the nasty flies, tormenting the baby's eyes. Who'd be fly-blow'd, by all the nasty blue-bottles, beetles, and flies?'

" People likes to buy of a boy as sings out well, 'cos it makes 'em laugh.

" I don't think I sell so many in town as I do in the borders of the country, about Highbury, Croydon, and Brentford. I've got some regular customers in town about the City-prison and the Caledonian-road; and after I've served them and the town custom begins to fall off, then I goes to the country.

" We goes two of us together, and we takes about three gross. We keep on silling before us all the way, and we comes back the same road. Last year we sould very well in Croydon, and it was the best place for gitting a price for· them; they'd give a penny a-piece for 'em there, for they didn't know nothing about them. I went off one day at tin o'clock and didn't come home till two in the morning. I sould eighteen dozen out in that d'rection the other day, and got rid of them before I had got half-way.

" But flies are very scarce at Croydon this year, and we haven't done so well. There ain't half as many flies this summer as last.

" Some people says the papers draws more flies than they ketches, and that when one gets in, there's twenty others will come to see him.

" It's according to the weather as the flies is about. If we have a fine day it fetches them out, but a cold day kills more than our papers.

" We sills the most papers to little cookshops and sweetmeat-shops. We don't sill so many at private-houses. The public-houses is pretty good customers, 'cos the beer draws the flies. I sould nine dozen at one house — a school — at Highgate, the other day. I sould 'em two for three-ha'pence. That was a good hit, but then t'other days we loses. If we can make a ha'penny each we thinks we does well.

" Those that sills their papers at three a-penny buys them at St. Giles's, and pays only three-ha'pence a dozen for them, but they an't half as big and good as those we pays tuppence-ha'penny a dozen for.

" Barnet is a good place for fly-papers; there's a good lot of flies down there. There used to be a man at Barnet as made 'em, but I can't say if he do now. There's another at Brentford, so it ain't much good going that way.

" In cold weather the papers keep pretty well, and will last for months with just a little warming at the fire; for they tears on opening when they are dry. You see we always carry them with the sticky sides doubled up together like a sheet of writing-paper. In hot wither, if you keep them folded up, they lasts very well; but if you opens them, they dry up. It's easy opening them in hot weather, for they comes apart as easy as peeling a horrange.

" We generally carries the papers in a bundle on our arm, and we ties a paper as is loaded with flies round our cap, just to show the people the way to ketch 'em. We get a loaded paper given to us at a shop.

" When the papers come out first, we used to do very well with fly-papers; but now it's hard work to make our own money for 'em. Some days we used to make six shillings a-day regular. But then we usen't to go out every day, but take a rest at home. If we do well one day, then we might stop idle another day, resting. You see, we had to do our twenty or thirty miles silling them to get that money, and then the next day we was tired.

" The silling of papers is gradual fallen off. I could go out and sill twenty dozen wonst where I couldn't sill one now.

" I think I does a very grand day's work if I yearns a shilling. Perhaps some days I may lose by them. You see, if it's a very hot day, the papers gets dusty; and beside, the stuff gets melted and oozes out; though that don't do much harm, 'cos we gets a bit of whitening and rubs 'em over.

" Four years ago we might make ten shillings a-day at the papers, but now, taking from one end of the fly-paper sason to the other, which is about three months, I think we makes about one shilling a-day out of papers, though even that aint quite certain. I never goes out without getting rid of mine, somehow or another, but then I am obleeged to walk quick and look about me.

" When it's a bad time for silling the papers, such as a wet, could day, then most of the fly-paper boys goes out with brushes, cleaning boots. Most of the boys is now out hopping. They goes reg'lar every year after the sason is give over for flies.

" The stuff as they puts on the paper is made out of boiled oil and turpentine and resin. It's seldom as a fly lives more than five minutes after it gets on the paper, and then it's as dead as a house. The blue-bottles is tougher, but they don't last long, though they keeps on fizzing as if they was trying to make a hole in the paper. The stuff is only p'isonous for flies, though I never heard of any body as ever eat a fly-paper."

The second lad I chose from among the group of applicants was of a middle age, and although the noisiest when among his companions, had no sooner entered the room with me, than his whole manner changed. He sat himself down, bent up like a monkey, and scarcely ever turned his eyes from me. He seemed as nervous as if in a witness-box, and kept playing with his grubby fingers till he had almost made them white.

" They calls me ' Curley.' I come from Ireland too. I'm about fourteen year, and have been in this line now, sir, about five year. I goes about the borders of the country. We general takes up the line about the beginning of June, that is, when we gets a good summer. When we gets a good close dull day like this, we does pretty well, but when we has first one day hot, and then another rainy and could, a' course we don't get on so well.

" The most I sould was one day when I went to Uxbridge, and then I sould a gross and a half. I paid half-a-crown a gross for them. I was living with mother then, and she give me the money to buy 'em, but I had to bring her back again all as I took. I al'us give her all I makes, except sixpence as I wants for my dinner, which is a kipple of pen'orth of bread and cheese and a pint of beer. I sould that gross and a half I spoke on at a ha'penny each, and I took nine shillings, so that I made five and sixpence. But then I'd to leave London at three or four o'clock in the morning, and to stop out till twelve o'clock at night. I used to live out at Hammersmith then, and come up to St. Giles's every morning and buy the papers. I had to rise by half-past two in the morning, and I'd get back again to Hammersmith by about six o'clock. I couldn't sill none on the road, 'cos the shops wasn't open.

" The flies is getting bad every summer. This year they a'n't half so good as they was last year or the year before. I'm sure I don't know why there aint so many, but they aint so plentiful like. The best year was three year ago. I know that by the quantity as my customers bought of me, and in three days the papers was swarmed with flies.

" I've got regular customers, where I calls two or three times a week to 'em. If I was to walk my rounds over I could at the lowest sell from six to eight dozen at ha'penny each at wonst. If it was nice wither, like to-day, so that it wouldn't come wet on me, I should make ten shillings a-week regular, but it depends on the wither. If I was to put my profits by, I'm sure I should find I make more than six shillings a-week, and nearer eight. But the season is only for three months at most, and then we takes to boot-cleaning. Near all the poor boys about here is fly-paper silling in the hot weather, and boot-cleaners at other times.

" Shops buys the most of us in London. In Barnet I sell sometimes as much as six or seven dozen to some of the grocers as buys to sell again, but I don't let them have them only when I can't get rid of 'em to t'other customers. Butchers is very fond of the papers, to catch the blue-bottles as gets in their meat, though there is a few butchers as have said to me, ' Oh, go away, they draws the flies more than they ketches 'em.' Clothes-shops, again, is very fond of 'em. I can't tell why they is fond of 'em, but I suppose 'cos the flies spots the goods.

" There's lots of boys going silling ' ketch 'em alive oh's' from Golden-lane, and White-chapel, and the Borough. There's lots, too, comes out of Gray's-inn-lane and St. Giles's. Near every boy who has nothing to do goes out with fly-papers. Perhaps it aint that the flies is falled off that we don't sill so many papers now, but because there's so many boys at it."

The most intelligent and the most gentle in his demeanour was a little boy, who was scarcely tall enough to look on the table at which I was writing. If his face had been washed, he would have been a pretty-looking lad; for, despite the black marks made by his knuckles during his last fit of crying, he had large expressive eyes, and his features were round and plump, as though he were accustomed to more food than his companions.

Whilst taking his statement I was interrupted by the entrance of a woman, whose fears had been aroused by the idea that I belonged to the Ragged School, and had come to look after the scholars. " It's no good you're coming here for him, he's off hopping to-morrow with his mother, as has asked me to look after him, and it's only your saxpence he's wanting."

It was with great difficulty that I could get rid of this lady's company; and, indeed, so great appeared to be the fear in the court that the object of my visit was to prevent the young gentlemen from making their harvest trip into the country, that a murmuring crowd began to assemble round the house where I was, determined to oppose me by force, should I leave the premises accompanied by any of the youths.

" I've been longer at it than that last boy, though I'm only getting on for thirteen, and he's older than I'm; 'cos I'm little and he's big, getting a man. But I can sell them quite as well as he can, and sometimes better, for I can holler out just as loud, and I've got reg'lar places to go to. I was a very little fellow when I first went out with them, but I could sell them pretty well then, sometimes three or four dozen a-day. I've got one place, in a stable, where I can sell a dozen at a time to countrypeople.

" I calls out in the streets, and I goes into the shops, too, and calls out, ' Ketch 'em alive, ketch 'em alive; ketch all the nasty black-beetles, blue-bottles, and flies; ketch 'em from teazing the baby's eyes.' That's what most of us boys cries out. Some boys who is stupid only says, ' Ketch 'em alive,' but people don't buy so well from them.

" Up in St. Giles's there is a lot of fly-boys, but they're a bad set, and will fling mud at gentlemen, and some prigs the gentlemen's pockets. Sometimes, if I sells more than a big boy, he'll get mad and hit me. He'll tell me to give him a halfpenny and he won't touch me, and that if I don't he'll kill me. Some of the boys takes an open fly-paper, and makes me look another way, and then they sticks the ketch 'em alive on my face. The stuff won't come off without soap and hot water, and it goes black, and looks like mud. One day a boy had a broken fly-paper, and I was taking a drink of water, and he come behind me and slapped it up in my face. A gentleman as saw him give him a crack with a stick and me twopence. It takes your breath away, until a man comes and takes it off. It all sticked to my hair, and I couldn't rack (comb) right for some time.

" When we are selling papers we have to walk a long way. Some boys go as far as Croydon, and all about the country; but I don't go much further than Copenhagen-fields, and straight down that way. I don't like going along with other boys, they take your customers away; for perhaps they'll sell 'em at three a-penny to 'em, and spoil the customers for you. I won't go with the big boy you saw 'cos he's such a blackgeyard; when he's in the country he'll go up to a lady and say, ' Want a fly-paper, marm?' and if she says ' No,' he'll perhaps job his head in her face — butt at her like.

" When there's no flies, and the ketch 'em alive's is out, then I goes tumbling. I can turn a cat'enwheel over on one hand. I'm going to-morrow to the country, harvesting and hopping—for, as we says, ' Go out hopping, come in jumping.' We start at three o'clock to-morrow, and we shall get about twelve o'clock at night at Dead Man's Barn. It was left for poor people to sleep in, and a man there was buried in a corner. The man had got six farms of hops; and if his son hadn't buried him there, he wouldn't have had none of the riches.

" The greatest number of fly-papers I've sold in a day is about eight dozen. I never sells no more than that; I wish I could. People won't buy 'em now. When I'm at it I makes, taking one day with another, about ten shilling a-week. You see, if I sold eight dozen, I'd make four shillings. I sell them at a penny each, at two for three-ha'pence, and three for twopence. When they gets stale I sells 'em at three a-penny. I always begin by asking a penny each, and perhaps they'll say, ' Give me two for three-ha'pence.' I'll say, ' Can't, ma'am,' and then they pulls out a purse full of money and gives a penny.

" The police is very kind to us, and don't interfere with us. If they sees another boy hitting us they'll take off their belts and hit 'em. Sometimes I've sold a ketch 'em alive to a policeman; he'll fold it up and put it in his pocket to take home with him. Perhaps he's got a kid, and the flies teazes its eyes.

" Some ladies like to buy fly-cages better than ketch 'em alive's, because sometimes when they're putting 'em up they falls in their faces, and then they screams."

THE FLY-PAPER MAKER.

IN a small attic-room, in a house near Drury-lane, I found the " catch 'em alive " manufacturer and his family busy at their trade.

Directly I entered the house where I had been told he lodged, I knew that I had come to the right address; for the staircase smelt of turpentine as if it had been newly painted, the odour growing more and more powerful as I ascended.

The little room where the man and his family worked was as hot as an oven; for although it was in the heat of summer, still his occupation forced him to have a fire burning for the purpose of melting and keeping fluid the different ingredients he spread upon his papers.

When I opened the door of his room, I was at first puzzled to know how I should enter the apartment; for the ceiling was completely hidden by the papers which had been hung up to dry from the many strings stretched across the place, so that it resembled a washerwoman's back-yard, with some thousands of red pocket-handkerchiefs suspended in the air. I could see the legs of the manufacturer walking about at the further end, but the other part of his body was hidden from me.

On his crying, " Come in !" I had to duck my head down, and creep under the forest of paper strips rustling above us.

The most curious characteristic of the apartment was the red colour with which everything was stained. The walls, floor, and tables were all smeared with ochre, like the pockets of a drover. The papers that were drying were as red as the pages of a gold-leaf book. This curious appearance was owing to part of the process of " catch 'em alive " making consisting in first covering the paper with coloured size, to prevent the sticky solution from soaking into it.

The room was so poorly furnished, that it was evident the trade was not a lucrative one. An old Dutch clock, with a pendulum as long as a walking-stick, was the only thing in the dwelling which was not indispensable to the calling. The chimneypiece — that test of "well-to-do" in the houses of the poorer classes — had not a single ornament upon it. The long board on which the family worked served likewise as the table for the family meals, and the food they ate had to be laid upon the red-smeared surface. There was but one chair, and that the wife occupied; and when the father or son wished to sit down, a tub of size was drawn out with its trembling contents from under the work-table, and on this they rested themselves.

"We are called in the trade," said the father, "fly-paper makers. They used to put a nice name to the things once, and call 'em Egyptian fly-papers, but now they use merely the word 'fly-papers,' or 'fly-destroyers,' or 'fly-catchers,' or 'catch 'em alive, oh.'

"I never made any calculation about flies, and how often they breeds. You see, it depends upon so many things how they're produced: for instance, if I was to put my papers on a dung-heap, I might catch some thousands; and if I was to put a paper in an ice-well, I don't suppose I should catch one.

"I know the flies produce some thousands each, because if you look at a paper well studded over with flies, you'll see — that is, if you look very carefully — where each fly has blown, as we call it, there'll be some millions on a paper, small grubs or little mites, like; for whilst struggling the fly shoots forth the blows, and eventually these blows would turn to flies.

"I have been at fly-catcher making for the last nine years. It's almost impossible to make any calculation as to the number of papers I make during the season, and this is the season. If it's fine weather, then flies are plentiful, and the lads who sell the papers in the streets keep me busy; but if it's at all bad weather, then they turn their attention to blacking boots.

"It's quite a speculation, my business is, for all depends upon the lads coming to me to buy, and there's no certainty beyond. I every season expect that these lads who bought papers of me the last year will come back and deal with me again. First of all, these lads will come for a dozen, or a kipple of dozen, of papers; and so it goes on till perhaps they are able to sell half a gross a-day, and then from that they will, if the weather is fine, get up to ten dozen, or perhaps a gross, but seldom or never over that.

"In the very busiest and hottest time as is, I have, for about two or three weeks, made as many as thirty-six gross of papers in a week. We generally begins about the end of June or the beginning of July, and then for five or six weeks we goes on very busy; after that it dies out, and people gets tired of laying out their money.

"It's almost impossible to get at any calculation of the quantity I make. You see, to-day I haven't sold a gross, and yesterday I didn't sell more than a gross; and the last three days I haven't sold a single paper, it's been so wet. But last week I sold more than five gross a-day,—it varies so. Oh yes, I sell more than a hundred gross during the season. You may say, that for a month I make about five gross a-day, and that—taking six days to the week, and thirty days to the month—makes a hundred and thirty gross: and then for another month I do about three gross a-day, and that, at the same calculation, makes seventy-eight gross, or altogether one hundred and ninety-eight gross, or 28,512 single papers, and that is as near as I can tell you.

"Sometimes our season lasts more than two months. You may reckon it from the latter end of June to the end of August, or if the weather is very hot, then we begins early in June, and runs it into September. The prime time is when the flies gets heavy and stings—that's when the papers sells most.

"There's others in the business besides myself; they lives up in St. Giles's, and they sells 'em rather cheaper. At one time the shopkeepers used to make the papers. When they first commenced, they was sold at twopence and threepence and fourpence a-piece, but now they're down to three a-penny in the streets, or a halfpenny for a single one. The boys when they've got back the money they paid me for their stock, will sell what papers they have left at anything they'll fetch, because the papers gets dusty and spiles with the dust.

"I use the very best 'Times' paper for my 'catch 'em alives.' I gets them kept for me at stationers' shops and liberaries, and such-like. I pays threepence a-pound, or twenty-eight shillings the hundred weight. That's a long price, but you must have good paper if you want to make a good article. I could get paper at twopence a-pound, but then it's only the cheap Sunday papers, and they're too slight.

"The morning papers are the best, and will stand the pulling in opening the papers; for we always fold the destroyers with the sticky sides together when finished. The composition I use is very stiff; if the paper is bad, they tear when you force them open for use. Some in the trade cut up their newspapers into twelve for the full sheet, but I cut mine up into only eight.

"The process is this. First of all the paper is sized and coloured. We colour them by putting a little red lead into the size, because if the sticky side is not made apparent the people wont buy 'em, 'cause they might spile the furniture by putting the composition-side downwards. After sizing the papers, they are hung up to dry, and then the composition is laid on. This composition is a secret, and I'm obligated to keep it so, for of course all the boys who come here would be trying to make 'em, and not only would it injure me, but I'd warrant they'd injure theirselves as well, by setting the house on fire. You may say that my composition is made from a mixture of resinous substances. Everything in making it depends upon using the proper proportions. There's some men who deal with me who know the substances to make the composition from, but because they haven't got the exact proportions of the quantities, they can't make it right.

"The great difficulty in making them is drying the papers after they are sized. Some days when it's fine they'll dry as fast as you can hang 'em up a'most, and other days they won't dry at all—in damp weather 'specially. There is some makers who sizes and colours their papers in the winter, and then puts 'em to dry; and when the summer comes, then they has only to put on the composition.

"I'm a very quick hand in the trade (if you can call it one, for it only lasts three months at most, and is a very uncertain one, too; indeed, I don't know what you can style our business—it ain't a purfession and it ain't a trade, I suppose it's a calling): I'm a quick hand I say at spreading the composition, and I can, taking the day through, do about two gross an hour—that is, if the papers was sized ready for me; but as it is, having to size 'em first, I can't do more than three gross a-day myself, but with my wife helping me we can do such a thing as five gross a-day.

"It's most important that the size should dry. Now those papers (producing some covered with a dead red coating of the size preparation) have been done four days, and yet they're not dry, although to you they appear so, but I can tell that they feel tough, and not crisp as they ought to. When the size is damp it makes them adhere to one another when I am laying the stuff on, and it sweats through and makes them heavy, and then they tears when I opens them.

"When I'm working, I first size the entire sheet. We put it on the table, and then we have a big brush and plaster it over. Then I gives it to my wife, and she hangs it up on a line. We can hang up a gross at a time here, and then the room is pretty full, and must seem strange to anybody coming in, though to us it's ordinary enough."

The man was about to exhibit to us his method of proceeding, when his attention was drawn off by a smell which the moving of the different pots had caused. "How strong this size smells, Charlotte!" he said to his wife.

"It's the damp and heat of the room does it," the wife replied; and then the narrative went on.

"Before putting on the composition I cut up the papers into slips as fast as possible, that don't take long."

"We can cut 'em in first style," interrupted the wife.

"I can cut up four gross an hour," said a boy, who was present.

"I don't think you could, Johnny," said the man. "Two gross is nearer the mark, to cut 'em evenly."

"It's only seventy sheets," remonstrated the lad, "and that's only a little more than one a minute."

A pile of entire newspapers was here brought out, and all of them coloured red on one side, like the leaves of the books in which gold-leaf is kept.

Judging from the trial at cutting which followed, we should conclude that the lad was correct in his calculation.

"When we put on the composition," continued the catch-'em-alive maker, "we has the cut slips piled up in a tall mound like, and then we have a big brush, and dips it in the pot of stuff and rubs it in; we folds each catcher up as we does it, like a thin slice of bread and butter, and put it down. As I said before, at merely putting on the composition I could do about two gross an hour.

"My price to the boys is twopence-halfpenny a dozen, or two-and-sixpence a gross, and out of that I don't get more than ninepence profit, for the paper, the resin, and the firing for melting the size and composition, all takes off the profit.

"This season nearly all my customers have been boys. Last season I had a few men who dealt with me. The principal of those who buys of me is Irish. A boy will sometimes sell his papers for a halfpenny each, but the usual price is three a-penny. Many of the blacking-boys deal with me. If it's a fine day it don't suit them at boot-cleaning, and then they'll run out with my papers; and so they have two trades to their backs—one for fine, and the other for wet weather.

"The first man as was the inventor of these fly-papers kept a barber's shop in St. Andrew-street, Seven Dials, of the name of Greenwood or Greenfinch, I forget which. I expect he diskivered it by accident, using varnish and stuff, for stale varnish has nearly the same effect as our composition. He made 'em and sold 'em at first at threepence and fourpence a-piece. Then it got down to a penny. He sold the receipt to some other par'es, and then it got out through their having to employ men to help 'em. I worked for a party as made 'em, and then I set to work making 'em for myself, and afterwards hawking them. They was a greater novelty then than they are now, and sold pretty well. Then men in the streets, who had nothing to do, used to ask me where I bought 'em, and then I used to give 'em my own address, and they'd come and find me."

OF BUGS AND FLEAS.

A NUMEROUS family of a large order of insects is but too well known, both in gardens and houses, under the general name of Bugs (*Cimicidæ*) most, if not all, of the species being distinguished by an exceedingly disagreeable smell, particularly when pressed or bruised.

The sucking instrument of these insects has been so admirably dissected and delineated by M. Savigny, in his "Theory of the Mouth of Six-legged (*hexapod*) Insects," * that we cannot do better than follow so excellent a guide.

The sucker is contained in a sheath, and this sheath is composed of four pieces, which, according to Savigny's theory, represent an under-lip much prolonged. The edges bend downwards, and form a canal receiving the four bristles, which he supposes to correspond with the two mandibles and the two lower jaws. It is probable that the two middle of these bristles act as piercers, while the other two, being curved at the extremity (though not at all times naturally so), assist in the process of suction.

The plant-bugs are all furnished with wings and membranous wing-cases, many of them being of considerable size, and decked in showy colours. These differ in all those points from their congener, the bed-bug (*Cimex lectularius*), which is small, without wings, and of a dull uniform brown. The name is of Welsh origin, being derived from the same root as *bug*-bear, and hence the passage in the Psalms, "thou shalt not be afraid for *the terror* by night," + is rendered in Matthew's Bible, "thou shalt not nede to be afraide of any *bugs* by night."

In earlier times this insect was looked upon with no little fear, no doubt because it was not so abundant as at present. "In the year 1503," says Mouffet, " Dr. Penny was called in great haste to a little village called Mortlake, near the Thames, to visit two noblemen who were much frightened by the appearance of bug-bites, and were in fear of I know not what contagion; but when the matter was known, and the insects caught, he laughed them out of all fear."‡ This fact, of course, disproves the statement of Southall, that bugs were not known in England before 1670.

Linnæus was of opinion, however, that the bug was not originally a native of Europe, but had been imported from America. Be this as it may, it seems to thrive but too well in our climate, though it multiplies less in Britain than in the warmer regions of the Continent, where it is also said to grow to a larger size, and to bite more keenly. This insect, it is said, is never seen in Ireland.§

"Commerce," says a learned entomologist, "with many good things, has also introduced amongst us many great evils, of which noxious insects form no small part; and one of her worst presents was, doubtless, the disgusting animals called bugs. They seem, indeed," he adds, "to have been productive of greater alarm at first than mischief,— at least, if we may judge from the change of name which took place upon their becoming common. Their original English name was *Chinche*, or *Wall-louse*; and the term *bug*, which is a Celtic word, signifying a ghost or goblin, was applied to them after Ray's time, most probably because they were considered as 'terrors by night.' Hence our English word *bug-bear*. The word in this sense often occurs in Shakspeare, *Winter's Tale*, act iii. sc. 2, 3; *Henry VI.* act v. sc. 2; *Hamlet*, act v. sc. 2. See Douce's *Illustrations of Shakspeare*, i. 329."

Even in our own island these obtrusive insects often banish sleep. "The night," says Goldsmith, in his *Animated Nature*, "is usually the season when the wretched have rest from their labour; but this seems the only season when the bug issues from its retreats to make its depredations. By day it lurks, like a robber, in the most secret parts of the bed, takes the advantage of every chink and cranny to make a secure lodgment, and contrives its habitation with so much art that it is no easy matter to discover its retreat. It seems to avoid the light with great cunning, and even if candles be kept burning, this formidable insect will not issue from its hiding-place. But when darkness promises security, it then issues from every corner of the bed, drops from the tester, crawls from behind the arras, and travels with great assiduity to the unhappy patient, who vainly wishes for rest. It is generally vain to destroy one only, as there are hundreds more to revenge their companion's fate; so that the person who thus is subject to be bitten (some individuals are exempt), remains the whole night like a sentinel upon duty, rather watching the approach of fresh invaders than inviting the pleasing approaches of sleep." *

Mouffet assures us, that against these enemies of our rest in the night our merciful God hath furnished us with remedies, which we may fetch out of old and new writers, either to drive them away or kill them.† The following is given as the best poison for bugs, by Mr. Brande, of the Royal Institution:—Reduce an ounce of corrosive sublimate (*perchloride of mercury*) and one ounce of white arsenic to a fine powder; mix with it one ounce of muriate of ammonia in powder, two ounces each of oil of turpentine and yellow wax, and eight ounces of olive oil; put all these into a pipkin, placed in a pan of boiling water, and when the wax is melted, stir the whole, till cold, in a mortar.‡ A strong solution of corrosive sublimate, indeed, applied as a wash, is a most efficacious bug-poison.

---

* " Mém. Anim. sans Vertébrat." i. 36.
† Ps. xci. 5. ‡ " Theatr. Insect." 270. § J. R.

* Goldsmith's " Animat. Nature," iv. 198.
† " Theatr. Insect." ‡ " Materia Medica," Index.

Though most people dislike this insect, others have been known to regard it with protecting care. One gentleman would never suffer the bugs to be disturbed in his house, or his bedsteads removed, till, in the end, they swarmed to an incredible degree, crawling up even the walls of his drawing-room; and after his death millions were found in his bed and chamber furniture.*

In the Banian hospital, at Surat, the overseers are said frequently to hire beggars from the streets, at a stipulated sum, to pass the night among bugs and other vermin, on the express condition of suffering them to enjoy their feast without molestation.†

The bed-bug is not the only one of its congeners which preys upon man. St. Pierre mentions a bug found in the Mauritius, the bite of which is more venomous than the sting of a scorpion, being succeeded by a swelling as big as the egg of a pigeon, which continues for four or five days.‡ Ray tells us that his friend Willoughby had suffered severe temporary pain, in the same way, from a water-bug. (*Notonecta glauca*, LINN.) §

The winged insects of the order to which the bed-bug belongs often inflict very painful wounds, and it is even stated, upon good authority, that an insect of the order, commonly known in the West Indies by the name of the *wheel-bug*, can communicate an electric shock to the person whose flesh it touches. The late Major-General Davies, R.A. (well known as a most accurate observer of nature and an indefatigable collector of her treasures, as well as a most admirable painter of them), having taken up this animal and placed it upon his hand, assures us that it gave him, with its legs, a considerable shock, as if from an electric jar, which he felt as high as his shoulders; and then dropping the creature, he observed six marks upon his hand where the six feet had stood.

Bugs are very voracious, and seem to bite most furiously in the autumn, as if determined to feast themselves before they retire to their winter quarters.

There is another pernicious bed insect— the flea (*Pulex irritans*, LINN.), which, being without wings, some of our readers may suppose to be nearly allied to the bed-bug, though it does not belong even to the same order, but to a new one (*Aphaniptera*, KIRBY), established on the principle that the wings are obsolescent or inconspicuous.

Fleas, it may be worth remarking, are not all of one species; those which infest animals and birds differing in many particulars from the common bed-flea (*Pulex irritans*). As many as twelve distinct sorts of fleas have been found in Britain alone.‖ The most annoying species, however, is, fortunately, not indigenous, being a native of the tropical latitudes, and variously named in the West Indies, chigoe, jigger, nigua, tungua, and pique (*Pulex penetrans*, LINN). According to Stedman, "this is a kind of small sand-flea, which gets in between the skin and the flesh without being felt, and generally under the nails of the toes, where, while it feeds, it keeps growing till it becomes of the size of a pea, causing no further pain than a disagreeable itching. In process of time its operation appears in the form of a small bladder, in which are deposited thousands of eggs, or nits, and which, if it breaks, produce so many young chigoes, which in course of time create running ulcers, often of very dangerous consequence to the patient. So much so, indeed, that I knew a soldier, the soles of whose feet were obliged to be cut away before he could recover; and some men have lost their limbs by amputation, nay, even their lives, by having neglected, in time, to root out these abominable vermin. Walton mentions that a Capuchin friar, in order to study the history of the chigoe, permitted a colony of them to establish themselves in his feet: but before he could accomplish his object his feet mortified and had to be amputated.* No wonder that Cardan calls the insect " a very shrewd plague."†

Several extraordinary feats of strength have been recorded of fleas by various authors, ‡ and we shall here give our own testimony to a similar fact. At the fair of Charlton, in Kent, 1830, we saw a man exhibit three fleas harnessed to a carriage in the form of an omnibus, at least fifty times their own bulk, which they pulled along with great ease; another pair drew a chariot. The exhibitor showed the whole first through a magnifying glass, and then to the naked eye, so that we were satisfied there was no deception. From the fleas being of large size they were evidently all females.§

It is rarely, however, that we meet with fleas in the way of amusement, unless we are of the singular humour of the old lady mentioned by Kirby and Spence, who had a liking to them; " because," said she, " I think they are the prettiest little merry things in the world; I never saw a dull flea in all my life."

When Ray and Willoughby were travelling, they found " at Venice and Augsburg fleas for sale, and at a small price too, decorated with steel or silver collars round their necks. When fleas are kept in a box amongst wool or cloth, in a warm place, and fed once a-day, they will live a long time. When these insects begin to suck they erect themselves almost perpendicularly, thrusting their sucker, which originates in the middle of the forehead, into the skin. The itching is not felt immediately,

* Nicholson's " Journal," xvii. 40.
† Forbes, " Oriental Mem." i.
‡ " Voyage to the Isle of France."
§ " Hist. Insect." 58.
‖ " Insect Transformations," p. 393.

* Walton's " Hispaniola."
† " Subtilia," lib. ix.
‡ " Insect Transformations," p. 180.
§ Introduction, i. 102.—J. R.

but a little afterwards. As soon as they are full of blood, they begin to void a portion of it; and thus, if permitted, they will continue for many hours sucking and voiding. After the first itching no uneasiness is subsequently felt. Willoughby had a flea that lived for three months, sucking in this manner the blood of his hand; it was at length killed by the cold of winter." *

According to Mouffet's account of the sucker of the flea, " the point of his nib is somewhat hard, that he may make it enter the better; and it must necessarily be hollow, that he may suck out the blood and carry it in." † Modern authors, particularly Straus and Kirby, show that Rösel was mistaken in supposing this sucker to consist of two pieces, as it is really made up of seven. First, there is a pair of triangular instruments, somewhat resembling the beak of a bird, inserted on each side of the mouth, under the parts which are generally regarded as the antennæ. Next, a pair of long sharp piercers (*scalpella*, KIRBY), which emerge from the head below the preceding instruments; whilst a pair of feelers (*palpi*), consisting of four joints, is attached to these near their base. In fine, there is a long, slender tongue, like a bristle, in the middle of these several pieces.

Mouffet says, " the lesser, leaner, and younger the fleas are, the sharper they bite,— the fat ones being more inclined to tickle and play. They molest men that are sleeping," he adds, " and trouble wounded and sick persons, from whom they escape by skipping; for as soon as they find they are arraigned to die, and feel the finger coming, on a sudden they are gone, and leap here and there, and so escape the danger; but so soon as day breaks they forsake the bed. They then creep into the rough blankets, or hide themselves in rushes and dust, lying in ambush for pigeons, hens, and other birds; also for men and dogs, moles and mice, and vex such as pass by. Our hunters report that foxes are of full them, and they tell a pretty story how they get quit of them. " The fox," say they, " gathers some handfuls of wool from thorns and briers, and wrapping it up, holds it fast in his mouth, then he goes by degrees into a cold river, and dips himself down by little and little; when he finds that all the fleas are crept so high as his head for fear of drowning, and ultimately for shelter crept into the wool, he barks and spits out the wool, full of fleas, and thus very froliquely being delivered from their molestations, he swims to land." ‡

This is a little more doubtful even than the story told of Christina, queen of Sweden, who is reported to have fired at the fleas that troubled her with a piece of artillery, still exhibited in the Royal Arsenal at Stockholm.§ Nor are fleas confined to the old continent, for

Lewis and Clarke found them exceedingly harassing on the banks of the Missouri, where it is said the native Indians are sometimes compelled to shift their quarters, to escape their annoyance. They are not acquainted, it would therefore seem, with the device of the shepherds in Hungary, who grease their clothes with hog's-lard to deter the fleas;* nor with the old English preventive:

"While wormwood hath seed, get a handful or twaine,
To save against March, to make fleas refrain.
Where chamber is swept, and wormwood is strown,
Ne'er flea for his life dare abide to be known."†

Linnæus was in error in stating that the domestic cat (*Felis maniculatus*, TEEMMINCK) is not infested with fleas; for on kittens in particular they abound as numerously as upon dogs.‡

HER MAJESTY'S BUG-DESTROYER.

THE vending of bug-poison in the London streets is seldom followed as a regular source of living. We have met with persons who remember to have seen men selling penny packets of vermin poison, but to find out the vendors themselves was next to an impossibility. The men seem merely to take to the business as a living when all other sources have failed. All, however, agree in acknowledging that there is such a street trade, but that the living it affords is so precarious that few men stop at it longer than two or three weeks.

Perhaps the most eminent firm of the bug-destroyers in London is that of Messrs. Tiffin and Son; but they have pursued their calling in the streets, and rejoice in the title of " Bug-Destroyers to Her Majesty and the Royal Family."

Mr. Tiffin, the senior partner in this house, most kindly obliged me with the following statement. It may be as well to say that Mr. Tiffin appears to have paid much attention to the subject of bugs, and has studied with much earnestness the natural history of this vermin.

" We can trace our business back," he said, " as far as 1695, when one of our ancestors first turned his attention to the destruction of bugs. He was a lady's stay-maker—men used to make them in those days, though, as far as that is concerned, it was a man that made my mother's dresses. This ancestor found some bugs in his house — a young colony of them, that had introduced themselves without his permission, and he didn't like their company, so he tried to turn them out of doors again, I have heard it said, in various ways. It is in history, and it has been handed down in my own family as well, that bugs were first introduced into England after the fire of London, in the timber that

* J. R.   † " Theatre of Insects," p. 1102.
‡ " Theatre of Insects," p. 1102.
§ Linnæus, " Lachesis Lapan." ii. 32, note.

* " Travels."
† Tusser, " Points of Goode Husbandry.
‡ J. R.

was brought for rebuilding the city, thirty years after the fire, and it was about that time that my ancestor first discovered the colony of bugs in his house. I can't say whether he studied the subject of bug-destroying, or whether he found out his stuff by accident, but he certainly *did* invent a compound which completely destroyed the bugs, and, having been so successful in his own house, he named it to some of his customers who were similarly plagued, and that was the commencement of the present connexion, which has continued up to this time.

" At the time of the illumination for the Peace, I thought I must have something over my shop, that would be both suitable for the event and to my business; so I had a transparency done, and stretched on a big frame, and lit up by gas, on which was written—

MAY THE

DESTROYERS OF PEACE

BE DESTROYED BY US.

TIFFIN & SON,

BUG-DESTROYERS TO HER MAJESTY.

" Our business was formerly carried on in the Strand, where both my father and myself were born; in fact, I may say I was born to the bug business.

" I remember my father as well as possible; indeed, I worked with him for ten or eleven years. He used, when I was a boy, to go out to his work killing bugs at his customers' houses with a sword by his side and a cocked-hat and bag-wig on his head— in fact, dressed up like a regular dandy. I remember my grandmother, too, when she was in the business, going to the different houses, and seating herself in a chair, and telling the men what they were to do, to clean the furniture and wash the woodwork.

" I have customers in our books for whom our house has worked these 150 years; that is, my father and self have worked for them and their fathers. We do the work by contract, examining the house every year. It's a precaution to keep the place comfortable. You see, servants are apt to bring bugs in their boxes; and, though there may be only two or three bugs perhaps hidden in the woodwork and the clothes, yet they soon breed if left alone.

" We generally go in the spring, before the bugs lay their eggs; or, if that time passes, it ought to be done before June, before their eggs are hatched, though it's never too late to get rid of a nuisance.

" I mostly find the bugs in the bedsteads. But, if they are left unmolested, they get numerous and climb to the tops of the rooms, and about the corners of the ceilings. They colonize anywhere they can, though they're very high-minded and prefer lofty places. Where iron bedsteads are used the bugs are more in the *rooms*, and that's why such things

are bad. They don't keep a bug away from the person sleeping. Bugs 'll come, if they're thirty yards off.

" I knew a case of a bug who used to come every night about thirty or forty feet—it was an immense large room—from a corner of the room to visit an old lady. There was only one bug, and he'd been there for a long time. I was sent for to find him out. It took me a long time to catch him. In that instance I had to examine every part of the room, and when I got him I gave him an extra nip to serve him out. The reason why I was so bothered was, the bug had hidden itself near the window, the last place I should have thought of looking for him, for a bug never by choice faces the light; but when I came to inquire about it, I found that this old lady never rose till three o'clock in the day, and the window-curtains were always drawn, so that there was no light like.

" Lord! yes, I am often sent for to catch a single bug. I've had to go many, many miles — even 100 or 200 — into the country, and perhaps catch only half-a-dozen bugs after all; but then that's all that are there, so it answers our employer's purpose as well as if they were swarming.

" I work for the upper classes only; that is, for carriage company and such-like approaching it, you know. I have noblemen's names, the first in England, on my books.

" My work is more method; and I may call it a scientific treating of the bugs rather than wholesale murder. We don't care about the thousands, it's the last bug we look for, whilst your carpenters and upholsterers leave as many behind them, perhaps, as they manage to catch.

" The bite of the bug is very curious. They bite all persons the same (?) but the difference of effect lays in the constitution of the parties. I've never noticed that a different kind of skin makes any difference in being bitten. Whether the skin is moist or dry, it don't matter. Wherever bugs are, the person sleeping in the bed is sure to be fed on, whether they are marked or not; and as a proof, when nobody has slept in the bed for some time, the bugs become quite flat; and, on the contrary, when the bed is always occupied, they are round as a ' lady-bird.'

" The flat bug is more ravenous, though even he will allow you time to go to sleep before he begins with you; or at least until he thinks you ought to be asleep. When they find all quiet, not even a light in the room will prevent their biting; but they are seldom or ever found under the bed-clothes. They like a clear ground to get off, and generally bite round the edges of the nightcap or the nightdress. When they are found *in* the bed, it's because the parties have been tossing about, and have curled the sheets round the bugs.

" The finest and the fattest bugs I ever saw were those I found in a black man's bed. He was the favourite servant of an Indian general. He didn't want his bed done by me; he didn't want it touched. His bed was full of 'em, no beehive was ever fuller. The walls and all were the same, there wasn't a patch that wasn't crammed with them. He must have taken them all over the house wherever he went.

"I've known persons to be laid up for months through bug-bites. There was a very handsome fair young lady I knew once, and she was much bitten about the arms, and neck, and face, so that her eyes were so swelled up she couldn't see. The spots rose up like blisters, the same as if stung with a nettle, only on a very large scale. The bites were very much inflamed, and after a time they had the appearance of boils.

"Some people fancy, and it is historically recorded, that the bug smells because it has no vent; but this is fabulous, for they *have* a vent. It is not the human blood neither that makes them smell, because a young bug who has never touched a drop will smell. They breathe, I believe, through their sides; but I can't answer for that, though it's not through the head. They haven't got a mouth, but they insert into the skin the point of a tube, which is quite as fine as a hair, through which they draw up the blood. I have many a time put a bug on the back of my hand, to see how they bite; though I never felt the bite but once, and then I suppose the bug had pitched upon a very tender part, for it was a sharp prick, something like that of a leech-bite.

"I once had a case of lice-killing, for my process will answer as well for them as for bugs, though it's a thing I should never follow by choice. Lice seem to harbour pretty much the same as bugs do. I found them in the furniture. It was a nurse that brought them into the house, though she was as nice and clean a looking woman as ever I saw. I should almost imagine the lice must have been in her, for they say there is a disease of that kind; and if the tics breed in sheep, why should not lice breed in us? for we're but live matter, too. I didn't like myself at all for two or three days after that lice-killing job, I can assure you; it's the only case of the kind I ever had, and I can promise you it shall be the last.

"I was once at work on the Princess Charlotte's own bedstead. I was in the room, and she asked me if I had found anything, and I told her no; but just at that minute I *did* happen to catch one, and upon that she sprang up on the bed, and put her hand on my shoulder, to look at it. She had been tormented by the creature, because I was ordered to come directly, and that was the only one I found. When the Princess saw it, she said, ' Oh, the nasty thing! That's what tormented me last night; don't let him escape.' I think he looked all the better for having tasted royal blood.

"I also profess to kill beetles, though you can never destroy them so effectually as you can bugs; for, you see, beetles run from one house to another, and you can never perfectly get rid of them; you can only keep them under. Beetles will scrape their way and make their road round a fireplace, but how they manage to go from one house to another I can't say, but they *do*.

"I never had patience enough to try and kill fleas by my process; it would be too much of a chivey to please me.

"I never heard of any but one man who seriously went to work selling bug-poison in the streets. I was told by some persons that he was selling a first-rate thing, and I spent several days to find him out. But, after all, his secret proved to be nothing at all. It was train-oil, linseed and hempseed, crushed up all together, and the bugs were to eat it till they burst.

"After all, secrets for bug-poisons ain't worth much, for all depends upon the application of them. For instance, it is often the case that I am sent for to find out one bug in a room large enough for a school. I've discovered it when the creature had been three or four months there, as I could tell by his having changed his jacket so often—for bugs shed their skins, you know. No, there was no reason that he should have bred; it might have been a single gentleman or an old maid.

"A married couple of bugs will lay from forty to fifty eggs at one laying. The eggs are oval, and are each as large as the thirty-second part of an inch; and when together are in the shape of a caraway comfit, and of a bluish-white colour. They'll lay this quantity of eggs three times in a season. The young ones are hatched direct from the egg, and, like young partridges, will often carry the broken eggs about with them, clinging to their back. They get their fore-quarters out, and then they run about before the other legs are completely cleared.

"As soon as the bugs are born they are of a cream colour, and will take to blood directly; indeed, if they don't get it in two or three days they die; but after one feed they will live a considerable time without a second meal. I have known old bugs to be frozen over in a horse-pond—when the furniture has been thrown in the water—and there they have remained for a good three weeks; still, after they have got a little bit warm in the sun's rays they have returned to life again.

"I have myself kept bugs for five years and a half without food, and a housekeeper at Lord H——'s informed me that an old bedstead that I was then moving from a store-room was taken down forty-five years ago, and had not been used since, but the bugs in it were still numerous, though as thin as living skeletons. They couldn't have lived upon the sap of the wood, it being worm-eaten and dry as a bone.

"A bug will live for a number of years, and we find that when bugs are put away in old furniture without food, they don't increase in number; so that, according to my belief, the bugs I just mentioned must have existed forty-five years : besides, they were large ones, and very dark-coloured, which is another proof of age.

" It is a dangerous time for bugs when they are shedding their skins, which they do about four times in the course of a year; then they throw off their hard shell and have a soft coat, so that the least touch will kill them; whereas, at other times they will take a strong pressure. I have plenty of bug-skins, which I keep by me as curiosities, of all sizes and colours, and sometimes I have found the young bugs collected inside the old ones' skins for warmth, as if they had put on their father's great-coat. There are white bugs — albinoes you may call 'em — freaks of nature like."

BLACK-BEETLES.

COCKROACHES are even more voracious than crickets. A small species (*Blatta Lapponica*, LINN.), occasionally met with about London, is said to swarm numerously in the huts of the Laplanders, and will sometimes, iu conjunction with a carrion-beetle (*Silpha Lapponica*, LINN.), devour, we are told, in a single day, their whole store of dried fish.

In London, and many other parts of the country, cockroaches, originally introduced from abroad, have multiplied so prodigiously as to be a great nuisance. They are often so numerous in kitchens and lower rooms in the metropolis as literally to cover the floor, and render it impossible for them to move, except over each other's bodies. This, indeed, only happens after dark, for they are strictly night insects, and the instant a candle is intruded upon the assembly they rush towards their hiding-places, so that in a few seconds not one of the countless multitude is to be seen.

In consequence of their numbers, independently of their carnivorous propensities, they are driven to eat anything that comes in their way; and, besides devouring every species of kitchen-stuff, they gnaw clothes, leather, and books. They likewise pollute everything they crawl over, with an unpleasant nauseous smell.

These "black-beetles," however, as they are commonly called, are harmless when compared with the foreign species, the giant cockroach (*Blatta gigantea*), which is not content with devouring the stores of the larder, but will attack human bodies, and even gnaw the extremities of the dead and dying. — (Drury's *Illustrations of Nat. Hist.* iii. *Pref.*)

Cockroaches, at least the kind that is most abundant in Britain, hate the light, and never come forth from their hiding-places till the lights are removed or extinguished (the *Blatta Germanica*, however, which abounds in some houses, is bolder, making its appearance in the day, and running up the walls and over the tables, to the great annoyance of the in-

habitants). In the London houses, especially on the ground-floor, they are most abundant, and consume everything they can find — flour, bread, meat, clothes, and even shoes. As soon as light, natural or artificial, appears, they all scamper off as fast as they can, and vanish in an instant.

These pests are not indigenous to this country, and perhaps nowhere in Europe, but are one of the evils which commerce has imported. In Captain Cook's last voyage, the ships, while at Husheine, were infested with incredible numbers of these creatures, which it was found impossible by any means to destroy. Every kind of food, when exposed only for a few minutes, was covered with them, and pierced so full of holes, that it resembled a honeycomb. They were so fond of ink that they ate out the writing on labels. Captain Cook's cockroaches were of two kinds — the *Blatta Orientalis* and *Germanica*.—(*Encyc. Britan.*)

The following fact we give from Mr. Douglas's *World of Insects* :—

" Everybody has heard of a haunted house ; nearly every house in and about London *is* haunted. Let the doubters, if they have the courage, go stealthily down to the kitchen at midnight, armed with a light and whatever other weapon they like, and they will see that beings of which Tam o'Shanter never dreamed, whose presence at daylight was only a myth, have here ' a local habitation and a name.' Scared from their nocturnal revels, the creatures run and scamper in all directions, until, in a short time, the stage is clear, and, as in some legend of *diablerie*, nothing remains but a most peculiar odour.

" These were no spirits, had nothing even of the fairy about them, but were veritable cockroaches, or ' black-beetles' — as they are more commonly but erroneously termed — for they are not beetles at all. They have prodigious powers of increase, and are a corresponding nuisance. Kill as many as you will, except, perhaps, by poison, and you cannot extirpate them — the cry is, ' Still they come.'

" One of the best ways to be rid of them is to keep a hedgehog, to which creature they are a favourite food, and his nocturnal habits make him awake to theirs. I have known cats eat cockroaches, but they do not thrive upon them."

" One article of their food would hardly have been suspected," says Mr. Newman, in a note communicated to the Entomological Society, at the meeting in February, 1855. " ' There is nothing new under the sun ;' so says the proverb. I believed, until a few days back, that I possessed the knowledge of a fact in the dietary economy of the cockroach of which entomologists were not cognisant, but I find myself forestalled; the fact is ' as old as the hills.' It is, that the cockroach seeks with diligence and devours with great gusto the common bed-bug.

"I will not mention names, but I am so confident of the veracity of the narrator, that I willingly take the entire responsibility of the following narrative :—

"'Poverty makes one acquainted with strange bedfellows ;' and my informant bears willing testimony to the truth of the adage. He had not been prosperous, and had sought shelter in a London boarding-house ; every night he saw cockroaches ascending his bed-curtains ; every morning he complained to his very respectable landlady, and invariably received the comforting assurance that there was not a 'black-beetle in the house.' Still he pursued his nocturnal investigations, and he not only saw cockroaches running along the tester of the bed, but, to his great astonishment, he positively observed one of them seize a bug, and he therefore concluded, and not without some show of reason, that the cockroach ascended the curtains with this especial object, and that the more odoriferous insect is a favourite food of the major one.

"The following extract from Mr. Webster's 'Narrative of Foster's Voyage,' corroborates this recent observation, and illustrates the proverb which I have taken as my text : 'Cockroaches, those nuisances of ships, are plentiful at St. Helena, and yet, bad as they are, they are more endurable than bugs. Previous to our arrival here in the Chanticleer we had suffered great inconvenience from the latter ; but the cockroaches no sooner made their appearance than the bugs entirely disappeared. The fact is, the cockroach preys upon them, and leaves no sign or vestige of where they have been. So far, the latter is a most valuable insect.' "

So great is the annoyance and discomfort arising from these insects in Cockney households, that the author of a paper in the *Daily News* discusses the best means of effecting their extirpation. The writer of the article referred to avows his conviction, that the ingenious individual who shall devise the means of effectually ridding our houses of these insect pests will deserve to be ranked amongst the benefactors of mankind. The writer details the various expedients resorted to — hedgehogs, cucumber-peel, red wafers, phosphoric paste, glazed basins or pie-dishes filled with beer, or a syrup of beer and sugar, with bits of wood set up from the floor to the edge, for the creatures to run up by, and then be precipitated into the fatal lake, but believes that "none of these methods are fundamental enough for the evil," which, so far as he is yet aware, can only be effectually cured by heating our houses by steam !

BEETLE DESTROYERS.

A FIRM, which has been established in London seven years, and which manufactures exclusively poison known to the trade as the "Phosphor Paste for the destruction of black-beetles, cockroaches, rats, mice," &c., were kind enough to give me the following information :—

"We have now sold this vermin poison for seven years, but we have never had an application for our composition from any street-seller. We have seen, a year or two since, a man about London who used to sell beetle-wafers ; but as we knew that kind of article to be entirely useless, we were not surprised to find that he did not succeed in making a living. We have not heard of him for some time, and have no doubt he is dead, or has taken up some other line of employment.

"It is a strange fact, perhaps ; but we do not know anything, or scarcely anything, as to the kind of people and tradesmen who purchase our poison—to speak the truth, we do not like to make too many inquiries of our customers. Sometimes, when they have used more than their customary quantity, we have asked, casually, how it was and to what kind of business-people they disposed of it, and we have always been met with an evasive sort of answer. You see tradesmen don't like to divulge too much ; for it must be a poor kind of profession or calling that there are no secrets in ; and, again, they fancy we want to know what description of trades use the most of our composition, so that we might supply them direct from ourselves.

"From this cause we have made it a rule not to inquire curiously into the matters of our customers. We are quite content to dispose of the quantity we do, for we employ six travellers to call on chemists and oilmen for the town trade, and four for the country.

"The other day an elderly lady from High-street, Camden Town, called upon us : she stated that she was overrun with black-beetles, and wished to buy some of our paste from ourselves, for she said she always found things better if you purchased them of the maker, as you were sure to get them stronger, and by that means avoided the adulteration of the shopkeepers. But as we have said we would not supply a single box to any one, not wishing to give our agents any cause for complaint, we were obliged to refuse to sell to the old lady.

"We don't care to say how many boxes we sell in the year ; but we can tell you, sir, that we sell more for beetle poisoning in the summer than in the winter, as a matter of course. When we find that a particular district uses almost an equal quantity all the year round, we make sure that that is a rat district ; for where there is not the heat of summer to breed beetles, it must follow that the people wish to get rid of rats.

"Brixton, Hackney, Ball's Pond, and Lower Road, Islington, are the places that use most of our paste, those districts lying low, and being consequently damp. Camden Town, though it is in a high situation, is very much infested with beetles ; it is a clayey soil, you understand, which retains moisture, and will not allow it to filter through like gravel. This is why in some very low districts, where the houses are built on gravel, we sell scarcely any of our paste.

"As the farmers say, a good fruit year is a good fly year; so we say, a good dull, wet summer, is a good beetle summer; and this has been a very fertile year, and we only hope it will be as good next year.

"We don't believe in rat-destroyers; they profess to kill with weasels and a lot of things, and sometimes even say they can charm them away. Captains of vessels, when they arrive in the docks, will employ these people; and, as we say, they generally use our composition, but as long as their vessels are cleared of the vermin, they don't care to know how it is done. A man who drives about in a cart, and does a great business in this way, we have reason to believe uses a great quantity of our Phosphor Paste. He comes from somewhere down the East-end or Whitechapel way.

"Our prices are too high for the street-sellers. Your street-seller can only afford to sell an article made by a person in but a very little better position than himself. Even our small boxes cost at the trade price two shillings a dozen, and when sold will only produce three shillings; so you can imagine the profit is not enough for the itinerant vendor.

"Bakers don't use much of our paste, for they seem to think it no use to destroy the vermin — beetles and bakers' shops generally go together."

CRICKETS.

THE house-cricket may perhaps be deemed a still more annoying insect than the common cockroach, adding an incessant noise to its ravages. Though it may not be unpleasant to hear for a short time "the cricket chirrup in the hearth," so constant a din every evening must greatly interrupt comfort and conversation.

These garrulous animals, which live in a kind of artificial torrid zone, are very thirsty souls, and are frequently found drowned in pans of water, milk, broth, and the like. Whatever is moist, even stockings or linen hung out to dry, is to them a *bonne bouche;* they will eat the skimmings of pots, yeast, crumbs of bread, and even salt, or anything within their reach. Sometimes they are so abundant in houses as to become absolute pests, flying into the candles and even into people's faces.— (Kirby and Spence's *Ent.* i. 206, 7.)

The house-cricket (*Acheta domestica*) is well known for its habit of picking out the mortar of ovens and fire-places, where it not only enjoys warmth, but can procure abundance of food. It is usually supposed that it feeds on bread. M. Latreille says it only eats insects, and it certainly thrives well in houses infested by the cockroach; but we have also known it eat and destroy lamb's-wool stockings, and other woollen stuffs, hung near a fire to dry. Although the food of crickets consists chiefly of vegetable substance, they exhibit a propensity to carnivorous habits. The house-cricket thrives best in the vicinity of a baker's oven, where there are plenty of bread crumbs.

Mouffet marvels at its extreme lankness, inasmuch as there is not "found in the belly any superfluity at all, although it feed on the moisture of flesh and fat of broth, to which, either poured out or reserved, it runs in the night; yea, although it feed on bread, yet is the belly always lank and void of superfluity." —(*Theatre of Insects,* p. 96.)

White of Selborne, again, says, " as one would suppose, from the burning atmosphere which they inhabit, they are a thirsty race, and show a great propensity for liquids, being frequently found dead in pans of water, milk, broth, or the like. Whatever is moist they are fond of, and therefore they often gnaw holes in wet woollen stockings and aprons that are hung to the fire. These crickets are not only very thirsty, but very voracious; for they will eat the scummings of pots, yeast, bread, and kitchen offal, or sweepings of almost every description."—(*Nat. Hist. of Selborne.*)

The cricket is evidently not fond of hard labour, but prefers those places where the mortar is already loosened, or at least is new, soft, and easily scooped out; and in this way it will dig covert channels from room to room. In summer, crickets often make excursions from the house to the neighbouring fields, and dwell in the crevices of rubbish, or the cracks made in the ground by dry weather, where they chirp as merrily as in the snuggest chimney-corner. Whether they ever dig retreats in such circumstances we have not ascertained, though it is not improbable they may do so for the purpose of making nests.

"Those," says Mr. Gough of Manchester, " who have attended to the manners of the hearth-cricket, know that it passes the hottest part of the summer in sunny situations, concealed in the crevices of walls and heaps of rubbish. It quits its summer abode about the end of August, and fixes its residence by the fireside of kitchens or cottages, where it multiplies its species, and is as merry at Christmas as other insects in the dog-days. Thus do the comforts of a warm hearth afford the cricket a safe refuge, not from death, but from temporary torpidity, though it can support this for a long time, when deprived by accident of artificial warmth.

"I came to a knowledge of this fact," continues Mr. Gough, " by planting a colony of these insects in a kitchen, where a constant fire was kept through the summer, but which is discontinued from November till June, with the exception of a day once in six or eight weeks. The crickets were brought from a distance, and let go in this room, in the beginning of September, 1806; here they increased considerably in the course of two months, but were not heard or seen after the fire was removed. Their disappearance led me to conclude that the cold had killed them; but in this I was mistaken; for a brisk fire being kept up for a whole day in the winter, the warmth of it invited my colony from their hiding-place, but not before the evening; after which they continued to skip about and chirp the greater part of the following day, when they again disappeared — being compelled, by the returning cold, to take refuge in their former retreats. They left the chimney-corner on the 25th of May, 1807, after a fit of very hot weather, and revisited their winter residence on the 31st of August. Here they spent the summer merely, and at present (January, 1808) lie torpid in the crevices of the chimney, with the exception of those days on which they are recalled to a temporary existence by the comforts of the fire."—(Reeve, *Essay on the Torpidity of Animals*, p. 84.)

M. Bery St. Vincent tells us that the Spaniards are so fond of crickets that they keep them in cages like singing-birds.—(*Dict. Classique d' Hist. Nat. Art.*, Grillon. Rennie's *Insect Architecture*, 4th edit. p. 242.)

Associated as is the chirping song of the cricket family of insects with the snug chimney-corner, or the sunshine of summer, it affords a pleasure which certainly does not arise from the intrinsic quality of its music. "Sounds," says White, "do not always give us pleasure according to their sweetness and melody; nor do harsh sounds always displease. Thus, the shrilling of the field-cricket (*Acheta campestris*), though sharp and stridulous, yet marvellously delights some hearers, filling their minds with a train of summer ideas of everything that is rural, verdurous, and joyous." —(*Nat. Hist. of Selborne*, ii. 73.)

> "Sounds inharmonious in themselves. and harsh,
> Yet heard in scenes where peace for ever reigns,
> And only there, please highly for their sake."
> COWPER, *Task*, Book I.

This circumstance, no doubt, causes the Spaniards to keep them in cages, as we do singing-birds. White tells us that, if supplied with moistened leaves, they will sing as merrily and loud in a paper cage as in the fields; but he did not succeed in planting a colony of them in the terrace of his garden, though he bored holes for them in the turf to save them the labour of digging.

The hearth-cricket, again, though we hear it occasionally in the hedge-banks in summer,

prefers the warmth of an oven or a good fire, and thence, residing as it were always in the torrid zone, is ever alert and merry — a good Christmas fire being to it what the heat of the dog-days is to others.

Though crickets are frequently heard by day, yet their natural time of motion is only in the night. As soon as darkness prevails the chirping increases, whilst the hearth-crickets come running forth, and are often to be seen in great numbers, from the size of a flea to that of their full stature.

Like the field-cricket, the hearth-crickets are sometimes kept for their music; and the learned Scaliger took so great a fancy to their song, that he was accustomed to keep them in a box in his study. It is reported that in some parts of Africa they are kept and fed in a kind of iron oven, and sold to the natives, who like their chirp, and think it is a good soporific.—(Mouffet, *Theat. Insect.* 136.)

Milton, too, chose for his contemplative pleasures a spot where crickets resorted :—

> "Where glowing embers through the room
> Teach light to counterfeit a gloom,
> Far from all resort of mirth,
> See the cricket on the hearth."—*Il Penseroso.*

Rennie, in his *Insect Miscellanies*, says, "We have been as unsuccessful in transplanting the hearth-cricket as White was with the field-crickets. In two different houses we have repeatedly introduced crickets, but could not prevail on them to stay. One. of our trials, indeed, was made in summer, with insects brought from a garden-wall, and it is probable they thought the kitchen fire-side too hot at that season."—(p. 82.)

The so-called *chirp* of the cricket is a vulgar error. The instrument (for so it may be styled) upon which the male cricket plays (the female is mute) consists of strong nervures or rough strings in the wing-cases, by the friction of which against each other a sound is produced and communicated to the membranes stretched between them, in the same manner as the vibrations caused by the friction of the finger upon the tambourine are diffused over its surface. It is erroneously stated in a popular work, that "the organ is a membrane, which in contracting, by means of a muscle and tendon placed under the wings of the insect, folds down somewhat like a fan;" and this, being "always dry, yields by its motion a sharp piercing sound."—(Bing, *Anim. Biog.* iv. 6th edit. Rennie's *Insect Miscellanies*, p. 62.)

OUR STREET FOLK.

I.—STREET EXHIBITORS.

PUNCH.

THE performer of Punch that I saw was a short, dark, pleasant-looking man, dressed in a very greasy and very shiny green shooting-jacket. This was fastened together by one button in front, all the other button-holes having been burst through. Protruding from his bosom, a corner of the pandean pipes was just visible, and as he told me the story of his adventures, he kept playing with the band of his very limp and very rusty old beaver hat. He had formerly been a gentleman's servant, and was especially civil in his manners. He came to me with his hair tidily brushed for the occasion, but apologised for his appearance on entering the room. He was very communicative, and took great delight in talking like Punch, with his call in his mouth, while some young children were in the room, and who, hearing the well-known sound of Punch's voice, looked all about for the figure. Not seeing the show, they fancied the man had the figure in his pocket, and that the sounds came from it. The change from Punch's voice to the man's natural tone was managed without an effort, and instantaneously. It had a very peculiar effect.

" I am the proprietor of a Punch's show," he said. " I goes about with it myself, and performs inside the frame behind the green baize. I have a pardner what plays the music—the pipes and drum; him as you see'd with me. I have been five-and-twenty year now at the business. I wish I'd never seen it, though it's *been* a money-making business—indeed, the best of all the street hex-hibitions I may say. I am fifty years old. I took to it for money gains—that was what I done it for. I formerly lived in service—was a footman in a gentleman's family. When I first took to it, I could make two and three pounds a-day—I could so. You see, the way in which I took first to the business was this here—there was a party used to come and ' cheer' for us at my master's house, and her son having a hexhibition of his own, and being in want of a pardner, axed me if so be I'd go out, which was a thing that I degraded at the time. He gave me information as to what the money-taking was, and it seemed to me that good, that it would pay me better nor service. I had twenty pounds a-year in my place, and my board and lodging, and two suits of clothes, but the young man told me as how I could make one pound a-day at the Punch-and-Judy business, after a little practice. I took a deal of persuasion, though, before I'd join him—it was beneath my dignity to fall from a footman to a showman. But, you see, the French gennelman as I lived with (he were a merchant in the city, and had fourteen clerks working for him) went back to his own country to reside, and left me with a written kerrackter ; but that was no use to me : though I'd fine recommendations at the back of it, no one would look at it ; so I was five months out of employment, knocking about—living first on my wages and then on my clothes, till all was gone but the few rags on my back. So I began to think that the Punch-and-Judy business was better than starving after all. Yes, I should think anything was better than that, though it's a business that, after you've once took to, you never can get out of—people fancies you know too much, and won't have nothing to say to you. If I got a situation at a tradesman's, why the boys would be sure to recognise me behind the counter, and begin a shouting into the shop (they *must* shout, you know): ' Oh, there's Punch and Judy—there's Punch a-sarving out the customers!' Ah, it's a great annoyance being a public kerrackter, I can assure you, sir; go where you will, it's ' Punchy, Punchy!' As for the boys, they'll never leave me alone till I die, I know; and I suppose in my old age I shall have to take to the parish broom. All our forefathers died in the workhouse. I don't know a Punch's showman that hasn't. One of my pardners was buried by the workhouse ; and even old Pike, the most noted showman as ever was, died in the workhouse—Pike and Porsini. Porsini was the first original street Punch, and Pike was his apprentice ; their names is handed down to posterity among the noblemen and footmen of the land. They both died in the workhouse, and, in course, I shall do the same. Something else *might* turn up, to be sure. We can't say what this luck of the world is. I'm obliged to strive very hard—very hard indeed, sir, now, to get a living ; and then not to get it after all—at times, compelled to go short, often.

" Punch, you know, sir, is a dramatic performance in two hacts. It's a play, you may say. I don't think it can be called a tragedy hexactly ; a drama is what we names it. There is tragic parts, and comic and sentimental parts, too. Some families where I performs will have it most sentimental—in the original style ; them families is generally sentimental theirselves. Others is all for the comic, and then I has to kick up all the games I can. To the sentimental folk I am obliged to perform werry steady and werry slow, and leave out all comic words and business. They won't have no ghost, no coffin, and no devil; and that's what I call spiling the performance entirely. It's the march of hintellect wot's a doing all this—it is, sir. But I was a going to tell you about my first jining the business. Well, you see, after a good deal of persuading, and being drew to it, I may say, I consented to go out with the young man as I were a-speaking about. He was to give me twelve shillings a-week and my keep, for two years certain, till I could get my own show things together, and for that I was to carry the show, and go round and *collect*. Collecting, you know, sounds better than begging; the pro-nounciation's better like. Sometimes the peo-ple says, when they sees us a coming round, ' Oh, here they comes a-begging'—but it can't be begging, you know, when you're a hexerting yourselves. I couldn't play the drum and pipes, so the young man used to do that himself, to call the people together before he got into the show. I used to stand outside, and patter to the figures. The first time that ever I went out with Punch was in the be-ginning of August, 1825. I did all I could to avoid being seen. My dignity was hurt at being hobligated to take to the streets for a living. At fust I fought shy, and used to feel queer somehow, you don't know how like, whenever the people used to look at me. I remember werry well the first street as ever I performed in. It was off Gray's Inn, one of them quiet, genteel streets, and when the mob began to gather round I felt all-overish, and I turned my head to the frame instead of the people. We hadn't had no rehearsals afore-hand, and I did the patter quite permiscuous. There was not much talk, to be sure, required then; and what little there was, consisted merely in calling out the names of the figures as they came up, and these my master prompted me with from inside the frame. But little as there was for me to do, I know I never could have done it, if it hadn't been for the spirits—the false spirits, you see (a little drop of gin), as my master guv me in the morning. The first time as ever I made my appearance in public, I collected as much as eight shillings, and my master said, after the performance was over, ' You'll do!' You see I was partly in livery, and looked a little bit decent like. After this was over, I kept on going out with my master for two years, as I had agreed, and at the end of that time I had saved enough to start a show of my own. I bought the show of old Porsini, the man as first brought Punch into the streets of Eng-land. To be sure, there was a woman over here with it before then. Her name was—— I can't think of it just now, but she never per-formed in the streets, so we consider Porsini as our real forefather. It isn't much more nor seventy years since Porsini (he was a werry old man when he died, and blind) showed the hexhibition in the streets of London. I've heerd tell that old Porsini used to take very often as much as ten pounds a-day, and he used to sit down to his fowls and wine, and

the very best of everything, like the first gennelman in the land; indeed, he made enough money at the business to be quite a tip-top gennelman, that he did. But he never took care of a halfpenny he got. He was that independent, that if he was wanted to perform, sir, he'd come at his time, not your'n. At last, he reduced himself to want, and died in St. Giles's workhouse. Ah, poor fellow! he oughtn't to have been allowed to die where he did, after amusing the public for so many years. Every one in London knowed him. Lords, dukes, princes, squires, and wagabonds —all used to stop to laugh at his performance, and a funny clever old fellow he was. He was past performing when I bought my show of him, and werry poor. He was living in the Coal-yard, Drury-lane, and had scarcely a bit of food to eat. He had spent all he had got in drink, and in treating friends,—aye, any one, no matter who. He didn't study the world, nor himself neither. As fast as the money came it went, and when it was gone, why, he'd go to work and get more. His show was a very inferior one, though it were the fust—nothing at all like them about now —nothing near as good. If you only had four sticks then, it was quite enough to make plenty of money out of, so long as it was Punch. I gave him thirty-five shillings for the stand, figures and all. I bought it cheap, you see, for it was thrown on one side, and was of no use to any one but such as myself. There was twelve figures and the other happa-ratus, such as the gallows, ladder, horse, bell, and stuffed dog. The characters was Punch, Judy, Child, Beadle, Scaramouch, Nobody, Jack Ketch, the Grand Senoor, the Doctor, the Devil (there was no Ghost used then), Merry Andrew, and the Blind Man. These last two kerrackters are quite done with now. The heads of the kerrackters was all carved in wood, and dressed in the proper costume of the country. There was at that time, and is now, a real carver for the Punch business. He was dear, but werry good and hexcellent. His Punch's head was the best as I ever seed. The nose and chin used to meet quite close together. A set of new figures, dressed and all, would come to about fifteen pounds. Each head costs five shillings for the bare carving alone, and every figure that we has takes at least a yard of cloth to dress him, besides ornaments and things that comes werry ex-pensive. A good show at the present time will cost three pounds odd for the stand alone —that's including baize, the frontispiece, the back scene, the cottage, and the letter cloth, or what is called the drop-scene at the theatres. In the old ancient style, the back scene used to pull up and change into a gaol scene, but that's all altered now.

" We've got more upon the comic business now, and tries to do more with Toby than with the prison scene. The prison is what we calls the sentimental style. Formerly

Toby was only a stuffed figure. It was Pike who first hit upon hintroducing a live dog, and a great hit it were—it made a grand alteration in the hexhibition, for now the performance is called Punch and Toby *as well.* There is one Punch about the streets at present that tries it on with three dogs, but that ain't much of a go—too much of a good thing I calls it. Punch, as I said before, is a drama in two hacts. We don't drop the scene at the end of the first—the drum and pipes strikes up instead. The first act we consider to end with Punch being taken to prison for the murder of his wife and child. The great difficulty in performing Punch consists in the speaking, which is done by a call, or whistle in the mouth, such as this here." (He then produced the call from his waistcoat pocket. It was a small flat instrument, made of two curved pieces of metal about the size of a knee-buckle, bound together with black thread. Between these was a plate of some substance (apparently silk), which he said was a secret. The call, he told me, was tuned to a musical instrument, and took a considerable time to learn. He afterwards took from his pocket two of the small metallic plates unbound. He said the composition they were made of was also one of the " secrets of the purfession." They were not tin, nor zinc, because " both of them metals were poisons in the mouth, and hinjurious to the constitution.") " These calls," he continued, " we often sell to gennelmen for a sovereign a-piece, and for that we give 'em a receipt how to use them. They ain't whistles, but calls, or unknown tongues, as we sometimes names 'em, because with them in the mouth we can pronounce each word as plain as any parson. We have two or three kinds — one for out-of-doors, one for in-doors, one for speaking and for singing, and another for selling. I've sold many a one to gennelmen going along, so I generally keeps a hextra one with me. Porsini brought the calls into this country with him from Italy, and we who are now in the purfession have all learnt how to make and use them, either from him or those as he had taught 'em to. I larnt the use of mine from Porsini himself. My master whom I went out with at first would never teach me, and was werry partickler in keeping it all secret from me. Porsini taught me the call at the time I bought his show of him. I was six months in perfecting myself in the use of it. I kept practising away night and morning with it, until I got it quite perfect. It was no use trying at home, 'cause it sounds quite different in the hopen hair. Often when I've made 'em at home, I'm obliged to take the calls to pieces after trying 'em out in the streets, they've been made upon too weak a scale. When I was practising, I used to go into the parks, and fields, and out-of-the-way places, so as to get to know how to use it in the hopen hair. Now I'm reckoned one of the best speakers in the whole purfession. When I made my first appearance as a regular performer of Punch on my own account, I did feel uncommon narvous, to be sure : though I know'd the people couldn't see me behind the baize, still I felt as if all the eyes of the country were upon me. It was as much as hever I could do to get the words out, and keep the figures from shaking. When I struck up the first song, my voice trembled so as I thought I never should be able to get to the hend of the first hact. I soon, however, got over that there, and at present I'd play before the whole bench of bishops as cool as a cowcumber. We always have a pardner now to play the drum and pipes, and collect the money. This, however, is only a recent dodge. In older times we used to go about with a trumpet—that was Porsini's ancient style ; but now that's stopped. Only her majesty's mails may blow trumpets in the streets at present. The fust person who went out with me was my wife. She used to stand outside, and keep the boys from peeping through the baize, whilst I was performing behind it ; and she used to collect the money afterwards as well. I carried the show and trumpet, and she the box. She's been dead these five years now. Take one week with another, all through the year, I should say I made then five pounds regular. I *have* taken as much as two pounds ten shillings in one day in the streets ; and I used to think it a bad day's business at that time if I took only one pound. You can see Punch has been good work—a money-making business—and beat all mechanics right out. If I could take as much as I did when I first began, what must my forefathers have done, when the business was five times as good as ever it were in my time ? Why, I leaves you to judge what old Porsini and Pike must have made. Twenty years ago I have often and often got seven shillings and eight shillings for one hexhibition in the streets : two shillings and three shillings I used to think low to get at one collection ; and many times I'd perform eight or ten times in a day. We didn't care much about work then, for we could get money fast enough ; but now I often show twenty times in the day, and get scarcely a bare living at it arter all. That shows the times, you know, sir—what things was and is now. Arter performing in the streets of a day we used to attend private parties in the hevening, and get sometimes as much as two pounds for the hexhibition. This used to be at the juvenile parties of the nobility ; and the performance lasted about an hour and a half. For a short performance of half-an-hour at a gennelman's house we never had less than one pound. A performance outside the house was two shillings and sixpence ; but we often got as much as ten shillings for it. I have performed afore almost all the nobility. Lord —— was particular partial to us, and one of our greatest patronizers. At the time of the Police Bill I met him at Cheltenham on my travels, and he told me as he had saved Punch's neck once more; and it's through him principally that we are allowed to exhibit in the streets. Punch is exempt from the Police Act. If you read the hact throughout, you won't find Punch mentioned in it. But all I've been telling you is about the business as it was. What it *is,* is a werry different consarn. A good day for us now seldom gets beyond five shillings, and that's between myself and my pardner, who plays the drum and pipes. Often we are out all day, and get a mere nuffing. Many days we have been out and taken nuffing at all—that's werry common when we dwells upon horders. By dwelling on horders, I means looking out for gennelmen what want us to play in front of their houses. When we strike up in the hopen street we take upon a haverage only threepence a show. In course we *may* do more, but that's about the sum, take one street performance with another. Them kind of performances is what we calls ' short showing.' We gets the halfpence and hooks it. A 'long pitch' is the name we gives to performances that lasts about half-an-hour or more. Them long pitches we confine solely to street corners in public thoroughfares; and then we take about a shilling upon a haverage, and more if it's to be got—we never turns away nuffing. 'Boys, look up your fardens, says the outside man; 'it ain't half over yet, we'll show it all through.' The short shows we do only in private by-streets, and of them we can get through about twenty in the day; that's as much as we can tackle —ten in the morning, and ten in the afternoon. Of the long pitches we can only do eight in the day. We start on our rounds at nine in the morning, and remain out till dark at night. We gets a snack at the publics on our road. The best hours for Punch are in the morning from nine till ten, because then the children are at home. Arter that, you know, they goes out with the maids for a walk. From twelve till three is good again, and then from six till nine; that's because the children are mostly at home at them hours. We make much more by horders for performance houtside the gennelmen's houses, than we do by performing in public in the hopen streets. Monday is the best day for street business; Friday is no day at all, because then the poor people has spent all their money. If we was to pitch on a Friday, we shouldn't take a halfpenny in the streets, so we in general on that day goes round for horders. Wednesday, Thursday, and Friday is the best days for us with horders at gennelmen's houses. We do much better in the spring than at any other time in the year, excepting holiday time, at Midsummer and Christmas. That's what we call Punch's season. We do most at hevening parties in the holiday time, and if there's a pin to choose

between them, I should say Christmas holidays was the best. For attending hevening parties now we generally get one pound and our refreshments—as much more as they like to give us. But the business gets slacker and slacker every season. Where I went to ten parties twenty years ago, I don't go to two now. People isn't getting tired of our performances, but stingier—that's it. Everybody looks at their money now afore they parts with it, and gennelfolks haggles and cheapens us down to shillings and sixpences, as if they was guineas in the holden time. Our business is werry much like hackney-coach work; we do best in vet vether. It looks like rain this evening, and I'm uncommon glad on it, to be sure. You see, the vet keeps the children in-doors all day, and then they wants something to quiet 'em a bit; and the mothers and fathers, to pacify the dears, gives us a horder to perform. It mustn't rain cats and dogs—that's as bad as no rain at all. What we likes is a regular good, steady Scotch mist, for then we takes double what we takes on other days. In summer we does little or nothing; the children are out all day enjoying themselves in the parks. The best pitch of all in London is Leicester-square; there's all sorts of classes, you see, passing there. Then comes Regent-street (the corner of Burlington-street is uncommon good, and there's a good publican there besides). Bond-street ain't no good now. Oxford-street, up by Old Cavendish-street, or Oxford-market, or Wells-street, are all favourite pitches for Punch. We don't do much in the City. People has their heads all full of business there, and them as is greedy arter the money ain't no friend of Punch's. Tottenham-court-road, the New-road, and all the henvirons of London, is pretty good. Hampstead, tho', ain't no good; they've got too poor there. I'd sooner not go out at all than to Hampstead. Belgrave-square, and all about that part, is uncommon good; but where there's many chapels Punch won't do at all. I did once, though, strike up hopposition to a street preacher wot was a holding forth in the New-road, and did uncommon well. All his flock, as he called 'em, left him, and come over to look at me. Punch and preaching is two different creeds—hopposition parties, I may say. We in generally walks from twelve to twenty mile every day, and carries the show, which weighs a good half-hundred, at the least. Arter great exertion, our woice werry often fails us; for speaking all day through the ' call ' is werry trying, 'specially when we are chirruping up so as to bring the children to the vinders. The boys is the greatest nuisances we has to contend with. Wherever we goes we are sure of plenty of boys for a hindrance; but they've got no money, bother 'em! and they'll follow us for miles, so that we're often compelled to go miles to awoid 'em. Many parts is swarming with boys, such as Vitechapel. Spitalfields,

PUNCH'S SHOWMEN.

[*From a Photograph.*]

that's the worst place for boys I ever come a-near; they're like flies in summer there, only much more thicker. I never shows my face within miles of them parts. Chelsea, again, has an uncommon lot of boys; and wherever we know the children swarm, there's the spots we makes a point of awoiding. Why, the boys is such a hobstruction to our performance, that often we are obliged to drop the curtain for 'em. They'll throw one another's caps into the frame while I'm inside on it, and do what we will, we can't keep 'em from poking their fingers through the baize and making holes to peep through. Then they *will* keep tapping the drum; but the worst of all is, the most of 'em ain't got a farthing to bless themselves with, and they *will* shove into the best places. Soldiers, again, we don't like, they've got no money—no, not even so much as pockets, sir. Nusses ain't no good. Even if the mothers of the dear little children has given 'em a penny to spend, why the nusses takes it from 'em, and keeps it for ribbins. Sometimes we can coax a penny out of the children, but the nusses knows too much to be gammoned by us. Indeed, servants in generally don't do the thing what's right to us—some is good to us, but the most of 'em will have poundage out of what we gets. About sixpence out of every half-crown is what the footman takes from us. We in generally goes into the country in the summer time for two or three months. Watering-places is werry good in July and August. Punch mostly goes down to the sea-side with the quality. Brighton, though, ain't no account; the Pavilion's done up with, and therefore Punch has discontinued his visits. We don't put up at the trampers' houses on our travels, but in generally inns is where we stays; because we considers ourselves to be above the other showmen and mendicants. At one lodging-house as I stopped at once in Warwick, there was as many as fifty staying there what got their living by street perform-ances—the greater part were Italian boys and girls. There are altogether as many as six-teen Punch-and-Judy frames in England. Eight of these is at work in London, and the other eight in the country; and to each of these frames there are two men. We are all acquainted with one another; are all sociable together, and know where each other is, and what they are a-doing on. When one comes home, another goes out; that's the way we proceed through life. It wouldn't do for two to go to the same place. If two of us happens to meet at one town, we jine, and shift pardners, and share the money. One goes one way, and one another, and we meet at night, and reckon up over a sociable pint or a glass. We shift pardners so as each may know how much the other has taken. It's the common practice for the man what per-forms Punch to share with the one wot plays the drum and pipes—each has half wot is

collected; but if the pardner can't play the drum and pipes, and only carries the frame, and collects, then his share is but a third of what is taken till he learns how to perform himself. The street performers of London lives mostly in little rooms of their own; they has generally wives, and one or two children, who are brought up to the business. Some lives about the Westminster-road, and St. George's East. A great many are in Lock's-fields—they are all the old school that way. Then some, or rather the principal part of the showmen, are to be found about Lisson-grove. In this neighbourhood there is a house of call, where they all assembles in the evening. There are a very few in Brick-lane, Spitalfields, now; that is mostly deserted by showmen. The West-end is the great resort of all; for it's there the money lays, and there the showmen abound. We all know one another, and can tell in what part of the country the others are. We have intelligence by letters from all parts. There's a Punch I knows on now is either in the Isle of Man, or on his way to it."

Punch Talk.

" ' Bona parlare ' means language ; name of patter. ' Yeute munjare '—no food. ' Yeute lente'—no bed. ' Yeute bivare '—no drink. I've ' yeute munjare,' and ' yeute bivare,' and, what's worse, 'yeute lente.' This is better than the costers' talk, because that ain't no slang at all, and this is a broken Italian, and much higher than the costers' lingo. We know what o'clock it is, besides.'

Scene with two Punchmen.

" ' How are you getting on ?' I might say to another Punchman. ' Ultra cateva,' he'd say. If I was doing a little, I'd say, ' Bonar.' Let us have a ' shant a bivare '—pot o' beer. If we has a good pitch we never tell one another, for business is business. If they know we've a ' bonar ' pitch, they'll oppose, which makes it bad.

" ' Co. and Co.' is our term for partner, or ' questa questa,' as well. ' Ultray cativa,'—no bona. ' Slumareys '—figures, frame, scenes, properties. ' Slum '—call, or unknown tongue. ' Ultray cativa slum '—not a good call. ' Tam-bora '—drum ; that's Italian. ' Pipares '— pipes. ' Questra homa a vardring the slum, scapar it, Orderly '—there's someone a looking at the slum. Be off quickly. ' Fielia ' is a child; ' Homa ' is a man; ' Dona,' a female; ' Charfering-homa '—talking-man, policeman. Policeman can't interfere with us, we're sanc-tioned. Punch is exempt out of the Police Act. Some's very good men, and some on 'em are tyrants; but generally speaking they're all werry kind to us, and allows us every privi-lege. That's a flattery, you know, because you'd better not meddle with them. Civility always gains its esteem."

The man here took a large clasp-knife out of his breeches pocket.

" This here knife is part of Punch's tools or materials, of great utility, for it cannot be done without. The knife serves for a hammer, to draw nails and drive them in again, and is very handy on a country road to cut a beefsteak—not a mistake—Well, ye cannot cut a mistake, can ye ?—and is a real poor man's friend to a certainty.

" This here is the needle that completes our tools (*takes out a needle from inside his waistcoat collar,*) and is used to sew up our cativa stumps, that is, Punch's breeches and Judy's petticoats, and his master's old clothes when they're in holes. I likes to have everything tidy and respectable, not knowing where I'm going to perform to, for every day is a new day that we never see afore and never shall see again ; we do not know the produce of this world, being luxurant (that's moral), being humane, kind, and generous to all our society of life. We mends our cativa and slums when they gets teearey (if you was to show that to some of our line they'd be horrified ; they can't talk so affluent, you know, in all kinds of black slums). Under the hedgeares, and were no care varder us questa—' questa' is a shirt—pronunciation for questra homa.

" Once, too, when I was scarpering with my culling in the monkey, I went to mendare the cativa slums in a churchyard, and sat down under the tombs to stitch 'em up a bit, thinking no one would varder us there. But Mr. Crookshank took us off there as we was a sitting. I know I'm the same party, 'cos Joe seen the print you know and draw'd quite nat'ral, as now in print, with the slumares a laying about on all the tombstones round us."

The Punchman at the Theatre.

" I used often when a youth to be very fond of plays and romances, and frequently went to theatres to learn knowledge, of which I think there is a deal of knowledge to be learnt from those places (that gives the theatres a touch —helps them on a bit). I was very partial and fond of seeing Romeau and Juliet ; Otheller ; and the Knights of St. John, and the Pretty Gal of Peerlesspool ; Macbeth and the Three Dancing Witches. Don Goovarney pleased me best of all though. What took me uncommon were the funeral purcession of Juliet—it affects the heart, and brings us to our nat'ral feelings. I took my ghost from Romeau and Juliet ; the ghost comes from the grave, and it's beautiful. I used to like Kean, the principal performer. Oh, admirable ! most admirable he were, and especially in Otheller, for then he was like my Jim Crow here, and was always a great friend and supporter of his old friend Punch. Otheller murders his wife, ye know, like Punch does. Otheller kills her, 'cause the green - eyed monster has got into his 'art, and he being so extremely fond on her ; but Punch kills his'n by accident, though he did not intend to do it, for the Act of Parliament against husbands

beating wives was not known in his time. A most excellent law that there, for it causes husbands and wives to be kind and natural one with the other, all through the society of life. Judy irritates her husband, Punch, for to strike the fatal blow, vich at the same time, vith no intention to commit it, not knowing at the same time, being rather out of his mind, vot he vas about. I hope this here will be a good example both to men and wives, always to be kind and obleeging to each other, and that will help them through the mainder with peace and happiness, and will rest in peace with all mankind (that's moral). It must be well worded, ye know, that's my beauty."

Mr. Punch's Refreshment.

" Always Mr. Punch, when he performs to any nobleman's juvenile parties, he requires a little refreshment and sperrits before commencing, because the performance will go far superior. But where teetotallers is he plays very mournful, and they don't have the best parts of the dramatical performance. Cos pump-vater gives a person no heart to exhibit his performance, where if any sperrits is given to him he woold be sure to give the best of satisfaction. I likes where I goes to perform for the gennelman to ring the bell, and say to the butler to bring this here party up whatever he chooses. But Punch is always moderate ; he likes one eye wetted, then the tother after ; but he likes the best : not particular to brandy, for fear of his nose of fading, and afeerd of his losing the colour. All theatrical people, and even the great Edmund Kean, used to take a drop before commencing performance, and Punch must do the same, for it enlivens his sperrits, cheers his heart up, and enables him to give the best of satisfaction imaginable."

The History of Punch.

" There are hoperas and romarnces. A romarnce is far different to a hopera, you know ; for one is interesting, and the other is dull and void of apprehension. The romance is the interesting one, and of the two I likes it the best ; but let every one speak as they find—that's moral. Jack Sheppard, you know, is a romarnce, and a fine one ; but Punch is a hopera—a huproar, we calls it, and the most pleasing and most interesting of all as was ever produced, Punch never was beat and never will, being the oldest performance for many hundred years, and now handed down to prosperity (there's a fine moral in it, too).

" The history or origination of Punch—(never put yerself out of yer way for me, I'm one of the happiest men in existence, and gives no trouble)—is taken from Italy, and brought over to England by Porsini, and exhibited in the streets of London for the first time from sixty to seventy years ago ; though he was not the first man who exhibited, for there was a female here before him, but not to perform at all in public—name unknown, but handed down to prosperity. She brought the figures and frame over with her, but never showed 'em—keeping it an unknown secret. Porsini came from Hitaly, and landed in England, and exhibited his performance in the streets of London, and realized an immense sum of money. Porsini always carried a rum-bottle in his pocket ('cause Punch is a rum fellow, ye see, and he's very fond of rum), and drinked out of this unbeknown behind the baize afore he went into the frame, so that it should lay in his power to give the audience a most excellent performance. He was a man as gave the greatest satisfaction, and he was the first man that brought a street horgan into England from Hitaly. His name is handed down to prosperity among all classes of society in life.

"At first, the performance was quite different then to what it is now. It was all sentimental then, and very touching to the feelings, and full of good morals. The first part was only made up of the killing of his wife and babby, and the second with the execution of the hangman and killing of the devil—that was the original drama of Punch, handed down to prosperity for 800 years. The killing of the devil makes it one of the most moral plays as is, for it stops Satan's career of life, and then we can all do as we likes afterwards.

"Porsini lived like the first nobleman in the land, and realized an immense deal of money during his lifetime; we all considered him to be our forefather. He was a very old man when he died. I've heard tell he used to take very often as much as 10l. a-day, and now it's come down to little more than 10d.; and he used to sit down to his fowls and wine, and the very best of luxuriousness, like the first nobleman in the world, such as a bottle of wine, and cetera. At last he reduced himself to want, and died in the workhouse. Ah! poor fellow, he didn't ought to have been let die where he did, but misfortunes will happen to all—that's moral. Every one in London knowed him: lords, dukes, squires, princes, and wagabones, all used to stop and laugh at his pleasing and merry interesting performance; and a funny old fellow he was, and so fond of his snuff. His name is writ in the annuals of history, and handed down as long as grass grows and water runs—for when grass ceases to grow, ye know, and water ceases to run, this world will be no utility; that's moral.

"Pike, the second noted street performer of Punch, was Porsini's apprentice, and he succeeded him after his career. He is handed down as a most clever exhibitor of Punch and showman—'cause he used to go about the country with waggons, too. He exhibited the performance for many years, and at last came to decay, and died in the workhouse. He was the first inventor of the live dog called Toby, and a great invention it was, being a great undertaking of a new and excellent addition to Punch's performance—that's well worded—we must place the words in a superior manner to please the public.

"Then if, as you see, all our forefathers went to decay and died in the workhouse, what prospect have we to look forward to before us at the present time but to share the same fate, unless we meet with sufficient encouragement in this life? But hoping it will not be so, knowing that there is a new generation and a new exhibition, we hope the public at large will help and assist, and help us to keep our head above water, so that we shall never float down the river Thames, to be picked up, carried in a shell, coroner's inquest held, taken to the workhouse, popped into the pithole, and there's an end to another poor old Punch—that's moral.

"A footman is far superior to a showman, 'cause a showman is held to be of low degrade, and are thought as such, and so circumstantiated as to be looked upon as a mendicant; but still we are not, for collecting ain't begging, it's only selliciting; 'cause parsons, you know (I gives them a rub here), preaches a sermon and collects at the doors, so I puts myself on the same footing as they—that's moral, and it's optional, ye know. If I takes a hat round, they has a plate, and they gets sovereigns where we has only browns; but we are thankful for all, and always look for encouragement, and hopes kind support from all classes of society in life.

"Punch has two kind of performances—short shows and long ones, according to denare. Short shows are for cativa denare, and long pitches for the bona denare. At the short shows we gets the ha'pence and steps it—scafare, as we say; and at the long pitches ve keeps it up for half an hour, or an hour, maybe—not particular, if the browns tumble in well—for we never leave off while there's a major solde (that's a halfpenny), or even a quartereen (that's a farden), to be made. The long pitches we fixes at the principal street-corners of London. We never turn away nothink.

"'Boys, look up your fardens,' says the outside man; 'it ain't half over yet, and we'll show it all through.'

"Punch is like the income-tax gatherer, takes all we can get, and never turns away nothink—that is our moral. Punch is like the rest of the world, he has got bad morals, but very few of them. The showman inside the frame says, while he's a working the figures, 'Culley, how are you a getting on?' 'Very inferior indeed, I'm sorry to say, master. The company, though very respectable, seems to have no pence among 'em.' 'What quanta denare have you chafered?' I say. 'Soldi major quartereen;' that means, three halfpence three fardens; 'that is all I have accumulated amongst this most respectable and numerous company.' 'Never mind, master, the showman will go on; try the generosity of the public once again.' 'Well, I think it's of very little utility to collect round again, for I've met with that poor encouragement.' 'Never mind, master, show away. I'll go round again and chance my luck; the ladies and gentlemen have not seen sufficient, I think. Well, master, I've got tres major'—that is, three half-pence—'more, and now it's all over this time. Boys, go home and say your prayers,' we says, and steps it. Such scenes of life we see! No person would hardly credit what we go through. We travel often yeute munjare (no food), and oftentimes we're in fluence, according as luck runs.

"We now principally dwells on orders at noblemen's houses. The sebubs of London pays us far better than the busy town of London. When we are dwelling on orders, we goes along the streets chirripping 'Roo-tooerovey ooey-ooey-ooerovey;' that means, Any more wanted? that's the pronounciation of the call in the old Italian style. Toorovey-to-roo-to-roo-toroo-torooey; that we does when we are dwelling for orders mostly at noblemen's houses. It brings the juvenials to the window, and causes the greatest of attractions to the children of noblemen's families, both rich and poor: lords, dukes, earls, and squires, and gentlefolks.

"'Call-hunting,'—that's another term for dwelling on orders—pays better than pitching; but orders is wery casual, and pitching is a certainty. We're sure of a brown or two in the streets, and noblemen's work don't come often. We must have it authentick, for we travels many days and don't succeed in getting one; at other times we are more fluent; but when both combine together, it's merely a living, after all's said and done, by great exertion and hard perseverance and asidity, for the business gets slacker and slacker every year, and I expect at last it will come to the dogs—not Toby, because he is dead and gone. People isn't getting tired with our performances; they're more delighted than ever; but they're stingier. Everybody looks twice at their money afore they parts with it.—That's a rub at the mean ones, and they wants it uncommon bad.

"And then, sometimes the blinds is all drawed down, on account of the sun, and that cooks our goose; or, it's too hot for people to stop and varder—that means, see. In the cold days, when we pitch, people stops a few minutes, drops their browns, and goes away about their business, to make room for more. The spring of the year is the best of the four seasons for us.

"A sailor and a lass half-seas over we like best of all. He will tip his mag. We always ensure a few pence, and sometimes a shilling, of them. We are fond of sweeps, too; they're a sure brown, if they've got one, and they'll give before many a gentleman. But what we can't abide nohow is the shabby genteel—them altray cativa, and no mistake: for they'll stand with their mouths wide open, like a nutcracker, and is never satisfied, and is too grand even to laugh. It's too much trouble to carry ha'pence, and they've never no change, or else they'd give us some; in fact, they've no money at all, they wants it all for, &c."

Mr. Punch's Figures.

"This is Punch; this his wife, Judy. They never was married, not for this eight hundred years—in the original drama. It is a drama in two acts, is Punch. There was a Miss Polly, and she was Punch's mistress, and dressed in silks and satins. Judy catches Punch with her, and there causes all the disturbance. Ah, it's a beautiful history; there's a deal of morals with it, and there's a large volume wrote about it. It's to be got now.

"This here is Judy, their only child. She's three years old come to-morrow, and heir to all his estate, which is only a saucepan without a handle.

"Well, *then* I brings out the Beadle.

"Punch's nose is the hornament to his face. It's a great walue, and the hump on his back is never to be got rid on, being born with him, and never to be done without. Punch was silly and out of his mind—which is in the drama—and the cause of his throwing his child out of winder, vich he did. Judy went out and left him to nurse the child, and the child gets so terrible cross he gets out of patience, and tries to sing a song to it, and ends by chucking it into the street.

"Punch is cunning, and up to all kinds of antics, if he ain't out of his mind. Artful like My opinion of Punch is, he's very incentric, with good and bad morals attached. Very good he was in regard to benevolence; because, you see, in the olden style there was a blind man, and he used to come and ax charity of him, and Punch used to pity him and give him a trifle, you know. This is in the olden style, from Porsini you know.

"The carving on his face is a great art, and there's only one man as does it reg'lar. His nose and chin, by meeting together, we thinks the great beauty. Oh, he's admirable!—He was very fond of hisself when he was alive. His name was Punchinello, and we calls him Punch. That's partly for short and partly on account of the boys, for they calls it Punch in hell O. 'Oh, there's Punch in hell,' they'd say, and gennelfolks don't like to hear them words.

"Punch has very small legs and small arms. It's quite out of portion, in course; but still it's nature, for folks with big bellies generally has thin pins of their own.

"His dress has never been altered; the use of his high hat is to show his half-foolish head, and the other parts is after the best olden fashion.

"Judy, you see, is very ugly. She represents Punch; cos, you see, if the two comes together, it generally happens that they're summat alike; and you see it's because his wife were so ugly that he had a mistress. You see, a head like that there wouldn't please most people.

The mistress, Polly, dances with Punch, just like a lady in a drawing-room. There ain't no grievance between him and Judy on account of Miss Polly, as she's called. That's the olden style of all, cos Judy don't know nothing about it.

"Miss Polly was left out because it wasn't exactly moral; opinions has changed: we ain't better, I fancy. Such things goes on, but people don't like to let it be seen now, that's the difference.

"Judy's dress, you see, is far different, bless you, than Miss Polly's. Judy's, you see, is bed-furniture stuff, and Polly's all silk and satin. Yes, that's the way of the world,—the wife comes off second-best.

"The baby's like his father, he's his pet all over and the pride of his heart; wouldn't take all the world for it, you know, though he does throw him out of window. He's got his father's nose, and is his daddy all over, from the top of his head to the tip of his toe. He never was weaned.

"Punch, you know, is so red through drink. He'd look nothing if his nose were not deep scarlet. Punch used to drink hard one time, and so he does now if he can get it. His babby is red all the same, to correspond.

"This is the Beadle of the parish, which tries to quell all disturbances but finds it impossible to do it. The Beadle has got a very reddish nose. He is a very severe, harsh man, but Punch conquers him. Ye see, he's dressed in the olden style—a brown coat, with gold lace and cock'd hat and all. He has to take Punch up for killing his wife and babby; but Punch beats the Beadle, for every time he comes up he knocks him down.

"This next one is the merry Clown, what tries his rig with Punch, up and down—that's a rhyme, you see. This is the merry Clown, that tries his tricks all round. This here's the new style, for we dwells more on the comical now. In the olden time we used to have a scaramouch with a chalk head. He used to torment Punch and dodge him about, till at last Punch used to give him a crack on the head and smash it all to pieces, and then cry out—'Oh dear, Oh dear; I didn't go to do it—it was an accident, done on purpose.' But now we do with Clown and the sausages. Scaramouch never talked, only did the ballet business, dumb motions; but the Clown speaks theatrical, comic business and sentimental. Punch being silly and out of his mind, the Clown persuades Punch that he wants something to eat. The Clown gets into the public-house to try what he can steal. He pokes his head out of the window and says, 'Here you are, here you are;' and then he asks Punch to give him a helping hand, and so makes Punch steal the sausages. They're the very best pork-wadding sausages, made six years ago and warranted fresh, and 'll keep for ever.

"This here's the poker, about which the Clown says, 'Would you like something hot?' Punch says 'Yes,' and then the Clown burns Punch's nose, and sits down on it himself and burns his breeches. Oh, it's a jolly lark when I shows it. Clown says to Punch, 'Don't make a noise, you'll wake the landlord up.' The landlord, you see, pretends to be asleep.

"Clown says, 'You mustn't hollar.' 'No,' says Punch, 'I wont;' and still he hollars all the louder.

"This is Jim Crow: ye see he's got a chain but he's lost his watch. He let it fall on Fish-street Hill, the other day, and broke it all to pieces. He's a nigger. He says, 'Me like ebery body;' not 'every,' but 'ebery,' cos that's nigger. Instead of Jim Crow we used formerly to show the Grand Turk of Sinoa, called Shallaballah. Sinoa is nowhere, for he's only a substance yer know. I can't find Sinoa, although I've tried, and thinks it's at the bottom of the sea where the black fish lays.

"Jim Crow sprung from Rice from America, he brought it over here. Then, ye see, being a novelty, all classes of society is pleased. Everybody liked to hear 'Jim Crow' sung, and so we had to do it. The people used to stand round, and I used to take some good money with it too, sir, on Hay-hill. Everybody's funny now-a-days, and they like comic business. They won't listen to anything sensible or sentimental, but they wants foolishness. The bigger fool gets the most money. Many people says, 'What a fool, you must look!' at that I put my head back. 'Come on.' 'I shan't. I shall stop a little longer.'

"This is the Ghost, that appears to Punch for destroying his wife and child. She's the ghost of the two together, or else, by rights, there ought to be a little ghost as well, but we should have such a lot to carry about. But Punch, being surprised at the ghost, falls into exstericks—represented as such. Punch is really terrified, for he trembles like a haspen leaf, cos he never killed his wife. He's got no eyes and no teeth, and can't see out of his mouth; or cannot, rather. Them cant words ain't grammatical. When Punch sees the Ghost he lays down and kicks the bucket, and represents he's dead.

"The Ghost is very effective, when it comes up very solemn and mournful-like in Romeau and Juliet. I took it from that, yer know: there's a ghost in that when she comes out of the grave. Punch sits down on his seat and sings his merry song of olden times, and don't see the Ghost till he gets a tap on the cheek, and then he thinks it's somebody else; instead of that, when he turns round, he's most terrible alarmed, putting his arms up and out. The drum goes very shaky when the Ghost comes up. A little bit of 'The Dead March in Saul,' or 'Home, sweet Home:' anything like that, slow. We none on us likes to be hurried to the grave.

"I now takes up the Doctor. This is the Doctor that cures all sick maids and says, 'Taste of my drugs before you die, you'll say they are well made.' The Doctor always wears a white ermine wig: rabbit skin wouldn't do, we can't go so common as that; it's most costly, cos it was made for him.

"After the Ghost has appeared Punch falls down, and calls loudly for the Doctor, and offers 50,000*l.* for one; then the Doctor feels his pulse and says, 'Very unfortunate misfortune! I have forgot my spectacles, cos I never had none. I can see all through it—the man's not dead.

"The Doctor gives Punch physic. That's stick-lickerish wot he subscribes for him; but Punch don't like it, though it's a capital subscription for a cure for the head-ache. (I dare say, Mr. Mayhew, sir, you thinks me a very funny fellow.) Punch tries to pay the Doctor back with his own physic, but he misses him every time. Doctors don't like to take their own stuff anyhow.

"This is the Publican as Punch steals the sausages from; he used to be the Grand Turk of Senoa, or Shallaballah, afore the fashion changed—for a new world always wants new things: the people are like babies, they must have a fresh toy ye know, and every day is a new day that we never seed before.—There's a moral for you; it'll make a beautiful book when you comes to have the morals explained. Ye see you might still fancy Punch was the Grand Turk, for he's got his moustaches still; but they're getting so fashionable that even the publicans wears 'em, so it don't matter.

"This tall figure is the hangman and finisher of the law, as does the business in the twinkling of a bed-post. He's like the income-tax gatherer, he takes all in and lets none out, for a guilty conscience needs no accusing. Punch being condemned to suffer by the laws of his country, makes a mistake for once in his life, and always did, and always will keep a-doing it. Therefore, by cunningness and artfulness, Punch persuades Jack Ketch to show him the way—which he very 'willingly doeth'—to slip his head into the noose, when Punch takes the opportunity to pull the rope, after he has shown him the way, and is exempt for once more, and quite free.

"Now this is the coffin, and this is the pall. Punch is in a great way, after he's hung the man, for assistance, when he calls his favourite friend Joey Grimaldi, the clown, to aid and assist him, because he's afeard that he'll be taken for the crime wot he's committed. Then the body is placed in the coffin; but as the undertaker ain't made it long enough, they have to double him up. The undertaker requests permission to git it altered. Ye see it's a royal coffin, with gold, and silver, and copper nails; with no plates, and scarlet cloth, cos that's royalty. The undertaker's forgot the lid of the coffin, ye see: we don't use lids, cos it makes them lighter to carry.

"This is the pall that covers him over, to keep the flies from biting him. We call it St. Paul's. Don't you see, palls and Paul's is the same word, with a *s* to it: it's comic. That 'ud make a beautiful play, that would. Then we take out the figures, as I am doing now, from the box, and they exaunt with a dance. 'Here's somebody a-coming, make haste!' the Clown says, and then they exaunt, you know, or go off.

"This here is the Scaramouch that dances without a head, and yet has got a head that'll reach from here to St. Paul's; but it's scarcely ever to be seen. Cos his father was my mother, don't ye see. Punch says that it's a beautiful figure. I've only made it lately. Instead of him we used to have a nobody. The figure is to be worked with four heads, that's to say one coming out of each arm, one from the body, and one from the neck. (He touches each part as he speaks.) Scaramouch is old-fashioned newly revived. He comes up for a finish, yer know. This figure's all for dancing, the same as the ghost is, and don't say nothing. Punch being surprised to see such a thing, don't know what to make on it. He bolts away, for ye see (whispering and putting up two hands first, and then using the other, as if working Scaramouch), I wants my two hands to work him. After Punch goes away the figure dances to amuse the public, then he exaunts, and Punch comes up again for to finish the remainder part of his performance. He sings as if he'd forgot all that's gone before, and wishes only to amuse the public at large. That's to show his silliness and simplicity. He sings comic or sentimental, such as 'God save the Queen;'— that's sentimental; or 'Getting up stairs and playing on the fiddle;' or 'Dusty Bob;' or 'Rory O'More, with the chill off;'—them's all comic, but 'the Queen's' sentimental.

"This here is Satan,—we might say the devil, but that ain't right, and gennelfolks don't like such words. He is now commonly called 'Spring-heeled Jack;' or the 'Roosian Bear,' —that's since the war. Ye see he's chained up for ever; for if yer reads, it says somewhere in the Scripture that he's bound down for two thousand years. I used to read it myself once; and the figure shows ye that he's chained up never to be let loose no more. He comes up at the last and shows himself to Punch, but it ain't continued long, yer know, the figure being too frightful for people to see without being frightened; unless we are on comic business and showing him as Spring-heeled Jack, or the Roosian Bear; and then we keeps him up a long time. Punch kills him, puts him on the top of his stick, and cries, 'Hooray! the devil's dead, and we can all do as we like! Good-by, farewell, and it's all over!' But the curtain don't come down, cos we haven't got none.

" This here's the bell. Stop a minute, I forgot: this is Punch's comic music, commonly called a peanner sixty,—not peanner forty, cos Punch wants something out of the common way,— and it plays fifty tunes all at once. This is the bell which he uses to rattle in the publican's ears when he's asleep, and wakes his children all up after the nuss as put 'em to bed. All this is to show his foolishness and simplicity; for it's one of his foolish tricks and frolics for to amuse himself : but he's a chap as won't stand much nonsense from other people, because his morals are true, just, right, and sound; although he does kill his wife and baby, knock down the Beadle, Jack Ketch, and the Grand Signor, and puts an end to the very devil himself."

Description of Frame and Proscenium.

" ' Ladies and gents,' the man says outside the show, afore striking up, ' I'm now going to exhibit a preformance worthy of your notice, and far superior to anythink you hever had a hopportunity of witnessing of before.' (I am a doing it now, sir, as if I was addressing a company of ladies and gentlemen, he added, by way of parenthesis.) ' This is the original preformance of Punch, ladies and gents ; and it will always gain esteem. I am going to hintroduce a preformance worthy of your notice, which is the dramatical preformance of the original and old-established preformance of Punch, experienced many year. I merely call your attention, ladies and gents, to the novel attraction which I'm now about to hintroduce to you.

" ' I only merely place this happyratus up to inform you what I am about to preform to you. The preformance will continue for upwards of one hour — *provising as we meets with sufficient encouragement.* (That's business, ye know, master ; just to give 'em to understand that we wants a little assistance afore we begins.) It will surpass anythink you've had the hopportunity of witnessing of before in all the hannuals of history. I hope, ladies and gents, I am not talking too grammatical for some of you.'

" That there is the address, sir," he continued, " what I always gives to the audience outside before I begins to preform—just to let the respectable company know that I am a working for to get my living by honest industry.

" ' Those ladies and gents,' he then went on, as if addressing an imaginary crowd, ' what are a-standing round, a-looking at the preformance, will, I hope, be as willing to give as they is to see. There's many a lady and gent now at the present moment standing around me, perhaps, whose hearts might be good though not in their power.' (This is Punch's patter, yer know, outside ; and when you has to say all that yourself, you wants the affluency of a methodist parson to do the talk, I can tell ye.) ' Now boys, look up yer ha'pence ! Who's got a farden or a ha'penny ? and I'll be the first brown towards it. I ain't particular if it's a half-crown. Now, my lads, feel in your pockets and see if you've got an odd copper. Here's one, and who'll be the next to make it even ? We means to show it all through, *provising we meets with sufficient encouragement.*' (I always sticks to them words, ' sufficient encouragement.') ' You'll have the pleasure of seeing Spring-heeled Jack, or the Roosian Bear, and the comical scene with Joey the clown, and the fryingpan of sassages !' (That's a kind of gaggery.)

" I'll now just explain to you, sir, the different parts of the frame. This here's the letter-cloth, which shows you all what we performs. Sometimes we has wrote on it—

THE DOMINION OF FANCY,
or,
PUNCH'S OPERA :

that fills up a letter-cloth; and Punch is a fancy for every person, you know, whoever may fancy it. I stands inside here on this footboard ; and if there's any one up at the winders in the street, I puts my foot longways, so as to keep my nob out of sight. This here is the stage front, or *proceedings* (proscenium), and is painted over with flags and banners, or any different things. Sometimes there's George and the Dragging, and the Rile Queen's Arms, (we can have them up when we like, cos we are sanctioned, and I've played afore the rile princes). But anything for freshness. People's tired of looking at the Rile Arms, and wants something new to cause attraction, and so on.

" This here's the playboard, where sits Punch. The scenes behind are representing a garding scene, and the side-scenes is a house and a cottage—they're for the exaunts, you know, just for convenience. The back scene draws up, and shows the prison, with the winders all cut out, and the bars showing, the same as there is to a gaol; though I never was in one in my life, and I'll take good care I never shall be.

" Our speaking instrument is an unknown secret, cos it's an ' unknown tongue,' that's known to none except those in our own purfession. It's a hinstrument like this which I has in my hand, and it's tuned to music. We has two or three kinds, one for out-doors, one for in-doors, one for speaking, one for singing, and one that's good for nothing, except selling on the cheap. They ain't whistles, but ' calls,' or ' unknown tongues ;' and with them in the mouth we can pronounce each word as plain as a parson, and with as much affluency.

" The great difficulty in preforming Punch consists in speaking with this call in the mouth — cos it's produced from the lungs : it's all done from there, and is a great strain, and requires sucktion—and that's brandy-and-water, or summat to moisten the whistle with.

"We're bound not to drink water by our purfession, when we can get anything stronger. It weakens the nerves, but we always like to keep in the bounds of propriety, respectability, and decency. I drinks my beer with my call in my mouth, and never takes it out, cos it exposes it, and the boys (hang 'em!) is so inquisitive. They runs after us, and looks up in our face to see how we speaks; but we drives 'em away with civility.

"Punch is a dramatical performance, sir, in two acts, patronised by the nobility and gentry at large. We don't drop the scene at the end of the first act, the drum and pipes strikes up instead. The first act we consider to end with Punch being took to prison for the murder of his wife and baby. You can pick out a good many Punch preformers, without getting one so well versed as I am in it; they in general makes such a muffing concern of it. A drama, or dramatical preformance, we calls it, of the original preformance of Punch. It ain't a tragedy; it's both comic and sentimental, in which way we think proper to preform it. There's comic parts, as with the Clown and Jim Crow, and cetera—that's including a deal more, yer know.

"It's a pretty play Punch is, when preformed well, and one of the greatest novelties in the world; and most ancient; handed down, too, for many hundred years.

"The prison scene and the baby is what we calls the sentimental touches. Some folks where I preforms will have it most sentimental, in the original style. Them families is generally sentimental theirselves. To these sentimental folks I'm obliged to preform werry steady and werry slow; they won't have no ghost, no coffin, and no devil; and that's what I call spiling the preformance entirely. Ha, ha!" he added, with a deep sigh, "it's the march of intellect that's a doing all this: it is, sir.

"Other folks is all for the comic, specially the street people; and then we has to dwell on the bell scene, and the nursing the baby, and the frying-pan, and the sassages, and Jim Crow.

"A few years ago Toby was all the go. Formerly the dog was only a stuffed figure, and it was Mr. Pike what first hit upon introducing a live animal; and a great hit it war. It made a surprising alteration in the exhibition, for till lately the preformance was called Punch and Toby as well. We used to go about the streets with three dogs, and that was admirable, and it did uncommon well as a new novelty at first, but we can't get three dogs to do it now. The mother of them dogs, ye see, was a singer, and had two pups what was singers too. Toby was wanted to sing and smoke a pipe as well, shake hands as well as seize Punch by the nose. When Toby was quiet, ye see, sir, it was the timidation of Punch's stick, for directly he put it down he flew at him, knowing at the same time that Punch was not his master.

"Punch commences with a song. He does roo-too-rooey, and sings the 'Lass of Gowrie' down below, and then he comes up, saying, 'Ooy-ey; Oh, yes, I'm a coming. How do you do, ladies and gents?'—ladies always first; and then he bows many times. 'I'm so happy to see you,' he says; 'Your most obedient, most humble, and dutiful servant, Mr. Punch.' (Ye see I can talk as affluent as can be with the call in my mouth.) 'Ooy-ey, I wishes you all well and happy.' Then Punch says to the drum-and-pipes man, as he puts his hand out, 'How do you do, master?—play up; play up a hornpipe: I'm a most hexcellent dancer;' and then Punch dances. Then ye see him a-dancing the hornpipe; and after that Punch says to the pipes, 'Master, I shall call my wife up, and have a dance; so he sings out, 'Judy, Judy! my pratty creetur! come up stairs, my darling! I want to speak to you'— and he knocks on the play-board.—'Judy! Here she comes, bless her little heart!'

Enter JUDY.

Punch. What a sweet creature! what a handsome nose and chin! (*He pats her on the face very gently.*)

Judy. (*Slapping him.*) Keep quiet, do!

Punch. Don't be cross, my dear, but give me a kiss.

Judy. Oh, to be sure, my love. [*They kiss.*

Punch. Bless your sweet lips! (*Hugging her.*) This is melting moments. I'm very fond of my wife; we must have a dance.

Judy. Agreed. [*They both dance.*

Punch. Get out of the way! you don't dance well enough for me. (*He hits her on the nose.*) Go and fetch the baby, and mind and take care of it, and not hurt it. [*Judy exaunts.*

Judy. (*Returning back with baby.*) Take care of the baby, while I go and cook the dumplings.

Punch. (*Striking Judy with his right hand.*) Get out of the way! I'll take care of the baby. [*Judy exaunts.*

Punch (*sits down and sings to the baby*)—

"Hush-a-by, baby, upon the tree-top,
When the wind blows the cradle will rock;
When the bough breaks the cradle will fall,
Down comes the baby and cradle and all."
[*Baby cries.*

Punch. (*Shaking it.*) What a cross boy! (*He lays it down on the play-board, and rolls it backwards and forwards, to rock it to sleep, and sings again.*)

"Oh, slumber, my darling, thy sire is a knight,
Thy mother's a lady so lovely and bright;
The hills and the dales, and the tow'rs which you see,
They all shall belong, my dear creature, to thee."

(*Punch continues rocking the child. It still cries, and he takes it up in his arms, saying,* What a cross child! I can't a-bear cross children. *Then he vehemently shakes it, and knocks its head up against the side of the proceedings several times, representing to kill it, and he then throws it out of the winder.*)

Enter JUDY.

Judy. Where's the baby?

Punch. (*In a lemoncholy tone.*) I have had a misfortune; the child was so terrible cross, I throwed it out of the winder. (*Lemontation of Judy for the loss of her dear child. She goes into asterisks, and then excites and fetches a cudgel, and commences beating Punch over the head.*)

Punch. Don't be cross, my dear: I didn't go to do it.

Judy. I'll pay yer for throwing the child out of the winder. (*She keeps on giving him knocks of the head, but Punch snatches the stick away, and commences an attack upon his wife, and beats her severely.*)

Judy. I'll go to the constable, and have you locked up.

Punch. Go to the devil. I don't care where you go. Get out of the way! (*Judy exaunts, and Punch then sings, "Cherry ripe," or "Cheer, boys, cheer." All before is sentimental, now this here's comic. Punch goes through his roo-too-to-rooey, and then the Beadle comes up.*)

Beadle. Hi! hallo, my boy!

Punch. Hello, my boy. (*He gives him a wipe over the head with his stick, which knocks him down, but he gets up again.*)

Beadle. Do you know, sir, that I've a special order in my pocket to take you up?

Punch. And I've a special order to knock you down. (*He knocks him down with simplicity, but not with brutality, for the juvenial branches don't like to see severity practised.*)

Beadle. (*Coming up again.*) D'ye know, my boy, that I've an order to take you up?

Punch. And I've an order I tell ye to knock you down. (*He sticks him. Punch is a tyrant to the Beadle, ye know, and if he was took up he wouldn't go through his rambles, so in course he isn't.*)

Beadle. I've a warrant for you, my boy.

Punch. (*Striking him.*) And that's a warrant for you, my boy. (*The Beadle's a determined man, ye know, and resolved to go to the ends of justice as far as possible in his power by special authority, so a quarrel enshoos between them.*)

Beadle. You are a blackguard.

Punch. So are you.

(*The Beadle hits Punch on the nose, and takes the law in his own hands. Punch takes it up momentary; strikes the Beadle, and a fight enshoos. The Beadle, faint and exhausted, gets up once more; then he strikes Punch over the nose, which is returned pro and con.*)

Beadle. That's a good 'un.

Punch. That's a better.

Beadle. That's a topper. (*He hits him jolly hard.*)

Punch. (*With his cudgel.*) That's a wopper. (*He knocks him out of his senses, and the Beadle exaunts.*)

Enter MERRY CLOWN.

Punch sings "Getting up Stairs," in quick time, while the Clown is coming up. Clown dances round Punch in all directions, and Punch with his cudgel is determined to catch him if possible.

Clown. No bono, allez tooti sweet, Mounseer. Look out sharp! Make haste! catch 'em alive! Here we are! how are you? good morning! don't you wish you may get it? Ah! coward, strike a white man! (*Clown keeps bobbing up and down, and Punch trying to hit all the time till Punch is exhausted nearly.*)

(The Clown, ye see, sir, is the best friend to Punch, he carries him through all his tricks, and he's a great favorite of Punch's. He's too cunning for him though, and knows too much for him, so they both shake hands and make it up.)

Clown. Now it's all fair; ain't it, Punch?

Punch. Yes.

Clown. Now I can begin again.

(You see, sir, the Clown gets over Punch altogether by his artful ways, and then he begins the same tricks over again; that is, if we wants a long performance; if not, we cuts it off at the other pint. But I'm telling you the real original style, sir.)

Clown. Good! you can't catch me.

(*Punch gives him one whack of the head, and Clown exaunts, or goes off.*)

Enter JIM CROW

Jim sings "Buffalo Gals," while coming up, and on entering Punch hits him a whack of the nose backhanded, and almost breaks it.

Jim. What for you do that? Me nigger! me like de white man. Him did break my nose.

Punch. Humbly beg your pardon, I did not go to help it.

(For as it had been done, you know, it wasn't likely he could help it after he'd done it — he couldn't take it away from him again, could he?)

Jim. Me beg you de pardon. (For ye see, sir, he thinks he's offended Punch.) Nebber mind, Punch, come and sit down, and we'll hab a song.

JIM CROW *prepares to sing.*

Punch. Bravo, Jimmy! sing away, my boy — give us a stunner while you're at it.

JIM *sings.*

"I'm a roarer on the fiddle,
  Down in the ole Virginny;
And I plays it scientific,
  Like Master Paganinni."

Punch. (*Tapping him on the head.*) Bravo! well done, Jimmy! give us another bit of a song.

Jim. Yes, me will.　　　　[*Sings again.*

"Oh, lubly Rosa, Sambo come;
  Don't you hear the banjo?
    Tum, tum, tum!"

Jim hits Punch with his head over the

nose, as if butting at him, while he repeats tum-tum-tum. Punch offended, beats him with the stick, and sings—

> "Lubly Rosa, Sambo come;
> Don't you hear the banjo?
> Tum, tum, tum!"

Jim. (*Rising.*) Oh mi! what for you strike a nigger? (*Holding up his leg.*) Me will poke your eye out. Ready—shoot—bang—fire. (*Shoves his leg into Punch's eye.*)

Punch. He's poked my eye out! I'll look out for him for the future.

Jim Crow excites, or exaunts. Exaunt we calls it in our purfession, sir,—that's going away, you know. He's done his part, you know, and ain't to appear again.

Judy has died through Punch's ill usage after going for the Beadle, for if she'd done so before she could'nt ha' fetched the constable, you know,—certainly not. The beholders only believe her to be dead though, for she comes to life again afterwards, because, if she was dead, it would do away with Punch's wife altogether—for Punch is doatingly fond of her, though it's only his fun after all's said and done.

The Ghost, you see, is only a repersentation, as a timidation to soften his bad morals, so that he shouldn't do the like again. The Ghost, to be sure, shows that she's really dead for a time, but it's not in the imitation; for if it was, Judy's ghost (the figure) would be made like her.

The babby's lost altogether. It's killed. It is supposed to be destroyed entirely, but taken care of for the next time when called upon to preform—as if it were in the next world, you know,—that's moral.

Enter Ghost. Punch sings meanwhile 'Home, sweet Home.' (This is original.) The Ghost repersents the ghost of Judy, because he's killed his wife, don't you see, the Ghost making her appearance; but Punch don't know it at the moment. Still he sits down tired, and sings in the corner of the frame the song of "Home, sweet Home," while the Sperrit appears to him.

Punch turns round, sees the Ghost, and is most terribly timidated. He begins to shiver and shake in great fear, bringing his guilty conscience to his mind of what he's been guilty of doing, and at last he falls down in a fit of frenzy. Kicking, screeching, hollaring, and shouting "Fifty thousand pounds for a doctor!" Then he turns on his side, and draws hisself double with the screwmatics in his gills.   [*Ghost excites.*

Enter DOCTOR.

Punch is represented to be dead. This is the dying speech of Punch.

Doctor. Dear me! bless my heart! here have I been running as fast as ever I could walk, and very near tumbled over a straw. I heard somebody call most lustily for a doctor. Dear me (*looking at Punch in all directions, and examining his body*), this is my pertickler friend Mr. Punch; poor man! how pale he looks! I'll feel his pulse (*counts his pulse*)—1, 2, 14, 9, 11. Hi! Punch, Punch, are you dead? are you dead? are you dead?

Punch. (*Hitting him with his right hand over the nose, and knocking him back.*) Yes.

Doctor. (*Rubbing his nose with his hand.*) I never heard a dead man speak before. Punch, you are not dead!

Punch. Oh, yes I am!

Doctor. How long have you been dead?

Punch. About six weeks.

Doctor. Oh, you're not dead, you're only poorly; I must fetch you a little reviving medicine, such as some stick-lickrish and balsam, and extract of shillalagh.

Punch. (*Rising.*) Make haste—(*he gives the Doctor a wipe on the nose*)—make haste and fetch it.   [*Doctor exaunts.*

Punch. The Doctor going to get me some physic! I'm very fond of brandy-and-water, and rum-punch. I want my physic; the Doctor never brought me no physic at all. I wasn't ill; it was only my fun. (*Doctor reappears with the physic-stick, and he whacks Punch over the head no harder than he is able, and cries*—"There's physic! physic! physic! physic! physic! pills! balsaam! stick-lickerish!"

Punch. (*Rising and rubbing his head against the wing.*) Yes; it is stick-lickrish.

(Ah! it's a pretty play, sir, when it's showed well—that it is—it's delightful to read the morals; I am wery fond of reading the morals, I am.)

Punch. (*Taking the stick from the Doctor.*) Now, I'll give you physic! physic! physic! (*He strikes at the Doctor, but misses him every time.*) The Doctor don't like his own stuff.

Punch. (*Presenting his stick, gun-fashion, at Doctor's head.*) I'll shoot ye—one, two, three.

Doctor. (*Closing with Punch.*) Come to gaol along with me.

(He saves his own life by closing with Punch. He's a desperate character is Punch, though he means no harm, ye know.) A struggle enshoos, and the Doctor calls for help, Punch being too powerful for him.

Doctor. Come to gaol! You shall repent for all your past misdeeds. Help! assistance! help, in the Queen's name!

(He's acting as a constable, the Doctor is, though he's no business to do it; but he's acting in self-defence. He didn't know Punch, but he'd heard of his transactions, and when he came to examine him, he found it was the man. The Doctor is a very sedate kind of a person, and wishes to do good to all classes of the community at large, especially with his physic, which he gives gratis for nothink at all. The physic is called 'Head-e-cologne, or a sure cure for the headache.')

Re-enter BEADLE. (*Punch and the Doctor still struggling together.*)

Beadle. (*Closing with them.*) Hi, hi! this is him; behold the head of a traitor! Come along! come to gaol!

Punch. (*A-kicking.*) I will not go.

Beadle. (*Shouting.*) More help! more help! more help! help! help! Come along to gaol! come along! come along! More help! more help!

(Oh! it's a good lark just here, sir, but tremendous hard work, for there's so many figures to work—and all struggling, too,—and you have to work them all at once. This is comic, this is.)

Beadle. More help! be quick! be quick!

Re-enter JIM CROW.

Jim Crow. Come de long! come de long! come de long! me nigger, and you beata me.

[*Exaunts all, Punch still singing out,* "I'll not go."

END OF FIRST ACT.

Change of Scene for Second Act.

Scene draws up, and discovers the exterior of a prison, with Punch peeping through the bars, and singing a merry song of the merry bells of England, all of the olden time. (That's an olden song, you know; it's old ancient, and it's a moral,—a moral song, you know, to show that Punch is repenting, but pleased, and yet don't care nothink at all about it, for he's frolicsome, and on the height of his frolic and amusement to all the juveniles, old and young, rich and poor. We must put all classes together.)

Enter Hangman Jack Ketch, or Mr. GRABALL.

That's Jack Ketch's name, you know; he takes all, when they gets in his clutches. We mustn't blame him for he must do his duty, for the sheriffs is so close to him.)

[*Preparation commences for the execution of Punch. Punch is still looking through the bars of Newgate.*

The last scene as I had was Temple-bar Scene; it was a prison once, ye know; that's the old ancient, ye know, but I never let the others see it, cos it shouldn't become too public. But I think Newgate is better, in the new edition, though the prison is suspended, it being rather too terrific for the beholder. It was the old ancient style; the sentence is passed upon him, but by whom not known; he's not tried by one person, cos nobody can't.

Jack Ketch. Now, Mr. Punch, you are going to be executed by the British and Foreign laws of this and other countries, and you are to be hung up by the neck until you are dead —dead—dead.

Punch. What, am I to die three times?

Jack. No, no; you're only to die once.

Punch. How is that? you said I was to be hung up by the neck till I was dead—dead—dead? You can't die three times.

Jack. Oh, no; only once.

Punch. Why, you said dead—dead—dead.

Jack. Yes; and when you are dead—dead—dead—you will be quite dead.

Punch. Oh! I never knowed that before.

Jack. Now, prepare yourself for execution.

Punch. What for?

Jack. For killing your wife, throwing your poor dear little innocent baby out of the window, and striking the Beadle unmercifully over the head with a mop-stick. Come on.

[*Exeunt Hangman behind Scene, and re-enter, leading Punch slowly forth to the foot of the gallows. Punch comes most willingly, having no sense.*

Jack. Now, my boy, here is the corfin, here is the gibbet, and here is the pall.

Punch. There's the corfee-shop, there's giblets, and there's St. Paul's.

Jack. Get out, young foolish! Now then, place your head in here.

Punch. What, up here?

Jack. No; a little lower down.

(There's quick business in this, you know; this is comic—a little comic business, this is.)

Punch. (*Dodging the noose.*) What, here?

Jack. No, no; in there (*showing the noose again*).

Punch. This way?

Jack. No, a little more this way; in there.

[*Punch falls down, and pretends he's dead.*

Jack. Get up, you're not dead.

Punch. Oh, yes I am.

Jack. But I say, no.

Punch. Please, sir, (*bowing to the hangman*) —(Here he's an hypocrite; he wants to exempt himself,)—do show me the way, for I never was hung before, and I don't know the way. Please, sir, to show me the way, and I'll feel extremely obliged to you, and return you my most sincere thanks.

(Now, that's well worded, sir; it's well put together; that's my beauty, that is; I am obliged to study my language, and not have any thing vulgar whatsoever. All in simplicity, so that the young children may not be taught anything wrong. There arn't nothing to be learnt from it, because of its simplicity.)

Jack. Very well; as you're so kind and condescending, I will certainly oblige you by showing you the way. Here, my boy! now, place your head in here, like this (*hangman putting his head in noose*); this is the right and the proper way; now, you see the rope is placed under my chin; I'll take my head out, and I will place yours in (that's a rhyme) and when your head is in the rope, you must turn round to the ladies and gentlemen, and say—Good-by; fare you well.

(Very slowly then—a stop between each of the words; for that's not driving the people out of the world in quick haste without giving 'em time for repentance. That's another moral, yer see. Oh, I like all the morals to it.)

Punch (*quickly pulling the rope*). Good-by; fare you well. (*Hangs the hangman.*) (What a hypocrite he is again, yer see, for directly he's done it he says: 'Now, I'm free again for frolic and fun;' calls Joey, the clown, his old friend, because they're both full of tricks and antics: 'Joey, here's a man hung nisself;'—that's his hypocrisy again, yer see, for he tries to get exempt after he's done it hisself.)

Enter CLOWN, *in quick haste, bobbing up against the gallows.*

Clown. Dear me, I've run against a milk-post! Why, dear Mr. Punch, you've hung a man! do take him down! How came you to do it?

Punch. He got wet through, and I hung him up to dry.

Clown. Dear me! why you've hung him up till he's dried quite dead!

Punch. Poor fellow! then he won't catch cold with the wet. Let's put him in this snuff-box. [*Pointing to coffin.*

[*Joey takes the figure down and gives it to Punch to hold, so as the body do not run away, and then proceeds to remove the gallows. In doing so he by accident hits Punch on the nose.*

Punch. Mind what you are about! (for Punch is game, yer know, right through to the back-bone.)

Clown. Make haste, Punch, here's somebody a-coming! (They hustle his legs and feet in; but they can't get his head in, the undertaker not having made the coffin large enough.)

Punch. We'd better double him up, place the pall on, and take the man to the brave,—not the grave, but the brave: cos he's been a brave man in his time may be.—Sings the song of 'Bobbing around,' while with the coffin he bobs Joey on the head, and exaunt.

Re-enter PUNCH.

Punch. That was a jolly lark, wasn't it? Sings,—

"I'd be a butterfly, born in a bower,
  Making apple-dumplings without any flour."

All this wit must have been born in me, or nearly so; but I got a good lot of it from Porsini and Pike—and gleanings, you know. [*Punch disappears and re-enters with bell.*

Punch. This is my pianner-sixty: it plays fifty tunes all at one time.

[*Goes to the landlord of the public-house painted on the side-scene, or cottage, represented as a tavern or hotel. The children of the publican are all a-bed. Punch plays up a tune and solicits for money.*

Landlord wakes up in a passion through the terrible noise; pokes his head out of window and tells him to go away.

(There's a little window, and a little door to this side-scene.) If they was to play it all through, as you're a writing, it 'ud open Drury-lane Theatre.

Punch. Go away? Yes, play away! Oh, you means, O'er the hills and far away. (He misunderstands him, wilfully, the hypocrite.) [*Punch keeps on ringing his bell violently. Publican, in a violent passion, opens the door, and pushes him away, saying, "Be off with you!"*]

Punch. I will not. (*Hits him over the head with the bell.*) You're no judge of music. (*Plays away.*)

Publican exaunts to fetch cudgel to pay him out. Punch no sooner sees cudgel than he exaunts, taking his musical instrument with him. It's far superior to anything of the kind you did ever see, except 'seldom.' You know it's silver, and that's what we says 'seldom;' silver, you know, is 'seldom,' because it's seldom you sees it.

Publican comes out of his house with his cudgel to catch old Punch on the grand hop. Must have a little comic.

Punch returns again with his bell, while publican is hiding secretly for to catch him. Publican pretends, as he stands in a corner, to be fast asleep, but keeps his eyes wide awake all the while, and says, 'If he comes up here, I'll be one upon his tibby.'

Punch comes out from behind the opposite side, and rings his bell violently. Publican makes a blow at him with his cudgel, and misses, saying, "How dare you intrude upon my premises with that nasty, noisy bell?"

Punch, while publican is watching at this side-scene, appears over at the other, with a hartful dodge, and again rings his bell loudly, and again the publican misses him; and while publican is watching at this side-scene, Punch re-enters, and draws up to him very slowly, and restes his pianner-sixty on the board, while he slowly advances to him, and gives him a whack on the head with his fist. Punch then disappears, leaving his bell behind, and the landlord in pursession of his music.)

Landlord (*collaring the bell*). Smuggings! pursession is nine points of the law! So this bell is mine, (*guarding over it with a stick*). Smuggings! this is mine, and when he comes up to take this bell away, I shall have him. Smuggings! it's mine.

Punch re-enters very slowly behind the publican as he is watching the bell, and snatching up the bell, cries out, 'That's mine,' and exaunts with it.

Publican. Dear me! never mind; I look after him; I shall catch him some day or other. (*Hits his nose up against the post as he is going away.*) (That's comic.) Oh, my nose! never mind, I'll have him again some time.

[*Excite* PUBLICAN.

CLOWN *re-enters with* PUNCH.

Clown. Oh, Punch, how are you?

Punch. I'm very glad to see you. Oh, Joey, my friend, how do you do?

Clown. Here, Punch, are you a mind for a lark? (*Peeping in at the cottage window, represented as a public-house.*) Are you hungry, Punch? would you like something to eat?

Punch. Yes.

Clown. What would you like?

Punch. Not peculiar.

(Not particular, he means, you know; that's a slip word.)

Clown. I'll go up into the landlord, and see if he's got anything to eat. (*Exaunt into cottage, and poking his head of the window.*) Here, Punch; here's the landlord fast asleep in the kitchen cellar; here's a lot of sausages hanging up here.

(Joey's a-thieving; don't you see, he's a robbing the landlord now?)

Would you like some for supper, eh, Punch?

Punch. Yes, to be sure.

Clown. Don't make a noise; you'll wake the landlord.

Punch (*whispering as loud as he can bawl through the window*). Hand 'em out here. (*Punch pulls them out of the window.*)

Clown. What are we to fry them in? I'll go and see if I can find a fryingpan.

[*Exaunt from window, and re-appears with fryingpan, which he hands out of window for Punch to cook sausages in, and then disappears for a moment; after which he returns, and says, with his head out of window, ' Would you like something hot, Punch?'*

Punch. Yes, to be sure.

(Punch is up to everything. He's a helping him to rob the publican. One's as much in the mud as the other is in the mire.)

Clown (*Thrusting red-hot poker out of window.*) Here, lay hold—Here's a lark—Make haste—Here's the landlord a coming. (*Rubs Punch with it over the nose.*)

Punch. Oh my nose!—that is a hot 'un. [*Takes poker.*

Clown. (*Re-enters, and calls in at window.*) Landlord, here's a fellow stole your sausages and fryingpan. (*Wakes up Landlord and exaunts.*)

Landlord. (*Appears at window.*) Here's somebody been in my house and axually stole my sausages, fryingpan, and red-hot poker!

(Clown exaunts when he has blamed it all to Punch. Joey stole 'em, and Punch took 'em, and the receiver is always worse than the thief, for if they was never no receivers there wouldn't never be no thieves.)

Landlord. Seizing the sausages in Punch's hand, says, How did you get these here?

Punch. Joey stole 'em, and I took 'em.

Landlord. Then you're both jolly thieves, and I must have my property. A scuffle ensues. Punch hollars out, Joey! Joey! Here's the landlord a stealing the sausages!

(So you see Punch wants to make the landlord a thief so as to exempt himself. He's a hypocrite there again, you see again—all through the piece he's the master-piece. Oh a most clever man is Punch, and such an hypocrite.)

(Punch, seizing the fryingpan, which has been on the play-board, knocks it on the

publican's head; when, there being a false bottom to it, the head goes through it, and the sausages gets about the Publican's neck, and Punch pulls at the pan and the sausages with veheminence, till the landlord is exhausted, and exaunts with his own property back again; so there is no harm done, only merely for the lark to return to those people what belongs to 'em—What you take away from a person always give to them again.)

Re-enter CLOWN.

Clown. Well, Mr. Punch, I shall wish you a pleasant good morning.

Punch. [*Hits him with his cudgel.*] Good morning to you, Joey.

Exaunt JOEY.

Punch sits down by the side of the poker, and Scaramouch appears without a head.

Punch looks, and beholds, and he's frightened, and exaunts with the poker.

Scaramouch does a comic dance, with his long neck shooting up and down with the actions of his body, after which he exaunts.

Punch re-enters again with the poker, and places it beside of him, and takes his cudgel in his hand for protection, while he is singing the National Anthem of " God save the Queen and all the Royal Family."

Satan then appears as a dream (and it is all a dream after all), and dressed up as the Roossian Bear (leave Politics alone as much as you can, for Punch belongs to nobody).

Punch has a dreadful struggle with Satan, who seizes the red-hot poker and wants to take Punch away, for all his past misdeeds, and frolic and fun, to the bottomless pit.

By struggling with Satan, Punch overpowers him, and he drops the poker, and Punch kills him with his cudgel, and shouts " Bravo! Hooray! Satan is dead," he cries (we must have a good conclusion): " we can now all do as we like!"—(That's the moral, you see.) " Good-by, Ladies and Gentlemen: this is the whole of the original performance of Mr. Punch; and I remain still your most obedient and most humble servant to command. Good-by, good-by, good-by. God bless you all. I return you my most sincere thanks for your patronage and support, and I hope you'll come out handsome with your gold and silver."

There is one Punch in France, but far different to the English Punch; they exhibiting their figures in a different way by performing them with sticks, the same as Scaramouch is done. They has a performing Punch sitivated at the Boulevards, in Paris, where he has a certain piece of ground allotted for him, with seats attached, being his own freehold property; the passers-by, if they wish to see the performance, they take their seat with the juveniles, sits down, and he performs to them for what they think proper to give him. I never was over in France, but I've heard talk of him a deal from foreigners who has given us inflammation about it, vich they was so kind to do. They shows the difference between English and French you know.

THE FANTOCCINI MAN.

EVERY one who has resided for any time in London must have noticed in the streets a large roomy show upon wheels, about four times as capacious as those used for the performance of Punch and Judy.

The proprietor of one of these perambulating exhibitions was a person of some 56 years of age, with a sprightly half-military manner; but he is seldom seen by the public, on account of his habit of passing the greater part of the day concealed within his theatre, for the purpose of managing the figures. When he paid me a visit, his peculiar erect bearing struck me as he entered. He walked without bending his knees, stamped with his heels, and often rubbed his hands together as if washing them with an invisible soap. He wore his hair with the curls arranged in a Brutus, à la George the Fourth, and his chin was forced up into the air by a high black stock, as though he wished to increase his stature. He wore a frock coat buttoned at waist, and open on his expanded chest, so as to show off the entire length of his shirt-front.

I could not help asking him, if he had ever served in the army. He, however, objected to gratify my curiosity on that point, though it was impossible from his reply not to infer that he had been in her majesty's service.

There was a mystery about his origin and parentage, which he desired should remain undisturbed. His relations were all of them so respectable, he said, that he did not wish to disgrace them by any revelations he might make; thus implying that he considered his present occupation a downfall in life.

"I followed it as my propensity," he proceeded, "and though I have run through three fortunes, I follow it still. I never knew the value of money, and when I have it in my pocket I cannot keep it there. I have spent forty-five pounds in three days."

He seemed to be not a little fond of exhibiting his dolls, and considered himself to be the only person living who knew anything of the art. He said orders were sent to him from all parts of the country to make the figures, and indeed some of them were so intricate, that he alone had the secret of their construction.

He hardly seemed to like the Marionettes, and evidently looked upon them as an interference with "the real original character" of the exhibition. The only explanation he could give of the difference between the Marionettes and the Fantoccini was, that the one had a French title, and referred to dolls in modern costume, whilst the other was an Italian word, and applied to dolls in fancy dresses.

He gave me the following interesting statement:—

"The Fantoccini," he said, "is the proper title of the exhibition of dancing dolls, though it has lately been changed to that of the 'Marionettes,' owing to the exhibition under that name at the Adelaide Gallery.

"That exhibition at the Adelaide Gallery was very good in its way, but it was nothing to be compared to the exhibition that was once given at the Argyll Rooms in Regent-street, (that's the old place that was burned down). It was called '*Le petit Théâtre Matthieu*,' and in my opinion it was the best one that ever come into London, because they was well managed. They did little pieces—heavy and light. They did Shakespeare's tragedies and farces, and singing as well; indeed, it was the real stage, only with dolls for actors and parties to speak for 'em and work their arms and legs behind the scenes. I've known one of these parties take three parts—look at that for clever work—first he did an old man, then an old woman, and afterwards the young man. I assisted at that performance, and I should say it was full twenty years ago, to the best of my recollection. After the Marionettes removed to the Western Institution, Leicester-square, I assisted at them also. It was a passable exhibition, but nothing out of the way. The figures were only modelled, not carved, as they ought to be. I was only engaged to exhibit one figure, a sailor of my own making. It was a capital one, and stood as high as a table. They wanted it for the piece called the 'Manager in Distress,' where one of the performers is a sailor. Mine would dance a hornpipe, and whip its hat off in a minute; when I had finished performing it, I took good care to whip it into a bag, so that they should not see how I arranged the strings, for they was very backwards in their knowledge. When we worked the figures it was very difficult, because you had to be up so high—like on the top of the ceiling, and to keep looking down all the time to manage the strings. There was a platform arranged, with a place to rest against.

"The first to introduce the Fantoccini into London—that is, into London streets, mind you, going about—was Gray, a Scotchman. He was a very clever fellow,—very good, and there was nothing but what was good that belonged to it—scenery, dresses, theatre and all. He had a frame then, no longer than the Punch frame now, only he had a labouring man to carry it for him, and he took with him a box no larger than a haberdasher's box, which contained the figures, for they were not more than nine inches high. Now my figures are two feet high, though they don't look it; but my theatre is ten feet high by six foot wide, and the opening is four feet high. This Gray was engaged at all the theatres, to exhibit his figures at the masquerades. Nothing went down but Mr. Gray, and he put poor Punch up altogether. When he performed at the theatres, he used to do it as a wind-up to the entertainment, after the dancing was over, and they would clear the stage on purpose for him, and then let down a scene with an opening in it, the size of his theatre. On these occasions his figures were longer, about two feet, and very perfect. There was juggling, and slack and tight rope-dancing, and Punches, and everything, and the performance was never less than one hour, and then it was done as quick as lightning, every morning, and no feat longer than two or three minutes. It didn't do to have silly persons there.

"This Gray performed at Vauxhall when Bish, the lottery-man in Cornhill, had it, and he went down wonderful. He also performed before George the Fourth. I've heard say that he got ten pounds a-week when he performed at Vauxhall, for they snatched him out of the streets, and wouldn't let him play there. It's impossible to say what he made in the streets, for he was a Scotchman and uncommon close. If he took a hatfull, he'd say, 'I've only got a few;' but he did so well he could sport his diamond rings on his fingers,—first rate—splendid.

"Gray was the first to exhibit gratis in the streets of London, but he was not the first to work fantoccini figures. They had always been exhibited at theatres before that, Old Porsini knowed nothing about them—it was out of his business all together, for he was Punch and nothing more. Gray killed Porsini and his Punch; regular shut him up. A man of the name of Flocton from Birmingham was, to the best of my knowledge, the first that ever had a fantoccini exhibition in England; but he was only for theatres.

"At this time I had been playing in the orchestra with some travelling comedians, and Mr. Seawood, the master, used among other things to exhibit the dancing figures. He had a proscenium fitted up so that he could open a twenty-foot theatre, almost large enough for living persons. He had the splendidest figures ever introduced into this country. He was an artist as well, splendid scene and transparent painter; indeed, he's worked for some of the first noblemen in Cheltenham, doing up their drawing-rooms. His figures worked their eyes and mouths by mechanism; according to what they had to say, they looked and moved their eyes and mouths according; and females, if they was singing, heaved their bosoms like Christians, the same as life. He had a Turk who did the tight-rope without anybody being seen. He always performed different pieces, and had a regular wardrobe with him—beautiful dresses—and he'd dress 'em up to their parts, and then paint their faces up with distemper, which dries in an hour. Somebody came and told me that Gray was in London, performing in the streets, and that's what brought me out. I had helped Mr. Seawood to manage the figures, and I knew something about them. They told me Gray had a frame, and I said, 'Well, it's a bit of genius, and is a fortune.' The only

figures they told me he had—and it was true—was a sailor, and a Turk, and a clown, and what we calls a Polander, that's a man that tosses the pole. I left Seawood directly, and I went to my father and got some money, and began instantly making my frame and figures. Mine was about sixteen inches high, and I had five of 'em. I began very strong. My fifth figure was a juggler. I was the second that ever came out in the streets of London. It was at the time that George the Fourth went to Scotland, and Gray went after him to try his luck, following the royal family. As the king went out of London I came in. I first of all put up at Peckham, just to lay to a bit and look about me. I'll tell you the reason. I had no one to play, and I couldn't manage the figures and do the music as well, consequently I had to seek after some one to do the pandean pipes. I didn't like to make my first appearance in London without music. At last I met a party that used to play the pipes at Vauxhall. I met him one day, and he says, 'What are you up to now?' so I told him I had the fantoccini figures. He was a beautiful pipe player, and I've never heard any one like him before or since. He wouldn't believe I had the figures, they was such a novelty. I told him where I was staying, and he and his partner came over to see me, and I performed the figures, and then we went on shares. He had worked for Gray, and he knew all his houses where he used to perform, and I knew nothing about these things. When Gray came back he found me performing before one of his houses in Harley-street, where he always had five shillings.

"They was a tremendous success—wonderful. If we had a call at a house our general price was two-and-sixpence, and the performance was, for a good one, twenty minutes. Then there was the crowd for the collection, but they was principally halfpence, and we didn't care about them much, though we have taken four shillings. We never pitched only to houses, only stopping when we had an order, and we hadn't occasion to walk far, for as soon as the tune was heard, up would come the servants to tell us to come. I've had three at me at once. I've known myself to be in Devonshire-place, when I was performing there, to be there for three hours and upwards, going from house to house. I could tell you how much we took a-day. It was, after taking expenses, from four to five pounds a-day. Besides, there was a labourer to whom we paid a guinea a-week to carry a frame, and he had his keep into the bargain. Where Punch took a shilling we've taken a pound.

"I recollect going down with the show to Brighton, and they actually announced our arrival in the papers, saying, that among other public amusements they had the Fantoccini figures from London. That's a fact. That was in the paper. We did well in Brighton.

We have, I can assure you, taken eighteen shillings and sixpence in half an hour, corner-pitching, as we call it; that is, at the corner of a street where there is a lot of people passing. We had such success, that the magistrates sent the head-constable round with us, to clear away the mob. If we performed before any gentleman's place, there was this constable to keep the place clear. A nasty busy fellow he was, too. All the time we was at Brighton we made twenty pounds a-week clear, for we then took only shillings and sixpences, and there was no fourpenny pieces or threepenny bits in them times. We had gentlemen come up many a time and offer to buy the whole concern, clear. What an idea, wasn't it? But we didn't want to sell it, they couldn't have given us our price.

"The crowd was always a great annoyance to us. They'd follow us for miles, and the moment we pitched up they'd come and gather about, and almost choke us. What was their ha'pence to us when we was taking our half-crowns? Actually, in London, we walked three and four miles to get rid of the mob; but, bless you! we couldn't get rid of them, for they was like flies after honey.

"We used to do a great business with evening parties. At Christmas we have had to go three and four times in the same evening to different parties. We never had less than a guinea, and I have had as much as five pounds, but the usual price was two pounds ten shillings, and all refreshments found you. I had the honour of performing before the Queen when she was Princess Victoria. It was at Gloucester-house, Park-lane, and we was engaged by the royal household. A nice berth I had of it, for it was in May, and they put us on the landing of the drawing-room, where the folding-doors opened, and there was some place close by where hot air was admitted to warm the apartments; and what with the heat of the weather and this 'ere ventilation, with the heat coming up the grating-places, and my anxiety performing before a princess, I was near baked, and the perspiration quite run off me; for I was packed up above, standing up and hidden, to manage the figures. There was the maids of honour coming down the stairs like so many nuns, dressed all in white, and the princess was standing on a sofa, with the Duke of Kent behind her. She was apparently very much amused, like others who had seen them. I can't recollect what we was paid, but it was very handsome and so forth.

"I've also performed before the Baroness Rothschild's, next the Duke of Wellington's, and likewise the Baron himself, in Grosvenor-place, and Sir Watkyn W. Wynne, and half the nobility in England. We've been in the very first of drawing-rooms.

"I shall never forget being at Sir Watkyn Wynne's, for we was very handsomely treated, and had the best of everything. It was in St. James's-square, and the best of mansions. It was a juvenile-party night, and there was a juggler, and a Punch and Judy, and our Fantoccini. One of the footmen comes up, and says he, 'Would any of you men like a jelly?' I told him I didn't care for none, but the Punch-and-Judy man says — 'My missus is very partial to them.' So the footman asks — 'How will you carry it home?' I suggested he should put it in his hat, and the foolish fellow, half silly with horns of ale, actually did, and wrapped it up in his pocket-handkerchief. There was a large tumbler full. By and by he cries — 'Lord, how I sweat!' and there was the stuff running down his hair like so much size. We did laugh, I can assure you.

"Fantoccini has fallen off now. It's quite different to what it was. I don't think the people's tired of it, but it ain't such a novelty. I could stop up a whole street if I liked, so that nothing could get along, and that shows the people ain't tired of it. I think it's the people that gave the half-crowns are tired of it, but those with the ha'pence are as fond of it as ever. As times go, the performance is worth two pounds a-week to me; and if it wasn't, I couldn't afford to stop with it, for I'm very clever on the violin, and I could earn more than thirty shillings a-week playing in bands. We still attend evening parties, only it isn't to princesses, but gentry. We depend more upon evening parties. It isn't street work, only if we didn't go round they'd think I was dead. We go to more than thirty parties a-year. We always play according to price, whether it's fifteen shillings, or ten shillings, or a guinea. We don't get many five-guinea orders now. The last one was six months ago, to go twenty-eight miles into Kent, to a gentleman's house. When we go to parties, we take with us a handsome, portable, fold-up frame. The front is beautiful, and by a first-rate artist. The gentleman who done it is at the head of the carriage department at a railway, and there's the royal arms all in gold, and it stands above ten feet high, and has wings and all, so that the music and everything is invisible. It shuts up like a portfolio. The figures are first-rate ones, and every one dressed according to the country, whatever it may be, she is supposed to represent. They are in the best of material, with satin and lace, and all that's good.

"When we perform in the streets, we generally go through this programme. We begins with a female hornpipe dancer; then there is a set of quadrilles by some marionette figures, four females and no gentleman. If we did the men we should want assistance, for four is as much as I can hold at once. It would require two men, and the street won't pay for it. After this we introduces a representation of Mr. Grimaldi the clown, who does tumbling and posturing, and a comic dance, and so forth, such as trying to catch a butterfly. Then comes the enchanted Turk. He comes on in the costume of a Turk, and he throws off his right and left arm, and then his legs, and they each change into different figures, the arms and legs into two boys and girls, a clergyman the head, and an old lady the body. That figure was my own invention, and I could if I like turn him into a dozen; indeed, I've got one at home, which turns into a parson in the pulpit, and a clerk under him, and a lot of little charity children, with a form to sit down upon. They are all carved figures, every one of them, and my own make. The next performance is the old lady, and her arms drop off and turn into two figures, and the body becomes a complete balloon and car in a minute, and not a flat thing, but round — and the figures get into the car and up they go. Then there's the tight-rope dancer, and next the Indian juggler — Ramo Samee, a representation — who chucks the balls about under his feet and under his arms, and catches them on the back of his head, the same as Ramo Samee did. Then there's the sailor's hornpipe — Italian Scaramouch (he's the old style). This one has a long neck, and it shoots up to the top of the theatre. This is the original trick, and a very good one. Then comes the Polander, who balances a pole and two chairs, and stands on his head and jumps over his pole; he dresses like a Spaniard, and in the old style. It takes a quarter of an hour to do that figure well, and make him do all his tricks. Then comes the Skeletons. They're regular first class, of course. This one also was my invention, and I was the first to make them, and I'm the only one that can make them. They are made of a particular kind of wood. I'm a first-rate carver, and can make my three guineas any day for a skull; indeed, I've sold many to dentists to put in their window. It's very difficult to carve this figure, and takes a deal of time. It takes full two months to make these skeletons. I've been offered ten pounds ten shillings for a pair, if I'd make 'em correct according to the human frame. Those I make for exhibiting in the streets, I charge two pounds each for. They're good, and all the joints is correct, and you may put 'em into what attitudes you like, and they walk like a human being. These figures in my show come up through a trap-door, and perform attitudes, and shiver and lie down, and do imitations of the pictures. It's a tragic sort of concern, and many ladies won't have 'em at evening parties, because it frightens the children. Then there's Judy Callaghan, and that 'livens up after the skeletons. Then six figures jump out of her pockets, and she knocks them about. It's a sort of comic business. Then the next is a countryman who can't get his donkey to go, and it kicks at him and throws him off, and all manner of comic antics, after Billy Button's style. Then I do the skeleton that falls to pieces, and then becomes whole again. Then there's another out of the-way comic figure that falls to pieces

similar to the skeleton. He catches hold of his head and chucks it from one hand to the other. We call him the Nondescript. We wind up with a scene in Tom and Jerry. The curtain winds up, and there's a watchman prowling the streets, and some of those larking gentlemen comes on and pitch into him. He looks round and he can't see anybody. Presently another comes in and gives him another knock, and then there's a scuffle, and off they go over the watch-box, and down comes the scene. That makes the juveniles laugh, and finishes up the whole performance merry like.

"I've forgot one figure now. I know'd there was another, and that's the Scotchman who dances the Highland fling. He's before the watchman. He's in the regular national costume, everything correct, and everything, and the music plays according to the performance. It's a beautiful figure when well handled, and the dresses cost something, I can tell you; all the joints are counter-sunk — them figures that shows above the knee. There's no joints to be seen, all works hidden like, something like Madame Vestris in Don Juan. All my figures have got shoes and stockings on. They have, indeed. If it wasn't my work, they'd cost a deal of money. One of them is more expensive than all those in Punch and Judy put together. Talk of Punch knocking the Fantoccini down! Mine's all show; Punch is nothing, and cheap as dirt.

"I've also forgot the flower-girl that comes in and dances with a garland. That's a very pretty figure in a fairy's dress, in a nice white skirt with naked carved arms, nice modelled, and the legs just the same; and the trunks come above the knee, the same as them ballet girls. She shows all the opera attitudes.

"The performance, to go through the whole of it, takes an hour and a half; and then you mustn't stand looking at it, but as soon as one thing goes off the music changes and another comes on. That ain't one third, nor a quarter of what I can do.

"When I'm performing I'm standing behind, looking down upon the stage. All the figures is hanging round on hooks, with all their strings ready for use. It makes your arms ache to work them, and especially across the loins. All the strength you have you must do, and chuck it out too; for those four figures which I uses at evening parties, which dance the polka, weighs six pounds, and that's to be kept dangling for twenty minutes together. They are two feet high, and their skirts take three quarters of a yard, and are covered with spangles, which gives 'em great weight.

"There are only two of us going about now with Fantoccini shows. Several have tried it, but they had to knock under very soon. They soon lost their money and time. In the first place, they must be musicians to make the figures keep time in the dances; and, again, they must be carvers, for it won't pay to put the figures out to be done. I had ten pounds the other day only to carve six figures, and the wood only come to three shillings; that'll give you some idea of what the carving costs.

"Formerly I used to make the round of the watering-places, but I've got quite enough to do in London now, and travelling's very expensive, for the eating and drinking is so very expensive. Now, at Ramsgate I've had to pay half-a-guinea for a bed, and that to a man in my position is more than I like. I always pays the man who goes along with me to play the music, because I don't go out every day, only when it suits me. He gets as good as his twenty-three shillings a-week, according to how business is, and that's on an average as good as four shillings a-day. If I'm very lucky I makes it better for him, for a man can't be expected to go and blow his life away into pandean pipes unless he's well paid for it."

Guy Fawkeses.

UNTIL within the last ten or twelve years, the exhibition of guys in the public thorough-fares every 5th of November, was a privilege enjoyed exclusively by boys of from 10 to 15 years of age, and the money arising there-from was supposed to be invested at night in a small pyrotechnic display of squibs, crackers, and catherine-wheels.

At schools, and at many young gentlemen's houses, for at least a week before the 5th arrived, the bonfires were prepared and guys built up.

At night one might see rockets ascending in the air from many of the suburbs of London, and the little back-gardens in such places as the Hampstead-road and Kennington, and, after dusk, suddenly illuminated with the blaze of the tar-barrel, and one might hear in the streets even banging of crackers mingled with the laughter and shouts of boys enjoying the sport.

In those days the street guys were of a very humble character, the grandest of them generally consisting of old clothes stuffed up with straw, and carried in state upon a kitchen-chair. The arrival of the guy before a window was announced by a juvenile chorus of "Please to remember the 5th of November." So diminutive, too, were some of these guys, that I have even seen dolls carried about as the representatives of the late Mr. Fawkes. In fact, none of these effigies were hardly ever made of larger proportions than Tom Thumb, or than would admit of being carried through the garden-gates of any suburban villa.

Of late years, however, the character of Guy Fawkes-day has entirely changed. It seems now to partake rather of the nature of a London May-day. The figures have grown to be of gigantic stature, and whilst clowns, musicians, and dancers have got to accompany them in their travels through the streets, the traitor Fawkes seems to have been almost

laid aside, and the festive occasion taken advantage of for the expression of any political feeling, the guy being made to represent any celebrity of the day who has for the moment offended against the opinions of the people. The kitchen-chair has been changed to the costermongers' donkey-truck, or even vans drawn by pairs of horses. The bonfires and fireworks are seldom indulged in; the money given to the exhibitors being shared among the projectors at night, the same as if the day's work had been occupied with acrobating or nigger singing.

The first guy of any celebrity that made its appearance in the London streets was about the year 1844, when an enormous figure was paraded about on horseback. This had a tall extinguisher-hat, with a broad red brim, and a pointed vandyked collar, that hung down over a smock frock, which was stuffed out with straw to the dimensions of a water-butt. The figure was attended by a body of some half-dozen costermongers, mounting many coloured cockades, and armed with for-midable bludgeons. The novelty of the ex-hibition ensured its success, and the "coppers" poured in in such quantities that on the following year gigantic guys were to be found in every quarter of the metropolis.

But the gigantic movement did not attain its zenith till the "No Popery" cry was raised, upon the division of England into papal bishoprics. Then it was no longer Fawkes, but Cardinal Wiseman and the Pope of Rome who were paraded as guys through the London thoroughfares.

The figures were built up of enormous pro-portions, the red hat of the cardinal having a brim as large as a loo-table, and his scarlet cape being as long as a tent. Guy Fawkes seated upon a barrel marked "Gunpowder" usually accompanied His Holiness and the Cardinal, but his diminutive size showed that Guy now played but a secondary part in the exhibition, although the lantern and the matches were tied as usual to his radishy and gouty fingers. According to the newspapers, one of these shows was paraded on the Royal Exchange, the merchants approving of the exhibition to such an extent that sixpences, shillings, and half-crowns were showered in to the hats of the lucky costers who had made the speculation. So excited was the public mind, that at night, after business was over, processions were formed by tradespeople and respectable mechanics, who, with bands of music playing, and banners flying, on which were inscribed anti-papal mottoes and devices, marched through the streets with flaming torches, and after parading their monster Popes and Cardinals until about nine o'clock at night, eventually adjourned to some open space — like Peckham-rye or Blackheath — where the guy was burned amid the most boisterous applauses.

Cardinal Wiseman and the Pope reappeared

for several years in succession, till at length the Russian war breaking out, the Guy-Fawkes constructors had a fresh model to work upon. The Emperor of Russia accordingly " came out " in the streets, in all forms and shapes ; sometimes as the veritable Nicholas, in jackboots and leather breeches, with his unmistakable moustache; and often as Old Nick, with a pair of horns and a lengthy appendage in the form of a tail, with an arrow-headed termination ; and not unfrequently he was represented as a huge bear crouching beneath some rude symbol of the English and French alliance.

On the 5th of November (1856) the guys were more of a political than a religious character. The unfortunate Pope of Rome had in some instances been changed for Bomba, though the Czar, His Holiness, and his British representative the Cardinal, were not altogether neglected. The want of any political agitation was the cause why the guys were of so uninteresting a character.

I must not, however, forget to mention a singular innovation that was then made in the recognised fashion of guy building—one of the groups of figures exhibited being (strange to say) of a complimentary nature. It consisted of Miss Nightingale, standing between an English Grenadier and a French foot-soldier, while at her feet lay the guy between two barrels marked " Gunpowder," and so equivocally attired that he might be taken for either the Emperor of Russia or the Pope of Rome.

At Billingsgate, a guy was promenaded round the market as early as five o'clock in the morning, by a party of charity-boys, who appeared by their looks to have been sitting up all night. It is well known to the boys in the neighbourhood of the great fish-market, that the guy which is first in the field reaps the richest harvest of halfpence from the salesmen; and indeed, till within the last three or four years, one fish-factor was in the habit of giving the bearers of the first effigy he saw a half-crown piece. Hence there were usually two or three different guy parties in attendance soon after four o'clock, awaiting his coming into the market.

For manufacturing a cheap guy, such as that seen at Billingsgate, a pair of old trousers and Wellington boots form the most expensive item. The shoulders of the guys are generally decorated with a paper cape, adorned with different coloured rosettes and gilt stars. A fourpenny mask makes the face, and a proper cocked hat, embellished in the same style as the cape, surrounds the rag head.

The general characteristics of all guys consists in a limpness and roundness of limb, which give the form a puddingy appearance. All the extremities have a kind of paralytic feebleness, so that the head leans on one side like that of a dead bird, and the feet have an unnatural propensity for placing themselves in every position but the right one; sometimes turning their toes in, as if their legs had been put on the wrong way, or keeping their toes turned out, as if they had been " struck so " while taking their first dancing-lesson. Their fingers radiate like a bunch of carrots, and the arms are as shapeless and bowed as the monster sausage in a cook-shop window. The face is always composed of a mask painted in the state of the most florid health, and singularly disagreeing with the frightful debility of the body. Through the holes for the eyes bits of rag and straw generally protrude, as though birds had built in the sockets. A pipe is mostly forced into the mouth, where it remains with the bowl downwards ; and in the hands it is customary to tie a lantern and matches. Whilst the guy is carried along, you can hear the straw in his interior rustling and crackling, like moving a workhouse mattrass. As a general rule, it may be added, that guys have a helpless, drunken look.

When, however, the monster Guy Fawkeses came into fashion, considerably greater expense was gone to in " getting up" the figures. Then the feet were always fastened in their proper position, and although the arrangement of the hands was never perfectly mastered, yet the fingers were brought a little more closely together, and approached the digital dexterity of the dummies at the cheap clothes marts.

For carrying the guys about, chairs, wheelbarrows, trucks, carts, and vans are employed. Chairs and wheelbarrows are patronised by the juvenile population, but the other vehicles belong to the gigantic speculations.

On the Surrey side a guy was exhibited in 1856 whose straw body was encased in a coachman's old great coat, covered with different colours, as various as the waistcoat patterns on a tailor's show-book. He was wheeled about on a truck by three or four young men, whose hoarse voices, when shouting " Please to remember the Guy," showed their regular occupation to be street-selling, for they had the same husky sound as the " Eight a-groat fresh herrens," in the Saturday night streetmarkets.

In the neighbourhood of Walworth, men dressed up as guys were dragged about on trucks. One of them was seated upon a barrel marked " Gunpowder," his face being painted green, and ornamented with an immense false nose of a bright scarlet colour. I could not understand what this guy was meant to represent, for he wore a sugarloaf hat with an ostrich feather in it, and had on a soldier's red coat, decorated with paper rosettes as big as cabbages. His legs, too, were covered with his own corduroy trowsers, but adorned with paper streamers and bows. In front of him marched a couple of men carrying broomsticks, and musicians playing upon a tambourine and a penny tin whistle.

The most remarkable of the stuffed figures of 1856 was one dressed in a sheet, intended to represent the Rev. Mr. Spurgeon in a sur-plice! It was carried about on a wooden stage by boys, and took very well with the mob, for no sooner did the lads cry out,—

> "Remember, remember,
> The fifth of November,
> Old Spurgeon's treason and plot!"

than a shout of laughter burst from the crowd, and the halfpence began to pour in. Without this alteration in the November rhyme, nobody would have been able to have traced the slightest resemblance between the guy and the reverend gentleman whose effigy it was stated to be.

Further, it should be added, that the guy exhibitors have of late introduced a new sys-tem, of composing special rhymes for the occa-sion, which are delivered after the well-known " Remember, remember." Those with the figures of the Pope, for instance, sing,—

> " A penn'orth of cheese to feed the pope,
> A twopenny loaf to choke him,
> A pint of beer to wash it down,
> And a good large fagot to smoke him!"

I heard a party of costermongers, who had the image of His Imperial Majesty the Em-peror of all the Russias wabbling on their truck, sing in chorus this home-manufactured verse,—

> " Poke an ingun in his eye —
> A squib shove up his nose, sirs;
> Then roast him till he's done quite brown,
> And Nick to old Nick goes, sirs."

With the larger guys little is usually said or done beyond exhibiting them. In the crowded thoroughfares, the proprietors mostly occupy themselves only with collecting the money, and never let the procession stop for a moment. On coming to the squares, however, a different course is pursued, for then they stop before every window where a head is visible and sing the usual " Remember, remember," winding up with a vociferous hurrah! as they hold out their hats for the halfpence.

At the West-end, one of the largest guys of 1856 was drawn by a horse in a cart. This could not have been less than fourteen feet high. Its face, which was as big as a shield, was so flat and good-humoured in expres-sion that I at once recognised it as a panto-mime mask, or one used to hang outside some masquerade costumier's shop door. The coat was of the Charles the Second's cut, and com-posed of a lightish coloured paper, ornamented with a profusion of Dutch metal. There was a sash across the right shoulder, and the legs were almost as long as the funnel to a penny steamer, and ended in brown paper cavalier boots. As the costermongers led it along, it shook like a load of straw. If it had not been for the bull's-eye lantern and lath matches, nobody would have recognised in the dandy figure the effigy of the wretched Fawkes.

By far the handsomest turn-out of the day, at this time, was a group of three figures, which promenaded Whitechapel and Bethnal-green. They stood erect in a van drawn by a blind horse, and accompanied by a "band" of *one* performer on the drum and pandean pipes. Four clowns in full costume made faces while they jumped about among the spectators, and collected donations. All the guys were about ten feet high. The centre one, intended for Fawkes himself, was attired in a flowing cloak of crimson glazed calico, and his black hat was a broad-brimmed sugar-loaf, the pointed crown of which was like a model of Langham-place church steeple, and it had a profusion of black hair streaming about the face. The figures on either side of this were intended for Lords Suffolk and Monteagle, in the act of arresting the traitor, and accord-ingly appeared to be gently tapping Mr. Fawkes on either shoulder. The bodies of their lordships were encased in gold scale-armour, and their legs in silver ditto, whilst their heads were covered with three-cornered cocked hats, surmounted by white feathers. In the front of the van were two white banners, with the following inscriptions in letters of gold:—

" APPREHENSION OF GUY FAWKES ON THE 5TH OF NOVEMBER, IN THE YEAR 1605."

And,—

" THE DISCOVERY OF THE GUNPOWDER PLOT ON THE 5TH OF NOVEMBER, 1605."

At the back of the van flaunted two flags of all nations. In addition to the four clowns, there were several other attendants; one in particular had the appearance of half a man and half a beast, his body being clad in a green frock-coat, whilst his legs and feet were shaggy, and made to imitate a bear's.

The most remarkable part of this exhibition was the expression upon the countenances of the figures. They were ordinary masks, and consequently greatly out of proportion for the height of the figures. There was a strong family resemblance between the traitor and his arrestors; neither did Fawkes's coun-tenance exhibit any look of rage, astonishment, or disappointment at finding his designs frus-trated. Nor did their lordships appear to be angry, disgusted, or thunderstruck at the con-spirator's bold attempt.

In the neighbourhood of Bond-street the guys partook of a political character, as if to please the various Members of Parliament who might be strolling to their Clubs. In one barrow was the effigy of the Emperor of the French, holding in his hands, instead of the lantern and matches, a copy of the *Times* newspaper, torn in half. I was informed that another figure I saw was intended to represent the form of Bomba.

In the neighbourhood of Lambeth Palace the guys were of an ecclesiastical kind, and such as it was imagined would be likely to flatter the Archbishop of Canterbury into giving at least a half-crown. One of these was drawn by two donkeys, and accompanied by drums and pipes. It represented Cardinal Wiseman in the company of four members of "the Holy Inquisition." The Cardinal was dressed in the usual scarlet costume, while the Inquisitors were robed in black with green veils over their faces. In front of the cart was a bottle, labelled "Holy Water," which was continually turned round, so that the people might discover that on the other side was printed "Whisky."

The practice of burning guys, and lighting bonfires, and letting off fireworks, is now generally discontinued, and particularly as regards the public exhibitions at Blackheath and Peckham Rye. The greatest display of fireworks, we are inclined to believe, took place in the public streets of the metropolis, for up to twelve o'clock at night, one might occasionally hear reports of penny cannons, and the jerky explosions of crackers.

GUY FAWKES (MAN).

"I'M in the crock'ry line, going about with a basket and changing jugs, and glass, and things, for clothes and that; but for the last eight years I have, every Fifth of November, gone out with a guy. It's a good job for the time, for what little we lay out on the guy we don't miss, and the money comes in all of a lump at the last. While it lasts there's money to be made by it. I used always to take the guy about for two days; but this last year I took him about for three.

"I was nineteen year old when I first went out with a guy. It was seeing others about with 'em, and being out of work at the time, and having nothing to sell, I and another chap we knocked up one between us, and we found it go on pretty well, so we kept on at it. The first one I took out was a very first-rater, for we'd got it up as well as we could to draw people's attention. I said, 'It ain't no good doing as the others do, we must have a tip-topper.' It represented Guy Fawkes in black velvet. It was about nine feet high, and he was standing upright, with matches in one hand and lantern in the other. I show'd this one round Clerkenwell and Islington. It was the first big 'un as was ever brought out. There had been paper ones as big, but ne'er a one dressed up in the style mine was. I had a donkey and cart, and we placed it against some cross-rails and some bits of wood to keep him steady. He stood firm because he had two poles up his legs, and being lashed round the body holding him firm to the posts —like a rock. We done better the first time we went out than we do lately. The guy must have cost a sovereign. He had a trunk-hose and white legs, which we made out of a pair of white drawers, for fleshings and yellow

boots, which I bought in Petticoat-lane. We took over 3*l.* with him, which was pretty fair, and just put us on again, for November is a bad time for most street trades, and getting a few shillings all at once makes it all right till Christmas.

"A pal of mine, of the name of Smith, was the first as ever brought out a big one. His wasn't a regular dressed-up one, but only with a paper apron to hang down the front and bows, and such-like. He put it on a chair, and had four boys to carry it on their shoulders. He was the first, too, as introduced clowns to dance about. I see him do well, and that's why I took mine in hand.

"The year they was chalking 'No Popery' all about the walls I had one, dressed up in a long black garment, with a red cross on his bosom. I'm sure I don't know what it meant, but they told me it would be popular. I had only one figure, with nine bows, and that tidiwated all about him. As we went along everybody shouted out 'No Popery!' Everybody did. He had a large brimmed hat with a low crown in, and a wax mask. I always had wax ones. I've got one at home now I've had for five year. It cost two-and-six-pence. It's a very good-looking face but rather sly, with a great horse-hair beard. Most of the boys make their'n devils, and as ugly as they can, but that wouldn't do for Christians like as I represent mine to be.

"One year I had Nicholas and his adviser. That was the Emperor of Russia in big top-boots and white breeches, and a green coat on. I gave him a good bit of mustachios— a little extra. He had a Russian helmet hat on, with a pair of eagles on the top. It was one I bought. I bought it cheap, for I only gave a shilling for it. I was offered five or six for it afterwards, but I found it answer my purpose to keep. I had it dressed up this year. The other figure was the devil. I made him of green tinsel paper cut out like scale armour, and pasted on to his legs to make it stick tight. He had a devil's mask on, and I made him a pair of horns out of his head. Over them was a banner. I was told what to do to make the banner, for I had the letters writ out first, and then I cut 'em out of tinsel paper and stuck them on to glazed calico. On this banner was these words:—

'What shall I do next?'
'Why, blow your brains out!'

That took immensely, for the people said 'That is wery well.' It was the time the war was on. I dare say I took between 3*l.* and 4*l.* that time. There was three of us rowed in with it, so we got a few shillings a-piece.

"The best one I ever had was the trial of Guy Fawkes. There was four figures, and they was drawn about in a horse and cart. There was Guy Fawkes, and two soldiers had hold of him, and there was the king sitting in a chair in front. The king was in a scarlet velvet cloak, sitting in an old arm-chair, papered over to make it look decent. There was green and blue paper hanging over the arms to hide the ragged parts of it. The king's cloak cost sevenpence a-yard, and there was seven of these yards. He had a gilt paper crown and a long black wig made out of some rope. His trunks was black and crimson, and he had blue stockings and red boots. I made him up out of my own head, and not from pictures. It was just as I thought would be the best way to get it up, out of my own head. I've seed the picture of Guy Fawkes, because I've got a book of it at home. I never was no scholar, not in the least. The soldiers had a breastplate of white steel paper, and baggy knee-breeches, and top boots. They had a big pipe each, with a top cut out of tin. Their helmets was the same as in the pictures, of steel paper, and a kind of a dish-cover shape, with a peak in front and behind. Guy was dressed the same kind as he was this year, with a black velvet dress and red cloak, and red boots turning over at top, with lace sewed on. I never made any of my figures frightful. I get 'em as near as I can to the life like.

"I reckon that show was the best as I ever had about. I done very well with it. They said it was a very good sight, and well got up. I dare say it cost me, with one thing and another, pretty nigh 4*l.* to get up. There was two of us to shove, me and my brother. I know I had a sovereign to myself when it was over, besides a little bit of merry-making.

This year I had the apprehension of Guy Fawkes by Lord Suffolk and Monteagle. I've followed up the hist'ry as close as I can. Next year I shall have him being burnt, with a lot of faggits and things about him. This year the figures cost about 3*l.* getting up. Fawkes was dressed in his old costume of black velvet and red boots. I bought some black velvet breeches in Petticoat-lane, and I gave 1*s.* 9*d.* for the two pair. They was old theatrical breeches. Their lordships was dressed in gold scale-armour like, of cut-out paper pasted on, and their legs imitated steel. They had three-corner cock'd hats, with white feathers in. I always buy fierce-looking masks with frowns, but one of them this year was a smiling—Lord Monteagle, I think. I took the figures as near as I can form from a picture I saw of Guy Fawkes being apprehended. I placed them figures in a horse and cart, and piled them up on apple-chests to the level of the cart, so they showed all, their feet and all. I bind the chests with a piece of table-cover cloth. The first day we went out we took 2*l.* 7*s.*, and the second we took 1*l.* 17*s.*, and the last day we took 2*l.* 1*s.* We did so well the third day because we went into the country, about Tottenham and Edmonton. They never witnessed such a thing down them parts. The drummer what I had with me was a blind man, and well known down

there. They call him Friday, because he goes there every Friday, so what they usually gave him we had. Our horse was blind, so we was obliged to have one to lead him in front and another to lead the blind drummer behind. We paid the drummer 16*s.* for the three days. We paid for two days 10*s.*, and the third one most of it came in, and we all went shares. It was a pony more than a horse. I think we got about a 1*l.* a-piece clear, when we was done on the Friday night. It took me six weeks getting up in my leisure time. There was the Russian bear in front. He wore a monkey dress, the same as in the pantomimes, and that did just as well for a bear. I painted his face as near as I could get it, to make it look frightful.

"When I'm building up a guy we first gits some bags and things, and cut 'em out to the shape of the legs and things, and then sew it up. We sew the body and arms and all round together in one. We puts two poles down for the legs and then a cross-piece at the belly and another cross-piece at the shoulder, and that holds 'em firm. We fill the legs with sawdust, and stuff it down with our hands to make it tight. It takes two sacks of sawdust for three figures, but I generally have it give to me, for I know a young feller as works at the wood-chopping. We stand 'em up in the room against the wall, whilst we are dressing them. We have lots of chaps come to see us working at the guys. Some will sit there for many hours looking at us. We stuff the body with shavings and paper and any sort of rubbish. I sew whatever is wanted myself, and in fact my fingers is sore now with the thimble, for I don't know how to use a thimble, and I feel awkward with it. I design everything and cut out all the clothes and the painting and all. They allow me 5*s.* for the building. This last group took me six weeks, —not constant, you know, but only lazy time of a night. I lost one or two days over it, that's all.

"I think there was more Guy Fawkeses out this year than ever was out before. There was one had Guy Fawkes and Punch and a Clown in a cart, and another was Miss Nightingale and two soldiers. It was meant to be complimentary to that lady, but for myself I think it insulting to bring out a lady like that as a guy, when she's done good to all.

"They always reckon me to be about the first hand in London at building a guy. I never see none like them, nor no one else I don't think. It took us two quire of gold paper and one quire of silver paper to do the armour and the banner and other things. The gold paper is 6*d.* a-sheet, and the silver is 1*d.* a sheet. It wouldn't look so noble if we didn't use the gold paper.

"This year we had three clowns with us, and we paid them 3*s.* a-day each. I was dressed up as a clown, too. We had to dance about, and joke, and say what we thought would be funny to the people. I had a child in my arms made of a doll stuffed with shavings, and made to represent a little boy. It. was just to make a laugh. Every one I went up to I told the doll to ask their uncle or their aunt for a copper. I had another move, too, of calling for 'Bill Bowers' in the crowd, and if I got into any row, or anything, I used to call to him to protect me. We had no time to say much, for we kept on moving, and it loses time to talk.

"We took the guy round Goswell-road and Pentonville the first day, and on the second we was round Bethnal-green way, among the weavers. We went that way for safety the second day, for the police won't interrupt you there. The private houses give the most. They very seldom give more than a penny. I don't suppose we got more than 3s. or 4s. in silver all the three days.

"Sometimes we have rough work with the Irish going about with guys. The 'No Popery' year there was several rows. I was up at Islington-gate, there, in the Lower-road, and there's loads of Irish live up there, and a rough lot they are. They came out with sticks and bricks, and cut after us. We bolted with the guy. If our guy hadn't been very firm, it would have been jolted to bits. We always nailed straps round the feet, and support it on rails at the waist, and lashed to the sides. We bolted from this Irish mob over Islington-green, and down John-street into Clerkenwell. My mate got a nick with a stone just on the head. It just give him a slight hurt, and drawed the blood from him. We jumped up in the donkey-cart and drove off.

"There was one guy was pulled out of the cart this year, down by Old Gravel-lane, in the Ratcliff-highway. They pulled Miss Nightingale out of the cart and ran away with her, and regular destroyed the two soldiers that was on each side of her. Sometimes the cabmen lash at the guys with their whips. We never say anything to them, for fear we might get stopped by the police for making a row. You stand a chance of having a feather knocked off, or such-like, as is attached to them.

"There's a lot of boys goes about on the 5th with sticks, and make a regular business of knocking guys to pieces. They're called guy-smashers. They don't come to us, we're too strong for that, but they only manage the little ones, as they can take advantage of. They do this some of them to take the money the boys have collected. I have had regular prigs following my show, to pick the pockets of those looking on, but as sure as I see them I start them off by putting a policeman on to them.

"When we're showing, I don't take no trouble to invent new rhymes, but stick to the old poetry. There's some do new songs. I usually sing out,—

'Gentlefolks, pray
Remember this day;
'Tis with kind notice we bring
The figure of sly
And villanous Guy,
Who wanted to murder the king.
By powder and store,
He bitterly swore,
As he skulk'd in the walls to repair,
The parliament, too,
By him and his crew,
Should all be blowed up in the air.

But James, very wise,
Did the Papists surprise,
As they plotted the cruelty great;
He know'd their intent,
So Suffolk he sent
To save both kingdom and state.
Guy Fawkes he was found
With a lantern underground,
And soon was the traitor bound fast:
And they swore he should die,
So they hung him up high,
And burnt him to ashes at last.
So we, once a-year,
Come round without fear,
To keep up remembrance of this day;
While assistance from you
May bring a review
Of Guy Fawkes a-blazing away.

So hollo, boys! hollo, boys!
Shout and huzza;
So hollo, boys! hollo, boys!
Keep up this day!
So hollo, boys! hollo, boys!
And make the bells ring!
Down with the Pope, and God save the Queen!'

"It used to be King, but we say Queen now, and though it don't rhyme, it's more correct.

"It's very seldom that the police say anything to us, so long as we don't stop too long in the gangway not to create any mob. They join in the fun and laugh like the rest. Wherever we go there is a great crowd from morning to night.

"We have dinner on Guy Fawkes' days between one and two. We go to any place where it's convenient for us to stop at, generally at some public-house. We go inside, and leave some of the lads to look after the guy outside. We always keep near the window, where we can look out into the street, and we keep ourselves ready to pop out in a minute if anybody should attack the guy. We generally go into some by-way, where there ain't much traffic. We never was interrupted much whilst we was at dinner, only by boys chucking stones and flinging things at it; and they run off as soon as we come out.

"There's one party that goes out with a guy that sells it afterwards. They stop in London for the first two days, and then they work their way into the country as far as Sheerness, and then they sells the guy to form part of the procession on Lord-mayor's day. It's the watermen and ferrymen mostly buy it, and they carry it about in a kind of merriment among themselves, and at night they burn it and let off fireworks. They don't make no charge for coming to see it burnt, but it's open to the air and free to the public.

"None of the good guys taken about on

the 5th are burnt at night, unless some gentlemen buy them. I used to sell mine at one time to the Albert Saloon. Sometimes they'd give me 15s. for it, and sometimes less, according to what kind of a one I had. Three years, I think, I sold it to them. They used to burn it at first in the gardens at the back, but after they found the gardens fill very well without it, so they wouldn't have any more.

" I always take the sawdust and shavings out of my guys, and save the clothes for another year. The clothes are left in my possession to be taken care of. I make a kind of private bonfire in our yard with the sawdust and shavings, and the neighbours come there and have a kind of a spree, and shove one another into the fire, and kick it about the yard, and one thing and another.

" When I am building the guy, I begin about six weeks before 5th of November comes, and then we subscribe a shilling or two each and buy such things as we wants. Then, when we wants more, I goes to my pals, who live close by, and we subscribe another shilling or sixpence each, according to how we gets on in the day. Nearly all those that take out guys are mostly street traders.

" The heaviest expense for any guy I've built was 4l. for one of four figures."

GUY FAWKES (BOY).

" I ALWAYS go out with a Guy Fawkes every year. I'm seventeen years old, and I've been out with a guy ever since I can remember, except last year; I didn't then, because I was in Middlesex Hospital with an abscess, brought on by the rheumatic fever. I was in the hospital a month. My father was an undertaker; he's been dead four months: mother carries on the trade. He didn't like my going out with guys, but I always would. He didn't like it at all, he used to say it was a disgrace. Mother didn't much fancy my doing it this year. When I was a very little un, I was carried about for a guy. I couldn't a been more than seven years old when I first begun. They put paper-hangings round my legs—they got it from Baldwin's, in the Tottenham Court-road; sometimes they bought, and sometimes got it give 'em; but they give a rare lot for a penny or twopence. After that they put me on a apron made of the same sort of paper—showy, you know—then they put a lot of tinsel bows, and at the corners they cut a sort of tail like there is to farriers' aprons, and it look stunnin'; then they put on my chest a tinsel heart and rosettes; they was green and red, because it shows off. All up my arms I had bows and things to make a show-off. Then I put on a black mask with a little red on the cheek, to make me look like a devil: it had horns, too. Always pick out a devil's mask with horns: it looks fine, and frightens the people a'most. The boy that dressed me was a very clever chap, and made a guy to rights. Why, he

made me a little guy about a foot high, to carry in my lap—it was piecings of quilting like, a sort of patch-work all sewn together,—and then he filled it with saw-dust, and made a head of shavings. He picked the shavings small, and then sewed 'em up in a little bag; and then he painted a face, and it looked wery well; and he made it a little tinsel bob-tail coat, and a tinsel cap with two feathers on the top. It was made to sit in a chair; and there was a piece of string tied to each of the legs and the arms, and a string come behind; and I used to pull it, and the legs and arms jumped up. I was put in a chair, and two old broom-handles was put through the rails, and then a boy got in front, and another behind, and carried me off round Holborn way in the streets and squares. Every now and then they put me down before a window; then one of 'em used to say the speech, and I used all the time to keep pulling the string of my little guy, and it amused the children at the winders. After they'd said the speech we all shouted hurrah! and then some of them went and knocked at the door and asked ' Please to remember the guy;' and the little children brought us ha'pence and pence; and sometimes the ladies and gentlemen chucked us some money out of the winder. At last they carried me into Russell-square. They put me down before a gentleman's house and begun saying the speech: while they was saying it, up comes a lot o' boys with sticks in their hands. One of our chaps knowed what they was after, and took the little guy out of my hand, and went on saying the speech. I kept all on sitting still. After a bit one of these 'ere boys says, ' Oh, it's a dead guy; let's have a lark with it!' and then one of 'em gives me a punch in the eye with his fist, and then snatched the mask off my face, and when he'd pulled it off he says, ' Oh, Bill, it's a live un!' We was afraid we should get the worst of it, so we run away round the square. The biggest one of our lot carried the chair. After we'd run a little way they caught us again, and says, ' Now then, give us all your money;' with that, some ladies and gentlemen that see it all came up to 'em and says, ' If you don't go we'll lock you up;' and so they let us go away. And so we went to another place where they sold masks; and we bought another. Then they asked me to be guy again, but I wouldn't, for I'd got a black-eye through it already. So they got another to finish out the day. When we got home at night we shared 2s. a-piece. There was five of us altogether; but I think they chisselled me. I know they got a deal more than that, for they'd had a good many sixpences and shillings. People usen't to think much of a shilling that time a-day, because there wasn't any but little guys about then; but I don't know but what the people now encourage little guys most, because they say that the chaps with the big ones ought to go to work.

"Next year I was out with a stuffed guy. They wanted me to be guy again, because I wasn't frightened easy, and I was lightish; but I told 'em 'No, I've had enough of being guy; I don't be guy any more: besides, I had such fine money for getting a whack in the eye!' We got on pretty well that year; but it gets wus and wus every year. We got hardly anything this year; and next I don't suppose we shall get anything at all. These chaps that go about pitchin' into guys we call 'guy smashers;' but they don't do it only for the lark of smashing the guys: they do it for the purpose of taking the boys' money away, and sometimes the clothes. If one of 'em has a hole in his boots, and he sees a guy with a good pair on, he pretty soon pulls 'em of the guy and hooks it off with 'em.

"After I'd been out with guys for three or four years, I got big enough to go to work, and I used to go along with my brother and help him at a coal-shed, carrying out coals. I was there ten months, and then one night — a bitter cold night, it was freezing hard — we had a naphtha lamp to light in the shop; and as me and my brother was doing it, either a piece of the match dropped in or else he poured it over, I can't say which, but all at once it exploded and blowed me across the road and knocked him in the shop all a-fire; and I was all a-fire, too — see how it's burnt my face and the hand I held the lucifer in. A woman run out of the next shop with some wet sacks, and throw'd 'em upon me, but it flared up higher then: water don't put it out, unless it's a mass of water like a engine. Then a milkman run up and pulled off his cape and throwed it over me, and that put it out; then he set me up, and I run home, though I don't know how I got there, and for two days after I didn't know anybody. Another man ran into the shop and pulled out my brother, and we was both taken to the University Hospital. Two or three people touched me, and the skin came off on their hands, and at nine o'clock the next morning my brother died. When they took me to the hospital they had no bed for me, and so they sent me home again, and I was seven months before I got well. But I've never been to say well since, and I shall never be fit for hard work any more.

"The next year I went out with a guy again, and I got on pretty well; and so I've done every year since, except last. I've had several little places since I got burnt, but they haven't lasted long.

'This year I made a stunning guy. First of all I got a pair of my own breeches — black uns — and stuffed 'em full of shavings. I tied the bottoms with a bit of string. Then I got a black coat — that belonged to another boy — and sewed it all round to the trousers; then we filled that with shavings, and give him a good corporation. Then we got a block, sich as the milliners have, and shoved that right in the neck of the coat, and then we shoved some more shavings all round, to make it stick in tight; and when that was done it looked just like a dead man. I know something about dead men, because my father was always in that line. Then we got some horsehair and some glue, and plastered the head all round with glue, and stuck the horse-hair on to imitate the hair of a man; then we put the mask on: it was a twopenny one — they're a great deal cheaper than they used to be, you can get a very good one now for a penny — it had a great big nose, and it had two red horns, black eyebrows, and red cheeks. I like devils, they're so ugly. I bought a good-looking un two or three years ago, and we didn't get hardly anything, the people said, 'Ah! it's too good-looking; it don't frighten us at all.' Well, then, after we put on his mask we got two gloves, one was a woollen un, and the other a kid un, and stuffed them full of shavings, and tied 'em down to the chair. We didn't have no lantern, 'cos it keeps on falling out of his hands. After that we put on an old pair of lace-up boots. We tied 'em on to the legs of the breeches. The feet mostly twistes round, but we stopped that; we shoved a stick up the leg of his breeches, and the other end into the boot, and tied it, and then it couldn't twist round very easy. After that we put a paper hanging-cap on his head; it was silk-velvet kind of paper, and decorated all over with tinsel bows. His coat we pasted all over with blue and green tinsel bows and pictures. They was painted theatrical characters, what we buy at the shop a ha'penny a sheet plain, and penny a sheet coloured: we bought 'em plain, and coloured them ourselves. A-top of his hat we put a hornament. We got some red paper, and cut it into narrow strips, and curled it with the blade of the scissors, and stuck it on like a feather. We made him a fine apron of hanging-paper, and cut that in slips up to his knees, and curled it with the scissors, the same as his feather, and decorated it with stars, and bows, and things, made out of paper, all manner of colours, and pieces of tinsel. After we'd finished the guy we made ourselves cock'd hats, all alike, and then we tied him in a chair, and wrote on his breast, '*Villanous Guy.*' Then we put two broomsticks under the chair and carried him out. There was four of us, and the two that wasn't carrying, they had a large bough of a tree each, with a knob at the top to protect the guy. We started off at once, and got into the squares, and put him in front of the gentlemen's houses, and said this speech:—

'Pray, gentlefolks, pray
Remember this day,
At which kind notice we bring
This figure of sly,
Old, villanous Guy,
He wanted to murder the king.

With powder in store,
He bitterly swore
By him in the vaults to compare,
By him and his crew,
And parliament, too,
Should all be blow'd up in the air.

So please to remember
The fifth of November,
The gunpowder treason and plot,
I see no reason
Why gunpowder treason
Should ever be forgot.

So hollo, boys! hollo, boys!
Shout out the day!
Hollo, boys! hollo, boys!
Hollo, Hurrah!

" After we'd finished our speech in one of the squares, and hollowed Hurrah! the beadle come out, and said he'd give us the stick about our backs, and the guy too, if we didn't go away. So we went away, and got into Russell-square and Bedford-square; but there was such a lot of small guys out, that we did worse than ever we'd done before. When we was in South-ampton-street, Holborn, I finished the speech with ' Down with the Pope, and God save the Queen;' so four shoe-black boys come up, and says, says they, ' What do you say, Down with the Pope and God save the Queen for?' And I says, ' I didn't mean no harm of it.' With that they makes use of some bad language, and told me they'd smash my head and the guy's too; and they was going to do it, when up comes a boy that I knew, and I says to him, ' They're going to knock me about;' so he says, ' No they won't;' so then the boys made their reply, and said they would. So I told 'em they was very fast about fighting, I'd fight one of them; so with that they all got ready to pitch upon me: but when they see this other boy stuck to me, they went off, and never struck a blow. When we got home I opened the money-box and shared the money; one had 5d., and two had 4½d. each, and I had 7d. because I said the speech. At night we pulled him all to pieces, and burnt his stuffing, and let off some squibs and crackers. I always used to spend the money I got guying on myself. I used to buy sometimes fowls, because I could sell the eggs. There is some boys that take out guys as do it for the sake of getting a bit of bread and butter, but not many as I knows of.

" It don't cost much to make a guy. The clothes we never burns—they're generally too good: they're our own clothes, what we wears at other times; and when people burn a guy they always pull off any of the things that's of use fust; but mostly the guy gets pulled all to pieces, and only the shavings gets burnt."

An Old Street Showman.

A SHORT, thick-set man, with small, puckered-up eyes, and dressed in an old brown velveteen shooting-jacket, gave me an account of some bygone exhibitions of the galantee show.

" My father was a soldier," he said, " and was away in foreign parts, and I and a sister lived with my mother in St. Martin's work-house. I was fifty-five last New-year's-day. My uncle, a bootmaker in St. Martin's-lane, took my mother out of the workhouse, that she might do a little washing, and pick up a living for herself; and we children went to live with my grandfather, a tailor. After his death, and after many changes, we had a lodging in the Dials, and there ——, the sweep, coaxed me with pudding one day, and encouraged me so well, that I didn't like to go back to my mother; and at last I was 'prenticed to him from Hatton-Garden on a month's trial, and I liked chimley-sweeping for that month; but it was quite different when I was regularly indentured. I was cruelly-treated then, and poorly fed, and had to turn out barefooted between three and four many a morning in frost and snow. In first climbing the chimleys, a man stood beneath me, and pushed me up, telling me how to use my elbows and knees, and if I slipped, he was beneath me and ketched me, and shoved me up again. The skin came off my knees and elbows; here's the marks now, you see. I suffered a great deal, as well as Dan Duff, a fellow-sweep, a boy that died. I've been to Mrs. Montague's dinner in the Square on the 1st of May, when I was a boy-sweep. It was a dinner in honour of her son having been stolen away by a sweep." (The man's own words.) " I suppose there were more than three hundred of us sweeps there, in a large green, at the back of her house. I run away from my master once, but was carried back, and was rather better used. My master then got me knee and ankle-pads, and bathed my limbs in salt and water, and I managed to drag on seven sorrowful years with him. I was glad to be my own man at last, and I cut the sweep-trade, bought pandean pipes, and started with an organ-man, as his mate. I saved money with the organ-man and then bought a drum. He gave me five shillings, a-week and my wittles and drink, washing and lodging; but there wasn't so much music afloat then. I left the music-man and went out with ' Michael,' the Italy bear. Michael was the man's name that brought over the bear from somewhere abroad. He was a Italy man; and he used to beat the bear, and manage her; they called her Jenny; but Michael was not to say roughish to her, unless she was obstro-pelous. If she were, he showed her the large mop-stick, and beat her with it—hard some-times—specially when she wouldn't let the monkey get a top on her head; for that was a part of the performance. The monkey was dressed the same as a soldier, but the bear had no dress but her muzzle and chain. The monkey (a clever fellow he was, and could jump over sticks like a Christian) was called Billy. He jumped up and down the bear, too, and on to his master's shoulders, where he set as Michael walked up and down the streets. The bear had been taught to roll and tumble. She rolled right over her head, all round a stick, and then she danced round about it. She did it at the word of command. Michael said to her, ' Round and round again.' We fed her on bread, a quartern-loaf every night after her work in half-a-pail of water, the same every morning; never any meat—nothing but bread, boiled 'tatoes, or raw carrots: meat would have made her savage. The monkey was fed upon nuts, apples, gingerbread, or anything. Besides them we had two dancing-dogs. The bear didn't like them, and they were kept on one side in performing. The dogs jumped through hoops, and danced on their hind legs; they're easyish enough trained. Sometimes the butchers set bull-dogs, two or three at a time, at Jenny; and Michael and me had to beat them off as well as the two other men that we had with us. Those two men collected the money, and I played the pipes and drum, and Michael minded the bear and the dogs and monkey. In London we did very well. The West-end was the best. Whitechapel was crowded for us, but only with ha'pence. I don't know what Michael made, but I had seven shillings a-week, with my wittles and lodging. Michael done well. We generally had twenty to thirty shillings every night in ha'pence, and used to give twenty-one shillings of it for a one-pound note; for they was in then. When we've travelled in the country, we've sometimes had trouble to get lodgings for the bear. We've had to sleep in outhouses with her, and have sometimes frightened people that didn't know as we was there, but nothing serious. Bears is well-behaved enough if they ain't aggravated. Perhaps no one but me is left in England now what properly understands a dancing-bear.

" Jenny wasn't ever baited, but offers was made for it by sporting characters.

" The country was better than London, when the weather allowed; but in Gloucester, Cheltenham, and a good many places, we weren't let in the high streets.

" The gentlefolk in the balconies, both in town and country, where they had a good sight, were our best friends.

" It's more than thirty years ago — yes, a good bit more now; at Chester races, one year, we were all taken, and put into prison: bear, and dogs, and musicianer, and all—every one—because we played a day after the races; that was Saturday.

" We were all in quod until Monday morning. I don't know how the authorities fed the bear. We were each in a separate cell, and I had bread and cheese, and gruel.

" On Monday morning we were discharged, and the bear was shot by the magistrate's orders. They wanted to hang poor Jenny at first, but she was shot, and sold to the hairdressers.

" I couldn't stay to see her shot, and had to go into an alehouse on the road. I don't know what her carcase sold for. It wasn't very fat.

" Michael and me then parted at Chester, and he went home rich to Italy, taking his monkey and dogs with him, I believe.

" He lived very careful, chiefly on rice and cabbage, and a very little meat with it, which he called ' manesta.' He was a very old man. I had ' manesta ' sometimes, but I didn't like it much. I drummed and piped my way from Chester to London, and there took up with another foreigner, named Green, in the clock-work-figure line.

" The figures were a Turk called Bluebeard, a sailor, a lady called Lady Catarina, and Neptune's car, which we called Nelson's car as well; but it was Neptune's car by rights.

" These figures danced on a table, when taken out of a box. Each had its own dance when wound up.

" First came my Lady Catarina. She, and the others of them, were full two feet high. She had a cork body, and a very handsome silk dress, or muslin, according to the fashion, or the season. Black in Lent, according to what the nobility wore.

" Lady Catarina, when wound up, danced a reel for seven minutes, the sailor a hornpipe, and Bluebeard shook his head, rolled his eyes, and moved his sword, just as natural as life. Neptune's car went either straight or round the table, as it was set.

" We often showed our performances in the houses of the nobility, and would get ten or twelve shillings at a good house, where there were children.

" I had a third share, and in town and country we cleared fifty shillings a week, at least, every week, among the three of us, after all our keep and expenses were paid.

" At Doncaster races we have taken three pounds in a-day, and four pounds at Lincoln races.

" Country, in summer, is better than town. There's now no such exhibition, barring the one I have; but that's pledged. It cost twenty pounds at Mr. ——'s for the four figures without dress. I saved money, which went in an illness of rheumatic gout. There's no bears at all allowed now. Times are changed, and all for the worser. I stuck to the clock-work concern sixteen years, and knows all parts of the country—Ireland, Scotland, Guernsey, Jersey, and the Isle of Wight.

" A month before Christmas we used to put the figures by, for the weather didn't suit; and then we went with a galantee show of a magic lantern. We showed it on a white sheet, or on the ceiling, big or little, in the houses of the gentlefolk, and the schools where there was a breaking-up. It was shown by way of a treat to the scholars. There was Harlequin, and Billy Button, and such-like. We had ten and sixpence and fifteen shillings for each performance, and did very well indeed. I have that galantee show now, but it brings in very little.

" Green's dead, and all in the line's dead, but me. The galantee show don't answer, because magic lanterns are so cheap in the shops. When we started, magic lanterns wasn't so common; but we can't keep hold of a good thing in these times. It was a reg'lar thing for Christmas once — the galantee shows.

"I can make, in a holiday time, twenty shillings a-week; but that's only at holiday times, and is just a mere casualty a few times a year.

"I do other jobs, when I can get 'em — at other times, I delivers bills, carries boards, and helps at funerals."

The Chinese Shades.

"The proper name of my exhibition," said a showman of this class to me, "is *Lez Hombres*, or the shades; that's the proper name for it, for Baron Rothschild told me so when I performed before him. We calls it the Chinese galantee show. It was invented over there with the Chinese, and some travellers went over there and see them doing it, and they come over here and tell us about it. They didn't do it as we do, you know. As for doing pieces, we lick them out of the field. Them only did the shadows, we do a piece with 'em.

"I should say, sir, — let me calculate — it is about twenty-six years since the ombres first come out. Reduce it if you like, but that's the time. Thomas Paris was the first as come out with them. Then Jim Macklin, and Paul Herring the celebrated clown, and the best showman of Punch in the world for pantomime tricks—comic business, you know, but not for showing in a gentleman's house—was the next that ever come out in the streets with the Chinese galantee show. I think it was his own ingenuity that first gave him the notion. It was thoughts of mind, you know,—you form the opinion in your own mind, you know, by taking it from the Chinese. They met a friend of theirs who had come from China, and he told him of the shadows. One word is as good as fifty, if it's a little grammatical—sound judgment. When it first come out, he began with the scene called 'Mr. Jobson the Cobbler,' and that scene has continued to be popular to the present day, and the best scene out. He did it just equally the same as they do it now, in a Punch-and-Judy frame, with a piece of calico stretched in front, and a light behind to throw the shadows on the sheet.

"Paul Herring did excellent well with it— nothing less than 30s. or 2l. a-night. He didn't stop long at it, because he is a stage clown, and had other business to attend to. I saw him the first time he performed. It was in the Waterloo-road, and the next night I were out with one of my own. I only require to see a thing once to be able to do it; but you must have ingenuity, or it's no use whatsumdiver. Every one who had a Punch-and-Judy frame took to it; doing the regular business in the day and at night turning to the shadows. In less than a week there were two others out, and then Paul Herring cut it. He only done

it for a lark. He was hard up for money and got it.

"I was the first that ever had a regular piece acted in his show. I believe there's nobody else as did, but only them that's copied me. They come and follow me, you understand, and copied me. I am the author of 'Cobbler Jobson,' and 'Kitty biling the Pot, or the Woodchopper's Frolic.' There's 'Billy Button's journey to Brentford on horseback, and his favorite servant, Jeremiah Stitchem, in want of a situation.' I'm the author of that, too. It's adapted from the equestrian piece brought out at Astley's. I don't know who composed 'the Broken Bridge.' It's too far gone by to trace who the first author is, but it was adapted from the piece brought out formerly at Drury-lane Theatre. Old ancient gentlemen has told me so who saw it, when it was first brought out, and they're old enough to be my grandfather. I've new revised it.

"We in general goes out about 7 o'clock, because we gets away from the noisy children —they place them to bed, and we gets respectable audiences. We choose our places for pitching: Leicester-square is a very good place, and so is Islington, but Regent-street is about the principal. There's only two of us about now, for it's dying away. When I've a mind to show I can show, and no mistake, for I'm better now than I was twenty years ago.

"'Kitty biling the Pot, or the Woodchopper's Frolic,' is this. The shadow of the fireplace is seen with the fire alight, and the smoke is made to go up by mechanism. The woodchopper comes in very hungry and wants his supper. He calls his wife to ask if the leg of mutton is done. He speaks in a gruff voice. He says, 'My wife is very lazy, and I don't think my supper's done. I've been chopping wood all the days of my life, and I want a bullock's head and a sack of potatoes.' The wife comes to him and speaks in a squeaking voice, and she tells him to go and chop some more wood, and in half-an-hour it will be ready. Exaunt. Then the wife calls the daughter Kitty, and tells her to see that the pot don't boil over; and above all to be sure and see that the cat don't steal the mutton out of the pot. Kitty says, 'Yes, mother, I'll take particular care that the mutton don't steal the cat out of the pot.' Cross-questions, you see—comic business. Then mother says, 'Kitty, bring up the broom to sweep up the room,' and Kitty replies, 'Yes, mummy, I'll bring up the room to sweep up the broom.' Exaunt again. It's regular stage business and cross-questions. She brings up the broom, and the cat's introduced whilst she is sweeping. The cat goes Meaw! meaw! meaw! and Kitty gives it a crack with the broom. Then Kitty gets the bellows and blows up the fire. It's a beautiful representation, for you see her working the bellows, and the fire get up, and the sparks fly up the chimney. She says, 'If I don't make haste the mutton will be sure to steal the cat out of the pot.' She blows the fire right out, and says, ' Why, the fire's blowed the bellows out! but I don't mind, I shall go and play at shuttlecock.' Child like, you see. Then the cat comes in again, and says, Meaw! meaw! and then gets up and steals the mutton. You see her drag it out by the claw, and she burns herself and goes, spit! spit! Then the mother comes in and sees the fire out, and says, ' Where my daughter? Here's the fire out, and my husband's coming home, and there isn't a bit of mutton to eat!' She calls ' Kitty, Kitty!' and when she comes, asks where she's been. ' I've been playing at shuttlecock.' The mother asks, ' Are you sure the cat hasn't stolen the mutton.' ' Oh, no, no, mother,' and exaunt again. Then the mother goes to the pot. She's represented with a squint, so she has one eye up the chimney and another in the pot. She calls out, ' Where's the mutton? It must be down at the bottom, or it has boiled away.' Then the child comes in and says, ' Oh! mother, mother, here's a great he-she-tom cat been and gone off with the mutton.' Then the mother falls down, and calls out, ' I shall faint, I shall faint! Oh! bring me a pail of gin.' Then she revives, and goes and looks in the pot again. It's regular stage business, and if it was only done on a large scale would be wonderful. Then comes the correction scene. Kitty comes to her, and her mother says, ' Where have you been?' and Kitty says, ' Playing at shuttlecock, mummy;' and then the mother says, ' I'll give you some shuttlecock with the gridiron,' and exaunt, and comes back with the gridiron; and then you see her with the child on her knee correcting of her. Then the woodchopper comes in and wants his supper, after chopping wood all the days of his life. ' Where's supper?' ' Oh, a nasty big he-she-tom cat has been and stole the mutton out of the pot.' ' What?' passionate directly, you see. Then she says, ' You must put up with bread and cheese.' He answers, ' That don't suit some people,' and then comes a fight. Then Spring-heeled Jack is introduced, and he carries off the fireplace and pot and all. Exaunt. That's the end of the piece, and a very good one it was. I took it from Paris, and improved on it. Paris had no workable figures. It was very inferior. He had no fire. It's a dangerous concern the fire is, for it's done with a little bit of the snuff of a candle, and if you don't mind you go alight. It's a beautiful performance.

" Our exhibition generally begins with a sailor doing a hornpipe, and then the tight-rope dancing, and after that the Scotch horn-pipe dancing. The little figures regularly move their legs as if dancing, the same as on the stage, only it's more cleverer, for they're made to do it by ingenuity. Then comes the piece called ' Cobbler Jobson.' We call it ' the laughable, comic, and interesting scene of old Father Jobson, the London cobbler; or, the old

Lady disappointed of her Slipper.' I am in front, doing the speaking and playing the music on the pandanean pipe. That's the real word for the pipe, from the Romans, when they first invaded England. That's the first music ever introduced into England, when the Romans first invaded it. I have to do the dialogue in four different voices. There is the child, the woman, the countryman, and myself, and there's not many as can do it besides me and another.

" The piece called Cobbler Jobson is this. It opens with the shadow of a cottage on one side of the sheet, and a cobbler's stall on the other. There are boots and shoes hanging up in the windows of the cobbler's stall. Cobbler Jobson is supposed at work inside, and heard singing:

'An old cobbler I am,
And live in my stall;
It serves me for house,
Parlour, kitchen, and all.
No coin in my pocket,
No care in my pate,
I sit down at my ease,
And get drunk when I please.
Hi down, hi derry down.

" Then he sings again:

'Last night I took a wife,
And when I first did woo her,
I vowed I'd stick through life
Like cobblers' wax unto her.
Hi down, derry down down down.'

" Then the figure of a little girl comes in and raps at the door: ' Mr. Jobson, is my mamma's slipper done?' ' No, miss, it's not done; but if you'll call in half-an-hour it shall be well done, for I've taken the soles off and put the upper leathers in a pail to soak.' ' What, in a pail?' ' Yes, my dear, without fail.' ' Then you won't disappint.' ' No, my dear, I'd sooner a pot than a pint.' ' Then I may depend?' ' Yes, and you won't have it.' He says this aside, so the girl don't hear him. Then Jobson begins to sing again. He comes in front and works. You see his lapstone and the hammer going. He begins to sing:

'T'other morning for breakfast on bacon and spin-nage,
Says I to my wife, ' I'm going to Greenwich;'
Says she, ' Dicky Hall, then I'll go too!'
Says I, ' Mrs. Hall, I'll be dished if you do.
Hi down, hi derry down.'

" Then the little girl comes in again to know if the slipper is done, and as it isn't, it's ' My dear, you must go without it.' Then she gets impertinent, and says, 'I shan't go with it, you nasty old waxy, waxy, waxy, waxy, waxy! Oh, you nasty old ball of bristles and bunch of wax!' Then he tries to hit her, and she runs into the house, and as soon as he's at work she comes out again: ' Ah, you nasty cobbler! who's got a lump of wax on his breeches? who sold his wife's shirt to buy a ha'porth of gin? Then the cobbler is regularly vexed, and he tries to coax her into the stall to larrup her. ' Here, my dear, here's a lump of pudden and a farden.' ' Oh, yes, you nasty old cobbler! you only want to give me a lump of pudden on my back.' ' Here's a penny, my dear, if you'll fetch it.' ' Chuck it here, and I'll fetch it.' At last she goes into the stall, and she gets a hiding with the hammer. She cries out, ' You nasty old cobbler waxy! waxy, waxy! I'll go and tell my mother all about it.' That's what we call the aggriwating scene; and next comes the passionate scene.

" He begins singing one of his songs. He thinks he's all right now he's got rid of the girl.

" Then comes in the old lady, shaking with rage. ' How dare you to strike my child in this here kind of a manner! Come out of the stall, or I'll pull you out neck and crop!' Then Jobson is in a funk, and expects a hiding. ' Oh, mum! I'm very sorry, but your child said, I skinned a cat for ninepence, and called me cobbler waxy, waxy, waxy.' ' I won't believe a word of it, Mr. Jobson.' ' Yes, mum, your child's very insaulting.' ' How dare you strike the chick? You nasty old villain! I'll tear the eyes out of you.'

" A fight then commences between them, and the old lady gets the worst of it. Then they make it up, and they'll have some gin. ' I'll be a penny to your threepence,' says the cobbler; and the old lady says, ' Oh, I can always treat myself.' Then there's another fight, for there's two fights in it. The old lady gets the worst of it, and runs into the cottage, and then old Jobson cries, ' I'd better be off, stall and all, for fear she should come back with the kitchen poker.' That finishes up the scene, don't you see, for he carries off the stall with him.

" Cobbler Jobson is up to the door, I think. It's first rate; it only wants elaborating. ' Billy Button' is a very laughable thing, and equally up to the door. There's another piece, called ' Billy Waters, the celebrated London Beggar;' and that's a great hit. There's the ' Bull-baiting.' That's all the scenes I know of. I believe I am the only man that knows the words all through. ' Kitty biling the pot' is one of the most beautifullest scenes in the world. It wants expounding, you know ; for you could open it the whole length of the theatre. I wanted to take Ramsgate Theatre, and do it there; but they wanted 2*l.* a-night, and that was too much for me. I should have put a sheet up, and acted it with real figures, as large as life.

" When I was down at Brighton, acting with the Chinese galantee show, I was forced to drop performing of them. Oh dear! oh dear! don't mention it. You'd have thought the town was on fire. You never saw such an uproar as it made; put the town in such an agitation, that the town authorities forced me to desist. I filled the whole of North-street, and the people was pressing upon me so, that I was obliged to run away. I was lodging at the Clarence Hotel in North-street, at the time. I ran off down a side-street. The next day the police come up to me and tell me that I mustn't exhibit that performance again.

" I shall calculate it at 5*s.* a-night, when I exhibit with the ombres. We don't go out every night, for it's according to the weather ; but when we do, the calculation is 5*s.* every night. Sometimes it is 10*s.*, or it may be only 2*s.* 6*d.*; but 5*s.* is a fair balance. Take it all the year round, it would come to 9*s.* a-week, taking the good weather in the bad. It's no use to exaggerate, for the shoe is sure to pinch somewhere if you do.

" We go out two men together, one to play the pipes and speak the parts, and the other to work the figures. I always do the speaking and the music, for that's what is the most particular. When we do a full performance, such as at juvenile parties, it takes one about one hour and a quarter. For attending parties we generally gets a pound, and, perhaps, we may get three or four during the Christmas holiday-time, or perhaps a dozen, for it's according to the recommendation from one to another. If you goes to a gentleman's house, it's according to whether you behave yourself in a superior sort of a manner ; but if you have any vulgarity about you you must exaunt, and there's no recommendation.

" Tom Paris, the first man that brought out the ombres in the streets, was a short, stout man, and very old. He kept at it for four or five years, I believe, and he made a very comfortable living at it, but he died poor ; what became of him I do not know. Jim Macklin I've very little knowledge of. He was a stage performer, but I'm not aware what he did do. I don't know when he died, but he's dead and gone ; all the old school is dead and gone—all the old ancient performers. Paul Herring is the only one that's alive now, and he does the clown. He's a capital clown for tricks; he works his own tricks : that's the beauty of him.

" When we are performing of an evening, the boys and children will annoy us awful. They follow us so that we are obliged to go miles to get away from them. They will have the best places ; they give each other raps on the head if they don't get out of each other's way. I'm obliged to get fighting myself, and give it them with the drumsticks. They'll throw a stone or two, and then you have to run after them, and swear you're going to kill them. There's the most boys down at Spital-fields, and St. Luke's, and at Islington ; that's where there's the worst boys, and the most audaciousest. I dare not go into St. Luke's ; they spile their own amusement by making a noise and disturbance. Quietness is everything ; they haven't the sense to know that. If they give us any money it's very trifling, only, perhaps, a farden or a halfpenny, and then it's only one out of a fifty or a hundred.

The great business is to keep them quiet. No; girls ain't better behaved than boys; they was much wus. I'd sooner have fifty boys round me than four girls. The impertinence of them is above bearing. They come carrying babies, and pushing, and crowding, and tearing one another to pieces. ' You're afore me—I was fust—No you wasn't—Yes I was'—and that's the way they go on. If a big man comes in front I'm obliged to ask him to go backwards, to let the little children to see. If they're drunk, perhaps they won't, and then there's a row, and all the children will join in. Oh, it's dreadful erksome!

" I was once performing on Islington-green, and some drunken people, whilst I was collecting my money, knocked over the concern from wanton mischief. They said to me, ' We haven't seen nothing, master.' I said, ' I can see you; and haven't you got a brown?' Then they begun laughing, and I turned round, and there was the show in a blaze, and my mate inside a kicking. I think it was two or three drunken men did it, to injure a poor man from gaining his livelihood from the sweat of his brow. That's eighteen years ago.

" I was up at Islington last week, and I was really obliged to give over on account of the children. The moment I put it down there was thousands round me. They was sarcy and impertinent. There was a good collection of people, too. But on account of the theatrical business we want quiet, and they're so noisy there's no being heard. It's morals is everything. It's shameful how parents lets their children run about the streets. As soon as they fill their bellies off they are, till they are hungry again.

" The higher class of society is those who give us the most money. The working man is good for his penny or halfpenny, but the higher class supports the exhibition. The swells in Regent-street ain't very good. They comes and looks on for a moment, and then go on, or sometimes they exempt themselves with ' I'm sorry, but I've got no pence.' The best is the gentlemen; I can tell them in a minute by their appearance.

" When we are out performing, we in generally burn three candles at once behind the curtain. One is of no utility, for it wants expansion, don't you see. I don't like naphtha or oil-lamps, 'cos we're confined there, and it's very unhealthy. It's very warm as it is, and you must have a eye like a hawk to watch it, or it won't throw the shadows. A brilliant light and a clean sheet is a great attraction, and it's the attraction is everything. In the course of the evening we'll burn six penny candles; we generally use the patent one, 'cos it throws a clear light. We cut them in half. When we use the others I have to keep a look-out, and tell my mate to snuff the candles when the shadows get dim. I usually say, ' Snuff the candles!' out loud, because

that's a word for the outside and the inside too, 'cos it let the company know it isn't all over, and leads them to expect another scene or two."

EXHIBITOR OF MECHANICAL FIGURES.

" I AM the only man in London—and in England, I think—who is exhibiting the figuer of méchanique; that is to say, leetle figuers, that move their limbs by wheels and springs, as if they was de living cretures. I am a native of Parma in Italy, where I was born; that is, you understand, I was born in the Duchy of Parma, not in the town of Parma—in the campagne, where my father is a farmer; not a large farmer, but a little farmer, with just enough land for living. I used to work for my father in his fields. I was married when I have 20 years of age, and I have a child aged 10 years. I have only 30 years of age, though I have the air of 40. Pardon, Monsieur! all my friends say I have the air of 40, and you say that to make me pleasure.

" When I am with my father, I save up all the money that I can, for there is very leetle business to be done in the campagne of Parma, and I determine myself to come to Londres, where there is affair to be done. I like Londres much better than the campagne of Parma, because there is so much affairs to be done. I save up all my money. I become very économique. I live of very leetle, and when I have a leetle money, I say adieu to my father and I commence my voyages.

" At Paris I buy a box of music. They are made at Genève these box of music. When I come to Londres, I go to the public-house—the palais de gin, you understand—and there I show my box of music—yes, musical box you call it—and when I get some money I live very économique, and then when it become more money I buy another machine, which I buy in Paris. It was a box of music, and on the top it had leetle figuers, which do move their eyes and their limbs when I mounts the spring with the key. And then there is music inside the box at the same time. I have three leetle figuers to this box: one was Judith cutting the head of the infidel chief—what you call him?—Holeferones. She lift her arm with the sword, and she roll her eyes, and then the other hand is on his head, which it lifts. It does this all the time the music play, until I put on another figuer of the soldat which mounts the guard—yes, which is on duty. The soldat goes to sleep, and his head falls on his bosom. Then he wake again and lift his lance and roll his eyes. Then he goes to sleep again, so long until I put on the other figuer of the lady with the plate in the hand, and she make salutation to the company for to ask some money, and she continue to do this so long as anybody give her money. All the time the music in the box continues to play.

" I take a great quantity of money with these

figuers, 3s. a-day, and I live very économique until I put aside a sum large enough to buy the figuers which I exhibit now.

"My most aged child is at Parma, with my father in the campagne, but my wife and my other child, which has only 18 months of age, are with me in Londres.

"It is two months since I have my new figuers. I did have them sent from Germany to me. They have cost a great deal of money to me; as much as 35l. without duty. They have been made in Germany, and are very clever figures. I will show them to you. They perform on the round table, which must be level or they will not turn round. This is the Impératrice of the French—Eugénie—at least I call her so, for it is not like her, because her cheveleure is not arranged in the style of the Impératrice. The infants like better to see the Impératrice than a common lady, that is why I call her the Impératrice. She holds one arm in the air, and you will see she turns round like a person waltzing. The noise you hear is from the wheels of the méchanique, which is under her petticoats. You shall notice her eyes do move as she waltz. The next figure is the carriage of the Emperor of the French, with the Queen and Prince Albert and the King de Sardaigne inside. It will run round the table, and the horses will move as if they gallop. It is a very clever méchanique. I attache this wire from the front wheel to the centre of the table, or it would not make the round of the table, but it would run off the side and break itself. My most clever méchanique is the elephant. It does move its trunk, and its tail, and its legs, as if walking, and all the time it roll its eyes from side to side like a real elephant. It is the cleverest elephant of méchanique in the world. The leetle Indian on the neck, who is the driver, lift his arm, and in the pavilion on the back the chieftain of the Indians lift his bow and arrow to take aim, and put it down again. That méchanique cost me very much money. The elephant is worth much more than the Impératrice of the French. I could buy two—three—Impératrice for my elephant. I would like sooner lose the Impératrice than any malheur arrive to my elephant. There are plenty more Impératrice, but the elephant is very rare. I have also a figuer of Tyrolese peasant. She go round the table a short distance and then turn, like a dancer. I must get her repaired. She is so weak in her wheels and springs, which wind up under her petticoats, like the Impératrice. She has been cleaned twice, and yet her méchanique is very bad. Oh, I have oiled her; but it is no good, she must be taken to pieces.

"When I sent to Germany to get these méchanique made for me, I told the mechanician what I desired, and he made them for me. I invented the figuers out of my own head, and he did the méchanique. I have voyaged in Holland, and there I see some méchanique, and I noticed them, and then I gave the order to do so and so. My elephant is the best of my leetle figures; there is more complication.

"I first come to England eighteen years ago, before I was married, and I stop here seven years; then I go back again to Parma, and then I come back again to England four years ago, and here I stop ever since.

"I exhibit my leetle figures in the street. The leetle children like to see my figuers méchanique dance round the table, and the carriage, with the horses which gallop; but over all they like my elephant, with the trunk which curls up in front, like those in the Jardin des Plantes, or what you call it Zoological Gardens.

"When I am in the street I have two men beside myself, one plays the organ, and the other carry the box with the méchanique figuers inside, and I carry the table. The box with the méchanique is in weight about 80 lbs. English, and there are straps at the back for the arms to go through. It is as large as a chest of drawers, for the leetle figures are eighteen inches high, and each has a compartment to itself. I pay my men 1l. a-month, besides lodge, clean, and grub him.

"The organ for the music is mine. I have another organ, with a horse to draw it, which I want to sell; for the horse, and the two men to play it, destroy all the profits.

"When I make my figuers to play in the street I must make the table level, for they will not mount up a hill, because the méchanique is not sufficiently strong for that. I go to the West-end to show my leetle figures to the gentlemans and ladies, and their families; and I go to the East-end to the families of the work-people. I also go to Brixton and Hoxton, where they are severe for religion. They like my figures because they are moral, and their children can see them without sinning. But everywhere my figures have much success. Of all the places, I prefer, rather, Regent-street, and there I go to the leetle streets, in the corners, close by the big street. If I calcule how much money I receive for all the year,—but I have only had them two months,—it is six shillings by day regularly. Sometime I take ten shillings, and sometimes four shillings, but it settles itself to six shillings a-day. After paying for my men, and to clean, lodge, and grub them, I have three shillings for myself.

"In wet weather, when it makes rain, or when there is fog, I cannot quit my house to show my figures, for the humidity attack the springs and wheels of the méchanique: besides, when it falls rain the dresses of my figuers are spoiled; and the robes of the Impératrice and the Tyrolese peasant are of silk and velvet bodies, with spangles, and they soon spoil. They cost me much money to repair their springs,—never less than eight shillings for each time: my peasant has been arranged twice in her springs. It was a watch-maker who arranged her, and he had to take all her inside out; and you know what those kind of people charge for their time.

" Sometimes, when I am out with my fi-guers, the ladies ask me to perform my figuers before their windows, to show them to their families. The leetle children look through the window, and then they cannot hear the movement of the méchanique, and the figuers look like living. When the organ play a valtz to the Impératrice, he has to turn the handle quick at the commencement, when the spring is strong in the méchanique, and she turn quick; and to make the music slow when she turn less often, when the spring get weak at the end. This makes it have the look of being true to one living,—as if she danced to the music, although the organ play to her dancing. I always mount the figures with the key myself.

" I have never performed to a school of young scholars, but I have visited evening-parties of children with my méchanique. For that they give me sometimes 8s., sometimes 10s., just as they are generous. My méchanique require nearly one hour to see them to perfection. The Impératrice of the French is what they admire more than the paysanne of Tyrol. The dress of the Impératrice has a long white veil behind her hairs, but her costume is not so soignée as the peasant's, for she has no spangles; but they like to see the Impératrice of the French, and they excuse her toilet be-cause she is noble. My elephant is the greatest delight for them, because it is more compli-cated in its méchanique. I have always to mount with the key the springs in its inside at least three times before they are fatigued with admiring it.

" I never perform in the streets during the night, because the air is damp, and it causes injures to my méchanique; besides, I must have lights to show off the costume of my figuers, and my table is not large enough.

" It is not only the leetle children that ad-mire my méchanique, but persons of a ripe age. I often have gentlemen and ladies stand round my table, and they say ' Very clever!' to see the lady figuers valtz, but above all when my elephant lift his trunk. The leetle children will follow me a long way to see my figuers, for they know we cannot carry the box far without exhibiting, on account of its weight. But my table is too high for them, unless they are at a distance to see the figuers perform. If my table was not 'high, the leetle children would want to take hold of my figuers. I always carry a small stick with me; and when the leetle children, who are being carried by other leetle children, put their hand to my figuers, I touch them with stick, not for to hurt them, but to make them take their hand away and prevent them from doing hurt to my méchanique.

" When the costume of my Impératrice is destroyed by time and wear, my wife makes new clothes for her. Yes, as you say, she is the dress-maker of the Impératrice of the French, but it is not the Emperor who pays the bill, but myself. The Impératrice—the one I have, not that of the Emperor—does not want more than half a yard of silk for a petti-coat. In the present style of fashion I make her petticoat very large and full, not for the style, but to hide the méchanique in her in-side."

THE TELESCOPE EXHIBITOR.

" It must be about eight years since I first exhibited the telescope. I have three tele-scopes now, and their powers vary from about 36 to 300. The instruments of the higher power are seldom used in the streets, because the velocity of the planets is so great that they must escape the eye before it can fix it. The opening is so very small, that though I can pass my eye on a star in a minute, an ordinary observer would have the orb pass away before he could accustom his eye to the instrument. High power is all very well for separating stars, and so forth; but I'm like Dr. Kitchener, I prefer a low power for street purposes. A street-passer likes to see plenty of margin round a star. If it fills up the opening he don't like it.

" My business is a tailor. I follow that business now. The exhibiting don't interfere with my trade. I work by day at tailoring, and then, at this time of the year (26th Oct. 1856), I go out with the instrument about six o'clock. You see I can, with a low power, see Jupiter rise. It is visible at about half-past five, but it gets above the horizon, out of the smoke, about a quarter past six. Saturn rises about ten.

" From a boy I was fond of philosophical instruments. I was left an orphan when I was ten years of age; indeed, I haven't a relation in the world that I'm aware of, only excepting my wife's family. My mother died the same year as the Princes Charlotte (1818) for I can remember her being in mourning for her. My name is a very peculiar one—it is Tregent. This will show you that it is. I some time ago advertised an instrument for sale, and I had a letter from gentleman living in Liver-pool. He said that he was sitting down to lunch and he took up the paper, and cried out, ' Good God! here's my name.' He sent for paper and pens and wrote off at once. He asked whether I was a relation of Tregent, the great chronometer maker. He said he always thought he was the only Tregent in England. He said he was a bachelor, and hoped I was too.' Perhaps he wanted the name to die out. His father, he told me, kept a paper-mill. We corresponded a long time, till I was tired, and then one day a friend of mine said, ' Let me write to him, and I'll tell him that if he wants any more informa-ation he must pay your expenses down to

Liverpool, and you'll pay him a visit. This letter was sent, and by and by comes an answer, telling me that I was no gentleman to make such a proposition, and then the matter dropped.

" When I was six years old I was brought up to tailoring. I was kept very close to work—always on the board, working. I even took my meals there. I don't consider it was hard, for it was done for my own benefit. If there was no work going on I used to be made to learn verses out of the Bible. I highly respected my master, for I consider this was done for my benefit. He died in the country, and I was sorry for it; for if I had known it, I would have gone anywhere to see him buried—ay, even if it had been a hundred miles off. I stopped with this party till I was ten years old.

" The next party I was with I was 'prenticed to, but he failed when I had been with him three or four years, and then I had more the keeping of him than he of me; I had that resolve in me even at that young age.

" After I finished my 'prentice articles I went with my society card on the tramp. I went all through Yorkshire, going to the tailors' houses of call, where the clubs are held, and a certain sum of money subscribed weekly, to relieve what are called tramps. In some towns I worked for months— such as Leeds. What is called ' a tramp' by tailors, means a man searching for work about the country. After I got back to London I went to my trade again, and I was particularly fortunate in getting good situations. Whenever I was out of work I'd start off to the country again. I was three years in Brighton, doing well, and I had six men under me.

" It's about eight years ago that I first exhibited in the streets. It was through a friend of mine that I did this. Me and my wife was at Greenwich-hill one Sunday. I was looking through a pocket-telescope of mine, and he says, ' Look through mine.' I did so, and it was a very good one; and then he says, ' Ah, you should see one I've got at home; it's an astronomical one, and this is terrestrial.' I did so, and went and saw it. The first planet I saw was Venus. She was in her horns then, like the moon. She exhibits the same phases as the moon, as does also Mercury; sometimes horns, sometimes half a sphere, and so on; but they're the only two planets that's known that does so. When I saw this, I said, ' Well, I must have something of this sort.' I went to a telescope-maker up at Islington, and I made a bargain with him, and he was to make me a day-and-night telescope for five suits of clothes. Well, I bought the cloth, and raised all the money to complete my part of the contract, and then, when the telescope was finished, it wasn't worth a d——. You might as well have looked through a blacking-bottle. When I told him of it he said he couldn't

help it. It was worth something to look at, but not to look through. I pawned it for 15*l*. and sold the ticket for 5*l*. The gentleman who bought it was highly satisfied with it till he found it out. I took this one out in the streets to exhibit with, but it was quite useless, and showed nothing; you could see the planetary bodies, but it defined nothing. The stars was all manner of colours and forks. The bodies look just like a drawing in chalk smudged out. The people who looked through complained, and wouldn't come and look again, and that's why I got rid of it.

" The next telescope I had made was by the manufacturer who made the one my friend first showed me. That maker has taken some hundred of pounds of me since then; indeed, I've had eleven five or six feet telescopes of him, and his name is Mr. Mull, of 13 Albion-place, Clerkenwell, and the value of each of the object-glasses was, on the average, 30*l*., though he charged me only trade-price, so I got them for less.

" The first telescope that was of any good that I exhibited with in the streets was worth to me 25*l*. If you was to go to Dollond he would have charged 105*l*. on a common tripod stand. I had it done under my own direction, and by working myself at it, I got it very cheap. It wasn't good enough for me, so I got rid of it. I've got so nice about object glasses and their distinct vision, and the power they bear, that I have never rested content until I have a telescope that would suit the first astronomer.

" I've got one now that will bear a magnifying power 300 times, and has an object-glass 4¼ inches diameter, with a focal length of 5 feet 6 inches. The stand is made of about 250 pieces of brass-work, and has ratchet action, with vertical and horizontal movement. It cost me 80*l*. and Ross, Featherstone-buildings, would charge 250*l*. for it. I'm so initiated into the sort of thing, that I generally get all my patterns made, and then I get the castings made, and then have them polished. The price of the object-glass is 30*l*. I'm going to take that one out next week. It will weigh about 1½ cwt. My present one is a very fine instrument indeed. I've nothing but what is excellent. You can see Jupiter and his satellites, and Saturn and his belt. This is a test for it. Supposing I want to see Polaris—that's the small star that revolves once in 180 years round the pole. It isn't the pole star. It isn't visible to the naked eye. It's one of the tests for a telescope. My instrument gives it as small as a pin's point. There's no magnifying power with a telescope upon stars. Of course they make them more brilliant, and give some that are not visible to the naked eye, for hundreds and thousands will pass through the field in about an hour. They also separate double stars, and penetrate into space, nebula, and so on; but they don't increase the size of stars, for the distance is too great.

" I've worked about five years with this last one that I've now. It weighs, with the stand, about 1 cwt., and I have to get somebody to help me along with it. One of my boys in general goes along with me.

" It depends greatly upon the weather as to what business I do. I've known the moon for a month not to be visible for twenty days out of the lunation. I've known that for three moons together, the atmosphere is so bad in London. When I do get a good night I have taken 35s.; but then I've taken out two instruments, and my boy has minded one. I only charge a penny a peep. Saturdays, and Mondays, and Sundays, are the best nights in my neighbourhood, and then I can mostly reckon on taking 20s. The other nights it may be 7s. or 8s., or even only 2s. 6d. Sometimes I put up the instrument when it's very fine, and then it'll come cloudy, and I have to take it down again and go home. Taking the year round, I should think I make 125l. a-year by the telescope. You see my business, as a tailor, keeps me in of a day, or I might go out in the day and show the sun. Now to-day the sun was very fine, and the spots showed remarkably well, and if I'd been out I might have done well. I sold an instrument of mine once to a fireman who had nothing to do in the day, and thought he could make some money exhibiting the telescope. He made 8s. or 10s. of an afternoon on Blackfriar's-bridge, showing the dome of St. Paul's at the time they were repairing it.

" When the instrument is equatoreally mounted and set to time, you can pick out the stars in the day-time, and they look like black specs. I could show them.

" People can't stop looking through the telescope for long at a time, because the object is soon out of the field, because of the velocity of the earth's motion and the rapidity at which the planets travel round the sun. Jupiter, for instance, 26,000 miles an hour, and Saturn 29,000, soon removes them from the field of the telescope. I have to adjust the telescope before each person looks through. It has, I fancy, hurt my eyes very much. My eyesight has got very weak through looking at the moon, for on a brilliant night it's like a plate of silver, and dazzles. It makes a great impression on the retina of the eye. I've seen when looking through the telescope a black spec, just as if you had dropped a blot of ink on a piece of paper. I've often had dancing lights before my eyes, too—very often. I find a homœopathic globule of belladonna very excellent for that.

" When I exhibit, I in general give a short lecture whilst they are looking through. When I am not busy I make them give me a description, for this reason : others are listening, and they would sooner take the word of the observer than mine. Suppose I'm exhibiting Jupiter, and I want to draw customers, I'll say, ' How many moons do you see?'

They'll answer, ' Three on the right, and one on the left,' as they may be at that time. Perhaps a rough standing by will say, ' Three moons ! that's a lie ! there's only one, everybody knows.' Then, when they hear the observer state what he sees, they'll want to have a peep.

" When I'm busy, I do a lecture like this. We'll suppose I'm exhibiting Saturn. Perhaps we had better begin with Jupiter, for the orbit of Saturn's satellites is so extensive that you can never see them all without shifting the glass : indeed it's only in very fine climates, such as Cincinnati, where the eight may be observed, and indeed up to a late period it was believed there were only seven.

" When the observer sees Jupiter, I begin : ' Do you see the planet, sir? ' Yes.' ' I introduce to you Jupiter with all his four satellites. It is distant 600 millions of miles from the sun, and its diameter is about 7900 miles. It travels round the sun at about 27,000 miles an hour, and its orbit is over four years, and of course its seasons are four times the length of ours, the summer lasting for a year instead of three months.' One night an Irishman, who was quite the gentleman, came to me rather groggy, and he says,—' Old boy, what are you looking at? ' ' Jupiter,' says I. ' What's that?' says he. ' A planet you may call it, sir,' says I ; ' and the price is one penny.' He paid me and had a look, and then he cries out, ' What a deception is this! By J—— it's a moon, and you call it a star!' ' There are four moons,' said I. ' You're another,' said he ; ' there's a moon and four stars. You ought to be took up for deception.' After a time he had another look, and then he was very pleased, and would bring out gin from a neighbouring public-house, and if he brought one, he brought seven.

" Another time, a man was looking through; and I had a tripod stand then, and one of the legs was out, and he pushed the tube and down it came right in his eye. He gave a scream and shouted out, ' My God ! there's a star hit me slap in the eye ! '

" Another night an old woman came up to me, and she says, ' God bless you, sir ; I'm so glad to see you. I've been looking for you ever such a time. You charge a penny, don't you ? I'm a charwoman, sir, and would you believe it, I've never had a penny to spare. What are you looking at ? The moon? Well, I must see it.' I told her she should see it for nothing, and up she mounted the steps. She was a heavy lusty woman, and I had to shove her up with my shoulder to get up the steps. When she saw the moon she kept on saying, ' Oh, that's beautiful ! well, it is beautiful ! And that's the moon, is it? Now, do tell me all about it.' I told her all about Mount Tycho, and about the light of the sun being seen on the mountain tops, and so on. When she'd looked for a time, she said, ' Well, your instrument is a finer one than my master's, but it don't show so much as his, for he says he can see the men fighting in it.' This made me laugh so, I very nearly let her tumble by taking my shoulder away from under her. But when she came down the steps, she said something quite moved me. She threw her hands up and cried, ' If this moon is so beautiful and wonderful, what must that God be like who made it?' And off she went. It was very fine, wasn't it?

"Sometimes when I'm exhibiting there is quite a crowd collects. I've seen them sitting down on the curb smoking and drinking, whilst they are waiting for their turns to have a peep. They'll send to the public-house for beer, and then they'll stop for hours. Indeed, I've had my business quite interfered with by the mob, for they don't go away after having their look. I seldom stop out after 12 o'clock at night.

"Sometimes when I have been exhibiting, the parties have said it was all nonsense and a deception, for the stars was painted on the glass. If the party has been anything agreeable, I've taken the trouble to persuade him. I've, for instance, placed the star on the very edge of the glass, and then they've seen it travel right across the field; and as I've told them, if it was painted it couldn't move and disappear from the lens.

"Most of the spectators go away quite surprised and impressed with what they have seen. Some will thank me a dozen times over. Some will say, 'Well, my penny is well laid out. I shouldn't have credited it with my own eyes.' Others, but there are very few of them, won't believe when they have looked. Some, when I can see the moon on their eye as they look in, swear they don't see it. Those I let go on and don't take their money, for the penny is no object. When I tell the people what the wonders of the heavens are, and how each of these planets is a world, they go away wonderfully grateful and impressed.

"I went down to Portsmouth with my telescope at the time the fleet sailed under Sir Charles Napier, and the Queen led them out in her yacht. I took a great deal of money there. I didn't exhibit in the day-time: I didn't trouble myself. I took two guineas showing the yacht the day she sailed, and at night with the moon. The other nights, with the moon and planets only, I took from 12s. to 14s. I refused 15s. for one hour, for this reason. A lady sent her servant to ask me to go to her house, and my price is one guinea for to go out, whether for an hour, or two, or three; but she first offered me 10s., and then the next night 15s. Then I found I should have to carry my instrument, weighing one cwt., two miles into the country, and up hill all the way; so, as I was sure of taking more than 10s. where I was, I wouldn't for an extra shilling give myself the labour. I took 12s. 6d. as it was. At Portsmouth a couple of sailors came up, and one had a look, and the other said ' What is there to see ? ' I told him the moon, and he asked the price. When I said ' One penny,' he says, ' I aint got a penny, but here's three halfpence, if that's the same to you ; ' and he gives it, and when I expected he was about to peep, he turns round and says, ' I'll be smothered if I'm going to look down that gallows long chimney ! You've got your money, and that's all your business.' So you see there are some people who are quite indifferent to scientific exhibitions.

"There are, to the best of my knowledge, about four men besides myself, going about with telescopes. I don't know of any more. Of these there's only one of any account. I've seen through them all, so I may safely say it. I consider mine the best in London exhibiting. Mine is a very expensive instrument. Everything depends upon the object-glass. There's glasses on some which have been thrown aside as valueless, and may have been bought for two or three pounds.

"The capital required to start a telescope in the streets all depends upon the quantity of the object-glass, from 3l. to 50l. for the object-glass alone.

"Nobody, who is not acquainted with telescopes, knows the value of object-glasses. I've known this offer to be made—that the object-glass should be placed in one scale and gold in the other to weigh it down, and then they wouldn't. The rough glass from Birmingham—before it is worked—only 12 inches in diameter, will cost 96l. Chance, at Birmingham, is the principal maker of crown and flint for optical purposes. The Swiss used formerly to be the only makers of optical metal of any account, and now Birmingham has knocked them out of the field: indeed they have got the Swiss working for them at Chance's.

"You may take a couple of plates of the rough glass to persons ignorant of their value, and they are only twelve inches in diameter, and he would think one shilling dear for them, for they only look like the bits you see in the streets to let light through the pavement. These glasses are half flint and half crown, the flint for the concave, and the crown for the convex side. Their beauty consists in their being pure metal and quite transparent, and not stringy. Under the high magnifying power we use you see this directly, and it makes the object smudgy and distorts the vision.

"After getting the rough metal it takes years to finish the object-glass. They polish it with satin and putty. The convex has to be done so correctly, that if the lens is the 100th part of an inch out its value is destroyed.

"The well-known object-glass which was shown in the Great Exhibition of 1851, was in Mr. Ross's hands (of Featherstone-buildings, Holborn,) for four years before it was finished. It was very good, and done him great credit. He is supposed to have lost by the job, for the price is all eat up by wages pretty near.

"The observatory on Wandsworth-common

STREET TELESCOPE EXHIBITOR.

[From a Photograph.]

STREET ACROBATS PERFORMING.

is a complete failure, owing to the object-glass being a bad one. It belongs to the Rev. Mr. Cragg. The tube is 72 feet long, I believe, and shaped like a cigar, bulging at the sides. He wanted to have a new object-glass put in, and what do you think they asked him at Birmingham for the rough metal alone?—2000*l.*! It is 24 inches in diameter. Mr. Ross asks 6000*l.*, I was told, to make a new one—finished for him.

"The making of object-glasses is dreadful and tedious labour. Men have been known to go and throw their heads under waggon wheels, and have them smashed, from being regularly worn out with working an object-glass, and not being able to get the convex right. I was told by a party that one object-glass was in hand for 14 years.

"The night of the eclipse of the moon, (the 13th October, 1856,) when it was so well seen in London, I took 1*l.* 1*d.* at 1*d.* each. I might as well have took 2*l.* by charging 2*d.*, but being so well known then I didn't make no extra charge. They were forty deep, for everybody wished to see. I had to put two lads under the stand to prevent their being trod to death. They had to stay there for two hours before they could get a peep, and so indeed had many others to do the same. A friend of mine didn't look at all, for I couldn't get him near. They kept calling to the one looking through the tube, 'Now, then, make haste, you there.' They nearly fought for their turns. They got pushing and fighting, one crying, 'I was first,' and, 'Now it's my turn.' I was glad when it was over, I can assure you. The buttons to my braces were dragged off my back by the pressure behind, and I had to hold up my breeches with my hand. The eclipse lasted from 21 minutes past 9 to 25 minutes past 12, and in that time 247 persons had a peep. The police were there to keep order, but they didn't interfere with me. They are generally very good to me, and they seem to think that my exhibition improves the minds of the public, and so pro-tect me.

"When I went to Portsmouth, I applied to Mr. Myers the goldsmith, a very opulent and rich man there, and chairman of the Espla-nade Committee at Southsea, and he instantly gave me permission to place my stand there. Likewise the mayor and magistrates of Ports-mouth, to exhibit in the streets."

EXHIBITOR OF THE MICROSCOPE.

"I EXHIBIT with a microscope that I wouldn't take fifty guineas for, because it suits my pur-pose, and it is of the finest quality. I earn my living with it. If I were to sell it, it wouldn't fetch more than 15*l.* It was presented to me by my dear sister, who went to America and died there. I'll show you that it is a valuable instrument. I'll tell you that one of the best lens-makers in the trade looked

through it, and so he said, 'I think I can im-prove it for you;' and he made me a present of a lens, of extreme high power, and the largest aperture of magnifying power that has ever been exhibited. I didn't know him at the time. He did it by kindness. He said, after looking through, 'It's very good for what it professes, but I'll make you a present of a lens made out of the best Swiss metal.' And he did so from the interest he felt in seeing such kinds of exhibitions in the streets. With the glass he gave me I can see cheese-mites as distinctly as possible, with their eight legs and transparent bodies, and heads shaped like a hedgehog's. I see their jaw moving as they eat their food, and can see them lay their eggs, which are as perfect as any fowl's, but of a bright blue colour; and I can also see them perform the duties of nature. I can also see them carry their young on their backs, showing that they have affection for their offspring. They lay their eggs through their ribs, and you can tell when they are going to lay for there is a bulging out just by the hips. They don't sit on their eggs, but they roll them about in action till they bring forth their ob-ject. A million of these mites can walk across a flea's back, for by Lardner's micrometer the surface of a flea's back measures 24 inches from the proboscis to the posterior. The micrometer is an instrument used for determining micro-scopic power, and it is all graduated to a scale. By Lardner's micrometer the mite looks about the size of a large black-beetle, and then it is magnified 100,000 times. This will give you some idea of the power and value of my in-strument. Three hundred gentlemen have viewed through it in one week, and each one delighted; so much so, that many have given double the money I have asked (which was a penny), such was the satisfaction my instru-ment gave.

"My father was a minister and local preacher in the Wesleyan Methodists. He died, poor fellow, at 27 years of age, therefore I never had an opportunity of knowing him. He was a boot and shoe maker. Such was the talent which he possessed, that, had it not been for his being lamed of one foot (from a fall off a horse), he would have been made a travelling minister. He was a wonderful clever man, and begun preaching when he was 21. He was the minister who preached on the occasion of laying the foundation-stone of Hoxton Chapel, and he drew thousands of people. I was only two years old when he died, and my mother was left with five of us to bring up. She was a visitor of the sick and the dying for the Strangers' Benevolent Fund, and much respected for her labours. After my father's death she was enabled to support her family of one son and four daughters by shoe-binding. She was married twice after my father's death, but she married persons of quite opposite principles and opinions to her own, and she was not comfortable with them, but left them, and always found shelter under her son's roof, where she died triumphantly happy.

"I was apprenticed when I was 13 years of age to a shoemaker, who was a profound philosopher, and very fond of making experiments and of lecturing on various branches of science. I could produce bills—I have them at home—such as that at the Friar's-mount Sunday-school, some six or seven years ago, where it states that William Knock, minister and lecturer, will lecture on zoology and natural history. He's about 70 now. Electricity is his favourite science. Whilst I was his apprentice, he had an observatory built at the top of his house in Underwood-street, Spitalfields, for the purpose of taking astronomical observations. My being in his house, and seeing him so busy with his instruments, gave me a great taste for science. I was his assistant when he went lecturing. I was apprenticed with him for five years. He was a kind and good master, and very affectionate. He encouraged me in my scientific studies, and gave me access to his library, which was immense, and consisted of 3000 volumes. Amongst other employment I used to copy out sermons for him, and he gave me a penny each, which by saving up enabled me to buy a watch of him for 5*l.* 5*s.* He was a shoemaker and manufacturer of ladies and children's boots and shoes, so that he might have made from his 2*l.* to 3*l.* a-week, for he was not a journeyman, but an employer.

"After I was out of my time I went to Mr. Children, a bootmaker of Bethnal-green-road, well known in that locality. My master had not sufficient employment for me. One night this Mr. Children went to hear a lecture on astronomy by Dr. Bird, and when he came home he was so delighted with what he had seen, that he began telling his wife all about it. He said, 'I cannot better explain to you the solar system, than with a mop,' and he took the mop and dipped it into a pail of water, and began to twirl it round in the air, till the wet flew off it. Then he said, 'This mop is the sun, and the spiral motion of the water gives the revolutions of the planets in their orbits.' Then, after a time, he cried out, 'If this Dr. Bird can do this, why shouldn't I?' He threw over his business directly, to carry out the grand object of his mind. He was making from 3*l.* to 4*l.* a-week, and his wife said, 'Robert, you're mad!' He asked me if I knew anything of astronomy, and I said, 'Sir, my old master was an astronomer and philosopher.' Then I got books for him, and I taught him all I knew of the science of astronomy. Then he got a magic-lantern with astronomical slides. The bull's-eye was six inches in diameter, so they were very large, so that they gave a figure of twelve feet. For the signs of the zodiac he had twelve separate small lanterns, with the large one in the centre to show the diverging rays of the

sun's light. He began with many difficulties in his way, for he was a very illiterate man, and had a vast deal to contend with, but he succeeded through all. He wrote to his father and got 500*l.*, which was his share of the property which would have been left him on his parent's death. At his first lecture he made many mistakes, such as, 'Now, gentlemen, I shall present to your notice the *consternations,*' at which expression the company cried, 'Hear, hear,' and one said, 'We are all in a consternation here, for your lamp wants oil.' Yet he faced all this out. I was his assistant. I taught him everything. When I told him of his mistake he'd say, 'Never mind, I'll overcome all that.' He accumulated the vast sum of 6000*l.* by lecturing, and became a most popular man. He educated himself, and became qualified. When, he went into the country he had Archbishops and Bishops, and the highest of the clergy, to give their sanction and become patrons of his lectures. He's now in America, and become a great farmer.

"After I left Mr. Children, I connected myself with a Young Men's Improvement Meeting. Previous to that, I had founded a Sunday-school in the New Kent-road. Deverell-street Sabbath-schools were founded by me, and I was for fourteen years manager of it, as well as performer of the funeral service in that place; for there was a chapel, and burying-ground and vaults, attached to the schools, and I became the officiating minister for the funeral service. Three thousand children have been educated at these schools, and for fourteen years I lectured to them every Sunday on religious subjects. With the tutors and the eldest scholars I formed a Young Men's Improvement Meeting. I became the president of that meeting, and their lecturer. I lectured on the following subjects,—Natural History, Electricity, Astronomy, and Phrenology.

"At this time I was a master-shoemaker, and doing a business of fifty guineas a-week, of which ten were profit. I built large workshops at the back of my house, which cost me 300*l.* Unfortunately, I lent my name to a friend for a very large amount, and became involved in his difficulties, and then necessity compelled me to have recourse to street-exhibitions for a living. When I was in affluent circumstances I had a library of 300 volumes, on scientific subjects mostly, and from them I have gleaned sufficient information to qualify me for street-exhibition, and thereby enable me to earn more money than most individuals in such circumstances.

"I began my street-life with exhibiting a telescope, and here is the origin of my doing so. I had a sister living at the west-end of the town who was a professed cook, and I used to visit her three times a-week. One night I saw a man in the Regent-circus exhibiting a telescope. I went up to him, and I said, 'Sir, what is the object to-night?' And he told me it was Jupiter. I was very much interested with looking at Jupiter, and I stopped with that man for two hours, conversing with him, and I saw exactly how much he took. Then I thought, 'Why shouldn't I do this?' So I wrote to my brother-in-law, and I told him this man was taking at the rate of 1*d.* per minute, and I offered, if he would provide me with a telescope, that I should be very happy and contented to take half of the receipts as my share, and give him the other for the use of his instrument. He did so, and bought a telescope which cost him 14*l.* I took up my stand on London-bridge, and did very well, taking on the average 6*s.* a-night. I gave up the telescope for this reason,—my brother-in-law was going to America, and was anxious to call in all his money. The telescope was sold, and my sister, the professed cook, fearing that I should be left without a means of living, bought for me a microscope out of her own earnings, which cost her 5*l.* She said to me, 'The microscope is better than the telescope, for the nights are so uncertain.' She was quite right, for when the telescopes have been idle for three months at a time, I can exhibit my microscope day and night. She gave it to me as a mark of her respect. She died in America, just after she arrived. That instrument has enabled me to support an afflicted and aged mother, and to bury her comfortably when she died.

"My microscope contains six objects, which are placed on a wheel at the back, which I turn round in succession. The objects are in cell-boxes of glass. The objects are all of them familiar to the public, and are as follows:—1. The flea. 2. The human hair, or the hair of the head. 3. A section of the old oak tree. 4. The animalculæ in water. 5. Cheese-mites. And 6. The transverse section of cane used by schoolmasters for the correction of boys.

"I always take up my stand in the day-time in Whitechapel, facing the London Hospital, being a large open space, and favourable for the solar rays—for I light up the instrument by the direct rays of the sun. At night-time I am mostly to be found on Westminster-bridge, and then I light up with the best sperm oil there is. I am never interfered with by the police; on the contrary, they come and have a look, and admire and recommend, such is the interest excited.

"The first I exhibit is the flea, and I commence a short lecture as follows:—'Gentlemen,' I says, 'the first object I have to present to your notice is that of a flea. I wish to direct your attention especially to the head of this object. Here you may distinctly perceive its proboscis or dart. It is that which perforates the cuticle or human skin, after which the blood ascends by suction from our body into that of the flea. Thousands of persons in London have seen a flea, have felt a flea, but have never yet been able by the human eye to discover that instrument which made them

sensible of the flea about their person, although they could not catch the old gentleman. This flea, gentlemen, by Dr. Lardner s micrometer, measures accurate 24 inches in length, and 11 across the back. My instrument, mark you, being of high magnifying power, will not show you the whole of the object at once. Mark you, gentlemen, this is not the flea of the dog or the cat, but the human flea, for each differ in their formation, as clearly proved by this powerful instrument. For they all differ in their form and shape, and will only feed upon the animal on which they are bred. Having shown you the head and shoulders, with its dart, I shall now proceed to show you the posterior view of this object, in which you may clearly discover every artery, vein, muscle and nerve, exact like a lobster in shape, and quite as large as one at 2*s.* 6*d.*' That pleases them, you know; and sometimes I add, to amuse them, 'An object of that size would make an excellent supper for half-a-dozen persons.' That pleases them.

"One Irishwoman, after seeing the flea, threw up her arms and screamed out, 'O J——! and I've had hundreds of them in my bed at once.' She got me a great many customers from her exclamations. You see, my lecture entices those listening to have a look. Many listeners say, 'Ain't that true, and philosophical, and correct?' I've had many give me 6*d.* and say, 'Never mind the change, your lecture is alone worth the money.'

"I'll now proceed to No. 2. 'The next object I have to present to your notice, gentlemen, is that of the hair of the human head. You perceive that it is nearly as large as yonder scaffolding poles of the House of Lords.' I say this when I am on Westminster-bridge, because it refers to the locality, and is a striking figure, and excites the listeners. 'But mark you, it is not, like them, solid matter, through which no ray of light can pass.' That's where I please the gentlemen, you know, for they say, 'How philosophical!' 'You can readily perceive, mark you, that they are all tubes, like tubes of glass; a proof of which fact you have before you, from the light of the lamp shining direct through the body of the object, and that light direct portrayed in the lens of your eye, called the retina, on which all external objects are painted.' 'Beautiful!' says a gentleman. 'Now, if the hair of the head be a hollow tube, as you perceive it is, then what caution you ought to exercise when you place your head in the hands of the hairdresser, by keeping your hat on, or else you may be susceptible to catch cold; for that which we breathe, the atmosphere, passing down these tubes, suddenly shuts to the doors, if I may be allowed such an expression, or, in other words, closes the pores of the skin and thereby checks the insensible perspiration, and colds are the result. Powdering the head is quite out of date now, but if a little was used on those occasions referred to, cold in the head would not be so frequent.' What do you think of that? I never had an individual complain of my lecture yet.

"Now comes No. 3. 'This, gentlemen, is the brave old oak, a section of it not larger than the head of a pin. Looking at it through this powerful instrument, you may accurately perceive millions of perforations, or pores, through which the moisture of the earth rises, in order to aid its growth. Of all the trees of the forest, none is so splendid as the brave old oak. This is the tree that braves the battle and the breeze, and is said to be in its perfection at 100 years. Who that looks at it would not exclaim, in the language of the song, 'Woodman, spare that tree, and cut it not down?' Such is the analogy existing between vegetable and animal physiology, that a small portion of the cuticle or human skin would present the same appearance, for there are millions of pores in the human skin which a grain of sand is said to cover; and here are millions of perforations through which the moisture of the earth is said to rise to aid the growth of the tree. See the similitude between the vegetable and animal physiology. Here is the exhibition of nature—see how it surpasses that of art. See the ladies at the Great Exhibition admiring the shawls that came from India : yet they, though truly deserving, could not compare with this bit of bark from the brave old oak. Here is a pattern richer and more deserving than any on any shawl, however wonderful. Where is the linendraper in this locality that can produce anything so beautiful as that on this bit of bark? Such are the works of art as compared with those of nature.'

"No. 4 is the animalculæ in water. 'Gentlemen, the object now before you is a drop of water, that may be suspended on a needle's point, teeming with millions of living objects. This one drop of water contains more inhabitants than the globe on which I stand. See the velocity of their motion, the action of their stomachs! the vertebræ is elegantly marked, like the boa-constrictor in the Zoological Gardens. They are all moving with perfect ease in this one drop, like the mighty monsters of the vast deep.'

"On one occasion a gentleman from St. Thomas's Hospital disputed my statement about it's being only one drop of water, so I said to the gent: 'If you will accompany me to some coffee-house the drop of water shall be removed, and perhaps what you see you may believe,' which he did, and he paid me 1s. for my experiment. He told me he was a doctor, and I told him I was surprised that he was not better acquainted with the instrument; for, said I, 'how can you tell the effects of inoculation on the cuticle, or the disease called the itch, unless you are acquainted with such an instrument?' He was quite ashamed as he paid me for my trouble. I tell this anecdote on the bridge, and I always conclude with,

'Now, gentlemen, whilst I was paid 1s. by the faculty for showing one object alone, I am only charging you 1d. for the whole six.' Then I address myself to the person looking into the microscope, and say, 'What do you think of this one drop of water, sir?' and he says, 'Splendid!' Then I add, 'Few persons would pass and re-pass this instrument without having a glance into it, if they knew the wonders I exhibit;' and the one looking says, 'That's true, very true.'

"The next object is the cheese-mite—No. 5. I always begin in this way,—'Those who are unacquainted with the study of entomology declare that these mites are beetles, and not mites; but could I procure a beetle with eight legs, I should present it to the British Museum as a curiosity.' This is the way I clench up the mouths of those sceptics who would try to ridicule me, by showing that I am philosophic. 'Just look at them. Notice, for instance, their head, how it represents the form of an hedgehog. The body presents that of the beetle shape. They have eight legs and eight joints. They have four legs forward and four legs back; and they can move with the same velocity forwards as they can back, such is their construction. They are said to be moving with the velocity of five hundred steps in one minute. Read Blair's 'Preceptor,' where you may see a drawing of the mite accurately given, as well as read the description just given.' A cheesemonger in Whitechapel brought me a few of these objects for me to place in my microscope. He invited his friends, which were taking supper with him, to come out and have a glance at the same objects. He gave me sixpence for exhibiting them to him, and was highly gratified at the sight of them. I asked him how he could have the impudence to sell them for a lady's supper at 10d. a-pound. The answer he gave me was,—'What the eye cannot see the heart never grieves.' Then I go on,—'Whilst this lady is extending her hand to the poor, and doing all the relief in her power, she is slaying more living creatures with her jaw-bone than ever Samson did with his.' If it's a boy looking through, I say, 'Now, Jack, when you are eating bread and cheese don't let it be said that you slay the mites with the jaw-bone of an ass. Cultivate the intellectual and moral powers superior to the passions, and then you will rise superior to that animal in intellect.' 'Good,' says a gentleman, 'good; here's sixpence for you;' and another says, 'Here's twopence for you, and I'm blessed if I want to see anything after hearing your lecture.' Then I continue to point out the affection of the mite for its young. 'You see fathers looking after their daughters, and mothers after their sons, when they are taking their walks; and such is their love for their young, that when the young ones are fatigued with their journey the parents take them up on their backs. Do you not see it?' And then some will say, 'I'll give a penny to see that;' and I've had four pennies put in my hand at once to see it. Excitement is everything in this world, sir.

" Next comes the cane—No. 6. ' The object before you, gentlemen, is a transverse section of cane,—common cane,—such, mark you, as is used by schoolmasters for the correction of boys who neglect their tasks, or play the wag.' I make it comic, you know. ' This I call the tree of knowledge, for it has done more for to learn us the rules of arithmetic than all the vegetable kingdom combined. To it we may attribute the rule of three, from its influence on the mind,'— that always causes a smile,—' just look at it for one moment. Notice, in the first place, its perforations. Where the human hand has failed to construct a micrometer for microscopic or telescopic purposes, the spider has lent its web in one case, and the cane in the other. Through the instrumentality of its perforations, we may accurately infer the magnifying power of other objects, showing the law of analogy. The perforations of this cane, apart from this instrument, would hardly admit a needle's point, but seem now large enough for your arm to enter. This cane somewhat represents a telescopic view of the moon at the full, when in conjunction with the sun, for instance. Here I could represent inverted rocks and mountains. You may perceive them yourself, just as they would be represented in the moon's disc through a powerful telescope of 250 times, such as I have exhibited to a thousand persons in St. Paul's Churchyard. On the right of this piece of cane, if you are acquainted with the science of astronomy, you may depicture very accurately Mount Tycho, for instance, representing a beautiful burning mountain, like Mount Vesuvius or Etany, near the fields of Naples. You might discover accurately all the diverging streaks of light emanating from the crater. Further on to the right you may perceive Mount St. Catherine, like the blaze of a candle rushing through the atmosphere. On the left you may discover Mount Ptolemy. Such is a similar appearance of the moon's mountainous aspect. I ask you, if the school-boy had but an opportunity of glancing at so splendid an object as the cane, should he ever be seen to shed a tear at its weight?'

" This shows that I am scientific, and know astronomy. The last part makes them laugh.

" This is the mode in which I exhibit my instrument, and such is the interest been excited in the public mind, that though a penny is the small charge which I make, that amount has been doubled and trebled by gentlemen who have viewed the instrument; and on one occasion a clergyman in the Commercial-road presented me with half-a-sovereign, for the interest he felt at my description, as well as the objects presented to his view. It has given universal satisfaction.

" I don't go out every night with my instru-ment. I always go on the Monday, Tuesday, Wednesday, and Saturday, for those are the nights when I take most money, especially on the Monday and Saturday. The Monday and Saturday are generally 6s., Tuesdays about 5s., and Wednesdays about 2s. 6d. Then the Thursday averages 1s. 8d., and the Fridays, in some localities, where the men are paid on that night, are equal to Saturday. Such are the benefits arising from night exhibition. In the day it comes to rather more. I've been to Greenwich, and on the One-tree Hill I've done more with the sun light than the night light. Taking the changes of weather, such as rain and cold bleak nights, and such weather as isn't suitable to such an exhibition, I may say safely that my income amounts to 80l. a-year. The capital required for such a business amounts to from 10l. to 20l. My instrument only cost 5l.; but it was parted with to raise money;—and I wouldn't take 50l. for it. It was my sister's son-in-law who sold it. It was a gift more than a sale. You can buy a very good microscope for 10l., but a great deal, of course, is required in choosing it; for you may buy a thing not worth 20s. You'd have an achromatic microscope for 20l. It costs me about 4d. a-week for oil, the best sperm, at 1s. 4d. the pint; and a quarter of a pint will last me the week. I get my specimens in London. I prepare them all myself, and always keep a stock by me. For the sake of any gentleman who may have any microscope, and wish to procure excellent living specimens of mites and animalculæ in water, may do so in this way. (This is a secret which I give from a desire which I feel to afford pleasure to gentlemen of a scientific mind.) Get mites from a cheesemonger. Mites differ in their shape and form, according to the cheese they are taken from. The Stilton-cheese differs from the Dutch-cheese mite, and so does that of the aristocratic Cheshire, as I call it. In order to rise them clear and transparent, take a wooden box, of 2½ inches deep and 2½ inches in diameter, with a thick screw-lid, and let the lid take off half-way down. Place the dust in the bottom of the box, damp the thread of the screw-lid, to make it air-tight. The mites will ascend to the lid of the box. Four or five hours afterwards unscrew the lid gently, and, removing it, let it fall gently on a piece of writing paper. The mites crawl up to the lid, and by this way you get them free from dust and clean. To make the animalculæ water, I draw from the bottom of the water-tub a small quantity of water, and I put about a handful of new hay in that water. I expose it to the influence of the solar light, or some gentle heat, for three or four hours. Skim off its surface. After washing your hands, take your finger and let one drop of the hay-water fall on the glass, and then add to it another drop of pure water to make it more transparent. This information took me some years of experience to discover. I never read it or learnt it from any one, but found it out myself; but all liberal scientific men like to share their information.

" It's impossible for me to say how many people have looked through my instrument, but they must be counted by tens of thousands. I have had 160 looking through in one night, or 13s. 4d. worth. This was on a peculiar occasion. They average about 6s. worth. If I could get out every night I should do well. As it is, I am obliged to work at my trade of shoemaking to keep myself: for you must take it into consideration, that there are some nights when I cannot show my exhibition. Very often I have a shilling or sixpence given to me as a present by my admirers. Many a half-crown I've had as well.

" One night I was showing over at the Elephant and Castle, and I saw a Quaker gentleman coming along, and he said to me, ' What art thee showing to night, friend ? ' So I told him; and he says, ' And what doth thee charge, friend ? ' I answered, ' To the working man, sir, I am determined to charge no more than a penny ; but to a gentleman, I always leave it to their liberality.' So he said, ' Well, I like that, friend; I'll give thee all I have.' And he put his hand into his pocket, and he pulled out five penny pieces. You see that is what I always do; and it meets with its reward."

PEEP-SHOWS.

CONCERNING these, I received the subjoined narrative from a man of considerable experience in the " profession :"—

" Being a cripple, I am obliged to exhibit a small peep-show. I lost the use of this arm ever since I was three months old. My mother died when I was ten years old, and after that my father took up with an Irishwoman, and turned me and my youngest sister (she was two years younger than me) out into the streets. My father had originally been a dyer, but was working at the fiddle-string business then. My youngest sister got employment at my father's trade, but I couldn't get no work, because of my crippled arms. I walked about till I fell down in the streets for want. At last a man, who had a sweetmeat-shop, took pity on me. His wife made the sweetmeats, and minded the shop while he went out a-juggling in the streets, in the Ramo Samee line. He told me as how, if I would go round the country with him, and sell prints while he was a-juggling in the public-houses, he'd find me in wittles and pay my lodging. I joined him, and stopped with him two or three year. After that, I went to work for a werry large waste-paper dealer. He used to buy up all the old back numbers of the cheap periodicals and penny publications, and send me out with them to sell at a farden a-piece. He used to give me fourpence out of every shilling, and I done very well with that, till the periodicals came

so low, and so many on 'em, that they wouldn't sell at all. Sometimes I could make 15s. on a Saturday night and a Sunday morning, a-selling the odd numbers of periodicals, such as ' Tales of the Wars,' ' Lives of the Pirates,' ' Lives of the Highwaymen,' &c. I've often sold as many as 2000 numbers on a Saturday night in the New Cut, and the most of them was works about thieves, and highwaymen, and pirates. Besides me there was three others at the same business. Altogether, I dare say, my master alone used to get rid of 10,000 copies of such works on a Saturday night and Sunday morning. Our principal customers was young men. My master made a good bit of money at it. He had been about 18 years in the business, and had begun with 2s. 6d. I was with him 15 year on and off, and at the best time I used to earn my 30s. a-week full at that time. But then I was foolish, and didn't take care of my money. When I was at the ' odd-number business,' I bought a peep-show. I gave 2l. 10s. for it. I had it second-hand. I was persuaded to buy it. A person as has got only one hand, you see, isn't like other folks, and the people said it would always bring me a meal of victuals, and keep me from starving. The peep-shows was a-doing very well then (that's about five or six years back), when the theaytres was all a shilling to go into them whole price, but now there's many at 3d. and 2d., and a good lot at a penny. Before the theaytres lowered, a peep-showman could make 3s. or 4s. a-day, at the least, in fine weather, and on a Saturday night about double that money. At a fair he could take his 15s. to 1l. a-day. Then there was about nine or ten peep-shows in London. These were all back-shows. There are two kinds of peep-shows, which we call ' back-shows ' and ' caravan-shows.' The caravan-shows are much larger than the others, and are drawn by a horse or a donkey. They have a green-baize curtain at the back, which shuts out them as don't pay. The showmen usually lives in these caravans with their families. Often there will be a man, his wife, and three or four children, living in one of these shows. These caravans mostly go into the country, and very seldom are seen in town. They exhibit principally at fairs and feasts, or wakes, in country villages. They generally go out of London between March and April, because some fairs begin at that time, but many wait for the fairs at May. Then they work their way right round, from village to town. They tell one another what part they're a-going to, and they never interfere with one another's rounds. If a new hand comes into the business, they're werry civil, and tells him what places to work. The carawans comes to London about October, after the fairs is over. The scenes of them carawan shows is mostly upon recent battles and murders. Anything in that way, of late occurrence, suits them. Theatrical plays ain't no good for country towns, 'cause they don't understand such things there. People is werry fond of the battles in the country, but a murder wot is well known is worth more than all the fights. There was more took with Rush's murder than there has been even by the Battle of Waterloo itself. Some of the caravan-shows does werry well. Their average taking is 30s. a-week for the summer months. At some fairs they'll take 5l. in the three days. They have been about town as long as we can recollect. I should say there is full 50 of these caravan-shows throughout the country. Some never comes into London at all. There is about a dozen that comes to London regular every winter. The business in general goes from family to family. The cost of a caravan-show, second-hand, is 40l.; that's without the glasses, and them runs from 10s. to 1l. a-piece, because they're large. Why, I've knowed the front of a peep-show, with the glasses, cost 60l.; the front was mahogany, and had 36 glasses, with gilt carved mouldings round each on 'em. The scenes will cost about 6l. if done by the best artist, and 3l. if done by a common hand. The back-shows are peep-shows that stand upon trussels, and are so small as to admit of being carried on the back. The scenery is about 18 inches to 2 foin in length, and about 15 inches high. They have been introduced about fifteen or sixteen years. The man as first brought 'em up was named Billy T——; he was lame of one leg, and used to exhibit little automaton figures in the New Cut. On their first coming out, the oldest back-showman as I know on told me they could take 15s. a-day. But now we can't do more than 7s. a-week, run Saturday and all the other days together,— and that's through the theayters being so low. It's a regular starving life now. We has to put up with the hinsults of people so. The back-shows generally exhibits plays of different kinds wot's been performed at the theayters lately. I've got many different plays to my show. I only exhibit one at a time. There's 'Halonzer the Brave and the Fair Himogen;' 'The Dog of Montargis and the Forest of Bondy;' 'Hyder Halley, or the Lions of Mysore;' 'The Forty Thieves' (that never done no good to me); 'The Devil and Dr. Faustus;' and at Christmas time we exhibit pantomimes. I has some other scenes as well. I've 'Napoleon's Return from Helba,' 'Napoleon at Waterloo,' 'The Death of Lord Nelson,' and also 'The Queen embarking to start for Scotland, from the Dockyard at Voolich.' We takes more from children than grown people in London, and more from grown people than children in the country. You see, grown people has such remarks made upon them when they're a-peeping through in London, as to make it bad for us here. Lately I have been hardly able to get a living, you may say. Some days I've taken 6d., others 8d., and sometimes 1s.—that's what I call a good day for any of the week-days. On a Saturday it runs from 2s. to 2s. 6d. Of the week-days, Monday or Tuesday is the best. If there's a fair on near London, such as Greenwich, we can go and take 3s., and 4s., or 5s. a-day, so long as it lasts. But after that, we comes back to the old business, and that's bad enough; for, after you've paid 1s. 6d. a-week rent, and 6d. a-week stand for your peep-show, and come to buy a bit of coal, why all one can get is a bit of bread and a cup of tea to live upon. As for meat, we don't see it from one month's end to the other. My old woman, when she is at work, only gets five fardens a-pair for making a pair of drawers to send out for the convicts, and three halfpence for a shirt; and out of that she has to find her own thread. There are from six to eight scenes in each of the plays that I shows; and if the scenes are a bit short, why I puts in a couple of battle-scenes; or I makes up a pannerammer for 'em. The children will have so much for their money now. I charge a halfpenny for a hactive performance. There is characters and all — and I explains what they are supposed to be a-talking about. There's about six back-shows in London. I don't think there's more. It don't pay now to get up a new play. We works the old ones over and over again, and sometimes we buys a fresh one of another showman, if we can rise the money — the price is 2s. and 2s. 6d. I've been obligated to get rid on about twelve of my plays, to get a bit of victuals at home. Formerly we used to give a hartist 1s. to go in the pit and sketch off the scenes and figures of any new play that was a-doing well, and we thought 'ud take, and arter that we used to give him from 1s. 6d. to 2s. for drawing and painting each scene, and 1d. and 1½d. each for the figures, according to the size. Each play costs us from 15s. to 1l. for the inside scenes and figures, and the outside painting as well. The outside painting in general consists of the most attractive part of the performance. The New-Cut is no good at all now on a Saturday night; that's through the cheap penny hexhibitions there. Tottenham-court-road ain't much account either. The street-markets is the best of a Saturday night. I'm often obliged to take bottles instead of money, and they don't fetch more than threepence a dozen. Sometimes I take four dozen of bottles in a day. I lets 'em see a play for a bottle, and often two wants to see for one large bottle. The children is dreadful for cheapening things down. In the summer I goes out of London for a month at a stretch. In the country I works my battle-pieces. They're most pleased there with my Lord Nelson's death at the battle of Trafalgar. 'That there is,' I tell 'em, 'a fine painting, representing Lord Nelson at the battle of Trafalgar.' In the centre is Lord Nelson in his last dying moments, supported by Capt. Hardy and the chaplain. On the left is the hexplosion of one of the enemy's ships by fire. That represents a fine painting, representing the death of Lord Nelson at the battle of Trafalgar, wot was fought on the 12th of October, 1805. I've got five glasses, they cost about 5s. a piece when new, and is about 3½ inches across, with a 3-foot focus."

Acrobat, or Street-Posturer.

A man who, as he said, "had all his life been engaged in the profession of Acrobat," volunteered to give me some details of the life led and the earnings made by this class of street-performers.

He at the present moment belongs to a "school" of five, who are dressed up in fanciful and tight-fitting costumes of white calico, with blue or red trimmings; and who are often seen in the quiet by-streets going through their gymnastic performances, mounted on each other's shoulders, or throwing somersaults in the air.

He was a short, wiry-built man, with a broad chest, which somehow or another seemed unnatural, for the bones appeared to have been forced forward and dislocated. His general build did not betoken the great muscular strength which must be necessary for the various feats which he has to perform; and his walk was rather slovenly and loutish than brisk and springy, as one would have expected. He wore the same brown Chesterfield coat which we have all seen him slip over his professional dress in the street, when moving off after an exhibition.

His yellow hair reached nearly to his shoulders, and not being confined by the ribbon he usually wears across his forehead in the public thoroughfare, it kept straggling into his eyes, and he had to toss it back with a jerk, after the fashion of a horse with his nose-bag.

He was a simple, "good-natured" fellow, and told his story in a straightforward manner, which was the more extraordinary, as he prefaced his statement with a remark, "that all in his 'school,' (the professional term for a gang or troop,) were terribly against his coming; but that as all he was going to say was nothing but the truth, he didn't care a fig for any of 'em."

It is a singular fact, that this man spoke fluently both the French and German languages; and, as will be seen in his statement, he has passed many years of his life abroad, performing in several circuses, or "pitching" (exhibiting in the streets) in the various large towns of Sweden, Denmark, Prussia, Switzerland, and France.

The following is the history of his life, from his earliest remembrance,—from two years old, indeed,—down to his present age, thirty-six:—

"I am what is known as a street-posturer, or acrobat. I belong to a school of five, and we go about the streets doing pyramids, bending, juggling, and la perche.

"I've been at acrobating for these thirty-five years, in London and all parts of England, as well as on the Continent, in France and Germany, as well as in Denmark and Sweden; but only in the principal towns, such as Copenhagen and Stockholm; but only a little, for we come back by sea almost directly. My father was a tumbler, and in his days very great, and used to be at the theatres and in Richardson's show. He's acted along with Joe Grimaldi. I don't remember the play it was in, but I know he's acted along with him at Sadler's Wells Theatre, at the time there was real water there. I have heard him talk about it. He brought me regular up to the profession, and when I first came out I wasn't above two years old, and father used to dance me on my hands in Risley's style, but not like Risley. I can just recollect being danced in his hands, but I can't remember much about it, only he used to throw me a somersault with his hand. The first time I ever come out by myself was in a piece called 'Snowball,' when I was introduced in a snowball; and I had to do the splits and strides. When father first trained me, it hurt my back awfully. He used to take my legs and stretch them, and work them round in their sockets, and put them up straight by my side. That is what they called being 'cricked,' and it's in general done before you eat anything in the morning. O, yes, I can remember being cricked, and it hurt me terrible. He put my breast to his breast, and then pulled my legs up to my head, and knocked 'em against my head and cheeks about a dozen times. It seems like as if your body was broken in two, and all your muscles being pulled out like India rubber.

"I worked for my father till I was twelve years of age, then I was sold for two years to a man of the name of Tagg, another showman, who took me to France. He had to pay father 5l. a-year, and keep me respectable. I used to do the same business with him as with father,—splits, and such-like,—and we acted in a piece that was wrote for us in Paris, called "Les deux Clowns anglais," which was produced at the Porte St. Antoine. That must have been about the year 1836. We were dressed up like two English clowns, with our faces painted and all; and we were very successful, and had plenty of flowers thrown to us. There was one Barnet Burns, who was showing in the Boulevards, and called the New Zealand Chief, who was tattooed all over his body. He was very kind to me, and made me a good many presents, and some of the ladies were kind to me. I knew this Barnet Burns pretty well, because my master was drunk all day pretty well, and he was the only Englishman I had to speak to, for I didn't know French.

"I ran away from Tagg in Paris, and I went with the 'Frères de Bouchett,' rope-dancers, two brothers who were so called, and I had to clown to the rope. I stopped with them three years, and we went through Belgium and Holland, and done very well with them. They was my masters, and had a large booth of their own, and would engage paraders to stand outside the show to draw the people; but they did all the performances themselves, and it was mostly at the fairs.

"From them I came to England, and began pitching in the street. I didn't much like it, after being a regular performer, and looked upon it as a drop. I travelled right down by myself to Glasgow fair. I kept company with Wombwell's show,— only working for myself. You see they used to stop in the towns, and draw plenty of people, and then I'd begin pitching to the crowd. I wasn't lonely because I knew plenty of the wild-beast chaps, and, besides, I've done pretty well, taking two or three shillings a day, and on a Saturday and Monday generally five or six. I had a suit of tights, and a pair of twacks, with a few spangles on, and as soon as the people came round me I began to work.

"At Glasgow I got a pound a day, for I went with Mr. Mumford, who had some dancing dolls showing at the bottom of the Stone buildings. The fair is a week. And after that one of our chaps wrote to me that there was a job for me, if I liked to go over to Ireland and join Mr. Batty, who had a circus there. They used to build wooden circuses in them days, and hadn't tents as now. I stopped a twelve-month with him, and we only went to four towns, and the troupe did wonders. Mr. Hughes was the manager for Mr. Batty. There was Herr Hengler, the great rope-dancer among the troupe, and his brother Alfred, the great rider, as is dead now, for a horse kicked him at Bristol, and broke his arm, and he wouldn't have it cut off, and it mortified, and he died.

"When I left Ireland I went back to Glasgow, and Mr. David Miller gave the school I had joined an engagement for three months. We had 6*l.* a-week between four of us, besides a benefit, which brought us 2*l.* each more. Miller had a large penny booth, and had taken about 12*l.* or 14*l.* a-night. There was acting, and our performances. Alexander, the lessee of the Theatre Royal, prevented him, for having acted, as he also did Anderson the Wizard of the North, who had the Circus, and acted as well, and Mumford; but they won the day.

"I left Glasgow with another chap, and we went first to Edinburgh and then to Hamburgh, and then we played at the Tivoli Gardens. I stopped abroad for fourteen years, performing at different places through France and Switzerland, either along with regular companies or else by ourselves, for there was four on us, in schools. After Hamburgh, we went to Copenhagen, and then we joined the brother Prices, or, as they call 'em there, Preece. We only did tumbling and jumping up on each other's shoulders, and dancing the the pole on our feet, what is called in French 'trankr.' From there we joined the brothers Layman,— both Russians they was,— who was very clever, and used to do the 'pierrot;' the French clown, dressed all in white,— for their clown is not like our clown,— and they danced the rope and all. The troupe was called the Russian pantomimists. There we met Herr Hengler again, as well as Deulan the dancer, who was dancing at the Eagle and at the theatres as Harlekin; and Anderson, who was one of the first clowns of the day, and a good comic singer, and an excellent companion, for he could make puns and make poems on every body in the room. He did, you may recollect, some few years ago, throw himself out of winder, and killed himself. I read it in the newspapers, and a mate of mine afterwards told me he was crazy, and thought he was performing, and said, "Hulloa, old feller! I'm coming!" and threw himself out, the same as if he'd been on the stage.

"In Paris and all over Switzerland we performed at the fairs, when we had no engagements at the regular theatres, or we'd pitch in the streets, just according. In Paris we was regular stars. There was only me and R——, and we was engaged for three months with Mr. Le Compte, at his theatre in the Passage Choiseul. It's all children that acts there; and he trains young actors. He's called the 'Physician to the King;' indeed, he is the king's conjurer.

"I'm very fond of France; indeed, I first went to school there, when I was along with Tagg. You see I never had no schooling in London, for I was so busy that I hadn't no time for learning. I also married in France. My wife was a great bender (used to throw herself backwards on her hands and make the body in a harch). I think she killed herself at it; indeed, as the doctors told me, it was nothing else but that. She would keep on doing it when she was in the family way. I've many a time ordered her to give over, but she wouldn't; she was so fond of it; for she took a deal of money. She died in childbed at St. Malo, poor thing!

"In France we take a deal more money than in England. You see they all give; even a child will give its mite; and another thing, anybody on a Sunday may take as much money as will keep him all the week, if they like to work. The most money I ever took in all my life was at Calais, the first Sunday cavalcade after Lent: that is the Sunday after Mardi-gras. They go out in a cavalcade, dressed up in carnival costume, and beg for the poor. There was me, Dick S——, and Jim C—— and his wife, as danced the Highland fling, and a chap they calls Polka, who did it when it first came up. We pitched about the streets, and we took 700 francs all in halfpence — that is, 28*l.* — on one Sunday: and you mustn't work till after twelve o'clock, that is grand mass. There were liards and centimes, and half-sous, and all kinds of copper money, but very little silver, for the Frenchmen can't afford it; but all copper money change into five-franc pieces, and it's the same to me. The other chaps didn't like the liards, so I bought 'em all up. They're like button-heads, and such-like; and they said they wouldn't have that bad money, so I got more than my share: for after we had shared I bought the heap of liards, and gave ten francs for the heap, and I think it brought me in sixty francs; but then I had to run about to all the little shops to get five-franc pieces. You see, I was the only chap that spoke French; so, you see, I'm worth a double share. I always tell the chaps, when they come to me, that I don't want nothink but my share; but then I says, 'You're single men, and I'm married, and I must support my children;' and so I gets a little out of the hôtel expenses, for I charges them 1s. 3d. a-day, and at the second-rate hôtels I can keep them for a shilling. There's three or four schools now want me to take them over to France. They calls me 'Frenchy,' because I can talk French and German fluently—that's the name I goes by.

"I used to go to all the fêtes in Paris along with my troupe. We have been four and we have been five in one troupe, but our general number is four, for we don't want any more than four; for we can do the three high and the spread, and that's the principal thing. Our music is generally the drum and pipes. We don't take them over with us, but gets Italians to do it. Sometimes we gets a German band of five to come for a share, for you see they can't take money as we can, for our performance will cause children to give, and with them they don't think about it, not being so partial to music.

"Posturing to this day is called in France 'Le Dislocation anglais;' and indeed the English fellows is the best in the world at posturing: we can lick them all. I think they eat too much bread; for though meat's so cheap in the south of France (2d. a-lb.), yet they don't eat it. They don't eat much potatoes either; and in the south they gives them to the pigs, which used to make me grumble, I'm so fond of them. Chickens, too, is 7d. the pair, and you may drink wine at 1d. the horn.

"At St. Cloud fête we were called 'Les Quatre Frères anglais,' and we used to pitch near the Cascade, which was a good place for us. We have shared our 30s. each a-day then easy; and a great deal of English money we got then, for the English is more generous out of England. There was the fête St. Germain, and St. Denis, and at Versailles, too; and we've done pretty well at each, as well as at the Champs Elysées on the 1st of May, as used to be the fête Louis-Philippe. On that fête we were paid by the king, and we had fifty francs a man, and plenty to eat and drink on that day; and every poor man in Paris has two pound of sausages and two pounds of

bread, and two bottles of wine. But we were different from that, you know. We had a déjeûné, with fish, flesh, and fowl, and a dinner fit for a king, both brought to us in the Champs Elysées, and as much as ever we liked to drink all day long—the best of wine. We had to perform every alternate half-hour.

"I was in Paris when Mr. Macready come to Paris. I was engaged with my troupe at the Porte St. Martin, where we was called the Bedouin Arabs, and had to brown our faces. I went to see him, for I knew one of the actors. He was very good, and a beautiful house there was—splendid. All my other partners they paid. The price was half-a-guinea to the lowest place. The French people said he was very good, but he was mostly supported by the English that was there. An engagement at the Porte St. Martin was 1000 francs a-week for five of us; but of course we had to leave the streets alone during the four weeks we was at the theatre.

"I was in Paris, too, at the revolution in 1848, when Louis-Philippe had to run off. I was in bed, about two o'clock in the morning, when those that began the revolution was coming round—men armed; and they come into everybody's bed-room and said, 'You must get up, you're wanted.' I told them I was English; and they said, 'It don't matter; you get your living here, and you must fight the same as we fight for our liberty.' They took us—four English as was in the same gang as I was with—to the Barrière du Trône, and made us pick up paving-stones. I had to carry them; and we formed four barricades right up to the Faubourg St. Antoine, close to the Bastille. We had sometimes a bit of bread and a glass of wine, or brandy, and we was four nights and three days working. There was a great deal of chaff going on, and they called me 'le petit Supplier' posturer, you know—but they was of all countries. We was put in the back-ground, and didn't fire much, for we was ordered not to fire unless attacked; and we had only to keep ground, and if anything come, to give warning; but we had to supply them with powder and ammunition of one sort and another. There was one woman—a very clever woman —from Normandy, who used to bring us brandy round. She died on the barricade; and there's a song about her now. I was present when part of the throne was burned. After that I went for a tour in Lorraine; and then I was confined in Tours for thirty-four days, for the Republicans passed a bill that all foreigners were to be sent home to their own countries; and, indeed, several manufactories where English worked had to stop, for the workmen was sent home.

"I came back to England in 1852, and I've been pitching in the streets ever since. I've changed gangs two or three times since then; but there's five in our gang now. There's three high for 'pyramids,' and 'the Arabs hang down;' that is, one a-top of his shoulders, and one hanging down from his neck; and ' the spread,' that's one on the shoulders, and one hanging from each hand; and ' the Hercules,' that is. one on the ground, supporting himself on his hands and feet; whilst one stands on his knees, another on his shoulders, and the other one a-top of them two, on their shoulders. There's loads of tricks like them that we do, that would a'most fill up your paper to put down. There's one of our gang dances, an Englishman, whilst the fifth plays the drum and pipes. The dances are mostly comic dances; or, as we call them, ' comic hops.' He throws his legs about and makes faces, and he dresses as a clown.

" When it's not too windy, we do the perch. We carry a long fir pole about with us, twenty-four feet long, and Jim the strong man, as they calls me, that is I, holds the pole up at the bottom. The one that runs up is called the sprite. It's the bottom man that holds the pole that has the dangerous work in la perche. He's got all to look to. Anybody, who has got any courage, can run up the pole; but I have to guide and balance it; and the pole weighs some 20 lbs., and the man about 8 stone. When it's windy, it's very awkward, and I have to walk about to keep him steady and balance him; but I'm never frightened, I know it so well. The man who runs up it does such feats as these; for instance, ' the bottle position,' that is only holding by his feet, with his two arms extended; and then ' the hanging down by one toe,' with only one foot on the top of the pole, and hanging down with his arms out, swimming on the top on his belly; and ' the horizontal,' as it is called, or supporting the body out sideways by the strength of the arms, and such-like, winding up with coming down head fust.

" The pole is fixed very tightly in a socket in my waistband, and it takes two men to pull it out, for it gets jammed in with his force on a-top of it. The danger is more with the bottom one than the one a-top, though few people would think so. You see, if he falls off, he is sure to light on his feet like a cat; for we're taught to this trick; and a man can jump off a place thirty feet high, without hurting himself, easy. Now if the people was to go frontwards, it would be all up with me, because with the leverage and its being fixed so tight to my stomach, there's no help for it, for it would be sure to rip me up and tear out my entrails. I have to keep my eyes about me, for if it goes too fur, I could never regain the balance again. But it's easy enough when you're accustomed to it.

" The one that goes up the pole can always see into the drawing-rooms, and he'll tell us where it's good to go and get any money, for he can see the people peeping behind the curtains; and they generally give when they find they are discovered. It's part of his work to glance his eyes about him, and then he calls out whilst he is up, ' to the right,' or ' the left,' as it may be; and although the crowd don't understand him, we do.

" Our gang generally prefer performing in the West-end, because there's more ' calls' there. Gentlemen looking out of window see us, and call to us to stop and perform; but we don't trust to them, even, but make a collection when the performance is half over; and if it's good we continue, and make two or three collections during the exhibition. What we consider a good collection is 7s. or 8s.; and for that we do the whole performance. And besides, we get what we call ' ringings' afterwards; that's halfpence that are thrown into the ring. Sometimes we get 10s. altogether, and sometimes more and sometimes less; though it's a very poor pitch if it's not up to 5s. I'm talking of a big pitch, when we go through all our ' slang,' as we say. But then we have our little pitches, which don't last more than a quarter of an hour—our flying pitches, as we call them, and for them 5s. is an out-and-outer, and we are well contented if we get half-a-crown. We usually reckon about twenty pitches a-day, that's eight before dinner and twelve after. It depends greatly upon the holidays as to what we makes in the days. If there's any fairs or feasts going on we do better. There's two days in the week we reckon nothing, that's Friday and Saturday. Friday's little good all day long, and Saturday's only good after six o'clock, when wages have been paid. My share may on the average come to this :—Monday, about 7s. or 8s., and the same for Tuesday. Then Wednesday and Thursday it falls off again, perhaps 3s. or 4s.; and Friday ain't worth much; no more is Saturday. We used to go to Sydenham on Saturdays, and we would find the gents there; but now it's getting too late, and the price to the Palace is only 2s. 6d., when it used to be 5s., and that makes a wonderful difference to us. And yet we like the poor people better than the rich, for it's the halfpence that tells up best. Perhaps we might take a half-sovereign, but it's very rare, and since 1853 I don't remember taking more than twenty of them. There was a Princess—I'm sure I've forgotten her name, but she was German, and she used to live in Grosvenor-square—she used to give us half-a-sovereign every Monday during three months she was in London. The servants was ordered to tell us to come every Monday at three o'cloc'., and we always did; and even though there was nobody looking, we used to play all the same; and as soon as the drum ceased playing, there was the money brought out to us. We continued playing to her till we was told she had gone away. We have also had sovereign calls. When my gang was in the Isle of Wight, Lord Y—— has often give us a sovereign, and plenty to eat and drink as well.

" I can't say but what it's as good as a

hundred a-year to me; but I can't say, it's the same with all posturers: for you see I can talk French, and if there's any foreigners in the crowd I can talk to them, and they are sure to give something. But most posturers make a good living, and if they look out for it, there are few but make 30*s.* a-week.

Posturing as it is called (some people call it contortionists, that's a new name; a Chinese nondescript — that's the first name it came out as, although what we calls posturing is a man as can sit upon nothing; as, for instance, when he's on the back of two chairs and does a split with his legs stretched out and sitting on nothing like) — posturing is reckoned the healthiest life there is, because we never get the rheumatics; and another thing, we always eat hearty. We often put on wet dresses, such as at a fair, when they've been washed out clean, and we put them on before they're dry, and that's what gives the rheumatism; but we are always in such a perspiration that it never affects us. It's very violent exercise, and at night we feels it in our thighs more than anywhere, so that if it's damp or cold weather it hurts us to sit down. If it's wet weather, or showery, we usually get up stiff in the morning, and then we have to 'crick' each other before we go out, and practise in our bed-rooms. On the Sunday we also go out and practise, either in a field, or at the 'Tan' in Bermondsey. We used to go to the 'Hops' in Maiden-lane, but that's done away with now.

"When we go out performing, we always take our dresses out with us, and we have our regular houses appointed, according to what part of the town we play in, if in London; and we have one pint of beer a man, and put on our costume, and leave our clothes behind us. Every morning we put on a clean dress, so we are obliged to have two of them, and whilst we are wearing one the other is being washed. Some of our men is married, and their wives wash for them, but them as isn't give the dress to anybody who wants a job.

"Accidents are very rare with posturers. We often put our hip-bone out, but that's soon put right again, and we are at work in a week. All our bones are loose like, and we can pull one another in, without having no pullies. One of my gang broke his leg at Chatham race-course, through the grass being slippery, and he was pitched down from three high; but we paid him his share, just the same as if he was out with us; — it wouldn't do if we didn't, as a person wouldn't mount in bad weather. That man is getting on nicely, — he walks with a crutch though, — but he'll be right in another month, and then he'll only be put to light work till he's strong. He ought not to be walking out yet, but he's so daring there's no restraining him. I, too, once broke my arm. I am a hand-jumper; that is, I a'most always light on my hands when I jump. I was on a chair on a top of a table,

and I had to get into the chair and do what we call the frog, and jump off it, coming down on my hands. Everything depends upon how you hold your arms, and I was careless, and didn't pay attention, and my arm snapped just below the elbow. I couldn't work for three months. I was at Beauvais, in France, at the time, but the circus I was with supported me.

"My father's very near seventy-six, and he has been a tumbler for fifty years; my children are staying with him, and he's angry that I won't bring them up to it: but I want them to be some trade or another, because I don't like the life for them. There's so much suffering before they begin tumbling, and then there's great temptation to drink, and such-like. I'd sooner send them to school, than let them get their living out of the streets. I've one boy and two girls. They're always at it at home, indeed; father and my sister-in-law say they can't keep them from it. The boy's very nimble.

"In the winter time we generally goes to the theatres. We are a'most always engaged for the pantomimes, to do the sprites. We always reckon it a good thirteen-weeks' job, but in the country it's only a month. If we don't apply for the job they come after us. The sprites in a pantomime is quite a new style, and we are the only chaps that can do it, — the posturers and tumblers. In some theatres they find the dresses. Last winter I was at Liverpool, and wore a green dress, spangled all over, which belonged to Mr. Copeland, the manager. We never speak in the play, but just merely rush on, and throw somersaults, and frogs, and such-like, and then rush off again. Little Wheeler, the greatest tumbler of the day, was a posturer in the streets, and now he's in France doing his 10*l.* a-week, engaged for three years."

THE STREET RISLEY.

THERE is but one person in London who goes about the street doing what is termed "The Risley performance," and even he is rarely to be met with.

Of all the street professionals whom I have seen, this man certainly bears off the palm for respectability of attire. He wore, when he came to me, a brown Chesterfield coat and black continuations, and but for the length of his hair, the immense size of his limbs, and the peculiar neatness of his movements, it would have been impossible to have recognized in him any of those characteristics which usually distinguish the street performer. He had a chest which, when he chose, he could force out almost like a pouter pigeon. The upper part of his body was broad and weighty-looking. He asked me to feel the muscle of his arm, and doubling it up, a huge lump rose, almost as if he had a cocoa-nut under his sleeve; in fact, it seemed as fully developed as the gilt arms placed as signs over the gold-beaters' shops.

Like most of the street professionals, he volunteered to exhibit before me some of his feats of strength and agility. He threw his head back (his long hair tossing about like an Indian fly-whisk) until his head touched his heels, and there he stood bent backward, and nearly double, like a strip of whalebone. Then he promenaded round the room, walking on his hands, his coat-tails falling about his shoulders, and making a rare jingle of halfpence the while, and his legs dangling in front of him as limp as the lash of a cart-whip. I refused to allow him to experiment upon me, and politely declined his obliging offer to raise me from the ground, " and hold me at arm's-length like a babby."

When he spoke of his parents, and the brothers who performed with him, he did so in most affectionate terms, and his descriptions of the struggles he had gone through in his fixed determination to be a tumbler, and how he had worked to gain his parents' consent, had a peculiarly sorrowful touch about them, as if he still blamed himself for the pain he had caused them. Farther, whenever he mentioned his little brothers, he always stopped for two or three minutes to explain to me that they were the cleverest lads in London, and as true and kind-hearted as they were talented.

He was more minute in his account of himself than my space will permit him to be; for as he said, " he had a wonderful rememory-ation, and could recollect anything."

With the omission of a few interesting details, the following is the account of the poor fellow's life :—

" My professional name is Signor Nelsonio, but my real one is Nelson, and my companions know me as 'Leu,' which is short for Lewis. I can do plenty of things beside the Risley business, for it forms only one part of my entertainment. I am a strong man, and a fire-king, and a stone-breaker by the fist, as well as being sprite, and posturer, and doing ' la perche.'

Last Christmas (1855) I was, along with my two brothers, engaged at the Theatre Royal, Cheltenham, to do the sprites in the pantomime. I have brought the bill of the performances with me to show it you. Here you see the pantomime is called ' THE IMP OF THE NORTH, or The Golden Bason; and Harlequin and the Miller's Daughter.' In the pantomimical transformations it says, ' SPRITES—by the Nelson Family :' that's me and my two brothers.

" The reason why I took to the Risley business was this. When I was a boy of seven I went to school, and my father and mother would make me go; but, unfortunately, I was stubborn, and would not. I said I wanted to do some work. ' Well,' said they, ' you shan't do any work not yet, till you're thirteen years old, and you shall go to school.' Says I, ' I will do work.' Well, I wouldn't; so I plays

the truant. Then I goes to amuse myself, and I goes to Haggerstone-fields in the Hackney-road, and then I see some boys learning to tumble on some dung there. So I began to do it too, and I very soon picked up two or three tricks. There was a man who was in the profession as tumbler and acrobat, who came there to practise his feats, and he see me tumbling, and says he, ' My lad, will you come along with me, and do the Risley business, and I'll buy you your clothes, and give you a shilling a-week besides?' I told him that perhaps mother and father wouldn't let me go; but says he, ' O, yes they will.' So he comes to our house; and says mother, ' What do you want along with my boy?' and he says, ' I want to make a tumbler of him.' But she wouldn't.

" My father is a tailor, but my uncle and all the family was good singers. My uncle was leader of the Drury-lane band, and Miss Nelson, who came out there, is my cousin. They are out in Australia now, doing very well, giving concerts day and night, and clearing by both performances one hundred and fifty pounds, day and night (and sooner, more than less), as advertised in the paper which they sent to us.

" One day, instead of going to school, I went along with this man into the streets, and then he did the Risley business, throwing me about on his hands and feet. I was about thirteen years old then. Mother asked me at night where I had been, and when I said I had been at school, she went and asked the master and found me out. Then I brought home some dresses once, and she tore them up, so I was forced to drop going out in the streets. I made some more dresses, and she tore those up. Then I got chucking about, à la Risley, my little brother, who was about seven years old; and says mother, ' Let that boy alone, you'll break his neck.' ' No, I shan't,' say I, and I kept on doing till I had learnt him the tricks.

" One Saturday night, father and mother and my eldest brother went to a concert-room. I had no money, so I couldn't go. I asked my little brother to go along with me round some tap-rooms, exhibiting with me. So I smuggled him out, telling him I'd give him lots of cakes; and away we went, and we got about seven shillings and sixpence. I got home before father and mother come home. When they returned, father says, 'Where have you been?' Then I showed the money we had got; he was regular astonished, and says he ' How is this? you can do nothing, you ain't clever!' I says, ' Oh, ain't I? and it's all my own learning :' so then he told me, that since he couldn't do nothing else with me, I should take to it as my profession, and stick to it.

" Soon after I met my old friend the swallower again, in Ratcliffe highway. I was along with my little brother, and both dressed up in tights and spangled trunks. Says he, ' Oh, you will take to tumbling will you? Well, then, come along with me, and we'll go in the country.' Then he took us down to Norwich (to Yarmouth); then he beat me, and would give me no clothes or money, for he spent it to go and get drunk. We not sending any money home, mother began to wonder what had become of me; so one night, when this man was out with a lot of girls getting drunk, I slipt away, and walked thirty miles that night, and then I began performing at different public-houses, and so worked my way till I got back to London again. My little brother was along with me, but I carried him on my shoulders. One day it came on to rain awful, and we had run away in our dresses, and then we was dripping. I was frightened to see little Johnny so wet, and thought he'd be ill. There was no shed or barn or nothing, and only the country road, so I tore on till we came to a roadside inn, and then I wrung his clothes out, and I only had fourpence in my pocket, and I ordered some rum and water hot, and made him drink. 'Drink it, it'll keep the cold out of you.' When we got out he was quite giddy, and kept saying, 'Oh, I'm so wet!' With all these misfortunes I walked, carrying the little chap across my shoulders. One day I only had a halfpenny, and Johnny was crying for hunger, so I goes to a fellow in a orchard and say I, 'Can you make me a ha'path of apples?' He would take the money, but he gave a cap-full of fallings. I've walked thirty-eight miles in one day carrying him, and I was awfully tired. On that same day, when we got to Colchester, we put up at the Blue Anchor, and I put Johnny into bed, and I went out myself and went the round of the public-houses. My feet was blistered, but I had my light tumbling slippers on, and I went to work and got sixteen pence-halfpenny. This got us bread and cheese for supper and breakfast, and paid threepence each for the bed; and the next day we went on and performed in a village and got three shillings. Then, at Chelmsford we got eight shillings. I bought Johnny some clothes, for he had only his tights and little trunks, and though it was summer he was cold, especially after rain. The nearer we got to London the better we got off, for they give us then plenty to eat and drink, and we did pretty well for money. After I passed Chelmsford I never was hungry again. When we got to Romford, I waited two days till it was market-day, when we performed before the country people and got plenty of money and beer; but I never cared for the beer. We took four shillings and sixpence. I wouldn't let Johnny take any beer, for I'm fond of him, and he's eleven now, and the cleverest little fellow in England; and I learnt him everything he knows out of my own head, for he never had no master. We took the train to London from Romford (one shilling and sixpence each), and then we went home.

"When we got back, mother and father said they knew how it would be, and laughed at us. They wanted to keep us at home, but I wouldn't, and they was forced to give way. In London I stopped still for a long time, at last got an engagement at two shillings a-night at a penny gaff in Shoreditch. It was Sambo, a black man, what went about the streets along with the Demon Brothers—acrobats—that got me the engagement.

"One night father and mother came to see me, and they was frightened to see me chucking my brother about; and she calls out, 'Oh, don't do that! you'll break his back.' The people kept hollaring out, 'Turn that woman out!' but she answers, 'They are my sons—stop 'em!' When I bent myself back'ards she calls out, 'Lord! mind your bones.'

"After this I noticed that my other brother, Sam, was a capital hand at jumping over the chairs and tables. He was as active as a monkey; indeed he plays monkeys now at the different ballets that comes out at the chief theatres. It struck me he would make a good tumbler, and sure enough he is a good one. I asked him, and he said he should; and then he see me perform, and he declared he would be one. He was at my uncle's then, as a carver and gilder. When I told father, says he, 'Let 'em do as they like, they'll get on.' I said to him one day, 'Sam, let's see what you're like: so I stuck him up in his chair, and stuck his legs behind his head, and kept him like that for five minutes. His limbs bent beautiful, and he didn't want no cricking.

"I should tell you, that before that he done this here. You've heard of Baker, the red man, as was performing at the City of London Theatre; well, Sam see the cut of him sitting in a chair with his legs folded, just like you fold your arms. So Sam pulls down one of the bills with the drawing on it, and he says, 'I can do that,' and he goes home and practises from the engraving till he was perfect. Then he showed me, and says I, 'That's the style! it's beautiful! you'll do.'

"Then we had two days' practice together, and we worked the double-tricks together. Then, I learned him style and grace, what I knowed myself; such as coming before an audience and making the obedience; and by and by says I to him, 'We'll come out at a theatre, and make a good bit of money.'

"Well, we went to another exhibition, and we came out all three together, and our salary was twenty-five shillings a-week, and we was very successful. Then we got outside Peter's Theatre at Stepney fair, the last as ever was, for it's done away with now; we did very well then; they give us twelve shillings a-day between us for three days. We did the acrobating and Risley business outside the parade, and inside as well. Sam got on wonderful, for his mind was up to it, and he liked the work. I and my brothers can do as well as any one in this business, I don't care who comes before us. I can do upwards of one hundred and twenty one different tricks in tumbling, when I'm along with those little fellows. We can do the hoops and glasses—putting a glass of beer on my forehead, and going through hoops double, and lying down and getting up again without spilling it. Then there's the bottle-sprite, and the short stilts, and globe running and globe dancing, and chair tricks; perform with the chairs; and the pole trick—*la perche*—with two boys, not one mind you.

"We've been continuing ever since at this Risley business. I lay down on a carpet, and throw then summersets from feet to feet. I tell you what the music plays to it,—it's the railway overtime, and it begins now and then quicker and quicker, till I throw them fast as lightning. Sam does about fifty-four or fifty-five of these summersets one after another, and Johny does about twenty-five, because he's littler. Then there's standing upright, and stand 'em one in one hand and one on the other. Then I throws them up in summersets, and catch 'em on my palm, and then I chuck 'em on the ground.

"The art with me lying on the ground is that it takes the strength, and the sight to see that I catch 'em properly; for if I missed, they might break their necks. The audience fancies that it's most with them tumbling, but every thing depends upon me catching them properly. Every time they jump, I have to give 'em a jerk, and turn 'em properly. It's almost as much work as if I was doing it myself. When they learn at first, they do it on a soft ground, so as not to hurt theirselves. It don't make the blood come to the head lying down so long on my back—only at first.

"I've done the Risley business first at penny exhibitions, and after that I went to fairs; then I went round the country with a booth—a man named Manly it was; but we dropped that, 'cos my little brother was knocked up, for it was too hard work for the little fellow building up and taking down the booth sometimes twice in a-day, and then going off twenty miles further on to another fair, and building up again the next day. Then we went pitching about in the main streets of the towns in the country. Then I always had a drum and pipes. As soon as a crowd collected I'd say, 'Gentlemen, I'm from the principal theatres in London, and before I begin I must have five shillings in the ring.' Then we'd do some, and after that, when half was over, I'd say, 'Now, gentlemen, the better part is to come, and if you make it worth my while, I go on with this here entertainment;' then, perhaps, they'd give me two shillings more. I've done bad and done good in the country. In one day I've taken two pounds five shillings, and many days we've not taken eight shillings, and there was four of us, me and my two brothers and the drummer, who had two-and-sixpence a-day, and a pot of beer besides. Take one

week with another we took regular two pounds five shillings, and out of that I'd send from twenty to thirty shillings a-week home to my parents. Oh, I've been very good to my parents, and I've never missed it. I've been a wild boy too, and yet I've always taken care of father and mother. They've had twelve in family and never a stain on their character, nor never a key turned on them, but are upright and honourable people.

"At a place called Brenford in Norfolk—where there's such a lot of wild rabbits—we done so well, that we took a room and had bills printed and put out. We charged threepence each, and the room was crowded, for we shared twenty-five shillings between us. When the people see'd me and my brothers come on dressed all in red, and tumble about, they actually swore we were devils, and rushed out of the place; so that, though there was a room full, there was only two stopped to see the performances. One old man called out, 'O wenches' —they call their wives wenches—'come out, they be devils.' We came out with red faces and horns and red dresses, and away they went screaming. There was one woman trampled on and a child knocked out of her arms. In some of these country towns they're shocking strict, and never having seen anything of the kind, they're scared directly.

"About six months ago I went to Woolwich with the boys, and there was a chap that wanted to fight me, because I wouldn't go along with him. So, I says, 'We won't have no fighting;' so I went along with him to Gravesend, and then we asked permission of the mayor, 'cos in country towns we often have to ask the mayor to let us go performing in the streets. There we done very well, taking twenty-five shillings in the day. Then we worked up by Chatham, and down to Herne-bay, and Ramsgate; and at Ramsgate we stopped a week, doing uncommon well on the sands, for the people on the chairs would give sixpence and a shilling, and say it was very clever, and too clever to be in the streets. We did Margate next, and then Deal, and on to Dover by the boat. At Dover, the mayor wouldn't let us perform, and said if he catched us in the streets he'd have us took up. We were very hard up. So I said to Sam, 'You must go out one way and I and Johnny the other, and busk in the public-house.' Sam got eight shillings and sixpence and I four shillings. But I had a row with a sailor, and I was bruised and had to lay up. When I was better we moved to Folkestone. There was the German soldiers there, and we did very well. I went out one day with our carpet to a village close by, and some German officers made us perform, and gave us five shillings, and then we went the round of the beer-shops, and altogether we cleared five pounds before we finished that day. We also went up to the camp, where the tents was, and I asked the colonel to let me perform before the men, and he said, 'Well it ain't usual, but you may if you like.' The officers we found was so pleased they kept on giving us two-shilling pieces, and besides we had a lot of foreign coin, which we sold to a jeweller for ten shillings.

"I worked my way on to Canterbury and Winchester, and then, by a deal, of persuasion I got permission to perform in the back-streets, and we done very well. Then we went on to Southampton. There was a cattle fair, on—Celsey fair is, I think, the name of it; and then I joined another troupe of tumblers, and we worked the fair, and after that went on to Southampton; and when we began working on the Monday, there was another troupe working as well. After we had pitched once or twice, this other troupe came and pitched opposition against us. I couldn't believe it at first, but when I see which was their lay, then says I, 'Now I'll settle this.' We was here, as it was, and they came right on to us—there, as it may be. So it was our dinner-time, and we broke up and went off. After dinner we came out again, and pitched the carpet in a square, and they came close to us again, and as soon as they struck up, the people run away to see the new ones. So I said 'I don't want to injure them, but they shan't injure us.' So I walked right into the middle of their ring, and threw down the carpet, and says I, 'Now, ladies and gentlemen, the best performance is the one that deserves best support, and I'll show you what I can do.' I went to work with the boys, and was two hours doing all my tumbling tricks. They was regularly stunned. The silver and the halfpence covered the carpet right over, as much as it would hold. I think there was three pounds. Then I says, 'Now you've seen the tumbling, now see the perche.' They had a perche, too; it was taller than mine; but, as I told them, it was because I couldn't get no higher a one. So I went to work again, and cries I, 'Now, both boys up;' though I had only stood one on up to that time, and had never tried two of 'em. Up they goes, and the first time they come over, but never hurt theirselves. It was new to me, you see. 'Up again, lads,' says I; and up they goes, and did it beautiful. The people regular applauded, like at a theatre. Down came the money in a shower, and one gentleman took his hat round, and went collecting for us. Says I to this other school, 'You tried to injure us, and what have you got by it? I beat you in tumbling, and if you can match the perche, do it.' Then they says, 'We didn't try to injure you; come and drink a gallon of beer.' So off we went, and the police told 'em to choose their side of the town and we would take ours. That settled the opposition, and we both done well.

"I've done the Risley in the streets of London, more so than at theatres and concerts. The stone paving don't hurt so much as you would think to lie down. We don't do it when it's muddy. The boys finds no difference whatsumever in springing off the stones. It pays very well at times, you know; but we don't like to do it often, because afterwards they don't like to appreciate you in concerts and theatres, and likewise penny exhibitions.

"My brother Sam can jump like a frog, on his hands, through his legs, out of a one-pair window; and little Johnny throws out of a one-pair-of-stairs window a back summerset.

"It's astonishing how free the bones get by practice. My brother Sam can dislocate his limbs and replace them again; and when sleeping in bed, I very often find him lying with his legs behind his neck. It's quite accidental, and done without knowing, and comes natural to him, from being always tumbling. Myself, I often in my dreams often frighten my wife by starting up and half throwing a summersault, fancying I'm at the theatre, and likewise I often lie with my heels against my head.

"We are the only family or persons going about the streets doing the Risley. I've travelled all through England, Scotland, and Wales, and I don't know anybody but ourselves. When we perform in the London theatres, which we do when we can get an engagement, we get six or seven pounds a-week between us. We've appeared at the Pavilion two seasons running; likewise at the City of London, and the Standard, and also all the cheap concerts in London. Then we are called 'The Sprites' by the Nelson family will appear; 'or, The Sprites of Jupiter;' or, 'Sons of Cerea;' cr, 'Air-climbers of Arabia!'

"Taking all the year round, I dare say my income comes to about thirty-five shillings or two pounds, and out of that I have to find dresses.'

THE STRONG MAN.

"I HAVE been in the profession for about thirteen years, and I am thirty-two next birthday. Excepting four years that I was at sea, I've been solely by the profession. I'm what is termed a strong man, and perform feats of strength and posturing. What is meant by posturing is the distortion of the limbs, such as doing the splits, and putting your leg over your head and pulling it down your back, a skipping over your leg, and such-like business. Tumbling is different from posturing, and means throwing summersets and walking on your hands; and acrobating means the two together, with mounting three stories high, and balancing each other. These are the definitions I make.

"I was nineteen before I did anything of any note at all, and got what I call a living salary. Long before that I had been trying the business, going in and out of these free concerts, and trying my hand at it, fancying I was very clever, but disgusting the audience, for they are mostly duffers at these free concerts;

which is clearly the case, for they only do it for a pint every now and then, and depend upon passing the hat round after their performance. I never got much at collections, so I must have been a duffer.

"My father is an architect and builder, and his income now is never less than a thousand a-year. Like a fool, I wouldn't go into his office: I wish I had. I preferred going to sea. I was always hankering after first one vessel and then another. I used to be fond of going down to the docks, and such-like, and looking at the vessels. I'd talk with the sailors about foreign countries, and such-like, and my ambition was to be a sailor. I was the scabby sheep of the family, and I've been punished for it. I never went into the governor's office; but when I was about fourteen I was put to a stonemason, for I thought I should like to be a carver, or something of that sort. I was two years there, and I should have done very well if I had stayed, for I earned a guinea a-week when I left.

"Before I went to the stonemason I was at the Victoria, taking checks—when there was any. I had an uncle there who kept the saloon there. I was always very partial to going to the theatre, for all our people are chapel people, and that I never liked. My father's parlour is always smothered with ministers, and mine with tumblers, and that's the difference. I used to go and see my uncle at the Vic., so as to get to the theatre for nothing. I wasn't paid for taking the checks, but I knew the check-taker, and he'd ask me to help him, and I was too glad to get inside a theatre to refuse the job. They were doing dreadful business. It was under Levi, and before Glossop's time. It was before the glass curtain come out. The glass curtain was a splendid thing. It went straight up, never wound. You can even now see where the roof was highered to receive it. Levi has got the Garrick now. They say he's not doing much.

"The first thing I did was at a little beer-shop, corner of Southwark-bridge-road and Union-street. I had seen Herbert do the Grecian statues at the Vic., in 'Hercules, King of Clubs,' and it struck me I could do 'em. So I knew this beer-shop, and I bought half-a-crown's worth of tickets to be allowed to do these statues. It was on a boxing-night, I remember. I did them, but they were dreadful bad. The people did certainly applaud, but what for, I don't know, for I kept shaking and wabbling so, that my marble statue was rather ricketty; and there was a strong man in the room, who had been performing them, and he came up to me and said that I was a complete duffer, and that I knew nothing about it at all. So I replied, that he knew nothing about his feats of strength, and that I'd go and beat him. So I set to work at it; for I was determined to lick him. I got five quarter-of-hundred weights, and used to practice throwing them at a friend's back-yard

in the Waterloo-road. I used to make myself all over mud at it, besides having a knock of the head sometimes. At last I got perfect chucking the quarter hundred, and then I tied a fourteen pound weight on to them, and at last I got up half-hundreds. I learnt to hold up one of them at arm's length, and even then I was obliged to push it up with the other hand. I also threw them over my head, as well as catching them by the ring.

"I went to this beer-shop as soon as I could do, and came out. I wasn't so good as he was at lifting, but that was all he could do; and I did posturing with the weights as well, and that licked him. He was awfully jealous, and I had been revenged. I had learnt to do a split, holding a half-hundred in my teeth, and rising with it, without touching the ground with my hands. Now I can lift five, for I've had more practice. I had tremendous success at this beer-shop.

"It hurt me awfully when I learnt to do the split with the weight on my teeth. It strained me all to pieces. I couldn't put my heels to the ground not nicely, for it physicked my thighs dreadful. When I was hot I didn't feel it; but as I cooled, I was cramped all to bits. It took me nine months before I could do it without feeling any pain.

"Another thing I learnt to do at this beer-shop was, to break the stone on the chest. This man used to do it as well, only in a very slight way — with thin bits and a cobbler's hammer. Now mine is regular flagstones. I've seen as many as twenty women faint seeing me do it. At this beer-shop, when I first did it, the stone weighed about three quarters of a hundred, and was an inch thick. I laid down on the ground, and the stone was put on my chest, and a man with a sledge hammer, twenty-eight pounds weight, struck it and smashed it. The way it is done is this. You rest on your heels and hands and throw your chest up. There you are, like a stool, with the weight on you. When you see the blow coming, you have to give, or it would knock you all to bits.

"When I was learning to do this, I practised for nine months. I got a friend of mine to hit the stone. One day I cut my chest open doing it. I wasn't paying attention to the stone, and never noticed that it was hollow; so then when the blow came down, the sharp edges of the stone, from my having nothing but a fleshing suit on, cut right into the flesh, and made two deep incisions. I had to leave it off for about a month. Strange to say, this stone-breaking never hurt my chest or my breathing; I rather think it has done me good, for I'm strong and hearty, and never have illness of any sort.

"The first time I done it I was dreadful frightened. I knew if I didn't stop still I should have my brains knocked out, pretty well. When I saw the blow coming I trembled a good bit, but I kept still as I was able. It was a hard blow, for it broke the bit of York-shire paving, about an inch thick, into about sixty pieces.

"I got very hard up whilst I was perform-ing at this beer-shop. I had run away from home, and the performances were only two nights a-week, and brought me in about six shillings. I wasn't engaged anywhere else. One night, a Mr. Emanuel, who had a benefit at the Salmon Saloon, Union-street, asked me to appear at his benefit. He had never seen me, but only heard of my performances. I agreed to go, and he got out the bills, and christened me Signor C——; and he had drawings made of the most extravagant kind, with me holding my arms out with about ten fifty-six-pound weights hanging to them by the rings. He had the weights, hammers, and a tremendous big stone chained outside the door, and there used to be mobs of people there all day long looking at it.

"This was the first success I made. Mr. Emanuel gave five shillings for the stone, and had it brought up to the saloon by two horses in a cart to make a sensation. It weighed from four to five hundred weight. I think I had such a thing as five men to lift it up for me.

"I had forgotten all about this engagement, and I was at the coffee-house where I lodged. The fact was, I was in rags, and so shabby I didn't like to go, and if he hadn't come to fetch me I should not have gone. He drove up in his chaise on the night in question to this coffee-shop, and he says, 'Signor C——, make haste; go and change your clothes, and come along.' I didn't know at first he was speaking to me, for it was the first time I had been Signor C——. Then I told him I had got my best suit on, though it was very ragged, and no mistake about it, for I remember there was a good hole at each elbow. He seemed astonished, and at last proposed that I should wear his great-coat; but I wouldn't, because, as I told him, his coat would be as well known at the saloon as he himself was, and that it didn't suit me to be seen in another's clothes. So he took me just as I was. When we got there, the landlady was regularly flab-bergastered to see a ragged fellow like me come to be star of the night. She'd hardly speak to me.

"There was a tremendous house, and they had turned above a hundred away. When I got into the saloon, Emanuel says, 'What'll you have to drink?' I said, 'Some brandy;' but my landlord of the coffee-house, who had come unbeknown to me, he grumbles out, 'Ask him what he'll have to eat, for he's had nothing since the slice of bread-and-butter for breakfast.' I trod on his toe, and says, 'Keep quiet, you fool!' Emanuel behaved like a regular brick, and no mistake. He paid for the supper and everything. I was regularly ashamed when the landlord let it out though. That supper put life into me,

for it almost had the same effect upon me as drink.

"It soon got whispered about in the saloon that I was the strong man, and everybody got handing me their glasses; so I was regularly tipsy when it was time to go on, and they had put me off to the last on purpose to draw the people and keep them there drinking.

"I had a regular success. When the women saw the five men put the stone on my chest, they all of them called out, 'Don't! don't!' It was a block like a curb, about a foot thick, and about a four feet six inches long. I went with Emanuel to buy it. I had never tried such a big one before. It didn't feel so heavy on the chest, for, you see, you've got such out-and-out good support on your hands and heels. I've actually seen one man raise a stone and another a waggon. It's the purchase done it. I've lifted up a cart-horse right off his legs.

"The stone broke after six blows with a twenty-eight pound sledge-hammer. Then you should have heard the applause. I thought it would never give over. It smashed all to atoms, just like glass, and there was the people taking away the bits to keep as a re-membrance.

"As I went out the landlady asked me to have a bottle of soda-water. The landlady was frightened, and told me she had felt sure I should be killed. I was the second that ever done stone-breaking in England or abroad, and I'm the first that ever did such a big one. The landlady was so alarmed that she wouldn't engage me, for she said I must be killed one of the nights. Her behaviour was rather different as I went out to when I came in.

"I, of course, didn't go on in my rags. I had a first-rate stage dress.

"After this grand appearance I got engaged at Gravesend fair by Middleton, and there I had eight shillings a-day, and I stopped with him three weeks over the fair. I used to do my performances outside on the parade, never inside. I had to do the stone-breaking about nine or ten times a-day. They were middling stones, some larger and some smaller, and the smaller ones about half-a-hundred weight, I suppose. Any man might bring his stone and hammer, and break it himself. The one who struck was generally chosen from the crowd; the biggest chap they could find. I've heard 'em say to me, 'Now, old chap, I'll smash you all to bits; so look out!' The fact is, the harder they strike the better for me, for it smashes it at once, and don't keep the people in suspense.

"It was at Gravesend that I met with my second and last accident. With the cutting of the chest, it is the only one I ever had. The feller who came up to break the stone was half tipsy and missed his aim, and obliged me by hitting my finger instead of the stone. I said to him, 'Mind what you are doing,' but

I popped my hand behind me, and when I got up I couldn't make out what the people was crying out about, till I looked round at my back and then I was smothered in blood. Middleton said, 'Good God! what's the matter?' and I told him I was hit on the finger. When the cry was given of 'All in to begin,' I went into a booth close by and had some brandy, and got a doctor to strap up the finger, and then I went on with the parade business just the same. It didn't pain me nothing like what I should have thought. It was too hard a knock to pain me much. The only time I felt it was when the doctor dressed it, for it gave me pepper taking the plaster off.

"I was at Gravesend some time, and I went to work again stone-masoning, and I had a guinea a-week, and in the evening I used to perform at the Rose Inn. I did just as I liked there. I never charged 'em anything. I lived in the house and they never charged me anything. It was a first-rate house. If I wanted five shillings I'd get it from the landlord. I was there about eleven months, and all that time I lived there and paid nothing. I had a benefit there, and they wouldn't even charge me for printing the bills, or cards, or anything. It was quite a clear benefit, and every penny taken at the doors was given to me. I charged a shilling admittance, and the room was crowded, and they was even on the stairs standing tip-toe to look at me. I wanted some weights, and asked a butcher to lend 'em to me, and he says, 'Lend 'em to you! aye, take the machine and all if it'll serve you.' I was a great favourite, as you may guess.

"After Gravesend I came up to London, and went and played the monkey at the Bower Saloon. It was the first time I had done it. There was all the monkey business, jumping over tables and chairs, and all mischievous things; and there was climbing up trees, and up two perpendicular ropes. I was dressed in a monkey's dress; it's made of some of their hearth-rugs; and my face was painted. It's very difficult to paint a monkey's face. I've a great knack that way, and can always manage anything of that sort.

"From the Bower I went on to Portsmouth. I'd got hard up again, for I'd been idle for three months, for I couldn't get any money, and I never appear under price. I walked all the way to Portsmouth, carrying a half-hundred weight, besides my dress, all the way; I played at the tap-rooms on the road. I did pretty middling, earned my living on the road, about two shillings a-day. When I got to Portsmouth I did get a job, and a good job it was, only one shilling and sixpence a-night; but I thought it better to do that than nothing. I only did comic singing, and I only knew two songs, but I set to and learnt a lot. I am very courageous, and if I can't get my money one way, I will another. With us, if you've got a shilling, you're a fool if you spend that before you have another. I stopped at this public-

house for two months, and then a man who came from Portsea, a town close by, came one night, and he asked me what I was doing. He had heard of what I could do, and he offered me two pounds a-week to go with him and do the strong business. He kept the Star Inn at Portsea. I stopped there such a thing as two years, and I did well. I had great success, for the place was cramm'd every night. For my benefit, Major Wyatt and Captain Holloway gave me their bespeak, and permission for the men to come. The admission was sixpence. Half the regiment marched down, and there was no room for the public. I was on the stage for two hours during my performances. I was tired, and fainted away as dead as a hammer after the curtain fell.

"Among other things I announced that I should, whilst suspended from the ceiling, lift a horse. I had this horse paraded about the town for a week before my night. There was such a house that numbers of people was turned away, and a comic singer who was performing at a house opposite, he put out an announcement that he too would lift a horse, and when the time came he brought on a clothes-horse.

"The way I did the horse was this: I was hanging by my ankles, and the horse was on a kind of platform under me. I had two sheets rolled up and tied round the horse like belly-bands, and then I passed my arms through them and strained him up. I didn't keep him long in the air, only just lifted him off his legs. In the midst of it the bandage got off his eyes, and then, what with the music and the applauding, the poor brute got frightened and begun plunging. I couldn't manage him at all whilst he was kicking. He got his two hind legs over the orchestra and knocked all the float-lights out. They kept roaring, 'Bring him out! bring him out!' as if they thought I was going to put him under my arm—a thundering big brute. I was afraid he'd crack his knees, and I should have to pay for him. The fiddler was rather uneasy, I can tell you, and the people began shifting about. I was frightened, and so I managed to pop part of the sheet over his head, and then I gave a tremendous strain and brought him back again.

"How the idea of lifting a horse ever came into my head, I don't know. It came in a minute; I had never tried it before. I knew I should have a tremendous purchase. The fact is, I had intended to do a swindle by having lines passed down my dress, and for somebody behind to pull the ropes and help me. The town was in an uproar when I announced I should do it.

"It was at my benefit that I first broke stones with my fist. I don't know whose original notion it was. I was not the first; there's a trick in it. It's done this way: anybody can do it. You take a cobbler's lapstone, and it's put on a half-hundred weight; you must hold it half an inch above, and then the concussion of the fist coming down smashes it all to bits. Any one can do it.

"I cleared about eight pounds by my benefit. I was a regular swell in those days. The white coats had just come up, and I had one made with two-shilling pieces for buttons, and with polished-leather Wellington's I'd walk about the town, the king of the place.

"I've been down to Manchester performing. I've been, too, to the Standard Theatre as well as the Victoria and the Marylebone. People won't believe I really do break the stone on my chest. Some ask me what I wear under my dress, though the fact is, that if I had anything hard there, it would just about kill me, for it's by yielding to the blow that I save myself. I actually gammoned one chap that the stones were made of small pieces stuck together with paste, and he offered to give me any sum to tell him what the paste was made of.

"When I'm engaged for a full performance I do this. All the weights, and the stone and the hammer, are ranged in front of the stage. Then I come on dressed in silk tights with a spangled trunk. Then I enter at the back of the stage, and first do several feats of posturing, such as skipping through my leg or passing it down my back, or splits. Then I take a ladder and mount to the top, and stand up on it, and hold one leg in my hand, shouldering it; and then I give a spring with the other leg, and shoot off to the other side of the stage and squash down with both legs open, doing a split. It's a very good trick, and always gets a round. Then I do a trick with a chair standing on the seat, and I take one foot in my hand and make a hoop of the leg, and then hop with one leg through the hoop of the other, and spring over the back and come down in a split on the other side. I never miss this trick, though, if the chair happens to be ricketty, I may catch the toe, but it doesn't matter much.

"Then I begin my weight business. I take one half-hundred weight and hold it up at arm's-length; and I also hold it out perpendicularly, and bring it up again and swing it two or three times round the head, and then throw it up in the air and catch it four or five times running; not by the ring, as others do, but in the open hand.

"The next trick is doing the same thing with both hands instead of one, that is with two weights at the same time; and then, after that, I take up a half-hundred by the teeth, and shouldering the leg at the same, and in that style I fall down into the splits. Then I raise myself up gradually, till I'm upright again. After I'm upright I place the weight on my forehead, and lay down flat on my back with it, without touching with the hands. I take it off when I'm down and place it in my mouth, and walk round the stage like a Greenwich-pensioner, with my feet tucked up like crossing the arms, and only using my

knees. Then I tie three together, and hold them in the mouth, and I put one in each hand. Then I stand up with them and support them. It's an awful weight, and you can't do much exhibiting with them.

"When I was at Vauxhall, Yarmouth, last year, I hurt my neck very badly in lifting those weights in the mouth. It pulled out the back of my neck, and I was obliged to give over work for months. It forced my head over one shoulder, and then it sunk, as if I'd got a stiff neck. I did nothing to it, and only went to a doctor-chap, who made me bathe the neck in hot water. That's all.

"One of my most curious tricks is what I call the braces trick. It's a thing just like a pair of braces, only, instead of a button, there's a half-hundred weight at each end, so that there are two behind and two in front. Then I mount on two swinging ropes with a noose at the end, and I stretch out my legs into a split, and put a half-hundred on each thigh, and take up another in my mouth. You may imagine how heavy the weight is, when I tell you that I pulled the roof of a place in once at Chelsea. It was a exhibition then. The tiles and all come down, and near smothered me. You must understand, that in these tricks I have to put the weights on myself, and raise them from the ground, and that makes it so difficult.

"The next, and the best, and most difficult trick of all is, I have a noose close to the ceiling, in which I place one of my ankles, and I've another loose noose with a hook at the end, and I place that on the other ankle. Two half-hundreds are placed on this hook, and one in each hand. The moment these weights are put on this ankle, it pulls my legs right apart, so that they form a straight line from the ceiling, like a plumb-line, and my body sticks out at the side horizontally, like a $\top$-square sideways. I strike an attitude when I have the other weights in my hand, and then another half-hundred is put in my mouth, and I am swung backwards and forwards for about eight or twelve times. It don't hurt the ankle, because the sling is padded. At first it pulls you about, and gives you a tremendous ricking. After this rope-performance I take a half-hundred and swing it round about fifty times. It goes as rapidly as a wheel, and if I was to miss my aim I should knock my brains out. I have done it seventy times, but that was to take the shine out of an opposition fellow.

"I always wind up with breaking the stone, and I don't mind how thick it is, so long as it isn't heavy enough to crush me. A common curb-stone, or a Yorkshire-flag, is nothing to me, and I've got so accustomed to this trick, that once it took thirty blows with a twenty-eight pound sledge-hammer to break the stone, and I asked for a cigar and smoked it all the while.

"I'll tell you another trick I've done, and

that's walking on the ceiling. Of course I darn't do it in the Professor Sands' style, for mine was a dodge. Professor Sands used an air-exhausting boot, on the model of a fly's foot, and it was a legitimate performance indeed; he and another man, to whom he gave the secret of his boots, are the only two who ever did it. The chap.that came over here wasn't the real Sands. The fact is well known to the profession, that Sands killed himself on his benefit night in America. After walking on the marble slab in the Circus, somebody bet him he couldn't do it on any ceiling, and he for a wager went to a Town-hall, and done it, and the ceiling gave way, and he fell and broke his neck. The chap that came over here was Sands' attendant, and he took the name and the boots, and came over as Professor Sands.

"The first who ever walked on the ceiling, by a dodge, was a man of the name of Herman, a wizard, who wound up his entertainment at the City of London by walking on some planks suspended in the air. I was there, and at once saw his trick. I knew it was a sleight-of-hand thing. I paid great attention and found him out.

"I then went to work in this way. I bought two planks about thirteen foot long, and an inch thick. In these planks I had small traps, about two inches long by one inch wide, let into the wood, and very nicely fitted, so that the cracks could not be seen. The better to hide the cracks, I had the wood painted marble, and the blue veins arranged on the cracks. These traps were bound on the upper side with iron hooping to strengthen them. Then I made my boots. They were something like Chinese boots, with a very thick sole, made on the principle of the bellows of an accordion. These bellows were round, about the size of a cheese-plate, and six inches deep. To the sole of the boot I had an iron plate and a square tenter-hook riveted in.

"Then came the performance. There was no net under me, and the planks was suspended about twenty feet from the stage. I went up on the ladder and inserted the hook on one boot into the first trap. The sucker to the boot hid the hook, and made it appear as if I held by suction. The traps were about six inches apart, and that gave me a very small step. The hooks being square ones—tenterhooks — I could slip them out easily. It had just the same appearance as Sands, and nobody ever taught me how to do it. I did this feat at the Albion Concert-rooms, just opposite the Effingham Saloon. I had eighteen shillings a-week there for doing it. I never did it anywhere else, for it was a bother to carry the planks about with me. I did it for a month, every night three times. One night I fell down. You see you can never make sure, for if you swung a little, it worked the hook off. I always had a chap walking along under me to catch me, and he broke my fall, so that I didn't hurt myself. I ran up again, and did it a second time without an accident. There was tremendous applause. I think I should have fallen on my hands if the chap hadn't been there.

"If the Secretary of State hadn't put down the balloon business, I should a made a deal of money. There is danger of course, but so there is if you're twenty or thirty feet. They do it now fifty feet high, and that's as bad as if you were two hundred or a mile in the air. The only danger is getting giddy from the height, but those who go up are accustomed to it.

"I sold the ceiling-walking trick to another fellow for two pounds, after I had done with it, but he couldn't manage it. He thought he was going to do wonders. He took a half-hundred weight along with him, but he swung like a pendulum, and down he come.

"Why this walking on the ceiling of mine was very near the same as what Harvey Leach did at the Surrey as the gnome fly. He was a tremendous clever fellow. His upper part of the body was very perfectly made, but his legs was so short, they weren't more than eighteen inches long. That's why he walked as much on his hands as his legs. That 'What is It,' at the Egyptian Hall killed him. They'd have made a heap of money at it if it hadn't been discovered. He was in a cage, and wonderfully got up. He looked awful. A friend of his comes in, and goes up to the cage, and says, 'How are you, old fellow?' The thing was blown up in a minute. The place was in an uproar. It killed Harvey Leach, for he took it to heart and died.

"I reckon Astley's is the worst money for any man. If a fellow wants to be finished up, let him go there. It doesn't pay so well as the cheap concerts, unless a man is a very great star, and they must give him his money.

"There are six men, including myself, who do the strong business. That's all I'm beware of in London, or England. Sometimes they change their names, and comes out as Herrs, or Signors, or Monsieurs, but they are generally the same fellows. Most of our foreigners in England come out of Tower-street. There was a house of call there for professionals of all nations, but that 'public' is done up now, and they mostly go to the Cooper's Arms now.

"If a strong man properly understands his business, and pays attention to his engagements, his average earnings will be about two pounds ten shillings a-week. As it is, they now make less than thirty shillings, but they spend it so readily that it doesn't go so far as a working man's pound. There's plenty of people to ask you, 'What'll you have?' but if you're anything of a man you're obliged to return the compliment at some time. The swells get hold of you. Perhaps a bottle of wine is called for, and then another; well, then a fellow must be no good if he doesn't pay for the third when it comes, and the day's money don't run to it, and you're in a hole."

THE STREET JUGGLER.

THE juggler from whom I received the following account, was spoken of by his companions and friends as "one of the cleverest that ever came out." He was at this time performing in the evening at one of the chief saloons on the other side of the water.

He certainly appears to have been successful enough when he first appeared in the streets, and the way in which he squandered the amount of money he then made is a constant source of misery to him, for he kept exclaiming in the midst of his narrative, "Ah! I might have been a gentleman now, if I hadn't been the fool I was then."

As a proof of his talents and success he assured me, that when Ramo Samee first came out, he not only learned how to do all the Indian's tricks, but also did them so dexterously, that when travelling "Samee has often paid him ten shillings not to perform in the same town with him."

He was a short man, with iron-grey hair, which had been shaved high upon the temples to allow him to assume the Indian costume. The skin of the face was curiously loose, and formed deep lines about the chin, whilst in the cheeks there were dimples, or rather hollows, almost as deep as those on a sofa cushion. He had a singular look, from his eyebrows and eyes being so black.

His hands were small and delicate, and when he took up anything, he did it as if he were lifting the cup with the ball under it.

"I'm a juggler," he said, "but I don't know if that's the right term, for some people call conjurers jugglers; but it's wrong. When I was in Ireland they called me a "manulist," and it was a gentleman wrote the bill out for me. The difference I makes between conjuring and juggling is, one's deceiving to the eye and the other's pleasing to the eye —yes, that's it—it's dexterity.

"I dare say I've been at juggling 40 years, for I was between 14 and 15 when I begun, and I'm 56 now. I remember Ramo Samee and all the first process of the art. He was the first as ever I knew, and very good indeed; there was no other to oppose him, and he must have been good then. I suppose I'm the oldest juggler alive.

"My father was a whitesmith, and kept a shop in the Waterloo-road, and I ran away from him. There was a man of the name of Humphreys kept a riding-school in the Waterloo-road (there was very few houses there then, only brick-fields—aye, what is the Victoria theatre now was then a pin-factory and a hatter's; it wasn't opened for performance then), and I used to go to this riding-school and practise tumbling when the horse-dung

was thrown out, for I was very ambitious to be a tumbler. When I used to go on this here dung-heap, sometimes father would want me to blow the fire or strike for him, and he'd come after me and catch me tumbling, and take off his apron and wallop me with it all the way home; and the leather strings used to hurt, I can tell you.

"I first went to work at the pin-factory, where the Coburg's built now, and dropped tumbling then. Then I went to a hatter's in Oakley-street, and there I took to tumbling again, and used to get practising on the wool-packs (they made the hats then out of wool stuff and hare-skins, and such-like, and you couldn't get a hat then under 25s.); I couldn't get my heart away from tumbling all the time I was there, for it was set on it. I'd even begin tumbling when I went out on errands, doing hand-spring, and starts-up (that's laying on your back and throwing yourself up), and round-alls (that's throwing yourself backwards on to your hands and back again to your feet), and walking on my hands. I never let any of the men see me practise. I had to sweep the warehouse up, and all the wool was there, and I used to have a go to myself in the morning before they was up.

"The way I got into my professional career was this: I used to have to go and get the men's beer, for I was kept for that. You see, I had to go to the men's homes to fetch their breakfasts, and the dinners and teas — I wish I had such a place now. The men gave me a shilling a-week, and there was twelve of them when in full work, and the master gave me 4s. 6d. Besides that they never worked on a Monday, but I was told to fetch their food just the same, so that their wives mightn't know; and I had all their twelve dinners, breakfasts, and so on. I kept about six of the boys there, and anybody might have the victuals that liked, for I've sometimes put 'em on a post for somebody to find.

"I was one day going to fetch the men's beer when I meets another boy, and he says, 'You can't walk on your hands.' 'Cant I!' says I, and I puts down the cans and off I started, and walked on my hands from one end of the street to the other, pretty nigh. Mr. Sanders, the rider, one of the oldest riders that was (before Ducrow's time, for Ducrow was a 'prentice of his, and he allowed Sanders 30s. a-week for all his lifetime), was passing by and he see me walking on my hands, and he come up and says, 'My boy, where do you belong to?' and I answers, 'My father;' and then he says, 'Do you think he'd let you come along with me?' I told him I'd go and ask; and I ran off, but never went to father—you'll understand—and then in a minute or two I came back and said, 'Father says yes, I may go when I thinks proper;' and then Mr. Sanders took me to Lock's-fields, and there was a gig, and he drove me down to Ware, in Hertfordshire.

" You may as well say this here. The circusses at that time wasn't as they are now. They used to call it in the profession moulding, and the public termed it mountebanking. Moulding was making a ring in a field, for there was no booths then, and it comes from digging up the mould to make it soft for the horses' feet. There was no charge for seeing the exhibition, for it was in a field open to the public; but it was worked in this way: there was prizes given away, and the tickets to the lottery were 1*s.* each, and most of the people bought 'em, though they weren't obligated to do so. Sometimes the prizes would be a five-pound note, or a silver watch, maybe, or a sack of flour, or a pig. They used to take the tickets round in a hat, and everybody saw what they drawed. They was all prizes — perhaps a penny ring — but there was no blanks. It was the last night that paid best. The first and second nights Sanders would give them a first-rate prize; but when the last night came, then a half-crown article was the highest he'd give away, and that helped to draw up. I've know'd him give 4*l.* or 5*l.* away, when he'd not taken 2*l.* Mr. Sanders put me to tumbling in the ring. I could tumble well before I went with him, for I'd practised on this dung-heap, and in this hatter's shop. I beat all his apprentices what he had. He didn't give me anything a-week, only my keep, but I was glad to run away and be a showman. I was very successful in the ring-tumbling, and from that I got to be clever on the stilts and on the slack-rope, or, as they call it in the profession, the waulting-rope. When I was ragged I used to run home again and get some clothes. I've many a time seen him burst out into tears to see me come home so ragged. ' Ah,' he'd say, ' where have you been now? — tumbling, I suppose.' I'd answer, ' Yes, father;' and then he'd say, ' Ah, your tumbling will bring you to the gallows.' I'd stop with him till he gave me some fresh clothes, and then I'd bolt again. You see I liked it. I'd go and do it for nothing. Now I dread it; but it's too late, unfortunately.

" I ran away from Sanders at last, and went back to father. One night I went to the theatre, and there I see Ramo Samee doing his juggling, and in a minute I forgot all about the tumbling, and only wanted to do as he did. Directly I got home I got two of the plates, and went into a back-room and began practising, making it turn round on the top of a stick. I broke nearly all the plates in the house doing this — that is, what I didn't break I cracked. I broke the entire set of a dozen plates, and yet couldn't do it. When mother found all her plates cracked, she said, ' It's that boy;' and I had a good hiding. Then I put on my Sunday suit and bolted away again. I always bolted in my best clothes. I then went about tumbling in the public-houses, till I had got money enough to have a tin plate made with a deep rim, and with this tin plate I learnt

it, so that I could afterwards do it with a crockery one. I kept on my tumbling till I got a set of wooden balls turned, and I stuck brass coffin-nails all over them, so that they looked like metal when they was up; and I began teaching myself to chuck them. It took a long time learning it, but I was fond of it, and determined to do it. I was doing pretty well with my tumbling, making perhaps my 3*s.* or 4*s.* a-night, so I was pretty well off. Then I got some tin knives made, and learnt to throw them: and I bought some iron rings, and bound them with red and blue tape, to make them look handsome; and I learnt to toss them the same as the balls. I practised balancing pipes, too. Every time I went into a public-house I'd take a pipe away, so it didn't cost me anything. I dare say I was a twelvemonth before I could juggle well. When I could throw the three balls middling tidy I used to do them on the stilts, and that was more than ever a man attempted in them days; and yet I was only sixteen or seventeen years of age. I must have been summut then, for I went to Oxford fair, and there I was on my stilts, chucking my balls in the public streets, and a gentleman came up to me and asked me if I'd take an engagement, and I said ' Yes, if it was a good un' — for I was taking money like smoke; and he agreed to give me a pound a-day during the fair; it was a week fair. I had so much money, I didn't know what to do with it. I actually went and bought a silk neckerchief for every day in the week, and flash boots, and caps, and everything I could see, for I never had so much money as in them days. The master, too, made his share out of me, for he took money like dirt.

" From Oxford I worked my way over to Ireland. I had got my hand into juggling now, but I kept on with my old apparatus, though I bought a new set in Dublin. I used to have a bag and bit of carpet, and perform in streets. I had an Indian's dress made, with a long horse-hair tail down my back, and white bag-trousers, trimmed with red, like a Turk's, tied right round at the ankles, and a flesh-coloured skull-cap. My coat was what is called a Turkish fly, in red velvet, cut off like a waistcoat, with a peak before and behind. I was a regular swell, and called myself the Indian Juggler. I used to perform in the barracks twice a-day, morning and evening. I used to make a heap of money. I have taken, in one pitch, more than a pound. I dare say I've taken 3*l.* a-day, and sometimes more indeed; I've saved a waggon and a booth there, — a very nice one, — and the waggon cost me 14*l.* second-hand; one of Vickry's it was, a wild-beast waggon. I dare say I was six months in Dublin, doing first-rate. My performances was just the same then as they is now; only I walked on stilts, and they was new then, and did the business. I was the first man ever seed in Ireland, either juggling or on the stilts.

"I had a drum and pipes, and I used to play them myself. I played any tune,—anythink, just what I could think of, to draw the crowd together; then I'd mount the stilts and do what I called ' a drunken frolic,' with a bottle in my hand, tumbling about and pretending to be drunk. Then I'd chuck the balls about, and the knives, and the rings, and twirl the plate. I wound up with the ball, throwing it in the air and catching it in a cup. I didn't do any balancing pipes on my nose, not whilst on the stilts.

"I used to go out one day on the stilts and one on the ground, to do the balancing. I'd balance pipes, straws, peacocks' feathers, and the twirling plate.

"It took me a long time learning to catch the ball in the cup. I practised in the fields or streets; anywhere. I began by just throwing the ball a yard or two in the air, and then went on gradually. The first I see do the ball was a man of the name of Dussang, who came over with Ramo Samee. It's a very dangerous feat, and even now I'm never safe of it, for the least wind will blow it to the outside, and spoil the aim. I broke my nose at Derby races. A boy ran across the ring, and the ball, which weighs a quarter of a pound, was coming right on him, and would have fallen on his head, and perhaps killed him, and I ran forward to save him, and couldn't take my aim proper, and it fell on my nose, and broke it. It bled awfully, and it kept on for near a month. There happened to be a doctor looking on, and he came and plastered it up; and then I chucked the ball up again, (for I didn't care what I did in them days), and the strain of its coming down made it burst out again. They actually gived me money not to throw the ball up any more. I got near a sovereign, in silver, give me from the Grand Stand, for that accident.

"At Newcastle I met with another accident with throwing the ball. It came down on my head, and it regularly stunned me, so that I fell down. It swelled up, and every minute got bigger, till I a'most thought I had a double head, for it felt so heavy I could scarce hold it up. I was obliged to knock off work for a fortnight.

"In Ireland I used to make the people laugh, to throw up raw potatoes and let them come down on my naked forehead and smash. People give more money when they laugh. No, it never hurt my forehead, it's got hardened; nor I never suffered from headaches when I was practicing.

"As you catch the ball in the cup, you are obliged to give, you know, and bend to it, or it would knock the brains out of you pretty well. I never heard of a man killing himself with the ball, and I've only had two accidents.

"I got married in Ireland, and then I started off with the booth and waggon, and she used to dance, and I'd juggle and balance. We went to the fairs, but it didn't answer, and

we lost all; for my wife turned out a very bad sort of woman. She's dead now, through drink. I went to the Isle of Man from Ireland; I had practised my wife in the stilts, and learnt her how to use them, and we did well there. They never see such a thing in their lives, and we took money like dirt. They christened us the ' Manx Giants.' If my wife had been like my present one, I should be a made gentleman by this time; but she drank away my booth, and waggon, and horse, and all.

"I saved up about 20l. in the Isle of Man; and from there we went to Scotland, and there my wife died,—through drink. That took away all the money I had saved. We didn't do much in Scotland, only in one particular town,—that's Edinburgh,— on New-year's day. We took a good deal of money, 2l. I think; and we carried coppers about in a stocking with me.

"I travelled about in England and Wales when I married my second wife. She's a strong woman, and lifts 700 lbs. by the hair of her head.

"When I got back to London I hadn't a shilling in my pocket, though my wife was very careful of me; but times got bad, and what not. We got a situation at 12s. a day, and all collections, at Stepney fair, which would sometimes come to a pound, and at others 30s.; for collections is better than salary any days: that set us up in a little house, which we've got now.

"I'm too old now to go out regularly in the streets. It tires me too much, if I have to appear at a penny theatre in the evening. When I do go out in the streets, I carry a mahogany box with me, to put my things out in. I've got three sets of things now, knives, balls, and cups. In fact, I never was so well off in apparatus as now; and many of them have been given to me as presents, by friends as have gi'n over performing. Knives, and balls, and all, are very handsome. The balls, some a pound, and some 2 lbs. weight, and the knives about 1½ lbs.

"When I'm out performing, I get into all the open places as I can. I goes up the Commercial-road and pitches at the Mile-end-gate, or about Tower-hill, or such-like. I'm well known in London, and the police knows me so well they very seldom interfere with me. Sometimes they say, ' That's not allowed, you know, old man!" and I say, ' I shan't be above two or three minutes,' and they say, ' Make haste, then!" and then I go on with the performance.

"I think I'm the cleverest juggler out. I can do the pagoda, or the canopy as some calls it; that is a thing like a parasol balanced by the handle on my nose, and the sides held up by other sticks, and then with a pea-shooter I blow away the supports. I also do what is called ' the birds and bush,' which is something of the same, only you knock off the birds with a pea-shooter. The birds is only made of cork, but it's very difficult, because you have to take your balance agin every bird as falls; besides, you must be careful the birds don't fall in your eyes, or it would take away your sight and spoil the balance. The birds at back are hardest to knock off, because you have to bend back, and at the same time mind you don't topple the tree off.

"These are the only feats we perform in balancing, and the juggling is the same now as ever it was, for there ain't been no improvements on the old style as I ever heerd on; and I suppose balls and knives and rings will last for a hundred years to come yet.

"I and my wife are now engaged at the 'Temple of Mystery' in Old Street-road, and it says on the bills that they are 'at present exhibiting the following new and interesting talent,' and then they calls me 'The Renowned Indian Juggler, performing his extraordinary Feats with Cups, Balls, Daggers, Plates, Knives, Rings, Balancing, &c. &c.'

"After the juggling I generally has to do conjuring. I does what they call 'the pile of mags,' that is, putting four halfpence on a boy's cap, and making them disappear when I say 'Presto, fly!' Then there's the empty cups, and making 'taters come under 'em, or there's bringing a cabbage into a empty hat. There's also making a shilling pass from a gentleman's hand into a nest of boxes, and such-like tricks: but it ain't half so hard as juggling, nor anything like the work.

"I and my missis have 5s. 6d. a-night between us, besides a collection among the company, which I reckon, on the average, to be as good as another pound a-week, for we made that the last week we performed.

"I should say there ain't above twenty jugglers in all England—indeed, I'm sure there ain't—such as goes about pitching in the streets and towns. I know there's only four others besides myself in London, unless some new one has sprung up very lately. You may safely reckon their earnings for the year round at a pound a-week, that is, if they stick to juggling; but most of us joins some other calling along with juggling, such as the wizard's business, and that helps out the gains.

"Before this year, I used to go down to the sea-side in the summer, and perform at the watering-places. A chap by the name of Gordon is at Ramsgate now. It pays well on the sands, for in two or three hours, according to the tides, we picks up enough for the day."

The Street Conjurer.

"I call myself a wizard as well; but that's only the polite term for conjurer; in fact, I should think that wizard meant an astrologer, and more of a fortune-teller. I was fifteen years of age when I first began my professional life; indeed I opened with Gentleman Cooke at the Rotunda, in Blackfriars'-road, and there I did Jeremiah Stitchem to his Billy Button.

"My father held a very excellent situation in the Customs, and lived at his ease, in very affluent circumstances. His library alone was worth two hundred pounds. I was only ten years of age when my father died. He was a very gay man, and spent his income to the last penny. He was a very gay man, very gay. After my mother was left a widow, the library was swept off for a year's rent. I was too young to understand it's value, and my mother was in too much grief to pay attention to her affairs. Another six-months' rent sold up the furniture. We took a small apartment close in the neighbourhood. My mother had no means, and we were left to shift for ourselves. I was a good boy, and determined to get something to do. The first day I went out I got a situation at four shillings a-week, to mind the boots outside a boot-maker's shop in Newington Causeway. The very first week I was there I was discharged, for I fell asleep on my stool at the door, and a boy stole a pair of boots. From there I went to a baker's, and had to carry out the bread, and for four years I got different employments, as errand boy or anything.

"For many years the mall opposite Bedlam was filled with nothing else but shows and show-people. All the caravans and swing-boats, and what not, used to assemble there till the next fair was on. They didn't perform there, it was only their resting-place. My mother was living close by, and every opportunity I had I used to associate with the boys belonging to the shows, and then I'd see them practising their tumbling and tricks. I was so fond of this that I got practising with these boys. I'd go and paint my face as clown, and although dressed in my ordinary clothes I'd go and tumble with the rest of the lads, until I could do it as well as they could. I did it for devilment, that's what I call it, and that it was which first made me think of being a professional.

"From there I heard of a situation to sell oranges, biscuits, and ginger-beer, at the Surrey Theatre. It was under Elliston's management. I sold the porter up in the gallery, and I had three-halfpence out of every shilling, and I could make one shilling and sixpence a-night; but the way I used to do it at that time was this: I went to fetch the beer, and then I'd get half-a-gallon of table-beer and mix it with the porter; and I tell you, I've made such a thing as fifteen shillings of a boxing-night. I alone could sell five gallons of a night; but then their pints at that time was tin measures, and little more than half-a-pint: besides, I'd froth it up. It was three-pence a pint, and a wonderful profit it must have been. From there I got behind the scenes as supernumerary, at the time Nelson Lee was manager of the supers.

"At this time the Rotunda in the Blackfriars'-road was an hotel kept by a Mr. Ford. Mr. Cook rented certain portions of the building, and went to a wonderful expense building a Circus there. The history of the Rotunda is that at one time it was a museum, and the lecture-hall is there to the present day. It's a beautiful building, and the pillars are said to be very valuable, and made of rice. It's all let to one party, a Frenchman, but he keeps the lecture-hall closed. When Cook took the Rotunda I asked him for an engagement, and he complied. I was mad for acting. I met with great success as Jeremiah Stitchem; and the first week he gave me one pound. Cook didn't make a good thing of it. Nobody could get their money, and the circus was closed. Then a Mr. Edwards took it. He was an optician, and opened it as a penny exhibition, with a magic lantern and a conjurer. Now comes how I became a conjurer. I couldn't tear myself away from the Rotunda. I went there and hovered about the door day and night. I wanted to get a situation there. He knew me when I was in the circus, and he asked me what I was a-doing of. I said, 'Nothing, sir.' Then he offered to give me one of the door-keeper's places, from ten in the morning till eleven at night, for three shillings a-day, and I took it. One day the conjurer that was there didn't come, but they opened the doors just the same, and there was an immense quantity of people waiting there. They couldn't do nothing without the conjurer. He always left his apparatus there of a night, in a bag. Well, this Edwards, knowing that I could do a few tricks, he came up to me and asks whether I knew where the wizard lived. I didn't, and Edwards says, 'What am I to do? I shall have to return this money: I shall go mad.' I said I could do a few tricks; and he says, 'Well, go and do it.' The people was making a row, stamping and calling out, 'Now then, is this here wizard coming?' When I went in, I give great satisfaction. I went and did all the tricks, just as the other had done it. At that time it was the custom to say after each performance, 'Ladies and gentlemen, allow me to inform you that I get no salary here, and only have to rely upon your generosity for a collection.' When the plate went round I got one shilling and sixpence. 'Hulloa!' I said to myself, 'is this the situation?' Then I sold some penny books, explaining how the tricks was done, and I got sixpence more. That was two shillings. I had four shillings a-day besides, and they would have sometimes twenty houses of a day, and I have seen thirty. The houses were not always very good. Sometimes we'd perform to seven or to twenty. It all told up. It was at night we did the principal work,—crowded upwards of two hundred there. We weren't in the Circus, but in the Rotunda. I'd make fifteen shillings a-night then. I got a permanent engagement then. I made too much

money. I went and bought a pack of cards and card-boxes, and a pea-caddy for passing peas from a handkerchief to a vase, and linking-rings, and some tape. That, with tying knots in a silk handkerchief, concluded the whole of my performances. In fact, it was all I knew. My talking helped me immensely, for I could patter well to them, and the other wizard couldn't.

"I left the Rotunda in consequence of the party having other novelties. He had Ambrosini, who done the sticks and string balls; but I was there three or four years, and that's a long time to be at one place. Then I joined a street-performer. He used to do the fire-proof business, such as eating the link, and the burning tow, and so on. Then I manufactured a portable table: it folded up, and I could carry it under my arm. It was as large as an ordinary dressing-table. We went in equal shares. I was dressed with ballet shirt, and braces, with spangled tights and fleshings. We pulled our coats off when we begun to perform. All the tricks we carried in a bag.

"The first pitch we made was near Bond-street. He began with his part of the performance whilst I was dressing up the table. It was covered with black velvet with fringe, and the apparatus ranged on it. After him I began my performance, and he went round for the nobbings. I did card tricks, such as the sautez-le-coup with the little finger. It's dividing the pack in half, and then bringing the bottom half to the top; and then, if there's a doubt, you can convey the top card to the bottom again; or if there's any doubt, you can bring the pack to its original position. It was Lord de Roos' trick. He won heaps of money at it. He had pricked cards. You see, if you prick a card at the corner, card-players skin their finger at the end, so as to make it sensitive, and they can tell a pricked card in a moment. Besides sautez-le-coup, I used to do innumerable others, such as telling a named card by throwing a pack in the air and catching the card on a sword point. Then there was telling people's thoughts by the cards. All card tricks are feats of great dexterity and quickness of hand. I never used a false pack of cards. There are some made for amateurs, but professionals never use trick cards. The greatest art is what is termed forcing, that is, making a party take the card you wish him to; and let him try ever so well, he will have it, though he's not conscious of it. Another feat of dexterity is slipping the card, that is, slipping it from top, bottom, or centre, or placing one or two cards from the top. If you're playing a game at all-fours and you know the ace of clubs is at the bottom, you can slip it one from the top, so that you know your partner opposite has it. These are the only two principal things in card tricks, and if you can do them dexteriously you can do a great part of a wizard's art. Sautez-le.

coup is the principal thing, and it's done by placing the middle finger in the centre of the pack, and then with the right hand working the change. I can do it with one hand.

"We did well with pitching in the streets. We'd take ten shillings of a morning, and then go out in the afternoon again and take perhaps fifteen shillings of nobbings. The footmen were our best customers in the morning, for they had leisure then. We usually went to the squares and such parts at the West-end. This was twenty years ago, and it isn't anything like so good now, in consequence of my partner dying of consumption; brought on, I think, by fire eating, for he was a very steady young fellow and not at all given to drink. I was for two years in the streets with the fire-eating, and we made I should say such a thing as fifty shillings a-week each. Then you must remember, we could have made more if we had liked; for some mornings, if we had had a good day before, we wouldn't go out if it was raining, or we had been up late. I next got a situation, and went to a wax-works to do conjuring. It was a penny exhibition in the New Cut, Lambeth. I had four shillings a-day and nobbings—a collection, and what with selling my books, it came to ten shillings a-day, for we had never less than ten and often twenty performances a-day. They had the first dissecting figure there — a Samson—and they took off the cranium and showed the brains, and also the stomach, and showed the intestines. It was the first ever shown in this country, and the maker of it had (so they say) a pension of one hundred pounds a year for having composed it. He was an Italian.

"We were burnt down at Birmingham, and I lost all my rattle-traps. However, the inhabitants made up a subscription which amply repaid me for my loss, and I then came to London, hearing that the Epsom races was on at the time, which I wouldn't have missed Epsom races, not at that time, not for any amount of money, for it was always good to one as three pounds, and I have had as much as seven pounds from one carriage alone. It was Lord Chesterfield's, and each gentleman in it gave us a sov. I went down with three acrobats to Epsom, but they were dealing unfair with me, and there was something that I didn't like going on; so I quarrelled with them and joined with another conjurer, and it was on this very occasion we got the seven pounds from one carriage. We both varied in our entertainments; because, when I had done my performance, he made a collection; and when he had done I got the nobbings. We went to Lord Chesterfield's carriage on the hill, and there I did the sovereign trick. 'My Lord, will you oblige me with the temporary loan of a sovereign?' 'Yes, old fellow: what are you going to do with it?' I then did passing the sovereign, he having marked it first; and then, though he held it tightly, I changed it for a farthing. I did this for Lord Waterford and Lord Waldegrave, and the whole of them in the carriage. I always said, 'Now, my Lord, are you sure you hold it?' 'Yes, old fellow.' 'Now, my Lord, if I was to take the sovereign away from you without you knowing it, wouldn't you say I was perfectly welcome to it?' He'd say, 'Yes, old fellow; go on.' Then, when he opened the handkerchief he had a farthing, and all of them made me a present of the sovereign I had performed with.

"Then we went to the Grand Stand, and then after our performance they'd throw us halfpence from above. We had our table nicely fitted up. We wouldn't take halfpence. We would collect up the coppers, perhaps five or six shillings worth, and then we'd throw the great handful among the boys. 'A bit of silver, your honours, if you please;' then sixpence would come, and then a shilling, and in ten minutes we would have a sovereign. We must have earned our six pounds each that Epsom Day; but then our expenses were heavy, for we paid three shillings a-night for our lodging alone.

"It was about this time that I took to busking. I never went into tap-rooms, only into parlours; because one parlour would be as good as a dozen tap-rooms, and two good parlours a-night I was quite satisfied with. My general method was this: If I saw a good company in the parlour, I could tell in a moment whether they were likely to suit me. If they were conversing on politics it was no good, you might as well attempt to fly. I have many a-time gone into a parlour, and called for my half-quartern of gin and little drop of cold water, and then, when I began my performances, it has been 'No, no! we don't want anything of that kind,' and there has been my half hour thrown away. The company I like best are jolly-looking men, who are sitting silently smoking, or reading the paper. I always got the privilege of performing by behaving with civility to my patrons. Some conjurers, when the company ain't agreeable, will say, 'But I will perform;' and then comes a quarrel, and the room is in future forbid to that man. But I, if they objected, always said, 'Very well, gentlemen, I'm much obliged to you all the same: perhaps another time. Bad to-night, better next night.' Then when I came again some would say, 'I didn't give you anything the other night, did I? Well, here's a fourpenny bit,' and so on.

"When I went into a parlour I usually performed with a big dice, three inches square. I used to go and call for a small drop of gin and water, and put this dice on the seat beside me, as a bit of a draw. Directly I put it down everybody was looking at it. Then I'd get into conversation with the party next to me, and he'd be sure to say, 'What the deuce is that?' I'd tell him it was a musical box, and he'd be safe to say, 'Well, I should like to hear it, very much.' Then I'd offer to perform, if agreeable, to the company; often the party would offer to name it to the company, and he'd call to the other side of the room, (for they all know each other in these parlours) 'I say, Mr. So-and-so, have you any objection to this gentleman showing us a little amusement?' and they are all of them safe to say, 'Not in the least. I'm perfectly agreeable if others are so;' and then I'd begin. I'd pull out my cards and card-boxes, and the bonus genius or the wooden doll, and then I'd spread a nice clean cloth (which I always carried with me) on the table, and then I'd go to work. I worked the dice by placing it on the top of a hat, and with a penknife pretending to make an incision in the crown to let the solid block pass through. It is done by having a tin covering to the solid dice, and the art consists in getting the solid block into the hat without being seen. That's the whole of the trick. I begin by striking the block to show it is solid. Then I place two hats one on the other, brim to brim. Then I slip the solid dice into the under hat, and place the tin covering on the crown of the upper one. Then I ask for a knife, and pretend to cut the hat-crown the size of the tin-can on the top, making a noise by dragging my nail along the hat, which closely resembles cutting with a knife. I've often heard people say, 'None of that!' thinking I was cutting their hat. Then I say, 'Now, gentlemen, if I can pass this dice through the crown into the hat beneath, you'll say it's a very clever deception,' because all conjurers acknowledge that they deceive; indeed, I always say when I perform in parlours, 'If you can detect me in my deceptions I shall be very much obliged to you by naming it, for it will make me more careful; but if you can't, the more credit to me.' Then I place another tin-box over the imitation dice; it fits closely. I say, 'Presto—quick—begone!' and clap my hands three times, and then lift up the tin-cases, which are both coloured black inside, and tumble the wooden dice out of the under hat. You see, the whole art consists in passing the solid block unseen into the hat.

"The old method of giving the order for the things to pass was this: 'Albri kira mumma tousha cocus co shiver de freek from the margin under the crippling hook,' and that's a language."

STATEMENT OF ANOTHER STREET CONJURER.

"In London I had a great quantity of parlours where I was known and allowed to perform. One night I'd take the West-end, and another the East-end. Sometimes I have done four or five houses of an evening, and I have had to walk miles for that—to Woolwich and back for instance, or to Edmonton and back—and occasionally I'd only come home with 1s. 6d. I have also had 8s. from one parlour only, and then I'd consider that a night's performance, and come home again.

"I remember one very peculiar circumstance which happened to me whilst I was out busking. There is a house at the bottom of York-street, Westminster, where they wouldn't allow any other conjurer but me. I was very friendly with the landlord, and I went there regularly every week, and I'd invariably take such a thing as 2s. or 3s. out of the room. If I found only a small muster in the parlour, I'd say, 'I'll come another evening,' and go off to another parlour in Pimlico. One night the company in the parlour said, after I had been performing, 'What a pity it is that one of your talent doesn't take a large room somewhere, and we'd patronise you.' 'Why,' says the landlord, 'he can have my large room up-stairs if he likes.' I agreed to it, and says, 'Well, gentlemen, we'll have it next Wednesday evening, if you think proper.' The landlord didn't tell his wife that there was a performance to take place on the Wednesday evening. When I went to this house to the appointment, there were about thirty assembled. The landlord was out. When we asked the landlady for the room, she wouldn't, and we had all the difficulty in the world before we got the apartment. I wanted a large table-cloth to dress up my stand, for I have, in order to perform some of my tricks, to make a bag with the end of the table-cloth to drop things into. We sent the waiter to ask for this cloth, and says she, 'I ain't going to lend no conjurers table-cloths.' Then a gentleman says, 'Oh, nonsense, I'll soon get you a table-cloth. She'll lend me one in a minute.' He goes to the bar, but the reply she made was, 'I'm surprised at Mr. W. having such a performance up there, and no table-cloth shall you have from me.' He came up-stairs, and said he had been grossly insulted at the bar; and then another gentleman said, 'Well, this young man shan't be disappointed, and we'll see if we can't find another house down the street, and move it to there, and we'll all go.' One went out, and came back and said he'd not only got a very large room and everything required, but the landlord had four friends in the bar who'd join our company. I made altogether about 1l. that night, for I made no charge, and it was altogether contribution. None of that company ever returned to that house again, so he lost the whole of his parlour customers. I could never go into that house again, and I really was sorry for the landlord, for it wasn't his fault. This is a very good proof that it is to the advantage of landlords to allow respectable performers to visit their parlours.

"At others times I have sometimes gone into a parlour and found the customers talking politics. If it was a very good company, and I saw good business, I'd try to break the thread of the discussion by saying when there was a pause in the debate, 'Gentlemen, would you like to see some of my performances, such as walking round the ceiling with my head down?' Then they'd say, 'Well, that's very curious; let's see you.' Of course I couldn't do this, and I only said it to attract notice. Then I'd do my card-tricks, and make a collection, and, after that, remark that as the ceiling-walking performance was a dangerous one, I must have a sovereign; of course they wouldn't give this, and I'd take my leave.

"One night, in Oxford-street, I met a singer, and he says, 'Where are you going?' I told him I was hunting for a good parlour, and he told me he had just left a good company at such and such a house. I thanked him, and I went there. It was up a long passage, and I entered the room without asking the landlord's permission, and I called for a glass of porter. As soon as I saw the waiter out of the room I made my appeal to the company. They were all of them agreeable and most happy to see my performances. After I'd done my performance I went to make a collection, and they said, 'Oh, certainly not; we thought you'd done it for your own amusement; we never give anything to anybody. I lost one hour of the best time of the night. I said, 'Very good, gentlemen, I'm satisfied if you are.' It was an agreed plan with the landlord, for he came into the room; and he says, 'What, another one!' and he seized me by the neck and pushed me out. As soon as I got outside I met another conjurer, and he asked where I'd been. I thought I'd let him be served the same as I was, so I showed him the house, and told him he could make a second 'nobbings' as we term it. I stopped outside peeping over the glass, and presently I see him being pushed out by the landlord as I had been. We had a hearty laugh, and then we started off to Regent-street, to one of our principal houses, but there wasn't a soul in the room. It was a house in a back-street, where none but grooms and footmen resort to. But we was determined to have some money that night, as both our families wanted it—both him and me did.

"Passing a tobacconist's shop in Regent-street, we saw three gents conversing with the lady behind the counter. I told him I'll go in, get a pickwick here, and see if I can't have a performance in the front of this counter. These things only wants an introduction; so I looks at my pickwick, and says I, 'This a pickwick? why I swallows such as these;' and I apparently swallowed it. One of them says, 'You don't mean to say you swallowed it?' 'Certainly I did, sir,' I replied; and then he makes me do it again. Then I told them I'd show them something more wonderful still, so I said, 'Have you gentlemen such a thing as a couple of half-crowns about you?' they gave me the money, and I did the trick of passing the money from hand to hand. I said to them, 'Can you tell me which hand the money's in?' says he, 'Why, anybody can see it's in that one.' 'No, sir,' says I, 'I think not.' 'If it

ain't,' says he, 'you may keep 'em.' Then I opened both hands, and they were in neither, and he asked where they was then; so I told him I'd given him them back again, which of course he denied, and appeared much surprised. Then I took 'em out of his cravat. It's a very clever trick, and appears most surprising, though it's as simple as possible, and all done by the way in which you take them out of the cravat; for you keep them palmed, and have to work 'em up into the folds. Of course I returned the half-crowns to him, but when I heard him say you may keep them I did feel comfortable, for that was something to the good. My friend outside was looking through the window, and I could see him rubbing his hands with glee; I got another half-crown out of them gentlemen before I'd done with them, for I showed 'em a trick with some walking-sticks which were lying on the counter, and also cut the tape in two and made it whole again, and such-like performances. When a fellow is on his beam-ends, as I was then, he must keep his eyes about him, and have impudence enough for anything, or else he may stop and starve. The great art is to be able to do tricks with anything that you can easily get hold of. If you take up a bit of string from a counter, or borrow a couple of shillings of a gentleman, your tricks with them startles him much more than if you had taken them out of your own pocket, for he sees there's been no preparation. I got ten shillings out of these two gents I spoke of, and then I and my mate went and busked in a parlour, and got fivepence more; so that we shared five and twopence-ha'penny each.

"I have often made a good deal of money in parlours by showing how I did my little tricks, such as cutting the tape and passing the half-crowns. Another thing that people always want to know is the thimble-rig trick. Of course it doesn't matter so much showing how these tricks are done, because they depend upon the quickness and dexterity of handling. You may know how an artist paints a picture, but you mayn't be able to paint one yourself.

"I never practised thimble-rigging myself, for I never approved of it as a practice. I've known lots of fellows who lived by it. Bless you! they did well, never sharing less than their 4*l.* or 5*l.* every day they worked. This is the way it's done. They have three thimbles, and they put a pea under two of 'em, so that there's only one without the pea. The man then begins moving them about and saying, 'Out of this one into that one,' and so on, and winds up by offering to 'lay anything, from a shilling to a pound,' that nobody can tell which thimble the pea is under. Then he turns round to the crowd, and pretends to be pushing them back, and whilst he's saying, 'Come, gentlemen, stand more backwarder,' one of the confederates, who is called 'a button,' lifts up one of the thimbles with a pea under it, and laughs to those around, as much as to say,

'We've found it out.' He shows the pea two or three times, and the last time he does so, he removes it, either by taking it up under his forefinger nail or between his thumb and finger. It wants a great deal of practice to do this nicely, so as not to be found out. When the man turns to the table again the button says, 'I'll bet you a couple of sovereigns I know where the pea is. Will any gentleman go me halves?' Then, if there's any hesitation, the man at the table will pretend to be nervous and offer to move the thimbles again, but the button will seize him by the arm, and shout as if he was in a passion, 'No, no, none of that! It was a fair bet, and you shan't touch 'em.' He'll then again ask if anybody will go him halves, and there's usually somebody flat enough to join him. Then the stranger is asked to lift up the thimble, so that he shouldn't suspect anything, and of course there's no pea there. He is naturally staggered a bit, and another confederate standing by will say calmly, 'I knew you was wrong; here's the pea;' and he lifts up the thimble with the second pea under it. If nobody will go shares in the 'button's' bet, then he lifts up the thimble and replaces the pea as he does so, and of course wins the stake, and he takes good care to say as he pockets the sovereign, 'I knew it was there; what a fool you was not to stand in.' The second time they repeat the trick there's sure to be somebody lose his money. There used to be a regular pitch for thimble-riggers opposite Bedlam, when the shows used to put up there. I saw a brewer's collector lose 7*l.* there in less than half-an-hour. He had a bag full of gold, and they let him win the three first bets as a draw. Most of these confederates are fighting-men, and if a row ensues they're sure to get the best of it.

"A very good place where I used to go busking was at Mother Emmerson's in Jermyn-street. There used to be all sorts of characters there, jugglers, and singers, and all sorts. It was a favourite house of the Marquis of Waterford, and he used to use it nearly every night. I've seen him buy a pipe of port, and draw tumblers of it for any body that came in, for his great delight was to make people drunk. He says to Mrs. Emmerson, 'How much do you want for that port, mother?' and then he wrote a cheque for the amount and had it tapped. He was a good-hearted fellow, was my Lord; if he played any tricks upon you, he'd always square it up. Many a time he's given me half-a-pint of brandy, saying, 'That's all you'll get from me.' Sometimes I'd say to him, 'Can I show you a few tricks, my Lord?' and then, when I'd finished, I knew he never gave money if you asked him for it, so I'd let him abuse me, and order me out of the house as a humbug; and then, just as I'd got to the door, he'd call me back and give me half-a-sovereign. I've seen him do some wonderful things. I've seen him jump into an old woman's crockeryware-basket, while she was carrying it along, and smash everything. Sometimes he'd get seven or eight cabs and put a lot of fiddlers and other musicians on the roofs, and fill 'em with anybody that liked, and then go off in procession round the streets, he driving the first cab as fast as he could and the bands playing as loud as possible. It's wonderful the games he'd be up to. But he always paid handsomely for whatever damage he did. If he swept all the glasses off a counter, there was the money to make 'em good again. Whenever I did any tricks before him, I took good care not to produce any apparatus that I cared for, or he'd be sure to smash it.

" One night I hadn't a penny in the world, and at home I knew they wanted food; so I went out to busk, and I got over in the Old Kent-road, and went to a house there called the Green Man. I walked into the parlour; and though I hadn't a penny in my pocket, I called for four pen'orth of rum and water. I put my big dice down upon the table by the side of me, and begun sipping my rum, and I could see everybody looking at this dice, and at last, just as I expected, somebody asked what it was. So I says— 'Gentlemen, I get my living this way, and if you like, I shall be happy to show you a few of my deceptions for your entertainment.' They said, 'Certainly, young man, we are perfectly agreeable.' Ah! I thought to myself, thank heaven that's all right, for I owed for the rum and water you see, and if they'd refused, I don't know what I should have done. I pulled out my nice clean cloth and laid it upon the table, and to work I went. I had only done one or two tricks, when in comes the waiter, and directly he sees me he cries out, 'We don't allow no conjurers or anything of that kind here,' and I had to pack up again. When he'd gone the company said, 'Go on, young man, it's all right now;' so I out with my cloth again; then in came the landlord, and says he, 'You've already been told we don't allow none of you conjurer fellows here,' and I had to put up a second time. When he'd gone, the gents told me to begin again. I had scarcely spread my cloth when in comes the landlord again, in a towering rage, and shouts out, 'What, at it again! Now you be off;' so I said, 'I only did it to oblige the company present, who were agreeable, and that I hadn't yet finished my rum and water, which wasn't paid for.' 'Not paid for?' says he; 'No,' says I: 'but I'm waiting here for a friend, and he'll pay for it.' You may imagine my feelings, without a penny in my pocket. 'Don't let me catch you at it again, or I'll give you in charge,' says he. Scarcely had he left again when the company began talking about it, and saying it was too bad to stop me; so one of them rings the bell, and when the landlord comes in he says, 'Mr. Landlord, this young person has been very civil, and conducted himself in a highly respectable manner, and has certainly afforded us a great deal of amusement; now why should you object to his showing us some tricks?' 'Thank heavens,' thought I to myself, 'I'm saved, and the rum will be paid for. The landlord's manner altered all of a sudden, and says he, ' Oh, certainly, gentlemen! certainly! if it's your wish, I don't mind the young man's being here; though I make it a rule to keep my parlour select.' Then I set to work and did all my tricks comfortably, and I made a collection of 7s. 6d. Then I rang the bell like a lord, and I put down a shilling to pay for the rum and water, and saying, ' Gentlemen, I'm very much obliged to you for your patronage,' to which they replied, ' Not at all, young man,' I walked past the bar to leave. Then the landlord comes up to me and says, shaking his fist, and blue in the face with rage, ' If ever I catch you here again, you d—— rogue, I'll give you to a policeman.' So, without more ado, I walks round to the other door, and enters the parlour again and tells the company, and they had in the landlord and blowed him well up. This will just show you the risks we have to run when out busking for a living, and what courage is wanted to speculate upon chances.

" There are very few conjurers out busking now. I don't know above four; one of 'em has had the best chances in the world of getting on; but he's a very uneducated man, and that has stood in his way, though he's very clever, and pr'aps the best hand at the cups and balls of any man in England. For instance, once he was at a nobleman's party, giving his entertainment, and he says such a thing as this:—' You see, my lords and ladies, I have a tatur in this hand, and a tatur in that; now I shall pass 'em into this handkercher,' Of course the nobleman said to himself, ' Tatur! handkercher! why, who's this feller?' You may depend upon it he was never asked there any more; for every thing in a wizard's business depends upon graceful action, and his style of delivery, so that he may make himself agreeable to the company.

" When a conjurer's out busking, he may reckon upon making his 20s. a-week, taking the year round; pr'aps, some weeks, he won't take more than 12s. or 15s.; but then, at other times, he may get 6s. or 8s. in one parlour alone, and I have taken as much as 1l. by teaching gentlemen how to do the tricks I had been performing. I have sometimes walked my twenty miles a-day, and busked at every parlour I came to, (for I never enter tap-rooms,) and come home with only 1s. 6d. in my pocket. I have been to Edmonton and back and only earned 1s., and then, pr'aps, at eleven the same night, when I was nearly done up, and quite dispirited with my luck, I've turned into one of the parlours in town and earned my 6s. in less than an hour, where I'd been twelve only earning one."

THE STREET FIRE-KING, OR SALAMANDER.

THIS person came to me recommended by one of my street acquaintances as the " pluckiest fire-eater going," and that as he was a little " down at heel," he should be happy for a consideration to give me any information I might require in the " Salamander line."

He was a tall, gaunt man, with an absent-looking face, and so pale that his dark eyes looked positively wild.

I could not help thinking, as I looked at his bony form, that fire was not the most nutritious food in the world, until the poor fellow explained to me that he had not broken his fast for two days.

He gave the following account of himself:—

" My father was a barber—a three-ha'penny one—and doing a good business, in Southwark. I used to assist him, lathering up the chins and shaving 'em—torturing, I called it. I was a very good light hand. You see, you tell a good shaver by the way he holds the razor, and the play from the wrist. All our customers were tradesmen and workmen, but father would never shave either coalheavers or fishermen, because they always threw down a penny, and said there was plenty of penny barbers, and they wouldn't give no more. The old man always stuck up for his price to the day of his death. There was a person set up close to him for a penny, and that injured us awful. I was educated at St. George's National and Parochial School, and I was a national lad, and wore my own clothes; but the parochials wore the uniform of blue bob-tailed coats, and a badge on the left side. When they wanted to make an appearance in the gallery of the church on charity-sermon days, they used to make all the nationals dress like the parochials, so as to swell the numbers up. I was too fond of entertainments to stick to learning, and I used to step it. Kennington common was my principal place. I used, too, to go to the outside of the Queen's-bench and pick up the racket-balls as they was chucked over, and then sell them for three-ha'pence each. I got promoted from the outside to the inside; for, from being always about, they took me at threepence a-day, and gave me a bag of whitening to whiten the racket-balls. When I used to hop the wag from school I went there, which was three times a-week, which was the reg'lar racket-days. I used to spend my threepence in damaged fruit—have a pen'orth of damaged grapes or plums—or have a ha'porth of wafers from the confectioner's. Ah, I've eat thousands and thousands of ha'porths. It's a kind of a paste, but they stick like wafers—my father's stuck a letter many a time with 'em. They goes at the bottom of the russetfees cake—ah, ratafees is the word.

" I got so unruly, and didn't attend to school, so I was turned out, and then I went to help father and assist upon the customers. I was confined so in the shop, that I only stopped there three months, and then I run away. Then I had no home to go to, but I found a empty cart, situated in Red-cross-street, near the Borough-market, and there I slept for five nights. Then Greenwich fair came on. I went round the fair, and got assisting a artist as was a likeness-cutter, and had a booth, making black profiles. I assisted this man in building his booth, and he took a great fancy to me, and kept me as one of his own. He was a shoemaker as well, and did that when fair was over. I used to fetch his bristles and leather, and nuss the child. He lived near the Kent-road; and one day as I was going out for the leather, I fell upon mother, and she solaced me, and took me home; and then she rigged me out, and kept me, till I run away again; and that was when Greenwich fair came on again, for I wanted to go back then. At the fair I got to be doorsman and grease-pot boy inside a exhibition, to let the people out and keep the lamps. I got a shilling a-day for my attendance during fair time, and I travelled with them parties for five months. That was Peterson's, the travelling comedian, or what we call a 'mumming concern.' When we got to Bexley, I thought I should like to see a piece called 'Tricks and Trials,' then being performed at the Surrey Theatre, so I cut away and come up to London again. There I got employment at a japanner, boiling up the stuff. I made a little bit of an appearance, and then I went home. I had learnt three or four comic songs, and I used to go singing at consart-rooms. I was a reg'lar professional. I went a busking at the free consart-rooms, and then go round with the cap. I principally sing 'The Four-and-nine,' or 'The Dark Arches,' or 'The Ship's Carpenter,' and 'The Goose Club.'

"It was at one of these free consart-rooms that I first saw a chap fire-eating. You see, at a free consart-room the professionals ain't paid, no more do the audience to come in, but the performers are allowed to go round with a cap for their remuneration. They are the same as the cock-and-hen clubs. This fire-eater was of the name of West, and I know'd him afore, and he used to ask me to prepare the things for him. His performance was, he had a link a-light in his hand, and he used to take pieces off with a fork and eat it. Then he would get a plate with some sulphur, light it, place it under his nose, and inhale the fumes that rose from it; and then he used to eat it with a fork whilst a-light. After that he'd get a small portion of gunpowder, put it in the palm of his hand, and get a fusee to answer for a quick-match, to explode the powder, and that concluded the performance —only three tricks. I was stunned the first time I see him do it; but when I come to prepare the things for him, I got enlightened into the business. When his back was turned, I used to sniff at the sulphur on the sly. I found it rather hard, for the fumes used to get up your head, and reg'lar confuse you, and lose your memory. I kept on the singing at consarts, but I practised the fire-eating at home. I tried it for the matter of two months, before I found the art of it. It used to make me very thick in my voice; and if I began it before breakfast it used to make you feel ill: but I generally began it after meals. I tried the link and sulphur till I got perfect in these two. It blistered my mouth swallowing the fire, but I never burnt myself seriously at it.

"After I learnt those, I got travelling again with a man that swallowed a poker, of the name of Yates. One of his tricks was with tow. He'd get some, and then get a fryingpan, and he'd put the tow in the fire-pan, and he'd get some ground rosin and brimstone together and put them on top of the tow in the pan. Then, when he'd set light to it, he used to bring it on the outside of the show and eat it with a knife and fork, while I held the pan. I learnt how to do the trick; this was when he had done with it, and I'd take it away. Then I used to eat the portion that was left in the pan, till I became the master of that feat.

"When I left Yates I practised again at home until I was perfect, and then I went about doing the performance myself. The first place that I attempted was at the Fox and Cock, Gray's-inn-lane, and I was engaged there at three shillings a-night, and with collections of what people used to throw to me I'd come away with about seven shillings and sixpence. I was very successful indeed, and I stopped there for about seven months, doing the fire-business; and I got another job at the same place, for one of the potmen turned dishonest, and the master gave me eight shillings a-week to do his work as well. I have continued ever since going to different concert-rooms, and giving my performances. My general demand for a night's engagement is four shillings and six pen'orth of refreshment. When I perform I usually have a decanter of ale and two glasses upon the table, and after every trick I sit down whilst an overture is being done and wash my mouth out, for it gets very hot. You're obliged to pause a little, for after tasting one thing, if the palate doesn't recover, you can't tell when the smoke is coming.

"I wore a regular dress, a kind of scale-armour costume, with a red lion on the breast. I do up my moustache with cork, and rouge a bit. My tights is brown, with black enamel jack-boots. On my head I wears a king's coronet and a ringlet wig, bracelets on my wrists, and a red twill petticoat under the armour dress, where it opens on the limps.

"For my performances I begin with eating the lighted link, an ordinary one as purchased at oil-shops. There's no trick in it, only confidence. It won't burn you in the inside, but if the pitch falls on the outside, of course it will hurt you. If you hold your breath the moment the lighted piece is put in your mouth, the flame goes out on the instant. Then we squench the flame with spittle. As we takes a bit of link in the mouth, we tucks it on one side of the cheek, as a monkey do with nuts in his pouch. After 1 have eaten sufficient fire I take hold of the link, and extinguish the lot by putting the burning end in my mouth. Sometimes, when I makes a slip, and don't put it in careful, it makes your moustache fiz up. I must also mind how I opens my mouth,'cos the tar sticks to the lip wherever it touches, and pains sadly. This sore on my hand is caused by the melted pitch dropping on my fingers, and the sores is liable to be bad for a week or eight days. I don't spit out my bits of link; I always swallow them. I never did spit 'em out, for they are very wholesome, and keeps you from having any sickness. Whilst I'm getting the next trick ready I chews them up and eats them. It tastes rather roughish, but not nasty when you're accustomed to it. It's only like having a mouthful of dust, and very wholesome.

" My next trick is with a piece of tow with a piece of tape rolled up in the interior. I begin to eat a portion of this tow—plain, not a-light —till I find a fitting opportunity to place the tape in the mouth. Then I pause for a time, and in the meantime I'm doing a little pantomime business—just like love business, serious—till I get the end of this tape between my teeth, and then I draws it out, supposed to be manufactured in the pit of the stomach. After that—which always goes immensely— I eat some more tow, and inside this tow there is what I call the fire-ball—that is, a lighted fusee bound round with tow and placed in the centre of the tow I'm eating—which I introduce at a fitting opportunity. Then I blows out with my breath, and that sends out smoke and fire. That there is a very hard trick, for it's according how this here fire-ball bustes. Sometimes it bustes on the side, and then it burns all the inside of the mouth, and the next morning you can take out pretty well the inside of your mouth with your finger; but if it bustes near the teeth, then it's all right, for there's vent for it. I also makes the smoke and flame—that is, sparks—come down my nose, the same as coming out of a blacksmith's chimney. It makes the eyes water, and there's a tingling; but it don't burn or make you giddy.

" My next trick is with the brimstone. I have a plate of lighted sulphur, and first inhale the fumes, and then devour it with a fork and swallow it. As a costermonger said when he saw me do it, ' I say, old boy, your game ain't all brandy.' There's a kind of a acid, nasty, sour taste in this feat, and at first it used to make me feel sick; but now I'm used to it, and it don't. When I puts it in my mouth it clings just like sealing-wax, and forms a kind of a dead ash. Of a morning, if I haven't got my breakfast by a certain time, there's a kind of a

retching in my stomach, and that's the only inconvenience I feel from swallowing the sulphur for that there feat.

" The next is, with two sticks of sealing-wax and the same plate. They are lit by the gas and dropped on one another till they are bodily a-light. Then I borrow either a ring of the company, or a pencil-case, or a seal. I set the sealing-wax a-light with a fork, and I press the impression of whatever article I can get with the tongue, and the seal is passed round to the company. Then I finish eating the burning wax. I always spits that out after, when no one's looking. The sealing-wax is all right if you get it into the interior of the mouth, but if it is stringy, and it falls, you can't get it off, without it takes away skin and all. It has a very pleasant taste, and I always prefer the red, as it's flavour is the best. Hold your breath and it goes out, but still the heat remains, and you can't get along with that so fast as the sulphur. I often burn myself, especially when I'm bothered in my entertainment; such as any person talking about me close by, then I listen to 'em perhaps, and I'm liable to burn myself. I haven't been able to perform for three weeks after some of my burnings. I never let any of the audience know anything of it, but smother up the pain, and go on with my other tricks.

" The other trick is a feat which I make known to the public as one of Ramo Samee's, which he used to perform in public-houses and tap-rooms, and made a deal of money out of. With the same plate and a piece of dry tow placed in it, I have a pepper-box, with ground rosin and sulphur together. I light the tow, and with a knife and fork I set down to it and eat it, and exclaim, ' This is my light supper.' There isn't no holding the breath so much in this trick as in the others, but you must get it into the mouth any how. It's like eating a hot beef-steak when you are ravenous. The rosin is apt to drop on the flesh and cause a long blister. You see, we have to eat it with the head up, full-faced; and really, without it's seen, nobody would believe what I do.

" There's another feat, of exploding the gunpowder. There's two ways of exploding it. This is my way of doing it, though I only does it for my own benefits and on grand occasions, for it's very dangerous indeed to the frame, for it's sure to destroy the hair of the head; or if anything smothers it, it's liable to shatter a thumb or a limb.

" I have a man to wait on me for this trick, and he unloops my dress and takes it off, leaving the bare back and arms. Then I gets a quarter of a pound of powder, and I has an ounce put on the back part of the neck, in the hollow, and I holds out each arm with an orange in the palm of each hand, with a train along the arms, leading up to the neck. Then I turns my back to the audience, and my man fires the gunpowder, and it blew up in a minute, and ran down the train and blew up that in my hands. I've been pretty lucky with this trick, for it's only been when the powder's got under my bracelets, and then it hurts me. I'm obliged to hold the hand up, for if it hangs down it hurts awful. It looks like a scurvy, and as the new skin forms, the old one falls off.

"That's the whole of my general performance for concert business, when I go busking at free concerts or outside of shows (I generally gets a crown a-day at fairs). I never do the gunpowder, but only the tow and the link.

"I have been engaged at the Flora Gardens, and at St. Helena Gardens, Rotherhithe, and then I was Signor Salamander, the great fire-king from the East-end theatres. At the Eel-pie-house, Peckham, I did the 'terrific flight through the air,' coming down a wire surrounded by fire-works. I was called Herr Alma, the flying fiend. There was four scaffold-poles placed at the top of the house to form a tower, just large enough for me to lie down on my belly, for the swivels on the rope to be screwed into the cradle round my body. A wire is the best, but they had a rope. On this cradle were places for the fireworks to be put in it. I had a helmet of fire on my head, and the three spark cases (they are made with steel-filings, and throw out sparks) made of Prince of Wales feathers. I had a sceptre in my hand of two serpents, and in their open mouths they put fire-balls, and they looked as if they was spitting fiery venom. I had wings, too, formed from the ankle to the waist. They was netting, and spangled, and well sized to throw off the fire. I only did this two nights, and I had ten shillings each performance. It's a momentary feeling coming down, a kind of suffocation like, so that you must hold your breath. I had two men to cast me off. There was a gong first of all, knocked to attract the attention, and then I made my appearance. First, a painted pigeon, made of lead, is sent down the wire as a pilot. It has moveable wings. Then all the fire-works are lighted up, and I come down right through the thickest of 'em. There's a trap-door set in the scene at the end, and two men is there to look after it. As soon as I have passed it, the men shut it, and I dart up against a feather-bed. The speed I come down at regularly jams me up against it, but you see I throw away this sceptre and save myself with my hands a little. I feel fagged for want of breath. It seems like a sudden fright, you know. I sit down for a few minutes, and then I'm all right.

"I'm never afraid of fire. There was a turner's place that took fire, and I saved that house from being burned. He was a friend of mine, the turner was, and when I was there, the wife thought she heard the children crying, and asked me to go up and see what it was. As I went up I could smell fire worse and worse, and when I got in the room it was full of smoke, and all the carpet, and bed-hangings, and curtains smouldering. I opened the window, and the fire burst out, so I ups with the carpet and throw'd it out of window, together with the blazing chairs, and I rolled the linen and drapery up and throw'd them out. I was as near suffocated as possible. I went and felt the bed, and there was two children near dead from the smoke; I brought them down, and a medical man was called, and he brought them round.

"I don't reckon no more than two other fire-kings in London beside myself. I only know of two, and I should be sure to hear of 'em if there were more. But they can only do three of the tricks, and I've got novelties enough to act for a fortnight, with fresh performances every evening. There's a party in Drury-lane is willing to back me for five, fifteen, or twenty pounds, against anybody that will come and answer to it, to perform with any other man for cleanness and cleverness, and to show more variety of performance.

"I'm always at fire-eating. That's how I entirely get my living, and I perform five nights out of the six. Thursday night is the only night, as I may say, I'm idle. Thursday night everybody's fagged, that's the saying—Got no money. Friday, there's many large firms pays their men on, especially in Bermondsey.

"I'm out of an engagement now, and I don't make more than eleven shillings a-week, because I'm busking; but when I'm in an engagement my money stands me about thirty-five shillings a-week, putting down the value of the drink as well—that is, what's allowed for refreshment. Summer is the worst time for me, 'cos people goes to the gardens. In the winter season I'm always engaged three months out of the six. You might say, if you counts the overplus at one time, and minus at other time, that I makes a pound a-week. I know what it is to go to the treasury on a Saturday, and get my thirty shillings, and I know what it is to have the landlord come with his ' Hallo! hallo! here's three weeks due, and another week running on.'

"I was very hard up at one time—when I was living in Friar-street—and I used to frequent a house kept by a betting-man, near the St. George's Surrey Riding-school. A man I knew used to supply this betting-man with rats. I was at this public-house one night when this rat-man comes up to me, and says he, ' Hallo! my pippin; here, I want you: I want to make a match. Will you kill thirty rats against my dog?' So I said, ' Let me see the dog first;' and I looked at his mouth, and he was an old dog; so I says, ' No, I won't go in for thirty; but I don't mind trying at twenty.' He wanted to make it twenty-four, but I wouldn't. They put the twenty in the rat-pit, and the dog went in first and killed his, and he took a quarter of an hour and two minutes. Then a fresh lot were put in the pit, and I began; my hands were tied behind me. They always make an allowance for a man, so the pit was made closer, for you see a man can't turn round like a dog; I had half the space of the dog. The rats lay in a cluster, and then I picked them off where I wanted 'em, and bit 'em between the shoulders. It was when they came to one or two that I had the work, for they cut about. The last one made me remember him, for he gave me a bite, of which I've got the scar now. It festered, and I was obliged to have it cut out. I took Dutch drops for it, and poulticed it by day, and I was bad for three weeks. They made a subscription in the room of fifteen shillings for killing these rats. I won the match, and beat the dog by four minutes. The wager was five shillings, which I had. I was at the time so hard up, I'd do anything for some money; though, as far as that's concerned, I'd go into a pit now, if anybody would make it worth my while."

THE SNAKE, SWORD, AND KNIFE-SWALLOWER.

HE was quite a young man, and, judging from his countenance, there was nothing that could account for his having taken up so strange a method of gaining his livelihood as that of swallowing snakes.

He was very simple in his talk and manner. He readily confessed that the idea did not originate with him, and prided himself only on being the second to take it up. There is no doubt that it was from his being startled by the strangeness and daringness of the act that he was induced to make the essay. He said he saw nothing disgusting in it; that people liked it; that it served him well in his "professional" engagements; and spoke of the snake in general as a reptile capable of affection, not unpleasant to the eye, and very cleanly in its habits.

"I swallow snakes, swords, and knives; but, of course, when I'm engaged at a penny theatre I'm expected to do more than this, for it would only take a quarter of an hour, and that isn't long enough for them. They call me in the perfession a 'Sallementro,' and that is what I term myself; though p'raps it's easier to say I'm a 'swallower.'

"It was a mate of mine that I was with that first put me up to sword-and-snake swallowing. I copied off him, and it took me about three months to learn it. I began with a sword first—of course not a sharp sword, but one blunt-pointed—and I didn't exactly know how to do it, for there's a trick in it. I see him, and I said, 'Oh, I shall set up master for myself, and practise until I can do it.'

"At first it turned me, putting it down my throat past my swallow, right down—about

eighteen inches. It made my swallow sore—very sore, and I used lemon and sugar to cure it. It was tight at first, and I kept pushing it down further and further. There's one thing, you mustn't cough, and until you're used to it you want to very bad, and then you must pull it up again. My sword was about three-quarters of an inch wide.

"At first I didn't know the trick of doing it, but I found it out this way. You see the trick is, you must oil the sword—the best sweet oil, worth fourteen pence a pint—and you put it on with a sponge. Then, you understand, if the sword scratches the swallow it don't make it sore, 'cos the oil heals it up again. When first I put the sword down, before I oiled it, it used to come up quite slimy, but after the oil it slips down quite easy, is as clean when it comes up as before it went down.

"As I told you, we are called at concert-rooms where I perform the 'Sallementro.' I think it's French, but I don't know what it is exactly; but that's what I'm called amongst us.

"The knives are easier to do than the sword because they are shorter. We puts them right down till the handle rests on the mouth. The sword is about eighteen inches long, and the knives about eight inches in the blade. People run away with the idea that you slip the blades down your breast, but I always hold mine right up with the neck bare, and they see it go into the mouth atween the teeth. They also fancy it hurts you; but it don't, or what a fool I should be to do it. I don't mean to say it don't hurt you at first, 'cos it do, for my swallow was very bad, and I couldn't eat anything but liquids for two months whilst I was learning. I cured my swallow whilst I was stretching it with lemon and sugar.

"I was the second one that ever swallowed a snake. I was about seventeen or eighteen years old when I learnt it. The first was Clarke as did it. He done very well with it, but he wasn't out no more than two years before me, so he wasn't known much. In the country there is some places where, when you do it, they swear you are the devil, and won't have it nohow.

"The snakes I use are about eighteen inches long, and you must first cut the stingers out, 'cos it might hurt you. I always keep two or three by me for my performances. I keep them warm, but the winter kills 'em. I give them nothing to eat but worms or gentles. I generally keep them in flannel, or hay, in a box. I've three at home now.

"When first I began swallowing snakes they tasted queer like. They draw'd the roof of the mouth a bit. It's a roughish taste. The scales rough you a bit when you draw them up. You see, a snake will go into ever such a little hole, and they are smooth one way.

"The head of the snake goes about an inch and a half down the throat, and the rest of it continues in the mouth, curled round like. I hold him by the tail, and when I pinch it he goes right in. You must cut the stinger out or he'll injure you. The tail is slippery, but you nip it with the nails like pinchers. If you was to let him go, he'd go right down; but most snakes will stop at two inches down the swallow, and then they bind like a ball in the mouth.

"I in generally get my snakes by giving little boys ha'pence to go and catch 'em in the woods. I get them when I'm pitching in the country. I'll get as many as I can get, and bring 'em up to London for my engagements.

"When first caught the snake is slimy, and I have to clean him by scraping him off with the finger-nail as clean as I can, and then wiping him with a cloth, and then with another, until he's nice and clean. I have put 'em down slimy, on purpose to taste what it was like. It had a nasty taste with it—very nasty.

"I give a man a shilling always to cut the stinger out—one that knows all about it, for the stinger is under the tongue. It was this Clark I first see swallow a snake. He swallowed it as it was when he caught it, slimy. He said it was nasty. Then he scraped it with his nail and let it crawl atween his hands, cleaning itself. When once they are cleaned of the slime they have no taste. Upon my word they are clean things, a'most like metal. They only lives on worms, and that ain't so nasty; besides, they never makes no mess in the box, only frothing in the mouth at morning and evening: but I don't know what comes from 'em, for I ain't a doctor.

"When I exhibit, I first holds the snake up in the air and pinches the tail, to make it curl about and twist round my arm, to show that he is alive. Then I holds it above my mouth, and as soon as he sees the hole in he goes. He goes wavy-like, as a ship goes,—that's the comparison. You see, a snake will go in at any hole. I always hold my breath whilst his head is in my swallow. When he moves in the swallow, it tickles a little, but it don't make you want to retch. In my opinion he is more glad to come up than to go down, for it seems to be too hot for him. I keep him down about two minutes. If I breathe or cough, he draws out and curls back again. I think there's artfulness in some of them big snakes, for they seem to know which is the master. I was at Wombwell's menagerie of wild beasts for three months, and I had the care of a big snake, as thick round as my arm. I wouldn't attempt to put that one down my throat, I can tell you, for I think I might easier have gone down his'n. I had to show it to the people in front of the carriages to draw 'em in, at fair time. I used to hold it up in both hands, with my arms in the air. Many a time it curled itself three or four times round my neck and about my body, and it never even so much as squeeged me the least bit. I had the feeding on it, and I used to

give it the largest worms I could find. Mr. Wombwell has often said to me, 'It's a dangerous game you're after, and if you don't give the snake plenty of worms and make it like you, it'll nip you some of these times.' I'm sure the snake know'd me. I was very partial to it, too. It was a furren snake, over spots, called a boa-constructor. It never injured me, though I'm told it is uncommon powerful, and can squeege a man up like a sheet of paper, and crack his bones as easy as a lark's. I'm tremendous courageous, nothing frightens me; indeed, I don't know what it is to be afraid.

"The one I was speaking of I have often held up in the air in both hands, and it was more than four yards long, and let it curl round my neck in five or six twirls. It was a boa-constructor, and I believe it know'd me, and that's why it didn't hurt me, for I feed him. He had nothing but long great worms, and he grew to know me.

"My performance with the snake is always very successful. The women is frightened at first, but they always stop to see, and only hide their eyes. There's no danger as long as you keep hold.

"I generally perform at concert-rooms, and penny theatres, and cheap circuses, and all round the country, such as in the street, or at farm-houses, or in tap-rooms. I have done it in the streets of London too, and then I'm dressed-up in fleshing tights, skin dress, and trunks. I carry the snake in a box. When I swallow it some holloa out, 'O my God, don't do that!' but when I'm finished, they say, 'It's hardly wonderful to be believed,' and give money.

"I generally mix up the sword-and-snake performances with my other ones; and it's the same in the streets.

"Sometimes I go out to tap-rooms in my every-day dress, with the snake in my pocket, and a sword. Then I go and offer to show my performance. First I'll do some tumbling, and throw a somerset over a table. Then I takes out the snake and say, 'Gentlemen, I shall now swallow a live snake, anybody is at liberty to feel it.' I have—according to the company, you know—made such a thing as five shillings, or one shilling and sixpence, or whatever it may be, by snake-swallowing alone.

"I'm the only one in London who can swallow a snake. There's nobody else besides me. It requires great courage. I've great courage. One night I was sleeping in a barn at a public-house, called the Globe, at Lewes, seven miles from Brighton. A woman who had cut her throat used to haunt the place. Well, I saw her walking about in a long white shroud, the doors opening and shutting before her. A man who was in the room with us jumped up in his bed and cried, 'Tumblers!'"

"I must tell you one thing before you finish, just to prove what tremendous courage

STREET CONJURER PERFORMING.

CIRCUS CLOWN AT FAIR.

I've got. I was out showing the sword-and-snake swallowing in the country, and I travelled down to near Lewes, which is seven miles from Brighton, and there I put up at a house called the Falcon. We slept in a barn, and at night, when all was asleep except myself, I see a figure all in white come into the room with her throat cut, and her face as white as chalk. I knowed she was a apperition, 'cos I'd been told the house was haunted by such. Well, in she come, and she stopped and looked at me, seeing that I was awake. The perspiration poured out of me like a shower; but I warn't afeard, I've that courage. I says, 'God help me!' for I knew I'd done no harm as I could call to mind; so I hadn't no fear of ghosts and such-like spirits. No, I'm certain it wern't no fancy of mine, 'cos others see it as well as me. There was a mate in the same room, and he woke up and sees the ghosts, and up he jumps in bed and cries out: 'Tumblers! Tumblers! here's a woman haunting us!' I told him to lie down and go to sleep, and hold his noise. Then I got out of bed, and it wanished past me, close as could be,—as near as I am to this table. The door opened itself to let her out, and then closed again. I didn't feel the air cold like, nor nothing, nor was there any smell or anythink. I'm sure I wasn't dreaming, 'cos I knows pretty well when I'm awake. Besides the doors kept bouncing open, and then slamming-to again for more than an hour, and woke everybody in the room. This kept on till one o'clock. Yet, you see, though the sweat run down me to that degree I was wetted through, yet I had that courage I could get out of bed to see what the spirit was like. I said, 'God help me! for I've done no harm as I knows of,' and that give me courage."

Whilst the "Salamentro" told me this ghost story, he spoke it in a half voice, like that of a nervous believer in such things. When he had finished he seemed to have something on his mind, for after a moment's silence he said, in a confidential tone, "Between ourselves, sir, I'm a Jew." I then asked him if he thought the ghost was aware of it, and had visited him on that account, and the following was his reply: "Well, it ain't unlikely; for, you see, some of our scholars know what to say to the poor things, and they know what to do to rest 'em. Now, pr'aps she thought I knew these secrets,—but, I'm no scholard—for, you see, we Jews always carry prayers about with us to keep off evil spirits. That's one reason why I was so bold as to go up to her."

STREET CLOWN.

HE was a melancholy-looking man, with the sunken eyes and other characteristics of semi-starvation, whilst his face was scored with lines and wrinkles, telling of paint and premature age.

I saw him performing in the streets with a school of acrobats soon after I had been questioning him, and the readiness and business-like way with which he resumed his professional buffoonery was not a little remarkable. His story was more pathetic than comic, and proved that the life of a street clown is, perhaps, the most wretched of all existence. Jest as he may in the street, his life is literally no joke at home.

"I have been a clown for sixteen years," he said, "having lived totally by it for that time. I was left motherless at two years of age, and my father died when I was nine. He was a carman, and his master took me as a stable-boy, and I stayed with him until he failed in business. I was then left destitute again, and got employed as a supernumerary at Astley's, at one shilling a-night. I was a 'super' some time, and got an insight into theatrical life. I got acquainted, too, with singing people, and could sing a good song, and came out at last on my own account in the streets, in the Jim Crow line. My necessities forced me into a public line, which I am far from liking. I'd pull trucks at one shilling a-day, rather than get twelve shillings a-week at my business. I've tried to get out of the line. I've got a friend to advertise for me for any situation as groom. I've tried to get into the police, and I've tried other things, but somehow there seems an impossibility to get quit of the street business. Many times I have to play the clown, and indulge in all kinds of buffoonery, with a terrible heavy heart. I have travelled very much, too, but I never did over-well in the profession. At races I may have made ten shillings for two or three days, but that was only occasional; and what is ten shillings to keep a wife and family on, for a month maybe? I have three children, one now only eight weeks old. You can't imagine, sir, what a curse the street business often becomes, with its insults and starvations. The day before my wife was confined, I jumped and labour'd doing Jim Crow for twelve hours—in the wet, too—and earned one shilling and threepence; with this I returned to a home without a bit of coal, and with only half-a-quartern loaf in it. I know it was one shilling and threepence; for I keep a sort of log of my earnings and my expenses; you'll see on it what I've earn'd as clown, or the funnyman, with a party of acrobats, since the beginning of this year."

He showed me this log, as he called it, which was kept in small figures, on paper folded up as economically as possible. His latest weekly earnings were, 12s. 6d., 1s. 10d., 7s. 7d., 2s. 5d., 3s. 11½d., 7s. 7½d., 7s. 9½d., 6s. 4½d., 10s. 10½d., 9s. 7d., 6s. 1½d., 15s. 6¼d., 6s. 5d., 4s. 2d., 12s. 10¼d., 15s. 5½d., 14s. 4d. Against this was set off what the poor man had to expend for his dinner, &c., when out playing the clown, as he was away from home and could not dine with his family. The ciphers intimate the weeks when there was no such expense, or in other words, those which had been passed without dinner. 0, 0, 0, 0, 2*s.* 2½*d.*, 3*s.* 9¼*d.*, 4*s.* 2*d.*, 4*s.* 5*d.*, 5*s.* 8¼*d.*, 5*s.* 11¼*d.*, 4*s.* 10½*d.*, 2*s.* 8¾*d.*, 3*s.* 7¾*d.*, 3*s.* 4¼*d.*, 6*s.* 5¼*d.*, 4*s.* 6¾*d.*, 4*s.* 3*d.* This account shows an average of 8*s.* 6½*d.* a-week as the gross gain, whilst, if the expenses be deducted, not quite six shillings remain as the average weekly sum to be taken home to wife and family.

"I dare say," continued the man, "that no persons think more of their dignity than such as are in my way of life. I would rather starve than ask for parochial relief. Many a time I have gone to my labour without breaking my fast, and played clown until I could raise dinner. I have to make jokes as clown, and could fill a volume with all I knows."

He told me several of his jests; they were all of the most venerable kind, as for instance:—"A horse has ten legs: he has two fore legs and two hind ones. Two fores are eight, and two others are ten." The other jokes were equally puerile, as, "Why is the City of Rome," (he would have it Rome), "like a candle wick? Because it's in the midst of Greece." "Old and young are both of one age: your son at twenty is young, and your horse at twenty is old: and so old and young are the same." "The dress," he continued, "that I wear in the streets consists of red striped cotton stockings, with full trunks, dotted red and black. The body, which is dotted like the trunks, fits tight like a woman's gown, and has full sleeves and frills. The wig or scalp is made of horse-hair, which is sown on to a white cap, and is in the shape of a cock's comb. My face is painted with dry white lead. I grease my skin first and then dab the white paint on (flake-white is too dear for us street clowns); after that I colour my cheeks and mouth with vermilion. I never dress at home; we all dress at public-houses. In the street where I lodge, only a very few know what I do for a living. I and my wife both strive to keep the business a secret from our neighbours. My wife does a little washing when able, and often works eight hours for sixpence. I go out at eight in the morning and return at dark. My children hardly know what I do. They see my dresses lying about, but that is all. My eldest is a girl of thirteen. She has seen me dressed at Stepney fair, where she brought me my tea (I live near there); she laughs when she sees me in my clown's dress, and wants to stay with me: but I would rather see her lay dead before me (and I had two dead in my place at one time, last Whitsun Monday was a twelvemonth) than she should ever belong to my profession."

I could see the tears start from the man's eyes as he said this.

"Frequently when I am playing the fool in the streets, I feel very sad at heart. I can't help thinking of the bare cupboards at home; but what's that to the world? I've often and often been at home all day when it has been wet, with no food at all, either to give my children or take myself, and have gone out at night to the public-houses to sing a comic song or play the funnyman for a meal—you may imagine with what feelings for the part—and when I've come home I've call'd my children up from their beds to share the loaf I had brought back with me. I know three or more clowns as miserable and bad off as myself. The way in which our profession is ruined is by the stragglers or outsiders, who are often men who are good tradesmen. They take to the clown's business only at holiday or fair time, when there is a little money to be picked up at it, and after that they go back to their own trades; so that, you see, we, who are obliged to continue at it the year through, are deprived of even the little bit of luck we should otherwise have. I know only of another regular street clown in London besides myself. Some schools of acrobats, to be sure, will have a comic character of some kind or other, to keep the pitch up; that is, to amuse the people while the money is being collected: but these, in general, are not regular clowns. They are mostly dressed and got up for the occasion. They certainly don't do anything else but the street comic business, but they are not pantomimists by profession. The street clowns generally go out with dancers and tumblers. There are some street clowns to be seen with the Jacks-in-the-greens; but they are mostly sweeps, who have hired their dress for the two or three days, as the case may be. I think there are three regular clowns in the metropolis, and one of these is not a professional: he never smelt the sawdust, I know, sir. The most that I have known have been shoemakers before taking to the business. When I go out as a street clown, the first thing I do is a comic medley dance; and then after that I crack a few jokes, and that is the whole of my entertainment. The first part of the medley dance is called 'the good St. Anthony' (I was the first that ever danced the polka in the streets); then I do a waltz, and wind up with a hornpipe. After that I go through a little burlesque business. I fan myself, and one of the school asks me whether I am out of breath? I answer, 'No, the breath is out of me.' The leading questions for the jokes are all regularly prepared beforehand. The old jokes always go best with our audiences. The older they are, the better for the streets. I know, indeed, of nothing new in the joking way; but even if there was, and it was in any way deep, it would not do for the public thoroughfares. I have read a great deal of 'Punch,' but the jokes are nearly all too high there; indeed, I can't say I think very much of them myself. The principal way in which I've got up my jokes is through associating with other clowns. We don't make our jokes ourselves; in fact, I never knew one clown who did. I must own that the street clowns like a little drop of spirits, and occasionally a good deal. They are in a measure obligated to it. I can't fancy a clown being funny on small beer; and I never in all my life knew one who was a teetotaller. I think such a person would be a curious character, indeed. Most of the street clowns die in the workhouses. In their old age they are generally very wretched and poverty-stricken. I can't say what I think will be the end of me. I daren't think of it, sir."

A few minutes afterwards I saw this man dressed as Jim Crow, with his face blackened, dancing and singing in the streets as if he was the lightest-hearted fellow in all London.

THE PENNY-GAFF CLOWN.

THE " professional" from whom I elicited my knowledge of penny-gaff clowning is known among his companions as " Funny Billy." He appeared not a little anxious to uphold the dignity of the penny theatre, frequently assuring me that " they brought things out there in a style that would astonish some of the big houses." His whole being seemed wrapped up in these cheap dramatic saloons, and he told me wonderful stories of first-class actors at " The Effingham," or of astonishing performers at " The Bower," or " Rotunda." He was surprised, too, that the names of several of the artistes there were not familiar to me, and frequently pressed me to go and see so-and-so's " Beadle," or hear so-and-so sing his " Oh ! don't I like my Father !"

Besides being a clown, my informant was also " an author," and several of the most successful ballets, pantomimes, and dramas, that of late years have been brought out at the City gaffs, have, I was assured, proceeded from " his pen."

In build, even in his every-day clothes, he greatly resembles a clown—perhaps from the broadness of his chest and high-buttoned waistcoat, or from the shortness and crookedness of his legs ; but he was the first I had seen whose form gave any indication of his calling.

Since the beginning of this year (1856) he has given up clowning, and taken to pantalooning instead, for " on last boxing-day," he informed me, " he met with an accident which dislocated his jaw, and caused a swelling in his cheek as if he had an apple inside his mouth." This he said he could conceal in his make-up as a pantaloon, but it had ruined him for clown.

His statement was as follows :—

" I'm a clown at penny gaffs and the cheap theatres, for some of the gaffs are twopence and threepence—that's as high as they run. The Rotunda in the Blackfriars'-road is the largest in London, and that will hold one thousand comfortably seated, and they give two in one evening, at one penny, twopence, and threepence, and a first-class entertainment it is, consisting of a variety of singing and dancing, and ballets, from one hour and a-half to two hours. There are no penny theatres where speaking is legally allowed, though they do do it to a great extent, and at all of 'em at Christmas a pantomime is played, at which Clown and Pantaloon speaks.

" The difference between a penny-gaff clown and a fair, or, as we call it, a canvas clown, is this,— at the fairs the principal business is outside on the parade, and there's very little done (seldom more than two scenes) inside. Now at the penny gaffs they go through a regular pantomime, consisting of from six to eight scenes, with jumps and all complete, as at a regular theatre ; so that to do clown to one of them, you must be equal to those that come out at the regular theatres ; and what's more, you must strain every nerve ; and what's more still, you may often please at a regular theatre when you won't go down at all at a penny gaff. The circus clown is as different from a penny-gaff clown as a coster is from a tradesman.

" What made me turn clown was this. I was singing comic songs at the Albion Saloon, Whitechapel, and playing in ballets, and doing the scene-painting. Business was none of the best. Mr. Paul Herring, the celebrated clown, was introduced into the company as a draw, to play ballets. The ballet which he selected was 'The Barber and Beadle;' and me being the only one who played the old men on the establishment, he selected me to play the Beadle to his Barber. He complimented me for what I had done, when the performance was over, for I done my uttermost to gain his applause, knowing him to be such a star, and what he said was—I think— deserved. We played together ballets for upwards of nine months, as well as pantomimes, in which I done the Pantaloon ; and we had two clear benefits between us, in which we realised three pounds each, on both occasions. Then Mr. Paul Herring was engaged by Mr. Jem Douglass, of the Standard, to perform with the great clown, Mr. Tom Matthews, for it was intended to have two clowns in the piece. He having to go to the Standard for the Christmas, left about September, and we was without a clown, and it was proposed that I should play the clown. I accepted the offer, at a salary of thirty-five shillings a-week, under Hector Simpson, the great pantomimist —who was proprietor, This gentl man was well known as the great dog-and-bear man of Covent Garden, and various other theatres, where he played Valentine and Orson with a living bear. He showed me various things that I were deficient in, and with what I knew myself we went on admiringly well; and I continued at it as clown for upwards of a year, and became a great favourite.

" I remember clowning last Christmas (1856) particularly, for it was a sad year for me, and one of the busiest times I have ever known. I met with my accident then. I was worked to death. First of all, I had to do my re-hearsals; then I had the scene-painting to go on with, which occupied me night and day, and what it brought me in was three shillings a-day and three shillings a-night. The last scene, equal to a pair of flats, was only given to me to do on Christmas-eve, to accomplish by the boxing-day. I got them done by five o'clock at Christmas morning, and then I had to go home and complete my dress, likewise my little boy's, who was engaged to sing and play in ballets at two shillings a-night; and he was only five years old, but very clever at singing, combating, and ballet performing, as also the illustrations of the Grecian statues, which he first done when he was two and a half years old.

"The pantomime was the original Statue Blanche, as performed by Joe Grimaldi, as Mr. Hector Simpson had produced it — for it was under his superintendence—at Govent Garden Theatre. It's title was, 'The Statue Blanche, or Harlequin and the Magic Cross.' I was very successful on the boxing-night, but on the second occasion of my acting in it I received an accident, which laid me up for three months, and I was not off my bed for ten weeks.

"I had, previous to this, played clown very often, especially on the Saturday evenings, for the Jews, for I was a great favourite with them; so far, that I knew they would go far and near to serve me. I had performed in 'Harlequin Blue Beard,' and 'Harlequin Merry Milliners, or The Two Pair of Lovers,' and several others, from eight to ten of them; but that was during the summer season. But I had never had a chance of coming out at Christmas before, and to me it was quite an event, and there's no doubt I should have prospered in it only for my accident.

"This accident was occasioned by this. During the comic scene—the scene of the stripping of the child—they allowed an in-experienced person to play the part of the Beadle, and the doll for the child was stuffed with oak sawdust, and weighed twenty-six pounds. He took it up by the leg and struck me a blow in the face, which dislocated the jaw-bone, and splintered it all to pieces. I went through the pantomime with the rem-nants of the broken jaw still in my face, having then four hours to perform, for we played sixteen houses that boxing-day, to upwards of from three to four thousand peo-ple, and we began at half-past eleven in the day, and terminated at twelve at night. I had met with great approbation the whole of the time, and it was a sad event for me. It was quite accidental was my accident, and of course I bore the man no malice for one, but more blamed the manager for letting him come on.

"When I had done that night, after my blow, I felt very fatigued, and my face was very sore. I was completely jaw-locked, and I imagined I had caught a cold. It hurt me awfully every time I closed my teeth, but I drowned my feelings in a little brandy, and so forth; and the next night I resumed my clowning. After I had done that evening, I found I was so very bad I could hardly move; and going home with my wife and children, I was obliged to sit down every other yard I took, which occupied me very near two hours to do the mile and a quarter. I went to bed, and never got up again for ten weeks, for it brought on fever again. Ah! what I have suffered, God, and God only, knows! When the doctor came, he said I were under a very severe fever, and he thought I had caught a cold, and that I had the erysiphilas, my face being so swollen that it hung on my shoulders as they propped me up with pillows. He knew nothing about it. He made 'em bathe my face with poppy-heads, and wash my mouth out with honey, which drove me out of my mind, for I was a fortnight deranged. My wife told me, that whilst I was mad I had behaved very ill to her—poor thing!—for I wouldn't let anybody come near me but her; and when she'd come I'd seize her by the hair, and fancy she was the man who had broke my jaw; and once I near strangled her. I was mad, you know. Ah! what I suffered then, nobody knows. Through that accident my wife and children has had many a time to go without victuals. Everything was sold then to keep me from the workhouse — even my poor little children's frocks. My poor wife saved my life, if anybody did, for three doctors gave me up. I don't believe they knew what I had. The teeth was loose, but the mouth was closed, and I couldn't open it. They thought I had an abscess there, and they cut me three or four times in the neck to open the gathering. At last they found out the jaw-bone was smashed. When I got better, the doctor told me he could do nothing for me, but give me a letter to Dr. Fergusson, at the King's College Hospital. I went to him, and he examined and probed the jaw through the incision under the gland of the neck, and then he said he must take the jaw out. I said I would consult my friends and hear what they said first; and with the idea of such an operation, and being so weak, I actually fainted down in the passage as I was leaving.

"Ah! fancy my distress to make such a hit, and everybody to compliment me as they did, and to see a prospect of almost coining money, and then suddenly to be thrown over, and be told it was either life or death for me!

"I wouldn't undergo the operation. So I went home, and here comes fortitude. I pulled out the teeth with a pair of cobbler's pincers, and cut open my face with a pen-knife to take out the bits of bone. If I hadn't been a prudent, sober man, I should have died through it.

"There was a friend of mine who was like a brother to me, and he stuck to me every inch. There was lots of professionals I had supported in their illness, and they never come near me; only my dear friend, and but for him I should have died, for he saved up his money to get me port wine and such things.

"Many a time I've gone out when I was better to sing comic songs at concerts, when I could feel the bits of bone jangling in my mouth. But, sir, I had a wife and family, and they wanted food. As it was, my poor wife had to go to the workhouse to be confined. At one time I started off to do away with myself. I parted with my wife and children, and went to say good-by to my good friend, and it was he who saved my life. If it hadn't been for him it would have been a gooser with me, for I was prepared to finish all. He walked about with me and reasoned me out of it, and says he, ' What on earth will become of the wife and the children?'

"I'm sufficiently well now to enable me to resume my old occupation, not as Clown but as Pantaloon.

"Altogether—taking it all in all—I was three years as clown, and very successful and a great favourite with the Jews. My standing salary for comic singing and clown was eighteen shillings a-week; but then at Christmas it was always rose to thirty shillings or thirty-five shillings. Then I did the writing and painting, such as the placards for the outside ; such as, ' This saloon is open this evening,' and such-like; and that, on the average, would bring me in eight shillings a-week.

"There was seven men and three females in my company when we played ' Harlequin Blue Beard,' for that's the one I shall describe to you, and that we played for a considerable time. I was manager at the time, and I always was liked by the company, for I never fined them or anything like that ; for, you see, I knew that to take sixpence from a poor man was to take a loaf of bread from the children.

"This pantomime was of my own writing, and I managed the chorus and the dances, and all. I painted the scenery, too, and moulded the masks—about six altogether—and then afterwards played clown. All this was included in my salary of eighteen shillings a-week, and that was the top price of the company.

"The first scene was with a cottage on the left hand and with the surrounding country in the back; three rows of waters, with the distant view of Blue Beard's castle. Enters the lover (he's the Harlequin) in a disguise dressed as a Turk; he explains in the pantomime that he should like to make the lady in the cottage his bride (which is Fatima, and afterwards Columbine). He goes to the cottage and knocks three times, when she appears at the window. She comes out and dances with him. At the end of the dance the old man comes in, to the tune of ' Roast Beef of Old England.' He wears a big mask, and is the father to Fatima, and afterwards Pantaloon.

He drives lover off stage, and is about to take Fatima back to cottage, when castle gates at back opens and discovers Blue Beard in gondola, which crosses the stage in the waters. Blue Beard wears a mask and a tremendous long sword, which takes two men to pull out. He's afterwards Clown, and I played the part.

"Several other gondolas cross stage, and when the last goes off the chorus begins in the distance, and increases as it approaches, and is thus :

' In fire or in water, in earth or in air :
Wake up, old Blue Beard, these good things to share :
Wake up ! wake up ! wake old up Blue Beard, these good things to share.'

"Then comes Blue Beard's march, and enter troops, followed by Shackaback in a hurry. He's Blue Beard's servant. He bears on his shoulder an immense key, which he places in the middle of stage. He then comes to the front with a scroll, which he exhibits, on which is written :

' Blue Beard comes this very day,
A debt of gratitude to pay :
Aye, you needn't trouble, it is all right,
He intends to wed Fatima this very night.'

At which they all become alarmed, and in an immense hurry of music enters Blue Beard majestically. He sings, to the tune of ' The Low-back Car :'

' When first I saw that lady,
As you may plainly see,
I thought she was the handsomest girl
As ever there could be ;
Such a cheerful chubby girl was she,
With such a pair of eyes,
With such a mouth, and such a nose,
That she did me so surprise :
Which made me cry out,
                              Ha ! Ha !'

"The lover from the side says :

' You're no credit to your dada.'

"Then Blue Beard looks round fiercely, and his mask is made with eyes to work with strings :

' But I shall him surprise
When I opens my eyes,'

(and he opens a tremendous pair of saucer eyes),

' That talks of my dear dada.'

Then the music goes ' Ha ! ha !' As he draws his sword into the army of four men, Shackaback gets it on the nose.

"Then Blue Beard goes direct to the old man and embraces him, and shows him a big purse of money. He then goes to the young lady, but she refuses him, and says she would sooner wed the young trooper. The old man gets in a rage, when enters Demon unseen by all; he waves over their heads; they then catch hold of hands and dance round the key again, to the tune of ' The Roast Beef of Old England.' Then begins a chorus which is thus, to the tune of ' Stoney Batter :'

'Round this magic key
    Gaily let us trudge it ;
    Hoping something new
Will be brought to our Christmas budget.

But a song about a key,
    Is but a doleful matter,
So we'll sing one of our own,
    And we'll call it Stoney Batter.
        Ri too loo ral loo.'

(Fairies from the side :)

'Ri too loo ral rido.'

(Others :)

'Ri too loo ral roo, loo ral lido.'

" After dancing round key, Blue Beard orders two of the troops to seize the girl and carry her to the castle. Then they catch hands and begin singing, to the tune of ' Fine Young Bachelors :'

'Here's a jolly lot of us,
    Fine Turkish gentlemen ;
With plenty of money in our purse,
    Fine Turkish gentlemen,' &c. &c.

" And the scene closes on this. Then the lover just crosses, so as to give time to arrange the back scene. He vows vengeance on Blue Beard. Then scene opens, and discovers a chamber with Fatima on couch, and Demon behind with a large heart, on the scene over which is in illuminated letters :

'Whosoe'er this dagger takes,
    The magic spells of Blue Beard breaks.'

The large key is placed at the foot of the couch on which she is laying. We don't introduce the haunted chamber scenes, as it would have been too lengthened ; but it was supposed that she had been there and examined it, and terror had overcome her and she had swooned. That's when the audience sees her. We couldn't do all the story at a penny gaff, it was too long. To return to the plot.

" Enter Fairy, who dances round the stage, and sees the heart. She goes and snatches the dagger ; then a loud crash, and the key falls to pieces on the stage.

" I had five shillings given me as a present for that scene, for I had painted the scene all arches, and round every pillar was a serpent with fire coming from the mouth. I produced that pantomime, so that altogether it did not cost thirty shillings, because each man found his own dress, don't you see.

" After the crash enters Blue Beard. He says the lady has broken the key, and he is about to kill her ; when enter lover, and he has a terrific combat, in which they never hit a blow (like a phantom-fight) ; but the lover is about to be struck to the ground, when enters Fairy, who speaks these words :

'Hold ! turn and turn is the Yorkshire way.
    You think ours. Now your dog shall have its day.
Behold !'

" Then the scene falls, and discovers a fairy palace at back, with fairies, who sing :

'Come, listen, gentle lover,
    Come, listen unto me ;
Be guided by our fairy queen,
    Who gained your liberty.'

" They all look dismayed at one another, and go to the sides ready for changing their dresses for the comic work.

" The Fairy Queen then says :

'You, the true lover, I think knows no sin,
    Therefore grace our pantomime as Harlequin.'

" And turning to the lady she adds :

'Nay, young lady, do not pine,
    But attend him as his faithful Columbine.'

" Turning to Blue Beard :

'You, Blue Beard, a man of great renown,
    Shall grace our pantomime as Christmas Clown.'

" Then Clown comes forward, and cries : 'Halla! ha, ha, ha! here we are ! Shobbus is out ;' (that's the Jewish Sunday) ; and, oh dear ! how they used to laugh at that !

" Then she turns to the old man :

'You, old man, you've been a silly loon,
    Attend him as slippery fidgetty Pantaloon !'

" Then as she's going off she says :

'Ah ! I'd almost forgotten ;
    Never mind, it is all right ;
Demon of the magic key,
    Attend as Sprite.'

" Then the fairies sing :

'We fairies dance, we fairies sing,
    Whilst the silver moon is beaming ;
We fairies dance, we fairies sing,
    To please our Fairy Queen.'

" Then there is blue fire, and the scene closes, and the comic business begins.

" Clown dances first with Harlequin, and at the end of trip hollars out : ' Ha, here we are !' Then he sings out, each time Harlequin beats him, ' A, E, I,' (Pantaloon drops in and gets a blow, O !) ; and Clown says, ' Tuppence ! all right, you owe me nothing ; I shan't give you no change.'

" Then there's a photography scene, and Clown comes on and says, ' Here, I say, what shall we do for a living ?' Then Pantaloon says, ' We'll become dancing-masters.' The Clown says, ' They'll take likenesses.'

" ' Ah, here's somebody coming !'

" Enter a swell with white ducks, and a blacking-boy follows, says, ' Clean your boots, sir ?' Clown asks him to clean his. As the boy is beginning, Harlequin bangs him, and he knocks the boy over. Next bang he gets he hits Pantaloon, and says he did it. Pantaloon says, 'I never touched you;' and Clown replies, 'Then don't do it again.' Then I'd give 'em a rub up on the smoking mania. I'd say to boy, 'Here, boy, take this farden to get yourself a pipe of tobacco, little boys is fond of smoking;' and Pantaloon would add, 'Yes, men's left off.' Boy goes off to buy the tobacco, and leaves his blacking-box, which Clown promises to take care of and clean the boots. He hollows out, 'Clean your boots?' and Pantaloon puts his foot down, and gets his toes rapped. Enter a lady, who asks where she can have her portrait taken,—Yes, marm; over there,—Clown steals parcel. When lady is gone, Clown discovers parcel to contain blank cards. This is what he takes the portraits on, and it was at a time when they was all the rage at a shilling. Clown then says, he's taking portraits, and makes a camera out of the blacking-box. He cuts a hole in the box, and sticks the blacking-bottle for a lens. Then he places the box on Pantaloon's back for a stand. Then, of course, Clown knocks him over, and he asks what that's for. 'Why, if you're a stand, what do you fall for? I never see such a stand.' Then ladies and gentlemen come in to have their portraits taken, and Clown smears the cards with blacking and gives it, and asks a shilling; when they grumble and won't pay, he rubs the blacking in their faces. General row, and the scene changes to a street-scene. There's another trip by Harlequin and Columbine, and enters Clown in a hurry with six fish, and he meets Pantaloon. 'Look'ee here, what I've found!' 'Oh, fair halves!' 'All right! sit down, and you shall have them.' Pantaloon declines, and Clown knocks him down, and they begin sharing fish. 'There's one for you and one for me, another for you and another for me, another for you and another for me.' 'How many have you got?' asks Clown, and Pantaloon says, 'One—two—three.' Clown says, 'No! you've got more than three.' Then, taking one up, he asks, 'How many is that?'—'One.' Taking another up, 'How many's that?' Pantaloon exclaims, 'Two!' Clown says, 'Then two and one is three,' and takes up another, and asks how many that is. Pantaloon exclaims, 'Three!' Clown says, 'Then three and three makes six.' Clown then counts his own, and says, 'I've only got three; you must give me these three to make me six. That's fair halves. Ain't you satisfied?' 'No!' 'Then take that,' and he knocks him over with a fish.

"The next scene is a public-house—'The Freemasons' Arms, a select club held here.' After trip by Harlequin and Columbine, enters Clown and Pantaloon. 'Look'ee here! it's a public-house! let's have half a pint of half-and-half.' Clown hollows, 'Now ramrod!' meaning landlord, and he comes on. 'Why don't you attend to gentlemen?' 'What's your pleasure, sir?' 'Half a pint of half-and-half for me and my friend.' He brings a tumbler, which Harlequin breaks, and it comes in half. 'Hallo!' cries Clown; 'this is rum half-and-half! Here's half for you and half for me.'

"Then they say, 'I say, here's somebody coming.' Enter two Freemasons, who give each other the sign by shaking both hands, bumping up against each other, whispering in each other's ear, and going into the public-house. Clown then calls the landlord, and says he belongs to the club. Landlord asks him for the sign. Clown says he's got it over the door. He then takes Pantaloon and shakes his hands, and bumps him, and asks if that is the sign. The landlord says 'No.' 'Is that it?' 'No, this is,' and he gives Clown a spank; and he passes it to Pantaloon, and knocks him down. 'That's the sign; now we've got it between us.' 'Yes, and I've got the best half.'

"Clown says, 'Never mind, we will get in;' and he goes to the door and knocks, when the club descends and strikes them on the head. Clown then tells Pantaloon to go and knock, and he'll watch and see where it comes from. The club comes down again, and knocks Pantaloon on the head; but Clown sees from whence it comes and pulls a man in fleshings out of the window. Clown and Pantaloon pursues him round stage, and he knocks them both over, and jumps through a trap in the window with a bottle on it, marked 'Old Tom,' and a scroll falls down, written 'Gone to blazes.' Pantaloon follows, and flap falls, on which is written, 'To be left till called for.' Clown is about to follow, when gun fires and scroll falls with 'Dead letter' on it. Pantaloon is bundled out by landlord and others; general row; policemen springing rattles, fireworks, &c.

"There are from four to five comic scenes like this. But it would take too long to describe them. Besides, we don't do the same scenes every evening, but vary them each night.

"Then comes the catch, or the dark scene, in which Clown, Pantaloon, Harlequin, and Columbine are in the dark, and seize one another.

'Hold! you've done your best with all your might;
And we'll give our friends a charge another night.'

"You see the poetry is always beautifully adapted to ourselves. They've very clever fairies.

"We in generally finale with that there:

'We fairies dance; we fairies sing,
Whilst the silver moon is beaming;
We fairies dance, we fairies sing,
And we have pleased our Fairy Queen.'

"Then the bell rings, and the man who keeps order cries out, 'Pass out! pass out!'

"The performance generally takes from one hour and a half to an hour and three-quarters, and we do three of 'em a night. It makes the perspiration run off you, and every house I have a wet shirt. The only rest I have is with my boy singing 'Hot codlins.' When they call for the song I say, 'Yes, yes; all right; you shall have them; only there's a chip of mine will sing it for me,' and I introduce my little boy—of four then—to sing.

"The general pay for Clowns at penny exhibitions is averaging from twenty to twenty-five shillings a-week. You can say without exaggeration, that there are twenty of these penny exhibitions in London. They always produce a new pantomime at Christmas; and all the year round, in summer as well as winter, they bring 'em out, when business is shy, for a draw, which they always find them answer.

"A Clown that can please at a penny gaff, is capable of giving satisfaction at any theatre, for the audience is a very difficult one to entertain. They have no delicacy in 'em, and will hiss in a moment if anything displeases them.

"A pantomime at a penny exhibition will run at Christmas three weeks or a month, if very successful; and during that time it's played to upwards of twelve hundred persons a-night, according to the size of the house, for few penny ones hold more than four hundred, and that's three times a-night. The Rotunda in the Blackfriars'-road, and the Olympic Circus in the Lower Marsh, Lambeth, do an immense business, for they hold near a thousand each, and that's three thousand spectators the night.

"When the pantomime is on we only do a little comic singing before it begins playing."

The Canvas Clown.

A TALL, fine-looking young fellow, with a quantity of dark hair, which he wore tucked behind his ears, obliged me with his experience as a clown at the fairs. He came to me dressed in a fashionable "paletot," of a ginger-bread colour, which, without being questioned on the subject, he told me he had bought in Petticoat Lane for three shillings.

I have seldom seen a finer-built youth than this clown, for he was proportioned like a statue. The peculiarity of his face was that, at the junction of the forehead with the nose there was a rising, instead of a hollow, somewhat like that which is seen in Roman antiquities.

His face, whilst talking, was entirely without emotion, and he detailed the business outside the show, on the parade, in a sing-song voice, like a child saying its lesson; and although he often said " This makes 'em shout with laughter," his own face remained as solemn as a parish clerk's.

He furnished me with the following particulars of his life:—

"On and off, I've been clowning these twelve year. Previous to that time, I have done busking in public-houses, and comic singing, and ballet performing at penny exhi-

bitions; as well as parading outside shows at fairs. I've done clowning at near every place, at fairs and in the streets, along with a school of acrobats, and at circuses, and at penny gaffs, and at the Standard, and such-like. I first commenced some twelve years ago, at Enfield fair. It was a travelling concern I was with,—the 'Thespian Temple,' or Johnson's Theatre,—where I was engaged to parade on the outside as a walking gentleman. There was no clown for the pantomime, for he had disappointed us, and of course they couldn't get on without one; so, to keep the concern going, old Johnson, who knew I was a good tumbler, came up to me, and said 'he had *nanti vampo*, and your *nabs* must *fake* it;" which means,—We have no clown, and you must do it. So I done the clowning on the parade, and then, when I went inside, I'd put on a pair of Turkish trousers, and a long cloak, and hat and feathers, to play 'Robert, duke of Normandy,' in the first piece.

"You see the performances consisted of all gag. I don't suppose anybody knows what the words are in the piece. Everybody at a show theatre is expected to do general business, and when you're short of people (as we was at Johnson's, for we played 'Robert, duke of Normandy,' with three men and two girls), Clown is expected to come on and slip a cloak over his dress, and act tragedy in the first piece. We don't make up so heavy for the clown for fairs, only a little dab of red on the cheeks, and powder on the face; so we've only just got to wipe off the 'slop' when it's in the way. You looks rather pale, that's all. The dress is hidden by the one we put over it.

"The plot of 'Robert, duke of Normandy,' is this : He and his slave Piccolo come in ; and after a little business between them, all gagging, he says, 'Slave! get back to the castle!' he answers, 'Your orders shall be attended to!' Then he says, 'At the peril of your life, and prevent the fair Angeline to escape!' That's the first scene. In the second, two of Robert's slaves attack his rival, and then Robert rushes in and pretends to save him. He cries 'Hold! two to one!' The men go off, saying, 'Well, we part as friends! when next we meet, we meet as foes!' As soon as Robert leaves the rival the lady comes in, and tells him she is flying from Robert's castle, and that Robert has seduced her, and seeks her life. She tells him that the man who just left him is he. 'It is false!' he says; 'that is my friend!' She cries, 'Test him!' 'But how?' he asks. She replies,' Follow me to the statue, at the bottom of the grove, and then I will tell you!' Then the third comes on. Enter Robert and slave, and the marble statue discovered: that is, it is supposed to be, but it is only Angeline dressed up. He gives the slave instructions to put a ring on the finger of the statue,—for he is supposed to have dealings with Old Nick, and that every time he put a ring on the statue he can demand a victim. He tells the slave to place a ring on the finger, and pronounce these words : ' When it may please your most gracious majesty to seek your husband, to find a victim, you will find him here !' 'No, no, not here — there !' pointing to Robert. The Duke half draws his sword, and exclaims, ' Slave! what ho !' without touching him. Enters the rival, who demands satisfaction of Robert ; who says, ' What can I do to satisfy you ?' for he's in a deuce of a go now. He then tells him to kneel to the statue, and swear he is not Robert, duke of Normandy. Instead of that he calls to the servant, and tells him to put the ring on; but Robert, the Duke, is in a deuce of a way, tearing his hair. The servant does it, and exclaims, ' I have done it; but would you believe it, when I placed it on the finger, the finger became collapsed !' Robert cries, ' Slave, thou art a liar ! if I find that it is false I will cleave thee to the earth !' Robert examines the finger, and exclaims, ' Alas ! it is too true !' and he kneels to the statue and says, ' I swear that I am '— and he's going to say, ' not duke of Normandy,' but the statue is too quick for him, and adds, ' Robert, duke of Normandy !' And then the comic slave pops his head round, and pronounces, ' Oh, the devil !' Then the rival stabs him, and he falls down wounded, and then he's triumphant; and a pen'orth of blue fire finishes the piece ; and then ding ! dong ! and down goes the curtain. We always have blue fire, — a pen'orth each house, — and that makes it go. Sometimes there are two friends in the piece ; but it all depends upon whether the piece is powerfully cast or not. We usually knocks the two friends into one, or does away with 'em all together. ' Robert, duke of Normandy,' is a never-failing fair piece, and we always does it every year. That and ' Blue Beard, or Female Curiosity,' and ' Fair Rosamond, or the Bower of Woodstock,' are our stock pieces. After the curtain has been down three minutes it goes up again, and the heavy goes in and says,—

> ' Elves of the mountain, dale, and dell,
> This young maid to please within her cell,
> Attend unto us, one and all —
> Listen to your potent master's call.'

" Then all of us at the sides put their fingers in their mouths and howl like Indians. There's generally a cue given of ' Now, demons.' After that the heavy man says :—

> ' You, young man, that knows no sin,
> Appear as russet-booted Harlequin.'

We called him russet-booted, because he had been playing the lover in the first piece. At Richardson's they called him ' Spangled Harlequin,' but old Johnson couldn't do that, he hadn't no wardrobe. Then the heavy man continues :—

> ' And you, young maid, no longer pine,
> Attend him as his faithful Columbine.'

Then he goes on :—

> ' Two more slaves will I rise from out the unfathomable deep,
> Who for a long time have been in perpetual sleep ;
> They, too, shall share my boon—
> Appear as Clown and tottering Pantaloon.
> Now away ! begin your magic sport,
> And bring me back a good report.'

Then I cried, ' Hulloa! here we are !' and the sports begin.

" The first *trip*, as we calls it—a dance, to use your terms—is Harlequin comes in with Columbine for a hornpipe. If he can't dance, Clown, as soon as he begins, cries, ' Here we are !' and rushes in and drives them off.

" After that, Clown runs on and says, ' Here we are !' and knocks Pantaloon down; who exclaims, ' Oh ! ain't I got the tooth-ache ! Clown says, ' Let me feel your tooth. Oh, it's quite loose ! I'll get a bit of string and soon have it out.' Clown goes off for string, Pantaloon singing out, ' Murder! murder !' Clown returns with string and a pistol, and then ties the string, and cries, ' Here goes one, and now it's two, and here goes three,' and fires and pulls a wooden tooth, as big as your fist, with four sharp prongs to it. I've had these teeth often as big as a quartern loaf, but I'm talking of my first appearance. Pantaloon says, ' Here, that's my tooth !' and Clown replies. ' So it is,' and hits him on the head with it. Then he asks Pantaloon if he's better ; but he answers, ' No, I'm worse. Oh! oh! I've got a cold in my gum !' Then a red-hot poker is introduced, and he burns him with it all round the stage. That concludes the first scene. Then there's another trip, a would-be polka or so ; and then comes the bundle-scene. Enter a Yorkshireman —it's mostly Harlequins do this, because most of the others are outside parading, to keep the crowd together — he's got a smockfrock on and russet boots at Johnson's, and he says, ' I've coome up here to Lunnon to see my Dolly. I feel rather dry, and I'll just gi' in here to get half-a-point of yale. I'll just leave my bunnel outside, and keep a strict eye on it, for they say as how Lunnon has plenty of thieves in it.' Enter Clown, very cautiously. He sees the bundle, and calls Pantaloon. He tells Pantaloon, ' I must have it, because I want it.' He goes and picks up the bundle, and says to Pantaloon, ' I shouldn't wonder but what this bundle belongs to——' ' Me,' the Yorkshireman says, and the Clown says, ' Ah, I thought so ;' and then he takes Pantaloon's hand, and says, ' Come along, little boy, we shall get into trouble,' and leads him off. They come on again, and this time Clown tells Pantaloon to get it ; so he goes and picks up the bundle, and Yorkshireman knocks him down. Clown runs off and Pantaloon after. Clown then returns on his belly, drawing himself on with his hands.

He gets the bundle in his mouth, and is just going off when Yorkshireman turns round, and Clown seeing him, gives the bundle to Pantaloon, and says, 'Hold this.' Yorkshireman seizes Clown and tells him he wants his bundle. Pantaloon having run away with it, Clown says, 'I haven't got it, starch me' (that means, 'search me'); and there is a regular run over the stage crying 'Hot beef! hot beef!' (instead of 'Stop thief!') The Yorkshireman collars Pantaloon, and says, 'I'll take you to the station-house,' and Clown exclaims, 'Yes, and I'll take this bundle down the lane' (meaning Petticoat-lane, because there is a sale for anything there). Then comes the catch-scene as we call it; that is, they all come on in the dark, Clown singing, 'Puss, puss! have you seen my pussy?' Then in pops the fairy, and cries, 'Hold! your magic sports is run, and thus I step between.' Pantaloon adds, 'Aye, it's all so gay;' and Clown cries, 'Yes, and all serene;' and the fairy says, 'And with my magic wand I change the scene.' Then everybody sings:—

> 'Now our pantomime's done,
> Here's an end to our fun,
> We shall shortly commence again:
> Our tricks are o'er,
> And we're friends once more,
> We shall shortly commence again.'

" Then the curtain falls, and Clown puts his head out on one side and exclaims, ' It's all,' and Pantaloon pops out at the other side and adds, ' over.'

" The handing man, who has done Robert, then shouts out from the top, ' Pass out!' in a sepulchral voice, and a door opens in the side of the stage for the people to leave by. That day I was with old Johnson — we used to call him 'Snuffy Johnson,' 'cos he carried a lot of snuff in his waistcoat pocket — we were very busy, and there was a good many people waiting on the outside to come in, so we only did about two of them regular performances; and then about six o'clock in the evening the crowd got so great, old Johnson used to hollow through the parade-door, over people's heads, ' John Aderley,' just as we had commenced playing, and that meant ' Cut it short.' We used to finish it up sharp then, and finish all up in six or seven minutes. We used to knock Robert the Devil into a very little space, doing the scenes, but cutting them short; and as for the pantomime, we had scarcely commenced with ' Two more slaves will I rise from out the unfathomable deep,' than we were singing, ' Our pantomime's done, here's an end to our fun.' Sometimes the people would grumble awful, and at others they laughed to see how they was swindled.

" I got on very fair on my first appearance as Clown, considering the circumstances, but I had, you see, four of the best parading comic men opposing me. There was Teddy W—— as Silly Billy, and Black Sambo as Black Fop, and Funny Felix as ring clown, and Steve

Sanderson, another clown, at Frazier's Circus, next door to us; and we didn't stand much chance at clowning alongside of them, as they're the best paraders out. Besides, Frazier's booth took nearly all the ground up; and as we drawed up on the ground (that is, with the parade-carriages) late on Sunday evening, we were obliged to have a plot next to the Circus, and we had the town pump right in the audience part, close to the first seat in the gallery, and the Obelisk — or rather a cross it is — took up one side of the stage, which next day we used as the castle in Blue Beard, when the girl gets up on a ladder to the top of the railings, which had a shutter on 'em, and that was Fatima looking out from the spire of the castle for her Salem. Ah! 'twas a great hit, for we put an old scene round it, and it had a capital effect.

"What we do when we go out clowning to a travelling theatre is this. This is what I did at Enfield: we arrived late and drawed up the parade-carriages on the ground, which the gov. had gone on a-head to secure. Then we went to sleep for awhile — pitched on a shutter underneath the parade-carriages, for it had been wet weather, and we couldn't sleep on the canvas for the booth, for it had been sopped with rain at Edmonton fair. As soon as it was break of day we begun getting up the booth, and being short-handed it took us till three o'clock before we was ready. First we had to measure our distances and fix the parade-waggons. Then we planted our king pole on the one in the centre; then we put our back-pole on the one near the parade; then we put on our ridge at top, and our side-rails; and then we put our side-ridges, and sling our rafters. We then roll the tilt up, which is for the roof, and it gets heavy with dirt, and we haul it up to the top and unroll it again and fasten it again; then we fix the sides up, with shutters about six feet square, which you see on the top of the travelling parade-carriages. We fixes up the theatre and the seats which we take with us. All the scenes roll up, and is done up in bundles. The performers drop under the parade-waggons, and there's a sacking up to divide the men's part from the women. There's a looking-glass — sometimes an old bit or a two-penny one starred, or any old thing we can get hold of — and the gov. gives you out your dress. We always provide our own slips and suchlike.

" When we parade outside, it all depends upon what kind of Pantaloon you've got with you, as to what business you can make. When we first come out on the parade all the company is together, and we march round, form a half-circle, or dress it, as we say, while the band plays ' Rule Britannia,' or some other operatic air. Then the manager generally calls out, ' Now, Mr. Merryman, state the nature of the performances to be given here to-day.' Then I come forward, and this is **the** dialogue: 'Well, Mr. Martin, what am I to tell them?' 'The truth, sir! what they'll see here to-day.' 'Well, if they stop long enough they'll see a great many people, I shouldn't wonder.' 'No, no, sir, I want you to tell them what they'll see inside our theatre.' 'Well, sir, they'll see a splendid drama by first-rate performers, of Robert Dooke of Normandy, with a variety of singing and dancing, with a gorgeous and comic pantomime, with new dresses and scenery, and everything combined to make this such an entertainment as was never before witnessed in this town, and all for the small charge of three shillings.' 'No, no, Mr. Merryman, threepence.' 'What! threepence? I shan't perform at a threepenny show.' And then I pretend to go down the steps as if leaving; he pulls me back, and says, 'Come here, sir; what are you going to do?' 'I shan't spoil my deputation playing for threepence.' 'But you must understand, Merryman, we intend giving them one and all a treat, that the working-classes may enjoy theirselves as well as noblemen.' 'Then if that's the case I don't mind, but only for this once.'

"Then I begin spouting again and again, always ending up with 'to be witnessed for the low charge of threepence.' Then Pantaloon comes up to say what he's going to do, and I give him the 'nap,' and knock him on his back. He cries 'I'm down,' and I turn him over and pick him up, and say, 'And now you're up.' Then the company form a half set and do a quadrille. When they have scrambled through that, Clown will do a comic dance, and then some burlesque statues. This is the way them statues are done: I go inside and get a birch-broom, and put a large piece of tilt or old cloth round me, and stand just inside the curtains at the entrance from the parade, ready to come out when wanted. Then the male portion of the company get just to the top of the steps, and Pantaloon says to one of them, 'Did you speak?' He says, 'When?' and Pantaloon says, 'Now;' and the whole lot make a noise, hollowing out, 'Oh, oh, oh!' as if they was astonished, but it's only to attract attention. Then the gong strikes, and the trumpets flourishes, and everybody shouts, 'Hi, hi! look here!' Then, naturally, all the people turn towards the caravan to see what's up. Then they clear a passage-way from the front to the entrance and back, and bring me forth with this bit of cloth before me. The music flourishes again, and they make a tremendous tumult, crying out, 'Look here! look here!' and when all are looking I drop the cloth, and then I stand in the position of Hercules, king of Clubs, with a birch-broom across my shoulders, and an old hat on a-top of my wig. Then the band strikes up the statue music, and I goes through the statues; such as Ajax defying the lightning, and Cain killing his brother Abel; and it finishes up with the fighting and dying Gladiator. As a

finale I do a back-fall, and pretend to be dead. The company then picks me up and carry me, lying stiff, on their shoulders round the parade. They carry me inside, and shout out, 'All in to begin; now we positively commence.' Then they drive everybody in off the parade. When the public have taken their seats then we come strolling out, one at a time, till we all get out on the parade again, because the place isn't sufficiently full. It's what we call 'making a sally.' The check-takers at the door prevent anybody leaving if they want to come out again.

"Then I get up to some nonsense again. Perhaps I'll get up a lot of boys out of the fair, and make 'em sit on the parade in a row, and keep a school, as I call it. I get an old property fiddle, and I tell them, when I play they must sing. Then I give out a hymn. The bow has a lot of notches in it, and there's a bit of wood sticking up in the fiddle; so that when I plays it goes 'ricketty, ricketty,' like. This is the hymn I gives out:—

> ' When I can shoot my rifle clear
>   At pigeons in the skies,
> I'll bid farewell to pork and peas,
>   And live on pigeon pies.'

"Of course, when they sings, they make a horrible noise, or even if they dont, I begin to wallop them with my bow. I then tell them I must teach them something easier first. Then I give them—

> ' Alas! old Grimes is dead and gone,
>   We ne'er shall see him more;
> He used to wear a old great coat
>   All buttoned down before.'

Then I finish up by putting on the boys a lot of masks, and some have old soldiers' coats; and I give them implements of war, such as old brooms or sticks, and then I put them through their military exercises. I stand in front, with the birch-broom as my gun, and I tell them they must do as I do. Then I cry, 'File arms,' and all mark their own muskets. I tell them to lay them all down; and after they have laid down their arms I tell them to shoulder arms, which makes a shout, because they haven't got no arms. One boy, who is put up to it, says, 'I've got no arms;' I go up to him and catch hold of his arms, and ask him what he calls 'these here.' Then I make him put them on his shoulders, and tell him, that's 'shoulder arms.' Then I tell them to ground arms, and I do it at the time, stooping down and putting my arms on the ground. I then call them to attention, and up comes the Pantaloon on a basket-horse, and I tell them they are going to be reviewed by the Duke. I give them all the implements again, and put them to stand attention. Pantaloon gallops round them, reviewing. He wears a large flap cocked-hat and soldier's old coat. He makes a bit of fun with his horse, making

it kick, and breaking the ranks of my soldiers. Then I quarrel with him about that,
and he says, ' He's a right to do as he likes,
because he's my superior horse-ifer.' Then
he orders me to the other end of the parade,
to stand attention, with my back towards
the boys. Then he tells them to ride about
face and charge, and they all run and charge
me in behind. They run two or three
times round the parade, still charging me,
until I run inside to the theatre, and all the
company shout out, ' All in to begin; we are
now positively to commence.' We then get
them in off the parade again, and if the place
is full begin; if not, we gradually crawl out
again one by one, and one of the girls dances
a hornpipe or a Highland fling. We then
make a sally, 'All in again,' and by that time
we generally begin.

" This is the parade business that is most
popular at fairs; we do a few other things,
but they are all much of a muchness. It's
very hard work; and I have worked, since
being with Snuffy Johnson, seventeen hours
of a-day; but then we have not had so much
to do on the outside. Sometimes I've been
so tired at night, that I've actually laid down
in my dress and never washed, but slept like
that all night.

" The general pay for a clown, during fair-
time, is 5s. or 6s. a-day, but that usually ends
in your moving on the first day; then 4s. on
the second, and, perhaps, 3s. on the third. The
reason is, that the second and third day is
never so good as the first. The excuse is,
that business is not so good, and expenses are
heavy; and if you don't like it, you needn't
come again. They don't stand about what
you agree for; for instance, if it's a wet day
and you don't open, there's no pay. Richardson's used, when the old man was alive, to
be more money, but now it's as bad as the
rest of 'em. If you go on shares with a
sharing company it averages about the same.
We always share at the drum-head at night,
when all's over. It's usually brought out
between the stage and the bottom seat of
the gallery. The master or missus counts
out the money. The money on the drum-
head may, if it's a good fair, come to 16l.
or 18l., or, as it most usually is, 9l. or 10l.
I have known us to share 1l. a-piece afore
now; and I've known what it is to take 10d.
for a share. We usually take two fairs a-
week, or we may stay a night or two after the
fair's over, and have a bespeak night. The
wages of a clown comes to—if you average
it—1l. a-week all the year round, and that's
puffing it at a good salary, and supposing
you to be continually travelling. Very likely,
at night we have to pull down the booth
after performing all day, and be off that night
to another fair—15 or 16 miles off it may
be—and have to build up again by the
next afternoon. The women always ride on
the top of the parade carriages, and the men

occasionally riding and shoving up behind the
carriages up hill. The only comfort in travelling is a short pipe, and many a time I've
drowned my woes and troubles in one.

" The scene of sharing at the drum-head is
usually this,—while the last performance is
going on the missus counts up the money; and
she is supposed to bring in all the money she
has taken, but that we don't know, and we
are generally fiddled most tremendous. When
the theatre's empty, she, or him, generally
says, ' Now lads, please, now ladies! it's getting late;' and when they have all mustered
it's generally the cry, ' We've had a bad fair!'
The people seldom speak. She then takes
the number of the company,—we generally
averages some sixteen performers,—and after
doing so she commences sharing, taking up
two or three shares, according to the ground-
rent; one then to herself for taking money; then
for the husband being there, (for they don't
often perform); then they takes shares for the
children, for they makes them go on for the
fairies, and on our parade. Snuffy Johnson
used to take two shares for the wardrobes and
fittings, and that is the most reasonable of
any of 'em, for they mostly take double that;
indeed, we always took six. Then there are
two shares for ground-rent, and two for travelling expenses. The latter two shares depend
entirely upon the fair; for the expenses are
just the same whether we takes money or not,
so that if it's a bad fair, more has to be deducted, and that's the worse for us, on both
sides. That makes twelve or thirteen shares
to be deducted before the men touch a penny
for themselves. Any strolling professional
who reads that will say, ' Well, 'tis very considerate; for it's under the mark, and not
over.'

" When we have finished at one fair, if we
want to go to another the next day, as soon
as the people have gone in for the last performance we commence taking down the pay-
box, and all the show-fittings on the outside,
and all that isn't wanted for the performance.
As soon as the mummers have done their first
slang, if they are not wanted in the pantomime they change themselves and go to work
pulling down. When the pantomime's over,
every one helps till all's packed up; then
sharing takes place, and we tramp on by night
to the next fair. We then camp as well as we
can till daylight, if it isn't morning already,
and to work we go building for the fair; and
in general, by the time we've done building,
it's time to open.

" I've travelled with ' Star's Theatre Royal,'
and ' Smith and Webster's,' (alias Richardson's), and ' Frederick's Theatre,' and ' Baker's
Pavilion,' and ' Douglass's travelling Shak-
spearian Saloon;' (he's got scenes from
Shakspear's plays all round the front, and it's
the most splendid concern on the road), and
I've done the comic business at all of them.
They are all conducted on the same principle,

and do the same kind of business, as that I've described to you.

"When we're travelling it depends upon the business as to what we eat. They talk of strolling actors living so jollily and well, but I never knew it fall to my share. What we call a mummer's feed is potatoes and herrings, and they always look out for going into a town where there's plenty of fresh herrings. A fellow we called Nancy Dawson was the best hand at herrings. I've known him go into a tavern and ask for the bill of fare, and shout out, 'Well, Landlord, what have you got for dinner? Perhaps he'd say, 'There's beef and veal, sir, very nice—just ready;' and then he'd say, 'No, I'm sick of meat; just get me a nice bloater!' and if it came to much more than a penny there was a row. If we are doing bad business, and we pass a field of swedes, there's a general rush for the pull. The best judges of turnips is strolling professionals. I recollect, in Hampshire, once getting into a swede field, and they was all blighted: we pulled up a hundred, I should think, but when we cut them open they was all flaxy inside, and we, after all, had to eat the rind. We couldn't get a feed. Sausages and fagots (that's made of all the stale sausages and savaloys, and unsightly bits of meat what won't sell) is what we gets hold of principally. The women have to make shifts as we do. We always get plenty of beer, even when we can't get money; for we can sing a song or so, and then the yokels stand something: besides, there's hardly a town we go into without some of the yokels being stage-struck, and they feel quite delighted to be among the professionals, and will give us plenty of beer if we'll talk to them about acting.

"It's impossible to say how many clowns there are working at canvas theatres. There's so many meddling at it,—not good uns, but trying to be. I can mention fifty, I am sure, by name. I shouldn't think you would exaggerate, if you was to say there was from one hundred and fifty to two hundred who call themselves clowns. Many of the first-rate clowns now in London have begun at strolling. There's Herring, and Lewis, and Nelson, and plenty more, doing well now.

"It's a hard life, and many's the time we squeedge a laugh out, when it's like killing us to do it. I've never known a man break down at a fair, done up, for, you see, the beer keeps us up; but I've known one chap to faint on the parade from exhaustion, and then get up, as queer as could be, and draw twopence and go and have a fish and bread. A woman at an oyster-stall alongside of the theatre give him a drop of beer. He was hearty and hungry, and had only joined lately,—regular hard up; so he went two days without food. When we shared at night he went and bought a ham-bone, and actually eat himself asleep, for he dropped off with the bone in his hand."

THE PENNY-CIRCUS JESTER.

A MAN who had passed many years of his life as jester at the cheap circuses, or penny equestrian shows frequenting the fairs in the neighbourhood of London, obliged me with the following details:—

"There are only two kinds of clowns, the stage and the circus clown, only there is different denominations: for instance, the clown at the fair and the clown at the regular theatre, as well as the penny gaff (when they give pantomimes there), are one and the same kind of clown, only better or worse, according to the pay and kind of performance; but it's the same sort of business. Now the circus clown is of the same kind as those that go about with schools of acrobats and negro serenaders. He is expected to be witty and say clever things, and invent anything he can for the evening's performance; but the theatre clown is expected to do nothing but what enters into the business of the piece. Them two are the main distinctions we make in the perfession.

"I've travelled along with only two circuses; but then it's the time you stop with them, for I was eighteen months along with a man of the name of Johnson, who performed at the Albion, Whitechapel, and in Museum-street, opposite Drury-lane (he had a penny exhibition then), and for above two years and a half along with Veale, who had a circus at the Birdcage, Hackney-road, and at Walworth.

"At Museum-street we only had one 'prad,' which is slang for pony, although we used to introduce all the circus business. We had jugglers, and globe-runners, and tight-rope dancers also. We never had no ring built, but only sawdust on the stage, and all the wings taken out. They used to begin with a chant and a hop (singing and dancing), after which there was tight-rope hopping. As soon as ever the rope was drawn up, Johnson, who had a whip in his hand, the same as if it was a regular circus, used to say, 'Now, Mr. Merryman.' Then I'd run on and answer, 'Here I am, sir, all of a lump, as the old man said what found the sixpence. I'm up and dressed, like a watchbox. What shall I have the pleasure for to come for to go, for to go for to fetch, for to fetch for to carry, to oblige you?' I usually wore a ring dress, with red rings round my trunks, and a fly to correspond. The tights had straight red lines. My wig was a white one with a red comb. Then Johnson would say, 'Have the pleasure to announce Madame Leone.' Then I give it: 'Ladies and gentlemen, this is Madame Leone, a young lady that threw her clothes into bed and hung herself upon the door-nail.' Then she just gets up on the rope, and I go and sit down as if I was going to sleep. Mr. Johnson then says, 'Come, sir, you're going to sleep; you've got your eyes shut.' I answer, 'I beg your pardon, sir, I was not asleep.' And then he says I was, and I contradict him, and add, 'If I had my eyes shut, I am the first of the family that went to sleep so.' Then he asks how that is? and I reply, 'Because they were afraid of having their pockets picked;' and he says, 'Nonsense! all your family was very poor, there was nothing in their pockets to pick;' and I add, 'Yes, but there was the stitches though.' All these puns and catches goes immense. 'Now, sir,' he continues, 'chalk the rope.' I say, 'Whose place is it?' and he replies, 'The fool's.' 'Then do it yourself,' I answer. And then we go on in this style. He cries, 'What did you say, sir?' 'I said I'd do it myself.' 'Now, Madame Leone, are you ready?' and she nods; and then I tell the music to toodelloo and blow us up. She then does a step or two—a little of the polka—and retires, and I am told to chalk the rope again, and this is our talk: ' Oh dear, oh dear! there's no rest for the wicked. Sir, would you be so kind, so obliging, as to inform me why I chalk the top of the rope?' 'To prevent the young lady from slipping down, sir.' 'Oh, indeed! then I'll chalk underneath the rope.' He then asks, 'What are you doing of, sir?' 'Why didn't you tell me when I chalked the top it's to prevent the young lady from slipping down?' 'Yes, sir.' ' Then I chalked underneath, to prevent her from slipping up again. Would you oblige me with your hand?' Then I look at it and say, ' Plenty of corns in it; you've done some hard work in your time.' 'I have, sir.' ' Beautiful nails, too;' and then I rub the chalk on his hand, and when he asks what I'm doing of, I say 'Chalking it.' 'What for, sir?' ' Why, sir, to keep it from slipping into other people's pockets.' Then he gives me a click of whip and says, ' Out of the way, sir! Now, Madame Leone, proceed.'

"When she's finished the dance I cry, ' Now I'll get on the rope and have a try,' and I mount very courageously, crying,

> ' I'd be a butcher's boy,
> Born in the Borough,
> Beef-steaks to-day
> And mutton chops to-morrow.'

" Then I find the rope move, and pretend to be frightened, and cry, ' O Lord, don't! it shakes.' Then I ask, ' Mr. Johnson, will you chalk my pulse and hand me up the barber's-pole?' and when I've got it I say, ' Here's a nice ornament on a twelfth-cake.' I also ask him, 'I say, sir, did you ever know some of my friends was first-rate rope-dancers?' ' No, sir.' ' Oh yes, sir, they danced to some of the large houses.' 'What house was that, sir? was it Victoria?' 'I know nothing about Victoria, sir; you must ask Albert.' ' Perhaps, sir, it was the Garrick.' ' Oh, catch my brother dancing in a garret.' ' Perhaps, sir, it was Covent Garden.' ' No, sir, he never danced in no garden, nor a lane neither.' ' Perhaps, sir, it was the Haymarket.' ' No, sir; nor the Corn-market.' ' I see, sir, you can't remember the house.' ' No, sir; I'll

tell you, sir, it's a high stone building between Holborn and Newgate-market.' ' Oh, you mean Newgate.' 'Yes, sir; don't you remember we were both in there for pot stealing?' ' Come down here, sir, and I'll give you a flogging.' 'You mean to say, sir, you'll give me a flogging if I come down?' ' Yes, sir.' ' Then, sir, I shall remain where I am.' I then tell the music to toodelloo and blow us up, and I attempt to dance, and he lets the rope down, which throws me on to my back. He asks, ' Are you hurt?' and I reply, ' No, I'm killed.' ' Get up, sir.' ' I'll not move, sir.' 'I'll give you the whip, sir.' ' That's no use, sir; I've made a bargain with it, that if I don't touch it it won't touch me. Oh, ain't I bad! I've got the cobbler's marbles, or else the hen-flew-out-of-the-window.' ' Here's a policeman coming!' and then I jumps up in a minute, and ask, 'Where?'

"Then I go to his whip, and touch it. 'What's this, Mr. Johnson?' ' My whip, sir.' ' I'll tell you what it is, Mr. Johnson, I'll bet you a bottle of blacking and a three-out brush, that you can't say 'my whip' to three questions that I shall put to you.' 'I'll take you, sir.' I then take the whip from him, and say, ' Providing, sir, you was to meet a poor blind old man, and you was to give him a ha'penny, and you was to meet me and make me a present of a 5l. note, what would you deserve?' He says, 'My whip, sir.' ' Yes, sir; that's one to you. I say, sir, you've got a daughter, and if she was to marry and get a great deal of money, what would you deserve?' 'My whip, sir.' 'Certainly, sir; that's two to you. Now, sir, providing you was a top of that rope, and I was to undo the rope and let you down, and I was to give you the cobbler's marbles with the hen-flew-out-of-the-window, and tell you that a policeman was a-coming, what should I deserve?' Then he don't like to say, ' My whip,' and stammers out; at last he says it, and then I beat him round the stage till he runs off. Then I lay it down and cry cock-a-doodle-do, crowing for victory, and he creeps in and gets the whip again, and then lashes me.

"After juggling and globes, we always did ' a laughable sketch entitled Billy Button's ride to Brentford,' and I used to be Jeremiah Stitchem, a servant of Billy Button's, that comes for a 'sitiation.' It opens this way. Jeremiah makes applications for this situation. He asks, 'What can you do?' 'Everythink and nothink.' ' Can you clean plates?' ' I can break 'em.' ' Can you run errands?' ' All ways.' He is engaged at 4s. a-week and his board; and then comes some comic business about a letter coming by post. Billy tells him to bring him a light to read this letter, and he sets fire to it. This letter is from Brentford, saying that his sister's ill and that he's wanted directly. He goes to a livery stable and asks for a lady's pony, at the same time saying he wants it quiet. The man says he's got three: one that is blind, and threw the last gentleman that rode it into a ditch, and Billy won't have that. The other is lame of one leg, and he don't like that, for he wants a lady's pony that is very quiet. Then this stable-keeper recommends this pony, saying it's very quiet, but it's a kicker. Then first he gets up the wrong way, and the head comes round to the tail of the horse; Jerry then tells him he's wrong, and then offers to give him a 'bung up,' and chucks him right over the pony's back on to the ground on the other side. He then gets on properly, ready for starting, and tells Jerry he may expect him home in a day or two. He tries to start the pony, but it won't go. Jerry takes a needle and pretends to stick it into the pony's flank, which causes it to kick and rear until he throws Billy Button off; and then the pony chases Jerry round the stage with his mouth open to bite him. Then there's a regular confusion, and that winds it up.

"If that pony catched you he'd give it you, too. He caught hold of me one night by my trousers, and nearly shook my life out of me. It hurt me, but everybody roared and thought it all right. After that I hit upon a dodge. I used to have a roll of calico tacked on to my back, and the pony would catch hold of it and pull out about four yards of what looked like a shirt. Those ponies are very playful, and may be taught anything.

"The stage-clown's dress is what we term full dresses, with a wig and a tail, but the circus clown's is merely the top-knot, and the ring dress, as if they are spangled they are always on the twist, something in the style of the serpent. They don't do the red half-moon on the cheek, like stage clowns, but they have just a dab, running up to the cheek-bone. A stage-clown's dress costs from from 5*l.* to 10*l.*; but a circus clown can make a suit complete, with pumps and all, for from 30*s.* to 35*s.* There's such a thing as fourteen or fifteen yards of canvas in a stage-clown's full dress; and that's without exaggerating.

"Veal's was the best circus I was at; there they had six prads (horses) and two ponies, and the performers were the best then of the day; for they had Monsieur Ludowic, a French-man, and the best bare-back juggler about. Mr. Moffat's troupe, and Mr. Emery's, was there also. Mr. Douglas was clown along with me, and little Ned and Sam was the tumblers. We had a large tent and regular circus, and could accommodate 1500 or 1600 people. I had 35*s.* a-week all the time I was there, (near 2½ years), and it wasn't much, considering the work, for I had to produce all the pantomimes and act as ballet-master as well.

"It is, and it ain't, difficult to ride round a circus standing up. I've known one man, who had never rode before in all his life, and yet went on one night, when they were short of hands, and done the Olympians to the best of his abilities, without falling off, though he felt very nervous. For these scenes they go slowly. You have to keep your eye fixed on the horse's head. I've been in a circus so long, and yet I can't ride. Even following the horse round the ring makes me feel so giddy at times, that I have had to catch hold of the tent-pole in the middle just to steady myself.

"I wasn't the regular principal clown at Veal's — only on occasions; I was the speak-ing clown and jester. I used to do such things as those :— For instance, there is a act—which is rode — called 'The Shipwrecked Sailors,' where he rides round the ring, introducing the shipwreck hornpipe, and doing a pantomime of giving a imitation of the sinking of the ship, and his swimming and returning safe on shore. Between the parts I used to say to the ring-master, 'Are you aware, sir, that I've been to sea?' He'd say, 'No, sir.' Then we'd go on : 'Yes, sir; I once took a voyage to the Ickney Nockney Islands, off Bulbusen, just by the Thames Tunnel, in the mud.' 'Indeed, sir!' 'Yes, sir; and I've seen some wonderful sights, sir, in my time.' 'Indeed, sir!' 'Yes, sir: on this occasion it come so cold, that as the captain was on the quarter-deck, as he gave the word of command to the men, the words dropped out of his mouth lumps of ice on the deck. The ship would have been lost, had I not had the presence of mind to pick the words up, put them into a fryingpan, and warm them over the galley-fire : and as they thawed, so I gave the word of command to the men.' 'Dear me, sir! that was a wonderful sight!' 'It was in-deed, sir!' 'I don't believe a word of it.' 'Ah, sir, if you'd have been there, you'd have seen it yourself.' 'I don't believe a word of it, Mr. Merryman.' 'Oh! come, sir, you must believe some.' 'Well, I believe a part it.' 'Then I believe the other part, sir, and so that makes the lot.' 'That's right, sir.' 'Well, sir, I went for another voyage; and going through the Needles our vessel sprung a leak; not an onion, a leak; and she got a hole in her side.' 'She, sir?' 'Yes, sir, the ship; so the pumps was put to work; but as fast as they pumped the water out it came in at the hole, and the ship was sink-ing, when the captain came on deck and asked if there was any man courageous enough to stop the hole. Of course, sir, I was there.' 'But you're not courageous.' 'Ain't I, sir? try me.' 'Now, says he, 'if there's any man will stop this hole, to him will I give the hand of my daughter and 150*l.* So away I went down in the hold, and there was more than about 15 foot of water, and I pops my head in the hole until they got the vessel ashore. So you see, sir, I had the hand of his daughter and the 150*l.*' 'That was a good job for you, Mr. Merryman.' 'No, sir; it was a bad job.' 'How was that, sir?' 'Because when I was married I found that she was a cream of tartar.' ' Then, sir, you had the money; that was a good job for you.' ' No, sir; that was a bad job, sir.' ' How so?' ' I bought some sheep and oxen, and they died of the rot.' ' Ah! that was a bad job, Mr. Merryman.' ' No, sir; it was a good job; for shoes were very dear, and I sold the hides for more than I gave for the cattle.' ' Well, that was a good job.' ' No, sir, that was a bad job: for I built houses with the money and they got burned down.' ' Indeed, sir! that was a *very* bad job for you.' ' Oh no, sir; it was a very good job, because my wife got burnt in them, and, you see, I got rid of a tormenting wife.'

" There's another famous gag ring-jesters always do, and I was very successful with it. After the act of horsemanship is over, when the ring-master is about leaving the ring, I say, ' Allow me to go first, sir;' and he replies, ' No, sir, I never follow a fool.' Then we go on:—' I always do,' meaning him. ' What did you say, sir?' ' That's quite true, sir.' ' I say, sir, did ever you see my sweetheart?' ' No, sir.' ' There she is, sir; that nice young girl sitting there.' ' I don't see her.' — ' Yes, there, sir, a-winking at me now. Ah! you little ducksey, ducksey, ducksey!' ' I don't see her, sir.' Then I gets him to the middle of the ring, and whilst he is pretending to stare in the direction I pointed to, I bolt off, saying, ' I never follows a fool.'

" At fairs we do pretty well, and a circus always pays better than an acting-booth. We are always on salaries, and never go upon shares. The actors often say we look down upon them, and think them beneath our notice; and I dare say it's true, to a great extent. I've heard our chaps cry out, ' Won't you be glad when herrings are cheap?' or, ' How were you off for bits of candle and lumps of coke last night at sharing?' Then, no doubt, we live better at circuses, for we do our steaks and onions, and all that sort of thing; and, perhaps, that makes us cheeky.'

" Some jesters at circuses get tremendous engagements. Mr. Barry, they say, had 10*l.* a-week at Astley's; and Stonalfe, with his dogs, is, I should think, equal to him. There's another, Nelson, too, who plays on the harmonicon, and does tunes on bits of wood — the same as went on the water in a tub drawn by geese, when the bridge broke down at Yarmouth—he's had as much as 15*l.* a-week on a regular travelling engagement.

" There ain't so many jesters as tumbling clowns. I think it's because they find it almost too much for them; for a jester has to be ready with his tongue if anything goes wrong in the ring. I shouldn't think there was more than from thirty to forty jesters in England. I reckon in this way. There are from ten to fifteen circuses, and that's allowing them two jesters each. In the three-penny circus, such as Clarke's or Frazier's,

the salary for a jester is about 2*l.* a-week, take the year round."

SILLY BILLY.

THE character of " Silly Billy " is a kind of clown, or rather a clown's butt; but not after the style of Pantaloon, for the part is comparatively juvenile. Silly Billy is supposed to be a schoolboy, although not dressed in a charity-boy's attire. He is very popular with the audience at the fairs; indeed, they cannot do without him. " The people like to see Silly Billy," I was told, " much more than they do Pantaloon, for he gets knocked about more though, but he gives it back again. A good Silly," said my informant, " has to imitate all the ways of a little boy. When I have been going to a fair, I have many a time stopped for hours watching boys at play, learning their various games, and getting their sayings. For instance, some will go about the streets singing:

' Eh, higgety, eh ho !
Billy let the water go ! '

which is some song about a boy pulling a tap from a water-butt, and letting the water run. There's another:

' Nicky nickey nite,
I'll strike a light !'

I got these both from watching children whilst playing. Again, boys will swear ' By the liver and lights of a cobbler's lapstone!' and their most regular desperate oath is,

' Ain't this wet? ain't it dry?
Cut my throat if I tells a lie.'

They'll say, too ' S'elp my greens!' and ' Upon my word and say so!' All these sayings I used to work up into my Silly Billy, and they had their success.

" I do such things as these, too, which is regularly boyish, such as ' Give me a bit of your bread and butter, and I'll give you a bit of my bread and treacle.' Again, I was watching a lot of boys playing at pitch-button, and one says, ' Ah, you're up to the rigs of this hole; come to my hole—you can't play there!' I've noticed them, too, playing at ring-taw, and one of their exclamations is ' Knuckle down fair, and no funking.' All these sayings are very useful to make the character of Silly Billy perfect. Bless you, sir, I was two years studying boys before I came out as Silly Billy. But then I persevere when I take a thing in hand; and I stick so close to nature, that I can't go far wrong in that line. Now this is a regular boy's answer: when somebody says ' Does your mother know you're out?' he replies, ' Yes, she do; but I didn't know the organ-man had lost his monkey!' That always went immense.

" It's impossible to say when Silly Billy first

come out at fairs, or who first supported the character. It's been popular ever since a fair can be remembered. The best I ever saw was Teddy Walters. He's been at all the fairs round the universe—England, Ireland, Scotland, Wales, and France. He belonged to a circus when he went abroad. He's done Silly Billy these forty year, and he's a great comic singer beside. I was reckoned very clever at it. I used to look it by making up so young for it. It tires you very much, for there's so much exertion attached to it by the dancing and capering about. I've done it at the fairs, and also with tumblers in the street; only, when you do it in the street, you don't do one-half the business.

"The make-up for a Silly Billy is this: Short white trousers and shoes, with a strap round the ankle, long white pinafore with a frill round the neck, and red sleeves, and a boy's cap. We dress the head with the hair behind the ears, and a dab of red on the nose and two patches of black over the eyebrows. When I went to the fair I always took three pairs of white trousers with me. The girls used to get up playing larks with me, and smearing my white trousers with gingerbread. It's a very favourite character with the women—they stick pins into you, as if you were a pin-cushion. I've had my thighs bleeding sometimes. One time, during Greenwich, a ugly old woman came on the parade and kissed me, and made me a present of a silver sixpence, which, I needn't say, was soon spent in porter. Why, I've brought home with me sometimes toys enough to last a child a fortnight, if it was to break one every day, such as carts and horses, cock and breeches, whistles, &c. You see, Silly Billy is supposed to be a thievish sort of a character, and I used to take the toys away from the girls as they were going into the theatre, and then I'd show it to the Clown and say, ' Oh, look what that nice lady's give me! I shall take it home to my mother.'

" I've done Silly Billy for Richardson's, and near every booth of consequence. The general wages is from 5s. to 7s. 6d. the day, but my terms was always the three half-crowns. When there's any fairs on, I can always get a job. I always made it a rule never to go far away from London, only to Greenwich or Gravesend, but not farther, for I can make it better in town working the concert-rooms. There are some who do nothing but Silly Billy; and then, if you take the year round, it comes to three days' work a-week. The regular salary doesn't come to more than a pound a-week, but then you make something out of those who come up on the parade, for one will chuck you 6d., some 1s. and 2s. 6d. We call those parties ' prosses.' I have had such a thing as 5s. give to me. We are supposed to share this among the company, and we generally do. These are the ' nobbings,' and may send up your earnings to as much as 25s. a-week, besides drink, which you can have more given to you than you want.

" When we go about the streets with tumblers, we mostly only sing a song, and dance, and keep the ring whilst the performance is going on. We also ' nob,' or gather the money. I never heard of a Silly Billy going out busking in tap-rooms and that. The tumblers like the Silly Billy, because the dress is attractive; but they are getting out of date now, since the grotesque clown is so much in the street. I went about with a school termed ' The Demons,' and very clever they was, though they've all broke up now, and I don't know what's become of them. There were four of them. We did middling, but we could always manage to knock up such a thing as 20s. each a-week. I was, on and off, about six months with them. After their tumbling, then my turn would begin. The drummer would say: ' Turn and turn about's fair play. Billy, now it's your turn. A song from Billy; and if we meet with any encouragement, ladies and gentlemen, the young man here will tie his legs together and chuck several summersets.' Then I'd sing such a song as ' Clementina Clements,' which begins like this:

' You talk of modest girls,
    Now I've seen a few,
But there's none licks the one
    I'm sticking up to.
But some of her faults
    Would make some chaps ill;
But, with all her faults,
    Yes, I love her still.
Such a delicate duck was Clementina Clements;
Such a delicate duck I never did see.'

" There's one verse where she won't walk over a potato-field because they've got eyes, and another when she faints at seeing a Dutch doll without clothes on. Then she doesn't like tables' legs, and all such as that, and that's why she is ' such a delicate duck.' That song always tells with the women. Then I used to sing another, called ' What do men and women marry for?' which was a very great favourite. One verse that went very well was:

' If a good wife you've got,
    (But there's very few of those,)
Your money goes just like a shot:
    They're everlasting wanting clothes.
And when you've bought 'em all you can,
    Of course you cannot buy them more;
They cry, Do you call yourself a man?
    Was this what we got married for?'

" When I danced, it was merely a comic dance—what we call a ' roley poley.' Sometimes, when we had been walking far, and pitching a good many times, the stones would hurt my feet awful with dancing.

" Pitching with tumblers is nothing compared to fair-parading. There you are the principal of the comic men after Clown, for he's first. We have regular scenes, which take twenty minutes working through. When the parade is slack, then comes the Silly Billy business. There's a very celebrated sketch, or whatever you call it, which Clown and Silly Billy do together, taking off mesmerism.

"Clown comes on, dressed up in a tall white hat, and with a cloak on. He says that he has just arrived from the island of Mititti, and that he's the great Doctor Bokanki, the most celebrated mesmeriser in the world. He says, 'Look at me. Here I am. Ain't I mesmerised elephants? Ain't I mesmerised monkeys? and ain't I going to mesmerise him?' He then tells Silly Billy to sit in the chair. Then he commences passing his hands across his eyes. He asks Billy, 'What do you see, Billy?' He turns his face, with his shut eyes, towards the crowd, and says, 'A man with a big nose, sir, and such a many pimples on his face.' 'And now what do you see, Billy?' 'Oh, ain't that gal a-winking at me! You be quiet, or I'll tell my mother.' 'Now what do you see, Billy?' 'Nothink.' Then the doctor turns to the crowd, and says, 'Now, ladies and gentlemen, I shall touch him on the fakement at the back of his head which is called a bump. Oh, my eyes! ain't Billy's head a-swelling! This bump, ladies and gentlemen, is called a organ—not a church nor yet a chapel organ, nor yet one of them they grind in the street. And here's another organ,' he says, putting his hand on Billy's stomach. 'This here is called his wittling department organ, or where he puts his grub. I shall now touch him on another fakement, and make him sing.' Then he puts his finger on Billy's head, and Billy sings:

'As I one day was hawking my ware,
I thought I'd invent something novel and rare;
For as I'm not green, and I know what's o'clock,
So I'll have a go in at the pine-apple rock.
Tol de ro lay, tol de ro lay.'

"Then Billy becomes quiet again, and the doctor says, 'I'll now, ladies and gentlemen, touch him on another fakement, and cause Billy to cry. This here is his organ of the handling department.' Then he takes Billy's finger and bites it, and Billy begins to roar like a town bull. Then the doctor says, 'I'll now, ladies and gentlemen, touch him on another fakement, whereby the youth can tell me what I've got in my hand.' He then puts his hand in his coat-tail pocket, and says, 'Billy, what have I got in my hand?' and Billy says, 'Ah, you nasty beast! why it's a—it's a—it's a —oh, I don't like to say!' They do this a lot of times, Billy always replying, 'Oh, I don't like to say!' until at last he promises that, if he won't tell his mother, he will; and then he says, 'It's a small-tooth comb.' 'Very right, Billy; and what's in it?' 'Why, one of them 'ere things that crawls.' 'Very right, Billy; and what is it?' 'Why, it's a—it's a black-beetle.' 'Very right, Billy; look again. Do you see anything else?' 'There's some crumbs.' Then he tells Billy, that as he is such a good boy he'll bring him to; and Billy says, 'Oh, don't, please, sir; one's quite enough.' Then he brings him to, and Billy says, 'Oh, ain't it

nice! Oh, it's so golly! Here, you young woman, I wish you'd let me touch your bumps.' Then, if the people laugh, he adds, 'You may laugh, but it gives you a all-over sort of a feeling, as if you had drunk three pints of pickling vinegar.'

"That's a very favourite scene; but I haven't give it you all, for it would fill a volume. It always makes a hit; and Billy has a rare chance of working comic attitudes and so on when the doctor touches his bumps.

"There's another very celebrated scene for Silly Billy. It's what we call the preaching scene. Silly Billy mounts up a ladder, and Clown holds it at the bottom, and looks through the steps. Clown has to do the clerk to Billy's parson. Billy begins by telling the clerk that he must say 'Barley sugar' at the end of every sentence he preaches. Billy begins in this way:—'Keyind brethren, and you fair damsels,' and he's supposed to be addressing the chaps and gals on the parade, 'I hope that the text I shall give you will be a moral to you, and prevent you from eating the forbidden sweets of—' 'Barley sugar!' 'No, you fool—sin! and that will put you in the right path as you walk through the fields of—' 'Barley sugar!' 'No; virtue, you fool! My text is taken from the epistle of Thomas to the Ethiopians, the first chapter, and two first slices off a leg of mutton, where it says so beautifully—' 'Barley sugar!' 'No, no; that's not it! Now it come to go along in the first year in the first month, two days before that, as we was journeying through the land of—' 'Barley sugar!' 'No, no, you fool! keep quiet. Flowerpotamia, we met a serpent, and from his mouth was issuing—' 'Barley sugar!' 'No, no! fire.' Then all the people on the parade jump up and shout, 'Where?' Then Billy says, 'Oh, my sister's tom-cat, here's a congregation! Sit down.' When they are all quiet again, Billy goes on: 'Now this I say unto you—' 'Barley sugar!' 'Keep quiet, will you!' and he hits Clown with his foot. 'Two shall be well and two shall be queer. Oh, ain't I ill! Go, men of little understanding, and inherit a basin of pea-soup at the cook-shop, together with—' 'Barley sugar!' 'No such thing!—my blessing. Unto you will I give nothing, and unto you just half as much—' 'Barley sugar!' 'Hold your tongue! You that have had nothing shall give it back again, and you that had nothing at all, you shall keep it. Now let us sing—' 'Barley sugar!' 'No; a song.' Then Billy tells them to get their books, and they take up pint pots, or whatever they can get. 'Let us sing,' and they all jump up, and they all begin:

'If I was a drayman's horse
One quarter of the year,
I'd put my tail where my head ought to be,
And I'd drink up all the—'

'Barley sugar!'—'Hold your tongue!—beer.'

After all of them have sung, Billy says, 'Now let us say,' and all of them howl, 'Aye, aye.'

> ' Now is the winter of our discontent—
> We have not enough money to pay our rent ;
> And by all the clouds that tip our house,
> We've not enough food to feed a ——'

'Barley sugar!' 'Yes, barley sugar,' says Billy. Then all the congregation cries—'O—o—o—o;' and Clown says, 'Bar—bar—bar—barley sugar,' and he is so much affected he weeps and goes to wipe his eyes, and lets the ladder fall, and down comes Billy. He gives sundry kicks, and then pretends to be dying. The congregation say, 'Peace be with you, Billy,' and he answers, 'Yes, peas-pudding and fried taters;' and the Clown howls out, 'Barley sugar!' When Billy is dead, if business isn't very good, they put the body on the ladder, and form a procession. The music goes at the head and plays a hornpipe, slowly, and then they leave the booth, and parade through the fair among the people, with Clown as chief mourner. The people are bursting their sides, and wherever we go they follow after. All the mourners keep crying, 'Oh, oh, oh, Billy's dead!' and then Billy turns round, and sometimes says, 'Don't be fools! it's only a lark:' or else, 'Don't tell mother; she'll give me a hiding.' This procession business always brings a flock behind us, and fills the theatre, or goes a great way towards it. When I have been Silly Billy, and representing this scene, and been carried through the fair, I've been black and blue from the girls coming up and pinching me through the ladder. The girls are wonderfully cheeky at fairs, and all for a lark. They used to get me so precious wild, I couldn't help coming to life, and say, 'Quiet, you hussies!' But it were no good, for they'd follow you all about, and keep on nipping a fellow.

"Another celebrated scene or sketch is the teetotal one, and a rich one it is. Billy is supposed to have joined the temperance parties. He calls for a tub to preach upon, and he says he will consider it a favour if they could let it be a water-butt. They lift Billy on to the tub, and a cove—Clown generally—sits under to take the chair of the meeting. Then the paraders stand about, and I begin: 'Ladies and gentlemen, waking friends, and lazy enemies, and Mr. Chairman, what I'm about to tell you I'm a stanch teetotaler.' 'Hear, hear, hear,' everybody cries. 'I have been so for now two—' and the Clown suggests 'Years.' 'No, minutes. I'd have you avoid water as you would avoid a bull that wasn't in a chaney-shop.' 'Hear, hear, hear.' 'I once knew a friend of mine who drank water till he was one solid mass of ice; and he drank tea till the leaves grew out of his nose.' 'Oh, oh, hear, hear.' 'He got so fat, you couldn't see him. This, my friends, comes of tea-drinking!' 'Hear, hear, hear.' 'I hope, kind friends, this will be a lesson to you to avoid

drinking too much'—Then the chairman jumps up and says, 'Beer!' 'No, no; tea. Drink in moderation, and never drink more than I do. Two pots of ale, three pints of porter, four glasses of gin, five of rum, and six of brandy, is enough for any man at one time. Don't drink more, please.' 'Hear, hear, hear.' 'That will cause you to be in the height of bloom. Your nose will blossom; your eyes will be bright as two burnt holes in a blanket; your head will swell till no hat will fit it. These are facts, my friends; undeniable facts, my kind friends.' 'Hear, hear, hear.' 'You will get so fat, you'll take up the pavement to walk. I believe, and I trust, that what I have said will not convince you that teetotalism and coffeetotalism are the best things ever invented. Sign the pledge. The pledge-book is here. You must all pay a penny; and if you don't keep up your payments, you will be scratched. With these few remarks I now conclude my address to you, hoping that every friend among you is so benevolent as to subscribe a pot of beer. I shall be happy to drink it, to show you how awful a thing it is not to become a teetotalier.' Then they all rush forward to sign the pledge, and they knock Clown over, and he tumbles Silly Billy into the barrel up to his neck. Then we all sing

> ' I likes a drop of good beer,
> I likes a drop of good beer ;
> And hang their eyes if ever they tries
> To rob a poor man of his beer.'

And that ends the meeting.

"I was in Greenwich fair, doing Silly Billy, when the celebrated disturbance with the soldiers took place. I was at Smith and Webster's booth (Richardson's that was), and our clown was Paul Petro. He had been a bit of a fighting man. He was bending down for Silly Billy to take a jump over him, and some of the soldiers ran up and took the back. They knocked his back as they went over, and he got shirtey. Then came a row. Four of them pitched into Paul, and he cries out for help. The mob began to pelt the soldiers, and they called out to their comrades to assist them. A regular confusion ensued. The soldiers tumbled us about, and took off their belts. They cut Paul's forehead right open. I was Silly Billy, and I got a broomstick, and when one of the soldiers gave me a lick over the face with his belt, I pitched him over on the mob with my broomstick. I was tumbled down the steps among the mob, and hang me if they didn't pitch into me too! I got the awfullest nose you ever see. There was I, in my long pinafore, a-wiping up the blood, and both my eyes going as black as plums. I cut up a side place, and then I sat down to try and put my nose to rights. Lord, how I did look about for plaster! When I came back there was all the fair a fighting. The fighting-men came out of their booths and let into the soldiers, who was going about flourishing their belts and hitting everybody. At last the police came; two of them was knocked down, and sent back on stretchers: but at last, when a picket was sent for, all the soldiers — there was about forty of them — were walked off. They got from six to nine months' imprisonment; and those that let into the police, eighteen months. I never see such a sight. It was all up with poor Silly Billy for that fair, for I had to wrap my face up in plaster and flannel, and keep it so for a week.

" I shouldn't think there were more than a dozen Silly Billys going about at the present time; and out of them there ain't above three first-raters. I know nearly all of them. When fairs ain't on they go about the streets, either with schools of tumblers or serenaders; or else they turn to singing at the concerts. To be a good Silly Billy, it requires a man with heaps of funniment and plenty of talk. He must also have a young-looking face, and the taller the man the better for it. When I go out I always do my own gag, and I try to knock out something new. I can take a candle, or a straw, or a piece of gingerbread, or any mortal thing, and lecture on it. At fairs we make our talk rather broad, to suit the audience.

" Our best sport is where a girl comes up on the parade, and stands there before going inside — we have immense fun with her. I offer to marry her, and so does Clown, and we quarrel as to who proposed to the young woman first. I swear she's my gal, and he does the same. Then we appeal to her, and tell her what we'll give her as presents. It makes immense fun. The girls always take it in good part, and seem to enjoy it as much as the mob in front. If we see that she is in any ways shy we drop it, for it's done for merriment, and not to insult; and we always strive to amuse and not to abuse our friends."

BILLY BARLOW.

" BILLY BARLOW," is another supposed comic character, that usually accompanies either the street-dancers or acrobats in their peregrinations. The dress consists of a cocked-hat and red feather, a soldier's coat (generally a sergeant's with sash), white trowsers with the legs tucked into Wellington boots, a large tin eye-glass, and an old broken and ragged umbrella. The nose and cheeks are coloured bright red with vermilion. The " comic business" consists of the songs of the " Merry Month of May," and " Billy Barlow," together with a few old conundrums and jokes, and sometimes (where the halfpence are very plentiful) a " comic " dance. The following statement concerning this peculiar means of obtaining a living I had from a man whom I had seen performing in the streets, dressed up for the part, but who came to me so thoroughly altered in appearance that I could hardly recognise him. In plain clothes he had almost a re-spectable appearance, and was remarkably clean and neat in his attire. Altogether, in his undress, he might have been mistaken for a better kind of mechanic. There was a humorous expression, however, about his mouth, and a tendency to grimace, that told the professional buffoon. " I go about now as Billy Barlow," he said; " the character of Billy Barlow was originally played at the races by a man who is dead. He was about ten years at the street business, doing nothing else than Billy Barlow in the public thoroughfares, and at fairs and races. He might have made a fortune had he took care on it, sir; but he was a great drunkard, and spent all he got in gin. He died seven years ago—where most of the street-performers ends their days—in the workhouse. He was formerly a potman at some public-house, and got discharged, and then took to singing comic songs about the streets and fairs. The song of ' Billy Barlow' (which was very popular then) was among the lot that he sung, and that gave his name. He used to sing, too, the song of ' I hope I don't intrude;' and for that he dressed up as Paul Pry, which is the reason of the old umbrella, the eye-glass, and the white trowsers tucked into the boots, being part of the costume at present. Another of his songs was the ' Merry Month of May,' or ' Follow the Drum;' and for that he put on the soldier's coat and cocked-hat and feather, which we wears to this day. After this he was called ' General Barlow.' When he died, one or two took to the same kerachter, and they died in the workhouse, like us all. Two months ago I thought I'd take to it myself, as there was a vacancy in the purfession. I have been for thirty years at the street business, off and on. I am fifty now. I was a muffin and biscuit-baker by trade; but, like the rest on us, I got fond of a roving life. My father was a tailor by trade, but took to being a supernumerary at Covent Garden Theayter, where my uncle was a performer, and when I was nine years old I played the part of the child in ' Pizarro,' and after that I was one of the devils what danced round my uncle in ' Mother Goose.' When I was fourteen year old my uncle apprenticed me to the muffin business, and I stuck to it for five years; but when I was out of my time I made up my mind to cut it, and take to performing. First I played clown at a booth, for I had always a taste for the comic after I had played the devil, and danced round my uncle in the Covent-garden pantomime. Some time after that I took to play the drum and pipes; and since then I have been chiefly performing as musicianer to different street exhibitions. When business is bad in the winter or wet weather, I make sweetmeats, and go about the streets and sell them. I never made muffins since I left the business; you see, I've no stove nor shop for that, and never had the means of raising them. Sweet-meats takes little capital—toffy, brandy-balls, and Albert rock isn't expensive to get up. Besides, I'm known well among the children in the streets, and they likes to patronise the purfession for sweetmeats, even though they won't give nothing while you're a performing; I've done much the same since I took to the Billy Barlow, as I did before at the street business. We all share alike, and that's what I did as the drum and pipes. I never dress at home. My wife (I'm a married man) knows the part I play. She came to see me once, and laughed at me fit to bust. The landlord nor the fellow-lodgers where I live—I have a room to myself—ain't aware of what I do; I sneaks my things out, and dresses at a public-house. It costs us a pot for dressing and a pot for undressing. We has the use of the tap-room for that. I'm like the rest of the world at home—or rather more serious, maybe,—though, thank God, I don't want for food; things is cheap enough now; and if I can't get a living at the buffoonery business, why I tries sweetmeats, and between the two I do manage to grab on somehow, and that's more than many of my purfession can do. My pardner (a street-dancer whom he brought with him) must either dance or starve; and there's plenty like him in the streets of London. I only know of one other Barlow but me in the business, and he's only taken to it after me. Some jokes ain't fit for ladies to listen to, but wot I says is the best-approved jokes—such as has been fashionable for many years, and can't give no offence to no one. I say to the musician, ' Well, master, can you tell me why are the Thames Tunnel and Hungerford Suspension Bridge like two joints badly done ?' He'll say, ' No, Mr. Barlow ;' and then I give him the answer: ' Because one is over-done, and the other is under-done.' Then I raise my umbrella, saying, ' I think I'm purwided against the weather ;' and as the umbrella is all torn and slit, it raises a laugh. Some days I get six shillings or seven shillings as my share; sometimes not a quarter of the money. Perhaps I may average full eighteen shillings a-week in the summer, or more; but not a pound. In the winter, if there's a subsistence, that's all. Joking is not natural to me, and I'm a steady man; it's only in the way of business, and I leave it on one side when I've got my private apparel on. I never think of my public character if I can help it, until I get my show-dress on, and I'm glad to get it off at night; and then I think of my home and children, and I struggle hard for them, and feel disgust oft enough at having been a tom-fool to street fools."

STROLLING ACTORS.

WHAT are called strolling actors are those who go about the country and play at the various fairs and towns. As long as they are acting in a booth they are called canvas actors; but supposing they stop in a town a few days after a fair, or build up in a town where there is no fair, that constitutes what is termed private business.

"We call strolling acting ' mumming,' and the actors ' mummers.' All spouting is mumming. A strolling actor is supposed to know something of everything. He doesn't always get a part given to him to learn, but he's more often told what character he's to take, and what he's to do, and he's supposed to be able to find words capable of illustrating the character; in fact, he has to ' gag,' that is, make up words.

"When old Richardson was alive, he used to make the actors study their parts regularly; and there's Thorne and Bennett's, and Douglas's, and other large travelling concerns, that do so at the present time ; but where there's one that does, there's ten that don't. I was never in one that did, not to study the parts, and I have been mumming, on and off, these ten years.

"There's very few penny gaffs in London where they speak; in fact, I only know one where they do. It ain't allowed by law, and the police are uncommon sewere. They generally play ballets and dumb acting, singing and dancing, and such-like.

"I never heard of such a thing as a canvas theatre being prosecuted for having speaking plays performed, so long as a fair is going on, but if it builds at other times I have known the mayor to object to it, and order the company away. When we go to pitch in a town, we always, if it's a quiet one, ask permission of the mayor to let us build.

"The mummers have got a slang of their own, which parties connected with the perfession generally use. It is called ' mummers' slang,' and I have been told that it's a compound of broken Italian and French. Some of the Romanee is also mixed up with it. This, for instance, is the slang for ' Give me a glass of beer,'— ' Your nabs sparkle my nabs,' ' a drop of beware.' ' I have got no money ' is, ' My nabs has nanti dinali.' I'll give you a few sentences.

" ' Parni' is rain; and ' toba' is ground.

" ' Nanti numgare' is—No food.

" ' Nanti fogare' is— No tobacco.

" ' Is his nabs a bona pross ?'—Is he good for something to drink ?

" ' Nanti, his nabs is a keteva homer '— No, he's a bad sort.

" ' The casa will parker our nabs multi' means,—This house will tumble down.

" Vada the glaze' is—Look at the window.

" These are nearly all the mummers' slang words we use; but they apply to different meanings. We call breakfast, dinner, tea, supper, all of them ' numgare ;' and all beer, brandy, water, or soup, are ' beware.' We call everybody ' his nabs,' or ' her nabs.' I went among the penny-ice men, who are Italian chaps, and I found that they were speaking a lot of mummers' slang. It is a good deal

Italian. We think it must have originated from Italians who went about doing panto-mimes.

"Now, the way we count money is nearly all of it Italian; from one farthing up to a shilling is this:—

"'Patina, nadsa, oni soldi, duey soldi, tray soldi, quatro soldi, chinqui soldi, say soldi, seter soldi, otter soldi, novra soldi, deshra soldi, lettra soldi, and a biouk.' A half-crown is a 'metsa carroon;' a 'carroon' is a crown; 'metsa punta' is half-a-sovereign; a 'punta' is a pound. Even with these few words, by mixing them up with a few English ones, we can talk away as fast as if we was using our own language.

"Mumming at fairs is harder than private business, because you have to perform so many times. You only wear one dress, and all the actor is expected to do is to stand up to the dances outside and act in. He'll have to dance perhaps sixteen quadrilles in the course of the day, and act about as often inside. The company generally work in shares, or if they pay by the day, it's about four or five shillings a-day. When you go to get engaged, the first question is, 'What can you do?' and the next, 'Do you find your own properties, such as russet boots, your dress, hat and feathers, &c?' Of course they like your dress the better if it's a showy one; and it don't much matter about its corresponding with the piece. For instance, Henry the Second, in 'Fair Rosamond,' always comes on with a cavalier's dress, and nobody notices the difference of costume. In fact, the same dresses are used over and over again for the same pieces. The general dress for the ladies is a velvet skirt with a satin stomacher, with a gold band round the waist and a pearl band on the forehead. They, too, wear the same dresses for all the pieces. A regular fair show has only a small compass of dresses, for they only goes to the same places once in a-year, and of course their costumes ain't remem-bered.

"The principal fair pieces are 'Blue Beard,' 'Robert, duke of Normandy,' and 'Fair Rosa-mond, or the Bowers of Woodstock.' I recol-lect once they played 'Maria Martin,' at a fair, in a company I was with, and we played that in cavalier costume; and so we did 'The Murder at Stanfield Hall,' Rush's affair, in dresses of the time of Charles the Second.

"An actor's share will average for a fair at five shillings a-day, if the fair is anything at all. When we don't work we don't get paid, so that if we only do one fair a-week, that's fifteen shillings, unless we stop to do a day or two private business after the fair.

"'Fair Rosamond' isn't so good a piece as 'Blue Beard,' for that's a great fair piece, and a never-failing draw. Five years ago I was with a company—Star and Lewis were the acting managers. Then 'Blue Beard' was our favourite piece, and we played it five fairs

out of six. 'Fair Rosamond' is too sentimen-tal. They like a comedy man, and the one in 'Fair Rosamond' isn't nothing. They like the secret-chamber scene in 'Blue Beard.' It's generally done by the scene rolling up and discovering another, with skeletons painted on the back, and blue fire. We always carried that scene with us wherever we went, and for the other pieces the same scenes did. At Star's, our scenes were somewhat about ten feet wide and eight feet high. They all rolled up, and there were generally about four in working order, with the drop curtain, which made five.

"You may put the price of a good fair theatrical booth down at from fifty pounds to two hundred and fifty pounds. There's some of them more expensive still. For instance, the paintings alone on the front of Douglas's Shakesperian theatre, must have cost seventy pounds; and his dress must have cost a deal, for he's got a private theatre at Bolton, and he works them there as well as at fairs.

"The 'Bottle Imp' is a very effective fair piece. It opens with a scene of Venice, and Willebald and Albert, which is the comedy man and the juvenile. The comic man's principal line is, 'I'll tell your mother,' every time Albert wants to go and see his sweet-heart, or if he's doing anything that he thinks improper. In the first act Albert goes to his sweetheart's house, and the father consents to their union, provided he can gain so many ducats. Albert then finds out a stranger, who is Nicolo, who asks him to gamble with him at dice: Albert says he is poor. Nicolo says he once was poor, but now he has great wealth. He then tells Albert, that if he likes he can be rich too. He says, 'Have you not heard of imps and bottle imps?' 'Stuff!' says Albert; 'me, indeed! a poor artist; I have heard of such things, but I heed them not.' 'But, boy,' says Nicolo, 'I have that in my possession will make you rich indeed; a drop of the elixir in this bottle, rubbed on the outside, will give you all you require; and if ever you wish to part with it, you must sell it for less than you gave.' He gives three ducats for it, and as he gives the money the demon laughs from the side, 'Ha! ha! ha! mine, mine!' Albert looks amazed. Nicolo says, 'Ah, youth! may you know more happiness than I have whilst I had that in my possession:' and then he goes off. Albert then tries the power of the bottle. He says, 'What, ho! I wish for wine,' and it's shoved on from the side. As he is drinking, Willebald exclaims, 'O dear, O dear! I've been looking for my master. O that I were only safe back again in Thread-needle-street! I'll never go hunting pretty girls again. Oh, won't I tell his mother!' 'How now, caitiff!—Leave me!' says Albert. 'All right,' says Willebald; 'I'll leave you—won't I tell your mother!'

"When Willebald goes, Albert wishes for sleep, and the Bottle Imp replies, 'All your wishes shall be gratified, excepting one. Sleep you cannot have while I am in your possession.' The demon then seizes him by the throat, and Albert falls on stage, demon exulting over him. Enter Willebald, who, seeing the demon, cries, ' Murder! murder! Oh, won't I tell their mothers!' and that ends the first act.

"In the second and last act, Albert gives Willebald instructions to sell the bottle; ' but it is to be for less than three ducats.' Willebald says, ' No marine-storekeeper would give three ducats for an old bottle;' but he goes off shouting, out 'Who'll buy a bottle? Who'll buy a bottle?' In the next scene, Willebald is still shouting his bottle for sale, with folks laughing off stage and dogs barking. He says, ' Ah! laugh away. It's well to be merry, but I'm obliged to cry—Who'll buy a bottle?' He then says he's 'not going walking about all day selling a bottle;' and then he says he's got two ducats, and he'll buy the bottle himself, sooner than trudge about Venice. Then he says, ' Oh, Mr. Bottle, here are the ducats; now you are mine.' Then the demon cries, ' Mine, mine!' He says it was only the wind. Then he says, ' Oh, how I wish I was at home again, and heard my little brothers and sisters singing!' And instantly from the sides you hear, ' Boys and girls come out to play!' Then Willebald says, 'I wish you'd hold your tongue, you little brutes!' and they cease. Next he complains that he's so poor, and he wishes it would rain gold on him, and then down comes a shower. Then in comes Albert, who asks whether the bottle has been sold; and Willebald replies that it's all right. ' Thank heavens,' cries Albert; ' but yet I pity the miserable wretch who has bought it.' ' What do you mean? O dear, O dear! to frighten one so! I'll tell your mother!' ' Know ye not, caitiff!' continues Albert, ' that that bottle contains a demon? O what a weight hast thou removed from my heart!' As Willebald is deploring his lot, enter a poor man, who asks for a drink of water; and Willebald tells him he can't give him any water, but he has an elixir he shall have very cheap. The old man replies that he hasn't got more than a petani, which is the sixtieth part of a farthing. However, Willebald sells him the bottle; and as it's the smallest coin in the world, and the bottle can't go no cheaper, the demon rushes in and seizes the beggar, who turns out to be Nicolo, the first who sold the bottle. As he is being carried off, Willebald cries out, ' For shame, you ugly devil! to treat the old gentleman like that! Won't I tell your mother!' and down comes the curtain.

"The ' Bottle Imp' is a very successful romantic drama. There's plenty of blue fire in it. The ' Bottle Imp' have it at every entrance that fellow do. There is some booths that are fonder of the ' Bottle Imp' than any other piece. We played it at Bill Weale's

theatre more than any other drama. The imp is always acted by a man in a cloak with a mask on. You can see his cavalier boots under his cloak, but that don't matter to holiday folk when once they know it's intended to be a demon.

"It's a very jolly life strolling, and I wouldn't leave it for any other if I had my choice. At times it's hard lines; but for my part I prefer it to any other. It's about fifteen shillings a-week for certain. If you can make up your mind to sleep in the booth, it ain't such bad pay. But the most of the men go to lodgings, and they don't forget to boast of it. ' Where do you lodge?' one 'll ask. ' Oh, I lodged at such a place,' says another; for we're all first-rate fellows, if you can get anybody to believe us.

"Mummers' feed is a herring, which we call a pheasant. After performance we generally disperse, and those who have lodgings go to 'em; but if any sleep in the booth, turn in. Perhaps there's a batch of coffee brought forwards, a subscription supper of three. The coffee and sugar is put in a kettle and boiled up, and then served up in what we can get: either a saucepan lid, or a cocoa-nut shell, or a publican's pot, or whatever they can get. Mummers is the poorest, flashest, and most independent race of men going. If you was to offer some of them a shilling they'd refuse it, though the most of them would take it. The generality of them is cobblers' lads, and tailors' apprentices, and clerks, and they do account for that by their having so much time to study over their work.

"Private business is a better sort of acting. There we do nearly the entire piece, with only the difficult parts cut out. We only do the outline of the story, and gag it up. We've done various plays of Shakspeare in this way, such as ' Hamlet' or ' Othello,' but only on benefit occasions. Then we go as near as memory will let us, but we must never appear to be stuck for words. Our prices of admission in the country for private business is threepence and sixpence, or sometimes sixpence or one shilling, for it all depends upon the town, but in London it's oftener one penny and twopence. We only go to the outskirts and act there, for they won't allow us in the streets. The principal parts for pitching the booth for private business in London, is about Lock's-fields, Walworth. We opened there about six years ago last Easter.

" Our rehearsals for a piece are the funniest things in the world. Perhaps we are going to play ' The Floating Beacon, or The Weird Woman of the Wreck.' The manager will, when the night's performance is over, call the company together, and he'll say to the low-comedyman, ' Now, you play Jack Junk, and this is your part: you're supposed to fetch Frederick for to go to sea. Frederick gets capsized in the boat, and gets aboard of the floating beacon. You go to search for him, and the smugglers tell you he's not aboard, and they give you the lie; then you say, 'What, the lie to a English sailor!' and you chuck your quid in his eye, saying, 'I've had it for the last fourteen days, and now I scud it with a full sail into your lubberly eye.' Then you have to get Frederick off.'

"Then the manager will turn to the juvenile, and say, 'Now, sir, you'll play Frederick. Now then, Frederick, you're in love with a girl, and old Winslade, the father, is very fond of you. You get into the boat to go to the ship, and you're wrecked and get on to the beacon. You're very faint, and stagger on, and do a back fall. You're picked up by the weird woman, and have some dialogue with her; and then you have some dialogue with the two smugglers, Ormaloff and Augerstoff. You pretend to sleep, and they're going to stab you, when the wild woman screams, and you awake and have some more dialogue. Then they bring a bottle, and you begin drinking. You change the cups. Then there's more dialogue, and you tackle Ormaloff. Then you discover your mother and embrace. Jack Junk saves you. Form a picture with your mother, the girl, and old Winslade, and Jack Junk over you.'

" That's his part, and he's got to put it together and do the talk.

"Then the manager turns to Ormaloff and Augerstoff, and says: 'Now, you two play the smugglers, do you hear? You're to try and poison the young fellow, and you're defeated.'

"Then he say to the wild woman: 'You're kept as a prisoner aboard the beacon, where your husband has been murdered. You have refused to become the wife of Ormaloff. Your child has been thrown overboard. You discover him in Frederick, and you scream when they are about to stab him, and also when he's about to drink. Make as much of it as you can, please; and don't forget the scream.'

"'Winslade, you know your part. You've only got to follow Junk.'

"'You're to play the lady, you Miss. You're in love with Frederick. You know the old business: 'What! to part thus? Alas! alas! never to this moment have I confessed I love you!''

"That's a true picture of a mumming rehearsal, whether it's fair or private business. Some of the young chaps stick in their parts. They get the stage-fever and knocking in the knees. We've had to shove them on to the scene. They keep on asking what they're to say. 'Oh, say anything!' we tell 'em, and push 'em on to the stage.

"If a man's not gifted with the gab, he's no good at a booth. I've been with a chap acting 'Mary Woodbine,' and he hasn't known a word of his part. Then, when he's stuck, he has seized me by the throat, and said, 'Caitiff! dog! be sure thou provest my wife unfaithful to me.' Then I saw his dodge, and I said, 'Oh, my lord!' and he continued—

'Give me the proof, or thou hadst best been born a dog.' Then I answered, 'My lord, you wrong your wife, and torture me;' and he said, 'Forward, then, liar! dog!' and we both rushed off.

"We were acting at Lock's-fields, Walworth, once, doing private business, when we got into trouble, and were all put into prison for playing without a license. We had built up in a piece of private ground—in a dust-yard known as Calf's—and we had been there eleven months doing exceedingly well. We treated the policeman every night, and gave him as much, with porter and money, that was equal to one shilling a-night, which was taken up from the company. It was something like a penny a-piece for the policeman, for we were rather afraid of something of the kind happening.

"It was about the time that 'Oliver Twist' was making such a success at the other theatres, and so we did a robbery from it, and brought out our version as 'The Golden Farmer.' Instead of having an artful dodge, we called our comic character Jimmy Twitcher, and made him do all the artful-dodgery business. We had three performances a-night in those days. We was in our second performance, and Jimmy Twitcher was in the act of getting through the window, and Hammer, the auctioneer, was asleep, saying in his sleep, 'Knock 'em down! going! going! gone!' when I saw the police in private clothes rising from the front seats, and coming towards the stage. They opened the side door, and let the other police in, about forty of them. Then the inspector said, 'Ladies and gentlemen, I forbid any of you to move, as I arrest those people for performing without a license.' Nobody moved. Three police took hold of me, one at each arm, and one at the back of the neck. They wouldn't allow us to change our dresses, nor to take our other clothes, though they were close by. They marched us off to the Walworth station, along with about a hundred of the spectators, for some of them got away. My wife went to fetch my clothes for me, and they took her, too, and actually locked her up all night, though she was so near her pregnancy that the doctor ordered her pillows to sleep on. In the morning they took us all before the magistrate. The audience were fined one shilling a-head, or seven days; but they paid the shilling. We were all fined twenty shillings, or fourteen days. Some paid, but I couldn't raise it, so I was walked off.

"We were all in an awful fright when we found ourselves in the police-cell that night. Some said we should get six months, others twelve, and all we could say was, 'What on earth will our old women do?'

"We were all in our theatrical costumes. I was Hammer, the auctioneer, dressed in a long white coat, with the swallow-tails touching the ground, and blue bottoms. I had a long figured chintz waistcoat, and a pair of drab knee-breeches, grey stockings, and low shoes, and my hat was a white one with a low crown and broad brim, like a Quaker's. To complete it, I wore a full bushy wig. As we were being walked off from Walworth to Kennington-lane, to go before the magistrate, the tops of the houses and the windows were full of people, waiting to see us come along in our dresses. They laughed more than pitied us. The police got pelted, and I caught a severe blow by accident, from a turnip out of a greengrocer's shop.

" I served all the time at Kingston, in my theatrical dress. I had nothing but bread and water all the time, with gruel for breakfast and supper. I had to pick oakum and make mats. I was only there two days before I was made deputy-wardsman, for they saw I was a decent sort of fellow. I was very much cut up, thinking of the wife so near her confinement. It was very hard, I thought, putting us in prison for getting our bread, for we never had any warning, whatever our master may have had. I can tell you, it was a nail in my coffin, these fourteen days, and one of us, of the name of Chau, did actually die through it, for he was of a very delicate constitution, and the cold laid hold of him. Why, fellows of our life and animation, to be shut up like that, and not allowed to utter a word, it was dreadful severe.

" At this time a little penny work came out, entitled the 'Groans of the Gallows.' I was working at an establishment in Whitechapel, and it was thought that something fresh would be a draw, and it was suggested that we should play this 'Groans of the Gallows,' for everything about hanging was always a hit. There was such a thing as ten people in the piece, and five were prominent characters. We got it written by one of the company, and it was called ' The Groans of the Gallows, or The Hangman's Career, illustrated with pictures.' This is how we brought it out. After an overture, the curtain rose and discovered a group on the stage, all with pots and pipes, gin measures, &c. They sing, 'We won't go home till morning,' and 'Kightly's a jolly good fellow.' Here the hangman is carousing with them, and his wife comes in and upbraids him with his intoxicating habits, and tells him that he spends all the money instead of purviding food for the children. A quarrel ensues, and he knocks her down with a quart pot and kills her. I was the hangman. There is then a picture of amazement from all, and he's repenting of what he's done. He then says, ' This comes of a little drinking. From the half-pint to the pint, from the pint to the pot, and so on, till ruin stares me in the face. Not content with starving my children, I have murdered my wife. Oh that this may be a moral to all !'

" The officers come in and arrest him, when enters the sheriff, who tells him that he has forfeited his life; but that there is a vacancy for the public executioner, and that if he will accept the office his life shall be spared. He accepts the office, and all the characters groan at him. This ends the first scene. In the second enters Kightly and two officers, who have got him and accuse him of murder. He is taken off proclaiming his innocence. Scene the third. Kightly discovered at table in condemned cell, a few months supposing to have elapsed. The bell is tolling, and the hour of seven is struck. Enter sheriffs with hangman, and they tell him to do his duty. They then leave him, and he speaks thus : ' At length, then, two little months only have elapsed, and you, my friend and pot-companion, aye, and almost brother, are the first victim that I have to execute for murder,'—and I shudder you know—' which I know you are innocent of. Am *I* not a murderer, and do I not deserve hanging more than you? but the law will have it's way, and I, the tool of that law, must carry it into force. It now becomes my painful duty to pinion your arms.' Then I do so, and it makes such a thrill through the house. ' I now take you from this place to your execution, where you will be suspended for one hour, and then it is my duty to cut you down. Have you any request to make ?' He cries ' None !' and I add, ' Then follow me.' I always come on to that scene with a white night-cap and a halter on my arm. All the audience was silent as death as I spoke, and with tears in their eyes. Scene the fourth. Gallows being erected by workmen. That's a picture, you know, our fixing the top beam with a hammer, another at the bottom, and a third arranging the bolt at the top. The bell still tolling, you know. Ah, it brought it home to one or two of them, I can tell you. As soon as the workmen have finished they go off. Enter procession of sheriff, parson, hangman, and the victim, with two officers behind. The parson asks the victim if he has any request to make, and he still says 'None,' only he is innocent. The sheriffs then tell the hangman to do his duty. He then places the white cap over the man's head, and the noose about his neck, and is about leaving to draw the bolt, when I exclaim, ' Something here tells me that I ought not to hang this man. He is innocent, and I know it. I cannot, and I will not take his life.' Enter officer in haste, with pardon for Kightly. I then say, ' Kightly, you are free ; live and be happy, and I am——' Here the sheriff adds, ' Doomed to the galleys for life.' That's because I refused to kill him, you know. I then exclaim, ' Then I shall be happy, knowing that I have not taken this man's life, and be thus enabled to give up the office of executioner and it's most horrid paraphernalia.' Then there's blue fire and end of piece.

" That piece was very successful, and run for three weeks. It drew in a deal of money. The boys used to run after me in the streets and call me Calcraft, so great was the hit I made in the part. On one occasion a woman was to be hung, and I was going along Newgate, past the prison, on the Sunday evening. There was a quantity of people congregated, and some of the lads then recognised me from seeing me act in the 'Groans from the Gallows,' and they sung out 'Here comes Calcraft!' Every eye was turned towards me. Some said, 'No, no; that ain't him;' but the boys replied, 'Oh, yes it is; that's the man that played it at the gaff.' Of course I mizzled, for fear of a stone or two.

"The pay of an actor in private business varies from two shillings and sixpence to three shillings, and each man is also supposed to sing two songs in each performance, which makes three performances a night besides performing a sketch. Your engagement lasts as long as you suit the audience; for if you're a favourite you may have such a thing as nine months at a time. Whenever we have a benefit it's a ticket one, which amounts to two hundred tickets and your night's salary, which generally brings you in a pound, with your pay included. There's one in the company generally has a benefit every Thursday, so that your turn comes once in about six months, for the musicians, and the checktakers, and all has their turn.

"The expense of putting a new piece on the stage is not more than a pound, and that includes new scenery. They never do such a thing as buy new dresses. Perhaps they pay such a thing as six shillings a-week for their wardrobe to hire the dresses. Some gives as much as ten shillings; but then, naturally, the costume is more showy. All that we are supposed to find is russet boots, a set of fleshings, a ballet shirt, and a wig.

"Town work is the more quiet and more general-business like. There's no casualty in it, for you're not in shares, but on salaries, and after your work there's your money, for we are paid nightly. I have known as much as thirty-five shillings a-week given at one of these theatres, when the admission is only a penny and twopence. Where I was at it would hold from six to seven hundred people, and there was three performances a-night; and, indeed, on Saturdays and Mondays generally four. We have no extra pay for extra performances. The time allowed for each representation is from one hour to an hour and three-quarters. If we find there is a likelihood of a fourth house, we leave out a song each singer, and that saves half an hour. As soon as one house is turned out another comes in, for they are always waiting outside the doors, and there is a rush immediately the house is empty. We begin at six and are over by a few minutes before twelve. When we do speaking pieces we have to do it on the sly, as we should be stopped and get into trouble."

BALLET PERFORMERS.

"THE Ballet," said a street-dancer to me, "is a very favourite amusement with the people who go to cheap penny theatres. They are all comic, like pantomimes; indeed, they come under that term, only there's no comic scenes or transformations. They're like the story of a pantomime, and nothing else. Nearly all the popular clowns are famous for their ballet performances; they take the comic parts mostly, and the pantaloons take the old men's parts. Ballets have been favourites in this country for forty or fifty year. There is always a comic part in every ballet. I have known ballets to be very popular for ever since I can remember,—and that's thirty years. At all the gaffs, where they are afraid to speak their parts, they always have a ballet. Every one in London, and there are plenty of them, have one every night, for it's very seldom they venture upon a talking play.

"In all ballets the costume is fanciful. The young ladies come on in short petticoats, like them at the opera. Some of the girls we have are the same as have been in the opera corps-de-ballet. Mr. Flexmore, the celebrated clown, is a ballet performer, and there's not a greater man going for the ballet that he appears in, called 'The Dancing Scotchman.' There's Paul Herring, too; he's very famous. He's the only man I know of that can play Punch, for he, works the speaker in his mouth; and he's been a great Punch-and-Judy man in his time. He's very clever in 'The Sprite of the Vineyard, or the Merry Devil of Como.' They've been playing it at Cremorne lately, and a very successful affair it was.

"When a professional goes to a gaff to get an engagement, they in general inquires whether he is a good ballet performer. Everything depends upon that. They also acts ballets at some of the concert-rooms. At the Rising Sun, Knightsbridge, as well as the Brown Bear, Knightsbridge, they play them for a week at a time, and then drop them for a fortnight for a change, and perhaps have tumblers instead; then they have them again for a week, and so on. In Ratcliffe Highway, at Ward's Hoop and Grapes, and also the Albion, and the Prince Regent, they always play ballets at stated intervals. Also the Effingham Saloon, Whitechapel, is a celebrated ballet-house. The admission to all these houses is 2d. I believe. At the Highway, when the ships are up and the sailors ashore, business is very brisk, and they are admitted to the rooms gratuitously; and a fine thing they make of them, for they are good hearted fellows and don't mind what money they spend. I've known one who was a little way gone to chuck half-a-crown on the stage to some actor, and I've known others to spend a pound at one bit,—standing to all round! One night, when I was performing ballets at the Rising Sun, Knightsbridge, Mr. Hill, the Queen's coachman, threw me two half-crowns on to the stage. We had been supposed to be fighting,— I and my mate,— and to have got so exhausted we fell down, and Mr. Hill came and poured three glasses of port-wine negus down our throats as we laid. I've repeatedly had 1s. and 6s. thrown to me by the grooms of the different people of nobility, such as the Russells and various other families.

" A good ballet performer will get averaging from a pound to 35s. a-week. They call Paul Herring a star, and he is one, for he always draws wherever he goes. I generally get my 25s., that's my running price, though I try for my 30s.; but 25s. is about my mark. I have always made Paul Herring my study, and I try to get to perform with him, for he's the best clown of the day, and a credit to work with.

" It's impossible to say how many ballet performers there are. There are such a host of them it's impossible to state that, for they change so. Then a great many are out of employment until Christmas, for that generally fills the vacancies up. My wife does a little in ballets, though she is principally a poses plastique girl. I married my wife off the table.

" One of the most successful ballets is the Statue Blanche. It has been performed at every theatre in London, both the cheap and the regular. The Surrey is an enormous place for it. It came out, I believe, in Grimaldi's time. It was played a fortnight ago at the Bower, and I took the part of the old man, and I was very successful; so far so, that I got a situation for Christmas. It's an excellent plot, and runs an hour and a quarter to play.

" It begins with a romantic view, with a cottage on the right hand, and white palings round it, and a quantity of straw laying on the stage. The villagers and the lover come on. Lover goes to cottage door and knocks three times, when lady appears at window. He ballets to her, ' Will you come down here and dance ?' She comes, and they all do a country dance. At the end of the dance the old man is heard to cough inside cottage. He opens the window and sees the girl outside, and shakes his fist at her. The lover hides behind the lady. He comes out and sends his daughter into cottage, and sends the lover off about his business. He refuses to do so. The old man makes a blow at him with his stick; he makes another, when lover bobs down and stick strikes Pierrot in the face, and knocks him down. This Pierrot is the Simpkin of the ballet, and he's dressed in white, with long sleeves, and a white face, and white scalp on his head. The ballet is from the French, and its real title is ' La Statue Blanche,' though we call it ' The Statue Blanche.'

" Lover is driven off stage, and old man picks up Simpkin, and ballets to him that he's very sorry but he thought it was the lover, and

tells him to hide under the straw which is on the stage, and that if the lover comes again to lay hold of him, to call assistance. He hides, and old man goes into cottage.

" Lover comes again with villagers carrying flails, and they begin to thresh this straw with Simpkin under it. They thresh him round stage. He knocks at door three times, and the third blow knocks old man in the face. Out he comes staggering. The old man threatens to sack lover. He goes into cottage and brings out lover's bundle, and throws it to lover, and sends him away. The lover appeals to old man, but all to no use. The lover then ballets to him that he has got no money, so the old man hands his purse, which Simpkin takes and carries up stage. The lover still asks for money, and the old man is astonished, and then turns round and sees Simpkin, and makes him return it. Exit old man and Simpkin into cottage, leaving lover on stage. He leans against wing very disconsolate, when an artist comes on with a scrap-book to sketch the scene. He asks the lover what is the matter, and then he tells him he has a plan if lover will become a sketcher; and if he likes to do so, he will make a statue of him and sell him to the old man, as he deals in antiquities, and by that plan he will be able to gain the girl. They go off, and another old man comes on and knocks at door, which old father opens, and thinking it is lover tumbles him over. He then says he's very sorry for mistaking him for the lover. They make it up, and the old man says he has plenty of money, and has come to marry the daughter. They embrace, and old father invites old man to step inside and have something to drink. As the second old man is going in, the Simpkin jumps over his head and hides; and old man swears it is the lover, and hunts for him, but can't find him, and enters cottage. The second scene has got the tea business in it, and the blacking of the old lover's face. The comic business here is, they are having tea, and Simpkin is waiting on them, and does every thing very clumsy. He carries on the old business of stirring the tea up with a candle, and then he puts the dirty kettle on the cloth and makes a mark; so he thinks for a minute, and then wipes the bottom of the kettle with the old lover's handkerchief when he is not looking. Then Simpkin steals the milk-jug, and as he is drinking the old father hits him on the stomach, and makes him sputter in old lover's face, who instantly snatches up the dirty handkerchief to wipe his face, and blacks it all over with the soot from the bottom of the kettle. Then there is some comic business about Simpkin breaking the tea-things, and bursting a coat in two; and then scene changes to a romantic view, with a pedestal in the centre, and statue on it. The old father comes on with the girl and Simpkin, and the villagers, who have all come to view the statue. The old man then calls the artist, and tells him to wind up the statue that he may see how it works. The statue does several positions, and the old man buys it. They all go off but Simpkin, the lady, and the old man. (The statue is still on the pedestal, you know.) The old man cautions Simpkin not to touch the statue, for he's going away. As soon as he is gone, Simpkin goes and winds it up until he breaks the spring. Then in comes the old man again, and the fool goes to a corner and pretends to be asleep. He is pulled up by the ear and shown what he has done, and is about to be beaten, when girl intercedes and puts the statue to rights. They go off, leaving Simpkin with the statue. Lady returns, and statue jumps down and embraces her. The statue then takes off his helmet and wig, and chucks it at Simpkin, and rushes off with girl, and the clown mounts the pedestal. Enter old man, who ballets that he'll have a turn as nobody is there. He goes and looks at statue, and perceives that he is in a different position. He turns the handle and Simpkin jumps about, burlesquing what the lover has done. Then Simpkin jumps down, and pushes the old man round stage with a club in his hand. Old man sings out ' Murder!' when lover returns with girl and stops Simpkin from knocking him down. They tell the old man they are married, and he joins their hands, and a general dance winds up the performance.

" That's one of the most successful ballets ever imagined, and in its time has drawn thousands and thousands to see it. I don't know who wrote the ballet, but I should imagine it was the property of Grimaldi's father, who was a great pantomimist.

" There's a new ballet, called ' The Dream before the Wedding, or the Ploughboy turned Sailor.' That one depends more upon the lover than the comic man. There's another, called ' The Boatman of the Ohio.' That's a comic nigger ballet, in which the banjo and bones are introduced; and there's a very funny duet song, to the tune of ' Roley poley.' They both hide in a clock-case to hide from the old man, and they frighten each other, for they put their ugly black faces out and take each other for the devil. Then there's ' The Barber and the Beadle.' The barber is one of Paul Herring's favourite characters. I've done the beadle to his barber. There's a very first-rate scene in it with the fop,—Jemmy Green he's called, a cockney sort of a fellow,—and this barber has to shave him, and cuts his nose, and ties him in a chair, and shoves the soap-suds in his mouth. This fop is arranging with the father about the daughter, and the barber ties a line to a pole and fishes off the old man's wig. The beadle is the father of the girl. It goes immense. I've played in it during my time more than 400 times.

" Another famous ballet is ' The Cobbler and the Tailor.' There's a celebrated fight in that, between the tailor with his sleeve-board and goose, and the cobbler with his clam and his awl. The tailor tries to burn me with the goose, and he hunts me all about. We are about twenty minutes fighting. It's a never-failing fight, that is. The sleeve-boards are split to make a noise at each knock, and so is the clam. There's one, two, three, four, and a crack on the nob. We keep it up till both are supposed to fall down exhausted. Then there's crowing ' Cock-a-doodle-doo ' at each other. We enjoy it just as much as the audience do, for it's very funny. Although the shirt is sticking to our backs with perspiration, we enter into the sport quite like them in front. We generally prefer winter for this ballet, for it's hot work; or if it's in the open air, like in gardens, then it's very delightful.

" One of the principal things in ballet performing is to be able to do the raps, or slaps, well and quickly. A fellow gives me a clap on the face in the piece, then I have to slap my hands together, and make a noise as if he had given me a tremendous knock down. Of course, the closer the sound is to the blow, the better is the effect; and the art is to do it close. That's what we call good working. The people, of course, follow with their eye the fist of the striker, and the one struck has his arms down in front, and claps them together. It is the same work as they do in the pantomimes. Another trick is hitting the knuckles when fighting, also striking on the head. That's done by holding the stick close to the pate, and that takes the blow. On the knuckles the striker aims just above the fingers. It wants a quick eye. A fellow caught me on the nose, at the Bower, the other night, and took the skin off the tip; and there's the mark now, you see. The principal distinction between pantomimes and ballets is that there are more cascades, and trips, and valleys in pantomimes, and none in ballets.

" A trip is a dance between Harlequin and the Columbine; and cascades and valleys are trundling and gymnastic performances, such as tumbling across the stage on wheels, and catching hold of hands and twirling round.

" We have done a kind of speaking ballet, where there is a little singing and talking just to help out the plot. It is a kind of pantomime sketch. It is entitled, ' The Magic Mirror, or how to reclaim a drunken Servant.' I was the author of it, for I'm generally engaged expressly to get up ballets, and occasionally they expect me to do a new one for them. I get from 25s. to 30s. a-week for such an engagement. The scene opens with a chamber in the front of the stage, with a candle on the table nearly burnt out. The clock strikes four. A servant in livery is waiting up for his other servant. He yawns and does the sleepy business. Then he says, ' Whenever it is Thomas's day out he stops so very late; master has threatened to discharge him, and he will get the sack. Would that I could reclaim him! I will endeavour to do so. I wish he would return.' And that's the cue for the other one off the stage to begin singing 'I've been roving, I've been roving,' &c. Then the honest servant says, 'He comes! Now then to form a magic looking-glass, wherein he can see his errors. Now to procure four pieces of timber.' He does so, and makes a square frame or strainer. 'Now for a few tacks.' He gets them, and then takes a gauze curtain down from the window, and places it on the back of the frame, which forms a looking-glass. Then lights is turned down on stage, and he puts a candle behind the mirror, which illuminates this gauze, you see. He then hides behind the glass.

"Thomas comes in very tipsy. He does the drunken business, and then says, 'I've had the best of cheer. I've been down to farmer Cheer's, and had the best of ale, and some good gin, and better brandy;' at which the man behind the frame echoes, 'Better brandy.' Thomas is alarmed. He looks around and says, 'That was the echo.' To which the voice replies, 'That was the echo.' Then they repeat this business; Thomas getting still more nervous. He says, 'Well, I declare, I'm getting quite melancholy. I'll see what singing can do to rouse me a little.' He then begins,—

> ' 'Tis love that rules the courts and the city,
> It rules both the high and the low;
> But sometimes—the more is the pity—
> Young Cupid won't rosin his bow.
> Won't rosin his bow.'

"The glass takes up 'Rosin his bo-o-o-o-w.' The time this is going on, the other servant is dressing himself to represent the other; combing his hair, and painting his face, and everything. Thomas gets quite I don't know how; and he says, 'I wonder if I look frightened?' And he goes to the glass, and the other appears at the same time, and it looks like the reflection in the glass. I've had some fools imagine it was the reflection. Thomas says 'Oh, I look very nice!' and as he speaks the other opens his mouth too. Then Thomas says, 'Why I've got some black on my nose!' and he goes to wipe it, and the form behind imitates him.

"He then goes down the stage and returns to glass again. There's a deal of business carried on. At last Thomas sees the figure turn round whilst he's looking in front, and then he exclaims, 'That's not me! My waistcoat ain't split up the back! I'll smash the glass.' He knocks down the gauze, and out pops the figure, yelling 'Ah! I'm the glass imp!' Thomas falls down on the stage, and as the imp walks about, one off the side at the wing thumps the ground at each step with a piece of wood, to mark the steps. Then the servant says, 'Fe fi fo fum, I smell the blood of an Englishman;' and Thomas answers, 'Oh no, Mr. Ghost, I ain't an Englishman; I'm a Irish woman;' and there's a shout at that, of course. The servant continues,—

'Let him be alive, let him be dead,'—and Thomas says 'I'm as dead as a red herring!' and there's another shout. The fellow-servant then catches hold of Thomas by the hair of the head, and tells him to follow him below. Thomas replies 'Oh don't! please, don't, Mr. Ghost! I'll do anything but follow you below, though you are so good-looking.' 'Will you promise to come home early for the future?' 'I will.' 'And never drink no more brandy nor stout?' 'I will.' The fellow-servant shouts in a hoarse voice, 'Nay, Slave! not I will, but I will not.' 'Not.' 'Enough! rise and look at me.' 'Oh, I wouldn't for the world.' 'Don't you know me?' 'Oh no! no! no! I never saw you before.' 'It's all right, I'm your friend James: your fellow-servant!' Then Thomas gets up and sees him, and begins laughing. 'Oh, I wasn't frightened: I knew you all the time.' The other cove then shouts, 'Fe fi fo fum;' and down goes Thomas on his face and screams 'Murder! murder!' Then James says, 'Oh, it's only me; look!' Then Thomas looks and says, 'Well, I declare I thought you was the glass imp.' 'No, I only played this prank to reclaim you. Has it had its effect?' 'It has.' 'Then I have gained my end, since you are reformed; and I hope you are reformed.' 'I am; and I hope it will be a lesson to my friends in front, and that they will never take a drop too much.' Then they sing together —

> 'Troubles all, great and small,
> You must think not of the past;
> For life is short, and mirth and sport
> Cannot ever last.
> Cannot ever last.
> Cannot ever last.'

"That pantomimic farce always goes down with wonderful success. It has a regular round of applause, which is everybody clapping as hard as they can. Some of the tavern-keepers, in whose concert-rooms we done this ballet pantomime, don't much like the wind-up to this piece,—about hoping our friends will take a lesson, and not drink too much. At one place the landlord happened to come just as that line was spoke, and he told me he'd fine me sixpence if I done it again. 'Why, I ain't sold a dozen pots of beer through it,' he says. So I agreed with him to alter the tag to this,— 'and not drink no more than you can carry, for that never did any one any harm, but more is injurious.' At some of these rooms, if a song is going too long and no drinking, the landlord will come in, and hold his hand up, as a cue for us to leave off and let the drinking begin again. Then the waiters looks the audience up again with their 'Give your orders, gentlemen; give your orders.'

"This ballet pantomime was quite an innovation, and isn't strictly ballet, but in the same line.

"Of all ballets, the one that has found the longest run is the 'Statue Blanche.' I've known it to go a month. All the young ladies in these pieces are regular ballet-girls, and all 'turned out;' that is, taught to stand with their dancing position. You know all of them is supposed to be able to kick their nose with their knees. You know they crick them when young, the same as a contortionist or acrobat. They are always practising. You see them in the green-room kicking their legs about. The men have to do the same, except the comic characters that don't dance. Paul Herring is very clever at these things, and don't want no practising. He can scratch his head with his foot. He's the finest clown that ever trod in shoe-leather.

"The green-rooms at the concert-rooms are very tidy. Even at the penny gaffs the men and women have separate rooms. The women there have got their decency the same as at a theatre, and they wouldn't go there if there wasn't separate dressing-rooms. In fact, they keep themselves more from the men than the men from them, for they are all madames; and though they only keep a wheelbarrow, they carry themselves as if they had a coach.

"At the concert-rooms they have always a useful set of scenery, about similar to that at the penny gaffs. At some of them you don't get so good scenery as at the gaffs. There's in general a romantic scene, and a cottage, and so forth, and that's all that's wanted. There's a regular proscenium to the theatres, with lights in front and all. The most usual manner is to have a couple of figures at the sides holding lights, and curtains behind them, because it answers for the ballets and also for the singing. At some of the concert-rooms there's no side-entrance to the stage, and then you have to go across the audience dressed in your costume, before you can get on to the stage. It's horrid, that is. I've done it many and many a time at Knightsbridge. It's very bad, for everything depends upon being discovered when the curtain draws up. Some of the people will say, 'Oh, that's nothing; I've seen him before.'

"I have repeatedly seen people in front go to the stage and offer their glass to the actor to drink. We are forbid to receive them, because it interferes with business; but we do take it. I've seen drink handed on to the stage from three to four times a-night.

"Sometimes, when a dance has pleased the audience, or an acrobat, or a bottle equilibrist, they'll throw halfpence on to the stage, to reward the performer. We sometimes do this for one another, so as to give the collection a start. We are forbidden to take money when it is thrown on to us, but we do. If a sixpence comes, we in general clap our foot on to it, and then your mate gives you a rap on the face, and we tumble down and put it in our mouth, so that the proprietor shan't see us. If he saw it done, and he could find it, he'd take it away if he could. I have known a man pick up as much as 3s. after a dance. Then there are generally some one who is not en-

gaged on the establishment, and he comes for what we term 'the nobbings,' that's what is throw'd to him. I've known a clog-dancer, of the name of Thompson, to earn as much as 10s. of a night at the various concert-rooms. He's very clever, and may be seen any night at the Hoop and Grapes, Ratcliffe-highway. He does 108 different steps, and 51 of them are on his toes.

"There's in general from five to six people engaged in a concert-room performances, and for professionals alone that'll come to from 30s. to 2l. a-night for expenses for actors and singers. That's putting down nothing for the conductor, or musicians, or gas. Some of them charge 2d. or 1d. admission, but then there's something extra put on to the drink. Porter is 5d. a pot, and fourpenny ale is charged 6d.; besides, you can't have less than 6d. worth of gin-and-water. At such a room as the Nag's Head in Oxford-street, I've known as many as from 200 to 300 go there in the evening; and the Standard, Pimlico, will hold from 400 to 450 people, and I've seen that full for nights together. There they only have merely a platform, and seldom do ballets, or Grecian statues, dancing, gymnastics, and various other entertainments, such as ventriloquism. There the admission is 4d., and on benefit occasions 6d."

THE TIGHT-ROPE DANCERS AND STILT-VAULTERS.

"I AM the father of two little girls who perform on the tight-rope and on stilts. My wife also performs, so that the family by itself can give an entertainment that lasts an hour and a half altogether. I don't perform myself, but I go about making the arrangements and engagements for them. Managers write to me from the country to get up entertainments for them, and to undertake the speculation at so much. Indeed I am a manager. I hire a place of amusement, and hire it at so much; or if they won't let it, then I take an engagement for the family. I never fancied any professional work myself, except, perhaps, a bit of sculpture. I am rather partial to the poses plastiques, but that's all.

"Both my little girls are under eight years of age, and they do the stilt-waltzing, and the eldest does the tight-rope business as well. Their mother is a tight-rope dancer, and does the same business as Madame Sayin used to appear in, such as the ascension on the rope in the midst of fireworks. We had men in England who had done the ascension before Madame Sayin came out at Vauxhall, but I think she was the first woman that ever did it in this country. I remember her well. She lodged at a relation of mine during her engagement at the Gardens. She was a ugly little woman, very diminutive, and tremendously pitted with the small-pox. She was what may be called a horny woman, very tough and bony. I've heard my father and mother say she had 20*l*. a-night at Vauxhall, and she did it three times a-week; but I can't vouch for this, as it was only hearsay.

"My eldest little girl first began doing the stilts in public when she was three-and a-half years old. I don't suppose she was much more than two-and-a-half years old when I first put her on the stilts. They were particularly short, was about four foot from the ground, so that she came to about as high as my arms. It was the funniest thing in the world to see her. She hadn't got sufficient strength in her knees to keep her legs stiff, and she used to wabble about just like a fellow drunk, and lost the use of his limbs. The object of beginning so soon was to accustom it, and she was only on for a few minutes once or twice a-day. She liked this very much, in fact so much, that the other little ones used to cry like blazes because I wouldn't let them have a turn at them. I used to make my girl do it, just like a bit of fun. She'd be laughing fit to crack her sides, and we'd be laughing to see her little legs bending about. I had a new dress made for her, with a spangled bodice and gauze skirt, and she always put that on when she was practising, and that used to induce her to the exercise. She was pleased as Punch when she had her fine clothes on. When she wasn't good, I'd say to her, 'Very well, miss, since you're so naughty, you shan't go out with us to perform; we'll teach your little sister, and take her with us, and leave you at home.' That used to settle her in a moment, for she didn't like the idea of having the other one take her place.

"Some people, when they teach their children for any entertainment, torture the little things most dreadful. There is a great deal of barbarity practised in teaching children for the various lines. It's very silly, because it only frightens the little things, and some children often will do much more by kindness than ill-usage. Now there are several children that I know of that have been severely injured whilst being trained for the Risley business. Why, bless your soul, a little thing coming down on it's head, is done for the remainder of it's life. I've seen them crying on the stage, publicly, from being sworn at and bullied, where they would have gone to it laughing, if they had only been coaxed and persuaded.

"Now my little things took to it almost naturally. It was bred and born in them, for my father was in the profession before me, and my wife's parents were also performers. We had both my little girls on the stilts before they were three years old. It's astonishing how soon the leg gets accustomed to the stilts, for in less than three months they can walk alone. Of course, for the first six weeks that they are put on we never leave go of their hands. The knees, which at first is weak and wabbly, gets strong, and when once that is used to the pad and stump (for the stilts are fastened on to just where the garter would come), then the child is all right. It does not enlarge the knee at all, and instead of croooking the leg, it acts in a similar way to what we see in a child born with the cricks, with irons on. I should say, that if any of my children have been born knock-kneed, or bow-legged, the stilts have been the means of making their legs straight. It does not fatigue their ankles at all, but the principal strain is on the hollow in the palm of the foot, where it fits into the tread of the still, for that's the thing that bears the whole weight. If you keep a child on too long, it will complain of pain there; but mine were never on for more than twenty minutes at a time, and that's not long enough to tire the foot. But one gets over this feeling.

"I've had my young ones on the stilts amusing themselves in my back-yard for a whole afternoon. They'll have them on and off three or four times in a hour, for it don't take a minute or two to put them on. They would put them on for play. I've often had them asking me to let them stop away from school, so as to have them on.

"My wife is very clever on the stilts. She does the routine of military exercise with them on. It's the gun exercise. She takes one stilt off herself, and remains on the other, and then shoulders the stilt she has taken off, and shows the gun practice. She's the only female stilt-dancer in England now. Those that were with her when she was a girl are all old women now. All of my family waltz and polka on stilts, and play tamborines whilst they dance. The little girls dance with their mother.

"It took longer to teach the children to do the tight-rope. They were five years old before I first began to teach them. The first thing I taught them to walk upon was on a pole passed through the rails at the back of two chairs. When you're teaching a child, you have not got time to go driving stakes into the ground to fix a rope upon. My pole was a bit of one of my wife's broken balance-poles. It was as thick as a broom handle, and not much longer. I had to lay hold of the little things' hands at first. They had no balance-pole to hold, not for some months afterwards. My young ones liked it very much; I don't know how other persons may. It was bred in them. They couldn't stand even upright when first they tried it, but after three months they could just walk across it by themselves. I exercised them once every day, for I had other business to attend to, and I'd give them a lesson for just, perhaps, half an hour at dinner time, or of an evening a bit after I came home. My wife never would teach them herself. I taught my wife rope-dancing, and yet I could not do it; but I understood it by theory, though not by experience. I never chalked my young ones' feet, but I put them on a little pair of canvas pumps, to get the feet properly formed to grasp the rope, and to bend round. My wife's feet, when she is on the rope, bend round from continual use, so that they form a hollow in the palm of the foot, or the waist of the foot as some call it. My girls' feet soon took the form. The foot is a little bit tender at first, not to the pole, because that is round and smooth, but the strands of the rope would, until the person has had some practice, blister the foot if kept too long on it. I never kept my young ones on the pole more than twenty minutes at a time, for it tired me more than them, and my arms used to ache with supporting them. Just when they got into the knack and habit of walking on the pole, then I shifted them to a rope, which I fixed up in my back-yard. The rope has to be a good cable size, about one-and-a-half inches in diameter. I always chalked the rope; chalk is of a very rough nature, and prevents slipping. The sole of the pump is always more or less hard and greasy. We don't rough the soles of the pumps, for the rope itself will soon make them rough, no matter how bright they may have been. My rope was three feet six inches from the ground, which was a comfortable height for me to go alongside of the children. I didn't give them the balance-pole till they were pretty perfect without it. It is a great help, is the pole. The one my wife takes on the rope with her is eighteen feet long. Some of the poles are weighted at both ends, but ours are not. My young ones were able to dance on the rope in a twelve-month's time. They wern't a bit nervous when I highered the rope in my yard. I was underneath to catch them. They seemed to like it.

"They appeared in public on the tight-rope in less than a twelvemonth from their first lesson on the broom-stick on the backs of the chairs. My girl had done the stilts in public when she was only three years and six months old, so she was accustomed to an audience. It was in a gardens she made her first performance on the rope, and I was under her in case she fell. I always do that to this day.

"Whenever I go to fairs to fulfil engagements, I always take all my own apparatus with me. There is the rope some twenty yards long, and then there's the pulley-blocks for tightening it, and the cross-poles for fixing it up, and the balance-poles. I'm obliged to have a cart to take them along. I always make engagements, and never go in shares, for I don't like that game. I could have lots of jobs at that game if I liked. There's no hold on the proprietor of the show. There's a share taken for this, and a share for this, so that before the company come to touch any money, twenty shares are gone out of thirty, and only ten left for the performers. I have had a pound a-day for myself and family at a fair. At the last one I went to, a week ago,

we took somewhere about 25s. a-day. When it isn't too far from London, we generally come home at night, but otherwise we go to a tavern, and put up there.

"I only go to circuses when we are at fairs. I never had a booth of my own. The young ones and my wife walk about the parade to make a show of the entire company, but unless business is very bad, and a draw is wanted, my little ones don't appear on the stilts. They have done so, of course, but I don't like them to do so, unless as a favour.

"In the ring, their general performance is the rope one time, and then reverse it and do the stilts. My wife and the girls all have their turns at the rope, following each other in their performances. The band generally plays quadrilles, or a waltz, or anything; it don't matter what it is, so long as it is the proper time. They dance and do the springs in the air, and they also perform with chairs, seating themselves on it whilst on the rope, and also standing up on the chair. They also have a pair of ladders, and mount them. Then again they dance in fetters. I am there underneath, in evening costume, looking after them. They generally wind up their tight-rope performance by flinging away the balance-pole, and dancing without it to quick measure.

"One of my little girls slipped off once, but I caught her directly as she came down, and she wasn't in the least frightened, and went on again. I put her down, and she curtsied, and ran up again. Did she scream? Of course not. You can't help having a slip off occasionally.

"When they do the stilts, the young ones only dance waltzes and polkas, and so on. They have to use their hands for doing the graceful attitudes. My wife, as I said before, does the gun exercise besides dancing, and it's always very successful with the audience, and goes down tremendously. The performances of the three takes about twenty minutes, I think, for I never timed it exactly. I've been at some fairs when we have done our performances eighteen times a-day, and I've been at some where I've only done it four or six, for it always depends upon what business is being done. That's the truth. When the booth is full, then the inside performance begins, and until it is, the parade work is done. There are generally persons engaged expressly to do the parade business.

" "I never knew my girls catch cold at a fair, for they are generally held in hot weather, and the heat is rather more complained of than the cold. My young ones put on three or four different dresses during a fair—at least mine do. I don't know what others do. Each dress is a different colour. There is a regular dressing-room for the ladies under the parade carriages, and their mother attends to them.

"Very often after their performances they get fruit and money thrown to them into the

STREET-PERFORMERS ON STILTS.

[*From a Sketch.*]

"OLD SARAH," THE WELL-KNOWN HURDY-GURDY PLAYER.

[*From a Daguerreotype by* BEARD.]

ring. I've known seven or eight shillings to be thrown to them in coppers and silver, but it's seldom they get more than a shilling or so. I've known ladies and gentlemen wait for them when they went to take off their dresses after they have done, and give them five or six shillings.

"When we go to fairs, I always pack the young ones off to bed about nine, and never later than ten. They don't seem tired, and would like to stop up all night, I should think. I don't know how it is with other kids.

"I send my young ones to school every day when there is no business on, and they are getting on well with their schooling. When we go to a country engagement, then I send them to a school in the town if we stop any time.

"Ours is, I think, the only family doing the rope-dancing and stilt-vaulting. I don't know of any others, nor yet of any other children at all who do it.

"Stilt-vaulting is dying out. You never see any children going about the streets as you did formerly. There never was so much money got as at that stilt-vaulting in the streets. My wife's family, when she was young, thought nothing of going out of an afternoon, after dinner, and taking their three or four pounds. They used to be as tall up as the first-floor windows of some of the houses. It must be very nearly twenty years since I remember the last that appeared. It isn't that the police would stop it, but there's nobody to do it. It's a very difficult thing to do, is walking about at that tremendous height. If you fall you're done for. One of my little ones fell once—it was on some grass, I think—but she escaped without any hurt, for she was light, and gathered herself up in a heap somehow.

"There used to be a celebrated Jellini family, with a similar entertainment to what I give. They were at the theatres mostly, and at public gardens, and so on. They used to do ballets on stilts, and had great success. That must be forty years ago. There used to be the Chaffs family too, who went about the streets on stilts. They had music with them, and danced in the public thoroughfares. Now there is nothing of the kind going on, and it's out of date.

"I have been abroad, in Holland, travelling with a circus company. I've also visited Belgium. The children and my wife were very much liked wherever they went. I was on an engagement then, and we had 11l. a-week, and I was with them seven weeks. They paid our travelling expenses there, and we paid them home."

STREET RECITER.

STREET reciters are somewhat scarce now-a-days, and I was a long time before meeting with one; for though I could always trace them through their wanderings about the streets, and learn where they had been seen the night before, still I could never find one myself. I believe there are not more than ten lads in London,—for they seem to be all lads,—who are earning a livelihood by street-reciting.

At length I heard that some street actors, as they call themselves, lived in a court in the City. There were two of them—one a lad, who was dressed in a man's ragged coat and burst boots, and tucked-up trowsers, and seemingly in a state of great want; and the other decently enough attired in a black paletot with a flash white-and-red handkerchief, or "fogle," as the costermongers call it, jauntily arranged so as to bulge over the closely-buttoned collar of his coat. There was a priggish look about the latter lad, while his manner was "'cute," and smacked of Petticoat-lane; and though the other one seemed to slink back, *he* pushed himself saucily forward, and at once informed me that he belonged "to the profession" of street declaimer. "I and this other boy goes out together," he said, as he took a short pipe from his mouth; and in proof of his assertion, he volunteered that they should on the spot give me a specimen of their histrionic powers.

I preferred listening to the modest boy. He was an extremely good-looking lad, and spoke in a soft voice, almost like a girl's. He had a bright, cheerful face, and a skin so transparent and healthy, and altogether appeared so different from the generality of street lads, that I felt convinced that he had not long led a wandering life, and that there was some mystery connected with his present pursuits. He blushed when spoken to, and his answers were nervously civil.

When I had the better-natured boy alone with me, I found that he had been well educated; and his statement will show that he was born of respectable parents, and the reason why he took to his present course of life. At first he seemed to be nervous, and little inclined to talk; but as we became better acquainted, he chatted on even faster than my pen could follow. He had picked up several of the set phrases of theatrical parlance, such as, "But my dream has vanished in air;" or, "I felt that a blight was on my happiness;" and delivered his words in a romantic tone, as though he fancied he was acting on a stage. He volunteered to show me his declamatory powers, and selected "Othello's Apology." He went to the back of the room, and after throwing his arms about him for a few seconds, and looking at the ceiling as if to inspire himself, he started off.

Whilst he had been chatting to us his voice was—as I said before—like a girl's; but no sooner did he deliver his, "Most potent, grave, and reverend Signiors," than I was surprised to hear him assume a deep stomachic voice—a style evidently founded upon the melo-dramatic models at minor theatres. His good-looking face, however, became flushed and excited during the delivery of the speech, his eyes rolled about, and he passed his hands through his hair, combing it with his fingers till it fell wildly about his neck like a mane.

When he had finished the speech he again relapsed into his quiet ways, and resuming his former tone of voice, seemed to think that an apology was requisite for the wildness of his acting, for he said, " When I act Shakspeare I cannot restrain myself,—it seems to master my very soul."

He had some little talent as an actor, but was possessed of more memory than knowledge of the use of words. Like other performers, he endeavoured to make his " points" by dropping his voice to almost a whisper when he came to the passage, " I' faith 'twas strange, 'twas passing strange."

In answer to my questions he gave me the following statement :—

" I am a street reciter, that is, I go about the streets and play Shakspeare's tragedies, and selections from poets. The boys in the streets call me Shakspeare. The first time they called me so I smiled at them, and was honoured by the name, though it's only passing ! it's only fleet !

" I was born in Dublin, and my father was in the army, and my mother was a lady's nurse and midwife, and used to go out on urgent business, but only to ladies of the higher classes. My mother died in Dublin, and my father left the army and became a turnkey in Dublin prison. Father left Dublin when I was about ten years of age, and went to Manchester. Then I went into an office—a herring-store, which had agents at Yarmouth and other fishing-ports ; and there I had to do writing. Summer-time was our busiest time, for we used to have to sit up at night waiting for the trains to come in with the fish. I used to get 3d. an hour for every hour we worked over, and 6d. in the morning for coffee, and 8s. 6d. standing wages, whether I worked or played. I know all about herrings and herring-packing, for I was two years there, and the master was like a father to me, and would give me money many times, Christmas-boxes, and new-years' gifts, and such-like. I might have been there now, and foreman by this time, in the Isle of Man, where we had a house, only I was too foolish—going to theatres and such-like.

" You see, I used, before I went out as clerk, to go to a school in Manchester, where the master taught recitation. We used to speak pieces from Uwin's ' Elocution,' and we had to get a piece off to elocution, and attitude, and position ; indeed, elocution may be said to be position and attitude. We used to do ' The Downfall of Poland,' and ' Lord Ullen's Daughter,' and ' My name is Norval,' and several others—' Rolla,' and all them. Then we used to speak them one at a time, and occasionally we would take different parts, such as the

' Quarrel of Brutus,' and ' Cassius,' and ' Rolla,' and the ' American Patriot,' and such-like. I will not boast of myself, but I was one of the best in the class, though since I have gone out in the streets it has spoiled my voice and my inclinations, for the people likes shouting. I have had as many as 500 persons round me in the Walworth-road at one time, and we got 4s. between us ; and then we lost several halfpence, for it was night, and we could not see the money that was thrown into the ring. We did the ' Gipsy's Revenge,' and ' Othello's Apology.'

" Whilst I was at the herring-stores I used to be very fond of the theatre, and I'd go there every night if I could, and I did nearly manage to be there every evening. I'd save up my money, and if I'd none I'd go to my master and ask him to let me have a few halfpence ; and I've even wanted to go to the play so much that, when I couldn't get any money, I'd sell my clothes to go. Master used to caution me, and say that the theatre would ruin me, and I'm sure it has. When my master would tell me to stop and do the books, I'd only just run them over at night and cast them up as quickly as I could, and then I'd run out and go to the twopenny theatre on the Victoria-bridge, Manchester. Sometimes I used to perform there for Mr. Row, who was the proprietor. It was what is called a travelling ' slang,' a booth erected temporarily. I did William Tell's son, and I've also done the ' Bloody Child' in Macbeth, and go on with the witches. It was a very little stage, but with very nice scenery, and shift-scenes and all, the same as any other theatre. On a Saturday night he used to have as many as six houses ; start off at three o'clock, after the factory hands had been paid off. I never had any money for acting, for though he offered me half-a-sovereign a-week to come and take a part, yet I wouldn't accept of it, for I only did it for my own amusement like. They used to call me King Dick.

" My master knew I went to the theatre to act, for he sent one of the boys to follow me, and he went in front and saw me acting in Macbeth, and he went and told master, because, just as the second act was over, he came right behind the scenes and ordered me out, and told me I'd have to get another situation if I went there any more. He took me home and finished the books, and the next morning I told him I'd leave, for I felt as if it was my sole ambition to get on to the stage, or even put my foot on it ; I was so enamoured of it. And it is the same now, for I'd do anything to get engaged—it's as if a spell was on me. Just before I left he besought me to remain with him, and said that I was a useful hand to him, and a good boy when I liked, and that he wanted to make a gentleman of me. He was so fond of me that he often gave me money himself to go to a theatre ; but he said too much of it was bad.

" After I left him I went with another boy to go to sea. I forgot all about the theatre, for it agitated my feelings when I left him, and I wished I had been back, for I'd been with him eighteen months, and he'd been like a father to me; but I was too ashamed to see him again. This boy and me started for Scarborough, and he had no money, and I had 5s., that was all between us; but I had a black suit of clothes cost 2l. 10s., which my master had made me a present of, for excelling the foreman in making up the books—for the foreman was 208 hands of herrings (five herrings make a hand) short in one week; and then I took the books the next week, and I was only four herrings short, and master was so pleased that he bestowed upon me a present of a new suit of clothes.

" I parted with my companion for this reason. One day, after we had been walking, we were so hungry we could eat anything, and I had been accustomed to never being hungry, so that I was very much exhausted from fatigue, for we had walked thirty miles that day, only eating one piece of bread, which I got at a public-house where I gave a recitation. We came to a farm-house at a place called Bishop Wilton, in Yorkshire, and he went inside the door to beg for something to eat. There was a young lady came out and talked to him and gave him some bread, and then she saw me and had compassion on me, because I looked respectable and was so miserable. We told her we were cousins, and had left our fathers and mothers (for we didn't like to say we had left our masters), and she said, ' Poor boys! your parents will be fretting after you; I'd go back, if I was you.' She gave him a large bit of bread, and then she gave me a big bit of cold plum-pudding. My companion wanted half my pudding besides his own bread, and I preferred to give him part of the pudding and not have any bread; but he wouldn't, and struck out at me. I returned it, and then we fought, and an old woman came out with a stick and beat us both, and said we were incorrigible young beggars, and couldn't be very hungry or we shouldn't fight that way. Then I parted from my companion, and he took the direct road to Scarborough, and I went to York. I saw him afterwards when I returned to Manchester. His father left him 200l., and he's doing very well in a good situation in a commercial office.

" I got bound for six years to sea to a shipowner at Scarborough, but the mate behaved very bad to me and used me brutally. I couldn't use the ropes as well as he thought I might, although I learned the compass and all the ropes very soon. The captain was a very good man, but I daren't tell him for fear of the mate. He used to beat me with the rope's end—sometimes the lead-rope—that was his usual weapon, and he used to leave marks on me. I took the part of Hamlet, and,

instead of complaining, I thought of that part where he says,

' And makes us rather bear those ills we have,
Than fly to others that we know not of.'

That's the best play of Shakspeare; he outdoes himself there.

" When the brig got to Scheidam, in Holland, five miles off Rotterdam, I ran away. The vessel was a collier, and whilst they were doing the one, two, three, and pulling up the coals, I slipped over the side and got to shore. I walked to Rotterdam, and there I met an Irish sailor and told him all, and he told me to apply to the British Consul and say that I had been left ashore by a Dutch galliot, which had sailed the day before for Jersey. The Consul put me in a boarding-house—a splendid place, with servants to wait on you, where they gave me everything, cigars and all, for everybody smokes there — little boys scarce higher than the table—and cigars are only a cent each—and five cents make a penny. I was like a gentleman then, and then they put me in the screw steamer, the Irwell, and sent me back to Hull.

" When I got to Manchester again, I went in my sailor-clothes to see my old master. He was very glad to see me, and asked me if I wanted anything to eat, and sent out for ale for me, and was so glad to see me that he gave me money. He took me back again at higher wages, 10s.—which was 1s. 6d. over—and I stopped there eight months, until they wrote to me from Dublin that father was very ill, and that I was to come over directly. So I went, and was by him when he died. He was sixty-two years of age, and left 400l. to my sister, which she is to have when she comes of age. He quarrelled with me because he was a Catholic, and I didn't follow that persuasion, and he disowned me; but, just before he died, he blessed me, and looked as if he wanted to say something to me, but he couldn't, for the breath was leaving him.

" When I returned to Manchester I found my master had taken another servant, as he expected I should stop in Dublin, and there was no vacancy; but he recommended me to another merchant, and there I was put in the yard to work among the herrings, as he didn't know my capabilities; but, in a short time I was put in the shop as boy, and then I was very much in favour with the master and the missus, and the son, and he used to bring me to concerts and balls, and was very partial to me; and I used to eat and drink with them at their own table. I've been foolish, and never a friend to myself, for I ran away from them. A lad told me that London was such a fine place, and induced me to sell my clothes and take the train; and here I've been for about eight months knocking about.

" As long as my money lasted I used to go to the theatre every night—to the Standard, and the City-road, and the Britannia; but when it was gone I looked then to see what I might do. At first I tried for a situation, but they wouldn't take me, because I couldn't get a recommendation in London. Then I formed a resolution of giving recitations from Shakspeare and the other poets in public-houses, and getting a living that way.

"I had learned a good deal of Shakspeare at school; and besides, when I was with my master I had often bought penny copies of Shakspeare, and I used to study it in the office, hiding it under the book I was writing in; and, when nobody was looking, studying the speeches. I used to go and recite before the men in the yard, and they liked it.

"The first night I went out I earned 4s., and that was a great cheer to my spirits. It was at a public-house in Fashion-street. I went into the tap-room and asked the gentlemen if they would wish to hear a recitation from Shakspeare, and they said, 'Proceed.' The first part I gave them was from Richard the Third: 'Now is the winter of our discontent;' and then they clapped me and made me do it over again. Then I performed Hamlet's 'Soliloquy on the Immortality of the Soul,' and they threw down 2s. in coppers, and one gentleman gave me sixpence.

"I've continued giving recitations from Shakspeare and selections from the poets ever since, and done very well, until I became ill with a cold, which made my voice bad, so that I was unable to speak. I've been ill now a fortnight, and I went out last night for the first time, along with another young fellow who recites, and we got 1s. 6d. between us in the 'Gipsy's Revenge.' We went to a public-house where they were having 'a lead,' that is a collection for a friend who is ill, and the company throw down what they can for a subscription, and they have in a fiddle and make it social. But it was not a good 'lead,' and poorly attended, so we did not make much out of the company.

"When I go out to recite, I generally go with another boy, and we take parts. The pieces that draw best with the public are, 'The Gipsy's Revenge,' 'The Gold Digger's Revenge,' 'The Miser,' 'The Robber,' 'The Felon,' and 'The Highwayman.' We take parts in these, and he always performs the villain, and I take the noble characters. He always dies, because he can do a splendid back-fall, and he looks so wicked when he's got the moustaches on. I generally draws the company by giving two or three recitations, and then we perform a piece; and whilst he goes round with the hat, I recite again. My favourite recitations are, 'Othello's Apology,' beginning with 'Most potent, grave, and reverend Signiors,' and those from Hamlet, Richard III., and Macbeth. Of the recitations I think the people prefer that from Othello, for the ladies have often asked me to give them that from Othello (they like to hear about Desdemona),

but the gentlemen ask for that from Hamlet, 'To be, or not to be?'

"My principal place for giving performances is the Commercial-road, near Limehouse, but the most theatrically inclined neighbourhood is the Walworth-road. The most money I ever took at one time in the streets was 4s. in the Walworth-road.

"The best receipts I ever had was got in a public-house near Brick-lane, for I took 12s., and I was alone. There was a 'lead' up there for a friend, and I knew of it, and I had my hair curled and got myself decently habited, I was there for about three or four hours, and in the intervals between the dances I used to recite. There were girls there, and they took my part, though they made me drink so much I was nearly tipsy.

"The only theatrical costume I put on is moustachios, and I take a stick to use as a sword. I put myself into attitudes, and look as fierce as I can. When first the people came to hear me they laughed, and then they became quiet; and sometimes you could hear a pin drop.

"When I am at work regularly—that's when I am in voice and will—I make about 10s. a-week, if there's not much rain. If it's wet, people don't go to the public-houses, and they are my best paying audiences. The least I have ever taken in a week is about 6s.

"There isn't many going about London reciting. It is a very rare class to be found; I only know about four who live that way, and I have heard of the others from hearsay—not that I have seen them myself.

"I'm very fond of music, and know most of the opera. That organ's playing something by Verdi; I heard it at the theatre at Dublin. I amuse them sometimes in the kitchen at my lodgings by playing on a penny tin whistle. I can do 'Still, so gently,' from 'La Sonnambula,' and hornpipes, and jigs, and Scotch airs, as well as 'Cheer boys, cheer,' and 'To the West,' and many others. They get me to play when they want to dance, and they pay me for them. They call me Shakspeare by name."

BLIND READER.

An intelligent man gave me the following account of his experience as a blind reader. He was poorly dressed, but clean, and had not a vulgar look.

"My father died when I was ten years old, and my mother in the coronation year, 1838. I am now in my thirty-eighth year. I was a clerk in various offices. I was not born blind, but lost my sight four years ago, in consequence of aneurism. I was a fortnight in the Ophthalmic Hospital, and was an out-patient for three months. I am a married man, with one child, and we did as well as we could, but that was very badly, until every bit of furniture (and I had a house full of good furniture up to that time) went. At last I thought I might earn a little by reading in the street. The Society for the Indigent Blind gave me the Gospel of St. John, after Mr. Freer's system, the price being 8s.; and a brother-in-law supplied me with the Gospel of St. Luke, which cost 9s. In Mr. Freer's system the regular alphabet letters are not used, but there are raised characters, thirty-four in number, including long and short vowels; and these characters express sounds, and a sound may comprise a short syllable. I learned to read by this system in four lessons. I first read in public in Mornington-crescent. For the first fortnight or three weeks I took from 2s. 6d. to 2s. 9d. a-day—one day I took 3s. My receipts than fell to something less than 18d. a-day, and have been gradually falling ever since. Since the 1st of January, this year, I haven't averaged more than 2s. 6d. a-week by my street reading and writing. My wife earns 3s. or 4s. a-week with her needle, slaving with a 'sweater' to a shirtmaker. I have never read anywhere but in Euston-square and Mornington-crescent. On Whit-Monday I made 2s. 0½d., and that, I assure you, I reckon real good holiday earnings; and I read until I was hoarse with it. Once I counted at Mornington-crescent, as closely as I could, just out of curiosity and to wile away the time, above 2000 persons, who passed and re-passed without giving me a halfpenny. The working people are my best friends, most decidedly. I am tired of the streets; besides, being half-starved. There are now five or six blind men about London, who read in the streets. We can read nothing but the Scriptures, as 'blind printing,'—so it's sometimes called—has only been used in the Scriptures. I write also in the streets, as well as read. I use Wedgwood's manifold writer. I write verses from Scripture. There was no teaching necessary for this. I trace the letters from my knowledge of them when I could see. I believe I am the only blind man who writes in the streets."

Gun-Exercise Exhibitor—One-legged Italian.

"I am an Italian, domiciled at Genoa, and I speak very little French, only just enough to ask for things—to get my life with, you know. Genoa is the most rich town of Piedmont, but it is not the most jolie. Oh no! no! no! Turin is the most beautiful, oh yes! It is a long street of palaces. You know Turin is where the King of Sardinia, with the long moustaches, lives. Has Monsieur been to Turin? No! Ah, it is a great sight! Perhaps Monsieur has seen Genoa? No! Ah you have a great pleasure to come. Genoa is very rich, but Turin is very beautiful. I prefer Turin.

"I was a soldier in my country. Oh, not an officer. I was in the 2nd battalion of the Bassolein, nearly the same as the Chasseurs de Vincennes in France. It is the first regiment in Piedmont. We had a green uniform with a roll collar, and a belt round one shoulder, and a short rifle. We had a feather one side of our hats, which are of felt. Ah, c'était bien joli ça! We use long bullets, Minié ones. All the army in my country are under four brothers, who are all generals, and Ferdinando Marmora is the commander-in-chief—the same that was in the Crimea. Nearly all my companions in the Bassolein regiment were from the Tyrol. Ah, they shoot well! They never miss. They always kill. Sacré Dieu!

"I was wounded at the bataille de Pescare, against the Austrians. We gained the battle and entered the town. The General Radetzky was against us. He is a good general, but Ferdinando Marmora beat him. Ferdinando was wounded by a ball in the cheek. It passed from left to right. He has the mark now. Ah, he is a good general. I was wounded. Pardon! I cannot say if it was a bal de canon or a bal de fusil. I was on the ground like one dead. I fell with my leg bent behind me, because they found me so. They tell me, that as I fell I cried, 'My God! my God!' but that is not in my memory. After they had finished the battle they took up the wounded. Perhaps I was on the ground twelve hours, but I do not know exactly. I was picked up with others and taken to the hospital, and then one day after my leg decomposed, and it was cut directly. All the bone was fracassé, vairy beaucoup. I was in the hospital for forty days. Ah! it was terrible. To cut the nerves was terrible. They correspond with the head. Ah, horrible! They gave me no chloroform. Rien! rien! No, nor any dormitore, as we call it in Italian, you know,—something in a glass to drink and make you sleep. Rien! rien! If I had gone into the Hôpital des Invalides, I should have had 20 sous a-day; but I would not, and now my pension is 12 sous a-day. I am paid that now; whether I am here or there, it is the same. My wife receives the 12 sous whilst I am here. I shall not stop here long. The langue is too difficult. No, I shall not learn it, because at the house where I lodge we speak Italian, and in the streets I speak to no one.

"I have been to France, but there the policemen were against me. They are bêtes, the policemen français. The gentlemen and ladies all all good. As I walked in the streets with my crutch, one would say, 'Here, poor fellow, are two sous;' or, 'Come with me and have some wine.' They are good hearts there. Whilst I was going to Paris I walk on my leg. I also even now and then find good occasions for mounting in a voiture. I say to them, 'Monsieur, accord me the relief of a ride?' and they say, 'Yes, come, come.'

"In England no police interfere with me. Here it is good. If the police say to me 'Go on, go on,' I say, 'Pardon, Monsieur,' and move away. I never ask any body for money. I work in the streets, and do my gun exercise, and then I leave it to the Bon Dieu to make them give me something. I never ask.

"I have been very unfortunate. I have a tumour come under the arm where I rest on my crutch. It is a tumour, as they call it in France, but I do not know what it is named in English. I went to the hospital of San Bartolommeo and they cut it for me. Then I have hurt my stomach, from the force of calling out the differing orders of commanding, whilst I am doing my gun exercises in the streets. I was two months in my bed with my arm and my stomach being bad. Some days I cannot go out, I am so ill. I cannot drink beer, it is too hot for me, and gets to my head, and it is bad for my stomach. I eat fish: that is good for the voice and the stomach. Now I am better, and my side does not hurt me when I cry out my commanding orders. If I do it for a long time it is painful.

"Ah, pauvre diable! to stop two months in my bed, June, August! The most beautiful months. It was ruin to me.

"After I have gone out for one day, I am forced to rest for the next one. Monday I go out, because I repose on the Sunday. Then all goes well, I am strong in my voice. But I cannot travailler two days following. It is not my leg, that is strong. It is my stomach, and the pains in my side from crying out my commandements. When I go out I make about 10s. a-week. Yes, it comes to that. It is more than 1s. a-day.

"I have a cold. I go out one day when it blew from the north, and the next day I was ill. It makes more cold here than at Genoa, but at Turin in the winter it is more cold than here. It is terrible, terrible. A servant brings in a jug of water, and by-and-by it has ice on its top. I find the bourgeois and not the militaires give the most money. All the persons who have voyagé in France and Italy will give me money — not much, you know, but to me fortune, fortune! If I see a foreigner in the crowd I speak to him. I know the face of an étranger tout-de-suite. Some say to me, 'Vous parlez Français?' 'Oui Monsieur.' Others ask me, 'You speak Italian?' 'Si, Signor.' I never, when I go through my exercise, begin by addressing the people. If I told them I had been a soldier in the army of Sardinia, they would not understand me. Yes, some of the words sound the same in French and English, such as army and soldat, but I have not the heart to beg. I have been soldier, and I cannot take off my cap and beg. I work for what they give me. They give me money and I give them my exercise. I sometimes have done my exercise before a great crowd of people, and when it is done nobody will give me money, and my heart sinks within me. I stand there honteux. One will then in pity throw a sou, but I cannot pick it up, for I will not sell my pride for a penny. If they hand it to me, then I take it, and am pleased with their kindness. But I have only one leg, and to throw the penny on the ground is cruel, for I cannot bend down, and it hurts my pride to put such money in my pocket.

"The little children do not annoy me in the streets, because I never do my exercise until they are at school. Between one and two I never do my exercise, because the little children they are going to their lessons. They never mock me in the streets, for I have been unfortunate to lose my legs, and nobody will mock a miserable infortuné. The carts of the butchers and the bakers, which carry the meat and the bread, and go so fast in the streets, they frighten me when I do my exercises. They nearly écrasé the gens. Tenez! Yesterday I go to the chemin de fer de Birmingham, to the open space before the station, and then I do my exercise. All the people come to their windows and collect about to see me. I walk about like a soldier —but only on my one leg, you know, hopping— and I do my exercise with my crutch for my gun. I stand very steady on one leg. There was a coachman of a cab, and he continued to drive his horse at me, and say, 'Go on! go on!' There was no policeman, or he would not have dared to do it, for the policemen protect me. Le bête! I turn upon him, and cry, 'Bête! take care, bête!' But he still say, 'Get on.' The cheval come close to my back whilst I hop on my one leg to avoid him. At last I was very tired, and he cried out always, 'Get on! get on!' So I cried out for help, and all the ladies run out from their houses and protect me. They said, 'Poor fellow! poor fellow!' and all gave me a half sou. If I had had five shillings in my pocket, I would have gone to a journal and reported that bête, and had the fellow exposed; but I had not five shillings, so I could not go to a journal.

"When I do my exercise, this what I do. I first of all stand still on one leg, in the position of a militaire, with my crutch shouldered like a gun. That is how I accumulate the persons. Then I have to do all. It makes me laugh, for I have to be the general, the capitaines, the drums, the soldiers, and all. Pauvre diable! I must live. It is curious, and makes me laugh.

"I first begin my exercises by doing the drums. I beat my hands together, and make a noise like this—'hum, hum! hum, hum, hum! hum, hum! hum, hum! hu-u-u-m!' and then the drums go away and I do them in the distance. You see I am the drummers then. Next I become the army, and make a noise with my foot, resembling soldiers on a march, and I go from side to side to imitate an army marching. Then I become the trumpeters, but instead of doing the trumpets I whistle their music, and the sound comes nearer and nearer, and gets louder and louder, and then gradually dies away in the distance, as if a bataillon was marching in front of its general. I make a stamping with my foot, like men marching past. After that I become the officiers, the capitaines and the lieutenants, as if the general was passing before them, and my crutch becomes my sword instead of my gun. Then I draw it from my side, and present it with the handle pointed to my breast. Then I become the general, and I gives this order: ' Separate bataillons three steps behind—un, deux, trois!' and I instantly turn to the army again and give three hops to the side, so that the general may walk up and down before me and see how the soldiers are looking. Then I in turn become the officier who gives the commands, and the soldiers who execute them. It hurts my voice when I cry out these commands. They must be very loud, or all the army would not hear them. I can be heard a long way off when I call them out. I begin with ' PORTEZ AR - R - R - MES!' that is, ' Carry arms,' in England. Then I lift my crutch up on my left side and hold it there. Then comes ' PRESENT AR - R - RMES!' and then I hold the gun—my crutch, you know—in front of me, straight up. The next is, ' REPOSE AR-R-RMES!' and I put to my hip, with the barrel leaning forwards. When I say, barrel, it's only my crutch, you understand. Then I shout, ' Un, deux, trois! GROUND AR-R-RMS!' and let the top of my crutch slide on to the road, and I stamp with my toes to resemble the noise. Afterwards I give the command, ' PORTEZ AR-R-RMES!' and then I carry my arms again in my left hand, and slap my other hand hard down by my right side, like a veritable soldier, and stand upright in position. Whilst I am so I shout, ' SEPARATE THE COLUMNS! UN, DEUX, TR-R-ROIS!' and instantly I hop on my one leg three times backwards, so as to let the general once more walk down the ranks and inspect the men. As soon as he is supposed to be near to me, I shout ' PRÉSENT AR-R-RMES!' and then I hold my gun—the crutch, you comprehend—in front of me. Then, as soon as the general is supposed to have passed, I shout out, ' REPOSE AR-R-RMES!' and I let the crutch slant from the right hip, waiting until I cry again ' GROUND AR - R - R - RMS! UN, DEUX, TR-R-ROIS!' and then down slides the crutch to the ground.

" Next I do the other part of the review. I do the firing now, only, you comprehend, I don't fire, but only imitate it with my crutch. I call out ' GROUND AR-R-RMS!' and let the top of my crutch fall to the earth. After that I shout, ' LOAD AR-R-RMS! UN, DEUX, TR-R-ROIS!' and I pretend to take a cartouche from my side, and bite off the end, and slip it down the barrel of my crutch. Next I give the command, ' Draw RAM-RODS! UN, DEUX, TR-R-ROIS!' and then I begin to ram the cartridge home to the breech of the barrel. Afterwards I give the com-

mand, ' COCK AR-R-RMS!' and then I pretend to take a percussion cap from my side-pocket, and I place it on the nipple and draw back the hammer. Afterwards I shout, ' POINT AR-R-RMS!' and I pretend to take aim. Next I shout, ' RECOVER AR-R-RMS!' that is, to hold the gun up in the air, and not to fire. Then I give orders, such as ' POINT TO THE LEFT,' or ' Point to the right,' and which-ever way it is, I have to twist myself round on my one leg, and take an aim that way. Then I give myself the order to ' FIRE!' and I imitate it by a loud shout, and then rattling my tongue as if the whole line was firing. As quickly as I can call out I shout, ' RECOVER AR-R-RMS!' and I put up my gun before me to resist with my bayonet any charge that may be made. Then I shout out, ' DRAW UP THE RANKS AND RECEIVE THE CAVALRY!' and then I work myself along on my one foot, but not by hopping; and there I am waiting for the enemy's horse, and ready to receive them. Often, after I have fired, I call out ' CHAR-R-RGE!' and then I hop forwards as fast as I can, as if I was rushing down upon the enemy, like this. Ah! I was nearly charging through your window; I only stopped in time, or I should have broken the squares in reality. Such a victory would have cost me too dear. After I have charged the enemy and put them to flight, then I draw myself up again, and give the order to ' FORM COLUMNS!' And next I ' CARRY AR-R-RMS,' and then ' PRESENT AR-R-RMS,' and finish by ' GROUNDING AR-R-RMS,' UN, DEUX, TR-R-ROIS.'

" Oh, I have forgotten one part. I do it after the charging. When I have returned from putting the enemy to flight, I become the general calling his troops together. I shout, ' AR-R-RMS ON THE SHOULDER!' and then I become the soldier, and let my gun rest on my shoulder, the same as when I am marching. Then I shout, ' MARCH!' and I hop round on my poor leg, for I cannot march, you comprehend, and I suppose my-self to be defiling before the general. Next comes the order ' Halt!' and I stop still.

" It does not fatigue me to hop about on one leg. It is strong as iron. It is never fatigued. I have walked miles on it with my crutch. It only hurts my chest to holloa out the com-mands, for if I do not do it with all my force it is not heard far off. Besides, I am supposed to be ordering an army, and you must shout out to be heard by all the men; and although I am the only one, to be sure, still I wish to make the audience believe I am an army.

" One day I was up where there is the Palace of the Regina, by the park, with the trees—a very pretty spot, with a park corner, you know. I was there, and I go by a street where the man marks the omnibus which pass, and I go down a short street, and I come to a large place where I do my exercises. A gentleman say to me, ' Come, my friend,' and

I go into his house, and he give me some bread, and some meat, and some beer, and a shilling, and I do my exercises for him. That is the only house where I was called to perform inside. He spoke Italian, and French, and English, so that I not know which country he belongs to. Another day I was doing my exercises and some little children called to their mamma, 'Oh, look! look! come here! the soldier! the soldier!' and the dame said to me, 'Come here and perform to my little boys;' and she gave me sixpence. Those are my fortunes, for to-day I may take two or three shillings, and to-morrow nothing but a few miserable sous; or perhaps I am ill in my stomach with shouting, and I cannot come out to work for my living.

"When it is cold it makes the end of my leg, where it's cut off, begin to tremble, and then it almost shakes me with its shivering, and I am forced to go home, for it is painful.

"I have been about fourteen months. They wanted 4s. to bring me from Boulogne to London; but I had no money, so at the bureau office they gave me a ticket for nothing. Then I came straight to London. When I came to London I couldn't speak English, and I knew no one; had no money, and didn't know where to lodge. That is hard — bien dur. I bought some bread and eat it, and then in the evening I met an Italian, who plays on the organ, you know; and he said, 'Come with me;' and he took me to his lodgings, and there I found Italians and Frenchmen, and I was happy. I began to work the next day at my exercises.

"One day I was in the quarter of the palaces, by the park, you know, and I began my exercises. I could not speak English, and a policeman came to me and said, 'Go on!' What's that? I thought. He said, 'Go on!' again, and I couldn't comprehend, and asked him, 'Parlate Italiano?' and he kept on saying, 'Go on!' This is drôle, I thought; so I said, 'Vous parlez Français?' and he still said, 'Go on!' What he meant I couldn't make out, for I didn't know English, and I had only been here a week. I thought he wanted to see my exercises, so I began, 'Portez ar-r-r-mes!' and he still said, 'Go on!' Then I laughed, and made some signs to follow him. Oh, I thought, it is some one else who wants to see my exercises; and I followed him, enchanted with my good fortune. But, alas! he took me to a police office. There I had an interpreter, and I was told I must not do my exercises in the street. When I told them I was a soldier in the army of the ally of England, and that I had been wounded in battle, and lost my leg fighting for my country, they let me go; and since the policemen are very kind to me, and always say, 'Go on,' with much politeness. I told the magistrate in Italian, 'How can England, so rich and so powerful, object to a pauvre diable like me earning a sou, by showing the exercises of the army of its ally?' The magistrate laughed, and so did the people, and I said, 'Good day,' and made my reverence and left. I have never been in a prison. Oh, no! no! no! no! no! What harm could I do? I have not the power to be a criminal, and I have the heart to be an honest man, and live by my exercises.

"I have travelled in the country. I went to Cheltenham and Bristol. I walked very little of the way. I did my exercises at one place, and then I got enough to go to another town. Ah, it is beautiful country out there. I went to Bristol. I made 7s. in two days there. But I don't like the country. It does not suit me. I prefer London.

"I one day did my exercises by — what do you call it? where the people go up — high, high — no, not St. Paul's — no, by a bridge, where there is an open space. Yes, the monument of Nelson; and then, O! what a crowd! To the right and the left, and to the front and behind, an immense crowd to see my exercises. I made a good deal of money that day. A great deal. The most that I ever did.

"I make about 8s. a-week regularly; I make more than that some weeks, but I often don't go out for a week, because in the rain nobody will come to see my exercises. Some weeks I make 15s., but others not 5s. But I must make 8s. to be able to pay for lodgings, and food, and washing, and clothes, and for my shoe; for I only want one. I give 3d. a-day for my lodgings; but then we have a kitchen, and a fire in it, where we go and sit. There are a great many paysans there, a great many boys, where I lodge, and that gives me pain to see them; for they have been brought over from their country, and here they are miserable, and cannot speak a word of English, and are made to work for their master, who takes the money. Oh! it's make me much pain.

"I cannot say if there are any others who do their exercises in the streets; but I have never seen any. I am, I think, the only stranger who does his exercises. It was my own idea. I did it in France whilst I was travelling; but it was only once or twice, for it was défendu to do it; and the policemen are very severe. Ils sont bêtes, les policemen en France. The gentlemens and ladies very good heart, and give a poor diable des sous, or offer wine to pauvre diable qui a perdu sa jambe en combattant pour sa patrie; mais les policemen sont bêtes. Ah, bêtes! so bêtes I can't tell you."

II.—STREET MUSICIANS.

CONCERNING street musicians, they are of multifarious classes. As a general rule, they may almost be divided into the tolerable and the intolerable performers, some of them trusting to their skill in music for the reward for their exertions, others only making a *noise*, so that whatever money they obtain is given them merely as an inducement for them to depart. The well-known engraving by Hogarth, of "the enraged musician," is an illustration of the persecutions inflicted in olden times by this class of street performers; and in the illustrations by modern caricaturists we have had numerous proofs, that up to the present time the nuisance has not abated. Indeed, many of these people carry with them musical instruments, merely as a means of avoiding the officers of the Mendicity Society, or in some few cases as a signal of their coming to the persons in the neighbourhood, who are in the habit of giving them a small weekly pension.

These are a more numerous class than any other of the street performers I have yet dealt with. The musicians are estimated at 1000, and the ballad singers at 250.

The street musicians are of two kinds, the skilful and the blind. The former obtain their money by the agreeableness of their performance, and the latter, in pity for their affliction rather than admiration of their harmony. The blind street musicians, it must be confessed, belong generally to the rudest class of performers. Music is not used by them as a means of pleasing, but rather as a mode of soliciting attention. Such individuals are known in the "profession" by the name of "pensioners;" they have their regular rounds to make, and particular houses at which to call on certain days of the week, and from which they generally obtain a "small trifle." They form, however, a most peculiar class of individuals. They are mostly well-known characters, and many of them have been performing in the streets of London for many years. They are also remarkable for the religious cast of their thoughts, and the comparative refinement of their tastes and feelings.

"Old Sarah."

One of the most deserving and peculiar of the street musicians was an old lady who played upon a hurdy-gurdy. She had been about the streets of London for upwards of forty years, and being blind, had had during that period four guides, and worn out three instruments. Her cheerfulness, considering her privation and precarious mode of life, was extraordinary. Her love of truth, and the extreme simplicity of her nature, were almost childlike. Like the generality of blind people, she had a deep sense of religion, and her charity for a woman in her station of life was something marvellous; for, though living on alms, she herself had, I was told, two or three little pensioners. When questioned on this subject, she laughed the matter off as a jest, though I was assured of the truth of the fact. Her attention to her guide was most marked. If a cup of tea was given to her after her day's rounds, she would be sure to turn to the poor creature who led her about, and ask, "You comfortable, Liza?" or "Is your tea to your liking, Liza?"

When conveyed to Mr. Beard's establishment to have her daguerreotype taken, she for the first time in her life rode in a cab; and then her fear at being pulled "back'ards" as she termed it (for she sat with her back to the horse), was almost painful. She felt about for something to lay hold of, and did not appear comfortable until she had a firm grasp of the pocket. After her alarm had in a measure subsided, she turned to her guide and said, "We must put up with those trials, Liza." In a short time, however, she began to find the ride pleasant enough. "Very nice, ain't it Liza?" she said; "but I shouldn't like to ride on them steamboats, they say they're shocking dangerous; and as for them railways, I've heard tell they're dreadful; but these cabs, Liza, is very nice." On the road she was continually asking "Liza" where they were, and wondering at the rapidity at which they travelled. "Ah!" she said, laughing, "if I had one of these here cabs, my 'rounds' would soon be over." Whilst ascending the high flight of stairs that led to the portrait-rooms, she laughed at every proposal made to her to rest. "There's twice as many stairs as these to our church, ain't there, Liza?" she replied when pressed. When the portrait was finished she expressed a wish to feel it.

The following is the history of her life, as she herself related it, answering to the variety of questions put to her on the subject:—

"I was born the 4th April, 1786 (it was Good Friday that year), at a small chandler's shop, facing the White Horse, Stuart's-rents, Drury-lane. Father was a hatter, and mother an artificial-flower maker and feather finisher. When I was but a day old, the nurse took me out of the warm bed and carried me to the window, to show some people how like I was to father. The cold flew to my eyes and I caught inflammation in them. Owing to mother being forced to be from home all day at her work, I was put out to dry-nurse when I was three weeks old. My eyes were then very bad, by all accounts, and some neighbours told the woman I was with, that Turner's cerate would do them good. She got some and put it on my eyes, and when poor mother came to suckle me at her dinner-hour, my eyes was all ' a gore of blood.' From that time I never see afterwards. She did it, poor woman, for the best; it was no fault of her'n, and I'm sure I bears her no malice for it. I stayed at home with mother until I was thirteen, when I was put to the Blind-school, but I only kept there nine months; they turned me out because I was not clever with my hands, and I could not learn to spin or make sash-lines; my hands was ocker'd like. I had not been used at home to do anything for myself—not even to dress myself. Mother was always out at her work, so she could not learn me, and no one else would, so that's how it was I was turned out. I then went back to my mother, and kept with her till her death. I well remember that; I heard her last. When she died I was just sixteen year old. I was sent to the Union—'Pancridge' Union it was—and father with me (for he was ill at the time). He died too, and left me, in seven weeks after mother. When they was both gone, I felt I had lost my only friends, and that I was all alone in the world and blind. But, take it altogether, the world has been very good to me, and I have much to thank God for and the good woman I am with. I missed mother the most, she was so kind to me; there was no one like her; no, not even father. I was kept in the Union until I was twenty; the parish paid for my learning the 'cymbal:' God bless them for it, I say. A poor woman in the workhouse first asked me to learn music; she said it would always be a bit of bread for me; I did as she told me, and I thank her to this day for it. It took me just five months to learn the—cymbal, if you please—the hurdy-gurdy ain't it's right name. The first tune I ever played was 'God save the King,' the Queen as is now; then 'Harlequin Hamlet,' that took me a long time to get off; it was three weeks before they put me on a new one. I then learnt 'Moll Brook;' then I did the 'Turnpike-gate' and 'Patrick's day in the morning:' all of them I learnt in the Union. I got a poor man to teach me the 'New-rigged ship.' I soon learnt it, because it was an easy tune. Two-and-forty years ago I played 'The Gal *I* left behind me.' A woman learnt it me: she played my cymbal and I listened, and so got it. 'Oh, Susannah!' I learnt myself by hearing it on the horgan. I always try and listen to a new tune when I am in the street, and get it off if I can: it's my bread. I waited to hear one to-day, quite a new one, but I didn't like it, so I went on. 'Hasten to the Wedding' is my favourite; I played it years ago, and play it still. I like 'Where have you been all the night?' it's a Scotch tune. The woman as persuaded me to learn the cymbal took me out of the Union with her; I lived with her, and she led me about the streets. When she died I took her daughter for my guide. She walked with me for more than five-and-twenty year, and she might have been with me to this day, but she took to drinking and killed herself with it. She behaved very bad to me at last, for as soon as we got a few halfpence she used to go into the public and spend it all; and many a time I'm sure she's been too tipsy to take me home. One night I remember she rolled into the road at Kensington, and as near pulled me with her. We was both locked up in the station-house, for she couldn't stand for liquor, and I was obligated to wait till she could lead me home. It was very cruel of her to treat me so, but, poor creature, she's gone, and I forgive her

I'm sure. I'd many guides arter her, but none of them was honest like Liza is : I don't think she'd rob me of a farden. Would you, Liza? Yes, I've my reg'lar rounds, and I've kept to 'em for near upon fifty year. All the children like to hear me coming along, for I always plays my cymbal as I goes. At Kentish-town they calls me Mrs. Tuesday, and at Kensington I'm Mrs. Friday, and so on. At some places they likes polkas, but at one house I plays at in Kensington they always ask me for 'Haste to the Wedding.' No, the cymbal isn't very hard to play; the only thing is, you must be very particular that the works is covered up, or the halfpence is apt to drop in. King David, they say, played on one of those here instruments. We're very tired by night-time; ain't we, Liza? but when I gets home the good woman I lodges with has always a bit of something for me to eat with my cup of tea. She's a good soul, and keeps me tidy and clean. I helps her all I can; when I come in, I carries her a pail of water up-stairs, and such-like. Many ladies as has known me since they was children allows me a trifle. One maiden lady near Brunswick-square has given me sixpence a week for many a year, and another allows me eighteenpence a fortnight; so that, one way and another, I am very comfortable, and I've much to be thankful for."

It was during one of old Sarah's journeys that an accident occurred, which ultimately deprived London of the well-known old hurdy-gurdy woman. In crossing Seymour-street, she and her guide Liza were knocked down by a cab, as it suddenly turned a corner. They were picked up and placed in the vehicle (the poor guide dead, and Sarah with her limbs broken), and carried to the University Hospital. Old Sarah's description of that ride is more terrible and tragic than I can hope to make out to you. The poor blind creature was ignorant of the fate of her guide, she afterwards told us, and kept begging and praying to Liza to speak to her as the vehicle conveyed them to the asylum. She shook her, she said, and intreated her to say if she was hurt, but not a word was spoken in answer, and then she felt how terrible a privation was her blindness; and it was not until they reached the hospital, and they were lifted from the cab, that she knew, as she heard the people whisper to one another, that her faithful attendant was dead. In telling us this, the good old soul forgot her own sufferings for the time, as she lay with both her legs broken beneath the hooped bed-clothes of the hospital bed; and when, after many long weeks, she left the medical asylum, she was unable to continue her playing on the hurdy-gurdy, her hand being now needed for the crutch that was requisite to bear her on her rounds.

The shock, however, had been too much for the poor old creature's feeble nature to rally against, and though she continued to hobble round to the houses of the kind people who had for years allowed her a few pence per week, and went limping along musicless through the streets for some months after she left the hospital, yet her little remaining strength at length failed her, and she took to her bed in a room in Bell-court, Gray's-inn-lane, never to rise from it again.

"Farm-yard" Player.

A QUIET-LOOKING man, half-blind, and wrapped in a large, old, faded black-cotton great-coat, made the following statement, having first given me some specimens of his art:—

"I imitate all the animals of the farm-yard on my fiddle : I imitate the bull, the calf, the dog, the cock, the hen when she's laid an egg, the peacock, and the ass. I have done this in the streets for nearly twelve years. I was brought up as a musician at my own desire. When a young man (I am now 53) I used to go out to play at parties, doing middling until my sight failed me; I then did the farm-yard on the fiddle for a living. Though I had never heard of such a thing before, by constant practice I made myself perfect. I studied from nature, I never was in a farm-yard in my life, but I went and listened to the poultry, anywhere in town that I could meet with them, and I then imitated them on my instrument. The Smithfield cattle gave me the study for the bull and the calf. My peacock I got at the Belvidere-gardens in Islington. The ass is common, and so is the dog; and them I studied anywhere. It took me a month, not more, if so much, to acquire what I thought a sufficient skill in my undertaking, and then I started it in the streets. It was liked the very first time I tried it. I never say what animal I am going to give; I leave that to the judgment of the listeners. They could always tell what it was. I could make 12s. a-week the year through. I play it in public-houses as well as in the streets. My pitches are all over London, and I don't know that one is better than another. Working-people are my best friends. Thursday and Friday are my worst days; Monday and Saturday my best, when I reckon 2s. 6d. a handsome taking. I am the only man who does the farm-yard."

Blind Performer on the Bells.

A HALE-looking blind man, with a cheerful look, poorly but not squalidly dressed, gave me the subjoined narrative. He was led by a strong, healthy-looking lad of 15, his step-son :—

"I have been blind since within a month of my birth," he said, "and have been 23 years a street performer. My parents were poor, but they managed to have me taught music. I am 55 years old. I was one of a street-band in my youth, and could make my 15s. a-week at it. I didn't like the band, for if you are steady yourself you can't get others to be steady, and so no good can be done. I next started a piano in the streets; that was 23 years ago. I bought a chaise big enough for an invalid, and having had the body removed, my piano was fitted on the springs and the axle-tree. I carried a seat, and could play the instrument either sitting or standing, and so I travelled through London with it. It did pretty well; in the summer I took never less than 20s., and I have taken 40s. on rare occasions, in a week; but the small takings in the winter would reduce my yearly average to 15s. a-week at the utmost. I played the piano, more or less, until within these three or four years. I started the bells that I play now, as near as I can recollect, some 18 years ago. When I first played them, I had my 14 bells arranged on a rail, and tapped them with my two leather hammers held in my hands in the usual way. I thought next I could introduce some novelty into the performance. The novelty I speak of was to play the violin with the bells. I had hammers fixed on a rail, so as each bell had its particular hammer; these hammers were connected with cords to a pedal acting with a spring to bring itself up, and so, by playing the pedal with my feet, I had full command of the bells, and made them accompany the violin, so that I could give any tune almost with the power of a band. It was always my delight in my leisure moments, and is a good deal so still, to study improvements such as I have described. The bells and violin together brought me in about the same as the piano. I played the violoncello with my feet also, on a plan of my own, and the violin in my hand. I had the violoncello on a frame on the ground, so arranged that I could move the bow with my foot in harmony with the violin in my hand. The last thing I have introduced is the playing four accordions with my feet. The accordions are fixed in a frame, and I make them accompany the violin. Of all my plans, the piano, and the bells and violin, did the best, and are the best still for a standard. I can only average 12s. a-week, take the year through, which is very little for two."

Blind Female Violin Player.

I HAD the following narrative from a stout blind woman, with a very grave and even meditative look, fifty-six years old, dressed in a clean cotton gown, the pattern of which was almost washed out. She was led by a very fine dog (a Scotch colley, she described it), a chain being affixed to the dog's leather collar A boy, poor and destitute, she said, barefooted, and wearing a greasy ragged jacket, with his bare skin showing through the many rents, accompanied her when I saw her. The boy had been with her a month, she supporting him. She said :—

"I have been blind twelve years. I was a servant in my youth, and in 1824 married a journeyman cabinet-maker. I went blind from an inflammation two years before my husband died. We had five children, all dead now—the last died six years ago; and at my husband's death I was left almost destitute. I used to sell a few laces in the street, but couldn't clear 2s. 6d. a-week by it. I had a little help from the parish, but very rarely; and at last I could get nothing but an order for the house. A neighbour—a tradesman— then taught me at his leisure to play the violin, but I'm not a great performer. I wish I was. I began to play in the streets five years ago. I get halfpennies in charity, not for my music. Some days I pick up 2s., some days only 6d., and on wet days nothing. I've often had to pledge my fiddle for 2s.—I could never get more on it, and sometimes not that. When my fiddle was in pledge, I used to sell matches and laces in the streets, and have had to borrow 1½d. to lay in a stock. I've sometimes taken 4d. in eight hours. My chief places, when I've only the dog to lead me, are Regent-street and Portland-place; and, really, people are very kind and careful in guiding and directing me,—even the cabmen! may God bless them!'

BLIND SCOTCH VIOLONCELLO PLAYER.

A STOUT, hale-looking blind man, dressed very decently in coloured clothes, and scrupulously clean, gave me the following details :—

"I am one of the three blind Scotchmen who go about the streets in company, playing the violoncello, clarionet, and flute. We are really Highlanders, and can all speak Gaelic; but a good many London Highlanders are Irish. I have been thirty years in the streets of London; one of my mates has been forty years, —he's sixty-nine;—the other has been thirty years. I became partially blind, through an inflammation, when I was fourteen, and was stone-blind when I was twenty-two. Before I was totally blind I came to London, travelling up with the help of my bagpipes, guided by a little boy. I settled in London, finding it a big place, where a man could do well at that time, and I took a turn every now and then into the country. I could make 14s. a-week, winter and summer through, thirty years ago, by playing in the streets; now I can't make 6s. a-week, take winter and summer. I met my two mates, who are both blind men, —both came to England for the same reason as I did,—in my journeyings in London; and at last we agreed to go together,—that's twenty years ago. We've been together, on and off, ever since. Sometimes, one of us will take a turn round the coast of Kent, and another round the coast of Devon; and then join again in London, or meet by accident. We have always agreed very well, and never fought. We,—I mean the street-blind,—

tried to maintain a burying and sick-club of our own; but we were always too poor. We live in rooms. I don't know one blind musician who lives in a lodging-house. I myself know a dozen blind men, now performing in the streets of London; these are not all exactly blind, but about as bad; the most are stone-blind. The blind musicians are chiefly married men. I don't know one who lives with a woman unmarried. The loss of sight changes a man. He doesn't think of women, and women don't think of him. We are of a religious turn, too, generally. I am a Roman Catholic; but the other Scotch blind men here are Presbyterians. The Scotch in London are our good friends, because they give us a little sum altogether, perhaps; but the English working-people are our main support: it is by them we live, and I always found them kind and liberal,—the most liberal in the world as I know. Through Marylebone is our best round, and Saturday night our best time. We play all three together. ' Johnny Cope' is our best-liked tune. I think the blind Scotch-men don't come to play in London now. I can remember many blind Scotch musicians, or pipers, in London : they are all dead now! The trade's dead too,—it is so! When we thought of forming the blind club, there was never more than a dozen members. These were two basket-makers, one mat-maker, four violin-players, myself, and my two mates; which was the number when it dropped for want of funds; that's now fifteen years ago. We were to pay 1s. a-month; and sick members were to have 5s. a-week, when they'd paid two years. Our other rules were the same as other clubs, I believe. The blind musicians now in London are we three; C—, a Jew, who plays the violin; R—, an Englishman, who plays the violin elegantly; W—, a harp player; T—, violin again; H—, violin (but he plays more in public-houses); R—, the flute; M—, bagpipes; C—, bagpipes; K—, violin : that's all I know myself. There's a good many blind who play at the sailors' dances, Wapping and Deptford way. We seldom hire children to lead us in the streets; we have plenty of our own, generally —I have five! Our wives are generally women who have their eyesight; but some blind men,—I know one couple,—marry blind women."

BLIND IRISH PIPER.

OF the Irish Pipers, a well-dressed, middle-aged man, of good appearance, wearing large green spectacles, led by a young girl, his daughter, gave me the following account:—

"I was eleven years old when I lost my sight from cold, and I was brought up to the musical profession, and practised it several years in Ireland, of which country I am a native. I was a man of private property,— small property—and only played occasionally at the gentle-people's places; and then more as a guest—yes, more indeed than professionally. In 1838 I married, and began to give concerts regularly; I was the performer, and played only on the union pipes at my concerts. I'm acknowledged to be the best performer in the world, even by my own craft,—excuse what seems self-praise. The union pipes are the old Irish pipes improved. In former times there was no chromatic scale; now we have eight keys to the chanter, which produce the chromatic scale as on the flute, and so the pipes are improved in the melody, and more particularly in the harmony. We have had fine performers of old. I may mention Caroll O'Daly, who flourished in the 15th century, and was the composer of the air that the Scotch want to steal from us, 'Robin Adair,' which is 'Alleen ma ruen,' or 'Ellen, my dear.' My concerts in Ireland answered very well indeed, but the famine reduced me so much that I was fain to get to England with my family, wife and four children; and in this visit I have been disappointed, completely so. Now I'm reduced to play in the streets, and make very little by it. I may average 15s. in the week in summer, and not half that in winter. There are many of my countrymen now in England playing the pipes, but I don't know one respectable enough to associate with; so I keep to myself, and so I cannot tell how many there are."

The English Street Bands.

Concerning these, a respectable man gave me the following details:—

"I was brought up to the musical profession, and have been a street-performer 22 years, and I'm now only 26. I sang and played the guitar in the streets with my mother when I was four years old. We were greatly patronised by the nobility at that time. It was a good business when I was a child. A younger brother and I would go out into the streets for a few hours of an evening, from five to eight, and make 7s. or 8s. the two of us. Ours was, and is, the highest class of street music. For the last ten years I have been a member of a street band. Our band is now four in number. I have been in bands of eight, and in some composed of as many as 25; but a small band answers best for regularity. With eight in the band it's not easy to get 3s. a-piece on a fine day, and play all day, too. I consider that there are 1000 musicians now performing in the streets of London; and as very few play singly, 1000 performers, not reckoning persons who play with niggers or such-like, will give not quite 250 street bands. Four in number is a fair average for a street band; but I think the greater number of bands have more than four in them. All the better sort of these bands play at concerts, balls, parties, processions, and water excursions, as well as in the streets. The class of

men in the street bands is, very generally, those who can't read music, but play by ear; and their being unable to read music prevents their obtaining employment in theatres, or places where a musical education is necessary; and yet numbers of street musicians (playing by ear) are better instrumentalists than many educated musicians in the theatres. I only know a few who have left other businesses to become musicians. The great majority—19-20ths of us, I should say—have been brought regularly up to be street-performers. Children now are taught very early, and seldom leave the profession for any other business. Every year the street musicians increase. The better sort are, I think, prudent men, and struggle hard for a decent living. All the street-performers of wind instruments are short-lived. Wind performers drink more, too, than the others. They must have their mouths wet, and they need some stimulant or restorative after blowing an hour in the streets. There are now twice as many wind as stringed instruments played in the streets; fifteen or sixteen years ago there used to be more stringed instruments. Within that time new wind instruments have been used in the streets. Cornopeans, or cornet-à-pistons, came into vogue about fourteen years ago; opheicleides about ten years ago (I'm speaking of the streets); and saxhorns about two years since. The cornopean has now quite superseded the bugle. The worst part of the street performers, in point of character, are those who play before or in public-houses. They drink a great deal, but I never heard of them being charged with dishonesty. In fact, I believe there's no honester set of men breathing than street musicians. The better class of musicians are nearly all married men, and they generally dislike to teach their wives music; indeed, in my band, and in similar bands, we wouldn't employ a man who was teaching his wife music, that she might play in the streets, and so be exposed to every insult and every temptation, if she's young and pretty. Many of the musicians' wives have to work very hard with their needles for the slop-shops, and earn very little in such employ; 3s. a-week is reckoned good earnings, but it all helps. The German bands injure our trade much. They'll play for half what we ask. They are very mean, feed dirtily, and the best band of them, whom I met at Dover, I know slept three in a bed in a common lodging-house, one of the very lowest. They now block us out of all the country places to which we used to go in the summer. The German bands have now possession of the whole coast of Kent and Sussex, and wherever there are watering-places. I don't know anything about their morals, excepting that they don't drink. An English street-performer in a good and respectable band will now average 25s. a-week the year through. Fifteen years ago he could have made 3*l.* a-week. Inferior performers make from 12*s.* to 15*s.* a-week. I consider Regent-street and such places our best pitches. Our principal patrons in the parties' line are tradesmen and professional men, such as attorneys: 10*s.* a-night is our regular charge."

The German Street Bands.

Next come the German Bands. I had the following statement from a young flaxen-haired and fresh-coloured German, who spoke English very fairly:—

"I am German, and have been six year in zis country. I was nearly fourteen when I come. I come from Oberfeld, eighteen miles from Hanover. I come because I would like to see how it was here. I heard zat London was a goot place for foreign music. London is as goot a place as I expect to find him. There was other six come over with me, boys and men. We come to Hull, and play in ze country about half a year; we do middling. And zen we come to London. I didn't make money at first when I come, I had much to learn; but ze band, oh! it did well. We was seven. I play ze clarionet, and so did two others; two play French horns, one ze tram-bone, and one ze saxhorn. Sometime we make 7*s.* or 8*s.* a-piece in a-day now, but the business is not so goot. I reckon 6*s.* a-day is goot now. We never play at fairs, nor for caravans. We play at private parties or public ball-rooms, and are paid so much a dance—sixpence a dance for ze seven of us. If zare is many dances, it is goot; if not, it is bad. We play sheaper zan ze English, and we don't spent so much. Ze English players insult us, but we don't care about that. Zey abuse us for playing sheap. I don't know what zair terms for dances are. I have saved money in zis country, but very little of it. I want to save enough to take me back to Hanover. We all live togeder, ze seven of us. We have three rooms to sleep in, and one to eat in. We are all single men, but one; and his wife, a Ger-man woman, lives wis us, and cooks for us. She and her husband have a bedroom to themselves. Anysing does for us to eat. We all join in housekeeping and lodging, and pay alike. Our lodging costs 2*s.* a-week each, our board costs us about 15*s.* a-week each; sometime rather less. But zat include beer; and ze London beer is very goot, and some-time we drink a goot deal of it. We drink very little gin, but we live very well, and have goot meals every day. We play in ze streets, and I zink most places are alike to us. Ladies and gentlemen are our best friends; ze work-ing people give us very little. We play opera tunes chiefly. We don't associate with any Englishmen. Zare are three public-houses kept by Germans, where we Germans meet. Sugar-bakers and other trades are of ze num-ber. There are now five German brass-bands, with thirty-seven performers in zem, reckon-

ing our own, in London. Our band lives near Whitechapel. I sink zare is one or two more German bands in ze country. I sink my countrymen, some of them, save money; but I have not saved much yet."

Of the Bagpipe Players.

A well-looking young man, dressed in full Highland costume, with modest manners and of slow speech, as if translating his words from the Gaelic before he uttered them, gave me these details:—

"I am a native of Inverness, and a Grant. My father was a soldier, and a player in the 42nd. In my youth I was shepherd in the hills, until my father was unable to support me any longer. He had 9*d.* a-day pension for seventeen years' service, and had been thrice wounded. He taught me and my brither the pipes; he was too poor to have us taught any trade, so we started on our own accounts. We travelled up to London, had only our pipes to depend upon. We came in full Highland dress. The tartan is cheap there, and we mak it up oursels. My dress as I sit here, without my pipes, would cost about 4*l.* in London. Our mithers spin the tartan in Inverness-shire, and the dress comes to maybe 30*s.*, and is better than the London. My pipes cost me three guineas new. It's between five and six years since I first came to London, and I was twenty-four last November. When I started, I thought of making a fortune in London; there was such great talk of it in Inverness-shire, as a fine place with plenty of money; but when I came I found the difference. I was rather a novelty at first, and did pretty well. I could make 1*l.* a-week then, but now I can't make 2*s.* a-day, not even in summer. There are so many Irishmen going about London, and dressed as Scotch Highlanders, that I really think I could do better as a piper even in Scotland. A Scotch family will sometimes give me a shilling or two when they find out I am a Scotchman. Chelsea is my best place, where there are many Scotchmen. There are now only five real Scotch Highlanders playing the bagpipes in the streets of London, and seven or eight Irishmen that I know of. The Irishmen do better than I do, because they have more face. We have our own rooms. I pay 4*s.* a-week for an empty room, and have my ain furniture. We are all married men, and have no connexion with any other street musicians. 'Tullochgorum,' 'Moneymusk,' 'The Campbells are comin',' and 'Lord Mac-donald's Reel,' are among the performances best liked in London. I'm very seldom insulted in the streets, and then mostly by being called an Irishman, which I don't like; but I pass it off just as well as I can."

Scotch Piper and Dancing-Girl.

"I was full corporal in the 93rd Southern Highlanders, and I can get the best of characters from my commanding officers. If I couldn't get a good character I wouldn't be orderly to the colonel; and wherever he and the lady went, I was sure to be with them. Although I used to wear the colonel's livery, yet I had the full corporal's stripes on my coat. I was first orderly to Colonel Sparkes of the 93rd. He belonged to Dublin, and he was the best colonel that ever belonged to a regiment. After he died I was orderly to Colonel Aynsley. This shows I must have been a good man, and have a good character. Colonel Aynsley was a good friend to me, and he always gave me my clothes, like his other private servants. The orderly's post is a good one, and much sought after, for it exempts you from regimental duty. Colonel Aynsley was a severe man on duty, but he was a good colonel after all. If he wasn't to be a severe man he wouldn't be able to discharge the post he had to discharge. Off duty he was as kind as anybody could be. There was no man he hated more than a dirty soldier. He wouldn't muddle a man for being drunk, not a quarter so much as for dirty clothing. I was reckoned the cleanest soldier in the regiment; for if I was out in a shower of rain, I'd polish up my brass and pipeclay my belt, to make it look clean again. Besides, I was very supple and active, and many's the time Colonel Aynsley has sent me on a message, and I have been there and back, and when I've met him he's scolded me for not having gone, for I was back so quick he thought I hadn't started.

"Whilst I was in the regiment I was attacked with blindness; brought on, I think, by cold. There was a deserter, that the policemen took up and brought to our barracks at Weedon, where the 93rd was stationed in 1852. It was very wet weather, and he was brought in without a stitch on him, in a pair of breeches and a miserable shirt—that's all. He was away two years, but he was always much liked. No deserters ever escape. We made a kit up for this man in less than twenty minutes. One gave him a kilt, another a coat, and I gave him the shoes off my feet, and then went to the regiment stores and got me another pair. Soldiers always help one another; it's their duty to such a poor, miserable wretch as he was.

"This deserter was tried by court-martial, and he got thirty-one days in prison, and hard labour. He'd have had three months, only he gave himself up. He was so weak with lying out, that the doctor wouldn't let him be flogged. He'd have had sixty lashes if he'd been strong. Ah! sixty is nothing. I've seen one hundred and fifty given. When this man was marched off to Warwick gaol I commanded the escort, and it was a very severe day's rain that day, for it kept on from six in the morning till twelve at night. It was a twenty-one miles' march; and we started at six in the morning, and arrived at Warwick by four in the afternoon. The prisoner was made to march the distance in the same clothes as when he gave himself up. He had only a shirt and waistcoat on his back, and that got so wet, I took off my greatcoat and gave it to him to wear to warm him. They wouldn't let him have the kit of clothes made up for him by the regiment till he came out of prison. From giving him my greatcoat I caught a severe cold. I stood up by a public-house fire and dried my coat and kilt, and the cold flew to the small of my back. After we had delivered our prisoner at Warwick we walked on to Coventry—that's ten miles more. We did thirty-one miles that day in the rain. After we got back to barracks I was clapped in hospital. I was there twenty-one days. The doctor told me I shouldn't leave it for twenty-eight days, but I left it in twenty-one, for I didn't like to be in that same place. My eyes got very blood-shot, and I lost the sight of them. I was very much afraid that I'd never see a sight with my eyes, and I was most miserable. I used to be, too, all of a tremble with a shiver of cold. I only stopped in the regiment for thirty-one days after I came out of hospital, and then I had my discharge. I could just see a little. It was my own fault that I had my discharge, for I thought I could do better to cure myself by going to the country doctors. The men subscribed for me all the extra money of their pay,—that's about 4d. each man,—and it made me up 10l. When I told Colonel Aynsley of this, says he, 'Upon my word, M'Gregor, I'm as proud of it as if I had 20,000l.' He gave me a sovereign out of his own pocket. Besides that, I had as many kilts given me as have lasted me up to this time. My boy is wearing the last of 'em now.

"At Oxford I went to a doctor, and he did me a deal of good; for now I can read a book, if the thread of it isn't too small. I can read the Prayer-book, or Bible, or newspaper, just for four hours, and then I go dim.

"I've served in India, and I was at the battles of Punjaub, 1848, and Moultan, 1849. Sir Colin Campbell commanded us at both, and says he, 'Now, my brave 93rd, none of your nonsense here, for it must be death and glory here to-day;' and then Serjeant Cameron says, 'The men are all right, Sir Colin, but they're afraid you won't be in the midst of them;' and says he, 'Not in the midst of them! I'll be here in ten minutes.' Sir Colin will go in anywhere; he's as brave an officer as any in the service. He's the first into the fight and the last out of it.

"Although I had served ten years, and been in two battles, yet I was not entitled to a pension. You must serve twenty-one years to be entitled to 1s. 0½d. I left the 93rd in 1852, and since that time I've been wandering about the different parts of England and Scotland, playing on the bagpipes. I take my daughter Maria about with me, and she dances whilst

I play to her. I leave my wife and family in town. I've been in London three weeks this last time I visited it. I've been here plenty of times before. I've done duty in Hyde-Park before the 46th came here.

"I left the army just two years before the war broke out, and I'd rather than twenty thousand pounds I'd been in my health to have gone to the Crimea, for I'd have had more glory after that war than ever any England was in. Directly I found the 93rd was going out, I went twice to try and get back to my old regiment; but the doctor inspected me, and said I wouldn't be fit for service again. I was too old at the time, and my health wasn't good, although I could stand the cold far better than many hundreds of them that were out there, for I never wear no drawers, only my kilt, and that very thin, for it's near worn. Nothing at all gives me cold but the rain.

"The last time I was in London was in May. My daughter dances the Highland fling and the sword-dance called 'Killim Callam.' That's the right Highland air to the dance — with two swords laid across each other. I was a good hand at it before I got stiff. I've done it before all the regiment. We'd take two swords from the officers and lay them down when they've been newly ground. I've gone within the eighth of an inch of them, and never cut my shoe. Can you cut your shoes? aye, and your toes, too, if you're not lithe. My brother was the best dancer in the army: so the Duke of Argyle and his lady said. At one of the prize meetings at Blair Athol, one Tom Duff, who is as good a dancer as from this to where he is, says he, 'There's ne'er a man of the Macgregor clan can dance against me to-day!' and I, knowing my brother Tom —he was killed at Inkermann in the 93rd—was coming, says I, 'Don't be sure of that, Tom Duff, for there's one come every inch of the road here to-day to try it with you.' He began, and he took an inch off his shoes, and my brother never cut himself at all; and he won the prize.

"My little girl dances that dance. She does it pretty, but I'd be rather doubtful about letting her come near the swords, for fear she'd be cutting herself, though I know she could do it at a pinch, for she can be dancing across two baccy-pipes without breaking them. When I'm in the streets, she always does it with two baccy-pipes. She can dance reels, too, such as the Highland fling and the reel Hoolow. They're the most celebrated.

"Whenever I go about the country I leave my wife and family in London, and go off with my girl. I send them up money every week, according to what I earn. Every farthing that I can spare I always send up. I always, when I'm travelling, make the first part of my journey down to Hull in Yorkshire. On my road I always stop at garrison towns, and they always behave very well to me. If they've a penny they'll give it to me, either English, Scotch, or Irish regiments; or I'd as soon meet the 23d Welsh Fusiliers as any, for they've all been out with me on service. At Hull there is a large garrison, and I always reckon on getting 3s. or 4s. from the barracks. When I'm travelling, it generally comes to 15s. a-week, and out of that I manage to send the wife 10s. and live on 5s. myself. I have to walk all the way, for I wouldn't sit on a rail or a cart for fear I should lose the little villages off the road. I can do better in many of them than I can in many of the large towns. I tell them I am an old soldier. I don't go to the cottages, but to the gentlemen's houses. Many of the gentlemen have been in the army, and then they soon tell whether I have been in service. Some have asked me the stations I have been at, and who commanded us; and then they'll say, 'This man is true enough, and every word of it is truth.'

"I've been in Balmoral many a dozen of times. Many a time I've passed by it when it was an old ruin, and fit for nothing but the ravens and the owls. Balmoral is the fourth oldest place in Scotland. It was built before any parts of Christianity came into the country at all. I've an old book that gives an account of all the old buildings entirely, and a very old book it is. Edinbro' Castle is the oldest building, and then Stirling Castle, and then Perth Castle, and then Balmoral. I've been there twice since the Queen was there. If I'd see any of the old officers that I knew at Balmoral, I'd play then, and they might give me something. I went there more for curiosity, and I went to see the Queen come out. She was always very fond of the 93rd. They'd fight for her in any place, for there isn't a man discharged after this war but they're provided for.

"I do pretty well in London, taking my 4s. a-day, but out of that I must pay 1s. 9d. a-week lodging-money, for I can't go into apartments, for if I did it would be but poorly furnished, for I've no beds, or furniture, or linen.

"I can live in Scotland much cheaper than here. I can give the children a good breakfast of oatmeal-porridge every morning, and that will in seven weeks make them as fat as seven years of tea and coffee will do here. Besides, in Scotland, I can buy a very pretty little stand-up bedstead for 2s., which here would come to 4s. I'm thinking of sending my family down to Scotland, and sending them the money I earn in London. They'll have to walk to Hull and then take the boat. They can get to Aberdeen from there. We shall have to work the money on the road.

"When I go out working with the little girl, I get out about nine in the summer and ten in the winter. I can't work much more than four hours a-day on the pipes, for the blowing knocks me up and leaves me very weak. No, it don't hurt my chest, but I'll be just quite weak. That's from my bad health. I've never had a day's health ever since I left the regiment. I have pains in my back and stitches in the side. My girl can't dance without my playing, so that when I give over she must give over too. I sometimes go out with two of my daughters. Lizzy don't dance, only Maria. I never ax anybody for money. Anybody that don't like to give we never ax them.

"I can't eat meat, for it won't rest on my stomach, and there's nothing I take that goes so well with me as soup. I live principally on bread, for coffee or tea won't do for me at all. If I could get a bit of meat that I like, such as a small fowl, or the like of that, it would do with me very well; but either bacon or beef, or the like of that, is too strong for me. I'm obliged to be very careful entirely with what I eat, for I'm sick. A lady gave me a bottle of good old foreign port about three months ago, and I thought it did me more good than all the meat in the world.

"When I'm in London I make about 4s. a-day, and when I'm in the country about 15s. a-week. My old lady couldn't live when I travel if it wasn't for my boy, who goes out and gets about 1s. a-day. Lord Panmure is very good to him, and gives him something whenever he meets him. I wouldn't get such good health if I stopped in London. Now there's Barnet, only eleven miles from St. Giles's, and yet I can get better health in London than I can there, on account of it's being on rising ground and fresh air coming into it every minute.

"I never be a bit bad with the cold. It never makes me bad. I've been in Canada with the 93d in the winter. In the year '43 was a very fearful winter indeed, and we were there, and the men didn't seem to suffer anything from the cold, but were just as well as in any other climate or in England. They wore the kilt and the same dress as in summer. Some of them wore the tartan trowsers when they were not on duty or parade, but the most of them didn't—not one in a dozen, for they looked upon it as like a woman. There's nothing so good for the cold as cold water. The men used to bathe their knees and legs in the cold water, and it would make them ache for the time, but a minute or two afterwards they were all right and sweating. I've many a time gone into the water up to my neck in the coldest days of the year, and then when I came out and dried myself, and put on my clothes, I'd be sweating afterwards. There can't be a better thing for keeping away the rheumatism. It's a fine thing for rheumatism and aches to rub the part with cold frosty water or snow. It makes it leave him and knocks the pains out of his limbs. Now, in London, when my hands are so cold I can't play on my pipes, I go to a pump and wash them in the frosty water, and then dry them and rub them together, and then they're as warm as ever. The more a man leans to the fire the worse he is after. It was leaning to a fire that gave me my illness.

"The chanter of the pipes I play on has been in my family very near 450 years. It's the oldest in Scotland, and is a heir-loom in our family, and they wouldn't part with it for any money. Many's a time the Museum in Edinburgh has wanted me to give it to them, but I won't give it to any one till I find myself near death, and then I'll obligate them to keep it. Most likely my youngest son will have it, for he's as steady as a man. You see, the holes for the fingers is worn as big round as sixpences, and they're quite sharp at the edges. The ivory at the end is the same original piece as when the pipe was made. It's breaking and splitting with age, and so is the stick. I'll have my name and the age of the stick engraved on the sole of the ivory, and then, if my boy seems neglectful of the chanter, I'll give it to the Museum at Edinburgh. I'll have German silver rings put round the stick, to keep it together, and then, with nice waxed thread bound round it, it will last for centuries yet.

"This chanter was made by old William McDonnall, who's been dead these many hundred years. He was one of the best pipe-makers that's in all Scotland. There's a brother of mine has a set of drones made by him, and he wouldn't give them for any sit of money. Everybody in Scotland knows William McDonnall. Ask any lad, and he'll tell you who was the best pipe-maker that ever lived in Scotland—aye, and ever will live. There's many a farmer in Scotland would give 30l. for a set of pipes by old William McDonnall, sooner than they'd give 30s. for a set of pipes made now. This chanter has been in our family ever since McDonnall made it. It's been handed down from father to son from that day to this. They always give it to the eldest. William McDonnall lived to be 143 years old, and this is the last chanter he made. A gentleman in London, who makes chanters, once gave me a new one, merely for letting him take a model of my old one, with the size of the bore and the place for the holes. You tell a good chanter by the tone, and some is as sweet as a piano. My old chanter has got rather too sharp by old age, and it's lost its tone; for when a stick gets too sharp a sound, it's never no good. This chanter was played by my family in the battles of Wallace and Bruce, and at the battle of Bannockburn, and every place whenever any of the Macgregor clan fought. These are the traditions given from family to family. I heard it from my father, and now I tell my lads, and they know it as well as I do myself. My great grandfather played on this stick when Charley Stuart, the Pretender, came over to Scotland from France, and he played on it before the Prince himself, at Stirling and the Island of Skye, and at Preston Pans and Culloden. It was at Preston Pans that the clans were first formed, and could be told by their tartans—the Macgregors, and the Stuart, and the Macbeths, and the Camerons, and all of them. I had three brothers older than me, but I've got this chanter, for I begged it of them. It's getting too old to play on, and I'll have a copper box made for it, and just carry it at my side, if God is good to me, and gives me health to live three weeks.

"About my best friends in London are the French people,—they are the best I can meet, they come next to the Highlanders. When I meet a Highlander he will, if he's only just a labouring man, give me a few coppers. A Highlander will never close his eye upon me. It's the Lowlander that is the worst to me. They never takes no notice of me when I'm passing: they'll smile and cast an eye as I pass by. Many a time I'll say to them when they pass, ' Well, old chap, you don't like the half-naked men, I know you don't!' and many will say, ' No, I don't!' I never play the pipes when I go through the Lowlands,—I'd as soon play poison to them. They never give anything. It's the Lowlanders that get the Scotch a bad name for being miserable, and keeping their money, and using small provision. They're a disgrace to their country.

"The Highlander spends his money as free as a duke. If a man in the 93rd had a shilling in his pocket, it was gone before he could turn it twice. All the Lowlanders would like to be Highlanders if they could, and they learn Gaelic, and then marry Highland lassies, so as to become Highlanders. They have some clever regiments composed out of the Lowlanders, but they have only three regiments and the Highlanders have seven; yet there's nearly three to one more inhabitants in the Lowlands. It's a strange thing, they'd sooner take an Irishman into a Highland regiment than a Lowlander. They owe them such a spleen, they don't like them. Bruce was a Lowlander, and he betrayed Wallace ; and the Duke of Buccleuch, who was a Lowlander, betrayed Stuart.

"I never go playing at public-houses, for I don't like such places. I am not a drinker, for as much whisky as will fill a teaspoon will lay me up for a day. If I take anything, it's a sup of porter. I went once into a public-house, and there was a woman drinking in it, and she was drunk. It was the landlord told me to come inside. She told me to leave the house, and I said the master told me to come: then she took up one of these pewter pots and hit me in the forehead. It was very sore for three weeks afterwards, and made a hole. I wouldn't prosecute her.

"My little boy that goes about is fourteen years old, and he's as straight and well-formed as if he was made of wax-work. He's the one that shall have the chanter, if anybody does; but I'm rather doubtful about it, for he's not steady enough, and I think I'll leave it to a museum.

"If I had a good set of pipes, there's not many going about the streets could play better ; but my pipes are not in good order. I've got three tunes for one that the Queen's piper plays ; and I can play in a far superior style, for he plays in the military style. McKay, the former piper to her majesty, he was reckoned as good a player as there is in Scotland. I knew him very well, and many and many a time I've played with him. He was took bad in the head and obliged to go back to Scotland. He is in the Isle of Skye now. I belong to Peterhead. If I had a good set of pipes I wouldn't be much afraid of playing with any of the pipers.

"In the country towns I would sometimes be called into Highland gentlemen's houses, to play to them, but never in London.

"I make all my reeds myself to put in the stick. I make them of Spanish cane. It's the outer glazed bark of it. The nearer you go to the shiny part, the harder the reed is, and the longer it lasts. In Scotland they use the Spanish cane. I have seen a man, at one time, who made a reed out of a piece of white thorn, and it sounded as well as ever a reed I saw sound; but I never see a man who could make them, only one."

ANOTHER BAGPIPE PLAYER.

"My father is a Highlander, and was born in Argyllshire, and there, when he was 14 or 15, he enlisted for a piper into the 92nd. They wear the national costume in that regiment — the Campbell tartan. Father married whilst he was in Scotland. We are six in family now, and my big brother is 17, and I'm getting on for 15 — a little better than 14. We and another brother of 10, all of us, go about the streets playing the bagpipes.

"Father served in India. It was after I was born (and so was my other brother of 10) that the regiment was ordered over there. Mother came up to England to see him off, and she has stopped in London ever since. Father lost a leg in the Punjaub war, and now he receives a pension of 1s. a-day. Mother had a very bad time of it whilst father was away ; I don't know the reason why, but father didn't send her any money. All her time was taken up looking after us at home, so she couldn't do any work. The parish allowed her some money. She used to go for some food every week. I can remember when we were so hard up. We lived principally on bread and potatoes. At last mother told Jim he had better go out in the streets and play the bagpipes, to see what he could pick up. Father had left some pipes behind him, small ones, what he learnt to play upon. Jim wasn't dressed up in the Highland costume as he is now. He did very well the first time he went out; he took about 10s. or so. When mother saw that she was very pleased, and thought she had the Bank of England tumbled into her lap. Jim continued going out every day until father came home. After father lost his leg he came home again. He had been absent about eighteen months. The pipers always go into action with the regiment. When they are going into the field they play in front of the regiment, but when the fighting begins they go to the side. He never talks about his wound. I never heard him talk about it beyond just what I've said; as to how they go into war and play the regiment into the field. I never felt much curiosity to ask him about it, for I'm out all day long and until about 10 o'clock at night, and when I get home I'm too tired to talk; I never think about asking him how he was wounded.

"When father came home from India he brought 10*l.* with him. He didn't get his pension not till he got his medal, and that was a good while after—about a year after, I should say. This war they gave the pension directly they got home, but the other war they didn't. Jim still continued playing in the streets. Then father made him a Highland suit out of his old regimentals. He did better then; indeed he one day brought home a pound, and never less than five, or nine or ten, shillings. Next, father made me a suit, and I used to go out with Jim and dance the fling to his bagpipes. I usen't to take no carpet with me, but dance in the middle of the road. I wear father's regimental-belt to this day, only he cut it down smaller for me. Here's his number at the end of it, 62, and the date, 1834—so it's twenty-two years old, and it's strong and good now, only it's been white buff leather, and my father's blacked it. We didn't take much more money going out together, but we took it quicker and got home sooner. Besides, it was a help to mother to get rid of me. We still took about 10*s.* a-day, but it got lesser and lesser after a time. It was a couple of years after we come out that it got lesser. People got stingier, or perhaps they was accustomed to see us, and was tired of the dancing. Whilst I was doing the dancing, father, when I got home of a night, used to teach me the bagpipes. It took me more than twelve months to learn to play. Now I'm reckoned a middling player.

"When I could play I went out with my big brother, and we played together; we did the tunes both together. No, I didn't do a bass, or anything of that; we only played louder when we was together, and so made more noise, and so got more attention. In the day-time we walked along the streets playing. We did better the two playing together than when I danced. Sometimes gentlemen would tell us to come to their houses and play to 'em. We've often been to General Campbell's and played to him, whilst he was at dinner sometimes, or sometimes after. We had 5*s.* or half-a-sovereign, according to the time we stopped there. There

was about six or seven gentlemen like this, and we go to their houses and play for them. We get from one shilling to five for each visit. When we go inside and play to them it's never less than 5*s.* They are all Scotch gentlemen that we go to see, but we have done it for one Englishman, but he's the only one.

"When my little brother John was old enough to go out, father made him a Highland suit, and then he went out along with my big brother and danced to his playing, and I went out by myself. I did pretty well, but not so well as when I was with Jim. We neither did so well as when we were together, but putting both our earnings together we did better, for the two separated took more than the two joined.

"My little sister Mary has been out with me for the last month. Father made her a suit. It's a boy's, and not a girl's costume, and she goes along with me. Whilst I play, she goes up to ladies and gentlemen and asks for the money. They generally give her something. She never says anything, only makes a bow and holds out her little hand. It was father's notion to send her out. He said, 'She may as well go out with one of you as be stopping at home.' She stops out as long as I do. She doesn't get tired, at least she never tells me she is. I always carry her home at night on my back. She is eight years old, and very fond of me. I buy her cakes as we go along. We dine anywhere we can. We have bread and cheese, and sometimes bread and meat. Besides, she's very often called over and given something to eat. I've got regular houses where they always give me dinner. There's one in Eaton-place where the servants are Scotch, and at the Duke of Argyle's, out Kensington way, and another at York-terrace, Camden-town. It's generally from Scotch servants I get the food, except at the Duke's, and he orders me a dinner whenever I come that way. It ain't the Lowland Scotch give me the food, only the Highland Scotch. Highlanders don't talk with a drawl, only Lowlanders. I can tell a Highlander in a minute. I speak a few words of Gaelic to him.

"So you see I never have occasion to buy my dinner, unless I'm out at a place where I am too far to go, but I generally work up to my eating places.

"It's about three years now since I've been out playing the pipe. Jim and Johnny go together, and I go with Mary. Between the two we take about 5*s.* a-day, excepting on Saturdays. I get home by ten, and have supper and then go to bed; but Jim he sometimes doesn't come till very late, about one in the morning. At night we generally go down to the Haymarket, and play before the public-houses. The ladies and gentlemen both give us money. We pick up more at night-time than in the day. Some of the girls then make the gentlemen give us money. They'll say, 'Give the little fellow a penny.' The highest I ever had given me at one time was a Scotch lady at a hotel in Jermyn-street, and she gave me a sovereign. I've often had half-a-crown give me in the Haymarket. It's always from Scotch gentlemen. English have given me a shilling, but never more; and nearly all we take is from Scotch people. Jim says the same thing, and I always found it so.

"I've had a whole mob round me listening. Some of them will ask for this tune, and some for that. I play all Scotch tunes. 'The Campbells are coming' is the chief air they like. Some ask for the 'Loch Harbour no more.' That's a sentimental air. 'The Highland Fling,' that is very popular; 'Money Musk,' and the 'Miss Drummond of Perth' is another they like very much. Another great favourite is 'Maggie Lauder.' That's a song. When I play in a gentleman's room I don't put the drone on, but only play on the chanter, or what you would call the flute part of it. I cut off the drone, by putting the finger in the tall pipe that stands up against the shoulder, which we call the drone pipe. The wind goes up there; and if you stop it up, it don't sound. A bagpipes has got five pipes—the chanter, the drone pipe, the two tenor pipes, and the blow-stick, through which you send the wind into the bag, which is of sheep-skin, covered with green baize. Every set of pipes is all alike. That's the true Highland pipe. When I'm playing in the streets I put the drone on, and I can be heard miles off. I've very often had a horse shy at me. He won't pass me sometimes, or if they do, they shy at me.

"I get the reeds which go inside my pipes, and which make the noise, from the Duke of Argyle's piper. He's a good friend to me, and very fond of me. They're made of thin pieces of split cane, and it's the wind going through them that makes them jar and give the music. Before I play, I have to wet them. They last me six or seven months, if I take care of them. The Duke of Argyle's piper never grumbles when I go for new ones. When I go to him he makes me play to him, to see how I've got on with my music. He's a splendid player, and plays from books. I play by ear. His pipes are of ebony, and with a silver chanter or flute-pipe. He plays every day to the Duke while he's at dinner. My pipes are made out of cocoa-nut wood.

"I know the Duke very well. He's very kind to his clan. He's Campbell clan, and so am I. He never spoke to me; but he told the servants to give me dinner every time I came that way. The servants told me the Duke had promised me my dinner every time I came. When I touch my bonnet, he always nods to me. He never gave me only a shilling once, but always my dinner. That's better for me.

"I wear the regular Highland costume, but

I don't wear the Campbell plaid, only the Stuart, because it's cheaper. My kilt ain't a regular one, because it's too dear for me. In a soldier's kilt it's reckoned there's thirty-two yards; mine has only got two and a half. My philibeg ought by rights to be of badgers' skin, with a badger's head on the top, and with tassels set in brass caps; but my philibeg is only sheep-skin. The centre is made up to look like the real one. Father makes all our clothes. He makes the jackets, and the belts even, down to the German silver buckles, with the slide and the tip. He cuts them out of sheet metal. He casts our buttons, too, in pewter. They are square ones, you see, with a Highlander on them. He makes our shoes, too, with the little buckle in front. Mother knits the stockings. They are mixed—red and blue mixed. I wear out about three a-year. She makes about twelve pairs a-year for us all. We buy our tartan and our bonnets, but make the pewter thistles at the side and the brooch which fastens the scarf on one shoulder. A suit of clothes lasts about twelve months, so that father has to make four suits a-year for us all; that is for Jim, myself, Johnny, and Mary. The shoes last, with repairing, twelve months. There's twenty buttons on each coat. Father has always got something to do, repairing our clothes. He's not able to go out for his leg, or else he'd go out himself; and he'd do well playing, for he's a first-rate piper, but not so good as the Duke's.

"We go about with our bare legs, and no drawers on. I never feel cold of my legs; only of my fingers, with playing. I never go cold in the legs. None of the Highlanders ever wear drawers; and none but the rich in Scotland wear stockings and shoes, so that their legs are altogether bare.

"When I'm marching through the streets, and playing on the pipes, I always carry my head high up in the air, and throw my legs out well. The boys will follow for miles—some of them. The children very often lose theirselves from following me such a way. Even when I haven't my pipes with me the boys will follow me in a mob. I've never been ill-treated by boys, but a drunken man, often on a Saturday night, gives me a push or a knock. You see, they'll begin dancing around me, and then a mob will collect, and that sets the police unto me; so I always play a slow tune when drunken men come up, and then they can't dance. They'll ask for a quick tune, and as I won't play one, they'll hit me or push me about. The police never interfere unless a mob collects, and then they are obliged, by their regulations, to interfere.

"I never carried a dirk, or a sword, or any thing of that. My brother used to have one in his stocking; but one day he was called up into a public house, where there was a lot of French butlers and footmen, and they would have him to play; and when he had for some time they begun to pull him about, and they broke his pipes and snapped the chanter in two; so Jim pulled out his dirk, and they got frightened. They tried to take it from him, but they couldn't. He's a bold fellow, and would do anything when he's in a passion. He'd have stuck one of the French fellows if he could. When father heard of it he took the dirk away, for fear Jim should get into mischief.

"When I've been playing the pipes for long I get very thirsty. It's continually blowing into the bag. I very seldom go and get any beer; only at dinner half-a-pint. I go to a pump and have a drink of water. At first it made me feel sick, blowing so much; but I very soon got used to it. It always made me feel very hungry, blowing all day long; I could eat every two or three hours. It makes your eyes very weak, from the strain on them. When I first went out with my brother, playing, I used to have to leave off every now and then and have a rest, for it made my head ache. The noise doesn't affect the hearing, nor has it Jim: but my father's quite deaf of the left ear, where the drones goes. I never have the drones on, only very seldom. When I have them on I can't hear anything for a few seconds after I leave off playing.

"Sometimes, of wet nights, I go into public-houses and play. Some publicans won't let you, for the instrument is almost too loud for a room. If there's a Scotchman in the tap-room he'll give me something. I do well when there's good company. I only go there when it rains, for my usual stand of an evening is in the Haymarket.

"The bagpipes I play on were sent from Edinburgh. Father wrote for them, and they cost 30s. They are the cheapest made. There are some sets go as high as a 100l. They are mounted with gold and silver. The Duke of Argyle's piper must have paid 100l. for his, I should say, for they are in silver. The bag is covered with velvet and silk fringe. There's eight notes in a long pipes. You can't play them softly, and they must go their own force.

"I know all those pipers who regular goes about playing the pipes in London. There's only four, with me and my brother—two men and us two. Occasionally one may pass through London, but they don't stop here more than a day or two. I know lots of them who are travelling about the country. There's about twenty in all. I take about 15s. a-week, and Jim does the same. That's clear of all expenses, such as for dinner, and so on. We sometimes take more, but it's very odd that we seldom has a good week both of us together. If he has a good week, most likely I don't. It comes, taking all the year round, to about 15s. a-week each. We both of us give whatever we may earn to father. We never go out on a Sunday. Whenever I can get home by eight o'clock I go to a night-school, and I am getting on pretty well with my reading and writing. Sometimes I don't go to school for a week together. It's generally on the Wednesday and Thursday nights that I can get to school, for they are the worst nights for working in the streets. Our best nights are Saturday and Monday, and then I always take about 5s. Tuesday it comes to about 3s.; but on Wednesday, and Thursday, and Friday, it don't come to more than 2s. 6d.; that's if I am pretty lucky; but some nights I don't take above 6d.; and that's how I put it down at 15s. a-week, taking the year round. Father never says anything if I don't take any money home, for he knows I've been looking out for it: but if he thought I'd been larking and amusing myself, most likely he'd be savage."

FRENCH HURDY-GURDY PLAYER, WITH DANCING CHILDREN.

"I PLAY on the same instrument as the Savoyards play, only, you understand, you can have good and bad instruments; and to have a good one you must put the price. The one I play on cost me 60 francs in Paris. There are many more handsome, but none better. This is all that there is of the best. The man who made it has been dead sixty years. It is the time that makes the value of it.

"My wife plays on the violin. She is a very good player. I am her second husband. She is an Italian by birth. She played on the violin when she was with her first husband. He used to accompany her on the organ, and that produced a very fine effect.

"The hurdy-gurdy is like the violin—it improves with age. My wife told me that she once played on a very old violin, and the difference between that and her own was curious for sound. She was playing, with her husband accompanying her on the organ, near the château of an old marquis; and when he heard the sound of the violin he asked them in. Then he said, 'Here, try my violin,' and handed her the old violin. My wife said that when she touched it with the bow, she cried, 'Ah, how fine it is!' It was the greatest enjoyment she had known for years. You understand, the good violins all bridge where the bridge is placed, but the new violins sink there, and the tune is altered by it. They call the violins that sink 'consumptive' ones.

"I am Dijon. The vineyard of Clos Nangent is near to Dijon. You have heard of that wine. Oh, yes, of course you have! That clos belongs to a young man of twenty-two, and he could sell it for 2,500,000 francs if he liked. At Dijon the bottles sell for 7 francs.

"My mother and father did not live happily together. My father died when I had three years, and then my mother, who had only twenty years of age, married again, and you know how it often happens, the second father does not love the first family of his wife. Some Savoyards passed through our village, and I was sold to them. I was their slave for ten years. I learnt to play the hurdy-gurdy with them. I used to accompany an organ. I picked out note for note with the organ. When I heard an air, too, which I liked, I used to go to my room and follow the air from my memory upon the instrument. I went to Paris afterwards.

"You see I play on only one string in my hurdy-gurdy. Those which the Savoyards play have several strings, and that is what makes them drone. The hurdy-gurdy is the same as the violin in principle. You see the wheel of wood which I turn with the handle is like its bow, for it grates on the string, and the keys press on the string like the fingers, and produce the notes. I used to play on a droning hurdy-gurdy at first, but one night I went into a café at Paris, and the gentlemen there cried out, 'Ah! the noise!' Then I thought to myself—I had fifteen years—if I play on one string it will not produce so much noise as on two. Then I removed one string, and when I went the next night the gentlemen said, 'Ah, that is much better!' and that is why I play on one string.

"I used to sing in Paris. I learnt all that of new in the style of romances, and I accompanied myself on my hurdy-gurdy. At Paris I met my wife. She was a widow then. I told her that I would marry her when her mourning was over, which lasted nine months. I was not twenty then. I went about playing at the cafés, and put by money. But when we went to be married, the priests would not marry us unless we had our parents' consents. I did not know whether my mother was dead. I hunted everywhere. As I could not find out, I lived with my wife the same as if we had been married. I am married to her now, but my children were all born before marriage. At last I went to the Catholic priest at Dover, and told him my life, and that I had four children, and wished to marry my wife, and he consented to marry us if I would get the consent of the priest of the place where I had lived last. That was Calais, and I wrote to the priest there, and he gave his consent, and now my children are legitimate. By the law of France, a marriage makes legitimate all the children born by the woman with whom you are united. My children were present at my marriage, and that produced a very droll effect. I have always been faithful to my wife, and she to me, though we were not married.

"When my wife is well, she goes out with me, and plays on the violin. It produces a very good effect. She plays the seconds. But she has so much to do at home with the children, that she does not come out with me much.

"My age is twenty-five, and I have voyaged for seventeen years. There are three months since I came in England. I was at Calais and at Boulogne, and it is there that I had the idea to come to England. Many persons who counselled us, told us that in England we should gain a great deal of money. That is why I came. It took three weeks before I could get the permission to be married, and during that time I worked at the different towns. I did pretty well at Dover; and after that I went to Ramsgate, and I did very well there. Yes, I took a great deal of money on the sands of a morning. I have been married a month now—for I left Ramsgate to go to be married. At Ramsgate they understood my playing. Unless I have educated people to play to, I do not make much success with my instrument. I play before a public-house, or before a cottage, and they say, 'That's all very well;' but they do not know that to make a hurdy-gurdy sound like a violin requires great art and patience. Besides, I play airs from operas, and they do not know the Italian music. Now if I was alone with my hurdy-gurdy, I should only gain a few pence; but it is by my children that I do pretty well.

"We came to London when the season was over in the country, and now we go everywhere in the town. I cannot speak English; but I have my address in my pocket, if I lose myself. *Je m'elance dans la ville.* To day I went by a big park, where there is a château of the Queen. If I lose my way, I show my written address, and they go on speaking English, and show me the way to go. I don't understand the English, but I do the pointed finger; and when I get near home, then I recognise the quarter.

"My little girl will have six years next February, and the little boy is only four years and a-half. She is a very clever little girl, and she notices everything. Before I was married, she heard me speaking to my wife about when we were to be married; and she'd say, constantly, 'Ah, papa, when are you going to be married to mamma?' We had a pudding on our marriage-day, and she liked it so much that now we very often says, 'Oh, papa, I should like a pudding like that I had when you married mamma.' That is compromising, but she doesn't know any better.

"It was my little girl Eugénie who taught her brother Paul to dance. He liked it very much; but he is young yet, and heavy in his movements; but she is graceful, and very clever. At Boulogne she was much beloved, and the English ladies would give her packets of sugar-plums and cakes. When they dance, they first of all polk together, and then they do the Varsovienne together, and after that she does the Cachuca and the Mazurka alone. I first of all taught my girl to do the Polka, for in my time I liked the dance pretty well. As soon as the girl had learnt it, she taught her brother. They like dancing above all, when I encourage them, for I say, 'Now, my children, dance well; and, above all, dance gracefully, and then I will buy you some cakes.' Then, if they take a fancy to anything, if it is not too dear, I buy it for them, and that encourages them. Besides, when she says 'Papa, when shall we go to France, and see my little brother who is out at nurse?' then I say, 'When we have earned enough money; so you must dance well, and, above all, gracefully, and when we have taken plenty of money we will be off.' That encourages them, for they like to see me take plenty of money. The little girl accompanies the music on the castanets in the Cachuca. It is astonishing how well she plays them. I have heard grown-up artists in the cafés chantants, who don't play them so well as she does. It is wonderful in so young a child. You will say she has learnt my style of playing on the hurdy-gurdy, and my movements; but it is the same thing, for she is as clever to other music. Sometimes, when she has danced, ladies come up and kiss her, and even carry her off into their houses, and I have to wait hours for her. When she sees that I gain money, she has much more courage. When the little girl has done dancing with my Paul, then he, when she is dancing alone, takes the plate and asks for money. He is very laughable, for he can already say, 'If you please, misses.' Sometimes the ladies begin to speak to him, he says, 'Yes! yes!' three or four times, and then he runs up to me and says, 'Papa, that lady speaks English;' and then I have to say, 'No speak English.' But he is contented if he hears anybody speak French. Then he runs up to me, and says, 'Papa, papa, Monsieur speaks French.'

"My little girl has embroidered trowsers and petticoats. You won't believe it, but I worked all that. The ends of the trowsers, the trimmings to her petticoats, her collars and sleeves, all I have worked. I do it at night, when we get home. The evenings are long and I do a little, and at the end of the week it becomes much. If I had to buy that it would cost too much. It was my wife who taught me to do it. She said the children must be well dressed, and we have no money to buy these things. Then she taught me: at first it seemed droll to me, and I was ashamed, but then I thought, I do it for my living and not for my pleasure, it is for my business; and now I am accustomed to do it. You would fancy, too, that the children are cold, going about in the streets dressed as they are, but they have flannel round the body, and then the jumping warms them. They would tell me directly if they were cold. I always ask them.

"The day I was married a very singular circumstance happened. I had bought my wife a new dress, and she, poor thing, sat up all night to make it. All night! It cost me five shillings, the stuff did. I had a very bad coat, and she kept saying, 'I shall be gay, but you, my poor friend, how will you look?' My coat was very old. I said, 'I shall do as I am;' but it made her sad that I had no coat to appear in style at our marriage. Our landlord offered to lend me his coat, but he was twice as stout as I am, and I looked worse than in my own coat. Just as we were going to start for the church, a man came to the house with a coat to sell—the same I have on now. The landlord sent him to me. It is nearly new, and had not been on more than three or four times. He asked 12s., and I offered 8s.; at last he took 9s. My wife, who is very religious, said, 'It is the good God who sent that man, to reward us for always trying to get married.'

"Since I have been here, my affairs have gone on pretty well. I have taken some days 5s., others 6s., and even 8s.; but then some days rain has fallen, and on others it has been wet under foot, and I have only taken 4s. My general sum is 5s. 6d. the day, or 6s. Every night when I get home I give my wife what I have taken, and I say, 'Here, my girl, is 3s. for to-morrow's food,' and then we put the remainder on one side to save up. We pay 5s. a-week for our room, and that is dear, for we are there very bad! very bad! for we sleep almost on the boards. It is lonely for her to be by herself in the day, but she is near her confinement, and she cannot go out.

"It makes me laugh, when I think of our first coming to this country. She only wore linen caps, but I was obliged to buy her a bonnet. It was a very good straw one, and cost 1s. It made her laugh to see everybody wearing a bonnet.

"When I first got to London, I did not know where to go to get lodgings. I speak Italian very well, for my wife taught me. I spoke to an Italian at Ramsgate, and he told me to go to Woolwich, and there I found an Italian lodging-house. There the landlord gave me a letter to a friend in London, and I went and paid 2s. 6d. in advance, and took the room, and when we went there to live I gave another 2s. 6d., so as to pay the 5s. in advance. It seems strange to us to have to pay rent in advance—but it is a custom.

"It costs me something to clothe my children. My girl has six different skirts, all of silk, of different colours, grey, blue, red, and yellow. They last the year. The artificial flowers on her head are arranged by her mamma. The boots cost the most money. She has a pair every month. Here they are 3s., but in France they are dearer. It is about the same for the little boy; only as he does not work so much as his sister, he is not dressed in so distinguished a style. He is clean, but not so elegant, for we give the best to the girl.

"My children are very good at home. Their mother adores them, and lets them do as they like. They are very good, indeed.

"On Sunday, they are dressed like other children. In the morning we go to mass, and then we go and walk a little, and see London. I have, as yet, made no friends in London. I know no French people. I have met some, but they don't speak to me. We confine ourselves to our family.

" When I am in the streets with good houses in them, and see anybody looking at the windows, then if I see them listening, I play pieces from the operas on my hurdy-gurdy. I do this between the dances. Those who go to the opera and frequent the theatres, like to hear distinguished music."

POOR HARP PLAYER.

A POOR, feeble, half-witted looking man, with the appearance of far greater age than he represented himself, (a common case with the very poor), told me of his sufferings in the streets. He was wretchedly clad, his clothes being old, patched, and greasy. He is well-known in London, being frequently seen with a crowd of boys at his heels, who amuse themselves in playing all kinds of tricks upon him.

" I play the harp in the streets," he said, " and have done so for the last two years, and should be very glad to give it up. My brother lives with me; we're both bachelors, and he's so dreadful lame, he can do nothing. He is a coach-body maker by business. I was born blind, and was brought up to music; but my sight was restored by Dr. Ware, the old gentleman in Bridge-street, Blackfriars, when I was nine years old, but it's a near sight now. I'm forty-nine in August. When I was young I taught the harp and the pianoforte, but that very soon fell off, and I have been teaching on or off these many years—I don't know how many. I had three guineas a-quarter for teaching the harp at one time, and two guineas for the piano. My brother and I have 1s. and a loaf a-piece from the parish, and the 2s. pays the rent. Mine's not a bad trade now, but it's bad in the streets. I've been torn to pieces; I'm torn to pieces every day I go out in the streets, and I would be glad to get rid of the streets for 5s. a-week. The streets are full of ruffians. The boys are ruffians. The men in the streets too are ruffians, and encourage the boys. The police protect me as much as they can. I should be killed every week but for them; they're very good people. I've known poor women of the town drive the boys away from me, or try to drive them. It's terrible persecution I suffer—terrible persecution. The boys push me down and hurt me badly, and my harp too. They yell and make noises so that I can't be heard, nor my harp. The boys have cut off my harp-strings, three of them, the other day, which cost me 6½d. or 7d. I tell them it's a shame, but I might as well speak to the stones. I never go out that they miss me. I don't make more than 3s. a-week in the streets, if I make that."

ORGAN MAN, WITH FLUTE HARMONICON ORGAN.

" WHEN I am come in this country I had nine or ten year old, so I know the English language better than mine. At that time there was no organ about but the old-fashioned one made in Bristol, with gold organ-pipe in front. Then come the one with figure-dolls in front; and then next come the piano one, made at Bristol too; and now the flute one, which come from Paris, where they make them. He is an Italian man that make them, and he is the only man dat can make them, because he paid for them to the government (patented them), and now he is the only one.

" I belong to Parma,—to the small village in the duchy. My father keep a farm, but I had three year old, I think, when he died. There was ten of us altogeder; but one of us he was died, and one he drown in the water. I was very poor, and I was go out begging there; and my uncle said I should go to Paris to get my living. I was so poor I was afraid to die, for I get nothing to eat. My uncle say, I will take one of them to try to keep him. So I go along with him. Mother was crying when I went away. She was very poor. I went with my uncle to Paris, and we walk all the way. I had some white mice there, and he had a organ. I did middling. The French people is more kind to the charity than the English. There are not so many beggar there as in England. The first time the Italian come over here we was took a good bit of money, but now——!

" When I was in Paris my uncle had to go home again on business. He ask me too if I would go with him. But I was afraid to be hungry again, for you see I was feel hungry again, and I wouldn't, for I got a piece of bread in France.

" My uncle was along with another man, who was a master like, you know; for he had a few instrument, but common thing. I don't know if he have some word wid my uncle, but they part. Den dis man say ' Come to England with me,' and he said 'you shall have five franc the month, and your victual.' We walk as far as Calais, and then we come in the boat. I was very sick, and I thought that I die then. 1 say to him plenty times ' I wish I never come,' for I never thought to get over.

" When we got to London, we go to a little court there, in Saffron-hill; and I was live there in the little public-house. I go out, sometime white mice, sometime monkey, sometime with organ—small one. I dare say I make 10s. a-week for him; but he wor very kind to me, and give me to eat what I like. He was take care of me, of course. I was very young at dat time.

" After I was in London a-year, I go back to Paris with my master. There I could have made my fortune, but I was so young I did not know what I do. There was an old lady who ask me to come as her servant. My master did not like very well to let me go. She say to me, 'You shall not have no hard work, only to go behind the carriage, or follow with the umbrella.' But I was so young I did not know my chance. I tell her I have my parent in Italy; and she say she go to Italy all the years, and I shall have two months to visit my mother. I did not go with this old lady, and I lose the chance; but I had only thirteen years, and I was foolish.

"Then I come to England again, and stop here three years. Where my master go, I was obliged to go too. Then I go to Italy, and I saw my moder. The most part of my family never know me when I went home, for I was grown much, and older. I stop there six weeks, and then I come back to England with anoder man. He give me 12 franc a-month, and very kind indeed he was. He had some broder in this country, so he take me along wid him. There was only me and him. My other master have two beside me.

"The master of organs send to Italy for boys to come here. Suppose I have a broder in Italy, I write to him to send me two boys, and he look out for them. They send money for the boy to come. Sometimes he send 3*l.*, sometimes 3*l.* 10*s.* or 4*l.* Then they walk, and live on the pear or the grape, or what is cheap; and if they put by any, then they keep what they put by. They generally tell them they shall have 12 francs a-month. But sometime they was cheap; but now they are dear, and it is sometime a pound a-month. They'd sooner have one who have been here before, because den they know the way to take care of the instrument, you know.

"I stop in England two year and six month, when I come over with my second master. He paid me like a bank, and I saved it up, and I take it over to Italy with me. When I had a bit of money I was obliged to send it home to my broder in Italy, for to keep him, you know. When I go home again I had a bit of money with me. I give it to the gentleman what support my mother and sister; but it was not enough, you know, not three part, so I was obliged to give him a good bit more.

"Then I came back to England again, to the same master. It take about a month to make the voyage. I was walk it all the way. I was cross the Alps. You must to come over here. I dare say I walk thirty miles a-day, sometime more dan that. I sleep at the public-house; but when you not get to the public-house, then when it begins dark, then I go to the farm-house and ask for a bit of straw to lodge. But I generally goes to the public-house when I get one. They charge 3*d.* or 2*d.*, or sometimes 1*d.* I never play anything on the road, or take de white mice. I never take nothing.

"After that time I have been to Italy and back three or four times; but I never been with no master, not after the second one. I bought an organ of my master. I think I give him 13*l.* No, sir, I not give the money down, but so much the week, and he trust me. It was according what I took, I paid him. I was trying to make up 1*l.* and bring him down. It take me about eighteen months to pay him, because I was obliged to keep me and one things and another. It was a middling organ. It was one was a piano, you know. I take about 1*s.* 3*d.* or 1*s.* 6*d.* a-day regularly with it.

"I have now an organ—a flute organ they call it—and it is my own. It cost me 20*l.* A man make it come from France. He knows an organ-maker in France, and he write for me, and make it come over for me. I suppose he had a pound profit for to make it come for me; for I think it cost less than 20*l.* in Paris.

"I have this organ this twelve months. It has worn out a little, but not much. It is not so good as when it come from France. An organ will wear twenty year, but some of them break. Then you must have it always repaired and tuned. You see, the music of it must be tuned every five or six months. Mine has never been tuned yet, the time I have it. It is the trumpet part that get out of tune sooner. I know a man who goes out with de big organ on the wheels, and he tune the organ for me. I go to him, and I say, 'My organ wants de repair;' and he come, and he never charge me anything. He make the base and tenor agree. He tune the first one to the base, you know, and then the second one to the second base. When the organ out of tune the pipe rattle.

"The organ fills with dust a good deal in the summer time, and then you must take it all to pieces. In London they can tune and repair it. They charge 10*s.* to clean and tune it. Sometime he have something to do with the pipes, and then it come to more. In winter the smoke get inside, and make it come all black. I am obliged to keep it all covered up when I am playing.

"My organ play eight tunes. Two are from opera, one is a song, one a waltz, one is hornpipe, one is a polka, and the other two is dancing tunes. One is from 'Il Lombardi,' of Verdi. All the organs play that piece. I have sold that music to gentlemens. They say to me, 'What is that you play?' and I say, 'From Il Lombardi.' Then they ask me if I have the music; and I say 'Yes;' and I sell it to them for 4*s.* I did not do this with my little organ; but when I went out with a big organ on two wheels. My little flute organ play the same piece. The other opera piece is 'Il Trovatore.' I have heard 'Il Lombardi' in Italy. It is very nice music; but never hear 'Il Trovatore.' It is very nice music, too. It go very low. My gentlemens like it very much. I don't understand music at all. The other piece is English piece, which we call the 'Liverpool Hornpipe.' There is two Liverpool Hornpipe. I know one these twenty years. Then come 'The Ratcatcher's Daughter;' he is a English song. It's get a little old; but when it's first come out the poor people do like it, but the gentlemens they like more the opera, you know. After that is what you call ' Minnie,' another English song. He is middling popular. He is not one of the new tune, but they do like it. The next one is a Scotch contre-danse. It is good tunes, but I don't know the name of it. The next one is, I think, a polka; but I think he's made from part of 'Scotische.' There is two or three tunes belongs to the 'Scotische.' The next one is, I think, a valtz of Vienna. I don't know which one, but I say to the organ-man, 'I want a valtz of Vienna;' and he say, 'Which one? because there is plenty of valtz of Vienna.' Of course, there is nine of them. After the opera music, the valtz and the polka is the best music in the organ.

"For doing a barrel of eight tune it come very near 14l., one thing and another. You can have a fresh tune put into an old barrel. But then he charge 10s. He's more trouble than to put only one. I have my tune changed once a-year. You see most of the people gets very tired of one tune, and I'm obliged to change them. You can have the new tune in three or four days, or a week's time, if he has nothing to do; but sometime it is three or four weeks, if he has plenty to do. It is a man who is called John Hicks who does the new tunes. He was born in Bristol. He has a father in Bristol. He live in Crockenwell, just at the back of the House of Correction. You know the prison? then it is just at the back, on the other side.

"It won't do to have all opera music in my organ. You must have some opera tunes for the gentlemen, and some for the poor people, and they like the dancing tune. Dere is some for the gentlemens, and some for the poor peoples.

"I have often been into the houses of gentlemens to play tunes for dancing. I have been to a gentleman's near Golden-square, where he have a shop for to make the things for the horse—a saddler, you call it. He have plenty customers; them what gets the things for the horse. There was carriage outside. It was large room, where you could dance thirty-two altogether. I think it's the boxing-day I go there. I have 10s. for that night. He have a farm in the country, and I go there too. He have the little children there—like a school, and there was two policemen at the door, and you couldn't get in without the paper to show. He had Punch and Judy. He has a English band as well.

"I have some two or three place where I go regular at Christmas-time, to play all night to the children. Sometime I go for an hour or two. When they are tired of dancing they sit down and have a rest, and I play the opera tune. I go to schools, too, and play to the little children. They come and fetch me, and say, ' You come such a time and play to the little children,' and I say, ' Very well,' and that's all right.

"My organ is like the organ, but he's got another part, and that is like a flute. Some organ is called de trompet, and that one he's called the flute-organ, because he's got de flute in it. When they first come out they make a great deal of money. I take 2s. 6d. or 3s., and sometimes 1s. 6d. You see, in our business, some has got his regular customer, and some they go up the street and down the street, and they don't take nothing. I have not got any regular customers much, sir.

"On the Monday when I goes out, I goes over the water up the Clapham-road. I have two or three regular there, and they give me plenty of beer and to eat. I know that family those twenty year. If I say to that lady, ' I am very ill,' he give me his card and say, ' Go to the doctor,' and I have nothing to pay. There was three sister, but one he died. They is very old, and one he can only come to the window. I dare say I have six houses in that neighbourhood where they give me some 1d. and some 2d. every time I go there. In the summer-time, when it is hot, I walk to Greenwich on the Monday. I have, I dare say, fifteen houses there where I go regular. I can make up 1s. I pay 4d. sometime to ride home in the boat. My organ weight more than fifty pounds, and that tire me. The first time when I'm not used to it, you know, I feel it more tired than when I'm used to it.

"On the Tuesday I go to Greenwich, now that it is cold, instead of the Monday. On Wednesday I ain't got no way to go. I try sometime down at Whitechapel, or some other way. On Thursday I goes out Islington way, and I go as far as Highbury Barn, but not further. There is a bill of the railway and a station there. I've got three or four regular customers there. The most I get at once is 2d. I never get 6d. One gentleman at Greenwich give me 6d., but only once. On the Friday I've got no way to go; I go where I like. On Saturday I go to Regent-street. I go to Leicester-square and the foreign hotels, where the foreign gentlemen is. Sometime I get the chance to get a few shilling; sometime not a halfpenny. The most I make is sometime at the fair-time. Sometime at Greenwich-fair I make 5s. all in copper, and that is the most I ever make; and the lowest is sometime 6d. When I see I can't make nothing, I go home. It is very bad in wet weather. I must sit at home, for the rain spoil the instrument. There is nothing like summer-times, for the regular money that I make for the year it come to between 9s. and 10s. the week. Sometimes it is 6d., sometimes 1s., or 1s. 6d. or 2s. the day. For 12s. the week it must be 2s. the day, and that is more than I take. I wish somebody pay me 12s.; there is no such chance.

" I live in a room by myself with three others, and we pay 1s. each, and there is two bed. If I go to lodging-house I pay 1s. 6d. the week. In the Italian lodging-house they give you clean shirt on the Sunday for the 1s. 6d. It is my own shirt, but they clean it. This is only in Italian house. In English house it is 1s. 6d. and no shirt. I have breakfast of coffee or what I like, and we club together. We have bread and butter, sometime herring, sometime bacon, what we likes. In the day I buy a pen'orth of bread and a pen'orth of cheese, and some beer, and at night I have supper. I make maccarone—what you call it?—or rice and cabbage, or I make soup or bile some taters; with all four together it come to about 9d. or 10d. a-day for living.

" In the house where I live they are all Italians. They are nearly all Italians that live about Leather-lane and Saffron-hill. There is a good bit of them live there. I should say 200: I dare say there is. The house where I live is my own. I let empty room; they bring their own things, you know. It is my lease, and I pay the rent.

" It is only the people say that the Italian boys are badly used: they are not so, the masters are very kind to them. If he make 1s. he bring it home; if 3s. or 4s. or 6d. he bring it home. He is not commandé to bring home so much; that is what the people say. I was with the magistrate of police in Marlborough-street four days ago, about a little Italian boy that the policemen take for asking money. Some one ask to buy his monkey and talk with him, and then he ask for a penny, and the police take him. A gentleman ask me about the boys. I tell him it is all nonsense what the people say. There is no more boys sent here now. If a boy comes over, and he is bad boys, he goes and play in the street instead of working; then, after paying so much for his coming to England, it is a loss. It does not pay the boys. If I was a master I would not have the boys, if they come here for nothing.

" Suppose I have two organs, then one is in the house doing nothing. Then some one come and say, ' Lend me the organ for to-day.' Then I say, ' Yes,' and charge him, some 4d., some 6d.; or if somebody ill and he cannot go out, then he's organ doing nothing, and he lend it out for 4d. or 6d. There is two or three in London who sends out men with organs, but I don't know who has got the most of us. Then they pay the men 1l. a-month and their keep, or some 15s. Then, some goes half and keep him: then, it's more profits to the man than the master.

" Christmas-time is nothing like the sum-mer-time. Sometimes they give you a Christ-mas-box, but it's not the time for Christmas-box now. Sometimes it's a glass of beer: ' Here's a Christmas-box for you.' Sometimes it's a glass of gin, or rum, or a piece of pud-ding : ' Here's a Christmas-box for you.' I have had 6d., but never 1s. for a Christmas-box. Sometimes on a boxing-day it is 3s., or 2s. 6d. for the day.

" I have never travelled in the country with my organ, only once when I was young, as far as Liverpool, but no further. Many has got his regular time out in the country. When I go out with the organ I should say it make altogether that I walk ten miles. I want two new pairs of boots every year. I start off in the morning, sometimes eight, sometimes nine or ten, whether I have far to go. I never stop out after seven o'clock at night. Some do, but I don't.

" I don't know music at all. I am middling fond of it. There is none of the Italians that I know that sings. The French is very fond of singing.

" When first you begins, it tries the wrist, turning the handle of the organ; but you soon gets accustomed to it. At first, the arm was sore with the work all day. When I am play-ing I turn the handle regularly. Sometimes there are people who say, ' Go a little quick,' but not often.

" If the silk in front of the organ is bad, I get new and put it in myself; the rain spoil it very much. It depend upon what sort of organ he is, as to the sort of silk he gets : sometimes 2s. 6d. a-yard, and he take about a yard and a half. Some like to do this once a-year; but some when he see it get a little dirty, like fresh things, you know, and then it is twice a-year.

" The police are very quiet to us. When anybody throw up a window and say, ' Go on,' I go. Sometime they say there is sick in the house, when there is none, but I go just the same. If I did not, then the policeman come, and I get into trouble. I have heard of the noise in the papers about the organs in the street, but we never talk of it in our quarter. They pay no attention to the subject, for they know if anybody say, ' Go,' then we must de-part. That is what we do."

ITALIAN PIPERS AND CLARIONET PLAYERS.

" THE companion I got about with me, is with me from Naples, not the city, but in the country. His is of my family; no, not my cousin, but my mother was the sister of his cousin. Yes! yes! yes! my cousin. Some one told me he was my nephew, but it's cousin. Naples is a pretty city. It is more pretty than Paris, but not so big. I worked on the ground at Naples, in the country, and I guarded sheep. I never was a domestic; but it was for my father. It was ground of his. It was not much. He worked the earth for yellow corn. He had not much of sheep, only fifteen. When I go out with the sheep I carry my bagpipes always with me. I play on them when I was sixteen years of age. I play them when I guard my sheep. In my country they call my instrument de 'zam-pogna.' All the boys in my country play on it, for there are many masters there who teach it. I taught myself to play it. I bought my own instrument. I gave the money myself for that affair. It cost me seven francs. The bag is made of a skin of goat. There are four clarionets to it. There is one for the high and one for the bass. I play them with different hands. The other two clarionets make a noise to make the accord; one makes high and the other the low. They drone to make harmony. The airs I play are the airs of my country. I did not invent them. One is 'La Tarentule Italien,' and another is what we call 'La Badend,' but I not know what you call it in French. Another is the 'Death of the Roi de France.' I know ten of these airs. The 'Pastorelle Naopolitan' is very pretty, and so is the 'Pastorelle Romaine.'

"When I go out to guard my sheep I play my zampogna, and I walk along and the sheep follow me. Sometimes I sit down and the sheep eat about me, and I play on my instrument. Sometimes I go into the moun-tains. There are plenty of mountains in my country, and with snow on them. I can hear the guardians of sheep playing all around me in the mountains. Yes, many at once,—six, ten, twelve, or fifteen, on every side. No, I did not play my instrument to keep my sheep together, only to learn the airs. I was a good player, but there were others who played much better than me. Every night in my village there are four or six who play together instruments like mine, and all the people dance. They prefer to dance to the 'Taren-tule Italien.' It is a pretty dance in our costume. The English do not dance like nous autres. We are not paid for playing in the village, only at fêtes, when gentlemen say, 'Play;' and then they give 20 sous or 40 sous, like that. There is another air, which is played only for singing. There is one only for singing chansons, and another for singing 'La Prière de la Vierge.' Those that play the zampogna go to the houses, and the candles are lighted on the altar, and we play while the bourgeois sing the prière.

"I am aged 23 years next March. I was sixteen when I learnt my instrument. The twelfth of this month I shall have left my country nine months. I have traversed the states of Rome and of France to come to England. I marched all the distance, playing my zampogna. I gain ten sous French whilst I voyage in the states of France. I march from Marseilles to Paris. To reach Marseilles by the boat it cost 15 frs. by head.

"The reason why we left our native land is this:—One of our comrades had been to Paris, and he had said he gained much money by painters by posing for his form. Then I had envy to go to Paris and gain money. In my country they pay 20 sous for each year for each sheep. I had 200 to guard for a

monsieur, who was very rich. There were four of us left our village at the same time. We all four played de zampogna. My father was not content that I voyage the world. He was very sorry. We got our passport ar-ranged tout de suite, two passport for us four. We all began to play our instruments together, as soon as we were out of the village. Four of our friends accompanied us on our road, to say adieu. We took bread of corn with us to eat for the first day. When we had finished that we played at the next village, and they give us some more bread.

"At Paris I posed to the artists, and they pay me 20 sous for the hour. The most I pose is four hours for the day. We could not play our instruments in the street, because the serjeant-de-ville catch us, and take us di-rectly to prison. I go to play in the courts be-fore the houses. I asked the concierge at the door if he would give me permission to play in the court. I gain 15 sous or 1 franc par jour. For all the time I rest in Paris I gain 2 francs for the day. This is with posing to artists to paint, and for playing. I also play at the barrière outside Paris, where the wine is cheap. They gave us more there than in the courts; they are more generous where they drink the wine.

"When I arrive at Paris my comrades have leave me. I was alone in Paris. There an Italian proposed to me to go to America as his servant. He had two organs, and he had two servants to play them, and they gave him the half of that which they gained. He said to me, that he would search for a piano organ for me, and I said I would give him the half of that which I gained in the streets. He made us sign a card before a notary. He told us it would cost 150 francs to go to America. I gave him the money to pay from Paris to Folkestone. From there we voyaged on foot to Londres. I only worked for him for eight days, because I said I would not go to Amérique. He is here now, for he has no money to go in Amérique.

"I met my cousin here in Londres. I was here fifteen days before I met him. We neither of us speak Anglais, and not French either, only a little very bad; but we under-stand it. We go out together now, and I play the zampogna, and he the 'biforc Italien,' or what the French call flageolet, and the English pipes. It is like a flageolet. He knows all the airs that I play. He play well the airs — that he does. He wears a cloak on his shoulders, and I have one, too; but I left it at home to-day. It is a very large cloak, with three yards of étoffe in it. He carry in his hat a feather of what you call here peacock, and a French lady give him the bright ribbon which is round his hat. I have also plume de peacock and flowers of stuff, like at the shops, round my hat. In my country we always put round our hat white and red flowers.

" Sometimes we go to pose to the artists, but it is not always. There are plenty of artists near Newman-street, but in other quarters there are none at all. It is for our costume they paint us. The colours they put on the pictures are those of our costume. I have been three times to a gentleman in a large street, where they took our portraits photographique. They give a shilling. I know the houses where I go to be done for a portrait, but I don't know the names of the messieurs, or the streets where they reside. At the artists' they pay 1s. par heure, and we pose two or three heures, and the most is four heures. When we go together we have 1s. each for the hour. My cousin is at an artist's to-day. They paint him more than me, because he carries a sash of silk round his waist, with ornaments on it. I haven't got one, because I want the money to buy one.

" We gain 1s. each the day. Ah! pardon, monsieur, not more than that. The artists are not for every day, perhaps one time for the week. When we first come here, we take 5s. between the two, but now it makes cold, and we cannot often play. Yesterday we play in the ville, and we take 7d. each. Plenty of persons look at us, but when my comrade touch his hat they give nothing. There is one month we take 2s. each the day, but now it is 1s. For the three months that we have been here, we have gained 12s. the week each, that is, if we count what we took when first we were arrived. For two months we took always a crown every day—always, always; but now it is only 1s., or 2s., or 7d. I had saved 72s., and I had it in my bourse, which I place under my head when I sleep. We sleep three in a bed—myself, my cousin, and another Italian. In the night this other take my bourse and run away. Now I have only 8s. in my bourse. It nearly broke the heart when I was robbed.

" We pay 2d. for each for our bed every night. We live in a house held by a Mossieu Italian. There are three who sleep in one bed—me, and my comrade, and another. We are not large. This mossieu let us lodge cheaper than others, because we are miserable, and have not much money. For breakfast we have a half-loaf each one. It is a loaf that you must pay 4d. or 4½d. We pay 2½d. each for that, and ½d. each for a cup of tea or coffee. In the day we eat 2d. or 3d. between both for some bread, and we come home the night at half-past eight, and we eat supper. It is of maccaroni, or potatoes boiled, and we pay 2½d. each. It costs us 9d. each the day to live. There are twenty-four Italian in the house where we live, and they have three kitchens. When one is more miserable than the others, then he is helped; and at another time he assists in his turn. We pay 2d. a-week to wash our shirt. I always share with my cousin what he makes in the day. If he goes to work and I stop at home, it is the same thing, and the same with me. He carries the money always, and pays for what we have want to eat; and then, if I wish to go back to my own country, then we share the money when we separate.

" The gentlemen give us more money than the ladies. We have never had anything to eat given to us. They have asked us to sing, but we don't know how. Only one we have sung to, an Italian mossieu, who make our portraits. We sang the ' Prayer of the Sainte Vierge.' They have also asked us to dance, but we did not, because the serjeant-de-ville, if we assemble a great mob, come and defend us to play.

" We have been once before the magistrate, to force the mossieu who brought us over to render the passport of my native village. He has not rendered to me my card. We shall go before a magistrate again some day.

" I can write and read Italian. I did not go much to the school of my native village, but the master taught me what I know. I can read better than I write, for I write very bad and slow. My cousin cannot read and write. I also know my numbers. I can count quickly. When we write a letter, we go to an Italian mossieu, and we tell him to say this and that, and he puts it down on the paper. We pay 1s. for the letter, and then at the post they make us pay 2s. 2d. When my parents get a letter from me, they take it to a mossieu, or the schoolmaster of the village, to read for them, because they cannot read. They have sent me a letter. It was well written by a gentleman who wrote it for them. I have sent my mother five pieces of five francs from Paris. I gave the money, and they gave me a letter; and then my mother went to the consul at Naples, and they gave her the money. Since I have been here I could send no money, because it was stolen. If I had got it, I should have sent some to my parents. When I have some more, I shall send it.

" I love my mother very much, and she is good, but my father is not good. If he gain a piece of 20 sous, he goes on the morrow to the marchand of wine, and play the cards, and spend it to drink. I never send my money to my father, but to my mother."

ITALIAN WITH MONKEY.

AN Italian, who went about with trained monkeys, furnished me with the following account.

He had a peculiar boorish, and yet good-tempered expression, especially when he laughed, which he did continually.

He was dressed in a brown, ragged, cloth jacket, which was buttoned over a long, loose, dirty, drab waistcoat, and his trowsers were of broad-ribbed corduroy, discoloured with long wearing. Round his neck was a plaid handkerchief, and his shoes were of the extreme " strong-men's" kind, and grey with dust and want of blacking. He wore the Savoy and broad-brimmed felt hat, and with it on his head had a very picturesque appearance, and the shadow of the brim falling on the upper part of his brown face gave him almost a Murillo-like look. There was, however, an odour about him,—half monkey, half dirt,—that was far from agreeable, and which pervaded the apartment in which he sat.

"I have got monkey," he said, "but I mustn't call in London. I goes out in countree. I was frightened to come here. I was frightened you give me months in prison. Some of my countrymen is very frightened what you do. No, sir, I never play de monkey in de town. I have been out vare dere is so many donkey, up a top at dat village—vat you call —I can't tell de name. Dey goes dere for pastime, — pleasure, — when it makes fine weather. Dere is two church, and two large hotel,—yes, I tink it is Blackheath! I goes dere sometime vid my monkey. I have got only one monkey now,—sometime I have got two;—he is dressed comme un soldat rouge, like one soldier, vid a red jacket and a Bonaparte's hat. My monkey only pull off his hat and take a de money. He used to ride a de dog; but dey stole a de dog,—some of de tinkare, a man vid de umbrella going by, stole a him. Dere is only tree months dat I have got my monkey. It is my own. I gave dirty-five shilling for dis one I got. He did not know no tricks when he come to me first. I did teach a him all he know. I teach a him vid de kindness, do you see. I must look rough for tree or four times, but not to beat him. He can hardly stir about; he is afraid dat you go to hit him, you see. I mustn't feed him ven I am teaching him. Sometimes I buy a happorth of nuts to give him, after he has done what I want him to do. Dis one has not de force behind; he is weak in de back. Some monkey is like de children at de school, some is very hard to teash, and some learn de more quick, you see. De one I had before dis one could do many tings. He had not much esprit pas grande chose; but he could play de drum,—de fiddle, too,— Ah! but he don't play de fiddle like de Christian, you know; but like de monkey. He used to fight vid de sword,—not exactly like de Christian, but like de monkey too,—much better. I beg your pardon to laugh, sir! He used to move his leg and jomp,—I call it danse,—but he could not do polka like de Christian.—I have seen the Christian though what can't danse more dan de monkey! I beg your pardon to laugh. I did play valtz to him on de organ. Non! he had not moosh ear for de musick, but I force him to keep de time by de jerk of de string. He commence to valtz vell when he die. He is dead the vinter dat is passed, at Sheltenham. He eat some red-ee paint. I give him some castor-oil, but no good: he die in great deal pain, poor fellow! I rather lose six pounds than lose my monkey.

I did cry!—I cry because I have no money to go and buy anoder monkey! Yes! I did love my monkey! I did love him for the sake of my life! I give de raisins, and bile dem for him. He have every ting he like. I am come here from Parma about fourteen or fifteen year ago. I used to work in my countree. I used to go and look at de ship in de montagnes: non! non! pas des vaisseaux, mais des moutons! I beg your pardon to laugh. De master did bring me up here,— dat master is gone to America now,—he is come to me and tell me to come to Angleterre. He has tell me I make plenty of money in dis country. Ah! I could get plenty of money in dat time in London, but now I get not moosh. I vork for myself at present. My master give me nine—ten shilling each veek, and my foot, and my lodging—yes! everyting ven I am first come here. I used to go out vid de organ,—a good one,—and I did get two, tree, and more shillan for my master each day. It was chance-work: sometimes I did get noting at all. De organ was my master's. He had no one else but me vid him. We used to travel about togeder, and he took all de money. He had one German piano, and play de moosick. I can't tell how moosh he did make,—he never tell to me,—but I did sheat him sometimes myself. Sometime when I take de two shillan I did give him de eighteen-pence! I beg your pardon to laugh! De man did bring up many Italians to dis country, but now it is difficult to get de passports for my countrymen. I was eighteen months with my master; after dat I vent to farm-house. I run away from my master. He gave me a slap of de face, you know, von time, so I don't like it, you know, and run away! I beg your pardon to laugh! I used to do good many tings at de farm-house. It was in Yorkshire. I used to look at de beasts, and take a de vater. I don't get noting for my vork, only for de sake of de belly I do it. I was dere about tree year. Dey behave to me very well. Dey give me de clothes and all I want. After dat I go to Liverpool, and I meet some of my countrymen dere, and dey lend me de monkey, and I teash him to danse, fight, and jomp, mush as I could, and I go vid my monkey about de country.

"Some day I make tree shillan vid my monkey, sometime only sixpence, and sometime noting at all. When it rain or snow I can get noting. I gain peut-être a dozen shillan a week vid my monkey, sometime more, but not often. Dere is long time I have been in de environs of London; but I don't like to go in de streets here. I don't like to go to prison. Monkey is defended, —*defendu*,—what you call it, London. But dere is many monkey in London still. Oh, non! not a dozen. Dere is not one dozen monkey wot play in Angleterre. I know dere is two monkey at Saffron hill, and one go in London; but he do no harm. I don't know dat de monkey was train to go down de area and steal a de silver spoons out of de kitchen. Dey would be great fool to tell dat; but every one must get a living de best dey can. Wot I tell you about de monkey I'm frightened vill hurt me!

" I tell you dey is defended in de streets, and dey take me up. I hope not. My monkey is very honest monkey, and get me de bread. I never was in prison, and I would not like to be. I play de moosick, and please de people, and never steal noting. Non! non! me no steal, nor my monkey too. Dey policemen never say noting to me. I am not beggar, but artiste!—every body know dat—and my monkey is artiste too! I beg your pardon to laugh."

THE DANCING DOGS.

I RECEIVED the following narrative from the old man who has been so long known about the streets of London with a troop of performing dogs. He was especially picturesque in his appearance. His hair, which was grizzled rather than grey, was parted down the middle, and hung long and straight over his shoulders. He was dressed in a coachman's blue greatcoat with many capes. His left hand was in a sling made out of a dirty pocket-handkerchief, and in his other he held a stick, by means of which he could just manage to hobble along. He was very ill, and very poor, not having been out with his dogs for nearly two months. He appeared to speak in great pain. The civility, if not politeness of his manner, threw an air of refinement about him, that struck me more forcibly from its contrast with the manners of the English belonging to the same class. He began :—

" I have de dancing dogs for de street—now I have nothing else. I have tree dogs—One is called Finette, anoder von Favorite, that is her nomme, an de oder von Ozor. Ah!" he said, with a shrug of the shoulders, in answer to my inquiry as to what the dogs did, " un danse, un valse, un jomp a de stick and troo de hoop—non, noting else. Sometime I had de four dogs—I did lose de von. Ah! she had beaucoup d'esprit—plenty of vit, you say—she did jomp a de hoop better dan all. Her nomme was Taborine! —she is dead dare is long time. All ma dogs have des habillements—the dress and de leetle hat. Dey have a leetel jackette in divers colours en étoffe—some de red, and some de green, and some de bleu. Deir hats is de rouge et noir—red and black, wit a leetle plume-fedder, you say. Dere is some 10 or 11 year I have been in dis country. I come from Italie — Italie — Oui, Monsieur, oui. I did live in a leetle ville, trento miglia, dirty mile, de Parma. Je travaille dans le campagne, I vork out in de countrie—je ne sais comment vous appellez la campagne. There is no commerce in de montagne. I am come in dis country here. I have leetel business to come. I thought to gagner ma vie—to gain my life wid my leetel dogs in dis countrie. I have dem déjà when I have come here from Parma—j'eu avait dix. I did have de ten dogs—je les apporte. I have carried all de ten from Italie. I did learn—yes—yes—de dogs to danse in ma own countrie. It did make de cold in de montagne in winter, and I had not no vork dere, and I must look for to gain my life some oder place. Après ça, I have instruct my dogs to danse. Yes, ils learn to danse; I play de music, and dey do jomp. Non, non—pas du tout! I did not never beat ma dogs; dare is a way to learn de dogs without no vip. Premièrement, ven I am come here I have gained a leetel monnaie—plus que now—beaucoup d'avantage—plenty more. I am left ma logement —my lodging, you say, at 9 hours in de morning, and am stay away vid ma dogs till 7 or 8 hours in de evening. Oh! I cannot count how many times de leetel dogs have danse in de day — twenty — dirty — forty peut-être—all depends : sometimes I would gain de tree shilling—sometime de couple—sometime not nothing—all depend. Ven it did make bad time, I could not vork; I could not danse. I could not gain my life den. If it make cold de dogs are ill—like tout de monde. I did pay plenty for de nouriture of de dogs. Sometime dey did get du pain de leetel dogs (de bread) in de street—sometime I give dem de meat, and make de soup for dem. Ma dogs danse comme les chiens, mais dey valtz comme les dames, and dey stand on dare back-legs like les gentilhommes. After I am come here to dis countrie two day, am terrible malade. I am gone to hospital, to St. Bartolomé, de veek before de Jour de Noël (Christmas-day). In dat moment I have de fevre. I have rested in l'hospital quatre semaine—four veek. Ma dogs vere at libertie all de time. Von compagnon of mine have promised me to take de care of ma dogs, and he have lose dem all—tout les dix. After dat I have bought tree oder dogs—one espanol, anoder von appellé ' Grifon,' and de oder vas de dog ordinaire,—non! non! not one ' pull dog.' He no good. I must have one month, or six semaine, to instruite ma dogs. I have rested in a logement Italien at Saffron-hill, ven I am come here to London. Dare vas plenty of Italiens dare. It was tout plein—quite full of strangers. All come dare—dey come from France, from Germany, from Italie. I have paid two shillings per semaine each veek—only pour le lit, for de bed. Every von make de kitchen for himself. Vot number vas dare, you say? Sometime dare is 20 person dere, and sometime dere is dirty person in de logement, sometime more dan dat. It is very petite maison. Dare is von dozen beds—dat is all—and two sleep demselves in each bed. Sometimes, ven dere arrive plenty, dey sleep demselves tree in von bed — but ordinairement dere is only two. Dey is all musicians dere — one play de organ, de piano, de guitar, de flute, yes, dare vos some vot played it, and de viol too. De great part vas Italiens. Some of dem have des monkeys, de oders des mice white, and des pigs d'Indes, (guinea-pigs) and encore oders have des dolls vid two heads, and des puppets vot danse vid de foot on de boards. Des animals are in an appartement apart vid de moosick. Dare vos sometime tree dancing dogs, one dozen of mice, five or six pigs d'Indes, and ma monkey, altogether vid de moosick, by demselves.

"Dare is all de actors vot vas dare. Ma tree dogs gained me sometime two shillan, sometime von shillan, and sometime I would rest on my feet all day, and not gain two sous. Sometimes de boys would ensault ma dogs vid de stones. Dare is long time I have rested in London. Dare is short time I vas in de campagne de countree here, not much. London is better dan de campagne for ma dogs — dare is always de vorld in London — de city is large — yes! I am always rested at Saffron-hill for 10, 11 years. I am malade at present, since the 15th of Mars; in ma arms, ma legs, ma tighs have de douleure — I have plenty of pains to march. Ma dogs are in de logement now. It is since the 15th of Mars dat I have not vent out vid ma dogs — yes, since de 15th of Mars I have done no vork. Since dat time I have not paid no money for ma logement — it is due encore. Non! non! I have not gained my life since the 15th of Mars. Plenty of time I have been vitout noting to eat. Des Italiens at de logement dey have given me pieces of bread and bouilli. Ah! it is very miserable to be poor, like me. I have sixty and tirteen years. I cannot march now but vith plenty of pains. Von doctor have give to me a letter for to present to de poor-house. He did give me my medicine for nothing — gratis. He is obliged, he is de doctor of de paroisse. He is a very brave and honest man, dat doctor dare. At de poor-house day have give to me a bread and six sous on Friday of de veek dat is past, and told me to come de Vednesday next. But I am arrive dere too late, and dey give me noting, and tell me to come de Vednesday next encore. Ma dogs dey march now in de street, and eat something dare. Oh! ma God, non! dey eat noting but what dey find in de street ven it makes good times; but ven it makes bad times dey have noting at all, poor dogs! ven I have it, dey have it,— but ven dere is noting for me to eat, dare is noting for dem, and dey must go out in de streets and get de nouriture for themselves. Des enfans vot know ma dogs vill give to dem to eat sometimes. Oh! yes, if I had de means, I would return to Italie, ma countree. But I have not no silver, and not no legs to walk. Vot can I do? Oh! yes, I am very sick at present. All my limbs have great douleur — Oh, yes! plenty of pain."

CONCERTINA PLAYER ON THE STEAMBOATS.

"I was always very fond of music, and if ever I heard any in the streets, I always followed it about. I'm nearly fifteen now; but I can remember when I was seven, being particularly taken with music. I had an uncle who was captain of a steamer that run to Richmond, and I was always on board with him; and they used to have a band on board. It wasn't in particular a passage-boat, but an excursion one, and let to private parties, and a band always went along with them. I was taken along to run after orders for the steward; and when I had nothing to do, I used to go and listen to them. I learn all their tunes by heart. They mostly played dances, and very seldom any sentimental songs, unless anybody asked them. For myself, I prefer lively tunes. I don't know much operatic music, only one or two airs; but they're easier to play on the concertina than lively music, because it's difficult to move the fingers very quickly. You can't hardly play a hornpipe. It makes the arm ache before you can play it all through, and it makes such a row with the valve working the bellows up and down, that it spoils the music.

"I had not got my instrument when I was in this steamboat. When I heard a tune, I used to whistle it. I asked my father to buy me a instrument, but he wouldn't. I was always on the steamboat, helping uncle; and I could have had lots of time to learn music there. When they, the musicians, put the harp down in the cabin, I'd get playing on it. There was a hole in the green baize cover of the harp, and I used to put my hand in and work away at it. I learnt myself several tunes, such as the 'Sultan Polka.' I must have been eight years old then. I didn't play it with both hands: I couldn't do the bass.

"I never had any lessons in music. I've done it all out of my own head. Before I had a concertina, I used to go about amusing myself with a penny tin whistle. I could play it pretty well, not to say all tunes, but all such as I knew I could play very well on it. The 'Red, White, and Blue' was my favourite tune.

"I have a brother, who is younger than I am, and he, before he was ten, was put out to a master to learn the violin. Father's a labourer, and does something of anything he can get to do; but bricklaying generally. He paid so much a quarter for having my brother Henry taught. I think it was about 16s. a-quarter. It was a great expense for father at first; but afterwards, when we was hard up, Henry could always fly to the fiddle to earn a crust. Henry never took to music, not to say well. I can play more out of my own head than he can by notes. He's a very good player now.

"I was about getting on for twelve when father first bought me a concertina. That instrument was very fashionable then, and everybody had it nearly. I had an accordion before; but it was only a 1s. 6d. one, and I didn't take a fancy to it somehow, although I could play a few tunes on it. I used to see boys about my own height carrying concertinas about the streets, and humming them. I always wanted one. There was a little boy I knew, he got one, and then I wanted one worse. He used to come to our house, and play all sorts of tunes, for he played very well. I liked the concertina, because it's like a full band. It's like having the fiddle and the harp together. I used to ask this little boy to lend me his instrument, and I'd work the keys about a little, but I couldn't do any airs.

"I play entirely out of my own head, for I never had any lessons at all. I learn the tunes from hearing other people playing of them. If I hear a street band, such as a fiddle and harp and cornopean playing a tune, I follow them and catch the air; and if it's any sort of a easy tune at all, I can pick it up after them, for I never want to hear it more than twice played on an instrument.

"At last, after bothering father a long time, he bought me a half-crown concertina. I was in bed when he brought it into my room, and he put it on the bed; when I woke up I see it. I instantly set to work, and before I had got up I had learnt 'Pop goes the Weasel.' I was just pleased. I was up and dressed, and playing it all day long. I never used to let anybody touch, not even my own father hardly, for fear he should break it. I did break it once, and then I was regular dull, for fear I should lose my tunes.

"It took me six months before I could play it well, and then I could play a'most any tune I heard. The fingers had learnt the keys, and knew where the notes was, so that I could play in the dark. My brother could play the fiddle well, long before I could do any tunes. We used to play together duets, such as 'A Boat, a Boat unto the Ferry.' We never hardly went out together in the streets and play together, only once or twice, because a fiddle and a concertina don't sound well together unless a harp's with it, and then it's beautiful.

"How I came to get on the steamboats was this: father went to take a trip up to Kew one day, so I wanted to go, and he said if I could earn my fare I might go. So I thought I'd take my concertina and try. So I went, and I earned that day about 9s., all in halfpence and 4d. bits. That was only by going up to Kew and coming back again. It was on a Whitsun-Monday. Then I thought I'd do it again the next day, and I think I took about the same. Then I kept on them all together. I didn't keep to the Kew boats, because they had got

their regular musicians, and they complained to the superintendent, and he forbid me going. Then I went to the Woolwich boats, and I used to earn a heap of money, as much as 10s. every day, and I was at it all the week for the season.

"I usen't to pay any fare, but I got a free pass. It was mostly the crew. When I got out at the pier, I used to tell them I'd been playing, and they would let me pass. Now I know near every man that is on the river, and they let me go on any boat I like. They consider I draw customers, and amuse them during the trip. They won't let some hardly play on board only me, because I've been on them such a long time—these three years. I know all the pier-masters, too, and they are all very kind to me. Sometimes, when I'm waiting for a boat to go up anywhere, I play on the piers, and I always do pretty fair.

"In winter I go on the boats all the same, and I play down in the cabin. Some of the passengers will object to it if they are reading, and then I have to leave off, or I should put my own self in a hobble, for they would go and tell the captain; and if he wouldn't say anything, then they would tell the superintendent. In winter and wet weather is my worst time; but even then I mostly take my 3s. In the winter time, my best time is between three o'clock and six, when the gentlemen are coming home from office; and I never hardly come out before two o'clock. In summer its good from twelve till eight o'clock. The passengers come to go to the Crystal Palace in the morning part. Those that are going out for pleasure are my best customers. In the summer I always take at the rate of about 6s. a-day. Pleasure-people mostly ask me for dancing tunes; and the gentlemen coming from business prefer song tunes. I have got a good many regular gentlemen, who always give me something when they are coming from business. There are some who give me 6d. every day I see them; but sometimes they go up by a different boat to what I'm in. There's one always gives me 6d., whether I'm playing or not; and it's about four o'clock or half-past that I mostly see him.

"In winter my hands gets very cold indeed, so that I can scarcely feel the keys. Sometimes I can't move them, and I have to leave off, and go down below and warm my hands at the cabin fire.

"In the summer I sometimes go out with a mate of mine, who plays the piccolo. He's very clever indeed, and plays most extraordinary. He's a little bigger than me. He lives by playing music in the boats. We don't play in the streets. I never played in the streets in my life. He don't play in the winter, but works with his father, who makes hair-oil and that, and sends it out in the country. He's a regular perfumer; and serves chandlers' shops and that like.

"There's a tune we play together called the

'Camp at Chobham.' It begins with my doing the bugle, and he answers it on his fife. Then we do it in the distance like. Then come all the different marches the soldiers march to. Some people are so fond of it, that when they see us they come up and ask us to give it them. It takes a good quarter of an hour to play it. When I'm with him, I earn about the same as when I'm alone; but I like to go with him, because it's company.

"One of the songs I play is, ' Mother, is the battle over?' That's lately come out. It is a lady's song, and they generally ask me for it. They also ask me for the Varsovienne. At the present time, the girls mostly ask me for 'Polly, won't you try me, oh!' They like anything that is new, if it is a very pretty tune like ' Polly, won't you try me, oh!' Sometimes I forget the tunes; they go right out of my head, and then, perhaps, a month afterwards they'll come back again. Perhaps I'll be fingering the keys, and I'll accidental do the beginning of the air I'd forgot, and then I remember it all of a sudden the same as before. Then I feel quite glad that I've got it back again, and I'll keep on playing it for a long time.

"When once I begin to play, I can scarcely leave off. I used at first to play as I went along the streets, but now I feel too tired to do it. If I haven't been out in the boats, I must have a play just the same. I like it very much. I don't like any of the other instruments, now I've learnt this one so well. The fiddle is pretty good, but nothing, to my fancy, like the concertina.

"The concertina I use now cost me 16s. It's got twenty double keys—one when I pull the bellows out and one when I close it. I wear out an instrument in three months. The edges of the bellows get worn out: then I have to patch them up, till they get so weak that it mostly doubles over. It costs me about 1s. a-week to have them kept in order. They get out of tune very soon. They file them, and put fresh notes in. I get all my repairs done trade price. I tune my instrument myself. The old instruments I sell to the boys, for about as much as I give for a new one. They are very dear; but I get them so cheap when I buy them, I only give 16s. for a 25s. instrument.

"I've got a beautiful instrument at home, and I give a pound for it, and it's worth two. Those I buy come from Germany, where they make them, and then they are took to this warehouse, where I buy them.

"Once I was turned off the penny steam-boats. There was such a lot of musicians come on board, and they got so cheeky, that when they was told not to play they would, just the same, and so a stop was put to all music on board. If one was stopped all must be stopped, so I was told not to go. I still had my fourpenny boats. I never used to go on the penny boats hardly, for I never used to get much money in them. Now I am allowed go on them just the same as before.

"I can't say how often I've been up the Thames. I never go as far as Chelsea hardly, only about twice a-day, for most of the people get out between London-bridge and Nine-elms. My general run is down to Hungerford and back to Blackfriars; and I do that about fifty times a-day.

"I never go out on the Sunday. I mostly go to a Sunday-school, and then take a walk. Father wants me to be a scholar: I can read and write. I'm a teacher at the Sunday-school, and make the children read their lessons. I know multiplication, and addition, and all them. I go to school every night at half-past six and come home at nine. Father makes me and my brother go to school every day, and we pay 1s. each a-week. It's a very good school, and the master is very kind. There are about 30 night scholars and 50 day ones, besides about 20 girls. His daughter teaches the girls.

"At night when I leave school I go and play music three nights a-week at a ball. My brother goes with me. We go to a place in the Westminster-road on Mondays, Wednesdays, and Thursdays. It's a very nice ball-room, and there are generally about 200 there. They pay 1s. each. There are four musicians, a fiddle, a harp, a fife, and a concertina. It isn't a Casino; it's an assembly-rooms. We teaches on three nights in the week, and the pupils assemble and practise on the other nights.

"The room is like a street almost, and the music sounds well in it. The other three play from notes, and I join in. I learnt their airs this way. My mother and father were very fond of dancing, and they used to go there nearly every night, and I'd go along with them, and then I'd listen and learn the tunes. My brother regularly played there. He was about ten years old when he first went to play there; but he could play any music that was put before him. In the day-time he blows the bellows at a blacksmith and engineer's. The first time I played in a orchestra I felt a little strange. I had been to rehearsal. I went twenty times before I was confident enough to appear at night. I could play the tunes well enough, but I didn't know when to leave off at the exact time they did. At last I learnt how to do it. I don't have any stand before me. I never look at any of the others' music. I look at the dancing. You've got to look at the time they're dancing at, and watch their figures when they leave off. The proprietor knew father, and that's how I came to have the job. I get 2s. 6d. a-night for playing there, and plenty to eat and drink. There's bread and cheese and a drop of beer. On the other three nights when I'm not at the ball I stop at home, and get a bit of rest. Father sends us to bed early, about half-past nine, when I come home from school. On ball-nights I'm sometimes up to two o'clock in the morning.

" I take all the money I earn home to father, and he gives me a few halfpence for myself. All the year round it comes to 5s. a-day. I buy my own food when I'm out on the boats. I go to a cookshop. I like pudding or pie better than anything, and next to that I like a bit of bread and butter as well as anything, except pie. I have meat or veal pies. They charge you 6d. a-plate, and you have potatoes and all. After that I have a couple of pen'orth of pudding with sugar. I drink water. My dinner comes to about 9d. a-day, for I generally have a pen'orth of apples as dessert. It makes you very hungry going about in the steam-boats — very much so.

" I'm the only boy that goes about the steam-boats with a concertina; indeed, I'm the only boy above-bridge that goes about with music at all on the boats. I know the old gentleman who plays the harp at the Essex pier. I often go and join in with him when I land there, and we go shares. He mostly plays there of a morning, and we mostly of an afternoon. We two are the only ones that play on the piers."

TOM-TOM PLAYERS.

WITHIN the last few years East Indians playing on the tom-tom have occasionally made their appearance in the London streets. The Indian or Lascar crossing-sweepers, who earned their living by alternately plying the broom and sitting as models to artists — the Indian converted to Christianity, who, in his calico clothes, with his brown bosom showing, was seen, particularly on cold days, crouching on the pavement and selling tracts, have lately disappeared from our highways, and in their stead the tom-tom players have made their appearance.

I saw two of these performers in one of the West-end streets, creeping slowly down the centre of the road, and beating their drums with their hands, whilst they drawled out a kind of mournful song. Their mode of parading the streets is to walk one following the other, beating their oyster-barrel-shaped drums with their hands, which they make flap about from the wrist like flounders out of water, whilst they continue their droning song, and halt at every twenty paces to look round.

One of these performers was a handsome lad, with a face such as I have seen in the drawings of the princes in the " Arabian Nights Entertainments." He had a copper skin and long black hair, which he brushed behind his ears. On his head was a white turban, made to cock over one ear, like a hat worn on one side, and its rim stood out like the stopper to a scent-bottle.

The costume of the man greatly resembled that of a gentleman wearing his waistcoat out-side his shirt, only the waistcoat was of green merino, and adorned with silk embroidery, his waist being bound in with a scarf. Linen trowsers and red knitted cuffs, to keep his wrists warm, completed his costume.

This man was as tall, slim, and straight, and as gracefully proportioned, as a bronze image. His face had a serious, melancholy look, which seemed to work strongly on the feelings of the nurses and the servant-girls who stopped to look at him. His companion, although dressed in the same costume, (the only difference being that the colour of his waistcoat was red instead of green,) formed a comical contrast to his sentimental Othello-looking partner, for he was what a Yankee would call " a rank nigger." His face, indeed, was as black and elastic-looking as a printer's dabber.

The name of the negro boy was Peter. Beyond " Yes" and " No," he appeared to be perfectly unacquainted with the English language. His Othello friend was 17 years of age, and spoke English perfectly. I could not help taking great interest in this lad, both from the peculiarity of his conversation, which turned chiefly upon the obedience due from children to their parents, and was almost fanatical in its theory of perfect submission, and also from his singularly handsome countenance; for his eyes were almond-shaped, and as black as elder-berries, whilst, as he spoke, the nostrils of his aquiline nose beat like a pulse.

When I attempted to repeat after them one of their Indian songs, they both burst out into uproarious merriment. Peter rolling about in his chair like a serenader playing " the bones," and the young Othello laughing as if he was being tickled.

In speaking of the duties which they owed to their parents, the rules of conduct which they laid down as those to be followed by a good son were wonderful for the completeness of the obedience which they held should be paid to a father's commands. They did not seem to consider that the injunctions of a mother should be looked upon as sacredly as those of the male parent. They told me that the soul of the child was damned if even he disputed to obey the father's command, although he knew it to be wrong, and contrary to God's laws. " Allah," they said, would visit any wickedness that was committed through such obedience upon the father, but he would bless the child for his submission. Their story was as follows:—

" Most of the tom-tom players are Indians, but we are both of us Arabs. The Arabs are just equally as good as the Indians at playing the tom-tom, but they haven't got exactly to the learning of the manufacture of them yet. I come from Mocha, and so does Peter, my companion; only his father belongs to what we call the Abshee tribe, and that's what makes him so much darker than what I am. The Abshee tribe are now outside of Arabia, up by the Gulf of Persia. They are much the same as the Mucdad people,—it's all the same tribe like.

" My name is Usef Asman, and my father has been over here twelve years now. He came here in the English army, I've heard him say, for he was in the 77th Bengal Native Infantry; but he wasn't an Indian, but enlisted in the service and fought through the Sikh war, and was wounded. He hasn't got a pension, for he sent his luggage through Paris to England, and he lost his writings. The East India Company only told him that he must wait un-til they heard from India, and that's been going on for now six years.

" Mother came home with father and me, and two brothers and a sister. I'm the second eldest. My brother is thirty-six, and he was in the Crimea, as steward on board the Royal Hydaspes, a steam screw she is. He was 17 and I was 6 years old when I came over. My brother is a fine strapping fellow, over six feet high, and the muscles in his arms are as big round as my thigh.

" I don't remember my native country, but Peter does, for he's only been here for two years and five months. He likes his own country better than England. His father left Arabia to go to Bombay, and there he keeps large coffee-shops. He's worth a little money. His shops are in the low quarter of the town, just the same as Drury Lane may be, though it's the centre of the town. They call the place the Nacopoora taleemoulla.

" Before father went into the army he was an interpreter in Arabia. His father was a horse-dealer. My father can speak eight or nine different languages fluently, besides a little of others. He was the interpreter who got Dr. Woolfe out of Bokhara prison, when he was put in because they thought he was a spy. Father was sent for by the chief to explain what this man's business was. It is the Mogul language they speak there. My father was told to get him out of the country in twenty-four hours, and my father killed his own horse and camel walking so hard to get him away.

" We was obliged to put ourselves up to going about the streets. Duty and necessity first compelled me to do it. Father couldn't get his pension, and, of course, we couldn't sit at home and starve; so father was obliged to go out and play the drum. He got his tom-toms from an Arab vessel which came over, and they made them a present to him.

" We used before now, father and myself, to go to artists or modelers, to have our like-nesses taken. We went to Mr. Armitage, when he was painting a battle in India. If you recollect, I'm leaning down by the rocks, whilst the others are escaping. I've also been to Mr. Dobson, who used to live in Newman-street. I've sat to him in my costume for several pictures. In one of them I was like a chief's son, or something of that, smoking a hubble-bubble. Father used to have a deal of

work at Mr. Gale's, in Fitzroy-square. I don't know the subjects he painted, for I wasn't there whilst father used to sit. It used to tire me when I had to sit for two or three hours in one position. Sometimes I had to strip to the waist. I had to do that at Mr. Dobson's in the winter time, and, though there was a good fire in the room, it was very wide, and it didn't throw much heat out, and I used to be very cold. He used to paint religious subjects. I had a shilling an hour, and if a person could get after-work at it, I could make a better living at it than in the streets; in fact, I'd rather do it any time, though it's harder work, for there is a name for that, but there is no name for going about playing the tom-tom; yet it's better to do that than sit down and see other people starving.

" Father is still sitting to artists. He doesn't go about the streets—he couldn't face it out.

" It's about eight years ago since father got the tom-toms. They are very good ones, and one of them is reckoned the best in England. They are made out of mango tree. It grows just the same as the bamboo tree; and they take a joint of it, and take out the pith—for it's pithy inside, just like elderberry wood, with the outside hard. Father had these tom-toms for a month before we went out with them.

" The first day father went out with me, and kept on until he got employ; and then I went out by myself. I was about for four years by myself, along with sister; and then I went with Peter; and now we go out together. My sister was only about seven years old when she first went out, and she used to sing. She was dressed in a costume with a short jacket, with a tight waistcoat, and white trowsers. She had a turban and a sash.

" When we first went out we done very well. We took 6, 7, or 8s. a-day. We was the first to appear with it; indeed there's only me and my cousin and another man that does it now. Peter is my cousin. His real name is Busha, but we call him Peter, because it's more a proper name like, because several people can call him that when they can't Busha. We are all turned Christians; we go to school every Sunday, in Great Queen-street, Lincoln's Inn, and always to chapel. They are joined together.

" I and Peter take now, on a fine day in summer-time, generally 5 or 6s., but coming on winter as it does now it's as much as we can do to take 2s. or 3s. Sometimes in winter we don't take more than 1s. 6d., and some-times 1s. Take the year round it would come, I should think, tc 3s. a-day. On wet days we can't do nothing.

" We were forced to become Christians when we came here. Of course a true Mus-sulman won't take anything to eat that has been touched by other people's hands. We were forced to break caste. The beasts were slaughtered by other people, and we wanted meat to eat. The bread, too, was made by Christians. The school-teachers used to come to father. We remained as Mussulmen as long as we could, but when winter came on, and we had no money, we was obliged to eat food from other people's hands.

"Persons wouldn't believe it, but little family as we are it takes 4s. a-day to keep us. Yet mother speaks English well. I'm sure father doesn't go out and drink not half-a pint a beer of a night, but always waits till we come home, and then our 3s. or 4s. go to get bread and rice and that, and we have a pot of beer between us.

"Peter's father married my father's sister, that's how we are cousins. He came over by ship to see us. He sent a message before to say that he was coming to see his uncle, and he expected to go back by the same ship, but he was used so cruelly on board that he preferred staying with us until we can all return together. Because he couldn't understand English and his duty, and coming into a cold country and all, he couldn't do his work, and they flogged him. Besides, they had to summon the captain to get their rights. He very much wants to get back to India to his father, and our family wants to get back to Mocha. I've forgot my Arabic, and only talk Hindostanee. I did speak French very fluently, but I've forgot it all except such things as Venez ici, or Voulez-vous danser? or such-like.

"When we are at home we mostly eat rice. It's very cheap, and we like it better than anything else, because it fills our bellies better. It wouldn't be no use putting a couple of half-quartern loaves before us two if we were hungry, for, thank God, we are very hearty-eating, both of us. Rice satisfies us better than bread. We mix curry-powder and a little meat or fish with it. If there's any fish in season, such as fresh herrings or mackerel, we wash it and do it with onions, and mix it with the curry-powder, and then eat it with rice. Plaice is the only fish we don't use, for it makes the curry very watery. We wash the rice two or three times after looking over it to take out any dirt or stones, and then we boil it and let it boil about five minutes. Rice-water is very strengthening, and the Arabs drink a deal of it, because whenever it lays in the stomach it becomes solid. It turns, when cold, as thick as starch, and with some salt it's not a bad thing.

"Our best places for playing the tom-tom is the West-end in summer-time, but in winter we goes round by Islington and Shoreditch, and such-like, for there's no quality at home, and we have to depend on the tradespeople. Sometimes we very often happen to meet with a gentleman—when the quality's in town —who has been out in India, and can speak the language, and he will begin chatting with us and give us a shilling, or sometimes more.

I've got two or three ladies who have taken a fancy to us, and they give me 6d. or 1s. whenever I go round. There's one old lady and two or three young ones, at several houses in different places, who have such kindness for us. I was in place once with Captain Hines, and he was very kind to me. He had been out in India, and spoke the language very fluently. I didn't leave him, he left me to go to the Crimea; and he told me he was very sorry, but he had a servant allowed him by the Government, and couldn't take me.

"Some of the servant-girls are very kind to us, and give us a 1d. or 2d. We in general tries to amuse the people as much as we can. All the people are very fond of Peter, he makes them laugh; and the same people generally gives us money when we goes round again.

"When we are out we walk along side by side beating the tom-toms. We keep on singing different songs,—foreign ones to English tunes. The most favourite tune is what we calls in Hindostanee,—

    ' Tasa bi tasa, no be no
    Mutra bakooch, no arber go ;
    Tasa bi tasa, no be no
    Attipa ho gora purgeen
    Mara gora gora chelopageen.
    Tasa bi tasa, no be no.
    O senna key taho baroo
    Dilla chungay gurrey kumahayroo.
    Tasa bi tasa, no be no
    Lutfellee karu basha bud
    Shibbe de lum sesta bud
    Tasa bi tasa, no be no.'

"This means :—

" ' I want something fresh (such as fish) in the value of nine. And after he went and bought these fresh goods he looked at them, and found them so good, that he was very pleased with them ('mutra bakooch' is pleased), that he says to his servant that he will give him leave to go about his business, because he's made such a good bargain.'

"That's all the meaning of that, sir, and we sing it to its original Indian tune. We sometimes sing Arab songs—one or two. They are very different, but we can't explain them so well as we can the Hindostanee. They're more melancholy, and towards the parents sentimental-like. There's one song they sing in Arabia, that it puts them in that way they don't know what they are doing of. They begin the song, and then they bend the body about and beat their knees, and keep on so until they tumble off their chairs. They nearly strangle themselves sometimes. It's about love to their parents, and as if they left them and went far away. It's a sort of a cutting song, and very sentimental. There's always a man standing in one corner, looking after those singing, and when he sees them get into a way, he reads a book and comes and rouses them. He's a kind of magician-like. Father sings it, and I know a verse or two of it. I've seen father and another man singing it, and they kept on see-sawing about, and at last they both fell off the chair. We got a little water and sprinkled their faces, and hit them on the back very hard, and said, ' Sallee a nabbee,' which is just the same as ' Rise, in the name of the Lord,' and they came to instantly, and after they got up was very calm — ah, very tame afterwards !

" The tom-tom hasn't got much music in it beyond beating like a drum. There are first-rate players in India, and they can make the tom-tom speak in the same way as if you was to ask a gentleman, ' How do you do?' and they'll answer you, ' Very well, thank you.' They only go to the feasts, which are called ' madggeless,' and then the noblemen, after hearing them, will give them great sums of money as a handsome present. The girls, too, dance to the tom-tom in India. Peter is a very good player, and he can make the tom-tom to answer. One side of the drum asks the question, that is the treble side, and the bass one answers it, for in a tom-tom each end gives a different note.

" Father makes all our clothes for us. We wear flannel under our shirts, which a lady made me a present of, or else we never used to wear them before. All through that sharp winter we never used to wear anything but our dress. All the Arab boys are brought up to respect their parents. If they don't they will be punished. For myself, I always obey mine. My father has often called shame on the laws of this country, to hear the children abusing their parents. In our country, if a son disobeys his father's command, he may, even though the child be as tall as a giant, take up his sword and kill him. My brother, who is on board ship, even though he has learnt the laws of this country, always obeys my father. One night he wouldn't mind what was said, so my father goes up and hit him a side slap on the chops, and my brother turned the other cheek to him, and said in Arabic, ' Father, hit this cheek, too; I have done wrong.' He was about 30 then. Father said he hoped he'd never disobey his orders again.

" The Arabs are very clean. In our country we bathe three times a-day; but over here we only go to the bath in Endell-street (a public one) twice a-week. We always put on clean things three times a-week.

" There's a knack in twisting the turban. A regular Arab always makes the rim bind over the right ear, like Peter's. It don't take more than five minutes to put the turban on. We do it up in a roll, and have nothing inside it to stiffen it. Some turbans have 30 yards in them, all silk, but mine is only 3½ yards, and is calico. The Arab waistcoat always has a pocket on each side of the breast, with a lengthways opening, and a bit of braid round the edge of the stuff, ending where the waist is, so that the flaps are not bound.

" The police are very kind to us, and never interfere with us unless there is somebody ill,

and we are not aware of it. The tom-tom makes a very humming sound, and is heard to a great distance."

ANOTHER " TOM-TOM " PLAYER.

A VERY handsome man, swarthy even for a native of Bengal, with his black glossy hair most picturesquely disposed, alike on his head and in his whiskers and moustache, gave me, after an Oriental salute, the following statement. His teeth were exquisitely white, and his laugh or smile lighted up his countenance to an expression of great intelligence. His dress was a garb of dark-brown cloth, fitting close to his body and extending to his knee. His trowsers were of the same coloured cloth, and he wore a girdle of black and white cotton round his waist. He was accompanied by his son, (whom he sometimes addressed in Hindoostanee), a round-faced boy, with large bright black eyes and rosy cheeks. The father said : —

" I was born in Calcutta, and was Mussulman — my parents was Mussulman — but I Christian now. I have been in dis contree ten year. I come first as servant to military officer, an Englishman. I lived wit him in Scotland six, seven mont. He left Scotland, saying he come back, but he not, and in a mont I hear he dead, and den I com London. London is very great place, and Indian city little if you look upon London. I use tink it plenty pleasure look upon London as de great government place, but now I look upon London, and it is plenty bad pleasure. I wish very often return to my own contree, where everyting sheap — living sheap, rice sheap. I suffer from climate in dis contree. I suffer dis winter more dan ever I did. I have no flannels, no drawer, no waistcoat, and have cold upon my chest. It is now near five year I come London. I try get service, but no get service. I have character, but not from my last master. He could not give me ; he dead ven I want it. I put up many insult in dis contree. I struck sometime in street. Magistrate punish man gave me blow dat left mark on my chin here. Gentlemen sometime save me from harm, sometime not. De boys call me black dis or de oder. Wen I get no service, I not live, and I not beg in street, so I buy tom-tom for 10s. De man want 30s. De 10s. my last money left, and I start to play in streets for daily bread. I beat tom-tom, and sing song about greatness of God, in my own language. I had den wife, Englishwoman, and dis little boy. I done pretty well first wid tom-tom, but it is very bad to do it now. Wen I began first, I make 3s., 4s., 5s., or 6s. a-day. It was someting new den, but nine or ten monts it was someting old, and I took less and less, until now I hardly get piece of bread. I sometime get few shilling from two or three picture-men, who draw me. It is call model. Anyting for honest bread. I must not be proud. I cannot make above 6s. a-week of tom-tom in street. Dare is, well as I know, about fifty of my contreemen playing and begging in streets of London. Dose who sweep crossing are Malay, some Bengal. Many are impostor, and spoil 'spectable men. My contreemen live in lodging-house; often many are plenty blackguard lodging-houses, and dere respectable man is always insult. I have room for myself dis tree mont, and cost me tree shilling and sixpennies a-week; it is not own furniture; dey burn my coke, coal, and candle too. My wife would make work wid needle, but dere is no work for her, poor ting. She servant when I marry her. De little boy make jump in my contree's way wen I play tom-tom—he too little to dance—he six year. Most of my contreemen in street have come as Lascar, and not go back for bosen and bosenmate, and flog. So dey stay for beg, or sweep, or anyting. Dey are never pickpocket dat I ever hear of."

PERFORMER ON DRUM AND PIPES.

A STOUT, reddish-faced man, who was familiar with all kinds of exhibitions, and had the coaxing, deferential manner of many persons who ply for money in the streets, gave me an account of what he called "his experience" as the "*drum and pipes :*"—

"I have played the pandean pipes and the drum for thirty years to street exhibitions of all kinds. I was a smith when a boy, serving seven years' apprenticeship; but after that I married a young woman that I fell in love with, in the music line. She played a hurdy-gurdy in the streets, so I bought pandean pipes, as I was always fond of practising music, and I joined her. Times for street-musicianers were good then, but I was foolish. I'm aware of that now; but I wasn't particularly partial to hard work; besides, I could make more as a street-musician. When I first started, my wife and I joined a fantoccini. It did well. My wife and I made from 9s. to 10s. a-day. We had half the profits. At that time the public exhibitions were different to what they are now. Gentlemen's houses were good then, but now the profession's sunk to street corners. Bear-dancing was in vogue then, and clock-work on the round board, and Jack-i'-the-green was in all his glory every May, thirty years ago. Things is now very dead indeed. In the old times, only sweeps were allowed to take part with the Jack; they were particular at that time; all were sweeps but the musicianers. Now it's everybody's money, when there's any money. Every sweep showed his plate then when performing. 'My lady' was anybody at all likely that they could get hold of; she was generally a watercress-seller, or something in the public way. 'My lady' had 2s. 6d. a-day and her keep for three days — that was the general hire. The boys, who were climbing-boys,

had 1s. or 6d., or what the master gave them; and they generally went to the play of a night, after washing themselves, in course. I had 6s. a-day and a good dinner —shoulder of mutton, or something prime—and enough to drink. 'My lord' and the other characters shared and shared alike. They have taken, to my knowledge, 5l. on the 1st of May. This year, one set, with two 'My ladies,' took 3l. the first day. The master of the lot was a teetotaler, but the others drank as they liked. He turned teetotaler because drink always led him into trouble. The dress of the Jack is real ivy tied round hoops. The sweeps gather the ivy in the country, and make the dresses at their homes. My lord's and the other dresses are generally kept by the sweeps. My lord's dress costs a mere trifle at the second-hand clothes shop, but it's gold-papered and ornamented up to the mark required. What I may call war tunes, such as 'The White Cockade,' the 'Downfall of Paris,' (I've been asked for that five or six times a-day—I don't remember the composer), 'Bonaparte's March,' and the 'Duke of York's March,' were in vogue in the old times. So was 'Scots wha hae' (very much), and 'Off she goes!' Now new tunes come up every day. I play waltzes and pokers now chiefly. They're not to compare to the old tunes; it's like playing at musicianers, lots of the tunes now-a-days. I've played with Michael, the Italy Bear. I've played the fife and tabor with him. The tabor was a little drum about the size of my cap, and it was tapped with a little stick. There are no tabors about now. I made my 7s. or 8s. a-day with Michael. He spoke broken English. A dromedary was about then, but I knew nothing of that or the people; they was all foreigners together. Swinging monkeys were in vogue at that time as well. I was with them, with Antonio of Saffron Hill. He was the original of the swinging monkeys, twenty years ago. They swing from a rope, just like slack-wire dancers. Antonio made money and went back to his own country. He sold his monkeys,—there was three of them,—small animals they were, for 70l. to another foreigner; but I don't know what became of them. Coarse jokes pleased people long ago, but don't now; people get more enlightened, and think more of chapel and church instead of amusements. My trade is a bad one now. Take the year through, I may make 12s. a-week, or not so much; say 10s. I go out sometimes playing single,— that's by myself,— on the drum and pipes; but it's thought nothing of, for I'm not a German. It's the same at Brighton as in London; brass bands is all the go when they've Germans to play them. The Germans will work at 2s. a-day at any fair, when an Englishman will expect 6s. The foreigners ruin this country, for they have more privileges than the English. The Germans pull the bells and knock at the doors for money, which an Englishman has hardly face for. I'm now with a fantoccini figures from Canton, brought over by a seaman. I can't form an exact notion of how many men there are in town who are musicianers to the street exhibitions; besides the exhibitions' own people, I should say about one hundred. I don't think that they are more drunken than other people, but they're liable to get top-heavy at times. None that I know live with women of the town. They live in lodgings, and not in lodging-houses. Oh! no, no, we've not come to that yet. Some of them succeeded their fathers as street-musicianers; others took it up casalty-like, by having learned different instruments; none that I know were ever theatrical performers. All the men I know in my line would object, I am sure, to hard work, if it was with confinement along with it. We can never stand being confined to hard work, after being used to the freedom of the streets. None of us save money; it goes either in a lump, if we get a lump, or in dribs and drabs, which is the way it mostly comes to us. I've known several in my way who have died in St. Giles's workhouse. In old age or sickness we've nothing but the parish to look to. The newest thing I know of is the singing dogs. I was with that as musician, and it answers pretty well amongst the quality. The dogs is three Tobies to a Punch-and-Judy show, and they sing,— that is, they make a noise,— it's really a howl,— but they keep time with Mr. Punch as he sings."

III.—STREET VOCALISTS.

The Street Vocalists are almost as large a body as the street musicians. It will be seen that there are 50 Ethiopian serenaders, and above 250 who live by ballad-singing alone.

Street Negro Serenaders.

At present I shall deal with the Ethiopian serenaders, and the better class of ballad-singers. Two young men who are of the former class gave the following account. Both were dressed like decent mechanics, with perfectly clean faces, excepting a little of the professional black at the root of the hair on the forehead :—

" We are niggers," said one man, " as it's commonly called; that is, negro melodists. Nigger bands vary from four to seven, and have numbered as many as nine; our band is now six. We all share alike. I (said the same man) was the first who started the niggers in the streets, abour four years ago. I took the hint from the performance of Pell and the others at the St. James's. When I first started in the streets I had five performers, four and myself. There were the banjo-player, the bones, fiddle, and tambourine. We are regu-

larly full-dressed, in fashionable black coats and trowsers, open white waistcoats, pumps (bluchers some had, just as they could spring them), and wigs to imitate the real negro head of hair. Large white wrists or cuffs came out after. It was rather a venturesome 'spec, the street niggers, for I had to find all the clothes at first start, as I set the school a-going. Perhaps it cost me 6s. a-head all round—all second-hand dress except the wigs, and each man made his own wig out of horse-hair dyed black, and sewn with black thread on to the skin of an old silk hat. Well, we first started at the top of the Liverpool-road, but it was no great success, as we weren't quite up in our parts and didn't play exactly into one another's hands. None of us were perfect, we'd had so few rehearsals. One of us had been a street singer before, another a street fiddler, another had sung nigger-songs in public-houses, the fourth was a mud-lark, and I had been a street singer. I was brought up to no trade regularly. When my father died I was left on the world, and I worked in Marylebone stone-yard, and afterwards sung about the streets, or shifted as I could. I first sung in the streets just before the Queen's coronation—and a hard life it was. But, to tell the truth, I didn't like the thoughts of hard labour—bringing a man in so little, too—that's where it is; and as soon as I could make any sort of living in the streets with singing and such-like, I got to like it. The first 'debew,' as I may say, of the niggers, brought us in about 10s. among us, besides paying for our dinner and a pint of beer a-piece. We were forced to be steady you see, sir, as we didn't know how it would answer. We sang from eleven in the morning till half-past ten at night, summer time. We kept on day after day, not rehearsing, but practising in the streets, for rehearsing in private was of little use — voices are as different in private rooms and the public streets as is chalk from cheese. We got more confidence as we went along. To be sure we had all cheek enough to start with, but this was a fresh line of business. Times mended as we got better at our work. Last year was the best year I've known. We start generally about ten, and play till it's dark in fine weather. We averaged 1l. a-week last year. The evenings are the best time. Regent-street, and Oxford-street, and the greater part of St. James's, are our best places. The gentry are our best customers, but we get more from gentlemen than from ladies. The City is good, I fancy, but they won't let us work it; it's only the lower parts, Whitechapel and Smithfield ways, that we have a chance in. Business and nigger-songs don't go well together. The first four days of the week are pretty much alike for our business. Friday is bad, and so is Saturday, until night comes, and we then get money from the working people. The markets, such as Cleveland-street, Fitzroy-square (Tottenham-court-road's no good at any time). Carnaby-market,

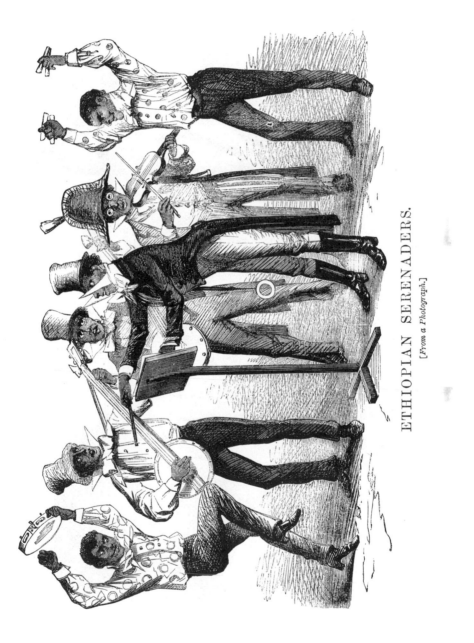

ETHIOPIAN SERENADERS.

[From a Photograph.]

PHOTOGRAPHIC SALOON, EAST END OF LONDON.

[*From a Sketch.*]

Newport-market, Great Marylebone-street, and the Edgeware-road, are good Saturday nights. Oxford-street is middling. The New-cut is as bad a place as can be. When we started, the songs we knew was 'Old Mr. Coon,' 'Buffalo Gals,' 'Going ober de Mountain,' 'Dandy Jim of Carolina,' 'Rowly Boly O,' and 'Old Johnny Booker.' We stuck to them a twelvemonth. The 'Buffalo Gals' was best liked. The 'bones'—we've real bones, rib-of-beef bones, but some have ebony bones, which sound better than rib-bones—they tell best in 'Going ober de Mountain,' for there's a symphony between every line. It's rather difficult to play the bones well; it requires hard practice, and it brings the skin off; and some men have tried it, but with so little success that they broke their bones and flung them away. The banjo is the hardest to learn of the lot. We have kept changing our songs all along; but some of the old ones are still sung. The other favourites are, or were, 'Lucy Neale,' 'O, Susannah,' 'Uncle Ned,' 'Stop dat Knocking,' 'Ginger Blue,' and 'Black-eyed Susannah.' Things are not so good as they were. We can average 1l. a-piece now in the week, but it's summer-time, and we can't make that in bad weather. Then there's so many of us. There's the Somer's-town 'mob' now in London; the King-street, the four St. Giles's mobs, the East-end (but they're white niggers), the two Westminster mobs, the Marylebone, and the Whitechapel. We interfere with one another's beats sometimes, for we have no arrangement with each other, only we don't pitch near the others when they're at work. The ten mobs now in London will have 50 men in them at least; and there's plenty of stragglers, who are not regular niggers: there's so many dodges now to pick up a living, sir. The Marylebone and Whitechapel lots play at nights in penny theatres. I have played in the Haymarket in 'the New Planet,' but there's no demand for us now at the theatres, except such as the Pavilion. There are all sorts of characters in the different schools, but I don't know any runaway gentleman, or any gentleman of any kind among us, not one; we're more of a poorer sort, if not to say a ragged sort, for some are without shoes or stockings. The 'niggers' that I know have been errand-boys, street-singers, turf-cutters, coalheavers, chandlers, paviours, mud-larks, tailors, shoemakers, tinmen, bricklayers' labourers, and people who have had no line in particular but their wits. I know of no connexion with pickpockets, and don't believe there is any, though pickpockets go round the mobs; but the police fling it in our teeth that we're connected with pickpockets. It's a great injury to us is such a notion. A good many of the niggers—both of us here likes a little drop—drink as hard as they can, and a good many of them live with women of the town. A few are married. Some niggers are Irish. There's Scotch niggers, too. I don't know a Welsh one, but one of the street nigger-singers *is* a real black—an African."

STATEMENT OF ANOTHER ETHIOPIAN SERENADER.

"It must be eight years ago," he commenced, "since the Ethiopian serenading come up—aye, it must be at least that time, because the twopenny boats was then running to London-bridge, and it was before the 'Cricket' was blown up. I know that, because we used to work the boats serenading. I used to wear a yellow waistcoat, in imitation of them at the St. James's Theatre.

"The first came out at St. James's Theatre, and they made a deal of money. There were five of them—Pell was bones, Harrington was concertina, I think, White was violin, Stanwood the banjo, and Germain the tambourine. I think that's how it was, but I can easy ascertain. After them sprang up the 'Lantum Serenaders' and the 'Ohio Serenaders,' the 'South Carolina Serenaders,' the 'Kentucky Minstrels,' and many other schools of them; but Pell's gang was at the top of the tree. Juba was along with Pell. Juba was a first class—a regular A 1—he was a regular black, and a splendid dancer in boots.

"As soon as I could get in to vamp the tunes on the banjo a little, I went at it, too. I wasn't long behind them, you may take your oath. We judged it would be a hit, and it was fine. We got more money at it then than we do at any game now. First of all we formed a school of three—two banjos and a tambourine, and after that we added a bones and a fiddle. We used to dress up just the same then as now. We'd black our faces, and get hold of a white hat, and put a black band round it, or have big straw hats and high collars up to the ears. We did uncommonly well. The boys would follow us for miles, and were as good as advertisements, for they'd shout, 'Here's the blacks!' as if they was trumpeting us. The first songs we came out with were 'Old Joe,' 'Dan Tucker,' and 'Going ober de Mountain,' and 'O come along, you sandy boys.' Our opening chorus was 'The Wild Racoon Track,' and we finished up with the 'Railway Overture,' and it was more like the railway than music, for it was all thumping and whistling, for nobody knowed how to play the banjo then.

"When I went out pitching first I could sing a good song; but it has ruined my voice now, for I used to sing at the top—tenor is the professional term.

"It wasn't everybody as could be a nigger then. We was thought angels then. It's got common now, but still I've no hesitation in saying that, keep steady and sober, and it works well to the present day. You can go and get a good average living now.

"We could then, after our 'mungare' and 'buvare' (that's what we call eat and drink, and I think it's broken Italian), carry home our

5s. or 6s. each, easy. We made long days, and did no night-work. Besides, we was always very indifferent at our business, indeed. I'd be blowed if I'd trust myself out singing as I did then: we should get murdered. It was a new thing, and people thought our blunders was intended. We used to use blacking then to do our faces—we got Messrs. Day and Martin to do our complexion then. Burnt cork and beer wasn't so popular then.

"I continued at the nigger business ever since. I and my mate have been out together, and we've gone out two, and three, or four, up to eleven in a school, and we've shared better when eleven than when we was two. The highest we've got in a day has been 1l. 6s. each, at the Portsmouth review, when Napier went out with the fleet, above two years ago. We walked down to Portsmouth a-purpose. We got 14s. 6d. each—and there was five of us—at the launch of the 'Albert.'

"The general dress of the nigger is a old white hat and a long-tailed coat; or sometimes, when we first come out, in white waistcoats and coats; or even in striped shirts and wigs, and no hats at all. It's all according to fancy and fashion, and what takes.

"When we go to a cheap concert-room, such as the Albion, Ratcliffe-highway, or the Ship and Camel, Bermondsey, our usual business is to open with a chorus, such as 'Happy are we,' though, perhaps, we haven't had a bit of grub all day, and been as wretched as possible; and then we do a song or two, and then 'crack a wid,' as we say, that is, tell an anecdote, such as this:—

"Three old niggers went to sea on a paving-stone. The first never had any legs, the next never had any arms, and the other was strip stark naked. So the one without any legs said, 'I see de bird; so the one without any arms took up a gun and shot it, and the one without any legs run after it, and the one that was strip stark naked put it in his pocket. Now, you tell me what pocket that was?'

"Then another says, 'In his wainscoat pocket.' Then I return, 'How can he if he was naked? Can you give the inflammation of that story? Do you give it up?' Then he says, 'No, won't give it up.' Then I say, 'Would you give it up if you had it.' Then he says, 'Yes!' and I reply, 'The inflammation of that is the biggest lie that ebber was told.'

"Sometimes we do conundrums between the songs. I ask, 'Can you tell me how to spell blind pig in two letters?' and then he, remembering the first story, answers, 'Yes, the biggest lie that ebber was told.' 'No, that's not it.' Then I continue, 'P, g; and if you leave the i out it must be a blind pig, Jim.'

"Then we go on with the concert, and sing perhaps, 'Going ober de Mountain' and 'Mary Blane,' and then I ask such conundrums as these:

"'Why is mahogany like flannel?' 'Because they are both used to manufacture into drawers;' and then we do this rhyme, 'Because mahogany makes drawers to put your clothes in, and flannel makes drawers to put your toes in.'

"Perhaps we do another conundrum, such as this:—' Supposing you nigger was dead, what would be the best time to bury you?' One says, 'I shan't suppose.' Another says, 'I don't know.' And then I say, 'Why, the latter end of the summer;' and one asks, 'Why, Jim?' 'Because it's the best time for black-berrying.' Then I cry out, 'Now, you niggers, go on with the consort;' and one of them will add, 'Now, Jim, we'll have that lemon-choly song of Dinah Clare, that poor girl that fell in the water-butt and got burnt to death.'

"Another of our dialogues is this one:— 'Did I ebber tell you about that lemoncholy occurrence, Mary Blane, the young girl that died last night in the house that was burned down this morning, and she's gone to live in a garret?' 'I shall call and see her.' 'You can't.' ''Cos why?' ''Cos she moved from where she lives now; she's gone to live where she used to come from.' 'Did you ever see her broder Bill?' 'No; he's dead.' 'What! broder Bill dead, too?' Yes; I seed him this morning, and axed him how he was.' 'Well, and what did he told you?' 'He told me he was wery well, thankye, and he was going to lib along with Dinah; and he'd only been married three weeks. So I asked him how many children he'd got. He said he'd only got one. So I said, 'Dere something very dark about that, and I don't think all goes right, if you was to have a son in three weeks.' So he said, 'Look you here, sir; if the world was made in six days, it's debblish hard if we can't make a son in three weeks.' 'Go on with the consort.'

"Another of our dialogues is this:— 'Did I ever tell you, Jim, about my going out a-riding?' 'Neber.' 'Well, then, I'll told you, I had two dollars in my pocket.' 'Had you?' 'And I thought I'd do it gentleman-tell-like.' 'Yes.' 'So I went to the libery dealer.' 'Who?' The libery dealer—the man that keeps the horses' stable.' 'Oh! golly! you mean the stable-man.' 'Yas. Well, I axed him if he could lend me a horse to ride on;' so he said, he'd only got one horse.' 'Wall?' 'And that was a grey mare. I thought that would do just as well. 'Of course.' 'And I axed him what that would cost me? and he said he should charge me two dollars for that—so I paid the two dollars.' 'Wall?' 'And he put me the spurs on my boots, and he put de bridle on the horse's back.' 'The bridle on the horse's back!—what did he do with the bit?' 'He neber had a bit at all; he put the stirrups in the mouth.' 'Now stop—you mean, he put the saddle on the back, and the bridle in the mouth.' 'I know it was something. Den they put me on the saddle, and my feet on the bridle.' 'You mean he put your foot in the stirrups.' 'So I went out very well.' 'So the mare begun for to gallop, so I caught hold of the turmel of the saddle.' 'The tummel!' 'Yes, Jim, the tummel.' 'No, no ; you means the pummel.' 'Wall, hab it the pummel—you knows—but, but, I know, I'm right. So I caught hold of the mane, and I got on berry well till I come to a hill, when the mare began to gollop hard down the hill, because she was shy.' 'What was she shy at?' 'She saw a new-found-out-land dog crossing the wood.' 'A new-found-out-land dog crossing the road!' 'Yes ; so I thought I'd try and stop her : so I stuck my knees into her side, and my spur into her, and by golly, she went too fast.' 'And did she now?' 'Till she falled down and broke her knees.' 'Poor thing!' 'Aye, and pitched poor nigger on his head ; so I got up and tought I'd take the debil of a mare back to the stable. So when I got back I told the libbery man about it.' 'Yas, the stable-man.' 'And he said I must pay 2*l*. 10*s*.' 'What for?' 'For re-pairing the mare ; so I said I wouldn't ; so he said he would take me before the court, and I said he might take me down the alley, if he liked ; so I thought I had better go and insult a man ob de law about it. So I went to the man ob the law's house and pulled at the servant, and out comed the bell.' 'No ; you means pulled the bell, and out comed the servant. Wall?' 'I said, Can you con-form me is de man ob de law at home?' so she told me he was out, but the man ob de law's wife was at home, so down she come. So I said I wanted to insult the man ob de law, and she said, Insult me ; I do just as well.' So she says, 'Plane yourself.' So I said, Well, den, supposing you was a gray mare, and I hired you for two dollars to ride you, and you was rader rusty, and went too fast for me, and I wanted to stop you, and I stuck my knees in your side, and my spur into you, and you falled down and broke your knees, how could I help it?' So she flung the door in my face and went in. So now go on with the consort.'

"Sometimes, when we are engaged for it, we go to concert-rooms and do the nigger-statues, which is the same as the tableaux vivants. We illustrate the adventures of Pompey, or the life of a negro slave. The first position is when he is in the sugar-brake, cutting the sugar cane. Then he is supposed to take it to be weighed, and not being weight, he is ordered to be flogged. My mate is then doing the orator and explaining the story. It's as nice a bit of business as ever was done, and goes out-and-out. You see, it's a new thing from the white ones. The next position is when he is being flogged, and then when he swears revenge upon the overseer, and after-wards when he murders the overseer. Then there's the flight of Pompey, and so on, and I conclude with a variety of sculptures

from the statues, such as the Archilles in Hyde-park, and so on. This is really good, and the finest bit of business out, and nobody does it but me ; indeed it says in the bill—if you saw it—'for which he stands un-rivalled.'

"We sometimes have a greenhorn wants to go out pitching with us—a 'mug,' we calls them ; and there's a chap of the name of 'Sparrow-back', as we called him, because he always wore a bob-tailed coat, and was a rare swell ; and he wished to go out with us, and we told him he must have his head shaved first, and Tom held him down while I shaved him, and I took every bit of hair off him. Then he underwent the operation of mugging him up with oil-colour paint, black, and not for-getting the lips, red. Ah, he carried the black marks on him for two months afterwards, and made a real washable nigger. We took him with us to Camberwell fair, and on the way he kept turning round and saying how strong he smelt of turps, and his face was stiff. Ah, he *was* a serenader! How we did scrub it into him with a stiff brush! When we washed at a horse-trough, coming home, he couldn't get a bit of the colour off. It all dried round his nose and eyes.

"When we are out pitching, the finest place for us is where there is anybody sick. If we can see some straw on the ground, or any tan, then we stays. We are sure to play up where the blinds are down. When we have struck up, we rattle away at the banjos, and down will come the servant, saying, 'You're to move on ; we don't want you.' Then I'll pretend not to understand what she says, and I'll say, 'Mary Blane did you ask for? O yes, cer-tainly, Miss ;' and off we'll go into full chorus. We don't move for less than a bob, for six-pence ain't enough for a man that's ill. We generally get our two shillings.

"Sometimes gents will come and engage us to go and serenade people, such as at wed-dings or anything of that sort. Occasionally young gents or students will get us to go to a house late in the morning, to rouse up some-body for a lark, and we have to beat away and chop at the strings till all the windows are thrown up. We had a sovereign given us for doing that.

"The Christmas time is very good for us, for we go out as waits, only we don't black, but only sing ; and that I believe—the singing, I mean—is, I believe, the original waits. With what we get for to play and to go away, and what we collect on boxing Monday, amounts to a tidy sum.

"There's very few schools of niggers going about London now. I don't think there are three schools pitching in the streets. There's the Westminster school—they have kettle-drums and music-stands, and never sings ; and there's the New Kent-road gang, or Houghton's mob, and that's the best singing and playing school out ; then a St. Giles's lot, but they are dicky—not worth much. The Spitalfields school is broke up. Of course there are other niggers going about, but to the best of my calculation there ain't more than 40 men scattered about.

"Houghton's gang make the tour of the watering-places every year. I've been to Brighton with them, and we did pretty well there in the fine season, making sure of 30s. a-week a man; and it's work that continues all the year round, for when it's fine weather we do pitching, and when it's wet we divide a school into parties of two, and go busking at the public-houses."

The following comic dialogue was composed by the "professional" who was kind enough to favour me with his statement:—

"We are finishing a song, and after the song we generally do a sympathy, as we calls it (a symphony, you know); and when I've finished, Jim, my mate, keeps on beating the tambourine, as if he couldn't leave off. Then I turn round to him and say, 'By golly, if you don't leave off, I'll broke you over de jaw.' He answers, 'Go on, dig a hole and bury yourself.' Then I say, 'Why don't you 'splain yourself properly.' Then he keeps on playing still, and I say, 'Can't you leave off, nigger?' and he replies, 'I'm trying to broke my trowsers.' Then he leaves off, and I say, 'What de debil do you do dat for?' and he says, 'Because I belong to de boulding (building) society.' Then I puts another question, and then begins this dialogue:—

"He says, 'I'm going to sustire from dis profession.' 'What shall you do den?' 'I'm going to be a boulder.' 'Go along! what shall you build?' 'I'm going to be a boulder of trousers.' 'By golly, you shall bould me a pair den.' 'Well, den, how would you like dem made? would you like dem with high-pointed collars, full bozomed, and nice wrist-bands?' 'What, de trowsems?' 'Made of lining nor calico?' 'What! lining or calico trowsems?' 'No! shirt!' 'Why, you neber said a word about shirt!' 'By golly, you did though.' 'Well, den, bould me a shirt.' 'Well, den, how would yer like it? will you like it with nice square toes, and bilingtary heels?' 'What! bilingtary heels shirts?' 'With a row of hobnails?' Then I turn round in a passion, and cry, 'By golly, I can't stand this! What! hobnails shirt?' 'No; I was talking about a pair of boots.' 'Now, you neber said a word about boots.' 'Oh yes, I did.' Then I get into a passion, and afterwards say, 'Well, bould me a pair of boots: now mind, you say a pair of boots.' 'Yes. Well, how would you like dem boulded? Newmarket cut, rolling collar, face of welwet?' Then I say, aside, 'What! rolling collar and faced with welwet boots?' and he continues, 'With pockets in de tail, and two row of gold buttons?' 'What! pockets in de tail, and two row of gold button boots? By golly, dat's a coat.' 'Yes; didn't

you say a coat?' 'Neber spoke a word about coat in all my life. Did I?' (that to the audience). 'Yes, ob course yer did.' Then I get into a passion again, but at last I say, 'Well, den, bould me a coat.' 'Well, how would yer like it? with a nice high crown?' Then I say, aside, 'What! a high-crowned coat?' 'With a nice cork body, patent Paris nap, and silk lining, with a return-up rim?' 'What! turn-up rim coat? Golly, dat's a hat!' 'Yas.' 'Neber spoked a work about a hat.' 'Oh, yer did now.' Then I get excited again; but at last say, 'Well, den, bould me a hat.' 'Well, den, how would you like it? Seben story high, with a nice green waterbutt behind, and de nice palings round the garden?' 'What! de palings round de garden of a hat?' 'No; I said de house.' 'By golly, you said hat!' 'No; I said de house.' 'By golly, you said hat!' Then we get into a terrific passion, and he gets up and hits my tambourine, and say, 'By golly, you said de house!' and I get up and hit him with the banjo on the head, and cry, 'By golly, you said a hat!' Then, in the height of my excitement, I turn to the people, and ask, 'Didn't he say a hat?' Of course they don't answer, and I conclude I must have made a mistake, so I reply, 'Well, den, bould me a house.' 'Well, den, how would you like it made? Of the best elm, with de inscription-plate on the lid, tree rows of nails, and handles at each side?' 'Well, by golly, dat's a coffin!' 'Yas, Jim.' 'What do yer tink I wants a coffin for?' 'Why, because you gets in such a passion, I thought you'd going to die.' Then I get sulky, and growl out, 'Well, den, go on wid de consort.'"

STREET GLEE-SINGERS.

An experienced street vocalist of the better kind, upon whose statements I satisfied myself that every reliance might be placed, described to me the present condition of his calling. He was accompanied by his wife.

"I have been in the profession of a vocalist," he said, "for twenty-five years. Before that I was a concert-singer. I was not brought up to the profession; I was a shipping agent, but I married a concert-singer, and then followed the profession. I was young, and a little stage-struck,"—("Rather," said his wife, smiling, "he was struck with those who were on the stage")—and so I abandoned the ship-agency. I have tried my fortune on the stage as a singer, and can't say but what I have succeeded. In fact, my wife and I have taken more than any two singers that have ever appeared in the humble way. We have been street vocalists for twenty-five years. We sing solos, duets, and glees, and only at night. When we started, the class of songs was very different to what it is now. We were styled 'the Royal Glee-singers.' 'Cherry ripe,' 'Meet me by moonlight,' 'Sweet home,' were popular then. Haynes Bailey's ballads were popular, and much of Bishop's music; as, indeed, it is still. Barnett's or Lee's music, however, is now more approved in the concert-rooms than Bishop's. Our plan was, and is, to inquire at gentlemen's houses if they wish to hear glee or solo singing, and to sing in the street or in the halls, as well as at parties. When we first commenced we have made 3*l.* and 3*l.* 10*s.* in a night this way; but that was on extraordinary occasions; and 3*l.* a-week might be the average earnings, take the year through. These earnings continued eight or ten years, and then fell off. Other amusements attracted attention. Now, my wife, my daughter, and I may make 25*s.* a-week by open-air singing. Concert-singing is extra, and the best payment is a crown per head a night for low-priced concerts. The inferior vocalists get 4*s.*, 3*s.*, 2*s.* 6*d.*, and some as low as 2*s.* Very many who sing at concerts have received a high musical education; but the profession is so overstocked, that excellent singers are compelled to take poor engagements." The better sort of cheap concert-singers, the man and wife both agreed in stating, were a well-conducted body of people, often struggling for a very poor maintenance, the women rarely being improper characters. " But now," said the husband, " John Bull's taste is inclined to the brutal and filthy. Some of the ' character songs,' such as ' Sam Hall,' ' Jack Sheppard,' and others, are so indelicate that a respectable man ought not to take his wife and daughters to see them. The men who sing character songs are the worst class of singers, both as regards character and skill; they are generally loose fellows; some are what is called ' fancy men,' persons supported wholly or partly by women of the town. I attempted once to give concerts without these low-character singings; but it did not succeed, for I was alone in the attempt. I believe there are not more than half-a-dozen street vocalists of the same class as ourselves. They are respectable persons; and certainly open-air singing, as we practise it, is more respectable than popular concert-singing as now carried on. No one would be allowed to sing such songs in the streets. The ' character' concerts are attended generally by mechanics and their families; there are more males than females among the audiences."

STREET BALLAD-SINGERS, OR CHAUNTERS.

THE street classes that are still undescribed are the lower class of street singers, the Street Artists, the Writers without Hands, and the Street Exhibition-keepers. I shall begin with the Street Singers.

Concerning the ordinary street ballad-singers, I received the following account from one of the class:—

" I am what may be termed a regular street ballad-singer—either sentimental or comic, sir, for I can take both branches. I have been, as near as I can guess, about five-and-twenty years at the business. My mother died when I was thirteen years old, and in consequence of a step-mother home became too hot to hold me, and I turned into the streets in consequence of the harsh treatment I met with. My father had given me no education, and all I know now I have picked up in the streets. Well, at thirteen years, I turned into the streets, houseless, friendless. My father was a picture-frame gilder. I was never taught any business by him—neither his own nor any other. I never received any benefit from him that I know. Well then, sir, there was I, a boy of thirteen, friendless, houseless, untaught, and without any means of getting a living— loose in the streets of London. At first I slept anywhere: sometimes I passed the night in the old Covent-garden-market; at others, in shutter-boxes; and at others, on door-steps near my father's house. I lived at this time upon the refuse that I picked up in the streets — cabbage-stumps out of the market, orange-peel, and the like. Well, sir, I was green then, and one of the Stamp-office spies got me to sell some of the *Poor Man's Guardians,* (an unstamped paper of that time), so that his fellow-spy might take me up. This he did, and I had a month at Coldbath-fields for the business. After I had been in prison, I got in a measure hardened to the frowns of the world, and didn't care what company I kept, or what I did for a living. I wouldn't have you to fancy, though, that I did anything dishonest. I mean, I wasn't particular as to what I turned my hand to for a living, or where I lodged. I went to live in Church-lane, St. Giles's, at a threepenny house; and having a tidy voice of my own, I was there taught to go out ballad-singing, and I have stuck to the business ever since. I was going on for fifteen when I first took to it. The first thing I did was to lead at glee-singing; I took the air, and two others, old hands, did the second and the bass. We used to sing the ' Red Cross Knight,' ' Hail, smiling Morn,' and harmonize ' The Wolf,' and other popular songs. Excepting when we needed money, we rarely went out till the evening. Then our pitches were in quiet streets or squares, where we saw, by the light at the windows, that some party was going on. Wedding-parties was very good, in general quite a harvest. Public-houses we did little at, and then it was always with the parlour company; the tap-room people have no taste for glee-singing. At times we took from 9*s.* to 10*s.* of an evening, the three of us. I am speaking of the business as it was about two or three-and-twenty years ago. Now, glee-singing is seldom practised in the streets of London: it is chiefly confined to the provinces, at present. In London, concerts are so cheap now-a-days, that no one will stop to listen to the street glee-singers; so most of the ' schools,' or sets, have gone to sing at the cheap concerts held at the public-houses. Many of the glee-singers have given up the business, and taken to the street Ethiopians instead. The street glee-singers had been some of them brought up to a trade, though some had not. Few were so unfortunate as me — to have none at all. The two that I was with had been a ladies' shoemaker and a paper-hanger. Others that I knew had been blacksmiths, carpenters, linendrapers' shopmen, bakers, French-polishers, pastrycooks, and such-like. They mostly left their business and took to glee-singing when they were young. The most that I knew were from nineteen to twenty-two years old; that had in general been a little rackety, and had got stage-struck or concert-struck at public-houses: they had got praised for their voices, and so their vanity led them to take to it for a living, when they got hard up. Twenty years ago there must have been at the east and west ends at least fourteen different sets, good and bad; and in each set there was, on an average, three singers: now I don't think there is one set at work in London streets. After I had been three years glee-singing in the streets, I took up with the ballad business, and found it more lucrative than the glee line. Sometimes I could take 5s. in the day, and not work heavily for it either; but at other times I couldn't take enough to pay my lodging. When any popular song came up, that was our harvest. 'Alice Gray,' 'The Sea,' 'Bridal Ring,' 'We met,' 'The Tartar Drum,' (in which I was well known,) 'The Banks of the Blue Moselle,' and such-like, not forgetting 'The Mistletoe Bough;' these were all great things to the ballad-singers. We looked at the bill of fare for the different concert-rooms, and then went round the neighbourhood where these songs were being sung, because the airs being well known, you see it eased the way for us. The very best sentimental song that ever I had in my life, and which lasted me off and on for two years, was Byron's 'Isle of Beauty.' I could get a meal quicker with that than with any other. 'The Mistletoe Bough' got me many a Christmas dinner. We always works at that time. It would puzzle any man, even the most exactest, to tell what they could make by ballad-singing in the street. Some nights it would be wet, and I should be hoarse, and then I'd take nothing. I should think that, take one week with another, my earnings were barely more than 10s. a-week: 12s. a-week on the average, I should think, would be the very outside. Street ballad-singers never go out in costume. It is generally supposed that some who appear without shoes and wretchedly clad are made up for the purpose of exciting charity; but this the regular street ballad-singer never does.

He is too independent to rank himself with the beggars. He earns his money, he fancies, and does not ask charity. Some of the ballad-singers may perhaps be called beggars, or rather pensioners — that is the term we give them; but these are of the worst de-scription of singers, and have money given to them neither for their singing nor songs, but in pity for their age and infirmities. Of these there are about six in London. Of the regular ballad-singers, sentimental and comic, there are not less than 250 in and about London. Occasionally the number is greatly increased by an influx from the country. I should say that throughout England, Wales, and Scotland, there is not less than 700 who live solely by ballad-singing, and selling ballads and song-books. In London the ballad-singers generally work in couples — especially the comic singers. The sentimental generally go alone; but there are very few in London who are merely sentimental ballad-singers — not more than a dozen at the very outside. The rest sing whatever comes up. The tunes are mostly picked up from the street bands, and sometimes from the cheap concerts, or from the gallery of the theatre, where the street ballad-singers very often go, for the express purpose of learning the airs. They are mostly utterly ignorant of music, and some of them get their money by the noise they make, by being paid to move on. There is a house in the Blackfriars'-road where the people has been ill for the last 16 years, and where the street ballad-singer always goes, because he is sure of getting 2d. there to move on. Some, too, make a point of beginning their songs outside of those houses where the straw is laid down in front; where the knockers are done up in an old glove the ballad-singer is sure to strike up. The comic songs that are popular in the street are never indecent, but are very often political. They are generally sung by two persons, one repeating the two first lines of the verse, and the other the two last. The street-ballads are printed and published chiefly in the Seven Dials. There are four ballad-publishers in that quarter, and three at the East-end. Many ballads are written expressly for the Seven-Dials press, especially the Newgate and the political ones, as well as those upon any topic of the day. There are five known authors for the Dials press, and they are all street ballad-singers. I am one of these myself. The little knowledge I have I picked up bit by bit, so that I hardly know how I have come by it. I certainly knew my letters before I left home, and I have got the rest off the dead walls and out of the ballads and papers I have been selling. I write most of the Newgate ballads now for the printers in the Dials, and, indeed, anything that turns up. I get a shilling for a 'copy of verses written by the wretched culprit the night previous to his execution.' I wrote Courvoisier's sorrowful lamentation. I called it, 'A Woice from the Gaol.' I wrote a pathetic ballad on the respite of Annette Meyers. I did the helegy, too, on Rush's execution. It was supposed, like the rest, to be written by the culprit himself, and was particular penitent. I didn't write that to order—I knew they would want a copy of verses from the culprit. The publisher read it over, and said, ' That's the thing for the street public.' I only got a shilling for Rush. Indeed, they are all the same price, no matter how popular they may be. I wrote the life of Manning in verse. Besides these, I have written the lament of Calcraft the hangman on the decline of his trade, and many political songs. But song and Newgate ballad-writing for the Dials is very poor work. I've got five times as much for writing a squib for a rag-shop as for a ballad that has taken me double the time."

THE WHISTLING MAN.

IT sometimes happens that a lad or a man, before being thrown for a living on the streets, has often sung a song to amuse his companions, or that he has been reckoned " a good whistler," so he resolves to start out and see if he cannot turn to pecuniary profits that which until now he had only regarded in the light of an amusement.

The young man from whom I elicited the annexed statement was one of this class. His appearance was rather ungainly, and when he walked across the room he moved in so slovenly a manner that one leg appeared to drag itself after the other with the greatest reluctance.

When telling me that he had never been guilty of stealing, nor imprisoned, all his life, he did so in such a manner, and with such a tone of voice, as left little doubt on my mind that he had been kept honest more by the fear of the gaol than by his own moral principle.

His face was long and thin, and his cheeks so hollowed by long whistling, that they appeared almost to have had a round piece of flesh scooped out of the centre of each of them. His large thick lips were generally kept half-an-inch apart, so that they gave the man a half-idiotic look; and when he rounded them for whistling, they reminded me somewhat of a lamb's kidney.

" I am a whistler—that is, I whistle merely with my lips, without the aid of anything besides. I have been at it about seven years. I am twenty next birthday. My father was, and is, a coach-painter. He is, I think, at the present time, working in Great Queen-street, Lincoln's-inn-fields. I had three sisters and one brother. I was the youngest but two. When I got to be about seven years old my mother died, and then I used to get into the streets and stop out all day playing with other boys, most of them older than myself; and they often persuaded me to ' hop the wag,' that is, play truant from school, and spend the money which my father gave me to take to the master. Sometimes they took me to Covent-garden or Farringdon Market, where they used to prig a lot of apples and pears, not with the idea of selling them, but to eat. They used to want me to do the same, but I never would nor never did, or else I dare say I should have been better off, for they say ' the biggest rogues get on best.' I was always afraid of being sent to prison, a place I was never in in all my life. At last I was persuaded by two young companions to stop out all night, so we all three went to Mrs. Reding's, Church-lane, and had a fourpenny lodging a-piece. My pals paid for me, because I'd got no money. I left them the next morning, but was afraid to go home; I had got nothing to eat, so I thought I'd see if I could get a few ha'pence by singing a song. I knew two or three, and began with the ' Mariner's Grave,' and then ' Lucy Neal.' I walked about all day, singing nearly the whole of the time, but didn't get a penny till about six o'clock. By nine o'clock I mustered 10d., and then I left off, and went to a lodging-house in Whitechapel, where I got something to eat, and paid my lodging for the night. It's a custom always to pay before-hand. The next morning I felt very down-hearted, and was half a mind to go home, but was afraid I should get a hiding. However, I at last plucked up my spirits, and went out again. I didn't get anything given me till about dinner-time, when a gentleman came up to me and asked me how so young a boy as me come to be in the streets? I told him I couldn't earn my living any other way. He asked my name, and where I lived. I gave him both a false name and address, for I was afraid lest he should go to my father. He said I had better go home with him, so he took me to his house in Grosvenor-square, which was a very fine un—for he was a very rich man, where he gave me plenty to eat, and made me wash myself, and put on a suit of his little boy's left-off clothes. I stayed here three months, being employed to clean knives and boots, and run of errands. He used to send me twice a-week to the Bank of England with a cheque, which he used to write upon and tear out of a book, and I used to bring back the money. They always tied it up safely for me in a bag, and I put it into my pocket. and never took my hand off it till I got safe back again. At the end of three months he called me one day, and told me he was going with his wife and family into the country, where, he was sorry to say, there'd be no room for me. He then gave me 3l., and told me to go and seek for my friends, and go and live with them if I could.

" I went home to my father, who was greatly pleased at seeing me again; and he asked what I had been doing all the time, and where I had got my clothes and money from. I told him all, and promised I would never run away again,—so he forgave me. However, for a long time he would not let me go out. At last, after a good deal of persuasion, he let me out to look after a place, and I soon got one at Mr. Cooper's, Surgeon, in Seven Dials, where I had 4s. a week. I used to be there from seven o'clock in the morning till nine at night, but I went home to my meals. After I'd been at my place four months, I by accident set fire to some naphtha, which I was stirring up in the back-yard, and it burnt off all my eyelashes, and so I 'got the sack.' When he paid me my wages,—as I was afraid to tell my father what had happened,—I started off to my old quarters in Whitechapel. I stopped there all day on Sunday, and the next three days I wandered about seeking work, but couldn't get none. I then give it up as a bad job, and picked up with a man named Jack Williams, who had no legs. He was an old sailor, who had got frost-bitten in the Arctic regions. I used to lead him about with a big painted board afore him. It was a picture of the place where he was froze in. We used to go all about Ratcliffe Highway, and sometimes work up as far as Notting Hill. On the average, we got from 8s. to 10s. a-day. My share was about a third. I was with him for fifteen months, till one night I said something to him when he was a-bed that didn't please him, and he got his knife out and stabbed my leg in two places,—here are the marks. I bled a good deal. The other lodgers didn't like to hit him for it, on account of his having no legs, but they kicked him out of the house, and would not let him back any more. They all wanted me to lock him up, but I wouldn't, as he was an old pal. Two or three silk handkerchiefs was tied round my leg, and the next day I was took to St. Thomas's Hospital, where I remained for about nine days. When I left the head-nurse gave me ten shillings on account of being so destitute—for I was without a ha'penny to call my own. As soon as I got out of the hospital I went down to Billingsgate, and bought some bread and pickled whelks at a stall, but when I pulled out my money to pay for 'em some costermongering chaps knocked me down, and robbed me of 5s. I was completely stunned by the blow. The police came up to see what was the matter, and took me to the station-house, where I stopped till the next morning, when the inspector made me tell where my father lived, and I was taken home to him. For about a month my father kept me under lock and key, and after I had been with him about three months more I 'stept it' again, and as I could always whistle very well, I thought I'd try it for a living; so I made a 'pitch' in New-street, Covent Garden, and began by whistling ' Will you love me then as now?' but there wasn't many in the world as loved me. I did very well though that day, for I got about 3s. 6d. or 4s., so I thought I'd practise it and stick to it. I worked all about town till I got well known. I used, sometimes, to go into public-houses and whistle upon a piece of 'bacco pipe, blowing into the bowl, and moving my fingers as if I was playing a

flute, and nobody could tell the difference if they had not seen me. Sometimes I used to be asked to stand outside hotels, taverns, and even club-houses, and give 'em a tune: I often had sixpences, shillings, and half-crowns thrown me. I only wish I had sich luck now, for the world's topsy-turvy, and I can't get hardly anything. I used then to earn 3s. or 4s. a-day, and now it don't amount to more than 1s. 6d.

" After I'd worked London pretty well, I sometimes would start off a few miles out to the towns and villages; but, generally, it wasn't much account. The country chaps like sich tunes as ' The Barley Stack,' or ' The Little House under the Hill.' I often used to whistle to them while they danced. They liked jigs mostly, and always paid me a penny a dance each.

" I recollect once when I was whistling before a gentleman's house down at Hounslow, he sent his servant and called me in. I was taken into a fine large room, full of looking-glasses, and time-pieces, and pictures. I was never in sich a room before, all my life. The gentleman was there with his family,—about six on 'em,— and he told me if I'd whistle, and learn his birds to sing, he'd give me a sovereign. He had three fine brass-wire cages, with a bird in each, slung all of a row from the ceiling. I set to work ' like a brick,' and the birds begun to sing directly, and I amused 'em very much. I stopped about an hour and a half, and let 'em have all sorts of tunes, and then he gave me a sovereign, and told me to call again when I come that way; but before I left he said the servants was to give me something to eat and drink, so I had dinner in the kitchen with the servants, and a jolly good dinner it was.

" From Hounslow I walked to Maidenhead, and took a lodging for the night at the Turk's Head. In the evening some countrymen come into the tap-room and kicked up a row with the missus because she couldn't lodge 'em. She run in to turn then away, when three of 'em pitched into her right and left; and if it hadn't been for me and another chap she'd have got killed. When they got her down I jumped upon the table and snatched up the only weapon I could find, a brass candlestick, and knocked one of 'em down senseless, and the other fellow got hold of a broomstick and give it 'em as hard as he could, till we beat 'em right out of the place. There happened to be some police outside, drilling, who came over and took three of them to the stocks, where they was locked in for twenty-four hours. The next day the magistrate sentenced 'em to three months' imprisonment each, and I started for London and never whistled a tune till I reached it, which was three days afterwards. I kept on at the old game, earning about 2s. 6d. a-day, till the militia was being called out, and then I joined them, for I thought it would be the best thing I could do. I was sworn in by Colonel Scrivens at Eton

Mews. We was taken into a stable, where there was three horses. Four of us laid hold of a book altogether; and then, after asking us if we had any complaints, or were lame, or any way unfit for service, or was married, or had any children; and when we had said No, he asked us if we was free, able, and willing to serve in her Majesty's militia, in either England, Ireland, Scotland, or Wales, for the term of five years, if so long her Majesty required our services; and when we said we was, we took the oath and kissed the book.

"The same day, which was the 11th of June, 1854, we was packed off from the Waterloo Station for Portsmouth. After being drilled for three weeks I was returned for duty, and went on guard. The first guard I mounted was at Detached Dock at Portsmouth—it's where the convicts are. I didn't do any whistling there, I can tell yer; I'd different sorts of work, for part of our duty was to bury the poor fellows that died after coming home invalided from the Crimea. The people through that used to call us the 'garrison undertakers.' I was there thirteen months, and never, the whole time, had more than two nights' bed a-week; and some part of the time the weather was very frosty, and we was often over our ankles in snow. I belonged to the 4th Middlesex, and no corps ever did so much duty, or went through so much hardships, as ours. From Portsmouth I was ordered, with my regiment, 950 strong, to Buttervant, county Cork, Ireland. When we reached the Irish Channel a storm arose, and we was all fastened under hatches, and not suffered to come upon deck for four days, by which time we reached the Cove of Cork: the Colonel's horse had to be thrown overboard, and they, more than once, had serious thoughts of throwing all the luggage into the sea as well. I was ten months in Ireland. I didn't do any whistling there; and then the regiment was ordered home again on account of the peace. But before we left we had a day's sport, consisting of greasy-pole climbing, jumping in sacks, racing after a pig with a greasy tail, and all them sort of things; and at night the officers had a grand ball. We landed at Portsmouth on a Monday morning at four o'clock, and marched through to the station, and reached Hounslow about four o'clock the same afternoon. A month after we were disembodied, and I came at once to London. I had about 1l. 5s. in my pocket, and I resolved in my own mind never to go whistling any more. I went to my father, but he refused to help me in any way. I tried for work, but couldn't get any, for the people said, they didn't like a militia man; so, after having spent all my money, I found that I must either starve or whistle, and so, you see, I'm once more on the streets.

"While I was in Ireland I absented myself from the barracks for twenty-one days, but fearing that a picket would get hold of me, I walked in one morning at six o'clock. I was instantly placed under arrest in the guard-room, where I remained four days, when I was taken before the Colonel, and to my great surprise I saw, sitting aside of him, the very gentleman who had given me the pound to whistle to his birds; his name was Colonel Bagot, as I found out afterwards, and he was deputy-magistrate for Middlesex. He asked me if I was not the chap as had been to his house; I told him I was, so he got me off with a good reprimand, and saved me being tried by a court-martial. When I first took to sleeping at lodging-houses they was very different to what they are now. I've seen as many as eighteen people in one cellar sleeping upon loose straw, covered with sheets or blankets, and as many as three in one bed; but now they won't take in any little boys like as I was, unless they are with their parents; and there's very few beds in a room, and never more than one in a bed. Married people have a place always parted off for themselves. The inspector comes in all times—often in the middle of the night—to see that the regulations ain't broken.

"I used, one time, to meet another man whistling, but like old Dick, who was the first at the profession, he's gone dead, and so I'm the only one at it now anywhere. It's very tiring work, and makes you precious hungry when you keep at it for two or three hours; and I only wish I could get something else to do, and you'd see how soon I'd drop it.

"The tunes that are liked best in the streets is sich as 'Ben Bolt' and 'Will you love me then as now?' but a year or two ago, nothin' went down like the 'Low-back Car.' I was always being asked for it. I soon gets hold of the new tunes that comes up. I don't think whistling hurts me, because I don't blow so hard as 'old Dick' used. A gentleman come up to me once in the street that was a doctor, and asked me whether I drunk much, and whether I drawed my breath in or blowed it out. I told him I couldn't get much to drink, and he said I ought at least to have three half-pints of beer a-day, or else I should go into a consumption; and when I said I mostly blowed out when I whistled, he said that was the best, because it didn't strain the lungs so much."

WHISTLING AND DANCING BOY.

At the present time there is only one English boy going about the streets of London dancing, and at the same time playing his own musical accompaniment on a tin whistle. There are two or three Italian boys who dance whilst they perform on either the flute or the hurdy-gurdy, but the lad who gave me the following statement assured me that he was the only Englishman who had made street whistling and dancing "his profession."

He was a red-headed lad, of that peculiar white complexion which accompanies hair of that colour. His forehead was covered with freckles, so thick, that they looked as if a quantity of cayenne pepper had been sprinkled over it; and when he frowned, his hair moved backwards and forwards like the twitching of a horse shaking off flies.

"I've put some ile on my hair, to make me look tidy," he said. The grease had turned his locks to a fiery crimson colour, and as he passed his hands through it, and tossed it backwards, it positively glittered with the fat upon it.

The lad soon grew communicative enough, and proceeded to show me a blue jacket which he had bought that morning for a shilling, and explained to me at the same time how artful he had been over the bargain, for the boy had asked eighteenpence.

I remarked that his shoes seemed in a bad state, for they were really as white as a baker's slippers from want of blacking, and the toe of one gaped like the opening to a tortoise-shell. He explained to me that he wore all his boots out dancing, doing the double shuffle.

"Now these 'ere shoes," he said, "cost me a shilling in Petticoat-lane not a week since, and looked as good as new then, and even now, with a little mending, they'll make a tidy pair of crab-shells again."

To give force to this remark, he lifted his leg up, but, despite his explanation, I could not see how the leather could possibly be repaired.

He went through his dances for me, at the same time accompanying himself on his penny whistle. He took his shoes off and did a hornpipe, thumping his feet upon the floor the while, like palms on a panel, so that I felt nervous lest there should be a pin in the carpet and he be lamed by it.

The boy seemed to have no notion of his age, for although he accounted for twenty-two years of existence, yet he insisted he was only seventeen "come two months." I was sorry to find, moreover, that he was in the habit of drinking, seldom going home after his night's work without being intoxicated; and, indeed, his thin body and pinched face bore evidence of his excess in this respect, though, but for his assertion that "he was never hungry, and food was no good to him," I should have imagined, at the first glance, that he was pining with want.

He seems to be among the more fortunate of those who earn their living in the streets, for although I questioned and cross-questioned him in every possible way, he still clung to his assertion that he made 2*l.* per week. His clothes, however, bore no evidence of his prosperity, for his outer garment was a washed-out linen blouse, such as glaziers wear, whilst his trousers were of coarse canvas, and as black on the thighs as the centre of a drum-head.

He brought with him a penny whistle to show me his musical talents, and, certainly, his execution of the tin instrument was rapid and certain.

The following is the statement he gave me :—

" WHISTLING BILLY.

That's my name, and I'm known all round about in the Borough as 'Whistling Billy,' though some, to be sure, calls me 'Whistling Bill,' but in general I'm 'Billy.' I'm not looking very respectable now, but you should see me when I'm going to the play; I looks so uncommon respectable, nobody knows me again. I shall go to the theatre next week, and I should just like you to see me. It's surprising.

"I ain't a very fat chap, am I? but I'm just meaty enough for my perfession, which is whistling and dancing in public-houses, where I gives 'em the hornpipe and the bandy jig, that's dancing with my toes turned in.

"My father was a barber. He only charged a penny for shaving, but he wouldn't cut your hair under twopence, and he used to do well—very well sometimes; I don't know whether he's alive now, for I ain't seen him these ten years, nor asked him for a halfpenny. Mother was alive when I left, and so was my two brothers. I don't know whether they're alive now. No, I don't want to go and see him, for I can get my own living. He used to keep a shop near Fitzroy-square.

"I was always fond of dancing, and I runned away from home for to follow it. I don't know my own age exactly: I was as tall then as I am now. I was twelve when I left home, and it must be ten years ago, but I ain't twenty-two: oh, dear no! Why, I ain't got no whiskers nor things. I drink such a lot of beer and stuff, that I can't grow no taller; gentlemen at the public-houses gives it me. Why, this morning I was near tipsy, dancing to some coalheavers, who gave me drink.

"I used, when I was at father's, to go to a ball, and that's where I learned to dance. It was a shilling ball in the New-road, where there was ladies, regular nice ones, beautifully dressed. They used to see me dancing, and say, when I growed up I should make a beautiful dancer; and so I do, for I'd dance against anybody, and play the whistle all the time. The ladies at these balls would give me money then for dancing before them. Ah! I'd get my entrance shilling back, and four or five into the bargain. I'd generally take it home to mother, after buying a little sweet-stuff, or such-like, and I think that's why mother would let me go, 'cos I picked up a good bit of money.

"It was another boy that put me up to running away from home. He axed me to go along with him, and I went. I dare say it troubled father a bit when he found I'd gone. I ain't troubled him for ten years now. If I was to go back to him, he'd only send me to work, and I make a better living by myself. I don't like work, and, to tell you the truth, I never did work, for it's like amusement to me to dance; and it must be an amusement, 'cos it amuses the people, and that's why I gets on so well.

"When I hooked it with that chap, we went to Croydon, in Surrey. We went to a lodging-house where there was men and women, and boys and chaps, and all like that; we all slept in one room. I had no money with me, only my clothes; there was a very nice velvet cap; and I looked very different then to what I do now. This young chap had some tin, and he kept me. I don't know how he earned his tin, for he'd only go out at night time, and then he'd come home and bring in money, and meat and bread, and such-like. He said to me, before I went pals with him, that he'd keep me, and that he'd make plenty of money. He told me he wanted a chum to mate with, so I went with him right off. I can't say what he was. He was about thirteen or fourteen, and I never seed him do no work. He might have been a prig for all I knows.

"After I'd been in the lodging-house, this chap bought a stock of combs and cheap jewels, and then we went out together, and he'd knock at the houses and offer the things for sale, and I'd stand by. There's a lot of gentlemen's houses, if you recollect, sir, round Croydon, on the London road. Sometimes the servants would give us grub instead of money. We had plenty to eat. Now you comes to speak of it, I do remember he used to bring back some old silver with him, such as old table-spoons or ladles, broke up into bits, and he'd make a deal selling them. I think he must have been a prig. At night we used to go to the public-houses and dance. He never danced, but sit down and looked on. He said he was my relation, and I always shared my drink with him, and the people would say, 'Feed me, feed my dog,' seeing me going halves with him.

"I kept along with him for three years, he working in the day, and I at night, dancing. We parted at Plymouth, and I took up with another mate, and worked on to Exeter. I think my new mate was a regular prig, for it was through his putting me up to prigging that I got into trouble there. This chap put me on to taking a brass cock from a foundry. It was in a big wooden butt, with 150 gallons of water in it. I got over a gate and pulled it out, and set all the foundry afloat. We cut away, but two hours afterwards the policeman come to the lodging-house, and though there was a lot of boys and girls, he picked me out, and I had two months for it, and all my hair was cut off, and I only had dry bread and gruel every day, and soup twice a-week. I was jolly sorry for that cock business when I was caught, and I made up my mind never to take nothing more. It's going to the lodging-

houses puts fellows up to prigging. The chaps brings in legs of beef, and puddens, and clothes, and then they sells 'em cheap. You can sometimes buy a pair of breeches, worth ten shillings, for two bob, for the chaps don't like to take 'em to sell at the shops, and would sooner sell 'em for a'most nothing rather than be found out.

"When I came out of quod I had a shilling give me, and I went and bought a penny whistle. I was always fond of music and dancing, and I know'd a little of playing the whistle. Mother and father was both uncom-mon fond of dancing and music, and used to go out dancing and to concerts, near every night pretty well, after they'd locked the shop up. I made about eleven bob the first week I was out, for I was doing very well of a night, though I had no hair on my head. I didn't do no dancing, but I knew about six tunes, such as 'Rory O'More,' and 'The Girl I left behind me,' two hornpipes, (the Fishers' and the Sailors') 'St. Patrick's Day,' and 'The Shells of the Ocean,' a new song as had just come up. I can play fifty tunes now. Whistles weren't so common then, they weren't out a quarter so much as now. Swinden had the making of them then, but he weren't the first maker of them. Clarke is the largest manufactory of them now, and he followed Swinden. People was asto-nished at seeing a tune played on a tin whistle, and gave pretty liberal. I believe I was the first as ever got a living on a tin whistle. Now there's more. It was at that time as I took to selling whistles. I carried 'em on a tin tray before me, and a lid used to shut on it, fixed. I'd pitch before a hotel amongst the gentlemen, and I'd get 2d. a-piece for the whistles, and some would give me sixpence or a shilling, just according. The young gents was them as bought most, and then they'd begin playing on them, and afterwards give them to the young ladies passing. They was very pleased with me, for I was so little, and I done well. The first two months I made about 17s. or 18s. a-week, but after that they got rather dull, so I gived up selling of them and took to dancing. It didn't pay me so well as the whistles, for it was pretty near all profit on them—they only cost me 3d. a-dozen. I tra-velled all round Devonshire, and down to Land's End, in Cornwall—320 miles from London, and kept on playing the whistle on the road. I knew all about them parts. I generally pitched before the hotels and the spirit-shops, and began whistling and dancing; but sometimes I'd give the cottagers a turn, and they'd generally hand over a ha'penny a-piece and some bread.

"I stopped travelling about the south of England, and playing and dancing, for a little better than four years and a half. I didn't do so well in winter as in summer. Harvest time was my best time. I'd go to the fields where they was working, and play and dance. Sometimes the master would hollar out, 'Here, you get cut of this!' but the men would speak up for me and say, 'Let him stop, master.' Many a chap's got the sack through me, by leaving off his work and beginning to dance. Sometimes, when the last load of hay was going home (you see, that's always considered the jolliest part of the work), they'd make me get up to the top of the load, and then whistle to them. They was all merry—as merry as could be, and would follow after dancing about, men, women, and boys. I generally played at the harvest suppers, and the farmer himself would give me 4s. 6d. or 5s. the night, besides my quart of ale. Then I'd pick up my 6s. or 7s. in ha'pence among the men. I've had as many as two harvest suppers a week for three weeks or a month following, for I used to ax the people round what time they was going to have a supper, and where, and set off, walking nine or ten miles to reach the farm, and after that we find another spot.

" It's very jolly among farm people. They give you plenty of cider and ale. I've drunk the cider hot, whilst they was brewing it—new cider, you know. You never want food neither, for there's more than you can eat, generally bread and cheese, or maybe a little cold biled pork. At night, the men and women used to sleep in a kind of barn, among the clean straw; and after the beer-shops had closed—they are all little beer-shops, 3d. a quart in your own jugs, and like that—they'd say to me, ' Come up to the doss and give us a tune,' and they'd come outside and dance in the open air, for they wouldn't let them have no candles nor matches. Then they'd make theirselves happy, and I'd play to 'em, and they'd club up and give me money, sometimes as much as 7s., but I've never had no higher than that, but never no less than 3s. One man used to take all the money for me, and I'd give him a pot o' ale in the morning. It was a penny a dance for each of 'em as danced, and each stand-up took a quarter of a hour, and there was generally two hours of it; that makes about seven dances, allowing for resting. I've had as many as forty dancing at a time, and sometimes there was only nine of 'em. I've seen all the men get up together and dance a hornpipe, and the women look on. They always did a hornpipe or a country dance. You see, some of 'em would sit down and drink during the dance, but it amounted to almost three dances each person, and generally there was about fifty present. Usually the men would pay for the women, but if they was hard up and been free with their money, the girls would pay for them. They was mostly Irish, and I had to do jigs for them, instead of a hornpipe. My country dance was to the tune ' Oh don't you tease me, pretty little dear.' Any fiddler knows that air. It's always played in the country for country dances. First they dances to each other, and then it's hands across, and then down the middle, and then it's back again and

turn. That's the country dance, sir. I used to be regular tired after two hours. They'd stick me up on a box, or a tub, or else they'd make a pile of straw, and stick me a-top of it; or if there was any carts standing by loaded with hay, and the horses out, I was told to mount that. There was very little drinking all this time, because the beer-shops was shut up. Perhaps there might be such a thing as a pint of beer between a man and his partner, which he'd brought in a can along with him. They only danced when it was moonlight. It never cost me nothing for lodgings all the harvest times, for they would make me stop in the barn along with them; and they was very good company, and took especial care of me. You mustn't think this dancing took place every night, but only three or four nights a-week. I find 'em out travelling along the road. Sometimes they've sent a man from one farm-house to bespeak me whilst I was playing at another. There was a man as played on the clarionet as used to be a favourite among haymakers, but they prefer the penny tin whistle, because it makes more noise, and is shriller, and is easier heard; besides, I'm very rapid with my fingers, and makes 'em keep on dancing till they are tired out. Please God, I'll be down among them again this summer. I goes down regular. Last year and the year before, and ever since I can recollect.

" When I'm in London I make a good living at dancing and playing, for I'm the only one that plays the whistle and dances at the same time. I'm reckoned the best hand at it of any man in town or country. I've often been backed by the company to dance and play against another man, and I generally win. I've been in hotels, and danced to gentlemen, and made plenty of money at it. I do all manner of tricks, just to make 'em laugh — capering, or ' hanky-panky,' as I term it. I once had half-a-sovereign given to me, but I think it was a mistake, for he says, ' Take that, and go on.' I went home to clean myself, and had my trousers washed, and my shoes blacked, and went half-price to the theatre—the ' Wic,' I think it was—and paid my shilling, and went in as tidy as a gentleman.

" When I first go into a public-house I go into the tap-room, and say, ' Would you like to hear a tune, gentlemen, or see a dance, or a little bit of amusement?' If they say ' No,' I stand still, and begin a talking, to make 'em laugh. I'm not to be choked off easy. I say, ' Come, gentlemen, can't you help a poor fellow as is the best dancer in England? I must have some pudden for breakfast, because I ain't had nothing for three weeks.' Then some say, ' Well, I will see the best dancer in England; I've got a mag.' Then after dancing I go to the gentleman who has given me most, and ask him six or seven times ' to give me a copper,' declaring he's the only one as has given me nothing, and that makes the others laugh. I also ask the landlord to give a half-pint of beer to grease my feet, and that makes 'em merry I generally gets good nobbings (that's a collection, you know). They likes the dancing better than music; but it's doing them together that takes. I ax them if they'll have the hornpipe or the Irish jig, and if they says the jig I do it with my toes turned in, like as if I was bandy; and that's very popular. I have been to as many as forty public-houses in a evening, and dance inside; or if they won't let me come in, they'll say, ' Dance outside as much as you like,' and that's very near as good for me. If I gets inside, I'll mop up 1s. if it's good company, or perhaps 3d. or 4d., and always plenty to drink—more than I can take, for I'm generally drunk before I can get home. They never gives me nothing to eat, but it don't matter, for I'm seldom hungry; but ' I like a drop of good beer,' as the song says.

" I've been engaged at concert-rooms to dance. I have pumps put on, and light trousers, and a Guernsey, dressed up as a sailor. That was in the country, at Canterbury, and I had 7s. and plenty to eat and drink. I've never appeared at a London concert-room, though I've been axed to come in and amuse the company; but I wasn't tidy enough, and didn't like.

" When I dance in a public-house I take my shoes off and say, ' Now, gentlemen, watch my steps.' For the hornpipe I begin with walking round, or ' twisting' as the term is; then I stands up, and does a double-shuffle—or the ' straight fives' as we calls it; then I walk round again before doing the back-snatches, another kind of double-shuffle. Then I does the rocks of Scilly, that's when you twists your feet and bends sideways; next comes the double steps and rattles, that is, when the heels makes a rattle coming down; and I finishes with the square step. My next step is to walk round and collect the money. The Irish like to see me do the jig better than the hornpipe. Them two are the only dances I know.

" I make regular 2l. a-week. Yesterday I made 7s. 3d., and it was rainy, so I couldn't get out till late. At Brighton Regatta I and my mate made 5l. 10s. between us, and at Dover Regatta we made 8l. between us. We squandered 2l. 10s. at the lodging-house in one night, betting and tossing, and playing at cards. We always follows up the regatta. We made only 2l. 10s. at Hastings Regatta. You see we pick up on a Saturday night our 11s. a-piece, and on other days perhaps 5s. or 8s., according to the day.

" I used to go about with a mate who had a wooden leg. He was a beautiful dancer, for he made 'em all laugh. He's a little chap, and only does the hornpipe, and he's uncommon active, and knocks his leg against the railings, and makes the people grin. He was very successful at Brighton, because he was pitied.

" I've also been about with a school of tumblers. I used to do the dancing between the posturing and likes of that. I've learnt tumbling, and I was cricked for the purpose, to teach me. I couldn't walk for three days. They put my legs round my neck, and then couldn't get 'em back again. I was in that state, regular doubled up, for two hours, and thought I was done for. Some of my mates said, ' There, you've been and spoiled that chap.' It's dreadful painful learning tumbling. When I was out with the posturers I used to play the drum and mouth-pipes; I had a old hat and coat on. Then when my turn come, I'd appear in my professional costume, and a young chap who was a fluter—not a whistler, like me,—would give a tune, and I'd go on the carpet and give the Irish jig or the hornpipe.

" There was four of us in the school, and we'd share a pound a-week each. We were down at Dover there, and put up at the Jolly Sailors. I left them there, and went alone on to the camp where the German Legion was—at Shorncliffe, that's the place. I stopped there for three weeks, and did very well, taking my 7s. or 8s. a-day.

" After that I got tired of dancing, and thought I'd like a change, so I went out on a fishing-boat. They didn't give me nothing a-week, only 4s. when we come home after two months, and your clothes, and victuals a-board. We first went fishing for plaice, and soles, and turbots, and we'd land them at Yarmouth, and they'd send them on to Lowestoft, and from there on to London. Then we went codding off the coast of Holland, for cod and haddock. It was just drawing on winter, and very cold. They set me with a line and I had to keep sawing it backwards and forwards till I felt a fish bite, then to hawl it up. One night I was a near froze, and suddenly I had two cods bite at once, and they nearly pulled me over, for they dart about like mad, and tug awful; so I said to the master, ' I don't like this work.' But he answers, ' You must like it the time you stops here.' So I made up my mind to bolt the first time I got to shore. I only did it as a change, to see if I liked it. You're right there, there ain't no drinking on board.

" When you hawl up a cod they bound about the deck, and they're as strong as a Scotch terrier dog. When we hold 'em down, we prick them under the fin, to let the wind out of them. It would choke them if we didn't let it out, for it hisses as it comes off. It's from dragging them up so quick out of fifteen-fathom water that gives 'em the wind. When they were pricked, we chucked them into the well in the hold, and let them swim about. We killed them when we got to Gravesend by hitting them on the head with tom-boys — the sticks we hauls the line through. After three or four blows they're stunned, and the blood comes, and they're killed.

"When I goes into the public-houses, part of my performance is to play the whistle up my nose. I don't do it in the streets, because if I did there'd be thousands looking at me, and then the police would make a row. Last night I did it. I only pitched at one place, and did my night's work right off. I took 4s. 3½d. and lots of beer in an hour, from the cabbies and the people and all. At last the police told me to move on. When I plays the whistle up my nose, I puts the end of it in my nostril, and blows down it. I can do that just as easy as with my mouth, only not as loud. I do it as a variety, first in my mouth, then in my nose, and then back again in my mouth. It makes the people laugh. I've got a cold now, so I can't do it so well as at times, but I'll let you see what it is like."

He then inserted the wooden tongue of the whistle into his nostril, and blowing down it, began a hornpipe, which, although not so shrill as when he played it with the mouth, was still loud enough to be heard all over the house.

IV.—STREET ARTISTS.

I now come to the Street Artists. These include the artists in coloured chalks on the pavements, the black profile - cutters, and others.

STREET PHOTOGRAPHY.

WITHIN the last few years photographic portraits have gradually been diminishing in price, until at the present time they have become a regular article of street commerce. Those living at the west-end of London have but little idea of the number of persons who gain a livelihood by street photography.

There may be one or two "galleries" in the New-road, or in Tottenham-court-road, but these supply mostly shilling portraits. In the eastern and southern districts of London, however, such as in Bermondsey, the New-cut, and the Whitechapel-road, one cannot walk fifty yards without passing some photographic establishment, where for sixpence persons can have their portrait taken, and framed and glazed as well.

It was in Bermondsey that I met with the first instance of what may be called pure street photography. Here a Mr. F——l was taking sixpenny portraits in a booth built up out of old canvas, and erected on a piece of spare ground in a furniture-broker's yard.

Mr. F——l had been a travelling showman, but finding that photography was attracting more attention than giants and dwarfs, he relinquished the wonders of Nature for those of Science.

Into this yard he had driven his yellow caravan, where it stood like an enormous Noah's ark, and in front of the caravan (by means of clothes-horses and posts, over which were spread out the large sail-like paintings (show-cloths), which were used at fairs to decorate the fronts of booths), he had erected his operating-room, which is about as long and as broad as a knife-house, and only just tall enough to allow a not particularly tall customer to stand up with his hat off: whilst by means of two window-sashes a glazed roof had been arranged for letting light into this little tent.

On the day of my visit Mr. F——l was, despite the cloudy state of the atmosphere, doing a large business. A crowd in front of his tent was admiring the photographic specimens, which, of all sizes and in all kinds of frames, were stuck up against the canvas-wall, as irregularly as if a bill-sticker had placed them there. Others were gazing up at the chalky-looking paintings over the door-way, and on which a lady was represented photographing an officer, in the full costume of the 11th Hussars.

Inside the operating room we found a crowd of women and children was assembled, all of them waiting their turn to be taken. Mr. F——l remarked, as I entered, that 'It was wonderful the sight of children that had been took;' and he added, 'when one girl comes for her portrait, there's a dozen comes along with her to see it took.'

The portraits I discovered were taken by Mrs. F——l, who, with the sleeves of her dress tucked up to the elbows, was engaged at the moment of my visit in pointing the camera at a lady and her little boy, who, from his wild nervous expression, seemed to have an idea that the operatress was taking her aim previous to shooting him. Mr. F——l explained to me the reason why his wife officiated. "You see," said he, "people prefers more to be took by a woman than by a man. Many's a time a lady tells us to send that man away, and let the missis come. It's quite natural," he continued; "for a lady don't mind taking her bonnet off and tucking up her hair, or sticking a pin in here and there before one of her own sect, which before a man proves objectionable."

After the portrait had been taken I found that the little square piece of glass on which it was impressed was scarcely larger than a visiting card, and this being handed over to a youth, was carried into the caravan at the back, where the process was completed. I was invited to follow the lad to the dwelling on wheels.

The outside of the caravan was very remarkable, and of that peculiar class of architecture which is a mixture of coach-and-ship building. In the centre of the front of the show were little folding-doors with miniature brass knockers, and glass let into the upper panels. On each side of the door were long windows, almost big enough for a shop-front, whilst the white curtains, festooned at their sides, gave them a pleasant appearance. The entire erection was coloured yellow, and the numerous little wooden joists and tie-beams, which framed and strengthened the vehicle, conferred upon it a singular plaid-like appearance.

I mounted the broad step-ladder and entered. The room reminded me of a ship's cabin, for it was panelled and had cross-beams to the arched roof, whilst the bolts and fastenings were of bright brass. If the windows had not been so large, or the roof so high, it would have resembled the fore-cabin of a Gravesend steamer. There were tables and chairs, as in an ordinary cottage room. At one end was the family bed, concealed during the day by chintz curtains, which hung down like a drop-scene before a miniature theatre; and between the openings of these curtains I could catch sight of some gaudily attired wax figures stowed away there for want of room, but standing there like a group of actors behind the scenes.

Along one of the beams a blunderbuss and a pistol rested on hooks, and the showman's speaking trumpet (as large as the funnel to a grocer's coffee-mill) hung against the wall, whilst in one corner was a kind of cabin stove of polished brass, before which a boy was drying some of the portraits that had been recently taken.

" So you've took him at last," said the proprietor, who accompanied us as he snatched the portrait from the boy's hand. " Well, the eyes ain't no great things, but as it's the third attempt it must do."

On inspecting the portrait I found it to be one of those drab-looking portraits with a light back-ground, where the figure rises from the bottom of the plate as straight as a post, and is in the cramped, nervous attitude of a patient in a dentist's chair.

After a time I left Mr. F——l's, and went to another establishment close by, which had originally formed part of a shop in the penny-ice-and-bull's-eye line—for the name-board over " Photographic Depôt" was still the property of the confectioner—so that the portraits displayed in the window were surmounted by an announcement of "Ginger beer 1*d*. and 2*d*."

A touter at the door was crying out " Hi! hi!—walk inside! walk inside! and have your c'rect likeness took, frame and glass complete, and only 6*d*.!— time of sitting only four seconds!"

A rough-looking, red-faced tanner, who had been staring at some coloured French lithographs which decorated the upper panes, and who, no doubt, imagined that they had been taken by the photographic process, entered, saying, " Let me have my likeness took."

The touter instantly called out, " Here, a shilling likeness for this here gent."

The tanner observed that he wanted only a sixpenny.

" Ah, very good, sir!" and raising his voice, the touter shouted louder than before — " A

sixpenny one first, and a shilling one afterwards."

" I tell yer I don't want only sixpennorth," angrily returned the customer, as he entered.

At this establishment the portraits were taken in a little alley adjoining the premises, where the light was so insufficient, that even the blanket hung up at the end of it looked black from the deep shadows cast by the walls.

When the tanner's portrait was completed it was nearly black; and, indeed, the only thing visible was a slight light on one side of the face, and which, doubtlessly, accounted for the short speech which the operator thought fit to make as he presented the likeness to his customer.

" There," he said, " there is your likeness, if you like! look at it yourself; and only eightpence"—" Only sixpence," observed the man.—"Ah! continued the proprietor, " but you've got a patent American preserver, and that's twopence more."

Then followed a discussion, in which the artist insisted that he lost by every sixpenny portrait he took, and the tanner as strongly protesting that he couldn't believe that, for they must get *some* profit any how. " You don't tumble to the rig," said the artist; " it's the half-guinea ones, you see, that pays us."

The touter, finding that this discussion was likely to continue, entered and joined the argument. " Why, it's cheap as dirt," he exclaimed indignantly; " the fact is, our governor's a friend of the people, and don't mind losing a little money. He's determined that everybody shall have a portrait, from the highest to the lowest. Indeed, next Sunday, he *do* talk of taking them for threepence-ha'penny, and if that ain't philandery, what is?"

After the touter's oration the tanner seemed somewhat contented, and paying his eightpence left the shop, looking at his picture in all lights, and repeatedly polishing it up with the cuff of his coat-sleeve, as if he were trying to brighten it into something like distinctness.

Whilst I was in this establishment a customer was induced to pay twopence for having the theory of photography explained to him. The lecture was to the effect, that the brass tube of the " camerer" was filled with clock-work, which carried the image from the lens to the ground glass at the back. To give what the lecturer called " hockeylar proof" of this, the camera was carried to the shop-door, and a boy who was passing by ordered to stand still for a minute.

" Now, then," continued the lecturer to the knowledge-seeker, " look behind here; there's the himage, you see;" and then addressing the boy, he added, " Just open your mouth, youngster;" and when the lad did so, the student was asked, " Are you looking down the young un's throat?" and on his nodding assent, he was informed, " Well, that's the way portraits is took."

Statement of a Photographic Man.

"I've been on and off at photographic-portrait taking since its commencement — that is to say, since they were taken cheap — two years this summer. I lodged in a room in Lambeth, and I used to take them in the back-yard — a kind of garden; I used to take a blanket off the bed, and used to tack it on a clothes-horse, and my mate used to hold it, if the wind was high, whilst I took the portrait.

"The reason why I took to photographing was, that I thought I should like it better than what I was at. I was out busking and drag-pitching with a banjo then. Busking is going into public-houses and playing, and singing, and dancing; and drag-pitching is going out in the day down the little courts — tidy places, little terraces, no thoroughfares, we call drags. I'm a very determined chap, and when I take a hidea into my head I always do it somehow or other. I didn't know anything about photographs then, not a mite, but I saved up my money; sometimes a 1s.; if I had a good day, 1s. 6d.; and my wife she went to work at day boot-binding, and at night dancing at a exhibition, or such-like (she's a tolerable good dancer — a penny exhibition or a parade dancer at fairs; that is, outside a show); sometimes she is Mademoiselle, or Madame, or what it may be. I got a loan of 3l. (and had to pay 4l. 3s. for it), and with what I'd saved, I managed to get together 5l. 5s., and I went to Gilbert Flemming's, in Oxford-street, and bought a complete apparatus for taking pictures; 6½ by 4¾, for 5l. 5s. Then I took it home, and opened the next day to take portraits for what we could get — 1s. and over. I never knew anything about taking portraits then, though they showed me when I bought the apparatus (but that was as good as nothing, for it takes months to learn). But I had cards ready printed to put in the window before I bought the apparatus. The very next day I had the camera, I had a customer before I had even tried it, so I tried it on him, and I gave him a black picture (for I didn't know how to make the portrait, and it was all black when I took the glass out), and told him that it would come out bright as it dried, and he went away quite delighted. I took the first Sunday after we had opened 1l. 5s. 6d., and everybody was quite pleased with their spotted and black pictures, for we still told them they would come out as they dried. But the next week they brought them back to be changed, and I could do them better, and they had middling pictures — for I picked it up very quick.

"I had one fellow for a half-guinea portrait, and he was from Woolwich, and I made him come three times, like a lamb, and he stood pipes and 'bacca, and it was a thundering bad one after all. He was delighted, and he swears now it's the best he ever had took, for it don't fade, but will stop black to the end of the world; though he remarks that I deceived him in one thing, for it don't come out bright.

"You see, when first photography come up I had my eye on it, for I could see it would turn me in something some time. I went and worked as a regular labourer, carrying pails and so on, so as to try and learn something about chemistry; for I always had a hankling after science. Me and Jim was out at Stratford, pitching with the banjo, and I saw some men coming out of a chemical works, and we went to 'nob' them (that's get some halfpence out of them). Jim was tambo beating, and we was both black, and they called us lazy beggars, and said we ought to work as they did. So we told them we couldn't get work, we had no characters. As we went home I and Jim got talking, and he says, 'What a fine thing if we could get into the berth, for you'd soon learn about them portraits if you get among the chemicals;' so I agreed to go and try for the situation, and told him that if I got the berth I'd 'nanti panka his nabs snide;' that means, I wouldn't turn him up, or act nasty to him, but would share money the same as if we were pitching again. That slang is mummers' slang, used by strolling professionals.

"I stopped there for near twelve months, on and off. I had 10s. at first, but I got up to 16s.; and if I'd stopped I've no doubt I should have been foreman of one of the departments, for I got at last to almost the management of the oxalic acid. They used to make sulphate of iron — ferri sulp is the word for it — and carbonate of iron, too, and I used to be like the red man of Agar then, all over red, and a'most thought of cutting that to go for a soldier, for I shouldn't have wanted a uniform. Then I got to charging the retorts to make carbonate of ammonia, and from that I went to oxalic acid.

"At night me and Jim used to go out with the banjo and tamborine, and we could manage to make up our shares to from 18s. to a guinea a-week each; that is, sharing my wages and all; for when we chum together we always panka each other bona (that is, share). We always made our ponta (that is, a pound) a-week, for we could average our duey bionk peroon a darkey,' or two shillings each, in the night.

"That's how I got an idea of chemicals, and when I went to photography many of the very things I used to manufacture was the very same as we used to take portraits, such as the hyposulphate of soda, and the nitrate of silver, and the sulphate of iron.

"One of the reasons why I couldn't take portraits was, that when I bought my camera at Flemming's he took a portrait of me with it to show me how to use it, and as it was a dull afternoon he took 90 seconds to produce the picture. So, you see, when I went to work

I thought I ought to let my pictures go the same time; and hang me if I didn't, whether the sun was shining or not. I let my plate stop 90 seconds, and of course they used to come out overdone and quite white, and as the evening grew darker they came better. When I got a good one I was surprised, and that picture went miles to be shown about. Then I formed an idea that I had made a miscalculation as to my time, and by referring to the sixpenny book of instructions I saw my mistake, and by the Sunday—that was five days after—I was very much improved, and by a month I could take a very tidy picture.

"I was getting on so well I got some of my portraits, when they was good ones, put in a chandler's shop; and to be sure I got first-rate specimens. I used to go to the different shilling portrait galleries and have a likeness of myself or friends done, to exhibit in my own window. That's the way I got my samples to begin with, and I believe it's done all over London.

"I kept at this all the winter, and all the time I suppose I earned 30s. a-week. When summer come again I took a place with a garden in the Old Kent-road, and there I done middling, but I lost the majority of my business by not opening on a Sunday, for it was a religious neighbourhood, and I could have earned my 5l. a-week comfortable, for as it was I cleared my 2l. regular. Then I had a regular tent built up out of clothes-horses. I stopped there till I had an offer of a good situation, and I accepted of it, at 2l. a-week.

" My new place was in Whitechapel, and we lowered the price from a shilling to sixpence. We did well there, that is the governor did, you know, for I've taken on the average from 60 to 100 a-day, varying in price from sixpence to half-a-guinea, and the majority was shilling ones. The greatest quantity I ever took was 146 in one day, and 124 was taken away as they was done. The governor used to take 20l. a-week, and of that 8l. clear profit, after paying me 2l. the men at the door 24s., a man and woman 29s., and rent 2l. My governor had, to my knowledge, 11 other shops, and I don't know all of his establishments; I managed my concern for him, and he never come near us sometimes for a month.

" I left on my own accord after four months, and I joined two others on equal shares, and opened a place of my own in Southwark. Unfortunately, I begun too late in the season, or I should have done well there; but at first we realised about 2l. a-week each, and up to last week we have shared our 25s. a-head.

" Sunday is the best day for shilling portraits; in fact, the majority is shilling ones, because then, you see, people have got their wages, and don't mind spending. Nobody knows about men's ways better than we do. Sunday and Monday is the Derby-day like, and then after that they are about cracked up and done. The largest amount I've taken at Southwark

on a Sunday is 80—over 4l. worth, but then in the week-days it's different; Sunday's 15s. we think that very tidy, some days only 3s. or 4s.

" You see we are obliged to resort to all sort of dodges to make sixpenny portraits pay. It's a very neat little picture our sixpenny ones is; with a little brass rim round them, and a neat metal inside, and a front glass; so how can that pay if you do the legitimate business? The glass will cost you 2d. a-dozen—this small size—and you give two with every picture; then the chemicals will cost quite a halfpenny, and varnish, and frame, and fittings, about 2d. We reckon 3d. out of each portrait. And then you see there's house-rent and a man at the door, and boy at the table, and the operator, all to pay their wages out of this 6d.; so you may guess where the profit is.

" One of our dodges is what we term ' An American Air-Preserver;' which is nothing more than a card,—old benefit tickets, or, if we are hard up, even brown paper, or any-think,—soap wrappings, just varnished on one side. Between our private residence and our shop, no piece of card or old paper escapes us. Supposing a party come in, and says ' I should like a portrait;' then I inquire which they'll have, a shilling or a sixpenny one. If they prefer a sixpenny one, I then make them one up, and I show them one of the air-preservers,—which we keep ready made up,—and I tell them that they are all chemicalized, and come from America, and that without them their picture will fade. I also tell them that I make nothing out of them, for that they are only 2d. and cost all the money; and that makes 'em buy one directly. They always bite at them; and we've actually had people come to us to have our preservers put upon other persons' portraits, saying they've been everywhere for them and can't get them. I charge 3d. if it's not one of our pictures. I'm the original inventor of the ' Patent American Air-Preserver.' We first called them the ' London Air-Preservers;' but they didn't go so well as since they've been the Americans.

" Another dodge is, I always take the portrait on a shilling size; and after they are done, I show them what they can have for a shilling,—the full size, with the knees; and table and a vase on it,—and let them understand that for sixpence they have all the back-ground and legs cut off; so as many take the shilling portraits as sixpenny ones.

" Talking of them preservers, it is astonishing how they go. We've actually had photographers themselves come to us to buy our ' American Air-Preservers.' We tells them it's a secret, and we manufacture them ourselves. People won't use their eyes. Why, I've actually cut up an old band-box afore the people's eyes, and varnished it and dried it on the hob before their eyes, and yet they still fancy they come from America! Why, we picks up the old paper from the shop-sweeping, and they make first-rate ' Patent American

Air-Preservers.' Actually, when we've been short, I've torn off a bit of old sugar-paper, and stuck it on without any varnish at all, and the party has gone away quite happy and contented. But you must remember it is really a useful thing, for it does do good and do preserve the picture.

"Another of our dodges,—and it is a splendid dodge, though it wants a nerve to do it,—is the brightening solution, which is nothing more than aqua distilled, or pure water. When we take a portrait, Jim, my mate, who stops in the room, hollows to me, 'Is it bona?' That is,—Is it good? If it is, I say, 'Say.' That is,—Yes. If not, I say 'Nanti.' If it is a good one he takes care to publicly expose that one, that all may see it, as a recommendation to others. If I say 'Nanti,' then Jim takes it and finishes it up, drying it and putting it up in its frame. Then he wraps it up in a large piece of paper, so that it will take sometime to unroll it, at the same time crying out 'Take sixpence from this lady, if you please.' Sometimes she says, 'O let me see it first;' but he always answers, 'Money first, if you please ma'am; pay for it first, and then you can do what you like with it. Here, take sixpence from this lady.' When she sees it, if it is a black one, she'll say, 'Why this ain't like me; there's no picture at all.' Then Jim says, 'It will become better as it dries, and come to your natural complexion.' If she still grumbles, he tells her that if she likes to have it passed through the brightening solution, it will come out lighter in an hour or two. They in general have it brightened; and then, before their face, we dip it into some water. We then dry it off and replace it in the frame, wrap it up carefully, and tell them not to expose it to the air, but put it in their bosom, and in an hour or two it will be all right. This is only done when the portrait come out black, as it doesn't pay to take two for sixpence. Sometimes they brings them back the next day, and says, 'It's not dried out as you told us;' and then we take another portrait, and charge them 3*d*. more.

"We also do what we call the 'bathing,'—another dodge. Now to-day a party came in during a shower of rain, when it was so dark it was impossible to take a portrait; or they will come in, sometimes, just as we are shutting up, and when the gas is lighted, to have their portraits taken; then we do this. We never turn business away, and yet it's impossible to take a portrait; so we ask them to sit down, and then we go through the whole process of taking a portrait, only we don't put any plate in the camera. We always make 'em sit a long time, to make 'em think it's all right,—I've had them for two-and-a-half minutes, till their eyes run down with water. We then tell them that we've taken the portrait, but that we shall have to keep it all night in the chemical bath

to bring it out, because the weather's so bad. We always take the money as a deposit, and give them a written paper as an order for the picture. If in the morning they come themselves we get them to sit again, and then we do really take a portrait of them; but if they send anybody, we either say that the bath was too strong and eat the picture out, or that it was too weak and didn't bring it out; or else I blow up Jim, and pretend he has upset the bath and broke the picture. We have had as many as ten pictures to bathe in one afternoon.

"If the eyes in a portrait are not seen, and they complain, we take a pin and dot them; and that brings the eye out, and they like it. If the hair, too, is not visible we takes the pin again, and soon puts in a beautiful head of hair. It requires a deal of nerve to do it; but if they still grumble I say, 'It's a beautiful picture, and worth half-a-crown, at the least;' and in the end they generally go off contented and happy.

"When we are not busy, we always fill up the time taking specimens for the window. Anybody who' sit we take him; or we do one another, and the young woman in the shop who colours. Specimens are very useful things to us, for this reason,—if anybody comes in a hurry, and won't give us time to do the picture, then, as we can't afford to let her go, we sit her and goes through all the business, and I says to Jim, 'Get one from the window,' and then he takes the first specimen that comes to hand. Then we fold it up in paper, and don't allow her to see it until she pays for it, and tell her not to expose it to the air for three days, and that if then she doesn't approve of it and will call again we will take her another. Of course they in general comes back. We have made some queer mistakes doing this. One day a young lady came in, and wouldn't wait, so Jim takes a specimen from the window, and, as luck would have it, it was the portrait of a widow in her cap. She insisted upon opening, and then she said, 'This isn't me; it's got a widow's cap, and I was never married in all my life!' Jim answers, 'Oh, miss! why it's a beautiful picture, and a correct likeness,'—and so it was, and no lies, but it wasn't of her.—Jim talked to her, and says he, 'Why this ain't a cap, it's the shadow of the hair,—for she had ringlets,—and she positively took it away believing that such was the case; and even promised to send us customers, which she did.

"There was another lady that came in a hurry, and would stop if we were not more than a minute; so Jim ups with a specimen, without looking at it, and it was the picture of a woman and her child. We went through the business of focussing the camera, and then gave her the portrait and took the 6*d*. When she saw it she cries out, 'Bless me! there's a child: I haven't ne'er a child!' Jim looked at her, and then at the picture, as if comparing, and says he, 'It is certainly a wonderful likeness, miss, and one of the best we ever took. It's the way you sat; and what has occasioned it was a child passing through the yard.' She said she supposed it must be so, and took the portrait away highly delighted.

"Once a sailor came in, and as he was in haste, I shoved on to him the picture of a carpenter, who was to call in the afternoon for his portrait. The jacket was dark, but there was a white waistcoat; still I persuaded him that it was his blue Guernsey which had come up very light, and he was so pleased that he gave us 9d. instead of 6d. The fact is, people don't know their own faces. Half of 'em have never looked in a glass half a dozen times in their life, and directly they see a pair of eyes and a nose, they fancy they are their own.

"The only time we were done was with an old woman. We had only one specimen left, and that was a sailor man, very dark—one of our black pictures. But she put on her spectacles, and she looked at it up and down, and says, 'Eh?' I said, 'Did you speak, ma'am?' and she cries, 'Why, this is a man! here's the whiskers.' I left, and Jim tried to humbug her, for I was bursting with laughing. Jim said, 'It's you ma'am; and a very excellent likeness, I assure you.' But she kept on saying, 'Nonsense, I ain't a man,' and wouldn't have it. Jim wanted her to leave a deposit, and come next day, but she never called. It was a little too strong.

"There was an old woman come in once and wanted to be taken with a favourite hen in her lap. It was a very bad picture, and so black there was nothing but the outline of her face and a white speck for the beak of the bird. When she saw it, she asked where the bird was? So Jim took a pin and scratched in an eye, and said, 'There it is, ma'am—that's her eye, it's coming out,' and then he made a line for the comb on the head, and she kept saying, 'Wonderful!' and was quite delighted.

"The only bad money we have taken was from a Methodist clergyman, who came in for a 1s. 6d. portrait. He gave us a bad sixpence.

"For colouring we charge 3d. more. If the portraits are bad or dark we tell them, that if they have them coloured the likeness will be perfect. We flesh the face, scratch the eye in, and blue the coat and colour the tablecloth. Sometimes the girl who does it puts in such a lot of flesh paint, that you can scarcely distinguish a feature of the person. If they grumble, we tell them it will be all right when the picture's dry. If it's a good picture, the colour looks very nice, but in the black ones we are obliged to stick it on at a tremendous rate, to make it show.

"Jim stands at the door, and he keeps on saying, 'A correct portrait, framed and glazed, for sixpence, beautifully enamelled.' Then, when they are listening, he shows the specimen in his hands, and adds, 'If not approved of, no charge made.'

"One morning, when we had been doing 'quisby,' that is, stopping idle, we hit upon another dodge. Some friends dropped in to see me, and as I left to accompany them to a tavern close by, I cried to Jim, 'Take that public-house opposite.' He brought the camera and stand to the door, and a mob soon collected. He kept saying, 'Stand back, gentlemen, stand back! I am about to take the public-house in front by this wonderful process.' Then he went over to the house, and asked the landlord, and asked some gentlemen drinking there to step into the road whilst he took the house with them facing it. Then he went to a policeman and asked him to stop the carts from passing, and he actually did. By this way he got up a tremendous mob. He then put in the slide, pulled off the cap of the camera, and focussed the house, and pretended to take the picture, though he had no prepared glass, nor nothing. When he had done, he called out, 'Portraits taken in one minute. We are now taking portraits for 6d. only. Time of sitting, two seconds only. Step inside and have your'n taken immediately.' There was a regular rush, and I had to be fetched, and we took 6s. worth right off.

"People seem to think the camera will do anything. We actually persuade them that it will mesmerise them. After their portrait is taken, we ask them if they would like to be mesmerised by the camera, and the charge is only 2d. We then focus the camera, and tell them to look firm at the tube; and they stop there for two or three minutes staring, till their eyes begin to water, and then they complain of a dizziness in the head, and give it up, saying they 'can't stand it.' I always tell them the operation was beginning, and they were just going off, only they didn't stay long enough. They always remark, 'Well, it certainly is a wonderful machine, and a most curious invention.' Once a coalheaver came in to be mesmerised, but he got into a rage after five or six minutes, and said, 'Strike me dead, ain't you keeping me a while!' He wouldn't stop still, so Jim told him his sensitive nerves was too powerful, and sent him off cursing and swearing because he couldn't be mesmerised. We don't have many of these mesmerism customers, not more than four in these five months; but it's a curious circumstance, proving what fools people is. Jim says he only introduces these games when business is dull, to keep my spirits up—and they certainly are most laughable.

"I also profess to remove warts, which I do by touching them with nitric acid. My price is a penny a wart, or a shilling for the job; for some of the hands is pretty well smothered with them. You see, we never turn money away, for it's hard work to make a living at sixpenny portraits. My wart patients seldom come twice, for they screams out ten thousand blue murders when the acid bites them.

" Another of my callings is to dye the hair. You see I have a good many refuse baths, which is mostly nitrate of silver, the same as all hair-dyes is composed of. I dyes the whiskers and moustache for 1s. The worst of it is, that nitrate of silver also blacks the skin wherever it touches. One fellow with carroty hair came in one day to have his whiskers died, and I went clumsily to work and let the stuff trickle down his chin and on his cheeks, as well as making the flesh at the roots as black as a hat. He came the next day to have it taken off, and I made him pay 3d. more, and then removed it with cyanide, which certainly did clean him, but made him smart awfully.

" I have been told that there are near upon 250 houses in London now getting a livelihood taking sixpenny portraits. There's ninety of 'em I'm personally acquainted with, and one man I know has ten different shops of his own. There's eight in the Whitechapel-rcad alone, from Butcher-row to the Mile-end turnpike. Bless you, yes! they all make a good living at it. Why, I could go to-morrow, and they would be glad to employ me at 2l. a-week—indeed they have told me so.

" If we had begun earlier this summer, we could, only with our little affair, have made from 8l. to 10l. a-week, and about one-third of that is expenses. You see, I operate myself, and that cuts out 2l. a-week."

The Penny Profile-Cutter.

The young man from whom the annexed statement was gathered, is one of a class of street-artists now fast disappearing from view, but which some six or seven years ago occupied a very prominent position.

At the period to which I allude, the steamboat excursionist, or visitor to the pit of a London theatre, whom Nature had favoured with very prominent features, oftentimes found displayed to public view, most unexpectedly, a tolerably correct profile of himself in black paper, mounted upon a white card. As soon as attention was attracted, the exhibitor generally stepped forward, offering, in a respectful manner, to " cut out any lady's or gentleman's likeness for the small sum of one penny;" an offer which, judging from the account below given as to the artist's takings, seems to have been rather favourably responded to.

The appearance presented by the profile-cutter from whom I derived my information bordered on the " respectable." He was a tall thin man, with a narrow face and long features. His eyes were large and animated. He was dressed in black, and the absence of shirt collar round his bare neck gave him a dingy appearance. He spoke as follows:—

" I'm a penny profile-cutter, or, as we in the profession call ourselves, a profilist. I commenced cutting profiles when I was 14 years of age, always acquiring a taste for cutting out ornaments, &c. My father's a very respectable man, and been in one situation 27 years. I left school against his wish when I was 10 years old, for I didn't like school much, though, mind you, I'm a good scholar. I can't write much, but I can read anything. After leaving school, I went arrand-boy to a printer, and was there nine months. I had 4s. 6d. per week. Then I went to a lithographic printer's, to turn a double-action press, but the work was too hard for a boy, and so I left it. I stopt there about nine weeks, and then I was out of work some time, and was living on my parents. I next went to work at a under-priced hatter's, termed a 'knobstick's,' but I was disgusted with the price paid for labour. I was a bodymaker. I learned my first task in four hours, and could do it as well as those who'd been at it for months. I earn'd good money, but I didn't like it, for it was boys keeping men out of employment who'd served their seven years to the trade. I left the hatter's after I'd been there two seasons, and then I was out of work for some months. One day I went to a fair at the Tenter-ground, Whitechapel. While I was walking about the fair, I see a young man I knew standing as 'doorsman' at a profile-cutter's, and he told me that another profile-cutter in the fair wanted an assistant, and thought I should do for it. He know'd I was handy at drawing, because he was at the hatter's along with me, and I used to chalk the men's likenesses on the shop door. So I went to this man and engaged. I had to talk at the door, or 'tout,' as we call it, and put or mount the likenesses on cards. I was rather backward at touting at first, but I got over that in the course of the day, and could patter like anything before the day was over. I had to shout out, 'Step inside, ladies and gentlemen, and have a correct likeness taken for one penny.' We did a very good business the two days of the fair that I attended, for I was not there till the second day. We took about 4l., but not all for penny likenesses, because, if we put the likeness on card we charged 2d., and if they was bronzed we charged 6d., and if they were framed complete, 1s. My pay was 4s. per day, and I was found in my keep.

" When the Tenter-ground fair was over, the profilist asked me if I'd travel with him, and I agreed upon stated terms. I was to have 4s. for working days, and 1s. and keep, and lodgings &c. for off-days. So we started next day for Luton ' Statties,' or Statues as it should be called. Luton is 32 miles from London, and this we walked, carrying with us the booth and every requisite for business the whole of the distance. I had not got my father's leave; I didn't ask for it, because I knew he'd object. We started for Luton at 12 o'clock in the day, and got there by 10 o'clock at night, and our load was not a very light un, for I'm sure the pair of us couldn't have had less than 3 cwt. to carry. I was so beat that I dropt down about a mile before we got to the town, but a stranger came up and offered to carry my load for me the rest of the journey. I went to sleep on the bank, though it was so late at night. While I was sleeping the horse-patrol came along and woke me up. He told me I'd better get on, as I'd only a mile to go. I got up and proceeded on, and turning the corner of the road, I distinctly saw the lights of Luton, which enlivened me very much. I reached the town about a half-an-hour after my mate. We had a very good fair. Fossett was there with his performing birds and mice, and a nice concern it was; but since then he's got a fust-rate circus. He travels the country still, and his concern is worthy a visit from any body. There was Frederick's theatrical booth there, and a good many others of the same sort.

" We did very well, having no opposition, for we cut out a great many likenesses, and most of them twopenny ones. It's a great place for the straw-plaiters, but there's about seven women to one man. There was plenty of agricultural men and women there as well, and most of the John and Molls had their profiles cut. If a ploughman had his cut, he mostly gave it to his sweetheart, and if his girl had hers cut out, she returned the compliment.

" From Luton we went to Stourbitch fair, Cambridge, and there we had very bad luck, for we had to build out of the fair, alongside of another likeness-booth, and it was raining all the while. We cut out very few likenesses, for we didn't take above a half a sovereign the whole three days.

" After leaving Stourbitch, we took the road for Peterborough-bridge fair. Being a cross-country road, there was no conveyance, and not liking the job of carrying our traps, we got a man who had a donkey and barrow to put our things aside of his own, and we agreed to pay him 4s. for the job. After we'd got about ten miles on the road, the donkey stopt short, and wouldn't move a peg. We didn't know what to do for the best. At last one of our party pulled off his hat and rattled a stick in it. The donkey pricked up his ears with fright, and darted off like one o'clock. After a bit he stopt again, and then we had to repeat the dose, and so we managed at last to get to Peterborough. We had out-and-out luck at this fair, for we cut out a great many likenesses, and a rare lot of 'em were bronzed. We took in the three days about 6l. This is supposed to be a great fair, and it's supported principally by respectable people. Some of the people that came for profiles were quite gentlefolks, and they brought their families with them; they're the people we like, because they believe we can cut a likeness, and stand still while we're doing it. But the lower orders are no good to anybody, for when they enter the booth they get larking, and make derisions, and won't stand still; and when that's the case. we don't take any trouble, but

cut out anything, and say it's like 'em, and then they often say, ' Ah, it's as much like me as it's like him.' But we always manage to get the money. There was a good many dashing young shop chaps came and had their portraits taken. They dress very fine, because they've got no other way to spend their money, for there's no theatre or concert-rooms in the place.

" We went, after leaving Peterborough, to two or three other fairs. At last we got to a fair in Huntingdonshire, and there I quarrelled with my mate, because he caught me practising with his scissors; so I went into a stall next to where we stood and bought a penny pair; but the pair I picked out was a sixpenny pair by rights, for they had fell off a sixpenny card by accident. I practised with them, whenever I got a chance. We got on pretty well, too, at this fair. We took about 3l. in the three days. When we got to our lodgings—the first night was at a public house—I got practising again, and my mate snatched my scissors out of my hand, and never gave them to me any more till we got on to the road for another fair. When he gave them to me I asked what he took 'em away for, and he said I'd no business to practise in a public-house ; and I told him I should do as I liked, and that I could cut as good a likeness as him, and I said, ' Give me my money and I'll go,'—for he'd only paid me a few shillings all the time I'd been with him—but he wouldn't pay me, and so we worked two or three more fairs together. One day, going along the road, we stopped at a public-house to get some dinner. There was a little boy playing with a ship. ' Now,' says I, ' I'll show you I can cut a better likeness than you, or, at all events, a more saleable one.' I took my scissors up for the first time in public, and cut out the little boy full length, with the ship in his hand and a little toy horse by his side, but could not bronze it, because I'd not practised the brush. I pencilled the little landscape scene behind, and when I showed it to my mate he was surprised, but he found many faults which he himself could not improve upon. I sold the likeness to the boy's mother for a shilling, before his face, and of course he was nettled. After dinner we started off again, making for Bedford fair; we'd sent our things on by the rail, and we soon begun talking about my cutting out. He wondered how I'd acquired it, and when I told him I'd practised hours unbeknown to him, he agreed that I should be a regular partner—pay half the expenses, and have half of the profits, and begin the next fair. When we got there the fair was very dull, and business very bad ; we only took 11s. ; he cut out all the busts, and I did all the full-lengths. He was very bad at full-lengths, because he'd got no idea of proportion, but I could always get my proportions right. I could always draw when I was a boy, and cut out figures for night-shades. Many a time, when I was only eight years old, I've amused a whole room full of people with 'Cobbler Jobson' and 'The Bridge is broken.'

"As things were so bad at Bedford, we agreed to come up to London, and not stop the other two days of the fair. When I came down stairs in the morning at 9 o'clock, I found my mate had bolted by the five-o'clock train, and left me in the lurch. He'd paid the reckoning, but he hadn't left me a shilling of the money that he owed me. I had very little money in my pocket, because he'd been cash-taker, and so I had to tramp the whole fifty miles to London. When I reached London, I found out where he lived, and succeeded in getting my money within a few shillings. The next thing I did was to join another man in opening a shop in London, in the profile line—he found capital and I found talent, and very well we did. Most of our customers were working people, and often they'd come and have two or three likenesses, to send to their friends who'd emigrated, because they'd go easy in a letter. There was one old gentleman that I had come to me regularly every morning, for nearly three months, and had three penny likenesses cut out, for which he would always pay sixpence. He had an excellent profile, and was easy to cut out; he was one of those club-nosed old men, with a deep brow and double chin. One morning he brought all of them back that I had taken, and asked us what we'd give for the lot. I told him they were no use to me, for if I had them for specimens, people would say that I could cut only one sort of face, because they were all alike. After chaffing for about half an hour, he said he had brought them all back to have shirt collars cut, and to have them put on cards. We put them all on cards and he paid us a penny for each one, and when he took 'em away he said he was going to distribute them among his friends. One day a gentleman rode up and asked us how much we'd charge to cut him out, horse and all. I told him we hadn't any paper large enough just then, but if he'd call another day we'd do it for 3s. 6d. He agreed to give it, and call the following morning. I knew I couldn't cut out a horse perfect, so I bought a picture of a race-horse for 6d., and cut it out in black profile paper, and when he came the next day as he sat on his horse outside, so I cut his likeness, and when I'd finished it I called him in, and he declared that it was the best likeness, both of him and his horse, too, that he'd ever seen; and it appears he had his horse painted in oil. When he paid us, instead of giving us 3s. 6d. as he'd agreed, he gave us 5s. After being at this shop for five months, trade got so bad we had to leave. The first month we took on the average 16s. a-day, but it gradually decreased till at last we didn't take more than about 2s. a-day. It was winter, to be sure. Before we left this shop we got another to go into, a mile or two off; but this turned out quite a failure,

and we only kept on a month, for we never got higher than three or four shillings a-day, and the rent alone was 8s. per week. The next shop we took was in a low neighbourhood, and we got a comfortable living in it. I always did the cutting out, and my partner the touting. We stopped in this place nine weeks, and then things begun to get slack here, so we thought we'd try the suburbs, such as Highgate, Clapham, and Kensington, places three or four miles out. We used to hang specimens outside the public-houses where we took our lodgings, and engage a room to cut in. In this way we managed to get the winter over very comfortable, but my partner was taken ill just as we'd knocked off, and had to go in the hospital, and so I now thought I'd try what is termed 'busking;' that is, going into public-houses and cutting likenesses of the company. I often met with rough customers; they used to despise the ingenuity of the art, and say, 'Why don't you go to work? I've got a chap that ain't so big as you, and he goes to work;' and things of that kind. On Saturday nights I'd take such a thing as 6s. or 8s., principally in pence, but on other nights not more than 2s. or 2s. 6d. : these were mostly tap-room customers, but when they'd let me go in a parlour I could do a good night's work in a little time, and the company would treat me better. I soon left off busking, because I didn't like the people I had to do with, and it was such a trouble to get the money when they were half tipsy. I never worked in theatres, because I didn't like the pushing about; but I've known a man to get a good living at the theatres and steamboats alone. I took to steam-boats myself when I left off public-houses, working mostly in the Gravesend boats on the Sunday, and the ha'penny boats on the week-days. I've taken before now 14s. of a Sunday, and I used to vary in the ha'penny boats from 2s. to 4s. a-day.

" I always attend Greenwich-park regularly at holiday times, but never have a booth at the fair, because I can do better moving about. I have a frame of specimens tied round a tree, and get a boy to hold the paper and cards. At this I've taken as much as 35s. in one day, and though there was lots of cheap photographic booths down there last Easter Monday, in spite of 'em all I took above 8s. 6d. in the afternoon. Battersea-fields and Chalk-farm used to be out-and-out spots on a Sunday, at one time. I've often taken such a thing as 30s. on a Sunday afternoon and evening in the summer. After I left the steam-boats I built myself a small booth, and travelled the country to fairs, 'statties,' and feasts, and got a very comfortable living; but now the cheap photographs have completely done up profiles, so I'm compelled to turn to that. But I think I shall learn a trade, for that'll be better than either of them.

" The best work I've had of late years has been at the teetotal festivals. I was at

Aylesbury with them, at St. Alban's, Luton, and Gore House. At Gore House last August, when the 'Bands of Hope' were there, I took about a pound."

BLIND PROFILE-CUTTER.

A CHEERFUL blind man, well known to all crossing Waterloo or Hungerford-bridges, gave me the following account of his figure-cutting:—

" I had the measles when I was seven, and became blind; but my sight was restored by Dr. Jeffrey, at old St. George's Hospital. After that I had several relapses into total blindness in consequence of colds, and since 1840 I have been quite blind, excepting that I can partially distinguish the sun and the gas-lights, and such-like, with the left eye only. I am now 31, and was brought up to house-painting. When I was last attacked with blindness I was obliged to go into St. Martin's workhouse, where I underwent thirteen operations in two years. When I came out of the workhouse I played the German flute in the street, but it was only a noise, not music, sir. Then I sold boot-laces and tapes in the street, and averaged 5s. a-week by it—certainly not more. Next I made little wooden tobacco-stoppers in the street, in the shape of legs—they're called 'legs.' The first day I started in that line—it was in Tottenham-court-road—I was quite elated, for I made half-a-crown. I next tried it by St. Clement's-church, but I found that I cut my hands so with the knives and files, that I had to give it up, and I then took up with the trade of cutting out profiles of animals and birds, and grotesque human figures, in card. I established myself soon after I began this trade by the Victoria-gate, Bayswater; that was the best pitch I ever had—one day I took 15s., and I averaged 30s. a-week for six weeks. At last the inspector of police ordered me off. After that I was shoved about by the police, such crowds gathered round me, until I at length got leave to carry on my business by Waterloo-bridge; that's seven years ago. I remained there till the opening of Hungerford-bridge, in May 1845. I sit there cold or fine, winter or summer, every day but Sunday, or if I'm ill. I often hear odd remarks from people crossing the bridge. In winter time, when I've been cold and hungry, and so poor that I couldn't get my clothes properly mended, one has said, ' Look at that poor blind man there;' and another (and oft enough, too) has answered, ' Poor blind man!—he has better clothes and more money than you or me; it's all done to excite pity!' I can generally tell a gentleman's or lady's voice, if they're the real thing. I can tell a purse-proud man's voice, too. He says, in a domineering, hectoring way, as an ancient Roman might speak to his slave, ' Ah, ha! my good fellow! how do you sell these things?'

Since January last, I may have averaged 8s. a-week—that's the outside. The working and the middling classes are my best friends. I know of no other man in my particular line, and I've often inquired concerning any."

WRITER WITHOUT HANDS.

THE next in order are the Writers without Hands and the Chalkers on Flag-stones.

A man of 61, born in the crippled state he described, tall, and with an intelligent look and good manners, gave me this account:—

" I was born without hands—merely the elbow of the right arm and the joint of the wrist of the left. I have rounded stumps. I was born without feet also, merely the ankle and heel, just as if my feet were cut off close within the instep. My father was a farmer in Cavan county, Ireland, and gave me a fair education. He had me taught to write, I'll show you how, sir.' (Here he put on a pair of spectacles, using his stumps, and then holding the pen on one stump, by means of the other he moved the two together, and so wrote his name in an old-fashioned hand.) 'I was taught by an ordinary schoolmaster. I served an apprenticeship of seven years to a turner, near Cavan, and could work well at the turning, but couldn't chop the wood very well. I handled my tools as I've shown you I do my pen. I came to London in 1814, having a prospect of getting a situation in the India-house; but I didn't get it, and waited for eighteen months, until my funds and my father's help were exhausted, and I then took to making fancy screens, flower-vases, and hand-racks in the streets. I did very well at them, making 15s. to 20s. a-week in the summer, and not half that, perhaps not much more than a third, in the winter. I continue this work still, when my health permits, and I now make handsome ornaments, flower-vases, &c. for the quality, and have to work before them frequently, to satisfy them. I could do very well but for ill-health. I charge from 5s. to 8s. for hand-screens, and from 7s. 6d. to 15s. for flower-vases. Some of the quality pay me handsomely—some are very near. I have done little work in the streets this way, except in very fine weather. Sometimes I write tickets in the street at a halfpenny each. The police never interfere unless the thoroughfare is obstructed badly. My most frequent writing is, ' Naked came I into the world, and naked shall I return.' ' The Lord giveth, and the Lord taketh away; blessed be the name of the Lord.' To that I add my name, the date sometimes, and a memorandum that it was the writing of a man born without hands or feet. When I'm not disturbed, I do pretty well, getting 1s. 6d. a-day; but that's an extra day. The boys are a great worry to me. Working people are my only friends at the writing, and women the best. My best pitches are Tottenham-court-road and the West-end thoroughfares. There's three men I know who write without hands. They're in the country chiefly, travelling. One man writes with his toes, but chiefly in the public-houses, or with showmen. I consider that I am the only man in the world who is a handicraftsman without hands or feet. I am married, and have a grown-up family. Two of my sons are in America, one in Australia, one a sailor, the others are emigrants on the coast of Africa, and one a cabinet-maker in London — all fine fellows, well made. I had fifteen in all. My father and mother, too, were a handsome, well-made couple."

CHALKER ON FLAG-STONES.

A SPARE, sad-looking man, very poorly dressed, gave me the following statement. He is well-known by his coloured drawings upon the flag-stones:—

"I was usher in a school for three years, and had a paralytic stroke, which lost me my employment, and was soon the cause of great poverty. I was fond of drawing, and colouring drawings, when a child, using sixpenny boxes of colours, or the best my parents could procure me, but I never had lessons. I am a self-taught man. When I was reduced to distress, and indeed to starvation, I thought of trying some mode of living, and remembering having seen a man draw mackerel on the flags in the streets of Bristol 20 years ago, I thought I would try what I could do that way. I first tried my hand in the New Kent-road, attempting a likeness of Napoleon, and it was passable, though I can do much better now; I made half-a-crown the first day. I saw a statement in one of your letters that I was making 1l. a-day, and was giving 14d. for a shilling. I never did: on the contrary, I've had a pint of beer given to me by publicans for supplying them with copper. It doesn't hurt me, so that you need not contradict it unless you like. The Morning Chronicle letters about us are frequently talked over in the lodging-houses. It's 14 or 15 years since I started in the New Kent-road, and I've followed up 'screeving,' as it's sometimes called, or drawing in coloured chalks on the flag-stones, until now. I improved with practice. It paid me well; but in wet weather I have made nothing, and have had to run into debt. A good day's work I reckon 8s. or 10s. A very good day's work? I should be glad to get it now. I have made 15s. in a day on an extraordinary occasion, but never more, except at Greenwich fair, where I've practised these 14 years. I don't suppose I ever cleared 1l. a-week all the year round at screeving. For 1l. a-week I would honestly work my hardest. I have a wife and two children. I would draw trucks or be a copying clerk, or do anything for 1l. a-week to get out of the streets. Or I would like regular employment as a painter in

crayons. Of all my paintings the Christ's heads paid the best, but very little better than the Napoleon's heads. The Waterloo-bridge-road was a favourite spot of mine for a pitch. Euston-square is another. These two were my best. I never chalked 'starving' on the flags, or anything of that kind. There are two imitators of me, but they do badly. I don't do as well as I did 10 years ago, but I'm making 15s. a-week all the year through."

V.—EXHIBITORS OF TRAINED ANIMALS.

THE HAPPY FAMILY EXHIBITOR.

"HAPPY Families," or assemblages of animals of diverse habits and propensities living amicably, or at least quietly, in one cage, are so well known as to need no further description here. Concerning them I received the following account:—

"I have been three years connected with happy families, living by such connexion. These exhibitions were first started at Coventry, sixteen years ago, by a man who was my teacher. He was a stocking-weaver, and a fancier of animals and birds, having a good many in his place — hawks, owls, pigeons, starlings, cats, dogs, rats, mice, guinea-pigs, jackdaws, fowls, ravens, and monkeys. He used to keep them separate and for his own amusement, or would train them for sale, teaching the dogs tricks, and such-like. He found his animals agree so well together, that he had a notion — and a snake-charmer, an old Indian, used to advise him on the subject —that he could show in public animals and birds, supposed to be one another's enemies and victims, living in quiet together. He did show them in public, beginning with cats, rats, and pigeons in one cage; and then kept adding by degrees all the other creatures I have mentioned. He did very well at Coventry, but I don't know what he took. His way of training the animals is a secret, which he has taught to me. It's principally done, however, I may tell you, by continued kindness and petting, and studying the nature of the creatures. Hundreds have tried their hands at happy families, and have failed. The cat has killed the mice, the hawks have killed the birds, the dogs the rats, and even the cats, the rats, the birds, and even one another; indeed, it was anything but a happy family. By our system we never have a mishap; and have had animals eight or nine years in the cage—until they've died of age, indeed. In our present cage we have 54 birds and animals, and of 17 different kinds; 3 cats, 2 dogs (a terrier and a spaniel), 2 monkeys, 2 magpies, 2 jackdaws, 2 jays, 10 starlings (some of them talk), 6 pigeons, 2 hawks, 2 barn fowls, 1 screech owl, 5 common-sewer rats, 5 white rats (a novelty), 8 guinea-pigs, 2 rabbits (1 wild and 1 tame), 1 hedgehog, and 1 tortoise. Of all these, the rat is the most difficult to make a member of a happy family: among birds, the hawk. The easiest trained animal is a monkey, and the easiest trained bird a pigeon. They live together in their cages all night, and sleep in a stable, unattended by any one. They were once thirty-six hours, as a trial, without food—that was in Cambridge; and no creature was injured; but they were very peckish, especially the birds of prey. I wouldn't allow it to be tried (it was for a scientific gentleman) any longer, and I fed them well to begin upon. There are now in London five happy families, all belonging to two families of men. Mine, that is the one I have the care of, is the strongest—fifty-four creatures: the others will average forty each, or 214 birds and beasts in happy families. Our only regular places now are Waterloo-bridge and the National Gallery. The expense of keeping my fifty-four is 12s. a-week; and in a good week—indeed, the best week—we take 30s.; and in a bad week sometimes not 8s. It's only a poor trade, though there are more good weeks than bad: but the weather has so much to do with it. The middle class of society are our best supporters. When the happy family—only one—was first in London, fourteen years ago, the proprietor took 1l. a-day on Waterloo-bridge; and only showed in the summer. The second happy family was started eight years ago, and did as well for a short time as the first. Now there are too many happy families. There are none in the country.'

The Original Happy Family.

" The first who ever took out a happy family to exhibit in the streets was a man of the name of John Austin, who lived in Nottingham. It was entirely his own idea, and he never copied it from any one. He was a very ingenious man indeed, and fond of all kinds of animals, and a fancier of all kinds of small birds. From what I have heard him say, he had a lot of cats he was very fond of, and also some white-mice, and the notion struck him that it would be very extraordinary if he could make his pets live together, and teach creatures of opposite natures to dwell in the same cage. In the commencement of his experiments he took the young, and learnt them to live happily together. He found it succeed very well indeed; and when he gets this to his liking he goes from Nottingham to Manchester, and exhibits them, for he was told that people would like to see the curious sight. He then had cats, mice, and all sorts of little birds. He was a weaver by trade, was Austin—a stocking-weaver. He didn't exhibit for money in Manchester. It was his hobby and amusement, and he only showed it for a curiosity to his friends. Then he was persuaded to come to London to exhibit. When he first came to London he turned to carpentering and cabinet-making work, for which he had a natural gift, and he laid the happy family aside. He didn't know London, and couldn't make his mind up to exhibiting in a strange place. At last he began to miss his pets; and then he gathered them together again, one here and one there, as he could get them into training. When he had a little stock round him he was advised by people to build a cage, and take them out to exhibit them.

" There was no bridge to the Waterloo-road in those days, but he took up his pitch in Waterloo-road, close to the Feathers public house, where the foot of Waterloo-bridge is now. He had a tremendous success. Everybody who passed gave him money. Noblemen and gentlepeople came far and near to see the sight. When first he went there he could go out at four o'clock in the afternoon, on any fine day as he thought proper to leave his work to go out, and he could take from his 14s. to 1l. He stopped on this same spot, opposite the Feathers public-house, from his first coming to the day he left it, a short space before he died, for 36 years all but 5 months. He's been dead for four years the 17th of last February, 1856, and then he wasn't getting 2s. 6d. a-day. Many had imitated him, and there was four happy family cages in London. When the old man saw people could do as much as he did himself, and rather got before him in their collections, it caused him to fret. He was too old to return to carpentering, and he had never been a prudent man, so he never saved anything. He was too generous to his friends when they were distressed, and a better man to his fellow-men never walked in two shoes. If he made 5l. in a week, there was money and food for them who wanted. He found that people were not so generous to him as he was to them; that he proved to his sorrow. He was a good man.

" In the year 1833 he had the honour of exhibiting before Her Majesty the Queen. She sent for him expressly, and he went to Buckingham Palace. He never would tell anybody what she gave him; but everybody considered that he had been handsomely rewarded. A few days after this there was a gentleman came to him at Waterloo-bridge (he was there all the time the bridge was building), and this party engaged him and his happy family, and took him dov n to exhibit at the Mechanics' Institution, down at Hull. I don't know what he got for the journey. After that he was engaged to go to the Mechanics' Institution in Liverpool. He travelled in this way all about the country, engaged at the different Institutions.

" I was with him as assistant for eight years before he died, and a better master there could not be living in the world. I had been travelling with him through Kent, showing the happy family, and business run bad and did not meet his approbation, so he at last said he would return to his station on Waterloo-bridge. Then I was left in the country, so I started a collection of animals for myself. It was a small collection of two monkeys, white rats and piebald ones, cats, dogs, hawks, owls, magpies, ferrets, and a cotamundi, a long-nosed animal from the Brazils. "I came to London after working in the country. He was perfectly agreeable to my exhibiting in the streets. He was a good old man, and I wish I knew how to be as good, for I can't know how to be as good. I took the West-end, and he kept to the bridge. For a time I did pretty well. I'd take about 6s. a-day, but then it cost me 1s. a-day for feeding the collection; and then I had a quantity of things given to me, such as bits of meat at the butchers', and so on. In 1851 my stand was in Regent-street, by the corner of Castle-street. I did there very well when the Exhibition was open, and as soon as it was done I fell from taking about 8s. a-day down to 1s., and that's speaking the truth. Then I shifted my post, and went and pitched upon Tower-hill. I done pretty well for the first 18 months as I was there. The sailors was the most generous people to me, and those I had most to depend upon whilst I was on Tower-hill. I've taken 8s. in one day on Tower-hill, and I've also been there, and stood there eight hours on Tower-hill and only taken 1½d. It was all casual as could be. I can say I took on the average 3s. a-day then, and then I had to feed the collection. I stayed at Tower-hill till I found that there wasn't positively a living to be made any longer there, and then I shifted from place to place, pitching at the corners of streets, and doing worse and worse, until I actually hadn't hardly strength to drag my cage about—for it's a tidy load. Then I returns to the old man's original spot, on Waterloo-bridge, to try that; for the old man was dead. The first five or six weeks as I was there, during the summer, I got a tolerable good living, and I continued there till I wasn't able to get a crust for myself. I was obliged to leave it off, and I got a situation to go to work for a firework-maker in the Westminster-road. Now I only take to the streets when I have no other employment. It isn't barely a living. I keep my collection always by me, as a resource when no other work is in hand, but if I could get constant employment I'd never go out in the streets no more.

"The animal that takes the longest to train is the ferret. I was the first that ever introduced one into a cage, and that was at Greenwich. It's a very savage little animal, and will attack almost anything. People have a notion that we use drugs to train a happy family; they have said to me, 'It's done with opium;' but, sir, believe me, there is no drugs used at all: it's only patience, and kindness, and petting them that is used, and nothing else of any sort. The first ferret as I had, it killed me about 2l. worth of things before I could get him in any way to get into the happy family. He destroyed birds, and rabbits, and guinea-pigs; and he'd seize them at any time, whether he was hungry or not. I watched that ferret till I could see that there was a better method to be used with a ferret, and then I sold my one to a rat-catcher, and then I bought two others. I tried my new system, and it succeeded. It's a secret which I used, so I can't mention it, but it's the simplest thing in the world. It's not drawing their teeth out, or operating on them; it's only kindness and such-like, and patience. I put my new ferrets into the cage, and there they have been ever since, as may have been seen on Tower-hill and such places as I've pitched on. My ferrets would play with the rats and sleep at night with them, while I've put them in the rat-box along with the rats, to carry them home together at night. My ferrets would come and eat out of my mouth and play with children, or anything. Now, I'll tell you this anecdote as a proof of their docility. They caught a rat one night at the Coopers' Arms public-house, Tower-hill, and they gave it to me, and I put it into the cage. The landlord and gentlemen in the parlour came out to see it, and they saw my ferrets hunt out the new-comer and kill him. They tossed over the white and brown and black rats that belonged to me, and seized the public-house rat and killed him. I always took the dead bodies away when they were killed, and didn't let the ferrets suck their blood, or anything of that. I've trained my animals to that state, that if I wasn't to feed them they'd sit down and starve by each other's side without eating one another.

"The monkey is almost as bad as a ferret for training for a happy family, for this reason—when they are playing they use their teeth. They are the best playfellows in the world, and never fall out or cry when they bite. They are the life and amusement of the company.

"Now, this is a curious thing with the ferret's nature. If he's ever so well trained for a happy family, he will always be avenged if he's crossed. For instance, if the ferret has a bit of meat, and the hawk comes near him and claws him, he'll, if it's months afterwards, kill that hawk. He'll wait a long time, but he's sure to kill the hawk, he's that spiteful. So that when he's crossed he never forgives. When the monkey and the ferret play, they always use their teeth, not to bite, but it's their nature in their play. Mr. Monkey, when he has played with Mr. Ferret till he has made him in a rage, will mount the perches and take Mr. Ferret by the tail and swing him backwards and forwards. The ferret gets into an awful rage, and he'll try all he knows to get hold of Mr. Monkey, but Mr. Monkey will pat him on the head, and knock him back as he tries to turn round and bite him. The ferret is the kindest of animals when at play. He don't bear no rancour to Mr. Monkey for this. He never cares for a bit of fun, but if it's an insult as is offered him, such as taking his food, he won't rest till he's revenged.

" The danger with a monkey is this. Now I've got a puppy as was give me by a friend of mine, and I both respects the gentleman as give it me and the mother of the little dog, and I've taken all the pains in the world to train this pup to the happy family, but he's a yelping, noising animal. Now, my monkey is the most pleasant and best-tempered one in the world, and the amusement and delight of all who see him, as many on Waterloo-bridge can testify. Whenever this monkey goes near the dog, it howls at him. So the monkey plays with him, pulling his tail and nibbling his ears and hair, and biting his toe, and so on. Anything that'll play with the monkey, it's all right, and they are the best friends in the world; but if they show any fear, then it's war, for the monkey won't be put upon. Now, there's another pup in the same cage which the monkey is just as fond of. They play open-mouthed together, and I've seen Mr. Monkey put his arms round the pup's neck and pull it down, and then they go to sleep together. I've actually seen when a lady has given the monkey a bit of biscuit, or what not, he's gone and crumbled some bits before the pup to give it its share. This is truth. My monkey is a lady monkey.

" The monkeys are very fond of cuddling the rats in their arms, like children. They also pull their tails and swing them. The rats are afraid, and then Mr. Monkey keeps on teasing them. If ever Mr. Rat do turn round and bite Mr. Monkey, he's sure to feel it by and by, for he'll get a swing by his tail, and he'll catch the tail whilst he's trying to run away, and bite the tip, and worry him near out of his life. A Monkey is the peace-maker and peace-breaker of a collection. He breaks peace first and then he'll go and caress afterwards, as much as to say, ' Never mind, it's only a lark.' He's very fond of the cat—for warmth, I think. He'll go and cuddle her for an hour at a time ; but if Miss Puss won't lay still to suit his comfort, he takes her round the neck, and tries to pull her down, and if then she turn's rusty, he's good to go behind her, for he's afraid to face her, and then he'll lay hold of the tip of her tail and give her a nip with his teeth. The cat and monkey are the best of friends, so long as Miss Puss will lie still to be cuddled and suit his convenience, for he will be Mr. Master, and have everything to suit his ways. For that reason I never would allow either of my cats to kitten in the cage, because Mr. Monkey would be sure to want to know all about it, and then it would be all war; for if he went to touch Miss Puss or her babies, there would be a fight. Now a monkey is always fond of any-

thing young, such as a kitten, and puss and he'd want to nurse the children. A monkey is kind to everything so long as it ain't afraid of him, but if so be as it is, then the bullying and teasing begins. My monkey always likes to get hold of a kitten, and hold it up in his arms, just the same as a baby.

" There's often very good amusement between the owl and the monkey in this way. The monkey will go and stare Mr. Owl in the face, and directly he does so Mr. Owl will begin swaying from side to side ; and then Mr. Monkey will pat him in the face or the nose. After he's bullied the owl till it's in a awful rage, the owl will take and dive at Mr. Monkey with his open claws, and perhaps get on his back. Then Mr. Monkey will go climbing all over the cage, chattering at the owl, and frightening him, and making him flutter all about. My owls can see well enough in the day-time, for they are used to be in the open air, and they get used to it.

" I compare my monkey to the clown of the cage, for he's mischievous, and clever, and good-natured. He'll never bully any of them very long after he sees they are in a regular passion, but leave them and go to some other bird or beast. One of my pups is my monkey's best friend, for neither of them are ever tired of playing.

" The cats and the birds are very good friends indeed ; they'll perch on her back, and I've even seen them come on her head and pick up the bits of dirt as you'll generally find in a cat's head. I've tried a very curious experiment with cats and birds. I've introduced a strange cat into my cage, and instantly she gets into the cage she gets frightened, and looks round for a moment, and then she'll make a dart upon almost the first thing that is facing her. If it's the owl, monkey, small birds, or any thing, she'll fly at it. It's in general then that the monkey is the greatest enemy to the strange cat of anything in the cage. He'll go and bite her tail, but he won't face her. Then the other cats will be all with their hairs up and their tails swelled up to fly at the stranger, but then I generally takes her out, or else there would be a fight. All the rats will be on the look-out and run away from the strange cat, and the little birds fly to the top of the cage, fluttering and chirriping with fear.

" The hawk I had a good deal of difficulty with to make him live happily with the small birds. When training a hawk, I always put him in with the large things first, and after he's accustomed to them, then I introduce smaller birds. He's always excited when he first comes amongst the smaller birds. I find Mr. Monkey is always the guard, as he doesn't hurt them. When he sees the hawk fluttering and driving about after the small birds, Mr. Monkey will go and pat him, as much as to say, ' You mustn't hurt them,' and also to take his attention off. After Mr. Hawk has been in the cage four, five, or six different times in training, the starlings gets accustomed to him, and will perch alongside of him; and it's as common as possible to see the starlings, when the hawk was feeding, go and eat off the same raw meat, and actually perch on his back and pick the bits off his bill as he is eating them.

"A magpie in a cage has as much as he can do to look after himself to keep his tail all right. It's a bird that is very scared, and here and there and everywhere, always flying about the cage. His time is taken up keeping out of Mr. Monkey's way. It's very rarely you see Mr. Monkey interfere with him. A magpie will pitch upon something smaller than himself, such as pigeons, which is inoffensive, or starlings, as is weaker; but he never attempts to tackle anything as is likely to be stronger than himself. He fights shy of the big animals.

"A good jackdaw, well trained to a happy family, is the life of the cage next to the monkey. He's at all the roguishness and mischief that it is possible for a man to be at. If he sees a cat or a dog, or anything asleep and quiet, he'll perch on its head, and peck away to rouse it. He's very fond of pitching on the top of the cat and turning the fur over, or pecking at the ears, till the cat turns round, and then he's off. If there's a rat in his way, he'll peck at its nose till it turns round, and then peck at its tail. If Mr. Rat gets spiteful he'll fly to the perches for it, and then follow out Jack Daw, as much as to say, 'I had the best of you.' The people are very fond of the jackdaw, too, and they like putting their fingers to the wires, and Jack'll peck them. He's very fond of stealing things and hiding them. He'll take the halfpence and conceal them. He looks round, as if seeing whether he was watched, and go off to some sly corner where there is nothing near him. If he can get hold of any of the others' food, that pleases him better than anything. My monkey and the jackdaw ain't very good company. When Mr. Jack begins his fun, it is generally when Mr. Monkey is lying still, cuddling his best friend, and that's one of the little dogs. If Mr. Monkey is lying down with his tail out, he'll go and peck him hard on it, and he'll hollow out 'Jackdaw,' and off he is to the perches. But Mr. Monkey will be after him, climbing after him, and he's sure to catch hold of him at last, and then Mr. Jack is as good as his master, for he'll hollow out to attract me, and I have to rattle my cane along the wires, to tell them to give over. Then, as sure as ever the monkey was gone, the jack would begin to crow.

"I had a heron once, and it died; I had it about fourteen months. The way as he met with his death was—he was all well in the cage, and standing about, when he took a false step, and fell, and lamed himself. I was obliged to leave him at home, and then he

pined and died. He was the only bird I ever had, or the only creature that ever was in a happy-family cage, that could keep Mr. Monkey at bay. Mr. Monkey was afraid of him, for he would give such nips with his long bill that would snip a piece out of Mr. Monkey, and he soon finds out when he would get the worst of it. I fed my heron on flesh, though he liked fish best. It's the most daintiest bird that is in its eating.

"The cotamundi was an animal as was civil and quiet with everything in the cage. But his propensity and habits for anything that was in a cage was a cat. It was always his bed-fellow; he'd fight for a cat; he'd bully the monkey for a cat. He and the cat were the best of friends, and they made common cause against Mr. Monkey. He was very fond of routing about the cage. He had very good teeth and rare claws, and a monkey will never stand against any thing as punishes him. Anything as is afraid of him he'll bully.

"I had an old crow once, who was a great favourite of mine, and when he died I could almost have cried. To tell you what he could do is a'most too much for me to say, for it was everything he was capable of. He would never stand to fight; always run away and hollow. He and the jackdaw was two birds as always kept apart from each other: they was both of a trade, and couldn't agree. He was very fond of getting on a perch next to any other bird—an owl, for instance—and then he'd pretend to be looking at nothing, and then suddenly peck at the feet of his neighbour on the sly, and then try and look innocent. After a time the other bird would turn round on him, and then he was off, screaming 'Caw' at the top of his beak, as I may say. He was a general favourite with everybody. It's a curious thing, but I never know a crow, or a jackdaw either, to be hungry, but what they'd come and ask for food by hollowing out the same as in their wild state. Mine was a carrion crow, and eat flesh. At feeding-time he'd always pick out the biggest pieces he could, or three or four of them, if he could lay hold of them in his beak, and then he'd be off to a corner and eat what he could and then hide the remainder, and go and fetch it out as he felt hungry again. He knew me perfectly well, and would come and perch on my shoulder, and peck me over the finger, and look at me and make his noise. As soon as he see me going to fetch the food he would, if he was loose in the court where I lived in, run to me directly, but not at other times. He was a knowing fellow. I had him about one year and nine months. I used to call him the pantaloon to Mr. Monkey's clown, and they was always at their pantomime tricks. Once an old woman came down our court when he was loose, and he cut after her and pecked at her naked feet, and she was so frightened she fell down. Then off he went, 'caw, caw,' as pleased as he could be. He always followed the children, picking at their heels. Nothing delighted him so much as all the roguishness and mischief as he could get into.

" For finding a happy family in good order, with 2 monkeys, 3 cats, 2 dogs, 16 rats, 6 starlings, 2 hawks, jackdaw, 3 owls, magpie, 2 guinea-pigs, one rabbit, will take about 1s. 4d. a-day. I buy leg of beef for the birds, about 1½lb., and the dogs have two pen'orth of proper dogs' meat; and there are apples and nuts for the monkey, about one pen'orth, and then there's corn of different kinds, and seeds and sopped bread for the rats, and hay and sand-dust for the birds. It all tells up, and comes to about 1s. 4d. a-day.

" There are two happy families in London town, including my own. I don't know where the other man stands, for he moves about. Now I like going to one place, where I gets known. It isn't a living for any man now. I wouldn't stick to it if I could get any work to do; and yet it's an ingenious exhibition and ought to be patronized. People will come and stand round for hours, and never give a penny. Even very respectable people will come up, and as soon as ever I hand the cup to them, they'll be off about their business. There are some gentlemen who give me regularly a penny or twopence a-week. I could mention several professional actors who do that to me. I make the most money when the monkey is at his tricks, for then they want to stop and see him at his fun, and I keep asking them for money, and do it so often, that at last they are obliged to give something.

" My cage has wire-work all round, and blinds to pull down when I change my pitch. There are springs under the cage to save the jolting over the stones.

" I forgot to tell you that I've had cats, whose kittens have been taken from them, suckle rats which have been put in their places when they are still blind, and only eight days old. She'll take to the rats instead of her kittens. I've not put them in the cage at this small age, but waited until they were old enough to run about. They'll keep on suckling at the cat till they get to a tidy size, till she gets annoyed with them and beats them off; but she'll caress them at other times, and allow them to come and lay under her belly, and protect them from Mr. Monkey. Many a time has a cat been seen suckling rats in my cage, but then they've been pretty old rats—of about eight or ten weeks old; and a rat will suckle then, and they'll follow her about and go and lie under her belly, just the same as chickens under a hen—just the same.

" At night I don't let my collection sleep together in the cage. It's four years since I first took to separating of them, for this reason: I had the cleverest monkey in London; there never was a better. I used to wheel the cage into the back-yard, and there let them sleep. One night somebody was so kind as to come and steal my monkey away. I found out my loss the same night. I had only gone into the house to fetch food, and when I came back Mr. Monkey was gone. He didn't run away, for he was too fond of the cage, and wouldn't leave it. I've often put him outside, and let him loose upon Tower-hill, and to run about gardens, and he'd come back again when I called him. I had only to turn his favourite dog out, and as soon as he see'd the dog he'd be on to his back and have a nice ride back to the cage and inside in a moment. Since that loss I've always carried the collection into the house, and let them sleep in the same room where I've slept in. They all know their beds now, and will go to them of their own accord, both the cats, the dogs, and the monkeys. I've a rat-box, too, and at night when I'm going home I just open the door of the cage and that of the rat-box, and the rats run into their sleeping-place as quick as possible, and come out again in the morning of their own accord.

" My family are fed on the best: they have as good as any nobleman's favourite dog. They've often had a deal more, and better, than their master.

" I don't know why happy families don't pay, for they all look at the cage, and seem as pleased as ever; but there's poverty or something in the way, for they don't seem to have any money. When I left off last—only a month ago—I wasn't taking 6d. a-day. It didn't pay for feeding my little stock. I went to firework-making. They are always busy with firework-making, ready for the 5th of November. I'm sick and tired of the other affair, and would do anything to get from it; but people are afraid to employ me, for they seem to fancy that after being in the streets we are no use for anything.

" I'm fond of my little stock, and always was from a child of dumb animals. I'd a deal sooner that anybody hurt me than any of my favourites."

EXHIBITOR OF BIRDS AND MICE.

A STOUT, acute-looking man, whom I found in a decently-furnished room with his wife, gave me an account of this kind of street-exhibition:—

" I perform," said he, " with birds and mice, in the open air, if needful. I was brought up to juggling by my family and friends, but colds and heats brought on rheumatism, and I left juggling for another branch of the profession; but I juggle a little still. My birds are nearly all canaries—a score of them sometimes, sometimes less. I have names for them all. I have Mr. and Mrs. Caudle, dressed quite in character: they quarrel at times, and that's self-taught with them. Mrs. Caudle is not noisy, and is quite amusing. They ride out in a chariot drawn by another bird, a goldfinch mule. I give him any name that comes into my head. The goldfinch harnesses himself to a little wire harness. Mr. and Mrs. Caudle and the mule is very much admired by people of taste. Then I have Marshal Ney in full uniform, and he fires a cannon, to keep up the character. I can't say that he's bolder than others. I have a little canary called the Trumpeter, who jumps on to a trumpet when I sound it, and remains there until I've done sounding. Another canary goes up a poll, as if climbing for a leg of mutton, or any prize at the top, as they do at fairs, and when he gets to the top he answers me. He climbs fair, toe and heel—no props to help him along. These are the principal birds, and they all play by the word of command, and with the greatest satisfaction and ease to themselves. I use two things to train them—kindness and patience, and neither of these two things must be stinted. The grand difficulty is to get them to perform in the open air without flying away, when they've no tie upon them, as one may say. I lost one by its taking flight at Ramsgate, and another at Margate. They don't and can't do anything to teach one another; not in the least; every bird is on its own account: seeing another bird do a trick is no good whatever. I teach them all myself, beginning with them from the nest. I breed most of them myself. To teach them to sing at the word of command is very difficult. I whistle to the bird to make it sing, and then when it sings I feed, and pet, and fondle it, until it gets to sing without my whistling—understanding my motions. Harshness wouldn't educate any bird whatsoever. I pursue the same system all through. The bird used to jump to be fed on the trumpet, and got used to the sound. To train Marshal Ney to fire his cannon, I put the cannon first like a perch for the bird to fly to for his food; it's fired by stuff attached to the touchhole that explodes when touched. The bird's generally frightened before he gets used to gunpowder, and flutters into the body of the cage, but after a few times he don't mind it. I train mice, too, and my mice fetch and carry, like dogs; and three of the little things dance the tight-rope on their hind legs, with balance-poles in their mouths. They are hard to train, but I have a secret way, found out by myself, to educate them properly. They require great care, and are, if anything, tenderer than the birds. I have no particular names for the mice. They are all fancy mice, white or coloured. I've known four or five in my way in London. It's all a lottery what I get. For the open-air performance, the West-end may be the best, but there's little difference. I have been ill seven months, and am just starting again. Then I can't work in the air in bad weather. I call 21s. a very good week's work; and to get that, every day must be fine—10s. 6d. is nearer the mark as an average for the year. An order to play at a private house may be extra; they give me what they please. My birds 'come with a whistle, and come with a call, and come with a good will, or they won't do at all'—for me. The police don't meddle with me—or nothing to notice. A good many of my birds and mice die before they reach any perfection—another expense and loss of time in my business. Town or country is pretty much the same to me, take it altogether. The watering-places are the best in the country, perhaps, for it's there people go for pleasure. I don't know any *best* place; if I did I'd stick to it. Ladies and children are my best friends generally."

The performance of the birds and mice above described is very clever. " Mr. and Mrs. Caudle " are dressed in red and blue cloaks, trimmed with silver lace and spangles; while Mr. Caudle, with an utter disregard of propriety, is adorned with a cocked hat.

SKILLED AND UNSKILLED LABOUR.

"Garret-Masters."

The Cabinet-makers, socially as well as commercially considered, consist, like all other operatives, of two distinct classes, that is to say, of society and non-society men, or, in the language of political economy, of those whose wages are regulated by custom and those whose earnings are determined by competition. The former class numbers between 600 and 700 of the trade, and the latter between 4000 and 5000. As a general rule I may remark, that I find the society-men of every trade comprise about one-tenth of the whole. Hence it follows, that if the non-society men are neither so skilful nor so well-conducted as the others, at least they are quite as important a body, from the fact that they constitute the main portion of the trade. The transition from the one class to the other is, however, in most cases, of a very disheartening character. The difference between the tailor at the west end, working for better shops at the better prices, and the poor wretch starving at starvation wages for the sweaters and slop-shops at the east end, has already been pointed out. The same marked contrast was also shown to exist between the society and non-society boot and shoemakers. The carpenters and joiners told the same story. There were found society men renting houses of their own—some paying as much as 70*l.* a-year—and the non-society men overworked and underpaid, so that a few weeks' sickness reduced them to absolute pauperism. Nor, I regret to say, can any other tale be told of the cabinet-makers; except it be, that the competitive men in this trade are even in a worse position than any other. I have already portrayed to the reader the difference between the homes of the two classes—the comfort and well-furnished abodes of the one, and the squalor and bare walls of the other. But those who wish to be impressed with the social advantages of a fairly-paid class of mechanics should attend a meeting of the Wood-carvers' Society. On the first floor of a small private house in Tottenham-street, Tottenham-court-road, is, so to speak, the museum of the working-men belonging to this branch of the cabinet-makers. The walls of the back-room are hung round with plaster casts of some of the choicest specimens of the arts, and in the front room the table is strewn with volumes of valuable prints and drawings in connexion with the craft. Round this table are ranged the members of the society—some forty or fifty were there on the night of my attendance —discussing the affairs of the trade. Among the collection of books may be found, "The Architectural Ornaments and Decorations of Cottingham," "The Gothic Ornaments" of Pugin, Tatham's "Greek Relics," Raphael's "Pilaster Ornaments of the Vatican," Le Pautre's "Designs," and Baptiste's "Collection of Flowers," large size; while among the casts are articles of the same choice description. The objects of this society are, in the words of the preface to the printed catalogue, "to enable wood-carvers to co-operate for the advancement of their art, and by forming a collection of books, prints, and drawings, to afford them facilities for self-improvement; also, by the diffusion of information among its members, to assist them in the exercise of their art, as well as to enable them to obtain employment." The society does not interfere in the regulation of wages in any other way than, by the diffusion of information among its members, to assist them in the exercise of their art, as well as to enable them to obtain employment; so that both employers and employed may, by becoming members, promote their own and each other's interests. The collection is now much enlarged, and with the additions that have been made to it, offers aid to the members which in many cases is invaluable. As a means of facilitating the use of this collection, the opportunities of borrowing from it have been made as general as possible. The meetings of the society are held at a place where attendance is unaccompanied by expense; and they are, therefore, says the preface, "free from all objection on account of inducements to exceed the time required for business." All this appears to be in the best possible taste, and the attention of the society being still directed to its improvement, assuredly gives the members, as they say, "good reason to hope that it will become one of which the wood-carver may be proud, as affording valuable assistance, both in the design and execution of any style of wood-carving." In the whole course of my investigations I have never experienced more gratification than I did on the evening of my visit to this society. The members all gave evidence, both in manner and appearance, of the refining character of their craft: and it was indeed a hearty relief from the scenes of squalor, misery, dirt, vice, ignorance, and discontent, with which these inquiries too frequently bring one into connexion, to find one's self surrounded with an atmosphere of beauty, refinement, comfort, intelligence, and ease.

The public, generally, are deplorably mis-informed as to the character and purpose of trade societies. The common impression is that they are combinations of working-men, instituted and maintained solely with the view of exacting an exorbitant rate of wages from their employers, and that they are necessarily connected with strikes, and with sundry other savage and silly means of attaining this object. It is my duty, however, to make known that the rate of wages which such societies are in-stituted to uphold has, with but few exceptions, been agreed upon at a conference of both masters and men, and that in almost every case I find the members as strongly opposed to strikes, as a means of upholding them, as the public themselves. But at all events the maintenance of the standard rate of wages is not the sole object of such societies — the ma-jority of them being organised as much for the support of the sick and aged as for the regulation of the price of labour; and even in those societies whose efforts are confined to the latter purpose alone, a considerable sum is devoted annually for the subsistence of their members when out of work. The general cabinet-makers, I have already shown, have contributed towards this object as much as 1000*l.* per annum for many years past. It is not generally known how largely the community is indebted to the trade and friendly societies of the working classes dispersed throughout the kingdom, or how much expense the public is saved by such means in the matter of poor-rates alone.

According to the last Government returns there are at present in England, Scotland, and Ireland, upwards of 33,000 such societies, 14,000 of which are enrolled and 8000 un-enrolled — the remaining 11,000 being secret societies, such as the Odd Fellows, Foresters, Druids, Old Friends, and Rechabites. The number of members belonging to these 33,000 societies is more than three millions. The gross annual income of the entire associations is 4,980,000*l.* and their accumulated capital 11,360,000*l.* The working people of this coun-try, and I believe of this country alone, con-tribute therefore to the support of their own poor nearly five millions of money every year, which is some thousands of pounds more than was dispensed in parochial relief throughout England and Wales in 1848. Hence it may be truly said, that the benefits conferred by the trade and friendly societies of the working classes are not limited to the individuals re-ceiving them, but are participated in by every ratepayer in the kingdom, for were there no such institutions the poor-rates must neces-sarily be doubled.

I have been thus explicit on the subject of trade societies in general, because I know there exists in the public mind a strong pre-judice against such institutions, and because it is the fact of belonging to some such society which invariably distinguishes the better class of workmen from the worse. The competitive men, or cheap workers, seldom or never are members of any association, either enrolled or unenrolled. The consequence is, that when out of work, or disabled from sickness or old age, they are left to the parish to support. It is the slop-workers of the different trades — the cheap men or non-society hands — who constitute the great mass of paupers in this country. And here lies the main social dis-tinction between the workmen who belong to societies and those who do not — the one maintain their own poor, the others are left to the mercy of the parish. The wages of the competitive men are cut down to a bare sub-sistence, so that, being unable to save anything from their earnings, a few days' incapacity from labour drives them to the workhouse for relief. In the matter of machinery, not only is the cost of working the engine, but the wear and tear of the machine, considered as a neces-sary part of the expense of production. With the human machine, however, it is different, slop-wages being sufficient to defray only the cost of keeping it at work, but not to compen-sate for the wear and tear of it. Under the allowance system of the old poor-law, wages, it is well known, were reduced far below sub-sistence-point, and the workmen were left to seek parish relief for the remainder; and so in the slop part of every trade, the underpaid workmen when sick or aged are handed over to the state to support.

As an instance of the truth of the above re-marks I subjoin the following statement, which has been furnished to me by the Chairmakers' Society concerning their outgoings:—

"Average number of members 110. Paid to unemployed members

from 1841 to 1850 . . £1256	10	0
Do. for insurance of tools . 211	10	6
Do. do. loss of time by fire . 19	2	8
Do. do. funerals of members . 120	15	0
Do. do. collections for sick . 60	4	0

"The objects which the London Chairmakers have in view by associating in a trade society," says the written statement from which the above account is extracted, "is to insure, as near as possible, one uniform price for the work they execute, so that the employer shall have a guarantee in making his calculations that he will not be charged more or less than his neighbours, who employ the same class of men: to assist their members in obtaining em-ployment, and a just remuneration for the work they perform: to insure their tools against fire: to provide for their funerals in the event of death: and to relieve their members when unemployed or in sickness — the latter being effected by paying persons to collect voluntary subscriptions for invalid members, such sub-scriptions producing on an average 5*l.* in each case. The members have, moreover, other modes of assisting each other when in diffi-culties."

I may as well here subjoin the statement I have received from this society concerning the circumstances affecting their business.

"Our trade," say they, in a written communication to me, "has suffered very materially from a change which took place about 30 years ago in the system of work. We were at that time chiefly employed by what we term 'trade-working masters,' who supplied the upholsterers with the frames of chairs and sofas; but since then we have obtained our work directly from the sellers. At first the change was rather beneficial than otherwise. The employer and his salesman, however, have now, in the greater number of instances, no knowledge of the manufacturing part of the business, and this is very detrimental to our interest, owing to their being unacquainted with the value of the labour part of the articles we make. Moreover, the salesman sends all the orders he can out of doors to be made by the middlemen, though the customer is led to believe that the work is executed on the premises, whereas only a portion of it is made at home, and that chiefly the odd and out-of-the-way work, because the sending of such work out of doors would not answer the end of cheapness. The middleman, who executes the work away from the premises, subdivides the labour to such an extent that he is enabled to get the articles made much cheaper, as well as to employ both unskilful workmen and apprentices.

"Placed in the position where the employer gets the credit of paying us the legitimate price for our labour, it would appear that we have no cause of complaint; but, owing to the system of things before stated, as well as to the number of linendrapers, carpet-makers, and others, who have recently entered the trade without having any practical knowledge of the business, together with the casualty of our employment, our social position has become scarcely any better, or so good, as that of the unskilful or the dissipated workman, while, from the many demands of our fellow-operatives upon us, in the shape of pecuniary assistance, we have a severe struggle to maintain anything like a respectable footing in the community. The principal source of regret with us is, that the public have no knowledge of the quality of the articles they buy. The sellers, too, from their want of practical acquaintance with the manufacturing part of the business, have likewise an injurious effect upon our interests, instead of seconding our efforts to keep up a creditable position in society.

"The subjoined is the amount of the capital of our society at the present time :—

"Property in the Funds . . £300
Out at use 175
Other available property, in the } 200
    shape of price-books, &c. }
                                    ————
                                    £675."

Such, then, is the state of the society men belonging to the cabinet-makers' trade. These, as I before said, constitute that portion of the workmen whose wages are regulated by custom, and it now only remains for me to set forth the state of those whose earnings are determined by competition. Here we shall find that the wages a few years since were from three to four hundred per cent better than they are at present, 20s. having formerly been the price paid for making that for which the operatives now receive only 5s., and this notwithstanding that the number of hands in the London trade from 1831 to 1841 declined 33 per cent relatively to the rest of the population. Nor can it be said that this extraordinary depreciation in the value of the cabinet-makers' labour has arisen from any proportionate decrease in the quantity of work to be done. The number of houses built in the metropolis has of late been considerably on the increase. Since 1839 there have been 200 miles of new streets formed in London, no less than 6405 new dwellings having been erected annually since that time : and as it is but fair to assume that the majority of these new houses must have required new furniture, it is clear that it is impossible to account for the decline in the wages of the trade in question upon the assumption of an equal decline in the quantity of work. How, then, are we to explain the fact that, while the hands have decreased 33 per cent, and work increased at a considerable rate, wages a few years ago were 300 per cent better than they are at present? The solution of the problem will be found in the extraordinary increase that has taken place within the last 20 years of what are called "garret-masters" in the cabinet trade. These garret-masters are a class of small "trade-working masters," supplying both capital and labour. They are in manufacture what the peasant-proprietors are in agriculture, their own employers and their own workmen. There is, however, this one marked distinction between the two classes,—the garret-master cannot, like the peasant-proprietor, eat what he produces: the consequence is, that he is obliged to convert each article into food immediately he manufactures it, no matter what the state of the market may be. The capital of the garret-master being generally sufficient to find him in the materials for the manufacture of only one article at a time, and his savings being barely enough for his subsistence while he is engaged in putting those materials together, he is compelled the moment the work is completed to part with it for whatever he can get. He cannot afford to keep it even a day, for to do so is generally to remain a day unfed. Hence, if the market be at all slack, he has to force a sale by offering his goods at the lowest possible price. What wonder, then, that the necessities of such a class of individuals should have created a special race of employers, known by the significant name of "slaughter-house men?"— or that these, being aware of the inability of the garret-masters to hold out against any offer, no matter how slight a remuneration it affords for their labour, should continually lower and lower their prices until the entire body of the competitive portion of the cabinet trade is sunk in utter destitution and misery? Moreover, it is well known how strong is the stimulus among peasant-proprietors, or indeed any class working for themselves, to extra production. So it is, indeed, with the garret-masters; their industry is indeed almost incessant, and hence a greater quantity of work is turned out by them, and continually forced into the market, than there would otherwise be. What though there be a brisk and a slack season in the cabinet-makers' trade, as in the majority of others? Slack or brisk, the garret-master must produce the same excessive quantity of goods. In the hope of extricating himself from his overwhelming poverty, he toils on, producing more and more; and yet the more he produces the more hopeless does his position become, for the greater the stock that he thrusts into the market the lower does the price of his labour fall, until at last he and his, own family work for less than he himself could earn, a few years back, by his own unaided labour.

Another cause of the necessity of the garret-master to part with his goods as soon as made is the large size of the articles he manufactures, and the consequent cost of conveying them from slaughter-house to slaughter-house till a purchaser be found. For this purpose a van is frequently hired; and the consequence is, that he cannot hold out against the slaughterer's offer, even for an hour, without increasing the expense of carriage, and so virtually decreasing his gains. This is so well known at the slaughter-houses, that if a man, after seeking in vain for a fair remuneration for his work, is goaded by his necessities to call at a shop a second time to accept a price which he had previously refused, he seldom obtains what was first offered him. Sometimes when he has been ground down to the lowest possible sum, he is paid late on a Saturday night with a cheque, and forced to give the firm a liberal discount for cashing it.

For a more detailed account, however, of the iniquities practised upon this class of operatives, I refer the reader to the statements given below. It will be there seen that all the modes by which work can be produced cheap are in full operation. The labour of apprentices and children is the prevailing means of production. I heard of one small trade-working master who had as many as eleven apprentices at work for him; and wherever the operative is blessed with a family they all work, even from 6 years old. The employment of any undue number of apprentices also tends to increase the very excess of hands from which the trade is suffering; and thus it is, that the lower wages become, the lower still they are

reduced. There are very few—some told me there were none, but there are a few who work as journeymen for little masters; but these men become little masters in their turn, or they must starve in idleness, for their employment is precarious. These men have no time for social intercommunication: the struggle to live absorbs all their energies, and confines all their aspirations to that one endeavour. Their labour is devoted, with the rarest exceptions, to the "slaughter-houses, linendrapers, 'polsterers, or warehouses." By all these names I heard the shopkeepers who deal in furniture of all kinds, as well as drapery goods, designated.

These men work in their own rooms, in Spitalfields and Bethnal-green; and sometimes two or three men in different branches occupy one apartment, and work together there. They are a sober class of men, but seem so perfectly subdued by circumstances, that they cannot or do not struggle against the system which several of them told me they knew was undoing them.

The subdivisions of this trade I need not give, they are as numerous as the articles of the cabinet-maker's calling.

I have mentioned that the black houses, or linendrapers at the west end of London, were principally supplied from the east end. In the neighbourhood of Tottenham-court-road and Oxford-street, for instance, most of my readers will have had their attention attracted by the dust-coloured appearance of some poor worker in wood carrying along his skeleton of an easy chair, or a sofa, or a couch, to dispose of in some shop. Often, too, a carter has to be employed for the same purpose, at the rate of 1s. 6d. an hour; and thus two hours will exhaust the very fullest value of a long day's labour. From a furniture-carter of this description I received some most shocking details of having to "busk" it, as this taking about goods for sale is called by those in the trade.

From a pale, feeble-looking man whom I met on a Saturday evening at the west end, carrying a mahogany chiffonier, I had the following statement:—

"I have dragged this chiffonier with me," he said, "from Spitalfields, and have been told to call again in two hours (it was then half-past 7). I am too tired to drag it to another linendraper's, and indeed I shouldn't have so good a chance there; for if we go late, the manager considers we've been at other places, and he'll say, 'You needn't bring me what others have refused.' I was brought up as a general hand at ——, but was never in society, which is a great disadvantage. I feel that now. I used to make my 25s. or 28s. a-week six or seven years back; but then I fell out of employ, and worked at chair-making for a slaughter-house, and so got into the system, and now I can't get out of it. I have no time to look about me, as, if I'm idle, I can't get bread for my family. I have a wife and two children. They're too young to do anything; but I can't afford to send them to school, except every now and then 1d. or 2d. a-week, and so they may learn to read, perhaps. The anxiety I suffer is not to be told. I've nothing left to pawn now; and if I don't sell this chiffonier I must take it back, and must go back to a house bare of everything, except, perhaps, 3s. or 2s. 6d. my wife may have earned by ruining her health for a tailor's sweater; and 1s. 6d. of that must go for rent. I ought to have 2l. for this chiffonier, for it's superior mahogany to the run of such things; but I ask only 35s., and perhaps may be bid 28s., and get 30s. ; and it may be sold, perhaps, by the linendraper for 3l. 3s. or 3l. 10s. Of course we're obliged to work in the slightest manner possible ; but, good or bad, there's the same fault found with the article. I have already lost 3½ hours ; and there's my wife anxiously looking for my return to buy bread and a bit of beast's head for to-morrow. It's hard to go without a bit o' meat on Sundays ; and, indeed, I must sell at whatever price — it don't matter, and that the linendraper depends upon."

I now subjoin a statement of a garret-master —a maker of loo tables—who was endeavouring to make a living by a number of apprentices :—

"I'm now 41," he said, " and for the last ten or twelve years have been working for a linendraper who keeps a slaughter-house. Before that I was in a good shop, Mr. D——'s, and was a general hand, as we were in the fair trade. I have often made my 50s. a-week on good work of any kind : now, with three apprentices to help me, I make only 25s. Work grew slack ; and rather than be doing nothing, as I'd saved a little money, I made loo tables, and sold them to a linendraper, a dozen.years back or so, and so somehow I got into the trade. For tables that, eighteen years ago, I had in a good shop 30s. for making, now 5s. is paid ; but that's only in a slaughterer's own factory, when he has one. I've been told often enough by a linendraper, ' Make an inferior article, so as it's cheap : if it comes to pieces in a month, what's that to you or me?' Now, a 4-foot loo is an average ; and if for profit and labour—and it's near two days' work—I put on 7s., I'm bid 5s. less. I've been bid less than the stuff, and have on occasions been forced to take it. That was four years ago ; and I then found I couldn't possibly live by my own work, and I had a wife and four children to keep ; so I got some apprentices. I have now three, and two of them are stiff fellows of 18, and can do a deal of work. For a 4-foot loo table I have only 1l., though the materials cost from 11s. to 13s., and it's about two days' work. There's not a doubt of it that the linendrapers have brought bad work into the market, and have swamped the good. For work that, ten or twelve years ago,

I had 3l. 5s. to 3l. 10s. from them, I have now 30s. Of course, it's inferior in quality in proportion, but it doesn't pay me half as well. I know that men like me are cutting one another's throats by competition. Fourteen years ago we ought to have made a stand against this system ; but, then, we must live."

A pale young man, working in a room with two others, but in different branches, gave me the following account:—

" I have been two years making looking-glass frames. Before that I was in the general cabinet line, but took to this when I was out of work. I make frames only ; the slaughter-houses put in the glasses themselves. If I had other work I couldn't afford to lose time going from one to another that I wasn't so quick at. I make all sizes of frames, from nine-sevens to twenty-four-eighteens (nine inches by seven, and twenty-four inches by eighteen). Nine-sevens are most in demand ; and the slaughter-houses give 10s. 6d. a-dozen for them. Two years back they gave 15s. All sizes has fallen 3s. to 4s. a-dozen. I find all the material. It's mahogany veneered over deal. There's only five or six slaughter-houses in my way ; but I serve the Italians or Jews, and they serve the slaughter-houses. There's no foreigners employed as I'm employed. It's not foreign competition as harms us—it's home. I almost ask more than I mean to take, for I'm always bid less than a fair price, and so we haggle on to a bargain. The best weeks I have had I cleared 25s. ; but in slack times, when I can hardly sell at all, only 12s. Carrying the goods for sale is such a loss of time. Things are very bad now ; but I must go on making, and get a customer when trade is brisker if I can. Glass has rose 1s. a-foot, and that's made a slack in the trade, for my trade depends greatly on the glass trade. I know of no women employed in my trade, and no apprentices. We are all little masters."

I shall now proceed to the other branch of the trade. The remarks I have made concerning the wretched social condition and earnings of fancy cabinet-makers who are in society, apply even more strongly to the non-society men. The society men are to be found chiefly in Clerkenwell ; the non-society men in Spitalfields and Bethnal Green. With these unfortunate workmen there is yet a lower deep. The underpaid men of Clerkenwell work generally to order, if the payment be never so inadequate. But the still more underpaid men of Spitalfields work almost universally on speculation. The Spitalfields cabinet-maker finds his own material, which he usually purchases of the great cabinet-makers or the pianoforte-makers, being the veneers which are the refuse of their work. The supply of the east-end warehousemen is derived from little masters—men who work at their own abodes, and have the assistance of their wives and children. It is very rarely that they, or their equally underpaid fellows in the general cabinet trade, employ an active journeyman. Almost every man in the trade works on his own account, finds his own material, and goes "on the busk to the slaughter-houses" for the chance of a customer.

I found the fancy cabinet-makers certainly an uninformed class, but patient, temperate, and resigned. Some few could neither read nor write, and their families were growing up as uninformed as the parents. The hawking from door to door of workboxes made by some of the men themselves, their wives assisting them with hawking, was far commoner than it is now; but it is still practised to a small extent.

I called on an old couple to whom I was referred, as to one of the few parties employed in working for the men who supplied the warehouses. The man's appearance was gaunt and wretched. He had been long unshorn; and his light blue eyes had that dull, half-glazed look, which is common to the old when spirit-broken and half-fed. His room, a small garret in Spitalfields, for which he paid 1s. 3d. a-week, was bare of furniture, except his work-bench and two chairs, which were occupied by his wife, who was at work lining the boxes her husband was making. A blanket rolled up was the poor couple's bed. The wife was ten years younger than her husband. She was very poorly clad in an old rusty black gown, tattered here and there; but she did not look very feeble.

"I am 63," the man said, and he looked 80, "and was apprenticed in my youth to the fancy cabinet trade. I could make 4l. 4s. a-week at it by working long hours when I was out of my time, forty-two years back. I have worked chiefly on workboxes. I didn't save money— I was foolish; but it was a hard-living and a hard-drinking time. I'm sorry for it now. Thirty years ago things weren't quite so good, but still very good; and so they were twenty years back. But since the slaughter-houses came in, men like me has been starving. Why here, sir, for a rosewood workbox like this, which I shall get 6d. for making, I used to give a brother of mine 6s. 6d. for making twenty years ago. I've been paid 22s. 6d. years ago for what I now get 2s. 6d. for. The man who employs me now works for a slaughter-house; and he must grind me down, or he couldn't serve a slaughter-house cheap enough. He finds materials, and I find tools and glue; and I have 6s. a-dozen for making these boxes, and I can only make a dozen a-week, and the glue and other odds and ends for them costs me 6d. a-dozen. That, with 9d. or 10d. a-week, or 1s., that my wife may make, as she helps me in lining, is all we have to live on. We live entirely on tea and bread and butter, when we can get butter; never any change—tea, and nothing else all day; never a bit of meat on a Sunday. As for beer, I haven't spent 4s. on it these last four years. When I'm not at work for a little master, I get stuff of one, and make a few boxes on my own account, and carry them out to sell. I have often to go three or four miles with them; for there's a house near Tottenham-court-road that will take a few from me, generally out of charity. When I'm past work, or can't meet with any, there's nothing but the workhouse for me."

The decline which has taken place within the last twenty years in the wages of the operative cabinet-makers of London is so enormous, and, moreover, it seems so opposed to the principles of political economy, that it becomes of the highest importance in an inquiry like the present to trace out the circumstances to which this special depreciation is to be attributed. It has been before shown that the number of hands belonging to the London cabinet trade decreased between 1831 and 1841 33 per cent in comparison with the rest of the metropolitan population; and that, notwithstanding this falling off, the workman's wages in 1831 were at least 400 per cent better than they are at present; 20s. having formerly been paid for the making of articles for which now only 5s. are given. To impress this fact, however, more strongly upon the reader's mind, I will cite here a few of many instances of depreciation that have come to my knowledge. "Twenty years ago," said a workman in the fancy cabinet line, "I had 6d. an inch for the making of 20-inch desks of solid mahogany; that's 10s. for the entire article: now I get 2s. 3d. for the same thing. Smaller desks used to average us 6s. each for wages: now they don't bring us more than 1s. Ladies' 12-inch workboxes twenty years ago were 3s. 6d. and 4s. a-piece making; now they are 5d. for the commoner sort and 7d. for those with better work." "I don't understand per cents," said another workman, "but this I do know, the prices that I get have within this twenty years fallen from 4s. to 5d., and in some cases to 4½d."

Here, then, we find that wages in the competitive portion of the cabinet trade — that is among the non-society hands — (the wages of the society men I have before explained are regulated, or rather fixed by custom) — were twenty years ago 400 per cent better in some cases, and in others no less than 900 per cent higher than they are at present, and this while the number of workmen has decreased as much as one-third relatively to the rest of the population. How, then, is this extraordinary diminution in the price of labour to be accounted for? Certainly not on the natural assumption that the quantity of work has declined in a still greater proportion than the number of hands to do it, for it has also been proved that the number of new houses built annually in the metropolis, and therefore the quantity of new furniture required has of late years increased very considerably.

GARRET-MASTER; OR CHEAP FURNITURE MAKER.

[*From a Sketch.*]

GANG OF COAL-WHIPPERS AT WORK BELOW BRIDGE.

[*From a Sketch.*]

In the cabinet trade, then, we find a collection of circumstances at variance with that law of supply and demand by which many suppose that the rate of wages is invariably determined. Wages, it is said, depend upon the demand and supply of labour; and it is commonly assumed that they cannot be affected by anything else. That they are, however, subject to other influences, the history of the cabinet trade for the last twenty years is a most convincing proof, for there we find, that while the quantity of work, or in other words, the demand for labour, has increased, and the supply decreased, wages, instead of rising, have suffered a heavy decline. By what means, then, is this reduction in the price of labour to be explained? What other circumstance is there affecting the remuneration for work, of which economists have usually omitted to take cognizance? The answer is, that wages depend as much on the distribution of labour as on the demand and supply of it. Assuming a certain quantity of work to be done, the amount of remuneration coming to each of the workmen engaged must, of course, be regulated, not only by the number of hands, but by the proportion of labour done by them respectively; that is to say, if there be work enough to employ the whole of the operatives for sixty hours a-week, and if two-thirds of the hands are supplied with sufficient to occupy them ninety hours in the same space of time, then one-third of the trade must be thrown fully out of employment: thus proving that there may be surplus labour without any increase of the population. It may, therefore, be safely asserted, that any system of labour which tends to make the members of a craft produce a greater quantity of work than usual, tends at the same time to over-populate the trade as certainly as an increase of workmen. This law may be summed up briefly in the expression that over-work makes under-pay.

Hence the next point in the inquiry is as to the means by which the productiveness of operatives is capable of being extended. There are many modes of effecting this. Some of these have been long known to students of political economy, while others have been made public for the first time in these letters. Under the former class are included the division and co-operation of labour, as well as the "large system of production;" and to the latter belongs "the strapping system," by which men are made to get through four times as much work as usual, and which I have before described. But the most effectual means of increasing the productiveness of labourers is found to consist, not in any system of supervision, however cogent, nor in any limitation of the operations performed by the work-people to the smallest possible number, nor in the apportionment of the different parts of the work to the different capabilities of the operatives, but in connecting the workman's interest directly with his labour; that is to say, by making the amount of his earnings depend upon the quantity of work done by him. This is ordinarily effected in manufacture by means of what is called piece-work. Almost all who work by the day, or for a fixed salary—that is to say, those who labour for the gain of others, not for their own—have, it has been well remarked, "no interest in doing more than the smallest quantity of work that will pass as a fulfilment of the mere terms of their engagement." Owing to the insufficient interest which day-labourers have in the result of their labour, there is a natural tendency in such labour to be extremely inefficient—a tendency only to be overcome by vigilant superintendance (such as is carried on under the strapping system among the joiners) on the part of the persons who are interested in the result. The master's eye is notoriously the only security to be relied on. But superintend them as you will, day labourers are so much inferior to those who work by the piece, that, as we before said, the latter system is practised in all industrial occupations where the work admits of being put out in definite portions, without involving the necessity of too troublesome a surveillance to guard against inferiority (or scamping) in the execution. But if the labourer at piece-work is made to produce a greater quantity than at day-work, and this solely by connecting his own interest with that of his employer, how much more largely must the productiveness of workmen be increased when labouring wholly on their own account! Accordingly, it has been invariably found, that whenever the operative unites in himself the double function of capitalist and labourer, making up his own materials or working on his own property, his productiveness single-handed is considerably greater than can be attained under the large system of production, where all the arts and appliances of which extensive capital can avail itself are brought into operation.

Of the industry of working masters or trading operatives in manufactures there are as yet no authentic accounts. We have, however, ample records concerning the indefatigability of their agricultural counterparts—the peasant-proprietors of Tuscany, Switzerland, Germany, and other countries where the labourers are the owners of the soil they cultivate. " In walking anywhere in the neighbourhood of Zürich," says Inglis, in his work on Switzerland, the South of France, and the Pyrenees, "one is struck with the extraordinary industry of the inhabitants. When I used to open my casement, between four and five o'clock in the morning, to look out upon the lake and the distant Alps, I saw the labourer in the fields; and when I returned from an evening walk, long after sunset, as late perhaps as half-past eight, there was the labourer mowing his grass or tying up his vines." The same state of thing exists among the French peasantry under the same circumstances. " The industry of the small proprietor," says Arthur Young, in his "Travels in France," "were so conspicuous and so meritorious, that no commendation would be too great for it. It was sufficient to prove that property in land is, of all others, the most active instigator to severe and incessant labour." If, then, this principle of working for one's self has been found to increase the industry, and consequently the productiveness of labourers, to such an extent in agriculture, it is but natural that it should be attended with the same results in manufactures, and that we should find the small masters and the peasant-proprietors toiling longer and working quicker than labourers serving others rather than themselves. But there is an important distinction to be drawn between the produce of the peasant-proprietor and that of the small master. Toil as diligently as the little farmer may, since he cultivates the soil not for profit, but as a means of subsistence, and his produce contributes directly to his support, it follows that his comforts must be increased by his extra-production; or, in other words, that the more he labours, the more food he obtains. The small master, however, producing what he cannot eat, must carry his goods to market and exchange them for articles of consumption. Hence, by over-toil he lowers the market against himself; that is to say, the more he labours the less food he ultimately obtains.

But not only is it true that over-work makes under-pay, but the converse of the proposition is equally true, that under-pay makes over-work; that is to say, it is true of those trades where the system of piece-work or small mastership admits of the operative doing the utmost amount of work that he is able to accomplish, for the workman in such cases seldom or never thinks of reducing his expenditure to his income, but rather of increasing his labour, so as still to bring his income, by extra production, up to his expenditure. This brings us to another important distinction which it is necessary to make between the peasant-proprietor and the small master. The little farmer cannot increase his produce by devoting a less amount of labour to each of the articles; that is to say, he cannot scamp his work without diminishing his future stock. A given quantity of labour must be used to obtain a given amount of produce. None of the details can be omitted without a diminution of the result: scamp the ploughing and there will be a smaller crop. In manufactures, however, the result is very different. There one of the principal means of increasing the productions of a particular trade, and of the cabinet trade especially, is by decreasing the amount of work in each article. Hence, in such cases, all kinds of schemes and impositions are resorted to to make the unskilled labour equal to the skilled, and thus the market is glutted with slop productions till the honourable part of the trade,

both workmen and employers, are ultimately obliged to resort to the same tricks as the rest.

There were, about twenty years ago, a numerous body of tradesmen, who were employers, though not workmen to the general public, known as "trade-working masters." These men, of whom there are still a few, confined their business solely to supplying the trade. They supplied the greater establishments where there were showrooms with a cheaper article than the proprietors of those greater establishments might be able to have had manufactured on their own premises. They worked not on speculation, but to order, and were themselves employers. Some employed, at a busy time, from twenty to forty hands, all working on their premises, which were merely adapted for making, and not for selling or showing furniture. There are still such trade-working masters, the extent of their business not being a quarter what it was; neither do they now generally adhere to the practice of having men to work on their premises, but they give out the material, which their journeymen make up at their own abodes.

"About twenty years ago," said an experienced man to me, "I dare say the small masters formed about a quarter of the trade. The slacker trade becomes, the more the small masters increase; that's because they can't get other work to do; and so, rather than starve, they begin to get a little stuff of their own, and make up things for themselves, and sell them as best they can. The great increase of the small masters was when trade became so dead. When was it that we used to have to go about so with our things? About five years since, wasn't it?" said he, appealing to one of his sons, who was at work in the same room with him. "Yes, father," replied the lad, "just after the railway bubble; nobody wanted anything at all then." The old man continued to say,—"The greater part of the men that couldn't get employed at the regular shops then turned to making up things on their account; and now, I should say, there's at least one half working for themselves. About twelve years ago masters wanted to cut the men down, and many of the hands, rather than put up with it, took to making up for themselves. Whenever there's a decrease of wages there's always an increase of small masters; for it's not until men can't live comfortably by their labour that they take to making things on their own account."

I now come to the amount of capital required for an operative cabinet-maker to begin business on his own account.

To show the readiness with which any youth out of his time, as it is called, can start in trade as a garret cabinet master, I have learned the following particulars:—This lad, when not living with his friends, usually occupies a garret, and in this he constructs a rude bench out of old materials, which may cost him 2s. If he be penniless when he ceases to be an apprentice, and can get no work as a journeyman, which is nearly always the case, for reasons I have before stated, he assists another garret-master to make a bedstead, perhaps; and the established garret-master carries two bedsteads instead of one to the slaughter-house. The lad's share of the proceeds may be about 5s.; and out of that, if his needs will permit him, he buys the article, and so proceeds by degrees. Many men, to start themselves, as it is called, have endured, I am informed, something like starvation most patiently. The tools are generally collected by degrees, and often in the last year of apprenticeship, out of the boy's earnings. They are seldom bought first-hand, but at the marine-store shops, or at the second-hand furniture brokers' in the New Cut. The purchaser grinds and sharpens them up at any friendly workman's where he can meet with the loan of a grindstone, and puts new handles to them himself out of pieces of waste wood. 10s. or even 5s. thus invested has started a man with tools, while 20s. has accomplished it in what might be considered good style. In some cases the friends of the boy, if they are not poverty-stricken, advance him from 40s. to 50s. to begin with, and he must then shift for himself.

When a bench and tools have been obtained, the young master buys such material as his means afford, and sets himself to work. If he has a few shillings to spare he makes himself a sort of bedstead, and buys a rug or a sheet and a little bedding. If he has not the means to do so he sleeps on shavings stuffed into an old sack. In some few cases he hires a bench alongside some other garret-master, but the arrangement of two or three men occupying one room for their labour is more frequent when the garrets where the men sleep are required for their wives' labour in any distinct business, or when the articles the men make are too cumbrous, like wardrobes, to be carried easily down the narrow stairs.

A timber merchant, part of whose business consists in selling material to little masters, gave me two instances, within his own knowledge, of journeymen beginning to manufacture on their own account.

A fancy cabinet-maker had 3s. 6d. at his command. With this he purchased material for a desk as follows :—

	s.	d.
3 ft. of solid ⅜ mahogany . . .	1s.	0d.
2 ft. of solid ⅜ cedar for bottom, &c. .	0	6
Mahogany top	0	3
Bead cedar for interior . .	0	6
Lining	0	4
Lock and key (no ward to lock) .	0	2
Hinges	0	1
Glue and springs . . .	0	1½
	2	11½

The making of the desk occupied four hours, as he bestowed extra pains upon it, and he sold it to a slaughterer for 3s. 6d. He then broke his fast on bread and water, bought material for a second desk and went to work again, and so he proceeds now; toiling and half-starving, and struggling to get 20s. a-head of the world to buy more wood at one time, and not pause so often in his work. "Perhaps," said my informant, "he'll marry, as most of the small masters do, some foolish servant-of-all-work, who has saved 3l. or 4l., and that will be his capital."

Another general cabinet-maker commenced business on 30s., a part of which he expended in the material for a 4-foot chest of drawers.

	s.	d.
3 ft. 6 inches of cedar for ends . .	4s.	0d.
Sets of mahogany veneers for three big and two little drawers }	2	4
Drawer sweep (deal to veneer the front upon) . . . }	2	6
Veneer for top	1	3
Extras (any cheap wood) for inside of drawers, partitioning, &c. }	5	0
5 locks	1	8
8 knobs, 1s., glue, sprigs, &c. . .	1	4
Set of four turned feet, beech-stained	1	6
	19	7

For the article when completed he received 25s., toiling at it for 27 or 28 hours. The tradesman from whom I derived this information, and who was familiar with every branch of the trade, calculated that three-fifths of the working cabinet-makers of London make for the warehouses—in other words, that there are 3000 small masters in the trade. The most moderate computation was that the number so employed exceed one half of the entire body of the 5000 metropolitan journeyman.

The next point in this inquiry is concerning the industry and productiveness of this class of workmen. Of over-work, as regards excessive labour, and of over-production from scamped workmanship, I heard the following accounts which different operatives, both in the fancy and general cabinet trade concurred in giving, while some represented the labour as of longer duration by at least an hour, and some by two hours a day, than I have stated.

The labour of the men who depend entirely on the slaughter-houses for the purchase of their articles, with all the disadvantages that I described in a former letter, is usually seven days a week the year through. That is seven days—for Sunday-work is all but universal—each of 13 hours, or 91 hours in all, while the established hours of labour in the honourable trade are six days of the week, each of 10 hours, or 60 hours in all. Thus 50 per cent is added to the extent of the production of low-priced cabinet work merely from over-hours, but in some cases I heard of 15 hours for seven days in the week, or 105 hours in all. The exceptions to this continuous toil are from one to three hours once or twice in the week, when the workman is engaged in purchasing his material of a timber merchant, who sells it in small quantities, and from six to eight hours when he is employed in conveying his goods to a warehouse, or from warehouse to warehouse for sale. Concerning the hours of labour I had the following minute particulars from a garret-master who was a chairmaker.

" I work from 6 every morning to 9 at night —some work till 10—I breakfast at 8, which stops me for 10 minutes. I can breakfast in less time, but it's a rest; my dinner takes me say 20 minutes at the outside, and my tea 8 minutes. All the rest of the time I'm slaving at my bench. How many minutes' rest is that, sir ? 38. Well, say three-quarters of an hour, and that allows a few sucks at a pipe when I rest; but I can smoke and work too. I have only one room to work and eat in, or I should lose more time. Altogether I labour 14¼ hours every day, and I must work on Sundays at least 40 Sundays in the year. One may as well work as sit fretting. But on Sundays I only work till it's dusk, or till five or six in summer. When it's dusk I take a walk; I'm not well-dressed enough for a Sunday walk when its light, and I can't wear my apron very well on that day to hide patches. But there's eight hours that I reckon I take up every week in dancing about to the slaughterers'. I'm satisfied that I work very nearly 100 hours a-week the year through, deducting the time taken up by the slaughterers and buying stuff —say eight hours a-week, it gives more than 90 hours a-week for my work, and there's hundreds labour as hard as I do just for a crust."

This excessive toil, however, is but one element of over-production. Scamping adds at least 200 per cent to the productions of the cabinet-maker's trade. I have ascertained several cases of this over-work from scamping, and adduce two. A very quick hand, a little master, working as he called it " at a slaughtering pace" for a warehouse, made 60 plain writing desks in a week of 90 hours, whilst a first-rate workman, also a quick hand, made 18 in a week of 70 hours. The scamping hand said he must work at the rate he did to make 14s. a-week from a slaughter-house, and so used to such style of work had he become, that though a few years back he did west-end work in the best style, he could not now make 18 desks in a week, if compelled to finish them in the style of excellence displayed in the work of the journeyman employed for the honourable trade. Perhaps, he added, he couldn't make them in that style at all. The frequent use of rosewood veneers in the fancy cabinet, and their occasional use in the general cabinet trade, gives, I was told, great facilities for scamping. If, in his haste, the scamping hand injure the veneer, or if it has been originally faulty, he takes a mixture of gum shellac and "colour," (colour being a composition of Venetian red and lamp black) which he has already by him, rubs it over the damaged part,

smooths it with a slightly heated iron, and so blends it with the colour of the rosewood that the warehouseman does not detect the flaw. Indeed, I was told that very few warehousemen are judges of the furniture they bought, and they only require it to look well enough for sale to the public, who know even less than themselves. In the general cabinet trade I found the same ratio of scamping, compared with the products of skilled labour in the honourable trade. A good workman made a 4-foot mahogany chest of drawers in five days, working the regular hours, and receiving at piece-work price 35s. A scamping hand made five of the same size in a week, and had time to carry them for sale to the warehouses, wait for their purchase or refusal, and buy material. But for the necessity of doing this the scamping hand could have made seven in the 91 hours of his week, of course in a very inferior manner. They would hold together for a time, I was assured, and that was all; but the slaughterers cared only to have them viewy and cheap. These two cases exceed the average, and I have cited them to show what can be done under the scamping system.

I now come to show how this scamp work is executed, that is to say, by what helps or assistants when such are employed. As in all trades where lowness of wages is the rule, the apprentice system prevails among the cheap cabinet-workers. It prevails, however, among the garret-masters, by very many of them having one, two, three, or four apprentices, and so the number of boys thus employed through the whole trade is considerable. This refers principally to the general cabinet trade. In the fancy trade the number is greater, as the boys' labour is more readily available, but in this trade the greatest number of apprentices is employed by such warehousemen as are manufacturers, as some at the east end are— or rather by the men that they constantly keep at work. Of these men one has now 8, and another 14 boys in his service, some apprenticed, some merely engaged and discharged at pleasure. A sharp boy, thus apprenticed, in six or eight months becomes handy, but four out of five of the workmen thus brought up can do nothing well but their own particular branch, and that only well as far as celerity in production is considered.

I have before alluded to the utter destitution of the cheap workers belonging to the cabinet trade, and I now subjoin the statement of a man whom I found last winter in the Asylum for the Houseless Poor.

" I have been out of work a twelvemonth, as near as I can reckon. When I was in work I was sometimes at piece-work and sometimes at day-work. When I first joined the trade (I never served my time, my brother learnt me) there was plenty of work to do. For this last twelvemonth I have not been able to get anything to do, not at my own trade. I have made up one dozen of mahogany chairs on my own account. The wood and labour of them cost me 1*l.* 5*s.*, I had to pay for a man to do the carving and sweeping of them, and I had to give 1*l.* for the wood. I could get it much cheaper now, but then I didn't know anything about the old broken ship-wood that is now used for furniture. The chairs I made I had to sell at a sacrifice. I was a week making them, and got only 2*l.* for the dozen when they were done. By right I should have had at least 50*s.* for them, and that would have left 25*s.* for my week's work, but as it was I had only 15*s.* clear money, and I have worked at them much harder than is usual in the trade. There are two large houses in London that are making large fortunes in this manner. About a fortnight after I found out that I couldn't possibly get a living at this work, and as I didn't feel inclined to make the fortunes of the large houses by starving myself, I gave up working at chair-making on my own account. I then made a few clothes-horses. I kept at that for about six months. I hawked them in the streets, but I was half-starved by it. Some days I sold them, and some I was without taking a penny. I never in one day got rid of more than half-a-dozen, and they brought 3*s.*, out of which there was the wood and the other materials to pay for, and they would be 1*s.* 6*d.* at least. If I could get rid of two or three in a day I thought I did pretty well, and my profit on these was about 9*d.*, not more. At last I became so reduced by the work that I was not able to buy any more wood, and the week after that I was forced to quit my lodging. I owed three weeks' rent, at 1*s.* 6*d.* a week, and was turned out in consequence. I had no things for them to seize, they had all gone long before. Then I was thrown upon the streets. I had no friends (my brothers are both out of the country) and no home. I was sleeping about anywhere I could. I used to go and sit at the coffee-houses where I knew my mates were in the habit of going, and they would give me a bit of something to eat, and make a collection to pay for a bed for me. At last this even began to fail me, my mates could do no more for me. Then I applied to some of the unions, but they refused to admit me into the casual ward on account of my not being a traveller. I was a whole week walking in the streets without ever lying to rest. I used to go to Billingsgate to get a nap for a few minutes, and then I used to have a doze now and then on a door-step and under the railway arches. At this time I had scarcely any food at all, not even bread. At last I was fairly worn out, and being in the neighbourhood, I applied at St. Luke's, and told them I was starving. They said they could do nothing for me, and advised me to apply at the Houseless Poor Asylum. I did so, and was admitted directly. I have been four nights in the Asylum already, and I don't know what I shall do when I leave. My tools are all gone; they are sold, and I have no money to buy new ones.

There are hundreds in the trade like me, walking about the streets with nothing to do and no place to put their heads in."

I shall now conclude with the following statement as to the effects produced by the slop cabinet business upon the honourable part of the trade. I derived my information from Mr. ——, one of the principal masters at the west-end, and who has the highest character for consideration for his men. "Since the establishment of slaughter-houses, and aptly indeed," said my informant, "from my knowledge of their effects upon the workmen, have they been named—the demand for articles of the best cabinet-work, in the manufacture of which the costliest woods and the most skilled labour London can supply are required, has diminished upwards of 25 per cent. The de-- mand, moreover, continues still to diminish gradually. The result is obvious. Only three men are now employed in this trade in lieu of four as formerly, and the men displaced may swell the lists of the underpaid, and even of the slop-workers. The expense incurred by some of the leading masters in the honourable trade is considerable, and for objects the designs of which inferior masters pirate from us. The designs for new styles of furniture add from 5 to 10 per cent to the cost of the most elaborate articles that we manufacture. The first time any of these novel designs comes to the hammer by the sale of a gentleman's effects they are certain of piracy, and so the pattern descends to the slaughter-houses. These great houses are frequently offered prices, and by very wealthy persons, that are an insult to a tradesman wishing to pay a fair price to his workmen. For instance, for an 8-foot mahogany bookcase, after a new design, and made to the very best style of art, the material being the choicest, and everything about in admirable keeping, the price is 50 guineas. 'O dear!' some rich customer will say, '50 guineas! I'll give you 20, or, indeed, I'll give you 25.'" (I afterwards heard from a journeyman that this would be the cost of the labour alone.) The gentleman I saw spoke highly of the intelligence and good conduct of the men employed, only society men being at work on his premises. He feared that the slop-trade, if not checked, would more and more swamp the honourable trade.

THE DOLL'S-EYE MAKER.

A curious part of the street toy business is the sale of dolls, and especially that odd branch of it, doll's-eye making. There are only two persons following this business in London, and by the most intelligent of these I was furnished with the following curious information:—

"I make all kinds of eyes," the eye-manufacturer said, "both dolls' and human eyes; birds' eyes are mostly manufactured in Birmingham, and as you say, sir, bulls' eyes at the confectioner's. Of dolls' eyes there are two sorts, the common and the natural, as we call it. The common are simply small hollow glass spheres, made of white enamel, and coloured either black or blue, for only two colours of these are made. The bettermost dolls' eyes, or the natural ones, are made in a superior manner, but after a similar fashion to the commoner sort. The price of the common black and blue dolls' eyes is five shillings for twelve dozen pair. We make very few of the bettermost kind, or natural eyes for dolls, for the price of those is about fourpence a pair, but they are only for the very best dolls. Average it throughout the year, a journeyman doll's-eye maker earns about thirty shillings a-week. The common dolls' eyes were twelve shillings the twelve dozen pairs twenty-five years ago, but now they are only five shillings. The decrease of the price is owing to competition, for though there are only two of us in the trade in London, still the other party is always pushing his eyes and underselling our'n. Immediately the demand ceases at all, he goes round the trade with his eyes in a box, and offers them at a lower figure than in the regular season, and so the prices have been falling every year. There is a brisk and a slack season in our business, as well as in most others. After the Christmas holidays up to March we have generally little to do, but from that time eyes begin to look up a bit, and the business remains pretty good till the end of October. Where we make one pair of eyes for home consumption, we make ten for exportation; a great many eyes go abroad. Yes, I suppose we should be soon over-populated with dolls if a great number of them were not to emigrate every year. The annual increase of dolls goes on at an alarming rate. As you say, sir, the yearly rate of mortality must be very high, to be sure, but still it's nothing to the rate at which they are brought into the world. They can't make wax dolls in America, sir, so we ship off a great many there. The reason why they can't produce dolls in America is owing to the climate. The wax won't set in very hot weather, and it cracks in extreme cold. I knew a party who went out to the United States to start as doll-maker. He took several gross of my eyes with him, but he couldn't succeed. The eyes that we make for Spanish America are all black. A blue-eyed doll wouldn't sell at all there. Here, however, nothing but blue eyes goes down; that's because it's the colour of the Queen's eyes, and she sets the fashion in our eyes as in other things. We make the same kind of eyes for the gutta-percha dolls as for the wax. It is true, the gutta-percha complexion isn't particularly clear; nevertheless, the eyes I make for the washable faces are all of the natural tint, and if the gutta-percha dolls look rather bilious, why I ain't a going to make my eyes look bilious to match.

"I also make human eyes. These are two cases; in the one I have black and hazel, and in the other blue and grey." [Here the man took the lids off a couple of boxes, about as big as binnacles, that stood on the table: they each contained 190 different eyes, and so like nature, that the effect produced upon a person unaccustomed to the sight was most peculiar, and far from pleasant. The whole of the 380 optics all seemed to be staring directly at the spectator, and occasioned a feeling somewhat similar to the bewilderment one experiences on suddenly becoming an object of general notice; as if the eyes, indeed, of a whole lecture-room were crammed into a few square inches, and all turned full upon you. The eyes of the whole world, as we say, literally appeared to be fixed upon one, and it was almost impossible at first to look at them without instinctively averting the head. The hundred eyes of Argus were positively insignificant in comparison to the 380 belonging to the human eye-maker.] "Here you see are the ladies' eyes," he continued, taking one from the blue-eye tray. "You see there's more sparkle and brilliance about them than the gentlemen's. Here's two different ladies' eyes; they belong to fine-looking young women, both of them. When a lady or gentleman comes to us for an eye, we are obliged to have a sitting just like a portrait-painter. We take no sketch, but study the tints of the perfect eye. There are a number of eyes come over from France, but these are generally what we call misfits; they are sold cheap, and seldom match the other eye. Again, from not fitting tight over the ball like those that are made expressly for the person, they seldom move 'consentaneously,' as it is termed, with the natural eye, and have therefore a very unpleasant and fixed stare, worse almost than the defective eye itself. Now, the eyes we make move so freely, and have such a natural appearance, that I can assure you a gentleman who had one of his from me passed nine doctors without the deception being detected.

"There is a lady customer of mine who has been married three years to her husband, and I believe he doesn't know that she has a false eye to this day.

"The generality of persons whom we serve take out their eyes when they go to bed, and sleep with them either under their pillow, or else in a tumbler of water on the toilet-table at their side. Most married ladies, however, never take their eyes out at all.

"Some people wear out a false eye in half the time of others. This doesn't arise from the greater use of them, or rolling them about, but from the increased secretion of the tears, which act on the false eye like acid on metal, and so corrodes and roughens the surface. This roughness produces inflammation, and then a new eye becomes necessary. The Scotch lose a great many eyes, why I cannot say; and the men in this country lose more eyes, nearly two to one. We generally make only one eye, but I did once make two false eyes for a widow lady. She lost one first, and we repaired the loss so well, that on her losing the other eye she got us to make her a second.

"False eyes are a great charity to servants. If they lose an eye no one will engage them. In Paris there is a charitable institution for the supply of false eyes to the poor; and I really think, if there was a similar establishment in this country for furnishing artificial eyes to those whose bread depends on their looks, like servants, it would do a great deal of good. We always supplies eyes to such people at half-price. My usual price is 2*l.* 2*s.* for one of my best eyes. That eye is a couple of guineas, and as fine an eye as you would wish to see in any young woman's head.

"I suppose we make from 300 to 400 false eyes every year. The great art in making a false eye is in polishing the edges quite smooth. Of dolls' eyes we make about 6000 dozen pairs of the common ones every year. I take it that there are near upon 24,000 dozen, or more than a quarter of a million, pairs of all sorts of dolls' eyes made annually in London."

THE COAL-HEAVERS.

THE transition from the artisan to the labourer is curious in many respects. In passing from the skilled operative of the west-end to the unskilled workman of the eastern quarter of London, the moral and intellectual change is so great, that it seems as if we were in a new land, and among another race. The artisans are almost to a man red-hot politicians. They are sufficiently educated and thoughtful to have a sense of their importance in the State. It is true they may entertain exaggerated notions of their natural rank and position in the social scale, but at least they have read, and reflected, and argued upon the subject, and their opinions are entitled to consideration. The political character and sentiments of the working classes appear to me to be a distinctive feature of the age, and they are a necessary consequence of the dawning intelligence of the mass. As their minds expand, they are naturally led to take a more enlarged view of their calling, and to contemplate their labours in relation to the whole framework of society. They begin to view their class, not as a mere isolated body of workmen, but as an integral portion of the nation, contributing their quota to the general welfare. If property has its duties as well as its rights; labour, on the other hand, they say, has its rights as well as its duties. The artisans of London seem to be generally well-informed upon these subjects. That they express their opinions violently, and often

savagely, it is my duty to acknowledge; but that they are the unenlightened and unthinking body of people that they are generally considered by those who never go among them, and who see them only as "the dangerous classes," it is my duty also to deny. So far as my experience has gone, I am bound to confess, that I have found the skilled labourers of the metropolis the very reverse, both morally and intellectually, of what the popular prejudice imagines them.

The unskilled labourers are a different class of people. As yet they are as unpolitical as footmen, and instead of entertaining violent democratic opinions, they appear to have no political opinions whatever; or, if they do possess any, they rather lead towards the maintenance of "things as they are," than towards the ascendancy of the working people. I have lately been investigating the state of the coalwhippers, and these reflections are forced upon me by the marked difference in the character and sentiments of these people from those of the operative tailors. Among the latter class there appeared to be a general bias towards the six points of the Charter; but the former were extremely proud of their having turned out to a man on the 10th of April, 1848, and become special constables for the maintenance of law and order on the day of the great Chartist demonstration. As to which of these classes are the better members of the state, it is not for me to offer an opinion; I merely assert a social fact. The artisans of the metropolis are intelligent, and dissatisfied with their political position: the labourers of London appear to be the reverse; and in passing from one class to the other, the change is so curious and striking, that the phenomenon deserves at least to be recorded in this place.

The labourers, in point of numbers, rank second on the occupation-list of the metropolis. The domestic servants, as a body of people, have the first numerical position, being as many as 168,000, while the labourers are less than one-third that number, or 50,000 strong. They, however, are nearly twice as many as the boot and shoemakers, who stand next upon the list, and muster 28,000 individuals among them; and they are more than twice as many as the tailors and breeches-makers, who are fourth in regard to their number, and count 23,500 persons. After these come the milliners and dressmakers, who are 20,000 in number.

According to the Criminal Returns of the metropolis (for a copy of which I am indebted to the courtesy of a gentleman who expresses himself most anxious to do all in his power to aid the inquiry), the labourers occupy a most unenviable pre-eminence in police history. One in every twenty-eight labourers, according to these returns, has a predisposition for simple larceny: the average for the whole population of London is one in every 266 individuals;

so that the labourers may be said to be more than nine times as dishonest as the generality of people resident in the metropolis. In drunkenness they occupy the same prominent position. One in every twenty-two individuals of the labouring class was charged with being intoxicated in the year 1848; whereas the average number of drunkards in the whole population of London is one in every 113 individuals. Nor are they less pugnaciously inclined; one in every twenty-six having been charged with a common assault, of a more or less aggravated form. The labourers of London are, therefore, nine times as dishonest, five times as drunken, and nine times as savage as the rest of the community. Of the state of their education as a body of people I have no similar means of judging at present; nor am I in a position to test their improvidence or their poverty in the same conclusive manner. Taking, however, the Government returns of the number of labourers located in the different unions throughout the country at the time of taking the last census, I find that one in every 140 of the class were paupers; while the average for all England and Wales was one in every 159 persons: so that, while the Government returns show the labourers generally to be extraordinarily dishonest, drunken, and pugnacious, their vices cannot be ascribed to the poverty of their calling; for, compared with other occupations, their avocation appears to produce fewer paupers than the generality of employments.

Of the moral and prudential qualities of the coalwhippers and coalporters, as a special portion of the labouring population, the crude, undigested, and essentially unscientific character of all the Government returns will not allow me to judge. Even the Census affords us little or no opportunity of estimating the numbers of the class. The only information to be obtained from that document—whose insufficiency is a national disgrace to us, for there the trading and working classes are all jumbled together in the most perplexing confusion, and the occupations classified in a manner that would shame the merest tyro in logic—is the following:—

Of coal and colliery agents and factors there are in London . . .	16
Ditto dealers and merchants . .	1541
Ditto labourers, heavers, and porters	1700
Ditto meters	136
Total in the coal trade in London .	3393
Deduct from this the number of merchants from the London Post Office Directory	565
Hence the coal labourers in the metropolis amount to . . .	2828

But this is far from being an accurate result.

There are at present in London upwards of 1900 (say 2000) registered coalwhippers, and as many more coalbackers or porters. These altogether would give as many as 4000 coal-labourers. Besides, there are 150 meters; so that, altogether, it may be safely said that the number engaged in the whipping and porterage of coals in London is 4000 and odd.

The following statistics, carefully collected from official returns, will furnish our readers with some idea of the amazing increase in the importation of coal:—

" About 300 years ago (say about 1550) one or two ships were sufficient for the demand and supply of London. In 1615, about 200 were equal to its demand; in 1705, about 600 ships were engaged in the London coal-trade; in 1805, 4856 cargoes, containing about 1,350,000 tons; in 1820, 5884 cargoes, containing 1,692,992 tons; in 1830, 7108 cargoes, containing 2,079,275 tons; in 1840, 9132 cargoes, containing 2,566,899 tons; in 1845, 2695 ships were employed in carrying 11,987 cargoes, containing 3,403,320 tons; and during the year 1848, 2717 ships, making 12,267 voyages, and containing 3,418,340 tons. The increase in the importation from the year 1838 to 1848, when the respective importations were 2,518,085 tons and 3,418,340 tons, is upwards of 90 per cent. Now, by taking 2700 vessels as the actual number now employed, and by calculating such vessels to average 300 tons burden per ship, and giving to a vessel of that size a crew of eight men, it will appear that at the present time 21,600 seamen are employed in the carrying department of the London coal-trade."

Before visiting the district of Wapping, where the greater part of the coal labour is carried on, I applied to the Clerk and Registrar of the Coal Exchange for the statistics connected with the body of which he is an officer. Such statistics—as to the extent of their great traffic, the weekly returns of sales, in short, the ramifications of an inquiry embracing maritime, mercantile, mining, and labouring interests, are surely the weekly routine of the business of the Registrar's office. I was promised a series of returns by the gentleman in question, but I did not receive and could not obtain them. Another officer, the Secretary of the Meters' Office, when applied to, with the sanction of his co-officer, the Clerk and Registrar, required a written application which should be attended to! I do not allude to these gentlemen with the slightest inclination unduly to censure them. The truth is, with questions affecting labour and the poor they have little sympathy. The labourer, in their eyes, is but a machine; so many labourers are as so many horse-power. To deny, or withhold, or delay information required for the purposes of the present inquiry is, however, unavailing. The matter I have given in fulness and in precision, without any aid from the gentlemen referred to shows that it was more through courtesy than through necessity that I applied to them in the first instance.

Finding my time, therefore, only wasted in dancing attendance upon city coal officials, I made the best of my way down to the Coalwhippers' Office, to glean my information among the men themselves. The following is the result of my inquiries :—

The coal-vessels are principally moored in that part of the river called the Pool.

The Pool, rightly so called, extends from Ratcliffe-cross, near the Regent's-canal, to Execution-dock, and is about a mile long, but the jurisdiction of the Coal Commissioners reaches from the Arsenal at Woolwich to London-bridge. The Pool is divided into the Upper and Lower Pool; it is more commonly called the North and South side, because the colliers are arranged on the Ratcliffe and Shadwell side, in the Lower Pool, and on the Redriff and Rotherhithe side, in the Upper. The Lower Pool consists of seven tiers, which generally contain each from fourteen to twenty ships; these are moored stern to stern, and lie from seven to ten abreast. The Upper Pool contains about ten tiers. The four tiers at Mill-hole are equally large with the tiers of the Lower Pool. Those of Church-hole, which are three in number, are somewhat smaller; and those of the fast tiers, which are also three in number, are single, and not double tiers like the rest. The fleet often consists of from 200 to 300 ships. In the winter it is the largest, many of the colliers in the summer season going foreign voyages. An easterly wind prevents the vessels making their way to London; and, if continuing for any length of time, will throw the whole of the coalwhippers out of work. In the winter, the coalwhipper is occupied about five days out of eight, and about three days out of eight in the summer; so that, taking it all the year round, he is only about half of his time employed. As soon as a collier arrives at Gravesend, the captain sends the ship's papers up to the factor at the Coal Exchange, informing him of the quality and quantity of coal in the ship. The captain then falls into some tier near Gravesend, and remains there until he is ordered nearer London by the harbourmaster. When the coal is sold and the ship supplied with the coal - meter, the captain receives orders from the harbour - master to come up into the Pool, and take his berth in a particular tier. The captain, when he has moored his ship into the Pool as directed, applies at the Coalwhippers' Office, and "the gang" next in rotation is sent to him.

There are upwards of 200 gangs of coalwhippers. The class, supernumeraries included, numbers about 2000 individuals. The number of meters is 150; the consequence is, that more than one-fourth of the gangs are unprovided with meters to work with them. Hence there are upwards of fifty gangs (of nine men each) of coalwhippers, or altogether 450 men more than there is any real occasion for. The consequence is, that each coalwhipper is necessarily thrown out of employ one-quarter of his time by the excess of hands. The cause of this extra number of hands being kept on the books is, that when there is a glut of vessels in the river, the coal merchants may not be delayed in having their cargoes delivered from want of whippers. When such a glut occurs, the merchant has it in his power to employ a private meter; so that the 450 to 500 men are kept on the year through, merely to meet the particular exigency, and to promote the merchant's convenience. Did any good arise from this system to the public, the evil might be overlooked; but since, owing to the combination of the coalfactors, no more coals can come into the market than are sufficient to meet the demand *without lowering the price*, it is clear that the extra 450 or 500 men are kept on and allowed to deprive their fellow-labourers of one-quarter of their regular work as whippers, without any advantage to the public.

The coalwhippers, previous to the passing of the Act of Parliament in 1843, were employed and paid by the publicans in the neighbourhood of the river, from Tower-hill to Limehouse. Under this system, none but the most dissolute and intemperate obtained employment; in fact, the more intemperate they were the more readily they found work. The publicans were the relatives of the northern shipowners; they mostly had come to London penniless, and being placed in a tavern by their relatives, soon became shipowners themselves. There were at that time seventy taverns on the north side of the Thames, below bridge, employing coalwhippers, and all of the landlords making fortunes out of the earnings of the people. When a ship came to be "made up," that is, for the hands to be hired, the men assembled round the bar in crowds and began calling for drink, and outbidding each other in the extent of their orders, so as to induce the landlord to give them employment. If one called for beer, the next would be sure to give an order for rum; for he who spent most at the public-house had the greatest chance of employment. After being "taken on," their first care was to put up a score at the public-house, so as to please their employer, the publican. In the morning before going to their work, they would invariably call at the house for a quartern of gin or rum; and they were obliged to take off with them to the ship "a bottle," holding nine pots of beer, and that of the worst description, for it was the invariable practice among the publicans to supply the coalwhippers with the very worst articles at the highest prices. When the men returned from their work they went back to the public-house, and there remained drinking the greater part of the night. He must have been a very steady man indeed, I am told, who could manage to return home sober to his wife and family. The consequence of this was, the men used to pass their days, and chief part of their nights, drinking in the public-house; and I am credibly informed that frequently, on the publican settling with them after leaving the ship, instead of having anything to receive they were brought in several shillings in debt; this remained as a score for the next ship: in fact, it was only those who were in debt to the publican who were sure of employment on the next occasion. One publican had as many as fifteen ships; another had even more; and there was scarcely one of them without his two or three colliers. The children of the coalwhippers were almost reared in the tap-room, and a person who has had great experience in the trade, tells me he knew as many as 500 youths who were transported, and as many more who met with an untimely death. At one house there were forty young robust men employed, about seventeen years ago, and of these there are only two living at present. My informant tells me that he has frequently seen as many as 100 men at one time fighting pell-mell at King James's-stairs, and the publican standing by to see fair play. The average money spent in drink by each man was about 12s. to each ship. There were about 10,000 ships entered the Pool each year, and nine men were required to clear each ship. This made the annual expenditure of the coalwhippers in drink, 54,000l., or 27l. a-year per man. This is considered an extremely low average. The wives and families of the men at this time were in the greatest destitution, the daughters invariably became prostitutes, and the mothers ultimately went to swell the number of paupers at the union. This state of things continued till 1843, when, by the efforts of three of the coalwhippers, the Legislature was induced to pass an Act forbidding the system, and appointing Commissioners for the registration and regulation of coalwhippers in the port of London, and so establishing an office where the men were in future employed and paid. Under this Act, every man then following the calling of a coalwhipper was to be registered. For this registration 4d. was to be paid; and every man desirous of entering upon the same business had to pay the same sum, and to have his name registered. The employment is open to any labouring man; but every new hand, after registering himself, must work for twenty-one days on half-pay before he is considered to be "broken in," and entitled to take rank and receive pay as a regular coalwhipper.

All the coalwhippers are arranged in gangs of eight whippers, with a basket-man or foreman. These gangs are numbered from 1 up to 218, which is the highest number at the present time. The basket-men, or foremen, enter their names in a rotation-book kept in the office, and as their names stand in that book so do they take their turn to clear the ship that is offered. On a ship being offered, a printed form of application, kept in the office, is filled up by the captain, in which he states the number of tons, the price, and time in which she is to be delivered. If the gang whose turn of work it is refuse the ship at the price offered, then it is offered to all the gangs, and if accepted by any other gang, the next in rotation may claim it as their right, before all others. In connexion with the office there is a long hall, extending from the street to the water-side, where the men wait to take their turn. There is also a room called the basket-men's room, where the foremen of the gang remain in attendance. There is likewise a floating pier called a dépôt, which is used as a receptacle for the tackle with which the colliers are unloaded. This floating pier is fitted up with seats, where the men wait in the summer. The usual price at present for delivering the colliers is 8d. per ton; but in case of a less price being offered, and the gangs all refusing it, then the captain is at liberty to employ any hands he pleases. According to the Act, however, the owner or purchaser of the coals is at liberty to employ his own servants, provided they have been in his service fourteen clear days previous, and so have become what the Act terms bonâ fide servants. This is very often taken advantage of, for the purpose of obtaining labourers at a less price. One lighterman, who is employed by the gas companies to "lighter" their coals to their various destinations, makes a practice of employing parties whom he calls the bonâ fide servants of the gas companies, to deliver the coals at a penny per ton less than the regular price. Besides this, he takes one man's pay to himself, and so stops one-tenth of the whole proceeds, thereby realizing, as he boasts, the sum of 300l. per annum. Added to this, a relative of his keeps a beer-shop, where the "bonâ fide servants" spend the chief part of their earnings, thereby bringing back the old system, which was the cause of so much misery and destitution to the work-people.

According to the custom of the trade, the rate at which a ship is to be delivered is forty-nine tons per day, and if the ship cannot be delivered at that rate, owing to the merchant failing to send craft to receive the coals, then the coalwhippers are entitled to receive pay at the rate of forty-nine tons per day, for each day they are kept in the ship over and above the time allowed by the custom of the trade for the delivery of the coals. The merchants, however, if they should have failed to send craft, and so keep the men idle on the first days of the contract, can, by the by-laws of the Commissioners, compel the coalwhippers to deliver the ship at the rate of ninety-eight tons per day: the merchants surely should be made to pay for the loss of time to the men at the same rate. The wrong done by this practice is rendered more apparent by the conduct of the merchants during the brisk and slack periods. When there is a slack, the merchants are all anxious to get their vessels delivered as fast as they can, because coals are wanting, and are consequently at a high price; then the men are taxed beyond their power, and are frequently made to deliver 150 to 200 tons per day, or to do four days' work in one. On the contrary, when there is a glut of ships, and the merchants are not particularly anxious about the delivery of the coals, the men are left to idle away their time upon the decks for the first two or three days of the contract, and then forced to the same extra exertion for the last two or three days, in order to make up for the lost time of the merchant, and so save him from being put to extra expense by his own neglect. The cause of the injustice of these by-laws may be fairly traced to the fact of there being several coal-merchants among the Commissioners, who are entrusted with the formation of bye-laws and regulations of the trade. The coalfactors are generally ship-owners, and occasionally pit-owners; and when a glut of ships come in they combine together to keep up the prices, especially in the winter time, for they keep back the cargoes, and only offer such a number of ships as will not influence the market. Since the passing of the Act, establishing the Coal-whippers' Office, and thus taking the employment and pay of the men out of the hands of the publicans, so visible has been the improvement in the whole character of the labourers, that they have raised themselves in the respect of all who know them.

Within the last few years they have established a Benefit Society, and they expended in the year 1847, according to the last account, 646l. odd, in the relief of the sick and the burial of the dead. They have also established a superannuation fund, out of which they allow 5s. per week to each member who is incapacitated from old age or accident. They are, at the present time, paying such pensions to twenty members. At the time of the celebrated Chartist demonstration, on the 10th of April, the coalwhippers were, I believe, the first class of persons who spontaneously offered their services as special constables.

Further than this they have established a school, with accommodation for six hundred scholars, out of their small earnings. On one occasion as much as 80l. was collected among the men for the erection of this institution.

The men are liable to many accidents; some fall off the plank into the hold of the vessel, and are killed; others are injured by large lumps of coal falling on them; and, indeed, so frequent are these disasters, that the Commissioners have directed that the indivisible fraction which remains, after dividing the earnings of the men into nine equal parts, should be applied to the relief of the injured;

and although the fund raised by these insignificant means amounts in the course of the year to 30l. or 40l., the whole is absorbed by the calamities.

Furnished with this information as to the general character and regulations of the calling, I then proceeded to visit one of the vessels in the river, so that I might see the nature of the labour performed. No one on board the vessel (the ——, of Newcastle) was previously aware of my visit or its object. I need not describe the vessel, as my business is with the London labourers in the coal trade. It is necessary, however, in order to show the nature of the labour of coal-whipping, that I should state that the average depth of coal in the hold of a collier, from ceiling to combing, is sixteen feet, while there is an additional seven feet to be reckoned for the basket-man's "boom," which makes the height that the coals have to be raised by the whippers from twenty-three to thirty feet. The complement of a gang of coalwhippers is about nine. In the hold are four men, who relieve each other in filling a basket—only one basket being in use with coal. The labour of these four men is arduous: so exhausting is it in hot weather that their usual attire is found to be cumbrous, and they have often to work merely in their trousers or drawers. As fast as these four men in the hold fill the basket, which holds 1¼cwt., four whippers draw it up. This is effected in a peculiar and, to a person unused to the contemplation of the process, really an impressive manner. The four whippers stand on the deck, at the foot of what is called "a way." This way resembles a short rude ladder: it is formed of four broken oars lashed lengthways, from four to five feet in height (giving a step from oar to oar of more than a foot), while the upright spars to which they are attached are called "a derrick." At the top of this "derrick" is a "gin," which is a revolving wheel, to which the ropes holding the basket, "filled" and "whipped," are attached. The process is thus one of manual labour with mechanical aid. The basket having been filled in the hold, the whippers correctly guessing the time for the filling—for they never look down into the hold—skip up the "way," holding the ropes attached to the basket and the gin, and pulling the ropes at two skips, simultaneously, as they ascend. They thus hoist the loaded basket some height out of the hold, and, when hoisted so far, jump down, keeping exact time in their jump, from the topmost beam of the way on to the deck, so giving the momentum of their bodily weight to the motion communicated to the basket. While the basket is influenced by this motion and momentum, the basket-man, who is stationed on a plank flung across the hold, seizes the basket, runs on with it (the gin revolving) to "the boom," and shoots the contents into the weighing-machine. The boom is formed of two upright poles, with a cross-pole attached by way of step, on to which the basket-man vaults, and rapidly reversing the basket, empties it. This process is very quickly effected, for if the basket-man did not avail himself of the swing of the basket, the feat would be almost beyond a man's strength, or, at least, he would soon be exhausted by it.

The machine is a large coal-scuttle or wooden box, attached to a scale connected with 2½ cwt. When the weight is raised by two deposits in the machine, which hangs over the side of the ship, it discharges it, by pulling a rope connected with it down a sliding wooden plane into the barge below. The machine holds 2½ cwt., and so the meter registers the weight of coal unladen. This process is not only remarkable for its celerity but for another characteristic. Sailors, when they have to " pull away " together, generally time their pulling to some rude chant; their " Yo, heave, yo," is thought not only to regulate but to mitigate the weight of their labour. The coalwhippers do their work in perfect silence: they do it indeed like work, and hard work, too. The basket-man and the meter are equally silent, so that nothing is heard but the friction of the ropes, the discharge of the coal from the basket into the machine, and from the machine into the barge. The usual amount of work done by the whippers in a day (but not as an average, one day with another) is to unload, or whip, ninety-eight tons! To whip one ton, sixteen basketfuls are required; so that to whip a single ton these men jump up and down 144 feet: for a day's work of ninety-eight tons, they jump up and down 13,088 feet, more in some instances; for in the largest ship the way has five steps, and ten men are employed. The coalwhippers, therefore, raise 1¼ cwt. very nearly four miles high, or twice as high as a balloon ordinarily mounts in the air: and, in addition to this, the coalwhippers themselves ascend very nearly 1½ mile perpendicularly in the course of the day. On some days they whip upwards of 150 tons —200 have been whipped, when double this labour must be gone through. The ninety-eight tons take about seven hours. The basket-man's work is the most critical, and accidents, from his falling into the hold, are not very unfrequent. The complement of men for the unlading of a vessel is, as I have said, nine: four in the hold, four whippers, and the basket-man — the meter forms a tenth, but he acts independently of the others. They seldom work by candlelight, and, whenever possible, avoid working in very bad weather; but the merchant, as I have shown, has great power in regulating their labour for his own convenience. The following statement was given to me by a coalwhipper on board this vessel:—

" We should like better wages, but then we have enemies. Now suppose you, sir, are a coalmerchant, and this gentleman here freights a ship of the captain — you understand me? The man who freights the ships that way is paid, by the captain, ninepence a-ton, for a gang of nine men, such as you've seen — nine coalwhippers — but these nine men, you understand me, are paid by the merchant (or buyer) only eightpence a ton ; so that by every ton he clears a penny, without any labour or trouble whatsomever. I and my fellows is dissatisfied, but can't help ourselves. This merchant, too, you understand me, finds there's rather an opening in the Act of Parliament about whippers. By employing a man as his servant on his premises for fourteen days, he's entitled to work as a coalwhipper. We call such made whipper ' boneyfides.' There's lots of them, and plenty more would be made if we was to turn rusty. I've heard, you understand me, of driving a coach through an Act of Parliament, but here they drive a whole fleet through it."

The coalwhippers all present the same aspect —they are all black. In summer, when the men strip more to their work, perspiration causes the coal-dust to adhere to the skin, and blackness is more than ever the rule. All about the ship partakes of the grimness of the prevailing hue. The sails are black; the gilding on the figurehead of the vessel becomes blackened, and the very visitor feels his complexion soon grow sable. The dress of the whippers is of every description; some have fustian jackets, some have sailors' jackets, some loose great coats, some Guernsey frocks. Many of them work in strong shirts, which once were white with a blue stripe: loose cotton neckerchiefs are generally worn by the whippers. All have black hair and black whiskers — no matter what the original hue; to the more stubbly beards and moustachios the coal-dust adheres freely between the bristles, and may even be seen, now and then, to glitter in the light amidst the hair. The barber, one of these men told me, charged nothing extra for shaving him, although the coal-dust must be a formidable thing to the best-tempered razor. In approaching a coal-ship in the river, the side has to be gained over barges lying alongside—the coal crackling under the visitor's feet. He must cross them to reach a ladder of very primitive construction, up which the deck is to be reached. It is a jest among the Yorkshire seamen that every thing is black in a collier, especially the soup. When the men are at work in whipping or filling, the only spot of white discernible on their hands is a portion of the nails.

There are no specific hours for the payment of these men : they are entitled to their money as soon as their work is reported to be completed. Nothing can be better than the way in which the whippers are now paid. The basket-man enters the office of the payclerk of the coal commission at one door, and hands over an adjoining counter an amount of money he has received from the captain. The pay-clerk ascertains that the amount is correct. He then divides the sum into nine portions, and, touching a spring to open a door, he cries out for "Gang such a number." The nine men, who, with many others, are in attendance in rooms provided for them adjacent to the pay-office, appear immediately, and are paid off. I was present when nine whippers were paid for the discharge of 363½ tons. The following was the work done and the remuneration received:—

	Day.	Tons.
Dec. 14th	1st	35
„ 15th	2nd	56
	Sunday intervenes.	
„ 17th	3rd	84
„ 18th	4th	98
„ 19th	5th	90½
		363½

These 363½ tons, at 8d. per ton, realized to each man, for five days' work, 1l. 6s. 4¼d.; 10s. of which had been paid to each as subsistence money during the progress of the work. In addition to the work so paid to each, there was deducted a farthing in every shilling as office fees, to defray the expenses of the office. From this farthing reduction, moreover, the basket-man is paid 1½d. in the pound, as commission for bringing the money from the captain. Out of the sum to be divided on the occasion I specify there was an indivisible fraction of 1¼d. This, as it cannot be shared among nine men, goes to what is called "The Fraction Fund," which is established for the relief of persons suffering from accidents on board coal-ships. These indivisible fractions realize between 30l. and 40l. yearly.

Connected with the calling of the whippers I may mention the existence of the Purlmen. These are men who carry kegs of malt liquor in boats, and retail it afloat, having a license from the Waterman's Company to do so. In each boat is a small iron grating, containing a fire, so that any customer can have the chill off, should he require that luxury. The purlman, rings a bell to announce his visit to the men on board. There are several purlmen, who keep rowing all day about the coal fleet; they are not allowed to sell spirits. In a fog the glaring of the fire in the purlmen's boats, discernible on the river, has a curious effect, nothing but the fire being visible.

I was now desirous of obtaining some information from the men collectively. Accordingly I entered the basket-men's waiting-room, where a large number of them were "biding their turn;" and no sooner had I made my appearance in the hall, and my object became known to the men, than a rush was made from without, and the door was obliged to be bolted to prevent the overcrowding of the room. As it was, the place was crammed so full, that the light was completely blocked by the men piled up on the seats and lockers, and standing before the windows. The room was thus rendered so dark that I was obliged to have the gas lighted, in order to see to take my notes; I myself was obliged to mount the opposite locker to take the statistics of the meeting.

There were eighty-six present. To show how many had no employment whatever last week, forty-five hands were held up. One had had no employment for a fortnight; twenty-four no work for eight days. Of those who had worked during the previous week, eight had received 20s.; sixteen between 15s. and seventeen between 10s. and 15s.; ten between 5s. and 10s.; one had received under 5s.; twelve had received nothing. The average of employment as to time is this:—None are employed for thirty weeks during the year; all for twenty-five weeks or upwards, realizing 12s. perhaps, yearly, per week—so many of the men said; but the office returns show 1s. 1½d. per day as the average for the last nine months. "Waterage" costs the whipper an average of 6d. a-week the year through. "Waterage" means the conveyance from the vessels to the shore. Fourteen of the men had wives or daughters who work at slop needlework, the husbands being unable to maintain the family by their own labour. A coalwhipper stated that there were more of the wives of the coalwhippers idle, because they couldn't get work, than were at work. All the wives and daughters would have worked if they could have got it. "Why, your honour," one man said, "we are better off in this office than under the old system. We were then compulsory drunkards, and often in debt to a publican after clearing the ship." The men employed generally spent 12s. to 15s. a-week. Those unemployed had abundant credit at the publican's. One man said, "I worked for a publican who was also a butcher; one week I had to pay 9s. for drink, and 11s. for meat, and he said I hadn't spent sufficient. I was one of his constant men." At the time a ship was cleared, the whipper had often nothing to take home. "Nothing but sorrow," said one. The publican swept all; and some publicans would advance 2s. 6d. towards the next job, to allow a man to live. Many of the whippers now do not drink at all. The average of the drinking among the men, when at hard work, does not exceed three half-pints a-day. The grievances that once afflicted the coalwhipper, are still felt by the ballast-men. The men all stated the fact as to the 9d. allowed, and the 8d. per ton paid for whipping. They all represented that a lighterman, engaged by the gas companies, was doing them great injury, by employing a number of 'bonafides,' and taking the best ships away from the regular office, and giving them to the 'bonafides' who "whip" the vessel at a lower rate of wages—about 6d. a-ton. He is connected with a beer-shop, and the men are expected to buy his beer.

If this man gets on with his system, (all this the men concurred in stating,) the bad state of things prevailing under the publican's management might be brought back. Sixteen years ago each whipper received 11¼d. per ton, prices steady, and the men in union. "If it wasn't for this office," one man said, "not one man who worked sixteen years ago would be alive now." The Union was broken up about twelve years ago, and prices fell and fluctuated down as low as 6d., and even 5½d., sometimes rising and falling 1¼d. a-week. The prices continued fluctuating until the present office was established, in 1844. The shipowners and merchants agreed, at the commencement of the office, to give the whippers 9d. a-ton, and in three months reduced it to 8d. The publicans, it was stated, formed themselves into a compact body for the purpose of breaking down the present system, and they introduced hundreds of fresh hands to undersell the regular workers. In 1847 wages rose again to 9d.; the whippers appealing to the trade, urging the high price of provisions, and their appeal being allowed. This 9d. a-ton continued until the 1st of June last. At that time the ' bonafides ' were generally introduced, and greatly increased, and getting three times the work the regular men did, they (the regular men) consented again to lower the prices. The ' bonafides ' are no better off than the regular hands; for though they have much more work they have less per ton, and have to spend more in drink. The coalwhippers represented themselves as benefited by the cheapness of provisions. With dear provisions they couldn't, at their present earnings, live at all. The removal of the backing system had greatly benefited the whippers. On being asked how many had things in pawn, there was a general laugh, and a cry of "All of us." It is common to pawn a coat on Monday and take it out on Saturday night, paying a month's interest. One man said, "I have now in pawn seven articles, all wearing apparel, my wife's or my own, from 15s. down to 9d." Four had in pawn goods to the amount of 5l. and upwards; five to 4l.; six to 3l.; thirteen to 2l.; thirteen to 1l.; under 1l. nineteen; five had nothing in pawn. When asked if all made a practice of pawning their coats during the week, there was a general assent. Some could not redeem them in time to attend church or chapel on a Sunday. One man said, that if all his effects were burnt in his absence, he would lose no wearing apparel. "Our children, under the old system, were totally neglected," they said; "the public-house absorbed everything." Under that system as many as 500 of the children of coalwhippers were transported; now that has entirely ceased; those charged with crime now were reared under the old system. "The legislature never did a better thing than to emancipate us," said the man; "they have

the blessing and prayers of ourselves, our wives, and children."

After the meeting I was furnished with the following accounts of a basket-man, of which I have calculated the averages :—

First Quarter.—January 2, 1849, to March 28.

Employed	.	.	.	.	.	50 days
Delivered	.	.	.	.	2570¼ tons
Amount earned at 9d. per ton	.	£10 15 2½
Deduct expenses of office 4s. 6d. }	0 12 10
Ditto waterage . . 8s. 4d. }	

£10 2 4½

Average weekly earnings about . 0 16 6

Second Quarter. — April 7 to June 30.

Employed	.	.	.	.	44 days
Delivered	.	.	.	.	2609 tons
Amount earned at 9d. per ton	£10 10 8
Deduct waterage . . 7s. 4d. }	0 11 8
Office expenses . 4s. 4d. }	

£9 19 0

Average weekly earnings . 0 15 3½

Third Quarter—July 4 to September 24.

Employed	.	.	.	.	42 days
Delivered	.	.	.	.	2485 tons
Amount earned at 8d. per ton	. £9 4 4¾
Deduct waterage . 7s. 0d. }	£0 10 10¼
Office expenses . 3s. 10¼d. }	

£8 13 6½

Average weekly earnings . 0 14 2

Fourth Quarter—Oct. 4 to Dec. 20.

Employed	.	.	.	.	49 days
Delivered	.	.	.	.	2858½ tons
Amount earned at 8d. per ton	. £9 16 4¾
Deduct waterage . . 8s. 2d. }	0 12 3¾
Office expenses . 4s. 1¾d. }	

£9 4 1

Average weekly earnings . 0 14 1¾

First Quarter	.	.	.	£10 2 4¼
Second Quarter	.	.	.	9 19 0
Third Quarter	.	.	.	8 13 6½
Fourth Quarter	.	.	.	9 4 1

£37 19 0

Average weekly earnings . 0 14 6

Employed—First Quarter	.	50 days.
Second Quarter	.	44 „
Third Quarter	.	42 „
Fourth Quarter	.	49 „

185 days.

Idle . . 180 days.

SECOND ACCOUNT.

Coalwhippers.

Employed	.	.	.	193 days
Delivered	.	.	.	11,573¾ tons
Amount earned at 9*d.* per ton	.	£46	15	10¼
Deduct waterage	.	.	1	12	2

£45 3 8¼

Average weekly earnings . 0 17 4½

THIRD ACCOUNT.

Employed	.	.	.	168 days
Delivered	.	.	.	9874½ tons
Amount earned	.	.	.	£37 19 0
Deduct waterage	.	.	1 8 0

Gross earnings . . £36 11 0

Average weekly earnings . 0 14 0½

The above accounts are rather above than under the average.

I then proceeded to take the statement of some of the different classes of the men. The first was a coalwhipper, whom the men had selected as one knowing more about their calling than the generality. He told me as follows:—

"I am about forty, and am a married man with a family of six children. I worked under the old system, and that to my sorrow. If I had been paid in money, according to the work I then did, I could have averaged 30*s.* a-week. Instead of receiving that amount in money, I was compelled to spend in drink 15*s.* to 18*s.* per week, when work was good; and the publican even then gave me the residue very grudgingly, and often kept me from eleven to twelve on Saturday night, before he would pay me. The consequences of this system were, that I had a miserable home to go to: I would often have faced Newgate as soon. My health didn't suffer, because I didn't drink the liquor I was forced to pay for. I gave most of it away. The liquors were beer, rum, and gin, all prepared the night before, adulterated shamefully for our consumption, as we dursn't refuse it,—dursn't even grumble. The condition of my poor wife and children was then most wretched. Now the thing is materially altered, thank God; my wife and children can go to chapel at certain times, when work is pretty good, and our things are not in pawn. By the strictest economy, I can do middling well—very well when compared with what things were. When the new system first came into operation, I felt almost in a new world. I felt myself a free man; I wasn't compelled to drink; my home assumed a better aspect, and keeps it still. Last Monday night I received 19*s.* 7*d.* for my work (five days) in the previous week. I shall now (Thursday) have to wait until Monday next before I can get to work at my business.

Sometimes I get a job in idle times at the docks, or otherwise, and wish I could get more. I may make, one week with another, by odd jobs, 1*s.* a-week. Perhaps for months I can't get a job. All that time I have no choice but to be idle. One week with another, the year through (at 8*d.* per ton), I may earn 14*s.* The great evil is the uncertainty of the work. We have all to take our rotation. This uncertainty has this effect upon many of the men— they are compelled to live on credit. One day a man may receive 19*s.*, and be idle for eight days after. Consequently, we go to the dealer where we have credit. The chandler supplies me with bread, to be paid for next pay-day, charging me a halfpenny a loaf more. A man with a wife and family of six children, as I have, will consume sixteen or seventeen quartern loaves a-week; consequently, he has to pay 8*d.* a-week extra on account of the irregularity or uncertainty. My rotation would come much oftener but for the backing system and the 'bonafides.' I also pay the butcher from a halfpenny to a penny per pound extra for credit when my family requires meat, sometimes a bit of mutton, sometimes a bit of beef. I leave that to the wife, who does it with economy. I this way pay the butcher 6*d.* a-week extra. The additional cost to me of the other articles, cheese, butter, soap, &c., which I get on credit, will be 6*d.* a-week. Altogether that will be 3*l.* 18*s.* a-year. My rent for a little house with two nice little rooms is 3*s.* per week; so that the extra charge for credit would just pay my rent. Many coalwhippers deal with tallymen for their wearing apparel, and have to pay enormous prices. I have had dealings with a tallyman, and suffered for it, but for all that I must make application for a supply of blankets from him for my family this winter. I paid him 45*s.* for wearing apparel—a shawl for my wife, some dresses for the children, a blanket, and other things. Their intrinsic value was 30*s.* Many of us— indeed most of us, if not all of us—are always putting things in and out of the pawnshops. I know I have myself paid more than 10*s.* a-year for interest to the pawnbroker. I know some of my fellow-workmen who pay nearly 5*l.* a-year. I once put in a coat that cost me 3*l.* 12*s.* I could only get 30*s.* on it. I was never able to redeem it, and lost it. The articles lost by the coalwhippers pledged at the pawnshop are three out of four. There are 2000 coalwhippers, and I am sure that each has 50*s.* in pawn, making 5000*l.* in a-year. Interest may be paid on one half this amount, 2500*l.* The other half of the property, at least, is lost. As the pawnbroker only advances one-third of the value, the loss in the forfeiture of the property is 7500*l.*, and in interest 2500*l.*, making a total of 10,000*l.* lost every year, greatly through the uncertainty of labour. A coalwhipper's life is one of debt and struggles—it is a round of relieving, paying, and credit. We very rarely have a halfpenny in the pocket when we meet our credit. If any system could possibly be discovered which would render our work and our earnings more certain, and our payments more frequent, it would benefit us as much as we have been benefited by the establishment of the office."

I visited this man's cottage, and found it neat and tidy. His children looked healthy. The walls of the lower room were covered with some cheap prints; a few old books, well worn, as if well used, were to be seen; and everything evinced a man who was struggling bravely to rear a large family well on small means. I took the family at a disadvantage, moreover, as washing was going on.

Hearing that accidents were frequent among the class, I was anxious to see a person who had suffered by the danger of the calling. A man was brought to me with his hand bound up in a handkerchief. The sleeve of his coat was ripped open and dangled down beside his injured arm. He walked lame; and on my inquiring whether his leg was hurt, he began pulling up his trousers and unlacing his boot, to show me that it had not been properly set. He had evidently once been a strong, muscular man, but little now remained as evidence of his physical power but the size of his bones. He furnished me with the following statement:—

"I was a coalwhipper. I had a wife and two children. Four months ago, coming off my day's work, my foot slipped, and I fell and broke my leg. I was taken to the hospital, and remained there ten weeks. At the time of my accident I had no money at all by me, but was in debt to the amount of 10s. to my landlord. I had a little furniture, and a few clothes of myself and wife. While I was in the hospital, I did not receive anything from our benefit society, because I had not been able to keep up my subscription. My wife and children lived while I was in the hospital by pawning my things, and going from door to door to every one she knowed to give her a bit. The men who worked in the same gang as myself, made up 4s. 6d. for me, and that, with two loaves of bread that they had from the relieving officer, was all they got. While I was in the hospital the landlord seized for rent the few things that my wife had not pawned, and turned her and my two little children into the street. One was a boy three years old, and the other a baby just turned ten months. My wife went to her mother, and she kept her and my little ones for three weeks, till she could do so no longer. My mother, poor old woman, was most as bad off as we were. My mother only works on the ground, out in the country, at gardening. She makes about 7s. a-week in the summer, and in the winter she has only 9d. a-day to live upon; but she had at least a shelter for her child, and she willingly shared that with her daughter and her daughter's children. She

pawned all the clothes she had, to keep them from starving; but at last everything was gone from the poor old woman, and then I got my brother to take my family in. My brother worked at garden-work, the same as my mother-in-law did. He made about 15s. a-week in the summer, and about half that in the winter time. He had a wife and two children of his own, and found it hard enough to keep them, as times go. But still he took us all in, and shared what he had with us, rather than let us go to the workhouse. When I was told to leave the hospital—which I was forced to do upon my crutches, for my leg was very bad still—my brother took me in too. He had only one room, but he got in a bundle of straw for me, and we lived and slept there for seven weeks. He got credit for more than a pound's worth of bread, and tea, and sugar for us; and now he can't pay, and the man threatens to summon him for it. After I left my brother's, I came to live in the neighbourhood of Wapping, for I thought I might manage to do a day's work at coalwhipping, and I couldn't bear to live upon his little earnings any longer—he could scarcely keep himself then. At last I got a ship to deliver; but I was too weak to do the work, and in pulling at the ropes my hands got sore, and festered for want of nourishment." [He took the handkerchief off and showed that it was covered with plaster. It was almost white from deficient circulation.] "After this I was obliged to lay up again, and that's the only job of work I've been able to do for these last four months. My wife can't do anything; she is a delicate, sickly little woman as well, and has the two little children to mind, and to look after me likewise. I had one pennyworth of bread this morning. We altogether had half-a-quartern loaf among the four of us, but no tea nor coffee. Yesterday we had some bread, and tea, and butter; but wherever my wife got it from I don't know. I was three days but a short time back without a taste of food." [Here he burst out crying.] "I had nothing but water that passed my lips. I had merely a little at home, and that my wife and children had. I would rather starve myself than let them do so: indeed, I've done it over and over again. I never begged: I'll die in the streets first. I never told nobody of my life. The foreman of my gang was the only one besides God that knew of my misery; and his wife came to me and brought me money and brought me food, and himself, too, many a time." ["I had a wife and five children of my own to maintain, and it grieved me to my heart," said the man who sat by, "to see them want, and I unable to do more for them."] "If any accident occurs to any of us who are not upon the society, they must be as bad off as I am. If I only had a little nourishment to strengthen me, I could do my work again; but, poor as I am, I can't get strength to do it, and not being totally incapacitated from ever resuming my labour, I cannot get any assistance from the superannuation fund of our men."

I told the man I wished to see him at his own home, and he and the foreman who had brought him to me, and who gave him a most excellent character, led me into a small house in a court near the Shadwell entrance to the London Docks. When I reached the place I found the room almost bare of furniture. A baby lay sprawling on its back on a few rags beside the handful of fire. A little shoeless boy, with only a light washed-out frock to cover him, ran shyly into a corner of the room as we entered. There was only one chair in the room, and that had been borrowed down stairs. Over the chimney hung to dry a few ragged infant's chemises that had been newly washed. In front of the fire, on a stool, sat the thinly-clad wife ; and in the corner of the apartment stood a few old tubs. On a line above these were two tattered men's shirts, hanging to dry, and a bed was thrown on some boxes. On a shelf stood a physic-bottle that the man had got from the parish doctor, and in the empty cupboard was a slice of bread—all the food, they said, they had in the world, and they knew not where on earth to look for more.

I next wished to see one of the improvident men, and was taken to the lodging of one who made the following statement :—

"I have been a coalwhipper for twenty years. I worked under the old publican's system, when the men were compelled to drink. In those days 18s. didn't keep me in drink. I have now been a teetotaler for five years. I have the bit of grub now more regular than I had. I earn less than 13s. a-week. I have four children, and have buried four. My rent is 1s. 6d." ["To-night," interrupted the wife, "if he won't part with his coat or boots, he must go without his supper."] "My wife," the man continued, "works at bespoke work—stay-making, but gets very little work, and so earns very little—perhaps 1s. 6d. a week."

This family resided in a wretched part of Wapping, called, appropriately enough, "the Ruins." Some houses have been pulled down, and so an open space is formed at the end of a narrow airless alley. The wet stood on the pavement of the alley, and the cottage in which the whipper I visited lived, seemed with another to have escaped when the other houses were pulled down. The man is very tall, and almost touched the ceiling of his room when he stood upright in it. The ceiling was as wet as a newly-washed floor. The grate was fireless, the children barefoot, and the bed-stead (for there was a bedstead) was bed-less, and all showed cheerless poverty. The dwelling was in strong contrast with that of the provident whipper whom I have described.

THE COALBACKERS.

I CONCLUDE with the statement of a coal-backer, or coalporter — a class to which the term coalheaver is usually given by those who are unversed in the mysteries of the calling. The man wore the approved fantail, and well-tarred short smock-frock, black velveteen knee breeches, dirty white stockings, and lace-up boots.

"I am a coalbacker," he said. "I have been so these twenty-two years. By a coal-backer, I mean a man who is engaged in carrying coals on his back from ships and craft to the waggons. We get $2\frac{1}{4}d$. for every fifth part of a ton, or $11\frac{1}{4}d$. per ton among five men. We carry the coals in sacks of 2 cwt., the sack usually weighs from 14 lbs. to 20 lbs., so that our load is mostly 238 lbs. We have to carry the load from the hold of the ship, over four barges, to the waggon. The hold of a ship is from sixteen to twenty feet deep. We carry the coals this height up a ladder, and the ship is generally from sixty to eighty feet from the waggon. This distance we have to travel over planks, with the sacks on our backs. Each man will ascend this height and travel this distance about ninety times in a day ; hence he will lift himself, with 2 cwt. of coals on his back, 1460 feet, or upwards of a quarter of a mile high, which is three times the height of St. Paul's, in twelve hours. And besides this, he will travel 6300 feet, or $1\frac{1}{4}$ miles, carrying the same weight as he goes. The labour is very hard—there are few men who can continue at it." My informant said it was too much for him ; he had been obliged to give it up eight months back ; he had over-strained himself at it, and been obliged to lay up for many months. "I am forty-five years of age," he continued, "and have as many as eight children. None of them bring me in a sixpence. My eldest boy did, a little while back, but his master failed, and he lost his situation. My wife made slop-shirts at a penny each, and could not do more than three a-day. How we have lived through all my illness, I cannot say. I occasionally get a little job, such as mending the hats of my fellow-workmen : this would sometimes bring me in about 2s. in the week, and then the parish allowed four quartern loaves of bread and 2s. 6d. a-week for myself, wife, and eight children. Since I have overstrained myself, I have not done more than two days' work alto-gether. Sometimes my mates would give me an odd seven tons to do for them, for I was not able to manage more." Such accidents as overstraining are very common among the coalbackers. The labour of carrying such a heavy weight from the ship's hold is so exces-sive, that after a man turns forty he is con-sidered to be past his work, and to be very liable to such accidents. It is usually reck-oned that the strongest men cannot last more than twenty years at the business. Many of the heartiest of the men are knocked up through the bursting of blood-vessels and other casualties, and even the strongest cannot continue at the labour three days together. After the second day's work, they are obliged to hire some unemployed mate to do the work for them. The coalbackers work in gangs of five men, consisting of two shovel-men and three backers, and are employed to deliver the ship by the wharfinger. Each gang is paid 11¼d. per ton, which is at the rate of 2¼d. per ton for each of the five men. The gang will do from thirty to forty tons in the course of the day. The length of the day depends upon the amount of work to be done, according to the wharfinger's orders. The coalbackers are generally at work at five o'clock in the morning, winter and summer. In the winter time, they have to work by the light of large fires in hanging caldrons, which they call bells. Their day's work seldom ends before seven o'clock in the evening. They are paid every night, and a man after a hard day's work will receive 6s. Strong, hearty men, who are able to follow up the work, can earn from 25s. to 30s. per week. But the business is a fluctuating one. In the summer time there is little or nothing to do. The earnings during the slack season are about one half what they are during the brisk. Upon an average, their earnings are 1l. a-week all the year round. The class of coalbackers is supposed to consist of about 1500 men. They have no provident or benefit society. Between seventeen and eighteen years ago, each gang used to have 1s. 0½d. per ton, and about a twelvemonth afterwards it fell to the present price of 11¼d. per ton. About six weeks back, the merchants made an attempt to take off the odd farthing; the reason assigned was the cheapness of provisions. They nearly carried it; but the backers formed a committee among themselves, and opposed the reduction so strongly that the idea was abandoned. The backers are paid extra for sifting, at the rate of 2d. per sack. For this office they usually employ a lad, paying him at the rate of 10s. per week. Upon this they will usually clear from 2s. to 4s. per week. The most injurious part of the backer's work is carrying from the ship's hold. That is what they object to most of all, and consider they get the worst paid for. They do a great injury to the coalwhippers, and the backers say it would be as great a benefit to themselves as to the coalwhippers, if the system was done away with. By bringing the ships up alongside the wharf, the merchant saves the expense of whipping and lightering, together with the cost of barges, &c. Many of the backers are paid at the public-house; the wharfinger gives them a note to receive their daily earnings of the publican, who has the money from the merchant. Often the backers are kept waiting an hour at the public-house for their money, and they have credit through the day for any drink they may choose to call for. While waiting, they mostly have two or three pots of beer before they are paid; and the drinking once commenced, many of them return home drunk, with only half their earnings in their pockets. There is scarcely a man among the whole class of backers, but heartily wishes the system of payment at the public-house may be entirely abolished. The coalbackers are mostly an intemperate class of men. This arises chiefly from the extreme labour and the over-exertion of the men, the violent perspiration and the intense thirst produced thereby. Immediately a pause occurs in their work, they fly to the public-house for beer. One coalbacker made a regular habit of drinking sixteen half-pints of beer, with a pennyworth of gin in each, before breakfast every morning. The sum spent in drink by the 'moderate' men varies from 9s. to 12s. per week, and the immoderate men on the average spend 15s. a-week. Hence, assuming the class of coalbackers to be 2000 in number, and to spend only 10s. a-week in drink each man, the sum that would be annually expended in malt liquors and spirits by the class would amount to no less than 52,000l. The wives and children of the coalbackers are generally in great distress. Sometimes no more than one quarter of the men's earnings is taken home at night.

"When I was moderate inclined," said one of them to me, " I used to have a glass of rum the first thing when I came out of a morning, just to keep the cold out — that might be as early as about five o'clock in the morning, and about seven o'clock I should want half a pint of beer with gin in it, or a pint without. After my work I should be warm, and feel myself dry; then I should continue to work till breakfast-time; then I should have another half pint with gin in it, and so I should keep on through the day, having either some beer or gin every two hours. I reckon that unless a man spent about 1s. 6d. to 2s. in drink, he would not be able to continue his labour through the day. In the evening, he is tired with his work, and being kept at the public-house for his pay, he begins drinking there, and soon feels unwilling to move, and he seldom does so until all his wages are gone." My informant tells me that he thinks the class would be much improved if the system of paying the men at the public-house was done away, and the men paid weekly instead of daily. The hard drinking he thinks a necessity of the hard labour. He has heard, he says, of coalbackers being teetotalers, but none were able to keep the pledge beyond two months. If they drink water and coffee, it will rather increase than quench their thirst. Nothing seems to quench the thirst of a hard-working man so well as ale.

"The only difference between the pay of the basketman and the whipper is the 1½d. in the pound which the former receives for carrying the money from the captain of the ship to the clerk of the pay-office. He has also for this sum to keep a correct account of the work done by the men every day, and to find security for his honesty to the amount of 10*l.* To obtain this, they usually pay 2*s.* 6*d.* a-year to the Guarantee Society, and they prefer doing this to seeking the security of some baker or publican in the neighbourhood, knowing that if they did so, they would be expected to become customers of the parties."

I now resume my inquiry whether stimulating drinks are necessary for the performance of severe labour.

I have already published the statement of a coalbacker, who declared that it was an absolute necessity of that kind of labour that the men engaged in backing coals from the hold of a ship should, though earning only 1*l.* per week, spend at least 12*s.* weekly in beer and spirits, to stimulate them for their work. This sum, the man assured me, was a moderate allowance, for 15*s.* was the amount ordinarily expended by the men in drink every week. Now if this quantity of drink be a necessity of the calling, it follows that the men pursuing the severest labour of all—doing work that cripples the strongest in from twelve to twenty years —are the worst paid of all labourers, their actual clear gains being only from 5*s.* to 8*s.* per week. This struck me as being so terrible a state of things that I could hardly believe it to be true, though I was assured by several coalwhippers who were present on the occasion, that the coalbacker who had made the statement had in no way exaggerated the account of the sufferings of his fellow-workmen. I determined, nevertheless, upon inquiring into the question myself, and ascertaining, by the testimony and experience of different classes of individuals engaged in this, the greatest labour, perhaps, performed by any men, whether drink was really a necessity or luxury to the working man.

Accordingly, I called a meeting of the coalwhippers, that I might take their opinion on the subject, when I found that out of eighty individuals only four were satisfied that fermented liquors could be dispensed with by the labouring classes. I was, however, still far from satisfied upon the subject, and I determined, as the question is one of the greatest importance to the working men,—being more intimately connected with their welfare, physical, intellectual, and moral, than any other,—to give the subject my most patient and unbiassed consideration. I was anxious, without advocating any opinion upon the subject, to collect the sentiments of the coal labourers themselves; and in order that I might do so as impartially as possible, I resolved upon seeing— 1st, such men as were convinced that stimulating liquors were necessary to the labouring man in the performance of his work; 2ndly, such men as once thought differently, and, in-

deed, had once taken the pledge to abstain from the use of all fermented liquors, but had been induced to violate their vow in consequence of their health having suffered; and 3rdly, such men as had taken the pledge and kept it without any serious injury to their constitutions. To carry the subject out with the fulness and impartiality that its importance seemed to me to demand, I further determined to prosecute the inquiry among both classes of coal labourers—the coalwhippers and coalbackers as well. The result of these investigations I shall now subjoin. Let me, however, in the first place, lay before the reader the following

COMPARATIVE TABLE OF DRUNKENNESS OF THE DIFFERENT TRADES IN LONDON.

Above the Average.

Button-makers, one individual in every	7·2
Tool-makers	10·1
Surveyors	11·8
Paper-makers and Stainers .	12·1
Brass-founders	12·4
Gold-beaters	14·5
Millers	16·6
French Polishers	17·3
Cutlers	18·2
Corkcutters	19·7
Musicians	22·0
Opticians	22·3
Bricklayers	22·6
Labourers	22·8
General and Marine-store Dealers	23·2
Brushmakers	24·4
Fishmongers	28·2
Coach and Cabmen . . .	28·7
Glovers	29·4
Smiths	29·5
Sweeps	32·2
Hairdressers	42·3
Tailors	43·7
Tinkers and Tinmen . . .	45·7
Saddlers	49·3
Masons	49·6
Glassmakers, &c. . . .	50·5
Curriers	50·6
Printers	52·4
Hatters and Trimmers . . .	53·1
Carpenters	53·8
Ironmongers	56·0
Dyers	56·7
Sawyers	58·4
Turners	59·3
Engineers	59·7
Butchers	63·7
Laundresses	63.8
Painters	66·1
Brokers	67·7
Medical Men	68·0
Brewers	70·2
Clerks	73·4
Shopkeepers	77·1
Shoemakers	78·0
Coachmakers	78·8

Milliners	.	.	.	.1 in every	81·4
Bakers .	.	.	.	.	.	. 82·0
Pawnbrokers	.	.	.	.	. 84·7
Gardeners	.	.	.	.	. 97·6
Weavers	.	.	.	.	. 99·3
Drapers	.	.	.	.	. 102·3
Tobacconists	.	.	.	.	. 103·4
Jewellers	.	.	.	.	. 104·5
Artists	.	.	.	.	. 106·3
Publicans	.	.	.	.	. 108·0
Average	.	.	.	113·8

Below the Average.

Carvers and Gilders	.	.	.	. 125·2
Artificial Flower Makers	.	.	. 128·1
Bookbinders .	.	.	.	. 148·6
Greengrocers	.	.	.	. 157·4
Watchmakers	.	.	.	. 204·2
Grocers	.	.	.	. 226·6
Clockmakers	.	.	.	. 286·0
Parish officers	.	.	.	. 373·0
Clergymen ·	.	.	.	. 417·0
Servants	.	.	.	. 585·7

The above calculations have been made from the Official Returns of the Metropolitan Police. The causes of the different degrees of intemperance here exhibited, I leave to others to discover.

After the meeting of coalwhippers just described, I requested some of the men who had expressed the various opinions respecting the necessity for drinking some kind of fermented liquor during their work to meet me, so that I might take down their sentiments on the subject more fully. First of all, came two of the most intelligent, who believed malt liquor to be necessary for the performance of their labour. One was a basketman or fireman, and the other an "up-and-down" man, or whipper; the first doing the lighter, and the second the heavier kind of work. The basketman, who I afterwards discovered was a good Greek and Latin scholar, said: "If I have anything like a heavy day's work to do, I consider three pints of porter a-day necessary. We are not like other labouring men, having an hour to dinner. Often, to save tide, we take only ten minutes to our meals. One thing I wish to remark is, that what renders it necessary to have the three pints of beer in winter, and two pots in summer, is the coal-dust arising from the work, which occasions great thirst. In the summer time the basketman is on the plank all day, and continually exposed to the sun, and in the winter to the inclemency of the weather. What with the labour and the heat, the perspiration is excessive. A basketman with a bad gang of men has no sinecure. In the summer he can wear neither coat nor waistcoat; very few can bear the hat on the head, and they wear nightcaps instead. The work is always done, in summer time, with only the shirt and trousers on. The basketman never takes off his shirt, like the whippers. The necessity for drink in the summer does not arise so much from the extent of the labour, as from the irritation caused by the coal-dust getting into the throat. There is not so much dust from the coals in the winter as in the summer, the coals being more damp in wet than in fine weather. It is merely the thirst that makes the drink requisite, as far as the basketman is concerned. Tea would allay the thirst, but there is no opportunity of having this on board ship. If there were an opportunity of having tea at our work, the basketman might manage to do with it as well as with beer. Water I don't fancy, especially the water of the river; it is very impure, and at the time of the cholera we were prohibited from drinking it. If we could get pure water, I do not think it would do as well for us, especially in winter time. In winter time it would be too cold, and too great a contrast to the heat of the blood. It would, in my opinion, produce stagnation in the circulation. We have had instances of men dying suddenly through drinking water when in a state of excitement." [He distinguishes between excitement and perspiration: he calls the basketman's labour an exciting one, and the whipper's work a heating one.] "The men who died suddenly were whippers. I never heard of a basketman dying from drinking cold water when at his work; I don't think they ever tried the experiment. The whippers have done so through necessity, not through choice. Tea is a beverage that I don't fancy, and I conceive it to be equally expensive, so I prefer porter. When I go off to my work early in the morning, I take about a pint of coffee with me in a bottle, and warm it up on board at the galley-fire for my breakfast; that I find quenches my thirst for the time as well porter. Porter would be too insipid the first thing in the morning; I never drank coffee through the day while at my work, so I cannot say what the effect would be. I drink porter when at my work, not as giving me greater strength to go through my labour, but merely as a means of quenching my thirst, it being as cheap as any other drink, with the exception of water, and less trouble to procure. Water I consider dangerous at our work, but I can't say that it is so from my own experience. I was in the hospital about seven years ago, and the doctor there asked me how many pints of beer I was in the habit of drinking per day. This was before the office was established. I told him, on the lowest calculation, six or seven; it was the case then under the old system; and he then ordered me two pints of porter a-day, as I was very weak, and he said I wanted a stimulus. I am not aware that it is the habit of the publicans to adulterate their porter with salt and water. If such is the case, it would, without a doubt, increase rather than diminish the thirst. I have often found that the beer sold by some of the publicans tends more to create than allay thirst. I am confident, that if the working men generally knew that salt and water was invariably mixed with the porter by the publicans, they would no longer hold to the notion that it could quench their thirst; but, to convince them of that, it would be almost necessary that they should see the publican adulterating the beer with their own eyes. If it really is the case that beer is adulterated with salt and water, it must be both injurious and heating to the labouring man. Some of the men who are in the habit of drinking porter at their work, very probably attribute the thirst created by the salt and water in the porter to the thirst created by the coal-dust or the work, and continue drinking it from the force of habit. The habit of drinking is doubtlessly the effect of the old system, when the men were forced to drink by the publicans who paid them. A most miraculous change, and one unparalleled in history, has been produced by altering the old mode of employing and paying the men: The reformation in the morals and character of the men is positively wonderful. The sons are no longer thieves, and the daughters are no longer prostitutes. Formerly it was a competition who could drink the most, for he who could do so got the most work. The introduction for a job was invariably, 'You know, Mr. So and So, I'm a good drinking man.' Seeing the benefit that has resulted from the men not drinking so much as formerly, I am of opinion that, though I take my beer every day myself, a great good would ensue if the men would drink even less than they do now, and eat more; it would be more conducive to their health and strength. But they have not the same facility for getting food over their work as there is for getting beer. You see, they can have credit for beer when they can't get a morsel of food on trust. There are no floating butchers or bakers, like there are floating publicans or purlmen. If there were, and men could have trust for bread and meat while at their work on the river, I am sure they would eat more and drink less, and be all the better for it. It would be better for themselves and for their families. The great evil of the drink is, that when a man has a little he often wants more, and doesn't know where to stop. When he once passes the 'rubi-can,' as I call it, he is lost. If it wasn't for this evil, I think a pint or two of porter would make them do their work better than either tea or water. Our labour is peculiar. The air is always full of coal-dust, and every nerve and muscle of the body is strained, and every pore of the body open, so that he requires some drink that will counteract the cold."

The next two that I saw were men who did the heaviest work; that is, " up-and-down men," or coalwhippers, as they are usually called. They had both of them been teetotalers. One had been so for eight years, and the other had tried it for three months. One who stood at least six feet and a half high, and was habited in a long blue great coat that reached to his heels, and made him look even taller than he was, said,—" I was a strict teetotaler for many years, and I wish I could be so now. All that time I was a coalwhipper at the heaviest work, and I have made one of a gang that have done as many as 180 tons in one day. I drank no fermented liquor the whole of the time; I had only ginger-beer and milk, and that cost me 1s. 6d. It was in the summer time. I didn't ' buff it' on that day; that is, I didn't take my shirt off. I did this work at the Regent's Canal; and there was a little milk-shop close on shore, and I used to run there when I was dry. I had about two quarts of milk and five bottles of ginger-beer, or about three quarts of fluid altgether. I found that amount of drink necessary. I perspired very violently; my shirt was wet through, and my flannels wringing wet with the perspiration over the work. The rule among us is, that we do 28 tons on deck, and 28 tons filling in the ship's hold. We go on in that way throughout the day, spelling at every 28 tons. The perspiration in the summer time streams down our foreheads so rapidly, that it will often get into our eyes before we have time to wipe it off. This makes the eyes very sore. At night, when we get home, we cannot bear to sit with a candle. The perspiration is of a very briny nature, for I often taste it as it runs down to my lips. We are often so heated over our work that the perspiration runs into the shoes; and often, from the dust and heat, jumping up and down, and the feet being galled with the small dust, I have had my shoes full of blood. The thirst produced by our work is very excessive; it is completely as if you had a fever upon you. The dust gets into the throat, and very nearly suffocates you. You can scrape the coal-dust off the tongue with the teeth; and do what you will it is impossible to get the least spittle into the mouth. I have known the coal-dust to be that thick in a ship's hold, that I have been unable to see my mate, though he was only two feet from me. Your legs totter under you, both before and after you are a teetotaler. I was one of the strongest men in the business; I was able to carry 7 cwt. on my back for fifty yards, and I could lift nine half-hundreds with my right-arm. After finishing my day's work I was like a child with weakness. When we have done 14 or 28 tons, we generally stop for a drop of drink, and then I have found that anything that would wet my mouth would revive me. Cold tea, milk, or ginger-beer, were refreshing, but not so much as a pint of porter. Cold water would give a pain in the inside, so that a man would have to lie down and be taken ashore, and, perhaps, give up work altogether. Many a man has been taken to the hospital merely through drinking cold water over his work.

They have complained of a weight and coldness in the chest; they say it has chilled the fat of the heart. I can positively state," continued the man, " that during the whole of eight years I took no fermented drink. My usual drink was cold tea, milk, ginger-beer, or coffee, whichever I could catch: the ginger-beer was more lively than the milk; but I believe I could do more work upon the milk. Tea I found much better than coffee. Cold tea was very refreshing; but if I didn't take it with me in a bottle, it wasn't to be had. I used to take a quart of cold tea with me in a bottle, and make that do for me all day, as well as I could. The ginger-beer was the most expensive, and would cost me a shilling, or more than that if I could get it. The milk would cost me sixpence or eight-pence. For tea and coffee the expense would be about twopence the day. But often I have done the whole day's work without any drink, because I would not touch beer, and then I was more fit to be carried home than walk. I have known many men scarcely able to crawl up the ladder out of the hold, they were so fatigued. For myself, being a very strong man, I was never so reduced, thank God. But often, when I've got home, I've been obliged to drink three pints of milk at a stretch, before I could touch a bit of victuals. As near as I can guess it used to cost me, when at work, a shilling a-day for ginger-beer, milk, and other teetotal drinks. When I was not at work my drink used to cost me little or nothing. For eight years I stuck to the pledge, but I found myself failing in strength and health; I found that I couldn't go through a day's work as clever as I used before I left off drink, and when first I was a teetotaler. I found myself failing in every inch of my carcase, my limbs, my body and all. Of my own free-will I gave it up. I did not do it in a fit of passion, but deliberately, because I was fully satisfied that it was injuring my health. Shortly after taking the pledge I found I could have more meat than I used to have before, and I found that I neither got strong nor weak upon it. After about five years my appetite began to fail, and then I found my strength leaving me; so I made up my mind to alter the system. When I returned to beer, I found myself getting better in health and stronger daily. Before I was a teetotaler I used to drink heavy, but after teetotalism I was a temperate man. I am sure it is necessary for a hard-working man that he should drink beer. He can't do his work so well without it as he can with it, in moderation. If he goes beyond his allowance he is better without any. I have taken to drinking beer again within the last twelve months. As long as a man does not go beyond his allowance in beer, his drink will cost him quite as much when he is teetotaler as it will when he has not taken the pledge. The difference between the teetotal and fermented drinks I find to be this :—When I drank milk it didn't make me any livelier; it quenched my thirst, but didn't give me any strength. But when I drank a pint or a quart of beer, it did me so much good after a day's labour, that after drinking it I could get up and go to my work again. This feeling would continue for a considerable time; indeed, I think the beer is much better for a hard-working man than any unfermented drink. I defy any man in England to contradict me in what I say, and that is—a man who takes his reasonable quantity of beer, and a fair share of food, is much better with it than without."

Another man, who had been a teetotaler for three months at one time, and seven years at another, was convinced that it was impossible for a hard-working man to do his work as well without beer as with. " He had tried it twice, and he spoke from his own experience, and he would say that a little—that is, two pints, or three for a very hard day's labour,—would never hurt no man. Beyond that a man has no right to go; indeed, anything extra only makes him stupid. Under the old system, I used to be obliged to buy rum; and, over and over again, I've had to pay fifteen-pence for half-a-pint of rum in a ginger-beer bottle; and have gone into the street and sold it for sixpence, and got a steak with the money. No man can say drink has ruined my constitution, for I've only had two penny-worth of antibilious pills in twenty-five years; and I will say, a little beer does a man more good than harm, and too much does a man more harm than good."

The next two " whippers " that I saw were both teetotalers. One had taken the pledge eight months before, and the other four years; and they had both kept it strictly. One had been cellarman at a public-house, and he said, " I neither take spruce nor any of the cordials: water is my beverage at dinner." The other had been an inveterate drunkard. The cellarman is now a basketman, and the other an up-and-down man, or whipper, in the same gang. The basketman said, " I can say this from my own experience,—that it is not necessary for a working man, doing the very hardest labour, to drink fermented liquors. I was an up-and-down man for two years, without tasting a drop of beer or spirits. I have helped to whip 189 tons of coal in one day, without any; and that in the heat of summer. What I had with me was a bottle of cocoa; and I took with that plenty of steak, potatoes, and bread. If the men was to take more meat and less beer, they would do much better. It's a delusion to think beer necessary. Often, the men who say the beer is necessary will deliver a ship, aye, and not half-a-dozen half-pints be drank aboard. The injury is done ashore. The former custom of our work—the compulsory system of drinking that we were under,—has so imbedded the idea of drink in the men, that they think it is actually necessary. It's not the least to be wondered at, that there's so many drunkards among them. I do not think we shall ever be able to undo the habit of drinking among the whippers in this generation. As far as I am concerned, since I've been a teetotaler, I have enjoyed a more regular state of health than I used before. Now that I am a basketman, I drink only water with my dinner; and during my work I take nothing. I have got a ship in hands — going to work on Monday morning. I shall have to run backwards and forwards on a one-and-twenty-foot plank, and deliver 300 tons of coals: and I shall do that upon water. That man," pointing to the teetotaler who accompanied him, "will be in it, and he'll have to help to pull the coals twenty foot above the deck; and he'll do it all upon water. When I was a coalwhipper myself, I used to drink cocoa. I took it cold with me of a morning, and warmed it aboard. They prophesied it would kill me in a week; and I know it's done me every good in life. I have drunk water when I was a-working up-and-down, and when I was in the highest perspiration, and never found it injure me. It allays the thirst more than anything. If it didn't allay the thirst I should want to drink often: but if I take a drink of water from the cask I find my thirst immediately quenched. Many of the men who drink beer will take a drink of water afterwards, because the beer increases their thirst, and heats them. That, I believe, is principally from the salt water in it: in fact, it stands to reason, that if beer is half brine it can't quench thirst. Ah! it's shocking stuff the purlmen make up for them on the river. When I was drinking beer at my employment, I used seldom to exceed three pints of beer a-day : that is what I took on board. What I had on shore was not, of course, to help me to do my labour. I know the beer used to inflame my thirst, because I've had to drink water after it over and over again. I never made a habit of drinking,— not since the establishment of the office. Previous to that, of course, I was obliged to drink. I've got 'jolly' now and then, but I never made a habit of it. It used to cost me about two shillings or two shillings and sixpence a-week, on the average, for drink, at the uttermost; because I couldn't afford more. Since I've taken the pledge, I'm sure it hasn't cost me sixpence a-week. A teetotaler feels less thirst than any other man. I don't know what natural thirst is, except I've been eating salt provisions. I belong to a total abstinence society, and there are about a dozen coalwhippers, and about the same number of coalbackers, members of it. Some have been total abstainers for twelve years, and are living witnesses that fermented drinks are not necessary for working men. There are about two hundred to two hundred and fifty coalwhippers, I have been given to understand,

who are teetotalers. Those coalwhippers who have been total abstainers for twelve years, are not weaker or worse in health for the want of beer." [This statement was denied by a person present; but a gentleman, who was intimately acquainted with the whole body, mentioned the names of several men who had been, some ten years, and some upwards of twelve years, strict adherents to the principles of teetotalism.] " The great quantity of drinking is carried on ashore. I should say the men generally drink twice as much ashore as they do afloat. Those who drink beer are always thirsty. Through drinking over their work, a thirst is created aboard, which they set to drinking, when ashore, to allay; and, after a hard day's labour, a very little overcomes a man. One or two pots of beer, and the man is loth to stir. He is tired; and the drink, instead of refreshing him, makes him sleepy and heavy. The next morning after drinking he is thirstier still; and then he goes to work drinking again. The perspiration will start out of him in large drops, like peas. You will see it stream down his face and his hands, with the coal-dust sticking to them, just like as if he had a pair of silk gloves on him. It's a common saying with us, about such a man, that ' he's got the gloves on.' The drunkards always perspire the most over their work. The prejudice existing among the men in favour of drink is such, that they believe they would die without it. I am quite astonished to see such an improvement among them as there is; and I do think that, if the clergymen of the neighbourhood did their duty, and exerted themselves, the people would be better still. At one time there were as many as five hundred coalwhippers total abstainers; and the men were much better clothed, and the homes and appearance of the whippers were much more decent. What I should do if I drank, I don't know. I got 1*l.* for clearing a ship last week, and shan't get any more till Monday night; and I have six children and a wife to keep out of that. For this last fortnight I have only made 10*s.* a-week, so I am sure I couldn't even afford a shilling a-week for drink, without robbing my family."

The second teetotaler, who had been an inveterate drunkard in his time, stated as follows. Like most of the coalwhippers, he thought once that he could not do his work without beer. He used to drink as much as he could get. He averaged two pots at his work, and when he came on shore he would have two pots more.

" He had been a coalwhipper for upwards of twenty years, and for nineteen years and three months of that time he was a hard drinker, — a regular stiff 'un," said he; " I not only used," he added, "to get drunk, but I taught my children to do so,— I have got sons as big as myself, coalbackers, and total abstainers. Often I have gone home on a Sunday morning drunk myself, and found two of my sons drunk,—they'd be unable to sit at the table. They were about fourteen then, and when they went out with me I used to teach them to take their little drops of neat rum or gin. I have seen the youngest 'mop up' his half-quartern as well as I did. Then I was always thirsty; and when I got up of a morning I used to go stalking round to the first public-house that was open, to see if I could get a pint or a quartern. My mouth was dry and parched, as if I had got a burning fever. If I had no work that day I used to sit in a public-house and spend all the money I'd got. If I had no money I would go home and raise it somehow. I would ask the old woman to give me the price of a pint, or perhaps the young uns were at work, and I was pretty safe to meet them coming home. Talk about going out of a Sunday! I was ashamed to be seen out. My clothes were ragged, and my shoes would take the water in at one end and let it out at the other. I keep my old rags at home, to remind me of what I was—I call them the regimentals of the guzzler. I pawned everything I could get at. For ten or twelve years I used a beer-shop regularly. That was my house of call. Now my home is very happy. All my children are teetotalers. My sons are as big as myself, and they are at work carrying 1¾ cwt. to 2 cwt. up a Jacob's ladder, thirty-three steps high. They do this all day long, and have been doing so for the last seven days. They drink nothing but water or cold tea, and say they find themselves the better able to do their work. Coalbacking is about the hardest labour a man can perform. For myself, too, I find I am quite as able to do my work without intoxicating drinks as I was with them. There's my basketman," said he, pointing to the other teetotaler, " and he can tell you whether what I say is true or not. I have helped to whip 147 tons of coal in the heat of summer. The other men were calling for beer every time they could see or hear a purlman, but I took nothing—I don't think I perspired so much as they did. When I was in the drinking custom, I have known the perspiration run down my arms and legs as if I'd been in a hot bath. Since I've taken the pledge I scarcely perspire at all. I'll work against any man that takes beer, provided I have a good teetotal pill—that is, a good pound of steak, with plenty of gravy in it. That's the stuff to work upon—that's what the working man wants—plenty of it, and less beer, and he'd beat a horse any day. I am satisfied the working man can never be raised above his present position until he can give over drinking. That is the reason why I am sticking to the pledge, that I may be a living example to my class that they can and may work without beer. It has made my home happy, and I want it to make every other working man's as comfortable. I tried the principle of teetotalism first on board a steam-

boat. I was stoker, and we burnt 27 cwt. of coals every hour we were at sea—that's very nearly a ton and a-half per hour. There, with the heat of the fire, we felt the effects of drinking strong brandy. Brandy was the only fermented drink we were allowed. After a time I tried what other stimulants we could use. The heat in the hold, especially before the fires, was awful. There were nine stokers and four coal-trimmers. We found that the brandy that we drank in the day made us ill, our heads ached when we got up in the morning, so four of us agreed to try oatmeal and water as our drink, and we found that suited us better than intoxicating liquor. I myself got as fat as a bull upon it. It was recommended to me by a doctor in Falmouth, and we all of us tried it eight or nine voyages. Some time after I left the company I went to strong drink again, and continued at it till the 1st of May last, and then my children's love of drink got so dreadful that I got to hate myself as being the cause of it. But I couldn't give up the drinking. Two of my mates, however, urged me to try. On the 1st of May I signed the pledge. I prayed to God on the night I went to give me strength to keep it, and never since have I felt the least inclination to return. When I had left off a fortnight I found myself a great deal better; all the cramps that I had been loaded with when I was drinking left me. Now I am happy and comfortable at home. My wife's about one of the best women in the world. She bore with me in all my troubles, and now she glories in my redemption. My children love me, and we club all our earnings together, and can always on Sunday manage a joint of sixteen or seventeen pounds. My wife, now that we are teetotalers, need do no work; and, in conclusion, I must say that I have much cause to bless the Lord that ever I signed the teetotal pledge.

"After I leave my work," added the teetotaler, " I find the best thing I can have to refresh me is a good wash of my face and shoulders in cold water. This is twice as enlivening as ever I found beer. Once a fortnight I goes over to Goulston-square, Whitechapel, and have a warm bath. This is one of the finest things that ever was invented for the working man. Any persons that use them don't want beer. I invited a coalwhipper-man to come with me once. 'How much does it cost?' he asked. I told him, 'A penny.' 'Well,' he said, 'I'd sooner have half-a-pint of beer. I haven't washed my body for these twenty-two years, and don't see why I should begin to have anything to do with these new-fangled notions at my time of life.' I will say, that a good wash is better for the working man than the best drink."

The man ultimately made a particular request that his statement might conclude with a verse that he had chosen from the Temperance Melodies:—

" And now we love the social cheer
　　Of the bright winter eve ;
We have no cause for sigh or tear,
　　We have no cause to grieve.

Our wives are clad, our children fed ;
　　We boast where'er we go —
'Twas all because we sign'd the pledge,
　　A long, long time ago."

At the close of my interview with these men I received from them an invitation to visit them at their own houses whenever I should think fit. It was clearly their desire that I should see the comforts and domestic arrangements of their homes. Accordingly on the morrow, choosing an hour when there could have been no preparation, I called at the lodgings of the first. I found the whole family assembled in the back kitchen, that served them for a parlour. As I entered the room the mother was busy at work, washing and dressing her children for the day. There stood six little things, so young that they seemed to be all about the same height, with their faces shining with the soap and water, and their cheeks burning red with the friction of the towel. They were all laughing and playing about the mother, who, with comb and brush in hand, found it no easy matter to get them to stand still while she made " the parting." First of all the man asked me to step up-stairs and see the sleeping-room. I was much struck with the scrupulous cleanliness of the apartment. The blind was as white as snow, half rolled up, and fastened with a pin. The floor was covered with patches of different coloured carpet, showing that they had been bought from time to time, and telling how difficult it had been to obtain the luxury. In one corner was a cupboard with the door taken off, the better to show all the tumblers, teacups, and coloured-glass mugs, that, with two decanters, well covered with painted flowers, were kept more for ornament than use. On the chimneypiece was a row of shells, china shepherdesses, and lambs, and a stuffed pet canary in a glass-case for a centre ornament. Against the wall, surrounded by other pictures, hung a half-crown water-colour drawing of the wife, with a child on her knee, matched on the other side by the husband's likeness, cut out in black paper. Pictures of bright-coloured ducks and a print of Father Moore the teetotaler completed the collection.

"You see," said the man, "we manages pretty well; but I can assure you we has a hard time of it to do it at all comfortably. Me and my wife is just as we stands—all our other things are in pawn. If I was to drink I don't know what I should do. How others manage is to me a mystery. This will show you I speak the truth," he added, and going to a secretary that stood against the wall he produced a handful of duplicates. There were seventeen tickets in all, amounting to 3l. 0s. 6d., the highest sum borrowed being 10s. "That'll

show you I don't like my poverty to be known, or I should have told you of it before. And yet we manage to sleep clean ;" and he pulled back the patchwork counterpane, and showed me the snow-white sheets beneath. " There's not enough clothes to keep us warm, but at least they are clean. We're obliged to give as much as we can to the children. Cleanliness is my wife's hobby, and I let her indulge in it. I can assure you last week my wife had to take the gown off her back to get 1s. on it. My little ones seldom have a bit of meat from one Sunday to another, and never a bit of butter."

I then descended into the parlour. The children were all seated on little stools that their father had made for them in his spare moments, and warming themselves round the fire, their little black shoes resting on the white hearth. From their regular features, small mouths, large black eyes, and fair skins, no one would have taken them for a labouring man's family. In answer to my questions, he said : " The eldest of them (a pretty little half-clad girl, seated in one corner) is ten, the next seven, that one five, that three, and this (a little thing perched upon a table near the mother) two. I've got all their ages in the Bible up-stairs." I remarked a strange look about one of the little girls. " Yes, she always suffered with that eye; and down at the hospital they lately performed an operation on it." An artificial pupil had been made.

The room was closed in from the passage by a rudely built partition. " That I did myself in my leisure," said the man; " it makes the room snugger.' As he saw me looking at the clean rolling-pin and bright tins hung against the wall, he observed : " That's all my wife's doing. She has got them together by sometimes going without dinner herself, and laying out the 2d. or 3d. in things of that sort. That is how she manages. To-day she has got us a sheep's head and a few turnips for our Sunday's dinner," he added, taking off the lid of the boiling saucepan. Over the mantelpiece hung a picture of George IV., surrounded by four other frames. One of them contained merely three locks of hair. The man, laughing, told me, " Two of them are locks of myself and my wife, and the light one in the middle belonged to my wife's brother, who died in India. That's her doing again," he added.

After this I paid a visit to the other teetotaler at his home, and there saw one of his sons. He had six children altogether, and also supported his wife's mother. If it wasn't for him, the poor old thing, who was seventy-five, and a teetotaler too, must have gone to the workhouse. Three of his six children lived at home; the other three were out at service. One of the lads at home was a coalbacker. He was twenty-four years of age, and on an average could earn 17s. 6d. It was four years since he had taken to backing. He said, " I am at work at one of the worst wharfs in London ; it is called 'the slaughter-house' by the men, because the work is so excessive. The strongest man can only last twelve years at the work there; after that he is overstrained and of no use. I do the hardest work, and carry the coals up from the hold. The ladder I mount has about thirty-five steps, and stands very nearly straight on end. Each time I mount I carry on my back 238 pounds. No man can work at this for more than five days in the week. I work three days running, then have a day's rest, and then work two days more. I myself generally do five days' work out of the six. I never drink any beer, and have not for the last eight months. For three years and four months I took beer to get over the work. I used to have a pint at eleven, a pot at dinner, a pint at four o'clock, and double allowance, or a couple of pots, after work. Very often I had more than double allowance. I seldom in a day drank less than that; but I have done more. I have drunk five pots in four minutes and a-half. So my expenditure for beer was 1s. 4d. a-day regularly. Indeed, I used to allow myself three half-crowns to spend in beer a-week, Sundays included. When a coal-worker is in full work, he usually spends 2s. a-day, or 12s. a-week, in beer. The trade calls these men temperate. When they spend 15s. the trade think they are intemperate. Before I took the pledge I scarcely ever went to bed sober after my labour. I was not always drunk, but I was heavy and stupid with beer. Twice within the time I was a coalbacker I have been insensibly drunk. I should say three-fourths of the coalbackers are drunk twice a-week. Coalbacking is as heavy a class of labour as any performed. I don't know any that can beat it. I have been eight months doing the work, and can solemnly state I have never tasted a drop of fermented liquor. I have found I could do my work better and brisker than when I drank. I never feel thirsty over my work now; before, I was always dry, and felt as if I could never drink enough to quench it. Now I never drink from the time I go to work till the time I have my dinner; then my usual beverage is either cold coffee or oatmeal and water. From that time I never drink till I take my tea. On this system I find myself quite as strong as I did with the porter. When I drank porter it used to make me go along with a sack a little bit brisker for half-an-hour, but after that I was dead, and obliged to have some more. There are men at the wharf who drink beer and spirits that can do six days' labour in the week. I can't do this myself. I have done as much when I took fermented liquors, but I only did so by whipping myself up with stimulants. I was obliged to drink every hour a pint of beer to force me along. That was only working for the publican; for I had less money at the week's end than when I did less work. Now I can keep longer and more steadily at my work. In a month I would warrant to back more coals than a drunkard. I think the drunkard

can do more for a short space of time than the teetotaler. I am satisfied the coalbackers as a class would be better off if they left off the drinking; and then masters would not force them to do so much work after dark as they do now. They always pay at public-houses. If that system was abandoned, the men would be greatly benefited by it. Drinking is not a necessity of the labour. All I want when I'm at work is a bit of coal in the mouth. This not only keeps the mouth cool, but as we go up the ladder we very often scrunch our teeth—the work's so hard. The coal keeps us from biting the tongue, that's one use; the other is, that by rolling it along in the mouth it excites the spittle, and it moistens the mouth. This I find a great deal better than a pot of porter."

In order to complete my investigations concerning the necessity of drinking in the coal-whipping trade, I had an interview with some of the more intelligent of the men who had been principally concerned in the passing of the Act that rescued the class from the "thraldom of the publican."

"I consider," said one, "that drink is not a necessity of our labour, but it is a necessity of the system under which we were formerly working. I have done the hardest work that any labouring man can do, and drank no fermented liquor. Nor do I consider fermented liquors to be necessary for the severest labour. This I can say of my own experience, having been a teetotaler for sixteen months. But if the working man don't have the drink, he must have good solid food, superior to what he is in the habit of having. A pot of coffee and a good beef dumpling will get one over the most severe labour. But if he can't have that he must have the stimulants. A pint of beer he can always have on credit, but he can't the beef dumpling. If there is an excuse for any persons drinking there is for the coalwhippers, for under the old system they were forced to become habitual drunkards to obtain work."

I also questioned another of the men, who had been a prime mover in obtaining the Act. He assured me, that before the "emancipation" of the men the universal belief of the coal-whippers, encouraged by the publicans, was, that it was impossible for them to work without liquor. In order to do away with that delusion, the three principal agents in procuring the Act became teetotalers of their own accord, and remained so, one for sixteen months and another for nine years, in order to prove to their fellow workmen that drinking over their labour could be dispensed with, and that they might have "cool brains to fight through the work they had undertaken."

Another of the more intelligent men who had been a teetotaler:—"I performed the hardest labour I ever did, before or after, with more ease and satisfaction than ever I did under the drinking system. It is quite a delusion to believe that with proper nutriment the health declines under principles of total abstinence."

After this I was anxious to continue my investigations among the coalporters, and see whether the more intelligent among them were as firmly convinced as the better class of coalwhippers were, that intoxicating drinks were not necessary for the performance of hard labour. I endeavoured to find one of each class, pursuing the same plan as I had adopted with the coalwhippers: viz. I sought first, one who was so firmly convinced of the necessity of drinking fermented liquors during his work, that he had never been induced to abandon them; secondly, I endeavoured to obtain the evidence of one who had tried the principle of total abstinence and found it fail; and thirdly, I strove to procure the opinion of those who had been teetotalers for several years, and who could conscientiously state that no stimulant was necessary for the performance of their labour. Subjoined is the result of my investigations.

Concerning the motives and reasons for the great consumption of beer by the coalporters, I obtained the following statement from one of them:—" I've been all my life at coalportering, off and on, and am now thirty-nine. For the last two years or so I've worked regularly as a filler to Mr. ——'s waggons. I couldn't do my work without a good allowance of beer. I can't afford so much now, as my family costs me more; but my regular allowance one time was three pots a-day. I have drank four pots, and always a glass of gin in the morning to keep out the cold air from the water. If I got off then for 7s. a week for drink I reckoned it a cheap week. I can't do my work without my beer, and no coalporter can, properly. It's all nonsense talking about ginger-beer, or tea, or milk, or that sort of thing; what body is there in any of it? Many a time I might have been choked with coal-dust, if I hadn't had my beer to clear my throat with. I can't say that I'm particularly thirsty like next morning, after drinking three or four pots of beer to my own work, but I don't get drunk." He frequently, and with some emphasis, repeated the words, "But I don't get drunk." " You see, when you're at such hard work as ours, one's tired soon, and a drop of good beer puts new sap into a man. It oils his joints like. He can lift better and stir about brisker. I don't care much for beer when I'm quiet at home on a Sunday; it sets me to sleep then. I once tried to go without to please a master, and did work one day with only one half-pint. I went home as tired as a dog. I should have been soon good for nothing if I'd gone on that way—half-pinting in a day. Lord love you! we know a drop of good beer. The coalporters is admitted to be as good judges of beer as any men in London—maybe, the best judges; better than publicans. No salt and water will go down with us. It's no use a publican trying to gammon us with any of his cag-mag stuff.

Salt and water for us! Sartainly, a drop of short (neat spirit) does one good in a cold morning like this; it's uncommon raw by the waterside, you see. Coalporters doesn't often catch cold—beer and gin keeps it out. Perhaps my beer and gin now cost me 5s. a-week, and that's a deal out of what I can earn. I dare say I earn 18s. a-week. Sometimes I may spend 6s. That's a third of my earnings, you say, and so it is; and as it's necessary for my work, isn't it a shame a poor man's pot of beer, and drop of gin, and pipe of tobacco, should be so dear? Taxes makes them dear. I can read, sir, and I understand these things. Beer—four pots a-day of it doesn't make me step unsteady. Hard work carries it off, and so one doesn't feel it that way. Beer's made of corn as well as bread, and so it stands to reason it's nourishing. Nothing'll persuade me it isn't. Let a teetotal gentleman try his hand at coal-work, and then he'll see if beer has no support in it. Too much is bad, I know, but a man can always tell how much he wants to help him on with his work. If beer didn't agree with me, of course I wouldn't drink it: but it does. Sartainly we drops into a beer-shop of a night, and does tipple a little when work's done; and the old women (our wives) comes for us, and they get a sup to soften them, and so they may get to like it overmuch, as you say, and one's bit of a house may go to rack and manger. I've a good wife myself, though. I know well enough all them things is bad—drunkenness is bad! All I ask for is a proper allowance at work; the rest is no good. I can't tell whether too much or no beer at coal-work would be best; perhaps none at all: leastways it would be safer. I shouldn't like to try either. Perhaps coalporters does get old sooner than other trades, and mayn't live so long; but that's their hard work, and it would be worse still without beer. But I don't get drunk."

I conversed with several men on the subject of their beer-drinking, but the foregoing is the only statement I met with where a coalporter could give any reason for his faith in the virtues of beer; and vague as in some points it may be, the other reasons I had to listen to were still vaguer. " Somehow we can't do without beer; it puts in the strength that the work takes out." " It's necessary for support." Such was the pith of every argument.

In order fully to carry out this inquiry, I obtained the address of a coalbacker from the ships, who worked hard and drank a good deal of beer, and who had the character of being an industrious man. I saw him in his own apartment, his wife being present while he made the following statement:—" I've worked at backing since I was twenty-four, and that's more than twelve years ago. I limit myself now, because times is not so good, to two pots of beer a-day; that is, when I'm all day at work. Some takes more. I reckon, that when times was better I drank fifteen pots a-week, for I was in regular work, and middlin' well off. That's 780 pots, or 195 gallons a-year, you say. Like enough it may be. I never calculated, but it does seem a deal. It can't be done without, and men themselves is the best judges of what suits their work—I mean, of how much to take. I'll tell you what it is, sir. Our work's harder than people guess at, and one must rest sometimes. Now, if you sit down to rest without something to refresh you, the rest does you harm instead of good, for your joints seem to stiffen; but a good pull at a pot of beer backs up the rest, and we start lightsomer. Our work's very hard. I've worked till my head's ached like to split; and when I've got to bed, I've felt as if I've had the weight on my back still, and I've started awake when I fell off to sleep, feeling as if something was crushing my back flat to my chest. I can't say that I ever tried to do without beer altogether. If I was to think of such a thing, my old woman there would think I was out of my head." The wife assented. "I've often done with a little when work's been slackish. First, you see, we bring the coal up from the ship's hold. There, sometimes, it's dreadful hot, not a mouthful of air, and the coal-dust sometimes as thick as a fog. You breathe it into you, and your throat's like a flue, so that you must have something to drink. I fancy nothing quenches you like beer. We want a drink that tastes. Then there's the coals on your back to be carried up a nasty ladder, or some such contrivance, perhaps twenty feet, and a sack full of coals weighs 2 cwt. and a stone, at least; the sack itself's heavy and thick: isn't that a strain on a man? No horse could stand it long. Then, when you get fairly out of the ship, you go along planks to the waggon, and must look sharp, 'specially in slippery or wet weather, or you'll topple over, and then there's the hospital or the workhouse for you. Last week we carried along planks sixty feet, at least. There's nothing extra allowed for distance, but there ought to be. I've sweat to that degree in summer, that I've been tempted to jump into the Thames to cool myself. The sweat's run into my boots, and I've felt it running down me for hours as I had to trudge along. It makes men bleed at the nose and mouth, this work does. Sometimes we put a bit of coal in our mouths, to prevent our biting our tongues. I do, sometimes, but it's almost as bad as if you did bite your tongue, for when the strain comes heavier and heavier on you, you keep scrunching the coal to bits, and swallow some of it, and you're half choked; and then it's no use, you must have beer. Some's tried a bit of tobacco in their mouths, but that doesn't answer; it makes you spit, and often spit blood. I know I can't do without beer. I don't think they 'dulterate it for us; they may for fine people, that just tastes it, and, I've heard, has wine and things. But we must have it good, and a publican knows

who's good customers. Perhaps a bit of good grub might be as good as beer to strengthen you at work, but the straining and sweating makes you thirsty, more than hungry; and if poor men must work so hard, and for so little, for rich men, why poor men will take what they feel will satisfy them, and run the risk of its doing them good or harm; and that's just where it is. I can't work three days running now without feeling it dreadful. I get a mate that's fresher to finish my work. I'd rather earn less at a trade that would give a man a chance of some ease, but all trades is overstocked. You see we have a niceish tidy room here, and a few middling sticks, so I can't be a drunkard."

I now give the statement of a coalporter who had been a teetotaler :—" I have been twenty-two years a coalheaver. When I began that work I earned 50s. a-week as backer and filler. I am now earning, one week with another, say 15s. We have no sick fund among us—no society of any sort—no club—no schools—no nothing. We had a kind of union among us before the great strike, more than fourteen years back, but it was just for the strike. We struck against masters lowering the pay for a ton to 2¼d. from 2½d. The strike only lasted two or three weeks, and the men were forced to give way; they didn't all give way at once, but came to gradual. One can't see one's wife and children without bread. There's very few teetotalers among us, though there's not many of us now that can be called drunken —they can't get it, sir. I was a teetotaler myself for two years, till I couldn't keep to it any longer. We all break. It's a few years back, I forget zactly when. At that time teetotalers might drink shrub, but that never did me no good; a good cup of tea freshened me more. I used then to drink ginger-beer, and spruce, and tea, and coffee. I've paid as much as 5s. a-week for ginger-beer. When I teetotaled, I always felt thirsty. I used to long for a drink of beer, but somehow managed to get past a public-house, until I could stand it no longer. A clerk of ours broke first, and I followed him. I certainly felt weaker before I went back to my beer; now I drink a pint or two as I find I want it. I can't do without it, so it's no use trying. I joined because I felt I was getting racketty, and giving my mind to nothing but drink, instead of looking to my house. There may be a few teetotalers among us, but I think not. I only knew two. We all break—we can't keep it. One of these broke, and the other kept it, because, if he breaks, his wife'll break, and they were both regular drunkards. A coalporter's worn out before what you may call well old. There's not very old men among us. A man's done up at fifty, and seldom lives long after, if he has to keep on at coalportering. I wish we had some sick fund, or something of that kind. If I was laid up now, there would be nothing but the parish for me, my wife, and four childer (here the poor man spoke in a broken voice). The masters often discharge old hands when they get feeble, and put on boys. We have no coals allowed for our own firesides. Some masters, if we buys of them, charges us full price, others a little cheaper."

I saw this man in the evening, after he had left his work, in his own room. It was a large and airy garret. His wife, who did not know previously of my visit, had in her domestic arrangements manifested a desire common to the better disposed of the wives of the labourers, or the poor—that of trying to make her " bit of place" look comfortable. She had to tend a baby four months old; two elder children were ill clad, but clean; the eldest boy, who is fifteen, is in the summer employed on a river steamboat, and is then of great help to his parents. There were two beds in the room, and the bedding was decently arranged so as to form a bundle, while its scantiness or worn condition was thus concealed. The solitary table had a faded green cloth cover, very threadbare, but still a cover. There were a few cheap prints over the mantelshelf, and the best description I can give is, in a phrase not uncommon among the poor, that the whole was an attempt to " appear decent." The woman spoke well of her husband, who was kind to her, and fond of his home, and never drank on Sundays.

Last of all, I obtained an interview with two coalporters who had been teetotalers for some years :—

" I have been a coalporter ever since I have been able to carry coals," said one. " I began at sixteen. I have been a backer all the time. I have been a teetotaler eight years on the 10th of next March. My average earnings where I am now is about 35s. per week. At some wharfs work is very bad, and the men don't average half that. They were paid every night where I worked last, and sometimes I have gone home with 2½d. Take one with the other, I should say the coalporter's earnings average about 1l. a-week. My present place is about as good a berth as there is along the waterside. There is only one gang of us, and we do as much work as two will do in many wharfs. Before I was a teetotaler, I principally drank ale. I judged that the more I gave for my drink, the better it was. Upon an average, I used to drink from three to four pints of ale per day. I used to drink a good drop of gin, too. The coalporters are very partial to 'dog's nose'—that is, half a pint of ale with a pennyworth of gin in it; and when they have got the money, they go up to what they term 'the lucky shop' for it. The coalporters take this every morning through the week, when they can afford it. After my work, I used to drink more than when I was at it. I used to sit as long as the house would let me have any. Upon an average, I should say I used to take three or four pints more of an evening; so that, altogether, I think I may fairly say I drank my four pots of ale regularly every day, and about half a pint of dog's nose. I reckon my drink used to cost me 13s. a-week when I was at work. At times I was a drunken, noisy gentleman then."

Another coalporter, who has been a teetaler ten years on the 25th of last August, told me, that before he took the pledge he used to drink a great deal after he had done his work, but while he was at work he could not stand it. " I don't think I used to drink above three pints and a half and a pennyworth of gin in the daytime," said this man. " Of an evening I used to stop at the publichouse, generally till I was drunk and unfit to work in the morning. I will vouch for it I used to take about three pots a-day after I had done work. My reckoning used to come to about 1s. 8d. a-day, or, including Sundays, about 10s. 6d. per week. At that time I could average all the year round about 30s. a-week, and I used to drink away 10s. of it regularly. I did, indeed, sir, more to my shame."

The other coalporter told me his earnings averaged about the same, but he drank more. " I should say I got rid of nearly one half of my money. I did like the beer then : I thought I could not live without it. It's between twelve and thirteen years since the first coalporter signed the pledge. His name was John Sturge, and he was looked upon as a madman. I looked upon him myself in that light. The next was Thomas Bailey, and he was my teetotal father. When I first heard of a coalporter doing without beer, I thought it a thing impossible. I made sure they wouldn't live long; it was part of my education to believe they couldn't. My grandfather brewed homebrewed beer, and he used to say to me, ' Drink, my lad, it'll make thee strong.' The coalporters say now, if we could get the genuine home-brewed, that would be the stuff to do us good; the publican's wash is no good. I drank for strength ; the stimulation caused by the alcohol I mistook for my own power."

" Richard Hooper ! He's been a teetotaler now about twelve years. He was the fourth of the coaleys as signed the pledge, and he first instilled teetotalism on my mind," said the other man. " Where he works now there's nine out of fifteen men is teetotalers. Seeing that he could do his work much better than when he drinked beer, induced me to become one. He was more regular in his work after he had given it up than whenever I knowed him before."

" The way in which Thomas Bailey put it into my head was this here," continued the other. " He invited me to a meeting : I told him I would come, but he'd never make a teetotaler of me, I knowed. I went with the intention to listen to what they could have to say. I was a little bit curious to know how they could make out that beer was no good for a body. The first man that addressed the meeting was a tailor. I thought it might do very well for him; but then, says I, if you had the weight of 238lbs. of coals on your back, my lad, you couldn't do it without ale or beer. I thought this here, because I was taught to believe I couldn't do without it. I cared not what any man said about beer, I believed it was life itself. After the tailor a coalporter got up to speak. Then I began to listen more attentively. The man said he once had a happy home and a happy wife, everything the heart could wish for, but through the intoxicating drinks he had been robbed of everything. The man pictured the drunkard's home so faithfully, that the arrows of conviction stuck fast in my heart, and my conscience said, Thou art a drunkard, too! The coalporter said his home had been made happy through the principle of total abstinence. I was determined to try it from that hour. My home was as miserable as it possibly could be, and I knowed intoxicating drink was the cause on it. I signed the pledge that night after the coalporter was done speaking, but was many months before I was thoroughly convinced I was doing right in abstaining altogether. I kept thinking on it after going home of a night, tired and fatigued with my hard work, some times scarcely able to get up-stairs through being so over-wrought; and not being quite satisfied about it, I took every opportunity to hear lectures upon the subject. I heard one on the properties of intoxicating drinks, which quite convinced me that I had been labouring under a delusion. The gentleman analysed the beer in my presence, and I saw that in a pint of it there was 14 ozs. of water that I had been paying 2d. for, 1 oz. of alcohol, and 1 oz. of what they call nutritious matter, but which is the filthiest stuff man ever set eyes upon. It looked more like cobblers' wax than anything else. It was what the lecturer called the—residyum, I think was the name he gave it. The alcohol is what stimulates a man, and makes him feel as if he could carry two sacks of coal while it lasts, but afterwards comes the depression; that's what the coalporters call the 'blues.' And then he feels that he can do no work at all, and he either goes home and puts another man on in his place, or else he goes and works it off with more drink. You see, where we coalporters have been mistaken is in believing alcohol was nutriment, and in fancying that a stimulant was strength. Alcohol is nothing strengthening to the body—indeed, it hardens the food in the stomach, and so hinders digestion. You can see as much any day if you go into the hospitals, and look at the different parts of animals preserved in spirits. The strength that alcohol gives is unnatural and false. It's food only that can give real strength to the frame. I have done more work since I've been a teetotaler in my eight years than I did in my ten or twelve years before. I have felt stronger. I don't say that I do my work better, but this I will

say, without any fear of contradiction, that I do my work with more ease to myself, and with more satisfaction to my employer, since I have given over intoxicating drinks. I scarcely know what thirst is. Before I took the pledge I was always dry, and the mere shadow of the potboy was quite sufficient to convince me that I wanted something. I certainly haven't felt weaker since I left off malt liquor. I have eaten more and drank less. I live as well now as any of the publicans do, and who has a better right to do so than the man who works? I have backed as many as sixty tons in a day since I took the pledge, and have done it without any intoxicating drink, with perfect ease to myself, and walked five miles to a temperance meeting afterwards. But before I became a teetotaler, after the same amount of work, I should scarcely have been able to crawl home; I should have been certain to have lost the next day's work at least: but now I can back that quantity of coals week after week without losing a day. I've got a family of six children under twelve years of age. My wife's a teetotaler, and has suckled four children upon the principle of total abstinence. Teetotalism has made my home quite happy, and what I get goes twice as far. Where I work now, four out of five of us are teetotalers. I am quite satisfied that the heaviest work that a man can possibly do may be done without a drop of fermented liquor. I say so from my own experience. All kind of intoxicating drinks is quite a delusion. They are the cause of the working man's wages being lowered. Masters can get the men who drink at their own price. If it wasn't for the money spent in liquor we should have funds to fall back upon, and then we could stand out against any reduction that the masters might want to put upon us, and could command a fair day's wages for a fair day's work: but as it is, the men are all beggars, and must take what the master offers them. The backing of coals out of the holds of ships is man-killing work. It's scandalous that men should be allowed to force their fellow-men to do such labour. The calves of a man's leg is as hard as a bit of board after that there straining work; they hardly know how to turn out of bed of a morning after they have been at that for a day. I never worked below bridge, thank God! and I hope I never shall. I've not wanted for a day's work since I've been a teetotaler. Men can back out of a ship's hold better without liquor than with it. We teetotalers can do the work better—that is, with more ease to ourselves—than the drinking men. Many teetotalers have backed coals out of the hold, and I have heard them say over and over again that they did their work with more comfort and ease than they did when they drank intoxicating drink. Coal-backing from the ship's hold is the hardest work that it is possible for a man to do.

Going up a ladder 16 feet high with 238 lbs. weight on a man's back is sufficient to kill any one; indeed, it does kill the men in a few years, they're soon old men at that work: and I do say that the masters below bridge should be stopped going on as they're doing now. And what for? Why, to put the money they save by it into their own pockets, for the public ain't no better off, the coals is just as dear. Then the whippers and lightermen are all thrown out of work by it; and what's more, the lives of the backers are shortened many years—we reckon at least ten years."

"I wish to say this much," said the other teetotaler: "it's a practice with some of the coal-merchants to pay their men in public-houses, and this is the chief cause of a great portion of the wages being spent in drink. I once worked for a master upon Bankside as paid his men at a public-house, and I worked a week there, which yearned me 28s. and some odd halfpence. When I went on Saturday night the publican asked me what I was come for. In reply, I said 'I'm come to settle.' He said, 'You're already settled with,' meaning I had nothing to take. I had drinked all my lot away, he said, with the exception of 5s. I had borrowed during the week. Then I told him to look back, and he'd find I'd something due to me. He did so, and said there was a halfpenny. I had nothing to take home to my wife and two children. I asked the publican to lend me a few shillings, saying my young un's had nothing to eat. His reply was, 'That's nothing to me, that's your business.' After that I made it my business. While I stood at the bar in came the three teetotalers, and picked up the 28s. each that was coming to them, and I thought how much better they was off than me. The publican stopped all my money for drink that I knowed I'd not had, and yet I couldn't help myself, 'cause he had the paying on me. Then something came over me as I stood there, and I said, 'From this night, with the help of God, I'll never taste of another drop of intoxicating liquors.' That's ten years ago the 25th of last August, and I've kept my pledge ever since, thank God! That publican has been the making of me. The master what discharged me before for getting drunk, when he heard that I was sober sent for me back again. But before that, the three teetotalers who was a working along with me was discharged by their master, to oblige the publican who stopped my money. The publican, you see, had his coals from the wharf. He was a 'brass-plate coal-merchant' as well as a publican, and had private customers of his own. He threatened to take his work away from the wharf if the three teetotalers wasn't discharged; and sure enough the master did discharge them, sooner than lose so good a customer. Many of the masters now are growing favourable to teetotalism. I can say that I've done more on the principle of total

abstinence than ever I done before. I'm better in health, I've no trembling when I goes to my work of a morning; but, on the contrary, I'm ready to meet it. I'm happier at home. We never has no angry words now," said the man, with a shake of the head, and a strong emphasis on the *now*. "My children never runs away from me as they used to before; they come and embrace me more. My money now goes for eatables and clothes, what I and my children once was deprived on through my intemperate habits. And I bless God and the publican that made me a teetotaler—that I do sincerely—every night as I go to bed. And as for men to hold out that they can't do their work without it, I'm prepared to prove that we have done more work without it than ever we have done or could do with it."

I have been requested by the coalwhippers to publish the following expression of gratitude on their part towards the Government for the establishment of the Coalwhippers' Office:—

"The change that the Legislature has produced in us, by putting an end to the thraldom of the publican by the institution of this office, we wish it to be generally known that we and our wives and children are very thankful for."

I shall now conclude with the following estimate of the number of the hands, ships, &c. engaged in the coal trade in London.

There are about 400 wharfs, I am informed, from Wapping to Chelsea, as well as those on the City-canal. A large wharf will keep about 50 horses, 6 waggons, and 4 carts; and it will employ constantly from 3 to 4 gangs of 5 men. Besides these, there will be 6 waggoners, 1 cart-carman, and about 2 trouncers —in all, from 24 to 29 men. A small wharf will employ 1 gang of 5 men, about 10 horses, 3 waggons, and 1 cart, 3 waggoners, 1 trouncer, and 1 cart-carman. At the time of the strike, sixteen years ago, there were more than 3000 coalporters, I am told, in London. It is supposed that there is an average of 1½ gang, or about 7 men employed in each wharf; or, in all, 2000 coalporters in constant employment, and about 200 and odd men out of work. There are in the trade about 4 waggons and 1 cart to each wharf, or 1600 waggons and 400 carts, having 5200 horses; to these there would be about 3 waggoners and 1 cart-carman upon an average to each wharf, or 1600 in all. Each wharf would occupy about 2 trouncers, or 900 in the whole.

Hence the statistics of the coal trade will be as follows:—

	No.
Ships	2,177
Seamen	21,600
Tons of coal entering the Port of London each year	3,418,140
Coalmeters	170

	No.
Coalwhippers	2,000
Coalporters	3,000
Coalfactors	25
Coalmerchants	502
Coaldealers	295
Coal waggons	1,600
Horses for ditto	5,200
Waggoners	1,600
Trimmers	800

I continue my inquiry into the state of the coal-labourers of the metropolis.

The coalheavers, properly so called, are now no longer known in the trade. The class of coalheavers, according to the vulgar acceptation of the word, is divided into coalwhippers, or those who whip up or lift the coals rapidly from the hold, and the coalbackers, or those who carry them on their backs to the wharf, either from the hold of the ship moored alongside the wharf, or from the lighter into which the coals have been whipped from the collier moored in the middle of the river, or " Pool." Formerly the coals were delivered from the holds of the ships by the labourers shovelling them on to a series of stages, raised one above the other·till they ultimately reached the deck. One or two men were on each stage, and hove the coals up to the stage immediately above them. The labourers engaged in this process were termed " coalheavers." But now the coals are delivered at once from the hold by means of a sudden jerk, which " whips " them on deck. This is the process of coalwhipping, and it is performed chiefly in the middle of the river, to fill the " rooms" of the barges that carry the coals from the ship to the wharf. Coals are occasionally delivered immediately from the ship on to the wharf by means of the process of " coalbacking," as it is called. This consists in the sacks being filled in the hold, and then carried on the men's backs up a ladder from the hold, along planks from the ship to the wharf. By this means, it will be easily understood that the ordinary processes of whipping and lightering are avoided. By the process of coalwhipping, the ship is delivered in the middle of the river, or the " Pool " as it is called, and the coals are lightered, or carried to the wharf, by means of barges, whence they are transported to the wharf by the process of backing. But when the coals are backed out of the ship itself on to the wharf, the two preliminary processes are done away with. The ship is moored alongside, and the coals are delivered directly from the ships to the premises of the wharfinger. By this means the wharfingers, or coalmerchants, below bridge, are enabled to have their coals delivered at a cheaper price than those above bridge, who must receive the cargoes by means of the barges. I am assured that the colliers, in being moored alongside the wharfs, receive considerable damage, and strain their timbers

severely from the swell of the steamboats passing to and fro. Again, the process of coalbacking appears to be of so extremely laborious a nature that the health, and indeed the lives, of the men are both greatly injured by it. Moreover, the benefit remains solely with the merchant, and not with the consumer, for the price of the coals delivered below bridge is the same as those delivered above. The expense of delivering the ship is always borne by the shipowner. This is, at present, 8d. per ton, and was originally intended to be given to the whippers. But the merchant, by the process of backing, has discovered the means of avoiding this process; and so he puts the money which was originally paid by the shipowner for whipping the coals into his own pocket, for the consumer is not a commensurate gainer. Since the merchant below bridge charges the same price to the public for his coals as the merchant above, it is clear that he alone is benefited at the expense of the public, the coalwhippers, and even the coalbackers themselves; for on inquiry among this latter class, I find that they object as much as the whippers to the delivery of a ship from the hold, the mounting of the ladders from the hold being of a most laborious and injurious nature. I have been supplied by a gentleman who is intimately acquainted with the expenses of the two processes with the following comparative account:—

Expenses of delivering a Ship of 360 tons by the process of Coalwhipping.

	£	s.	d.
For whipping 360 tons at 8d. per ton	12	0	0
Lighterman's wages for 1 week engaged in lightering the said 360 tons from ship to wharf . .	1	10	0
Expenses of backing the said coals from craft to wharf at 11¼d. per ton	16	17	6
	£30	7	6

Expense of delivering a Ship of 360 tons by the process of Coalbacking.

For backing a ship of 360 tons directly from the ship to the wharf	£16	17	6

By the above account it will be seen, that if a collier of 360 tons is delivered in the Pool, the expense is 30l. 7s. 6d., but if delivered at the wharf-side the expense is 16l. 17s. 6d., the difference between the two processes being 13l. 10s. Hence, if the consumer were the gainer, the coals should be delivered below bridge 9d. a ton cheaper than they are above bridge. The nine coalwhippers ordinarily engaged in the whipping of the coals would have gained 1l. 6s. 8d. each man if they had not been "backed" out of the ship; but as the coals delivered by backing below bridge are not cheaper, and the whippers have not received any money, it follows that the 12*l.* which has been paid by the shipowner to the merchant for the expense of whipping has been pocketed by the merchant, and the expense of lightering, 1*l.* 10*s.*, saved by him; making a total profit of 13*l.* 10*s.*, not to mention the cost of wear and tear, and interest of capital sunk in barges. This sum of money is made at the expense of the coalbackers themselves, who are seldom able to continue the labour (so extreme is it) for more than twenty years at the outside, the average duration of the labourers being only twelve years. After this period, the men, from having been overstrained by their violent exertion, are unable to pursue any other calling; and yet the merchants, I am sorry to say, have not even encouraged them to form either a benefit society, a superannuation fund, or a school for their children.

Wishing to perfect the inquiry, I thought it better to see one of the seamen engaged in the trade. Accordingly, I went off to some of the colliers lying in Mill Hole, and found an intelligent man, ready to give me the information I sought. His statement was, that he had been to sea between twenty-six and twenty-seven years altogether. "Out of that time," he said, "I've had nine or ten years' experience at the coal-trade. I've been to the East Indies and West Indies, and served my apprenticeship in a whaler. I have been to the Mediterranean, and to several parts of France. I think that, take the general run, the living and treatment of the men in the coal-trade is better than in any other going. It's difficult to tell how many ships I've been in, and how many owners I've served under. I have been in the same ship for three or four years, and I have been only one voyage in one ship. You see, we are obliged to study our own interest as much as we can. Of course the masters won't do it for us. Speaking generally, of the different ships and different owners I've served under, I think the men are generally well served. I have been in some that have been very badly victualled: the small stores in particular, such as tea, sugar, and coffee, have been very bad. They, in general, nip us very short. There is a regular allowance fixed by Act of Parliament; but it's too little for a man to go by. Some owners go strictly by the Act, and some give more; but I don't know one that gives under. Indeed, as a general rule, I think the men in the trade have nothing to complain of. The only thing is, the wages are generally small; and the ships are badly manned. In bad weather there is not enough hands to take the sail off her, or else there wouldn't be so many accidents as there are. The average tonnage of a coal-ship is from 60 up to about 250 tons. There are sometimes large ships; but they come seldom, and when they do, they carry but part coal cargo. They only load a portion with coals that they may be able to come across the bar-harbours in the north. If they were loaded altogether with coals, they couldn't get over the bar: they would draw too much water. For a ship of about from 100 to 130 tons, the usual complement is generally from five to six hands, boys, captain, and men all included together. There might be two men before the mast—a master, a mate, and a boy. This is sadly too little. A ship of this sort shouldn't, to my mind, have less than seven hands: that is the least to be safe. In rough weather, you see, perhaps the ship is letting water: the master takes the 'hellum,' one hand, in general, stops on deck to work the pumps, and three goes aloft. Most likely one of the boys has only been to sea one or two voyages; and if there's six hands to such a ship, two of them is sure to be 'green-boys,' just fresh from the shore, and of little or no use to us. We haven't help enough to get the sail off the yards in time,— there's no one on deck looking out,—it may be thick weather,—and, of course, it's properly dangerous. About half the accidents at sea occur from the ships being badly manned. The ships generally, throughout the coal-trade, have one hand in six too little. The colliers, mostly, carry double their registered tonnage. A ship of 250 tons carrying 500, will have ten hands, when she ought to have twelve or thirteen; and out of the ten that she does have, perhaps four of them is boys. All sailors in the coal-trade are paid by the voyage. They vary from 3*l.* 10*s.* up to 4*l.* for able-bodied seamen. The ships from the same port in the north give all alike for a London journey. In the height of summer, the wages is from 3*l.* 5*s.* to 3*l.* 15*s.*; and in the winter they are 4*l.* Them's the highest wages given this winter. The wages are increased in the winter, because the work's harder and the weather's colder. Some of the ships lay up, and there's a greater demand for those that are in the trade. It's true that the seamen of those that are laying up are out of employ; but I can't say why it is that the wages don't come down in consequence. All I know is they go up in the winter. This is sadly too little pay, this 4*l.* a journey. Probably, in the winter, a man may make only two journeys in four months; and if he's got a wife and family, his expenses is going on at home all the while. The voyage I consider to last from the time of sailing from the north port, to the time of entering the north port again. The average time of coming from the north port to London is from ten to eleven days. Sometimes the passage has been done in six: but I'm speaking of the average. We are generally about twenty-two days at sea, making the voyage from the north and back. The rest of the time we are discharging cargo, or lying idle in the Pool. On making the port of London, we have to remain in 'the Section' till the cargo is sold. 'The Section' is between Woolwich and Gravesend. I have remained there as much as five weeks. I have been there, too, only one market-day—that is, three days. It is very seldom this occurs. The average time that we remain in 'the Section' is from two to three weeks. The cause of this delay arises from the factors not disposing of the coals, in order to keep up the prices. If a large fleet comes, the factors will not sell immediately, because the prices would go down; so we are kept in 'the Section,' for their convenience, without no more wages. When the cargo is sold we drop down into the Pool; and there we remain about two days more than we ought, for want of a meter. We are often kept, also, a day over the day of delivery. This we call a 'balk day.' The owners of the ship receive a certain compensation for every one of these balk days. This is expressed in the charter-party, or ship's contract. The whippers and meters, too, receive a certain sum for these balk days, the same as if they were working; but the seamen of the colliers are the only parties who receive nothing. The delay arises entirely through the merchant, and he ought to pay us for it. The coal-trade is the only trade that pays by the voyage; all others paying by the month : and the seamen feel it as a great grievance, this detention not being paid for. Very often, while I have been laying in 'the Section,' because the coalfactor would not sell, other seamen that entered the port of London with me have made another voyage and been back again, whilst I was stopping idle; and been been 3*l.* 10*s.*, or 4*l.*, the better for it. Four or five years since the voyage was 1*l.* or 2*l.* better paid for. I have had, myself, as much as 6*l.* the voyage, and been detained much less. Within the last three years our wages have decreased 30 per cent, whilst the demand for coals and for colliers has increased considerably. I never heard of such a thing as supply and demand; but it does seem to me a very queer thing that, whilst there's a greater quantity of coals sold, and more colliers employed, we poor seamen should be paid worse. In all the ships that I have been in, I've generally been pretty well fed; but I have been aboard some ships, and heard of a great many more, where the food is very bad, and the men are very badly used. On the passage, the general rule is to feed the men upon salt meat. The pork they in general use is Kentucky, Russian, Irish, and, indeed, a mixture of all nations. Any kind of offal goes aboard some ships; but the one I'm on now there's as good meat as ever went aboard; aye, and plenty of it—no stint."

A basketman, who was present whilst I was taking the above statement, told me that the foreman of the coalwhippers had more chances of judging of the state of the provisions supplied to the colliers than the men had themselves; for the basketmen delivered many different ships, and it was the general rule for them to get their dinner aboard, among the sailors. The basketman here referred to told me that he had been a butcher, and was consequently well able to judge of the quality of the meat. "I have no hesitation," said he, "in stating, that one half the meat supplied to the seamen is unfit for human consumption. I speak of the pork in particular. Frequently the men throw it overboard to get it out of the way. Many a time when I've been dining with the men I wouldn't touch it. It fairly and regularly stinks as they takes it out of the coppers."

THE COALMETERS.

I NOW come to the class called Coalmeters. These, though belonging to the class of " clerks," rather than labourers, still form so important a link in the chain, that I think it best to give a description of their duty here.

The coalmeters weigh the coals on board ship. They are employed by a committee of coalfactors and coalmerchants—nine factors and nine merchants forming such committee. The committee is elected by the trade. They go out every year, and consequently two new members are elected annually. They have the entire patronage of the meter's office. No person can be an official coalmeter without being appointed by the coal-committee. There were formerly several bye-meters, chosen by the merchants from among their own men, as they pleased. This practice has been greatly diminished since April last. The office of the coalmeter is to weigh out the ship's cargo, as a middle-man between the factor and the merchant. The cargo is consigned by the pit-owner or the shipowner to the coalfactor. The number of coalfactors is about twenty-five. These men dispose of all the coals that are sold in London. As soon as the ship arrives at Gravesend, her papers are transmitted to an office appointed for that purpose, and the factor then proceeds to the Coal Exchange to sell them. Here the merchants and the factors assemble three times a-week. The purchasers are divided into large and small buyers. Large buyers consist of the higher class coalmerchants, and they will sometimes buy as many as three or four thousand tons in a-day. The small buyers only purchase by multiples of seven—either fourteen, twenty-one, or twenty-eight tons, as they please. The rule of the market is, that the buyers pay one half of the purchase-money the first market-day after the ship is cleared, and for the remainder a bill at six weeks is given. After the ship is sold she is admitted from the Section into the Pool, and a meter is appointed to her from the coalmeter's office. This office is maintained by the committee of factors and merchants, and the masters appointed by them are registered there. According as a fresh ship is sold, the next meter in rotation is sent down to her. There are in all 170 official meters, divided into three classes, called respectively "placemen," "extra men," and "supernumeraries." The placeman has the preference of the work. If there is more than the placeman can do the extra man takes it, and if both classes are occupied then the supernumerary steps in. Should the earnings of the latter class not amount to 25s. weekly, that sum is made up to them. Before " breaking bulk," that is, before beginning to work the cargo of the ship, the City dues must, under a penalty, be paid by the factor. These amount to 1s. 1d. per ton. The 1s. goes to the City, and the 1d. to the Government. Formerly the whole of the dues went to the City, but within a short period the odd 1d. has been claimed by Government. The coal dues form one of the principal revenues of the city. The dues are collected by the clerk of the Coal Exchange. All the harbour dues and light dues are paid by the shipowner. After the City dues have been paid, the meter receives his papers and goes on board to deliver the cargo, and see that each buyer registered on the paper gets his proper complement. The meter's hours of attendance are from seven to four in winter, and from seven to five in summer. The meter has to wait on board the ship until such time as the purchasers send craft to receive their coals. He then weighs them previously to their delivery into the barge. There are eight weighs to the ton. The rate of payment to the meter is 1¼d. per ton, and the merchant is compelled to deliver the cargo at the rate of forty-nine tons per day, making the meter's wages amount to 6s. 1¼d. per day. If there is a necessity or demand for more coals, we can do double that amount of work. On the shortest day in the year we can do ninety-eight tons." One whom I saw said, " I myself have done 112 tons to-day. That would make my earnings to-day 15s., but as I did nothing on Saturday, of course that reduces them one half."

Upon an average, a place-meter is employed about five days in the week. An extra meter is employed about four days in the week, and a supernumerary about half his time, but he has always his 25s. weekly secured to him, whether employed or not. Two pounds a-week would be a very fair average for the wages of a place-meter, since the reduction on the 1st of April. Many declare they don't earn 36s. a-week, but many do more. The extra man gets very nearly the same money as the place-man, under the present arrangement. The supernumerary generally makes his 30s. weekly. As the system at present stands, the earnings of the meters generally are not so much as those of superior mechanics. It is an office requiring interest to obtain it: a man must be of known integrity; thousands and thousands of pounds of property pass through his hands, and he is the man appointed to see justice between factor and merchant. Before the Act directing all coals to be sold by weight, the meter measured them in a vat, holding a quarter of a chaldron.

In those days a first-class meter could reckon upon an income of from 400l. to 500l. a-year, and the lowest salary was not under 300l. per annum. The meter's office was then entirely a city appointment, and none but those of considerable influence could obtain it. This system was altered eighteen years ago, when the meter's office was placed in the hands of a committee of coalfactors and coalmerchants. Immediately after this time the salaries decreased. The committee first agreed to pay the meters at the rate of 2d. per ton, undertaking that that sum should produce the place-meter an income of 120l. One gentleman assured me that he never exceeded 114l., but then he was one of the juniors. Under the old system the meters were paid at a rate that would have been equivalent to 3d. a ton under the present one. In the year 1831 the salary was reduced to 2d., and on the 1st of April in the present year, the payment has again been cut down to 1¼d. per ton. Besides this, the certificate money, which was 2s. per ship, and generally amounted to 30s. per quarter, was entirely disallowed, making the total last reduction of their wages amount to full 30 per cent. No corresponding reduction has taken place in the price of coals to the consumer. At the same time the price of whipping has been reduced 1d. per ton, so that, within the last year, the combined factors and merchants have lowered the price of delivery 1½d. per ton, and they (the merchants and factors) have been the sole gainers thereby. This has been done, too, while the demand for coals has been increasing every year. Now, according to the returns of the clerk of the Coal Exchange, there were 3,418,340 tons of coals delivered in the port of London in the year 1848, and assuming that amount to have remained the same in the present year, it follows that the factors and merchants have gained no less than 21,364l. 12s. 6d. per annum, and that out of the earnings of the meters and the whippers.

The coalwhippers, already described, whip the coals by means of a basket and tackle from the hold to the deck of the ship. The coalmeters weigh the coals when so whipped from the hold, previously to their being delivered into the barge alongside. The " coalbacker" properly carries the coals in sacks upon his back from the barges, when they have reached the premises of the coal-merchants, on to the wharfs.

I will now proceed to speak of

THE COALPORTERS.

COALPORTERS are employed in filling the waggons of the merchants at their respective wharfs, and in conveying and delivering the coal at the residence of the customers. Their distinguishing dress is a fantail hat, and an outer garment—half smock-frock and half jacket—heavy and black with coal-dust: this garment is often left open at the breast, especially, I am told, on a Monday, when the porter generally has a clean shirt to display. The narrative I give, will show how the labour of these men is divided. The men themselves have many terms for the same employment. The man who drives the waggon I heard styled indifferently, the " waggoner," " carman," or " shooter." The man who accompanies him to aid in the delivery of the coals was described to me as the " trimmer," " trouncer," or " pull back." There are also the " scurfs " and the " sifters," of whom a description will be given presently. The coalporters form a rude class; not, perhaps, from their manners being ruder than those of other classes of labourers, whose labour cannot be specified under the description of " skilled," (it is, indeed, but the exertion of animal strength—the work of thew and muscle), but from their being less educated. I was informed that not one man in six—the manager in a very large house in the coal-trade estimated it at but one in eight—could read or write, however imperfectly. As a body, they have no fellowship or " union " among themselves, no general sick fund, no organization in rules for their guidance as an important branch (numerically) of an important traffic; indeed, as it was described to me by one of the class, " no nothing." The coalporters thus present a striking contrast to the coalwhippers, who, out of means not exceeding those of the porters, have done so much for the sick among them, and for the instruction of their children. The number of men belonging to the Benefit Society of Coalwhippers is 436; and there are about 200 coalwhippers belonging to another society, that was instituted before the new office. There are 200 more in connexion with other offices. There were 130 sick men relieved by the Coalwhippers' Society last year. There were 14 deaths out of the 436 members. Each sick man receives 10s. a-week, and on death there is a payment of 5l. a man, and 3l. in the case of a wife. The amount of subscription to the fund is 3d. per week under forty years of age, 4d. to fifty, 5d. to sixty, and above that, 6d. On account of the want of any organization among the coalporters, it is not easy to get at their numbers with accuracy. No apprenticeship is necessary for the coalporter, no instruction even; so long as he can handle a shovel, or lift a sack of coals with tolerable celerity, he is perfect in his calling. The concurrent testimony of the best-informed parties, gave me the number of the porters (exclusive of those known as sifters, scurfs, or odd men,) as 1500; that is, 1500 employed thus: in large establishments on " the waterside," five men are employed as backers and fillers—two to fill the sacks, and three to carry them on their backs from the barge to the waggon, (in smaller establishments there are only two to carry). There are two more then employed to conduct the load of coal to

the residence of the purchaser—the waggoner (or carman), and the trimmer (or trouncer). Of these the waggoner is considered the picked man, for he is expected to be able to write his name. Sometimes he can write nothing else, and more frequently not even so much, carrying his name on the customer's ticket ready written; and he has the care of the horses as driver, and frequently as groom.

At one time, when their earnings were considerable, these coalporters spent large sums in drink. Now their means are limited, and their drunkenness is not in excess. The men, as I have said, are ill-informed. They have all a pre-conceived notion that beer sometimes in large quantities (one porter said he limited himself to a pint an hour, when at work), is necessary to them "for support." Even if facts were brought conclusively to bear upon the subject to prove that so much beer, or any allowance of beer, was injurious, it would, I think, be difficult to convince the porters, for an ignorant man will not part with a pre-conceived notion. I heard from one man, more intelligent than his fellows, that a temperance lecturer once went among a body of the coalporters and talked about " alcohol " and " fermentation," and the like, until he was pronounced either mad or a Frenchman.

The question arises, Why is this ignorance allowed to continue, as a reproach to the men, to their employers, and to the community? Of the kindness of masters to the men, of discouragement of drunkenness, of persuasions to the men to care for the education of their children, I had the gratification of hearing frequently. But of any attempt to establish schools for the general instruction of the coalporters' children, of any talk of almshouses for the reception of the worn-out labourer, of any other provision for his old age, which is always premature through hard work,—of any movement for the amelioration of this class, I did not hear. Rude as these porters may be, machines as they may be accounted, they are the means of wealth to their employers, and deserve at least some care and regard on their part.

The way in which the barges are unladen to fill the waggons is the same in the rivers as in the canals. Two men standing in the barge fill the sacks, and three (or two) carry them along planks, if the barge be not moored close ashore to the waggon, which is placed as near the water as possible. In the canals, this work is carried on most regularly, as the water is not influenced by the tide, and the work can go on all day long. I will describe, therefore, what I saw in the City Basin, Regent's Canal. This canal has been opened about twenty years. It commences at the Grand Junction at Paddington, and falls into the Thames above the Limehouse Dock. Its course is circuitous, and in it are two tunnels—one at Islington, three-quarters of a mile long; the other at the Harrow Road a quarter

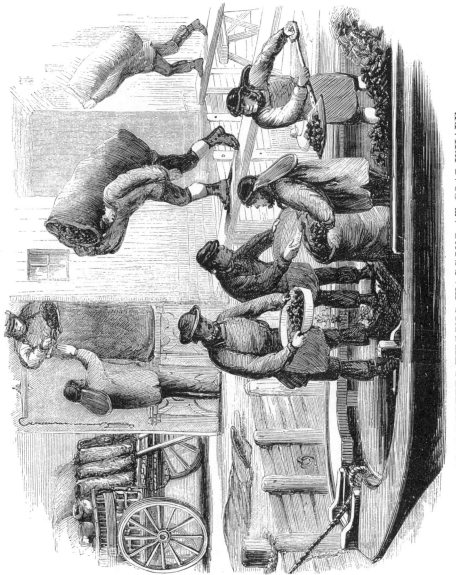

COAL-PORTERS FILLING WAGGONS AT COAL-WHARF.

[*From a Sketch.*]

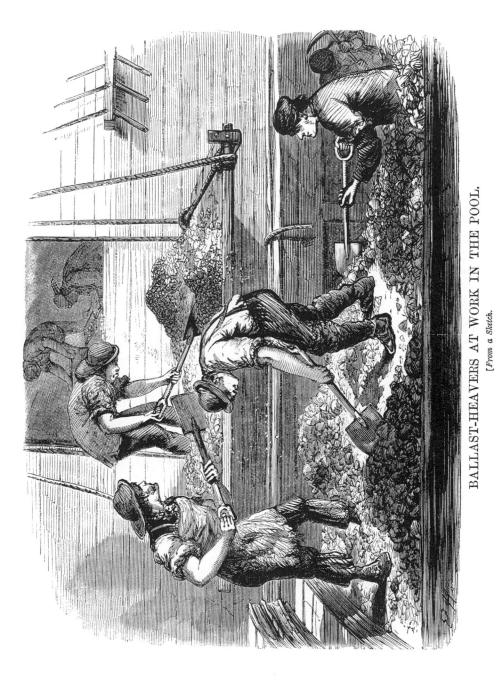

BALLAST-HEAVERS AT WORK IN THE POOL.

[*From a Sketch.*]

of a mile long. If a merchant in the Regent's Canal has purchased the cargo of a collier, such cargo is whipped into the barge. For the conducting of this laden barge to the Limehouse Basin of the canal, the merchant has to employ licensed lightermen, members of the Waterman's Company, as none else are privileged to work on the river. The canal attained, the barge is taken into charge by two men, who, not being regular "watermen," confine their labours to the canal. These men (a steerer and a driver) convey the barge,—suppose to the City Basin, Islington, which, as it is about midway, gives a criterion as to the charge and the time when other distances are concerned. They go back with an empty barge. Each of these bargemen has 2s. a barge for conveyance to the City Basin. The conveyance of the loaded barge occupies three hours, sixty-four tons of coal being an average cargo. Two barges a-day, in fine weather, can be thus conducted, giving a weekly earning to each man in full work of 24s. This is subject to casualties and deductions, but it is not my present intention to give the condition of these bargemen. I reserve this for a future and more fitting occasion. In frosty weather, when the ice has caused many delays, as much as 6s. a-barge per man has been paid; and, I was told, hard-earned money, too. A barge at such times has not been got into the City Basin in less than forty-eight hours. The crowded state of the canal at the wharfs at this time of the year, gives it the appearance of a crowded thoroughfare, there being but just room for one vessel to get along.

From the statement with which I was favoured by a house carrying on a very extensive business, it appears that the average earnings of the men in their employ was, the year through, upwards of 28s. I give the payments of twelve men regularly employed as the criterion of their earnings, on the best paid description of coalporters' labour, for four weeks at the busiest time:—

December 22	. .	£21 5 5
„ 15	. .	21 17 3
„ 8	. .	22 10 1
November 17	. .	28 8 0

This gives an average of more than 1l. 19s. per man a-week for this period; but the slackness of trade in the summer, when coals are in smaller demand, reduces the average to the amount I have stated. In the two weeks omitted in the above statement, viz. those ending December 1st and November 24th, fourteen men had to be employed, on account of the briskness of trade. Their joint earnings were 39l. 12s. 5d. one week, and 33l. 6s. 7d. the other. By this firm each waggoner is paid 1l. a-week, and 6s. extra if he "do" 100 tons; that is, 6s. between him and the trimmer. For every ton above 100 carried out by their waggoner and trimmer, 1d. extra is paid,

and sometimes 130 are carried out, but only at a busy time; 142 have been carried out, but that only was remembered as the greatest amount at the wharf in question. For each waggon sent out, the waggoner and the trimmer together receive 4d. for "beer money" from their employers. They frequently receive money (if not drink) from the customers, and so the average of 28s. and upwards is made up. I saw two waggoners fully employed, and they fully corroborated this statement. Such payment, however, is not the rule. Many give the waggoner 21s. a-week, and employ him in doing whatever work may be required. A waggoner at what he called "poor work," three or four days a-week, told me he earned about 13s. on the average.

The scurfs are looked upon as, in many respects, the refuse of the trade. They are the men always hanging about the wharfs, waiting for any "odd job." They are generally coalporters who cannot be trusted with full and regular work, who were described to me as "tonguey, or drunken," anxious to get a job just to supply any pressing need, either for drink or meat, and careless of other consequences. Among them, however, are coalporters seeking employment, some with good characters. These scurfs, with the sifters, number, I understand, more than 500; thus altogether making, with the coalbackers and other classes of coalporters, a body of more than 2000.

I now come to the following statement, made by a gentleman who for more than thirty years has been familiar with all matters connected with the coal-merchants' trade. "I cannot say," he began, "that the condition of the coalporter (not referring to his earnings, but to his moral and intellectual improvement) is much amended now, for he is about the same sort of man that he was thirty years ago. There may be, and I have no doubt is, a greater degree of sobriety, but I fear chiefly on account of the men's earnings being now smaller, and their having less means at their command. Thirty-five years ago, before the general peace, labourers were scarce, and the coalporters then had full and ready employment, earning from 2l. to 3l. a-week. I have heard a coalporter say that one week he earned 5l.; indeed, I have heard several say so. After the peace, the supply of labour for the coal-trade greatly increased, and the coalporters' earnings fell gradually. The men employed in a good establishment thirty years ago, judging from the payments in our own establishment as a fair criterion, were in the receipt of nearly 3l. a-week on the average. At that time coal was delivered by the chaldron. A chaldron was composed of 12 sacks containing 36 bushels, and weighing about 25 cwt. (a ton and a-quarter). For the loading of the waggons a gang of four men, called 'fillers,' was, and is, employed. They were paid 1s. 4d. per chaldron; that is, 4*d*. per man. This was for measuring the coal, putting it into sacks, and putting the sacks into the waggon. The men in this gang had nothing to do with the conveyance of the coal to the customers. For that purpose two other men were employed; a 'waggoner,' and a man known as a 'trimmer,' or 'trouncer,' who accompanied the waggoner, and aided him in carrying the sacks from the waggon to the customers' coal-cellar, and in arranging the coal when delivered, so as properly to assort the small with the large, or indeed making any arrangement with them required by the purchaser. The waggoner and the trimmer were paid 1*s*. 3*d*. each per chaldron for delivery, but when the coal had to be carried up or down-stairs any distance, their charge was an extra shilling—2*s*. 3*d*. Many of the men have at that time, when work was brisk, filled and delivered fifteen chaldrons day by day, provided the distance for delivery was not very far. Drink was sometimes given by the customers to the waggoner and trimmer who had charge of the coal sent to their houses— perhaps generally given; and I believe it was always asked for, unless it happened to be given without asking. At that time I did not know one teetotaler; I do not know one personally among those parties now. Some took the pledge, but I believe none kept it. In this establishment we discourage drunkenness all that we possibly can. In 1832, wages having varied from the time of the peace until then, a great change took place. Previous to that time a reduction of 4*d*. per ton had been made in the payment of the men who filled the waggons (the fillers), but not in that of the waggoner or the trimmer. The change I allude to was that established by Act of Parliament, providing for the sale of all coal by the merchant being by weight instead of by measure. This change, it was believed, would benefit the public, by ensuring them the full quantity for which they bargained. I think it has benefited them. Coal was, under the former system, measured by the bushel, and there were frequently objections as to the way in which the bushel was filled. Some dealers were accused of packing the measure, so as to block it up with large pieces of coal, preventing the full space being filled with the coal. The then Act provided that the bushel measure should be heaped up with the coal so as to form a cone six inches above the rim of the measure. When the new Act came into operation the coalporters were paid 10*d*. a-ton among the gang of four fillers, and the same to the waggoner and trimmer. Before two years this became reduced generally to 9*d*. The gang could load twenty-five tons a-day without extra toil; forty tons, and perhaps more, have been loaded by a gang: but such labour continued would exhaust strong men. With extra work there was always extra drink, for the men fancy that their work requires beer 'for support.' My opinion is that a moderate allowance of good malt liquor, say three pints a-day when work is going on all day, is of advantage to a coalporter. In the winter they fancy it necessary to drink gin to warm them. At one time all the men drank more than now. I estimate the average earnings of a coalporter fully employed now at 1*l*. a-week. There are far more employed at present than when I first knew the trade, and the trade itself has been greatly extended by the new wharfs on the Regent's Canal, and up and down the river."

I had heard from so many quarters that "beer" was a necessity of the coal-labourers' work, that finding the coalwhippers the most intelligent of the whole class, I thought it best to call the men together, and to take their opinion generally on the subject. Accordingly I returned to the basketmen's waiting-room at the coalwhippers' office, and, as before, it was soon crowded. There were eighty present. Wishing to know whether the coalbacker's statement already given, that the drinking of beer was a necessity of hard labour, was a correct one, I put the question to the men there assembled: "Is the drinking of fermented liquors necessary for performing hard work? How many present believe that you can work without beer?" Those who were of opinion that it was necessary for the performance of their labour, were requested to hold up their hands, and *four* out of the eighty did so.

A basketman who had been working at the business for four years, and for two of those years had been a whipper, and so doing the heaviest labour, said that in the course of the day he had been one of a gang who had delivered as many as 189 tons. For this he had required no drink at all; cocoa was all he had taken. Three men in the room had likewise done without beer at the heaviest work. One was a coalwhipper, and had abstained for six years. Some difference of opinion seemed to exist as to the number in the trade that worked without beer. Some said 250, others not 150. One man stated that it was impossible to do without malt liquor. "One shilling a day properly spent in drink would prolong life full ten years," he said. This was received with applause. Many present declared that they had tried to do without beer, and had injured themselves greatly by the attempt. Out of the eighty present, fourteen had tried teetotalism, and had thrown it up after a time on account of its injuring their health. One man, on the other hand, said he had given the total-abstinence principle a fair trial for seven months, and had never found himself in such good health before. Another man stated, that to do a day's work of ninety-eight turns, three pints of beer were requisite. All but three believed this. The three pints were declared to be requisite in winter time, and four pints, or two pots, were considered to be not too much in a hot summer's day. Before the present office was instituted, each man, they told me, drank half-a-pint of gin and six pots of beer daily. That was the average—many drank more. Then they could not do their work so well; they were weaker from not having so much food. The money went for drink instead of meat. They were always quarrelling on board a ship. Drunken men could never agree. A portion of beer is good, but too much is worse than none at all." This was the unanimous declaration.

Since this meeting I have been at considerable pains to collect a large amount of evidence in connexion with this most important question. The opinion of the most intelligent of the class seems to be, that no kind of fermented drink is necessary for the performance of the hardest labour; but I have sought for and obtained the sentiments of all classes, temperate and intemperate, with the view of fairly discussing the subject. These statements I must reserve till my next letter. At present I shall conclude with the following story of the sufferings of the wife of one of the intemperate class :—

"I have been married nineteen or twenty years. I was married at Penton, in Oxfordshire. We came to London fifteen years ago. My husband first worked as a sawyer. For eleven years he was in the coal-trade. He was in all sorts of work, and for the last six months he was a 'scurf.' What he earned all the time I never knew. He gave me what he liked, sometimes nothing at all. In May last he only gave me 2s. 8d. for the whole month, for myself and two children. I buried four children. I can't tell how we lived then. I can't express what we've suffered, all through drink. He gave me twenty years of misery through drink. [This was repeated four or five times.] Some days that May we had neither bit nor sup; the water was too bad to drink cold, and I had to live on water put through a few leaves in the teapot—old leaves. Poor people, you know, sir, helps poor people; and but for the poor neighbours we might have been found dead some day. He cared nothing. Many a time I have gone without bread to give it to the children. Was he ever kind to them, do you say, sir? No; they trembled when they heard his step; they were afraid of their very lives, he knocked them about so; drink made him a savage; drink took the father out of him." This was said with a flush and a rapid tone, in strong contrast with the poor woman's generally subdued demeanour. She resumed :—" Twenty miserable years through drink! I've often gone to bring him from the public-house, but he seldom would come. He would abuse me, and would drink more because I'd gone for him. I've often whispered to him that his children was starving: but I durstn't say that aloud when his mates was by. We seldom had a fire. He often beat me. I've 9s. in pawn now. Since we came to London I've lost 20l. in the pawnshop."

This man had died a fortnight before, having ruptured a blood-vessel. He lay ill six days. The parish doctor attended him. His comrades "gathered" for his burial, but the widow had still some funeral expenses to pay by instalments. The room she and the children occupied was the same as in the husband's lifetime. There was about the room a cold damp smell, arising from bad ventilation and the chilliness of the weather. Two wretched beds almost filled the place. No article was worth a penny, nor could a penny have been obtained at a sale or a pawnshop. The woman was cleanly clad, but looked sadly pinched, miserable, and feeble. She earns a little as a washerwoman, and did earn it while her husband lived. She bears an excellent character. Her repetition of the words, "_twenty years of misery through drink_," was very pitiful. I refrained from a prolonged questioning, as it seemed to excite her in her weak state.

BALLAST-MEN.

HAVING finished with the different classes of coal-labourers in London — the whippers, backers, pull-backs, trimmers, and waggoners —I purpose now dealing with the ballast-men, including the ballast-getters, the ballast-lightermen, and the ballast-heavers of the metropolis. My reason for pasing from the coal to the ballast-labourers is, because the latter class of the work-people are suffering under the same iniquitous and pernicious system of employment as that from which the coal-labourers have recently been emancipated, and the transition will serve to show not only the present condition of the one class of men, but the past state of the other.

After treating of the ballast-labourers, I purpose inquiring into the condition and income of the stevedores, or men engaged in the stowing or unstowing of vessels; and of the lumpers and riggers, or those engaged in the rigging and unrigging of them. It is then my intention to pass to the corn-labourers, such as the corn-porters, corn-runners, and turners, touching incidentally upon the corn-meters. After this, I mean to devote my attention to the timber-labourers engaged at the different timber-docks — as, for instance, the Commercial, the Grand Surrey, and the East Country Docks. Then, in due course, I shall come to the wharf-labourers and porters, or men engaged at the different wharfs in London; thence I shall digress to the bargemen and lightermen, or men engaged in the transit of the different cargoes from the ships to their several points of destination up or down the river; and finally, I shall treat of the watermen, the steamboat-men, and pier-men, or those engaged in the transit of passengers along the Thames. These, with the dock-labourers, of whom I have before treated, will, I believe, exhaust the subject of the longshore labourers; and the whole will, I trust, form, when completed, such a body of facts and information, in connexion with this particular branch of labour, as has never before been collected. I am happy to say, that, with some few exceptions, I have received from the different official gentlemen not only every courtesy and consideration, but all the assistance and co-operation that it lay in their power to afford me. Every class seems to look upon the present inquiry as an important undertaking, and all, save the Clerk of the Coal Exchange and the Deputy-Superintendent of the London Docks, have shown themselves not only willing, but anxious, to lend a hand towards expediting the result.

Before quitting the subject of the coal-market, let me endeavour to arrive at an estimate as to the amount of wealth annually brought into the port of London by means of the colliers, and to set forth, as far as possible, the proportion in which it is distributed. I have already given some statistics, which, notwithstanding the objections of a coal-merchant, who, in a letter to a journal, stated that I had reckoned the number of ships at twice the real quantity, were obtained from such sources, and, I may add, with so much care and caution, as to render them the most accurate information capable of being procured at present on the subject. The statistics of the number of tons of coals brought into the port of London in the year 1848, the number of vessels employed, of the voyages made by those vessels collectively, and of the seamen engaged in the traffic, were furnished by the Clerk of the Coal Exchange at the time of the opening of the new building. Had the coal-merchant, therefore, made it his duty to devote the same time and care to the investigation of the truth of my statements that I have to the collection of them, he would not only have avoided committing the very errors he condemns, but would have displayed a more comprehensive knowledge of his business.

In 1848 there were imported into the London coal market 3,418,340 tons of coal. These were sold to the public at an average rate all the year round of 22s. 6d. a ton. Hence the sum expended in the metropolis for coal in that year was 3,845,632l. 10s.

There are 21,600 seamen engaged in the coal trade, and getting on an average 3l. 10s. per man per voyage. Each of these men makes between 4 and 5 voyages in the course of the year. Hence the average earnings of each man per year will be 15l. 18s., exclusive of his keep; calculating that at 5s. per week, or 13l. per year, we have 28l. 18s. for the expense of each of the seamen employed. Hence, as there are 21,600 sailors in the coal trade, the total yearly cost would be . £624,240 0 0

There are 170 coal-meters, earning, on an average, 2l. per week, or 104l. per year each man. This would make the total sum paid in the year to the coal-meters . . . 17,680 0 0

There are 2000 coal-whippers, earning 15s. 1½d. each per week, or 39l. 6s. 6d. per man. Hence the total sum paid in the course of last year to the coal-whippers was . . 78,650 0 0

There are 3000 coal-porters earning, on an average, 1l. per week, or 52l. per year per man, so that they receive annually 156,000 0 0

Hence the total amount paid per year to the working-men engaged in bringing and delivering coals in the London market is £876,570 0 0

The area of all the coal-fields of Great Britain has been roughly estimated at 9000 square miles. The produce is supposed to be about 32,000,000 tons annually, of which 10,000,000 tons are consumed in the iron-works, 8,500,000 tons are shipped coastwise, 2,500,000 tons are exported to foreign countries, and 11,000,000 tons distributed inland for miscellaneous purposes. Near upon 4,000,000 tons were brought to London by ships and otherwise in the year 1848, and it is computed that about one-eighth part of this, or 500,000 tons, were consumed by the gas-works.

The price of coals as quoted in the London market is the price up to the time when the coals are whipped from the ships to the merchants' barges. It includes, 1st. the value of the coals; 2d. the expense of transit from the pit to the ship; 3d. the freight of the ship to London; 4th. the Thames' dues; and 5th. the whipping. The difference between the market price and that paid by the consumer is made up of the expense incurred by the coal-merchant for barges, wharfs, waggons, horses, wages, coal-porters, &c., to his profit and risk. In 1836 the expenses incurred by the merchant from the time he bought a ship-load of coals to the deposition of them in the cellars of his customers amounted, on an average, it was said, to 7s. a ton. These expenses comprise commission, lighterage, porterage, cartage, shooting, metage, market-dues, land-metage, and other items. At the present time the expenses must be considerably lower, the wages of the labourers and the meters having been lowered full 50 per cent, though the demand for and consumption of coal has increased at nearly the same rate; indeed the law of the coal-market appears to be, that in proportion as the demand for the article rises, so do the wages of the men engaged in the supply of it fall.

As the ballast-heavers are under the thraldom of the same demoralising and oppressive system as that which the coal-whippers recently suffered under, it may be as well, before going further, to lay before the reader the following concise account of the terms on which the latter were engaged before the Coal-whippers' Office was established.

Until the last few years the coal-whippers suffered themselves to be duped in an extraordinary way by publicans and petty shopkeepers on shore. The custom was, for the captain of a coal-ship, when he required a cargo to be whipped, to apply to one of these publicans for a gang; and a gang was accordingly sent from the public-house. There was no professed or pre-arranged deduction from the price paid for the work; the captain paid the publican, and the publican paid the coal-whippers; but the middleman had his profit another way. The coal-whipper was expected to come to the public-house in the morning; to drink while waiting for work, to take drink with him to the ship, to drink again when the day's work was over, and to linger about and in the public-house until almost bed-time before his day's wages were paid. The consequence was, that an enormous ratio of his earnings went every week to the publican. The publicans were wont to divide their dependants into two classes — the constant men and the stragglers, of whom the former were first served whenever a cargo was to be whipped; in return for this they were expected to spend almost the whole of their spare time in the public-house, and even to take up their lodgings there.

The captains preferred applying to the publicans to engaging the men themselves, because it saved them trouble; and because (as was pretty well understood) the publicans curried favour with them by indirect means; grocers and small shopkeepers did the same, and the coal-whippers had then to buy bad and dear groceries instead of bad and dear beer and gin. The Legislature tried by various means to protect the coal-whippers, but the publicans contrived means to evade the law. At length, in 1843, an Act was passed, which has placed the coal-whippers in a far more advantageous position.

The transition from coal-labour to ballast-labour is gradual and easy, and would be even if the labourers were not kindred in suffering.

The coal-ships, when discharged by the whippers, must get back to the north; and as there are not cargoes enough from London to freight them, they must take in ballast to make the ships heavy enough to sail in safety. This ballast is chiefly ballast or sand, dredged up from the bed of the Thames at and near Woolwich Reach. The Trinity House takes upon itself this duty. The captain, when he requires to sail, applies to the Ballast Office, and the required weight of ballast is sent to the ship in lighters belonging to the Trinity House, the captain paying so much a ton for it. About 80 tons on an average are required for each vessel, and the quantity thus supplied by the Trinity House is about 10,000 tons per week. Some of the ships are ballasted with chalk taken from Purfleet; all ballast taken from higher up the river than that point must be supplied by the Trinity House. When the ship reaches the Tyne, the ballast is of no further use, but it must not be emptied into that river; it has, therefore, to be deposited on the banks, where huge mounds are now collected two or three hundred feet high.

New places on the banks of the river have to be discovered for this deposit as the ballast mounds keep increasing, for it must be recollected that the vessels leave these ports — no matter for what destination — with coal, and may return in ballast. Indeed a railway has been formed from the vicinity of South Shields to a waste place on the sea-shore, hard by the mouth of the Tyne, where the ballast may be conveyed at small cost, its further accumulation on the river bank being found an incumbrance. "It is really something more than a metaphor," it has been said, "to designate this a transfer of the bed of the Thames to the banks of the Tyne." We may add as another characteristic, that some of the older ballast mounds are overgrown with herbage. As the vessels from foreign ports returning to the coal-ports in ballast, have not unfrequently to take soil on board for ballast, in which roots and seeds are contained, some of there struggle into vegetation, so that Italian flowers not unfrequently attempt to bloom in Durham, Yorkshire, or Northumberland, while some have survived the climate and have spread around; and thus it is that botanists trace the history of plants which are called indigenous to the ballast-hills.

Before treating of the ballast labourers themselves I shall give a brief history of the ballast laws.

Ships are technically said to be in ballast when they sail without a cargo, having on board only the stores and other articles requisite for the use of the vessel and crew, as well as of any passengers who may be proceeding with her upon the voyage. In favour of vessels thus circumstanced it is usual to dispense with many formalities at the custom-houses of the ports, and to remit the payment of the dues and charges levied upon ships having cargoes on board. A foreign vessel proceeding from a British port may take chalk on board as ballast. Regulations have at various times been made in different ports and countries, determining the modes in which ships may be supplied with ballast, and in what manner they may discharge the same, such regulations being necessary to prevent injury to harbours.

Charles I. published a proclamation in 1636, ordering that none shall buy any ballast out of the river Thames but a person appointed by him for that purpose. And this appointment was sold for the king's profit. Since then the soil of the river Thames has been vested in the corporation of the Trinity House, and a fine of 10*l.* may be recovered for every ton of ballast taken out of the river without the authority of the corporation. Ships may take on board land-ballast from any quarries or pits east of Woolwich by paying 1*d.* per ton to the Trinity House. For river-ballast the corporation are authorised by Act of Parliament to make other charges. The receipts of the Trinity House from this source were 33,591*l.* in the year 1840, and their expenses were 31,622*l.*, leaving a clear profit of 1969*l.* The ballast of all ships or vessels coming into the Thames must be unladen into a lighter, and if any ballast be thrown into the river the master of the vessel whence it is thrown is liable to a fine of 20*l.* Some such regulation is usually enforced at every port.

Before proceeding further with my present subject, it is proper that I should express my acknowledgments of the ready courtesy with which the official information necessary for the full elucidation of my subject was supplied to me by the Secretary of the principal Ballast Office at Trinity House, Tower Hill. I have always observed, that when the heads of a department willingly supply information to go before the public, I find in the further course of my investigations that under such departments the claims of the labourer are not only acknowledged but practically allowed. On the other hand, if official gentlemen neglect (which is to refuse) to supply the returns and other information, it is because the inquiry is unpalatable to them, as the public may find that in their departments the fair claims of the labourers are *not* allowed. Were the poor ballast-heavers taken under the protection of the corporation of the Trinity House (something in the same way that Parliament has placed the coal-whippers under the guardianship of a board of commissioners) the good done would be great indeed, and the injury would be none: for it cannot be called an injury to prevent a publican forcing a man to buy and swallow bad drink.

By charter of Queen Elizabeth in the 36th year of her reign, the lastage and ballastage, and office of lastage and ballastage, of all ships and other vessels betwixt the bridge of the city of London and the main sea, I am informed by the Secretary of the Trinity Company, was granted to the Master Wardens and Assistants of the Trinity House of Deptford Strond. This was renewed, and the gravel, sand, and soil of the river Thames granted to the said master wardens, &c. for the ballasting of ships and vessels in the 15th year of Charles II., and again in the 17th year of the reign of that monarch. This last-named charter remains

in force, and has been confirmed by Acts of Parliament at different times; by which Acts also various regulations in relation to the conduct of the ballast service, the control of the persons employed therein, and the prices of the ballast supplied, have been established. The Act now in force is the 6th and 7th Vict. cap. 57.

The number of men employed in lighters as ballast-getters, or in barges conveying it from the dredgers, is 245, who are paid by the ton raised.

The number of vessels entered for ballast in the year 1848 was:

Colliers	6,480
British merchant vessels .	3,690
Aliens	1,054
Total vessels .	11,224

The total quantity of ballast supplied to shipping in the year 1848 was 615,619 tons, or thereabouts; such ballast being gravel raised from the bed of the river Thames and delivered alongside of vessels, either lying in the different docks or being afloat in the stream between London-bridge and Woolwich.

The number of vessels employed in this service is 69, viz:—

	Men.
3 steam dredging-vessels, having 8 men in each . . .	24
43 lighters, having 4 men in each .	172
9 lighters, having 5 men in each .	45
14 barges, having 2 men in each .	28
69	Total 269

The ballast is delivered into the vessels from the lighters and barges by men called ballast-heavers, who are employed by the vessel, and are not in the service of the Trinity House.

I now come to the nature of the ballast labour itself. This is divisible into three classes: that performed by the ballast-getters, or those who are engaged in raising it from the bed of the Thames; by the ballast-lighters, or those who are engaged in carrying it from the getters to the ships requiring it; and by the ballast-heavers, or those who are engaged in putting it on board of such ships. The first and second of these classes have, according to their own account, "nothing to complain of," being employed by gentlemen who, judging by the wanton neglect of labouring men by their masters, so general in London, certainly exhibit a most extraordinary consideration and regard for their work-people; and the change from the indifference and callousness of the coal-merchants to the kindness of the corporation of the Trinity House is most gratifying. The ballast-heavers constitute an entirely different class. They have every one, to a man, deep and atrocious wrongs to complain of, such as I am sure are unknown, and which, when once made public, will at once demand some remedy.

I must, however, first deal with

THE BALLAST-GETTERS.

OF these there are two sub-classes, viz. those engaged in obtaining the ballast by steam power, and those who still procure it as of old by muscular power.

Of seven dredging-engines employed in the collecting of ballast from the bed of the Thames there are three, the Hercules, the Goliath, and the Samson. These are now stationed respectively in Barking Reach, Half Reach near Dagenham, and the bottom of Half-way Reach off Rainham. Most persons who have proceeded up or down the Thames will have perceived black unshapely masses, with no visible indications that they may be classed with steam-vessels except a chimney and smoke. These are the dredging-vessels; they are of about 200 tons burden. The engines of the Hercules and the Samson are of 20-horse power,—those of the Goliath are 25. When the process of dredging is carried on, the use of the dredging-vessel is obvious to any spectator; but I believe that most persons imagine the object to be merely to deepen the river by removing inequalities in its bed, and so to render its navigation easier by equalizing its depth, and in some degrees checking the power of cross-currents. Few are aware that an ulterior object is gained. I visited one of these steam-dredgers, and was very courteously shown over it. The first feeling was an impression of the order, regularity, and trimness that prevailed. In the engineers' department, too, there was an aspect, as well as a feeling, of extreme snugness, the more perceptible both to the eye and the body from its contrast with the intense cold on the muddy river outside, then running down in very strong ebb. In the engineers' department there was more than cleanliness; there was a brightness about the brass-handles attached to the machinery, and, indeed, about every portion of the apparatus at all susceptible of brightness, which indicated a constant and systematic attention by well-skilled hands. Each dredger carries eight men, the master (called the captain, commonly enough, on the river), two engineers, an engineer's assistant, two legsmen (who attend to the ladders), and three men for general purposes. They are all called engine-men. The master of the dredger I visited had the weather-beaten look of the experienced seaman, and the quiet way of talking of past voyages which is found generally in men who have really served, whether in the merchant service or royal navy. He resided on board the dredger with his wife and family, the principal cabin being a very comfortable parlour. All the men live on board, having their turns for visit to the shore from Saturday morning, noon, or evening (as their business permits), to Monday morning. Their sleeping-places are admirable for cleanliness. All the dredgers are under the control of the corporation of the Trinity House. They are, as it was worded to me, as strong as wood and iron can make them. But for secure anchorage these dredgers would soon go adrift. Colliers beating up or down occasionally run against the dredgers: this happens mostly in light winds, when the masters of these colliers are afraid to let go their anchors. The machinery consists of a steam-engine and spur-gear for directing the buckets. The application of the steam-power I need not minutely describe, as it does not differ from other applications where motion has to be communicated. It is connected with strong iron beams, having cogged and connected wheels, which when put into operation give upward and downward motion to the buckets. These buckets are placed on ladders as they are called, one on each side the vessel. These ladders (or shafts) consist of three heavy beams of wood, firmly bolted together and fitted with friction-wheels. To each ladder 29 buckets are attached, each bucket holding 2½ cwt. of gravel. Each bucket is attached by joints to the next, and a series of holes permits the water drawn up with the deposit to ooze out. When the bucket touches the bottom of the river it dips, as it is called. A rotary motion being communicated, the construction ensures the buckets being brought up flat on the ladder until a due height is attained, when the rotary (or circular) motion again comes into play, and the contents of the bucket are emptied into a lighter moored alongside, and the empty bucket is driven down to be refilled. The contents so drawn up are disposed of for ballast, which is the ulterior purpose I have alluded to. Upon an average the buckets revolve once in two minutes. That time, however, varies, from the nature of the bed of the river. The Goliath and the Samson being fitted up with marine engines drive the fastest. The three vessels have for the last year worked within a circle of a mile. The quantity of ballast raised depends upon the demand, as well as upon the character of the deposit at the bottom of the river. Between 900 and 1000 tons have been raised in 7½ hours, sometimes in a like period less than 300 tons have been raised. The dredger I was on board of has taken in a year from 180,000 to 190,000 tons. A stratum of mud 2½ feet had been raised, then 3 feet of gravel, and a chalk bottom was anticipated. In some places 15 feet have been so cleared away to a chalk bottom. In others 15 feet have been so worked off, and no bottom but gravel reached. The gravel lies in shoals. Sometimes the dredgers come to hard conglomerate gravel, as compact as a rock. No fossils have been found. In a few places a clay bottom has been met with. The men in the dredgers are paid according to the number of tons raised, the proceeds being duly apportioned. They work as frequently by night as by day, their labour depending upon the time when an order for a supply of ballast is received. Each lighter holds 60 tons of ballast. The dredgers above bridge are the property of individuals working with the concurrence of the civic corporation of London. Those below bridge are, as I have said, under the control of the corporation of the Trinity House. The Hercules was the first Trinity House dredger worked by steam. Private individuals, however, employed steam sooner than the Trinity House authorities to draw up materials to mix with lime for building purposes. The first Trinity House steam-dredger was started in 1827.

I had some conversation with a man employed on one of the steam-dredgers. He described the process carried on there as I have given it, estimating the tons of ballast raised at about 4000 a-week. He expressed a sense of his good fortune in having the employment he had; he was well used, and wouldn't like to change. He declined stating his earnings (otherwise than that he had his fair share) until he saw his master, and of course I did not press him further on the subject.

The ballast-getters are men employed in raising ballast from the bed of the river by bodily labour. The apparatus by which this is effected consists of a long staff or pole, about thirty-five feet in length. At the end of this is an iron "spoon" or ring, underneath which is a leathern bag holding about 20 cwt. The ballast is raised on board the working-lighters by means of this spoon. The working-lighters carry six hands: that is, a staffsman whose duty it is to attend to the staff; a bagman, who empties the bag; a chainsman, who hauls at the chain; a heelsman, who lets go the pall of the winch; and two trimmers, who trim the ballast in the lighter as fast as it comes in. Previous to the men getting at work, the staffsman takes hold of the spoon to feel whereabout the ballast-bed lies. When this is found, he puts down his "sets," as it is termed,—that is to say, he drives the iron-tipped spars that he has with him in the lighter into the ground, so as to steady the craft. This done, the staffsman seizes hold of the middle of the staff, while the bargeman takes the bag and the chainsman the chain, which is fastened to the iron ring or spoon; the staff is thus thrown overboard into the water, about midway of the lighter, and the tide carries the spoon down towards the stern. The staffsman then fastens the staff to the lighter by means of the gaff-string or rope attached to the side of the vessel. At the same time the men go forward to heave at the winch, round the roll of which the chain attached to the spoon itself is wound. All the men, with the exception of the staffsman, then heave away, and so drag the spoon along the bed of the river. When the staffsman feels that the bag is full, he leaves go of the gaff-string and goes forward to heave with the men as well. Immediately the gaff-string is undone the top part of the staff falls back on an oar that projects from the after-part of the vessel, and the bag is then raised by means of the winch and chain to the level of the gunwale of the craft; then the bagsman hauls it in and empties it into the lighter, while the two trimmers spread the ballast discharged. The spoon can only be worked when the tide is nearly down, because the water would be too deep for the set to bring the craft steady. To hoist the 20 cwt. of ballast in the bag will require the whole force of the six men; and none but the very strongest are of use. The ballast-getters are all very powerful men; they are mostly very tall, big-boned, and muscular. Many of them are upwards of six feet high, and have backs two feet broad. " I lifted seven half-hundredweights with one of my hands," said one whom I saw. He was a man of thirty-nine years of age, and stood half an inch over six feet, while another was six feet two inches. They were indeed extraordinarily fine specimens of the English labourer, making our boasted Life-guardsman appear almost weak and effeminate in comparison with them. Before the steam dredging-engines were introduced, I am informed the ballast-getters were even bigger and heavier men than they are now. The ballast-getters seldom or never fish up anything besides ballast. Four or five years back they were lucky enough to haul up a box of silver plate; but they consider a bit of old iron or a bit of copper very good luck now. The six men generally raise sixty tons eighteen feet high in the course of the tide, which is at the rate of 22,400lbs. each man in three hours: this makes the quantity raised per hour by each man upwards of 7400 lbs. The price paid is 8d. per ton, or 2l. for sixty tons; this is shared equally among five of the men, who receive 8s. a-piece as their proportion, and out of this they pay 3s. 6d. a tide to the stern-trimmer, whom they employ—the Trinity Company allowing only five men and the ballast-getters engaging the sixth man themselves. Upon an average the ballast-getters do about three loads in the week throughout the year, —this, deducting the money paid to the sixth man, makes the earnings of each ballast-getter come to about 22s. throughout the year. The staffsman is allowed 20l. a-year to keep the craft in gear. The ballast-getters usually work above the dredging-engines, mostly about Woolwich; there the cleanest ballast is to be got. The Trinity Company they speak most highly of; indeed the corporation are universally spoken of as excellent masters: the men say they have nothing to complain of. They get their money on every Friday night, and have no call to spend a farthing of their earnings otherwise than as they please. They only wish, they add, that the ballast-heavers were as well off. " It would be a good job if they was, poor men," say one and all.

The second class of ballast-labourers are

THE BALLAST-LIGHTERMEN.

THESE are men engaged by the Trinity Company to carry the ballast in the company's barges and lighters from the steam dredging-engines to the ship's side. The corporation has fifty-two lighters and fourteen barges, all sixty-ton craft. Each lighter carries four men, and there are two men in each barge; so that altogether 108 lightermen and 28 bargemen are employed in bringing the ballast from the engines. These men are not required to have a license from the Waterman's Company, like other lightermen and bargemen on the Thames, and that is one of the reasons for my dealing with them at present. They form a class of labourers by themselves, and I treat of them here because it appears the fittest place for a statement of their condition and earnings. Besides the lightermen and bargemen engaged in carrying the ballast from the steam dredging-machines, there are others employed on board what are called the working-lighters; these are vessels in which ballast is got up from the bed of the river by muscular labour. There are ten of these working-lighters, and six men engaged in each, or in all sixty men employed in raising ballast by such means. There are three steam dredging-engines employing each eight men, or twenty-four in all; so that there are altogether 220 labouring men engaged in the ballast service of the Trinity Company. Each of the carrying lighters has a staffsman or master and three men. The lighters all carry sixty tons of ballast, and make upon an average between three and four voyages a-week, or about seven in the fortnight. There is no place of deposit for the ballast brought up the river from the engines; it is left in the lighter until required. The ballast chiefly consists of gravel; indeed the ships will mostly refuse anything else. When there is a plentiful supply of ballast they will refuse clay in particular. Clayey ballast is what is termed bad ballast. Upon an average there are thirty loads, or 1800 tons of ballast, brought up by the lighters every day from the engines. In the course of the year there are between 550,000 and 600,000 tons of ballast supplied by the three steam dredging-machines. "It is about three-and-twenty years since the steam dredging-engine first came out," said the party who gave me the above information. "For the last twenty years I should think the company have been raising about 500,000 tons of gravel from the bed of the river. Thirty years ago I thought the ballast would soon be out, but there appears to be little or no difference; and yet the shoals do not fill up again after being once taken away. In Barking Reach I am sure there is six feet more water now than there was thirty years ago; there was at that time a large shoal in that part of the river,

called Barking Shelf; it was certainly a mile long and half a mile wide. The vessels would ground upon it long before low water. At some tides it used to strip dry, and at low tide generally there was about six foot of water over it. That part of the river is now the deepest about Barking, and as deep as the best of places in the Thames. When I first came to London we were prevented from getting the ballast from anywhere else than Barking, on account of the great shoals there; but now the great ballast-bed is between four and five miles lower down. The river has been very nearly cleared of shoals by the dredging-engines, from Limehouse Reach to the bottom of Half Reach. The only shoal in the way of the navigation below the Pool is what is called Woolwich Shelf: there is indeed another shoal, but this consists of stiff clay or conglomerate, and the engines cannot work through it. The men on board the carrying-lighters are paid 5d. a-ton for bringing the ballast from the dredging-engines to the ships; this is equally divided among the four men. The staffsman, in addition to his fourth share, receives 10l. a-year for his extra duties; but out of this he has to buy oars for the boat and lighter, locks, fenders, and shovels. Upon an average the cost of these will be about 30s. a-year. Each man's share of the sixty-ton load is 6s. 3d.; and there are about seven loads brought up by each lighter in the fortnight. Some weeks the men can earn as much as 37s., but at others they cannot get more than 12s. 6d. "I did myself only two load last week," said my informant. "When there is little or no 'vent,' as we call it, for the ballast—that is, but a slight demand for it—we have but little work. Upon an average, each lighterman makes from 21s. to 22s. a-week. At the time of the strike among the pitmen in the North, the lightermen, generally, only did about two load a-week throughout the year; but then the following year we had as much as we could do. The Trinity Company, whom I serve, and have served for thirty years, are excellent masters to us when we are sick or well. The corporation of the Trinity House allow the married lightermen in their service 10s. and the single ones 7s. 6d. a-week, as long as they are ill. I have known the allowance given to men for two years, and for this we pay nothing to any benefit society or provident fund. If we belong to any such society we have our sick money from them independent of that. The superannuation money is now 6l. a-year; but I understand," continued the man, "that the company intend increasing it next Tuesday. Some of the old men were ordered up to the house a little while ago, and were asked what they could live comfortably upon, and one of the gentlemen there promised them that no more of us should go to the workhouse. They do not provide any school for our children; a great many of the lightermen neither read nor write. I never heard any talk of the company erecting a school, either for the instruction of their men or their men's families. All I can say is, that in all my dealings with the Trinity Corporation I have found them very kind and considerate masters. They are always ready to listen to the men, and they have hospitals for the sick in their employ and midwives for the wives of the labourers; and they bury, free of expense, most of the men that die in their service. To the widows of their deceased servants they allow 6l. a-year; and if there be any children, they give 2s. a-month to each under fourteen years old. I never knew them to reduce the lightermen's wages; they have rather increased than lowered them. After the introduction of the steam-dredging machines we were better off than we were before. Previous to that time the lightermen were getters as well, and then the labour was so hard that the expenses of the men for living were more than they are now."

I now come in due order to

THE BALLAST-HEAVERS.

OF these I can at present give but a general description. The individual instances of oppression that I have sought out I must reserve for a subsequent page, when I most heartily hope that the publication of the iniquity of which these poor fellows are the victims, will be at least instrumental in putting an end to a most vile and wicked plan for the degradation and demoralization of our fellow-creatures. The tales I have to tell are such as must rouse every heart not positively indurated by the love of gain. I must, however, be here content, as I said before, with merely describing the system.

The duty of the ballast-heaver is to heave into the holds of the ship the ballast brought alongside the vessel by the Trinity-lighters from the dredging-engines. The ships take in ballast either in the docks or in the Pool. When the ship is cranky-built, and cannot stand steady after a portion of her cargo has been discharged, she usually takes in what is called shifting or stiffening ballast. The ballast is said to stiffen a cranky vessel, because it has the effect of making her firm or steady in the water. The quantity of ballast required by cranky vessels depends upon the build of the ships. Sixty tons of cargo will stiffen the most cranky vessel. I am informed by those who have been all their lives at the business, that they never knew a vessel, however cranky, but what 60 tons' weight would stiffen her. Some vessels are so stiff-built, that they can discharge the whole of their cargo without taking in any ballast at all. These are generally flat-bottomed vessels, whereas cranky vessels are built sharp towards the keel. The colliers are mostly flat-bottomed vessels, and could in calm weather return to the north without either ballast or cargo in them. This, how-

ever, is not allowed by the owners. The generality of ships discharge all their cargo before they take in any ballast. The cranky-built ships form the exception, and begin taking in ballast when they are about three-parts discharged. When a ship requires ballast, the owner or one of his agents or servants applies to the Trinity House for the quantity needed. If the ship belong to the merchant service, and is lying in any of the docks, the owner has to pay 1s. 7d. per ton to the Trinity Company for the ballast supplied: but if the merchant vessel be lying in the Pool, then the price is 1s. 3d. per ton, and if the vessel be a collier, the price is 1s. per ton. On application being made at the Ballast Office, the party is supplied with a bill, specifying the name and situation of the vessel, the quantity of ballast required for her, and the price that has been paid for it. The bill is then taken to the Ruler's Office, where it is entered in a book, and the ship supplied with the ballast, according to the place that she has on the books. If the weather is rough, a ship has often to remain three or four days without receiving the ballast she wants. The application for ballast is seldom made directly from the captain or shipowner himself. There are parties living in the neighbourhood of Wapping and Ratcliffe who undertake, for a certain sum per score of tons, to have the requisite quantity of ballast put aboard the ship. These parties are generally either publicans, grocers, butchers, lodging-house keepers or watermen, and they have a number of labourers dealing with them whom they employ to heave the ballast on board. The publicans, butchers, grocers, or lodging-house-keepers, are the ballast-contractors, and they only employ those parties who are customers at their houses. It is the owner or captain of the vessel who contracts with these "truckmen" for the ballasting of the ship at a certain price per score of tons, and the truckmen for that sum undertake not only to procure the ballast from the Trinity Company, and save the owner or captain all the trouble of so doing, but also to carry it from the Trinity-lighters on board the ship. The reason of the publicans, grocers, butchers, or lodging-house-keepers, undertaking the job is to increase the custom at their shops, for they make it a rule to employ no heavers but those who purchase their goods from them. The price paid to these truckmen varies considerably. Their principal profit, however, is made out of the labourers they employ. The highest price paid to the contractors for putting the ballast on board colliers (exclusive of the cost of the ballast itself) is 10s. per score tons. Many contractors charge less than this—not a few indeed undertake to do it for 9s., and there are one or two who will do it for 8s. the score. But these, I am informed, "are men who are trying to get the work away from the other contractors." The highest price paid to the contractors for ballasting small merchant vessels is 12s. per score as well. For large vessels the price varies according to their size, and, consequently, the number of heavers required to put the ballast on board. The lowest price paid per score to the contractors for small merchant vessels is 10s. Eight or nine years ago the price for ballasting small merchant vessels was much higher. Then the highest price paid to the contractor was 15s. Since that time the prices both for merchant vessels and colliers have been continually falling. This, I am told, arises from the number of contractors increasing, and their continual endeavours to underwork one another. Before the establishment of the Coal-whippers' Office, the contractors for ballast were solely publicans; and they not only undertook to put ballast on board, but to deliver the coals from the ships as well. At this time the publicans engaged in the business made rapid and large fortunes, and soon became shipowners themselves, but after the institution of the Coal-whippers' Office, the business of the publicans, who had before been the contractors, declined. Since that period the contracts for ballasting ships have been undertaken by butchers and grocers, as well as publicans, and the number of these has increased every year, and according as the number of the contractors has increased, so have the prices decreased, for each one is anxious to undersell the other. In order to do this, the contractors have sought everywhere for fresh hands, and the lodging-house-keepers in particular have introduced labouring men from the country, who will do the work at a less price than those who have been regularly brought up to the business: and I am credibly informed, that whereas nine or ten years ago every ballast-heaver was known to his mates, now the strangers have increased to such an extent that at least two-thirds of the body are unacquainted with the rest. There is treble the number of hands at the work now, I am told, to what there was but a few years back. The prices paid by the contractors to the ballast-heavers are very little below what the owners pay to them, indeed some of the publicans pay the heavers the same price that they themselves receive, and make their profit solely out of the beer and spirits supplied to the workmen. The butchers and grocers generally pay the men 6d. and some 1s. in the score less than they themselves get; but, like the publican, their chief profit is made out of the goods they supply. The lodging-house-keepers seldom contract for the work. They are generally foremen employed by the publican, butcher, or grocer contracting, and they make it a rule that the ballast-heavers whom they hire shall lodge at their house, as well as procure their beer, meat, or grocery, as the case may be, from the shop of the contractor by whom they are employed. All the English ships that enter the port of London are supplied with ballast in this manner. The owners always make it a rule to contract with some publican, butcher, grocer, or lodging-house-keeper for the ballasting of their vessels, and it is impossible for the ballast-heaver to obtain employment at his calling but by dealing at the shops of some or other of these parties. According to the Government returns there were 170 ballast-heavers in the metropolis in 1841, and I am assured that there are more than double that number at present, or nearly 400 labourers engaged in the business. There are now 27 publicans who make a regular business of contracting for the supply of ballast. Besides these there are four butchers, the same number of grocers, and as many lodging-house keepers. Further than this, there is a foreman attached to each of the public-houses, or butchers' or grocers' shops, and these foremen are mostly lodging-house-keepers as well. The foremen in general have the engagement of the heavers, and the first hands they employ are those who lodge at their houses: these hands are expected also to deal with the contractor under whose foreman they serve. The heavers generally, therefore, are obliged to lodge at the house of some foreman, and to obtain their meat, beer, and grocery from the different ballast-contractors, in order to obtain work; indeed, with the exception of clothing, the heaver is compelled to obtain almost every article he consumes through the medium of some contractor. The greater the number of contractors the heaver deals with, the greater is his chance of work. The rule with each of the contractors is to give credit to the hands they employ, and those who are the most in debt with them have the preference in labour. The butchers and grocers generally charge 1d. per lb. extra for everything they sell to the heavers, and the publicans make it up in adulteration. Each of the publicans, butchers, and grocers, who make a rule of contracting for the supply of ballast, has, on an average, two gangs of men dealing at his house, and if he have more ships to supply than his regular hands are capable of doing, then he sends the foreman to either of the places of call where the unemployed men wait for hire throughout the day. Each ship requires from four to six heavers to put the ballast on board, and the men generally ship about 50 tons in the course of the day. They often do as much as 100 tons, and sometimes only 20 in the day. The heavers are divided into constant and casualty men.

"The constant men are the first gang working out of the public-house, or butchers' or grocers' shops. The constant men with the publicans are those that are the best customers. "If they didn't drink," said my informant, "they'd be thought of very little use. These constant men make three times as much as the casualty men, or, in other words, they have three times as much to drink. Generally, one-fifth part of what the publican's constant men earn is spent in drink. The casualty men are those who belong to no regular houses; but these, if taken on by a publican, are expected to spend the same amount in drink as the constant men. There are no ballast-heavers who are teetotalers. "Indeed it would be madness," says my informant, "for a man to think of it, for to sign the pledge would be entirely to deprive himself and his family of bread."

To complete the different classes of ballast-labourers, I will conclude with the statement of a casualty man :—

"I am about 57," (said my informant, who was 6 feet high, and looked like a man far older than 57,) "and have been 35 years a ballast-heaver, with the exception of seven or eight years, when I had the care of some horses used in coal-waggons. When I first knew the trade, earnings was good. I might clear my 1l. a-week. On that I brought up four sons and one daughter—all now married. At that time, I mean when I first worked at ballast-heaving, the men were not so much employed by publicans and other tradesmen. A gang of men could then get work on their own account, a good deal easier than they can get it now through the tradesmen who supply the ballast. As the trade got more and more into the hands of the publicans and such-like, it grew worse and worse for such as me. We earned less, and were not anything like to call free men. Instead of my 1l. I had to stir myself to make 15s. or as low as 12s. a-week. Lately I have been what is called a casualty man. There's constant men and casualties. Each publican has a foreman to look out, and get men, and see after them. These foremen —all of them that I know of—keeps lodgers, charging them 2s. 6d. or 3s. a-week for a room they could get but for this tie, for 2s. — ay, that they could. Suppose now a publican has a ship to supply with ballast, he acquaints his foreman, and the foreman calls on his lodgers, and sets them to work. These are the constant men. They have always the first turn out of the house. If they return from work at 4, and there's another job at 5, they get it. That's interest you see, sir. The more such men earn this way, the more they're expected to spend with the publican. It's only bad stuff they have to drink at a full price. It's only when all the constant men are at work, and a job must be done at once, that me, and such as me, can get work. If I hear of a chance of a job I call on the foreman. If I have money, why, I must drink myself, and treat the foreman with a drop of gin, or what he fancies. If I haven't the money, I have the worse chance for a job. Suppose I get a job and earn 6s. out of 60 tons of ballast; out of that 6s. I may have 4s., or, at most, 4s. 6d. to take home with me, after paying for what I must drink at the publican's —what I'm forced to spend. Casualty men have sad trouble to get any work. Those that belong to the houses have all the call. Last week I was on the look-out every day, and couldn't get a single job, nor earn a single farthing. Last night I had to get a bite of supper at my son's, and a bite of breakfast this morning as well, and I had to borrow a pair of shoes to come out in. The best week's work I've had this winter was 15s. I had five days in one ship. For that five days I was entitled, I fancy, to 20s., or may be 21s., so that the difference between that and the 15s. went for drink. I only wanted a pint of beer now and then at my work—two or three a day. The worst of it is, we don't get drink at our work so much as at the public-house we're employed from. If we want to go home, some of the constant men want to have more and more, and so the money goes. Other weeks I have carried home 10s., 8s., 5s., and many a week nothing, living as I could. It would be a deal better for poor men, like me, if trades-men had nothing to do with ballast work. If the men that did the work were paid by the gentlemen what wants the ballast, there might then be a living for a poor man. As it is, it's a very bad, hateful system, and makes people badly off. A ballast-man may sit in a tap-room, wet, and cold, and hungry, (I've felt it many a time,) and be forced to drink bad stuff, waiting to be paid. It always happens, unless they're about shutting up, that we have to wait. We have no sick-fund or benefit societies. I declare to you, that if anything happened to me—if I was sick—I have nothing to call my own but what I've on; and not all that, as I've told you—and there's nothing but the parish to look to. (Here the man somewhat shuddered.) I pay 2s. a-week rent.

"Then again, sir, there's the basket-men at the docks—all the docks. They're as bad to the poor man as the publican, or worse. The way they do is this. They're not in any trade, and they make it their business to go on board ships—foreign ships—American generally. In better times, twenty or twenty-five years ago, there used to be 1s., and as high as 1s. 6d. paid for a ton from such ships to a gang of six ballast-men. I've earned six, seven, and eight shillings a-day myself then. We heaved the ballast out of the lighters with our shovels on to a stage, and from that it was heaved into the hold. Two men worked in the lighter, two on the stage, and two in the hold of the vessel. The basket-men manage to fill the hold now by heaving the ballast up from the lighter in baskets by means of a windlass. The basket-man contracts with the captain, and then puts us poor men at the lowest rate he can get; he picks them up any-where, anything in the shape of men. For every half-crown he pays these men he'll get 9s. for himself, and more. An American liner may require 300 tons of ballast, and, maybe, a captain will give a basket-man 8d. a-ton: that would be 10l. The basket-man employs six men, and he makes another. He never works himself—never—not a blow : but he goes swaggering about the ship when his men are at work, and he's on the look-out in the streets at other times. For the 10*l.* he'll get for the 300 tons, he'll pay his men each 2*s.* 6*d.* for 60 tons, that is 3*l.* 15*s.*, and so there's 6*l.* 5*s.* profit for him. Isn't that a shame, when so many poor men have to go without dinner or breakfast? There's five basket-men to my knowledge. They are making money all out of poor men that can't help themselves. The poor suffers for all."

In order to assure myself of the intensity of the labour of ballast-heaving, of which I heard statements on all sides, I visited a gang of men at work, ballasting a collier in the Pool. My engagements prevented my doing this until about six in the evening. There was a very dense fog on the river, and all along its banks; so thick was it, indeed, that the water, which washed the steps where I took a boat, could not be distinguished, even with the help of the adjacent lights. I soon, however, attained the ballast-lighter I sought. The ballast-heavers had established themselves alongside a collier, to be filled with 43 tons of ballast, just before I reached them, so that I observed all their operations. Their first step was to tie pieces of old sail, or anything of that kind, round their shoes, ankles, and half up their legs, to prevent the gravel falling into their shoes, and so rendering their tread painful. This was rapidly done; and the men set to work with the quiet earnestness of those who are working for the morrow's meal, and who know that they must work hard. Two men stood in the gravel (the ballast) in the lighter; the other two stood on " a stage," as it is called, which is but a boarding placed on the partition-beams of the lighter. The men on this stage, cold as the night was, threw off their jackets, and worked in their shirts, their labour being not merely hard, but rapid. As one man struck his shovel into the ballast thrown upon the stage, the other hove his shovelful through a small porthole in the vessel's side, so that the work went on as continuously and as quickly as the circumstances could possibly admit. Rarely was a word spoken, and nothing was heard but an occasional gurgle of the water, and the plunging of the shovel into the gravel on the stage by one heaver, followed instantaneously by the rattling of the stones in the hold shot from the shovel of the other. In the hold the ballast is arranged by the ship's company. The throwing of the ballast through the porthole was done with a nice precision. A tarpaulin was fixed to prevent any of the ballast that might not be flung through the porthole being wasted by falling into the river, and all that struck merely the bounds of the porthole fell back into the lighter; but this was the merest trifle. The men pitched the stuff through most dexterously. The porthole might be six feet above the stage from which they hove the ballast; the men in the lighter have an average heave of six feet on to the stage. The two men on the stage and the two on the lighter fill and discharge their shovels twelve times in a minute; that is, one shovelful is shot by each man in every alternate five seconds; so that every one of the four men engaged at the work flings the height of 36 feet every minute, or 2160 feet in an hour; and in that time, according to the concurrent computation of the heavers, the four men may easily fling in 10 tons, or 5600 lbs. a man. The men work with the help of large lanterns, being employed mostly by night.

I shall now state the sentiments of the men generally, and then individually, upon the subject of their grievances.

To be certain as to the earnings of the men, to see their condition, and to hear from a large number of them their own statements as to the hardships they suffered, and the sums they gained, I met two bodies of the ballast-heavers, assembled without pre-arrangement. At one station 50 were present, at the other 30. The men were chiefly clad in coarse, strong jackets; some of them merely waistcoats, with strong, blue flannel sleeves, and coarse trowsers, thick with accumulated grease from long wear. They had, notwithstanding their privations, generally a hardy look. There was nothing squalid in their appearance, as in that of men who have to support life on similar earnings with in-door employment. Their manners were quiet, and far from coarse. At the first meeting 50 were present. One man said, " Well, I think I am the oldest man at present, and I don't get above 5*s.* a-week; but that's because I'm an old man, and cannot work with the young ones." Upon an average the common men earned 10*s.* a-week the year through, and took home 5*s.* I inquired, " Are you all compelled to spend a great part of all you earn in drink with the publican?" The answer was simultaneously, " All of us—all—all!" Of the remainder of their earnings, after the drink deductions, the men were all satisfied they spent so much, that many only took 2*s.* 6*d.* a-week home to their wives and families on an average. Last week two earned 20*s.*, the publican taking 10*s.* from each. Three earned 15*s.*; one of these took 1*s.* 6*d.* home, the other 3*s.*, both working for publicans; the third, who worked for a grocer, took home 13*s.*; the other 2*s.* being spent in tea and sugar, he being a single man. Three earned 10*s.*; one, working for a publican, carried home 6*s.*, the difference going in compulsory drink; another 4*s.*, and another 5*s.* Six did one load of ballast, receiving 7*s.* 6*d.* each for it; one took home 4*s.* 11*d.*; another 6*s.* 6*d.* (a private job); another, who did a load for 5*s.* 3*d.*, took home 2*s.* 3*d.*; the other two took home 5*s.* each. One man earned 3*s.*, and took it all home, having worked at a private job for a foreigner. Fifteen earned nothing in the course of the last week. For the last fortnight nine had earned nothing. There were nine present that had earned something in the last three weeks. " The fortnight before Christmas," said one, " I didn't earn 5s. all that fortnight." " Nor I, nor I," said several others. On being asked, " Are you compelled to spend half of your earnings in drink?" there was a general cry of, " More than that, sir; more than that." I asked if men were forced to become drunkards under this system; there was a general cry of, " We are; and blackguards, too." Seventeen were married men. Of them, 3 had no children; 3 had one child; 4 had 2 children; 2 had 3; 3 had 4; one had 5; one had 6. The men all said, that to get away from the publican would be " a new life to them— all to their benefit—no force to waste money in drink—and the only thing that would do them good." Many threw away the drink they had from the publicans, it was so bad; they drank Thames water rather. They were all satisfied " they earned 10s. a-week the year through, spending of that sum what they *must* spend, and what they were induced to spend, from 5s. to 7s. 6d. a-week." " Another thing," they said, " if you get a job, the publican will advance 1s.—now and then he may. They hate to give money; there's trust for as much grog as you like." All hailed with delight the least possible chance of being freed from the publican. One man said he was compelled often enough to pawn something of his own or his wife's to go and spend it at the public-house, or he would have no chance of a job. All declare " such a system never was known to have been carried on for years." Many said, " We shall be discharged if they know we have told you the truth." They stated that the ballast-heavers numbered between 300 and 400. There were 60 craft, each requiring 4 heavers; and many men were idle when all the others were at work. Thirty were present when I counted the other meeting. A man said there might be three times that number looking for work then, and as many at work belonging to that station alone. In 1841 the census returns showed that there were 170 ballast-heavers; the men assembled declared that their numbers had more nearly trebled than doubled since then. Within the last two or three years many new hands had got to work, on account of the distress in Ireland. The men agreed with the others I had seen that they earned, one week with another, 10s., taking home but 5s. at the outside, and often only 2s. 6d. In answer to my questions they said, the winter is the best season; the trade is very slack in summer. Earnings in winter are pretty well double what they are in summer. Many agricultural labourers work among the heavers in winter, when they cannot be employed on the land. Of this body all said they were sober men till they took to

ballast-heaving, and would like to become sober men again. (A general assent.) Three of the men had taken the pledge before becoming ballast-heavers, and were obliged to break it to get work. They had to drink five pots of beer, they declared, where, if they were free men, they would only drink one. When asked if the present system made drunkards, they answered with one voice, " All; every ballast-heaver in it." Twenty were married men. All their wives and children suffered (this was affirmed generally with a loud murmur), and often had nothing to eat or drink while their husbands had but the drink. It was computed (with general concurrence) that 150 ballast-heavers paid foremen for lodgings, not half of them ever seeing the bed they paid for. About twelve years ago they could earn twice or three times as much as they can now; but prices were higher (12s. per score, for what is now 8s.), and the men were far less numerous. The following is a precise statement of the sums to which each ballast-heaver present was entitled, followed by the amount he had carried home the week before, after payment of his compulsory drinkings, and of what he might be induced to drink at the house of his employer while waiting to be paid:—

Earned.			Took home.		
£0	12	0	£0	7	6
0	7	0	0	3	6
0	15	0	0	9	0
0	12	0	0	6	0
0	13	0	0	4	0
0	11	0	0	5	0
0	5	0	0	2	6
0	8	0	0	5	0
0	9	6	0	5	0
1	0	0	0	10	0
0	12	6	0	3	6
1	0	0	0	9	0
0	12	0	0	4	0
0	15	0	0	9	0
0	15	0	0	8	6
0	16	0	0	6	0
0	15	0	0	5	0
Nothing			Nothing		
"			"		
"			"		
"			"		
0	12	0	0	2	6
0	9	0	0	5	0
1	0	0	0	4	6
1	0	0	0	10	0
0	10	0	0	3	0
0	10	0	0	5	0
0	12	0	0	2	6
0	8	0	0	3	6
0	14	0	0	9	0
£16	13	0	£7	7	0

This statement shows, out of 11s. 1½d. earnings, a receipt of less than 5s. a-week.

According to the returns of the Trinity

House, there were 615,619 tons of ballast put on board 11,234 ships in the year 1848. The ballast-heavers are paid at the rate of 6*d.* per ton for shovelling the ballast out of the Trinity Company's lighters into the holds of vessels. Hence, the total earnings of the ballast-heavers in that year were 15,390*l.* 9*s.* 6*d.* And calculating two-thirds (the men say they always get rid of a half, and often three-fourths, of their earnings in drink) of this sum to have been spent in liquor, it follows that as much as 10,260*l.* 6*s.* 4*d.* went to the publican, and only 5,130*l.* 3*s.* 2*d.* to the labouring men. According to this estimate of their gross earnings, if we calculate the body of the ballast-heavers as numbering 350 men, the average wages of the class are about 16*s.* 6*d.* per week each man; or if we reckon the class at 400, then the average wages of each person would be about 14*s.* 6*d.* per week. From all I can learn this appears to be about the truth—the earnings of the men being about 15*s.* a-week, and their real income about 5*s.*

The men shall now speak for themselves.

The first that I saw were two of the better class of foremen, who volunteered to give me an account of the system.

"I am a foreman or ganger of the ballast-heavers," said one. "I work under a man who is a publican and butcher; and I also work under another who is only a butcher. I, moreover, work under a grocer. I engage the different gangs of men for the parties under whom I work. I also pay the men. The publican, butcher, or grocer, as the case may be, agrees to give me 9*s.* a score tons. The foremen often give the men the same money as they themselves receive, barring a pot of beer or a quartern of gin that they may have out of the job. Some foremen take much more."

Another foreman, who was present while I was taking the statement of this man, here observed, that "Many foremen claim tow-tow, or a 'fifth-handed' proportion — that is, they will have 10*s.* when the working men have only 5*s.* There is a great deal of imposition on the working-classes here, I can assure you; the general thing, when we go to a job out of a public-house is, that the publican expects the men to drink to the amount of 4*s.* out of every 1*l.*, and 6*s.* out of every 30*s.* that's coming to them — that is, one-fifth part of the men's money must be spent in liquor. The drink is certainly not the best; indeed, if there is any inferior stuff they have it: it's an obligation on them that they drink. If they refuse to drink, they won't get employed, and that's the plain truth of it. Oh, it's long wanted looking to; and I'm glad at last to find some one inquiring into it. If they went to get the regular beer from the fair public-houses they would have to pay 3*d.* a pot for it; and at the contracting publicans' they must give 4*d.* a pot, and have short measure, and the worst of stuff

too. Every six pots of beer they give to the men is only five pots fair measure; and the rum they charge them 2*d.* half-a-pint more than the regular public-houses would, and far worse rum into the bargain. Besides the profit on their drink, some publicans charge 6*d.* per score tons as well. Out of the money coming to the men after the publican has been paid his score, many foremen claim one-fifth part over and above their regular share; or, in other words, the foremen takes two shares, and the men only one each. When the men have been paid, the publican paying them expects them to spend a further sum in drink, looking black at the man who goes away without calling for his pint or his pot, and not caring if they drink away the whole of their earnings. There's a good many would be glad if the men sat in their houses and spent their last farthing, and then had to go home penniless to their wives and families."

"I am a 'ganger' to a butcher as well as a publican," said one of the foremen. "His practice is just the same as the publican's. He receives 10*s.* per score tons, and pays me for the men 9*s.* The men and myself are all expected to spend about one-half of our earnings with the butcher in meat. He charges 6½*d.* per lb.; and at other houses, with ready money, I and the men might get it for 4*d.* as good. His meat is at least one-third dearer than other butchers'. I am also ganger to a grocer, and he gets about the same profit out of the men he employs—that is to say, the articles he supplies the men with are at least one-third dearer than at other shops. If anything, he makes more out of the men than the butcher; for if any man goes a score (which he always encourages) he stops the whole out the man's earnings, and often leaves him without a penny after the job is done. When the publican, grocer, butcher, or lodging-house keeper has a contract for ballast, he directs the foreman working under him to get together the gang that regularly work from his house. This gang are men who always deal at the shop, and the contractor would dismiss me if I was to engage any other men than those who were his regular customers. Many a time a publican has told me that some man was a good, hard drinker, and directed me to engage him whenever I could. If a man sticks up a score, he also tells me to put him on first of all: the grocer and the butcher do the same. This system is the cause, I know, of much distress and misery among the men; the publicans make the men drunkards by forcing them to drink. I know many wives and children who starve half their time through it. They haven't a bit of shoe or clothing, and all through the publican compelling the men to spend their earnings in drink. After the gang is paid, at least three out of the four get drunk; and, often, the whole four. Many a time I have seen the whole of the men reel-ing home without a penny to bless themselves, and the wife and children have to suffer for all this; they are ill-treated and half-starved: this I can safely say from my own knowledge."

I next saw two men, who stated that they were oppressed by the publican, and the foreman also. The first said, "I work under a publican, and have to pay the foreman one-fifth of my earnings; I only have fourpence out of every shilling I earn, and I must be a sober man indeed to get that. Both the publican and the foreman get eightpence out of a shilling, and make their money out of my sweat. Nine years ago I was left, to my sorrow, with nine motherless children, and I am the slave of the publican. He is my destruction, and such are my sufferings, that I don't care what I do if I can destroy the system; I shall die happy if I can see an end to it. I would go to bed supperless to-night, and so should my children, if I could stop it. After I have had a job of work, many's the time I have not had a penny to take home to my children, it has all gone betwixt the foreman and the publican; and what is more, if I had brought anything home I should have stood a worse chance of work the next day. If I had gone away with sixpence in my pocket, the work that should have come to me would have gone to those who had spent all in the house. I can solemnly say that the men are made regular drunkards by the publicans. I am nine-and-twenty years dealing with this oppression, and I wish from my heart I could see an end to it, for the sake of my children and my fellow-creatures' children as well. But I suffer quite as much from the foreman as I do from the publican. I am obliged to treat him before I can get a job of work. The man who gives him the most drink he will employ the first. Besides this, the foreman has two-fifth parts of the money paid for the job; he has twice as much as the men if he does any of the work; and if he does none of the work he takes one-fifth of the whole money: besides this, the men do three times the foreman's labour. If I could get the full value of my sweat, I could lay by to-morrow, and keep my family respectably. In the room of that, now, my family want bread often—worse luck, for it hurts my feelings. I have been idle all to-day; for hearing of this, I came to make my statement, for it was the pride of my heart to do all that I could to put an end to the oppression. The publicans have had the best of me, and when the system is done away with I shan't be much the better for it. I have been nine-and-twenty years at it, and it has ruined me both body and soul; but I say what I do for the benefit of others, and those who come after me."

The other man said that he worked under a publican, and a grocer as well, and lodged with a foreman. "I pay 2s. a week for my lodgings," he said; "there are two beds in the room, and two men in each. The room where we all sleep is not more than seven feet long by five feet wide, and barely seven feet high. There is no chimney in it. It is a garret, with nothing in it but the two beds. There hadn't need be much more, for it wouldn't hold even a chair besides. There's hardly room, in fact, for the door to open. I find it very close sleeping there at night-time, with no ventilation, but I can't help myself. I stay there for the job of work. I must stay; I shouldn't get a day's work if I didn't. The lodgings are so bad, I'd leave them to-morrow if I could. I know I pay twice as much as I could get them for elsewhere. That's one way in which I, for one, am robbed. Besides this, I am obliged to treat the foreman; I am obliged to give him two glasses of rum, as well as lodging at his house, in order to get employment. I have also to drink at the public-house; one-fifth of my money is kept, first and foremost, by the publican. That goes for the compulsory drink—for the swash which he sends us on board, and that we think the Thames-water is sweet and wholesome to it. It is expressly adulterated for our drink. If we speak a word against it we should be left to walk the streets, for a week and more forward. Even if we were known to meet a friend, and have a pint or a pot in another public-house, we should be called to an account for it by the publican we worked under, and he would tell us to go and get work where we spent our money; and, God knows, very little money we would have coming out of his house after our hard sweat. After the compulsory drink, and the publican has settled with us, and his fifth part of our hard-earned money for the swash—it's nothing else—that he has given us to drink, then I should be thought no man at all if I didn't have two pots of beer, or half-a-pint of gin, so that I would count myself very lucky indeed if I had a couple of shillings to take home, and out of that I should have to spend two-thirds of it to get another job. I am a married man, and my wife and three children are in Ireland. I can't have them over, for it is as much as I can do to support myself. I came over here thinking to get work, and to send them money to bring them over after me, but since I have been here I have been working at the ballast-work, and I have not been able to keep myself. I don't complain of what is paid for the work; the price is fair enough; but we don't get a quarter of what we earn, and the Irish ballast-heavers suffer more here than in their own country. When I came over here I had a good suit of clothes to my back, and now I'm all in rags and tatters, and yet I have been working harder, and earning more money, that I did in all my life. We are robbed of all we get by the foremen and publicans. I was eight years a teetotaler before I went to ballast-work, and now I am forced to be a drunkard, to my sorrow, to get a job of work. My wife and children have a bit of land in Ireland to keep them, and they're badly off enough, God knows. I can neither help them, nor send money to bring them over to me; nor can I get over to them myself. The grocers whom we work under rob us in the same manner. I have worked under one. He supplied bread, butter, tea, sugar, coffee, candles, tobacco, cheese, &c. It is a larger kind of chandlers' shop. He charges us 5½d. for the same bread as I can buy for 4½d. at other shops. The tea, sugar, and other articles he supplies us with are at the same rate; they are either worse or dearer than at other shops. They generally manage to get a fifth part of our earnings wherever we go; but the grocers are best of all, for they don't ruin our health, as what they give us don't make us sick. I work for these two houses because the foreman that I lodge with has work out of both houses, and we are obliged to deal at the houses that he works under; if we didn't we shouldn't get the job, so that if we are not robbed by the publican we are by the grocer. They will have it out of the poor hard-working man, and the foreman must have the gain out of it as well. I only wish to God it was done away with, for it is downright oppression to us all, and if I never have another stroke of work I will strive all I can to have it done away with for the sake of my fellow-men.

After these two cases came one who said,— " I have been three years a ballast-heaver. Just before that I came to this country. When I came I got to be a lodger with a foreman to a publican. I paid him 2s. 6d. a-week. My family, a wife and two children, came over when I had got work as a ballast-heaver. I couldn't take them to the lodgings I then had; they were all for single men: so I had to take another place, and there I went to live with my family; but to keep my work I had to pay the foreman of the publican — him that lets these lodgings to the ballast-heaver— 2s. 6d. a-week all the same as if I had been living there. That I had, and I had to do it for two years. Yes, indeed. I didn't earn enough to pay for two lodgings, so two or three months back I refused to pay the 2s. 6d. a-week for a place I hadn't set my foot in for two years, and so I lost my work under that foreman and his publican. If me and my children was starving for want of a bite of bread, neither of them would give me a farthing. There's plenty as bad as them, too, and plenty used like me, and it's a murdering shame to tax poor men's labour for nothing."

This man reiterated the constant story of being compelled to drink against his will, hating the stuff supplied to him, being kept for hours waiting before he was paid, and being forced to get drunk, whether he would or no. The man also informed me that he now works under a butcher, who pays 8s. a score to the hands he employs, he (the butcher) receiving from the captain 10s.

" Suppose," he said, " I have a 60-ton job, I'd be entitled to 7s. 6d. without beer, or such-like; but under this butcher I get only 5s. 3d., and out of that 5s. 3d. — that's all I get in hard money — I'm expected to spend 4s. or thereabouts in meat, such as he chooses to give. I have no choice; he gives what he likes, and charges me 6½d. a-pound for what I could buy at 4d. in a regular way. Very inferior stuff he keeps. Working under a butcher, we must all live on this poor meat. We can't afford bread or vegetables to it."

This same butcher, I was afterwards informed, had been twice fined for using false weights to customers, such as the man whose statement I have given; he even used wooden weights made to look like lead.

The following is an instance of the injustice done to the men by those who contract to whip rather than to heave the ballast on board.

" I now work," said the man, whom I was referred to as an exponent of the wrong, " for Mr. ——, a publican who contracts to supply ships with ballast by the lump. He'll contract to supply a ship with all the ballast she'll want by the lump — that is, so much money for all she wants, instead of so much by the ton; or he may contract with a ship at 2s. 6d. a-ton. We — that is a gang of eight men — may put two loads or 120 tons on board in the course of a day. For those 120 tons he will receive 120 half-crowns, that's 15l. For putting in those 120 tons we— that is, the eight ballast-heavers employed— receive 2s. 6d. a-day of 12 or 14 hours; that is 8 half-crowns or 20 shillings, with 3s. 6d. a-day for a basket-man, in addition to the eight, so leaving the publican a profit of 13l. 16s. 6d." I could hardly believe in the existence of such a system — yielding a mere pittance to the labourer, and such an enormous profit to the contractor, and I inquired further into the matter. I found the statement fully corroborated by many persons present; but that was not all I learned. When the men, by incessant exertion, get in 120 tons in a day, as they often do, nothing is charged them for the beer they have had, four or five pints a-day each; but if only 60 tons be got in, as sometimes happens, through the weather and other circumstances, then the men employed on the half-a-crown a-day must pay for their own beer and pay their private scores for treating a friend, or the like. " There's no chance of a job," said my informant; " not a bit of it." He continued : " Very bad drink it is — the worst — it makes me as sick as a dog. There's two brothers there what they call blood-hounds; they're called so because they hunt up the poor men to get them to work, and to see that they spend their money at their employer's public-house when work's done. If you don't spend something, no bread to cut the next morning—not a bit of it—and no chance of another job there. He employs us ballast-heavers, when we are not at the ballast, in backing coals into the steamers."

I have given the statement of a ballast-heaver as to the system pursued by those whom he called basket-men. The employer here alluded to is one of that class, the difference being, that the ballast-heavers shovel the ballast out of the lighter on to the stage, and from the stage through a port-hole into the hold. Four men are thus employed, two on the lighter, and two on the stage. With a large ship five men are employed, and two stages. When the basket-man or the man contracting by the lump is employed, this process is observed :—There are two men in the lighter alongside the vessel to be ballasted, whose business it is to fill five baskets. There are five men at the winch aboard ship employed heaving up these baskets, and a basket-man to turn them over and empty out their contents.

To ascertain that there was no provident fund — no provision whatever for sickness — I investigated the case of a man who, in consequence of illness occasioned by his trade, was afflicted with a pulmonary complaint. This man was formerly one of the wine-cellarmen in the London Dock ; he was then made a permanent man at the St. Katherine's Dock, and was dismissed for having taken a lighted pipe in while at his work; and for the last fourteen years and upwards he has been a ballast-heaver. I now give his wife's statement :—" My husband has been ill for three months, and he has been six weeks in Guy's Hospital, and I am afraid he'll never get out again, for he kept up as long as he could for the sake of the children. We have five at home; one of them (twelve years old) I hope to get to sea, having two older sons at sea, and being the mother of twelve children altogether. I will tell you what led to my poor husband's illness; he was a kind husband to me. I consider it was his hard work that made him ill, and his not getting his rights—not his money when entitled to it. After doing a heavy day's work he had to go and sit in a cold tap-room, drinking bad beer; but it wasn't beer—muck, I call it—and he had to wait to be paid, ay, and might have had to wait till the day after, and then come home cold and have to go to bed without a bit of victuals. His illness is owing to that; no horse could stand it long. Ballast-men are worse than slaves in the West Indies. When at work he earned what the others did. He only drank what he couldn't help—the worst of stuff. No drink, no work. Six weeks ago she went to the hospital, I conveying him. When I returned home I found three strange men had turned my four children into the street, doing it in a brutal way. I rushed

into the house, and one said, ' Who are you ?' I seized the fellow who said this by the hand kerchief, and put him out. One of them said, ' Be off, you old Irish hag, you have no business here ; we have possession.' When I saw the children in the street, passion made me strong, and so I put him out. The collector of the rent, who employed the broker, is a publican, for whom my husband worked as a ballast-heaver until he was unable to work from illness. I was given into custody for an assault, and taken before Mr. Yardley. He considered the assault proved, and as an honest woman I couldn't deny it, and so I had fourteen days with bread and water. The children were placed in the workhouse, where they were well treated. I was very glad they were so taken care of. As soon as I got out I went to see about my children; that was the first thing I did. I couldn't rest till I did that. I brought them home with me, though it was only to bread and water, but I was with them. I only owed about 15s. rent, and had been four years in the house at the time the publican put the broker in. We paid 6s. 6d. a-week; it was no use asking such a man as that any mercy. He was in the habit of employing ballast-heavers for many years ; and if that doesn't harden a man's heart, nothing will. In general these ballast publicans are cruel and greedy. At present I go out washing or charing, or doing anything I can to maintain my children, but work's very slack. I've had a day and a-half this fortnight, earning 2s. 6d., that's all for a fortnight; the parish allows me four loaves of bread a-week. The children, all boys, just get what keeps a little life in them. They have no bed at night, and are starved almost to death, poor things. I blame the system under which my husband had to work — his money going in drink — for leaving me destitute in the world. On Christmas-day we lived on a bit of workhouse bread —nothing else, and had no fire to eat it by. But for the money gone in drink we might have had a decent home, and wouldn't so soon have come to this killing poverty. I have been tenderly reared, and never thought I should have come to this. May God grant the system may be done away with, for poor people's sake."

I now give the statement of two women, the wives of ballast-heavers, that I may further show how the wives and families of these men are affected by the present system.

" I have been 11 years married," said one, " and have had five children, four being now living."

The other woman had been married 23 years, but has no children living.

" We are very badly off," said the woman with a family, " my husband drinking hard. When I first knew him—when we were sweethearts in a country part of Ireland—he was a farm-labourer and I was a collier's daughter, he was a sober and well-behaved man. Two years after we were married, and he was a sober man those two years still. We came to London to better ourselves, worse luck. The first work he got was ballast-heaving. Then he was obligated to drink or he couldn't get work; and so, poor man, he got fond of it. This winter oft enough he brings me and the children home 2s. or 1s. 6d. after a job; and on that we may live for two or three days,—we're half starved, in course. The children have nothing to eat. It's enough to tear any poor woman's heart to pieces. What's gone into the publican's till would get the children bread, and bedding. and bits of clothes. Nothing but his being employed at ballast-heaving made him a drunkard, for he *is* a drunkard now. He often comes home and ill-uses me, but he doesn't ill-use the children. He beats me with his fists; he strikes me in the face; he has kicked me. When he was a sober man he was a kind, good husband; and when he's sober now, poor man, he's a kind, good husband still. If he was a sober man again with his work, I'd be happy and comfortable to what I am now. Almost all his money goes in drink."

"We can't get shoes to our feet," said the second woman.

"When my husband is sober and begins to think," (continued the first,) "he wishes he could get rid of such a system of drinking,—he really does wish it, for he loves his family, but when he goes out to work he forgets all that. It's just the drink that does it. I would like him to have a fair allowance at his work, he requires it; and beyond that it's all waste and sin: but he's forced to waste it, and to run into sin, and so we all have to suffer. We are often without fire. Much in the pawn-shop do you say, sir? Indeed I haven't much out."

"We," interposed the elder woman, "haven't a stitch but what's in pawn except what wouldn't be taken. We have 50s. worth in pawn altogether—all for meat and fire."

"I can't, I daren't," the younger woman said, "expect anything better while the present system of work continues. My husband's a slave, and we suffer for it."

The elder woman made a similar statement. After his score is paid, she said, her husband has brought her 4s., 3s., 2s., 1s., and often nothing, coming home drunk with nothing at all. Both women stated that the drink made their husbands sick and ill, and for sickness there was no provision whatever. They could have taken me to numbers of women situated and used as they were. The rooms are four bare walls, with a few pieces of furniture and bedding such as no one would give a penny for. The young woman was perfectly modest in manner, speech, and look, and spoke of what her husband was and still might be with much feeling. She came to me with a half-clad and half-famished child in her arms.

I then took, for the sake of avoiding repe-

tition, the statements of two ballast-heavers together—*constant men*—working under different publicans. The account they gave me of the way in which the publicans contracted to ballast a ship was the same as I have given elsewhere.

"I have been twenty years a ballast-heaver," said one, "and all that time I have worked for a publican, and haven't a coat to my back. Twenty years ago the publicans had the same number of hands, but had more work for them, and I might then earn 20s. a-week; but I couldn't fetch that home from the publican. He expected me to spend one-half of my earnings with him; and when I left his house drunk, I might spend the other half. I've drunk gallons of drink against my will. I've drunk stuff that was poison to me. I turned teetotaler about six months ago, and the publican, my employer, *sacked* me when he found it out, saying, ' He'd be d——d if he'd have such men as me—he didn't make his living by teetotalers.' "

"Yes," added the other man, "and so *my* publican told me; for I turned teetotaler myself somewhere about seven years ago, and took the pledge from Father Mathew in the Commercial-road. The publican told me, that if Father Mathew chose to interfere with me, why Father Mathew might get employment for me, for he—that's the publican—wouldn't. So I was forced to break my pledge to live—me and my youngsters—I had six then, and I've buried two since."

"Work," resumed the man who first gave me the statement, "keeps getting worse. Last week I carried only 8s. home, and if I'd got paid by the captain of the ship for the amount of work I did, and on the same terms as the publican, I should have taken home at the very least 16s. The publican that employs us gives us only 8s. a-score, and receives 10s. from the captain. All the publicans don't do this; some give what they get from the captain, but some publicans takes two-thirds, and that's the truth. (The second man assented.) One week with another I've taken home, this winter, from 12s. to 13s., and but for this shameful starvation system, having to work for a publican's profit, and to drink his drink, I'd take home my 20s. every week. It makes a man feel like a slave; indeed, I'm not much better. We should be in heaven if we got away from the publican or butcher either; it's compulsion one's life through. Some of the publicans have as many as sixty single men lodging in their houses, paying half-a crown a-week; ay, and men that don't lodge with them, when the house is full, must pay half-a-crown all the same, to get a job of work, as well as paying for the places where they do lodge."

The first man continued:—

"The gin and rum is the worst that can be supplied; but we must drink it or waste it. We often spill it on the ballast, it's that bad "—[" Often, often," was the response of the other man.] "And that's not the worst. When we get a job of putting sixty tons of ballast on board, we are forced to take six pots of beer with us to our work; but only four pots are supplied, and we must pay for six. We are robbed on every side. I cannot describe how bad it is; a man would hardly believe it; but all will tell you the same—all the men like us." [So, indeed, the poor fellows did afterwards.] "When we call to be paid, we are kept for hours in a cold tap-room, forced to drink cold stuff without being let have a strike of fire to take the chill off it."

The other man then made a further statement.

"I've been forced to put my sticks in pawn—what I had left—for I was better off once, though I was always a ballast-heaver and have worked for the same publican fourteen years. I have 3*l.* in pawn now, I blame this present system for being so badly off—sorrow a thing else! Now just look at this: A single man, a lodger, will go into a publican's and call for 1*s.* worth of rum, and the publican will call me a scaly fellow, if I don't do the same; that will be when I'd rather be without his rum, if I got it for nothing." One publican (the men gave me this account concurrently, and it was fully confirmed by a host of others,) married the niece of a waterman employed to pull the harbour-master about the river. He kept a public-house, and carried on the system of lodgers for ballast-heaving, making a great deal of money out of them; by this means he got so much work at his command, that the rest of the publicans complained to the harbour-master, and the man was forced to give up his public-house. When he had to give it up he made it over to his niece's husband, and that man allowed him 1*s.* for every ship he brought him to ballast. I've known him—that's the publican that succeeded the man I've been telling you of—have 40 ships in a day: one week with another he has had 100 ships; that's 5*l.*, and he has them still. It's the same now. We've both worked for him. His wife's uncle (the harbour-master's waterman) says to the captains, and he goes on board to see them after the harbour-master's visit to them,—Go to ——; get your ballast of him, and I'll give you the best berth in the river.'"

I next obtained an interview with a young man who was the victim of a double extortion. He made the following statement:—

"I work under a publican, and lodge in his house. I have done so for five years. I pay 2*s.* 6*d.* a-week, there being ten of us in two rooms. We're all single men. These two rooms contain four beds, three in the larger room and one in the other. We sleep two in a bed, and should have to sleep three in some; only two of the men don't occupy the lodgings

they pay for. The bigger room may be 16 feet by 10; the smaller about a quarter that size. You cannot turn in it—the bed cannot be brought out of the room without being taken to pieces. We must cook in the tap-room, which is a room for the purpose; it contains forms and an old table, with a large grate. We are found fryingpans and gridirons, and pans, and fire, and candle; but we must find our own knives and forks. The room is shamefully dirty—I mean the tap (cooking) room. It looks as if it hadn't been washed for years. It's never been washed to my knowledge. The bed-rooms are very little better. The bedding is very bad—a flock bed, with a pair of blankets and quilt, and a sort of sheet clean once a-fortnight. There's very bad ventilation and very unpleasant smells. It's a horrid den altogether. None of us would stop there if we could help it—but we can't help it, for if we leave we get no work. We are forced to find locks for our rooms, to keep our bits of things from being stolen. One man was robbed; my clothes was in the box with his; the box was broken open, but the clothes was left, and a few halfpence put away in the box was taken. There's lots of bugs; we can only sleep after hard work, and we must drink when we're at work. I've poured my beer into the river many a time, it was so bad—it tasted poisonous. We've drank Thames water rather than the bad beer we're all forced to drink. To show how we're treated I'll tell you this: I owe so much, and so much a week's stopped to pay it; but it never gets less, I am always charged the same. There it is, the same figures are on the slate, keep paying, paying off as you will. They won't rub it off, or if they do rub it off it's there again the next time. Only last week a man was discharged for grumbling, because he objected to paying twice over. He hasn't had a day's work since."

Then came one who was the *employé* of a publican and grocer. He said:

"I work under a publican and grocer. I'm any man's man. I stand with my fingers in my mouth at Ratcliff-cross watching, and have done it these last nine years. Half of us is afraid to come and speak to you. When I volunteered, the big-whiskered and fat-faced men (foremen) were looking at me and threatening me for coming to you. No matter, I care for nobody. Worse nor I am I can't be. No more I can't. I go to one publican's to work 60 tons, and for that I get 4*s.*, but 6*s.* is my rights. The remainder 2*s.* is left—I'm forced to leave it—for me to drink out on Sunday night. If I was in a fair house the publican would pay me 7*s.* 6*d*; as it is I get 4*s.* and 2*s.* must be drunk,—it's the rule at that house—he's in opposition and works low. If I was at liberty it wasn't to his house I'd go for a drink. The hardest-drinking man gets work first, and when a man's drunk he doesn't care what stuff he puts into his belly.

Before we go to a job the four of us are expected to drink half-a-pint of rum or gin; the publicans expect it. If I was a teetotaler I must pay my whack and the other men may drink it, for the score against the ship is divided among the men equal.

"Suppose two foremen were to meet and have a drop of rum or brandy together, and a little talk about a ship's ballast, that's charged to us poor fellows—it's stuck up to us—but we mustn't say nothing, though we know we never had a sup of it; but if we say a word it's all up—no more work.

"Once on a time I worked for a publican close by here, and when I came to the house I had nothing to drink. My oldest mate whispered to me as we were on our way from the London Dock, and told me to speak my mind, for he knew there was a false score chalked against the ship; and the others was afraid to say a word. Well, I did speak when I got into the house, and the foreman was there, and he asked me what business I had to speak more than another? There was 6s. charged to the score for drink that we never touched or ever saw,—not a sup of it. He—that's the foreman—told me I shouldn't go to finish the ship; I said I would, in spite of him. I told the missus I expected she wouldn't give any more drink but what we had ourselves, or would get when we came home; and she said she wouldn't; and that's two years ago; but I haven't had a job from them parties since.

"Suppose I get to the public-house for my money at six in the evening, I am forced to wait there till eleven, until I am drunk very often—drunk from vexation; stopt when I'm hungry after five or six hours' work on the river, and not let take the money home to my wife and family, nor let have anything to eat, for I'm waiting for that money to get a bit of grub; but when I'm half drunk the hunger goes off just for a time. I must go and drink in a morning if my children go without breakfast, and starve all day till I come home at night. I can get nothing from my employers but *drink*. If I ask them for a shilling I can't get it. I've finished my load of ballast without breaking my fast but on the beer we're forced to take with us.

"I've found grocers better to work under than publicans,—there's a great deal more honesty in them. They charge a middling fair price; but they'll have tow-row out of it, —that's dry money—so much a score. They'll stop 6d. a score only for giving us a job. I can get as good sugar as I get them at 4d. for 3½d.; but then the difference between the grocer and publican is, that the wife and family can have a bit of something to eat under the grocer, but not under the publican. All goes in drink with the publican; but we cannot carry drink home. When I go home drunk from the publican's, I tumble on the floor, perhaps, and say, 'Is there anything to eat for me?' and my old woman says, 'Where's the money? give me that and I'll give you something to eat.' Then a man gets mad with vexation, and the wife and children runs away from him; they are glad to get away with their lives, they're knocked about so. It makes a man mad with vexation to see a child hungry,—it kills me; but what the foreman gives me I *must* take; I dare never say no. If I get nothing—if all is gone in drink—I must go from him with a blithe face to my starving children, or I need never go back to him for another job."

I shall now set forth as fully as possible the nature of the system by which the ballast-heaver is either forced by the fear of losing all chance of future employment, or induced by the hope of obtaining the preference of work from the publican, his employer, to spend at least one half of his earnings every week in intoxicating drinks. Let me, however, before proceeding directly to the subject of my present communication, again lay before the reader the conclusions which I lately drew from the Metropolitan Police returns for 1848, concerning the intemperance of the labouring classes of London. It is essential that I should first prove the fact, and show its necessary consequences. This done, the public will be more ready to perceive the cause, and to understand that until this and similar social evils are removed, it is worse than idle to talk of "the elevation of the masses," and most unjust, to use the mildest term, to condemn the working men for sins into which they are positively forced. To preach about the virtues of teetotalism to the poor, and yet to allow a system to continue that compels them to be drunk before they can get work—not to say bread—is surely a mockery. If we would really have the industrious classes sober and temperate men, we must look first, it seems, to their *employers*. We have already seen that the intemperance of the coal-labourer is the fault of the employer, rather than the man; but we have only to go among the ballast-labourers to find the demoralization of the working man arising, not from any mere passive indifference, but from something like a positive conspiracy on the part of the master.

According to the criminal returns for the metropolis, there were 9197 males and 7264 females, making altogether a total of 16,461 individuals, charged with drunkenness in the year 1848. This makes one in every 110 individuals in London a drunkard—a proportion which, large as it seems, is still less than one-half what it was some ten or fifteen years back.

For the sake of comparison I subjoin, in the following page, a Table, taken from the Government Report on Drunkenness; being a return of the number of charges of drunkenness which have been entered upon the books of the Metropolitan Police in the years 1831,

NUMBER OF CHARGES OF DRUNKENNESS EACH YEAR IN THE YEARS 1831, 1832, 1833.

Locality of each Division.	No. of Officers employed in each Division.	Computed Population in each Division, according to the Parliamentary Returns.	1831.			1832.			1833.			Public-Houses and Beer-Shops in each Division.		
			Males.	Females.	Total.	Males.	Females.	Total.	Males.	Females.	Total.	Public Houses.	Beer-Shops.	Total.
A. Whitehall	120	6,238	406	230	636	384	243	627	371	228	599	32	5	37
B. Westminster .	168	53,147	1,596	800	2,396	1,829	831	2,660	1,864	1,193	3,057	186	58	244
C. St. James's ..	188	105,862	2,290	1,127	3,417	2,119	1,055	3,174	2,208	1,256	3,464	302	20	322
D. St.Marylebone	106	122,206	1,375	727	2,102	1,300	650	1,950	1,019	605	1,624	148	54	202
E. Holborn	168	75,241	1,785	1,079	2,864	1,241	897	2,138	879	618	1,497	249	19	368
F. Covent Garden	168	41,010	2,238	1,555	3,793	2,165	1,617	3,782	1,665	1,388	3,053	309	28	332
G. Finsbury	236	115,266	2,141	1,423	3,564	2,192	1,440	3,632	1,916	1,270	3,186	368	100	468
H. Whitechapel .	191	119,042	1,253	812	2,065	1,631	1,268	2,899	1,803	1,295	3,098	359	102	461
K. Stepney	296	143,137	899	574	1,473	1,387	732	2,119	1,125	762	1,887	437	131	568
L. Lambeth	191	101,561	1,732	1,271	3,003	1,581	1,234	2,815	1,291	944	2,235	183	70	153
M. Southwark ..	189	107,537	1,655	1,050	2,705	1,470	982	2,452	1,284	843	2,127	321	66	387
N. Islington	269	140,407	850	373	1,223	1,165	573	1,738	826	409	1,235	267	144	311
P. Camberwell ..	243	77,825	256	87	343	201	75	276	203	80	283	138	96	234
R. Greenwich ..	212	58,778	363	137	500	513	240	753	418	210	628	283	51	334
S. Hampstead ..	223	112,136	573	301	874	613	326	939	697	319	1,016	138	74	212
T. Kensington ..	184	70,296	124	24	148	303	109	412	464	137	601	220	93	313
V. Wandsworth .	186	62,039	212	35	247	210	60	270	235	55	290	133	76	209
Total..	3,398	1,511,728	19,748	11,605	31,353	20,304	12,332	32,636	18,268	11,612	29,880	4,073	1,187	5,155

1832, and 1833, with the number of officers employed in, and the locality of, each division: also the amount of population in each, according to the Parliamentary returns of 1831.

Now, comparing these returns with those of the year before last, we find that the decrease of intemperance in the metropolis has been most extraordinary. In the year 1831, 1 in every 48 individuals was drunk; in 1832 the number increased to 1 in 46; whereas in 1833 it decreased to 1 in 50; and in 1848 the average had again fallen to 1 individual to every 110. This decrease of intemperance was attended with a similar decrease in the number of metropolitan beer-shops. In 1833 there were 1182, and in 1848 only 779 beer-shops in London. Whether this decrease preceded or succeeded, and so was the cause or the consequence of the increased sobriety of the people, it is difficult to say. The number of public-houses in London, however, had increased during the same period from 4073 to 4275. Upon the cause and effect of this I leave others to speculate.

Of the total, 16,461 persons, male and female, who were charged with being intoxicated in the year 1848, no less than one individual in every seven belonged to the labouring class: and, excluding the females from the number, we shall find that, of the males, every fourth individual that was taken up for drunkenness was a labouring man. Taking the whole population of London, temperate and intemperate, only 1 in every 110 is a drunkard; but with the labouring classes the average is as high as 1 in every 22. Of course, where the habit of drinking is excessive, we may expect to find also excessive pugnacity. That it is the tendency of all intoxicating liquors to increase the irritability of the individual is well known. We might infer therefore, *à priori*, that the greater number of common assaults would be committed by the greatest drunkards. In 1848 there were 7780 individuals assaulted in London, and nearly one-fourth of these, or 1882, were attacked by labouring men, one in every 26 of the entire body of labourers having been charged with this offence. The "simple larceny," of which the labouring classes appear, by the same returns, to be more guilty than any other body of individuals, is also explained by their inordinate intemperance. When a man's bodily energy is destroyed by drink, labour is so irksome to him that he would sooner peril his liberty than work. What wonder, then, that as many as 1 in every 28 labourers should be charged with theft? Whereas, of the rest of the population there are only 1 in every 226 individuals. Thus, of the labouring classes, 1 in every 22 is charged with being drunk; 1 in every 26 with committing an assault; and 1 in every 28 with being guilty of simple larceny.

For the truth of the connexion existing between drink, pugnacity, and theft, I would refer to the statement of one of the most intelligent and experienced of the coal whippers,— one, indeed, to whose unceasing and heroic exertions that class principally owe their redemption:— " The children of the coal-whippers," he told me, " were, under the old system, almost reared in the tap-room." He himself had known as many as 500 youths that were transported; and this, be it remembered, out of a class numbering only 2000 men.

Such, then, are the proved consequences of an inordinate use of intoxicating liquors. It becomes, therefore, the duty of every one who is anxious for the well-being of the people, to diminish the occasions for drinking wherever possible. To permit the continuance of certain systems of employment and payment, which are well known, both to tempt and compel the men to indulge in intoxicating liquors, is at once to breed the very crimes that it is the office of Government to suppress. The custom pursued by the coal-merchants of paying the labourers in their employ in public-houses, as I lately exposed, appeared bad enough. The "backer," jaded and depressed with his excessive work through the day, was entrapped into the public-house in the evening, under the pretence of receiving his wages. Once inside he was kept waiting there hour after hour by the publican (who of course was out of silver, and had to send some distance for it). Beer is called for by the men in the meantime. Under the influence of the stimulant, the fatigue and the depression begin to leave the labourers, the burden that is still on their backs (it will be remembered that such is the description of the men themselves) is shaken off, and their muscles no longer ache and are stiff, but relax, while their flagging spirits gradually revive under the potent charm of the liquor. What wonder, then, that the poor creatures finding it so easy, and when the habit is once formed, so pleasant, a cure for their ills, should be led to follow up one draught with another and another? This system appeared to me to be vicious enough, and to display a callousness on the part of the employers that quite startled me. But the system under which the ballast-labourers are now suffering, is an infamy hardly to be credited as flourishing in these days. I have, therefore, been at considerable pains to establish such a mass of evidence upon the subject as shall make all earnest men look upon the continuance of such a system as a national dishonour.

MEETING OF THE BALLAST-HEAVERS' WIVES.

BEFORE dealing with the Lumpers, or those who discharge the timber from ships — in contradistinction to the stevedores, or those who stow the cargoes of vessels,—I will give the following report of a meeting of the ballast-heavers' wives. It is the wife and children who are the real sufferers from the intemperance of the working-man; and being anxious to give the public some idea of the amount of misery entailed upon these poor creatures by the compulsory and induced drunkenness of the husbands, I requested as many as could leave their homes to meet me at the British and Foreign School, in Shakespeare-walk, Shadwell. The meeting consisted of the wives of ballast-heavers and coal-whippers. The wives of the coal-whippers had come there to contrast their present state with their past, with a view of showing the misery they had endured when their husbands were under the same thraldom to the publican as the ballast-heavers are now, and the comparative happiness which they have experienced since they were freed from it. They had attended unsolicited, in the hope, by making their statements public, of getting for the ballast-heavers the same freedom from the control of the publican which the coal-whippers had obtained.

The meeting consisted of the wives of ballast-heavers and coal-whippers, thirty-one were present. Of the thirty-one, nine were the wives of coal-whippers, the remaining twenty-two the wives of ballast-heavers. Many others, who had expressed a desire to attend, were prevented by family cares and arrangements; but, small as the meeting was comparatively, it afforded a very fair representation of the circumstances and characters of their husbands. For instance, those who were coal-whippers' wives appeared comfortable and "well to do." They wore warm gowns, had on winter-bonnets and clean tidy caps underneath; the ballast-heavers' wives, on the contrary, were mostly ragged, dejected, and anxious-looking.

An endeavour was made to ascertain in the first instance how many children each person had. This was done by questioning them separately; and from the answers it appeared that they all had families. Eight had one child each, the rest varied from two to eight, and one woman stated that she had twelve children, all of whom were living, but that only four resided now with her and her husband. Five had infants in their arms, and several had children sick, either at home or in some hospital.

In the next place the ballast-heavers' wives were asked whether their husbands worked under publicans? "All of them," was the reply, "work under publicans;" and, said one, "Worse luck for us,"—a sentiment that was very warmly concurred in by all the rest.

This fact having been specifically ascertained from each woman, we proceeded to inquire from them separately how much their husbands earned, and how much of their earnings was spent at the publicans' houses through which they obtained work, or where they were paid.

"My husband," said the first woman, "works under a publican, and I know that he earns now 12s. or 13s. a-week, but he brings home to me only half-a-crown, and sometimes not so much. He spends all the rest at a public-house where he gets his jobs, and often comes home drunk."

"My husband," exclaimed the second, "will sometimes get from 24s. to 28s. a-week, but I never see anything the likes o' that money from him. He spends it at the publican's. And when he has earned 24s. he will sometimes bring home only 2s. or 2s. 6d. We are badly off, you may be sure, when the money goes in this way. But my husband cannot help spending it, for he is obliged to get his jobs at the public-house."

"Last week," interposed another, "we had not one penny coming into our house; and the week before—which was Christmas week—my husband got two jobs which would come, he told me, to 8s. or 9s. if he had brought it all home; but he only brought me 1s. This was all the money I had to keep me and my five children for the whole week; and I'm sure I don't know how we got through. This is all owing to the public-house. And when we go to fetch our husbands at eleven or twelve o'clock at night they shut us out, and say they are not there, though we know very well they are inside in a back place. My husband has been kept in that back place many a time till two or three in the morning—then he has been turned out and come home drunk, without 6d. in his pocket, though the same day he has received 8s. or 9s. at the same public-house."

"They go to the public-house," added another woman, "to get jobs, and to curry favour they spend their money there, because if they did not spend their money they would never get a job. The men who will drink the greatest quantity of money will get the most jobs. This leaves their families and their wives miserable, and I am sure me and my poor family are miserable enough."

"But this," interposed a quiet, elderly woman, "is the beginning of the tenth week, in all of which my husband has only had four jobs, and all I have received of him during that time is 1s. 3½d. a-week, and we stand in 2s. 6d. a-week rent. I am sure I don't know how we get along. But our publicans are very civil, for my husband works for two. Still, if he does not drink a good part of it away we know very well he will get no more work."

"It is very little," said a female with an infant in her arms, "that my husband earns; and of what little he does earn he does not fetch much to me. He got one job last week, heaving 45 tons, and he fetched me home 1s. 6d. for it. I was then in lodgings at 1s. 6d. a-week, but I could not afford them, but now I'm in lodgings at 9d. a-week. This week he has no work yet. In Christmas week my man told me he earned 25s., and I believe he did, but he only fetched me home 8s. or 9s. on Saturday. My husband works for a publican, and it was at his house he spent his money. One day last week he asked the publican to give him a job, and he said, 'I cannot give you a job, for there is nothing against you on the slate but 1s.,' and so he got none there. My infant is six weeks old to-day, and this woman by me (appealing to the female next to her) knows well it is the truth that I tell—that for two nights in last week my child and myself were obliged to go to bed breadless. We had nothing neither of those two days. It was the same in one night the week before Christmas, though my husband received that night 8s., but all was spent at the public-house. On Christmas night we could not get any supper. We had no money, and I took the gown off my back and pawned it for 2s. to provide something for us to eat. I have nothing else to say but this—that whatever my husband earns I get little or nothing of it, for it goes to the public-house where he gets his jobs."

An infirm woman, approaching fifty years of age, who spoke in a tone of sorrowful resignation, said,—"We have had very little money coming in of late. My husband has been very bad for ten weeks back. He throws up blood; I suppose he has strained himself too much. All the money I have had for six weeks to keep us both has been 8s. If he was earning money he would bring it to me."

Another woman, "Not without the publican's allowance, I am sure."

The first woman, "No; the publican's allowance would be taken off; but the publican, you see, must have a little—I do not know how much it is, but they must have something if they give us their jobs."

This woman was here asked if her husband ever came home drunk?

"Yes," she replied; "many a time he comes home drunk; but he must have the drink to get the jobs."

A number of other women having made statements confirmatory of the above:—

"Do you think," the meeting was asked, "your husbands would be sober as well as industrious men if they could be got away from the public-house system of employment and payment of wages?"

"God Almighty bless you!" exclaimed one woman, "they would love us and their families all the better for it! We should all be much the better for it."

"And so say all of us!" was the next and perfectly unanimous exclamation.

"If we could see that day," said one who had spoken before, "our families would have little to complain of."

Another added, "The night-houses ought to be closed. That would be one good thing."

Some inquiries were then made as to whe-ther these poor women were ill-treated by their husbands when they came home in a state of intoxication. There was a good deal of hesitation before any answers could be obtained. At last one woman said, "her husband did certainly beat her, of course; but then," she added, "he did not know what he was doing."

"I," said another, "should not know what it was to have an angry word with my husband if he was always sober. He is a quiet man—very, when the drink is out of him; but we have many words together when he is tipsy; and ——" she stopped without completing the sentence.

Several others gave similar testimony; and many declared that it was the public-house system which led their husbands to drink.

One woman here said that the foremen of gangs, as well as the publican, helped to reduce the ballast-heaver's earnings; for they gave work to men who took lodgings from them, though they did not occupy them.

This was confirmed by another woman, who spoke with great warmth upon the subject. She said that married men who could not afford to spend with the publican and lodge with the foremen in the manner pointed out, would be sure to have no work. Other men went straight from one job to another, while her own husband and other women's husbands had been three or four weeks without lifting a shovelful of ballast. She considered this was very hard on men who had families.

A question was here asked, whether any women were present whose husbands, in order to obtain work, were obliged to pay for lodgings which they did not use?

One immediately rose and said, "They do it regularly at a publican's in Wapping; and I know the men that have paid for them have had six jobs together, when my husband has had none for weeks." "There are now," added another, "fourteen at that very place who never lodge there, though they are paying for lodgings."

They were next asked, who had suffered from want owing to their husbands drinking their earnings, as described at the public-houses in question?

"Starvation has been my lot," said one. "And mine," added another. "My children," said a third, "have often gone to bed at night without breaking their fast the whole length of the day." "And mine," said one, "have many a time gone without a bit or sup of anything all the day, through their father working for the publican."

"I cannot," exclaimed the next, "afford my children a ha'porth of milk a-day."

"Many a time," said one, who appeared to be very much moved, "have I put my four children to bed, when the only meal they have had the whole day has been 1lb. of bread; but it's of no use opening my mouth."

" 1,' said the last, " have been in London twenty-seven years, and during that time I can safely say I have never taken myself a single glass of spirits or anything else ; but in that time I have suffered the martyrdom of forty years — all through my husband and the public-house. I have two children who bring me in, one of them 2s. 6d. and the other 6s. 6d. a-week, which is all we have, for my husband gets nearly nothing. If he could bring his earnings home, instead of spending them at a public-house, we should be very comfortable."

These questions led to one concerning the late-hour system at the public-houses frequented by the ballast-heavers.

" I often go for my husband," said one, " at one or two o'clock in the morning, after I know he has been paid ; but they have kept him in a back apartment away from me, till I have threatened to smash the windows if they did not let him out. I threatened to smash the windows because my children were wanting the money for bread, which he was spending there. If our husbands were inclined to come home sober there is little chance, for they have cards and bagatelle to keep them till they become heady, and when they are become heady, there is nothing left for their families — then the publicans kick our poor men out, and lock the doors."

This statement was confirmed, and after several other persons had described their feelings,—

The coal-whippers' wives were asked whether or not their condition and that of their families had been improved since the system of carrying on the trade had been altered by the Legislature ?

The answer was a most decisive affirmative. Their husbands, they said, used to spend all, or very nearly all, their earnings with the publicans ; but now, when they got a good ship, they brought home the greatest part of their earnings, which was sufficient to make their families comfortable. Their husbands had become quite different men. They used to ill-treat them when they were paid at a public-house — very much so, because of the drink ; but now they were very much altered, because they were become sober men to what they were. None were now distressed to provide for their families, and if there was plenty of work they would be quite happy. The improvement, one woman said, must be very great, otherwise there would not be so many institutions and benefit societies, pension societies, and schools or their children.

This declaration was very warmly applauded by the wives of the ballast-heavers. They declared that similar measures would produce similar benefits in their case, and they hoped the day would soon come when they should be secure in the enjoyment of them.

So terminated the proceedings.

LUMPERS.

THE " Lumpers" are, if possible, in a more degraded state than the ballast-heavers ; they are not, it is true, under the same amount of oppression from the publican, but still they are so besotted with the drink which they are tempted to obtain from the publicans who employ them, as to look upon the man who tricks them out of their earnings rather as a friend than an enemy.

The lumpers make, I am informed, during six months in the year, as much as 24s. ; and during the other six months they have nothing to do. Of the 24s. that they earn in their busy time, 20s. it will be seen is spent in the public-house. One master-lumper, who is a publican, employs as many as 100 men. This information I have, not only from the men themselves, but from the managers of the Commercial Docks, where the greater number of the lumpers are engaged. The 100 men in the publican's employ, as will be seen from the evidence of the wives, spend upon an average 1l. a-week in the house, taking generally but 4s. home to their wives and families : so that no less a sum than 100l. a-week is squandered in the publican-contractor's house by the working men in drink. There is not only a pay-night, but two " draw-nights" are appointed in the week, as a means of inveigling the men to their master's tap-room ; and indeed the same system, which gives the greatest drunkard the best chance of work, prevails among the lumpers as among the ballast-heavers. The effect of this is, that the lumpers are the most drunken, debased, and poverty-stricken of all the classes of labouring men that I have yet seen ; for, earning more than the ballast-heavers, they of course have more to spend in the public-house.

I made it a point of looking more minutely into the state of these men on the Sunday, for I have found that on that day it is easy to tell the habits of men by their external appearance. The greater part that I saw were either intoxicated, or else reeking of liquor as early as eleven o'clock on the Sunday morning. One foreman was decently dressed, it was true ; but then he was sent to me, I was credibly informed, by the master-publican, who had heard of my previous investigations, to give me a false impression as to the state of the labourers ; the rest of the men that I saw were unwashed and unshaven, even up to five and six in the afternoon of that day. Their clothes were the same tattered and greasy garments that I had seen them in the day before ; indeed the wives of the lumpers appeared to be alone alive to the degradation of their husbands. At one house that I visited late on the Sunday evening, I found two of the children in one corner of the small close room on the bare boards, covered with a piece of old carpet, and four more boys and girls stowed away at the top and bottom of the one bed in which the rest of the family slept. Dirty wet clothes were hanging to dry on lines across the room; and the face of the wife, who was alone, in all her squalid misery, was black and gashed with cuts and bruises. Not a step I took but I was dogged by some foreman or other, in the hopes of putting me on the wrong scent. I had arranged with the men on Saturday morning to have a meeting with them on that night after their labour, but on going to the appointed place I found not one labouring man there; and I learnt the next day that the publican had purposely deferred paying them till a late hour, so that they might have no chance of meeting me. On Monday morning, while at the office of the Superintendent of the Commercial Dock Company, one of the lumpers staggered drunk into the room, intent upon making some insolent demand or other. That this drunkenness, with all its attendant vices, is not the fault of the lumpers, but the necessary consequence of the system under which they are employed, no man who has seen the marked difference between the coal-whippers and that class of labourers who still work out of the public-house, can for a moment doubt. The sins of the labouring man, so far as I have seen, are, in this instance, most indisputably the sins of his employer. If he is drunken, it is his master who makes him so: if he is poor, his house bare, his wife ragged, his children half-clothed, half-fed, and wholly uneducated, it is mainly because his master tricks him out of his earnings at the public-house.

Let me now give a description of the lumpers' labour, and then of their earnings. The timber-trade is divided by the custom of the trade into two classes, called timber and deals. By "timber" is meant what is brought in uncut logs; this is American red pine, yellow pine, elm, ash, oak, and birch. The teak-trade is more recent, and seems to be an exception to the classification I have mentioned: it is generally described as teak; mahogany and dye-woods again are not styled timber. The deals are all sawn ready for the carpenter or joiner's use. At the Custom-house the distinctions are, hewn and sawn woods; that is, timber and deals. On timber there is now a duty of 1s. per load (a load being fifty cubic feet) and on deals of 2s. The deals are sawn in Canada, where immense steam-mills have been erected for the purpose. The advantage to the trader in having this process effected in Canada rather than in this country, seems to be this: the deals brought over prepared, as I have described, of different lengths, varying from six feet to twenty, while three inches is a usual thickness, are ready for the workman's purpose, and no refuse-matter forms a part of them. Were the pine brought in logs, the bark and the unevenness of the tree would add to the freight for what

was only valueless. Timber and deals require about the same time for their discharge. The largest vessels that enter into this trade in the port of London are to be found in the West India South Dock, formerly the City Canal. On one occasion in this dock a vessel of 800 tons, containing 24,000 deals and ends, was discharged in twenty-six working hours—forty-five men being employed. I am informed that twenty men would discharge a ship of 600 tons of timber and deals in seven days. Forty men will do it in four days. In order to become acquainted with the system of lumping, I went on board a vessel in the river where a gang of twenty men were at work. She was a vessel of 600 tons, from Quebec. She lay alongside the Flora, a Norwegian vessel—the first timber-ship that had reached the port of London since the change in the Navigation Laws had come into operation. The Flora's cargo was 900 pieces of timber, which would be discharged by her crew, as the lumpers are only employed in British vessels. The vessel that I visited, and which lay next the Flora, had her hold and the between-decks (which might be thirty-eight yards in length) packed closely with deals. She held between 17,000 and 18,000 deals. She was being lightened in the river before going into dock; twenty men were at work in two barges, well moored alongside, close to two portholes in the stern of the ship. There were three men in each barge who received and packed the deals into the barge as they were thrust out of the portholes; the larger deals were carried along by two men as soon as a sufficient clearance had been made to enable them to run along—at first, bent half-double. The two men who carried the deals ran along in a sort of jog-trot motion, keeping time, so that the motion relieved the pressure of the weight; the men all said it was easier to run than to walk with the deals: the shorter deals (ends) were carried, one by each man, who trotted on in the same measured steps,—each man, or each two men employed, delivering his or their deal to one especial man in the barge, so that a constant communication from the ship to the barge was kept up, and the work went on without hitch or stoppage. This same vessel, on a former occasion, was discharged in thirty-six hours, which shows (as there were between 17,000 and 18,000 carryings and deliverings of the deals) how rapidly the work is conducted. The timber is all dragged from the holds or the between-decks of the ship by machines; the lumpers house it from its place in the ship by means of winches, tackles, and dogs—which latter are iron links to lay hold of the logs. Three of these winches and tackles are stationed at equal distances on each side of a large ship, and thus with the aid of crowbars the several pieces of timber are dragged along the hold and then dropped gently into the water, either in the dock or in the river, and floated in rafts to its destination. All "timber" is floated, as a rule. Sometimes when the ship is discharged in dock, timber or deals are let down a slide on to a platform, and so carried to the pile or the waggon. Contractors are employed by the ship-owners in the West India Docks, as they will do some ships cheaper by 10*l.* than the company could afford to do it. The ship-owners bear the expense of discharging the ship.

The following evidence of a lumper was given unwillingly, indeed it was only by a series of cross-questionings that any approximation to the truth could be extracted from him. He was evidently in fear of losing his work; and the tavern to which I had gone to take his statement was filled with foremen watching and intimidating him. He said:

" I am a working lumper, or labourer at discharging timber or deal-ships. I have been sixteen years at the work. I should think that there are more than two hundred men at Deptford who are constantly engaged at the work: there are a great many more working lumpers living at Limehouse, Poplar, and Blackwall. These do the work principally of the West India Docks; and when the work is slack there and brisk at the Commercial, East Country, or Grand Surrey Canal Docks, the men cross the water and get a job on the Surrey side of the river. In the summer a great many Irish labourers seek for work as lumpers. They come over from Ireland in the Cork boats. I should say there are altogether upwards of 500 regular working lumpers; but in the summer there are at least 200 more, owing to the number of Irish who come to England to look for work at that time of the year. The wages of the regular lumpers are not less when the Irish come over in the summer, nor do the men get a less quantity of work to do. There are more timber and deal-ships arriving at that season, so more hands are required to discharge them. The ships begin to arrive in July, and they continue coming in till January. After that time they lay up till March, when they sail for the foreign ports. Between January and July the regular working lumpers have little or nothing to do. During that time there are scarcely any timber or deal ships coming in; and the working lumpers then try to fall in with anything they can, either ballasting a ship, or carrying a few deals to load a timber-carriage, or doing a little ' tide work.' Between July and January the work is very brisk. We are generally employed every day for those six months. Sometimes we lose a day after lightening a ship in the river, while the vessel is going into dock. We call it lightening a ship when she is laden too heavy, and draws too much water to enter the docks. In such a case we generally begin discharging the timber or deals in the river, either off Deptford or Blackwall, according as the ship may be for the docks on the Middlesex or Surrey side. In the river we discharge the deals into lighters, whereas when the ship is in the dock we generally discharge along a stage on to the shore. Timber we put overboard in both cases, and leave it for the raftsmen to put together into rafts, and float into the timber-ponds of the different docks. The deals we merely land. It is our duty to put them ashore and nothing more. After that the deal-porters take them and sort them, and pile them. They sort the white from the yellow deals, and each kind into different lengths, and then arrange them in piles all along the dock.

" Our usual time of working is from six to six in the summer time and from daylight to dark in the winter. We always work under a foreman. There are two foremen lumpers to almost every ship that we discharge; and they engage the men, who work in gangs under them. Each gang consists of from 4 to 12 men, according as the size of the ship is large, or she is wanted to be discharged quickly. I have known as many as 30 lumpers engaged on one ship; she was 1000 tons, and wanted to be got out quick, so that she might make another voyage before the winter set in abroad.

" The foreman and men are employed by the master-lumper. Some of the master-lumpers are publicans; some others keep chandlers' shops, and others do nothing else that I know of. The master pays the working men 3*s.* 6*d.* a-day, and the foreman 1*s.* extra. We are settled with every Saturday night. We have two draw-nights in each week; that is, the master advances either a part or the whole of our earnings, if we please, on Tuesday and Thursday nights. I work under a publican. My master has only gone into the public line very lately. I don't think he's been at it more than eighteen months. He has been a master-lumper I should say for these 10 or 12 years past. I worked under him before he had a public-house. Then he paid every Tuesday, Thursday, and Saturday nights, at the same house he is now proprietor of. The master-lumper always pays the men he employs at the public-house, whether they are publicans or not.

" My master employs, I should say, in the spring season, from 80 to 100 hands regularly: and most of these meet at his house on Tuesday and Thursday nights, and all of them on Saturday night, either to be settled with in full or have a part of their wages advanced. We are usually paid at 7 o'clock in the evening. I have been paid as late as 3 o'clock on Sunday morning; but that was some years ago, and I was all that time in the public-house. We go straight to the public-house after we have done our work.

" At this time of the year we knock off work at dark, that is, at five [I am informed at the Commercial Docks that the usual hour is four] o'clock, and we remain at our master's until pay-time, that is 7 o'clock. This we do for three nights a-week certain; and after our work at other nights we mostly meet at our master's public-house. The men generally draw from 2s. to 4s., and on a Thursday night the same sum is advanced to them. The men are not enforced to spend anything in the house. Each man has a little beer while the master is getting ready to pay him on the draw-nights; and he generally remains in the house after he has received his money some time, as he thinks proper. On a draw-night in the brisk season many out of the hundred he employs will stop drinking till 10 o'clock. Some go away immediately after they have drawn their money. At least half stop for some time, that is, till 10 o'clock. Some sit there and spend all they draw. All the beer that the lumpers have on board ship is supplied by the master. He supplies any quantity that is wanted. The reason why he keeps the public-house is to have the right of supplying the men with beer. He wouldn't, of course, like to see us take beer from any other house than his; if we did he would give us the sack. Every master-lumper works out of a public-house, and the men must have their beer from the house that he works out of; and if they don't, why they ain't wanted. We generally take about two pots per man a-day from the house when we go to our work in the morning. On a Saturday night we mostly stop longer than on the draw-nights. Upon an average, the working lumpers I should say spend about 2s. a-day in the season in the public-house. [It will have been seen, that the lumpers' wives whom I saw declare that the men spend 20s. out of every 24s.] After a hard week's work I think they have generally 8s. or 9s. out of the 1l. 4s. that they earn at the busiest time of the year. I myself have taken home as little as 5s. [According to this statement, assuming that there are 100 hands—many say that there are more—regularly employed out of this public-house in the spring season, and spending each upon an average from 12s. to 20s., or say 16s. a-week, as much as 80l. a-week is squandered in beer.] I should say, taking all the year round, the men make 10s. 6d. a-week. For at least four months in the year there is no work at all; and for two months more it is very slack. I am a married man with one child: when I am in full work I take home 5s. a-week at the least. My wife and child has to suffer for it all."

Let me now cite the following table, which I have been at considerable trouble in obtaining, as the only means of arriving at a correct estimate as to the collective earnings of the "journeymen lumpers," or men generally engaged in discharging the cargoes of the British timber and deal ships. The information has in the three principal instances been derived directly from the books of the Dock Companies, through the courtesy and consideration of the superintendents and directors, to whom I am greatly indebted.

NUMBER OF SHIPS WOOD-LADEN DISCHARGED AT THE DIFFERENT DOCKS IN 1849.

	By the Dock Company.		By Lumpers.		By Crews.		Total.	
	Ships.	Tonnage.	Ships.	Tonnage.	Ships.	Tonnage.	Ships.	Tonnage.
West India Docks	36	22,556	69	24,347	24	6,796	129	53,699
Commercial Docks	2	1,186	154	63,213	259	75,096	415	139,495
Grand Surrey Canal	..	..	153	45,900	59	17,000	212	62,900
East Country Docks	..	..	11	3,400	64	19,091	75	22,500
Regent's Canal	..	..	2	600	..	..	2	600
	38	23,742	389	137,469	406	117,983	833	279,194

By the above returns it will be seen, that in the course of that year 389 timber and deal ships, of 137,469 tons burthen collectively, were discharged by lumpers. This at 9d. per ton, which is the price usually given by the Dock Companies, would give 5,155l. 1s. 9d. as the gross amount paid to the contractors. The master-lumper derives little or no profit out of this sum directly. This will be evident from the subjoined statement. A gentleman at the West India Docks, who has been all his life connected with the timber trade, informs us that twenty men will discharge a wood-laden ship in seven days. Now,—

	£	s.	d.
20 men at 3s. 6d. per day for seven days, comes to . .	24	10	0
And 600 tons at 9d. per ton, to	22	10	0
So that the master-lumper, by this account, would lose by the job at the very least .	2	0	0

This statement is fully borne out by the fact that the master-lumpers will often agree to discharge a ship for 10l. less than the company could possibly afford to do it for with their own men. The question then arises, How is it that the master-lumper is enabled to do this and live? This is easily answered. He is generally either a publican himself or connected with one, and the journeymen in his employ spend at his public-house, according to the account of the wives, five-sixths of their wages in drink, or 1*l.* out of every 24*s.* they earn. Say, however, that only four-fifths of the gross earnings are thus consumed, then four thousand and odd out of the 5,155*l.* will go to the publican, and one thousand and odd pounds to the men.

TIMBER-DOCK LABOURERS.

Having already given an account of the supply and consumption of timber throughout the country generally, I shall now speak of the importations into London, and more especially of the condition of the labourers connected with the foreign and colonial timber trade.

The quantity of colonial and foreign timber that has been brought into the port of London since the year 1843 has been as follows :—

	1844.	1845.	1846.	1847.	1848.	1849.
Colonial deals and battens (in pieces) . . .	2,025,000	2,349,000	2,355,000	3,339,000	2,740,000	2,722,000
Foreign ditto (in ditto)	2,130,000	2,290,000	1,242,000	1,996,000	2,044,000	1,903,000
Total pieces .	4,155,000	4,639,000	3,597,000	5,335,000	4,784,000	4,625,000
Colonial timber (in loads)	57,200	55,800	53,600	49,600	38,300	38,600
Foreign ditto (in do.) .	58,200	68,100	86,000	79,100	69,000	61,400
Total loads .	115,400	123,900	139,600	128,700	107,300	100,000

The consumption of the metropolis has been little less than the quantity imported. In the six years above enumerated the total importation of foreign and colonial deals and battens was 27,135,000 pieces, of which 26,695,573 were consumed in London; and the total importation of foreign and colonial timber was 714,900 loads, of which 644,224 were consumed. This gives an average annual importation of 4,522,500 deals and battens, of which only 73,238 have been sent out of the country every year. Of timber, the average annual importation is 119,150 loads, and the average annual exportation only 11,779 loads.

The number of wood-laden ships that have entered the port of London since 1840, together with the countries whence they came, is given below. By this we shall perceive that our trade with Norway in this respect has sunk to exactly one-half of what it was ten years back, while that with Sweden and Finland has been very nearly doubled in the same time. The timber-ships from the Prussian ports have increased little less than one-third, while those from Russia have decreased in the same proportion. The trade with Quebec and Montreal also appears to be much greater than it was in 1840, though compared with 1841 there has been a considerable falling off; that of New Brunswick and Nova Scotia remains very nearly the same as it was at the beginning of the decennial period. Altogether the great change appears to have been the decline of the Norwegian and Russian timber-trade, and the increase of that with Sweden and Prussia. It is also worthy of notice, that notwithstanding the increase of population, the number of wood-laden ships entering the port of London every year has not materially increased within the last ten years.

THE NUMBER OF CARGOES OF TIMBER, DEALS, AND BATTENS, IMPORTED INTO LONDON IN THE FOLLOWING YEARS.

	1840.	1841.	1842.	1843.	1844.	1845.	1846.	1847.	1848.	1849.
Christiana and Christiansund .	49	50	47	27	36	27	22	32	39	23
Other ports of Norway . .	52	43	38	36	49	39	17	28	25	27
Gothenburg	61	64	49	59	59	66	30	67	55	41
Swedish ports and Finland .	85	84	85	102	90	149	103	101	138	154
Russian ports	181	108	130	119	163	115	146	91	113	134
Prussian ports . . .	70	70	52	104	143	124	109	167	108	100
Quebec and Montreal . .	168	224	188	230	206	206	166	216	179	195
New Brunswick and Nova Scotia	104	97	62	134	90	102	127	145	108	105
Sierra Leone, Maulmein, &c. .	16	20	29	31	5	10	20	21	13	20
	786	760	681	842	841	838	740	868	778	799

The next step in our inquiry is, What becomes of the 800 wood-laden ships that annually enter the port of London? Whither do they go to be unladen? to what docks, or places of "special security," are they consigned to be discharged and to have their cargoes delivered or bonded?

For this purpose there are five docks, three of which lie on the Surrey side of the river. These three are the Commercial Docks, the Grand Surrey Canal Dock, and the East Country Dock, and they are almost contiguous to each other, the Surrey Canal Dock lying immediately alongside the Commercial, and the East Country at the upper end of it. They are situated in, and indeed occupy, nearly the whole of that small cape of land which is formed by the bending of the river between the Pool and Limehouse Reach. The docks on the Middlesex side of the river, which are used for the reception and unlading of timber-ships, are the West India and the Regent's Dock, or the entrance to the Regent's Canal.

The number of wood-laden ships that have entered the three principal docks for the last ten years is given below. I am informed by Mr. Jones of the Commercial Docks, that for every ship above 100 tons six men are required to sort and pile away. Rafting from ships of the above burden requires one or two men daily, according to circumstances.

THE NUMBER OF WOOD-LADEN SHIPS WHICH ENTERED THE DIFFERENT DOCKS UNDERMENTIONED IN THE FOLLOWING YEARS.

Year.	West India Docks.		Commercial Docks.		Grand Surrey Docks.	
	Vessels.	Tons.	Vessels.	Tons.	Vessels.	Tons.
1840	155	62,024	211	65,809	135	40,447
1841	201	82,196	265	70,438	114	34,594
1842	136	54,931	250	87,124	100	29,596
1843	169	71,211	368	121,846	108	31,299
1844	121	53,581	480	142,223	173	48,896
1845	149	70,514	424	137,047	155	43,211
1846	182	88,308	351	111,189	195	50,908
1847	228	124,114	423	143,966	226	62,433
1848	138	76,650	412	132,406	195	53,423
1849	138	67,860	410	136,329	212	58,780
Total	1,617	751,389	3,544	1,148,377	1,613	453,587
Average Number of Ships per Year, and their Average Tonnage	161	4464	354	324	161	281

The foreign and colonial timber trade is, then, confined to five of the seven docks belonging to the port of London. Of these five, three—the Commercial, the Grand Surrey Canal, and the East Country—are situate on the Surrey side of the river, occupying altogether an area of 172½ acres, of which 100½ are water and 72 land, and offering accommodation and protection for no less than 678 vessels. Here the principal part of the timber and deal trade is carried on, the Commercial receiving the greatest number of wood-laden vessels, perhaps greater than any other dock in the world. These, together with that portion of the West India Dock which is devoted to the same purpose, make the entire extent of the timber docks attached to the port of London about 250 acres, of which upwards of 140 are water—a space sufficient to give berths to no less than 940 ships.

I now come to speak of the condition and earnings of the labourers connected with the timber and hard-wood trade. Of these, it appears there are 1030 men casually employed at all the timber docks, of whom only 132 obtain work all the year round. How the 900 casual deal-porters and rafters live during the six months of the year that the slack season usually lasts in the timber trade, I cannot conceive. As not a sixpence of their earnings is saved in the brisk season, their fate in the winter is to suffer privations and afflictions which they only know.

I shall begin with the state of the dock-labourers employed at the foreign and hard-wood trade. This trade is confined mainly, if not solely, to the West India Dock.

Concerning this branch of the wood trade, I give below the statement of a man who has worked at it for many years, and in doing so, I wish to draw attention to the latter part of the narrative, as a proof of what I have repeatedly asserted respecting the regard exhibited by the authorities of the West India

Dock, and in particular by Mr. Knight, the superintendent, for the welfare of all the men, whether directly or even indirectly employed by them.

This indirect employment of workmen, however, is the great bane of the industrious classes. Whether the middleman goes by the name of sweater, chamber-master, lumper, or contractor, it is this trading operative who is the great means of reducing the wages of his fellow working-men. To make a profit out of the employment of his brother-operatives he must obtain a lower-class labour. He cares nothing about the quality of the work, so long as the workmen can get through it somehow, and will labour at a cheaper rate. Hence it becomes a business with him to hunt out the lowest grades of working men—the drunken, the dishonest, the idle, the vagabond, and the unskilful men—because these, being unable to obtain employment at the regular wages of the sober, honest, industrious, and skilful portion of the trade, he can obtain their labour at a lower rate than what is usually paid. " Boy-labour or thief-labour," said a middleman on a large scale, " what do I care, so long as I can get my work done cheap." I have already shown that the wives of the sweaters not only parade the streets of London on the look-out for youths raw from the country, but that they make periodical trips to the poorest provinces of Ireland, in order to obtain workmen at the lowest possible rate. I have shown, moreover, that foreigners are annually imported from the Continent for the same purpose, and that among the chamber-masters in the shoe trade, the child-market at Bethnal-green, as well as the workhouses, are continually ransacked for the means of obtaining a cheaper kind of labour. All my investigations go to prove that it is chiefly by means of the middleman-system that the wages of the working men are reduced. This contractor—this trading operative—uses the most degraded of the class as a means of underselling the worthy and skilful labourers, and of ultimately dragging the better down to the abasement of the worst. If men cannot subsist on lower prices, then he takes apprentices or hires children; or if workmen of character and worth refuse to work at less than the ordinary rate, then he seeks out the moral refuse of the trade, those whom none else will employ; or else he flies to the workhouse and the gaol to find labour meet for his purpose. Backed by this cheap and refuse labour, he offers his work at lower prices, and so keeps on reducing and reducing the wages of his brethren until all sink in poverty, wretchedness, and vice. I am therefore the more anxious to impress upon the minds of those gentlemen who are actuated by a sincere regard for the interests and comforts of the men in their employ, the evils of such a system; for, however great may be the saving of trouble effected by it, yet, unless it be strictly watched (as I must confess it is at the West India and Commercial Docks) it can only be maintained by the employment of a cheaper and worse class labourer, and therefore must result in the degradation of the workmen. I have said thus much, because I find this contract system the general practice at all the wood-docks, and because I am convinced that the gentlemen to whom the management of those docks is entrusted, Mr. Knight, Mr. Jones, and Mr. Cannan, have the welfare of the men in their employ sincerely at heart.

Of the evils of lumping, or discharging wood-ships by contract, I have already treated at considerable length. Under that system, it will be remembered, I showed that the contractor, who is commonly a publican, makes his profit, not by cheapening the labourer, but by intoxicating him. Like the contractor for ballast, he gets his money out of the drunkenness of the workmen, and by this means is enabled to undersell the dock proprietors; or, in other words, to discharge the wood-laden ships at a less rate than they could possibly afford to do it for by the fair and honourable employment of their men. Of the effects of this system—the drunkenness of the men, the starvation of the wives, the squalor and ignorance of the children, the wretchedness and desolation of the homes, I have already treated at some length: and it will be seen hereafter that in those docks where the supervision that is maintained at the West India and Commercial is not kept up, the labourers are reduced to almost the same state of poverty and destitution.

But to return. A man living in a small room in a poor neighbourhood, but in a tidy apartment, and with a well-kept little garden at the back, gave me the following account of his earnings and labour in the mahogany department of the West India Docks :—

"I have worked in the West India Docks for eleven years, and for the last half of that time in the mahogany part of the wood-yard. Before that, I was eleven years in the merchant service as able seaman; but I got married, and thought I could do better in the docks; for, after all, what is 18*l.* a-year, supposing I had the luck to be at sea nine months every year at 2*l.* a-month—what is 18*l.* a-year, sir, to keep a wife and family on, as well as a man himself when he's ashore? At the West India Docks, we unload the mahogany, or logwood, or fancy wood from the ships, and pile them wherever they're ordered. We work in gangs of six or seven, with a master at the head of the gang; the logs are got out of the hold with a purchase and a jigger, and heaved ashore by a crane on to a truck, and we drag the truck to the place to stow the timber. In the wood-yards a machine lifts the timber up, by us men turning handles to work the machine, and puts it into its place in the warehouse. We are paid 2*s.* 6*d.* a-day, working from eight to four. If only employed for four hours—and we're not

set to work for less than four hours—we have
1s. 4d. If I could get 2s. 6d. a-day all the year
through, I'd be a happy man; but I can't.
Me, and such as me, earns 10s., 11s., or as far
as 15s. a-week when we are wanted. But take
the year through, I make between 9s. and 10s.
a-week; out of that I have to keep a wife and
four children. I've lost one child, and my wife
can get little or nothing most times to do with
her needle; and if she does get work, what can
she make at five farthings or three-halfpence
a shirt for the slop-shops? My eldest child,
however, does make 1s. or 1s. 6d. a-week. I
live on bread and butter, with a drop of beer
now and then, six days out of the seven. On
Sundays we mostly have a shilling's worth of
meat—bullock's head generally. Sometimes
our work is very hard, with heavy lifting. A
weakly man's no use, and I've wondered how I
have the strength I have on bread and butter.
We are all paid in the dock, and there's nobody
allowed to get the men to drink, or to traffic
with them anyhow, but in a fair, regular way.
There's plenty hang about every day who would
work a day's work for 2s.: there's a good many
Irish. I don't know that there's any foreigners,
without it be on the sugar side. Sometimes a
hundred men are employed in our part of the
business; to-day there was from forty to fifty
at work, and a hundred more was to be had if
they'd been wanted. Jobs often come in in a
lump—all at once, or none at all; very often
with the wind. We run backwards and forwards to the sugar-side or the Surrey Dock, as
we expect to be wanted. We don't know what
the foremen of the gangs get, but the company
won't allow them to underpay us; and I have
nothing to complain about, either of them or
the company, though we're bad off. The foreman can pick his men. Many of us has to go
to the parish. Once I earned only 3s. in three
weeks. Our best time is from June or July,
continuing on for two, three, four, or five
months, as happens. We live half the year
and starve the t'other. There's very few teetotalers among us—men want beer if they
live upon bread and butter; there's many I
know lives on a meal a-day, and that's bread
and butter. There's no drunkards among our
men. We're mostly married men with families; most poor men is married, I think.
Poor as I am, a wife and family's something
to cling to like."

The Timber and Deal Trade.

I now come to the timber and deal trade.
The labourers connected with this portion of
the trade are rafters or raftsmen, and deal or
stave-porters; these are either permanently or
casually employed. I shall give an account of
each, as well as of the system pursued at each
of the docks, beginning with the Commercial,
because it does the most extensive business in
this branch of the wood-trade; and here let
me acknowledge the obligations I am under
to Mr. Jones, the intelligent and courteous
superintendent, for much valuable information.

The working lumpers, as I before explained,
are the labourers employed to discharge all
wood-laden vessels, except foreign ships, which
are discharged by their own crews; the vessels
unladen by the lumpers are discharged sometimes in the dock, and sometimes (when too
heavily laden) in the river. The cargoes of
wood-laden vessels are termed either landed
or rafted goods; the "landed" goods are deals,
battens, sleepers, wainscot logs, and indeed all
but hewn timber, which is "rafted." When a
vessel is unladen in the river, the landed goods
are discharged by lumpers, who also load the
lighters, whereas in dock the lumpers discharge them into the company's barges, which
are loaded by them as well. With smaller
vessels, however, which occasionally go alongside, the lumpers discharge directly to the
shore, where the goods are received by the
company's porters. The lumpers never work
on shore. Of the porters working on shore
there are two kinds, viz. deal and stave-porters,
whose duty it is to receive the landed goods
and to pile and sort them, either along the
quay or in the building ground, if duty has to
be paid upon them.

The hewn-timber, or rafted goods, the lumpers thrust through the porthole into the water,
and there the raftsman receives them, puts
them into lengths and sizes, and then arranges
them in floats—there being eighteen pieces to
a float. If the ship is discharged in the river,
the rafter floats the timber to the docks, and
then to the ponds of the company. If, however, the ship is discharged in dock, then the
raftman floats the timber only from the main
dock to the ponds.

The rafters are all freemen, for otherwise
they could not work on the river; they must
have served seven years to a waterman, and
they are obliged to pay 3s. a-year to the Waterman's Company for a license. There are sixteen or seventeen rafters (all preferable men)
employed by the Commercial Dock Company,
and in busy times there are occasionally as
many as forty casual rafters, or "pokers," as
they are called, from their poking about the
docks for a job: these casual men are not
capable of rafting a ship, nor are they free
watermen, they are only employed to float the
timber from the ship up to the ponds and stow
it, or to attend to deliveries. The skill of the
rafter lies in gauging and sorting the timber
according to size, quality, and ownership, and
making it up into floats. It is only an experienced rafter who can tell the different sizes,
qualities, and owners of the timber; this the
pokers, or casual rafters, are unable to do.
The pokers, again, cannot float the timber
from the river to the ponds; this is owing to
two reasons: first, they are not allowed to do
so on account of not being free watermen;
and, secondly, they are unable to do so from

the difficulty of navigation. The pokers work exclusively in the docks; neither the rafters nor pokers work under contractors, but the deal and stave-porters invariably do.

The following statement of a rafter at the Commercial Dock I had from a prudent, well-behaved, sober man. He was in company with another man, employed in the same capacity at the same docks, and they both belonged to the better class of labouring men:—

"I am a rafter at the Commercial Dock. I have been working at that dock for the last six years, in the same capacity, and before that I was rafter at the Surrey Dock for between five and six years. I served my apprenticeship to a waterman. I was bound when I was sixteen. We are not allowed to work till we have served two years. In my apprenticeship I was continually engaged in timber-towing, lightering, and at times sculling; but that I did only when the other business was slack. After my time was out I went lightering; and about a dozen years after that I took to rafting. I had been a rafter at the Surrey Canal before then —while I was in my apprenticeship indeed. I had 18s. a-week when I first commenced rafting at the Surrey Canal; but that, of course, all went to my master. I was with the Surrey Canal about two years as rafter, and then I joined another party at 30s. a-week in the same capacity; this party rented a wharf of the Surrey Canal Company, and I still worked in the dock. There I worked longer time— four hours longer; the wages would have been as good at the Surrey Canal at outside work as they were with the second party I joined. The next place that I went to as rafter was the Commercial Dock, where I am now, and have been for the last six years. I am paid by the week. When I work at the dock I have 1l. 1s. a-week, and when I am rafting short-hour ships (i.e. ships from which we work only from eight till four) I get 4s. per day. When I am working long-hour ships (i.e. ships at which the working lasts from six till six) I get 5s. a-day; the other rafters employed by the company are paid the same. Our wages have remained the same ever since I have been in the business; all the other men have been lowered, such as carpenters, labourers, watchmen, deal-porters and the like; but we are not constant men, or else I dare say ours would have been reduced too. They have lowered the wages of the old hands, who have been there for years, 1s. a-week. Formerly they had 1l. 1s., now they get 1l.; the men are dissatisfied. The wages of the casual dock-labourers have been reduced a great deal more than those of the constant men; three months ago they all had 18s. a-week, and now the highest wages paid to the casual labourers is 15s. The reason why the wages of the rafters have not been lowered is, I take it, because we are freemen, and there are not so many to be had who could supply our places. Not one of a hundred lightermen and watermen are able

to raft. We are only employed at certain times of the year. Our busy time begins at July, and ends in October. We are fully employed about four months in the year, and get during that time from 1l. 1s. to 30s. a-week, or say 25s. upon an average. The rest of our time we fills up as we can. Some of the rafters has boats, and they look out for a job at sculling; but that's poor enough now."

"Ah, very poor work, indeed," said an old weather-beaten man who was present, and had had 40 years' experience at the business. "When I first joined it, it was in the war time," he added, "and then I was scarcely a day idle, and now I can't get work for better than half my time."

"For the other eight months," continued the other man, "I should think the rafters upon an average make 5s. a-week. Some of them has boats, and some gets a job at timber-towing; but some (and that's the greatest number) has nothing at all to turn their hands to excepting the casual dock labour; that is, anything they can chance to get hold of. I don't think those who depend upon the casual labour of the docks after the fall season is over (the fall ships are the last that come) make 5s. a-week, take one man with another. I should say, more likely, their weekly earnings is about 4s. There are about 16 rafters at the Commercial Docks, and only one single man among the number. They none of them save any money during the busy season. They are in debt when the brisk time comes, and it takes them all the summer to get clear; which perhaps they does by the time the fall ships have done, and then, of course, they begin going on in the old strain again. A rafter's life is merely getting into debt and getting clear of it,— that is it—and that is a great part of the life of all the labourers along shore."

He then produced the following account of his earnings for the last year:—

				£	s.	d.
1st week	.	.	.	£1	1	0
2d „	.	.	.	1	8	0*
3d „	.	.	.	1	4	0
4th „	.	.	.	1	5	6
5th „	.	.	.	0	0	0
6th „	.	.	.	1	1	0
7th „	.	.	.	0	0	0
8th „	.	.	.	1	1	0
9th „	.	.	.	0	0	0
10th „	.	.	.	1	1	0
11th „	.	.	.	0	4	0†
12th „	.	.	.	1	1	0
13th „	.	.	.	0	4	0†
14th „	.	.	.	0	7	6
15th „	.	.	.	0	0	0
16th „	.	.	.	0	0	0
17th „	.	.	.	1	1	0
18th „	.	.	.	0	10	0†
19th „	.	.	.	1	4	0
20th „	.	.	.	0	17	6†

* Outside work.   † Jobbing.

				£	s.	d.	
21st week	.	.	.	£0	13	0	
22d „	.	.	.	0	7	0	
23d „	.	.	.	1	1	0	
24th „	.	.	.	0	10	0†	
25th „	.	.	.	0	2	6	
26th „	.	.	.	0	4	0	
27th „	.	.	.	0	1	0	
28th „	.	.	.	1	1	0‡	
29th „	.	.	.	1	4	0	
30th „	.	.	.	1	3	0	
31st „	.	.	.	1	1	0	
32d „	.	.	.	1	6	0	
33d „	.	.	.	1	3	0	
34th „	.	.	.	1	1	0	
35th „	.	.	.	0	14	0	
36th „	.	.	.	1	7	0	
37th „	.	.	.	2	0	0	
38th „	.	.	.	1	5	0§	
39th „	.	.	.	1	0	6	
40th „	.	.	.	1	4	0	
41st „	.	.	.	1	10	0	
42d „	.	.	.	1	4	0	
43d „	.	.	.	1	10	0	
44th „	.	.	.	1	14	0	
45th „	.	.	.	1	5	6	
46th „	.	.	.	1	10	4	
47th „	.	.	.	0	5	0	
48th „	.	.	.	1	10	0	
49th „	.	.	.	1	10	0	
50th „	.	.	.	1	10	0	
51st „	.	.	.	1	7	0	
52d „	.	.	.	1	1	0	

1850.

				£	s.	d.	
1st week	.	.	.	£1	10	0	
2d „	.	.	.	0	10	6	
3d „	.	.	.	1	1	0	
4th „	.	.	.	0	12	6	
5th „	.	.	.	2	10	6‖	
6th „	.	.	.	1	1	0	
7th „	.	.	.	1	7	0	
8th „	.	.	.	1	8	0	
9th „	.	.	.	0	19	0	
10th „	.	.	.	1	1	0¶	
11th „	.	.	.	0	3	0†	
12th „	.	.	.	0	18	0¶	
13th „	.	.	.	0	10	0†	
14th „	.	.	.	0	0	0	
15th „	.	.	.	1	0	0	
16th „	.	.	.	0	12	0	
17th „	.	.	.	1	1	0	
18th „	.	.	.	1	5	0¶	
19th „	.	.	.	1	0	0	
20th „	.	.	.	0	0	0	

This gives an average for the seventy-two weeks above cited of 18s. 6¼d. per week.

"Where I get 1l." the man continued, after I had copied his accounts, "many don't get 5s. I know many friends on the river, and I get a number of odd jobs which others can't. In the last six years my earnings have been much about the same; but others, I am sure, don't make half what I do—I have earned

† Jobbing. ‡ Busy time begins.
§ Working Sunday and nights.
‖ Contract job on river. ¶ Dock work.

1l. 8s. when I know they have been walking about and not earned a penny. In busy times, as many as forty pokers are employed; sometimes for as many as five weeks in the year. They get 3s. 6d. a-day from six to six. After they are out of work they do as best they can. It's impossible to tell how one-half of them live. Half their time they are starving. The wives of the rafters go some of them charing; some are glove-makers, and others dressmakers. None that I know of do slopwork."

I now come to the deal and stave-porters. First, as to those employed at the Commercial Docks.

From a man who has an excellent character given to him by his employers I had the following account:—

"At our dock," he said, "timber and corn are the principal articles; but they are distinct branches and have distinct labourers. I am in the deal part; when a foreign timber-ship comes to the dock, the timber is heaved out of the porthole by the crew themselves. The deal ships, too, are sometimes unloaded by the foreigners themselves, but not often; three or four out of a dozen may. Ours is very dangerous work: we pile the deals sometimes ninety deals high—higher at the busiest time, and we walk along planks, with no hold, carrying the deals in our hands, and only our firm tread and our eye to depend upon. We work in foggy weather, and never stop for a fog; at least, we haven't for eight or nine years, to my knowledge. In that sort of weather accidents are frequent. There was last year, I believe, about thirty-five falls, but no deaths. If it's a bad accident, the deal-porters give 6d. a-piece on Saturday night, to help the man that's had it. There's no fund for sickness. We work in gangs of five usually, sometimes more. We are paid for carrying 100 of 12-feet deals, 1s. 9d.; 14 feet, 2s. 2d.; 20 and 21 feet, 3s.; 22 feet, 3s. 8d.; and from 24 to 27 feet, 4s. 3d. That's at piece-work. We used to have 3d. per 100 more for every sort, but it was reduced three or four months back,—or more, may be. In a general way we are paid nothing extra for having to carry the deals beyond an average distance, except for what we call long runs: that's as far, or about as far, as the dock extends from the place we start to carry the deals from. One week with another, the year through, we make from 12s. to 15s.; the 15s. by men who have the preference when work is slack. We're busiest from July to Christmas. I'm the head of a gang or team of five, and I'm only paid as they are; but I have the preference if work is slack, and so have the men in my team. Five men must work at the Commercial, or none at all. We are paid in the dock at the contractor's office (there are three contractors), at four o'clock every Saturday evening. Drinking is kept down in our dock, and with my contractor drunkards are discharged. The men are all satisfied but for the lowering of their wages. No doubt they can get labour cheaper still, there's so many idlers about. A dozen years back, or so, they did pay us in a public-house. Our deal-porters are generally sober men. The beer-men only come into the dock twice a-day—ten in the morning, and half-past three in the afternoon—and the men never exceed a pint at a time."

An older man, in the same employ, said:—

"I've known deal-portering for twenty years back, and then, at the Commercial Dock, men was paid in a public-house, and there was a good deal of drunkenness. The men weren't compelled to drink, but was expected to. In that point it's far better now. When I was first a deal-porter I could make half as much more as I do now. I don't complain of any body about the dock; it ain't their fault; but I do complain uncommon about the times, there's so little work and so many to snap at it."

From a stave-porter at the same dock I had the following account:—

"We are paid by the piece, and the price varies according to size from 1s. 6d. to 10s. the thousand. Quebec staves, 6 feet long by 2 inches thick and a few inches broad, are 10s. the thousand; and other sizes are paid in the same proportion, down to 1s. 6d. We pack the bigger staves about our shoulders, resting one stave on another, more like a Jack-in-the-green than anything else, as our head comes out in the middle of 'em. Of the biggest, five is a good load, and we pack all sizes alike, folding our arms to hold the smaller staves better. Take it altogether, we make at stave-work what the deal-porters do at their work; and, indeed, we are deal-porters when staves isn't in. There's most staves comes to the Surrey Canal Dock."

A man who had worked at the West India Dock as a deal-porter informed me that the prices paid were the same as were paid by the Commercial and East Country Dock Companies before the reduction; but the supply of labour was uncertain and irregular, chiefly at the spring and fall, and in British-American ships. As many as 100 men, however, my informant stated, had been so employed at this dock, making from 15s. to 25s. a-week, or as much as 30s. on occasions, and without the drawback of any compulsory or "expected drinking." Such, as far as I could learn, is the condition of the labourers employed at these timber docks, where the drinking system and the payment of men in public-houses are not allowed. Concerning the state of the men employed at the other docks where the public-house system still continues, I had the following details.

A deal-porter at the Surrey Canal Dock stated: "I have worked a good many years in the Surrey Dock. There were four contractors at the Surrey Canal, but now there's one, and he pays the publican where we gets our beer all that's owing to us deal-porters, and the

publican pays us every Saturday night. I can't say that we are compelled to take beer, certainly not when at our work in the dock, but we're expected to take it when we're waiting. I can't say either that we are discharged if we don't drink, but if we don't we are kept waiting late on a Saturday night, on an excuse of the publican's having no change, or something like that; and we feel that, somehow or other, if we don't drink we'll be left in the back-ground. Why don't the superintendent see us paid in the dock? He pays the company's labourers in the dock; they're corn-turners and rafters, and they are paid early, too. We now have 4s. 4d. a day of from 8 to 4, and 5s. 8d. from 6 to 6. It used to be, till four months back, I think, 4s. 10d. and 6s. 4d. In slack times, say six months in the year, we earns from 10s. to 12s. a-week; in the brisk time 30s., and sometimes more; but 30s. is about the average. We are all paid at the public-house. We gathers from after five or so on the Saturday night. We are kept now and then till 12, and after 12, and it has been Sunday morning before we've got paid. There is more money spent, in course, up to 12 than up to 10. To get away at ½ past 9 is very early. I should say that half our earnings, except in our best weeks, goes to the publican for drink—more than half oft enough; if it's a bad week, all our earnings, or more. When it waxes late the wives, who've very likely been without Saturday's dinner or tea, will go to the publi- can's for their husbands, and they'll get to scold very likely, and then they'll get beaten very likely. We are chiefly married men with families. Pretty well all the deal-porters at the dock are drunkards; so there is misery enough for their families. The publican gives credit two following weeks, and encourages drinking, in course; but he does it quietly. He'll advance any man at work 1s. a night in money, besides trusting him for drink. I don't know how many we are; I should say from 50 to 200. In old age or accident, in course, we comes to the parish."

Other men whom I saw corroborated this statement, and some of their wives expressed great indignation at the system pursued in paying the labourers. None of them objected to their husbands having four pints of beer when actually at their work in the dock; it was against the publicans' temptations on Saturday and other nights that they bitterly inveighed.

At the earnest entreaty of a deal-porter's wife, I called on Saturday evening at the public house where the men were waiting to be paid. I walked into the tap-room as if I had called casually, and I was then unknown to all the deal-porters. The tap-room I found small, dark, dirty, and ill-ventilated. What with the tobacco-smoke and the heat of the weather, the room was most disagreeably close and hot. As well as I could count—for although it was a bright summer's evening the smoke and gloom rendered it somewhat difficult—there

LUMPERS DISCHARGING TIMBER-SHIP IN COMMERCIAL DOCKS.

[*From a Sketch.*]

A DINNER AT A CHEAP LODGING-HOUSE.

were 24 men in this tap-room, which is fitted up with boxes, and the number completely filled the apartment. In an adjoining room, where was a small bar, there were some six or eight more deal-porters lounging about. These numbers, however, fluctuated, for men kept coming in and going out; but all the time I was present there might have been thirty men in the two hot, dirty little rooms. They were strong-looking men enough, and all sun-burnt; but amongst them were some with pinched features and white lips. There they sat, each man with his beer before him; there was not the slightest hilarity amongst them: there was not the least semblance of a convivial Saturday-night's gathering. The majority sat in silence. Some dozed; others drank or sipped at their pint measures, as if they must do it to while away the time. These deal-porters were generally dressed in corduroy, fustian, or strong, coarse, blue woollen jackets, with trousers of similar material, open big woollen waistcoats, and with coloured cotton handkerchiefs rolled round some thick substance in the way of a stock, and tied loosely round their necks over a striped cotton or loose linen shirt. All had rough bristly beards, intimating that their shaving was confined to the Sunday mornings. With respect to the system pursued at this dock in the payment of the deal-porters, it is right that I should state that I heard from many deal-porters praises of the superintendent, though certainly not of the contractor or the publican. I am glad to be able to state, however, that it is the determination of the company to attempt— and that, indeed, they are now attempting — the abolition of the system of public-house payment. Mr. M'Cannan, the superintendent of these docks, to whom I am indebted for many favours and courtesies, informed me that an arrangement was once made for the payment of the deal-porters in " an old box" (a sort of wooden office) within the dock; but the impatience and struggling of the men who had to wait a little while for their week's earnings almost demolished the frail timbers of the old box, and the attempt was abandoned. Within the dock the supply of beer is now limited to three times a-day, with a " vend" of half-a-pint a man each visit.

A middle-aged man, sunburnt and with much of the look of a seaman, gave me an account of his labour as a deal-porter at the East Country Dock. His room, and he with his wife and children had but one, was very sparely furnished, the principal article being a large clean bed. He complained that his poverty compelled him to live in the neighbourhood of some low lodging-houses, which caused all sorts of bad characters to resort to the locality, while cries of " murder" were not uncommon in the night.

" I have been a deal-porter," he said, " nearly twenty years, and for the last few years I have worked at the East Country Dock. Sometimes we work single-handed, sometimes in gangs of two, three, or four. The distance the deals have to be carried has a good deal to do with it, as to the number of the gang. We're paid nothing extra for distance. Mr. —— contracts with the Dock Company to do all the deal-portering. There are three gangs regularly employed, each with a master or foreman, or ganger, over them. They have always the preference. If three ships was to unload in one day, there would be one for each gang, and when more hands are wanted the men of the regular gangs are put over deal-porters such as me, who are not regularly employed, but on the look-out for piece-work or a day's work. We reckon when that happens that the gangers' men have 9s. for our 4s. We are paid at a public-house. The house belongs to the company. We pay 4d. a-pot for our beer, and we're expected to drink not less than four pints a-day. We're not obliged, you understand, but we're expected to drink this; and if we don't do as we're expected, why we're not wanted next time, that's all. But we're only expected to take our regular beer when work's brisk. We're not encouraged to run into debt for drink and work it out. Indeed, if a man be 1s. or 1s. 6d. in debt to the publican, he can't get credit for a bit of bread and cheese, or a drink of beer. We have good beer, but sometimes we'd rather be without it. But we can't do without some. Many deal-porters, I know, are terrible drunkards. We are paid the same as at the Commercial Dock, and were reduced about the same time. If I had a regular week's work now and no stop, I could make 26s., less by 8d. a-day, or 4s. a-week, for beer. We're not expected to drink any gin. Before wages came down I could have made 30s. Our beer-money is stopped out of our earnings by the masters and paid to the publican. It's very seldom, indeed, we get a regular week's work, and take it the year through I don't clear 12s. a-week. To-day, there was only 16 men at work, but sometimes there's 80. From June to Christmas is the best time. Sometimes we may wait three or four days for a job. The regular pay for the Custom-house hours, from 8 to 4, is 4s. a-day to a deal-porter, but there's plenty to do it for what they can catch. Lots of Irish, sir? they'll work for anything, and is underselling all of us, because an Englishman and his family can't live like them. In the winter my family and me lived on 4s. or 5s. a-week, but I kept clear of the parish, though plenty of us have to come on the parish. Much in pawn, sir? I have so; look at my place. It was a nice place once. Most of what you may call the regular hands has been brought up as deal-porters. I don't know how many you may call regular at our dock, it varies; working and waiting for a turn; but we've no regular turn at work; there's 100 perhaps, or near about it. Ours is very hard and very dangerous work. Last year one man was killed by a fall, and two had broken legs, and two had broken thighs; but it was an easy year for accidents. There is no fund to help or to bury us, only the parish. In a bad case we're carried to the Dreadnought, or some hospital. We are all of us dissatisfied. I wish I could have 2s. 6d. a-day for regular work, and I'd live 20 years longer than I shall now, with nothing to do one day and tearing my soul out with slaving work the others."

The result of all my inquiries shows that the deal-porters in nowise exaggerated the hardness or the danger of their labours. I saw them at work, walking along planks, some sloping from an elevated pile of timber to one somewhat more elevated, the plank vibrating as two men carrying a deal trod slowly and in measure along it, and so they proceed from one pile to another, beginning, perhaps, from the barge until the deals have been duly deposited. From a distance, when only the diminished thickness of the plank is visible, they appear to be walking on a mere stick; the space so traversed is generally short, but the mode of conveyance seems rude and primitive.

ACCOUNT OF THE CASUAL LABOURERS.

In the foregoing narratives frequent mention has been made of the Casual Labourers at the timber-docks; and I now proceed to give some short account of the condition and earnings of this most wretched class. On the platform surrounding the Commercial Dock basins are a number whom I have heard described as "idlers," "pokers," and "casual labourers." These men are waiting in hopes of a job, which they rarely obtain until all the known hands have been set to work before them. The casual labourers confine themselves to no particular dock, but resort to the one which they account the most likely to want hands; and some even of the more regularly employed deal-porters change their docks occasionally for the same reason. These changes of locality puzzle the regular deal-porters in the estimation of the number of hands in their calling at the respective docks. On my visits the casual labourers were less numerous than usual, as the summer is the season when such persons consider that they have the best chance in the country. But I saw groups of 10 and 20 waiting about the docks; some standing alone, and some straggling in twos and threes, as they waited, all looking dull and listless. These men, thus wearisomely waiting, could not be called ragged, for they wore mostly strong canvas or fustian suits—large, and seemingly often washed jackets, predominating; and rents, and tatters are far less common in such attire than in woollen-cloth garments. From a man dressed in a large, coarse, canvas jacket, with worn corduroy trousers, and very heavy and very brown laced-leather boots, I had the

following statement, in a somewhat provincial tone:—

"My father was a small farmer in Dorsetshire. I was middling educated, and may thank the parson for it. I can read the Bible and spell most of the names there. I was left destitute, and I had to shift for myself—that's nine year ago, I think. I've hungered, and I've ordered my bottle of wine since, sir. I got the wine when railways was all the go; and I was a navvy; but I didn't like wine-drinking; I drank it just for the fun of the thing, or mayhap because gentlemen drink it. The port was like rather rough beer, but stronger, certainly. Sherry I only had once or twice, and liked good ale better. I shifted my quarters every now and then till within two or three years ago, and then I tried my hand in London. At first Mr. —— (a second cousin of my father he was) helped me now and then, and he gave me odd jobs at portering for himself, as he was a grocer, and he got me odd jobs from other people besides. When I was a navvy I should at the best time have had my 50s. a-week, and more if it hadn't been for the tommy-shops; and I've had my 15s. a-week in portering in London for my cousin; but sometimes I came down to 10s., and sometimes to 5s. My cousin died sudden, and I was very hard up after that. I made nothing at portering some weeks. I had no one to help me; and in the spring of last year—and very cold it often was—I've walked after 10, 11, or 12 at night, many a mile to lie down and sleep in any bye-place. I never stole, but have been hard tempted. I've thought of drowning myself, and of hanging myself, but somehow a penny or two came in to stop that. Perhaps I didn't seriously intend it. I begged sometimes of an evening. I stayed at lodging-houses, for one can't sleep out in bad weather, till I heard from one lodger that he took his turn at the Commercial Dock. He worked at timber, or corn, or anything; and so I went, about the cholera time last year, and waited, and run from one dock to another, because I was new and hadn't a chance like the old hands. I've had 14s. a-week sometimes; and many's the week I've had three, and more's the week I've had nothing at all. They've said, 'I don't know you.' I've lived on penny loaves—one or two a-day, when there was no work, and then I've begged. I don't know what the other people waiting at any of the docks got. I didn't talk to them much, and they didn't talk much to me."

THE DOCK-LABOURERS.

I SHALL now pass to the labourers at the docks. This transition I am induced to make, not because there is any affinity between the kinds of work performed at the two places; but because the docks constitute, as it were, a sort of home colony to Spitalfields, to which the unemployed weaver migrates in the hope of bettering his condition. From this it would be generally imagined that the work at the docks was either better paid, less heavy, or more easily, and therefore more regularly, obtained. So far from such being the fact, however, the labour at the docks appears to be not only more onerous, but doubly as precarious as that of weaving; while the average earnings of the entire class seems to be less. What, then, it will be asked, constitutes the inducement for the change? Why does the weaver abandon the calling of his life, and forsake an occupation that at least appears to have, and actually had in the days of better prices, a refining and intellectual tendency? Why does he quit his graceful art for the mere muscular labour of the human animal? This, we shall find, arises purely from a desire for some out-of-door employment. And it is a consequence of all skilled labour—since the acquirement of the skill is the result of long practice—that if the art to which the operative has been educated is abandoned, he must take to some unskilled labour as a means of subsistence. I pass, then, to the consideration of the incomings and condition of the dock-labourers of the metropolis, not because the class of labour is similar to that of weaving, but because the two classes of labourers are locally associated. I would rather have pursued some more systematic plan in my inquiries; but in the present state of ignorance as to the general occupation of the poor, system is impossible. I am unable to generalise, not being acquainted with the particulars; for each day's investigation brings me incidentally into contact with a means of living utterly unknown among the well-fed portion of society. All I can at present assert is, that the poor appear to admit of being classified according to their employments under three heads—artizans, labourers, and petty traders; the first class consisting of skilled, and the second of unskilled workmen; while the third comprises hawkers, costermongers, and such other small dealers, who are contradistinguished from the larger ones by bringing their wares to the consumer instead of leaving the consumer to seek the wares. Of the skilled workmen few are so poorly paid for their labour as not to obtain a sufficiency for the satisfaction of their wants. The amount of wages is generally considered above the sum required for the positive necessaries of life; that is to say, for appeasing an appetite or allaying a pain, rather than gratifying a desire. The class of Spitalfields weavers, however, appear to constitute a striking exception to the rule, from what cause I do not even venture to conjecture. But with the unskilled labourer the amount of remuneration is seldom much above subsistence-point, if it be not very frequently below it. Such a labourer, commercially considered, is, as it were, a human steam-engine, supplied with so much fuel in the shape of food, merely to set him in motion.

If he can be made to perform the same amount of work with half the consumption, why a saving of one-half the expense is supposed to be effected. Indeed, the grand object in the labour-market of the present day appears to be to economise human fuel. If the living steam-engine can be made to work as long and as well with a less amount of coal, just so much the better is the result considered.

The dock-labourers are a striking instance of mere brute force with brute appetites. This class of labour is as unskilled as the power of a hurricane. Mere muscle is all that is needed; hence every human locomotive is capable of working there. All that is wanted is the power of moving heavy bodies from one place to another. Mr. Stuart Mill tells us that labour in the physical world is always and solely employed in putting objects in motion; and assuredly, if this be the principle of physical labour, the docks exhibit the perfection of human action. Dock-work is precisely the office that every kind of man is fitted to perform, and there we find every kind of man performing it. Those who are unable to live by the occupation to which they have been educated, can obtain a living there without any previous training. Hence we find men of every calling labouring at the docks. There are decayed and bankrupt master-butchers, master-bakers, publicans, grocers, old soldiers, old sailors, Polish refugees, broken-down gentlemen, discharged lawyers' clerks, suspended government clerks, almsmen, pensioners, servants, thieves—indeed, every one who wants a loaf, and is willing to work for it. The London Dock is one of the few places in the metropolis where men can get employment without either character or recommendation, so that the labourers employed there are naturally a most incongruous assembly. Each of the docks employs several hundred hands to ship and discharge the cargoes of the numerous vessels that enter; and as there are some six or seven of such docks attached to the metropolis, it may be imagined how large a number of individuals are dependent on them for their subsistence. At a rough calculation, there must be at least 20,000 souls getting their living by such means.

THE LONDON DOCK.

BEFORE proceeding to give an account of the London Dock itself, let me thus publicly tender my thanks to Mr. Powles, the intelligent and obliging secretary, for the ready manner in which he placed the statistics of the company at my service. Had I experienced from the deputy-superintendent the same courtesy and consideration, the present exposition of the state of the labourers employed in the London Dock would, doubtless, have been more full and complete. But the one gentleman seemed as anxious to withhold information as the other was to impart it. Indeed, I found in the first instance, that the orders given by the deputy-superintendent throughout the dock to each of the different officers were, that no answers should be made to any inquiries I might put to them; and it was not until I had communicated my object to the secretary that I was able to obtain the least information concerning even the number of hands employed at different times, or the amount of wages paid to them.

I shall now give a brief statement of the character, condition, and capacity of the London Dock. After which, the description of the kind of labour performed there; and then the class of labourers performing it will follow in due order.

The London Dock occupies an area of ninety acres, and is situated in the three parishes of St. George, Shadwell, and Wapping. The population of those three parishes in 1841 was 55,500, and the number of inhabited houses 8000, which covered a space equal to 338 acres. This is in the proportion of twenty-three inhabited houses to an acre and seven individuals to each house. The number of persons to each inhabited house is, despite of the crowded lodging-houses with which it abounds, not beyond the average for all London. I have already shown that Bethnal-green, which is said to possess the greatest number of low-rented houses, had only, upon an average, seventeen inhabited houses to each acre, while the average through London was but 5·5 houses per acre. So that it appears that in the three parishes of St. George's-in-the-East, Shadwell, and Wapping, the houses are more than four times more crowded than in the other parts of London, and more numerous by half as many again than those even in the low-rented district of Bethnal-green. This affords us a good criterion as to the character of the neighbourhood, and, consequently, of the people living in the vicinity of the London Dock.

The courts and alleys round about the dock swarm with low lodging-houses; and are inhabited either by the dock-labourers, sackmakers, watermen, or that peculiar class of the London poor who pick up a living by the water-side. The open streets themselves have all more or less a maritime character. Every other shop is either stocked with gear for the ship or for the sailor. The windows of one house are filled with quadrants and bright brass sextants, chronometers, and huge mariners' compasses, with their cards trembling with the motion of the cabs and waggons passing in the street. Then comes the sailors' cheap shoe-mart, rejoicing in the attractive sign of "Jack and his Mother." Every public-house is a "Jolly Tar," or something equally taking. Then come sailmakers, their windows stowed with ropes and lines smelling of tar. All the grocers are provision-agents, and exhibit in their windows the cases of meat and biscuits; and every article is warranted to keep in any climate. The corners of the streets, too, are

mostly monopolised by slopsellers; their windows parti-coloured with bright red-and-blue flannel shirts; the doors nearly blocked up with hammocks and " well-oiled nor'-westers;" and the front of the house itself nearly covered with canvas trousers, rough pilot-coats, and shiny black dreadnoughts. The passengers alone would tell you that you were in the maritime districts of London. Now you meet a satin-waistcoated mate, or a black sailor with his large fur cap, or else a Custom-house officer in his brass-buttoned jacket.

The London Dock can accommodate 500 ships, and the warehouses will contain 232,000 tons of goods. The entire structure cost 4,000,000*l.* in money: the tobacco warehouses alone cover five acres of ground. The wall surrounding the dock cost 65,000*l.* One of the wine-vaults has an area of seven acres, and in the whole of them there is room for stowing 60,000 pipes of wine. The warehouses round the wharfs are exposing from their extent, but are much less lofty than those at St. Katherine's; and being situated at some distance from the dock, goods cannot be craned out of the ship's hold and stowed away at one operation. According to the last half-yearly report, the number of ships which entered the dock during the six months ending the 31st of May last was 704, measuring upwards of 195,000 tons. The amount of earnings during that period was 230,000*l.* and odd, and the amount of expenditure nearly 121,000*l.* The stock of goods in the warehouses last May was upwards of 170,000 tons.

As you enter the dock the sight of the forest of masts in the distance, and the tall chimneys vomiting clouds of black smoke, and the many coloured flags flying in the air, has a most peculiar effect; while the sheds with the monster wheels arching through the roofs look like the paddle-boxes of huge steamers. Along the quay you see, now men with their faces blue with indigo, and now gaugers, with their long brass-tipped rule dripping with spirit from the cask they have been probing. Then will come a group of flaxen-haired sailors chattering German; and next a black sailor, with a cotton handkerchief twisted turban-like round his head. Presently a blue-smocked butcher, with fresh meat and a bunch of cabbages in the tray on his shoulder; and shortly afterwards a mate, with green paroquets in a wooden cage. Here you will see sitting on a bench a sorrowful-looking woman, with new bright cooking tins at her feet, telling you she is an emigrant preparing for her voyage. As you pass along this quay the air is pungent with tobacco; on that it overpowers you with the fumes of rum; then you are nearly sickened with the stench of hides, and huge bins of horns; and shortly afterwards the atmosphere is fragrant with coffee and spice. Nearly everywhere you meet stacks of cork, or else yellow bins of sulphur, or lead-coloured copper-ore. As you enter this warehouse, the flooring is sticky, as if it had been newly tarred, with the sugar that has leaked through the casks; and as you descend into the dark vaults, you see long lines of lights hanging from the black arches, and lamps flitting about midway. Here you sniff the fumes of the wine, and there the peculiar fungus-smell of dry rot; then the jumble of sounds as you pass along the dock blends in anything but sweet concord. The sailors are singing boisterous nigger songs from the Yankee ship just entering; the cooper is hammering at the casks on the quay; the chains of the cranes, loosed of their weight, rattle as they fly up up again; the ropes splash in the water; some captain shouts his orders through his hands; a goat bleats from some ship in the basin; and empty casks roll along the stones with a heavy drum-like sound. Here the heavily-laden ships are down far below the quay, and you descend to them by ladders; whilst in another basin they are high up out of the water, so that their green copper sheathing is almost level with the eye of the passenger; while above his head a long line of bowsprits stretches far over the quay; and from them hang spars and planks as a gangway to each ship.

This immense establishment is worked by from one to three thousand hands, according as the business is either brisk or slack. Out of this number there are always 400 to 500 permanent labourers, receiving on an average 16s. 6d. per week, with the exception of coopers, carpenters, smiths, and other mechanics, who are paid the usual wages of those crafts. Besides these are many hundred — from 1000 to 2500 — casual labourers, who are engaged at the rate of 2s. 6d. per day in the summer and 2s. 4d. in the winter months. Frequently, in case of many arrivals, extra hands are hired in the course of the day, at the rate of 4d. per hour. For the permanent labourers a recommendation is required; but for the casual labourers no character is demanded. The number of the casual hands engaged by the day depends, of course, upon the amount of work to be done; and I find that the total number of labourers in the dock varies from 500 to 3000 and odd. On the 4th May, 1849, the number of hands engaged, both permanent and casual, was 2794; on the 26th of the same month it was 3012; and on the 30th it was 1189. These appear to be the extreme of the variation for that year: the fluctuation is due to a greater or less number of ships entering the dock. The lowest number of ships entering the dock in any one week last year was 29, while the highest number was 141. This rise and fall is owing to the prevalence of easterly winds, which serve to keep the ships back, and so make the business slack. Now, deducting the lowest number of hands employed from the highest number, we have no less than 1823 individuals who obtain so precarious a subsistence by their labour at the docks, that by the mere shifting of the wind

they may be all deprived of their daily bread. Calculating the wages at 2s. 6d. per day for each, the company would have paid 376l. 10s. to the 3012 hands employed on the 26th of May 1849; while only 148l. 12s. 6d. would have been paid to the 1189 hands engaged on the 30th of the same month. Hence, not only would 1823 hands have been thrown out of employ by the chopping of the wind, but the labouring men dependent upon the business of the docks for their subsistence would in one day have been deprived of 227l. 17s. 6d. This will afford the reader some faint idea of the precarious character of the subsistence obtained by the labourers employed in this neighbourhood, and, consequently, as it has been well proved, that all men who obtain their livelihood by irregular employment are the most intemperate and improvident of all.

It will be easy to judge what may be the condition and morals of a class who to-day, as a body, may earn near upon 400l., and to-morrow only 150l. I had hoped to have been able to have shown the fluctuations in the total amount of wages paid to the dock-labourers for each week throughout the whole year; and so, by contrasting the comparative affluence and comfort of one week with the distress and misery of the other, to have afforded the reader some more vivid idea of the body of men who are performing, perhaps, the heaviest labour, and getting the most fickle provision of all. But still I will endeavour to impress him with some faint idea of the struggle there is to gain the uncertain daily bread. Until I saw with my own eyes this scene of greedy despair, I could not have believed that there was so mad an eagerness to work, and so biting a want of it, among so vast a body of men. A day or two before I had sat at midnight in the room of the starving weaver; and as I heard him tell his bitter story, there was a patience in his misery that gave it more an air of heroism than desperation. But in the scenes I have lately witnessed the want has been positively tragic, and the struggle for life partaking of the sublime. The reader must first remember what kind of men the casual labourers generally are. They are men, it should be borne in mind, who are shut out from the usual means of life by the want of character. Hence, you are not astonished to hear from those who are best acquainted with the men, that there are hundreds among the body who are known thieves, and who go to the docks to seek a living; so that, if taken for any past offence, their late industry may plead for some little lenity in their punishment.

He who wishes to behold one of the most extraordinary and least-known scenes of this metropolis, should wend his way to the London Dock gates at half-past seven in the morning. There he will see congregated within the principal entrance masses of men of all grades, looks, and kinds. Some in half-fashioned surtouts burst at the elbows, with the dirty shirts showing through. Others in greasy sporting jackets, with red pimpled faces. Others in the rags of their half-slang gentility, with the velvet collars of their paletots worn through to the canvas. Some in rusty black, with their waistcoats fastened tight up to the throat. Others, again, with the knowing thieves' curl on each side of the jaunty cap; whilst here and there you may see a big-whiskered Pole, with his hands in the pockets of his plaited French trousers. Some loll outside the gates, smoking the pipe which is forbidden within; but these are mostly Irish.

Presently you know, by the stream pouring through the gates and the rush towards particular spots, that the "calling foremen" have made their appearance. Then begins the scuffling and scrambling forth of countless hands high in the air, to catch the eye of him whose voice may give them work. As the foreman calls from a book the names, some men jump up on the backs of the others, so as to lift themselves high above the rest, and attract the notice of him who hires them. All are shouting. Some cry aloud his surname, some his christian name, others call out their own names, to remind him that they are there. Now the appeal is made in Irish blarney — now in broken English. Indeed, it is a sight to sadden the most callous, to see thousands of men struggling for only one day's hire; the scuffle being made the fiercer by the knowledge that hundreds out of the number there assembled must be left to idle the day out in want. To look in the faces of that hungry crowd is to see a sight that must be ever remembered. Some are smiling to the foreman to coax him into remembrance of them; others, with their protruding eyes, eager to snatch at the hoped-for pass. For weeks many have gone there, and gone through the same struggle —the same cries; and have gone away, after all, without the work they had screamed for.

From this it might be imagined that the work was of a peculiarly light and pleasant kind, and so, when I first saw the scene, I could not help imagining myself. But, in reality, the labour is of that heavy and continuous character that you would fancy only the best fed could stand it. The work may be divided into three classes. 1. Wheel-work, or that which is moved by the muscles of the legs and weight of the body; 2. jigger, or winch-work, or that which is moved by the muscles of the arm. In each of these the labourer is stationary; but in the truck work, which forms the third class, the labourer has to travel over a space of ground greater or less in proportion to the distance which the goods have to be removed.

The wheel-work is performed somewhat on the system of the treadwheel, with the exception that the force is applied inside instead of outside the wheel. From six to eight men enter a wooden cylinder or drum, upon which are nailed battens, and the men laying hold of ropes commence treading the wheel round,

occasionally singing the while, and stamping time in a manner that is pleasant, from its novelty. The wheel is generally about sixteen feet in diameter and eight to nine feet broad; and the six or eight men treading within it, will lift from sixteen to eighteen hundred weight, and often a ton, forty times in an hour, an average of twenty-seven feet high. Other men will get out a cargo of from 800 to 900 casks of wine, each cask averaging about five hundred weight, and being lifted about eighteen feet, in a day and a half. At trucking each man is said to go on an average thirty miles a-day, and two-thirds of that time he is moving 1½ cwt. at six miles and a-half per hour.

This labour, though requiring to be seen to be properly understood, must still appear so arduous that one would imagine it was not of that tempting nature, that 3000 men could be found every day in London desperate enough to fight and battle for the privilege of getting 2s. 6d. by it; and even if they fail in "getting taken on" at the commencement of the day, that they should then retire to the appointed yard, there to remain hour after hour in the hope that the wind might blow them some stray ship, so that other gangs might be wanted, and the calling foreman seek them there. It is a curious sight to see the men waiting in these yards to be hired at 4d. per hour, for such are the terms given in the after part of the day. There, seated on long benches ranged against the wall, they remain, some telling their miseries and some their crimes to one another, whilst others doze away their time. Rain or sunshine, there can always be found plenty ready to catch the stray 1s. or 8d. worth of work. By the size of the shed you can tell how many men sometimes remain there in the pouring rain, rather than run the chance of losing the stray hours' work. Some loiter on the bridges close by, and presently, as their practised eye or ear tells them that the calling foreman is in want of another gang, they rush forward in a stream towards the gate, though only six or eight at most can be hired out of the hundred or more that are waiting there. Again the same mad fight takes place as in the morning. There is the same jumping on benches, the same raising of hands, the same entreaties, and the same failure as before. It is strange to mark the change that takes place in the manner of the men when the foreman has left. Those that have been engaged go smiling to their labour. Indeed, I myself met on the quay just such a chuckling gang passing to their work. Those who are left behind give vent to their disappointment in abuse of him whom they had been supplicating and smiling at a few minutes before. Upon talking with some of the unsuccessful ones, they assured me that the men who had supplanted them had only gained their ends by bribing the foreman who had engaged them. This I made a point of inquiring into, and the deputy-warehousekeeper, of whom I sought the information, soon assured me, by the production of his book, that he himself was the person who chose the men, the foreman merely executing his orders: and this, indeed, I found to be the custom throughout the dock.

At four o'clock the eight hours' labour ceases, and then comes the paying. The names of the men are called out of the muster-book, and each man, as he answers to the cry, has half-a-crown given to him. So rapidly is this done that, in a quarter of an hour, the whole of the men have had their wages paid them. They then pour towards the gate. Here two constables stand, and as each man passes through the wicket, he takes his hat off, and is felt from head to foot by the dock-officers and attendant: and yet, with all the want, misery, and temptation, the millions of pounds of property amid which they work, and the thousands of pipes and hogsheads of wines and spirits about the docks, I am informed, upon the best authority, that there are on an average but thirty charges of drunkenness in the course of the year, and only eight of dishonesty every month. This may, perhaps, arise from the vigilance of the superintendents; but to see the distressed condition of the men who seek and gain employment in the London Dock, it appears almost incredible, that out of so vast a body of men, without means and without character, there should be so little vice or crime. There still remains one curious circumstance to be added in connexion with the destitution of the dock-labourers. Close to the gate by which they are obliged to leave, sits on a coping-stone the refreshment man, with his two large canvas pockets tied in front of him, and filled with silver and copper, ready to give change to those whom he has trusted with their dinner that day until they were paid.

As the men passed slowly on in a double file towards the gate, I sat beside the victualler, and asked him what constituted the general dinner of the labourers. He told me that he supplied them with pea-soup, bread and cheese, saveloys, and beer. "Some," he said, "had twice as much as others. Some had a pennyworth, some had eatables and a pint of beer; others, two pints, and others four, and some spend their whole half-crown in eating and drinking." This gave me a more clear insight into the destitution of the men who stood there each morning. Many of them, it was clear, came to the gate without the means of a day's meal, and, being hired, were obliged to go on credit for the very food they worked upon. What wonder, then, that the calling foreman should be often carried many yards away by the struggle and rush of the men around him seeking employment at his hands! One gentleman assured me that he had been taken off his feet and hurried a distance of a quarter of a mile by the eagerness of the impatient crowd around him.

Having made myself acquainted with the character and amount of the labour performed, I next proceeded to make inquiries into the condition of the labourers themselves, and thus to learn the average amount of their wages from so precarious an occupation. For this purpose, hearing that there were several cheap lodging-houses in the neighbourhood, I thought I should be better enabled to arrive at an average result by conversing with the inmates of them, and thus endeavouring to elicit from them some such statements of their earnings at one time and at another, as would enable me to judge what was their average amount throughout the year. I had heard the most pathetic accounts from men in the waiting-yard; how they had been six weeks without a day's hire. I had been told of others who had been known to come there day after day in the hope of getting sixpence, and who lived upon the stray pieces of bread given to them in charity by their fellow-labourers. Of one person I was informed by a gentleman who had sought out his history in pure sympathy, from the wretchedness of the man's appearance. The man had once been possessed of 500l. a-year, and had squandered it all away; and through some act or acts that I do not feel myself at liberty to state, had lost caste, character, friends, and everything that could make life easy to him. From that time he had sunk and sunk in the world, until, at last, he had found him, with a lodging-house for his dwelling-place, the associate of thieves and pickpockets. His only means of living at this time was bones and rag-grubbing; and for this purpose the man would wander through the streets at three every morning, to see what little bits of old iron, or rag, or refuse bone he could find in the roads. His principal source of income I am informed, from such a source as precludes the possibility of doubt, was by picking up the refuse ends of cigars, drying them, and selling them at one-halfpenny per ounce, as tobacco, to the thieves with whom he lodged.

However, to arrive at a fair estimate as to the character and the earnings of labourers generally, I directed my guide, after the closing of the docks, to take me to one of the largest lodging-houses in the neighbourhood. The young man who was with me happened to know one of the labourers who was lodging there, and having called him out, I told him the object of my visit, and requested to be allowed to obtain information from the labourers assembled within. The man assented, and directing me to follow him, he led me through a narrow passage into a small room on the ground floor, in which sat, I should think, at least twenty or thirty of the most wretched objects I ever beheld. Some were shoeless — some coatless — others shirtless; and from all these came so rank and foul a stench, that I was sickened with a moment's inhalation of the fetid atmosphere.

Some of the men were seated in front of a table, eating soup out of yellow basins. As they saw me enter, they gathered round me; and I was proceeding to tell them what information I wished to gather from them, when in swaggered a drunken man, in a white canvas suit, who announced himself as the landlord of the place, asking whether there had been a robbery in the house, that people should come in without saying "with your leave" or "by your leave." I explained to him that I had mistaken the person who had introduced me for the proprietor of the house, when he grew very abusive, and declared I should not remain there. Some of the men, however, swore as lustily that I should; and after a time succeeded in pacifying him. He then bade me let him hear what I wanted, and I again briefly stated the object of my visit. I told him I wished to publish the state of the dock-labourers in the newspapers, on which the man burst into an ironical laugh, and vowed with an oath that *he* knowed me, and that the men were a set of b——y flats to be done in that way. "I know who you are well enough," he shouted. I requested to be informed for whom he took me. "Take you for!" he cried; "why, for a b——y spy! You come here from the Secretary of State, you know you do, to see how many men I've got in the house, and what kind they are." This caused a great stir among the company, and I could see that I was mistaken for one of the detective police. I was located in so wretched a court, and so far removed from the street, with a dead wall opposite, that I knew any atrocity might be committed there almost unheard: indeed, the young man who had brought me to the house had warned me of its dangerous character before I went; but, from the kind reception I had met with from other labourers, I had no fear. At last the landlord flung the door wide open, and shouted from his clenched teeth, "By G—! if you ain't soon mizzled, I'll crack your b——y skull open for you!" And so saying, he prepared to make a rush towards me, but was held back by the youth who had brought me to the place. I felt that it would be dangerous to remain; and rising, informed the man that I would not trouble him to proceed to extremities.

It was now so late that I felt it would be imprudent to venture into another such house that night; so, having heard of the case of a dock-labourer who had formerly been a clerk in a Government office, I made the best of my way to the place where he resided.

He lived in a top back-room in a small house, in another dismal court. I was told by the woman who answered the door to mount the steep stairs, as she shrieked out to the man's wife to show me a light. I found the man seated on the edge of a bed, with six young children grouped round him. They were all shoeless, and playing on the bed was an infant with only a shirt to cover it. The room was about 7 feet square, and, with the man and his wife, there were eight human creatures living in it. In the middle of the apartment, upon a chair, stood a washing-tub foaming with fresh suds, and from the white crinkled hands of the wife it was plain that I had interrupted her in her washing. On one chair, close by, was a heap of dirty linen, and on another was flung the newly-washed. There was a saucepan on the handful of fire, and the only ornaments on the mantelpiece were two flat-irons and a broken shaving-glass. On the table at which I took my notes there was the bottom of a broken ginger-beer bottle filled with soda. The man was without a coat, and wore an old tattered and greasy black satin waistcoat. Across the ceiling ran strings to hang clothes upon. On my observing to the woman that I supposed she dried the clothes in that room, she told me that they were obliged to do so, and it gave them all colds and bad eyes. On the floor was a little bit of matting, and on the shelves in the corner one or two plates. In answer to my questionings the man told me he had been a dock-labourer for five or six years. He was in Her Majesty's Stationery Office. When there he had 150*l*. a-year. Left through accepting a bill of exchange for 871*l*. He was suspended eight years ago, and had petitioned the Lords of the Treasury, but never could get any answer. After that he was out for two or three years, going about doing what he could get, such as writing letters. "Then," said the wife, "you went into Mr. What's-his-name's shop." "Oh, yes," answered the man, "I had six months' employment at Camberwell. I had 12*s*. a-week and my board there."

Before this they had lived upon their things. He had a good stock of furniture and clothing at that time. The wife used to go out for a day's work when she could get it. She used to go out shelling peas in the pea season — washing or charing — anything she could get to do. His father was a farmer, well to do. He should say the old man was worth a good bit of money, and he would have some property at his death.

"Oh, sir," said the woman, "we have been really very bad off indeed; sometimes without even food or firing in the depth of winter. It is not until recently that we have been to say very badly off, because within the last four years has been our worst trouble. We had a very good house — a seven-roomed house in Walworth—and well furnished and very comfortable. We were in business for ourselves before we went there. We were grocers, near Oxford-street. We lived there at the time when Aldis the pawnbroker's was burnt down. We might have done well if we had not given so much credit."

"I've got," said the husband, "about 90*l*. owing me down there now. It's quite out of character to think of getting it. At Clerkenwell I got a job at a grocer's shop. The master was in the Queen's-bench Prison, and the mistress employed me at 12s. a-week until he went through the Insolvent Debtor's Court. When he passed the Court the business was sold, and of course he didn't want me after that. I've done nothing else but this dock-labouring work for this long time. Took to it first because I found there was no chance of anything else. The character with the bill transaction was very much against me : so, being unable to obtain employment in a whole-sale house, or anywhere else, I applied to the docks. They require no character at all there. I think I may sometimes have had 7 or 8 days altogether. Then I was out for a fortnight or three weeks perhaps ; and then we might get a day or two again, and on some occasion such a thing as — well, say July, August, September, and October. I was in work one year almost the whole of those months — three years ago I think that was. Then I did not get any-thing, excepting now and then, not more than about three days' work until the next March ; that was owing to the slack time. The first year I might say that I might have been em-ployed about one-third of the time. The second year I was employed six months. The third year I was very unfortunate. I was laid up for three months with bad eyes and a quinsey in the throat, through working in an ice ship. I ve scarcely had anything to do since then. That is nearly 18 months ago ; and since then I have had casual employment, perhaps one, and sometimes two days a-week. It would average 5s. a-week the whole year. Within the last few weeks I have, through a friend, applied at a shipping-merchant's, and within the month I have had five days' work with them, and nothing else, except writing a letter, which I had 2d. for—that's all the em-ployment I've met with myself. My wife has been at employment for the last three months, she has a place she goes to work at. She has 3s. a-week for washing, for charing, and for mangling : the party my wife works for has a mangle, and I go sometimes to help ; for if she has got 6d. worth of washing to do at home, than I go to turn the mangle for an hour in-stead of her,—she's not strong enough."

"We buy most bread," said the wife, " and a bit of firing, and I do manage on a Saturday night to get them a bit of meat for Sunday if I possibly can ; but what with the soap, and one thing and another, that's the only day they do get a bit of meat, unless I've a bit given me. As for clothing, I'm sure I can't get them any unless I have that given me, poor little things."

"Yes, but we have managed to get a little bread lately," said the man. " When bread was 11d. a loaf, that was the time when we was worse off. Of course we had the seven children alive then. We buried one only three months ago. She was an afflicted little creature for 16 or 17 months : it was one person's work to attend to her, and was very badly off for a few months then. We've known

what it was sometimes to go without bread and coals in the depth of winter. Last Christ-mas two years we did so for the whole day, until the wife came home in the evening and brought it might be 6d. or 9d. according how long she worked. I was looking after them. I was at home ill. I have known us to sit several days and not have more than 6d. to feed and warm the whole of us for the whole of the day. We'll buy half-a-quartern loaf, that'll be 4½d. or sometimes 5d., and then we have a penny for coals, that would be pretty nigh all that we could have for our money. Sometimes we get a little oatmeal and make gruel. We had hard work to keep the children warm at all. What with their clothes and what we had, we did as well as we could. My children is very contented ; give 'em bread, and they're as happy as all the world. That's one comfort. For instance, to-day we've had half-a quartern loaf, and we had a piece left of last night's after I had come home. I had been earning some money yesterday. We had 2 oz. of butter, and I had this afternoon a quarter of an oz. of tea and a pennyworth of sugar. When I was ill I've had two or three of the children round me at a time, fretting for want of food. That was at the time I was ill. A friend gave me half a sovereign to bury my child. The parish provided me with a coffin, and it cost me about 3s. besides. We didn't have her taken away from here, not as a parish funeral exactly. I agreed that if he would fetch it, and let it stand in an open space that he had got there, near his shop, until the Saturday, which was the time, I would give the under-taker 3s. to let a man come with a pall to throw over the coffin, so that it should not be seen exactly it was a parish funeral. Even the people in the house don't know, not one of them, that it was buried in that way. I had to give 1s. 6d. for a pair of shoes before I could follow my child to the grave, and we paid 1s. 9d. for rent, all out of the half sovereign. I think there s some people at the docks a great deal worse off than us. I should say there's men go down there and stand at that gate from 7 to 12, and then they may get called in and earn 1s., and that only for two or three days in the week, after spending the whole of their time there."

The scenes witnessed at the London Dock were of so painful a description, the struggle for one day's work—the scramble for twenty-four hours' extra-subsistence and extra-life were of so tragic a character, that I was anxious to ascertain if possible the exact number of individuals in and around the metropolis who live by dock labour. I have said that at one of the docks alone I found that 1823 stomachs would be deprived of food by the mere chop-ping of the breeze. "It's an ill wind," says the proverb, "that blows nobody good ;" and until I came to investigate the condition of the dock-labourer I could not have believed it possible that near upon 2000 souls in one place alone lived, chameleon-like, upon the air, or that an easterly wind, despite the wise saw, could deprive so many of bread. It is indeed " a nipping and an eager air." That the sustenance of thousands of families should be as fickle as the very breeze itself; that the weathercock should be the index of daily want or daily ease to such a vast number of men, women, and children, was a climax of misery and wretchedness that I could not have imagined to exist; and since that I have witnessed such scenes of squalor, and crime, and suffering, as oppress the mind even to a feeling of awe.

The docks of London are to a superficial observer the very focus of metropolitan wealth. The cranes creak with the mass of riches. In the warehouses are stored goods that are as it were ingots of untold gold. Above and below ground you see piles upon piles of treasure that the eye cannot compass. The wealth appears as boundless as the very sea it has traversed. The brain aches in an attempt to comprehend the amount of riches before, above, and beneath it. There are acres upon acres of treasure, more than enough, one would fancy, to stay the cravings of the whole world, and yet you have but to visit the hovels grouped round about all this amazing excess of riches to witness the same amazing excess of poverty. If the incomprehensibility of the wealth rises to sublimity, assuredly the want that co-exists with it is equally incomprehensible and equally sublime. Pass from the quay and warehouses to the courts and alleys that surround them, and the mind is as bewildered with the destitution of the one place as it is with the superabundance of the other. Many come to see the riches, but few see the poverty, abounding in absolute masses round the far-famed port of London.

According to the official returns, there belonged to this port on the 31st of December, 1842, very nearly 3000 ships, of the aggregate burden of 600,000 tons. Besides that there were 239 steamers, of 50,000 tons burden; and the crews of the entire number of ships and steamers amounted to 35,000 men and boys. The number of British and foreign ships that entered the port of London during the same year was 6400 and odd, whose capacity was upwards of a million and a quarter of tons, and the gross amount of customs duly collected upon their cargoes was very nearly 12,000l. of money. So vast an amount of shipping and commerce, it has been truly said, was never concentrated in any other single port.

Now, against this we must set the amount of misery that co-exists with it. We have shown that the mass of men dependent for their bread upon the business of only one of the docks are, by the shifting of the breeze, occasionally deprived in one day of no less than 220l., the labourers at the London Dock earning as a body near upon 400l. to-day, and

to-morrow scarcely 150l. These docks, however, are but one of six similar establishments —three being on the north and three on the south side of the Thames—and all employing a greater or less number of hands, equally dependent upon the winds for their subsistence. Deducting, then, the highest from the lowest number of labourers engaged at the London Dock—the extremes according to the books are under 500 and over 3000—we have as many as 2500 individuals deprived of a day's work and a living by the prevalence of an easterly wind; and calculating that the same effect takes place at the other docks— the East and West India for instance, St. Katherine's, Commercial, Grand Surrey, and East Country, to a greater or less extent, and that the hands employed to load and unload the vessels entering and quitting all these places are only four times more than those required at the London Dock, we have as many as 12,000 individuals or families whose daily bread is as fickle as the wind itself; whose wages, in fact, are one day collectively as much as 1500l. and the next as low as 500l., so that 8000 men are frequently thrown out of employ, while the earnings of the class to day amount to 1000l. less than they did yesterday.

It would be curious to take an average number of days that easterly winds prevail in London throughout the year, and so arrive at an estimate of the exact time that the above 8000 men are unemployed in the course of twelve months. This would give us some idea of the amount of their average weekly earnings. By the labourers themselves I am assured that, taking one week with another, they do not gain 5s. weekly throughout the year. I have made a point of visiting and interrogating a large number of them, in order to obtain some definite information respecting the extent of their income, and have found in only one instance an account kept of the individual earnings. In that case the wages averaged within a fraction of 13s. per week, the total sum gained since the beginning of the year being 25l. odd. I should state, however, that the man earning thus much was pointed out to me as one of the most provident of the casual labourers, and one, moreover, who is generally employed. " If it is possible to get work, he'll have it," was said of him; " there's not a lazy bone in his skin." Besides this he had done a considerable quantity of piece-work, so that altogether the man's earnings might be taken as the very extreme made by the best kind of " extra hands."

The man himself gives the following explanation as to the state of the labour-market at the London Dock. " He has had a good turn of work," he says, since he has been there. " Some don't get half what he does. He's not always employed, excepting when the business is in anyway brisk, but when a kind of a slack comes the recommended men get the prefer ence of the work, and the extras have nothing to do. This is the best sumner he has had since he has been in London. Has had a good bit of piece-work. Obliged to live as he does because he can't depend on work. Isn't certain of the second day's work. He's paid off every night, and can't say whether or not they'll want him on the morrow." The account of his wages was written in pencil on the cover of an old memorandum-book, and ran as follows:

	£. s. d.		£. s. d.	
Earned by day-work from 1st Jan. to 1st Aug. 1849	16 11 6	averaging	0 11 10	per week
By piece-work in August . . .	5 5 8	„	1 6 5	„
By day work from 1st Sept to 1st Oct.	3 8 7	„	0 17 1¾	„
Total . . .	£25 5 9	„	£2 15 4¾	„

If, then, 13s. be the average amount of weekly earnings by the most provident, industrious, and fortunate of the casual labourers at the docks — and that at the best season — it may be safely asserted that the lowest grade of workmen there do not gain more than 5s. per week throughout the year. It should be remembered that the man himself says " some don't get half what he does," and from a multiplicity of inquiries that I have made upon the subject this appears to be about the truth. Moreover, we should bear in mind that the average weekly wages of the dock-labourer, miserable as they are, are rendered even more wretched by the uncertain character of the work on which they depend. Were the income of the casual labourer at the docks 5s. per week from one year's end to another the workman would know exactly how much he had to subsist upon, and might therefore be expected to display some little providence and temperance in the expenditure of his wages. But where the means of subsistence occasionally rise to 15s. a-week, and occasionally sink to nothing, it is absurd to look for prudence, economy, or moderation. Regularity of habits are incompatible with irregularity of income; indeed, the very conditions necessary for the formation of any habit whatsoever are, that the act or thing to which we are to become habituated should be repeated at frequent and regular intervals. It is a moral impossibility that the class of labourers who are only occasionally employed should be either generally industrious or temperate — both industry and temperance being habits produced by constancy of employment and uniformity of income. Hence, where the greatest fluctuation occurs in the labour, there, of course, will be the greatest idleness and improvidence; where the greatest want generally is, there we shall find the greatest occasional excess; where from the uncertainty of the occupation prudence is most needed, there, strange to say, we shall meet with the highest imprudence of all. " Previous to the formation of a canal in the north of Ireland," says Mr. Porter, in " The Progress of the Nation," " the men were improvident even to recklessness. Such work as they got before came at uncertain intervals, the wages insufficient for the comfortable sustenance of their families were wasted at the whis-

key-shop, and the men appeared to be sunk in a state of hopeless degradation. From the moment, however, that work was offered to them which was constant in its nature and certain in its duration, men who before had been idle and dissolute were converted into sober, hard-working labourers, and proved themselves kind and careful husbands and fathers; and it is said that, notwithstanding the distribution of several hundred pounds weekly in wages, the whole of which must be considered as so much additional money placed in their hands, the consumption of whisky was absolutely and permanently diminished in the district. Indeed it is a fact worthy of notice, as illustrative of the tendency of the times of pressure, and consequently of deficient and uncertain employment, to increase spirit-drinking, that whilst in the year 1836 — a year of the greatest prosperity — the tax on British spirits amounted only to 2,390,000l.; yet, under the privations of 1841, the English poorer classes paid no less than 2,600,000l. in taxes upon the liquor they consumed — thus spending upwards of 200,000l. more in drink at a time when they were less able to afford it, and so proving that a fluctuation in the income of the working-classes is almost invariably attended with an excess of improvidence in the expenditure. Moreover, with reference to the dock-labourers, we have been informed, upon unquestionable authority, that some years back there were near upon 220 ships waiting to be discharged in one dock alone; and such was the pressure of business then, that it became necessary to obtain leave of Her Majesty's Customs to increase the usual time of daily labour from eight to twelve hours. The men employed, therefore, earned 50 per cent more than they were in the habit of doing at the briskest times; but so far from the extra amount of wages being devoted to increase the comforts of their homes, it was principally spent in public-houses. The riot and confusion thus created in the neighbourhood were such as had never been known before, and indeed were so general among the workmen, that every respectable person in the immediate vicinity expressed a hope that such a thing as " overtime " would never occur again.

It may then be safely asserted, that though the wages of the casual labourer at the docks average 5s. per week, still the weekly earnings are of so precarious and variable a nature, that when the time of the men is fully employed, the money which is gained over and above the amount absolutely required for subsistence is almost sure to be spent in intemperance, and that when there is little or no demand for their work, and their gains are consequently insufficient for the satisfaction of their appetites, they and those who depend upon their labour for their food must at least want, if not starve. The improvidence of the casual dock-labourer is due, therefore, not to any particular malformation of his moral constitution, but to the precarious character of his calling. His vices are the vices of ordinary human nature. Ninety-nine in every hundred similarly circumstanced would commit similar enormities. If the very winds could whistle away the food and firing of wife and children, I doubt much whether, after a week's or a month's privation, we should many of us be able to prevent ourselves from falling into the very same excesses.

It is consoling to moralise in our easy chairs, after a good dinner, and to assure ourselves that we should do differently. Self-denial is not very difficult when our stomachs are full and our backs are warm; but let us live a month of hunger and cold, and assuredly we should be as self-indulgent as they.

I have devoted some time to the investigation of the state of the casual labourers at the other docks, and shall now proceed to set forth the result of my inquiries.

The West India Docks.

The West India Docks are about a mile and a-half from the London Docks. The entire ground that they cover is 295 acres, so that they are nearly three times larger than the London Docks, and more than twelve times more extensive than those of St. Katherine's. Hence they are the most capacious of all the great warehousing establishments in the port of London. The export dock is about 870 yards, or very nearly half-a-mile in length by 135 yards in width; its area, therefore, is about 25 acres. The import dock is the same length as the export dock, and 166 yards wide. The south dock, which is appropriated both to import and export vessels, is 1,183 yards, or upwards of two-thirds of a mile long, with an entrance to the river at each end; both the locks, as well as that into the Blackwall basin, being forty feet wide, and large enough to admit ships of 1,200 tons burden. The warehouses for imported goods are on the four quays of the import dock. They are well contrived and of great extent, being calculated to contain 180,000 tons of merchandise; and there has been at one time on the quays, and in the sheds, vaults, and warehouses, colonial produce worth 20,000,000l. sterling. The East India Docks are likewise the property of the West India Dock Company, having been purchased by them of the East India Company at the time of the opening of the trade to India. The import dock here has an area of 18 acres, and the export dock about 9 acres. The depth of water in these docks is greater, and they can consequently accommodate ships of greater burden than any other establishment on the river. The capital of both establishments, or of the united company, amounts to upwards of 2,000,000 of money. The West India import dock can accommodate 300 ships, and the export dock 200 ships of 300 tons each; and the East India import dock 84 ships, and the export dock 40 ships, of 800 tons each. The number of ships that entered the West India Dock to load and unload last year was 3008, and the number that entered the East India Dock 298. I owe the above information, as well as that which follows, to the kindness of the secretary and superintendent of the docks in question. To the politeness and intelligence of the latter gentleman I am specially indebted. Indeed his readiness to afford me all the assistance that lay in his power, as well as his courtesy and gentlemanly demeanour, formed a marked contrast to that of the deputy-superintendent of the London Docks, the one appearing as anxious for the welfare and comfort of the labouring men as the other seemed indifferent to it.

The transition from the London to the West India Docks is of a very peculiar character. The labourers at the latter place seem to be more civilised. The scrambling and scuffling for the day's hire, which is the striking feature of the one establishment, is scarcely distinguishable at the other. It is true there is the same crowd of labourers in quest of a day's work, but the struggle to obtain it is neither so fierce nor so disorderly in its character. And yet, here the casual labourers are men from whom no character is demanded as well as there. The amount of wages for the summer months is the same as at the London Docks. Unlike the London Docks, however, no reduction is made at the East and West India Docks during the winter.

The labour is as precarious at one establishment as at the other. The greatest number of hands employed for any one day at the East and West India Docks in the course of last year was nearly 4000, and the smallest number about 1300. The lowest number of ships that entered the docks during any one week in the present year was 28, and the highest number 209, being a difference of 181 vessels, of an average burden of 300 tons each. The positive amount of variation, however, which occurred in the labour during the briskest and slackest weeks of last year was a difference of upwards of 2500 in the number of extra workmen employed, and of about 2000l. in the amount of wages paid for the six days' labour. I have been favoured with a return of the number of vessels that entered the East and West India Docks for each week in the present year, and

I subjoin a statement of the number arriving in each of the first fourteen of those weeks. In the 1st week of all there were 86, the 2d 47, the 3d 43, the 4th 48, the 5th 28, the 6th 49, the 7th 46, the 8th 37, the 9th 42, the 10th 47, the 11th 42, the 12th 131, the 13th 209, and the 14th 85. Hence it appears, that in the second week the number of ships coming into dock decreased nearly one-half; in the fifth week they were again diminished in a like proportion, while in the sixth week they were increased in a similar ratio; in the twelfth week they were more than three times what they were in the eleventh, in the thirteenth the number was half as much again as it was in the twelfth, and in the fourteenth it was down below half the number of the thirteenth, so that it is clear that the subsistence derived from dock labour must be of the most fickle and doubtful kind.

THE ST. KATHERINE'S DOCK.

NOR are the returns from St. Katherine's Dock of a more cheerful character. Here it should be observed that no labourer is employed without a previous recommendation; and, indeed, it is curious to notice the difference in the appearance of the men applying for work at this establishment. They not only have a more decent look, but seem to be better behaved than any other dock-labourers I have yet seen. The "ticket" system is here adopted—that is to say, the plan of allowing only such persons to labour within the docks as have been satisfactorily recommended to the company, and furnished with a ticket by them in return—this ticket system, says the statement which has been kindly drawn up expressly for me by the superintendent of the docks, may be worth notice, at a time when such efforts are making to improve the condition of the labourers. It gives an identity and *locus standi* to the men which casual labourers cannot otherwise possess, it connects them with the various grades of officers under whose eyes they labour, prevents favouritism, and leads to their qualifications being noted and recorded. It also holds before them a reward for activity, intelligence, and good conduct; because the vacancies in the list of preferable labourers, which occur during the year, are invariably filled in the succeeding January by selecting, upon strict inquiry, the best of the extra-ticket labourers, the vacancies among the permanent men being supplied in like manner from the list of preferable labourers, while from the permanent men are appointed the subordinate officers, as markers, samplers, &c.

Let us, however, before entering into a description of the class and number of labourers employed at St. Katherine's give a brief description of the docks themselves. The lofty walls, which constitute it in the language of the Custom-house a place of special security, enclose an area of 23 acres, of which 11 are water, capable of accommodating 120 ships, besides barges and other craft; cargoes are raised into the warehouses out of the hold of a ship, without the goods being deposited on the quay. The cargoes can be raised out of the ship's hold into the warehouses of St. Katherine's in one-fifth of the usual time. Before the existence of docks, a month or six weeks was taken up in discharging the cargo of an East-Indiaman of from 800 to 1200 tons burden, while 8 days were necessary in the summer and 14 in the winter to unload a ship of 350 tons. At St. Katherine's, however, the average time now occupied in discharging a ship of 250 tons is twelve hours, and one of 500 tons two or three days, the goods being placed at the same time in the warehouse: there have been occasions when even greater despatch has been used, and a cargo of 1100 casks of tallow, averaging from 9 to 10 cwt. each, has been discharged in seven hours. This would have been considered little short of a miracle on the legal quays less than fifty years ago. In 1841, about 1000 vessels and 10,000 lighters were accommodated at St. Katherine's Dock. The capital expended by the dock company exceeds 2,000,000 of money.

The business of this establishment is carried on by 35 officers, 105 clerks and apprentices, 135 markers, samplers, and foremen, 250 permanent labourers, 150 preferable ticket-labourers, proportioned to the amount of work to be done. The average number of labourers employed, permanent, preferable, and extras, is 1096; the highest number employed on any one day last year was 1713, and the lowest number 515, so that the extreme fluctuation in the labour appears to be very nearly 1200 hands. The lowest sum of money that was paid in 1848 for the day's work of the entire body of labourers employed was 64*l*. 7*s*. 6*d*., and the highest sum 214*l*. 2*s*. 6*d*., being a difference of very nearly 150*l*. in one day, or 900*l*. in the course of the week. The average number of ships that enter the dock every week is 17, the highest number that entered in any one week last year was 36, and the lowest 5, being a difference of 31. Assuming these to have been of an average burden of 300 tons, and that every such vessel would require 100 labourers to discharge its cargo in three days, then 1500 extra hands ought to have been engaged to discharge the cargoes of the entire number in a week. This, it will be observed, is very nearly equal to the highest number of the labourers employed by the company in the year 1848.

The remaining docks are the Commercial Docks and timber ponds, the Grand Surrey Canal Dock at Rotherhithe, and the East Country Dock. The Commercial Docks occupy an area of about 49 acres, of which four-fifths are water. There is accommodation for 350 ships, and in the warehouses for 50,000 tons of merchandise. They are appropriated to vessels engaged in the European timber and corn trades, and the surrounding warehouses are used chiefly as granaries—the timber remaining afloat in the dock until it is conveyed to the yard of the wholesale dealer and builder. The Surrey Dock is merely an entrance basin to a canal, and can accommodate 300 vessels. The East Country Dock, which adjoins the Commercial Docks on the South, is capable of receiving 28 timber-ships. It has an area of 6½ acres, and warehouse-room for 3700 tons.

In addition to these there is the Regent's Canal Dock, between Shadwell and Limehouse, and though it is a place for bonding timber and deals only, it nevertheless affords great accommodation to the trade of the port by withdrawing shipping from the river.

The number of labourers, casual and permanent, employed at these various establishments is so limited, that, taken altogether, the fluctuations occurring at their briskest and slackest periods may be reckoned as equal to that of St. Katherine's. Hence the account of the variation in the total number of hands employed, and the sum of money paid as wages to them, by the different dock companies, when the business is brisk or slack, may be stated as follows :—

At the London Dock the difference between the greatest and smallest number is . } 2000 hands
At the East and West India Dock 2500 ,,
At the St. Katherine's Dock . 1200 ,,
At the remaining docks say . . 1300 ,,
Total number of dock labourers thrown out of employ by the prevalence of easterly winds } 7000

The difference between the highest and lowest amount of wages paid at the London Dock is . . } £. 1500
At the East and West India Dock . 1875
At the St. Katherine Dock . . . 900
At the remaining docks . . . 975
————
£5250

From the above statement then it appears, that by the prevalence of an easterly wind no less than 7000 out of the aggregate number of persons living by dock labour may be deprived of their regular income, and the entire body may have as much as 5250l. a week abstracted from the amount of their collective earnings, at a period of active employment. But the number of individuals who depend upon the quantity of shipping entering the port of London for their daily subsistence is far beyond this amount. Indeed we are assured by a gentleman filling a high situation in St. Katherine's Dock, and who, from his sympathy with the labouring poor, has evidently given no slight attention to the subject, that taking into consideration the number of wharf-labourers, dock-labourers, lightermen, riggers and lumpers, shipwrights, caulkers, ships'

carpenters, anchor-smiths, corn-porters, fruit and coal-meters, and indeed all the multifarious arts and callings connected with shipping, there are no less than from 2500 to 30,000 individuals who are thrown wholly out of employ by a long continuance of easterly winds. Estimating then the gains of this large body of individuals at 2s. 6d. per day, or 15s. per week, when fully employed, we shall find that the loss to those who depend upon the London shipping for their subsistence amounts to 20,000l. per week, and, considering that such winds are often known to prevail for a fortnight to three weeks at a time, it follows that the entire loss to this large class will amount to from 40,000l. to 60,000l. within a month,—an amount of privation to the labouring poor which it is positively awful to contemplate. Nor is this the only evil connected with an enduring easterly wind. Directly a change takes place a glut of vessels enters the metropolitan port, and labourers flock from all quarters; indeed they flock from every part where the workmen exist in a greater quantity than the work. From 500 to 800 vessels frequently arrive at one time in London after the duration of a contrary wind, and then such is the demand for workmen, and so great the press of business, owing to the rivalry among merchants, and the desire of each owner to have his cargo the first in the market, that a sufficient number of hands is scarcely to be found. Hundreds of extra labourers, who can find labour nowhere else, are thus led to seek work in the docks. But, to use the words of our informant, two or three weeks are sufficient to break the neck of an ordinary glut, and then the vast amount of extra hands that the excess of business has brought to the neighbourhood are thrown out of employment, and left to increase either the vagabondism of the neighbourhood or to swell the number of paupers and heighten the rates of the adjacent parishes.

CHEAP LODGING-HOUSES.

I NOW come to the class of cheap lodging-houses usually frequented by the casual labourers at the docks. It will be remembered, perhaps, that I described one of these places, as well as the kind of characters to be found there. Since then I have directed my attention particularly to this subject; not because it came first in order according to the course of investigation I had marked out for myself, but because it presented so many peculiar features that I thought it better, even at the risk of being unmethodical, to avail myself of the channels of information opened to me rather than defer the matter to its proper place, and so lose the freshness of the impression it had made upon my mind.

On my first visit, the want and misery that I saw were such, that, in consulting with the gentleman who led me to the spot, it was arranged that a dinner should be given on the following Sunday to all those who were present on the evening of my first interview; and, accordingly, enough beef, potatoes, and materials for a suet-pudding, were sent in from the neighbouring market to feed them every one. I parted with my guide, arranging to be with him the next Sunday at half-past one. We met at the time appointed, and set out on our way to the cheap lodging-house. The streets were alive with sailors, and bonnetless and capless women. The Jews' shops and public-houses were all open, and parties of "jolly tars" reeled past us, singing and bawling on their way. Had it not been that here and there a stray shop was closed, it would have been impossible to have guessed it was Sunday. We dived down a narrow court, at the entrance of which lolled Irish labourers smoking short pipes. Across the court hung lines, from which dangled dirty-white clothes to dry; and as we walked on, ragged, unwashed, shoeless children scampered past us, chasing one another. At length we reached a large open yard. In the centre of it stood several empty costermongers' trucks and turned-up carts, with their shafts high in the air. At the bottom of these lay two young girls huddled together, asleep. Their bare heads told their mode of life, while it was evident, from their muddy Adelaide boots, that they had walked the streets all night. My companion tried to see if he knew them, but they slept too soundly to be roused by gentle means. We passed on, and a few paces further on there sat grouped on a door-step four women, of the same character as the last two. One had her head covered up in an old brown shawl, and was sleeping in the lap of the one next to her. The other two were eating walnuts; and a coarse-featured man in knee-breeches and "ankle-jacks" was stretched on the ground close beside them.

At length we reached the lodging-house. It was night when I had first visited the place, and all now was new to me. The entrance was through a pair of large green gates, which gave it somewhat the appearance of a stable-yard. Over the kitchen door there hung a clothes-line, on which were a wet shirt and a pair of ragged canvas trousers, brown with tar. Entering the kitchen, we found it so full of smoke that the sun's rays, which shot slanting down through a broken tile in the roof, looked like a shaft of light cut through the fog. The flue of the chimney stood out from the bare brick wall like a buttress, and was black all the way up with the smoke; the beams, which hung down from the roof, and ran from wall to wall, were of the same colour; and in the centre, to light the room, was a rude iron gas-pipe, such as are used at night when the streets are turned up. The floor was unboarded, and a wooden seat projected from the wall all round the room. In front of this were ranged a series of tables, on which lolled dozing men. A number of the inmates were grouped around the fire;

some kneeling toasting herrings, of which the place smelt strongly; others, without shirts, seated on the ground close beside it for warmth; and others drying the ends of cigars they had picked up in the streets. As we entered the men rose, and never was so motley and so ragged an assemblage seen. Their hair was matted like flocks of wool, and their chins were grimy with their unshorn beards. Some were in dirty smock-frocks; others in old red plush waistcoats, with long sleeves. One was dressed in an old shooting-jacket, with large wooden buttons; a second in a blue flannel sailor's shirt; and a third, a mere boy, wore a long camlet coat reaching to his heels, and with the ends of the sleeves hanging over his hands. The features of the lodgers wore every kind of expression: one lad was positively handsome, and there was a frankness in his face and a straightforward look in his eye that strongly impressed me with a sense of his honesty, even although I was assured he was a confirmed pickpocket. The young thief who had brought back the 11½d. change out of the shilling that had been entrusted to him on the preceding evening, was far from prepossessing, now that I could see him better. His cheek-bones were high, while his hair, cut close on the top, with a valance of locks, as it were, left hanging in front, made me look upon him with no slight suspicion. On the form at the end of the kitchen was one whose squalor and wretchedness produced a feeling approaching to awe. His eyes were sunk deep in his head, his cheeks were drawn in, and his nostrils pinched with evident want, while his dark stubbly beard gave a grimness to his appearance that was almost demoniac; and yet there was a patience in his look that was almost pitiable. His clothes were black and shiny at every fold with grease, and his coarse shirt was so brown with long wearing, that it was only with close inspection you could see that it had once been a checked one: on his feet he had a pair of lady's side-laced boots, the toes of which had been cut off so that he might get them on. I never beheld so gaunt a picture of famine. To this day the figure of the man haunts me.

The dinner had been provided for thirty, but the news of the treat had spread, and there was a muster of fifty. We hardly knew how to act. It was, however, left to those whose names had been taken down as being present on the previous evening to say what should be done; and the answer from one and all was that the new-comers were to share the feast with them. The dinner was then half-portioned out in an adjoining outhouse into twenty-five platefuls — the entire stock of crockery belonging to the establishment numbering no more — and afterwards handed into the kitchen through a small window to each party, as his name was called out. As he hurried to the seat behind the bare table, he commenced tearing the meat asunder with his fingers, for knives and forks were unknown there. Some, it is true, used bits of wood like skewers, but this seemed almost like affectation in such a place : others sat on the ground with the plate of meat and pudding on their laps; while the beggar-boy, immediately on receiving his portion, danced along the room, whirling the plate round on his thumb as he went, and then, dipping his nose in the plate, seized a potato in his mouth. I must confess the sight of the hungry crowd gnawing their food was far from pleasant to contemplate; so, while the dinner was being discussed, I sought to learn from those who remained to be helped, how they had fallen to so degraded a state. A sailor lad assured me he had been robbed of his mariner's ticket; that he could not procure another under 13s.; and not having as many pence, he was unable to obtain another ship. What could he do? he said. He knew no trade : he could only get employment occasionally as a labourer at the docks ; and this was so seldom, that if it had not been for the few things he had, he must have starved outright. The good-looking youth I have before spoken of wanted but 3l. 10s. to get back to America. He had worked his passage over here; had fallen into bad company; been imprisoned three times for picking pockets; and was heartily wearied of his present course. He could get no work. In America he would be happy, and among his friends again. I spoke to the gentleman who had brought me to the spot, and who knew them all well. His answers, however, gave me little hope. The boy, whose face seemed beaming with innate frankness and honesty, had been apprenticed by him to a shoe-stitcher. But, no! he preferred vagrancy to work. I could have sworn he was a trustworthy lad, and shall never believe in "looks" again.

The dinner finished, I told the men assembled there that I should come some evening in the course of the week, and endeavour to ascertain from them some definite information concerning the persons usually frequenting such houses as theirs. On our way home, my friend recognised, among the females we had before seen huddled on the step outside the lodging-house, a young woman whom he had striven to get back to her parents. Her father had been written to, and would gladly receive her. Again the girl was exhorted to leave her present companions and return home. The tears streamed from her eyes at mention of her mother's name; but she would not stir. Her excuse was, that she had no clothes proper to go in. Her father and mother were very respectable, she said, and she could not go back to them as she was. It was evident, by her language, she had at least been well educated. She would not listen, however, to my friend's exhortations; so, seeing that his entreaties were wasted upon her, we left her, and wended our way home.

Knowing that this lodging-house might be

taken as a fair sample of the class now abounding in London, and, moreover, having been informed by those who had made the subject their peculiar study, that the characters generally congregated there constituted a fair average of the callings and habits of those who resort to the low lodging-houses of London, I was determined to avail myself of the acquaintances I made in this quarter, in order to arrive at some more definite information upon those places than had yet been made public. The only positive knowledge the public have hitherto had of the people assembling in the cheap lodging-houses of London is derived chiefly from the Report of the Constabulary Commissioners, and partly from the Report upon Vagrancy. But this information, having been procured through others, was so faulty, that having now obtained the privilege of personal inspection and communication, I was desirous of turning it to good account. Consequently I gave notice that I wished all that had dined there on last Sunday to attend me yesterday evening, so that I might obtain from them generally an account of their past and present career. I found them all ready to meet me, and I was assured that, by adopting certain precautions, I should be in a fair way to procure information upon the subject of the cheap lodging-houses of London that few have the means of getting. However, so as to be able to check the one account with another, I put myself in communication with a person who had lived for upwards of four months in the house. Strange to say, he was a man of good education and superior attainments—further than this I am not at liberty to state. I deal with the class of houses, and not with any particular house, be it understood.

The lodging-house to which I more particularly allude makes up as many as 84 "bunks," or beds, for which 2d. per night is charged. For this sum the parties lodging there for the night are entitled to the use of the kitchen for the following day. In this a fire is kept all day long, at which they are allowed to cook their food. The kitchen opens at 5 in the morning, and closes at about 11 at night, after which hour no fresh lodger is taken in, and all those who slept in the house the night before, but who have not sufficient money to pay for their bed at that time, are turned out. Strangers who arrive in the course of the day must procure a tin ticket, by paying 2d. at the wicket in the office, previously to being allowed to enter the kitchen. The kitchen is about 40 feet long by about 40 wide. The "bunks" are each about 7 feet long, and 1 foot 10 inches wide, and the grating on which the straw mattress is placed is about 12 inches from the ground. The wooden partitions between the "bunks" are about 4 feet high. The coverings are a leather or a rug, but leathers are generally preferred. Of these "bunks" there are five rows, of about 24 deep; two rows being placed head to head, with a gangway between each of such two rows, and the other row against the wall. The average number of persons sleeping in this house of a night is 60. Of these there are generally about 30 pickpockets, 10 street-beggars, a few infirm old people who subsist occasionally upon parish relief and occasionally upon charity, 10 or 15 dock-labourers, about the same number of low and precarious callings, such as the neighbourhood affords, and a few persons who have been in good circumstances, but who have been reduced from a variety of causes. At one time there were as many as 9 persons lodging in this house who subsisted by picking up dogs' dung out of the streets, getting about 5s. for every basketful. The earnings of one of these men were known to average 9s. per week. There are generally lodging in the house a few bone-grubbers, who pick up bones, rags, iron, &c., out of the streets. Their average earnings are about 1s. per day. There are several mud-larks, or youths who go down to the water-side when the tide is out, to see whether any article of value has been left upon the bank of the river. The person supplying this information to me, who was for some time resident in the house, has seen brought home by these persons a drum of figs at one time, and a Dutch cheese at another. These were sold in small lots or slices to the other lodgers.

The pickpockets generally lodging in the house consist of handkerchief-stealers, shop-lifters — including those who rob the till as well as steal articles from the doors of shops. Legs and breasts of mutton are frequently brought in by this class of persons. There are seldom any housebreakers lodging in such places, because they require a room of their own, and mostly live with prostitutes. Besides pickpockets, there are also lodging in the house speculators in stolen goods. These may be dock-labourers or Billingsgate porters, having a few shillings in their pockets. With these they purchase the booty of the juvenile thieves. "I have known," says my informant, "these speculators wait in the kitchen, walking about with their hands in their pockets, till a little fellow would come in with such a thing as a cap, a piece of bacon, or a piece of mutton. They would purchase it, and then either retail it amongst the other lodgers in the kitchen or take it to some 'fence,' where they would receive a profit upon it." The general feeling of the kitchen — excepting with four or five individuals — is to encourage theft. The encouragement to the "gonaff," (a Hebrew word signifying a young thief, probably learnt from the Jew "fences" in the neighbourhood) consists in laughing at and applauding his dexterity in thieving; and whenever anything is brought in, the "gonaff" is greeted for his good luck, and a general rush is made towards him to see the produce of his thievery. The "gonaffs" are generally young boys; about 20 out of 30 of these lads are under 21 years of age. They almost all of them love idleness, and will only work for one or two days together, but then they will work very hard. It is a singular fact that, as a body, the pickpockets are generally very sparing of drink. They are mostly libidinous, indeed universally so, and spend whatever money they can spare upon the low prostitutes round about the neighbourhood. Burglars and smashers generally rank above this class of thieves. A burglar would not condescend to sit among pickpockets. My informant has known a housebreaker to say with a sneer, when requested to sit down with the "gonaffs," "No, no! I may be a thief, sir; but, thank God, at least I'm a respectable one." The beggars who frequent these houses go about different markets and streets asking charity of the people that pass by. They generally go out in couples; the business of one of the two being to look out and give warning when the policeman is approaching, and of the other to stand "shallow;" that is to say, to stand with very little clothing on, shivering and shaking, sometimes with bandages round his legs, and sometimes with his arm in a sling. Others beg "scran" (broken victuals) of the servants at respectable houses, and bring it home to the lodging-house, where they sell it. You may see, I am told, the men who lodge in the place, and obtain an honest living, watch for these beggars coming in, as if they were the best victuals in the City. My informant knew an instance of a lad who seemed to be a very fine little fellow, and promised to have been possessed of excellent mental capabilities if properly directed, who came to the lodging-house when out of a situation as an errand-boy. He stayed there a month or six weeks, during which time he was tampered with by the others, and ultimately became a confirmed "gonaff." The conversation among the lodgers relates chiefly to thieving and the best manner of stealing. By way of practice, a boy will often pick the pocket of one of the lodgers walking about the room, and if detected declare he did not mean it.

The sanitary state of these houses is very bad. Not only do the lodgers generally swarm with vermin, but there is little or no ventilation to the sleeping-rooms, in which 60 persons, of the foulest habits, usually sleep every night. There are no proper washing utensils, neither towels nor basins, nor wooden bowls. There are one or two buckets, but these are not meant for the use of the lodgers, but for cleaning the rooms. The lodgers never think of washing themselves. The cleanliest among them will do so in the bucket, and then wipe themselves with their pocket-handkerchiefs, or the tails of their shirts.

A large sum to be made by two beggars in one week is 20s.; or 10s. a-piece, one for looking out, and the other for "standing shallow." The average earnings of such persons are certainly below 8s. per week. If the Report of the Constabulary Force Commissioners states that 20s. per week is the average sum earned, I am told the statement must have been furnished by parties who had either some object in overrating the amount, or else who had no means of obtaining correct information on the subject. From all my informant has seen as to the earnings of those who make a trade of picking pockets and begging, he is convinced that the amount is far below what is generally believed to be the case. Indeed, nothing but the idle, roving life that is connected with the business, could compensate the thieves or beggars for the privations they frequently undergo.

After obtaining this information, I attended the lodging-house in pursuance of the notice I had given, in order to ascertain from the lodgers themselves what were the callings and earnings of the different parties there assembled. I found that from 50 to 60 had mustered purposely to meet me, although it was early in the evening, and they all expressed themselves ready to furnish me with any information I might require. The gentleman who accompanied me assured me that the answers they would give to my questionings would be likely to be correct, from the fact of the number assembled, as each would check the other. Having read to them the account (in the *Morning Chronicle*) of my previous interview with them, they were much delighted at finding themselves in print, and immediately arranged themselves on a seat all round the room. My first question was as to the age of those present. Out of 55 assembled, I found that there were; 1 from 60 to 70 years old, 4 from 50 to 60, 1 from 40 to 50, 15 from 30 to 40, 16 from 20 to 30, and 18 from 10 to 20. Hence it will be seen that the younger members constituted by far the greater portion of the assembly. The 18 between 10 and 20 were made up as follows : — There were 3 of 20 years, 8 of 19 years, 3 of 18 years, 4 of 17 years, 1 of 16 years, and 2 of 15 years. Hence there were more of the age of 19 than of any other age present.

My next inquiry was as to the place of birth. I found that there were 16 belonging to London, 9 to Ireland, 3 to Bristol, 3 to Liverpool, 2 were from Norfolk, 2 from Yorkshire, 2 from Essex, 2 from Germany, and 2 from North America. The remaining 14 were born respectively in Macclesfield, Bolton, Aylesbury, Seacomb, Deal, Epping, Hull, Nottinghamshire, Plumstead, Huntingdonshire, Plymouth, Shropshire, Northamptonshire, and Windsor. After this I sought to obtain information as to the occupations of their parents, with a view of discovering whether their delinquencies arose from the depraved character of their early associations. I found among the number, 13 whose fathers had been labouring men, 5 had been carpenters, 4 millers and farmers, 2 dyers, 2 cabinet-makers, a tallow-chandler, a wood-turner, a calico-glazer, a silversmith, a compositor, a cotton-spinner, a hatter, a grocer,

a whip-maker, a sweep, a glover, a watchmaker, a madhouse-keeper, a bricklayer, a shipbuilder, a cow-keeper, a fishmonger, a millwright, a coast-guard, a ropemaker, a gunsmith, a collier, an undertaker, a leather-cutter, a clerk, an engineer, a schoolmaster, a captain in the army, and a physician.

I now sought to learn from them the trades that they themselves were brought up to. There were 17 labourers, 7 mariners, 3 weavers, 2 bricklayers, and 2 shoemakers. The rest were respectively silversmiths, dyers, blacksmiths, wood-turners, tailors, farriers, caulkers, French polishers, shopmen, brickmakers, sweeps, ivory-turners, cowboys, stereotype-founders, fishmongers, tallow-chandlers, ropemakers, miners, bone-grubbers, engineers, coal-porters, errand-boys, beggars, and one called himself "a prig."

I next found that 40 out of the 55 could read and write, 4 could read, and only 11 could do neither.

My next point was to ascertain how long they had been out of regular employment, or to use their own phrase, "had been knocking about." One had been 10 years idle; one, 9; three, 8; two, 7; four, 6; five, 5; six, 4; nine, 3; ten, 2; five, 1; three, 6 months, and one, 2 months out of employment. A bricklayer told me he had been eight summers in, and eight winters out of work; and a dock-labourer assured me that he had been 11 years working at the dock, and that for full three-fourths of his time he could obtain no employment there.

After this, I questioned them concerning their earnings for the past week. One had gained nothing, another had gained 1s, eleven had earned 2s. ; eight, 3s. ; nine, 4s. ; five, 5s. ; four, 6s. ; four, 7s. ; six, 8s. ; one, 10s. ; one, 11s. ; and one, 18s. From three I received no answers. The average earnings of the 52 above enumerated are 4s. 11d. per week.

Respecting their clothing, 14 had no shirts to their backs, 5 had no shoes, and 42 had shoes that scarcely held together.

I now desired to be informed how many out of the number had been confined in prison ; and learnt that no less than 34 among the 55 present had been in gaol once, or oftener. Eleven had been in once; five had been in twice; five, in 3 times ; three, 4 times ; four, 6 times ; one, 7 times ; one, 8 times ; one, 9 times ; one, 10 times ; one, 14 times ; and one confessed to having been there at least 20 times. So that the 34 individuals had been imprisoned altogether 140 times ; thus averaging four imprisonments to each person. I was anxious to distinguish between imprisonment for vagrancy and imprisonment for theft. Upon inquiry I discovered that seven had each been imprisoned once for vagrancy ; one, twice ; one, 3 times ; two, 4 times ; one, 5 times ; two, 6 times ; two, 8 times ; and one, 10 times ; making in all 63 imprisonments under the Vagrant Act. Of those who had been confined in gaol for theft, there were eleven who had been in once; seven, who had been in twice; two, 3 times; three, 6 times; one, 8 times, and two, 10 times; making a total of 77 imprisonments for thieving. Hence, out of 140 incarcerations, 63 of those had been for vagrancy, and 77 for theft; and this was among 34 individuals in an assemblage of 55.

The question that I put to them after this was, how long they had been engaged in thieving? and the following were the answers: one had been 15 years at it; one, 14 years; two, 12 years; three, 10 years; one, 9 years; one, 8 years; two, 7 years; one, 6 years; two, 5 years; three, 4 years; and one, 3 years; one, 18 months; one, 7 months; two, 6 months; and one, 2 months. Consequently, there were, of the half-hundred and odd individuals there assembled, thieves of the oldest standing and the most recent beginning.

Their greatest gains by theft, in a single day, were thus classified. The most that one had gained was 3*d.*, the greatest sum another had gained was 7*d.*; another, 1*s.* 6*d.*; another, 2*s.* 6*d.*; another, 6*s.*; five had made from 10*s.* to 15*s.*; three from 1*l.* to 2*l.*; one from 2*l.* to 3*l.*; six from 3*l.* to 4*l.*; one from 4*l.* to 5*l.*; two from 20*l.* to 30*l.*; and two from 30*l.* to 40*l.* Of the latter two sums, one was stolen from the father of the thief, and the other from the till of a counter when the shop was left unoccupied, the boy vaulting over the counter and abstracting from the till no less than seven 5*l.* notes, all of which were immediately disposed of to a Jew in the immediate neighbourhood for 3*l.* 10*s.* each.

The greatest earnings by begging had been 7*s.* 6*d.*, 10*s.* 6*d.*, and 1*l.*; but the average amount of earnings was apparently of so precarious a nature, that it was difficult to get the men to state a definite sum. From their condition, however, as well as their mode of living whilst I remained among them, I can safely say begging did not seem to be a very lucrative or attractive calling, and the lodgers were certainly under no restraint in my presence.

I wanted to learn from them what had been their motive for stealing in the first instance, and I found upon questioning them, that ten did so on running away from home; five confessed to have done so from keeping flash company, and wanting money to defray their expenses; six had first stolen to go to theatres; nine, because they had been imprisoned for vagrants, and found that the thief was better treated than they; one because he had got no tools to work with; one because he was "hard up;" one because he could not get work; and one more because he was put in prison for begging.

The following is the list of articles that they first stole: six rabbits, silk shawl from home, a pair of shoes, a Dutch cheese, a few shillings from home, a coat and trousers, a bullock's heart, four "tiles" of copper, fifteen and sixpence from master, two handkerchiefs, half a quartern loaf, a set of tools worth 3*l.*, clothes from a warehouse, worth 22*l.*, a Cheshire cheese, a pair of carriage lamps, some handkerchiefs, five shillings, some turnips, watchchain and seals, a sheep, three and sixpence, and an invalid's chair. This latter article, the boy assured me he had taken about the country with him, and amused himself by riding down hill.

Their places of amusement consisted, they told me, of the following: The Britannia Saloon, the City Theatre, the Albert Saloon, the Standard Saloon, the Surrey and Victoria Theatres when they could afford it, the Penny Negroes, and the Earl of Effingham concerts.

Four frequenters of that room had been transported, and yet the house had been open only as many years, and of the associates and companions of those present, no less than 40 had left the country in the same manner. The names of some of these were curious. I subjoin a few of them. The Banger, The Slasher, The Spider, Flash Jim, White-coat Mushe, Lankey Thompson, Tom Sales [he was hung], and Jack Sheppard.

Of the fifty-five congregrated, two had signed the temperance pledge, and kept it. The rest confessed to getting drunk occasionally, but not making a practice of it. Indeed, it is generally allowed that, as a class, the young pickpockets are rather temperate than otherwise; so that here, at least, we cannot assert that drink is the cause of the crime. Nor can their various propensities be ascribed to ignorance, for we have seen that out of 55 individuals 40 could read and write, while 4 could read. It should be remembered, at the same time, that out of the 55 men only 34 were thieves. Neither can the depravity of their early associations be named as the cause of their delinquencies, for we have seen that, as a class, their fathers are men rather well to do in the world. Indeed their errors seem to have rather a physical than either an intellectual or a moral cause. They seem to be naturally of an erratic and self-willed temperament, objecting to the restraints of home, and incapable of continuous application to any one occupation whatsoever. They are essentially the idle and the vagabond; and they seem generally to attribute the commencement of their career to harsh government at home.

According to the Report of the Constabulary Force Commissioners, there were in the metropolis in 1839, 221 of such houses as the one at present described, and each of these houses harboured daily, upon an average, no less than eleven of such characters as the foregoing, making in all a total of 2431 vagrants and pickpockets sheltered by the proprietors of the low lodging-houses of London. The above twopenny lodging-house has, on an average, from fifty to sixty persons sleeping in it nightly, yielding an income of nearly 3*l.* per week. The three-penny lodging-houses in the same neighbourhood average from fifteen to twenty persons per night, and produce a weekly total of from 20s. to 25s. profit, the rent of the houses at the same time being only from 5s. to 6s. per week.

There is still one question worthy of consideration. Does the uncertainty of dock labour generate thieves and vagabonds, or do the thieves and vagabonds crowd round the docks so as to be able to gain a day's work when unable to thieve? According to returns of the metropolitan police force, the value of the property stolen in this district in the year 1848 was 200l., of which only 365l. were recovered. The number of robberies was 521, the average amount of each robbery being 3l. 17s. 0½d. The amount recovered averaged 14s. on each robbery.

ON THE TRANSIT OF GREAT BRITAIN AND THE METROPOLIS.

As the entire transit system of Great Britain, with all its railroads, turnpike-roads, canals, and navigable rivers, converges on London, I propose to make it the subject of the present section, by way of introduction to my inquiry into the condition of the metropolitan labourers connected therewith.

"There is a very great amount of labour employed," says Mr. Stewart Mill, "not only in bringing a product into existence, but in rendering it, when in existence, accessible to those for whose use it is intended. Many important classes of labourers find their sole employment in some functions of this kind. There is the whole class of carriers by land and water — waggoners, bargemen, sailors, wharfmen, porters, railway officials, and the like. Good roads," continues the same eminent authority, "are equivalent to good tools, and railways and canals are virtually a diminution of the cost of production of all things sent to market by them."

In order to give the public as comprehensive an idea of this subject as possible, and to show its vastness and importance to the community, I shall, before entering upon the details of that part of it which more immediately concerns me; viz. the transit from and to the different parts of the metropolis, and the condition and earnings of the people connected therewith — I shall, I say, furnish an account of the extent of the external and internal transit of this country generally. Of the provisions for the internal transit I shall speak in due course — first speaking of the grand medium for carrying on the traffic of Great Britain with the world, and showing how, within the capital of an island which is a mere speck on the map of the earth, is centered and originated, planned and executed, so vast a portion of the trade of all nations. I shall confine my observations to the latest returns and the latest results.

THE MERCANTILE MARINE.

THE number of vessels belonging to the United Kingdom was, in 1848, nearly 25,000, having an aggregate burden of upwards of 3000 tons, and being manned by 180,000 hands. To give the reader, however, a more vivid idea of the magnitude of the "mercantile marine" of this kingdom, it may be safely asserted, that in order to accommodate the whole of our merchant vessels, a dock of 15,000 square acres would be necessary; or, in other words, there would be required to float them an extent of water sufficient to cover four times the area of the city of London, while the whole population of Birmingham would be needed to man them. But, besides the 20,000 and odd British, with their 180,000 men, that are thus engaged in conveying the treasures of other lands to our own, there are upwards of 13,000 foreign vessels, manned by 100,000 hands, that annually visit the shores of this country.

Of the steam-vessels belonging to the United Kingdom in 1848, there were 1100. Their aggregate length was 125,283 feet; their aggregate breadth, 19,748 feet; their aggregate tonnage, 255,371; and their aggregate of horse-power, 92,862. It may be added, that they are collectively of such dimensions, that by placing them stem to stern, one after the other, they would reach to a distance of 23½ miles, or form one continuous line from Dover to Calais; while, by placing them abreast, or alongside each other, they would occupy a space of 3¾ miles wide.

According to the calculations of Mr. G. F. Young, the eminent shipbuilder, the entire value of the vessels belonging to the mercantile marine of the British empire is upward of 38,000,000l. sterling. The annual cost of the provisions and wages of the seamen employed in navigating them, 9,500,000l. The sum annually expended in the building and outfitting of new ships, as well as the repairing of the old ones, is 10,500,000l., while the amount annually received for freight is 28,500l.

The value of the merchandise thus imported or exported has still to be set forth. By this we learn not only the vast extent of the international trade of Great Britain, but the immense amount of property entrusted annually to the merchant-seaman. It would, perhaps, hardly be credited, that the value of the articles which our mercantile marine is engaged in transporting to and from the shores of this kingdom, amounts to upwards of one hundred million pounds sterling.

Such, then, is the extent of the external transit of this country. There is scarcely a corner of the earth that is not visited by our vessels, and the special gifts and benefits conferred upon the most distant countries thus diffused and shared among even the humblest members of our own. To show the connexion of the metropolis with this vast amount of trade, involving so many industrial interests, I shall conclude with stating, that the returns prove that one-fourth of the entire maritime commerce of this country is carried on at the port of London.

As a sad contrast, however, to all this splendour, I may here add, that the annual loss of property in British shipping wrecked or foundered at sea may be assumed as amounting to nearly three million pounds sterling per annum. The annual loss of life occasioned by the wreck or foundering of British vessels may be fairly estimated at not less than one thousand souls in each year; so that it would appear, that the annual loss by shipwreck amongst the vessels belonging to the United Kingdom is, on an average, 1 ship in every 42; and the annual loss of property engaged therein 1*l*. in every 42*l*.; while the average number of sailors drowned amounts to 1 in every 203 persons engaged in navigation.

I now come to speak of the means by which the vast amount of wealth thus brought to our shores is distributed throughout the country. I have already said that there are three different modes of internal communication:—1, to convey the several articles coastwise from one port to another; 2, to carry them inland from town to town; and 3, to remove them from and to the different parts of the same town. I shall deal first with the communication along the coast.

In 1849, the coasting vessels employed in the intercourse between Great Britain and Ireland made upwards of 26,000 voyages, and the gross burden of the vessels thus engaged amounted to more than 3,500,000 tons. The " coasters " engaged in the carrying trade between the different ports of Great Britain in 1849, made no less than 255,000 voyages, and possessed collectively a capacity for carrying upwards of 20,000,000 tons of goods. Of the steam-vessels employed coastwise in the United Kingdom, the number that entered inwards, including their repeated voyages, was 17,800, having an aggregate burden of upwards of 4,000,000 tons, while 14,500 and odd steam-vessels, of not quite the same amount of tonnage, were cleared outwards. This expresses the entire amount of the coasting trade in connexion with the several ports of Great Britain. London, as I have before shown, has four times the number of sailing vessels, and ten times the amount of tonnage, over and above any port in the kingdom, whilst of steam-impelled coasting vessels it has but little more than one-third, compared with Liverpool.

TURNPIKE-ROADS AND STAGE-COACHES.

THE next branch of my subject that presents itself in due order is the means by which the goods thus brought to the several ports of the kingdom are carried to the interior of the country. There are two means of effecting this; that is to say, either by land or water-carriage. Land-carriage consists of transit by rail and transit by turnpike roads; the water-carriage of transit by canals and navigable rivers, I shall begin with the first-mentioned of these, viz. turnpike-roads, and then proceed in due order to the others.

The turnpike-roads of England present a perfect network of communication, connecting town with town, and hamlet with hamlet. It was only within the present century, however, that these important means of increasing commerce and civilization were constructed according to scientific data. Before that, portions of what were known as the great coaching roads were repaired with more than usual care: but until Mr. M'Adam's system was generally adopted, about forty years back, all were more or less defective. It would be wearisome were I to add to the number of familiar instances of the difficulties and dilatoriness of travelling in the old days, and to tell how the ancient " heavy coaches " were merged in the " fast light coaches," which, in their turn, yielded to the greater speed of the railways.

In 1818, according to the Government Report on the turnpike-roads and the railways of England and Wales, there existed—

	Miles.
In England and Wales, paved streets and turnpike-roads to the extent of	19,725
Other public highways . . .	95,104
Total . . .	114,829

Other parliamentary returns show, that in 1829 the length of only the turnpike-roads in England and Wales was 20,875 miles, or upwards of 1000 miles more than they (together with the paved streets) extended to 10 years before. In 1839, the length of the turnpike-roads and paved streets throughout England and Wales amounted to 22,534 miles, while all other highways 96,993 miles long; making in all, 119,527 miles of road. By this it appears, that in the course of 20 years upwards of 4500 miles of highway had been added to the resources of the country. As these are the latest returns on the subject, and it is probable that, owing to the establishment of railways, there has been no great addition since that period to the aggregate extent of mileage above given, it may be as well to set forth the manner in which these facilities for intercommunication were distributed among the different parts of the country at that time. The counties containing the greatest length of turnpike-road, according to their size, were Derby, Worcester, Flint, Gloucester, Somerset, Monmouth, Stafford, Hereford, Southampton, &c., which severally contained one mile of turnpike-road to about each thousand statute acres, the average for the entire country being nearly double that amount of acres to each mile of road. Those counties, on the other hand, which contained the shortest length of turnpike-roads in relation to their size, were Anglesey (in which there were only five miles of road to 173,000 statute acres, being in the proportion of one mile to 34,688 acres); then Westmoreland, Suffolk, Essex, Norfolk, Pembroke, and Cumberland. The counties containing the greatest length of paved streets at the above period were, first, Middlesex, where there was one mile of street to every 774 acres; second, Suffolk; third, Lancaster; fourth, Warwick; fifth, Surrey; and sixth, Chester. The average number of acres to each mile of paved street was 12,734, and in the districts above specified the number of acres to the mile ranged from 3600 to 6900. Those counties, on the contrary, which contained the shortest length of streets, were Radnor and Anglesey, in which there were no paved streets whatever; Brecon, which has only one mile, and Carnarvon which has only two; whereas Middlesex, the county of the capital, has as many as 232 miles of streets extending through it. The cost of the repairs of the roads and streets in the different counties is equally curious. In Merioneth, the rate of the expenditure is 12s. 11¾d. per mile; in Montgomery, 1l.14s.2½d.; in Radnor, 1l. 18s. 1d.; in Brecon, 2l. 6s. 6½d.; in Carnarvon, 2l. 10s. 1¾d.; in Anglesey, 3l. 8s.; in Cardigan, 3l. 3s. 0½d.; whereas in Middlesex the cost amounts to no less than 87l. 1s. 6½d. per mile; in Lancashire, the next most expensive county, it is 32l. 2s. 6d.; in the West Riding of Yorkshire it comes to 23l. 4s. 3d.; and in Surrey, the other metropolitan county, to 19l. 1s. 1½d.; the average for the whole country being 10l. 12s. 1½d. per mile, or, 1,267,848l. for the maintenance of 119,527 miles of public highways throughout England and Wales.

These roads were used for a threefold purpose,—the conveyance of passengers, letters, and goods. The passengers, letters, and parcels, were conveyed chiefly by the mail and stage-coaches, the goods by waggons and vans. Of the number of passengers who travelled by the mail and stage-coaches no return was ever made. I am indebted, however, to Mr. Porter, for the following calculation as to the number of stage-coach travellers before their vehicles (to adopt their own mode of expression) were run off the roads by the steam-engine:—

"In order to obtain some approximation to the extent of travelling by means of stage-coaches in England, a careful calculation has been made upon the whole of the returns to the Stamp Office, and the licenses for which coaches were in operation at the end of the year 1834. The method followed in making the application has been to ascertain the performance of each vehicle, supposing that performance to have been equal to the full amount of the permission conveyed by the license, reducing the power so given to a number equal to the number of miles which one passenger might be conveyed in the course of the year. For example: a coach is licensed to convey 15 passengers daily from London to Birmingham, a distance of 112 miles. In order to ascertain the possible performance of this carriage during the year, if the number of miles is multiplied by the number of journeys, and that product multiplied again by the number of passengers, we shall obtain, as an element, a number equal to the number of miles along which one person might have been conveyed; viz. 112 × 365 × 15 = 613,200. In this case the number of miles travelled is 40,880, along which distance 15 persons might have been carried during the year: but for the simplification of the calculation, the further calculation is made, which shows that amount of travelling to be equal to the conveyance of one person through the distance of 613,200 miles. Upon making this calculation for the whole number of stage-coaches that possessed licenses at the end of the year 1834, it appears that the means of conveyance thus provided for travelling were equivalent to the conveyance during the year of one person for the distance of 597,159,420 miles, or more than six times between the earth and the sun. Observation has shown, that the degree in which the public avail themselves of the accommodation thus provided is in the proportion of 9 to 15, or three-fifths of its utmost extent. Following this proportion, the sum of all the travelling by stage-coaches in Great Britain may be represented by 385,295,652 miles. We shall probably go the utmost extent in assuming that not more than two millions of persons travel in that manner. It affords a good measure of the relative importance of the metropolis to the remainder of the country, that of the above number of 597,159,420, the large proportion of 409,052,644 is the product of stage-coaches which are licensed to run from London to various parts of the kingdom."

In this calculation the stage-coach travelling of Ireland is not included, nor is that of Scotland, when confined to that kingdom; but when part of the communication is with England it is included. Of course, only public conveyances are spoken of: all the travelling in private carriages, or post-chaises, or hired gigs, is additional.

The number of stage-coachmen and guards in 1839 were 2619; in 1840, 2507; in 1841, 2239; in 1842, 2107; in 1843, 146.

The expenditure on account of these roads in 1841 amounted to 1,551,000l.; the revenue derived from them for the same year having been 1,574,000l.

A great change has been induced in the character of the turnpike-roads of England. The liveliness imparted to many of the lines of road by the scarlet coats of the drivers and guards, and by the sound of the guard's bugle as it announced to all the idlers of the country place that "the London coach was coming in," these things exist no longer. Now, on very few portions of the 1448 miles of the turnpike-road in Yorkshire, or the 840 of Gloucestershire, is a stage-coach-and-four to be seen: and the great coaching inns by the wayside, with the tribes of ostlers and helpers "changing horses" with a facility almost marvellous, have become farmhouses or mere wayside taverns.

The greatest rate of speed attained by any of the mail-coaches was eleven miles an hour, including stoppages; that is, eleven miles notwithstanding the delay incurred in changing horses, which was the work of from one minute to three, depending upon whether any passenger was "taken up" or set down at that stage (the word "station" is peculiar to railways). If there was merely a change of horses, about a minute was consumed. The horses were not unfrequently unsuccessful racehorses, and they were generally of "good blood." Some would run daily on the same stages 8 and 10 years. About 10⅝ miles was an average rate for the mail, and 8½ to 9 miles for the stage-coaches. They often advertised 10 miles an hour, but that was only an advertisement.

So rapid, so systematic, and so commended was the style of stage-coach travelling, that some of the great coach proprietors dreaded little from the competitive results of railway travelling. One of these proprietors on "the Great North Road" used to say, "Railways are just a bounce—all speculation. People will find it out in time, and there'll be more coaching than ever; railways can never answer!"

So punctual, too, were these carriages, that one gentleman used to say he set his watch by the Glasgow mail, as "she passed his door by the roadside, at three minutes to ten."

Nor is it only in the discontinuance of stage-coaches that the roads of the kingdom have experienced a change in character. Until the prevalence of railways, "posting" was common. A wealthy person travelled to London in his own carriage, which was drawn by four horses, almost as quickly as by the mail. The horses were changed at the several stages; the ostler's cry of "first turn out," summoning the stablemen and the postilions with a readiness second only to that in the case of the passengers' coaches. The horses, however, were ridden by postilions in red or light blue jackets, with white buttons, light-coloured breeches, and brown top-boots, instead of being driven four-in-hand. This was the aristocratic style of travelling, and its indulgence was costly. For a pair of good horses 1s. 6d. a-mile was an average charge, and 3d. a-mile had to be given in the compulsory gratuities of those days to the postilion; 3s. a-mile was the charge for four horses, but sometimes rather less. Thus, supposing that 500 noblemen and gentlemen "posted" to London on the opening of Parliament, each, as was common, with two carriages-and-four, and each posting 200 miles, the aggregate expenditure, without any sum for meals or for beds —and to "sleep on the road" was common when ladies were travelling—would be 35,000l., and to this add five per cent for the turnpike-tolls, and the whole cost would be 36,750l.; an average of 73l. 10s. for each nobleman and gentleman, with his family and the customary members of his household. The calculation refers merely to a portion of the members of the two houses of legislature, and is unquestionably within the mark; for though many travelled shorter distances and by cheaper modes, many travelled 400 miles, and with more carriages than three. No "lady" condescended to enter a stage-coach at the period concerning which I write. As the same expense was incurred in returning to the castle, hall, park, abbey, wood, or manor, the annual outlay for this one purpose of merely a fraction of the posters to London was 73,500l. It might not be extravagant to assert, that more than five times this outlay was annually incurred, including "pairs" and "fours," or a total of 367,500l. This mode of travelling I believe is now almost wholly extinct, if indeed it be not impossible, since there are no horses now kept on the road for the purpose. I have been informed that the late Duke of Northumberland was the last, or one of the last, who, in dislike or dread of railways, regularly "posted" to and from Alnwick Castle to London.

THE RAILWAYS.

THE next branch of the transit by land appertains to the conveyance of persons and goods per rail. The railways of the United Kingdom open, in course of construction, or authorised to be constructed, extend over upwards of 12,000 miles, or four times the distance across the Atlantic. The following is the latest return on the subject, in a Report printed by order of the House of Commons, the 22nd of March last :—

	Miles.	Chains.	Persons employed.
Total length of railway open on June 30, 1849, and persons employed thereon	5447	10¾	55,968
Total length of railway in course of construction on June 30, 1849, and persons employed thereon	1504	20½	
Total length of railway neither open nor in course of construction on June 30, 1849	5132	38¾	103,846
Total length of railway authorised to be used for the conveyance of passengers on June 30, 1849, and the total number of persons employed thereon	12,083	70	159,784

There are now upwards of 6000 miles of railroad open for traffic in the three kingdoms, 549 miles having been opened in the course of the half-year following the date of the above return. At that date 111 miles of railroad were open for traffic, irrespective of their several branches. 266 railways, including branches, were authorised to be constructed, but had not been commenced.

The growth of railways was slow, and not gradual. They were unknown as modes of public conveyance before the present century, but roads on a similar principle, irrespective of steam, were in use in the Northumberland and Durham collieries, somewhere about the year 1700. The rails were not made of iron but of wood, and, with a facility previously unknown, a small cart, or a series of small carts, was dragged along them by a pony or a horse, to any given point where the coal had to be deposited. In the lead mines of the North Riding of Yorkshire the same system was adopted, the more rapidly and with the less fatigue, to convey the ore to the mouth of the mine. Some of these "tramways," as they are called, were and are a mile and more in length; and visitors who penetrate into the very bowels of the mine are conveyed along those tramways in carts, drawn generally by a pony, and driven by a boy (who has to duck his head every here and there to avoid collision) into the galleries and open spaces where the miners are at work.

In the year 1801, the first Act of Parliament authorising the construction of a railway was passed. This was the Surrey, between Wandsworth and Croydon, nine miles in length, and constructed at a cost, in round numbers, of 60,000*l*. In the following twenty years, sixteen such Acts were passed, authorising the construction of 124⅜ miles of railway, the cost of which was 971,232*l*., or upwards of 7500*l*. a-mile. In 1822 no such Act was passed. In 1823, Parliament authorised the construction of the Stockton and Darlington; and on that short railway, originated and completed in a great measure through the exertions of the wealthy Quakers of the neighbourhood, and opened on the 27th of December, 1825, steam-power was first used as a means of propulsion and locomotion on a railway. It was some little time before this that grave senators and learned journalists laughed to scorn Mr. Stephenson's assertion, that steam "could be made to do twenty miles an hour on a railway." In the following ten years, thirty railway bills were passed by the legislature; and among these, in 1826, was the Liverpool and Manchester, which was opened on the 16th September, 1830—an opening rendered as lamentable as it is memorable by the death of Mr. Huskisson. In 1834, seven railway bills were passed; ten in 1835; twenty-six in 1836; eleven in 1837; one in 1838; three in 1839; none again till 1843, and then only one—the Northampton and Peterborough, which extends along 44½ miles, and which cost

429,409*l*. The mass of the other railways have been constructed, or authorised, and the Acts of Parliament authorising their construction shelved, since the close of 1843. I find no official returns of the dates of the several enactments.

The following statement, in averages of four years, shows the amount of the sums which Parliament authorised the various companies to raise from 1822 to 1845. Upwards of one-half of the amount of the aggregate sum expended in 1822-6 was spent on the Manchester and Liverpool Railway, 1,832,375*l*. The cost of the Stockton and Darlington, (450,000*l*.), is also included:

From 1822 to 1825 inclusive		£451,465
„ 1826 „ 1829	„	816,846
„ 1830 „ 1833	„	2,157,136
„ 1834 „ 1837	„	10,880,431
„ 1838 „ 1841	„	3,614,428
„ 1842 „ 1845	„	20,895,128

Of these years, 1845 presents the era when the rage for railway speculation was most strongly manifested, as in that year the legislature sanctioned the raising, by new railway companies, of no less than 59,613,536*l*. more than the imperial taxes levied in the United Kingdom, while in 1844 the amount so sanctioned was 14,793,994*l*. The total sum to be raised for railway purposes for the last twenty years of the above dates was 153,455,837*l*., with a yearly average of 7,672,792*l*. For the four years preceding the yearly average was but 112,866*l*.

The parliamentary expenses attending the incorporation of sixteen of the principal railway companies were 683,498*l*., or an average per railway of 42,718*l*. It will be seen from the following table, that the greatest amount thus expended was on the incorporation of the Great Western. On that undertaking an outlay not much short of 90,000*l*. was incurred, before a foot of sod could be raised by the spade of the "navvy."

Birmingham and Gloucester	£22,618
Bristol and Gloucester	25,589
Bristol and Exeter	18,592
Eastern Counties	39,171
Great Western	89,197
Great North of England	20,526
Grand Junction	22,757
Glasgow, Paisley, and Greenock	23,481
London and Birmingham	72,868
London and South-Western	41,467
Manchester and Leeds	49,166
Midland Counties	28,776
North Midland	41,349
Northern and Eastern	74,166
Sheffield, Ashton, and Manchester	31,473
South-Eastern	82,292

It must be borne in mind that these large sums were all for parliamentary expenses alone, and were merely the disbursements of the railway proprietors, whose applications to Parliament were successful. Probably as large an amount was expended in opposition to the several bills, and in the fruitless advocacy of rival companies. Thus above a million and a-quarter of pounds sterling was spent as a preliminary outlay.

Of the railway lines, the construction of the Great Western, 117½ miles in length, was the most costly, entailing an expenditure of nearly eight millions; the London and Birmingham, 112½ miles, cost 6,073,114*l.*; the South-Eastern, 66 miles, 4,306,478*l.*; the Manchester and Leeds, 53 miles, 3,372,240*l.*; the Eastern Counties, 51 miles, 2,821,790*l.*; the Glasgow, Paisley, Kilmarnock, and Ayr, 57½ miles, 1,071,263*l.*; an amount which was exceeded by the outlay on only the 3½ miles of the London and Blackwall, first opened, which cost 1,078,851*l.* I ought to mention, that the lengths in miles are those of the portions first opened to the public in the respective lines, and first authorised by parliamentary enactments. "Junctions," "continuations," and the blending of companies, have been subsequent measures, entailing, of course, proportionate outlay. The length of line of the Great Western, for instance, with its immediate branches, opened on the 30th of June, 1849, was 225 miles; that of the South-Eastern, 144 miles; and that of the Eastern Counties, 309 miles. It is stated in Mr. Knight's "British Almanac" for the current year, that the "London and North-Western is almost the only company which has maintained in 1849 the same dividend even as in the preceding year, viz. seven per cent. The Great Western, the Midland, the Lancashire and Yorkshire, the York and Newcastle, the York and North Midland, the Eastern Counties, the South-Eastern, the South-Western, Brighton, the Manchester and Lincolnshire, all have suffered a decided diminution of dividend. These ten great companies, whose works up to the present time have cost over one hundred millions sterling, have on an average declared for the half year ending in the summer of 1849, a dividend on the regular non-guaranteed shares of between three and four per cent per annum. The remaining companies, about sixty in number, can hardly have reached an average of two per cent per annum in the same half year."

The following Table gives the latest returns of railway traffic from 1845. Previous to that date no such returns were published in parliamentary papers:—

COMPARATIVE STATEMENT OF THE TRAFFIC ON ALL THE RAILWAYS IN THE UNITED KINGDOM FOR THE FIVE YEARS ENDING JUNE 30, 1845, 1846, 1847, 1848, 1849, TOGETHER WITH THE LENGTH OF RAILWAY OPEN ON DECEMBER 31 AND JUNE 30 IN EACH YEAR.

	Length open on June 30 in each year.	Total Number of Passsengers.	Total Receipts from Passengers.			Receipts from Goods, Cattle, Parcels, Mails, &c.			TOTAL RECEIPTS.		
Year ending	Miles.		£	s.	d.	£	s.	d.	£	s.	d.
June 30, 1845	2343	33,791,253	3,976,341	0	0	2,233,373	0	0	6,209,714	0	0
„ 1846	2765	43,790,983	4,725,215	11	8½	2,840,353	16	6¼	7,565,569	8	2¾
„ 1847	3603	51,352,163	5,148,002	5	0½	3,362,883	19	6¾	1,510,886	4	7¼
„ 1848	4478	57,965,070	5,720,382	9	1¾	4,213,169	14	5½	9,933,552	3	7¼
„ 1849	5447	60,398,159	6,105,975	7	7¾	5,094,025	18	11	11,200,901	6	6¾

This official table shows a conveyance for the year ending June, 1849, of 60,398,159 passengers. It may be as well to mention that every distinct trip is reckoned. Thus a gentleman travelling from and returning to Greenwich daily, figures in the return as 730 passengers. Of the number of individuals who travel in the United Kingdom I have no information. Thousands of the labouring classes travel very rarely, perhaps not more than once on some holiday trip in the course of a twelvemonth. But assuming every one to travel, and the population to be thirty millions, then we have two railway trips made by every man, woman, and child in the kingdom every year.

There are no data from which to deduce a precisely accurate calculation of the number of miles travelled by the 60,398,159 passengers who availed themselves of railway facilities in the year cited. Official lists show that seventy-eight railways comprise the extent of mileage given, but these railways vary in extent. The shortest of them open for the conveyance of passengers is the Belfast and County Down, which is only 4 miles 35 chains in length, and the number of passengers travelling on it 81,441. The Midland and the London and North-Western, on the other hand, are respectively 465 and 477 miles in length, and their complement of passengers is respectively 2,252,984 and 2,750,541½. The average length of the 78 railways is 70 miles, but as the stream of travel flows more from intermediate station to station along the course of the line, than from one extremity to the other, it may be reasonable to compute that each individual passenger has travelled one-fourth of the entire distance, or $17\frac{1}{2}$ miles—a calculation confirmed by the amount paid by each individual, which is something short of 2s., or rather more than $1\frac{1}{4}d.$ per mile.

Thus we may conclude that each passenger has journeyed $17\frac{1}{2}$ miles, and that the grand aggregate of travel by all the railway passengers of the kingdom will be $1,052,327,632\frac{1}{2}$ miles, or nearly eleven times the distance between the earth and the sun every year.

The Government returns present some curious results. The passengers by the second-class carriages have been more numerous every year than those by any other class, and for the year last returned were more than three times the number of those who indulged in the comforts of first-class vehicles. Notwithstanding nearly 1000 new miles of railway were opened for the public transit and traffic between June 1848-9, still the number of first-class passengers decreased no fewer than 112,000 and odd, while those who resorted to the humbler accommodation of the second class increased upwards of 170,000. The numerical majority of the second-class passengers over the first was :—

Year ending June, 1845 .. 8,851,662
,,   ,,   1846 .. 10,770,712
,,   ,,   1847 .. 12,126,574
,,   ,,   1848 .. 14,499,730
,,   ,,   1849 .. 16,313,760

These figures afford some criterion as to the class or character of the travelling millions who are the supporters of the railways.

The official table presents another curious characteristic. The originators of railways, prior to the era of the opening of the Manchester and Liverpool, depended for their dividends far more upon the profits they might receive in the capacity of common carriers, upon the conveyance of manufactured goods, minerals, or merchandise, than upon the transit of passengers. It was the property in canals and in heavy carriage that would be depreciated, it was believed, rather than that in the stage-coaches. Even on the Manchester and Liverpool, the projectors did not expect to realise more than 20,000l. a-year by the conveyance of passengers. The result shows the fallacy of these computations, as the receipts for passengers for the year ending June, 1849, exceeded the receipts from "cattle, goods, parcels, and mails," by 1,011,050l. In districts, however, which are at once agricultural and mineral, the amount realised from passengers falls short of that derived from other sources. Two instances will suffice to show this : The Stockton and Darlington is in immediate connexion with the district where the famous short-horn cattle were first bred by Mr. Collins, and where they are still bred in high perfection by eminent agriculturists. It is in

connexion, moreover, with the coal and lead-mining districts of South Durham and North Yorkshire, the produce being conveyed to Stockton to be shipped. For the last year, the receipts from passengers were 8000l. and odd, while for the conveyance of cattle, coal, &c., no less than 62,000l. was paid. From their passengers the Taff Vale, including the Aberdale Railway Company, derived, for the same period, in round numbers, an increase of 6500l., and from their "goods" conveyance, 45,941l. In neither instance did the passengers pay one-seventh as much as the "goods."

I now present the reader with two "summaries" from returns made to Parliament. The first relates to the number and description of persons employed on railways in the United Kingdom, and the second to the number and character of railway accidents.

Concerning the individuals employed upon the railways, the Table on the opposite page contains the latest official information.

Of the railways in full operation, the London and North-Western employs the greatest number of persons, in its long and branching extent of 477 miles, $35\frac{1}{4}$ chains, with 153 stations. The total number employed is 6194, and they are thus classified :—

Secretaries or managers	.	.	. 8
Engineers	.	.	. 5
Superintendents	.	.	. 40
Storekeepers	.	.	. 8
Accountants or cashiers	.	.	. 4
Inspectors or timekeepers	.	.	. 83
Draughtsmen	.	.	. 11
Clerks	.	.	. 775
Foremen	.	.	. 130
Engine-drivers	.	.	. 334
Assistant-drivers or firemen	.	.	. 318
Guards or breaksmen	.	.	. 207
Artificers	.	.	. 1891
Switchmen	.	.	. 363
Gatekeepers	.	.	. 76
Policemen or watchmen	.	.	. 241
Porters or messengers	.	.	. 1456
Platelayers	.	.	. 14
Labourers	.	.	. 30

On the Midland there were employed 4898 persons; on the Lancashire and Yorkshire, 3971 ; Great Western, 2997 ; Eastern Counties, 2939 ; Caledonian, 2409 ; York, Newcastle, and Berwick, 2731 ; London and South-Western, 2118 ; London, Brighton, and South-Coast, 2053 ; York and North Midland, 1614 ; North British, 1535 ; and South-Eastern, 1527. Thus the twelve leading companies retain permanently in their service 35,735 men, supplying the means of maintenance, (reckoning that a family of three is supported by each man employed) to 122,940 individuals. Pursuing the same calculation, as 159,784 men were employed on all the railways "open and unopen," we may conclude that 739,136 indi-

TOTAL NUMBER AND DESCRIPTION OF PERSONS EMPLOYED ON RAILWAYS.

	Secretaries and Managers.	Treasurers.	Engineers.	Superintendents.	Storekeepers.	Accountants and Cashiers.	Inspectors and Timekeepers.	Station Masters.	Draughtsmen.	Clerks.	Foremen.	Engine Drivers.	Assistant Engine Drivers and Firemen.	Guardsmen and Breaksmen.	Switchmen.	Gatekeepers.	Policemen or Watchmen.	Porters and Messengers.	Platelayers.	Artificers.	Labourers.	Miscellaneous employment.	Total.
Total number of persons employed upon railways open for traffic on the 30th June, 1849	156	32	107	314	120	138	490	1300	103	4021	709	1839	1871	1631	1540	1361	1508	8238	5508	10,809	14,829	144	55,968
Total number of persons employed upon railways not open for traffic on the 30th June, 1849	142	7	269	419	182	144	821	—	153	421	1421	—	—	—	—	—	481	118	—	16,144	83,052	42	103,816
Total number and description of persons employed on all railways (open and unopen) authorised to be used for the conveyance of passengers	298	39	376	733	302	282	1311	1300	256	4442	2130	1839	1871	1631	1540	1361	1989	8356	5508	26,953	97,081	186	159,784

viduals were dependent, more or less, upon railway traffic for their subsistence.

The other summary to which I have alluded is one derived from a return which the House of Commons ordered to be printed on the 8th of April last. It is relative to the railway accidents that occurred in the United Kingdom during the half-year ending the 31st December, 1849, and supplies the following analysis :—

" 54 passengers injured from causes beyond their own control.

11 passengers killed and 10 injured, owing to their own misconduct or want of caution.

2 servants of companies or of contractors killed, and 3 injured, from causes beyond their own control.

62 servants of companies or of contractors killed, and 37 injured, owing to their own misconduct or want of caution.

28 trespassers and other persons, neither passengers nor servants of the company, killed, and 7 injured, by improperly crossing or standing on the railway.

1 child killed and 1 injured, by an engine running off the rails and entering a house.

2 suicide.

Total, 106 killed and 112 injured.

The total number of passengers conveyed during the half-year amounted to 34,924,469."

The greatest number of accidents was on the Lancashire and Yorkshire : 2,793,764 passengers were conveyed in the term specified, and 17 individuals were killed and 24 injured. On the York, Newcastle, and Berwick, 15 were killed and injured, 1,613,123 passengers having been conveyed. On the Midland, 2,658,903 having been the number of passengers, 9 persons were killed and 7 injured. On the Great Western, conveying 1,220,507½ passengers, 2 individuals were killed and 1 injured. On the London and Blackwall, with 1,200,514 passengers, there was 1 man killed and 16 injured. The London and Greenwich supplied the means of locomotion to 1,126,237 persons, and none were killed and none were injured. These deaths on the railway, for the half-year cited above, are in the proportion of 106 to to 34,924,469, or 1 person killed to every 329,476 ; and the 106 killed include 2 suicides and the deaths of 28 trespassers and others. The total number of persons who suffered from accidents was 218, which is in the proportion of 1 accident to every 160,203 persons travelling ; and when the injuries arising from this mode of conveyance are contrasted with the loss of life by shipwreck, which, as before stated, amounts to 1 in every 203 individuals, the comparative safety of railway over marine travelling must appear most extraordinary. Mr. Porter's calculation as to the number of stage-coach travellers (which I cite under that head) shows that my estimates are far from extravagant.

INLAND NAVIGATION.

THE next part of my subject is the "water-carriage," carried on by means of canals and rivers. The means of inland navigation in England and Wales are computed to comprise more than 4000 miles, of which 2200 miles are in navigable canals and 1800 in navigable rivers. In Ireland, such modes of communication extend about 500 miles, and in Scotland about 350. As railways have been the growth of the present half-century, so did canals owe their increase, if not their establishment, in England, to the half-century preceding —from 1750 to 1800 ; three-fourths of those now in existence having been established during that period. Previously to the works perfected by the Duke of Bridgewater and his famous and self-taught engineer, James Brindley, the efforts made to improve our means of water-transit were mainly confined to attempts to improve the navigation of rivers. These attempts were not attended with any great success. The current of the river was often too impetuous to be restrained in the artificial channels prepared for the desired improvements, and the forms and depths of the channels were gradually changed by the current, so that labour and expense were very heavily and continuously entailed. Difficulties in the way of river navigation," says Mr. M'Culloch, "seem to have suggested the expediency of abandoning the channels of most rivers, and of digging parallel to them artificial channels, in which the water may be kept at the proper level by means of locks. The Act passed by the legislature in 1755 for improving the navigation of Sankey Brook on the Mersey, gave rise to a lateral canal of this description about 11¼ miles in length, which deserves to be mentioned as the earliest effort of the sort in England. But before this canal had been completed, the Duke of Bridgewater and James Brindley had conceived a plan of canalisation independent altogether of natural channels, and intended to afford the greatest facilities to commerce by carrying canals across rivers and through mountains, wherever it was practicable to construct them."

The difficulties which Brindley overcame were considered insurmountable until he did overcome them. In the construction of a canal from Worsley to Manchester it was necessary to cross the river Irwell, where it is navigable at Barton. Brindley proposed to accomplish this by carrying an aqueduct 39 feet above the surface of the Irwell. This was considered so extravagant a proposition that there was a pause, and a gentleman eminent for engineering knowledge was consulted. He treated Brindley's scheme as the scheme of a visionary, declaring that he had often heard of castles in the air, but never before heard where one was to be erected. The duke, however, had confidence in his engineer; and a successful, serviceable, and profitable aqueduct, instead of a castle in the air, was the speedy and successful result. The success of Brindley's plans and the spirited munificence of the Duke of Bridgewater, who, that he might have ample means to complete his projects, at one time confined his mere personal expenses to 400*l.* a-year—laid the foundations of the large fortunes enjoyed by the Duke of Sutherland and his brother the late Earl of Ellesmere.

The canals which have been commenced and completed in the United Kingdom since the year 1800 are 30 in number, and extend 582¾ miles in length.

Mr. M'Culloch gives a list of British canals, with the number of shareholders in the proprietary of each, the amount and cost of shares, and the price on the 27th June, 1843. The Erewash, with 231 shares, each 100*l.* returned a dividend of 40*l.*, each share being then worth 675*l.* The Loughborough, with only 70 100*l.* shares, the average cost of each share having been 142*l.* 17*s.*, had a dividend of 80*l.* and a selling price per share of 1400*l.* The Stroudwater, with 200 shares of 150*l.*, returned a dividend of 24*l.*, with a price in the market of 490*l.* On the other hand, the 50*l.* shares of the Crinau were then selling at 2*l.* The 50*l.* shares of the North Walsham and Dillon were of the same almost nominal value in the market; and the shares of the Thames and Medway, with an average cost of 30*l.*4*s.*3*d.*, were worth but 1*l.* Of the cost expended in construction of the canals of England, I have no means of giving a precise account; but the following calculation seems sufficiently accurate for my present purpose. I find that, if in round numbers the 250,000 shares of the 40 principal canals averaged an expenditure of 100*l.* per share—the result would be 25,000,000*l.*, and perhaps we may estimate the canals of the United Kingdom to have cost 35,000,000*l.*, or one-tenth as much as the railways.

The foregoing inquiries present the following gigantic results:—There are employed in the yearly transit of Great Britain, abroad and along her own shores, 33,672 sailing-vessels and 1110 steam-vessels, employing 236,000 seamen. Calculating the value of each ship and cargo as the value has been estimated before Parliament, at 5000*l.*, we have an aggregate value — sailing-vessels, steamers, and their cargoes included — of 173,910,000*l.* Further, supposing the yearly wages of the seamen, including officers, to be 20*l.* per head, the amount paid in wages would be 4,720,000*l.*

The railways now in operation in the United Kingdom extend 6000 miles, the cost of their construction (paid and to be paid) having been estimated at upwards of 350,000,000*l.* Last year they supplied the means of rapid travel to above 63,000,000 of passengers, who tra-versed above a billion of miles. Their receipts for the year approached 11,250,000*l.* of money, and nearly three-quarters of a million of persons are dependent upon them for subsistence.

The turnpike and other roads of Great Britain alone (independently of Ireland) present a surface 120,000 miles in length, for the various purposes of interchange, commerce, and recreation. They are maintained by the yearly expenditure of a million and a half.

For similar purposes the navigable canals and rivers of Great Britain and Ireland furnish an extent of 4850 miles, formed at a cost of probably 35,000,000*l.* Adding all these together, we have of turnpike-roads, railways, and canals, no less than 130,000 and odd miles, formed at an aggregate cost of upwards of 386,000,000*l.* If we add to this the 54,250,000*l.* capital expended in the mercantile marine, we have the gross total of more than 440,000,000 of money sunk in the transit of the country. If the number of miles traversed by the natives of this country in the course of the year by sea, road, rail, river, and canal, were summed up, it would reach to a distance greater than to the remotest planet yet discovered.

LONDON WATERMEN, LIGHTERMEN, AND STEAMBOAT-MEN.

Of all the great capitals, London has least the appearance of antiquity, and the Thames has a peculiarly modern aspect. It is no longer the "silent highway," for its silence is continually broken by the clatter of steamboats. This change has materially affected the position and diminished the number of the London watermen, into whose condition and earnings I am now about to examine.

The character of the transit on the river has, moreover, undergone a great change, apart from the alteration produced by the use of steam-power. Until the more general use of coaches, in the reign of Charles II., the Thames supplied the only mode of conveyance, except horseback, by which men could avoid the fatigue of walking; and that it was made largely available, all our older London chroniclers show. From the termination of the wars of the Roses, until the end of the 17th century, for about 200 years, all the magnates of the metropolis, the king, the members of the royal family, the great officers of state, the Archbishop of Canterbury, the noblemen whose mansions had sprung up amidst trees and gardens on the north bank of the Thames, the Lord Mayor, the City authorities, the City Companies, and the Inns of Court, all kept their own or their state barges, rowed by their own servants, attired in their respective liveries. In addition to the river conveyances of these functionaries, private boats or barges were maintained by all whose wealth permitted, or whose convenience required their use, in the same way as carriages and horses are kept by them in our day. The Thames, too, was then the principal arena for the display of pageants. These pageants, however, are now reduced to one—the Lord Mayor's show. The remaining state barges are but a few, viz. the Queen's, the Lord Mayor's, and such as are maintained by the City Companies, and even some of these are rotting to decay.

Mr. Charles Knight says in his "London:"—" In the time of Elizabeth and the first James, and onward to very recent days, the north bank of the Thames was studded with the palaces of the nobles; and each palace had its landing-place, and its private retinue of barges and wherries; and many a freight of the brave and beautiful has been borne, amidst song and merriment, from house to house, to join the masque and the dance, and many a wily statesman, muffled in his cloak, has glided along unseen in his boat, to some dark conference with his ambitious neighbour. Upon the river itself, busy as it was, fleets of swans were ever sailing; and they ventured unmolested into that channel which is now narrowed by vessels from every region. Paulus Jovius, who died in 1552, describing the Thames, says : ' This river abounds in swans, swimming in flocks, the sight of whom, and their noise, are vastly agreeable to the fleets that meet them in their course.' The only relics of the palatial 'landing-places' above alluded to, which is now to be seen, is the fine arch, or water-gate, the work of Inigo Jones, at the foot of Buckingham-street. This was an adornment of the landing-place from York House, once the town abode of the archbishops of that see, but afterwards the property of George Villiers, duke of Buckingham. In front of this gate, or nearly so, the Hungerford steam-boat piers are now stationed; and in place of stately barges, directed by half-a-dozen robust oarsmen, in gorgeous liveries, approaching the palace, or lying silently in wait there, we have halfpenny, penny, twopenny, and other steam-boats, hissing, spluttering, panting, and smoking."

Moreover, in addition to the state and private barges of the olden times, there were multitudes of boats and watermen always on hire. Stow, who was born in 1525, and died at eighty years of age, says that in his time 49,000 watermen were employed on the Thames. This, however, is a manifest exaggeration, when we consider the population of London at that time; still it is an over-estimate common to old chroniclers, by whom precise statistical knowledge was unattainable. That Stow represents the number of these men at 40,000, shows plainly that they were very numerous; and one proof of their great number, down to the middle of the last century, is, that until one hundred years ago, the cities of London and

Westminster had but one bridge—the old London-bridge—which was commenced in 1176, completed in thirty-one years, and after standing 625 years, was pulled down in 1832. The want of bridges to keep pace with the increase of the population caused the establishment of numerous ferries. It has been computed, that in 1760 the ferries across the Thames, taking in its course from Richmond to Greenwich, were twenty-five times as numerous as they are at present. Westminster-bridge was not finished until 1750; Blackfriars was built in 1769; Battersea in 1771; Vauxhall in 1816; Waterloo in 1817; Southwark in 1819; the present London-bridge in 1831; and Hungerford in 1844.

THE THAMES WATERMEN.

THE character of the Thames watermen in the last century was what might have been expected from slightly-informed, or uninformed, and not unprosperous men. They were hospitable and hearty one to another, and to their neighbours on shore; civil to such fares as were civil to them, especially if they hoped for an extra sixpence; but often saucy, abusive, and even sarcastic. Their interchange of abuse with one another, as they rode on the Thames, down to the commencement of the present century, if not later, was remarkable for its slang. In this sort of contest their fares not unfrequently joined; and even Dr. Johnson, when on the river, exercised his powers of objurgation to overwhelm some astonished Londoner in a passing boat. During the greater part of the last century the Thames watermen were employed in a service now unknown to them. They were the carriers, when the tide and the weather availed, of the garden-stuff and the fruit grown in the neighbourhood of the river from Woolwich and Hampton to the London markets. The green and firmly-packed pyramids of cabbages that now load the waggons were then piled in boats : and it was the same with fruit. One of the most picturesque sights Sir Richard Steele ever enjoyed was when he encountered, at the early dawn of a summer's day, " a fleet of Richmond gardeners," of which " ten sail of apricot-boats" formed a prominent and fragrant part. Turnpike-roads and railways have superseded this means of conveyance, which could only be made available when the tide served.

The observances on the Thames customary in the olden time still continue, though on a very reduced scale. The Queen has her watermen, but they have only been employed as the rowers of her barge twice since her accession to the throne; once when Her Majesty and Prince Albert visited the Thames Tunnel; and again when Prince Albert took water at Whitehall, and was rowed to the city to open the Coal-exchange. Besides the Queen's watermen, there are still extant the dukes' and lords' watermen; the Lord Mayor's and the City Companies', as well as those belonging to the Admiralty. The above constitute what are called the privileged watermen, having certain rights and emoluments appertaining to them which do not fall to the lot of the class generally.

The Queen's watermen are now only eighteen in number. They have no payment except when actually employed, and then they have 10s. for such employment. They have, however, a suit of clothes; a red jacket, with the royal arms on the buttons, and dark trousers, presented to them once every two years. They have also the privileges of the servants of the household, such as exemption from taxes, &c. Most of them are proprietors of lighters, and are prosperous men.

The privileges of the retainers of the nobles in the Stuart days linger still among the lords' and dukes' watermen, but only as a mere shadow of a fading substance. There are five or six men now who wear a kind of livery. I heard of no particular fashion in this livery being observed, either now or within the memory of the waterman. Their only privilege is that they are free from impressment. In the war time these men were more than twenty-five times as numerous as they are at present; in fact they are dying out, and the last "dukes," and the last "lord's" privileged watermen are now, as I was told, "on their last legs."

The Lord Mayor's watermen are still undiminished in number, the complement being thirty-six. Of these, eight are water-bailiffs, who, in any procession, row in a boat before the Lord Mayor's state-barge. The other twenty-eight are the rowers of the chief magistrate's barge on his aquatic excursions. They are all free from impressment, and are supplied with a red jacket and dark trousers every two years, the city arms being on the buttons.

One of these men told me that he had been a Lord Mayor's man for some years, and made about eight journeys a-year, " swan-hopping and such-like," the show being, as he said, a regular thing: 10s. a voyage was paid each man. It was jolly work, my informant stated, sometimes, was swan-hopping, though it depended on the Lord Mayor for the time being whether it was jolly or not. He had heard say, that in the old times the Lord Mayor's bargemen had spiced wine regularly when out. But now they had no wine of any sort—but sometimes, when a Lord Mayor pleased; and he did not always please. My informant was a lighterman as well as a Lord Mayor's waterman, and was doing well.

Among other privileged classes are the " hog-grubbers " (as they are called by the other watermen), but their number is now only four. These hog-grubbers ply only at the Pelican stairs; they have been old sailors in the navy, and are licensed by the Trinity house. No apprenticeship or freedom of the

Waterman's Company in that case being necessary. " There was from forty to fifty of them, sir," said a waterman to me, " when I was a lad, and I am not fifty-three, and fine old fellows they were. But they're all going to nothing now."

The Admiralty watermen are another privileged class. They have a suit of clothes once every two years, a dark-blue jacket and trousers, with an anchor on the buttons. They also wear badges, and are exempt from impressment. Their business is to row the officials of the Admiralty when they visit Deptford on Trinity Monday, and on all occasions of business or recreation. They are now about eighteen in number. They receive no salary, but are paid per voyage at the same rate as the Lord Mayor's watermen. There was also a class known as " the navy watermen," who enjoyed the same privileges as the others, but they are now extinct. Such of the city companies as retain their barges have also their own watermen, whose services are rarely put into requisition above twice a-year. The Stationers' Company have lately relinquished keeping their barge.

The present number of Thames watermen (privileged and unprivileged) is, I am informed by an officer of the Waterman's Hall, about 1600. The Occupation Abstract of 1841 gives the number of London boat, barge, and watermen as 1654. The men themselves have very loose notions as to their number. One man computed it to me at 12,000; another at 14,000. This is evidently a traditional computation, handed down from the days when watermen were in greater requisition. To entitle any one to ply for hire on the river, or to work about for payment, it is provided by the laws of the City that he shall have duly and truly served a seven-years' apprenticeship to a licensed waterman, and shall have taken up his freedom at Waterman's Hall. I heard many complaints of this regulation being infringed. There were now, I was told, about 120 men employed by the Custom-house and in the Thames Police, who were not free watermen. " There's a good many from Rochester way, sir," one waterman said, " and down that way. They've got in through the interest of members of Parliament, and such-like, while there's many free watermen, that's gone to the expense of taking up their freedom, just starving. But we are going to see about it, and it's high time. Either give us back the money we've paid for our rights, or let us have our proper rights—that's what I say. Why, only yesterday, there was two accidents on the river, though no lives were lost. Both was owing to unlicensed men."

" It's neither this nor that," said an old waterman to me, alluding to the decrease in their number and their earnings, " people may talk as they like about what's been the ruin of us—it's nothing but new London Bridge. When my old father heard that the old bridge was to come down, 'Bill,' says he, 'it'll be up with the watermen in no time. If the old bridge had stood, how would all these steamers have shot her? Some of them could never have got through at all. At some tides, it was so hard to shoot London Bridge (to go clear through the arches), that people wouldn't trust themselves to any but watermen. Now any fool might manage. London-bridge, sir, depend on it, has ruined us.'"

The places where the watermen now ply, are, on the Middlesex shore, beginning from London Bridge, down the river, Somers Quay, Upper Custom-house Quay, Lower Custom-house Quay, Tower Stairs, Irongate Stairs, St. Katharine's, Alderman's Stairs, Hermitage Stairs, Union Stairs, Wapping Old Stairs, Wapping New Stairs, Execution Dock, Wapping Dock, New Crane Stairs, Shadwell Dock Stairs, King James's Stairs, Cold Stairs, Stone Stairs, Hanover Stairs, Duke's Shore, Limehouse Hole, Chalk Stones, Masthouse, and Horseferry. On the Surrey side, beginning from Greenwich, are Greenwich, Lower Watergate, Upper Water-gate, George's Stairs, Deptford Stairs, Dog-and-Duck Stairs, Cuckold's Point, Horseferry Road, Globe Stairs, King-and-Queen Stairs, Surrey Canal Stairs, Hanover Row, Church Stairs, Rotherhithe Stairs, Prince's Stairs, Cherry Garden, Fountain High Stairs, East Lane, Mill Stairs, Horse and Groom New Stairs, George's Stairs, Horse and Groom Old Stairs, Pickle Herring Stairs, Battle Bridge Stairs, and London Bridge Stairs.

Above London Bridge, the watermen's stairs or stations on the Middlesex shore are, London Bridge, All Hallows, Southwark Bridge, Paul's Wharf, Blackfriars, Fox-under-the-Hill, Adelphi, Hungerford, Whitehall-Stairs, Westminster Bridge, Horseferry, Vauxhall, and Hammersmith. On the opposite shore are London Bridge, Horseshoe Alley, Bankside, Southwark Bridge, Blackfriars Hodges, Waterloo Bridge, Westminster Bridge, Stangate Stairs, Lambeth Stairs, Vauxhall Bridge, Nine Elms, and the Red House, Battersea. Beyond, at Putney, and on both sides of the river up to Richmond, boats are to be had on hire, but the watermen who work them are known to their London brethren as "up-country watermen"—men who do not regularly ply for hire, and who are not in regular attendance at the river side, though duly licensed. They convey passengers or luggage, or packages of any kind adapted to the burden of a boat of a light draught of water. When they are not employed, their boats are kept chained to piles driven into the water's edge. These men occasionally work in the market gardens, or undertake any job within their power; but, though they are civil and honest, they are only partially employed either on or off the river, and are very poor. Sometimes, when no better employment is in prospect, they stand at the toll-bridges of Putney,

Hammersmith, or Kew, and offer to carry passengers across for the price of the toll. Since the prevalence of steam-packets as a means of locomotion along the Thames, the " stairs," (if so they may be called), above bridge, are for the most part almost nominal stations for the watermen. At London Bridge stairs (Middlesex side), there now lie but three boats, while, before the steam era, or rather before the removal of the old London Bridge, ten times that number of boats were to be " hailed " there. At Waterloo and Southwark bridges, a man stands near the toll-gate offering a water conveyance no dearer than the toll; but it is hopeless to make this proposition when the tide is low, and these men, I am assured, hardly make eightpence a-day when offering this futile opposition. The stairs above bridge most frequented by the watermen, are at the Red House, Battersea, where there are many visitors to witness or take part in shooting-matches, or for dinner or picnic parties.

Down the river, the Greenwich stairs are the most numerously stocked with boats. Ordinarily about thirty boats are to be engaged there, but the business of the watermen is not one-twentieth so much to convey passengers as to board any sailing vessels beating up for London, and to inquire with an offer of their services (many of them being pilots) if they can be of any use, either aboard or ashore.

The number of " stairs " which may be considered as the recognised stations of watermen plying for hire, are, as I have shown by the foregoing enumeration, 75. The watermen plying at these places, I am told, by the best-informed men, average seventy a " stairs." This gives 525 men and boats, but that, however, as we shall presently see, presents no criterion of the actual number of persons authorised to act as watermen.

Near the stairs below bridge the watermen stand looking out for customers, or they sit on an adjacent form, protected from the weather, some smoking and some dozing. They are weather-beaten, strong-looking men, and most of them are of, or above, the middle age. Those who are not privileged work in the same way as the privileged, wear all kinds of dresses, but generally something in the nature of a sailor's garb, such as a strong pilot-jacket and thin canvas trousers. The present race of watermen have, I am assured, lost the sauciness (with occasional smartness) that distinguished their predecessors. They are mostly patient, plodding men, enduring poverty heroically, and shrinking far more than many other classes from any application for parish relief. " There is not a more independent lot that way in London," said a waterman to me, " and God knows it isn't for want of all the claims which being poor can give us, that we don't apply to the workhouse." Some, however, are obliged to spend their old age, when incapable of labour, in the union. Half or more than one-half of the Thames watermen, I am credibly informed, can read and write. They used to drink quantities of beer, but now, from the stress of altered circumstances, they are generally temperate men. The watermen are nearly all married, and have families. Some of their wives work for the slop-tailors. They all reside in the small streets near the river, usually in single rooms, rented at from 1s. 6d. to 2s. a-week. At least three-fourths of the watermen have apprentices, and they nearly all are sons or relatives of the watermen. For this I heard two reasons assigned. One was, that lads whose childhood was passed among boats and on the water contracted a taste for a waterman's life, and were unwilling to be apprenticed to any other calling. The other reason was, that the poverty of the watermen compelled them to bring up their sons in this manner, as the readiest mode of giving them a trade; and many thus apprenticed become seamen in the merchant service, and occasionally in the royal navy, or get employment as working-lightermen, or on board the river steamers.

At each stairs there is what is called a "turnway and causeway club," to which the men contribute each 2s. per quarter. One of the regulations of these clubs is, that the oldest men have the first turn on Monday, and the next oldest on Tuesday, and so on, through the several days of the week, until Saturday, which is the apprentices' day. The fund raised by the 2s. subscription is for keeping the causeway clean and in repair. There is also a society in connexion with the whole body of watermen, called the "Protection Society," to proceed against any parties who infringe upon their privileges. To this society they pay 1d. per week each. The Greenwich watermen are engaged generally as pilots to colliers, and other small crafts.

From one of the watermen, plying near the Tower, I had the following statement:—

"I have been a waterman eight-and-twenty years. I served my seven years duly and truly to my father. I had nothing but my keep and clothes, and that's the regular custom. We must serve seven years to be free of the river. It's the same now in our apprenticeship. No pay; and some masters will neither wash, nor clothe, nor mend a boy: and all that ought to be done by the master, by rights. Times and masters is harder than ever. After my time was out I went to sea, and was pretty lucky in my voyages. I was at sea in the merchant service five years. When I came back I bought a boat. My father helped me to start as a waterman on the Thames. The boat cost me twenty guineas, it would carry eight fares. It cost 2l. 15s. to be made an apprentice, and about 4l. to have a license to start for myself. In my father's time—from what I know when I was his apprentice, and what I've heard him

say—a waterman's was a jolly life. He earned 15s. to 18s. a-day, and spent it accordingly. When I first started for myself, twenty-eight years ago, I made 12s. to 14s. a-day, more than I make in a week now, but that was before steamers. Many of us watermen saved money then, but now we're starving. These good times lasted for me nine or ten years, and in the middle of the good times I got married. I was justified, my earnings was good. But steamers came in, and we were wrecked. My father was in the River Fencibles, which was a body of men that agreed to volunteer to serve on board ships that went on convoys in the war times. The watermen was bound to supply so many men for that and for the fleet. I can't call to mind the year, but the full number wasn't supplied, and there was a press. Some of my neighbours, watermen now, was of the press-gang. When the press was on there was a terrible to do, and all sorts of shifts among the watermen. The young ones ran away to their mothers, and kept in hiding. I was too young then,—I was an apprentice, too,—to be pressed. But a lieutenant once put his hand on my poll, and said, 'My fine red-headed fellow, you'll be the very man for me when you're old enough.' Mine's a very bad trade—I make from 10s. to 12s. a-week, and that's all my wife and me has to live on. I've no children—thank the Lord for it: for I see that several of the watermen's children run about without shoes or stockings. On Monday I earned 1s. 9d., on Tuesday, 1s. 7d., on Wednesday, which was a very wet day, 1s., and yesterday, Thursday, 1s. 6d., and up to this day, Friday noon, I've earned nothing as yet. We work Sundays and all. My expenses when I'm out isn't much. My wife puts me up a bit of meat, or bacon and bread, if we have any in the house, and if I've earned anything I eat it with half-a-pint of beer, or a pint at times. Ours is hard work, and we requires support if we can only get it. If I bring no meat with me to the stairs, I bring some bread, and get half-a-pint of coffee with it, which is 1d. We have to slave hard in some weathers when we're at work, and indeed we're always either slaving or sitting quite idle. Our principal customers are people that want to go across in a hurry. At night—and we take night work two and two about, two dozen of us, in turn—we have double fares. There's very few country visitors take boats now to see sights upon the river. The swell of the steamers frightens them. Last Friday a lady and gentleman engaged me for 2s. to go to the Thames Tunnel, but a steamer passed, and the lady said, 'Oh, look what a surf! I don't like to venture;' and so she wouldn't, and I sat five hours after that before I'd earned a farthing. I remember the first steamer on the river; it was from Gravesend, I think. It was good for us men at first, as the passengers came ashore in boats. There was no steam-piers then, but now the big foreign steamers can come alongside, and ladies and cattle and all can step ashore on platforms. The good times is over, and we are ready now to snap at one another for 3*d.*, when once we didn't care about 1*s.* We're beaten by engines and steamings that nobody can well understand, and wheels."

"Rare John Taylor," the water-poet in the days of James I. and Charles I., with whose name I found most of the watermen familiar (at least they had heard of him), complained of the decay of his trade as a waterman, inasmuch as in his latter days "every Gill Turn-tripe, Mistress Tumkins, Madame Polecat, my Lady Trash, Froth the tapster, Bill the tailor, Lavender the broker, Whiff the tobacco-seller, with their companion trulls, must be coached." He complained that wheeled conveyances ashore, although they made the casements shatter, totter, and clatter, were preferred to boats, and were the ruin of the watermen. And it is somewhat remarkable that the watermen of our day complain of the same detriment from wheeled conveyances on the water.

THE LIGHTERMEN AND BARGEMEN.

THESE are also licensed watermen. The London watermen rarely apply the term bargemen to any persons working on the river; they confine the appellation to those who work in the barges in the canals, and who need not be free of the river, though some of them are so, many of them being also seamen or old men-of-war's men. The river lightermen (as the watermen style them all, no matter what the craft) are, however, so far a distinct class, that they convey goods only, and not passengers: while the watermen convey only passengers, or such light goods as passengers may take with them in the way of luggage. The lighters are the large boats used to carry the goods which form the cargo to the vessels in the river or the docks, or from the vessels to the shore. The barge is a kind of larger lighter, built deeper and stronger, and is confined principally to the conveyance of coal. Two men are generally employed in the management of a barge. The lighters are adapted for the conveyance of corn, timber, stone, groceries and general merchandise: and the several vessels are usually confined to such purposes—a corn lighter being seldom used, for instance, to carry sugar. The lighters and barges in present use are built to carry from 6 to 120 tons, the greater weight being that of the huge coal barges. A lighter carrying fourteen tons of merchandise costs, when new, 120*l.*—and this is an average size and price. Some of these lighters are the property of the men who drive them, and who are a prosperous class compared with the poor watermen. The lightermen cannot be said to apply for hire in the way of the watermen, but they are always what they call "on the look out." If a vessel arrives, some of them go on board and offer their services to the captain in case he be concerned in having his cargo transported ashore; or they ascertain to what merchant or grocer goods may be consigned, and apply to them for employment in lighterage, unless they know that some particular lighterman is regularly employed by the consignee. There are no settled charges—each tradesman has his regular scale, or drives his own bargains for lighterage, as he does for the supply of any other commodity. I heard no complaints of underselling among the lightermen, but the men who drive their own boats themselves sometimes submit to very hard bargains. Laden lighters, I was told on all hands, ought not, in "anything like weather," to be worked by fewer than two men; but the hard bargains I have spoken of induce some working lightermen to attempt feats beyond their strength, in driving a laden lighter unassisted. Sometimes the watermen have to put off to render assistance, when they see a lighter unmanageable. Lighters can only proceed with the tide, and are often moored in the middle of the river, waiting the turn of the tide, more especially when their load consists of heavy articles. The lighters, when not employed, are moored alongshore, often close to a waterman's stairs. Most master-lightermen have offices by the waterside, and all have places where "they may always be heard of." Many lightermen are capitalists, and employ a number of hands. The "London Post Office Directory" gives the names of 175 master-lightermen. If a ship has to be laden or unladen in a hurry, one of them is usually employed, and he sets a series of lighters "on the job," so that there is no cessation in the work. Most lightermen are occasionally employers; sometimes engaging watermen to assist them, sometimes hiring a lighter, in addition to their own, from some lighterman. A man employed occasionally by one of the greater masters made the following statement:—

"I work for Mr. ——, and drive a lighter that cost above 100*l.*, mostly at merchandise. I have 28*s.* a-week, and 2*s.* extra every night when there's nightwork. I should be right well off if that lasted all the year through, but it don't. On a Saturday night, when we've waited for our money till ten or eleven perhaps, master will say, 'I have nothing for you on Monday, but you can look in.' He'll say that to a dozen of us, and we may not have a job till the week's half over, or not one at all. That's the mischief of our trade. I haven't means to get a lighter of my own, though I can't say I'm badly off, and I'm a single man; and if I had a lighter I've no connexion. There's very few of the great lightermen that one has a regular berth under. I suppose I make 14*s.* or 15*s.* the year through, lumping it all like."

The lightermen who are employed in the conveyance of goods chargeable with duty are licensed by the Excise Office, as a check against the conveyance of contraband articles. Both the proprietors of the lighter and the persons he employs must be licensed for this conveyance, the cost being 5s. yearly. A licensed man thus employed casually by the master-lighterman is known as a jobber, and has 6s. a-day; the average payment of the regular labourers of the lighterman is 25s. a-week; but some employers, whom I heard warmly extolled as the old masters, give 30s. a-week. In addition to this 25s. or 30s., as the case may be, nightwork ensures 2s. or 2s. 6d. extra. Thus the permanent labourers under the lightermen appear to be fairly paid.

The master-lightermen, as I said before, are, according to the " Post Office Directory," 175 in number. I am told that the number may be taken (as the Directory gives only those that have offices) at 200 at the least, and that of this number one half employ, on an average, one man each. The proprietors of the lighters who average ten hands in their employ cannot be reckoned among men working on the river, except perhaps one-fourth of their number, but of the other class all work themselves. The annual number of actual labourers in this department of metropolitan industry will thus be 125 proprietors to 1100 non-proprietors, or 1225 in all, driving 1100 lighters at the least. The bargemen, who are also employed, when convenience requires, as lightermen, are 400 or 500, driving more than half that number of barges; but in these are not included many coal barges, which are the property of the coal-merchants having wharfs. The number of London boat-bargemen and lightermen given in the Occupation Abstract of 1841 was 1503, which, allowing for the increase of population, will be found to differ but slightly from the numbers above given.

The lightermen differ little in character from the watermen, but, as far as their better circumstances have permitted them, they have more comfortable homes. I speak of the working lightermen, who are also proprietors; and they can all, with very few exceptions, read and write. They all reside near the river, and generally near the Docks—the great majority of them live on the Middlesex side. They are a sober class of men, both the working masters and the men they employ. A drunken lighterman, I was told, would hardly be trusted twice. The watermen and lightermen are licensed by the by-laws of the City, passed for the regulation of the freemen of the Company of Master, Wardens, and Commonalty of Watermen and Lightermen of the River Thames, their widows and apprentices, to row or work boats, vessels, and other craft, in all parts of the river, from New Windsor, Berks, to Yantlet Creek (below Gravesend), Kent, and in all docks, canals, creeks, and harbours, of or out of the said river, so far as the tide flows therein. A rule of the corporation, in 1836, specifies the construction and dimensions of the boats to be built, after that date, for the use of the watermen. A wherry to carry eight persons, was to be 20½ feet in length of keel, 4½ feet breadth in the midships, and of the burden of 21 cwt. A skiff to carry four persons was to be 14 feet length of keel, 5 feet breadth in the midships, and 1 ton burden. · The necessity of improved construction in the watermen's boats, since the introduction of steamers caused swells on the river, was strongly insisted on by several of the witnesses before Parliament, who produced plans for improved craft, but the poverty of the watermen has made the regulations of the authorities all but a dead letter. These river labourers are unable to procure new boats, and they patch up the old craft.

The census of 1841 gives the following result as to the number of those employed in boatwork in the metropolis :—

Boat and barge-men and women	2516
Lightermen	1503
Watermen	1654
	5673

The boat and barge-men and women thus enumerated are, I presume, those employed on the canals which centre in the metropolis; so that, deducting these from the 5673 labourers above given, we have 3157, the total number of boat, bargemen, lightermen, and watermen, belong to the Thames.

STEAM NAVIGATION.

I HAVE now to speak of the last great change in river transit—the introduction of steam navigation on the river Thames. The first steamboat used in river navigation, or, indeed, in any navigation, was one built and launched by Fulton, on the river Hudson, New York, in 1807. It was not until eleven years later, or in 1818, that the first English river steamboat challenged the notice of the citizens as she commenced her voyage on the Thames, running daily from the Dundee Arms, Wapping, to Gravesend and back. She was called " Margery," and was the property of a company, who started her as an experiment. She was about the burden of the present Gravesend steamers, but she did not possess covered paddle-wheels, being propelled by uncovered wheels (which were at the time compared to ducks' feet,) projecting from the extremity of the stern. The splashing made by the strokes of the wheels was extreme, and afforded a subject for all the ridicule and wit the watermen were masters of. Occasionally, too, the steamer came into contact with a barge, and broke one or more of her duck feet, which might cause a delay of an hour or so (as it was worded to me) before a jury duck-foot could be fitted, and perhaps, before another mile was done, there was another break and another stoppage. These delays, which would now be intolerable, were less regarded at that period, when the average duration of a voyage from Wapping to Gravesend by the " Margery " was about 5½ hours, while at present, with favouring wind and tide, the distance from London-bridge to Gravesend, thirty-one miles by water, is done in less than one hour and a half. The fares by the first river steamer were 3s. for the best, and 2s. 6d. for the fore cabin. Sailing-packets, at that time, ran from the Dundee Arms to Gravesend, the fare being 1s. 6d.; and these vessels were sometimes a day, and sometimes a day and a-half in accomplishing the distance. The first river steamboat, after running less than three months of the summer, was abandoned as a failure. A favourite nickname, given by the watermen and the river-side idlers to the unfortunate " Margery " was " the Yankee Torpedo." About that time there had been an explosion of an American steamer, named the " Torpedo," with loss of life, and the epithet, doubtless, had an influence in deterring the timid from venturing on a voyage down the Thames in so dangerous a vessel. The construction of the " Margery " was, moreover, greatly inferior to the steamers of the present day, as when she shot off her steam she frequently shot off boiling water along with it. One waterman told me that he had his right hand so scalded by the hot water, as he was near the " Margery," in his boat, that it was disabled for a week.

In the following summer another steamer was started by another company—the " Old Thames." The " Old Thames " had paddle-wheels, as in the present build, her speed was better by about one mile in ten than that of her predecessor, and her success was greater. She ran the same route, at the same prices, until the " Majestic," the third river steamer, was started in the same year by a rival company, and the fares were reduced to 2s. 6d. and 2s. The " Majestic" ran from the Tower to Gravesend. At this time, and twenty years afterwards, the watermen had to convey passengers in boats to and from the steamers, as one of the watermen has stated in the narrative I have given. This was an additional source of employment to them, and led to frequent quarrels among them as to their terms in conveying passengers and luggage; and these quarrels led to frequent complaints from the captains of the steamers, owing to their passengers being subject to annoyances and occasional extortions from the watermen. In 1820, two smaller boats, the " Favourite " and the " Sons of Commerce " were started, and the distance was accomplished in half the time. It was not until 1830, however, that steam navigation became at all general above bridge.

The increase of the river steamboats from 1820 is evinced by the following Table :—

Years.	Number of River Steamers.	Number of Voyages.
1820	4	227
1830	20	2344
1825	43	8843

Thus we have an increase in the ten years from 1820 to 1830 of 16 steamers; and in the five years from 1830 to 1835, of 23 over the number employed in 1830; and of 39 over the number of 1820.

During the next thirty years—that is from 1820 to 1850,—there was an increase of 65 steamers.

The diminution in the time occupied by the river steamboats in executing their voyages, is quite as remarkable as the increase in their numbers. In 1820, four boats performed 227 voyages; or presuming that they ran, at that period, 26 weeks in the year, 56¾ voyages each, or about two a-week. In 1830, following the same calculation, 20 steamers accomplished 2344 voyages, being 117 each, or between 4 and 5 voyages a-week. In 1835, 43 steamers made 8843 voyages, being 205 voyages each, or about 8 a-week. During this time some of the steamers going the longer distances, such as to Richmond, Gravesend, &c. ran only one, two, or three days in the week, which accounts for the paucity of voyages compared with the number of vessels.

In 1820, only 227 voyages were accomplished during the season of twenty-six weeks; in 1850, half that number of voyages were accomplished daily during a similar term, and during the whole of that term the river steamboats conveyed 27,955,200 passengers. The amount expended in this mode of transit exceeds a quarter of a million sterling, or upwards of half-a-crown a-head for the entire metropolitan population.

The consequences of the increase of steam-navigation commanded the attention of Parliament in the year 1831, when voluminous evidence was taken before a Committee of the House of Commons, but no legislative enactments followed, the management of the steam traffic, as well as that of all other river traffic, being left in the hands of the Navigation Committee of the Corporation of London, of the composition of which body I have already spoken. " Collisions have taken place," said Sir John Hall, in 1836; " barges, boats, and craft, have been swamped, and valuable property destroyed, from the crowded and narrow space of the passage through the Pool; and human life has, in some instances, also fallen a sacrifice from such collisions, and in others, from the effect of the undulations of the water produced by the action of the paddle-wheels of the steamboats, — circumstances which have been aggravated by the unnecessary velocity with which some of those vessels have been occasionally pro-

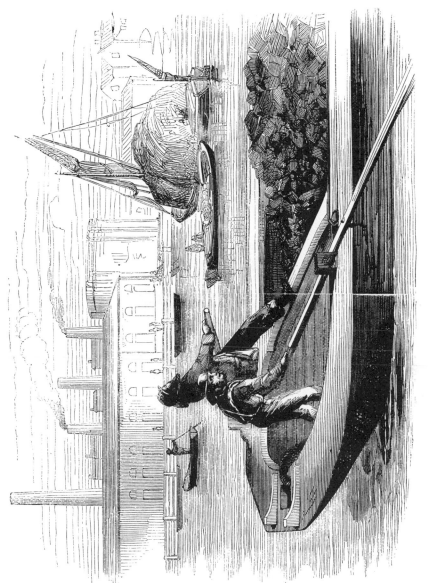

THAMES LIGHTERMEN.

[From a Sketch.]

CAB DRIVER.

[*From a Photograph.*]

pelled." The returns laid before Parliament show three deaths, in 1834, attributable to steam craft. In the year 1835, the number of deaths from the same causes was no less than ten. In all these cases inquests were held. In 1834, the number of deaths, from all causes, whether of accident or suicide on the river, as investigated by the coroner, was fifty-four; the deaths caused by steamboats being one-eighteenth that number; while, in 1835, the deaths from all causes were forty-one, the steamboats having occasioned loss of life to nearly one-fourth of that number.

To obviate the danger and risk to boats, it was suggested to the committee that the steamers should not be propelled beyond a certain rate, and that an indicator should be placed on board, which, by recording the number of revolutions of the paddle-wheels, should show the speed of the steam-vessel, while excessive speed, when thus detected, was to entail punishment. It was shown, however, that the number of times the wheel revolves affords no criterion of the speed of the vessel, as regards the space traversed in a given period. Her speed is affected by depth of water, weight of cargo, number of passengers, by her superior or inferior construction and handling, and most especially by her going with or against the tide; while, in all these circumstances of varying speed, as regards rates of progress, the revolutions of the paddle-wheels might, in every fifteen minutes, vary little in number. The tide moves, ebb and flow, on the average, three miles an hour. Mr. Rowland, the harbour-master, has said, touching the proper speed of steam-vessels on the river:—" Four miles an hour through the water against the tide, and seven with the tide, would give ample speed for the steamboats. An opportunity would thus be afforded of travelling over the ground against the tide at the rate of about four miles an hour, and with the tide they would positively pass over the ground at the rate of about seven miles." The rate at which the better class of river steamers progress, when fairly in motion, is now from eight to nine miles an hour.

Although no legislative enactments for the better regulation of the river steam navigation took place after the Report of the Committee, accidents from the cause referred to are now unfrequent. In the present year, I am informed, there has been no loss of life on the Thames occasioned by steamboats. This is attributable to a better and clearer "water way" being kept, and to a greater efficiency on the part of the captains and helmsmen of the river steam fleet.

It is common for people proceeding from London-bridge to Gravesend to exclaim about the "crowds of shipping!" The fact is, however, that notwithstanding the great increase in the commerce and traffic of the capital, the Thames is less crowded with shipping than it was at the beginning of the century. Mr.

Banyon, clerk to the Waterman's Company, in his evidence before a Committee of the House of Commons, described himself as a " practical man twenty-two years before 1811." He says, " There is a wonderful difference since my time. I was on the river previous to any docks being made, when all the trade of the country was laying out in the river. . . . . The river was then so crowded that the tiers used to overlap one another, and we used to be obliged to bring up so as to prevent getting athwart hawse." I mention this fact to show that, without the relief afforded by the docks, steam navigation would be utterly impracticable.

The average tonnage of a steam-vessel, of a build adapted to run between London and Greenwich, or Woolwich, is 70 or 80 tons; one adapted to run to Gravesend or beyond is about 180 tons; and those merely suitable for plying between London-bridge and Westminster, 40 or 50 tons. What is the number of persons, per ton, which may safely be entrusted to the conveyance of steamboats, authorities are not agreed upon. Mr. W. Cunningham, the captain of a Woolwich steamer, represented it to the committee as four or five to the ton, though he admits that five to the ton inconvenienced the passengers by crowding them. The tonnage of Mr. Cunningham's vessel was 77; his average number of passengers, " on extreme freights," was 200; yet he once carried 500 persons, though, by his own admission, 385 would involve crowding.

The changes wrought in the appearance of the river, and in the condition of the waterman, by the introduction of steamers, have been rapid and marked. Not only since the steam era have new boats and new companies gradually made their appearance, but new piers have sprung up in the course of the Thames from Gravesend to Richmond. Of these piers, that at Hungerford is the most remarkable, as it is erected fairly in the river; and on a fine summer's day, when filled with well-dressed persons, waiting " for their boat," it has a very animated appearance. A long, wooden framework, which rises into a kind of staircase at high water, and is a sloping platform at low water, connects the pier with Hungerford-bridge. At Southwark and Vauxhall bridges the piers are constructed on the abutments of an arch, and a staircase conducts the passenger to the bridge. On the north side of the river are, three at London-bridge, one at Southwark-bridge, at Paul's-wharf (Blackfriars), Temple, Arundel-street, Waterloo-bridge, Fox-under-the-hill, George-street, Adelphi, Hungerford, Pimlico, Cadogan-pier, Chelsea, Battersea-bridge, Hammersmith, and Kew. On the other side are, two at Richmond, one at Putney, Red House, Battersea; Nine Elms, Lambeth, Westminster-bridge, and London-bridge. Below bridge, on the Middlesex side, the piers are, the Tunnel,

Limehouse-hole, Brunswick, North Woolwich, and Purfleet. On the Surrey side there are two piers at Gravesend, one at Rosherville, Erith, Woolwich, East Greenwich, Greenwich, and the Commercial-docks, Rotherhithe.

The piermen at the pier belonging to the Gravesend Diamond Company (the oldest company now flourishing, as it was started in June 1828), and to others of similar character, are seven in number. At Hungerford, however, there are eleven piermen; and taking the steamboat-piers altogether, it may be safely said there are four men to each on an average, or 168 men to 42 such piers. The piermen are of three classes as regards the rates of remuneration.

The piermaster, who is the general superintendent of the station, has 35s. a-week; the others have 25s. and 21s. These men are not confined to any one duty; as the man who takes the tickets from the passengers one day may assist merely in mooring, or in "touting" the next—though a good touter is not often changed. The colour of the tickets is changed daily, unless a colour is "run out," in which case another colour must be substituted until a supply can be obtained. The majority of the piermen have been watermen, or seamen, or in some way connected with river work. They are, for the most part, married men, supporting families in the best manner that their means will admit.

From a gentleman connected with a Steam-packet Company I had the pleasure of hearing a very good character of these men, while by the men themselves I was informed that they were, as a body, fairly treated, never being dismissed without reasons assigned and due inquiry. The directors of such vessels as are in the hands of companies meet weekly, and among their general business they then investigate any complaints by or against the men, who are sometimes suspended as a punishment, though such cases are unfrequent. All the men employed on board the river-steamers are free watermen, excepting those working in the engine-room. In the winter some of them return to the avocation of watermen—hiring a boat by the month or week, if they do not possess, as many do, boats of their own. In the course of my inquiries among the merchant seamen, I heard not a few contemptuous opinions expressed of the men on board the river-craft. There is no doubt, however, that the captain of a river-steamer, who is also the pilot, must have a quick and correct eye to direct his vessel out of the crowd of others about London-bridge, for instance, without collision. The helmsman is frequently the mate of the steamer—sometimes, but rarely, one of the crew—while sometimes the captain himself relieves the mate at the helm, and then the mate undertakes the piloting of the vessel. During the season, when a steam-boat is "made safe" for the

night, one of the crew usually sleeps on board to protect what property may be kept there, and to guard against fire. The crew go on board about two hours before the vessel starts, to clean her thoroughly; the engineer and his people must be in attendance about that time to get the steam up; and the captain about half-an-hour or an hour before the boat leaves her mooring, to see that everything is in order.

The river-steamers generally commence running on Good Friday or Easter Monday, and continue until the 1st of October, or a little later if the weather be fine. Each steamer carries a captain, a mate, and three men as crew, with an engineer, a stoker, and a call-boy—or eight hands altogether on board. The number daily at work on the river-steamers is thus 552; so that including the piermen, the clerks, and the "odd men," between 700 and 800 persons are employed in the steam navigation of the Thames. Calculating each voyage to average six miles, the extent of steam navigation on the Thames, performed daily in the season, is no less than 8280 miles. The captains receive from 2l. to 3l. per week; the mates, from 30s. to 35s.; the crew, 25s. each; the call-boy, 7s.; the engineer, from 2l. to 3l.; and the stokers, 30s.

The class of persons travelling by these steamboats is mixed. The wealthier not unfrequently use them for their excursions up or down the river; but the great support of the boats is from the middle and working classes, more especially such of the working class (including the artisans) as reside in the suburbs, and proceed by this means of conveyance to their accustomed places of business: in all, or nearly all, the larger steamers, a band of music adds to the enjoyment of the passengers; but with this the directors of the vessel have nothing to do beyond giving their consent to gratuitous conveyance of the musicians who go upon speculation, their remuneration being what they can collect from the passengers.

LONDON OMNIBUS DRIVERS AND CONDUCTORS.

THE subject of omnibus conveyance is one to the importance of which the aspect of every thoroughfare in London bears witness. Yet the dweller in the Strand, or even in a greater thoroughfare, Cheapside, can only form a partial notion of the magnitude of this mode of transit, for he has but a partial view of it; he sees, as it were, only one of its details.

The routes of the several omnibuses are manifold. Widely apart as are their starting-points, it will be seen how their courses tend to common centres, and how generally what may be called the great trunk-lines of the streets are resorted to.

The principal routes lie north and south,

east and west, through the central parts of London, to and from the extreme suburbs. The majority of them commence running at eight in the morning, and continue till twelve at night, succeeding each other during the busy part of the day every five minutes. Most of them have two charges — 3*d.* for part of the distance, and 6*d.* for the whole distance.

The omnibuses proceeding on the northern and southern routes are principally the following:—

The Atlases run from the Eyre Arms, St. John's Wood, by way of Baker-street, Oxford-street, Regent-street, Charing-cross, Westminster-bridge and road, and past the Elephant and Castle, by the Walworth-road, to Camberwell-gate. Some turn off from the Elephant (as all the omnibus people call it) and go down the New Kent-road to the Dover railway-station; while others run the same route, but to and from the Nightingale, Lisson-grove, instead of the Eyre Arms. The Waterloos journey from the York and Albany, Regent's-park, by way of Albany-street, Portland-road, Regent-street, and so over Waterloo-bridge, by the Waterloo, London, and Walworth-roads, to Camberwell-gate. The Waterloo Association have also a branch to Holloway, *viâ* the Camden Villas. There are likewise others which run from the terminus of the South-Western Railway in the Waterloo-road, *viâ* Stamford-street, to the railway termini on the Surrey side of London-bridge, and thence to that of the Eastern Counties in Shoreditch.

The Hungerford-markets pursue the route from Camden Town along Tottenham Court-road, &c. to Hungerford; and many run from this spot to Paddington.

The Kentish Town run from the Eastern Counties station, and from Whitechapel to Kentish Town, by way of Tottenham Court-road, &c.

The Hampsteads observe the like course to Camden Town, and then run straight on to Hampstead.

The King's-crosses run from Kennington-gate by the Blackfriar's-road and bridge, Fleet-street, Chancery-lane, Gray's-inn-lane, and the New-road, to Euston-square, while some go on to Camden Town.

The Great Northerns, the latest route started, travel from the railway terminus, Maiden-lane, King's-cross, to the Bank and the railway-stations, both in the city and across the Thames; also to Paddington, and some to Kennington.

The Favourites' route is from Westminster Abbey, along the Strand, Chancery-lane, Gray's-inn-lane, and Coldbath-fields, to the Angel, Islington, and thence to Holloway; while some of them run down Fleet-street, and so past the General Post-office, and thence by the City-road to the Angel and to Holloway. The Favourites also run from Holloway to the Bank.

The Islington and Kennington line is from Barnsbury-park, by the Post-office and Blackfriars-bridge, to Kennington-gate.

The Camberwells go from Gracechurch-street, over London-bridge, to Camberwell, while a very few start from the west end of the town, and some two or three from Fleet-street; the former crossing Westminster and the latter Blackfriars-bridge, while some Nelsons run from Oxford-street to Camberwell or to Brixton.

The Brixtons and Claphams go, some from the Regent-circus, Oxford-street, by way of Regent-street, over Westminster-bridge; and some from Gracechurch-street, over London-bridge, to Brixton or Clapham, as the case may be.

The Paragons observe the same route, and some of these conveyances go over Blackfriar's-bridge to Brixton.

The Carshaltons follow the track of the Mitchams, Tootings, and Claphams, and go over London-bridge to the Bank.

The Paddingtons go from the Royal Oak, Westbourne-Green, and from the Pine-apple-gate by way of Oxford-street and Holborn to the Bank, the London-bridge, Eastern Counties, or Blackwall railway termini; while some reach the same destination by the route of the New-road, City-road, and Finsbury. These routes are also pursued by the vehicles lettered "New-road Conveyance Association," and "London Conveyance Company;" while some of the vehicles belonging to the same proprietors run to Notting-hill, and some branches to St. John's Wood and elsewhere.

The Wellingtons and Marlboroughs pursue the same track as the Paddingtons, but some of them diverge to St. John's Wood.

The Kensall-greens go from the Regent-circus, Oxford-street, to the Cemetery.

The course of the Bayswaters is from Bayswater *viâ* Oxford-street, Regent-street, and the Strand, to the Bank.

The Bayswaters and Kensingtons run from the Bank *viâ* Finsbury, and then by the City-road and New-road, down Portland-road, and by Oxford-street and Piccadilly to Bayswater and Kensington.

The Hammersmith and Kensingtons convey their passengers from Hammersmith, by way of Kensington, Knightsbridge, Piccadilly, &c. to the Bank.

The Richmond and Hampton Courts, from St. Paul's-churchyard to the two places indicated.

The Putneys and Bromptons run from Putney-bridge *viâ* Brompton, &c. to the Bank and the London-bridge railway station.

The Chelseas proceed from the Man in the Moon to the Bank, Mile-end-road, and City railway stations.

The Chelsea and Islingtons observe the route from Sloane-square to the Angel, Islington, travelling along Piccadilly, Regent-street, Portland-road, and the New-road.

The Royal Blues go from Pimlico *viâ*

Grosvenor-gate, Piccadilly, the Strand, &c. to the Blackwall railway station.

The direction of the Pimlicos is through Westminster, Whitehall, Strand, &c. to Whitechapel.

The Marquess of Westminsters follow the route from the Vauxhall-bridge *viâ* Millbank, Westminster Abbey, the Strand, &c. to the Bank.

The Deptfords go from Gracechurch-street, and over London-bridge, and some from Charing-cross, over Westminster-bridge, to Deptford.

The route of the Nelsons is from Charing-cross, over Westminster-bridge, and by the New and Old Kent-roads to Deptford, Greenwich, and Woolwich; some go from Gracechurch-street, over London-bridge.

The Shoreditches pursue the direction of Chelsea, Piccadilly, the Strand, &c. to Shoreditch, their starting-place being Battersea-bridge.

The Hackneys and Claptons run from Oxford-street to Clapton-square.

Barber's run from the Bank, and some from Oxford-street, to Clapton.

The Blackwalls run some from Sloane-street to the Docks, and the Bow and Stratfords from different parts of the West-end to their respective destinations.

I have enumerated these several conveyances from the information of persons connected with the trade, using the terms they used, which better distinguish the respective routes than the names lettered on the carriages, which would but puzzle the reader, the principal appellation giving no intimation of the destination of the omnibus.

The routes above specified are pursued by a series of vehicles belonging to one company or to one firm, or one individual, the number of their vehicles varying from twelve to fifty. One omnibus, however, continues to run from the Bank to Finchley, and one from the Angel to Hampton Court.

The total number of omnibuses traversing the streets of London is about 3000, paying duty including mileage, averaging 9*l.* per month each, or 324,000*l.* per annum. The number of conductors and drivers is about 7000 (including a thousand "odd men,"—a term that will be explained hereafter), paying annually 5*s.* each for their licenses, or 1750*l.* collectively. The receipts of each vehicle vary from 2*l.* to 4*l.* per day. Estimating the whole 3000 at 3*l.*, it follows that the entire sum expended annually in omnibus hire by the people of London amounts to no less than 3,285,000*l.*, which is more than 30*s.* a-head for every man, woman, and child, in the metropolis. The average journey as regards length of each omnibus is six miles, and that distance is in some cases travelled twelve times a-day by each omnibus, or, as it is called, "six there and six back." Some perform the journey only ten times a-day (each omnibus), and some, but a minority, a less number of times.

Now taking the average as between forty-five and fifty miles a-day, travelled by each omnibus, and that I am assured on the best authority is within the mark, while sixty miles a-day might exceed it, and computing the omnibuses running daily at 3000, we find "a travel," as it was worded to me, upwards of 140,000 miles a-day, or a yearly travel of more than 50,000,000 of miles : an extent that almost defies a parallel among any distances popularly familiar. And that this estimate in no way exceeds the truth is proved by the sum annually paid to the Excise for "mileage," which, as before stated, amounts on an average to 9*l.* each "bus," per month, or, collectively, to 324,000*l.* per annum, and this at 1½*d.* per mile (the rate of duty charged) gives 51,840,000 miles as the distance travelled by the entire number of omnibuses every year.

On each of its journeys experienced persons have assured me an omnibus carries on the average fifteen persons. Nearly all are licensed to carry twenty-two (thirteen inside and nine out), and that number perhaps is sometimes exceeded, while fifteen is a fair computation; for as every omnibus has now the two fares, 3*d.* and 6*d.*, or, as the busmen call them, "long uns and short uns," there are two sets of passengers, and the number of fifteen through the whole distance on each journey of the omnibus is, as I have said, a fair computation: for sometimes the vehicle is almost empty, as a set-off to its being crammed at other times. This computation shows the daily "travel," reckoning ten journeys a-day, of 450,000 passengers. Thus we might be led to believe that about one-fourth the entire population of the metropolis and its suburbs, men, women, and children, the inmates of hospitals, gaols, and workhouses, paupers, peers, and their families all included, were daily travelling in omnibuses. But it must be borne in mind, that as most omnibus travellers use that convenient mode of conveyance at least twice a-day, we may compute the number of individuals at 225,000, or, allowing three journeys as an average daily travel, at 150,000. Calculating the payment of each passenger at 4½*d.*, and so allowing for the set-off of the "short uns" to the "long uns," we have a daily receipt for omnibus fares of 8,439*l.*, a weekly receipt of 58,073*l.*, and a yearly receipt of 2,903,650*l.*; which it will be seen is several thousands less than the former estimate: so that it may be safely assured, that at least three millions of money is annually expended on omnibus fares in London.

The extent of individual travel performed by some of the omnibus drivers is enormous. One man told me that he had driven his "bus" seventy-two miles (twelve stages of six miles) every day for six years, with the exception of twelve miles less every second Sunday, so that this man had driven in six years 179,568 miles.

ORIGIN OF OMNIBUSES.

This vast extent of omnibus transit has been the growth of twenty years, as it was not until the 4th July, 1829, that Mr. Shillibeer, now the proprietor of the patent mourning coaches, started the first omnibus. Some works of authority as books of reference, have represented that Mr. Shillibeer's first omnibus ran from Charing-cross to Greenwich, and that the charge for outside and inside places was the same. Such was not the case; the first omnibus, or rather, the first pair of those vehicles (for Mr. Shillibeer started two), ran from the Bank to the Yorkshire Stingo. Neither could the charge out and in be the same, as there were no outside passengers. Mr. Shillibeer was a naval officer, and in his youth stepped from a midshipman's duties into the business of a coach-builder, he learning that business from the late Mr. Hatchett, of Long Acre. Mr. Shillibeer then established himself in Paris as a builder of English carriages, a demand for which had sprung up after the peace, when the current of English travel was directed strongly to France. In this speculation Mr. Shillibeer was eminently successful. He built carriages for Prince Polignac, and others of the most influential men under the dynasty of the elder branch of the Bourbons, and had a bazaar for the sale of his vehicles. He was thus occupied in Paris in 1819, when M. Lafitte first started the omnibuses which are now so common and so well managed in the French capital. Lafitte was the banker (afterwards the minister) of Louis Philippe, and the most active man in establishing the Messageries Royales. Five or six years after the omnibuses had been successfully introduced into Paris, Mr. Shillibeer was employed by M. Lafitte to build two in a superior style. In executing this order, Mr. Shillibeer thought that so comfortable and economical a mode of conveyance might be advantageously introduced in London. He accordingly disposed of his Parisian establishment, and came to London, and started his omnibus as I have narrated. In order that the introduction might have every chance of success, and have the full prestige of respectability, Mr. Shillibeer brought over with him from Paris two youths, both the sons of British naval officers; and these young gentlemen were for a few weeks his "conductors." They were smartly dressed in "blue cloth and togs," to use the words of my informant, after the fashion of Lafitte's conductors, each dress costing 5*l.* Their addressing any foreign passenger in French, and the French style of the affair, gave rise to an opinion that Mr. Shillibeer was a Frenchman, and that the English were indebted to a foreigner for the improvement of their vehicular transit, whereas Mr. Shillibeer had served in the British navy, and was born in Tottenham-court-road. His speculation was particularly and at once successful. His two vehicles carried each twenty-two, and were filled every journey. The form was that of the present omnibus, but larger and roomier, as the twenty-two were all accommodated inside, nobody being outside but the driver. Three horses yoked abreast were used to draw these carriages.

There were for many days, until the novelty wore off, crowds assembled to see the omnibuses start, and many ladies and gentlemen took their places in them to the Yorkshire Stingo, in order that they might have the pleasure of riding back again. The fare was one shilling for the whole and sixpence for half the distance, and each omnibus made twelve journeys to and fro every day. Thus Mr. Shillibeer established a diversity of fares, regulated by distance; a regulation which was afterwards in a great measure abandoned by omnibus proprietors, and then re-established on our present threepenny and sixpenny payments, the "long uns" and the "short uns." Mr. Shillibeer's receipts were 100*l.* a-week. At first he provided a few books, chiefly magazines, for the perusal of his customers; but this peripatetic library was discontinued, for the customers (I give the words of my informant) "boned the books." When the young-gentlemen conductors retired from their posts, they were succeeded by persons hired by Mr. Shillibeer, and liberally paid, who were attired in a sort of velvet livery. Many weeks had not elapsed before Mr. Shillibeer found a falling off in his receipts, although he ascertained that there was no falling off in the public support of his omnibuses. He obtained information, however, that the persons in his employ robbed him of at least 20*l.* a-week, retaining that sum out of the receipts of the two omnibuses, and that they had boasted of their cleverness and their lucrative situations at a champagne supper at the Yorkshire Stingo. This necessitated a change, which Mr. Shillibeer effected, in his men, but without prosecuting the offenders, and still it seemed that defalcations continued. That they continued was soon shown, and in " a striking manner," as I was told. As an experiment, Mr. Shillibeer expended 300*l.* in the construction of a machine fitted to the steps of an omnibus which should record the number of passengers as they trod on a plate in entering and leaving the vehicle, arranged on a similar principle to the tell-tales in use on our toll-bridges. The inventor, Mr. ——, now of Woolwich, himself worked the omnibus containing it for a fortnight, and it supplied a correct index of the number of passengers : but at the fortnight's end, one evening after dark, the inventor was hustled aside while waiting at the Yorkshire Stingo, and in a minute or two the machine was smashed by some unknown men with sledge-hammers. Mr. Shillibeer then had recourse to the use of such clocks as were used in the French omnibuses as a check. It was publicly notified that it was the business of the conductor to move the hand of the clock a given distance when a passenger entered the vehicle, but this plan did not succeed. It is common in France for a passenger to inform the proprietor of any neglect on the part of his servant, but Mr. Shillibeer never received any such intimation in London.

In the meantime Mr. Shillibeer's success continued, for he insured punctuality and civility; and the cheapness, cleanliness, and smartness of his omnibuses, were in most advantageous contrast with the high charges, dirt, dinginess, and rudeness of the drivers of many of the "short stages." The short-stage proprietors were loud in their railings against what they were pleased to describe as a French innovation. In the course of from six to nine months Mr. Shillibeer had twelve omnibuses at work. The new omnibuses ran from the Bank to Paddington, both by the route of Holborn and Oxford-street, as well as by Finsbury and the New-road. Mr. Shillibeer feels convinced, that had he started fifty omnibuses instead of two in the first instance, a fortune might have been realised. In 1831-2, his omnibuses became general in the great street thoroughfares; and as the short stages were run off the road, the proprietors started omnibuses in opposition to Mr. Shillibeer. The first omnibuses, however, started after Mr. Shillibeer's were not in opposition. They were the Caledonians, and were the property of Mr. Shillibeer's brother-in-law. The third started, which were two-horse vehicles, were foolishly enough called "Les Dames Blanches;" but as the name gave rise to much low wit in *équivoques* it was abandoned. The original omnibuses were called "Shillibeers" on the panels, from the name of their originator; and the name is still prevalent on those conveyances in New York, which affords us another proof that not in his own country is a benefactor honoured, until perhaps his death makes honour as little worth as an epitaph.

The opposition omnibuses, however, continued to increase as more and more short stages were abandoned; and one oppositionist called his omnibuses "Shillibeers," so that the real and the sham Shillibeers were known in the streets. The opposition became fiercer. The "busses," as they came to be called in a year or two, crossed each other and raced or drove their poles recklessly into the back of one another; and accidents and squabbles and loitering grew so frequent, and the time of the police magistrates was so much occupied with "omnibus business," that in 1832 the matter was mentioned in Parliament as a nuisance requiring a remedy, and in 1833 a Bill was brought in by the Government and passed for the "Regulation of Omnibuses (as well as other conveyances) in and near the metropo-

lis." Two sessions after, Mr. Alderman Wood brought in a bill for the better regulation of omnibuses, which was also passed, and one of the provisions of the bill was that the drivers and conductors of omnibuses should be licensed. The office of Registrar of Licenses was promised by a noble lord in office to Mr. Shillibeer (as I am informed on good authority), but the appointment was given to the present Commissioner of the City Police, and the office next to the principal was offered to Mr. Shillibeer, which that gentleman declined to accept. The reason assigned for not appointing him to the registrarship was that he was connected with omnibuses. At the beginning of 1834, Mr. Shillibeer abandoned his metropolitan trade, and began running omnibuses from London to Greenwich and Woolwich, employing 20 carriages and 120 horses; but the increase of steamers and the opening of the Greenwich Railway in 1835 affected his trade so materially, that Mr. Shillibeer fell into arrear with his payments to the Stamp Office, and seizures of his property and reseizures after money was paid, entailed such heavy expenses, and such a hindrance to Mr. Shillibeer's business, that his failure ensued.

I have been thus somewhat full in my detail of Mr. Shillibeer's career, as his procedures are, in truth, the history of the transit of the metropolis as regards omnibuses. I conclude this portion of the subject with the following extracts from a parliamentary paper, "Supplement to the Votes and Proceedings, Veneris, 7° die Julii, 1843," containing the petition of George Shillibeer.

"That in 1840, and after several years of incessant application, the Lords of the Treasury caused Mr. Gordon, their then financial secretary, to enquire into your petitioner's case; and so fully satisfied was that gentleman with the hardships and cruel wrongs which the department of Stamps and Taxes had inflicted upon your petitioner, that he (Mr. Gordon) promised, on behalf of the Lords of the Treasury, early redress should be granted to your petitioner, either by a Government appointment adequate to the loss he had sustained, or pecuniary compensation for the injustice which, upon a thorough investigation of the facts, Mr. Gordon assured your petitioner he had fully established, to the satisfaction of the Lords of the Treasury.

"That in proof of the sincerity of Mr. Gordon, he, in his then official capacity of secretary to the said Lords of her Majesty's Treasury, applied, in April 1841, to the then heads of two Government departments, viz. the Marquess of Normanby and the Right Hon. Henry Labouchere, to appoint your petitioner 'Inspector General of Public Carriages,' or some appointment in the Railway department at the Board of Trade; but these applications being unsuccessful, Mr. Gordon applied and obtained for your petitioner the promise of one of the twenty-five appointments of Receiver-General of County Courts (testimonials of your petitioner's fitness being at the Treasury), the bill for establishing which was then in progress through Parliament.

"That shortly after your petitioner's claims had been admitted, and redress promised by the Lords of the Treasury, Mr. Gordon resigned his situation of secretary, and on the 6th May, 1841, your petitioner again saw Mr. Gordon, who assured your petitioner that but for the fact of the miscellaneous estimates being made up and passed for that year, your petitioner's name should have been placed in them for a grant of 5000*l*., further observing that your petitioner's was a case of very great hardship and injustice, and assuring your petitioner that he (Mr. Gordon) would not quit the Treasury without stating to his successor that your petitioner's case was one of peculiar severity, and deserved immediate attention and redress."

And so the matter remains virtually at an end.

I will now give the regulations and statistics of the French omnibuses, which I am enabled to do through the kindness of a gentleman to whom I am indebted for much valuable information.

As the regulations of the French public conveyances (*des voitures faisant le transport en commun*) are generally considered to have worked admirably well, I present a digest of them. The earlier enactments provide for the numbering of the conveyances and for the licensing of all connected with them.

The laws which provide the regulations are of the following dates: I enumerate them to show how closely the French Government has attended to the management of hired vehicles. Dec. 14, 1789; Aug. 14, 1790; 9 Vendemiaire, An VI. (Sep. 30, 1797); 11 Frimaire, An VII. (Dec. 1, 1798); 12 Messidor, An VIII. (July 1, 1800; 3 Brumaire, An IX. (Oct. 29, 1800); Dec. 30, 1818; July 22, 1829; Aug. 1, 1829; March 29, 1836; Sep. 15, 1838, and Jan. 5, 1846. The 471st, 474th, 479th, and 484th Articles of the Penal Code also relate to this subject.

The principal regulations now in force are the following :—

The proprietors of all public conveyances (for hire) shall be numbered, licensed, and find such security as shall be satisfactory to the authorities. Every proprietor, before he can change the locality of his establishment, is bound to give forty-eight hours' notice of his intention to remove. The sale of such establishments can only be effected by undertakers (*entrepreneurs*), duly authorised for the purpose; and the privilege of the undertaker is not transferable, either wholly or partially, without the sanction of the authorities. The proprietors cannot employ any conductors, drivers, or porters, but such as have a license or permit (*permis de conduire*, &c). Neither can a master retain or transfer any such permit if the holder of it

have left his service; it must be given up within twenty-four hours at the prefecture (chief office) of police, and the date of the man's entering and leaving his employ must be inscribed by his late master on the back of the document. Proprietors must keep a register of the names and abodes of their drivers and conductors, and of their numbers as entered in the books of the prefecture; also a daily entry of the numbers of the vehicles in use, as engraved on the plates affixed to them, and a record of the conduct of the men to whom they have been entrusted. No proprietor to be allowed to employ a driver or conductor whose permit through ill-conduct or any cause has been withdrawn. In case of the contravention of this regulation by any one, the plying (*la circulation*) of his carriage is to be stopped, either temporarily or definitely. No carriage shall be entrusted to either driver or conductor, if either be in a state of evident uncleanliness (*malpropreté*). No horse known to be vicious, diseased, or incapable of work, is to be employed.

The conductors are to maintain order in their vehicles, and to observe that the passengers place themselves so as not to incommode one another. They are not to take more persons than they are authorised to convey, which number must be notified in the interior and on the exterior of the omnibus. They are also forbidden to admit individuals who may be drunk, or clad in a manner to disgust or annoy the other passengers; neither must they admit dogs, or suffer persons who may drink, sing, or smoke to remain in the carriages; neither must they carry parcels which, from their size, or the nature of their contents, may incommode the passengers. Conductors must not give the coachman the word to go on until each passenger leaving the omnibus shall have quitted the footstep, or until each passenger entering the omnibus shall have been seated. Every person so entering is to be asked where he wishes to be set down. All property left in the omnibus to be conveyed to the prefecture of police. It is, moreover, the conductor's business to light the carriage lamps after night-fall.

The drivers, before they can be allowed to exercise their profession, must produce testimonials as to their possessing the necessary skill. They are not to gallop their horses under any circumstances whatever. They are required, moreover, to drive slowly, or at a walk (*au pas*), in the markets and in the narrow streets where only two carriages can pass abreast, at the descent of the bridges, and in all parts of the public ways where there may be a stoppage or a rapid slope. Wherever the width of the streets permits it, the omnibus must be driven at least three feet from the houses, where there is no footpath (*trottoir*); and where there is a footpath, two feet from it. They must, as much as possible, keep the wheels of their vehicle out of the gutters.

No driver or conductor can exercise his profession under the age of eighteen; and before being authorised to do so, he must show that his morals and trustworthiness are such as to justify his appointment. (The *ordonnance* then provides for the licensing, at the cost of 70c., of these officers, by the police, in the way I have already described.) They are not permitted to smoke while at their work, nor to take off their coats, even during the sultriest weather. The omnibuses are to pull up on the right-hand side of the street; but if there be any hindrance, then on the left.

The foregoing regulations (the infractions of which are punishable through the ordinary tribunals) do not materially differ from those of our own country, though they may be more stringently enforced. The other provisions, however, are materially different. The French Government fixes the amount of fare, prescribes the precise route to be observed and the time to be kept, and limits the number of omnibuses. On the 12th August, 1846, they were 387 in number, running along 36 lines, which are classed under the head of 12 routes (*entreprises*), in the following order :—

Routes.	No. of Lines.	No. of Carriages.	Nos. according to the Licenses.
1 Omnibus Orléanaises and Diligentes	13	151	1 to 151
2 Dames réunies	3	29	152 to 180
3 Tricyles	1	11	181 to 191
4 Favorites	4	47	192 to 238
5 Béarnaises	2	19	239 to 257
6 Citadines	2	13	258 to 270
7 Batignolles—gazelles	2	19	271 to 289
8 Hirondelles	2	30	290 to 319
9 Parisiennes	3	33	320 to 352
10 Constantines	1	12	353 to 364
11 Excellentes	2	15	365 to 379
12 Gauloises.........	1	8	380 to 387
	36	387	

In order to prevent the inconvenience of too rigidly defined routes, a system of inter-communication has been established. At a given point (*bureau des correspondances*), a passenger may always be transferred to another omnibus, the conductor giving him a free ticket; and so may reach his destination, or the nearest point to it, from any of the starting-places. This system now exists, but very partially, on some of the London lines.

The number conveyed by a Parisian omnibus is fixed at 16; each vehicle is to be drawn by two horses, and is to unite "all the conditions of solidity, commodiousness, and elegance that may be desirable." In order to ensure these conditions, the French Government directs in what manner every omnibus shall be built. Those built prior to the promulgation of the ordonnance (Aug. 12, 1846), regulating the construction of these vehicles, are still allowed to be "in circulation;" but after the 1st of January, 1852, no omnibus not constructed in exact accordance with the details laid down will be allowed "to circulate." The height of the omnibus is fixed, as well as the length and the width; the circumference of the wheels, the adjustment of the springs, the hanging of the body, the formation of the ventilators, the lining and cushioning of the interior, the dimensions of the footsteps, and the disposition of the lamps, which are three in number.

The arrangements, where a footpath is not known in the streets of Paris, and a gutter is in existence, are tolerably significant of distinctions between the streets of the French and English capitals.

I shall now pass to the consideration of the English vehicles as they are at present conducted.

OMNIBUS PROPRIETORS.

THE "labourers" immediately connected with the trade in omnibuses are the proprietors, drivers, conductors, and time-keepers. Those less immediately but still in connexion with the trade are the "odd men" and the horsekeepers.

The earlier history of omnibus proprietors presents but a series of struggles and ruinous lawsuits, one proprietor with another, until many were ruined; and then several opposed companies or individuals coalesced or agreed; and these proprietaries now present a united, and, I believe, a prosperous body. They possess in reality a monopoly in omnibus conveyance; but I am assured it would not be easy under any other plan to serve the public better. All the proprietors of omnibuses may be said to be in union, as they act systematically and by arrangement, one proprietary with another. Their profits are, of course, apportioned, like those of other joint-stock companies, according to the number of shares held by individual members. On each route one member of the proprietary is appointed ("directed") by his co-proprietors. The directory may be classed as the "executive department" of the body. The director can displace a driver on a week's notice: but by some directors, who pride themselves on dealing summarily, it seems that the week's notice is now and then dispensed with. The conductor he can displace at a day's notice. The "odd men" sometimes supply the places of the officials so discharged until a meeting of the proprietary, held monthly for the most part, when new officers are appointed; there being always an abundance of applicants, who send or carry in testimonials of their fitness from persons known to the proprietors, or known to reside on the line of the route. The director may indeed appoint either driver or conductor at his discretion, if he see good reason to do so. The driver, however, is generally appointed and paid by the proprietor, while the conductor is more particularly the servant of the association. The proprietaries have so far a monopoly of the road, that they allow no new omnibuses to be started upon it. If a speculator should be bold enough to start new conveyances, the pre-existing proprietaries put a greater number of conveyances on the route, so that none are well filled; and one of the old proprietaries' vehicles immediately precedes the omnibus of the speculator, and another immediately follows it; and thus three vehicles are on the ground, which may yield only customers for one: hence, as the whole number on the route has been largely increased, not one omnibus is well filled, and the speculator must in all probability be ruined, while the associated proprietors suffer but a temporary loss. So well is this now understood, that no one seems to think of embarking his money in the omnibus trade unless he "buys his times," that is to say, unless he arranges by purchase; and a "new man" will often pay 400*l.* or 500*l.* for his "times," to have the privilege of running his vehicles on a given route, and at given periods; in other words, for the privilege of becoming a recognised proprietor.

The proprietors pay their servants fairly, as a general rule; while, as a universal rule, they rigidly exact sobriety, punctuality, and cleanliness. Their great difficulty, all of them concur in stating, is to ensure honesty. Every proprietor insists upon the excessive difficulty of trusting men with uncounted money, if the men feel there is no efficient check to ensure to their employers a knowledge of the exact amount of their daily receipts. Several plans have been resorted to in order to obtain the desired check. Mr. Shillibeer's I have already

given. One plan now in practice is to engage a well-dressed woman, sometimes accompanied by a child, and she travels by the omnibus; and immediately on leaving it, fills up a paper for the proprietor, showing the number of insides and outs, of short and long fares. This method, however, does not ensure a thorough accuracy. It is difficult for a woman, who must take such a place in the vehicle as she can get, to ascertain the precise number of outsides and their respective fares. So difficult, that I am assured such a person has returned a *smaller* number than was actually conveyed. One gentleman who was formerly an omnibus proprietor, told me he employed a "ladylike," and, as he believed, trusty woman, as a "check;" but by some means the conductors found out the calling of the "ladylike" woman, treated her, and she made very favourable returns for the conductors. Another lady was observed by a conductor, who bears an excellent character, and who mentioned the circumstance to me, to carry a small bag, from which, whenever a passenger got out, she drew, not very deftly it would seem, a bean, and placed it in one glove, as ladies carry their sixpences for the fare, or a pea, and placed it in the other. This process, the conductor felt assured, was "a check;" that the beans indicated the "long uns," and the peas the "short uns:" so, when the unhappy woman desired to be put down at the bottom of Cheapside on a wintry evening, he contrived to land her in the very thickest of the mud, handing her out with great politeness. I may here observe, before I enter upon the subject, that the men who have maintained a character for integrity regard the checks with great bitterness, as they naturally feel more annoyed at being suspected than men who may be dishonestly inclined. Another conductor once found a memorandum-book in his omnibus, in which were regularly entered the "longs" and "shorts."

One proprietor told me he had once employed religious men as conductors; "but," said he, "they grew into thieves. A Methodist parson engaged one of his sons to me— it's a good while ago—and was quite indignant that I ever made any question about the young man's honesty, as he was strictly and religiously brought up; but he turned out one of the worst of the whole batch of them." One check resorted to, as a conductor informed me, was found out by them. A lady entered the omnibus carrying a brown-paper parcel, loosely tied, and making a tear on the edge of the paper for every "short" passenger, and a deeper tear for every "long." This difficulty in finding a check where an indefinite amount of money passes through a man's hands—and I am by no means disposed to undervalue the difficulty—has led to a summary course of procedure, not unattended by serious evils. It appears that men are now discharged suddenly, at a moment's notice, and with no reason assigned. If a reason be demanded, the answer is, "You are not wanted any longer." Probably, the discharge is on account of the man's honesty being suspected. But whether the suspicion be well founded or unfounded, the consequences are equally serious to the individual discharged; for it is a rule observed by the proprietors not to employ any man discharged from another line. He will not be employed, I am assured, if he can produce a good character; and even if the "'bus he worked" had been discontinued as no longer required on that route. New men, who are considered unconnected with all versed in omnibus tricks, are appointed; and this course, it was intimated to me very strongly, was agreeable to the proprietors for two reasons — as widely extending their patronage, and as always placing at their command a large body of unemployed men, whose services can at any time be called into requisition at reduced wages, should "slop-drivers" be desirable. It is next to impossible, I was further assured, for a man discharged from an omnibus to obtain other employ. If the director goes so far as to admit that he has nothing to allege against the man's character, he will yet give no reason for his discharge; and an inquirer naturally imputes the withholding of a reason to the mercy of the director.

OMNIBUS DRIVERS.

THE driver is paid by the week. His remuneration is 34s. a-week on most of the lines. On others he receives 21s. and his box —that is, the allowance of a fare each journey for a seat outside, if a seat be so occupied. In fine weather this box plan is more remunerative to the driver than the fixed payment of 34s.; but in wet weather he may receive nothing from the box. The average then the year through is only 34s. a-week; or, perhaps, rather more, as on some days in sultry weather the driver may make 6s., "if the 'bus do twelve journeys," from his box.

The omnibus drivers have been butchers, farmers, horsebreakers, cheesemongers, old stage-coachmen, broken-down gentlemen, turfmen, gentlemen's servants, grooms, and a very small sprinkling of mechanics. Nearly all can read and write, the exception being described to me as a singularity; but there are such exceptions, and all must have produced good characters before their appointment. The majority of them are married men with families; their residences being in all parts, and on both sides of the Thames. I did not hear of any of the wives of coachmen in regular employ working for the slop-tailors. "We can keep our wives too respectable for that," one of them said, in answer to my inquiry. Their children, too, are generally sent to school; frequently to the national schools. Their work is exceedingly hard, their lives

being almost literally spent on the coach-box. The most of them must enter "the yard" at a quarter to eight in the morning, and must see that the horses and carriages are in a proper condition for work; and at half-past eight they start on their long day's labour. They perform (I speak of the most frequented lines), twelve journeys during the day, and are so engaged until a quarter-past eleven at night. Some are on their box till past midnight. During these hours of labour they have twelve "stops;" half of ten and half of fifteen minutes' duration. They generally breakfast at home, or at a coffee-shop, if unmarried men, before they start; and dine at the inn, where the omnibus almost invariably stops, at one or other of its destinations. If the driver be distant from his home at his dinner hour, or be unmarried, he arranges to dine at the public-house; if near, his wife, or one of his children, brings him his dinner in a covered basin, some of them being provided with hot-water plates to keep the contents properly warm, and that is usually eaten at the public-house, with a pint of beer for the accompanying beverage. The relish with which a man who has been employed several hours in the open air enjoys his dinner can easily be understood. But if his dinner is brought to him on one of his shorter trips, he often hears the cry before he has completed his meal, "Time's up!" and he carries the remains of his repast to be consumed at his next resting-place. His tea, if brought to him by his family, he often drinks within the omnibus, if there be an opportunity. Some carry their dinners with them, and eat them cold. All these men live "well;" that is, they have sufficient dinners of animal food every day, with beer. They are strong and healthy men, for their calling requires both strength and health. Each driver, (as well as the timekeeper and conductor), is licensed, at a yearly cost to him of 5s. From a driver I had the following statement:—

"I have been a driver fourteen years. I was brought up as a builder, but had friends that was using horses, and I sometimes assisted them in driving and grooming when I was out of work. I got to like that sort of work, and thought it would be better than my own business if I could get to be connected with a 'bus; and I had friends, and first got employed as a time-keeper; but I've been a driver for fourteen years. I'm now paid by the week, and not by the box. It's a fair payment, but we must live well. It's hard work is mine; for I never have any rest but a few minutes, except every other Sunday, and then only two hours; that's the time of a journey there and back. If I was to ask leave to go to church, and then go to work again, I know what answer there would be—'You can go to church as often as you like, and we can get a man who doesn't want to go there.' The cattle I drive are equal to gentlemen's carriage-horses. One I've driven five years, and I believe she was worked five years before I drove her. It's very hard work for the horses, but I don't know that they are over-worked in 'busses. The starting after stopping is the hardest work for them; it's such a terrible strain. I've felt for the poor things on a wet night, with a 'bus full of big people. I think that it's a pity that anybody uses a bearing rein. There's not many uses it now. It bears up a horse's head, and he can only go on pulling, pulling up a hill, one way. Take off his bearing rein, and he'll relieve the strain on him by bearing down his head, and flinging his weight on the collar to help him pull. If a man had to carry a weight up a hill on his back, how would he like to have his head tied back? Perhaps you may have noticed Mr. ——'s horses pull the 'bus up Holborn Hill. They're tightly borne up; but then they are very fine animals, fat and fine: there's no such cattle, perhaps, in a London 'bus—least-ways there's none better—and they're borne up for show. Now, a jib-horse won't go in a bearing rein, and will without it. I've seen that myself; so what can be the use of it? It's just teasing the poor things for a sort of fashion. I must keep exact time at every place where a time-keeper's stationed. Not a minute's excused—there's a fine for the least delay. I can't say that it's often levied; but still we are liable to it. If I've been blocked, I must make up for the block by galloping; and if I'm seen to gallop, and anybody tells our people, I'm called over the coals. I must drive as quick with a thunder-rain pelting in my face, and the roads in a muddle, and the horses starting — I can't call it shying, I have 'em too well in hand,—at every flash, just as quick as if it was a fine hard road, and fine weather. It's not easy to drive a 'bus; but I can drive, and must drive, to an inch: yes, sir, to half an inch. I know if I can get my horses' heads through a space, I can get my splinter-bar through. I drive by my pole, making it my centre. If I keep it fair in the centre, a carriage must follow, unless it's slippery weather, and then there's no calcu-lating. I saw the first 'bus start in 1829. I heard the first 'bus called a Punch-and-Judy carriage, 'cause you could see the people inside without a frame. The shape was about the same as it is now, but bigger and heavier. A 'bus changes horses four or five times a-day, according to the distance. There's no cruelty to the horses, not a bit, it wouldn't be allowed. I fancy that 'busses now pay the proprietors well. The duty was 2½d. a-mile, and now it's 1½d. Some companies save twelve guineas a-week by the doing away of toll-gates. The 'stablishing the threepennies—the short uns —has put money in their pockets. I'm an unmarried man. A 'bus driver never has time to look out for a wife. Every horse in our stables has one day's rest in every four; but it's no rest for the driver."

OMNIBUS CONDUCTORS.

THE conductor, who is vulgarly known as the "cad," stands on a small projection at the end of the omnibus; and it is his office to admit and set down every passenger, and to receive the amount of fare, for which amount he is, of course, responsible to his employers. He is paid 4s. a-day, which he is allowed to stop out of the monies he receives. He fills up a waybill each journey, with the number of passengers. I find that nearly all classes have given a quota of their number to the list of conductors. Among them are grocers, drapers, shopmen, barmen, printers, tailors, shoe-makers, clerks, joiners, saddlers, coach-build-ers, porters, town-travellers, carriers, and fish-mongers. Unlike the drivers, the majority of the conductors are unmarried men; but, per-haps, only a mere majority. As a matter of necessity, every conductor must be able to read and write. They are discharged more frequently than the drivers; but they require good characters before their appointment. From one of them, a very intelligent man, I had the following statement:—

"I am 35 or 36, and have been a conductor for six years. Before that I was a lawyer's clerk, and then a picture-dealer; but didn't get on, though I maintained a good character. I'm a conductor now, but wouldn't be long behind a 'bus if it wasn't from necessity. It's hard to get anything else to do that you can keep a wife and family on, for people won't have you from off a 'bus. The worst part of my business is its uncertainty, I may be dis-charged any day, and not know for what. If I did, and I was accused unjustly, I might bring my action; but it's merely, 'You're not wanted.' I think I've done better as a con-ductor in hot weather, or fine weather, than in wet; though I've got a good journey when it's come on showery, as people was starting for or starting from the City. I had one master, who, when his 'bus came in full in the wet, used to say, 'This is prime. Them's God Almighty's customers; he sent them.' I've heard him say so many a time. We get far more ladies and children, too, on a fine day; they go more a-shopping then, and of an evening they go more to public places. I pay over my money every night. It runs from 40s. to 4l. 4s., or a little more on extraordinary occasions. I have taken more money since the short uns were established. One day before that I took only 18s. There's three riders and more now, where there was two formerly at the higher rate. I never get to a public place, whether it's a chapel or a play-house, unless, indeed, I get a holiday, and that is once in two years. I've asked for a day's holiday and been refused. I was told I might take a week's holiday, if I liked, or as long as I lived. I'm quite ignorant of what's passing in the world, my time's so taken up. We only know what's going on from hearing people talk in the 'bus. I never care to read the paper now, though I used to like it. If I have two minutes to spare, I'd rather take a nap than anything else. We know no more politics than the backwoodsmen of America, because we haven't time to care about it. I've fallen asleep on my step as the 'bus was going on, and almost fallen off. I have often to put up with insolence from vulgar fellows, who think it fun to chaff a cad, as they call it. There's no help for it. Our masters won't listen to complaints : if we are not satisfied we can go. Conductors are a sober set of men. We must be sober. It takes every farthing of our wages to live well enough, and keep a wife and family. I never knew but one teetotaller on the road. He's gone off it now, and he looked as if he was going off altogether. The other day a teetotaller on the 'bus saw me take a drink of beer, and he began to talk to me about its being wrong ; but I drove him mad with argument, and the passengers took part with me. I live one and a half mile off the place I start from. In summer I sometimes breakfast before I start. In winter, I never see my three children, only as they're in bed ; and I never hear their voices, if they don't wake up early. If they cry at night it don't disturb me ; I sleep so heavy after fifteen hours' work out in the air. My wife doesn't do anything but mind the family, and that's plenty to do with young children. My business is so uncertain. Why, I knew a conductor who found he had paid 6d. short—he had left it in a corner of his pocket ; and he handed it over next morning, and was discharged for that—he was reckoned a fool. They say the sharper the man the better the 'busman. There's a great deal in understanding the business, in keeping a sharp look-out for people's hailing, and in working the time properly. If the conductor's slow the driver can't get along ; and if the driver isn't up to the mark the conductor's bothered. I've always kept time except once, and that was in such a fog, that I had to walk by the horses' heads with a link, and could hardly see my hand that held the link ; and after all I lost my 'bus, but it was all safe and right in the end. We're licensed now in Scotland-yard. They're far civiller there than in Lancaster-place. I hope, too, they'll be more particular in granting licenses. They used to grant them day after day, and I believe made no inquiry. It'll be better now. I've never been fined : if I had I should have to pay it out of my own pocket. If you plead guilty it's 5s. If not, and it's very hard to prove that you did display your badge properly if the City policeman— there's always one on the look-out for us— swears you didn't, and summons you for that : or, if you plead not guilty, because you weren't guilty, you may pay 1l. I don't know of the checks now ; but I know there are such people. A man was discharged the other day because

he was accused of having returned three out of thirteen short. He offered to make oath he was correct ; but it was of no use—he went."

OMNIBUS TIMEKEEPERS.

ANOTHER class employed in the omnibus trade are the timekeepers. On some routes there are five of these men, on others four. The timekeeper's duty is to start the omnibus at the exact moment appointed by the proprietors, and to report any delay or irregularity in the arrival of the vehicle. His hours are the same as those of the drivers and conductors, but as he is stationary his work is not so fatiguing. His remuneration is generally 21s. a week, but on some stations more. He must never leave the spot. A timekeeper on Kennington Common has 28s. a week. He is employed 16 hours daily, and has a box to shelter him from the weather when it is foul. He has to keep time for forty 'busses. The men who may be seen in the great thoroughfares noting every omnibus that passes, are not timekeepers ; they are employed by Government, so that no omnibus may run on the line without paying the duty.

A timekeeper made the following statement to me :—

"I was a grocer's assistant, but was out of place and had a friend who got me a timekeeper's office. I have 21s. a week. Mine's not hard work, but it's very tiring. You hardly ever have a moment to call your own. If we only had our Sundays, like other working-men, it would be a grand relief. It would be very easy to get an odd man to work every other Sunday, but masters care nothing about Sundays. Some 'busses do stop running from 11 to 1, but plenty keep running. Sometimes I am so tired of a night that I dare hardly sit down, for fear I should fall asleep and lose my own time, and that would be to lose my place. I think timekeepers continue longer in their places than the others. We have nothing to do with money-taking. I'm a single man, and get all my meals at the —— Inn. I dress my own dinners in the tap-room. I have my tea brought to me from a coffee-shop. I can't be said to have any home—just a bed to sleep in, as I'm never ten minutes awake in the house where I lodge."

The "odd men" are, as their name imports, the men who are employed occasionally, or, as they term it, "get odd jobs." These form a considerable portion of the unemployed. If a driver be ill, or absent to attend a summons, or on any temporary occasion, the odd man is called upon to do the work. For this the odd man receives 10d. a journey, to and fro. One of them gave me the following account :—

"I was brought up to a stable life, and had to shift for myself when I was 17, as my parents died then. It's nine years ago. For two or three years, till this few months, I drove a 'bus. I was discharged with a week's notice, and don't know for what—it's no use asking for a reason : I wasn't wanted. I've been put to shifts since then, and almost everything's pledged that could be pledged. I had a decent stock of clothes, but they're all at my uncle's. Last week I earned 3s. 4d., the week before 1s. 8d., but this week I shall do better, say 5s. I have to pay 1s. 6d. a week for my garret. Im' a single man, and have nothing but a bed left in it now. I did live in a better place. If I didn't get a bite and sup now and then with some of my old mates I think I couldn't live at all. Mine's a wretched life, and a very bad trade."

HACKNEY-COACH AND CABMEN.

I HAVE how described the earnings and conditions of the drivers and conductors of the London omnibuses, and I proceed, in due order, to treat of the Metropolitan Hackney-coach and Cabmen. In official language, an omnibus is "a Metropolitan Stage-carriage," and a "cab" a "Metropolitan Hackney" one : the legal distinction being that the stage-carriages pursue a given route, and the passengers are mixed, while the fare is fixed by the proprietor; whereas the hackney-carriage plies for hire at an appointed "stand," carries no one but the party hiring it, and the fare for so doing is regulated by law. It is an offence for the omnibus to stand still and ply for hire, whereas the driver of the cab is liable to be punished if he ply for hire while his vehicle is moving.

According to the Occupation Abstract of 1841, the number of "Coachmen, Coach-guards, and Postboys" in Great Britain at that time was 14,469, of whom 13,013 were located in England, 1123 in Scotland, 295 in Wales, and only 138 in the whole of the British Isles. The returns for the metropolis were as follows :—

Coach, cab, and omnibus owners	650
Coachmen, coach and omnibus guards, and postboys	5428
Grooms and ostlers	2780
Horse-dealers and trainers	246
Total	9104

In 1831 the number of "coachowners, drivers, grooms, &c.," was only 1322, and the "horse-dealers, stable, hackney-coach, or fly-keepers," 655, or 2047 in all; so that, assuming these returns to be correct, it follows that this class must have increased 7027, or more than quadrupled itself in ten years.

The returns since the above-mentioned periods, however, show a still more rapid extension of the class. For these I am again indebted to the courtesy of the Commissioners of Police, for whose consideration and assistance I have again to tender my warmest thanks.

A RETURN OF THE NUMBER OF PERSONS LICENSED AS HACKNEY-DRIVERS, STAGE-DRIVERS, CONDUCTORS, AND WATERMEN, FROM THE YEARS 1843 TO 1850.

Year.	Hackney Drivers.	Stage Drivers.	Conductors.	Watermen.	Total.
1843	4,627	1,740	1,854	371	8,592
1844	4,927	1,833	1,961	390	9,111
1845	5,199	1,825	1,930	363	9,317
1846	5,356	1,865	2,051	354	9,626
1847	5,109	1,830	2,009	342	9,290
1848	5,231	1,736	2,017	352	9,836
1849	5,487	1,731	2,026	375	9,619
1850*	5,114	1,463	1,484	352	8,413
Totals.	41,050	14,023	17,332	2,899	73,804

By this it will be seen that the drivers and conductors of the metropolitan stage and hackney carriages were in 1849 no less than 9619, whereas in 1841, including coachmen of all kinds, guards and postboys, there were only 5428 in the metropolis ; so that within the last ten years the class, at the very least, must have more than doubled itself.

HACKNEY-COACHES AND CABS.

I SHALL now proceed to give an account of the rise and progress of the London hackney-

* From 1st May to 4th September, inclusive.

cabs, as well as the decline and fall of the London hackney-coaches.

Nearly all the writers on the subject state that hackney-coaches were first established in London in 1625 ; that they were not then stationed in the streets, but at the principal inns, and that their number grew to be considerable after the Restoration. There seems to be no doubt that these conveyances were first kept at the inns, and sent out when required—as post-chaises were, and are still, in country towns. It may very well be doubted, however, whether the year 1625 has been correctly fixed upon as that in which hackney-carriages were established in London. It is so asserted in Macpherson's "Annals of Commerce," but it is thus loosely and vaguely stated : " Our historiographers of the city of London relate that it was in this year (1625) that hackney-coaches first began to ply in London streets, or rather at the inns, to be called for as they are wanted ; and they were, at this time, only twenty in number." One of the City " historiographers," however, if so he may be called, makes a very different statement. John Taylor, the waterman and the water-poet, says in 1623 (two years before the era usually assigned), " I do not inveigh against any coaches that belong to persons of worth and quality, but only against the caterpillar swarm of hirelings. They have undone my poor trade, whereof I am a member; and though I look for no reformation, yet I expect the benefit of an old proverb, ' Give the losers leave to speak.' . . . This infernal swarm of tradespellers (hackney-coachmen) have so overrun the land that we can get no living upon the water ; for I dare truly affirm that in every day in any term, especially if the Court be at Whitehall, they do rob us of our livings, and carry 500 fares daily from us.'

Of the establishment of hackney-coach "stands," we have a more precise account. The Rev. Mr. Garrard, writing to Lord Stafford in 1638, says, " Here is one Captain Baily, he hath been a sea-captain but now lives on land, about this city, where he tries experiments. He hath erected, according to his ability, some four hackney-coaches, put his men in livery, and appointed them to stand at the Maypole in the Strand, giving them instructions at what rate to carry men into several parts of the town, where all day they may be had. Other hackney-men, seeing this way, they flocked to the same place, and perform the journeys at the same rate. So that sometimes there is twenty of them together, which disperse up and down, that they and others are to be had everywhere, as watermen are to be had at the water-side. Everybody is much pleased with it." The site of the Maypole that once " o'erlooked the Strand,'' is now occupied by St. Mary's church.

There were after this many regulations passed for the better management of hackney-coaches. In 1652 their number was ordered to be limited to 200; in 1654, to 300; in 1661, to 400; in 1694, to 700. These limitations, however, seem to have been but little regarded. Garrard, writing in 1638, says, " Here is a proclamation coming forth about the reformation of hackney-coaches, and ordering of other coaches about London. One thousand nine hundred was the number of hackney-coaches of London, bare lean jades, unworthy to be seen in so brave a city, or to stand about a king's court." As within the last twenty-seven years, when cabs and omnibuses were unknown, the number of hackney-carriages was strictly limited to 1200, it seems little likely that nearly two centuries earlier there should have been so many as 1900. It is probable that " glass" and " hackney-coaches" had been confounded somehow in the enumeration.

It was not until the ninth year of Queen Anne's reign that an Act was passed appointing Commissioners for the licensing and superintending of hackney-coachmen. Prior to that they seem to have been regulated and licensed by the magistracy. The Act of Anne authorised the number of hackney-coaches to be increased to 800, but not until the expiration of the existing licenses in 1715. In 1771 there was again an additional number of hackney-coach licenses granted—1000; which was made 1200 in 1799. In the last-mentioned year a duty was for the first time placed on hired carriages of all descriptions. It was at first 5s. a-week, but that sum was not long after raised to 10s. a-week, to be paid in advance ; while the license was raised from 2l. 10s. to 5l. The duties upon all hackney-carriages is still maintained at the advanced rate.

The hackney-carriages, when their number became considerable after the Restoration, were necessarily small, though drawn by two horses. The narrowness of the streets before the great fire, and the wretched condition of the pavement, rendered the use of large and commodious vehicles impossible. Davenant says of hackney-carriages, "They are unusually hung, and so narrow that I took them for sedans on wheels.'' The hackney-coachman then rode one of his horses, postilion-fashion ; but when the streets were widened, he drove from his seat on the box. In the latter days of London hackney-coaches they were large enough without being commodious. They were nearly all noblemen's and gentlemen's disused family coaches, which had been handed over to the coachmaker when a new carriage was made. But it was not long that these coaches retained the comfort and cleanliness that might distinguish them when first introduced into the stand. The horses were, as in the Rev. Mr. Garrard's time, sorry jades, sometimes cripples, and the harness looked as frail as the carriages. The exceptions to this description were few, for the hackney-coachmen possessed a monopoly and thought it unchangeable. They were of the same class of men—nearly all gentlemen's servants or their sons. The obtaining of a license for a hackney-coach was generally done through interest. It was one way in which many peers and members of Parliament provided for any favourite servant, or for the servant of a friend. These " patrons," whether peers or commoners, were not uncommonly called " lords;" a man was said to be sure of a license if he had " a great lord for his friend.'

The " takings " of the London hackney-coachmen, as I have ascertained from some who were members of the body, were 10l. 10s. a-week the year through, the months of May,

June, and July, being the best, when their earnings were from 15*l.* to 18*l.* a-week. Out of this three horses had to be maintained. During the war times the quality of oats which are now 18*s.* a quarter were 60*s.*, while hay and the other articles of the horses' consumption were proportionately dear. The expense of repair to the coach or harness was but trifling, as they were generally done by the hackney-man himself, or by some hanger-on at the public-houses frequented by the fraternity.

Of the personal expenditure of hackney-coachmen when "out for the day" I had the following statement from one of them:—"We spent regular 7*s.* a-day when we was out. It was before coffee-shops and new-fangled ways came in as the regular thing that I'm speaking of; breakfast 1*s.*, good tea and good bread-and-butter, as much as you liked always, with a glass of rum in the last cup for the 'lacing' of it—always rum, gin weren't so much run after then. Dinner was 1*s.* 6*d.*, a cut off some good joint; beer was included at some places and not at others. Any extras to follow was extras to pay. Two glasses of rum-and-water after dinner 1*s.*, pipes found, and most of us carried our own 'baccy-boxes. Tea the same as breakfast, and 'laced' ditto. Supper the same as dinner, or 6*d.* less; and the rest to make up the 7*s.* went for odd glasses of ale, or stout, or 'short'—but 'short' (neat spirits) was far less drunk then than now—when we was waiting, or to treat a friend, or such-like. We did some good in those days, sir. Take day and night, and 1200 of us was out, and perhaps every man spent his 7*s.*, and that's 1200 times 7*s.*." Following out this calculation we have 420*l.* per day (and night), 2940*l.* a-week, and 152,880*l.* a-year for hackney-coachmen's personal expenses, merely as regards their board.

The old hackney-coachmen seem to have been a self-indulgent, improvident, rather than a vicious class; neither do they seem to have been a drunken class. They acted as ignorant men would naturally act who found themselves in the enjoyment of a good income, with the protection of a legal monopoly. They had the sole right of conveyance within the bills of mortality, and as that important district comprised all the places of public resort, and contained the great mass of the population, they may be said to have had a monopoly of the metropolis. Even when the cabs were first established these men exhibited no fear of their earnings being affected. "But," said an intelligent man, who had been a hackney-coachman in his younger days, and who managed to avoid the general ruin of his brethren, "but when the cabs got to the 100 then they found it out. The cabs was all in gentlemen's hands at first. I know that. Some of them was government-clerks too: they had their foremen, to be sure, but they was the real proprietors, the gentlemen *was; they* got the licenses. Well, it's easy to understand how

100 cabs was earning money fast, and people couldn't get them fast enough, and how some hundreds of hackney-coachmen was waiting and starving till the trade was thrown open, and then the hackney-coachmen was clean beat down. They fell off by degrees. I'm sure I hardly know what became of most of them, but I do know that a many of them died in the workhouses. They hadn't nothing aforehand. They dropped away gradual. You see they weren't allowed to transfer their plates and licenses to a cab, or they'd have done it—plenty would. They were a far better set of men than there's on the cabs now. There was none of your fancy-men, that's in with women of the town, among the old hackney-coachmen. If you remember what they was, sir, you'll say they hadn't the cut of it."

The hackney-coachmen drove very deliberately, rarely exceeding five, and still more rarely achieving six miles an hour, unless incited by the hope or the promise of an extra fare. These men resided very commonly in mews, and many of them I am assured had comfortable homes, and were hospitable fellows in their way, smoking their pipes with one another when "off the stones," treating their poorer neighbours to a glass, and talking over the price of oats, hay, and horses, as well as the product of the past season, or the promise of the next. The majority of them could neither read nor write, or very imperfectly, and, as is not uncommon with uninformed men who had thriven tolerably well without education, they cared little about providing education for their children. Politics they cared nothing about, but they prided themselves on being "John-Bull Englishmen." For public amusements they seem to have cared nothing. "Our business," said one of them, "was with the outside of play-houses. I never saw a play in my life."

As my informant said, "they dropped away gradual." Eight or ten years ago a few old men, with old horses and old coaches, might be seen at street stands, but each year saw their numbers reduced, and now there is not one; that is to say, not one in the streets, though there are four hackney-coaches at the railway-stations.

One of the old fraternity of hackney-coachmen, who had, since the decline of his class, prospered by devoting his exertions to another department of business, gave me the following account:—

"My father," said he, "was an hackney-coachman before me, and gave me what was then reckoned a good education. I could write middling and could read the newspaper. I've driven my father's coach for him when I was fourteen. When I was old enough, seventeen I think I was, I had a hackney-coach and horses of my own, provided for me by my father, and so was started in the world. The first time I plied with my own coach was when Sir

Francis Burdett was sent to the Tower from his house in Piccadilly. Sir Francis was all the go then. I heard a hackney-coachman say he would be glad to drive him for nothing. The hackney-coachmen didn't like Pitt. I've heard my father and his mates say many a time 'D——n Pitt!' that was for doubling of the duty on hackney-carriages. Ah, the old times was the rackety times! I've often laughed and said that I could say what perhaps nobody, or almost nobody in England can say now, that I'd been driven by a king. He grew to be a king afterwards, George IV. One night you see, sir, I was called off the stand, and told to take up at the British Coffee-house in Cockspur Street. I was a lad then, and when I pulled up at the door, the waiter ran out and said, 'You jump down and get inside, the Prince is a-going to drive hisself.' I didn't much like the notion on it, but I didn't exactly know what to do, and was getting off my seat to see if the waiter had put anything inside, for he let down the glass, and just as I was getting down, and had my foot on the wheel, out came the Prince of Wales, and four or five rattlebrained fellows like himself. I think Major Hanger was one, but I had hardly time to see them, for the Prince gripped me by the ankle and the waistband of my breeches, and lifted me off the wheel and flung me right into the coach, through the window, and it was opened, as it happened luckily. I was little then, but he must have been a strong man. He didn't seem so very drunk either. The Prince wasn't such a bad driver. Indeed, he drove very well for a prince, but he didn't take the corners or the crossings careful enough for a regular jarvey. Well, sir, the Prince drove that night to a house in King Street, Saint James's. There was another gentleman on the box with him. It was a gaming-house he went to that night, but I have driven him to other sorts of houses in that there neighbourhood. He hadn't no pride to such as me, hadn't the Prince of Wales. Then one season I used to drive Lord Barrymore in his rounds to the brothels—twice or thrice a-week sometimes. He used always to take his own wine with him. After waiting till near daylight, or till daylight, I've carried my lord, girls and all—fine dressed-up madams—to Billingsgate, and there I've left them to breakfast at some queer place, or to slang with the fishwives. What times them was, to be sure! One night I drove Lord Barrymore to Mother Cummins's in Lisle Street, and when she saw who it was she swore out of the window that she wouldn't let him in—he and some such rackety fellows had broken so many things the last time they were there, and had disgraced her, as she called it, to the neighbourhood. So my lord said, 'Knock at the door, tiger; and knock till they open it.' He knocked and knocked till every drop of water in the house was emptied over us, out of the windows, but my lord didn't like to be beaten, so he

stayed and stayed, but Mother Cummins wouldn't give way, and at last he went home. A wet opera-night was the chance for us when Madame—I forget her name—Catalini?—yes, I think that was it, was performing. Many a time I've heard it sung out—'A guinea to Portman Square'—and I've had it myself. At the time I'm speaking of hackney-coachmen took 30s. a-day, all the year round. Why, I myself have taken 16l. and 18l. a-week through May, June, and July. But then you see, sir, we had a monopoly. It was in the old Tory times. Our number was limited to 1200. And no stage-carriage could then take up or set down on the stones, not within the bills as it was called—that's the bills of mortality, three miles round the Royal Exchange, if I remember right. It's a monopoly that shouldn't have been allowed, I know that, but there was grand earnings under it; no glass-coaches could take people to the play then. Glass coaches is what's now called flies. They couldn't set down in the mortality, it was fine and imprisonment to do it. We hadn't such good horses in our coaches then, as is now in the streets, certainly not. It was war-time, and horses was bought up for the cavalry, and it's the want of horses for the army, and for the mails and stages arter'ards, that's the reason of such good horses being in the 'busses and cabs. We drove always noblemen or gentlemen's old carriages, family coaches they was sometimes called. There was mostly arms and coronets on them. We got them of the coachmakers in Long Acre, who took the noblemen's old carriages, when they made new. The Duke of —— complained once that his old carriage, with his arms painted beautiful on the panels, was plying in the streets at 1s. a mile; his arms ought not to be degraded that way, he said, so the coachmaker had the coach new painted. When the cabs first came in we didn't think much about it; we thought, that is, most of us did, that things was to go on in the old way for ever; but it was found out in time that it was not. When the clarences, the cabs that carry four, come in, they cooked the hackney-coachmen in no time."

INTRODUCTION OF CABS.

For the introduction of hackney-*cabriolets* (a word which it now seems almost pedantic to use) we are indebted — as for the introduction of the omnibuses — to the example of the Parisians. In 1813 there were 1150 *cabriolets de place* upon the hackney-stands of Paris: in 1823, ten years later, there were twelve upon the hackney-stands of London, but the vested right of the hackney-coachmen was an obstacle. Messrs. Bradshaw and Rotch, however, did manage in 1823 to obtain licenses for twelve cabriolets, starting them at 8d. a mile. The number was subsequently increased to 50, and then to 100, and in less than nine years after the first cab plied in the streets of London all restriction as to their number was abolished.

The form of cab first in use was that of a hooded chaise, the leather head or hood being raised or lowered at pleasure. In wet, windy weather, however, it was found, when raised, to present so great a resistance to the progress of the horse that the head was abandoned. In these cabs the driver sat inside, the vehicle being made large enough to hold two persons and the cabman. The next kind had a detached seat for the driver alongside his fare. On the third sort the driver occupied the roof, the door opening at the back. These were called " back-door cabs." The " covered cab," carrying two inside with the driver on a box in front, was next introduced, and it was a safer conveyance, having four wheels — the preceding cabs had but two. The clarences, carrying four inside, came next ; and almost at the same time with them the Hansom's, which are always called " showfulls" by the cabmen. " Showfull," in slang, means counterfeit, and the " showfull" cabs are an infringement on Hansom's patent. There are now no cabs in use but the two last-mentioned. A clarence built in the best manner costs from 40*l.* to 50*l.*, a good horse to draw it is worth 18*l.* to 20*l.*, and the harness 4*l.* 10*s.* to 5*l.* This is the fair price of the carriage and harness when new, and from a good shop. But second-hand cabs and harness are sold and re-sold, and are repaired or fitted up by jobbing coachmakers. Nearly all the greater cab proprietors employ a coachbuilder on their premises. A cab-horse has been purchased in Smithfield for 40*s.*

Some of the cabmen have their own horse and vehicle, while others, and the great majority, rent a cab and horse from the proprietor, and pay him so much a day or night, having for their remuneration all they can obtain for the amount of rent. The rent required by the most respectable masters is 14*s.* in the season — out of the season, the best masters expect the drivers to bring home about 9*s.* a-day. For this sum two good horses are found to each cab. Some of the cab proprietors, especially a class known as " contractors," or " Westminster masters," of whom a large number are Jews, make the men hiring their cabs " sign " for 16*s.* a-day in the season, and 12*s.* out of it. This system is called signing instead of agreeing, or any similar term, because the 6th & 7th Victoria provides that no sum shall be recovered from drivers " on account of the earnings of any hackney-carriage, unless under an agreement in writing, signed in presence of a competent witness." The steadiest and most trusty men in the cabdriving trade, however, refuse to sign for a stipulated sum, as in case of their not earning so much they may be compelled summarily, and with the penalties of fine and imprisonment, to pay that stipulated sum. I

was informed by a highly respectable cab proprietor, that in the season 12*s.* 6*d.* a-day would be a fair sum to sign for, and 9*s.*, or even less, out of the season. In this my informant cannot be mistaken, for he has practical experience of cab-driving, he himself often driving on an emergency. There are plenty, however, who will sign for 16*s.*, and the consequence of this branch of the contract system is, that the men so contracting resort to any means to make their guinea. They drive swell-mobsmen, they are connected with women of the town, they pick up and prey upon drunken fellows, in collusion with these women, and resort to any knavery to make up the necessary sum. On this subject I give below the statement of an experienced proprietor.

CHARACTER OF CABDRIVERS.

AMONG the present cabdrivers are to be found, as I learned from trustworthy persons, quondam greengrocers, costermongers, jewellers, clerks, broken-down gentlemen, especially turf gentlemen, carpenters, joiners, saddlers, coach-builders, grooms, stable-helpers, footmen, shopkeepers, pickpockets, swell-mobsmen, housebreakers, innkeepers, musicians, musical-instrument makers, ostlers, some good scholars, a good number of broken-down pawnbrokers, several ex-policemen, draper's assistants, barmen, scene-shifters, one baronet, and as my informant expressed it, " such an uncommon sight of folks that it would be uncommon hard to say what they was." Of the truthfulness of the list of callings said to have contributed to swell the numbers of the cabmen there can be no doubt, but I am not so sure of " the baronet." I was told his name, but I met with no one who could positively say that he knew Sir V—— C—— as a cabdriver. This baronet seems a tradition among them. Others tell me that the party alluded to is merely nicknamed the Baron, owing to his being a person of good birth, and having had a college education. The " flashiest " cabman, as he is termed, is the son of a fashionable master-tailor. He is known among cabdrivers as the " Numpareil," and drives one of the Hansom cabs. I am informed on excellent authority, a tenth, or, to speak beyond the possibility of cavil, a twelfth of the whole number of cabdrivers are " fancy men." These fellows are known in the cab trade by a very gross appellation. They are the men who live with women of the town, and are supported, wholly or partially, on the wages of the women's prostitution.

These are the fellows who, for the most part, are ready to pay the highest price for the hire of their cabs. One swell-mobsman, I was told, had risen from " signing " for cabs to become a cab proprietor, but was now a prisoner in France for picking pockets.

The worse class of cabmen which, as I have before said, are but a twelfth of the whole, live in Granby Street, St. Andrew's Place, and similar localities of the Waterloo Road; in Union Street, Pearl Row, &c., of the Borough Road; in Princes Street, and others, of the London Road; in some unpaved streets that stretch from the New Kent Road to Lock's Fields; in the worst parts of Westminster, in the vicinity of Drury Lane, Whitechapel, and of Lisson Grove, and wherever low depravity flourishes. "To get on a cab," I was told, and that is the regular phrase, "is the ambition of more loose fellows than for anything else, as it's reckoned both an idle life and an exciting one." Whetstone Park is full of cabmen, but not wholly of the fancy-man class. The better sort of cabmen usually reside in the neighbourhood of the cab-proprietors' yards, which are in all directions. Some of the best of these men are, or rather have been mechanics, and have left a sedentary employment, which affected their health, for the open air of the cab business. Others of the best description have been connected with country inns, but the majority of them are London men. They are most of them married, and bringing up families decently on earnings of from 15s. to 25s. a-week. Some few of their wives work with their needles for the tailors.

Some of the cab-yards are situated in what were old inn-yards, or the stable-yards attached to great houses, when great houses flourished in parts of the town that are now accounted vulgar. One of those I saw in a very curious place. I was informed that the yard was once Oliver Cromwell's stable-yard; it is now a receptacle for cabs. There are now two long ranges of wooden erections, black with age, each carriage-house opening with large folding-doors, fastened in front with padlocks, bolts, and hasps. In the old carriage-houses are the modern cabs, and mixed with them are superannuated cabs, and the disjointed or worn-out bodies and wheels of cabs. Above one range of the buildings, the red-tiled roofs of which project a yard and more beyond the exterior, are apartments occupied by the stable-keepers and others. Nasturtiums with their light green leaves and bright orange flowers were trained along light trellis-work in front of the windows, and presented a striking contrast to the dinginess around.

Of the cabdrivers there are several classes, according to the times at which they are employed. These are known in the trade by the names of the "long-day men," "the morning-men," the "long-night men," and the "short-night men," and "the bucks." The long-day man is the driver who is supposed to be driving his cab the whole day. He usually fetches his cab out between 9 and 10 in the morning, and returns at 4 or 5, or even 7 or 8, the next morning; indeed it is no matter at what hour he comes in so long as he brings the money that he signs for; the long-day men are mostly employed for the contractors, though some of the respectable masters work their

cabs with long-day men, but then they leave the yard between 8 and 9 and are expected to return between 12 and 1. These drivers when working for the contractors sign for 16s. a-day in the season, as before stated, and 12s. out of the season; and when employed by the respectable masters, they are expected to bring home 14s. or 9s., according to the season of the year. The long-day men are the parties who mostly employ the "bucks," or unlicensed drivers. They are mostly out with their cabs from 16 to 20 hours, so that their work becomes more than they can constantly endure, and they are consequently glad to avail themselves of the services of a buck for some hours at the end of the day, or rather night. The morning man generally goes out about 7 in the morning and returns to the yard at 6 in the evening. Those who contract sign to bring home from 10s. to 11s. per day in the season, and 7s. for the rest of the year, while those working for the better class of masters are expected to give the proprietor 8s. a-day, and 5s. or 6s. according to the time of the year. The morning man has only one horse found him, whereas the long-day man has two, and returns to the yard to change horses between three and six in the afternoon. The long-night man goes out at 6 in the evening and returns at 10 in the morning. He signs when working for contractors for 7s. or 8s. per night, at the best time of the year, and 5s. or 6s. at the bad. The rent required by the good masters differs scarcely from these sums. He has only one horse found him. The short-night man fetches his cab out at 6 in the evening and returns at 6 in the morning, bringing with him 6s. in the season and 4s. or 5s. out of it. The contractors employ scarcely any short-night men, while the better masters have but few long-day or long-night men working for them. It is only such persons as the Westminster masters who like the horses or the men to be out so many hours together, and they, as my informant said, "don't care what becomes of either, so long as the day's money is brought to them." The bucks are unlicensed cabdrivers, who are employed by those who have a license to take charge of the cab while the regular drivers are at their meals or enjoying themselves. These bucks are generally cabmen who have been deprived of their license through bad conduct, and who now pick up a living by "rubbing up" (that is, polishing the brass of the cabs) on the rank, and "giving out buck" as it is called amongst the men. They usually loiter about the watering-houses (the public-houses) of the cab-stands, and pass most of their time in the tap-rooms. They are mostly of intemperate habits, being generally "confirmed sots." Very few of them are married men. They have been fancy-men in their prime, but, to use the words of one of the craft, "got turned up." They seldom sleep in a bed. Some few have a bedroom in some obscure part of the town, but the most of them loll about and doze in the tap-rooms by day, and sleep in the cabs by night. When the watering-houses close they resort to the night coffee-shops, and pass the time there till they are wanted as bucks. When they take a job for a man they have no regular agreement with the driver, but the rule is that they shall do the best they can. If they take 2s. they give the driver one and keep the other for themselves. If 1s. 6d. they usually keep only 6d. The Westminster men have generally got their regular bucks, and these mostly take to the cab with the second horse and do all the night-work. At three or four in the morning they meet the driver at some appointed stand or watering-place. Burleigh Street in the Strand, or Palace Yard, are the favourite places of rendezvous of the Westminster men, and then they hand over to the long-day man " the stuff" as they call it. The regular driver has no check upon these men, but unless they do well they never employ them again. For "rubbing up" the cabs on the stand these bucks generally get 6d. in the season, and for this they are expected to dishclout the whole of the panels, clean the glasses, and polish the harness and brasses, the cabdriver having to do these things himself or having to pay for it. Some of the bucks in the season will make from 2s. to 2s. 6d. a-day by rubbing up alone, and it is difficult to say what they make by driving. They are the most extortionate of all cab-drivers. For a shilling fare they will generally demand 2s. and for a 3s. fare they will get 5s. or 6s., according to the character of the party driven. Having no licenses, they do not care what they charge. If the number of the cab is taken, and the regular driver of it summoned, the party overcharged is unable to swear that the regular driver was the individual who defrauded him, and so the case is dismissed. It is supposed that the bucks make quite as much money as the drivers, for they are not at all particular as to how they get their money. The great majority, indeed 99 out of 100, have been in prison, and many more than once, and they consequently do not care about revisiting gaol. It is calculated that there are at least 800 or 1000 bucks, hanging about the London cab-stands, and these are mostly regular thieves. If they catch any person asleep or drunk in a cab, they are sure to have a dive into his pockets; nor are they particular if the party belong to their own class, for I am assured that they steal from one another while dozing in the cabs or tap-rooms. Very few of the respectable masters work their cabs at night, except those who do so merely because they have not stable-room for the whole of their horses and vehicles at the same time. Some of the cabdrivers are the owners of the vehicles they drive. It is supposed that out of the 5000 drivers in London, at least 2000, or very nearly half, are small masters, and they are amongst the most respectable men of the ranks. Of the other half of the

cabdrivers about 1500 are long-day men, and about 150 long-night men (there are only a few yards, and they are principally at Islington, that employ long-night men). Of the morning-men and the short-night men there are, as near as I can learn, about 500 belonging to each class, in addition to the small masters.

THE WATERMEN.

THE Waterman is an important officer at the cab-stand. He is indeed the master of the rank. At some of the larger stands, such as that at the London and Birmingham Railway terminus, there are four watermen, two being always on duty day and night, fifteen hours by day and nine by night, the day-waterman becoming the night-waterman the following week. On the smaller stands two men do this work, changing their day and night labour in the same way. The waterman must see that there is no "fouling" in the rank, that there is no straggling or crowding, but that each cab maintains its proper place. He is also bound to keep the best order he can among the cabmen, and to restrain any ill-usage of the horses. The waterman's remuneration consists in the receipt of 1d. from every cabman who joins his rank, for which the cabman is supplied with water for his horse, and ½d. for every cabman who is hired off the rank. There are now 350 odd watermen, and they must be known as trusty men, a rigid inquiry being instituted, and unexceptional references demanded before an appointment to the office takes place. At some stands the supply of water costs these officers 4l. a-year, at others the trustees of the waterworks, or the parishes, supply it gratuitously. All the watermen, I am informed, on good authority, have been connected with the working part of it. They must all be able to read and write, for as one of them said to me, "We're expected to understand Acts of Parliament." They are generally strong, big-boned, red-faced men, civil and honest, married (with very few exceptions), and bringing up families. They are great readers of newspapers, and in these they devote themselves first of all to the police reports.

One of the body said, "I have been a good many years a waterman, but was brought up a coachbuilder in a London firm. I then got into the cab-trade, and am now a waterman. I make my 24s. a-week the year through : but there's stands to my knowledge where the waterman doesn't make more than half as much; and that for a man that's expected to be respectable. He can give his children a good schooling— can't he, sir?— on 12s. a-week, and the best of keep, to be sure. Why, my comings-in—it's a hard fight for me to do as much. I have eight children, sir. I pay 16l. a year for three tidy rooms in a mews—that's rather more than 6s. a-week; but I have the carriage place below, and that brings me in a little. Six of my children don't earn a halfpenny now. My eldest daughter, she's 17, earns 6*d.* a-day from a slop-tailor. I hate to see her work, work, work away, poor lass! but it's a help, and it gets them bits of clothes. Another boy earns 6*d.* a-day from a coach-builder, and lives with me. Another daughter would try her hand at shirtmaking, and got work from a shirtmaker near Tabernacle Square; and in four days and a half she made five bodies, and they came to 1*s.* 10½*d.*; and out of that she had to pay 7½*d.* for her thread and that, and so there was 1*s.* 3*d.* for her hard work; but they gave satisfaction, her employer said, as if that was a grand comfort to her mother and me. But I soon put a stop to that. I said, 'Come, come, I'll keep you at home, and manage somehow or anyhow, rather than you shall pull your eyes out of your head for 3½*d.* a-day, and less; so it's no more shirts.' Why, sir, the last time bread was dear—1847, was it?—I paid 19*s.* and 20*s.* a-week for bread: it's now about half what it was then; rather more, though. But there's one thing's a grand thing for poor men, and that's such prime and such cheap fish. The railways have done that. In Tottenham-court-road my wife can buy good soles, as many pairs for 6*d.* of a night, as would have been 3*s.* 6*d.* before railways. That's a great luxury for a poor man like me, that's fonder of fish than meat. They are a queer set we have to do with in the ranks. The 'pounceys,' (the class I have alluded to as fancy-men, called 'pounceys' by my present informant), are far the worst. They sometimes try to bilk me, and it's always hard to get your dues from contractors. That's the men what sign for heavy figures. Credit them once, and you're never paid—never. None signs for so much as the pounceys. They'd sign for 18*s.* Why, if a pouncey's girl, or a girl he knows, seems in luck, as they call it—that is, if she picks up a gentleman, partickler if he's drunk, the pouncey—I've seen it many a time—jumps out of the ranks, for he keeps a look-out for the spoil, and he drives to her. It's the pounceys, too, that mostly go gagging where the girls walk. It's such a set we have to deal with. Only yesterday an out-and-out pouncey called me such names about nothing. Why, it's shocking for any female that may be passing. Aye, and of a busy night in the Market (Haymarket), when it's an opera-night and a play-night, the gentlemen's coachmen's as bad for bad language as the cabmen; and some gentlemen's very clever at that sort of language, too. It's not as it was in Lord ——'s days. Swells now think as much of one shilling as they did of twenty then. But there's some swells left still. One young swell brings four quarts of gin out of a public-house in a pail, and the cabmen must drink it out of pint pots. He's quite master of bad language if they don't drink fairly. Another swell gets a gallon of gin always from Carter's,

and cabmen must drink it out of quart pots—no other way. It makes some of them mad drunk, and makes them drive like mad; for they might be half drunk to begin with. Thank God, no man can say he's seen me incapable from liquor for four-and-twenty years. There's no racketier place in the world than the Market. Houses open all night, and people going there after Vauxhall and them places. After a masquerade at Vauxhall I've seen cabmen drinking with lords and gentlemen—but such lords get fewer every day; and cockney tars that was handy with their fists wanting to fight Highlanders that wasn't; and the girls in all sorts of dresses here and there and everywhere among them, the paint off and their dresses torn. Sometimes cabmen assaults us. My mates have been twice whipped lately. I haven't, because I know how to humour their liquor. I give them fair play; and more than that, perhaps, as I get my living out of them. Any customer can pick his own cab; but if I'm told to call one, or none's picked, the first on the rank, that's the rule, gets the fare. I take my meals at a coffee-shop; and my mate takes a turn for me when I'm at dinner, and so do I for him. My coffee-shop cuts up 150lbs. a-meat a-day, chiefly for cabmen. A dinner is 6½*d.* without beer: meat 4*d.*, bread 1*d.*, vegetables 1*d.*, and waiter ½*d.*; at least I give him a halfpenny. At ——'s public-house I can dine capitally for 8½*d.*, and that includes a pint of beer. On Sundays there's a dessert of puddings, and then it's 1*s.* A waterman's berth when it's one of the best isn't so good, I fancy, as a privileged cabman's."

Suggestions for Regulating the Trade.

I SHALL now conclude with some statements of sundry evils connected with the cab business, under the old and also under the new system, and shall then offer suggestions for their rectification.

One cab proprietor, after expressing his opinion that the new police arrangements for the regulation of the trade would be a decided improvement, suggested it would be an excellent plan to make policemen of the watermen; for then, he said, the cabmen thieves would be reluctant to approach the ranks. He also gave me the following statement of what he considered would be greater improvements. "I think," he said, "it would do well for those in the cab-trade if licenses were made 10*l.* instead of 5*l.*, with a regulation that 5*l.* should be returned to any one on bringing his plates in previous to leaving the trade, and so not wanting his license any longer. This would, I believe, be a check to any illegal transfer, as men wouldn't be so ready to hand over their plates to other parties when they disposed of their cabs, if they were sure of 5*l.* in a regular and legal way. I would also," he said, "reduce the duty from 10*s.* a-week to 5*s.*, and that would allow cabs to ply for 6*d.* a-mile. As everything is cheaper, I wonder people don't want cheaper cabs. 'Busses don't at all answer the purpose; for if it's a wet day, almost every one has to walk some way to his 'bus, and some way to the house he's going to. Sunday visitors particularly; and they like the wet least of all. Now, if cabs ran at 6d., they could take a man and his wife and two children, and more, two miles for 1s., or four miles for 2s., about what the 'busses would charge four persons for those distances : and the persons could go from door to door as cheap ; or, if not quite so cheap, they'd save it in not having their clothes spoiled by the weather, and go far more comfortably than in a 'bus full of wet people and dripping um brellas. I know most cabmen don't like to hear of this plan; and why? Because, by the present system they reckon upon getting a shilling a-mile ; and they almost always do get it for an 8d. fare, and for longer distances oft enough. But it wouldn't be so easy to overcharge when there's a fixed coin a-mile for the fare. It would be one, two, three, four, five, or as many sixpences as miles. Now it's 1s. 4d. for two miles, and that's 1s. 6d. —1s. 8d. for over two miles, and that means 2s.—of course cabmen don't carry change unless for an even sum ; 2s. 4d. for over three miles and a half, and that's 2s. 6d. if not 3s., and so on. The odd coppers make cabmen like the present way."

I now give a statement concerning "foul plates" and informers. It may, however, be necessary to state first, that every cab proprietor must be licensed, at a cost to him of 5l., and that he must affix a plate, with his number, &c., to his cab, to show that he is duly licensed : while every driver and waterman is licensed at a cost to each of 5s. a-year, and is bound to wear a metal ticket showing his number. The law then provides, that in case of *unavoidable necessity*, which must be proved to the satisfaction of the magistrate, a proprietor may be allowed to employ an unlicensed person for twenty-four hours ; with this exception, every unlicensed person acting as driver, and every licensed person lending his license, or permitting any other person to use or wear his ticket, is to be fined 5l. The same provision applies to any proprietor "lending his license," but with a penalty of 10l. I now give the statement :—

" You see, sir, if a man wants to dispose of his cab, why he must dispose of it as a cab. Well, if it ain't answered for him, he'll get somebody or other willing to try it on. And the new hand will say, ' I'll give you so much, and work your plates for you ;' and so he does when a bargain's made. Well, this thing's gone on till there's 1000 or 1200 ' foul plates' in the trade ; and then government says, ' What a lot of foul plates ! There must be a check to this.' And a nice check they found. Mister —— (continued my informant, laying a peculiar emphasis on the mister), the informer, was set to work, and he soon ferreted

out the foul plates, and there was a few summonses about them at first ; but it's managed different now. Suppose I had a foul plate in my place here, though in course I wouldn't, but suppose I had, Mister —— would drop in some day and look about him, and say little or nothing, but it's known what he's up to. In a day or two comes Mister —— No. 2, he's Mister —— No. 1's friend; and he'll look about and say, ' Oh, Mister ——, I see you've got so-and-so—it's a foul plate. I'll call on you for 2s. in a day or two. He calls sure enough; and he calls for the same money, perhaps, every three months. Some pays him 5s. a-year regular ; and if he only gets that on 1000 plates, he makes a good living of it—only 250l. a-year, 5l. a-week, that's all. In course Mister —— No. 1 has nothing to do with Mister —— No. 2, not he : it's always Mister —— No. 2 what's paid, and never Mister —— No. 1. But if Mister —— No. 2 ain't paid, then Mister —— No. 1 looks in, and lets you know there may be a hearing about the foul plate ; and so he goes on.'

This same Mister —— No. 1, I am informed by another cab proprietor, is employed by the Excise to see after the duty, which has to be paid every month. Should the proprietor be behind with the 10s. a-week, the informer is furnished with a warrant for the month's money; and this he requires a fee of from 10s. to 1l. (according to the circumstances of the proprietor), to hold over for a short time. It is difficult to estimate how many fees are obtained in this way every month ; but I am assured that they must amount to something considerable in the course of the year.

It is proper that I should add that my informants in this and other matters refer to the systems with which they had been long familiar. The new regulations when I was engaged in this inquiry, had been so recently in force, that the cab proprietors said they could not yet judge of their effect; but it was believed that they would be beneficial. An experienced man complained to me that the clashing of the magistrates' decisions, especially when the police were mixed up with the complaints against cabmen, was an evil. My informant also pointed out a clause in the 2d and 3d Victoria, cap. 71, enacting that magistrates should meet once a quarter, each furnishing a report of his proceedings as respects the " Act for regulating the Police Courts in the Metropolis." Such a meeting, and a comparison of the reports, might tend to a uniformity in decisions; but the clause, I am told, is a dead letter, no such meeting taking place. Another cab proprietor said it would be a great improvement if an authorised officer of the police, or a government officer, had the fixing of plates on carriages, together with the inspection and superintendence of them afterwards. These plates, it was further suggested to me, should be metallic seals, and easily perceptible inside or out. Some of the cab proprietors complain of the stands in

Oxford-street (the best in all London, they say), being removed to out-of-the-way places.

Among the matters I heard complained of, that of privileged cabs was much dwelt upon. These are the cabs which are privileged to stand within a railway terminus, waiting to be hired on the arrival of the trains. For this privilege 2s. a-week is paid by the cabmen to some of the railway companies, and as much as 5s. a-week to others. The cabmen complain of this as a monopoly established to their disadvantage, and with no benefit to the public, but merely to the railway companies; for there are cab-stands adjacent to all the railway stations, at which the public would be supplied with conveyances in the ordinary way. The horses in the cabs at the railway stations are, I am informed, amongst the hardest-worked of any in London; the following case being put to me:—"Suppose a man takes a fare of four persons and heavy luggage from the Great Western Terminus to Mile End, which is near upon seven miles, he must then hurry back again all the way, because he plies only at the railway. Now, if he didn't, he would go to the nighest cab-stand, and his horse would be far sooner relieved. Then, perhaps, he gets another fare to Finsbury, and must hurry back again; and then another below Brompton; and he may live at Whitechapel, and have to go home after all; so that his poor horse gets 'bashed' to bits."

Another cab proprietor furnished me with the following statement in writing of his personal experience and observation concerning the working of the 23d clause in the Hackney Carriage Act, or that concerning the signing before alluded to. "A master is in want of drivers. A, B, and C apply. The only questions asked are, 'Are you a driver? Where is your license? Well! here, sign this paper; my money is so much.' In very few large establishments is more caution used as to real character of the driver than this; the effect of which is, that a man with a really good character has no better claim to employ ment than one of the worst. Then, as to the feeling of a man who has placed himself under such a contract. 'I must get my money,' he says, 'I will do anything to obtain it; and as a gaol hangs over my head, what matters about my breaking the law?' and so every unfair trick is resorted to: and the means used are 'gagging,' that is to say, driving about and loitering in the thoroughfares for jobs. It is known that some men very seldom put on the ranks at all. Some masters have told their drivers not to go on the stand, as they well know that the money is not to be obtained by what is termed 'ranking it.' Now, the effect of this is, that the thoroughfares are troubled with empty cabs. It has also this effect: it causes great cruelty and overdriving to the horses; and drivers under such circumstances frequently agree to go for very much less than the fare, and then, as they

term it, take it out by insulting and bullying their customers. It may be said that the law in force is sufficient to counteract this; but it may not be known that a great many protection-clubs exist, by contributions from cabmen, and which clubs are, in fact, premiums for breaking the law; for by them a man is borne harmless of the consequences of being fined. Now, these clubs exist sometimes at public-houses, but in many cases in the proprietors' yards, the proprietors themselves being treasurers, and so becoming agents to induce their servants to infringe the law, for the purpose of obtaining for themselves a large return. The moral consequence of all this is, that men being dealt with and made to suffer as criminals, that is to say, being sent to gaol to experience the same treatment, save indignity, as convicted felons, and all this for what they after all believe to be a debt, a simple contract between man and man; the consequence, I repeat, is, that the driver having served his time, as it is called, in prison, returns to the trade a degraded character and a far worse man. Be it observed, also, that the fact of a driver having been imprisoned is no barrier to his being employed again if he will but sign—that's the test."

ACCOUNT OF CRIME AMONGST CABMEN.

I HAVE now but to add a comparative statement of the criminality of the London coach and cabmen in relation to that of other callings.

The metropolitan criminal returns show us that crime among this class has been on the decline since 1840. In that year the number taken into custody by the London police was 1319; from which time until 1843 there was a gradual decrease, when the number of coach and cabmen taken into custody was 820. After this the numbers fluctuated slightly; till, in 1848, there were 972 individuals arrested for various infractions of the law.

For the chief offences given in the police returns, I find, upon taking the average for the last ten years, that the criminality of the London coach and cabmen stands as follows: For murder there has been annually 1 individual in every 29,710 of this body taken into custody; for manslaughter, 1 in every 2829; for rape, 1 in 8488; for common assaults, 1 in 40; for simple larceny, 1 in 92; for wilful damage, 1 in 285; for uttering counterfeit coin, 1 in 612; for drunkenness, 1 in 46; for vagrancy, 1 in 278; for the whole of the offences mentioned in the returns, 1 in every 5 of their number. On comparing these results with the criminality of other classes, we arrive at the following conclusions:—The tendency of the metropolitan coach and cabmen for murder is less than that of the weavers (who appear to have the greatest propensity of all classes to commit this crime), as well as sailors (who are the next criminal in this respect), and labourers, sawyers, and carpenters. On the other hand, however, the coach and cabmen would seem to be more inclined to this species of atrocity than the turners, coachmakers, shoemakers, and tailors ; the latter, according to the metropolitan police returns for the last ten years, being the least murderous of all classes. For manslaughter, the coach and cabmen have a stronger predisposition than any other class that I have yet estimated. The average crime in this respect for ten years is 1 in 20,000 individuals of the entire population of London ; whereas the average for the same period among the London coach and cabmen has been as high as 1 in every 2800 of their trade. In rape they rank less criminal than the labourers, carpenters, and weavers, but still much higher than the general average, and considerably above the tailors, sawyers, turners, shoemakers, or coachmakers. In the matter of common assaults they stand the highest of all ; even the labourers being less pugnacious than they. Their honesty seems, nevertheless, to be greater than common report gives them credit for ; they being, according to the same returns, less disposed to commit simple larceny than either labourers, sailors, or weavers, though far more dishonest than the generality of the London population. Nor are they so intemperate as, from the nature of their calling, we should be led to imagine. The sailors (who seem to form the most drunken of all trades, there being 1 in every 13 of that body arrested for this offence), and the labourers (who come next), are both much more addicted to intoxication than the coach and cabmen ; although the latter class appear to be nearly twice as intemperate as the rest of the people, the general average being 1 drunkard in every 81 of the entire residents of the metropolis, and 1 in every 46 of the London coach and cabmen. Hence it may be said, that the great vices of the class at present under consideration are a tendency to manslaughter and assault.

The cause of this predisposition to violence against the person on the part of the London coach and cabmen I leave others to explain.

CARMEN AND PORTERS.

HAVING dealt with the social condition of the conductors and drivers of the London omnibuses and cabs, I now, in due order, proceed to treat of the number, state, and income of the men connected with the job and glass-coaches, as well as the flies for the conveyance of persons, and the waggons, carts, vans, drays, &c., for the conveyance of goods from one part of the metropolis to another ; also of the porters engaged in conveyance by hand.

The metropolitan carriages engaged in the conveyance of passengers are of two classes,—ticketed and unticketed ; that is to say, those who ply for passengers in the public streets, carry a plate inscribed with a certain number, by which the drivers and owners of them may be readily known. Whereas those who do not ply in public, but are let out at certain yards or stables, have no badge affixed to them, and are, in many cases, scarcely distinguishable from private vehicles. The ticketed carriages include the stage and hackney-coaches, or, in modern parlance, the 'busses and cabs of London. The unticketed carriages, on the other hand, comprise the glass-coaches and flies that, for a small premium, may be converted into one's own carriage for the time being. But besides these there is another large class of hired conveyances, such as the job-carriages, which differ from the glass-coaches principally in the length of time for which they are engaged. The term of lease for the glass-coach rarely exceeds a day ; while the fly is often taken by the hour ; the job-carriage, however, is more commonly engaged by the month, and not unfrequently by the year. Hence the latter class of conveyances may be said to partake of the attributes of both public and private carriages. They are public, in so far as they are let to hire for a certain term ; and private, inasmuch as they are often used by the same party, and by them only, for several years.

The tradesmen who supply carriage-horses (and occasionally carriages) by the day, week, month, or year, to all requiring such temporary or continuous accommodation, are termed job-masters, of whom, according to the Post-office Directory, there are 154 located in London ; 51 being also cab proprietors, and 28 the owners of omnibuses. They boast, and doubtlessly with perfect truth, that in their stables are the major part of the finest carriage horses in the world. The powerful animals which are seen to dash proudly along the streets, a pair of them drawing a large carriage with the most manifest ease, are, in nine cases out of ten, not the property of the nobleman whose silver crest may adorn the glittering harness, but of the job-master. One of those masters has now 400 horses, some of which are worth 120 guineas, and the value is not less than 60l. per horse, or 24,000l. in all. The premises of some of the job-masters are remarkable for their extent, their ventilation, and their scrupulous cleanliness. All those in a large way of business have establishments in the country as well as in town, and at the latter are received the horses that are lame, that require rest, or that are turned out to grass. The young horses that are brought up from the country fairs, or have been purchased of the country breeders (for job-masters or their agents attend at Horncastle, Northallerton, and all the great horse-fairs in Yorkshire and Lincolnshire), are generally conducted in the first instance to the country establishment of the town master, which may be at Barnet or any place of a like distance. These agents have what is called the pick of the market, not unfrequently visiting the premises of the country horse-dealer and there completing purchases without subjecting the farmer (for country horse-breeders and dealers are nearly all farmers) to the trouble and expense of sending his cattle to the fair; and it is thus that the London dealers secure the best stock in the kingdom. Until within twenty or thirty years ago some of the wealthier of the nobility or gentry, as I have previously intimated, would vie with each other during the London season in the display of their most perfect Cleveland bays, or other description of carriage-horses. The animals were at that period walked to London under the care of the coachman and his subordinates, the family travelling post to town. Such a procedure is now never resorted to. Very few noblemen at present bring their carriage-horses to town, even if within a short railway distance; they nearly all job, as it is invariably called: that is, they hire carriage-horses by the month at from twenty to thirty guineas a pair, the job-master keeping the animals by sending the quantity of provender to his customer's premises, and they are groomed by his own servants. "Why sir," said a job-master to me, "everybody jobs now. A few bishops do, and lords, and dukes, and judges. Lord D—— jobs, and lots of parsons and physicians; yes lots, sir. The royal family job, all but the Queen herself. The Duchess of Kent jobs. The late Duke of C—— jobbed, and no doubt the present duke will. The Queen Dowager jobbed regularly. It's a cheaper and better plan for those that must have good horses and handsome carriages. I dare say all the gentlemen in the Albany job, for I know a many that do. By jobbing, rich people can always secure the best horses in the world." I may add, that any of the masters of whom I have spoken will job a carriage duly emblazoned (if ordered to provide one); he will job harness, too, with the proper armorial bearings about it, and job coachmen and grooms as well. For the use of a first-class carriage 80 guineas a year is paid. A brougham with one horse and a driver is jobbed at 16s. a-day. But these vehicles are usually supplied by jobbing coach-masters: but the jobbing in carriages is not so common as in horses, gentlemen preferring to have their own chariots or broughams, while the jobbing in servants is confined principally to bachelors or gentlemen keeping no establishments.

The job trade I am assured has increased fivefold since the general establishment of railways. In this trade there is no "slop" supply. Even the smaller masters supply horses worth the money; for to furnish bad horses would be at once to lose custom. "Gentlemen are too good judges of horse-flesh," a small job-master said to me, "to put up with poor cattle, even though they may wear slop coats themselves, and rig their servants out in slop liveries. Nothing shows a gentleman

more than his horse; and they can't get first-rate horses in the country as they can in London, because they're bought up for the metropolis."

The men employed in the job-masters' yards do not live in the yards, except a few of the higher servants, to whom can be entrusted the care of the premises and of the costly animals kept there. Nearly all the men in these yards have been brought up as grooms, and must, in stable phraseology, "know a horse well." None of them in the better yards receive less than 20s. a-week in wages; nor will any master permit his horses to be abused in any manner. Cruelty to a horse is certain dismissal if detected, and is now, I am glad to be informed on good authority, very rare I may here mention the rather amusing reply of a rough old groom out of place to my remark that Mr. —— would not allow any of his horses to be in any way abused. "*Abused!*" said my respondent, confining the meaning of the word to one signification: "Abused! you mayn't so much as swear at them." Another rough-spoken person, who was for a time a foreman to a job-master, told me that he had never, or rarely, any difficulty in making a bargain with gentlemen who were judges of horses; "but," said he, "ladies who set up for judges are dreadful hard to please, and talk dreadful nonsense. What do they know about the points of a horse? But of all of 'em, a—— is the worst to please in a horse or a carriage; she is the very devil, sir."

The people employed by the job-masters are strong, healthy-looking men, with no lack of grey hairs—always a good sign among them. Their amusements, I am told, are confined to an odd visit to the play, more especially to Astley's, and to skittle-playing. These enjoyments, however, are rare, as the groom cannot leave his labours for a day and then return to it as a mechanic may. Horses must be tended day and night, Sunday and work-day, so that it is only "by leave" that they can enjoy any recreation. Nearly all of them, however, take great interest in horse-races, steeple-chases, and trotting-matches. Many of them dabble in the Derby and St. Leger lotteries, and some "make a book," risking from two or three half-crowns to 5l., and sometimes more than they can pay. These parties, however, belong as much to the class of servants as they do to the labourers engaged in connexion with the transit of the metropolis.

I am informed that each of the 150 job-masters resident in London may be said to employ six or seven men in their yards or stables, some having at least double that number in their service, and others, again, only two or three; the latter, however, is the exception rather than the rule. According to this estimate there must be from 900 to 1000 individuals engaged in the job business of London. Their number is made up of stablemen, washers, ostlers, job-coachmen, and glass-coachmen or flymen, besides a few grooms for the job cabriolets. The stableman attends only to the horses in the stables, and gets 2*s.* 6*d.* a-day, or 17*s.* 6*d.* a-week, standing wages. The washer has from 18*s.* to 1*l.* a-week, and is employed to clean the carriages only in the best yards, for those of a second-rate character the stableman washes the carriages himself. The ostler attends to the yard, and seldom or never works in the stables. He answers all the rings at the yard bell, and takes the horses and gigs, &c. round to the door. He is, as it were, the foreman or superintendent of the establishment. He usually receives 1*l.* 1*s.* a-week standing wages at the best yards, while at those of a lower character only 15*s.* is given. The job-coachman is distinct from the glass-coachman or flyman. "He often goes away from the yard on a job," to use the words of my informant, "for three or six months at a stretch." He is paid by the job-master, and gets 30*s.* a-week standing wages. He has to drive and attend to his horses in the stable. The glass-coachman or flyman goes out merely by the day or by the hour. He gets 9*s.* a-week from the job-master, and whatever the customers think proper to give him. Some persons give 6*d.* an hour to the glass-coachman, and others 5*s.* a-day for a pair of horses, and from 3*s.* to 3*s.* 6*d.* a-day for one horse. A glass coach, it may be as well to observe, is a carriage and pair hired by the day, and a fly a one-horse carriage hired in a similar manner. The job-coachman and the glass-coachman have for the most part been gentlemen's servants, and have come to the yard while seeking for another situation. They are mostly married men, having generally wedded either the housemaid, nurse, or cook, in some family in which they have lived. "The lady's maid," to quote from my informant, "is a touch among them. The cooks are in general the coachman's favourite, in regard of getting a little bit of lunch out of her."

The job-coachman's is usually a much better berth than that of the glass-coachman or flyman. The gentlefolks who engage the glass-coaches and flies are, I am told, very near, and the flies still nearer than the glass-coaches. The fly people, as the customers were termed to me, generally live about Gower-street and Burton-crescent, Woburn-place, Tavistock-square, Upper Baker-street, and other "shabby-genteel" districts. The great majority of the persons using flies, however, live in the suburbs, and are mostly citizens and lawyers. The chief occasions for the engagement of a fly are visits to the theatre, opera, or parties at night, or else when the wives of the above-named gentry are going out a-shopping; and then the directions, I am told, are generally to draw two or three doors away from the shops, so that the shopmen may not see them drive up in a carriage and charge accordingly. A number of flies are engaged to carry the re-

ligious gentry in the suburbs to Exeter Hall during the May meetings; and it is they, I am assured, who are celebrated for over-crowding the vehicles. "Bless you," said one man whom I saw, "them folks never think there can be too many behind a hoss—six is nothing for them,—and it is them who is the meanest of all to the coachman; for he never, by no chance, receives a glass at their door." The great treat of the glass-coachman or flyman, however, is a wedding; then they mostly look for 5*s*; "but," said my informant, "brides and bridegrooms is getting so stingy that now they seldom gets more than three." Formerly, I am assured, they used to get a glass of wine to drink the health of the happy pair; but now the wine has declined to gin, "and even this," said one man to me, "we has to bow and scrape for before we gits it out of 'em." There is but little call for glass-coaches compared with flies now. Since the introduction of the broughams and clarences, the glass-coaches have been almost all put on one side, and they are now seldom used for anything but taking a party with a quantity of luggage from the suburbs to the railway. They were continued at weddings till a short time back, but now the people don't like them. "They have got out of date," said a flyman; "besides, a clarence or brougham, even with a pair of horses, is one-third cheaper." There are no glass-coaches now kept in the yards, if they are wanted they are hired at the coachmaker's. Take one job-master with another, I am informed that they keep on an average six flies each, so that the total number of hack clarences and broughams in the metropolis may be said to be near upon 1000. Postboys are almost entirely discontinued. The majority of them, I am told, have become cabmen. The number of job-horses kept for chance-work in the metropolis may be estimated at about 1000, in addition to the cab and omnibus horses, many of which frequently go out in flies. One lady omnibus proprietor at Islington keeps, I am told, a large number of flies, and so do many of the large cab-proprietors.

According to the Government returns, the total number of carriages throughout Great Britain, in 1848, was 149,000 and odd, which is in the proportion of 1 carriage to every 33 males of the entire population above twenty years of age. Of these carriages upwards of 97,000 were charged with duty, and yielded a revenue of more than 434,000*l.* while 52,000 were exempt from taxation. Those charged with duty consisted of 67,000 four-wheeled carriages, (of which 26,000 were private conveyances, and 41,000 let to hire,) and 30,000 two-wheeled carriages, of which 24,500 were for private use, and 5,500 for the use of the public:—

The 41,000 four-wheeled carriages let to hire were subdivided in round numbers as follows:—

Four-wheeled carriages, let to hire without horses	500	
Pony-phaetons, &c. drawn by a pair .	2,000	
Broughams, flies, &c. drawn by one horse	30,000	
Hearses	1,700	
Post-chaises	5,550	
Carriers' conveyances . . .	1,250	
	41,000	

Of the 52,000 carriages exempt from taxation there was the following distribution :—

Private pony-phaetons . . .	7,000
Ditto pony-chaises	4,500
Chaise-carts	39,000
Conveyances for paupers and criminals	1,500
	52,000

The owners of four-wheeled private carriages were, it appears from the same returns, 20,739 : of whom,

16,349 persons kept 1 carriage.			
3,685	„	2	„
495	„	3	„
116	„	4	„
58	„	5	„
19	„	6	„
6	„	7	„
11	„	8 and upwards.	

Now the total number of persons returned as of independent means, at the time of taking the last census, was 500,000 and odd : of these very nearly 490,000 were twenty years of age and upwards. Hence it would appear that only 1 person in every 23 of those who are independent keep their carriage.

Such are the statistics of carriages, both public and private, of Great Britain. What proportion of the vehicles above enumerated belong to the metropolis I have no means of ascertaining with any accuracy.

The number of horses throughout the country is equally curious. In 1847 there were no less than 800,000 horses in Great Britain, which is in the proportion of five horses to each carriage, and of one horse to every six males of the entire population of twenty years of age and upwards. Of these 800,000 horses, upwards of 320,000 were charged with duty, while nearly 500,000 were exempt from it. Among the 320,000 horses charged with duty were comprised—

Private riding and carriage-horses .	143,000
Draught-horses used in trade . .	147,000
Ponies	22,000
Butchers' horses . . .	4,750
Job horses	1,750
Race-horses	1,500
	320,000

The horses not charged with duty were in round numbers as under :—

Horses used in husbandry . .	330,500
„ belonging to small farmers .	61,000
„ belonging to poor clergymen .	1,250
„ belonging to poor traders .	10,500
„ belonging to volunteers .	13,000
„ used in untaxed carriages .	15,000
„ used by waggoners for their own riding . . .	2,000
„ used by bailiffs, shepherds, &c.	1,000
„ used by masters, ditto . .	3,700
„ used by market-gardeners .	2,000
„ in conveying paupers and criminals	250
„ kept for sale	7,000
„ kept for breeding . . .	4,500
Colts not used	16,000
Post-horses	8,500
Stage-coach horses	9,600
London hackney-coach horses . .	3,600
	496,000

The owners of the 140,000 private riding and carriage-horses were 100,000 in number, and of these,

78,335 persons kept .	.	.	.	1
17,358	„	.	.	2
4,080	„	.	.	3
1,624	„	.	.	4
622	„	.	.	5
380	„	.	.	6
328	„	.	.	7 to 8
81	„	.	.	9
107	„	.	.	10 to 12
54	„	.	.	13 to 16
6	„	.	.	17
8	„	.	.	18
6	„	.	.	19
67	„	.	.	20
	And upwards.			

From this it will appear, that two persons in every seven of those who are of independent means keep a riding or carriage-horse. The increase and decrease in the number of carriages and horses, within the last ten years, is a remarkable sign of the times. Since 1840, the number of all kinds of horses throughout Great Britain has decreased 43,000. But while some have declined, others have increased in number. Of private riding and carriage-horses (where only one is kept) there has been a decrease of 12,000, and of ponies, 700. Stage-coach horses have declined 4000; post-horses, 2500; horses used in husbandry, 57,000; breeding mares, 1300; colts, 7000; and horses kept for sale, 500. The London hackney-coach horses, on the other hand, have increased in the same space of time no less than 2000, and so have the draught-horses used in trade, to the extent of 17,000; while those kept by small farmers are 13,000 more, and the race-horses 400 more, than they were in 1840.

Of carriages, those having two wheels, and drawn by one horse (gigs, &c.), have decreased 15,000, and the post-chaises 700;

whereas the four-wheel carriages, drawn by one horse, and let to hire (broughams, clarences, &c.), have increased 6000, the pony-phaetons 3000, pony-chaises 2000, and the chaise-carts 19,000.

The total revenue derived from the transit of this country, by means of carriages and horses, amounted in 1848 to upwards of 1,190,000*l.* This sum is made up of the following items:—

Duty on carriages	.	.	£434,334
„	horses	.	395,041
„	horses let to hire	.	155,721
„	stage-carriages	.	96,218
„	hackney-coaches	.	28,926
Licenses to let horses to hire	.	6,968
„	stage-coaches	.	9,606
„	hackney-carriages	.	435

£1,127,249

From the foregoing accounts, then, it would appear, that the number of carriages and horses for the use of the public throughout Great Britain, two years ago, was as follows:

Job carriages	500
Broughams, clarences, flies, &c.	
drawn by one horse . .	30,000
Pony-phaetons and pair . .	2,000
Post-chaises	5,500

Total carriages let to hire .	38,000
Job horses	1,750
Post horses	8,500
Stage-coach horses . . .	9,600
London hackney-coach horses .	3,600

Total horses for public carriages 23,450

THE CARRYING TRADE.

THE next part of the subject that presents itself is the conveyance of goods from one part of the metropolis to another. This, as I have before said, is chiefly effected by vans, waggons, carts, drays, &c. It has already been shown that the number of carriers' waggons, throughout Great Britain, in 1848, was 1,250, while the carriers' carts were no less than 17,000 odd, or very nearly 3000 in all. This was 800 more than they were in 1840.

Of the number of horses engaged in the "carrying trade," or rather that particular branch of it which concerns the removal of goods, there are no returns, unless it be that there were 2000 horses under 13 hands high ridden by the waggoners of this kingdom.

The number of carriers, carters, and waggoners throughout Great Britain, at the time of taking the last census, was 34,296, of whom 25,411 were located in England, 7802 in Scotland, 940 in Wales, and 143 in the British Isles. Of the 34,296 carriers, carters, and waggoners, throughout Great Britain, in 1841, 30,972 were males of 20 years of age and upwards, while, in 1831, the number was only 18,859, or upwards of 10,000 less; so that between these two periods the trade must have increased at the rate of 1000 per annum at least. I am informed, however, that the next returns will show quite as large a decrease in the trade, owing to the conveyance of goods having been mainly transferred from the road to the rail since the last-mentioned period. The number of carriers, carters, and waggoners engaged in the metropolis in 1841 was 3899, of whom 3667 were males of twenty years of age and upwards. In 1831 there were but 871 individuals of the same age pursuing the same occupation; and I am assured, that owing to the increased facilities for the conveyance of goods from the country to London, the trade has increased at even a greater rate since the last enumeration of the people. The London carriers, carters, and waggoners, may safely be said to be now nearer 8000 than 4000 in number.

THE LONDON CARMEN

ARE of two kinds, public and private. The private carmen approximate so closely to the character of servants, that I purpose dealing at present more particularly with the public conveyers of goods from one part of the metropolis to another. The metropolitan public master-carmen are 207 in number, of whom fifteen are licensed to ply on the stands in the city. The carmen here enumerated must be considered more in the light of the owners of vans and other vehicles for the removing of goods than working men. It is true that some drive their own vehicles; but many are large proprietors, and belong to the class of employers rather than operatives.

I shall begin my account of the London carmen with those appertaining to the unlicensed class, or those not resident in the city. The modern spring van is, as it were, the landau, or travelling carriage of the working classes. These carriages came into general use between twenty and thirty years ago, but were then chiefly employed by the great carriers for the more rapid delivery of the lighter bales of goods, especially of drapery and glass goods and of parcels. They came into more general use for the removal of furniture in 1830, or thereabouts; and a year or two after were fitted up for the conveyance of pleasure-parties. The van is usually painted yellow, but some are a light brown or a dark blue picked out with red. They are fourteen feet in length on the average, and four and a half feet in breadth, and usually made so as, by the adjustment of the shafts, to be suitable for the employment of one, two, three, or four horses, —the third horse, when three are used, being yoked in advance of the pair in the shafts. The seats are generally removable, and are ranged along the sides of the vehicle, across the top, and at the two corners at the end, as the extremity of the van from the horses is called, the entrance being at the end, usually by means of iron steps, and through a kind of gate which is secured by a strong latch. The driver sits on a box in front, and on some vans seems perched fearfully high. A wooden framework surmounts the body of the carriage, and over it is spread an awning, sometimes of strong chintz patterned, sometimes of plain whity-brown calico—the side portions being made to draw like curtains, so as to admit the air and exclude the sun and rain at pleasure. If there be a man in attendance besides the driver, he usually sits at the end of the vehicle close to the gate, or rides on the step or on a projection fixed behind. A new van costs from 50l. to 80l. The average price of a good van-horse is from 16l. to 18l. The harness, new and good, costs from 5l. to 5l. 10s. for two horses. The furniture-van of the latter end of the week is the pleasure-van of the Sunday, Monday, and Tuesday—those being the days devoted to excursions, unless in the case of a club or society making their "annual excursion," and then any day of the week is selected except Sunday; but Sunday on the whole is the principal day. The removal of the seats and of the apparatus for the awning converts the pleasure into the furniture-van. The uses to which the same vehicle is put are thus many a time sadly in contrast. On the Saturday the van may have been used to convey to the brokers or the auctioneers the furniture seized in some wretched man's dwelling, leaving behind bare walls and a wailing family; and on the Sunday it rings with the merriment of pleasure-seekers, who loudly proclaim that they have left their cares behind them.

The owners usually, perhaps, I might say always, unite some other calling along with the business of van-proprietorship; they are for the most part greengrocers, hay and corn-dealers, brokers, beershop-keepers, chandlers, rag - and - bottle shopkeepers, or dairymen. Five-sixths of them, however, are greengrocers, or connected with that trade. It is not unusual for these persons to announce that, besides their immediate calling of a greengrocer, they keep a furniture-van, go pleasure-excursions, beat carpets (if in the suburbs), and attend evening parties. Many of them have been gentlemen's servants. They are nearly all married men or widowers with families, and are as a body not unprosperous. Their tastes are inexpensive, though some drink pretty freely; and their early rising necessitates early going to bed, so there is little evening expenditure. I am told their chief enjoyments are a visit to Astley's, and to the neighbouring horse-races. Their enjoyment of the turf, however, is generally made conducive to their profits, as they convey vans full to Hampton, Egham, and Epsom races. A few van-men, however, go rather further in turf-business, and bet a little; but these, I am assured, are the exceptions. The excursions are more frequently to Hampton Court than to any other place. The other favourite resorts are High Beach, Epping Forest, and Rye House, Hertfordshire. Windsor is but occasionally visited; and the shorter distances, such as Richmond, are hardly ever visited in pleasure-vans. Indeed the superior cheapness of the railway or the steamboat has confined the pleasure-excursions I am speaking of to the longer distances, and to places not so easily accessible by other means.

The van will hold from twenty to thirty grown persons. "Twenty, you see, sir," I was told, "is a very comfortable number, not reckoning a few little 'uns over; but thirty, oh, thirty's quite the other way." The usual charge per head for "a comfortable conveyance to Hampton Court and back," including all charges connected with the conveyance, is 2s. (children going for nothing, unless they are too big for knees, and then sometimes half price). Instead of 2s. perhaps the weekly-payment speculator receives 2s. 6d. or 2s. 3d.; and if he can engage a low-priced van he may clear 9d. or 1s. per head, or about 1l. in all. On this subject and on that of under-selling, as it was described to me, I give the statement of a very intelligent man, a prosperous van-proprietor, who had the excellent characteristic of being proud of the kindly treatment, good feeding, and continued care of his horses, which are among the best employed in vans.

The behaviour of these excursionists is, from the concurrent testimony of the many van-proprietors and drivers whom I saw, most exemplary, and perhaps I shall best show this by at once giving the following statement from a very trustworthy man:—

"I have been in the van-trade for twenty years, and have gone excursions for sixteen years. Hampton Court has the call for excursions in vans, because of free-trade in the palace: there's nothing to pay for admission. A party makes up an excursion, and one of them bargains with me, say for 2l. It shouldn't be a farthing less with such cattle as mine, and everything in agreement with it. Since I've known the trade, vans have increased greatly. I should say there's five now where there was one sixteen years ago, and more. There's a recommendable and a respectable behaviour amongst those that goes excursions. But now on an excursion there's hardly any drunkenness, or if there is, it's through the accident of a bad stomach, or something that way. The excursionists generally carry a fiddler with them, sometimes a trumpeter, or else some of them is master of an instrument as goes down. They generally sings, too, such songs as, 'There's a Good Time coming,' and, 'The Brave Old Oak.' Sometimes a nigger-thing, but not so often. They carry always, I think, their own eatables and drinkables; and they take them on the grass very often. Last Whit-Monday I counted fifty vans at Hampton, and didn't see anybody drunk there. I reckoned them earlyish, and perhaps ten came after, at least; and every van would have twenty and more." Sixty vans would, at this moderate computation, convey 1200 persons. "They walk through the Palace at Hampton, and sometimes dance on the grass after that, but not for long. It soon tires, dancing on the grass. A school often goes, or a club, or a society, or any party. I generally do Hampton Court in three hours with two horses. I reckon it's fourteen miles, or near that, from my place. If I go to High Beach there's the swings for the young ones, and the other merry-makings. At Rye House it's country enjoyment—mere looking about the real country. The Derby day's a great van-day. I'm sure I couldn't guess to one hundred—not, perhaps, to twice that—how many pleasure-vans go to the Derby. It's extra charge—3*l.* 10*s.* for the van to Epsom and back. It's a long distance ; but the Derby has a wonderful draw. I've taken all sorts of excursions, but it's working-people that's our great support. They often smoke as they come back, though it's against my rules. They often takes a barrel of beer with them."

It is not easy to ascertain the number of vans used for pleasure-excursions, but the following is the best information to be obtained on the subject. There is not more than one-sixth of the greengrocers who have their own vans : some keep two vans and carts, besides two or three trucks ; others, three vans and carts and trucks. These vans, carts, and trucks are principally used in the private transactions of their business. Sometimes they are employed in the removal of furniture. The number of vans employed in the metropolis is as follows :—

Those kept by greengrocers, about	450
By others for excursions . .	1000
Total	1450

The season for the excursion trips commences on Whit-Monday, and continues till the latter end of September.

Table showing the average number of pleasure-vans hired each week throughout the season, and the decrease since railway excursions.

		Before the Railway. Excursion trips.	Since the Railway, Excursion trips.
Hampton Court,	Sunday .	50	10
„	Monday .	80	30
„	Tuesday .	20	10
Rye House, weekly	. .	35	12
High Beach „	. .	40	20
		225	82

From this it appears that before the railway trips there were 225 pleasure-excursions by vans every week during five months of the year (or 4500 such excursions in the course of the twelve months), and only 1640 since that time.

This is exclusive of those to Epsom-races, at which there were nearly 200 more.

When employed in the removal of furniture the average weight carried by these vans is about two tons, and they usually obtain about two loads on an average per week. The party engaged to take charge of the van is generally a man employed by the owner, in the capacity of a servant. The average weekly salary of these servants is about 18*s.* Some van-proprietors will employ one man, and some as many as nine or ten. These men look after the horses and stables of their employers. A van proprietor takes out a post-horse license, which is 7*s.* 6*d.* a-year; and for excursions he is also obliged to take out a stage-carriage license for each van that goes out with pleasure-parties. Such license costs 3*l.* 3*s.* per year ; and besides this they have to pay to the excise 1½*d* per mile for each excursion they take. The van-horses number about three to each van, so that for the whole 1450 vans as many as 4350 horses are kept.

Calculating the pleasure-excursions by van in the course of the year at from 1500 to 2000—and that twenty persons is the complement carried on each occasion—we have a pleasure-excursion party of between 30,000 and 40,000 persons annually : and supposing that each excursionist spends 3*s.* 6*d.*, the sum spent every year by the working-classes in pleasure-excursions by spring-vans alone will amount to very nearly 7000*l.*

The above account relates only to the conveyance of persons by means of the London vans. Concerning the removal of goods by the same means, I obtained the following information from the most trustworthy and experienced members of the trade.

" The charge for the use of spring-vans for the conveyance of furniture and other damageable commodities is 1*s.* 6*d.* an hour, when one man is employed assisting in packing, unpacking, conveying the furniture into its place of destination, and sometimes helping to fix it. If two men are employed in this labour, 2*s.* an hour is the charge. If the furniture is conveyed a considerable distance the carman's employer may at his option pay 6*d.* a mile instead of 1*s.* 6*d.* an hour, but the engagement by the hour ensues in nine cases out of ten."

The conveyance of people on pleasure excursions and the removal of furniture constitute the principal business of the west-end and suburb carmen. The city carmen, however, constitute a distinct class. They are the licensed carmen, and none others are allowed by the city authorities to take up in the precincts of the city of London, though any one can put down therein; that is to say, the unlicensed carman may convey a houseful of furniture from the Strand to Fleet-street, but he may not legally carry an empty box from Fleet-street to the Strand. The city carmen, as I have said, must be licensed, and the law sanctions the following rates of payment for carriage ·

" By order of Quarter Sessions, held at Guildhall, Midsummer, 49th George III., all goods, wares, and merchandise whatsoever, weighing 14 cwt. or under, shall be deemed half a load ; and from 14 cwt. to 26 cwt. shall be deemed a load; from any part of the city of London the rates for carrying thereof shall be as follow. For any place within and to the extension of half a mile, for half a load and under, 2s. 7d.; above half a load and not exceeding a load, 4s. 2d.; from half a mile to a mile, for half a load or under, 3s. 4d.; for above half a load and not exceeding a load, 5s. 2d.; a mile, to one mile and a half, for half a load or under, 4s. 2d.; for above half a load and not exceeding a load, 5s. 11d.; and so on, according to distance."

The other distances and weights are in relative proportion. These regulations, however, are altogether disregarded; as are those which limit the cartage for hire within the city to the carmen licensed by the city, who must be freemen of the Carmen's Company, the only company in London whose members are all of the trade incorporated. Instead of the prices I have cited, the matter is now one of bargain. Average charges are 1s. 6d. an hour for vans, and 1s. for carts, or 4s. and 4s. 6d. per ton from the West India Docks to any part of the city; and in like proportion from the other docks and localities. The infringers of the city carmen's privileges are sometimes called pirates; but within these three or four years no strenuous attempts have been made to check them. One carman told me that he had complained to the City Chamberlain, who told him to punish the offenders; but as it was left to individual efforts nothing was done, and the privileges, except as regards standings, are almost or altogether a dead letter. Fourteen years ago it cost 100l. to become free of the Carmen's Company. Ten years ago it cost 32l. odd; and within these five years the cost has been reduced to 11l. The carmen who resort to the stands pay 5s. yearly for that privilege. The others are not required to do so; but every year they have to register the names of their servants, with a bond of security, who are employed on goods " under bond;" and it is customary on these occasions to give the toll-keeper 5s., which is equal to a renewal of the license. Until ten years ago there were only 400 of these conveyances licensed in the city. The figures called " carroons" ran from 1 to 400; and were sold by their possessors, on a disposal of their property and privilege, as if freehold property, being worth about 100l. a carroon. No compensation was accorded when the restriction as to numbers was abolished. The principal standings are in Coleman-street, Bread-street, Bishopsgate-street, Dowgate-hill, Thames-street, and St. Mary Axe. The charges do not differ from those I have given; but some of the employers of these carmen drive very hard bargains.

A car of the best build costs from 60l. to 70l. The best horses cost 40l.; the average price being 20l. at the least. The wages of the carmen's servants vary from 16s. to 21s. a-week, under the best masters; and from 12s. to 14s. under the inferior. These men are for the most part from the country.

THE PORTERS, &c.

I now approach the only remaining part of this subject, viz. the conveyance of goods and communications by means of the porters, messengers, and errand-boys of the metropolis. The number of individuals belonging to this class throughout Great Britain in 1841 amounted to 27,552, of whom 24,092 were located in England; 3,296 in Scotland; 113 in Wales; and 51 in the British isles. Of the 27,500 porters, messengers, and errand-boys in Great Britain, very nearly one-fifth, or 4,965, were lads under 20 years of age. The number of individuals engaged in the same occupation in the metropolis was, in 1841, no less than 13,103, or very nearly half the number of porters, &c. throughout Great Britain. Of this number 2,726, or more than a fifth of the class, may be considered to represent the errand-boys, these being lads under 20 years of age.

At present, however, I purpose dealing solely with the public porters of the metropolis. Those belonging to private individuals appear to partake (as I said of the carmen's assistants) more of the character of servants paid out of the profits of the trade than labourers whose wages form an integral portion of the prime cost of a commodity.

The metropolitan porters are, like the carmen, of two classes; the ticketed, and unticketed. I shall begin with the former.

The privileged porters of the city of London were at one period, and until within these twenty years, a numerous, important, and tolerably prosperous class. Prescriptive right, and the laws and by-laws of the corporation of the city of London, have given to them the sole privilege of porterage of every description, provided it be carried on in the precincts of the city. The only exception to this exclusive right is, that any freeman may employ his own servants in the porterage of his own goods, and even that has been disputed. The first mention of the privileged porters is in the early part of the 16th century.

It is almost impossible to classify the especial functions of the different classes of porters; for they seem to have become especial functions through custom and prescriptive right, and they are not defined precisely in any legitimate or municipal enactment. Even at the present time, what constitutes the business of a fellowship-porter, what of a ticket-porter, and on what an unprivileged porter (known as a foreigner, because a non-freeman) may be employed, are matters of dispute

STREET PORTER WITH KNOT.

[*From a Photograph.*]

VAGRANTS IN THE CASUAL WARD OF WORKHOUSE.

[*From a Sketch.*]

A reference to city enactments, and the aid of a highly intelligent member of the fraternity of ticket-porters, enables me to give the following account, which is the more interesting, as it relates to a class of labourers whose numbers, with the exception of the fellowship-porters, have been limited since 1838, and who must necessarily die out from want of renewal. In the earliest common council enactments (June 27, 1606) on the subject of porterage, the distinctions given, or rather intimated incidentally, are—" Tackle-house porter, porter-packer of the gooddes of English merchants, streete-porter, or porter to the packer for the said citie for strangers' goods." As regards the term ticket porter, not mentioned in this enumeration, I have to observe that all porters are necessarily ticket-porters, which means that they can produce a ticket or a document, showing that they are duly qualified, and have been " admitted and allowed to use the feate of a porter," by being freemen of the city and members of a porter's company or fellowship. In some of the older city documents tackle and ticket-porters are mentioned as if constituting one class; and they did constitute one class when their labour was identical, as to a great extent it was. In 1712 they are mentioned or indicated as one body, although the first clause of the common council enactment sets out that several controversies and quarrels have lately arisen between the tackle-house porters and the ticket-porters touching the labour or work to them respectively belonging, notwithstanding the several acts of this court heretofore made. As these acts were vague and contradictory, the controversies were a natural consequence.

The tackle-porters were employed in the weighing of goods for any purpose of shipping, duty, or sale, which was formerly carried on in public in the city. But there was a city officer known as the master-weigher, styled " Mr. Weigher," in the old acts, and the profits of the weighing thus carried on publicly in the city went to the hospitals. In 1607 it was enacted (I give the old orthography, with its many contractions), " that no p'son or p'sons usinge the feate of a porter, or being a forreynor, inholder, wharfinger, or keye-keeper, where any merchaunts' gooddes are to bee landed or laidd, or such-like, shall at any time after the making and publishing of this acte, have, use, keepe, or use within the said citie or l'b'ties thereof, any manner triangle, with beams, scales, and weightes, or any other balance, in any sorte, to weigh any the goods, wares, or merchandize, of any merchant or merchants, p'son or p'sons whatsoever, within the said citie or lib'ties thereof, whereby the proffyte cominge and growinge to the hospitals of the said cytie, by weighinge at the yron beams or at the great beame at the weigh-house, or the proffytes of the Mr. Weigher and porters of the same weigh-

house, may in anywise be impeached, hindered, or diminished." The privilege of " weighinge" fell gradually into desuetude; but there is no record of the precise periods. However, a vestige of it still remains; as I shall show in my account of the markets, as it properly comes under that head. There were 24 tackle-porters appointed; each of the 12 great city companies appointing two. These 12 companies are — the Mercers', Grocers', Drapers', Fishmongers', Goldsmiths', Skinners', Ironmongers', Vintners', and Clothworkers'. The 24 appointed porters were known, it appears, as " maister-porters ;" but as it was impossible that they could do all the work required, they called to them the aid of " fellowes," freemen of the city, and members of their society, who in time seem to have been known simply as ticket-porters. If a sufficiency of these fellows, or ticket-porters, could not be made available on any emergency, the maisters could employ any " foreign porter not free of this cyttie, using the feate of a porter-packer of the goods of English merchants, or the feate of a streete-porter, at the tyme of the making of this acte (1607), and which at this present is commemorante in the same citye or suburbes thereof, charged with familye, or, being a single man, bringing a good certificate in the wryting, under the handes of the churchwardens of the parish where he is resident, or other substantiall neighbours, to the number of fower, of his good conversacon and demeanor." This employment, however, was not to be to the prejudice of the privileged porters; and that the employment of foreigners was resorted to jealously, and only through actual necessity, is sufficiently shown by the whole tenor of the enactments on the subject. The very act which I have just cited, as permitting the employment of foreigners, contains a complaint in its preamble that the toleration of these men caused many " of badd and lewde condition daylie to resorte from the most parte of this realme to the said cytie, suburbs and places adjoining, procuring themselves small habytacons, namely, one chamber-roome for a poor foreignere and his familye in a small cottage, with some other as poore as himself, to the great increase and pestringe of this cyttie with poor people; many of them provinge shifters, lyvinge by cozeninge, stealinge and imbeazellinge men's goods, as opportunity may serve them." A somewhat curious precedent as regards the character of the dwellings, being in " one chamber-roome," &c., for the abodes of the workmen, for the slop-tailors and others in our day, as I have shown in my previous letters.

The ticket-porters in 1846 are described as 3000 persons and upwards, which sufficiently shows their importance; and in 1712 a Common Council enactment provides that they shall have and enjoy the work or labour of unshipping, landing, carrying and housing of pitch, tar, soap, ashes, clapboards, wainscot, fir-poles, masts, deals, oars, chests, tables, flax and hemp, brought hither from Dantzic, Melvyn, or any other part or place of the countries commonly called the east countries. Also of the imports from Ireland, "from any of the plantations belonging to Great Britain, and of all manner of coast-goods, (except lead)." The tackle-house porters were, by the same enactment, to "have and enjoy the work and labour of the shipping and all goods imported and belonging to the South Sea Company, or to the Company of Merchants trading to the East Indies, and of all other goods and merchandizes coming from other ports not before mentioned. The functions of the tackle-house and ticket-porters are by this regulation in 1712 made identical as to labour, with merely the distinction as to the place from which the goods were received: and as the number of tackle-house porters was properly 24, with them must be included, I presume, all such ticket-porters, but not to the full number; nor is it likely that they will be renewed in case of death. The tackle-house porters that are still in existence, I was told, are gentlemen. One is a wharfinger, and claims and enjoys the monopoly of labour on his own wharf. "The tackle-house porters, or most of them, were labourers within these twenty years." The tackle-house and ticket-porters still enjoy, by law, the right to man the work, wherever porterage is required; or, in other words, to execute the labour themselves, or to engage men to do it, no matter whether the work relate to shipping, to the markets, or to mere street-porterage, such as the conveyance of parcels for hire by men's labour. The number of the ticket-porters was, 20 years ago, about 600. At that time to become free of the company, which has no hall but assembles at Guildhall, cost upwards of 40*l.*, but soon afterwards the expense was reduced to 6*l.* 3*s.* 4*d.* By a resolution of the Common Council, no new ticket-porters have been appointed since 1838. Previously to becoming a ticket-porter a man must have taken up his freedom, no matter in what character, and must produce certificates of good character and security of two freemen, householders of good credit, each in 100*l.*, so that the owner of any articles entrusted to the ticket-porter may be indemnified in case of loss. The ticket-porters are not the mere labourers people generally imagine they are, but are, or were, for their number does now not exceed 100, decayed tradesmen, who resorted to this means of livelihood when others had failed. They are also the sons of ticket-porters. Any freeman of the city, by becoming a member of the Tackle-House and Ticket-Porters' Company, was entitled to act as a ticket-porter. They are still recognised at the markets and the wharfs, but their privileges are constantly, and more and more infringed.

From a highly intelligent member of their body I had the following statement:—

"It may be true, or it may not, that ticket-porters are not wanted now; but 15 or 16 years ago a committee of the Common Council, the Market Committee I believe it was, resolved that the ticket-porters ought to be upheld, and that 50*l.* should be awarded to us; but we never got it, it was stopped by some after-resolution. Put it this way, sir. To get bread for myself and my children I became a ticket-porter, having incurred great expense in taking up my freedom and all that. Well, for this expense I enjoyed certain privileges, and enjoy them still to some extent; but that's only because I'm well known, and have had great experience in porterage, and quickness, as it is as much art as strength. But, supposing that railways have changed the whole business of the times, are the privileges I have secured with my own money, and under the sanction of all the old laws of the city, to be taken from me? If the privileges, though they may not be many, of the rich city companies are not to be touched, why are mine? Every day they are infringed. A railway-waggon, for instance, carries a load of meat to Newgate Market. Ticket-porters have the undoubted right to unload the meat and carry it to its place of sale; but the railway servants do that, though only freemen employ their own servants in porterage, and that only with their own goods, or goods they are concerned in. I fancy that railway companies are not freemen, and don't carry their own property to market for sale. If we complain to the authorities, we are recommended to take the law of the offenders, and we can only take it of the person committing the actual offence. And so we may sue a beggar, whom his employers may send down their line an hour after to Hull or Halifax, as the saying is. If we are of no further use, don't sacrifice, but compensate us, and let us make the best of it, though we are none of us so young as we were; some are very old, and none are under 40, because no new members have been made for some years. If a man's house be a hindrance to public business, he must be paid a proper price for it before it can be removed, and so ought we. The Palace Court people were compensated, and ought not we, who work hard for an honest living, and have bought the right to work in our portering, according to the laws of the city, that secure the goldsmiths in their right of assaying, and all the rich companies in possession of their lands and possessions? and so it ought to be with our labour."

The porter-packers have been unknown in the business of the city for some years; their avocation "in the packinge and shippinge of strangers' gooddes," having barely survived the expiring of the East India Company's charter in 1834.

The street porters, or men who occupy, or

rather did occupy (for they are not now always to be found there,) the principal business parts of the city, are of course ticket-porters, and by the law have exclusive right of all porterage by hire from " aliens or foreigners" in the streets, (a freeman may employ his own servant), even to the carrying of a parcel of the burden of which any one may wish to relieve himself. They usually, but not always, wear white aprons, and display their tickets as badges. They do not confine themselves to the streets, but resort to the wharfs in the fruit or any busy season, and to the meat and fish-markets, whenever they think there is the chance of a job, and the preference, as is not unfrequently the case, likely to fall to them, for they are known to be trusty and experienced men. This shifting of labour from one place to another renders it impossible to give the number of ticket-porters working in any particular locality.

The fellowship-porters seem to have sprung into existence in consequence of the misunderstandings of the tackle and ticket-porters, and in this way, fellowships, or gangs of porters, were confined, or confined themselves, to the porterage of coal, corn, malt and indeed, all grain, salt, fruit, and wet fish (conceded to them after many disputes by the ticket-porters of Billingsgate), and their privileges are not infringed to any such extent as those of the ticket-porters.

The payments of ticket porters were settled in 1799.

To or from any of the quays, wharfs, stairs, lanes, or alleys at the waterside, between the Tower and London Bridge to any part of Lower Thames-street, Beer-lane, Water-lane, Harp-lane, St. Dunstan's-hill, St. Mary-hill, Love-lane, Botolph-lane, Pudding-lane, and Fish-street-hill :

For any load or parcel by knot or hand —

Not exceeding	½ cwt.	.	.	0s. 4d.
„	1	„	.	. 0 6
„	1½	„	.	. 0 9
„	2	„	.	. 1 0

For the like weights, and not exceeding Poplar, Bow-church, Bishop Bonner's Farm, Kingsland-turnpike, Highbury-place, (Old) Pancras-church, Portman-square, Grosvenor-square, Hyde-park-corner, Buckingham-gate, Westminster Infirmary, Tothill-fields Bridewell, Strutton-ground, Horseferry, Vauxhall, Walworth-turnpike, and places of the like distance—

Not exceeding	½ cwt.	.	.	2s. 9d.
„	1	„	.	. 3 3
„	1½	„	.	. 3 9
„	2	„	.	. 5 0

I cite these regulations to show the distances to which porters were sent half a century ago, and the charges. These charges, however, were not always paid, as the persons employing parties often made bargains with them, and some twenty years ago the legalised charges were reduced 1d. in every 3d. The street-porters complain that any one may now, or at all events does now, ply for hire in the city, and get higher prices than them.

All ticket-porters pay 8s. yearly towards the funds of their society, which is called quarterage. Out of this a few small pensions are granted to old women, the widows of ticket-porters.

The difference of the functions of the ticket and fellowship-porters seems to be this—that the ticket-porters carry dry goods, or those classed by weight or bulk, the fellowship-porters carry measured goods.

LONDON VAGRANTS.

THE evils consequent upon the uncertainty of labour I have already been at considerable pains to point out. There is still one other mischief attendant upon it that remains to be exposed, and which, if possible, is greater than any other yet adduced. Many classes of labour are necessarily uncertain or fitful in their character. Some work can be pursued only at certain seasons; some depends upon the winds, as, for instance, dock labour; some on fashion; and nearly all on the general prosperity of the country. Now, the labourer who is deprived of his usual employment by any of the above causes, must, unless he has laid by a portion of his earnings while engaged, become a burden to his parish, or the state, or else he must seek work, either of another kind or in another place. The mere fact of a man's seeking work in different parts of the country, may be taken as evidence that he is indisposed to live on the charity or labour of others; and this feeling should be encouraged in every rational manner. Hence the greatest facility should be afforded to all labourers who may be unable to obtain work in one locality, to pass to another part of the country where there may be a demand for their labour. In fine, it is expedient that every means should be given for extending the labour-market for the working classes; that is to say, for allowing them as wide a field for the exercise of their calling as possible. To do this involves the establishment of what are called the " casual wards" of the different unions throughout the country. These are, strictly speaking, the free hostelries of the unemployed workpeople, where they may be lodged and fed, on their way to find work in some more active district. But the establishment of these gratuitous hotels has called into existence a large class of wayfarers, for whom they were never contemplated. They have been the means of affording great encouragement to those vagabond or erratic spirits who find continuity of application to any task specially irksome to them, and who are physically unable or mentally unwilling to remain for any length of time in the same place, or at the same work—creatures who are vagrants in disposition and principle; the wandering tribe of this country; the nomads of the present day.

" The right which every person apparently destitute possesses, to demand food and shelter, affords," says Mr. Pigott, in the Report on Vagrancy, " great facilities and encouragement to idle and dissolute persons to avoid labour, and pass their lives in idleness and pillage.

There can be no doubt that of the wayfarers who, in summer especially, demand admission into workhouses, the number of those whom the law contemplates under the titles of ' idle and disorderly,' and ' rogues and vagabonds,' greatly exceeds that of those who are honestly and *bonâ fide* travelling in search of employment, and that it is the former class whose numbers have recently so increased as to require a remedy."

It becomes almost a necessary result of any system which seeks to give shelter and food to the industrious operative in his way to look for work, that it should be the means of harbouring and fostering the idle and the vagabond.

To refuse an asylum to the vagrant is to shut out the traveller; so hard is it to tell the one from the other.

The prime cause of vagabondism is essentially the non-inculcation of a habit of industry; that is to say, the faculty of continuous application at a particular form of work, has not been engendered in the individual's mind, and he has naturally an aversion to any regular occupation, and becomes erratic, wandering from this thing to that, without any settled or determined object. Hence we find, that the vagrant disposition begins to exhibit itself precisely at that age when the first attempts are made to inculcate the habit of continuous labour among youths. This will be seen by the table in the opposite page (taken from the Returns of the Houseless Poor), which shows the greatest number of inmates to be between the ages of fifteen and twenty-five.

The cause of the greater amount of vagrancy being found among individuals between the ages of fifteen and twenty-five (and it is not by the table alone that this fact is borne out), appears to be the irksomeness of any kind of sustained labour when first performed. This is especially the case with youth; and hence a certain kind of compulsion is necessary, in order that the habit of doing the particular work may be engendered. Unfortunately, however, at this age the self-will of the individual begins also to be developed, and any compulsion or restraint becomes doubly irksome. Hence, without judicious treatment, the restraint may be entirely thrown off by the youth, and the labour be discarded by him, before any steadiness of application has been produced by constancy of practice. The cause of vagrancy then resolves itself, to a great extent, into the harshness of either parents or employers; and this it will be found is generally the account given by the vagrants themselves. They have been treated with severity, and being generally remarkable for their self-will, have run away from their home or master to live while yet mere lads in some of the low lodging-houses. Here they find companions of the same age and character as themselves, with whom they ultimately set out on a vagabond excursion through the country, begging or plundering on their way.

Another class of vagrants consists of those who, having been thrown out of employment, have travelled through the country, seeking work without avail, and who, consequently, have lived on charity so long, that the habits of wandering and mendicancy have eradicated their former habits of industry, and the industrious workman has become changed into the habitual beggar.

THE AGES OF APPLICANTS FOR SHELTER AT THE CENTRAL ASYLUM, PLAYHOUSE-YARD, WHITECROSS-STREET, IN THE YEAR 1849.

Age. Months.	No. of Applicants.	Age. Years.	No. of Applicants.	Age. Years.	No. of Applicants.
Children under 1	17	17	380	49	84
Children of 1	4	18	336	50	108
„ 2	42	19	385	51	28
„ 3	21	20	296	52	46
„ 4	14	21	335	53	44
„ 5	14	22	386	54	21
„ 6	26	23	295	55	49
„ 7	30	24	399	56	35
„ 8	7	25	122	57	27
„ 9	14	26	238	58	35
„ 10	7	27	219	59	27
„ 11	5	28	238	60	35
	—	29	84	61	7
	201	30	294	62	14
Age. Years.	**No. of Applicants.**	31	56	63	7
1	28	32	91	64	14
2	22	33	105	65	12
3	28	34	98	66	6
4	30	35	186	67	10
5	36	36	98	68	7
6	39	37	63	69	4
7	56	38	56	70	7
8	38	39	42	71	4
9	92	40	117	72	6
10	108	41	63	73	7
11	104	42	91	74	6
12	107	43	49	75	7
13	177	44	42	76	6
14	102	45	91	77	2
15	268	46	28	78	4
16	259	47	35	79	0
		48	56	80	2

" Having investigated the general causes of depredation, of vagrancy, and mendicancy," say the Constabulary Commissioners, in the Government Reports of 1839 (p. 181), as developed by examinations of the previous lives of criminals or vagrants in the gaols, we find that scarcely in any cases is it ascribable to the pressure of unavoidable want or destitution, and that in the great mass of cases it arises from the temptation of obtaining property with a less degree of labour than by regular industry." Again, in p. 63 of the same Report, we are told that "the inquiries made by the most experienced officers into the causes of vagrancy manifest, that in all but three or four per cent the prevalent cause was the impatience of steady labour." My investigations into this most important subject lead me, I may add, to the same conclusions. In order to understand the question of vagrancy thoroughly, however, we must not stop here; we must find out what, in its turn, is the cause of this impatience of steady labour; or, in other words, we must ascertain whence comes the desire to obtain property with a less degree of labour than by regular industry. Now, all "steady labour"—that is to say, the continuance of any labour for any length of time— is naturally irksome to us. We are all innately erratic—prone to wander both in thought and action; and it is only by a vigorous effort, which is more or less painful to us at first, that we can keep ourselves to the steady prosecution of the same object, to the repeated performance of the same acts, or even to continuous attention to the same subject. Labour and effort are more or less irksome to us all. There are, however, two means by which this irksomeness may be not only removed, but transformed into a positive pleasure. One is, by the excitement of some impulse or purpose in the mind of the workman; and the other, by the inculcation of a habit of working. Purpose and habit are the only two modes by which labour can be rendered easy to us; and it is precisely because the vagrant is deficient in both that he has an aversion to work for his living, and wanders through the country without an object, or, indeed, a destination. A love of industry is not a gift, but a habit; it is an accomplishment rather than an endowment; and our purposes and principles do not arise spontaneously from the promptings of our own instincts and affections, but are the mature result of education, example, and deliberation. A vagrant, therefore, is an individual applying himself continuously to no one thing, nor pursuing any one aim for any length of time, but wandering from this subject to that, as well as from one place to another, because in him no industrial habits have been formed, nor any principle or purpose impressed upon his nature.

Pursuing the subject still further, we shall find that the cause of the vagrant's wandering through the country—and indeed through life —purposeless, objectless, and *unprincipled*, in the literal and strict meaning of the term, lies mainly in the defective state of our educational institutions; for the vagrants, as a class, it should be remembered, are not "educated." We teach a lad reading, writing, and arithmetic, and believe that in so doing we are developing the moral functions of his nature; whereas it is often this ability to *read merely*— that is to say, to read without the least moral perception—which becomes the instrument of the youth's moral depravity. The "Jack Sheppard" of Mr. Harrison Ainsworth is borrowed from the circulating library, and read aloud in the low lodging-houses in the evening by those who have a little education, to their companions who have none; and because the thief is there furbished up into the hero—because the author has tricked him out with a sort of brute insensibility to danger, made "noble blood flow in his veins," and tinselled him over with all kinds of showy sentimentality—the poor boys who listen, unable to see through the trumpery deception, are led to look up to the paltry thief as an object of admiration, and to make his conduct the *beau idéal* of their lives. Of all books, perhaps none has ever had so baneful an effect upon the young mind, taste, and principles as this. None has ever done more to degrade literature to the level of the lowest licentiousness, or to stamp the author and the teacher as guilty of pandering to the most depraved propensities. Had Mr. Ainsworth been with me, and seen how he had vitiated the thoughts and pursuits of hundreds of mere boys—had he heard the names of the creatures of his morbid fancy given to youths at an age when they needed the best and truest counsellors—had he seen these poor little wretches, as I have seen them, grin with delight at receiving the degrading titles of "Blue skin," "Dick Turpin," and "Jack Sheppard," he would, I am sure, ever rue the day which led him to paint the most degraded and abandoned of our race as the most noble of human beings. What wonder, then, that—taught either in no school at all, or else in that meretricious one which makes crime a glory, and dresses up vice as virtue—these poor lads should be unprincipled in every act they do— that they should be either literally actuated by no principles at all, or else fired with the basest motives and purposes, gathered from books which distort highway robbery into an act of noble enterprise, and dignify murder as justifiable homicide?

Nor are the habits of the young vagrant less cultivated than his motives. The formation of that particular habit which we term industry, and by which the youth is fitted to obtain his living as a man, is perhaps the most difficult part of all education. It commences at an age when the will of the individual is beginning to develope itself, and when the docile boy is changed into the impatient young man. Too great lenity, or too strict severity of government, therefore, becomes at this period of life dangerous. If the rule be too lax, the restless youth, disgusted with the monotony of pursuing the same task, or performing the same acts, day by day, neglects his work—till habits of indolence, rather than industry, are formed, and he is ultimately thrust upon the world, without either the means or the disposition of labouring for his living. If, on the other hand, the authority of the parent or master be too rigidly exercised, and the lad's power of endurance be taxed too severely, then the self-will of the youth is called into action; and growing restless and rebellious under the tyranny of his teachers, he throws off their restraint, and leaves them—with a hatred, instead of a love of labour engendered within him. That these are two of the primary causes of vagrancy, all my inquiries have tended to show. The proximate cause certainly lies in the impatience of steady labour; but the cause of this impatience is referable to the non-formation of any habit of industry in the vagrant, and the absence of this habit of industry is usually due to the neglect or the tyranny of the lad's parent or master. This is no theory be it remembered. Whether it be the master of the workhouse, where the vagrants congregate every night— whether it be the young vagrant himself, or the more experienced tramp—that speaks upon the subject, all agree in ascribing the vagabondism of youth to the same cause. There is, however, another phase of vagrancy still to be explained; viz. the transition of the working man into the regular tramp and beggar. This is the result of a habit of dependence, produced in the operative by repeated visits to the casual wards of the unions. A labouring man, or mechanic, deprived of employment in a particular town, sets out on a journey to seek work in some other part of the country. The mere fact of his so journeying to seek work shows that he has a natural aversion to become a burden to the parish. He is no sooner, however, become an inmate of the casual wards, and breakfasts and sups off the bounty of the workhouse, than he learns a most dangerous lesson — he learns how to live by the labour of others. His sense of independence may be shocked at first, but repeated visits to the same places soon deaden his feelings on this score; and he gradually, from continual disuse, loses his habit of labouring, and ultimately, by long custom, acquires a habit of "tramping" through the country, and putting up at the casual wards of the unions by the way. Thus, what was originally designed as a means of enabling the labouring man to obtain work, becomes the instrument of depriving him of employment, by rendering it no longer a necessity for him to seek it ; and the independent workman is transformed after a time into the habitual tramper, and finally into the professional beggar and petty thief. Such characters, however, form but a small proportion of the great body of vagabonds continually traversing the country.

The vagrants are essentially the non-working, as distinguished from the hard-working, men of England. They are the very opposite to the industrious classes, with whom they are too often confounded. Of the really destitute working-men, among the vagrants seeking relief at the casual wards, the proportion is very small; the respectable mechanics being deterred by disgust from herding with the filth, infamy, disease, and vermin congregated in the tramp-wards of the unions, and preferring the endurance of the greatest privations before subjecting themselves to it. " I have had this view confirmed by several unfortunate persons," says Mr. Boase, in the Poor-law Report on Vagrancy: " they were apparently mechanics out of employment, who spoke of the horrors passed in a tramp-ward, and of their utter repugnance at visiting such places again." " The poor mechanic," says the porter at the Holborn workhouse, " will sit in the casual wards like a lost man — *scared*. It's shocking to think a decent mechanic's houseless," he adds; " when he's beat out, he's like a bird out of a cage : he doesn't know where to go, or how to get a bit." But the highest tribute ever paid to the sterling honesty and worth of the working men of this country, is to be found in the testimony of the master of the Wands-

worth and Clapham Union. "The destitute mechanics," he says, " are entirely a different class from the regular vagrant ; they have different habits, and, indeed, different features. They are strictly honest. During the whole of my experience, I never knew a distressed artisan who applied for a night's shelter commit an act of theft; and I have seen them," he adds, " in the last stage of destitution. Occasionally they have sold the shirt and waistcoat off their backs, before they applied for admittance into the workhouse; while some of them have been so weak from long starvation, that they could scarcely reach the gate, and, indeed, had to be kept for several days in the infirmary, before their strength was recruited sufficiently to continue their journey." For myself, I can safely say, that my own experience fully bears out this honourable declaration of the virtues of our working men. Their extreme patience under the keenest privations is a thing that the wisest philosophers might envy; their sympathy and charity for their poorer brethren far exceeds, in its humble way, the benevolence and bounty of the rich ; while their intelligence, considering the little time they have for study and reflection, is almost marvellous. In a word, their virtues are the spontaneous expressions of their simple natures; and their vices are the comparatively pardonable excesses, consequent upon the intensity of their toil. I say thus much in this place, because I am anxious that the public should no longer confound the honest, independent working men, with the vagrant beggars and pilferers of the country ; and that they should see that the one class is as respectable and worthy, as the other is degraded and vicious.

CHARACTERISTICS OF THE VARIOUS CLASSES OF VAGRANTS.

I NOW come to the characteristics of vagrant life, as seen in the casual wards of the metropolitan unions. The subject is one of the most important with which I have yet had to deal, and the facts I have collected are sufficiently startling to give the public an idea of the great social bearings of the question; for the young vagrant is the budding criminal.

Previously to entering upon my inquiry into this subject, I consulted with a gentleman who had long paid considerable attention to the question, and who was, moreover, in a position peculiarly fitted for gaining the greatest experience, and arriving at the correctest notions upon the matter. I consulted, I say, with the gentleman referred to, as to the Poor-law officers, from whom I should be likely to obtain the best information; and I was referred by him to Mr. Knapp, the master of the Wandsworth and Clapham Union, as one of the most intelligent and best-informed upon the subject of vagrancy. I found that gentleman all that he had been represented to me as being, and obtained from him the following statement, which, as an analysis of the vagrant character, and a description of the habits and propensities of the young vagabond, has, perhaps, never been surpassed.

He had filled the office of master of the Wandsworth and Clapham Union for three years, and immediately before that he was the relieving officer for the same union for upwards of two years. He was guardian of Clapham parish for four years previously to his being elected relieving officer. He was a member of the first board of guardians that was formed under the new Poor-law Act, and he has long given much attention to the habits of the vagrants that have come under his notice or care. He told me that he considered a casual ward necessary in every union, because there is always a migratory population, consisting of labourers seeking employment in other localities, and destitute women travelling to their husbands or friends. He thinks a casual ward is necessary for the shelter and relief of such parties, since the law will not permit them to beg. These, however, are by far the smaller proportion of those who demand admittance into the casual ward. Formerly, they were not five per cent of the total number of casuals. The remainder consisted of youths, prostitutes, Irish families, and a few professional beggars. The youths formed more than one-half of the entire number, and their ages were from twelve to twenty. The largest number were seventeen years old—indeed, he adds, just that age when youth becomes disengaged from parental control. These lads had generally run away, either from their parents or masters, and many had been reared to a life of vagrancy. They were mostly shrewd and acute youths; some had been very well educated. Ignorance, to use the gentleman's own words, is certainly not the prevailing characteristic of the class; indeed, with a few exceptions, he would say it is the reverse. These lads are mostly distinguished by their aversion to continuous labour of any kind. He never knew them to work—they are, indeed, essentially the idle and the vagabond. Their great inclination is to be on the move, and wandering from place to place; and they appear, he says, to receive a great deal of pleasure from the assembly and conversation of the casual ward. They are physically stout, healthy lads, and certainly not emaciated or sickly. They belong especially to the able-bodied class, being, as he says, full of health and mischief. When in London, they live in the day-time by holding horses, and carrying parcels from the steam-piers and railway termini. Some loiter about the markets in the hope of a job, and others may be seen in the streets picking up bones and rags, or along the water-side searching for pieces of old metal, or anything that may be sold at the marine-store shops. They have nearly all been in prison more than once,

and several a greater number of times than they are years old. They are the most dishonest of all thieves, having not the least respect for the property of even the members of their own class. He tells me he has frequently known them to rob one another. They are very stubborn and self-willed. They have often broken every window in the oakum-room, rather than do the required work. They are a most difficult class to govern, and are especially restive under the least restraint; they can ill brook control, and they find great delight in thwarting the authorities of the workhouse. They are particularly fond of amusements of all kinds. My informant has often heard them discuss the merits of the different actors at the minor theatres and saloons. Sometimes they will elect a chairman, and get up a regular debate, and make speeches from one end of the ward to the other. Many of them will make very clever comic orations; others delight in singing comic songs, especially those upon the workhouse and gaols. He never knew them love reading. They mostly pass under fictitious names. Some will give the name of "John Russell," or "Robert Peel," or "Richard Cobden." They often come down to the casual wards in large bodies of twenty or thirty, with sticks hidden down the legs of their trousers, and with these they rob and beat those who do not belong to their own gang. The gang will often consist of a hundred lads, all under twenty, one-fourth of whom regularly come together in a body; and in the casual ward they generally arrange where to meet again on the following night. In the winter of 1846, the guardians of Wandsworth and Clapham, sympathising with their ragged and wretched appearance, and desirous of affording them the means of obtaining an honest livelihood, gave my informant instructions to offer an asylum to any who might choose to remain in the workhouse. Under this arrangement, about fifty were admitted. The majority were under seventeen years of age. Some of them remained a few days—others a few weeks—none stopped longer than three months; and the generality of them decamped over the wall, taking with them the clothes of the union. The confinement, restraint, and order of the workhouse were especially irksome to them. This is the character of the true vagrant, for whom my informant considers no provision whatsoever should be made at the unions, believing as he does that most of them have settlements in or around London. The casual wards, he tells me, he knows to have been a great encouragement to the increase of these characters. Several of the lads that have come under his care had sought shelter and concealment in the casual wards, after having absconded from their parents. In one instance, the father and mother of a lad had unavailingly sought their son in every direction: he discovered that the youth had ran away, and he sent him home in the custody of one of the inmates; but when the boy got to within two or three doors of his father's residence, he turned round and scampered off. The mother afterwards came to the union in a state of frantic grief, and said that he had disappeared two years before. My informant believes that the boy has never been heard of by his parents since. Others he has restored to their parents, and some of the young vagrants who have died in the union have, on their death-beds, disclosed the names and particulars of their families, who have been always of a highly respectable character. To these he has sent, and on their visits to their children scenes of indescribable grief and anguish have taken place. He tells me he is convinced that it is the low lodging-houses and the casual wards of the unions that offer a ready means for youths absconding from their homes, immediately on the least disagreement or restraint. In most of the cases that he has investigated, he has found that the boys have left home after some rebuke or quarrel with their parents. On restoring one boy to his father, the latter said that, though the lad was not ten years old, he had been in almost every workhouse in London; and the father bitterly complained of the casual wards for offering shelter to a youth of such tender years. But my informant is convinced that, even if the casual wards throughout the country were entirely closed—the low lodging-houses being allowed to remain in their present condition—the evil would not be remedied, if at all abated. A boy after running away from home, generally seeks shelter in one of the cheap lodging-houses, and there he makes acquaintance with the most depraved of both sexes. The boys at the house become his regular companions, and he is soon a confirmed vagrant and thief like the rest. The youths of the vagrant class are particularly distinguished for their libidinous propensities. They frequently come to the gate with a young prostitute, and with her they go off in the morning. With this girl, they will tramp through the whole of the country. They are not remarkable for a love of drink,—indeed, my informant never saw a regular vagrant in a state of intoxication, nor has he known them to exhibit any craving for liquor. He has had many drunkards under his charge, but the vagrant is totally distinct, having propensities not less vicious, but of a very different kind. He considers the young tramps to be generally a class of lads possessing the keenest intellect, and of a highly enterprising character. They seem to have no sense of danger, and to be especially delighted with such acts as involve any peril. They are likewise characterised by their exceeding love of mischief. The property destroyed in the union of which my informant is the master has been of considerable value, consisting of windows broken, sash-frames demolished, beds and bedding torn to pieces, and rags burnt. They will frequently come down in large gangs, on purpose to destroy the property in the union. They generally are of a most restless and volatile disposition. They have great quickness of perception, but little power of continuous attention or perseverance. They have a keen sense of the ridiculous, and are not devoid of deep feeling. He has often known them to be dissolved to tears on his remonstrating with them on the course they were following—and then they promise amendment; but in a few days, and sometimes hours, they would forget all, and return to their old habits. In the summer they make regular tours through the country, visiting all places that they have not seen, so that there is scarcely one that is not acquainted with every part within 100 miles of London, and many with all England. They are perfectly organised, so that any regulation affecting their comforts or interests becomes known among the whole body in a remarkably short space of time. As an instance, he informs me that on putting out a notice that no able-bodied man or youth would be received in the casual ward after a certain day, there was not a single application made by any such party, the regular vagrants having doubtless informed each other that it was useless seeking admission at this union. In the winter the young vagrants come to London, and find shelter in the asylums for the houseless poor. At this season of the year, the number of vagrants in the casual wards would generally be diminished one-half. The juvenile vagrants constitute one of the main sources from which the criminals of the country are continually recruited and augmented. Being repeatedly committed to prison for disorderly conduct and misdemeanour, the gaol soon loses all terrors for them; and, indeed, they will frequently destroy their own clothes, or the property of the union, in order to be sent there. Hence they soon become practised and dexterous thieves, and my informant has detected several burglaries by the property found upon them. The number of this class is stated, in the Poor-law Report on Vagrancy, to have been, in 1848, no less than 16,086, and they form one of the most restless, discontented, vicious, and dangerous elements of society. At the period of any social commotion, they are sure to be drawn towards the scene of excitement in a vast concourse. During the Chartist agitation, in the June quarter of the year 1848, the number of male casuals admitted into the Wandsworth and Clapham Union rose from 2501 to 3968, while the females (their companions) increased from 579 to 1388.

Of the other classes of persons admitted into the casual wards, the Irish generally form a large proportion. At the time when juvenile vagrancy prevailed to an alarming extent, the Irish hardly dared to show themselves in the casual wards, for the lads would beat them and plunder them of whatever they might have—either the produce of their begging, or the ragged kit they carried with them. Often my informant has had to quell violent disturbances in the night among these characters. The Irish tramp generally makes his appearance with a large family, and frequently with three or four generations together—grandfather, grandmother, father, and mother, and children—all coming at the same time. In the year ending June, 1848, the Irish vagrants increased to so great an extent that, of the entire number of casuals relieved, more than one-third in the first three quarters, and more than two-thirds in the last quarter, were from the sister island. Of the Irish vagrants, the worst class—that is the poorest and most abject—came over to this country by way of Newport, in Wales. The expense of the passage to that port was only 2*s.* 6*d.* ; whereas the cost of the voyage to Liverpool and London was considerably more, and consequently the class brought over by that way were less destitute. The Irish vagrants were far more orderly than the English. Out of the vast number received into the casual ward of this union during the distress in Ireland, it is remarkable that not one ever committed an act of insubordination. They were generally very grateful for the relief afforded, and appeared to subsist entirely by begging. Some of them were not particularly fond of work, but they were invariably honest, says my informant—at least so far as his knowledge went. They were exceedingly filthy in their habits, and many diseased.

These constitute the two large and principal classes of vagrants. The remainder generally consist of persons temporarily destitute, whereas the others are habitually so. The temporarily destitute are chiefly railway and agricultural labourers, and a few mechanics travelling in search of employment. These are easily distinguishable from the regular vagrant; indeed, a glance is sufficient to the practised eye. They are the better class of casuals, and those for whom the wards are expressly designed, but they only form a very small proportion of the vagrants applying for shelter. In the height of vagrancy, they formed not one per cent of the entire number admitted. Indeed, such was the state of the casual wards, that the destitute mechanics and labourers preferred walking through the night to availing themselves of the accommodation. Lately, the artisans and labourers have increased greatly in proportion, owing to the system adopted for the exclusion of the habitual vagrant, and the consequent decline of their number. The working man travelling in search of employment is now generally admitted into what are called the receiving wards of the workhouse, instead of the tramp-room, and he is usually exceedingly grateful for the accommodation. My informant tells me that persons of this class seldom return to the workhouse after one night's shelter, and this is a conclusive proof that the regular working-man seldom passes into an habitual beggar. They are an entirely distinct class, having different habits, and, indeed, different features, and I am assured that they are strictly honest. During the whole experience of my informant, he never knew one who applied for a night's shelter commit one act of dishonesty, and he has seen them in the last stage of destitution. Occasionally they have sold the shirt and waistcoat off their backs before they applied for admittance into the workhouse, while some of them have been so weak from long starvation, that they could scarcely reach the gate. Such persons are always allowed to remain several days to recruit their strength. It is for such as these that my informant considers the casual wards indispensable to every well-conducted union—whereas it is his opinion that the habitual vagrant, as contradistinguished from the casual vagrant or wayfaring poor, should be placed under the management of the police, at the charge of the union.

Let me, however, first run over, as briefly as possible, the several classes of vagrants falling under the notice of the parish authorities. The different kinds of vagrants or tramps to be found in the casual wards of the unions throughout the country, may be described as follows:—" The more important class, from its increasing numbers," says Mr. Boase, in the Poor-law Report upon Vagrancy, "is that of the regular young English vagabond, generally the native of a large town. He is either a run-away apprentice, or he has been driven from home by the cruelty of his parents, or allowed by them to go wild in the streets: in some cases he is an orphan, and has lost his father and mother in early life. Having no ties to bind him, he travels about the country, being sure of a meal, and a roof to shelter him at night. The youths of this class are principally of from fifteen to twenty-five years of age. They often travel in parties of two or three—frequently in large bodies, with young women, as abandoned as themselves, in company."

Approaching these in character are the young countrymen who have absconded—perhaps for come petty poaching offence—and to whom the facility for leading an idle vagabond life has proved too great a temptation.

The next class of vagrants is the sturdy English mendicant. He, though not a constant occupant of the tramp-ward in the workhouse, frequently makes his appearance there to partake of the shelter, when he has spent his last shilling in dissipation.

Besides these, there are a few calling themselves agricultural labourers, who are really such, and who are to be readily distinguished. There are also a few mechanics—chiefly tailors, shoemakers, and masons, who are occasionally destitute. The amount of those really destitute, however, is very small in proportion to the numbers relieved.

Of the age and sex of tramps, the general proportion seems to be four-fifths male and one-fifth female.

Of the female English tramps, little can be said, but that they are in great part prostitutes of the lowest class. The proportion of really destitute women in the tramp-wards (generally widows with young children) is greater than that of men—probably from the ability to brave the cold night wind being less in the female, and the love of the children getting the shelter, above dread of vile association. Girls of thirteen or fourteen years old, who run away from masters or factory employment, often find shelter in the tramp-ward.

The Irish, who, till very recently, formed the majority of the applicants for casual relief, remain to be described. These can scarcely be classified in any other way than as those who come to England to labour, and those who come to beg. The former class, however, yield readily to their disposition to idleness—the difficulties of providing supper, breakfast, and lodging for themselves being removed by the workhouse. This class are physically superior to the mass of Irish vagrants. It appears that for very many years considerable numbers of these have annually come to England in the spring to work at hay-harvest, remaining for corn-harvest and hop-picking, and then have carried home their earnings in the autumn, seldom resorting to begging. Since the failure of the potato crop greater numbers have come to England, and the tramp-ward has been their principal refuge, and an inducement to many to remain in the country. A great many harvest men land at Newport and the Welsh ports; but by far the greater proportion of the Irish in Wales are, or were, women with small children, old men apparently feeble, pregnant women, and boys about ten years old. They are brought over by coal-vessels as a return cargo (living ballast) at very low fares, (2s. 6d. is the highest sum), huddled together like pigs, and communicating disease and vermin on their passage.

Harriet Huxtable, the manager of the tramp-house at Newport, says:—"There is hardly an Irish family that came over and applied to me, but we have found a member or two of it ill, some in a shocking filthy state. They don't live long, diseased as they are. They are very remarkable; they will eat salt by basins' full, and drink a great quantity of water after. I have frequently known those who could not have been hungry, eat cabbage-leaves and other refuse from the ash-heap. I really believe they would eat almost anything."

"A remarkable fact is, that all the Irish whom I met on my route between Wales and London," says Mr. Boase, "said they came from Cork county. Mr. John, the relieving officer at Cardiff, on his examination, says, 'that not 1 out of every 100 of the Irish come from any other county than Cork.'"

In the township of Warrington, the number of tramps relieved between the 25th of March, 1847, and the 25th of March, 1848, was:—

Irish	12,038
English	4,701
Scotch	427
Natives of other places	156
Making a total of	17,322

Of the original occupations or trades of the vagrants applying for relief at the different unions throughout the country, there are no returns. As, however, a considerable portion of these were attracted to London on the opening of the Metropolitan Asylums for the Houseless Poor, we may, by consulting the Society's yearly Reports, where an account of the callings of those receiving shelter in such establishments is always given, be enabled to arrive at some rough estimate as to the state of destitution and vagrancy existing among the several classes of labourers and artisans for several years.

The following table, being an average drawn from the returns for seventeen years of the occupation of the persons admitted into the Asylums for the Houseless Poor, which I have been at considerable trouble in forming, exhibits the only available information upon this subject, synoptically arranged:—

Factory employment	1 in every 3
Hawkers	4
Labourers (agricultural)	12
Seamen	12
Charwomen and washerwomen	13
Labourers (general)	17
Waddingmakers	35
Smiths and ironfounders	36
Weavers	38
Brickmakers	39
Ropemakers	41
Braziers	55
Papermakers and stainers	58
Skindressers	58
Basketmakers	62
Bricklayers, plasterers, and slaters	62
Gardeners	67
Filecutters	70
Sawyers	73
Turners	74
Wireworkers	75
Cutlers	77
Harnessmakers and saddlers	80
Stonemasons	88
Dyers	94
Chimneysweeps	97
Errand boys	99
Porters	99
Painters, plumbers, and glaziers	119
Cabinetmakers and upholsterers	128
Shoemakers	130
Compositors and printers	142
Brushmakers	145
Carpenters, joiners, and wheelwrights	150
Bakers	167

Brassfounders . . .	1 in every 177
Tailors	177
Combmakers	178
Coopers	178
Surveyors	198
Fellmongers	203
Glasscutters	229
Bedsteadmakers	235
Average for all London . .	219
Butchers	248
Bookbinders	255
Mendicants	256
Engineers	265
Miners	267
Lacemakers	273
Poulterers	273
Furriers	274
Straw-bonnetmakers . . .	277
Trimming and buttonmakers . .	277
Ostlers and grooms . . .	286
Drovers	297
Hairdressers	329
Pipemakers	340
Clerks and shopmen . . .	346
Hatters	350
Tinmen	354
Tallowchandlers . . .	364
Servants	377
Corkcutters	380
Jewellers and watchmakers . .	411
Umbrella-makers . . .	415
Sailmakers	455
Carvers and gilders . . .	500
Gunsmiths	554
Trunkmakers	569
Chairmakers	586
Fishmongers	643
Tanners	643
Musicians	730
Leatherdressers and curriers . .	802
Coachmakers	989
Engravers	1,133
Shipwrights	1,358
Artists	1,374
Drapers	2,047
Milliners and dressmakers . .	10,390

Of the disease and fever which mark the course of the vagrants wheresoever they go, I have before spoken. The "tramp-fever," as the most dangerous infection of the casual wards is significantly termed, is of a typhoid character, and seems to be communicated particularly to those who wash the clothes of the parties suffering from it. This was likewise one of the characteristics of cholera. That the habitual vagrants should be the means of spreading a pestilence over the country in their wanderings will not be wondered at, when we find it stated in the Poor-law Report on Vagrancy, that "in very few workhouses do means exist of drying the clothes of these paupers when they come in wet, and it often happens that a considerable number are, of necessity, placed together wet, filthy, infested with vermin, and diseased,

in a small, unventilated space." "The majority of tramps, again," we are told, "have a great aversion to being washed and cleaned. A regular tramper cannot bear it; but a distressed man would be thankful for it."

The cost incurred for the cure of the vagrant sick in 1848, was considerably more than the expense of the food dispensed to them. Out of 13,406 vagrants relieved at the Wandsworth and Clapham Union in 1848, there were 332 diseased, or ill with the fever.

The number of vagrants relieved throughout England and Wales in the same year was 1,647,975; and supposing that the sickness among these prevailed to the same extent as it did among the casuals at Wandsworth (according to the Vagrancy Report, it appears to have been much more severe in many places), there would have been as many as 40,812 sick in the several unions throughout the country in 1848. The cost of relieving the 332 sick at Wandsworth was 300*l.*; at the same rate, the expense of the 40,812 sick throughout the country unions would amount to 36,878*l.* According to the above proportion, the number of sick relieved in the metropolitan unions would have been 7678, and the cost for their relief would amount to 6931*l.*

Of the tide of crime which, like that of pestilence, accompanies the stream of vagrants, there are equally strong and conclusive proofs. "The most prominent body of delinquents in the rural districts," says the Report of the Constabulary Commissioners, "are vagrants, and these vagrants appear to consist of two classes : first, the habitual depredators, housebreakers, horse-stealers, and common thieves ; secondly, of vagrants, properly so called, who seek alms as mendicants. Besides those classes who travel from fair to fair, and from town to town, in quest of dishonest gains, there are numerous classes who make incursions from the provincial towns upon the adjacent rural districts."

"The classes of depredators who perambulate the country (says the same Report) are the vagrants, properly so called. Upwards of 18,000 commitments per annum of persons for the offence of vagrancy, mark the extent of the body from which they are taken.

"It will be seen that vagrancy, or the habit of wandering abroad, under colour of either of distress, or of some ostensible, though illegal occupation, having claims on the sympathies of the uninformed, constitutes one great source of delinquency, and especially of juvenile delinquency. The returns show that the vagrant classes pervade every part of the country, rendering property insecure, propagating pernicious habits, and afflicting the minds of the sensitive with false pictures of suffering, and levying upon them an offensive impost for the relief of that destitution for which a heavy tax is legally levied in the shape of poor's rates.

"Mr. Thomas Narrill, a sergeant of the

Bristol police, was asked — ' What proportion of the vagrants do you think are thieves, that make it a point to take anything for which they find a convenient opportunity?' ' We have found it so invariably.' ' Have you ever seen the children who go about as vagrants turn afterwards from vagrancy to common thieving,—thieving wholly or chiefly?' ' We have found it several times.' ' Therefore the suppression of vagrancy or mendicity would be to that extent the suppression of juvenile delinquency?' ' Yes, of course.'

Mr. J. Perry, another witness, states:—" I believe vagrancy to be the first step towards the committal of felony, and I am supported in that belief by the number of juvenile vagrants who are brought before the magistrates as thieves."

An officer, appointed specially to take measures against vagrancy in Manchester, was asked,—" Does your experience enable you to state that the large proportion of vagrants are thieves too, whenever they come in the way of thieving?" " Yes, and I should call the larger proportion there thieves." " Then, from what you have observed of them, would you say that the suppression of vagrancy would go a great way to the suppression of a great quantity of depredation?" " I am sure of it."

The same valuable Report furnishes us with a table of the numbers and character of the known depredators and suspected persons frequenting five of the principal towns; from which it appears that in these towns alone there are 28,706 persons of known bad character. According to the average proportion of these to the population, there will be in the other large towns nearly 32,000 persons of a similar character, and upwards of 69,000 of such persons dispersed throughout the rest of the country. Adding these together, we shall have as many as 130,000 persons of known bad character living in England and Wales, without the walls of the prisons. To form an accurate notion of the total number of the criminal population, we must add to the above amount the number of persons resident within the walls of the prisons. These, according to the last census, are 19,888, which, added to the 130,000 above enumerated, gives within a fraction of 150,000 individuals for the entire criminal population of the country.

In order to arrive at an estimate of the number of known depredators, or suspected persons, continually tramping through the country, we must deduct from the number of persons of bad character without the walls of the prisons, such as are not of migratory habits; and it will be seen on reference to the table above given, that a large proportion of the classes there specified have usually some fixed residence (those with an asterisk set before them may be said to be non-migratory). As many as 10,000 individuals out of the 20,000 and odd above given certainly do not belong to the tramping tribe; and we may safely say that there must be as many as 35,000 more in the country, who, though of known bad character, are not tramps like the rest. Hence, in order to ascertain the number of depredators and suspected persons belonging to the tramping or vagrant class, we must deduct 10,000 + 35,000 from 85,000, which gives us 40,000 for the number of known bad characters continually traversing the country.

This sum, though arrived at in a very different manner from the estimate given in my last letter, agrees very nearly with the amount there stated. We may therefore, I think, without fear of erring greatly upon the matter, assert that our criminal population, within and without the walls of the prisons, consists of 150,000 individuals, of whom nearly one-third belong to the vagrant class; while, of those without the prison walls, upwards of one half are persons who are continually tramping through the country.

The number of commitments for vagrancy throughout the country is stated, in the Constabulary Report, at upwards of 18,000 per annum. This amount, large as it is, will not surprise when we learn from Mr. Pigott's Report on Vagrancy to the Poor-law Commissioners, that " it is becoming a system with the vagrants to pass away the cold months by fortnightly halts in different gaols. As soon as their fourteen days have expired they make their way to some other union-house, and commit the same depredation there, in order to be sent to gaol again."

" There are some characters," say the officers of the Derby Union, in the same Report, " who come on purpose to be committed, avowedly. These have generally itch, venereal disease, and lice, all together. Then there are some who tear their clothes for the purpose of being committed."

I shall now give as full an account as lies in my power of the character and consequences of vagrancy. That it spreads a moral pestilence through the country, as terrible and as devastating as the physical pest which accompanies it wherever it is found, all the evidence goes to prove. Nevertheless, the facts which I have still to adduce in connexion with that class of vagrancy which does not necessarily come under the notice of the parish authorities, are of so overpowering a character, that I hope and trust they may be the means of rousing every earnest man in the kingdom to a sense of the enormous evils that are daily going on around him.

The number of vagrants taken into custody by the police, according to the Metropolitan Criminal Returns for 1848, was 5598; they belonged to the trades cited in the subjoined table, where I have calculated the proportionate number of vagrants furnished by each of the occupations, according to the total number of individuals belonging to the class.

Toolmakers	1 in every 33·9	Hatters and trimmers.	250·4	Glassmakers, &c.	580·5
Labourers .	. 45·9	Musicians .	292·0	Butchers .	608·0
Weavers .	. 75·6	Turners, &c.	308·8	Laundresses .	623·8
Cutlers .	. 82·1	Shoemakers	310·5	Coachmakers .	709·3
French polishers	. 109·7	Surveyors .	326·5	Grocers .	712·2
Glovers, &c.	. 112·8	Average for all London	334·7	General and marine	
Corkcutters	. 114·2	Gardeners .	341·8	storedealers .	721·2
Brassfounders .	. 119·1	Tobacconists	344·6	Jewellers .	922·7
Smiths .	. 129·1	Painters .	359·5	Artificial flowermakers	1025·0
Bricklayers	. 143·4	Bakers .	364·4	Brushmakers .	1077·5
Papermakers, stainers,		Tailors .	373·2	Ironmongers .	1177·0
&c..	. 188·1	Milliners .	451·7	Watchmakers .	1430·0
Fishmongers	. 207·3	Clerks .	453·7	Engineers .	1433·3
Curriers .	. 211·6	Printers .	461·6	Dyers. .	1930·0
Masons .	. 231·4	Sweeps .	516·5	Servants .	2444·9
Tinkers and tinmen	. 236·3	Opticians .	536·0	Drapers .	2456·5
Sawyers .	. 248·1	Saddlers .	542·7	Bookbinders .	2749·5
Carvers and gilders	. 250·3	Coach and cabmen	542·8		

The causes and encouragements of vagrancy are two-fold,—*direct* and *indirect.* The roving disposition to which, as I have shown, vagrancy is *directly* ascribable, proceeds (as I have said) partly from a certain physical conformation or temperament, but mainly from a non-inculcation of industrial habits and moral purposes in youth. The causes from which the vagabondism of the young *indirectly* proceeds are:—

1. The neglect or tyranny of parents or masters. (This appears to be a most prolific source.)

2. Bad companions.

3. Bad books, which act like the bad companions in depraving the taste, and teaching the youth to consider that approvable which to all rightly constituted minds is morally loathsome.

4. Bad amusements — as penny-theatres, where the scenes and characters described in the bad books are represented in a still more attractive form. Mr. Ainsworth's "Rookwood," with Dick Turpin "in his habit as he lived in," is now in the course of being performed nightly at one of the East-end saloons.

5. Bad institutions — as, for instance, the different refuges scattered throughout the country, and which, enabling persons to live without labour, are the means of attracting large numbers of the most idle and dissolute classes to the several cities where the charities are dispensed. Captain Carroll, C.B., R.N., chief of police, speaking of the Refuges for the Destitute in Bath, and of a kindred institution which distributes bread and soup, says,—"I consider those institutions an attraction to this city for vagrants." At Liverpool, Mr. Henry Simpson said of a Night Asylum, supported by voluntary contributions, and established for several years in this town — "This charity was used by quite a different class of persons from those for whom it was designed. A vast number of abandoned characters, known thieves and prostitutes, found nightly shelter there." "The chief inducement to vagrancy in the town," says another Report, speaking of a certain part of the North Riding of York, "is the relief given by mistaken but benevolent individuals, more particularly by the poorer class. Instances have occurred where the names of such benevolent persons have been found in the possession of vagrants, obtained, no doubt, from their fellow-travellers."

6. Vagrancy is largely due to, and, indeed, chiefly maintained by the low lodging-houses.

STATEMENTS OF VAGRANTS.

The first vagrant was one who had the thorough look of a "professional." He was literally a mass of rags and filth. He was, exactly what in the Act of Henry VIII. is denominated a "valiant beggar." He stood near upon six feet high, was not more than twenty five, and had altogether the frame and constitution of a stalwart labouring man. His clothes, which were of fustian and corduroy, tied close to his body with pieces of string, were black and shiny with filth, which looked more like pitch than grease. He had no shirt, as was plain from the fact that, where his clothes were torn, his bare skin was seen. The ragged sleeves of his fustian jacket were tied like the other parts of his dress, close to his wrists, with string. This was clearly to keep the bleak air from his body. His cap was an old, brimless "wide-awake," and when on his head gave the man a most unprepossessing appearance. His story was as follows:—

"I am a carpet-weaver by trade. I served my time to it. My father was a clerk in a shoe-thread manufactory at ——. He got 35s. a-week, and his house, coals, and candles found him. He lived very comfortably; indeed, I was very happy. Before I left home, I knew none of the cares of the world that I have known since I left him. My father and mother are living still. He is still as well off as when I was at home. I know this, because I have heard from him twice, and seen him once. He won't do anything to assist me. I have transgressed so many times, that he won't take me in hand any more. I will tell you the truth, you may depend upon it; yes, indeed, I would, even if it were to injure myself. He has tried me many times, but now he has given me up. At the age of twenty-one he told me to go from home and seek a living for myself. He said he had given me a home ever since I was a child, but now I had come to manhood I was able to provide for myself. He gave me a good education, and I might have been a better scholar at the present time, had I not neglected my studies. He put me to a day-school in the town when I was eight years old, and I continued there till I was between twelve and thirteen. I learnt reading, writing, and ciphering. I was taught the catechism, the history of England, geography, and drawing. My father was a very harsh man when he was put out of his way. He was a very violent temper when he was vexed, but kind to us all when he was pleased. I have five brothers and six sisters. He never beat me more than twice, to my remembrance. The first time he thrashed me with a cane, and the last with a horsewhip. I had stopped out late at night. I was then just rising sixteen, and had left school. I am sure those thrashings did me no good, but made me rather worse than before. I was a self-willed lad, and determined, if I couldn't get my will in one way, I would have it another. After the last thrashing he told me he would give me some trade, and after that he would set me off and get rid of me. Then I was bound apprentice as a carpet-weaver for three years. My master was a very kind one. I runned away once. The cause of my going off was a quarrel with one of the workmen that was put over me. He was very harsh, and I scarce could do anything to please him; so I made up my mind to leave. The first place I went when I bolted was to Crewkerne, in Somersetshire. There I asked for employment at carpet-weaving. I got some, and remained there three days, when my father found out where I was, and sent my brother and a special constable after me. They took me from the shop where I was at work, and brought me back to ———, and would have sent me to prison had I not promised to behave myself, and serve my time out as I ought. I went to work again; and when the expiration of my apprenticeship occurred, my father said to me, 'Sam, you have a trade at your fingers' ends: you are able to provide for yourself.' So then I left home. I was twenty-one years of age. He gave me money, 3*l.* 10*s.*, to take me into Wales, where I told him I should go. I was up for going about through the country. I made my father believe I was going into Wales to get work; but all I wanted was, to go and see the place. After I had runned away once from my apprenticeship, I found it very hard to stop at home. I couldn't bring myself to work somehow. While I sat at the

work, I thought I should like to be away in the country: work seemed a burden to me. I found it very difficult to stick to anything for a long time; so I made up my mind, when my time was out, that I'd be off roving, and see a little of life. I went by the packet from Bristol to Newport. After being there three weeks, I had spent all the money that I had brought from home. I spent it in drinking—most of it, and idling about. After that I was obliged to sell my clothes, &c. The first thing I sold was my watch; I got 2*l.* 5*s.* for that. Then I was obliged to part with my suit of clothes. For these I got 1*l.* 5*s.* With this I started from Newport to go farther up over the hills. I liked this kind of life much better than working, while the money lasted. I was in the public-house three parts of my time out of four. I was a great slave to drink. I began to like drink when I was between thirteen and fourteen. At that time my uncle was keeping a public-house, and I used to go there, backwards and forward, more or less every week. Whenever I went to see my uncle he gave me some beer. I very soon got to like it so much, that, while an apprentice, I would spend all I could get in liquor. This was the cause of my quarrels with my father, and when I went away to Newport I did so to be my own master, and drink as much as I pleased, without anybody saying anything to me about it. I got up to Nant-y-glô, and there I sought for work at the iron-foundry, but I could not get it. I stopped at this place three weeks, still drinking. The last day of the three weeks I sold the boots off my feet to get food, for all my money and clothes were now gone. I was sorry then that I had ever left my father's house; but, alas! I found it too late. I didn't write home to tell them how I was off; my stubborn temper would not allow me. I then started off barefoot, begging my way from Nant-y-glô to Monmouth. I told the people that I was a carpet-weaver by trade, who could not get any employment, and that I was obliged to travel the country against my own wish. I didn't say a word about the drink—that would never have done. I only took 2½*d.* on the road, 19 miles long; and I'm sure I must have asked assistance from more than a hundred people. They said, some of them, that they had 'nout' for me; and others did give me a bit of ' bara caws,' or ' bara minny' (that is, bread and cheese, or bread and butter). Money is very scarce among the Welsh, and what they have they are very fond of. They don't mind giving food; if you wanted a bagful you might have it there of the working people. I inquired for a night's lodging at the union in Monmouth. That was the first time I ever asked for shelter in a workhouse in my life. I was admitted into the tramp-room. Oh, I felt then that I would much rather be in prison than in such a place, though I never knew what the inside of a prison was—no, not then. I thought of the kindness of my father and mother. I would have been better, but I knew that, as I had been carrying on, I never could expect shelter under my father's roof any more; I knew he would not have taken me in had I gone back, or I would have returned. Oh, I was off from home, and I didn't much trouble my head about it after a few minutes; I plucked up my spirits and soon forgot where I was. I made no male friends in the union; I was savage that I had so hard a bed to lie upon; it was nothing more than the bare boards, and a rug to cover me. I knew very well it wasn't my bed, but still I thought I ought to have a better. I merely felt annoyed at its being so bad a place, and didn't think much about the rights of it. In the morning I was turned out, and after I had left I picked up with a young woman, who had slept in the union over-night. I said I was going on the road across country to Birmingham, and I axed her to go with me. I had never seen her before. She consented, and we went along together, begging our way. We passed as man and wife, and I was a carpet-weaver out of employment. We slept in unions and lodging-houses by the way. In the lodging-houses we lived together as man and wife, and in the unions we were separated. I never stole anything during all this time. After I got to Birmingham I made my way to Wolverhampton. My reason for going to Wolverhampton was, that there was a good many weavers there, and I thought I should make a good bit of money by begging of them. Oh, yes, I have found that I could always get more money out of my own trade than any other people. I did so well at Wolverhampton, begging, that I stopped there three weeks. I never troubled my head whether I was doing right or wrong by asking my brother-weavers for a portion of their hard earnings to keep me in idleness. Many a time I have given part of my wages to others myself. I can't say that I would have given it to them if I had known they wouldn't work like me. I wouldn't have worked sometimes if I could have got it. I can't tell why, but somehow it was painful to me to stick long at anything. To tell the truth, I loved a roving, idle life. I would much rather have been on the road than at my home. I drank away all I got, and feared and cared for nothing. When I got drunk over-night, it would have been impossible for me to have gone to work in the morning, even if I could have got it. The drink seemed to take all the work out of me. This oftentimes led me to think of what my father used to tell me, that 'the bird that can sing and won't sing ought to be made to sing.' During my stay in Wolverhampton I lived at a tramper's house, and there I fell in with two men well acquainted with the town, and they asked me to join them in breaking open a shop. No, sir, no, I didn't give a thought whether I was doing right or wrong at it. I didn't think my father would ever know anything at all about it, so I didn't care. I liked my mother best,

much the best. She had always been a kind, good soul to me, often kept me from my father's blows, and helped me to things unknown to my father. But when I was away on the road I gave no heed to her. I didn't think of either father or mother till after I was taken into custody for that same job. Well, I agreed to go with the other two; they were old hands at the business — regular housebreakers. We went away between twelve and one at night. It was pitch dark. My two pals broke into the back part of the house, and I stopped outside to keep watch. After watching for about a quarter of an hour, a policeman came up to me and asked what I was stopping there for. I told him I was waiting for a man that was in a public-house at the corner. This led him to suspect me, it being so late at night. He went to the public-house to see whether it was open, and found it shut, and then came back to me. As he was returning he saw my two comrades coming through the back window (that was the way they had got in). He took us all three in custody; some of the passers-by assisted him in seizing us. The other two had six months' imprisonment each, and I, being a stranger, had only fourteen days. When I was sent to prison, I thought of my mother. I would have written to her, but couldn't get leave. Being the first time I ever was nailed, I was very downhearted at it. I didn't say I'd give it up. While I was locked up, I thought I'd go to work again, and be a sober man, when I got out. These thoughts used to come over me when I was 'on the stepper,' that is, on the wheel. But I concealed all them thoughts in my breast. I said nothing to no one. My mother was the only one that I ever thought upon. When I got out of prison, all these thoughts went away from me, and I went again at my old tricks. From Wolverhampton I went to Manchester, and from Manchester I came to London, begging and stealing wherever I had a chance. This is not my first year in London. I tell you the truth, because I am known here; and if I tell you a lie, you'll say 'You spoke an untruth in one thing, and you'll do so in another.' The first time I was in London, I was put in prison fourteen days for begging, and after I had a month at Westminster Bridewell, for begging and abusing the policeman. Sometimes I'd think I'd rather go anywhere, and do anything, than continue as I was; but then I had no clothes, no friends, no house, no home, no means of doing better. I had made myself what I was. I had made my father and mother turn their backs upon me, and what could I do, but go on? I was as bad off then as I am now, and I couldn't have got work then if I would. I should have spent all I got in drink then, I know. I wrote home twice. I told my mother I was hard up; had neither a shoe to my foot, a coat to my back, nor a roof over my head. I had no answer to my first letter, because it fell into the hands of my brother, and he tore it up, fearing that my mother might see it. To the second letter that I sent home my mother sent me an answer herself. She sent me a sovereign. She told me that my father was the same as when I first left home, and it was no use my coming back. She sent me the money, bidding me get some clothes and seek for work. I didn't do as she bade. I spent the money—most part in drink. I didn't give any heed whether it was wrong or right. Soon got, soon gone; and I know they could have sent me much more than that if they had pleased. It was last June twelvemonth when I first came to London, and I stopped till the 10th of last March. I lost the young woman when I was put in prison in Manchester. She never came to see me in quod. She cared nothing for me. She only kept company with me to have some one on the road along with her; and I didn't care for her, not 'I. One half of my time last winter I stopped at the ' Straw-yards,' that is, in the asylums for the houseless poor here and at Glasshouse. When I could get money I had a lodging. After March I started off through Somerset-shire. I went to my father's house then. I didn't go in. I saw my father at the door, and he wouldn't let me in. I was a little better dressed than I am now. He said he had enough children at home without me, and gave me 10s. to go. He could not have been kind to me, or else he would not have turned me from his roof. My mother came out to the garden in front of the house, after my father had gone to his work, and spoke to me. She wished me to reform my character. I could not make any rash promises then. I had but very little to say to her. I felt myself at that same time, for the very first time in my life, that I was doing wrong. I thought, if I could hurt my mother so, it must be wrong to go on as I did. I had never had such thoughts before. My father's harsh words always drove such thoughts out of my head; but when I saw my mother's tears, it was more than I could stand. I was wanting to get away as fast as I could from the house. After that I stopped knocking about the country, sleeping in unions, up to November. Then I came to London again, and remained up to this time. Since I have been in town I have sought for work at the floor-cloth and carpet manufactory in the Borough, and they wouldn't even look at me in my present state. I am heartily tired of my life now altogether, and would like to get out of it if I could. I hope at least I have given up my love of drink, and I am sure, if I could once again lay my hand on some work, I should be quite a reformed character. Well, I am altogether tired of carrying on like this. I haven't made 6d. a-day ever since I have been in London this time. I go tramping it across the country just to pass the time, and see a little of new places. When the summer comes I want to be off. I am sure have seen enough of this country now, and I should like to have a look at some foreign land. Old England has nothing new in it now for me. I think a beggar's life is the worst kind of life that a man can lead. A beggar is no more thought upon than a dog in the street, and there are too many at the trade. I wasn't brought up to a bad life. You can see that by little things —by my handwriting; and, indeed, I should like to have a chance at something else. I have had the feelings of a vagabond for full ten years. I know, and now I am sure, I'm getting a different man. I begin to have thoughts and ideas I never had before. Once I never feared nor cared for anything, and I wouldn't have altered if I could; but now I'm tired out, and if I haven't a chance of going right, why I must go wrong.'

The next was a short, thick-set man, with a frequent grin on his countenance, which was rather expressive of humour. He wore a very dirty smock-frock, dirtier trousers, shirt, and neckerchief, and broken shoes. He answered readily, and as if he enjoyed his story.

" I never was at school, and was brought up as a farm labourer at Devizes," he said, " where my parents were labourers. I worked that way three or four years, and then ran away. My master wouldn't give me money enough—only 3s. 6d. a-week,—and my parents were very harsh; so I ran away, rather than be licked for ever. I'd heard people say, ' Go to Bath,' and I went there; and I was only about eleven then. I'm now twenty-three. I tried to get work on the railway there, and I did. I next got into prison for stealing three shovels. I was hard-up, having lost my work, and so I stole them. I was ten weeks in prison. I came out worse than I went in, for I mixed with the old hands, and they put me up to a few capers. When I got out I thought I could live as well that way as by hard work; so I took to the country. I began to beg. At first I took ' No ' for an answer, when I asked for ' Charity to a poor boy;' but I found that wouldn't do, so I learned to stick to them. I was forced, or I must have starved, and that wouldn't do at all. I did middling; plenty to eat, and sometimes a drop to drink, but not often. I was forced to be merry, because it's no good being down-hearted. I begged for two years,—that is, steal and beg together: I couldn't starve. I did best in country villages in Somersetshire; there's always odds and ends to be picked up there. I got into scrapes now and then. Once, in Devonshire, me and another slept at a farm-house, and in the morning we went egg-hunting. I must have stowed three dozen of eggs about me, when a dog barked, and we were alarmed and ran away, and in getting over a gate I fell, and there I lay among the smashed eggs. I can't help laughing at it still : but I got away. I was too sharp for them. I have been twenty or thirty times in prison. I have been in for stealing bread, and a side of bacon, and cheese, and shovels, and other things; generally provisions. I generally learn something new in prison. I shall do no good while I stop in England. It's not possible a man like me can get work, so I'm forced to go on this way. Sometimes I haven't a bit to eat all day. At night I may pick up something. An uncle of mine once told me he would like to see me transported, or come to the gallows. I told him I had no fear about the gallows; I should never come to that end: but if I were transported I should be better off than I am now. I can't starve, and I won't; and I can't 'list, I'm too short. I came to London the other day, but could do no good. The London hands are quite a different set to us. We seldom do business together. My way's simple. If I see a thing, and I'm hungry, I take it if I can, in London or anywhere. I once had a turn with two Londoners, and we got two coats and two pair of trousers; but the police got them back again. I was only locked up one night for it. The country's the best place to get away with anything, because there's not so many policemen. There's lots live as I live, because there's no work. I can do a country policeman, generally. I've had sprees at the country lodging-houses — larking, and drinking, and carrying on, and playing cards and dominoes all night for a farthing a game; sometimes fighting about it. I can play at dominoes, but I don't know the cards. They try to cheat one another. Honour among thieves! why there's no such thing; they take from one another. Sometimes we dance all night—Christmas time, and such times. Young women dance with us, and sometimes old women. We're all merry; some's lying on the floor drunk; some's jumping about, smoking; some's dancing; and so we enjoy ourselves. That's the best part of the life. We are seldom stopped in our merry-makings in the country. It's no good the policemen coming among us; give them beer, and you may knock the house down. We have good meat sometimes; sometimes very rough. Some are very particular about their cookery, as nice as anybody is. They must have their pickles, and their peppers, and their fish-sauces (I've had them myself), to their dishes. Chops, in the country, has the call; or ham and eggs—that's relished. Some's very particular about their drink, too; won't touch bad beer; same way with the gin. It's chiefly gin (I'm talking about the country), very little rum; no brandy: but sometimes, after a good day's work, a drop of wine. We help one another when we are sick, where we're knowed. Some's very good that way. Some lodging-house keepers get rid of anybody that's sick, by taking them to the relieving-officer at once."

A really fine-looking lad of eighteen gave me the following statement. He wore a sort of frock-coat, very thin, buttoned about him, old cloth trousers, and bad shoes. His shirt was tolerably good and clean, and altogether he had a tidy look and an air of quickness, but not of cunning :—

"My father," he said, "was a bricklayer in Shoreditch parish, and my mother took in washing. They did pretty well; but they're dead and buried two years and a half ago. I used to work in brick-fields at Ball's-pond, living with my parents, and taking home every farthing I earned. I earned 18s. a-week, working from five in the morning until sunset. They had only me. I can read and write middling; when my parents died, I had to look out for myself. I was off work, attending to my father and mother when they were sick. They died within about three weeks of each other, and I lost my work, and I had to part with my clothes before that I tried to work in brick-fields, and couldn't get it, and work grew slack. When my parents died I was thirteen; and I sometimes got to sleep in the unions; but that was stopped, and then I took to the lodging-houses, and there I met with lads who were enjoying themselves at push-halfpenny and cards; and they were thieves, and they tempted me to join them, and I did for once—but only once. I then went begging about the streets and thieving, as I knew the others do. I used to pick pockets. I worked for myself, because I thought that would be best. I had no fence at all—no pals at first, nor anything. I worked by myself for a time. I sold the handkerchiefs I got to Jews in the streets, chiefly in Field-lane, for 1s. 6d., but I have got as much as 3s. 6d. for your real fancy ones. One of these buyers wanted to cheat me out of 6d., so I would have no more dealings with him. The others paid me. The 'Kingsmen' they call the best handkerchiefs—those that have the pretty-looking flowers on them. Some are only worth 4d. or 5d., some's not worth taking. Those I gave away to strangers, boys like myself, or wore them myself, round my neck. I only threw one away, but it was all rags, though he looked quite like a gentleman that had it. Lord-mayor's day and such times is the best for us. Last Lord-mayor's day I got four handkerchiefs, and I made 11s. There was a 6d. tied up in the corner of one handkerchief; another was pinned to the pocket, but I got it out, and after that another chap had him, and cut his pocket clean away, but there was nothing in it. I generally picked my men—regular swells, or good-humoured looking men. I've often followed them a mile. I once got a purse with 3s. 6d. in it from a lady when the Coal Exchange was opened. I made 8s. 6d. that day—the purse and handkerchiefs. That's the only lady I ever robbed. I was in the crowd when Manning and his wife were hanged. I wanted to see if they died game, as I heard them talk so much about them at our house. I was there all night. I did four good handkerchiefs and a rotten one not worth picking up. I saw them hung. I was right under the drop. I was a bit startled when they brought him up and put the rope round his neck and the cap on, and then they brought her out. All said he was hung innocently; it was she that should have been hung by herself. They both dropped together, and I felt faintified, but I soon felt all right again. The police drove us away as soon as it was over, so that I couldn't do any more business; besides, I was knocked down in the crowd and jumped upon, and I won't go to see another hung in a hurry. He didn't deserve it, but she did, every inch of her. I can't say I thought, while I was seeing the execution, that the life I was leading would ever bring me to the gallows. After I'd worked by myself a bit, I got to live in a house where lads like me, big and little, were accommodated. We paid 3d. a-night. It was always full; there was twenty or twenty-one of us. We enjoyed ourselves middling. I was happy enough: we drank sometimes, chiefly beer, and sometimes a drop of gin. One would say, 'I've done so much,' and another, 'I've done so much;' and stand a drop. The best I ever heard done was 2l. for two coats from a tailor's, near Bow-church, Cheapside. That was by one of my pals. We used to share our money with those who did nothing for a day, and they shared with us when we rested. There never was any blabbing. We wouldn't do one another out of a farthing. Of a night some one would now and then read hymns, out of books they sold about the streets—I'm sure they were hymns; or else we'd read stories about Jack Sheppard and Dick Turpin, and all through that set. They were large thick books, borrowed from the library. They told how they used to break open the houses, and get out of Newgate, and how Dick got away to York. We used to think Jack and them very fine fellows. I wished I could be like Jack (I did then), about the blankets in his escape, and that old house in West-street —it is a ruin still. We played cards and dominoes sometimes at our house, and at pushing a halfpenny over the table along five lines. We struck the halfpenny from the edge of the table, and according to what line it settled on was the game—like as they play at the Glasshouse—that's the 'model lodging-house' they calls it. Cribbage was always played at cards. I can only play cribbage. We have played for a shilling a game, but oftener a penny. It was always fair play. That was the way we passed the time when we were not out. We used to keep quiet, or the police would have been down upon us. They knew of the place. They took one boy there. I wondered what they wanted. They catched him at the very door. We lived pretty well; anything we liked to get, when we'd money: we cooked it ourselves. The master of the house was always on the look-out to keep out those who had no business there. No girls were admitted. The master of the house had nothing to do with what we got. I don't know of any other such house in London; I don't

think there are any. The master would sometimes drink with us—a larking like. He used us pretty kindly at times. I have been three times in prison, three months each time; the Compter, Brixton, and Maidstone. I went down to Maidstone fair, and was caught by a London policeman down there. He was dressed as a bricklayer. Prison always made me worse, and as I had nothing given me when I came out, I had to look out again. I generally got hold of something before I had been an hour out of prison. I'm now heartily sick of this life. I wish I'd been transported with some others from Maidstone, where I was tried."

A cotton-spinner (who had subsequently been a soldier), whose appearance was utterly abject, was the next person questioned. He was tall, and had been florid-looking (judging by his present complexion). His coat—very old and worn, and once black—would not button, and would have hardly held together if buttoned. He was out at elbows, and some parts of the collar were pinned together. His waistcoat was of a match with his coat, and his trousers were rags. He had some shirt, as was evident by his waistcoat, held together by one button. A very dirty handkerchief was tied carelessly round his neck. He was tall and erect, and told his adventures with heartiness.

"I am thirty-eight," he said, "and have been a cotton-spinner, working at Chorlton-upon-Medlock. I can neither read nor write. When I was a young man, twenty years ago, I could earn 2l. 10s., clear money, every week, after paying two piecers and a scavenger. Each piecer had 7s. 6d. a-week—they are girls; the scavenger—a boy to clean the wheels of the cotton-spinning machine—had 2s. 6d. I was master of them wheels in the factory. This state of things continued until about the year 1837. I lived well and enjoyed myself, being a hearty man, noways a drunkard, working every day from half-past five in the morning till half-past seven at night—long hours, that time, master. I didn't care about money as long as I was decent and respectable. I had a turn for sporting at the wakes down there. In 1837, the 'self-actors' (machines with steam power) had come into common use. One girl can mind three pairs—that used to be three men's work—getting 15s. for the work which gave three men 7l. 10s. Out of one factory 400 hands were flung in one week, men and women together. We had a meeting of the union, but nothing could be done, and we were told to go and mind the three pairs, as the girls did, for 15s. a-week. We wouldn't do that. Some went for soldiers, some to sea, some to Stopport (Stockport), to get work in factories where the 'self-actors' wern't agait. The masters there wouldn't have them—at least, some of them. Manchester was full of them; but one gentleman in Hulme still won't have them, for he says he won't turn the men out of bread. I 'listed for a soldier in the 48th. I liked a soldier's life very well until I got flogged—100 lashes for selling my kit (for a spree), and 150 for striking a corporal, who called me an English robber. He was an Irishman. I was confined five days in the hospital after each punishment. It was terrible. It was like a bunch of razors cutting at your back. Your flesh was dragged off by the cats. Flogging was then very common in the regiment. I was flogged in 1840. To this day I feel a pain in the chest from the triangles. I was discharged from the army about two years ago, when the reduction took place. I was only flogged the times I've told you. I had no pension and no friends. I was discharged in Dublin. I turned to, and looked for work. I couldn't get any, and made my way for Manchester. I stole myself aboard of a steamer, and hid myself till she got out to sea, on her way from Dublin to Liverpool. When the captain found me there, he gave me a kick and some bread, and told me to work, so I worked for my passage twenty-four hours. He put me ashore at Liverpool. I slept in the union that night—nothing to eat and nothing to cover me—no fire; it was winter. I walked to Manchester, but could get nothing to do there, though I was twelve months knocking about. It wants a friend and a character to get work. I slept in unions in Manchester, and had oatmeal porridge for breakfast, work at grinding logwood in the mill, from six to twelve, and then turn out. That was the way I lived chiefly; but I got a job sometimes in driving cattle, and 3d. for it, —or 2d. for carrying baskets in the vegetable markets; and went to Shoedale Union at night. I would get a pint of coffee and half-a-pound of bread, and half-a-pound of bread in the morning, and no work. I took to travelling up to London, half-hungered on the road—that was last winter—eating turnips out of this field, and carrots out of that, and sleeping under hedges and haystacks. I slept under one haystack, and pulled out the hay to cover me, and the snow lay on it a foot deep in the morning. I slept for all that, but wasn't I froze when I woke? An old farmer came up with his cart and pitchfork to load hay. He said: 'Poor fellow! have you been here all night?' I answered, 'Yes.' He gave me some coffee and bread, and one shilling. That was the only good friend I met with on the road. I got fourteen days of it for asking a gentleman for a penny; that was in Stafford. I got to London after that, sleeping in unions sometimes, and begging a bite here and there. Sometimes I had to walk all night. I was once forty-eight hours without a bite, until I got hold at last of a Swede turnip, and so at last I got to London. Here I've tried up and down everywhere for work as a labouring man, or in a foundry. I tried London Docks, and Blackwall, and every place; but no job. At one foundry, the boiler-makers made a collection of 4s. for me. I've walked the streets for three nights together. Here, in this fine London, I was refused a night's lodging in Shoreditch and in Gray's-inn-lane. A policeman, the fourth night, at twelve o'clock, procured me a lodging, and gave me 2d. I couldn't drag on any longer. I was taken to a doctor's in the street. I fell in the street from hunger and tiredness. The doctor ordered me brandy and water, 2s. 6d., and a quartern loaf, and some coffee, sugar, and butter. He said, what I ailed was hunger. I made that run out as long as I could, but I was then as bad off as ever. It's hard to hunger for nights together. I was once in 'Steel' (Coldbath-fields) for begging. I was in Tothill-fields for going into a chandler's shop, asking for a quartern loaf and half a pound of cheese, and walking out with it. I got a month for that. I have been in Brixton for taking a loaf out of a baker's basket, all through hunger. Better a prison than to starve. I was well treated because I behaved well in prison. I have slept in coaches when I had a chance. One night on a dunghill, covering the stable straw about me to keep myself warm. This place is a relief. I shave the poor people and cut their hair, on a Sunday. I was handy at that when I was a soldier. I have shaved in public-houses for halfpennies. Some landlords kicks me out. Now, in the days, I may pick up a penny or two that way, and get here of a night. I met two Manchester men in Hyde Park on Saturday, skating. They asked me what I was. I said, 'A beggar.' They gave me 2s. 6d., and I spent part of it for warm coffee and other things. They knew all about Manchester, and knew I was a Manchester man by my talk."

The statement I then took was that of a female vagrant—a young girl with eyes and hair of remarkable blackness. Her complexion was of the deepest brunette, her cheeks were full of colour, and her lips very thick. This was accounted for. She told me that her father was a mulatto from Philadelphia. She was short, and dressed in a torn old cotton gown, the pattern of which was hardly discernible from wear. A kind of half-shawl, patched and mended in several places, and of very thin woollen texture, was pinned around her neck; her arms, which, with her hands, were full and large, were bare. She wore very old broken boots and ragged stockings. Her demeanour was modest.

"I am now eighteen," she stated. "My father was a coloured man. He came over here as a sailor, I have heard, but I never saw him; for my mother, who was a white woman, was not married to him, but met him at Oxford; and she married afterwards a boxmaker, a white man, and has two other children. They are living, I believe, but I don't know where they are. I have heard my mother say that my father—that's my own father—had become a missionary, and had been sent out to America from England as a missionary, by Mr. ——. I believe that was fifteen years ago. I don't know who Mr. —— was, but he was a gentleman, I've heard my mother say. She told me, too, that my father was a good scholar, and that he could speak seven different languages, and was a very religious man. He was sent out to Boston, but I never heard whether he was to stay or not, and I don't know what he was to missionary about. He behaved very well to my mother, I have heard her say, until she took up with the other man (the box-maker), and then he left her, and gave her up, and came to London. It was at Oxford that they all three were then; and when my father got away, or came away to London, my mother followed him (she told me so, but she didn't like to talk about it), as she was then in the family way. She didn't find him; but my father heard of her, and left some money with Mr. —— for her, and she got into Poland-street workhouse through Mr. —— I've heard. While there, she received 1s. 6d. a-week, but my father never came to see her or me. At one time, my father used to live by teaching languages. He had been in Spain, and France, and Morocco. I've heard, at any rate, that he could speak the Moors' language, but I know nothing more. All this is what I've heard from my mother and my grandmother—that's my mother's mother. My grandfather and grandmother are dead. He was a sawyer. I have a great grandmother living in Oxford, now ninety-two, supported by her parish. I lived with my grandmother at Oxford, who took me out of pity, as my mother never cared about me, when I was four months old. I remained with her until I was ten, and then my mother came from Reading, where she was living, and took me away with her. I lived with her and my step-father, but they were badly off. He couldn't get much to do at his trade as a box-maker, and he drank a great deal. I was with them about nine months, when I ran away. He beat me so; he never liked me. I couldn't bear it. I went to Pangbourne, but there I was stopped by a man my stepfather had sent—at least I suppose so—and I was forced to walk back to Reading—ten miles, perhaps. My father applied to the overseer for support for me, and the overseer was rather harsh, and my father struck him, and for that he was sent to prison for three months. My mother and her children then got into the workhouse, but not until after my stepfather had been some time in prison. Before that she had an allowance, which was stopped; I don't know how much. I was in the workhouse twenty-one days. I wasn't badly treated. My mother sweared my parish, and I was removed to St. James's, Poland-street, London. I was there three weeks, and then I was sent to New Brentford—it was called the Juvenile Establishment—and I went to school. There was about 150 boys and girls; the boys were sent to Norwood when they were fifteen. Some of the girls were eighteen, kept there until they could get a place. I don't know whether they all belonged to St. James's, or to different parishes, or how. I stayed there about two years. I was very well treated, sufficient to eat; but we worked hard at scrubbing, cleaning, and making shirts. We made all the boys' clothes as well, jackets and trousers, and all. I was then apprenticed a maid-of-all-work, in Duke-street, Grosvenor-square, for three years. I was there two years and a half, when my master failed in business, and had to part with me. They had no servant but me. My mistress was sometimes kind, pretty well. I had to work very hard. She sometimes beat me if I stopped long on my errands. My master beat me once for bringing things wrong from a grocer's. I made a mistake. Once my mistress knocked me down-stairs for being long on an errand to Pimlico, and I'm sure I couldn't help it, and my eye was cut. It was three weeks before I could see well. [There is a slight mark under the girl's eye still.] They beat me with their fists. After I left my master, I tried hard to get a place; I'm sure I did, but I really couldn't; so to live, I got watercresses to sell up and down Oxford-street. I stayed at lodging-houses. I tried that two or three months, but couldn't live. My mother had been 'through the country,' and I knew other people that had, through meeting them at the lodging-houses. I first went to Croydon, begging my way. I slept in the workhouse. After that I went to Brighton, begging my way, but couldn't get much, not enough to pay my lodgings. I was constantly insulted, both in the lodging-houses and in the streets. I sung in the streets at Brighton, and got enough to pay my lodgings, and a little for food. I was there a week, and then I went to the Mendicity, and they gave me a piece of bread (morning and night) and a night's lodging. I then went to Lewes and other places, begging, and got into prison at Tunbridge Wells for fourteen days, for begging. I only used to say I was a poor girl out of place, could they relieve me? I told no lies. I didn't pick my oakum one day, it was such hard stuff; three and a half pounds of it to do from nine to half-past three: so I was put into solitary for three days and three nights, having half a pound of bread and a pint of cold water morning and night; nothing else, and no bed to sleep on. I'm sure I tell you the truth. Some had irons on their hands if they were obstropolous. That's about two months ago. I'm sorry to say that during this time I couldn't be virtuous. I know very well what it means, for I can read and write, but no girl can be so circumstanced as I was. I seldom got money for being wicked; I hated being wicked, but I was tricked and cheated. I am truly sorry for it, but what could a poor girl do? I begged my way from London to Hastings, and got here on Saturday last, and having no money, came here. I heard of this asylum from a girl in Whitechapel, who had been here. I met her in a lodging-house, where I called to rest in the daytime. They let us rest sometimes in lodging-houses in the daytime. I never was in any prison but Tunbridge Wells, and in Gravesend lock-up for being out after twelve at night, when I had no money to get a lodging. I was there one Saturday night, and got out on Sunday morning, but had nothing given me to eat—I was in by myself. It's a bad place—just straw to sleep on, and very cold. I told you I could read and write. I learnt that partly at Oxford, and finished my learning at the Juvenile Establishment at Brentford. There I was taught, reading, writing, sums, marking, sewing, and scrubbing. Once I could say all the multiplication table, but I've forgot most of it. I know how to make lace, too, because I was taught by a cousin in Oxford, another grandchild of my grandmother's. I can make it with knitting-needles. I could make cushion-lace with pins, but I'm afraid I've forgot how now. I should like, if I could to get into service again, here or abroad. I have heard of Australia, where I have a cousin. I am sure I could and would conduct myself well in service, I have suffered so much out of it. I am sure of it. I never stole anything in my life, and have told all I have done wrong."

STATEMENT OF A RETURNED CONVICT.

I SHALL now give the statement of a man who was selected at random from amongst a number such as himself, congregated in one of the most respectable lodging-houses. He proved, on examination, to be a returned convict, and one who had gone through the severest bodily and mental agony. He had lived in the bush, and been tried for his life. He was an elderly-looking man, whose hair was just turning grey, and in whose appearance there was nothing remarkable, except that his cheek-bones were unusually high, and that his face presented that collected and composed expression which is common to men exposed to habitual watchfulness from constant danger. He gave me the following statement. His dress was bad, but differed in nothing from that of a long-distressed mechanic. He said :—

"I am now 43 (he looked much older), and had respectable parents, and a respectable education. I am a native of London. When I was young I was fond of a roving life, but cared nothing about drink. I liked to see 'life,' as it was called, and was fond of the company of women. Money was no object in those days; it was like picking up dirt in the streets. I ran away from home. My parents were very kind to me; indeed, I think I was used too well, I was petted so, when I was between 12 and 13. I got acquainted with some boys at Bartlemy-fair a little before

that, and saw them spending lots of money and throwing at cock-shies, and such-like; and one of them said, 'Why don't you come out like us ?' So afterwards I ran away and joined them. I was not kept shorter of money than other boys like me, but I couldn't settle. I couldn't fix my mind to any regular business but a waterman's, and my friends wouldn't hear of that. There was nine boys of us among the lot that I joined, but we didn't all work together. All of 'em came to be sent to Van Dieman's Land as transports except one, and he was sent to Sydney. While we were in London it was a merry life, with change of scene, for we travelled about. We were successful in nearly all our plans for several months. I worked in Fleet Street, and could make 3*l*. a-week at handkerchiefs alone, sometimes falling across a pocket-book. The best handkerchiefs then brought 4*s*. in Field-lane. Our chief enjoyments were at the 'Free and Easy,' where all the thieves and young women went, and sang and danced. I had a young woman for a partner then; she went out to Van Dieman's Land. She went on the lift in London (shopping and stealing from the counter). She was clever at it. I carried on in this way for about 15 months, when I was grabbed for an attempt on a gentleman's pocket by St. Paul's Cathedral, on a grand charity procession day. I had two months in the Old Horse (Bridewell). I never thought of my parents at this time—I wouldn't. I was two years and a half at this same trade. One week was very like another,—successes and escapes, and free-and-easies, and games of all sorts, made up the life. At the end of the two years and a half I got into the way of forged Bank-of-England notes. A man I knew in the course of business, said, 'I would cut that game of 'smatter-hauling,' (stealing handkerchiefs), and do a little soft,' (pass bad notes). So I did, and was very successful at first. I had a mate. He afterwards went out to Sydney, too, for 14 years. I went stylishly dressed as a gentleman, with a watch in my pocket, to pass my notes. I passed a good many in drapers' shops, also at tailors' shops. I never tried jewellers, they're reckoned too good judges. The notes were all finnies, (5*l*. notes), and a good imitation. I made more money at this game, but lived as before, and had my partner still. I was fond of her; she was a nice girl, and I never found that she wronged me in any way. I thought at four months' end of retiring into the country with gambling-tables, as the risk was becoming considerable. They hung them for it in them days, but that never daunted me the least in life. I saw Cashman hung for that gunsmith's shop on Snow-hill, and I saw Fauntleroy hung, and a good many others, but it gave me no uneasiness and no fear. The gallows had no terror for people in my way of life. I started into the country with another man and his wife—his lawful wife—

for I had a few words with my own young woman, or I shouldn't have left her behind me, or, indeed, have started at all. We carried gambling on in different parts of the country for six months. We made most at the E. O. tables,—not those played with a ball, they weren't in vogue then, but throwing dice for prizes marked on a table. The highest prize was ten guineas, but the dice were so made that no prize could be thrown; the numbers were not regular as in good dice, and they were loaded as well. If anybody asked to see them, we had good dice ready to show. All sorts played with us. London men and all were taken in. We made most at the races. My mate and his wife told me that at the last Newmarket meeting we attended, 65*l.* was made, but they rowed in the same boat. I know they got a deal more. The 65*l.* was shared in three equal portions, but I had to maintain the horse and cart out of my own share. We used to go out into the roads (highway robbery) between races, and if we met an 'old bloke' (man) we 'propped him' (knocked him down), and robbed him. We did good stakes that way, and were never found out. We lived as well as any gentleman in the land. Our E. O. table was in a tilted cart. I stayed with this man and his wife two months. She was good-looking, so as to attract people. I thought they didn't use me altogether right, so at Braintree I gave another man in the same way of business 25*l.* for his kit—horse, harness, tilted-cart, and table. I gave him two good 5*l.* notes and three bad ones, for I worked that way still, not throwing much of a chance away. I came to London for a hawker's stock, braces and such-like, to sell on the road, just to take the down off (remove suspicion). In the meantime, the man that I bought the horse, &c., of, had been nailed passing a bad note, and he stated who he got it from, and I was traced. He was in a terrible rage to find himself done, particularly as he used to do the same to other people himself. He got acquitted for that there note after he had me 'pinched' (arrested). I got 'fullied' (fully committed). I was tried at the 'Start' (Old Bailey), and pleaded guilty to the minor offence, (that of utterance, not knowing the note to be forged), or I should have been hanged for it then. It was a favourable sessions when I was tried. Thirty-six were cast for death, and only one was 'topped' (hanged), the very one that expected to be 'turned up' (acquitted) for highway robbery. I was sentenced to 14 years' transportation. I was ten weeks in the Bellerophon hulk at Sheerness, and was then taken to Hobart Town, Van Dieman's Land, in the Sir Godfrey Webster. At Hobart Town sixty of us were picked out to go to Launceston. There (at Launceston) we lay for four days in an old church, guarded by constables; and then the settlers came there from all parts, and picked their men out. I

got a very bad master. He put me to harvest work that I had never even seen done before, and I had the care of pigs as wild as wild boars. After that I was sent to Launceston with two letters from my master to the superintendent, and the other servants thought I had luck to get away from Red Barks to Launceston, which was 16 miles off. I then worked in a Government potato-field; in the Government charcoal-works for about 11 months; and then was in the Marine department, going by water from Launceston to George Town, taking Government officers down in gigs, provisions in boats, and such-like. There was a crew of six (convicts) in the gigs, and four in the watering-boats. All the time I consider I was very hardly treated. I hadn't clothes half the time, being allowed only two slop-suits in a year, and no bed to lie on when we had to stay out all night with the boats by the river Tamar. With 12 years' service at this my time was up, but I had incurred several punishments before it was up. The first was 25 lashes, because a bag of flour had been burst, and I picked up a capfull. The flogging is dreadfully severe, a soldier's is nothing to it. I once had 50 lashes, for taking a hat in a joke when I was tipsy; and a soldier had 300 the same morning. I was flogged as a convict, and he as a soldier; and when we were both at the same hospital after the flogging, and saw each other's backs, the other convicts said to me, 'D— it, you've got it this time;' and the soldier said, when he saw my back, 'You've got it twice as bad I have.' 'No,' said the doctor, 'ten times as bad—he's been flogged; but you, in comparison, have only had a child's whipping.' The cats the convicts were then flogged with were each six feet long, made out of the logline of a ship of 500 tons burden; nine over-end knots were in each tail, and nine tails whipped at each end with wax-end. With this we had half-minute lashes; a quick lashing would have been certain death. One convict who had 75 lashes was taken from the triangles to the watch-house in Launceston, and was asked if he would have some tea,—he was found to be dead. The military surgeon kept on saying in this case, ' Go on, do your duty.' I was mustered there, as was every hand belonging to the Government, and saw it, and heard the doctor. When I was first flogged, there was inquiry among my fellow-convicts, as to ' How did D— (meaning me) stand it—did he sing ?' The answer was, 'He was a pebble;' that is, I never once said, ' Oh !' or gave out any expression of the pain I suffered. I took my flogging like a stone. If I had sung, some of the convicts would have given me some lush with a locust in it (laudanum hocussing), and when I was asleep would have given me a crack on the head that would have laid me straight. That first flogging made me ripe. I said to myself, 'I can take it like a bullock.' I could have taken the flogger's life at the time, I felt such revenge. Flogging always gives that feeling; I know it does, from what I've heard others say who had been flogged like myself. In all I had 875 lashes at my different punishments. I used to boast of it at last. I would say, ' I don't care, I can take it till they see my backbone.' After a flogging, I've rubbed my back against a wall, just to show my bravery like, and squeezed the congealed blood out of it. Once I would not let them dress my back after a flogging, and I had 25 additional for that. At last I bolted to Hobart Town, 120 miles off. There I was taken before Mr. H——, the magistrate, himself a convict formerly, I believe from the Irish Rebellion; but he was a good man to a prisoner. He ordered me 50, and sent me back to Launceston. At Launceston I was 'fullied' by a bench of magistrates, and had 100. Seven years before my time was up I took to the bush. I could stand it no longer, of course not. In the bush I met men with whom, if I had been seen associating, I should have been hanged on any slight charge, such as Brittan was and his pals."

I am not at liberty to continue this man's statement at present: it would be a breach of the trust reposed in me. Suffice it, he was in after days tried for his life. Altogether it was a most extraordinary statement; and, from confirmations I received, was altogether truthful. He declared that he was so sick of the life he was now leading, that he would, as a probation, work on any kind of land anywhere for nothing, just to get out of it. He pronounced the lodging-houses the grand encouragements and concealments of crime, though he might be speaking against himself, he said, as he had always hidden safely there during the hottest search. A policeman once walked through the ward in search of him, and he was in bed. He knew the policeman well, and was as well known to the officer, but he was not recognised. He attributed his escape to the thick, bad atmosphere of the place giving his features a different look, and to his having shaved off his whiskers, and pulled his nightcap over his head. The officer, too, seemed half-sick, he said.

It ought also to be added, that this man stated that the severity of the Government in this penal colony was so extreme, that men thought little of giving others a knock on the head with an axe, to get hanged out of the way. Under the discipline of Captain Macconochie, however, who introduced better order with a kindlier system, there wasn't a man but what would have laid down his life for him.

LIVES OF THE BOY INMATES OF THE CASUAL WARDS OF THE LONDON WORKHOUSES.

AN intelligent-looking boy, of sixteen years of age, whose dress was a series of ragged coats, three in number—as if one was to obviate the deficiency of another, since one would not button, and another was almost sleeveless—gave me the following statement. He had long and rather fair hair, and spoke quietly. He said:—

" I'm a native of Wisbeach, in Cambridgeshire, and am sixteen. My father was a shoemaker, and my mother died when I was five years old, and my father married again. I was sent to school, and can read and write well. My father and step-mother were kind enough to me. I was apprenticed to a tailor three years ago, but I wasn't long with him; I runned away. I think it was three months I was with him when I first runned away. It was in August—I got as far as Boston in Lincolnshire, and was away a fortnight. I had 4s. 6d. of my own money when I started, and that lasted two or three days. I stopped in lodging-houses until my money was gone, and then I slept anywhere—under the hedges, or anywhere. I didn't see so much of life then, but I've seen plenty of it since. I had to beg my way back from Boston, but was very awkward at first. I lived on turnips mainly. My reason for running off was because my master ill-used me so; he beat me, and kept me from my meals, and made me sit up working late at nights for a punishment: but it was more to his good than to punish me. I hated to be confined to a tailor's shopboard, but I would rather do that sort of work now then hunger about like this. But you see, sir, God punishes you when you don't think of it. When I went back my father was glad to see me, and he wouldn't have me go back again to my master, and my indentures were cancelled. I stayed at home seven months, doing odd jobs, in driving sheep, or any country work, but I always wanted to be off to sea. I liked the thoughts of going to sea far better than tailoring. I determined to go to sea if I could. When a dog's determined to have a bone, it's not easy to hinder him. I didn't read stories about the sea then, not even ' Robinson Crusoe,'—indeed I haven't read that still, but I know very well there is such a book. My father had no books but religious books; they were all of a religious turn, and what people might think dull, but they never made me dull. I read Wesley's and Watts's hymns, and religious magazines of different connexions. I had a natural inclination for the sea, and would like to get to it now. I've read a good deal about it since—Clark's ' Lives of Pirates,' ' Tales of Shipwrecks,' and other things in penny numbers (Clark's I got out of a library though). I was what people called a deep boy for a book; and am still. Whenever I had a penny, after I got a bellyful of victuals, it went for a book, but I haven't bought many lately. I did buy one yesterday —the 'Family Herald'—one I often read when I can get it. There's good reading in it; it elevates your mind—anybody that has a mind for studying. It has good tales in it. I never read 'Jack Sheppard,'—that is, I haven't read the big book that's written about him; but I've often heard the boys and men talk about it at the lodging-houses and other places. When they haven't their bellies and money to think about they sometimes talk about books; but for such books as them—that's as 'Jack'—I haven't a partiality. I've read 'Windsor Castle,' and 'The Tower,'—they're by the same man. I liked 'Windsor Castle,' and all about Henry VIII. and Herne the hunter. It's a book that's connected with history, and that's a good thing in it. I like adventurous tales. I know very little about theatres, as I was never in one.

"Well, after that seven months—I was kindly treated all the time—I runned away again to get to sea; and hearing so much talk about this big London, I comed to it. I couldn't settle down to anything but the sea. I often watched the ships at Wisbeach. I had no particular motive, but a sort of pleasure in it. I was aboard some ships, too; just looking about, as lads will. I started without a farthing, but I couldn't help it. I felt I must come. I forgot all I suffered before—at least, the impression had died off my mind. I came up by the unions when they would take me in. When I started, I didn't know where to sleep any more than the dead; I learned it from other travellers on the road. It was two winters ago, and very cold weather. Sometimes I slept in barns, and I begged my way as well as I could. I never stole anything then or since, except turnips; but I've been often tempted. At last I got to London, and was by myself. I travelled sometimes with others as I came up, but not as mates—not as friends. I came to London for one purpose just by myself. I was a week in London before I knew where I was. I didn't know where to go. I slept on door-steps, or anywhere. I used often to stand on London-bridge, but I didn't know where to go to get to sea, or anything of that kind. I was sadly hungered, regularly starved; and I saw so many policemen, I durstn't beg—and I dare not now, in London. I got crusts, but I can hardly tell how I lived. One night I was sleeping under a railway-arch, somewhere about Bishopsgate-street, and a policeman came and asked me what I was up to? I told him I had no place to go to, so he said I must go along with him. In the morning he took me and four or five others to a house in a big street. I don't know where; and a man—a magistrate, I suppose he was—heard what the policeman had to say, and he said there was always a lot of lads there about the arches, young thieves, that gave him a great deal of trouble, and I was one associated with them. I declare I didn't know any of the other boys, nor any boys in London—not a soul; and I was under the arch by myself, and only that night. I never saw the policeman himself before that, as I know of. I got fourteen days of it, and they took me in an omnibus,

but I don't know to what prison. I was committed for being a rogue and something else. I didn't very well hear what other things I was, but 'rogue' I know was one. They were very strict in prison, and I wasn't allowed to speak. I was put to oakum some days, and others on a wheel. That's the only time I was ever in prison, and I hope it will always be the only time. Something may turn up—there's nobody knows. When I was turned out I hadn't a farthing given to me. And so I was again in the streets, without knowing a creature, and without a farthing in my pocket, and nothing to get one with but my tongue. I set off that day for the country. I didn't try to get a ship, because I didn't know where to go to ask, and I had got ragged, and they wouldn't hear me out if I asked any people about the bridges. I took the first road that offered, and got to Greenwich. I couldn't still think of going back home. I would if I had had clothes, but they were rags, and I had no shoes but a pair of old slippers. I was sometimes sorry I left home, but then I began to get used to travelling, and to beg a bit in the villages. I had no regular mate to travel with, and no sweetheart. I slept in the unions whenever I could get in—that's in the country. I didn't never sleep in the London workhouses till afterwards. In some country places there were as many as forty in the casual wards, men, women, and children; in some, only two or three. There used to be part boys, like myself, but far more bigger than I was; they were generally from eighteen to twenty-three: London chaps, chiefly, I believe. They were a regularly jolly set. They used to sing and dance a part of the nights and mornings in the wards, and I got to sing and dance with them. We were all in a mess; there was no better or no worse among us. We used to sing comic and sentimental songs, both. I used to sing 'Tom Elliott,' that's a sea song, for I hankered about the sea, and 'I'm Afloat.' I hardly know any but sea-songs. Many used to sing indecent songs; they're impudent blackguards. They used to sell these songs among the others, but I never sold any of them, and I never had any, though I know some, from hearing them often. We told stories sometimes; romantic tales, some; others blackguard kind of tales, about bad women; and others about thieving and roguery; not so much about what they'd done themselves, as about some big thief that was very clever at stealing, and could trick anybody. Not stories such as Dick Turpin or Jack Sheppard, or things that's in history, but inventions. I used to say when I was telling a story—for I've told one story that I invented till I learnt it,—

[I give this story to show what are the objects of admiration with these vagrants.]

"'You see, mates, there was once upon a time, and a very good time it was, a young man, and he runned away, and got along with a gang of thieves, and he went to a gentleman's house, and got in, because one of his mates sweethearted the servant, and got her away, and she left the door open.' [" But don't," he expostulated, " take it all down that way; it's foolishness. I'm ashamed of it — it's just what we say to amuse ourselves."] ' And the door being left open, the young man got in and robbed the house of a lot of money, 1000*l.*, and he took it to their gang at the cave. Next day there was a reward out to find the robber. Nobody found him. So the gentleman put out two men and a horse in a field, and the men were hidden in the field, and the gentleman put out a notice that anybody that could catch the horse should have him for his cleverness, and a reward as well; for he thought the man that got the 1000*l.* was sure to try to catch that there horse, because he was so bold and clever, and then the two men hid would nab him. This here Jack (that's the young man) was watching, and he saw the two men, and he went and caught two live hares. Then he hid himself behind a hedge, and let one hare go, and one man said to the other, ' There goes a hare,' and they both run after it, not thinking Jack's there. And while they were running he let go the t'other one, and they said, ' There's another hare,' and they ran different ways, and so Jack went and got the horse, and took it to the man that offered the reward, and got the reward; it was 100*l.*; and the gentleman said ' D——n it, Jack's done me this time.' The gentleman then wanted to serve out the parson, and he said to Jack, ' I'll give you another 100*l.* if you'll do something to the parson as bad as you've done to me.' Jack said, ' Well, I will;' and Jack went to the church and lighted up the lamps, and rang the bells, and the parson he got up to see what was up. Jack was standing in one of the pews like an angel, when the parson got to the church. Jack said, ' Go and put your plate in a bag; I'm an angel come to take you up to heaven.' And the parson did so, and it was as much as he could drag to church from his house in a bag; for he was very rich. And when he got to the church Jack put the parson in one bag, and the money stayed in the other; and he tied them both together, and put them across his horse, and took them up hills and through water to the gentleman's, and then he took the parson out of the bag, and the parson was wringing wet. Jack fetched the gentleman, and the gentleman gave the parson a horsewhipping, and the parson cut away, and Jack got all the parson's money and the second 100*l.*, and gave it all to the poor. And the parson brought an action against the gentleman for horsewhipping him, and they both were ruined. That's the end of it.' That's the sort of story that's liked best, sir. Sometimes there was fighting in the casual-wards. Sometimes I was in it, I was like the rest. We jawed each other often, calling names. and coming to fight at last. At

Romsey a lot of young fellows broke all the windows they could get at, because they were too late to be admitted. They broke them from the outside. We couldn't get at them from inside. I've carried on begging, and going from union to union to sleep, until now. Once I got work in Northampton with a drover. I kept working when he'd a job, from August last to the week before Christmas. I always tried to get a ship in a seaport, but couldn't. I've been to Portsmouth, Plymouth, Bristol, Southampton, Ipswich, Liverpool, Brighton, Dover, Shoreham, Hastings, and all through Lincolnshire, Nottinghamshire, Cambridgeshire, and Suffolk—not in Norfolk—they won't let you go there. I don't know why. All this time I used to meet boys like myself, but mostly bigger and older; plenty of them could read and write, some were gentlemen's sons, they said. Some had their young women with them that they'd taken up with, but I never was much with them. I often wished I was at home again, and do now, but I can't think of going back in these rags; and I don't know if my father's dead or alive (his voice trembled), but I'd like to be there and have it over. I can't face meeting them in these rags, and I've seldom had better, I make so little money. I'm unhappy at times, but I get over it better than I used, as I get accustomed to this life. I never heard anything about home since I left. I have applied at the Marine Society here, but it's no use. If I could only get to sea, I'd be happy; and I'd be happy if I could get home, and would, but for the reasons I've told you."

The next was a boy with a quiet look, rather better dressed than most of the vagrant boys, and far more clean in his dress. He made the following statement :—

" I am now seventeen. My father was a cotton-spinner in Manchester, but has been dead ten years; and soon after that my mother went into the workhouse, leaving me with an aunt; and I had work in a cotton factory. As young as I was, I earned 2*s.* 2*d.* a-week at first. I can read well, and can write a little. I worked at the factory two years, and was then earning 7*s.* a-week. I then ran away, for I had always a roving mind; but I should have stayed if my master hadn't knocked me about so. I thought I should make my fortune in London—I'd heard it was such a grand place. I had read in novels and romances,—halfpenny and penny books,—about such things, but I've met with nothing of the kind. I started without money, and begged my way from Manchester to London, saying I was going up to look for work. I wanted to see the place more than anything else. I suffered very much on the road, having to be out all night often; and the nights were cold, though it was summer. When I got to London all my hopes were blighted. I could get no further. I never tried for work in London, for I believe there are no cotton factories in it; besides, I wanted to see life. I begged, and slept in the unions. I got acquainted with plenty of boys like myself. We met at the casual wards, both in London and the country. I have now been five years at this life. We were merry enough in the wards, we boys, singing and telling stories. Songs such as 'Paul Jones' was liked, while some sung very blackguard songs; but I never got hold of such songs, though I have sold lots of songs in Essex. Some told long stories, very interesting; some were not fit to be heard; but they made one laugh sometimes. I've read 'Jack Sheppard' through, in three volumes; and I used to tell stories out of that sometimes. We all told in our turns. We generally began,—'Once upon a time, and a very good time it was, though it was neither in your time, nor my time, nor nobody else's time.' The best man in the story is always called Jack."

At my request, this youth told me a long story, and told it very readily, as if by rote. I give it for its peculiarity, as it is extravagant enough, without humour.

"A farmer hired Jack, and instructed him over-night. Jack was to do what he was required, or lose his head. 'Now, Jack,' said the farmer, [I give the conclusion in the boy's words,] 'what's my name?' 'Master, to be sure,' says Jack. 'No,' said he, 'you must call me Tom Per Cent.' He showed his bed next, and asked, 'What's this, Jack?' 'Why, the bed,' said Jack. 'No, you must call that, He's of Degree.' And so he bid Jack call his leather breeches 'forty cracks;' the cat, 'white-faced Simeon;' the fire, 'hot coleman;' the pump, the 'resurrection;' and the haystack, the 'little cock-a-mountain.' Jack was to remember these names or lose his head. At night the cat got under the grate, and burned herself, and a hot cinder struck her fur, and she ran under the haystack and set it on fire. Jack ran up-stairs to his master, and said:—

'Tom Per Cent, arise out of he's of degree,
Put on your forty cracks, come down and see;
For the little white-faced Simeon
Has run away with hot coleman
Under the little cock-a-mountain,
And without the aid of the resurrection
We shall be damned and burnt to death.'

So Jack remembered his lesson, and saved his head. That's the end. Blackguard stories were often told about women. There was plenty told, too, about Dick Turpin, Sixteen-string Jack, Oxford Blue, and such as them; as well as about Jack Sheppard; about Bamfylde Moore Carew, too, and his disguises. We very often had fighting and quarrelling among ourselves. Once, at Birmingham, we smashed all the windows, and did all the damage we could. I can't tell exactly why it was done, but we must all take part in it, or we should be marked. I believe some did it to get into prison, they were so badly off. They piled up the rugs; there was no straw;

and some put their clothes on the rugs, and then the heap was set fire to. There was no fire, and no light, but somebody had a box of lucifers. We were all nearly suffocated before the people of the place could get to us. Seventeen of us had a month a-piece for it: I was one. The rugs were dirty and filthy, and not fit for any Christian to sleep under, and so I took part in the burning, as I thought it would cause something better. I've known wild Irishmen get into the wards with knives and sticks hidden about their persons, to be ready for a fight. I met two young men in Essex who had been well off—very well,—but they liked a tramper's life. Each had his young woman with him, living as man and wife. They often change their young women; but I never did travel with one, or keep company with any more than twelve hours or so. There used to be great numbers of girls in the casual wards in London. Any young man travelling the country could get a mate among them, and can get mates—partners they're often called,—still. Some of them are very pretty indeed; but among them are some horrid ugly—the most are ugly; bad expressions and coarse faces, and lame, and disgusting to the eye. It was disgusting, too, to hear them in their own company; that is, among such as themselves;—beggars, you know. Almost every word was an oath, and every blackguard word was said plain out. I think the pretty ones were worst. Very few have children. I knew two who had. One was seventeen, and her child was nine months old; the other was twenty-one, and her child was eighteen months. They were very good to their children. I've heard of some having children, and saying they couldn't guess at the fathers of them, but I never met with any such myself. I didn't often hear them quarrel,—I mean the young men and young women that went out as partners,—in the lodging-houses. Some boys of fifteen have their young women as partners, but with young boys older women are generally partners—women about twenty. They always pass as man and wife. All beggar-girls are bad, I believe. I never heard but of one that was considered virtuous, and she was always reading a prayer-book and a testament in her lodging-house. The last time I saw her was at Cambridge. She is about thirty, and has traces of beauty left. The boys used to laugh at her, and say, 'Oh! how virtuous and righteous we are! but you get your living by it.' I never knew her to get anything by it. I don't see how she could, for she said nothing about her being righteous when she was begging about, I believe. If it wasn't for the casual wards, I couldn't get about. If two partners goes to the same union, they have to be parted at night, and join again the morning. Some of the young women are very dirty, but some's as clean. A few, I think, can read and write. Some boasts of their wickedness, and others tell them in derision it's wrong to do that, and then a quarrel rages in the lodging-house. I liked a roving life, at first, being my own master. I was fond of going to plays, and such-like, when I got money; but now I'm getting tired of it, and wish for something else. I have tried for work at cotton factories in Lancashire and Yorkshire, but never could get any. I've been all over the country. I'm sure I could settle now. I couldn't have done that two years ago, the roving spirit was so strong upon me, and the company I kept got a strong hold on me. Two winters back, there was a regular gang of us boys in London. After sleeping at a union, we would fix where to meet at night to get into another union to sleep. There were thirty of us that way, all boys; besides forty young men, and thirty young women. Sometimes we walked the streets all night. We didn't rob, at least I never saw any robbing. We had pleasure in chaffing the policemen, and some of us got taken up. I always escaped. We got broken up in time, —some's dead, some's gone to sea, some into the country, some home, and some lagged. Among them were many lads very expert in reading, writing, and arithmetic. One young man—he was only twenty-five,—could speak several languages: he had been to sea. He was then begging, though a strong young man. I suppose he liked that life: some soon got tired of it. I often have suffered from cold and hunger. I never made more than 3d. a-day in money, take the year round, by begging; some make more than 6d.: but then, I've had meat and bread given besides. I say nothing when I beg, but that I am a poor boy out of work and starving. I never stole anything in my life. I've often been asked to do so by my mates. I never would. The young women steal the most. I know, least, I did know, two that kept young men, their partners, going about the country with them, chiefly by their stealing. Some do so by their prostitution. Those that go as partners are all prostitutes. There is a great deal of sickness among the young men and women, but I never was ill these last seven years. Fevers, colds, and venereal diseases, are very common."

The last statement I took was that of a boy of thirteen. I can hardly say that he was clothed at all. He had no shirt, and no waist-coat; all his neck and a great part of his chest being bare. A ragged cloth jacket hung about him, and was tied, so as to keep it together, with bits of tape. What he had wrapped round for trousers did not cover one of his legs, while one of his thighs was bare. He wore two old shoes; one tied to his foot with an old ribbon, the other a woman's old boot. He had an old cloth cap. His features were distorted somewhat, through being swollen with the cold. " I was born," he said, " at a place called Hadley, in Kent. My father died when I was three days old, I've heard my mo-

ther say. He was married to her, I believe, but I don't know what he was. She had only me. My mother went about begging, some-times taking me with her; at other times she left me at the lodging-house in Hadley. She went in the country, round about Tunbridge and there, begging. Sometimes she had a day's work. We had plenty to eat then, but I haven't had much lately. My mother died at Hadley a year ago. I didn't know how she was buried. She was ill a long time, and I was out begging; for she sent me out to beg for myself a good while before that, and when I got back to the lodging-house they told me she was dead. I had sixpence in my pocket, but I couldn't help crying to think I'd lost my mother. I cry about it still. I didn't wait to see her buried, but I started on my own ac-count. I met two navvies in Bromley, and they paid my first night's lodging; and there was a man passing, going to London with po-tatoes, and the navvies gave the man a pot of beer to take me up to London in the van, and they went that way with me. I came to Lon-don to beg, thinking I could get more there than anywhere else, hearing that London was such a good place. I begged; but sometimes wouldn't get a farthing in a day; often walking about the streets all night. I have been beg-ging about all the time till now. I am very weak—starving to death. I never stole any-thing: I always kept my hands to myself. A boy wanted me to go with him to pick a gen-tleman's pocket. We was mates for two days, and then he asked me to go picking pockets; but I wouldn't. I know it's wrong, though I can neither read nor write. The boy asked me to do it to get into prison, as that would be better than the streets. He picked pockets to get into prison. He was starving about the streets like me. I never slept in a bed since I've been in London: I am sure I haven't: I generally slept under the dry arches in West-street, where they're building houses—I mean the arches for the cellars. I begged chiefly from the Jews about Petticoat-lane, for they all give away bread that their children leave—pieces of crust, and such-like. I would do anything to be out of this misery."

INCREASE AND DECREASE OF NUMBER OF AP-PLICANTS TO CASUAL WARDS OF LONDON WORKHOUSES.

THE vagrant applying for shelter is admitted at all times of the day and night. He applies at the gate, he has his name entered in the va-grant book, and he is then supplied with six ounces of bread and one ounce of cheese. As the admission generally takes place in the even-ing, no work is required of them until the fol-lowing morning. At one time every vagrant was searched and bathed, but in the cold sea-son of the year the bathing is discontinued; neither are they searched unless there are grounds for suspecting that they have property secreted upon them. The males are conducted to the ward allotted to them, and the females to their ward. These wards consist each of a large chamber, in which are arranged two large guard-beds, or inclined boards, similar to those used in soldiers' guard-rooms; between these there is a passage from one end of the chamber to the other. The boards are strewn with straw, so that, on entering the place in the daytime, it has the appearance of a well-kept stable. All persons are supplied with two, and in the cold season with three, rugs to cover them. These rugs are daily placed in a fumigating oven, so as to decompose all infectious matter. Formerly beds were supplied in place of the straw, but the habitual vagrants used to amuse themselves with cutting up the mattresses, and strewing the flock all over the place; the blankets and rugs they tore into shreds, and wound them round their legs, under their trousers. The windows of the casual ward are protected on the inside with a strong guard, similar to those seen in the neighbourhood of racket-grounds. No lights are allowed in the casual ward, so that they are expected to retire to rest immediately on their entrance, and this they invariably are glad to do. In the morning they are let out at eight in the winter, and seven in the summer. And then another six ounces of bread and one ounce of cheese is given to them, and they are discharged. In return for this, three hours' labour at the hand corn-mill was formerly exacted; but now the numbers are so few, and the out-door paupers so numerous, and so different from the class of vagrants, that the latter are allowed to go on their road immediately the doors of the casual ward are opened. The labour formerly exacted was not in any way remunerative. In the three hours that they were at work, it is supposed that the value of each man's labour could not be expressed in any coin of the realm. The work was demanded as a test of destitution and industry, and not as a matter of compensation. If the vagrants were very young, they were put to oakum-picking instead of the hand-mill. The women were very rarely employed at any time, because there was no suitable place in the union for them to pick oakum, and the master was unwilling to allow them, on account of their bad and immoral characters, as well as their filthy habits, to communicate with the other inmates. The female vagrants generally consist of prostitutes of the lowest and most miserable kind. They are mostly young girls, who have sunk into a state of dirt, disease, and almost nudity. There are few of them above twenty years of age, and they appear to have commenced their career of vice frequently as early as ten or twelve years old. They mostly are found in the company of mere boys.

The above descriptions apply rather to the state of the vagrants some two or three years back, than to things as they exist at present. In the year 1837, a correspondence took place between the Commissioners of Police and the Commissioners of the Poor-law, in which the latter declare that "if a person state that he has no food, and that he is destitute, or otherwise express or signify that he is in danger of perishing unless relief be given to him, then any officer charged with the administration of relief is bound, unless he have presented to him some reasonable evidence to rebut such statement, to give relief to such destitute person in the mode prescribed by law." The Poor-law Commissioners further declare in the same document, that they will feel it their duty to make the officers responsible in their situations for any serious neglect to give prompt and adequate relief in any case of real destitution and emergency. The consequence of this declaration was, that Poor-law officers appeared to feel themselves bound to admit all vagrants upon their mere statement of destitution, whereas before that time parties were admitted into the casual wards either by tickets from the ratepayers, or else according to the discretion of the master. Whether or not the masters imagined that they were compelled to admit every applicant from that period my informant cannot say, but it is certain that after the date of that letter vagrancy began to increase throughout the country; at first gradually, but after a few years with a most enormous rapidity; so that in 1848, it appeared from the Poor-law Report on Vagrancy (presented to both Houses of Parliament in that year) that the number of vagrants had increased to upwards of 16,000. The rate of increase for the three years previous to that period is exhibited in the following table:—

I.—Summary of the Number of Vagrants in Unions and Places under Local Acts, in England and Wales, at different periods, as appears from the Returns which follow:—

Average number relieved in one night in 603 Unions, &c., in the week ending 20th December, 1845.......	1,791
Average number relieved in one night in 603 Unions, &c., in the week ending 19th December, 1846......	2,224
Average number relieved in one night in 596 Unions, &c., in the week ending 18th December, 1847......	4,508
Total number relieved, whether in or out of the workhouse in 626 Unions, &c., on the 25th March, 1848.......	16,086

Matters had reached this crisis, when the late Mr. C. Buller, President of the Poor-law Board, issued, in August 1848, a minute, in which—after stating that the Board had received representations from every part of England and Wales respecting the continual and rapid increase of vagrancy—he gives the following instructions to the officers employed in the administration of the Poor-law:—

"With respect to the applicants that will thus come before him, the relieving officer will have to exercise his judgment as to the truth of their assertions of destitution, and to ascertain by searching them whether they possess any means of supplying their own necessities. He will not be likely to err in judging from their appearance whether they are suffering from want of food. He will take care that women and children, the old and infirm, and those who, without absolutely serious disease, present an enfeebled or sickly appearance, are supplied with necessary food and shelter. As a general rule, he would be right in refusing relief to able-bodied and healthy men; though in inclement weather he might afford them shelter, if really destitute of the means of procuring it for themselves. His duties would necessarily make him acquainted with the persons of the habitual vagrants; and to these it would be his duty to refuse relief, except in case of evident and urgent necessity.

"It was found necessary by the late Poor-law Commissioners at one time to remind the various unions and their officers of the responsibility which would be incurred by refusing relief where it was required. The present state of things renders it necessary that this Board should now impress on them the grievous mischiefs that must arise, and the responsibilities that may be incurred, by a too ready distribution of relief to tramps and vagrants not entitled to it. Boards of guardians and their officers may, in their attempts to restore a more wise and just system, be subjected to some obloquy from prejudices that confound poverty with profligacy. They will, however, be supported by the consciousness of discharging their duty to those whose funds they have to administer, as well as to the deserving poor, and of resisting the extension of a most pernicious and formidable abuse. They may confidently reckon on the support of public opinion, which the present state of things has aroused and enlightened; and those who are responsible to the Poor-law Board may feel assured that, while no instance of neglect or hardship to the poor will be tolerated, they may look to the Board for a candid construction of their acts and motives, and for a hearty and steadfast support of those who shall exert themselves to guard from the grasp of imposture that fund which should be sacred to the necessities of the poor."

Thus authorised and instructed to exercise their own discretion, rather than trust to the mere statements of the vagrants themselves, the officers immediately proceeded to act upon the suggestions given in the minute above quoted, and the consequence was, that the number of vagrants diminished more rapidly even than they had increased throughout the country. In the case of one union alone—the Wandsworth and Clapham—the following returns will show both how vagrancy was fostered under the one system, and how it has declined under the other:—

The number of vagrants admitted into the casual ward of Wandsworth and Clapham was,

In 1846	. . .	6,759
1847	. . .	11,322
1848	. . .	14,675
1849	. . .	3,900

In the quarter ending June 1848, previously to the issuing of the minute, the number admitted was 7325, whereas, in the quarter ending December, after the minute had been issued, the number fell to 1035.

The cost of relief for casuals at the same union in the year 1848 was 94l. 2s. 9½d.; in 1849 it was 24l. 10s. 1½d.

The decrease throughout all London has been equally striking. From the returns of the Poor-law Commissioners, as subjoined, I find that the total number of vagrants relieved in the metropolitan unions in 1847–48 was no less than 310,058, whereas, in the year 1848–49, it had decreased to the extent of 166,000 and odd, the number relieved for that year being only 143,064.

During the great prevalence of vagrancy, the cost of the sick was far greater than the expense of relief. In the quarter ending June 1848, no less than 322 casuals were under medical treatment, either in the workhouse of the Wandsworth and Clapham union or at the London Fever Hospital. The whole cost of curing the casual sick in 1848 was near upon 300l., whereas, during 1849 it is computed not to have exceeded 30l.

Another curious fact, illustrative of the effect of an alteration in the administration of the law respecting vagrancy, is to be found in the proportion of vagrants committed for acts of insubordination in the workhouses. In the year 1846, when those who broke the law were committed to Brixton, where the diet was better than that allowed at the workhouse—the cocoa and soup given at the treadmill being especial objects of attraction, and indeed the allowance of food being considerably higher there—the vagrants generally broke the windows, or tore their clothes, or burnt their beds, or refused to work, in order to be committed to the treadmill; and this got to such a height in that year, that no less than 467 persons were charged and convicted with disorderly conduct in the workhouse. In the year following, however, an alteration was made in the diet of prisoners sentenced to not more than fourteen days, and the prison of Kingston, of which they had a greater terror, was substituted for that of Brixton, and then the number of committals decreased from 467 to 57; while in 1848, when the number of vagrants was more than double what it had been in 1846, the committals again fell to 37; and in 1849, out of 3900 admissions, there were only 10 committed for insubordination.

VAGRANTS, OR TRAMPS, ADMITTED INTO THE WORKHOUSES OF THE METROPOLITAN DISTRICTS DURING THE YEARS 1847-8 AND 1848-9.

WORKHOUSES.	Population.	First Quarter, ending Christmas.		Second Quarter, ending Lady-day.		Third Quarter, ending Midsummer.		Fourth Quarter, ending Michaelmas.		TOTAL.	
		1847	1848	1848	1849	1848	1849	1848	1849	1848	1849
Kensington	26,830	3,502	2,667	1,369	1,233	5,580	7	4,125	10	14,866	3,917
Chelsea	40,177	2,480	4,507	1,985	4,146	2,604	5,189	2,849	1,357	9,918	15,199
Fulham	22,772	2,014	162	805	157	1,352	452	1,137	246	5,308	9,017
St. George, Hanover-square ...	66,453	50	...	10	...	...	...	...	...	60	...
St. Margaret's, Westminster...	56,481	1,514	2,575	2,973	1,809	2,100	1,815	2,339	1,211	8,926	7,410
St. Martin-in-the-Fields	25,195	3,875	847	3,637	428	2,718	536	...	12	10,230	1,823
St. James, Westminster	37,398	96	139	127	86	104	86	79	61	416	371
Marylebone	138,164	...	...	...	...	...	...	...	...	...	...
Paddington	25,173	48	1,450	566	1,455	1,438	1,525	1,176	948	3,228	5,378
Hampstead	10,093	...	...	...	...	...	...	...	...	...	...
St. Pancras	128,479	3,762	7,427	2,982	4,439	6,097	3,911	7,422	4,082	20,263	19,859
Islington	55,690	944	944	823	374	2,439	2,518	1,148	725	6,079	4,561
Hackney	42,274	89	210	76	123	280	308	245	192	690	833
St. Giles	54,292	106	174	106	132	100	86	244	189	556	581
Strand	43,894	663	62	1,063	6	3,040	...	63	...	4,829	68
Holborn	53,045	4,309	1,808	3,346	2,234	4,302	2,708	3,072	1,197	15,029	7,947
Clerkenwell	56,756	115	43	42	5	115	26	25	14	297	88
St. Luke's	49,829	691	575	841	1,086	1,258	1,251	1,293	497	4,083	3,409
East London	39,655	1,720	962	1,116	1,390	1,863	1,975	1,176	585	5,875	4,912
West London	33,629	3,915	2,481	2,873	2,279	3,966	2,914	3,264	2,103	14,018	9,777
London City	55,967	8,703	5,709	8,181	1,476	11,090	384	9,732	256	36,706	6,825
Shoreditch	83,432	959	1,585	721	1,274	1,121	1,954	1,399	1,108	4,200	5,921
Bethnal-green	74,087	291	441	315	227	454	538	501	415	1,561	1,620
Whitechapel	71,758	4,654	1,074	4,454	612	4,552	1,123	3,744	495	17,404	3,304
St. George-in-the-East	41,351	5,228	31	4,572	...	7,977	...	5,713	...	23,290	31
Stepney	90,657	4,229	4,801	4,318	3,428	6,564	3,984	6,243	1,656	21,354	12,869
Poplar	31,091	2,838	835	3,463	474	5,019	278	2,516	150	13,836	1,737
St. Saviour, Southwark	32,980	30	7	7	8	...	...	...	...	37	15
St. Olave	18,427	...	...	...	...	...	...	...	...	...	...
Bermondsey	34,947	...	...	...	...	...	...	...	...	...	...
St. George, Southwark	46,622	272	2,673	1,176	2,316	1,240	1,810	1,484	919	4,172	6,918
Newington	54,606	2,196	3,796	4,022	1,841	5,025	132	4,217	206	15,460	5,975
Lambeth	115,883	10,221	483	7,530	674	4,917	873	3,358	486	26,026	2,516
Wandsworth	39,853	2,444	784	3,374	1,257	5,730	1,344	1,858	463	13,406	3,848
Camberwell	39,867	907	768	706	463	1,625	793	1,122	80	4,360	2,104
Rotherhithe	13,916	375	445	161	439	309	917	353	826	1,288	2,627
Greenwich	80,811	2,977	283	2,436	384	4,761	481	4,908	256	15,082	1,404
Lewisham	23,013	13	2	4	...	18	7	43	3	78	12
Total		76,230	51,700	70,180	35,255	99,846	38,325	77,198	20,748	310,058	143,064

Of the character of the vagrants frequenting the unions in the centre of the metropolis, and the system pursued there, one description will serve as a type of the whole.

At the Holborn workhouse (St. Andrew's) there are two casual wards, established just after the passing of the Poor-law Amendment Act in 1834. The men's ward will contain 40, and the women's 20. The wards are underground, but dry, clean, and comfortable. When there was a "severe pressure from without," as a porter described it to me, as many as 106 men and women have been received on one night, but some were disposed in other parts of the workhouse away from the casual wards.

"Two years and a half ago, 'a glut of Irish'" (I give the words of my informant) "came over and besieged the doors incessantly; and when above a hundred were admitted, as many were remaining outside, and when locked out they lay in the streets stretched along by the almshouse close to the workhouse in Gray's-inn-lane." I again give the statement (which afterwards was verified) verbatim :—" They lay in camps," he said, "in their old cloaks, some having brought blankets and rugs with them for the purpose of sleeping out; pots, and kettles, and vessels for cooking when they camp; for in many parts of Ireland they do nothing—I've heard from people that have been there—but wander about; and these visitors to the workhouse behaved just like gipsies, combing their hair and dressing themselves. The girls' heads, some of them, looked as if they were full of caraway seeds—vermin, sir—shocking! I had to sit up all night; and the young women from Ireland—fine-looking young women; some of them finer-looking women than the English, well made and well formed, but uncultivated—seemed happy enough in the casual wards, singing songs all night long, but not too loud. Some would sit up all night washing their clothes, coming to me for water. They had a cup of tea, if they were poorly. They made themselves at home, the children did, as soon as they got inside; they ran about like kittens used to a place. The young women were often full of joke; but I never heard an indecent word from any of them, nor an oath, and I have no doubt, not in the least, that they were chaste and modest. Fine young women, too, sir. I have said, 'Pity young women like you should be carrying on this way' (for I felt for them), and they would say, 'What can we do? It's better than starving in Ireland, this workhouse is.' I used to ask them how they got over, and they often told me their passages were paid, chiefly to Bristol, Liverpool, and Newport, in Monmouthshire. They told me that was done to get rid of them. They told me that they didn't know by whom; but some said, they believed the landlord paid the captain. Some declared they knew it, and that it was done just to get rid of them. Others told me the captain would bring them over for any trifle they had; for he would say, 'I shall have to take you back again, and I can charge my price then.' The men were uncultivated fellows compared to the younger women. We have had old men with children who could speak English, and the old man and his wife could not speak a word of it. When asked the age of their children (the children were the interpreters), they would open the young creatures' mouths and count their teeth, just as horse-dealers do, and then they would tell the children in Irish what to answer, and the children would answer in English. The old people could never tell their own age. The man would give his name, but his wife would give her maiden name. I would say to an elderly man, 'Give me your name.' 'Dennis Murphy, your honour.' Then to his wife, 'And your name?' 'The widdy Mooney, your honour.' 'But you're married?' 'Sure, then, yes, by Father——.' This is the case with them still. Last night we took in a family, and I asked the mother—there was only a woman and three children—her name. 'The widdy Callaghan, indeed, then, sir.' 'But your Christian name?'' 'The widdy,' (widow,)' was the only answer. It's shocking, sir, what ignorance is, and what their sufferings is. My heart used to ache for the poor creatures, and yet they seemed happy. Habit's a great thing—second nature, even when people's shook. The Irishmen behaved well among themselves; but the English cadgers were jealous of the Irish, and chaffed them, as spoiling their trade—that's what the cadging fellows did. The Irish were quiet, poor things, but they were provoked to quarrel, and many a time I've had to turn the English rips out. The Irish were always very thankful for what they had, if it was only a morsel; the English cadger is never satisfied. I don't mean the decent beat-out man, but the regular cadger, that won't work, and isn't a good beggar, and won't starve, so they steal. Once, now and then, there was some suspicion about the Irish admitted, that they had money, but that was never but in those that had families. It was taken from them, and given back in the morning, They wouldn't have been admitted again if they had any amount. It was a kind-

ness to take their money, or the English rascals would have robbed them. I'm an Englishman, but I speak the truth of my own countrymen, as I do of the Irish. The English we had in the casual wards were generally a bad cadging set, as saucy as could be, particularly men that I knew, from their accent, came from Nottinghamshire. I'd tell one directly. I've heard them, of a night, brag of their dodges—how they'd done through the day—and the best places to get money. They would talk of gentlemen in London. I've often heard them say, ——, in Piccadilly, was good; but they seldom mentioned names, only described the houses, especially club-houses in St. James's-street. They would tell just where it was in the street, and how many windows there was in it, and the best time to go, and 'you're sure of grub,' they'd say. Then they'd tell of gentlemen's seats in the country—sure cards. They seldom give names, and, I believe, don't know them, but described the houses and the gentlemen. Some were good for bread and money, some for bread and ale. As to the decent people, we had but few, and I used to be sorry for them when they had to mix with the cadgers; but when the cadgers saw a stranger, they used their slang. I was up to it. I've heard it many a night when I sat up, and they thought I was asleep. I wasn't to be had like the likes o' them. The poor mechanic would sit like a lost man—scared, sir. There might be one deserving character to thirty cadgers. We have had gipsies in the casual wards; but they're not admitted a second time, they steal so. We haven't one Scotch person in a month, or a Welshman, or perhaps two Welshmen, in a month, among the casuals. They come from all counties in England. I've been told by inmates of 'the casual,' that they had got 2s. 6d. from the relieving officers, particularly in Essex and Suffolk — different unions—to start them to London when the 'straw-yards' (the asylums for the houseless) were opened; but there's a many very decent people. How they suffer before they come to that! you can't fancy how much; and so there should be straw-yards in a Christian land—we'll call it a Christian land, sir. There's far more good people in the straw-yards than the casuals; the dodgers is less frequent there, considering the numbers. It's shocking to think a decent mechanic's houseless. When he's beat out, he's like a bird out of a cage; he doesn't know where to go, or how to get a bit—but don't the cadgers!" The expense of relieving the people in the casual ward was twopence per head, and the numbers admitted for the last twelve months averaged only twelve nightly."

I will now give the statements of some of the inmates of the casual wards themselves. I chose only those at first who were habitual vagrants.

ESTIMATE OF NUMBERS AND COST OF VAGRANTS.

LET me first endeavour to arrive at some estimate as to the number and cost of the vagrant population.

There were, according to the returns of the Poor-law Commissioners, 13,547 vagrants relieved in and out of the workhouses of England and Wales, on the 1st of July, 1848. In addition to these, the Occupation Abstract informs us that, on the night of the 6th of June, 1841, when the last census was taken, 20,348 individuals were living in barns and tents. But in order to arrive at a correct estimate of the total number of vagrants throughout the country, we must add to the above numbers the inmates of the trampers' houses. Now, according to the Report of the Constabulary Commissioners, there were in 1839 a nightly average of very nearly 5000 vagrants infesting some 700 mendicants' lodging-houses in London and six other of the principal towns of England and Wales. (See " London Labour," Vol. I. p. 408.) Further, it will be seen by the calculations given at the same, that there are in the 3823 postal towns throughout the country (averaging two trampers' houses to each town, and ten trampers nightly to each house), and 76,400 other vagrants distributed throughout England and Wales.

Hence the calculation as to the total number of vagrants would stand thus :—

In the workhouses . . .	13,547
In barns and tents (according to census)	20,348
In the mendicants' houses of London, and six other principal towns of England and Wales, according to Constabulary Commissioners' Report . . .	4,813
Ditto in 3820 other postal towns, averaging each two mendicants' houses, and ten lodgers to each house	76,400
	115,108
Deduct five per cent for characters really destitute and deserving .	5,755
Total number of habitual vagrants in England and Wales	109,353

The cost of relieving these vagrants may be computed as follows : — On the night of the 1st of July, 1848, there were 13,547 vagrants relieved throughout England and Wales ; but I am informed by the best authorities on the subject, that one-third of this number only can be fairly estimated as receiving relief every night throughout the year at the different unions. Now, the third of 13,547 is 4515,

and this, multiplied by 365, gives 1,647,975 as the total number of cases of vagrancy relieved throughout England and Wales during the year 1848. The cost of each of these is estimated at twopence per head per night for food, and this makes the sum expended in their relief amount to 13,733*l.* 7*s.* 8*d.*

In addition to this, we must estimate the sum given in charity to the mendicants, or carried off surreptitiously by the petty thieves frequenting the tramping-houses. The sums thus abstracted from the public may be said to amount at the lowest to 6*d.* per day for each of the trampers not applying for relief at the workhouses. In the Constabulary Report, p. 11, the earnings of the petty thieves are estimated at 10*s.* per week, and those of the beggars at 3*s.* 6*d.* per day (p. 24). Hence we have the following account of the total cost of the vagrants of England and Wales :—

	£	s.	d.
Sum given in relief to the vagrants at the workhouses	13,733	7	8
Sum abstracted by them, either by begging or pilfering on the road . .	138,888	11	8
	£152,621	19	4
As five per cent must be taken off this for the truly deserving . . .	7,631	1	8
The total cost will be .	£144,990	17	8

By this it appears that the total number of professional vagrants dispersed throughout England and Wales amounts to 47,669. These live at the expense of the industrious classes, and cost the country no less than 144,990*l.* 17*s.* 8*d.* per annum. And if the 13,000 and odd vagrants relieved in the workhouses constitute merely the twentieth dispersed throughout the country, we have in round numbers nearly 3,000,000*l.* for the cost of the whole.

There are, then, no less than 100,000 individuals of the lowest, the filthiest, and most demoralised classes, continually wandering through the country ; in other words, there is a stream of vice and disease—a tide of iniquity and fever, continually flowing from town to town, from one end of the land to the other.

" One of the worst concomitants of vagrant mendicancy," says the Poor-law Report, " is the fever of a dangerous typho:.. character, which has universally marked the path of the mendicants. There is scarcely a workhouse in which this pestilence does not prevail in a greater or less degree, and numerous union officers have fallen victims to it." Those who are acquainted with the exceeding filth of the persons frequenting the casual wards, will not wonder at the fever which follows in the wake of the vagrants. "Many have the itch. I have seen," says Mr. Boase, "a party of twenty almost all scratching themselves at once, before settling into their rest in the straw. Lice exist in great numbers upon them."

That vagrancy is the nursery of crime, and that the habitual tramps are first the beggars, then the thieves, and, finally, the convicts of the country, the evidence of all parties goes to prove. There is, however, a curious corroboration of the fact to be found, by referring to the period of life at which both crime and vagrancy seem to be in their youth. The ages of the vagrants frequenting the asylums for the houseless poor, are chiefly between fifteen and twenty-five years old; and the tables of the ages of the criminals, given in the Government Returns, show that the majority of persons convicted of crime are equally young.

The total number of vagrants in the metropolis may be calculated as follows:—There were 310,058 vagrants relieved at the metropolitan unions during the year 1848. (I take the metropolitan returns of 1848, because those for England and Wales published as yet only extend to that year.) As the vagrants never remain two days in the same place, we must divide this number by 365, in order to ascertain the number of vagrants resident at one and the same time in London. This gives us 849 for the average number relieved each night in the whole of the metropolitan unions. To this we must add the 2431 tramps residing in the 221 metropolitan mendicants' lodging-houses (averaging 11 inmates each); and the sum of these must be further increased by the 750 individuals relieved nightly at the asylums for the houseless poor (including that of Market-street, Edgeware-road), for the majority of these seldom or never make their appearance in the casual wards of the metropolis, but are attracted to London solely by the opening of the asylums. Hence the account will stand as follows:—

Average number of vagrants relieved night in the metropolitan unions	849
Average number of vagrants resident in the mendicants' lodging-houses in London	2431
Average number of individuals relieved at the metropolitan asylums for the houseless poor	750
	4030

Now, as 5 per cent of this amount is said to consist of characters really destitute and deserving, we arrive at the conclusion that there are 3829 vagrants in London, living either by mendicancy or theft.

The cost of the vagrants in London in the year 1848 may be estimated as follows:—

	£	s.	d.
310,058 vagrants relieved at the metropolitan unions, at the cost of 2*d.* per head	2,584	13	0
67,500 nights' lodgings afforded to the houseless poor at the metropolitan asylums, including the West-end Asylum, Market-street, Edgeware road	3,134	1	4½
2,431 inmates of the mendicants' lodging-houses in London, gaining upon an average 1*s.* per day, or altogether per year	44,365	15	0
	£59,084	9	4½
Deduct 5 per cent for the cost of the relief of the truly deserving	2,504	4	5

The total will then be . £47,580 4 11½

It appears, then, that there are 3829 habitual vagrants in the metropolis, and the cost for their support annually amounts to 47,580*l.* 4*s.* 11½*d.*

The number of metropolitan beggars is considerably increased on the eve of any threatened disturbances, or any large open-air meeting in London. For several days previous to the Chartist display in 1848, there was an influx of 100 tramps over and above the ordinary quantity, each day, at one union alone in the suburbs of London; and the master assured me that on the night of the meeting on Kennington Common, he overheard the inmates of the casual ward boasting how they had assisted in pillaging the pawnbroker's house that had been broken into that afternoon.

Well might the master of the Wandsworth and Clapham Union say, therefore, that the vagrants form one of the most restless, discontented, vicious, and dangerous elements of society. Of these we have seen that there are about 100,000 dispersed throughout the country, 4000 of whom, in round numbers, are generally located in London. These constitute, in the words of the same gentleman, the main source from which the criminals are continually recruited and augmented.

ROUTES OF THE VAGRANTS.

I was desirous of ascertaining some information concerning the routes of the vagrants, and the reason why they frequent one district or county more than another. It will be seen from the following table, computed from the Poor-Law Returns for the 1st July, 1848, that the vagrants were far from equally distributed over the country at that period.

NUMBER OF VAGRANTS RELIEVED IN THE DIFFERENT COUNTIES OF ENGLAND AND WALES ON THE 1st OF JULY, 1848.

Durham	.	. 1425	Essex .	. .	. 147	Oxfordshire . . .	46
Middlesex	.	. 1393	Northamptonshire		. 136	Carmarthenshire . .	46
Lincolnshire	.	. 1355	Wiltshire	.	. 135	Radnorshire . . .	46
West Riding	.	. 1197	Westmoreland	.	. 130	Denbighshire . .	45
Cumberland	.	. 1087	Nottinghamshire .		. 129	Dorsetshire . . .	43
Lancashire	.	. 673	Norfolk .	. .	. 128	Cardiganshire . .	39
Southampton	.	. 648	North Riding	.	. 105	Carnarvonshire . .	38
Derbyshire .	.	. 541	Bedfordshire	.	. 102	Buckinghamshire . .	28
Warwickshire	.	. 509	Hertfordshire	.	. 100	Suffolk	21
Monmouthshire	.	. 475	Devonshire .	.	. 94	Cambridgeshire . .	20
Staffordshire	.	. 351	Cheshire	.	. 92	Brecknockshire . .	17
Surrey .	.	. 319	Somersetshire	.	. 88	Pembrokeshire . .	15
Glamorganshire	.	. 244	Shropshire .	.	. 80	Montgomeryshire . .	14
Worcestershire	.	. 227	Huntingdonshire .		. 75	Anglesea . . .	11
Kent .	. .	. 179	Leicestershire	.	. 72	Flintshire . . .	10
Berkshire	.	. 175	Cornwall	. .	. 63	Rutlandshire . .	6
Northumberland	.	. 172	Merionethshire	.	. 54		
East Riding .	.	. 152	Gloucestershire	.	. 52	Total . .	13,547
Sussex .	. .	. 150	Herefordshire	.	. 48		

In order to discover the cause of this unequal distribution, I sought out a person, whom I knew to be an experienced tramper, and who had offered to give any information that I might require upon the subject. There was a strange mystery about the man. It was evident, both from his manner and his features, that he had once been well to do in the world. He was plainly not of the common order of vagrants, though his dress was as filthy and ragged as that of the generality of the class.

"I have been right through the country on the tramp," he said, "about six or seven summers. What I was formerly I do not wish to state. I have been much better off. I was, indeed, in receipt of a very large income at one time; but it matters not how I lost it. I would rather that remained a secret. You may say that I lost it through those follies and extravagancies that are incident both to the higher and the lower classes; but let it pass. You want to know about the habits and characters of the vagrants generally, and there is no necessity for my going into my private history, further than saying, I was a gentleman once, and I am a vagrant now. I have been so for the last six years. I generally start off into the country about April or May. I stay, after the refuges are closed, until such time as I have tired out all the unions in and around London. I go into the country because I am known at all the casual wards in the metropolis, and they will not let a tramper in a second time if they know it, except at the City of London, and there I have been allowed to stay a month together. The best of the casual wards used to be in Bermondsey, but they are closed there now, I believe, as well as many of the others ; however, the vagrants seldom think of going to the London unions

until after the refuges are closed, because at the refuges the accommodation is better, and no work is required. I know that the vagrants come purposely to London in large bodies about the end of December, on purpose to sleep at the refuges for the winter. I myself always make it a point to come up to town every winter, so as to have my lodgings for nothing at the refuge, not being able to get it by any other means. There are at the refuges, of course, many worthy objects of charity. I have met with men who have become destitute, certainly not through any fault of their own; a good many of such persons I have found. But still the greater number at such places are persons who are habitual vagabonds and beggars, and many thieves. As the refuges are managed at present, I consider they do more harm than good. If there were no such places in London in the winter, of course I, and such as are like me, would have been driven to find shelter at our parishes; whereas the facilities they afford for obtaining a night's shelter—to the vagabond as well as to the destitute—are such that a large number of the most depraved and idle classes are attracted to London by them. I believe some such places to be necessary, in order to prevent persons dying of cold and starvation in the streets, but they should be conducted on a different plan. You see I tell you the truth, although it may be against my own interest. After these refuges are closed, and the unions round the suburbs are shut against me, as far as Richmond, Kingston, Bromley, Romford, Stratford, Greenwich, and similar distances from the metropolis, I generally proceed upon my travels for the summer. Those who make a practice of sleeping at the casual wards are vagrants either by nature, by habit, or by force of circumstances. They generally support themselves by begging or thieving, and often by both. They are mostly boys, from about nine up to twenty years of age. The others are principally Irish beggars, and a very few are labourers and mechanics out of work. The youths I believe to be, with some exceptions, naturally bad, and almost irreclaimable. I know that many of them have been made vagrants by harsh treatment at home; they have run away. They have been threatened to be punished, generally for going to some place of amusement, as Greenwich fair, or 'penny gaffs,'—that is, to the low theatres; and, being afraid to return, they have sought shelter, first at the low lodging-houses, and when they have had no money left, they have gone to the casual wards of the unions. Other boys have contracted bad habits from being allowed by their parents to run about the streets and pick up vagabond companions. These soon initiate them into their mode of life, and they then leave their homes in order to follow it. This is the way that most of the lads are depraved. I am sure that the fault lies more with the parents than with the boys themselves. The lads are either neglected or ill-treated in their youth. Some of the lads are left destitute; they are left orphans — probably to the care of some distant relation or friend — and the lads very soon find that they are not treated or cared for like the other members of the family, and they take to the streets. The majority of the vagrants are very sharp, intelligent lads, and I believe they are induced to take to a vagabond life by the low lodging-houses, the casual wards, and the refuges. These make shelter and provision so easy to them, that they soon throw off the restraint of their parents or guardians. Were there a greater difficulty of obtaining food and lodging, I am sure that there would certainly not be the number of juvenile vagrants that there are. The Irish people who resort to the casual wards are beggars at heart and soul. Many of them I know have lodgings of their own, and they will give them up at the time the refuges are open. Some I have known to go into the refuge with the whole of their family on the Saturday night, and stop all Sunday, till the Monday morning, for the express purpose of obtaining the bread and cheese which is given away there on the Sunday. The children have the same allowance as the parents, and the mother and father take all the young ones they can into the place, to get the greater quantity. This they take back home with them, and it serves to keep them the greater part of the week. The Irish, I think, do not make a point of travelling the country so much as the English vagrants. When they go into the provinces, it is generally to get work at harvesting, or 'tato getting, or hop-picking; not like the English, for the mere sake of vagabondising.

"The low Irish do better in London. They are the best beggars we have. They have more impudence and more blarney, and therefore they do much better than we can at it. A very large portion of the Irish beggars in London are in possession of money, which they have secreted about them in some way or other. I recollect seeing one Irishman have 8s. taken from him by the vagrant boys in the casual ward of St. George's Workhouse, in the Borough. The boys generally suspect the Irish vagrants of having money on their persons; and I have often seen a number of them hold, or, as they call it, 'small-gang,' an Irish beggar in the darkness of the casual wards, while some of the other boys rifled the Irishman's pockets. The labourers and mechanics are generally the only parties to be found in casual wards who are driven there through destitution. I have known many an honest, industrious, working man, however, made a regular beggar and vagrant by continued use of the casual wards. They are driven there first by necessity, and then they learn that they can live in such places throughout the year without working for their livelihood. Many a hard-working man, I am convinced, is made idle and dishonest by such means: yes, that is the case. There are some that I know now, who have been going the round of the different refuges for not less than seven — ay, you may say for nine years. They were originally labouring men, or mechanics, and had given over all thoughts of working, finding that there was no necessity to do so in order to live.

"The regular vagrant leaves town every year about April, or the beginning of May. A very large portion of the wandering beggars and thieves would remain in town if they were allowed to remain longer in their nightly haunts; but after the closing of the refuges, the system of not permitting them more than one night in the same union forces them to be continually on the move: so they set off immediately they have made themselves known at all the workhouses. The boys will mostly go in small gangs of twos and threes. Before they start, they generally pick up from some other gang whom they meet in the London wards, the kind of treatment and relief they will receive at the country unions, and they regulate their journey accordingly; and they will very often go one or two days' march out of their way, in order to avoid some union that has a bad character among them, or to get to some other union where the accommodation is good, and the work required of them very slight. Often they will go miles round to get to some gentleman's seat or hall where provisions are known to be distributed. I have heard boys not twelve years of age tell every union between London and Newcastle. The majority of them seldom go further than there; some will go on to Edinburgh, but not many. They would know what kind of treatment and provision would be obtained at each union, and what form of application was necessary in order to gain admittance. Very many of them will go from London, first into Essex (the unions are good there, and the stages not long); then perhaps through Suffolk, keeping tolerably near the coast, because the shipping is attractive to most boys of their age ; thence they will proceed, by long or short stages, according to the distance of the unions, through Lincolnshire and Yorkshire. Few of the vagrants miss Leeds, there being a Mendicity Asylum in the town, where a good night's lodging is given to them, and threepence or fourpence, and in some cases sixpence (according to the apparent worthiness of the applicant) is bestowed upon each. I believe the habitual vagrants will go three or four stages out of the direct road to make Leeds in their way. From here they will go in different directions towards Durham and Northumberland, or, perhaps, to Manchester, where there is a society of the same kind as at Leeds, supported by the Quakers, where similar relief is afforded. At Northumberland, the body of vagrants generally turn back and begin to steer southwards. Some, indeed, will go as far as Berwick; but as the relief afforded in Scotland is not obtained so readily as in England, they seldom, as I have said, proceed northward beyond that point. The Scotch are 'too far north' for the regular English tramps. It is true they sometimes give them a little barley-cake, but, from all I have heard, the vagrants fare very poorly beyond Berwick. From Northumberland, they turn off towards Cumberland, Westmoreland, and Lancashire; and then many will go off through Cheshire into North Wales, and thence come round again into Shropshire. Others will wander through Staffordshire and Derbyshire, but most of them centre in Birmingham ; that is a favourite meeting-place for the young vagrants. Here they make a point of tearing up their clothes, because for this offence they are committed to Warwick gaol for a month, and have a shilling on being discharged from the prison. It is not the diet of Warwick gaol that induces them to do this, but the shilling. Frequently they tear up their clothes in order to get a fresh supply. You see, sir, from continually sleeping in their clothes, and never washing their bodies, or changing their shirts—even if they have such things to change—they get to swarm with vermin, to such an extent that they cannot bear them upon their bodies. Oh ! I have seen such sights sometimes—such sights as any decent, cleanly person would not credit. I have seen the lice on their clothes in the sunshine, as thick as blight on the leaves of trees. When their garments, from this cause, get very uncomfortable to them, they will tear them up, for the purpose of forcing the parish officers to give them some fresh ones. From Birmingham they will come up, generally through Northampton and Hertford, to London ; for by this time either the

refuges will be about opening, or the lads will have been forgotten at the unions in and around the metropolis. They say that London is fresh to them, when, owing either to long absence, or some alteration in their appearance, they are looked upon as strangers by the masters or porters of the workhouses. London, on the other hand, they say, is dead to them, when they have become too well known at such places. Some will make only a short turn out of London, going across the country through Sussex, Hampshire, or Wiltshire. Hampshire they are attracted to in large numbers, in consequence of the charity distributed at Winchester." [It will be seen by the table above given, that Southampton stands very high among the places upon the vagrant list.] " In these parts the vagrants keep crossing the country to various 'reliefs,' as they call it, and so manage to spin out nearly two months in the autumn. The vagrants mostly go down with the fashionables to the sea-side in the latter part of the year—the practised beggars in particular. In the spring they generally make for the north of England. I believe there are more beggars and tramps in Durham, Lincolnshire, and Yorkshire, than in half of the other parts of England put together." . . . . . " Begging is more profitable there than in any other quarter of the kingdom. A man may pick up more provisions in the day-time in those counties than anywhere else. The farmers are more liberal in those parts, which are great places for pudding, pies, and cakes ; and of these the young tramps are remarkably fond. Round about these parts the tramps pass the summer. If the weather is fine and mild, they prefer ' skippering it,' that is, sleeping in an outhouse or hay-field, to going to a union. They have no trouble in getting ' scran,' or provisions there, and they object to the work connected with the casual wards. In the autumn, they are mostly in Sussex or Kent; for they like the hop-picking. It is not hard work, and there are a great many loose girls to be found there. I believe many a boy and man goes hop-picking who never does anything else during the year but beg. The female tramps mostly go down to Kent to pick up their ' young chaps,' as they call them ; and with them they travel through the country as long as they can agree, or until either party meets with some one they are better pleased with, and then they leave the other, or bury them, as they term it.

" The Irish vagrants are mostly to be found on the roads from Liverpool or from Bristol to London. I should think that at the end of June the roads must be literally covered with the Irish families tramping to London. They come over in boatsful, without a penny in their pockets, to get a little work during the harvesting and hop-picking. Such of them as make up their minds to return to their country after the autumn, contrive, by some means, to send their money to Ireland, and then they apply to the English parishes to send them home. It is very rare indeed that the low Irish go to the expense of paying for their lodging, even when they have money. They make a point of going to the unions, where they not only get a nightly shelter, but a pound of bread for nothing. Whatever money they have, they generally give to some countryman, who is their banker, and he sleeps in another place, for fear he should be searched or robbed at the casual wards. The Irish are mostly very filthy and diseased. They live upon little or nothing, and upon the worst kind of provision that can be bought, even though it be not fit for human food. They will eat anything. The Irish tramp lives solely by begging. It has often astonished me, sir, that there are scarcely any Welsh tramps. I suppose this comes from the industry of the people. The English tramp lives by begging and stealing, —I think, mostly by stealing; a thorough tramp gets more that way than the other. If he goes to the back-door of a house on the pretence of begging, and sees any linen, or brushes, or shoes, or, indeed, even a bit of soap, he will be off with it, and sell it, mostly to the keeper of some low lodging-house where he may put up for the night. They seldom commit highway robberies, and are generally the very lowest and meanest of thieves. No one can imagine, but those who have gone through it, the horror of a casual ward of a union; what with the filth, the vermin, the stench, the heat, and the noise of the place, it is intolerable. The usual conversation is upon the adventures of the day. One recounts how he stole this thing, and another that. Some tell what police are stationed in the different towns; others, what places to go to either to beg, rob, or sleep; and others, what places to beware of. I have passed seven years of my life in this way, and I have been so used to tramping about, that when the spring comes round I must be on the move. In the winter there is more food to be picked up in London than in the country, and the beggars seldom fail to make a good thing of it in the cold weather. I have met with beggars in Carnarvon who had come all the way from London for the express purpose of begging from the visitors to the Snowdon mountains. There are very few houses round about, but a good deal is picked up from the company coming to the hotels."

I shall now conclude this account of the numbers, cost, and character of the country and the metropolis, with the narratives of two female tramps.

The first—a young woman 20 years of age —gave me the following statement. Her face was what the vulgar would call "good-looking," as her cheeks were full and deep-coloured, and her eyes tolerably bright, and her teeth good. She was very stout, too. Her dress was tolerably clean and good, but sat close about her, as if she had no under-clothing. She said:—

"I am a native of ——, where my father was a woolcomber. I was an only child. I can't remember my mother, she died when I was so young. My father died more than four years ago. I've heard as much since I left home. I was sent to the National School. I can read, but can't write. My father went to work at Wellington, in Somersetshire, taking me with him, when I was quite a little girl. He was a good father and very kind, and we had plenty to eat. I think of him sometimes: it makes me sorrowful. He would have been sadly distressed if he had seen me in this state. My father married again when I was 12, I suppose. He married a factory-woman. She was about 30. She wasn't good to me, She led me a dreadful life, always telling my father stories of me,— that I was away when I wasn't, and he grumbled at me. He never beat me, but my stepmother often beat me. She was very bad-tempered, and I am very bad-tempered, too—very passionate; but if I'm well treated my passion doesn't come out. She beat me with anything that came first to hand, as the hearth-brush, and she flung things at me. She disliked me, because she knew I hated my father marrying again. I was very happy before that, living with my father. I could cook dinner for him, young as I was, make his bed, and do all those sort of things, all but his washing. I had a bed to myself. My father was a good man. He came home drunk sometimes, but not often. It never made any difference in him, he was always kind. He seemed comfortable with my stepmother, but I wasn't. I used to tell my father how she used me, but he said it was nonsense. This went on till I was 15, when I ran away. I'm sure I had been a good girl till then. I never slept out of my father's house up to that time, and didn't keep company with any young men. I could stand my stepmother's treatment no longer. If she had been kind I wouldn't have run away. I was almost as big then as I am now. I had 4s. or 5s. with me, I don't remember just how much, I started in such a passion; but it was money I had saved up from what my father had given me. I took no clothes with me but what I had on. I was tidily dressed. It was in the haymaking time, and I made straight away to London. I was so young and in such a rage, I couldn't think of nothing but getting away. When I cooled I began to think of my father, but at home I had heard of young girls being sent out to Australia and having done well, and I thought I could easily get sent out from London, and so I went on. I slept in lodging-houses. I was shocked the first night I got into Bridgewater, men, women, and boys, all sleeping in the same room. I slept with another young woman, a travelling-woman, but married. I couldn't think of going back. I couldn't humble myself before that stepmother. I thought anything would be better than that. I couldn't sleep at all the first night I was out. I never was in such a bed before. A young man who saw me there wanted me to live with him; he was a beggar, and I didn't like a beggar, and I wouldn't have nothing to say to him. He wasn't impudent; but he followed me to Bristol, all the time, whenever I met with him, teasing me to live with him. I lived on my money as long as I could, and then had to go and sleep in a union. I don't know where. It was a dreadful place. The rats ran over my head while I slept; and I prayed for daylight—for I used to pray then. I don't now. I don't like the thoughts of it. At last I got to London. I was sitting in Hyde-park thinking where I should go—I know it was in Hyde-park, for I was taken up from it since. The park-keeper took me up for making a noise—that's a disturbance—in the park; me and some other young women: we were only washing ourselves where the horses drink, near the canteen. In Hyde-park, while I was sitting, as I've told you, some girls and some young men, and some older men, passed me, carrying rakes. I was sitting with three other girls I'd got acquainted with on the road, all Irish girls. The people that passed me said, 'We are going half-way to Watford a-haymaking. Go with us?' We all went. Each of those Irish girls soon took up with a mate. I think they had known each other before. I had a fortnight at haymaking. I had a mate at haymaking, and in a few days he ruined me. He told the master that I belonged to him. He didn't say I was his wife. They don't call us their wives. I continued with him a long time, living with him as his wife. We next went into Kent harvesting, then a-hopping, and I've been every summer since. He was kind to me, but we were both pas-sionate — fire against fire — and we fought sometimes. He never beat me but once, for contradicting him. He wasn't jealous, and he had no reason to be so. I don't know that he was fond of me, or he wouldn't have run away. I liked him, and would have gone through trouble for him. I like him still. We never talked about marrying. I didn't care, for I didn't think about it. I lived with him, and was true to him, until he ran away in hay-making time in 1848. He ran away from me in Kent, where we were hopping. We hadn't quarrelled for some days before he started. I didn't think he was going, for he was kind to me just before. I left him once for a fort-night myself, through some quarrel, but he got me back again. I came up to London in a boat from Gravesend, with other hoppers. I lived on fifteen shillings I had saved up. I lived on that as long as it lasted—more than a week. I lodged near the Dials, and used to go drinking with other women I met with there, as I was fond of drink then. I don't like it so much now. We drank gin and beer. I kept to myself until my money was gone, and then I looked out for myself. I had no particular friends. The women I drank with were some bad and some good. I got ac-quainted with a young girl as I was walking along the Strand looking out for my living by prostitution — I couldn't starve. We walked together. We couldn't stay in the Strand, where the girls were well-dressed, and so we kept about the Dials. I didn't think much about the life I was leading, because I got hardened. I didn't like it, though. Still I thought I should never like to go home. I lodged in a back-street near the Dials. I couldn't take anybody there. I didn't do well. I often wanted money to pay my lodgings, and food to eat, and had often to stay out all night perishing. Many a night out in the streets I never got a farthing, and had to walk about all day because I durstn't go back to my room without money. I never had a fancy man. There was all sorts in the lodging-house— thirty of them—pickpockets, and beggars, and cadgers, and fancy men, and some that wanted to be fancy men, but I never saw one that I liked. I never picked pockets as other girls did; I was not nimble enough with my hands. Sometimes I had a sovereign in my pocket, but it was never there a day. I used to go out a-drinking, treating other women, and they would treat me. We helped one another now and then. I was badly off for clothes. I had no illness except colds. The common fellows in the streets were always jeering at me. Sometimes missionaries, I think they're called, talked to me about the life I was leading, but I told them, 'You mind yourself, and I'll mind myself. What is it to you where I go when I die?' I don't steal anything. I swear some-times now. When I was at home and good, I was shocked to hear such a thing. Me and the other girls used to think it clever to swear hard, and say bad words one to another or to anybody—we're not particular. If I went into the Magdalen, I know I couldn't stay there. I have not been there, but I know I couldn't, from what I've heard of it from the other girls, some of whom said they'd been; and I suppose they had, as there was no motive at all for them to tell lies about it. I have been in the casual wards at Holborn and Kensington when I was beat out. It was better than walk-ing the streets. I think, by the life I lead— and without help I must lead it still, or starve —I sometimes get twenty shillings a-week, sometimes not more than five shillings. I would like best to go to Australia, where no-body would know me. I'm sure I could be-have myself there. There's no hope for me here: everybody that knows me despises me. I could take a service in Sydney. I could get rid of my swearing. I only swear now when I'm vexed—it comes out natural-like then. I could get rid of my love of drink. No one— no girl can carry on the life I do without drink. No girl's feelings would let her. I never met one but what said so, and I know they all told the truth in that. I am strong and healthy, and could take a hard place with country work. That about Australia is the best wish I have. I'm sure I'm sick of this life. It has only drink and excitement to recommend it. I haven't a friend in the world. I have been told I was a fool not to pick pockets like other girls. I never begged but once, and that was as I was coming to London, and a woman said, 'You look better than I do!' so I never begged again—that checked me at once. But I've got tickets for the 'straw-yards,' or the 'leather-houses,' as some call them (asylums for the houseless). The old women all say it was far better when they were young. I think what a change it is from my country life; but when I get sad, I go and get a glass of gin, if I have the money. I can get a pennyworth in some houses. I can't do much at my needle. The idleness of the life I lead is terrible. There is nothing to interest me."

The next was a mere girl, who had lost all traces of feminine beauty. There was an impudence in her expression that was utterly repulsive; and even in her most serious moments it was evident that she had the greatest difficulty to restrain her inward levity. Her dress consisted principally of a ragged red and green plaid shawl, pinned tight over her neck, and a torn straw-bonnet, worn back upon her head.

" I have a father alive," she said; " I have got no mother. I have been away these three years. I came away with a chap. I was living, sir, when I was at home, with my father in Maidstone. My father was a gardener, and I used to work at shirt-making when I was at home with my father. My mother has been dead eight years, I think. I can't say how old I was then. I am twenty now. My father, after my mother's death, married again. She was dead seven years before he got another wife. He didn't marry again while I was at home. My mother was a very good mother. I was very fond of my mother, for she was a very good mother; but not of my father, for he was a bad father. Why, sir, he used to treat us three girls so ill, my biggest sister was obliged to go to Australia from him. My next sister was younger than me, and I don't know whether she is at home now; but I don't believe that she can stop at home, because I have been down as far as Maidstone since I went away with my young man, and I've heard that she's almost dead between the pair of them. By the pair of them, I mean my father and stepmother. My mother-in-law is the worst to my sister. My father was bad before she came; he was such a drunkard. We went to school, where we paid nothing a-week, in Maidstone; it's a free school. I can read. I can't write. All the money my father used to earn he used to drink, and leave us without any food. I went to the shirt-making when I was twelve years of age, and that used to

bring me about 4d. a-day, and with that I used to buy bread, for we never got a halfpenny from my father to keep us. My father used to work for a gentleman, and got pretty good wages. The young chap that I first took up with was a carpenter. He was apprenticed to the trade. He enticed me away. He told me if I'd come to London with him he'd do anything for me. I used to tell him how badly my father treated me, and he used to tell me not to stop at home. I have been knocking about three years, and I'm twenty now, so I leave you to say how old I was then. No, I can't say. I'm twenty now, and I've been away these three years, and I don't know how old that would make me. I never learnt any ciphering. My father used to beat us and knock us about when he came home drunk. I liked the young man that came a-courting on me very well. I thought all he said was true, and I thought he would make me much happier than I was at home." [Here she shook her head with apparent regret.] " Yes, sir, he promised he would marry me; but when I came over to London he ruined me, and then ran away and left me. I knew it was wrong to go away and live with him without being married; but I was wretched at home, and he told me he would make me his wife, and I believed him. He brought me up to London with him, into the Borough. He took me to a low lodging-house there. The charge was 6d. a-night for the two of us. There were six sleeping in the same room beside us two. They were men and women. Some of 'em were married, and some were not. He had 4s. 6d. when he came up to London with me, and I had none. He stopped with me. He stopped with me in the same house a week. He was 22 years of age, or 23, I can't say which. While he was with me he was very kind to me: oh, yes, sir, much kinder than my father, and I loved him a great deal more, I'm sure. I hadn't many clothes when I left my father's home. I had nothing but what I stood upright in. I had no more clothes when I was at home. When my young man left me there was another young girl in the same lodging-house, who advised me to turn out upon the streets. I went and took her advice. I did like the life for a bit, because I see'd there was money getting by it. Sometimes I got 4s. or 5s. a-day, and sometimes more than that. I still kept at the same house. There were a lot of girls like me at the same place. It was not a bad house, but they encouraged us like. No tramps used to come there, only young chaps and gals that used to go out thieving. No, my young man didn't thieve, not while he was with me, but I did afterwards. I've seen young chaps brought in there by the girls merely to pay their lodging-money. The landlady told us to do that; she said I could do better than knocking about with a man. If I hadn't had enough to pay for my lodging, I couldn't have had a bed to lie on. We used to be all in the same room, chaps and girls, sometimes nine or ten couples in the same room—only little bits of girls and chaps. I have seen girls there 12 years of age. The boys was about 15 or 16. They used to swear dreadful. I fell out with the gal as first told me to go on the streets, and then I got with another at another house. I moved to Paddington. I lived at a little public-house there—a bad house; and I used to go out shoplifting with my pal. I used to take everything I could lay my hands on. We went one night, and I stole two dresses, at a linendraper's shop, and had two months a-piece for it. Yes, sir, I liked prison very well, because I had such bad clothes; and was glad to be out of the way. Some days we hardly had a bit to put in our mouths. Sometimes we used to get nothing shoplifting; the men, perhaps, would notice—the fly-men, as we called them. They used to be too wide-awake for us. Sometimes we used to make 5s. in the day; but then we used to spend it all in waste —why, spending it in anything. We'd buy fish, and meat, and baked potatoes, and pudding. No, sir, very little drink we had. We didn't care for gin, nor any liquor at all. There was none among us but one that cared for drink, and she used to pawn all her clothes for it. I dare say there was upwards of twelve or thirteen gals; the kitchen used to be full. The mistress used to treat us well if we paid her; but she used to holler at us if we didn't. The chaps used to serve her out so. They used to take the sheets, and blankets, and everything away from her. She was deaf. They was mostly all prigs that used to come to see us. They used to go out nailing—that's thieving. There was one that they used to call Fogerty was transported: another got seven months; and another got a twelvemonth. I had one fancy-man. He was a shoplifter and a pickpocket: he has got two years now. I went to see him once in quod; some calls it 'the Steel.' I cried a good deal when he got nailed, sir: I loved him. A little time after he went away, I went down into the country; down into Essex. I saw I couldn't get him off, 'cause it was for a watch, and the gentleman went so hard against him. I was with him at the time he stole it, but I didn't know he'd got it till I saw him run. I got the man down by a saw-mill; he was tipsy. He was a gentleman, and said he would give me five shillings if I would come along with him. My fancy-man always kept near to me whenever I went out of a night. I usen't to go out to take the men home; it was only to pick them up. My young man used to tell me how to rob the men. I'd get them up in a corner, and then I used to take out of their pockets whatever I could lay my hands on; and then I used to hand it over to him, and he used to take the things home and 'fence' them. We used to do a good deal this way sometimes: often we'd get enough to keep us two or three days. At last he got caught for the watch; and when I see'd I couldn't get him off, I went down into the country—down into Essex, sir. I travelled all parts, and slept at the unions on the road. I met a young girl down in Town Malling, in Kent. I met her, and then we used to go begging together, and tramp it from one union to another. At last we got so ragged and dirty, and our things all got so bad, that we made up our minds to go in for three months into prison, at Battle, down in Sussex. We used to meet a great many on the road boiling their kettle, and sometimes we used to stop and skipper with them of a night. Skippering is sleeping in barns or under hedges, if it's warm weather. They weren't gipsies. We usen't to stop to speak to the gipsies—not much—unless we went to fairs or horse-races. Then we used to sit with them for a little while, if they had their tent. We generally used to steal on the way. If we could see anything, we used to take it. At last, when our clothes got bad, I and the other girl—she still kept with me—determined to break the parson's windows at Battle. We broke one because the house was good for a cant—that's some food—bread or meat, and they wouldn't give it us, so we got savage, and broke all the glass in the windows. For that we got three months. After we got out, the parson sent word for us to come to his house, and he gave us half-a-crown a-piece to take us on our road. He would have given us some clothes—we had no shoes and stockings: we was very bad off; but his wife was in London. So we went on the road tramping again, and I have been tramping it about the country ever since. I was all last winter in Town Malling union with the fever, and when I got well I set off tramping again. I didn't have no more chaps since I left my fancy-man—I mean, I never took up with no others, not to keep their company. I have been about two years tramping altogether; out of that I had five months in prison for stealing and breaking windows. I like the tramping life well enough in the summer, 'cause there's plenty of victuals to be had then, but it's the winter that we can't stand. Then we generally come to London, but we can't call at house to house here as we do in the country, so we make but a poor thing of it. I never was so bad off as I am now, excepting when I was at Battle, for I had no shoes or stockings then. The police is too sharp for us in London. I'm very fond of going through the country in fine weather. Sometimes we don't make much freedom with the chaps in the union, and sometimes we do. They tells us to go along with them, for they knows good houses to call at. What you make is all according to whether you're in a lonesome road. I've travelled a day, and not seen a house that I could get anything at. Some days I've got a shilling given to me, and some days as much as half-a-crown. We can always get plenty of bread and meat, for countryfolks is very good. If I had some good things—that is, good boots—I should like to go into the country again. Sometimes we gets so much scran we sells it among ourselves. I should sell my lot to some travellers on the road. They gives us 3d. or 4d., but we must give them a good lot for that. I can't say which is the best of the unions now, for they are all shut up. They used to be good at one time, but the Irish ruined them; they came in such swarms, the people, I knew, would never stand it. We used often to say of a night that them Irish Greeks would ruin the business. They are much better beggars than we are, though they don't get as much as the English, because they go in such swarms up to the door. Now, down in Hawkhurst, there used to be a two-penny loaf allowed to everybody that called at the parson's house, little and big; it was allowed by a lady, till the pigs of Irish came in such lots, that they spoilt all the game. The parson won't give it to no one now, except eight travelling-men in the morning. I know all the good houses, and the tidy grubbikens,—that's the unions where there's little or nothing to do for the food we gets. We walk mostly eleven miles a-day. If it's hot we walk only six miles, and turn in under a hedge if we've got our things with us to make a tent. We go all right round the country, up to Yorkshire, and as far as Northumberland. We don't try Warwick gaol, because the shilling they used to give on being discharged is stopped, excepting to those that's not been there before, and there's very few of the trampers, boys or girls, that hasn't. Then there's the twopenny-house down in High-field, in Kent. I'm blowed if they ain't been and stopped that! I can't tell what's come to the country of late. It's got very bad and scaly, there's no hospitality going on. I've been two years at the business, and I've seen it grow worse and worse, meaner and meaner, every day before my very eyes. I don't know, I'm sure, what poor trampers will do if it gets any worse. Some do talk of the good old times, when there was plenty of money-getting in them days. I shouldn't like to give it up just yet. I do like to be in the country in the summer-time. I like haymaking and hopping, because that's a good bit of fun. Still, I'm sick and tired of what I'm doing now. It's the winter that sickens me. I'm worn out now, and I often sits and thinks of the life that I've led. I think of my kind, dear mother, and how good I would have been if my father had taught me better. Still, if I'd clothes I'd not give up my present life. I'd be down in the country now. I do love roving about, and I'm wretched when I'm not at it. After my mother died I never liked to be at home. I've seen many an unhappy day since I've been away; still, I wouldn't go back to my home, because it's no home to me."

LONDON VAGRANTS' ASYLUMS FOR THE HOUSELESS.

To give the reader an idea of the motley assemblage to be found in these places, I subjoin the following table (taken from the Report), by which it will be seen that almost every quarter of the globe contributes its quota of wretchedness :—

PLACES TO WHICH THE INDIVIDUALS SHELTERED BY THE HOUSELESS POOR SOCIETY DURING THE WINTER 1848-49 APPEARED TO BELONG.

Africa	12	Hampshire	414	Russia	7
America	78	Herefordshire	45	Rutlandshire	24
Bedfordshire	55	Hertfordshire	181	Scotland	230
Berkshire	267	Huntingdonshire	25	Shropshire	42
Buckinghamshire	88	Ireland	8068	Somersetshire	246
Cambridgeshire	88	Italy	7	Spain	10
Cheshire	40	Jersey	15	St. Helena	8
Cornwall	32	Kent	523	Staffordshire	129
Cumberland	12	Lancashire	811	Suffolk	133
Derbyshire	48	Leicestershire	75	Surrey	204
Denmark	6	Lincolnshire	85	Sussex	147
Devonshire	209	London	343	Wales	122
Dorsetshire	46	Middlesex	214	Warwickshire	160
Durham	54	Norfolk	163	West Indies	25
East Indies	19	Northamptonshire	67	Westmoreland	6
Essex	392	Northumberland	72	Wiltshire	87
France	14	Nottinghamshire	68	Worcestershire	36
Germany	53	Oxfordshire	100	Yorkshire	126
Gibraltar	3	Poland	4	Unknown	29
Gloucestershire	163	Portugal	5	Born at sea	5
Guernsey	32				

VAGRANT FROM THE REFUGE IN PLAYHOUSE
YARD, CRIPPLEGATE.

[*From a Photograph.*]

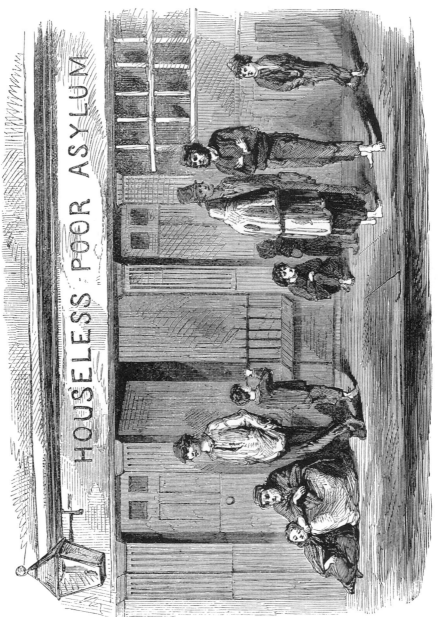

ASYLUM FOR THE HOUSELESS POOR, CRIPPLEGATE.

[*From a Sketch.*]

These places of shelter for the houseless are only open at certain periods of the year; and at this season a large proportion of the country labourers who are out of employ flock to London, either to seek for work in the winter-time, or to avail themselves of the food and lodging afforded by these charitable institutions. Others, again, who are professional vagrants, tramping through the country, and sleeping at the different unions on their road, come to town as regularly as noblemen every winter, and make their appearance annually in these quarters. Moreover, it is at this season of the year that the sufferings and privations of the really poor and destitute are rendered tenfold more severe than at any other period; and it is at the houses of refuge that the great mass of London, or rather English and Irish, poverty and misery, is to be met with.

The congregation at the Refuges for the Destitute is, indeed, a sort of ragged congress of nations—a convocation of squalor and misery—a synopsis of destitution, degradation, and suffering, to be seen, perhaps, nowhere else.

Nor are the returns of the bodily ailments of the wretched inmates of these abodes less instructive as to their miserable modes of life, their continual exposure to the weather, and their want of proper nutriment. The subjoined medical report of the diseases and bodily afflictions to which these poor creatures are liable, tells a tale of suffering which, to persons with even the smallest amount of pathological knowledge, must need no comment. The catarrh and influenza, the rheumatism, bronchitis, ague, asthma, lumbago— all speak of many long night's exposure to the wet and cold; whereas the abscesses, ulcers, the diarrhœa, and the excessive debility from starvation, tell, in a manner that precludes all doubt, of the want of proper sustenance and extreme privation of these, the very poorest of all the poor.

Medical Report for 1848–49. *Of the persons who applied at the general asylum, there were afflicted with—*

Catarrh and influenza	149
Incipient fever	52
Rheumatism	50
Atrophy	3
Dropsy	3
Incised wounds	3
Diarrhœa	60
Cholera	2
Bronchitis	13
Abscess	15
Ulcers	11
Affections of the head	12
Ague	13
Excessive debility from starvation	17
Inflammation of lungs	2
Asthma	10
Epilepsy	4
Diseased joints	4
Erysipelas	3
Rupture	3
Cramps and pains in bowels	2
Spitting of blood	4
Lumbago	1
Rheumatic ophthalmia	2
Strumous disease	2
Sprains	1
Fractures	4
Pregnant	30

The returns of the different callings of the individuals seeking for the shelter of the refuges are equally curious and worthy of study. These, however, I shall reserve for my next letter, as, by comparing the returns for each year since the opening of the institution, now thirty years ago, we shall be enabled to arrive at almost an historical account of the distress of the different trades since the year 1820. These tables I am now preparing from the valuable yearly reports of the Society, one of the most deserving among all our charitable institutions, and one which, especially at this bitter season, calls for the support of all those who would give a meal and a bed to such as are too poor to have either.

I will now proceed to a description of the Refuge itself.

The only refuge for the houseless now open which is really a home for the homeless, is that in Playhouse-yard, Cripplegate. The doors open into a narrow by-street, and the neighbourhood needs no other announcement that the establishment is open for the reception of the houseless, than the assembly of a crowd of ragged shivering people, certain to be seen on the night of opening, as if they knew by instinct where they might be housed under a warm and comfortable roof. The crowd gathers in Playhouse-yard, and many among them look sad and weary enough. Many of the women carry infants at the breast, and have children by their sides holding by their gowns. The cries of these, and the wrangling of the hungry crowds for their places, is indeed disheartening to hear. The only sounds of merriment come from the errand-boys, as they call themselves, whom even starvation cannot make sorrowful for two hours together. The little struggle that there usually is among the applicants is not for a rush when the doors are opened, but for what they call the "front rank." They are made to stand clear of the footpath; and when five o'clock—the hour of admission—comes, an officer of the Refuge steps out, and quietly, by a motion of his hand, or a touch on the shoulder, sends in about 150 men and boys, and about 50 women and girls. He knows the great majority of those who have tickets which entitle them to one or two nights' further lodging (the tickets are generally for three nights), and these are commonly in the foremost rank. The number thus admitted show themselves more or less at home. Some are quiet and abashed; but some proceed briskly, and in a business-like way, to the first process, to wash themselves. This is done in two large vessels, in what may be called the hall or vestibule of the building. A man keeps pumping fresh water into the vessels as fast as that used is drained off, and soap and clean towels are supplied when thought necessary; the clean towels, which are long, and attached to rollers, soon becoming, in truth, exceedingly dirty. I noticed some little contention—whether to show an anxiety to conform to the rules of the Refuge, or to hurry through a disagreeable but inevitable task, or really for the comfort of ablution, I will not pretend to determine — but there was some little contention for the first turn among the young men at the washing. To look down upon them from the main staircase, as I did, was to survey a very motley scene. There they were—the shirtless, the shoeless, the coatless, the unshaven, the uncouth, ay, and the decent and respectable. There were men from every part of the United Kingdom, with a coloured man or two, a few seamen, navigators, agricultural labourers, and artizans. There were no foreigners on the nights that I was there; and in the returns of those admitted there will not be found one Jew. It is possible that Jews may be entered under the heads of "Germans" or "Poles"—I mean, foreign Jews; but on my visits I did not see so much as any near approach to the Hebrew physiognomy. To attempt to give an account of anything like a prevailing garb among these men is impossible, unless I described it as rags. As they were washing, or waiting for a wash, there was some stir, and a loud buzz of talk, in which "the brogue" strongly predominated. There was some little fun, too, as there must be where a crowd of many youths is assembled. One in a ragged, coarse, striped shirt, exclaimed as he shoved along, "By your leave, gentlemen!" with a significant emphasis of his "gentlemen." Another man said to his neighbour, "The bread's fine, Joe; but the sleep, isn't that plummy?" Some few, I say, seemed merry enough, but that is easily accounted for. Their present object was attained, and your real professional vagabond is always happy by that—for a forgetfulness of the past, or an indifference to it, and a recklessness as to the future, are the primary elements of a vagrant's enjoyment. Those who had tickets were of course subjected to no further examination, unless by the surgeon subsequently; but all the new candidates for admission — and the officers kept admitting fresh batches as they were instructed — were not passed before a rigid examination, when a ticket for three nights was given to each fresh applicant. On the right hand, as you enter the building, is the office. The assistant-superintendant sits before a large

ledger, in which he enters every name and description. His questions to every fresh candidate are:—"Your name?" "How old are you?" "What trade?" "How do you live (if no trade)?" "Where did you sleep last night?" "To what parish do you belong?" In order to answer these questions, each fresh applicant for admission stands before the door of the office, a portion of the upper division of the door being thrown open. Whilst I was present, there was among a portion of the male applicants but little hesitation in answering the inquiries glibly and promptly. Others answered reluctantly. The answers of some of the boys, especially the Irish boys, were curious. "Where did you sleep last night?" "Well, then, sir, I sleep walking about the streets all night, and very cowld it was, sir." Another lad was asked, after he had stated his name and age, how he lived? "I beg, or do anything," he answered. "What's your parish?" "Ireland." (Several pronounced their parish to be the "county Corruk.") "Have you a father here?" "He died before we left Ireland." "How did you get here, then?" "I came with my mother." "Well, and where's she?" "She died after we came to England." So the child had the streets for a stepmother.

Some of the women were as glib and systematic in their answers as the men and boys. Others were much abashed. Among the glib-tongued women, there seemed no shamefacedness. Some of the women admitted here, however, have acquitted themselves well when provided (through charitable institutions) with situations. The absence of shame which I have remarked upon is the more notable, because these women were questioned by men, with other men standing by. Some of the women were good-looking; and when asked how old they were, they answered at once, and, judging by their appearance, never understated their years. Many I should have pronounced younger than they stated. Vanity, even with silliness and prettiness, does not seem to exist in their utter destitution.

All the regular processes having been observed (and the women have a place for their ablutions after the same fashion as the men), the applicants admitted enter their several wards. The women's ward is at the top of the building. It supplies accommodation, or berths, for 95 women in an apartment 35 yards in length and 6 in width. At one corner of this long chamber, a few steps lead down to what is called "the nursery," which has 30 berths. Most of these berths may be described as double, and are large enough to accommodate a mother and her children. The children, when I saw them, were gambolling about in some of the berths as merry as children elsewhere, or perhaps merrier, for they were experiencing the unwonted luxuries of warmth and food. The matron can supply these women and their children with gruel at her discretion; and it appeared to be freely given. Some who had children seemed to be the best of all there in point of physiognomy. They had not, generally, the stolid, stupid, indifferent, or shameless look of many of the other women; it was as though the motherly feeling had somewhat humanized them. Some of the better sort of women spoke so low as to be hardly audible. Among them were, indeed, many decent-looking females.

The men's wards are the Chapel Ward (for the better sort of persons), containing 90 berths, one line being ranged 2 berths deep; the Lower Ward, containing 120 berths; the Boys' Ward, containing 60 berths; and the Straw Loft, 40. There is a walk alongside the berths in each ward. What is called the Boys' Ward is not confined to boys: it used to be so, but they were found so noisy that they could no longer be allowed a separate apartment. They are now scattered through the several wards with the men, the officers arranging them, and varying the arrangements as they consider best. Before there can be any retirement to rest, each man, woman, and child must be examined by a surgeon. Whilst I was present, a young assistant conducted the investigation in a careful, yet kindly and gentlemanly manner. Indeed, I was much struck with the sympathy and gentleness he displayed; and it was evident from the respect of the people, that kindness and consideration are the very qualities to impress and control the class he has to deal with. All afflicted with cutaneous disorders (and there were but five men so afflicted) were lodged apart from the others. Bronchitis and rheumatism are the prevalent disorders, occasioned by their exposure to the weather, and their frequent insufficiency of food. Ninety per cent of them, I was told by Mr. Gay, the intelligent surgeon of the establishment, might have coughs at some periods, but of that they thought nothing. Women advanced in pregnancy, and men with any serious (especially any infectious) ailment, are not permitted to sleep in the Refuge; but the institution, if they have been admitted, finds them lodgings elsewhere.

Each person admitted receives in the evening half-a-pound of the best bread. Every child has the same allowance. If a woman be admitted with four children, she receives two half-pounds of bread — a half-pound for every one, no matter if one be at the breast, as is not unfrequently the case. The same quantity of bread is given in the mornings. In the night that I was present, 430 were admitted, and consequently (including the evening and morning allowances), 430 lbs. of bread were disposed of. On Sundays, when Divine Service is celebrated by a clergyman of the Church of England, three half-pounds of bread and three ounces of cheese are distributed to each inmate, children and babies included. I witnessed a number of young men eating the bread administered to them. They took it with a keen appetite; nothing was heard among them but the champing of the teeth, as they chewed large mouthfuls of the food.

The berths, both in the men's and women's wards, are on the ground, and divided one from another only by a wooden partition about a foot high; a similar partition is at the head and feet; so that in all the wards it looks as if there were a series of coffins arranged in long catacombs. This burial-like aspect is the more striking when the inmates are all asleep, as they were, with the rarest exceptions, when I walked round at ten o'clock at night. Each sleeper has for covering a large basil (dressed sheep-skin), such as cobblers use for aprons. As they lie in long rows, in the most profound repose, with these dark brown wrappers about them, they present the uniform look and arrangement of a long line of mummies. Each bed in the coffin, or trough-like division, is made of waterproof cloth, stuffed with hay, made so as to be easily cleaned. It is soft and pleasant to the touch. Formerly the beds were plain straw, but the present plan has been in use for seven years. In this Refuge only three men have died since it was established, thirty years ago. One fell dead at the sink-stone while washing himself; the other two were found dead in their berths during the prevalence of the cholera.

Every part of the building was scrupulously clean. On the first night of the opening, the matron selects from the women who have sought an asylum there, three, who are engaged for the season to do the household work. This is done during the day when the inmates are absent. All must leave by eight in the morning, the doors being open for their departure at five, in case any wish to quit early — as some do for the chance of a job at Covent-garden, Farringdon, or any of the early markets. The three women-helpers receive 7s. a-week each, the half of that sum being paid them in money every Saturday, and the other half being retained and given to each of them, in a round sum, at the closing of the Refuge. The premises in which this accommodation to the houseless is now supplied were formerly a hat manufactory on a large scale; but the lath and plaster of the ceilings, and the partitions, have been removed, so that what was a suite of apartments on one floor is now a long ward. The rafters of the ceilings are minutely whitewashed, as are the upright beams used in the construction of the several rooms before the place was applied to its present charitable end. Those now are in the nature of pillars, and add to the catacomb-like aspect that I have spoken of. In different parts of each ward are very large grates, in which bright fires are kept glowing and crackling; and as these are lighted some time before the hour of opening, the place has a warmth and cosiness which must be very grateful to those who have encountered the cold air all the day, and perhaps all the night before.

In order to arrive at a correct estimate as to the number of the really poor and houseless who availed themselves of the establishment (to afford nightly shelter to whom the refuge was originally instituted by the benevolent founder, Mr. Hick, the City mace-bearer) I consulted with the superintendent as to the class of persons he found most generally seeking refuge there. These were — among the men — mostly labourers out of work—agricultural, railway, and dock; discharged artisans, chiefly carpenters and painters; sailors, either cast away or without their registry tickets; broken-down tradesmen, clerks, shopmen, and errand-boys, who either through illness or misfortune had been deprived of their situations; and, above all, Irish immigrants, who had been starved out of their own country. These he considered the really deserving portion of the inmates for whom the institution was designed. Among the females, the better and largest class of poor were needlewomen, servants, charwomen, gardenwomen, sellers of laces in the street, and occasionally a beggar-woman. Under his guidance I selected such as appeared the most meritorious among the classes he had enumerated, and now subjoin the statements of a portion of the number.

The first of the houseless that I saw was a railway navigator. He was a fine, stoutly-built fellow, with a fresh-coloured open countenance, and flaxen hair—indeed, altogether a splendid specimen of the Saxon labourer. He was habited in a short blue smockfrock, yellow in parts with clay, and he wore the heavy high lace-up boots, so characteristic of the tribe. These were burst, and almost soleless with long wear.

The poor fellow told the old story of the labourer compelled to squander the earnings at the public-house of his master :—

"I have been a navvy for about eighteen years. The first work that I done was on the Manchester and Liverpool. I was a lad then. I used to grease the railway waggons, and got about 1s. 6d. a-day. There we had a tommy-shop, and we had to go there to get our bit of victuals, and they used to charge us an extra price. The next place I had after that was on the London and Brummagem. There I went as horse-driver, and had 2s. 6d. a-day. Things was dear then, and at the tommy-shop they was much dearer; for there was tommy-shops on every line then ; and indeed every contractor and sub-contractor had his shop that he forced his men to deal at, or else he wouldn't have them in his employ. At the tommy-shop we was charged half as much again as we should have had to pay elsewhere ; and it's the same now, wherever these tommy-shops is. What the contractors, you see, can't make out of the company, they fleeces out of the men. Well,

sir, I worked on that line through all the different contracts till it was finished: sometimes I was digging, sometimes shovelling. I was mostly at work at open cuttings. All this time I was getting from 2s. 6d. to 3s. and 3s. 6d. a-day ; that was the top price ; and if I'd had the ready-money to lay out myself, I could have done pretty well, and maybe have put a penny or two by against a rainy day : but the tommy-shop and the lodging-house took it all out of us. You see, the tommy-shop found us in beer, and they would let us drink away all our earnings there if we pleased, and when pay-time came we should have nothing to take. If we didn't eat and drink at the tommy-shop we should have no work. Of an evening, we went to the tommy-shop after the drink, and they'd keep drawing beer for us there as long as we'd have anything coming to us next pay-day (we were paid every fortnight, and sometimes every month), and when we had drunk away all that would be coming to us, why they'd turn us out. The contractor, who keeps these tommy-shops, is generally a gentleman, a man of great property, who takes some four, five, or seven lengths to do. Well, with such goings on, in course there wasn't no chance in the world for us to save a halfpenny. We had a sick fund among ourselves, but our masters never cared nothing about us further than what they could get out of us at their tommy-shops. They were never satisfied if a man didn't spend all his money with them; if we had a penny to take at the month's end, they didn't like it; and now the half of us has to walk about and starve, or beg, or go to the union. After I left the Brummagem line, I went on to the Great Western. I went to work at Maidenhead. There it was on the same system, and on the same rules — the poor man being fleeced and made drunk by his master. Sometimes the contractor would lot the work out to some sub-contractor, and he, after the men had worked for a month, would run away, and we should never see the colour of his money. After the Great Western, I went into Lancashire, on the Manchester and Oldham branch. I started there to work at nights, and there I worked a month for the contractors, when they went bankrupt, and we never received a farthing but what we had got out of the tommy-shop. Well, I came away from there, and got on to the London and Brighton, and I worked all up and down that, saving the tunnels ; and it was the same there — the tommy-shop and imposition was wherever we went. Well, from there I went on to the London and Dover. It was monthly payments on that. There, too, I worked for a month, when the sub-contractor runned away with all the men's money—900l., sir, it were calculated. After that another party took it, and it was the same all the way up and down — the tommy-shop and beer as much as we liked, on credit. Then I went on to the London and Cambridge, and there it was the same story over and over again. Just about this time, railway work began to get slack, and then farmers' work was slack too; and you see that made things worse for the navvies, for all came to look for employment on the railroads. This is about seven years ago. After that some more fresh lines started throughout Lancashire and Yorkshire, and trade being bad in them parts, all the weavers applied for work on the railways, and the regular navvies had a hard time of it then. But we managed to get on somehow—kept lingering on—till about three years agone, when trade got a little bit better. That was about the time when things was very dear, and our wages was rose to 3s. 6d. a-day.: they'd been only 2s. 6d. and 3s. before that; and we did much better when our pay was increased, because we had the ready-money then, and there was no tommy-shops that summer, for the company wouldn't have them on that line. At the end of that year the work was all stopped, on account of the Chartist rising, and then there was hundreds of men walking about begging their bread from door to door, with nothing to do. After this, (that's two years ago, the back end of this year,) I went to work on the London and York. Here we had only 2s. 9d. a-day. and we had only four days' work in the week to do besides; and then there was a tommy-shop, where we were forced to get our victuals and drink: so you see we were very bad off then. I stopped on this line (for work was very scarce, and I thought myself lucky to have any) till last spring. Then all the work on it stopped, and I dare say 2000 men were thrown out of employ in one day. They were all starving, the heap of them, or next door to it. I went away from there over to the Brummagem and Beechley branch line. But there I found things almost as bad as what I left before. Big, strong, able-bodied men were working for 1s. 8d. a-day, and from that to 2s.: that was the top price; for wages had come down, you see, about one-half, and little or no work to do at that price; and tommy-shop and beer, sir, as before, out of the little we did get. The great cause of our wages being cut down was through the work being so slack in the country; everybody was flocking to them parts for employment, and the contractors, seeing a quantity of men walking backwards and forwards, dropped the wages: if one man wouldn't work at the price, there was hundreds ready to do it. Besides, provisions was very cheap, and the contractors knew we could live on less, and do their work quite as well. Whenever provisions goes down our wages does, too; but when they goes up, the contractors is very slow in rising them. You see, when they find so many men walking about without work, the masters have got the chance of the poor man. Three year agone this last winter—I think it was '46—provisions was high and wages was good; and in the summer of the very same year, food got

cheap again, and our wages dropped from 3s. 6d. to 3s. and 2s. 9d. The fall in our wages took place immediately the food got cheaper. The contractors said, as we could live for less, we must do the work for less. I left the Brummagem and Beechley line, about two months before the Christmas before last, and then I came to Copenhagen-fields, on the London and York—the London end, sir; and there I was till last March, when we were all paid off, about 600 on us; and I went back to Barnet, and there I worked till the last seven weeks, and had 2s. 9d. a-day for what, four years ago, I had 3s. 6d. for; and I could only have three or four days' work in the week then. Whilst I was there, I hurted my leg, and was laid up a month. I lived all that time on charity; on what the chaps would come and give me. One would give a shilling, another sixpence, another a shilling, just as they could spare it; and poorly they could do that, God knows! I couldn't declare on to the sick fund, because I hadn't no bones broken. Well, when I come to look for work, and that's three weeks agone, when I could get about again, the work was all stopped, and I couldn't get none to do. Then I come to London, and I've looked all about for a job, and I can't find nothing to do. I went to a lodging-house in the Borough, and I sold all my things—shovel and grafting-tool and all, to have a meal of food. When all my things was gone, I didn't know where to go. One of my mates told me of this Refuge, and I have been here two nights. All that I have had to eat since then is the bread night and morning they gives us here. This will be the last night I shall have to stop here, and after that I don't know what I shall do. There's no railway work—that is, there's none to speak of, seeing the thousands of men that's walking about with nothing to do, and not knowing where to lay their heads. If I could get any interest, I should like to go away as an emigrant. I shouldn't like to be sent out of my native country as a rogue and a vagabone; but I'm tired of stopping here, and if I can't get away, why I must go home and go to the parish, and it's hard for a young man that's willing and able like me to work, and be forced to want because he can't get it. I know there is thousands—thousands, sir, like I am—I know there is, in the very same condition as I am at this moment: yes, I know there is." [This he said with very great feeling and emphasis.] "We are all starving. We are all willing to work, but it ain't to be had. This country is getting very bad for labour; it's so overrun with Irish that the Englishman hasn't a chance in his own land to live. Ever since I was nine years old I've got my own living, but now I'm dead beat, though I'm only twenty-eight next August."

The next man to whom I spoke was tall and hale-looking, except that his features were pinched, and his eyes had a dull lack-lustre look, common to men suffering from cold and hunger. His dress was a coarse jacket, fustian trousers, and coarse, hard-worn shoes. He spoke without any very provincial accent.

"I am now forty-eight, and have been a farm-labourer all my life. I am a single man. When I was a boy of twelve, I was put to dig, or see after the birds, or break clods, or anything, on a farm at Croland, in Lancashire. I had very little school before that, and can neither read nor write. I was then living with my parents, poor people, who worked on the land whenever they could get a day's work. We had to live very hard, but at hay and harvest times we had meat, and lived better. I had 3s. a-week as a boy. When I grew up to fourteen I left home. I thought my father didn't use me well: perhaps it was my own fault. I might have been a bad boy; but he was severe when he did begin with me, though he was generally quiet. When his passion was up, there was no bearing it. Anyhow, I started into the world at fourteen to do the best I could for myself—to make my fortune if I could. Since then, I have had work in all sorts of counties; Midland counties, principally. When a boy, I got employment readily enough at bird-scaring, or hay-making; but I soon grew up, and took a man's place very early, and I could then do any kind of farmer's work, except ploughing or seeding. They have men on purpose for that. Farm work was far better in my younger days than it is now. For a week, when hired by the day, I never get more than 15s., regular work. For taken work (by the job), I have made as much as 42s. in a week; that is, in reaping and mowing, when I could drop on such jobs in a difficult season, when the weather was uncertain. I talk of good times. The last good job I had was three years ago, come next summer. Now I should be glad to get 9s. a-week, constant work: anything but what I'm doing now. As I went about from place to place, working for farmers, I generally lodged at the shepherds' houses, or at some labourer's. I never was in a lodging-house when I was in work, only when money runs low one must have shelter. At some lodging-houses I've had a good feather-bed; others of them are bad enough: the best, I think, are in Norfolk. I have saved a bit of money several times—indeed, year after year, until the last three or four years; but what I saved in the summer, went in the winter. In some summers, I could save nothing. It's how the season comes. I never cared for drink. I've done middling till these last two seasons. My health was good, to be sure; but when a man's in health his appetite is good also; and when I'm at regular work I don't eat half so much as when I'm knocking about idle, and get hold of a meal. I often have to make up for three or four days then. The last job I had was six weeks before Christmas, at Boston, in Lincolnshire. I couldn't make 1s. 6d. a-day

on account of the weather. I had 13s., however, to start with, and I went on the road, not standing for a straight road, but going where I heard there was a chance of a job, up or down anywhere, here or there, but there was always the same answer, 'Nobody wanted —no work for their own constant men.' I was so beat out as soon as my money was done—and it lasted ten days—that I parted with my things one by one. First my waistcoat, then my stockings (three pair of them), then three shirts. I got 2s. 4d. for three shirts, and 6d. a pair for my stockings. My clothes were done, and I parted with my pocket-knife for 2d., and with my 'bacco-box for 1½d. After I left Boston, I got into Leicestershire, and was at Cambridge, and Wisbeach, and Lynn, and Norwich; and I heard of a job among brickmakers at Low Easthrop, in Suffolk, but it was no go. The weather was against it, too. It was when the snow set in. And then I thought I would come to London, as God in his goodness might send me something to do. I never meant anything slinking. I'm only happy when I'm at work, but here I am destitute. Some days as I walked up I had nothing to eat. At others I got half-pennies or pennies from men like myself that I saw at work. I've given shillings away that way myself at times. Sometimes I had to take to the road, but I'm a very poor beggar. When I got to London I was a stranger, and lodged here the first night—that's a week ago. A policeman sent me here. I've tried every day to get work—labouring-work for builders, or about manure-carts, or anything like that, as there's no farming in London, but got none; so but for this place I had starved. When this place is closed I must tramp into the country. There are very many farm-labourers now going from farm to farm, and town to town, to seek work, more than ever I saw before. I don't know that the regular farm-workmen come so much to London. As I travelled up from Suffolk I lay rough often enough. I got into stables, or any places. Such places as this save many a man's life. It's saved mine, for I might have been found dead in the street, as I didn't know where to go."

This man appeared to me to be a very decent character.

The large number of Irish found among the inmates of these establishments is one of the peculiar features of the Refuges. By the returns above given, it will be seen that they constitute more than one-half of the total applicants. Such being the fact, I selected two from the more decent, as types of the better class of immigrants, and subjoin their narratives.

One of these men had a half-shrewd, half-stolid look, and was clad in very dirty fustian. His beard was some days old, and he looked ill-fed and wretched. His children—for he had two boys with him, ten and twelve years old—were shoeless, their white skins being a contrast to their dirty dress, as the former appeared through the holes in their jackets. They looked on with a sort of vacant wonder, motionless, and without a word. The father said :—

" I've been knocking about in England these four years from place to place. I'm telling you the truth, sir. [This he often repeated.] I came here to betther myself, to knock out something betther; but I wish to God I'd been buried before I buried my wife and children. I do, indeed, sir. I was a labourer in Ireland, working in farms and gardens for anybody. My wages warn't much, only 3s. a-week, and my datal house (that is, a house rent-free), and two meals of victuals a-day, sometimes 'taties and milk for meals, and sometimes 'taties and fish, and sometimes— aye, often—'taties and nothing. My wife and me, and four children, came from Cork—it was in the county Cork I lived—to Wales. I don't know the name of the part; they've such queer names there; sure, then, they have, sir. It cost me half-a-crown a-piece for the six of us. I raised the money partly by digging up a garden I had, and selling what stuff there was, and the rest was made up by the farmers in the neighbourhood giving their 3d. or 6d. a-piece to me, so that I might lave. I wasn't on the poor-law rate, but I soon might. When I got to Wales, I had only 6d. left. I went to the workhouse for a night's lodging, to be sure—what else? I started next day for London with my wife and children, begging as we came, and going from workhouse to work-house; and very badly we got along. It finished a fortnight to get to London. When we got to London (that's about four years agone) we got work at peas-picking, my wife and me, in the gardens about. That is for the summer. In the winter we sold oranges in the streets while she lived, and we had nothing from the parishes. I can't complain of the living till this time, sir; it was better than I knew in Ireland. I don't know what we got, she managed all. Last autumn we went into the hop county, to Ellis's farm. I don't know the town nearest; and there my wife and two children died of the cholera at the farm. The three of them wern't a week ill. The parish kept them and buried them. Since that I've been worse off than ever, and will always be worse off than ever, for I've lost a good wife. Since her death I jobbed about in the country, living very bare, me and the children, till the frost came, and then we came to London. I was knocking about for a fortnight, and begged a little; but sorrow a much I got by that. How did I know of this place? Musha, all the neighbours know about it."

The younger man, who was tall and gaunt, more intelligent than the other, and less squalid in his appearance, said :— " I have been in England two years in August. I came to better my living. I tilled a portion of land in Ireland. It was 30l. a-year rent, and forty acres. That was in the county Cork, parish of Kilmeen. I rented the land of a middleman, and he was very severe. My family and I couldn't live under him. I had a wife and three children. We all came to England, from Cork to Bristol. I kept a little substance back to pay my way to England. The voyage cost 25s. From Bristol I went to Cardiff, as I got no work at Bristol. At Cardiff I worked on the railway at 2s. 6d. a-day. I did well for a couple of months. I would like to continue at that, or at 1s. a-day here, better than in Ireland these times. I worked in Cardiff town with a bricklayer, after I'd done on the railway, at 12s. a-week. I next year had a twelvemonth's work, on and off, with a farmer near Bristol, at 10s. a-week, and was still plenty comfortable. I made for London at the hay-harvest. I had a little money to start with, but I got no hay-work, only a trifle of work at the Docks. In corn-harvest, near Brighton, I worked for six weeks, making 10s. an acre for cutting wheat by piece-work, and 7s. for oats, and 2s. for any day's work. I made 4l. altogether. I got back to London with 40s. I could get no work at all, but five days' work at a stone-yard, at 1s. a-day. I sold a few things in the streets, oranges and apples; so did my wife. It helped to keep us. All was gone at last, so I got in here with one child (a fine boy). My wife's got three with her. She's in a lodging in Gray's-inn-lane. She's starving, I'm afraid; but she wished me to come in here with the child, as I could do nothing at night-time. I don't know how many came over about the time I did. The gentry give poor men money, or did give it to them, to send them over here, to free the land from its expenses."

To complete the picture of this Irish desti-tution, I add the following.

One wretched creature had come to the Refuge with her four children. She herself was habited in a large blue cloth cloak, her toes were through the end of her shoes, and her gown clung tight to her limbs, telling that she was utterly destitute of under clothing. In her arms she carried an infant, round which were wound some old woollen rags. As the little thing sucked at its mother's breast, it breathed so hard that it needed no words to tell of its long exposure to the cold. Though the mother was half-clad, still there was the little bit of clean net inside the old rusty straw bonnet. The children were respectively eleven, six, and three years old. The eldest (a good-looking grey-eyed girl, who stood with her forefinger in her mouth, half simple) was covered with a tattered plaid shawl. This, at her mother's bidding, she drew from her shoulder with an ostentation of poverty, to show that what had before appeared a gown beneath was nothing more than a bombazine petticoat. On her feet were a pair of women's old fashionable shoes, tied on with string. These had been given in charity to her by a servant a week back. The next child—a boy —laughed as I looked at him, and seemed, though only six years old, to have been made prematurely "knowing" by his early street education. He put out his foot as he saw my eye glance downward to his shoes, to show me that he had one boot and one shoe on. He was clad in all kinds of rags, and held in his hand a faded velvet cap. The youngest boy was almost a dwarf. He was three years old, but so stunted that he seemed scarce half that age.

"I come from the county of Corruk, the worst and the poorest part of it—yes, indeed, sir, it is," said the woman; "and the gintlemen know that I do. When I had it to do, I manufactured at flax and wool. I knit and sewed, to be sure I did; but God Almighty was plazed to deprive me of it. It was there I was married. My husband was a miner. Distress and want, and hunger and poverty— nothing else—druv us to this counthry. It was the will of God—glory be to his holy and blessed name!—to fail the 'taties. To be sure, I couldn't dig one out of the ground not fit to ate. We lived on 'taties, and milk, and fish, and eggs. We used to have hins then. And the mining failed, too; and the captains came over here. Yes, to be sure; for here they lived, sir. Yes, sir, indeed; and I could tell you that I used to be eight days—yes, that I did—before I could get one ha'porth to ate—barring the wather I boiled and drank to keep the life in myself and children. It was Doctor O'Donovan that paid for our passage. When he see all the hunger, and distress, and want—yes, indeed, sir—that I went through, he gave a letther to the stame-packet office, and then they brought me and my three childer over. It was here that this baby was borrun. My husband was here before me, he was, about seven or eight months. He hadn't sent me any money, for he couldn't a penny. He wrote home to see if I lived, for he didn't think I lived; and then I showed the letther to Dr. O'Donovan. My husband niver got a day's work since he came over; indeed, he couldn't give the childer their breakfast the next morning after they came. I came to London-bridge, and met my husband there. Well, indeed, that is nearly three years agone. Oh, thin, I had nothing to do since but what little we done at the harvest. It was tin weeks before Christmas that I came over, and I don't know what month it was, for I don't read or write, you know. Oh, thin, indeed, we had to live by begging from that up to harvest time. I had to beg for him sooner than let him die with the hunger. He didn't do any work, but he'd be glad of a sixpence he'd earn. He'd rather have it that way than if he'd begged tin pound—it would be more plisure. Never a day's work could he get; and many beside him. Oh, Lord, there is

many, sir. He never does anything but at the harvest-time, and then he works at raping the corrun. I know nothing else that he does; and I bind the shaves afther him. Why, indeed, we get work then for about a fortnight or three weeks—it don't howld a month. Oh no, sir, no; how could my children do anything, but as fast as we'd earn it to ate it? I declare I don't know how much we'd make a-week then. They got only eight shillings an acre last year for it. I declare I don't know what we made; but whatever we had, we hadn't two shillings laving it. Ah, indeed, I had to beg all the rest of my time. My husband doesn't beg—I'll tell you the thruth. The thruth is the best. When he has e'er a penny, he tries to sell a handful of oranges; and, indeed, he had to lave off silling, for he couldn't buy half a hundred of 'em to sill back. He done pritty well when the onions were in season, he did, sir; but there's so many silling oranges, he can't sill one of 'em. Now he does nothing, for he has nothing to reach half a hundred of limons with, and that isn't much. When I gets a pinny to pay for the lodgings, then we lodges and sleeps together; but when I can't, I must go about this way with my children. When I go out begging, he remains at home in the lodging-house; he has nothing else to do, sir. I always go out with my childer; sure I couldn't look at 'em die with hunger. Where's the use of laving them with the husband; what has he to give them? Indeed, if I had left them last night with him, he couldn't have give them as much as they'd put in their mouths onced. Indeed, I take them out in the cowld to big with me to get a bit of victuals for 'em. Sure God knows I can't hilp it—he knows I can't —glory be to his holy name! Indeed, I have a part of the brid I got here last night to carry to my poor husband, for I know he wanted it. Oh, if I'm to go to the gallows, I'm telling you the thruth. Oh, to be sure, yes, sir; there's many a one would give a bit to the childer when they wouldn't to me— sure the world knows that; and maybe the childer will get ha'pence, and that will pay my lodging or buy a loaf of brid for 'em. Oh, sir, to be sure, you know I'd get more with all my little childer out than I would with one, and that's the rason indeed. Yes, indeed, that's why I take them out! Oh, then, that's what you want to know! Why, there's some people wouldn't believe I'd have so many. Maybe, some days I wouldn't get a pinny, and maybe I'd git a shilling. I met a gintleman the other day that gave me a shilling together. I'd all my childer out with me then. The sister carries the little fellow on her back, no more would he stop afther me nayther. Only twice I've left him at home. Oh thin, indeed, he do cry with the cowld, and often again with the hunger; and some of the people says to me it's myself that makes him cry; but thin, indeed, it ain't. Maybe I've no home to give my husband, maybe it's at some union he slept last night. My husband niver goes bigging, he didn't, sir—I won't tell a lie—he didn't, indeed; but he sinds me out in the cowld, and in the wit, and in the hate, too: but thin he can't help it. He's the best man that iver put a hat on his hid, and the kindest."

She persisted in asseverating this, being apparently totally incapable of perceiving the inhumanity of her husband's conduct.

" He don't force me—he don't, indeed—but he sits idle at home while I go out. Ah, if you knew what I suffers! Oh, yes, he'd rather work, if I'd got a guinea in gowld for him to-night; and yesterday morning he prayed to God Almighty to put something in his way to give him a day's work. I was in prison onced for bigging. My children was taken away from me, and sint to some union. I don't know the name of it. That was the time my husband was silling the limons. He niver came to spake for me when I was going to prison, and he doesn't know whether I'm in prisin to-night. Ah, I beg your honour's pardon, he would care, but he can't help me. I thought I'd ind my life in the prisin, for I wouldn't be allowed to spake a word. The poor man, my husband, can't help it. He was niver counted lazy in his counthry; but God Almighty plazed to deprive him of his work, and what can he do?"

The next was a rather tall and well-spoken woman of fifty-eight.

"When I was young," she said, " I used to go out to day's works, or charing, and sometimes as a laundress. I went charing till five years ago, sometimes doing middling, often very badly, when I burst a blood-vessel in lifting a weight—a pail of water to fill a copper. I fell down all at once, and bled at the ears and nose. I was taken to St. Bartholomew's, and was there four months. When I came out, I took to sell things in the street. I could do nothing else. I have no friends in London—none in the world. Sometimes I picked up a living by selling laces, and iron-holders, and memorandum-books, in the City. I made the memorandum-books myself—penny books. The pincushions I made myself. I never had anything from my parish, or rather my husband's—that's Bristol. He was a bricklayer, but I chared when he was out of work. He died eighteen years ago. I was known by ladies and others in the City, who would sometimes give me a sixpence for a lace. I was working two months back—it was the general thanksgiving-day—when I was working at a fishmonger's in Gresham-street, and fell down the cellar stairs and broke my arm. I was again three weeks in Bartholomew's hospital. I have been destitute ever since. I have made away with everything. A little quilt is all I have left, and that would have gone last night if I hadn't got in here."

The poor woman whom I next accosted was a widow (her husband having died only a few months before). She had altogether what I may call a faded look; even her widow's cap was limp and flat, and her look was miserably subdued. She said:—

" My husband was a journeyman shoemaker. Sometimes he would earn 20s. a-week; but we were badly off, for he drank; but he did not ill-use me—not much. During his last illness we raised 5l. on a raffle for a silk handkerchief among the shoemakers, and 10s. from the Mendicity Society, and a few shillings from the clergyman of the parish. The trade buried him. I didn't get 1s. as his widow—only 5l. to bury him; but there was arrears of rent to pay, and about a month after his death I hadn't a farthing, and I took the cholera, and was eight days in St. Bartholomew's, the parish officers sending me there in a cab. I lived in furnished lodgings before that, and had nothing to call my own, when I had pawned my black for my husband. When I got out I helped a neighbour at shoe-binding. One time I have earned 15s. a-week at shoe-binding for ——, Regent-street. Now I can only earn 5s. with full work. I have seldom earned 3s. of late weeks. I had to leave my neighbour, because I felt that I was a burden, and was imposing upon her. I then had a shelter with a young woman I once lodged with, but I couldn't stay there any longer. She was poor, and had nothing for me to do. So, on Saturday last, I had no work, no money, no friends, and I thought I would try and get in here, as another poor woman had done. Here I've had a shelter."

A pretty, pleasant-spoken young woman, very tidy in her poor attire, which was an old cloak wrapped close round her, to cover her scanty dress, gave me the following statement very modestly:—

" I am twenty-two; my mother died six years ago; my father I never knew, for I'm an unlawful child. My mother had a small income from my father, and kept me at school. I can't even guess who my father was. I am an only child. I was taken from school to wait upon my mother; very kind indeed she was to me, but she died in three weeks after I came from school. She'd been in a consumption for six years; she fretted sadly about me. She never told me I was an unlawful child. My aunt, my mother's sister, told me one day afterwards. My mother always said my father lived in the country. I loved my mother, so I seldom spoke of my father, for she would say, ' I don't wish to hear about him.' There was nothing for me at my mother's death, so I put myself to learn fancy-box-making for grocers and pastrycooks, for their sweetmeats, and for scents. My aunt assisted me. She is now poor, and a widow. I could never earn more than 3s. or 4s. a-week at box-making, the pay is so bad. I lived this way for four or five years, lodging with my aunt, and giving her all I earned, and she kept me for it. I then went to learn the

Macintosh-coat-making. I went into lodgings, my aunt being unable to help me any longer, as at my uncle's death she could only keep a room for herself and children. She makes pill-boxes. I could earn at the Macintoshes only 4s. a-week and my tea, when in full work, and when work was bad, I earned only 2s. 6d. It was 8d. a-day and my tea. I parted with a good box of clothes to keep myself; first one bit of dress went, and another. I was exposed to many a temptation, but I have kept my character, I am happy to say. On Monday night I was in the streets all night—I hardly knew in what part, I was so miserable—having no place to put my head in, and frightened to death almost. I couldn't pay my lodgings, and so lost them—I was locked out. I went to the station-house, and asked to sit there for a shelter, but the policeman said it was no place for me, as I was not guilty of any offence; they could do nothing for me: they were all very civil. I walked the streets all that cold night; I feel the cold of that night in my limbs still. I thought it never would be over. I wasn't exposed to any insults. I had to walk about all Tuesday, without a bite either Monday or Tuesday. On Tuesday evening I got admitted into this place, and was very thankful. Next day I tried for work, but got none. I had a cup of tea from my aunt to live on that day."

This girl wished to get into the parish, in order to be sent out as an emigrant, or any-thing of that kind; but her illegitimacy was a bar, as no settlement could be proved.

It was not difficult to see, by the looks of the poor woman whom I next addressed, the distress and privation she had endured. Her eyes were full of tears, and there was a plaintiveness in her voice that was most touching. She was clad in rusty black, and had on a black straw bonnet with a few old crape flowers in it; but still, in all her poverty, there was a neatness in her appearance that told she was much unused to such abject misery as had now come upon her. Hers was, in-deed, a wretched story—the victim of her husband's ill-treatment and neglect:—"I have been working at needlework ever since the end of August. My husband is living; but he has deserted me, and I don't know where he is at present. He had been a gen-tleman's servant, but he could attend to a garden, and of late years he had done so. I have been married nine years next April. I never did live happily with him. He drank a very great deal, and when tipsy he used to beat me sorely. He had been out of work for a long time before he got his last situa-tion, and there he had 18s. a-week. He lost his place before that through drink. Oh, sir, perhaps he'd give me all his money at the end of the week within three shillings; but then he'd have more than half of it back again—not every week alike, of course, but that was mostly the case—and in particular,

for the last year and a half, for since then he had been worse. While he was with me I have gone out for a day's charing occasion-ally, but then I found I was no for'arder at the week's end, and so I didn't strive so much as I might have done, for if I earned two shillings he'd be sure to have it from me. I was a ser-vant, before he married me, in a respectable tradesman's family. I lived three years and a half at my master's house out of town, and that was where I fell in with my husband. He was a shopman then. I lived with him more than eight years, and always acted a wife's part to him. I never drank myself, and was never untrue to him; but he has been too untrue to me, and I have had to suffer for it. I bore all his unkindness until August last, when he treated me so badly. I cannot mention to you how—but he de-ceived me and injured me in the worst pos-sible manner. I have one child, a boy, seven years old last September; but this boy is with him, and I don't know where. I have striven to find him out, but cannot. When I found out how he had deceived me we had words, and he then swore he wouldn't come home any more to me, and he has kept to his oath, for I haven't set eyes on him since. My boy was down at a friend's house at Cam-bridge, and they gave him up to the father without my knowledge. When he went away I had no money in the house. Nothing but a few things—tables, and chairs, and a bed in a room. I kept them as long as I could, but at last they went to find me in food. After he had gone I got a bit of needle-work. I worked at the dress-making and several different kinds of work since he left me. Then I used to earn about five shillings a-week; sometimes not so much. Sometimes I have made only two shillings, and lately—that is, within the last six weeks—I have earned scarcely anything. About October last I was obliged to sell my things to pay off my rent and get myself something to eat. After that I went to lodge with a person, and there I stopped till very lately, when I had scarce nothing, and couldn't afford to pay my rent. Then I was turned out of there, and I went and made shift with a friend by lying down on the boards, beside her children. I lay down with my clothes on. I had nothing to cover me, and no bed under me. They was very poor people. At last my friend and her husband didn't like to have people about in the room where they slept; and besides, I was so poor I was obliged to beg a bit of what they had, and they was so poor they couldn't afford to spare it to me. They were very good and kind to me so long as they could hold out anyhow, but at last I was obliged to leave, and walk about the streets. This I did for two whole nights—last Sunday and Monday nights. It was bitter cold, and freezing sharp. I did go and sit on the stairs of a lodging-house on Monday night, till I was that cold I could scarcely move a limb. On Tuesday night I slept in the Borough: A lady in the street gave me threepence. I asked her if she could give me a ticket to go anywhere. I told her I was in the deepest distress, and she gave me all the halfpence she had, and I thought I would go and have a night's lodging with the money. All these three days and nights I had only a piece of bread to keep down my hunger. Yesterday I was walking about these parts, and I see a lot of people standing about here, and I asked them if there was anything being given away. They told me it was the Refuge, or else I shouldn't have known there was such a place. Had I been aware of it, I shouldn't have been out in the streets all night as I was on Sunday and Monday. When I leave here (and they'll only keep me for three nights) I don't know what I shall do, for I have so parted with my things that I ain't respectable enough to go after needlework, and they do look at you so. My clothes are all gone to live upon. If I could make myself look a little decent, I might perhaps get some work. I wish I could get into service again. I wish I'd never left it, indeed : but I want things. If I can't get any things, I must try in such as I have got on : and if I can't get work, I shall be obliged to see if the parish will do anything for me; but I'm afraid they won't. I am thirty-three years old, and very miserable indeed."

From the opening of the Refuges for the Houseless in 1820, until 1852, as many as 189,223 homeless individuals received "nightly shelter" there, being an average of upwards of 6000 a-year. Some of these have remained three or four nights in the same establishment; so that, altogether, no less than 1,141,558 nights' lodgings were afforded to the very poor, and 2,778,153 lbs., or nearly 25,000 cwt. of bread distributed among them.

Asylum for the Houseless Poor.

There is a world of wisdom to be learnt at the Asylum for the Houseless Poor. Those who wish to be taught in this, the severest school of all, should pay a visit to Playhouse-yard, and see the homeless crowds gathered about the Asylum, waiting for the first opening of the doors, with their bare feet, blue and ulcerous with the cold, resting for hours on the ice and snow in the streets, and the bleak stinging wind blowing through their rags. To hear the cries of the hungry, shivering children, and the wrangling of the greedy men, scrambling for a bed and a pound of dry bread, is a thing to haunt one for life. There are 400 and odd creatures utterly destitute—mothers with infants at their breasts—fathers with boys holding by their side—the friendless —the penniless—the shirtless, shoeless, breadless, homeless ; in a word, the very poorest of this the very richest city in the world.

The Asylum for the Houseless is the con-fluence of the many tides of poverty that, at this period of the year, flow towards the metropolis. It should be remembered that there are certain callings, which yield a subsistence to those who pursue them only at particular seasons. Brickmakers, agricultural labourers, garden-women, and many such vocations, are labours that admit of being performed only in the summer, when, indeed, the labourer has the fewest wants to satisfy. The privations of such classes, then, come at a period when even the elements conspire to make their destitution more terrible. Hence, restless with want, they wander in hordes across the land, making, in vain hope, for London, as the great emporium of wealth — the market of the world. But London is as overstocked with hands as every other nook and corner of the country. And then the poor creatures, far away from home and friends, find at last to their cost, that the very privations they were flying from pursue them here with a tenfold severity. I do not pretend to say that all found within the walls of these asylums are such as I have described; many, I know, trade upon the sympathy of those who would ease the sufferings of the destitute labourers, and they make their appearance in the metropolis at this especial season. Winter is the beggar's harvest. That there are hundreds of professional vagabonds drawn to London at such a time, I am well aware ; but with them come the unemployed workmen. We must not, therefore, confound one with the other, nor let our indignation at the vagabond who will not work, check our commiseration for the labourer or artisan who cannot get work to do.

The table on the following page, which has been made up with considerable care and no little trouble, shows the number of persons from different counties sheltered at the Asylum for the Houseless Poor in the Metropolis for fourteen years.

A homeless painter gave me the following statement. His appearance presented nothing remarkable. It was merely that of the poor artisan. There was nothing dirty or squalid about him :—

" I was brought up a painter," he said, " and I am now 27. I served my apprenticeship in Yorkshire, and stayed two years after my term was out with the same master. I then worked in Liverpool, earning but little through illness, and working on and off as my health permitted. I got married in Liverpool, and went with my wife to Londonderry, in Ireland, of which place she was a native. There she died of the cholera in 1847. I was very ill with diarrhœa myself. We lived with her friends, but I got work, though wages are very low there. I never earned more than 2s. 6d. a-day there. I have earned 5s. 6d. a-day in Liverpool, but in Londonderry provisions are very cheap—the best meat at 4d. a-pound. It was an advantage to me being

	1829 to 1830	1830 to 1831	1831 to 1832	1832 to 1833	1834 to 1835	1840 to 1841	1841 to 1842	1842 to 1843	1843 to 1844	1844 to 1845	1845 to 1846	1846 to 1847	1847 to 1848	1848 to 1849	Total.	Average for each year for 14 years.
NORTH MIDLAND AGRICULTURAL.																
Lincolnshire	142	40	47	50	17	80	147	110	167	89	43	204	81	85	1302	93·0
Rutlandshire	...	...	...	...	1	5	13	13	8	10	2	24	8	24	108	7·7
Northamptonshire	17	20	31	15	14	77	144	108	125	124	50	227	115	67	1135	81·0
Shropshire	142	36	27	23	11	32	75	74	105	60	41	79	80	42	827	50·0
Herefordshire	18	19	...	...	9	28	61	28	85	43	18	65	54	45	445	31·8
SOUTH MIDLAND EASTERN AGRICULTURAL.																
Norfolk	82	94	73	53	37	125	167	226	268	267	135	364	161	163	2215	158·2
Suffolk	53	57	35	29	21	79	164	210	239	188	81	385	100	133	1783	127·2
Cambridgeshire	141	49	44	33	20	70	84	106	150	90	88	204	114	88	1281	91·5
Huntingdonshire	13	5	6	9	2	24	46	41	44	14	8	34	22	25	293	20·9
Essex	101	176	165	17	44	206	324	406	715	519	133	1034	567	392	4799	342·8
Oxfordshire	71	66	15	21	9	75	127	154	234	193	99	303	136	100	1603	114·5
Berkshire	142	93	43	51	33	153	264	382	641	366	244	767	342	287	3788	270·5
Wiltshire	53	62	58	34	21	99	193	201	262	202	97	377	205	87	1951	139·3
SOUTH AGRICULTURAL AND MARITIME.																
Kent	160	242	150	120	53	271	467	539	989	649	412	1458	845	523	6878	491·3
Sussex	52	64	47	54	27	135	170	175	322	230	136	506	230	147	2195	15·7
Hampshire	129	134	...	...	47	134	286	341	544	406	226	730	441	414	3832	273·7
Dorsetshire	40	27	17	23	11	37	71	62	99	79	25	126	57	46	720	51·4
Devonshire	122	118	141	153	70	83	180	206	375	225	135	453	237	209	2697	192·6
SOUTH MIDLAND AGRICULTURAL, WITH DISPERSED DOMESTIC MANUFACTURES.																
Bedfordshire	44	48	27	35	12	43	116	114	131	92	55	171	109	55	1052	75·1
Hertfordshire	93	104	33	24	31	164	240	262	199	259	182	592	377	181	2741	19·6
Buckinghamshire	40	42	24	31	11	84	190	147	258	246	187	314	168	88	1830	130·7
Somersetshire	158	153	195	181	75	210	345	262	535	327	247	871	556	246	4361	311·5
NORTHERN AND MIDLAND MANUFACTURING AND MINING.																
Lancashire	85	221	230	195	100	285	490	716	404	604	408	1272	748	811	6509	469·2
Cheshire	60	21	20	35	12	37	91	100	108	53	32	170	51	40	830	59·3
Derbyshire	29	19	25	17	6	43	79	70	91	60	39	97	46	48	669	47·8
Nottinghamshire	71	40	16	21	17	43	77	52	128	51	39	107	62	68	784	56·0
Staffordshire	48	50	25	28	7	94	175	136	270	123	50	256	121	129	1521	108·6
Leicestershire	40	44	20	23	14	55	11x	81	168	96	41	163	69	79	1007	71·9
Warwickshire	78	112	72	60	28	163	295	384	51	242	188	562	256	160	2760	197·1
Worcestershire	62	12	27	...	12	49	96	72	114	43	33	128	74	36	758	53·4
Gloucestershire	119	110	32	39	18	82	137	232	352	281	138	267	147	163	2048	146·3
NORTHERN MINING AND AGRICULTURAL.																
Northumberland	9	32	24	15	11	24	49	49	88	74	19	69	51	72	586	41·8
Durham	...	16	6	9	8	19	68	80	134	126	26	110	71	54	727	41·9
Cumberland	18	27	23	33	6	28	35	29	45	48	10	66	32	12	412	29·4
Westmoreland	...	...	5	9	1	10	24	20	24	7	4	19	14	6	143	10·2
Yorkshire	98	120	49	31	52	180	330	306	282	215	121	427	298	126	2635	188·2
WESTERN MINING AND AGRICULTURAL.																
Wales	117	115	593	887	280	138	137	103	160	559	210	878	726	343	5236	374·0
Cornwall	20	29	29	31	5	29	54	67	82	47	22	82	52	32	581	41·5
METROPOLITAN.																
London	107	115	593	887	280	138	137	103	160	559	210	878	726	343	5236	374·0
Middlesex	1742	1251	195	217	150	774	862	576	807	390	227	1065	538	214	9008	643·4
Surrey	263	119	151	127	38	211	294	193	355	195	151	572	329	204	3202	22·9
Ireland	1371	1311	547	403	300	896	1108	1305	1712	1253	772	7576	10756	5068	34378	2455·5
Scotland	213	914	241	210	139	77	136	240	299	400	294	172	623	344	4331	309·3
Guernsey and Jersey	5	14	...	2	3	5	...	7	22	8	8	1	25	47	147	10·5
France	1	...	3	7	7	...	...	1	...	10	2	8	24	14	77	5·5
Italy	2	2	...	...	...	...	...	5	13	1	...	9	5	7	44	3·1
Germany	...	...	7	5	...	24	36	59	60	25	27	38	36	53	370	26·4
Holland	11	9	2	4	...	...	...	4	6	2	...	...	...	...	38	2.7
Prussia	7	9	3	...	...	...	...	6	24	8	2	4	5	...	68	4·0
Spain	6	6	...	...	...	...	...	4	21	13	...	...	...	10	60	4·3
Portugal	7	7	2	11	1	...	...	...	...	...	...	...	2	5	35	2·5
Russia	1	5	3	...	...	...	...	...	4	10	...	2	10	7	42	3·0
Sweden	7	22	4	9	...	...	...	8	...	...	...	...	...	...	50	3·6
Norway	16	8	3	5	1	...	...	6	3	26	4	...	3	...	75	5·3
Australia	...	...	...	...	...	...	...	2	...	6	...	2	4	...	14	1·0
America	2	31	42	32	8	20	52	80	67	56	50	65	76	78	679	48·5
East Indies	9	1	5	3	6	22	39	40	57	12	200	24	38	19	475	33·9
West Indies	20	22	26	11	4	16	21	57	83	44	34	53	25	25	446	31·8
Africa	4	11	6	7	...	...	...	5	50	24	6	2	6	12	132	9·4
															130,625	87·496

an Englishman. English workmen seem to be preferred in Ireland, so far as I can tell, and I have worked in Belfast and Coleraine, and a short time in Dublin, as well as in Londonderry. I came back to Liverpool early in 1848, and got work, but was again greatly distressed through sickness. I then had to travel the country again, getting a little employment at Hemel Hempstead, and St. Alban's, and other places about, for I aimed at London, and at last I got to London. That was in November, 1848. When in the country I was forced to part with my clothes. I had a beautiful suit of black among them. I very seldom got even a trifle from the painters in the country towns; sometimes 2*d*. or 3*d*. from a master. In London I could get no work, and my shirts and my flannel-shirts went to keep me. I stayed about a month, and having nothing left, was obliged to start for the country. I got a job at Luton, and at a few other places. Wages are very low. I was always a temperate man. Many a time I have never tasted drink for a week together, and this when I had money in my pocket, for I had 30*l*. when I got married. I have, too, the character of being a good workman. I returned to London again three weeks back, but could find no work. I had again to part with any odd things I had. The last I parted with was my stopping-knife and diamond, for I can work as a glazier and plumber; country painters often can—I mean those apprenticed in the country. I have no clothes but what I have on. For the last ten days, I declare solemnly, I have had nothing but what I picked up in the streets. I picked up crusts that I saw in the streets, put out on the steps by the mistresses of the houses for the poor like myself. I got so weak and ill that I had to go to King's College Hospital, and they gave me medicine which did me good. I often had to walk the streets all night. I was so perished I could hardly move my limbs. I never asked charity, I can't; but I could have eaten anything. I longed for the fried fish I saw; yes, I was ravenous for that, and such-like, though I couldn't have touched it when I had money, and was middling well off. Things are so different in the country that I couldn't fancy such meat. I was brought to that pitch, I had the greatest mind to steal something to get into prison, where, at any rate, I said to myself, I shall have some food and shelter. I didn't—I thought better of it. I hoped something might turn up next day; besides, it might have got into the papers, and my friends might have seen it, and I should have felt I disgraced them, or that they would think so, because they couldn't know my temptations and my sufferings. When out all night, I used to get shelter, if I could, about Hungerford Market, among the straw. The cold made me almost dead with sleep; and when obliged to move, I couldn't walk at first, I could only crawl along. One night I had a penny given me, all I had gotten in five bitter nights in the streets. For that penny I got half a pint of coffee; it made me sick, my stomach was so weak. On Tuesday I asked a policeman if he couldn't recommend me to some workhouse, and he told me to come here, and I was admitted, and was very thankful to get under shelter.'

The next was a carpenter, a tall, fine-built man, with a pleasing expression of countenance. He was dressed in a flannel jacket and fustian trousers, with the peculiar little side-pocket for his foot-rule, that told you of his calling. He was about 40 years of age, and had the appearance, even in his destitution, of a most respectable mechanic. It is astonishing to mark the difference between the poor artisan and the labourer. The one seems alive to his poverty, and to feel it more acutely than the other. The labourer is more accustomed to "rough it," as it is called; but the artisan, earning better wages, and used to better ways, appears among the houseless poor as a really pitiable character. Carpenters are among the classes of mechanics in which there appears to be the greatest amount of destitution, and I selected this man as a fair average specimen of the body. He said,—

" I have been out of work nearly three months. I have had some little work in the mean time, an odd job or two at intervals, but nothing regular. When I am in full work, on day work, I can make 5*s*. a-day in London; but the masters very generally wishes the men to take piece-work, and that is the cause of men's work being cut down as it is, because men is obliged to take the work as they offers. I could get about 30*s*. a-week when I had good employment. I had no one but myself to keep out of my earnings. I have saved something when I have been on day-work; but then it went again as soon as I got to piece-work. This is generally the case with the carpenters. The last job I had was at Cobham, in Surrey, doing joiners' work, and business with my master got slack, and I was discharged. Then I made my way to London, and have been about from place to place since then, endeavouring to get work from every one that I knew or could get recommended to. But I have not met with any success. Well, sir, I have been obliged to part with all I had, even to my tools; though they're not left for much. My tools are pawned for 12*s*., and my clothes are all gone. The last I had to part with was my rule and chalk-line, and them I left for a night's lodging. I have no other clothes but what you see me in at present. There are a vast many carpenters out of work, and like me. It is now three weeks since the last of my things went, and after that I have been about the streets, and gone into bakers' shops, and asked for a crust. Sometimes I have got a penny out of the tap-room of a public-house. It's now more than a fortnight since I quitted my lodgings. I have been in the Asylum eight nights. Before that, I was out in the streets for five nights together. They were very cold nights ; yes, *very.*" [The man shivered at the recollection.] " I walked up one street, and down another. I sometimes got under a doorway, but it was impossible to stand still long, it was so cruel cold. The sleet was coming down one night, and freezed on my clothes as it fell. The cold made me stiff more than sleepy. It was next day that I felt tired ; and then, if I came to sit down at a fireside, I should drop asleep in a minute. I tried, when I was dead-beat, to get into St. Giles's union, but they wouldn't admit me. Then the police sent me up to another union: I forget the name, but they refused me. I tried at Lambeth, and there I was refused. I don't think I went a day without some small bit of bread. I begged for it. But when I walked from St. Alban's to London, I was two days without a bit to put in my mouth. I never stole, not a particle, from any person, in all my trials. I was brought up honest, and, thank God, I have kept so all my life. I would work willingly, and am quite capable : yes, and I would do my work with all my heart, but it's not to be got at."

This the poor fellow said with deep emotion ; and, indeed, his whole statement appeared in every way worthy of credit. I heard afterwards that he had offered to " put up the stairs of two houses" at some man's own terms, rather than remain unemployed. He had told the master that his tools were in pawn, and promised, if they were taken out of pledge for him, to work for his bare food. He was a native of Somerset, and his father and mother were both dead.

I then took the statement of a seaman, but one who, from destitution, had lost all the distinguishing characteristics of a sailor's dress of the better description. He wore a jacket, such as seamen sometimes work in, too little for him, and very thin and worn ; a waistcoat, once black; a cotton shirt; and a pair of canvas trousers. He had an intelligent look enough, and spoke in a straightforward manner. He stated : — " I am now thirty-five, and have been a seaman all my life. I first went to sea, as a cabin-boy, at Portsmouth. I was left an orphan at fourteen months, and don't know that I have a single relation but myself. I don't know what my father was. I was brought up at the Portsea workhouse. I was taught to read and write. I went to sea in 1827. I have continued a seaman ever since — sometimes doing pretty well. The largest sum I ever had in my possession was 38*l.* when I was in the Portuguese service, under Admiral Sartorius, in the ' Donna Maria' frigate. He hadn't his flag aboard, but he commanded the fleet, such as it was ; but don't call it a fleet, say a squadron. Captain Henry was my last captain there ; and after him I served under Admiral Napier ; he was admiral out there, with his

flag in the 'Real,' until Don Miguel's ships were taken. The frigate I was in, (the ' Donna Maria,') took the ' Princessa Real;' she was a 44-gun ship, and ours was a 36. It was a stiffish thing while it lasted, was the fight; but we boarded and carried the ' Princessa.' I never got all my prize-money. I stopped in Lisbon some time after the fight; and then, as I couldn't meet with a passage to England, I took service on board the 'Donegal,' 74 guns, Captain Fanshawe. I liked Lisbon pretty well; they're not a very tidy people — treacherous, too, but not all of them. I picked up a very little Portuguese. Most of my thirty-eight pounds went in Lisbon. The ' Donegal' brought Don Carlos over, and we were paid off in Plymouth; that was in 1834. Since then I have been in the merchant service. I like that best. My last voyage was in the ' Richard Cobden,' a barque of 380 tons, belonging to Dundee ; but she sailed from Gloucester for Archangel, and back from Archangel to Dundee, with a cargo of hemp and codilla. We were paid off in Dundee, and I received 4*l.* 8*s.* on the 13th of October." [He showed me his discharge from the ' Richard Cobden,' and his register ticket.] " I went to Glasgow and got a vessel there, an American, the ' Union ;' and before that I stayed at a lodging-house in Dundee that sailors frequent. There was a shipmate of mine there, a carpenter, and I left my things in his charge, and I went on board the ' Union' at Glasgow, and stayed working on board eighteen days ; she was short of men. The agreement between me and my old shipmate was, that he should send my things when I required them. My clothes were worth to me more than 5*l.* The ship was to sail on Friday, the 15th of November. Sailors don't mind getting under weigh on a Friday now ; and I got 10*s.* from the skipper to take me to Dundee on Thursday, the 14th ; but when I got to Dundee for my clothes, I found that the carpenter had left a fortnight before, taking all my things with him. I couldn't learn anything as to where he had gone. One man told me he thought he had gone to Derry, where some said he had a wife. The skipper paid me for what days I had been employed, and offered to let me work a passage to New York, but not on wages; because I had no clothes, he couldn't take me. I tried every ship in the Broomilaw, but couldn't get a job, nor a passage to London ; so me and two other seamen set off to walk to London. I started with 3*s.* One seaman left us at Carlisle. We didn't live on the way — we starved. It took us a month to get to London. We slept sometimes at the unions ; some wouldn't admit us. I was very lame at last. We reached London a month ago. I got three days' work as a rigger, at 2*s.* 6*d.* a-day, and a week's shelter in the Sailors' Asylum. I had five days' work also on stevedore's work in the 'Margaret West,' gone to Batavia. That brought me 12*s.*

those five days' work. Since that I've done nothing, and was so beat out that I had to pass two days and nights in the streets. One of those days I had a bit of bread and meat from an old mate. I had far rather be out in a gale of wind at sea, or face the worst storm, than be out two such nights again in such weather, and with an empty belly. My mate and I kept on trying to get a ship, but my old jacket was all against me. They look at a man's clothes now. I passed these two nights walking about Tower-hill, and to London-bridge and back, half dead, and half asleep, with cold and hunger. I thought of doing something to get locked up, but I then thought that would be no use, and a disgrace to a man, so I determined to bear it like a man, and try to get a ship. The man who left us at Carlisle did no better than me, for he's here too, beat out like me, and he told me of this Asylum. The other man got a ship. I'm not a drinking man, though I may have had a spree or two, but that's all over. I could soon get a ship if I had some decent clothes. I bought these trousers out of what I earned in London. I spun out my money as fine as any man could."

The poor fellow who gave me the following narrative was a coloured man, with the regular negro physiognomy, but with nothing of the lighthearted look they sometimes present. His only attire was a sadly soiled shirt of coarse striped cotton, an old handkerchief round his neck, old canvas trousers, and shoes. "I am twenty," he said, in good English, "and was born in New York. My father was a very dark negro, but my mother was white. I was sent to school, and can read a little, but can't write. My father was coachman to a gentleman. My mother spoke Dutch chiefly; she taught it to my father. She could speak English, and always did to me. I worked in a gentleman's house in New York, cleaning knives and going errands. I was always well treated in New York, and by all sorts of people. Some of the 'rough-uns' in the streets would shout after me as I was going to church on a Sunday night. At church I couldn't sit with the white people. I didn't think that any hardship. I saved seven dollars by the time I was sixteen, and then I went to sea as a cabin-boy on board the 'Elizabeth,' a brigantine. My first voyage was to St. John's, New Brunswick, with a cargo of corn and provisions. My second voyage was to Boston. After that I was raised to be cook. I had a notion I could cook well. I had cooked on shore before, in a gentleman's house, where I was shown cooking. Pretty many of the cooks in New York are coloured people—the men more than the women. The women are chiefly chambermaids. There was a vacancy, I was still in the 'Elizabeth,' when the cook ran away. He was in a bother with the captain about wasting tea and sugar. We went some more voyages, and I then got engaged as cook on board a new British ship, just off the stocks, at St. John's, New Brunswick, the 'Jessica.' About four months ago I came in her to Liverpool, where we were all paid off. We were only engaged for the run. I received 5*l*. I paid 2*l*. 10*s*. to my boarding mistress for two months' board. It was 5*s*. and extras a-week. I laid out the rest in clothes. I had a job in Liverpool, in loading hay. I was told I had a better chance for a ship in London. I tramped it all the way, selling some of my clothes to start me. I had 6*s*. to start with, and got to London with hardly any clothes, and no money. That's two months back, or nearly so. I couldn't find a ship. I never begged, but I stood on the highways, and some persons gave me twopences and pennies. I was often out all night, perishing. Sometimes I slept under the butchers' stalls in Whitechapel. I felt the cold very bitter, as I was used to a hot climate chiefly. Sometimes I couldn't feel my feet. A policeman told me to come here, and I was admitted. I want to get a ship. I have a good character as a cook; my dishes were always relished; my pea-soup was capital, and so was my dough and pudding. I often wished for them when I was starving." [He showed his white teeth, smiling as he spoke.] "Often under the Whitechapel stalls I was so frozen up I could hardly stir in the morning. I was out all the night before Christmas that it snowed. That was my worst night, I think, and it was my first. I couldn't walk, and hardly stand, when the morning came. I have no home to go to."

The next was a brickmaker, a man scarce thirty, a stout, big-boned man, but a little pale, evidently from cold and exhaustion. His dress was a short smockfrock, yellow with dry clay, and fustian trousers of the same colour, from the same cause. His statement was as follows:—

"I have been out of work now about seven weeks. Last work I done was on the Middle Level Drainage, in Cambridgeshire. Brick-making generally begins (if the weather's fine) about February, or the beginning of March, and it ends about September, and sometimes the latter end of November. If the weather's frosty, they can't keep on so long. I was at work up to about the middle of November last, making bricks at Northfleet, in Kent. I was with the same party for three years before. After that, brickmaking was done for the season, and I was discharged with 'five stools' of us beside. Each stool would require about six people to work it; so that altogether thirty hands were thrown out of work. After that I went to look for work among the 'slop' brick-makers. They makes bricks 'slop-way' right through the winter, for they're dried by flues. I am by rights a sand-stock brickmaker. Howsomever, I couldn't get a job at brickmaking slop-way, so I went down on the Middle Level, and there I got a job at river-cutting; but the wet weather came, and the water was so strong upon us that we got drownded out. That's the last job I've had. At brickmaking I had 3*s*. 10*d*. a thousand, this last summer. I have had my 4*s*. 6*d*. for the very same work. Two years ago I had that. Six of us could make about 35,000 in a-week, if it was fine. On an average, we should make, I dare say, each of us about 1*l*. a-week, and not more, because if it was a showery day we couldn't do nothing at all. We used to join one among another in the yard to keep our own sick. We mostly made the money up to 14*s*. a-week when any mate was bad. I did save a few shillings, but it was soon gone when I was out of work. Not many of the brickmakers save. They work from seventeen to eighteen hours every day when it's fine, and that requires a good bit to eat and drink. The brickmakers most of them drink hard. After I got out of work last November, I went away to Peterborough to look for employment. I thought I might get a job on the London and York Railway, but I couldn't find none. From there I tramped it to Grimsby : 'perhaps,' I said, 'I may get a job at the docks;' but I could get nothing to do there, so I came away to Grantham, and from there back to Peterborough again, and after that to Northampton, and then I made my way to London. All this time I had laid either in barns at night-times, or slept in the casual wards of the unions—that is, where they would have me. Often I didn't get nothing to eat for two or three days together, and often I have had to beg a bit to keep body and soul together. I had no other means of living since November last but begging. When I came to town I applied at a large builder's office for work. I heard he had something to do at the Isle of Dogs, but it was the old story—they were full, and had plenty of hands till the days got out longer. Then I made away to Portsmouth. I knew a man there who had some work, but when I got there he had none to give me at the present time. From there I went along the coast, begging my way still, to Hastings, in hope of getting work at the railway ; but all to no good. They had none, too, till the days got longer. After that I came round to London again, and I have been here a fortnight come next Monday. I have done no work. I have wandered about the streets any way. I went to the London Docks to see for a job, and there I met with a man as I knowed, and he paid for my lodging for one or two nights. I walked the streets for two whole nights before I came here. It was bitter cold, freezing sharp, indeed, and I had nothing to eat all the time. I didn't know there was such a place as this till a policeman told me. A gentleman gave me 6*d*., and that's all I've had since I've been in this town. I have been for the last three nights at the Asylum. I don't suppose they'll take my ticket away till after to-morrow night, and then I thought of making my way down home

till my work starts again. I have sought for work all over the country, and can't get any. All the brickmakers are in the same state as myself. They none of them save, and must either starve or beg in-the winter. Most times we can get a job in the cold weather, but this year, I don't know what it is, but I can't get a job at all. Former years I got railway work to do, but now there's nothing doing, and we're all starving. When I get down home I shall be obliged to go into the union, and that's hard for a young man like me, able to work, and willing; but it ain't to be had, it ain't to be had."

Then came a tailor, a young man only twenty-one years old, habited in a black frock-coat, with a plaid shawl twisted round his neck. His eyes were full and expressive, and he had a look of intelligence superior to any that I had yet seen. He told a story which my inquiries into the " slop trade " taught me was " ower true."

" I have been knocking about for near upon six weeks," he replied, in answer to my inquiries. " I was working at the slop-trade at the West-end. I am a native of Scotland. I was living with a sweater. I used to board and lodge with him entirely. At the week's end I was almost always in debt with him—at least he made it out so. I had very often to work all night, but let me slave as hard as I might I never could get out of debt with the sweater. There were often as many as six of us there, and we slept two together in each bed. The work had been slack for some time, and he gave me employment till I worked myself out of his debt, and then he turned me into the streets. I had a few clothes remaining, and these soon were sold to get food and lodging. I lived on my other coat and shirts for a week or two, and at last all was gone, and I was left entirely destitute. Then I had to pace the streets all day and night. The two nights before I came here I never tasted food nor lay down to rest. I had been in a four-penny lodging before then, but I couldn't raise even that; and I knew it was no good going there without the money. You must pay before you go to bed at those places. Several times I got into a doorway, to shelter from the wind and cold, and twice I was roused by the policeman, for I was so tired that I fell asleep standing against a shop near the Bank. What with hunger and cold, I was in a half-stupid state. I didn't know what to do : I was far from home and my mother. I have not liked to let her know how badly I was off." [The poor lad's eyes flooded with tears at the recollection of his parent.] " I thought I had better steal something, and then at least I should have a roof over my head. Then I thought I'd make away with myself. I can't say how; it was a sort of desperation ; and I was so stupid with cold and want, that I can hardly remember what I thought. All I wanted was to be allowed to sit down on some doorstep and die; but the police did not allow this. In the daytime I went up and lay about the parks most part of the day, but I couldn't sleep then; I hardly know why, but I'd been so long without food, that I couldn't rest. I have purposely kept from writing to my mother. It would break her heart to know my sufferings. She has been a widow this ten years past. She keeps a lodging-house in Leith, and has two children to support. I have been away eight months from her. I came to London from a desire to see the place, and thinking I could better my situation. In Edinburgh, I had made my 1*l*. a-week regularly; often more, and seldom less. When I came to London, a woman met me in the street, and asked me if I wasn't a tailor? On my replying in the affirmative, she informed me if I would come and work for her husband, I should have good wages, and live with her and her husband, and they would make me quite comfortable. I didn't know she was the wife of a sweater at that time. It was a thing I had never heard of in Edinburgh. After that time, I kept getting worse and worse off, working day and night, and all Sunday, and still always being in debt to them I worked for. Indeed, I wish I had never left home. If I could get back, I'd go in a moment. I have worked early and late, in the hope of accumulating money enough to take me home again, but I could not even get out of debt, much more save, work as hard as I would."

I asked if he would allow me to see some letters of his mother's, as vouchers for the truth of his story, and he produced a small packet, from which, with his permission, I copied the following:—

" My dear Son,—I have this moment received your letter. I was happy to hear from you, and trust you are well. Think of that God who has carried you in safety over the mighty deep. We are all much as you left us. I hope you will soon write. Ever believe me,
" Your affectionate mother,
" —— ——."

This was the first letter written after his absence from home. Since then his mother, who is aged and rheumatic (his letters vouched for this), had been unable to write a line. His brother, a lad of 16, says, in one of his letters,—

" I am getting on with my Greek, Hebrew, Latin, and French, only I am terribly ill off for want of books. My mother was saying that you would be bringing me a first-rate present from London. I think the most appropriate present you can bring me will be a Greek and English, or a Hebrew and English Lexicon; or some Hebrew, Greek, or Latin book."

A letter from his sister, a girl of 18, ran as follows:—

" My dear brother,—I take this opportunity of writing you, as you wrote that you would like to have a letter from me. I am very sorry you have been ill, but I hope you are keeping better. I trust also that affliction will be the means of leading you only more closely to the only true source of happiness. Oh, my dear brother, you are still young, and God has told us in His word, that those who seek Him early shall find Him. My dear brother, we get many a sad and solemn warning to prepare to meet our God: and oh! my dear brother, 'what is a man profited, if he shall gain the whole world, and lose his own soul?'"

The last letter was dated the 5th of December last, and from his brother:—

" We received your kind letter," it ran, " this instant, and we hasten to answer it. It has given my mother and me great relief to hear from you, as my mother and I were very miserable about you, thinking you were ill. We trust you will take care of yourself, and not get any more cold. We hope you will be able to write on receipt of this, and let us know how you are, and when we may expect you home, as we have daily expected you since the month of October."

These letters were shown to me at my request, and not produced by the young man himself, so that it was evident they were kept by the youth with no view of being used by him as a means of inducing charity; indeed, the whole manner of the young man was such as entirely precluded suspicion. On my asking whether he had any other credentials as to character, he showed me a letter from a Scotch minister, stating that " he had been under his charge, and that from his conduct he had been led to form a favourable opinion of his talents and moral character; and that he believed him to be a deserving, industrious young man."

Of the class of distressed tradesmen seeking shelter at this asylum, the two following may be taken as fair types. One was a bankrupt linendraper, and appeared in a most destitute state. When he spoke of his children, his eyes flooded with tears:—

" I have been in business in the linendrapery line—that's five years ago. I had about 600*l*. worth of stock at first starting, and used to take about 65*l*. every week. My establishment was in a country village in Essex. I went on medium well for the first two or three years, but the alteration of the poor-laws and the reduction of the agricultural labourers' wages destroyed my business. My customers were almost all among the working classes. I had dealings with a few farmers, of whom I took butter, and cheese, and eggs, in exchange for my goods. When the poor-laws were altered, the out-door relief was stopped, and the paupers compelled to go inside the house. Before that, a good part of the money given to the poor used to be expended at my shop. The overseers used to have tickets for flannels, blankets, and shirtings, and other goods; with these they used to send the paupers to my house. I used to take full 8*l*. or 10*l*. a-week in this manner; so that when the poor-laws were altered, and the previous system discontinued, I suffered materially. Besides, the wages of the agricultural labourers being lowered, left them less money to lay out with me. On a market-day they were my chief customers. I would trust them one week under the other, and give them credit for 7*s*. or 10*s*., if they wanted it. After their wages came down, they hadn't the means of laying out a sixpence with me; and where I had been taking 65*l*. a-week, my receipts dwindled to 30*l*. I had been in the habit of keeping two shopmen before, but after the reduction I was obliged to come down to one. Then the competition of the large houses in other towns was more than I could stand against. Having a larger capital, they could buy cheaper, and afford to take a less profit, and so of course they could sell much cheaper than I could. Then, to try and keep pace with my neighbours, I endeavoured to extend my capital by means of accommodation bills, but the interest I had to pay on these was so large, and my profits so little, that it soon became impossible for me to meet the claims upon me. I was made a bankrupt. My debts at the time were 300*l*. This is about six years ago. After that I took a public-house. Some property was left me. I came into about 1000*l*.; part of this went to my creditors, and I superseded my bankruptcy. With the rest I determined upon starting in the publican line. I kept at this for about ten months, but I could do nothing with it. There was no custom to the house. I had been deceived into taking it. By the time I got out of it all my money was gone. After that I got a job as a referee at the time of the railway mania, and when that was over, I got appointed as a policeman on the Eastern Union line. There I remained two years and upwards, but then they began reducing their establishment, both in men and in wages. I was among the men who were turned off. Since that time, which is now two years this Christmas, I have had no constant employment. Occasionally I have got a little law-writing to do; sometimes I have got a job as under-waiter at a tavern. After I left the waiter's place, I got to be very badly off. I had a decent suit of clothes to my back up to that time, but then I became so reduced, I was obliged to go and live in a low lodging-house in Whitechapel. I was enabled to get along somehow; I know many friends, and they gave me a little money now and then. But at last I had exhausted these. I could get nothing to do of any kind. I have been to Shoreditch station to try to pick up

a few pence at carrying parcels, but there were so many there that I could not get a crust that way. I was obliged to pawn garment after garment to pay for my food and lodging; and when they were all gone, I was wholly destitute. I couldn't even raise twopence for a night's lodging, so I came here and asked for a ticket. My wife is dead. I have three children; but I would rather you would not say anything about them, if you please."

I assured the man that his name should not be printed, and he then consented to his children being mentioned.

"The age of my eldest child is fourteen, and my youngest nine. They do not know of the destitution of their father. They are staying with one of my relations, who has supported them since my failure. I wouldn't have them know of my state on any account. None of my family are aware of my misery. My eldest child is a girl, and it would break her heart to know where I am, and see the state of distress I am in. My boy, I think, would never get over it. He is eleven years old. I have tried to get work at carrying placard-boards about, but I can't. My clothes are now too bad for me to do anything else. I write a good hand, and would do anything, I don't care what, to earn a few pence. I can get a good character from every place I have been in."

The other tradesman's story was as follows:—

"I am now thirty-three, and am acquainted with the grocery trade, both as master and assistant. I served a five-years' apprenticeship in a town in Berkshire. The very late hours and the constant confinement made me feel my apprenticeship a state of slavery. The other apprentices used to say they felt it so likewise. During my apprenticeship I consider that I never learnt my trade properly. I knew as much at the year's end as at the five years' end. My father gave my master fifty pounds premium; the same premium, or more, was paid with the others. One, the son of a gentleman at ——, paid as much as eighty pounds. My master made an excellent thing of his apprentices. Nearly all the grocers in the part of Berkshire I'm acquainted with do the same. My master was a severe man to us, in respect of keeping us in the house, and making us attend the Methodist Chapel twice, and sometimes thrice, every Sunday. We had prayers night and morning. I attribute my misfortunes to this apprenticeship, because there was a great discrepancy between profession and practice in the house; so there could be no respect in the young men for their employer, and they grew careless. He carried on his business in a way to inspire anything else than respect. On the cheesemongery side we were always blamed if we didn't keep the scale well wetted, so as to make it heavier on one side than the other—I mean the side of the scale where the butter was put—that was filled or partly filled with water, under pretence of preventing the butter sticking, and so the customer was wronged half an ounce in every purchase. With regard to the bacon, which, on account of competition, we had to sell cheap—at no profit sometimes—he used to say to us, 'You must make the ounces pay;' that is, we were expected to add two or more ounces, calculating on what the customer would put up with, to every six odd ounces in the weight of a piece. For instance, if a hock of bacon weighed six pounds seven ounces, at 4½d. per pound, we were to charge 2s. 3d. for the six pounds, and (if possible) adding two ounces to the seven which was the actual weight, charge each ounce a halfpenny, so getting 2s. 7½d. instead of 2s. 5d. This is a common practice in all the cheap shops I am acquainted with. With his sugars and teas, inferior sorts were mixed. In grinding pepper, a quantity of rice was used, it all being ground together. Mustard was adulterated by the manufacturers, if the price given showed that the adulterated stuff was wanted. The lowest priced coffee was always half chiccory, the second quality one-third chiccory; the best was one pound of chiccory to three pounds of coffee, or one-fourth. We had it either in chiccory-nibs, which is the root of the endive cultivated in Yorkshire, Prussia, &c., or else a spurious chiccory powdered, twopence per pound cheaper, the principal ingredient being parsnips and carrots cut in small pieces, and roasted like chiccory. A quart of water is the allowance to every twenty-eight pounds of tobacco. We had to keep pulling it, so as to keep it loose, for if left to lie long it would mould, and get a very unpleasant smell. In weighing sugar, some was always spilt loose in the scale opposite the weight, which remains in the scale, so that every pound or so is a quarter of an ounce short. This is the practice only in cutting shops. Often enough, after we have been doing all these rogueries, we were called into prayers. In my next situation, with an honourable tradesman in Yorkshire, I found I had to learn my business over again, so as to carry it on fairly. In two or three years I went into business in the town where I was apprenticed; but I had been subjected to such close confinement, and so many unnecessary restrictions, without any opportunity of improving by reading, that when I was my own master, and in possession of money, and on the first taste of freedom, I squandered my money foolishly and extravagantly, and that brought me into difficulties. I was 150l. deficient to meet my liabilities, and my friends advanced that sum, I undertaking to be more attentive to business. After that, a man started as a grocer in the same street, in the 'cutting' line, and I had to compete with him, and he sold his sugar a halfpenny a pound less than it cost, and I was obliged to do the same. The preparing of the sugar for the market-day is a country grocer's week's work, and all at a loss.

That's the ruin of many a grocer. My profits dwindled year by year, though I stuck very close to business; and in eighteen months I gave it up. By that time other 'cutting' shops were opened — none have done any good. I was about 100l. bad, which my friends arranged to pay by instalments. After that I hawked tea. I did no good in that. The system is to leave it at the working men's houses, giving a week's credit, the customers often taking more. Nothing can be honestly made in that trade. The Scotchmen in the trade are the only men that can do any good in it. The charge is six shillings for what's four shillings in a good shop. About nine months ago my wife—I had been married seven years — was obliged to go and live with her sister, a dressmaker, as I was too poor to keep her or myself either. I then came to London, to try for employment of any kind. I answered advertisements, and there were always forty or fifty young men after the same situation. I never got one, except for a short time at Brentford. I had also a few days' work at bill delivery—that is, grocers' circulars. I was at last so reduced that I couldn't pay for my lodgings. Nobody can describe the misery I felt as I have walked the streets all night, falling asleep as I went along, and then roused myself up half-frozen, my limbs aching, and my whole body trembling. Sometimes, if I could find a penny, I might sit up in a coffee-shop in Russell-street, Covent-garden, till five in the morning, when I had to roam the streets all day long. Two days I was without food, and determined to commit some felony to save me from starvation, when, to my great joy—for God knows what it saved me from, as I was utterly careless what my fate would be—I was told of this refuge by a poor man who had been there, who found me walking about the Piazzas in Covent-garden as a place of shelter. I applied, and was admitted. I don't know how I can get a place without clothes. I have one child with my wife, and she supports him and herself very indifferently by dressmaking."

A soldier's wife, speaking with a strong Scotch accent, made the following statement. She had altogether a decent appearance, but her features—and there were the remains of prettiness in her look—were sadly pinched. Her manners were quiet, and her voice low and agreeable. She looked like one who had "seen better days," as the poor of the better sort not unfrequently say in their destitution, clinging to the recollection of past comforts. She wore a very clean checked cotton shawl, and a straw bonnet tolerably entire. The remainder of her dress was covered by her shawl, which was folded closely about her, over a dark cotton gown.

"I was born twenty miles from Inverness, (she said), and have been a servant since I was eleven. I always lived in good places— the best of places. I never was in inferior places. I have lived as cook, housemaid, or servant-of-all-work, in Inverness, Elgin, and Tain, always maintaining a good character. I thank God for that. In all my distress I've done nothing wrong, but I didn't know what distress was when in service. I continued in service until I married; but I was not able to save much money, because I had to do all I could for my mother, who was a very poor widow, for I lost my father when I was two years old. Wages are very low in Scotland to what they are in England. In the year 1847 I lived in the service of the barrack-master of Fort George, twelve miles below Inverness. There I became acquainted with my present husband, a soldier, and I was married to him in March, 1847, in the chapel at Fort George. I continued two months in service after my marriage. My mistress wouldn't let me away; she was very kind to me; so was my master: they all were. I have a written character from my mistress." [This, at my request, she produced.] "Two months after, the regiment left Fort George for Leith, and there I lived with my husband in barracks. It is not so bad for married persons in the artillery as in the line (we were in the artillery), in barracks. In our barrack-rooms no single men were allowed to sleep where the married people were accommodated. But there were three or four married families in our room. I lived two years in barracks with my husband, in different barracks. I was very comfortable. I didn't know what it was to want anything I ought to have. My husband was a kind, sober man." [This she said very feelingly.] "His regiment was ordered abroad, to Nova Scotia. I had no family. Only six soldiers' wives are allowed to go out with each company, and there were seventeen married men in the company to which my husband belonged. It's determined by lot. An officer holds the tickets in his cap, and the men draw them. None of the wives are present. It would be too hard a thing for them to see. My husband drew a blank." She continued:—

"It was a sad scene when they embarked at Woolwich last March. All the wives were there, all crying and sobbing, you may depend upon that; and the children, too, and some of the men; but I couldn't look much at them, and I don't like to see men cry. My husband was sadly distressed. I hoped to get out there and join him, not knowing the passage was so long and expensive. I had a little money then, but that's gone, and I'm brought to misery. It would have cost me 6l. at that time to get out, and I couldn't manage that, so I stayed in London, getting a day's work at washing when I could, making a very poor living of it; and I was at last forced to part with all my good clothes after my money went; and my husband, God bless him! always gave me his money to do what I thought best with it. I used to earn a little in barracks with my needle, too. I was taken ill with cholera

at the latter end of August. Dear, dear, what I suffered! And when I was getting better I had a second attack, and that was the way my bit of money all went. I was then quite destitute; but I care nothing for that, and would care nothing for anything if I could get out to my husband. I should be happy then. I should never be so happy since I was born before. It's now a month since I was entirely out of halfpence. I can't beg; it would disgrace me and my husband, and I'd die in the streets first. Last Saturday I hadn't a farthing. I hadn't a thing to part with. I had a bed by the night, at 3d. a-night, not a regular lodging-house; but the mistress wouldn't trust me no longer, as I owed her 2s. 6d., and for that she holds clothes worth far more than that. I heard of this Asylum, and got admitted, or I must have spent the night in the street—there was nothing else for me; but, thank God! I've been spared that. On Christmas day I had a letter from my husband."

This she produced. It contained the following passage:—

"I am glad this letter only costs you a penny, as your purse must be getting very low; but there is a good time coming, and i trust in God it will not be long, my deir wife. i hope you will have got a good place before this raches you. I am dowing all in my power to help you. i trust in good in 3 months more, if you Help me, between us we make it out."

She concluded:—

"I wouldn't like him to know how badly I am off. He knows I would do nothing wrong. He wouldn't suspect me; he never would. He knows me too well. I have no clothes but what are detained for 2s. 6d., and what I have on. I have on just this shawl and an old cotton gown, but it's not broke, and my under-clothing. All my wish is to get out to my husband. I care for nothing else in this world."

Next comes the tale of a young girl who worked at velvet embossing. She was comely, and modestly spoken. By her attire it would have been difficult to have told that she was so utterly destitute as I afterwards discovered. She was scrupulously neat and clean in her dress; indeed it was evident, even from her appearance, that she belonged to a better class than the ordinary inmates of the Asylum. As she sat alone in the long, unoccupied wards, she sighed heavily, and her eyes were fixed continually on the ground. Her voice was very sorrowful. Her narrative was as follows:—

"I have been out of work for a very long while, for full three months now, and all the summer I was only on and off. I mostly had my work given out to me. It was in pieces of 100 yards, and sometimes less, and I was paid so much for the dozen yards. I generally had 3½d., and sometimes 1½d., according to what it was; 3½d. was the highest price that I had. I could, if I rose at five in the morning, and sat up till twelve, earn between 1s. and 1s. 3d. in a day. I had to cut the velvet after it had been embossed. I could, if a diamond pattern, do five dozen yards in a-day, and if a leaf pattern, I could only do three dozen and a-half. I couldn't get enough of it to do, even at these prices. Sometimes I was two days in the week without work, and sometimes I had work for only one day in the week. They wanted, too, to reduce the 1½d. diamond work to 1d. the dozen yards; and so they would have done, only the work got so slack that we had to leave it altogether. That is now seven weeks ago. Before that, I did get a little to do, though it was very little, and since then I have called almost every week at the warehouse, but they have put me off, telling me to come in a fortnight or a week's time. I never kept acquaintance with any of the other young women working at the warehouse, but I dare say about twenty-five were thrown out of work at the same time as I was. Sometimes I made 6s. a-week, and sometimes only 3s., and for the last fortnight I got 1s. 6d. a-week, and out of that I had my own candles to find, and 1s. 6d. a-week to pay for my lodgings. After I lost my work, I made away with what little clothes I had, and now I have got nothing but what I stand upright in." [The tears were pouring down the cheeks of the poor girl; she was many minutes afterwards before she could answer my questions, from sobbing.] "I can't help crying," she said, "when I think how destitute I am. Oh, yes, indeed, [she cried through her sobs,] I have been a good girl in all my trials. I might have been better off if I had chosen to take to that life. I need not have been here if I had chosen to part with my character. I don't know what my father was. I believe he was a clerk in one of the foreign confectionery houses. He deserted my mother two months before I was born. I don't know whether he is dead or not, for I never set eyes on him. If he is alive, he is very well off. I know this from my aunt, who was told by one of his fellow-clerks that he had married a woman of property and gone abroad. He was disappointed with my mother. He expected to have had a good bit of money with her; but after she married him, her father wouldn't notice her. My mother died when I was a week old, so I do not recollect either of my parents. When my aunt, who was his own sister, wrote to him about myself, my brother and sister, he sent word back that the children might go to the workhouse. But my aunt took pity on us, and brought us all up. She had a little property of her own. She gave us a decent education, as far as lay in her power. My brother she put to sea. My father's brother was a captain, and he took my brother with him. The first voyage he went (he was fourteen), a part of the rigging fell on him and the first mate, and they were both killed on the spot. My sister went as lady's-maid to Lady ——, and went abroad with her, now eighteen months ago, and I have never heard of her since. The aunt who brought me up is dead now. She was carried off two years and three months ago. If she had lived I should never have wanted a friend. I remained with her up to the time of her death, and was very happy before that time. After that I found it very hard for a poor lone girl like me to get an honest living. I have been struggling on ever since, parting with my clothes, and often going for two days without food. I lived upon the remainder of my clothes for some little time after I was thrown entirely out of work; but at last I got a fortnight in debt at my lodgings, and they made me leave; that's a week and three days ago now. Then I had nowhere but the streets to lay my head. I walked about for three days and nights without rest. I went into a chapel. I went there to sit down and pray; but I was too tired to offer up any prayers, for I fell asleep. I had been two nights and three days in the streets before this, and all I had during that time was a penny loaf, and that I was obliged to beg for. On the day that I was walking about, it thawed in the morning, and froze very hard at night. My shoes were very bad, and let in water; and as the night came on, my stockings froze to my feet. Even now I am suffering from the cold of those nights. It is as much as I can do to bend my limbs at present. I have been in the Asylum a week, and to-night is my last night here. I have nowhere to go, and what will become of me the Lord God only knows." [Again she burst out crying most piteously.] "My things are not fit to go into any respectable workroom, and they won't take me into a lodging either, unless I've got clothes. I would rather make away with myself than lose my character." [As she raised her hand to wipe away her tears, I saw that her arms were bare; and on her moving the old black mantle that covered her shoulders, I observed that her gown was so ragged that the body was almost gone from it, and it had no sleeves.] "I shouldn't have kept this," she said, "if I could have made away with it." She said that she had no friend in the world to help her, but that she would like much to emigrate.

I afterwards inquired at the house at which this poor creature had lodged, as to whether she had always conducted herself with propriety while living there. To be candid, I could hardly believe that any person could turn a young friendless girl into the streets because she owed two weeks' rent; though the girl appeared too simple and truthful to fabricate such a statement. On inquiry, I found her story true from the beginning to the end. The landlady, an Irishwoman, acknowledged that the girl was in her debt but 3s.; that she had lodged with her for several months, and always paid her regularly when she had money; but she couldn't afford, she said, to keep people for nothing. The girl had been a good, well-behaved, modest girl with her.

Description of the Asylum for the Houseless.

The Asylum for the Houseless Poor of London is opened only when the thermometer reaches freezing-point, and offers nothing but dry bread and warm shelter to such as avail themselves of its charity.

To this place swarm, as the bitter winter's night comes on, some half-thousand penniless and homeless wanderers. The poverty-stricken from every quarter of the globe are found within its wards; from the haggard American seaman to the lank Polish refugee, the pale German "out-wanderer," the tearful black sea-cook, the shivering Lascar crossing-sweeper, the helpless Chinese beggar, and the half-torpid Italian organ-boy. It is, indeed, a ragged congress of nations—a convocation of squalor and misery—of destitution, degradation, and suffering, from all the corners of the earth.

Nearly every shade and grade of misery, misfortune, vice, and even guilt, are to be found in the place; for characters are not demanded previous to admission, want being the sole qualification required of the applicants. The Asylum for the Houseless is at once the beggar's hotel, the tramp's town-house, the outcast's haven of refuge—the last dwelling, indeed, on the road to ruin.

It is impossible to mistake the Asylum if you go there at dark, just as the lamp in the wire cage over the entrance-door is being lighted. This is the hour for opening; and ranged along the kerb is a kind of ragged regiment, drawn up four deep, and stretching far up and down the narrow lane, until the crowd is like a hedge to the roadway. Nowhere in the world can a similar sight be witnessed.

It is a terrible thing, indeed, to look down upon that squalid crowd from one of the upper windows of the institution. There they stand shivering in the snow, with their thin, cobwebby garments hanging in tatters about them. Many are without shirts; with their bare skin showing through the rents and gaps of their clothes, like the hide of a dog with the mange. Some have their greasy coats and trousers tied round their wrists and ankles with string, to prevent the piercing wind from blowing up them. A few are without shoes; and these keep one foot only to the ground, while the bare flesh that has had to tramp through the snow is blue and livid-looking as half-cooked meat.

It is a sullenly silent crowd, without any of the riot and rude frolic which generally ensue upon any gathering in the London streets; for the only sounds heard are the squealing of the beggar infants, or the wrangling of the vagrant boys for the front ranks, together with a continued succession of hoarse coughs, that seem to answer each other like the bleating of a flock of sheep.

To each person is given half-a-pound of the best bread on coming in at night, and a like quantity on going out in the morning; and children, even if they be at the breast, have the same, which goes to swell the mother's allowance. A clerk enters in a thick ledger the name, age, trade, and place of birth of the applicants, as well as where they slept the night before.

As the eye glances down the column of the register, indicating where each applicant has passed the previous night, it is startled to find how often the clerk has had to write down, "in the streets;" so that "ditto," "ditto," continually repeated under the same head, sounded as an ideal chorus of terrible want in the mind's ear.

The sleeping-wards at the Asylum are utterly unlike all preconceived notions of a dormitory. There is not a bedstead to be seen, nor is even so much as a sheet or blanket visible. The ward itself is a long, bare, whitewashed apartment, with square post-like pillars supporting the flat-beamed roof, and reminding the visitor of a large unoccupied store-room—such as are occasionally seen in the neighbourhood of Thames-street and the Docks. Along the floor are ranged what appear at first sight to be endless rows of large empty orange chests, packed closely side by side, so that the boards are divided off into some two hundred shallow tanpit-like compartments. These are the berths, or, to speak technically, the "bunks" of the institution. In each of them is a black mattress, made of some shiny waterproof material, like tarpauling stuffed with straw. At the head of every bunk, hanging against the wall, is a leather—a big "basil" covering—that looks more like a wine-cooper's apron than a counterpane. These "basils" are used as coverlids, not only because they are strong and durable, but for a more cogent reason—they do not retain vermin.

Around the fierce stove, in the centre of the ward, there is generally gathered a group of the houseless wanderers, the crimson rays tinting the cluster of haggard faces with a bright lurid light that colours the skin as red as wine. One and all are stretching forth their hands, as if to let the delicious heat soak into their half-numbed limbs. They seem positively greedy of the warmth, drawing up their sleeves and trousers so that their naked legs and arms may present a larger surface to the fire.

Not a laugh nor sound is heard, but the men stand still, munching their bread, their teeth champing like horses in a manger. One poor wretch, at the time of my visit, had been allowed to sit on a form inside the railings round the stove, for he had the ague; and there he crouched, with his legs near as a roasting-joint to the burning coals, as if he were trying to thaw his very marrow.

Then how fearful it is to hear the continued coughing of the wretched inmates! It seems to pass round the room from one to another, now sharp and hoarse as a bark, then deep and hollow as a lowing, or—with the old—feeble and trembling as a bleat.

In an hour after the opening the men have quitted the warm fire and crept one after another to their berths, where they lie rolled round in their leathers—the rows of tightly-bound figures, brown and stiff as mummies, suggesting the idea of some large catacomb.

The stillness is broken only by the snoring of the sounder sleepers and the coughing of the more restless.

It is a marvellously pathetic scene. Here is a herd of the most wretched and friendless people in the world, lying down close to the earth as sheep; here are some two centuries of outcasts, whose days are an unvarying round of suffering, enjoying the only moments when they are free from pain and care—life being to them but one long painful operation as it were, and sleep the chloroform which, for the time being, renders them insensible.

The sight sets the mind speculating on the beggars' and the outcasts' dreams. The ship's company, starving at the North Pole, dreamt, every man of them, each night, of feasting; and are those who compose this miserable, frozen-out beggar crew, now regaling themselves, in their sleep, with visions of imaginary banquets?—are they smacking their mental lips over ideal beef and pudding? Is that poor wretch yonder, whose rheumatic limbs rack him each step he takes—is *he* tripping over green fields with an elastic and joyous bound, that in his waking moments he can never know again? Do that man's restlessness and heavy moaning come from nightmare terrors of policemen and treadwheels?—and which among those runaway boys is fancying that he is back home again, with his mother and sisters weeping on his neck?

The next moment the thoughts shift, and the heart is overcome with a sense of the vast heap of social refuse—the mere human street-sweepings—the great living mixen—that is destined, as soon as the spring returns, to be strewn far and near over the land, and serve as manure to the future crime-crops of the country.

Then come the self-congratulations and the self-questionings! and as a man, sound in health and limb, walking through a hospital, thanks God that he has been spared the bodily ailments, the mere sight of which sickens him, so in this refuge for the starving and the homeless, the first instinct of the well-to-do visitor is to breathe a thanksgiving (like the Pharisee in the parable) that " he is not as one of these."

But the vain conceit has scarcely risen to the tongue before the better nature whispers in the mind's ear, " By what special virtue of your own are you different from them? How comes it that you are well clothed and well fed, whilst so many go naked and hungry?" And if you in your arrogance, ignoring all the accidents that have helped to build up your wordly prosperity, assert that you have been the " architect of your own fortune," who, let us ask, gave you the genius or energy for the work?

Then get down from your moral stilts, and confess it honestly to yourself, that you are what you are by that inscrutable grace which decreed your birthplace to be a mansion or a cottage rather than a "padding-ken," or which granted you brains and strength, instead of sending you into the world, like many of these, a cripple or an idiot.

It is hard for smug-faced respectability to acknowledge these dirt-caked, erring wretches as brothers, and yet, if from those to whom little is given little is expected, surely, after the atonement of their long suffering, they will make as good angels as the best of us.

CHARITIES AND SUMS GIVEN TO THE POOR.

ACCORDING to the last Report of the Poor-law Commissioners, the paupers receiving in- and out-door relief was, in 1848, no less than 1,870,000 and odd. The number of criminals in the same year was 30,000 and odd. In 1844, the number of lunatics in county asylums was 4000 and odd; while according to the Occupation Abstract of the returns of the population there were, in 1841, upwards of 5000 almspeople, 1000 beggars, and 21,000 pensioners: these formed into one sum, give us no less than two millions and a quarter individuals who pass their time without applying to any gainful occupation, and consequently live in a state of inactivity and vice upon the income of the remainder of the population. By the above computation, therefore, we see that out of a total of 16,000,000 souls, one-seventh, or 14 per cent of the whole, continue their existence either by pauperism, mendicancy, or crime. Now the cost of this immense mass of vice and want is even more appalling than the number of individuals subsisting in such utter degradation. The total amount of money levied in 1848 for the relief of England and Wales was seven millions four hundred thousand pounds; but, exclusive of this amount, the magnitude of the sum that we give voluntarily towards the support and education of the poor classes is unparalleled in the history of any other nation or any other time.

According to the summary of the returns annexed to the voluminous Reports of the Charity Commissioners, the rent of the land and other fixed property, together with the interest of the money left for charitable pur- poses in England and Wales, amounts to 1,200,000*l.* a year; and it is believed, by proper management, this return might be increased to an annual income of at least two millions of money; and yet, says Mr. M'Cul- loch, "there can be no doubt that even this large sum falls far below the amount expended every year in voluntary donations to charitable establishments. Nor can any estimate be formed," he adds, "of the money given in charity to individuals; but in the aggregate cannot fail to amount to an immense sum." All things considered, therefore, we cannot be very far from the truth, if we assume that the sums voluntarily subscribed towards the re- lief of the poor equal, in the aggregate, the total amount raised by assessment for the same purpose; so that it appears that the well-to-do amongst us expend the vast sum of fifteen million pounds per annum in mitigating the miseries of their less fortunate brethren.

But though we give altogether fifteen mil- lion pounds a year to alleviate the distress of those who want or suffer, we must remember that this vast sum expresses not only the liberal extent of our sympathy, but likewise the fearful amount of want and suffering, of excess and luxury, that there must be in the land, if the poorer classes require fifteen mil- lions to be added in charity every year to their aggregate income, in order to relieve their pains and privations, and the richer can afford to have the same immense sum taken from theirs, and yet scarcely feel the loss, it shows at once how much the one class must possess and the other want.

MEETING OF TICKET-OF-LEAVE MEN.

A meeting of ticket-of-leave men, convened by Mr. H. Mayhew, was held some time since at the National Hall, Holborn, with the view of affording to persons of this class, who are anxious to lead a reformed life, an opportunity of stating the difficulties they have to encounter in their endeavour to obtain a honest livelihood. About fifty mem- bers of the body responded to Mr. Mayhew's invitation. The men were admitted on pre- senting their tickets of leave, and were re- quired on entrance to fill up the columns of a register, setting forth their ages, their occu- pations, the offence for which they were last convicted, their sentences, and the amount of instruction they had severally received. From the information thus collected, it appears that only 3 out of the 50 present were above the age of 40, the large majority ranging between 18 and 35, the highest age of all being 68; that they consisted of labourers, hawkers, cos- termongers, blacksmiths, shoemakers, carpen- ters, and other handicraftsmen; that their previous punishments varied from 2 years to

14 years' transportation; and that more than one-half of them had been educated either at day schools or Sunday schools. Suspecting that the men would be unwilling to attend if the police presented themselves, either in the hall or at its entrance, Mr. Mayhew took the precaution to apply beforehand to the Metro- politan Commissioners on the subject. The authorities at once acceded to the request thus made to them, and not a solitary constable was permitted to overawe the meeting."

Mr. Mayhew, in opening the proceedings, said:—"The object of this meeting is three- fold. In the first place, I wish society to know more about you as a distinct class; secondly, I wish the world to understand the working of the ticket-of-leave system; and, thirdly, I want to induce society to exert itself to assist you, and extricate you from your dif- ficulties. When I first went among you, it was not very easy for me to make you compre- hend the purpose I had in view. You at first fancied that I was a Government spy, or a person in some way connected with the police. I am none of these, nor am I a clergyman wishing to convert you to his particular creed, nor a teetotaler anxious to prove the source of all evil to be over-indulgence in intoxi- cating drink; but I am simply a literary man, desirous of letting the rich know something more about the poor. (Applause.) Some persons study the stars, others study the ani- mal kingdom, others again direct their re- searches into the properties of stones, devoting their whole lives to these particular vocations. I am the first who has endeavoured to study a class of my fellow-creatures whom Providence has not placed in so fortunate a position as myself, my desire being to bring the extremes of society together—the poor to the rich, and the rich to the poor. (Applause.) I wish to get bodies of men together in a mass, their influence by that means being more sensibly felt than if they remain isolated. I know you, perhaps, nearly as well as many of you know yourselves. I have had many of you in my house with my wife and children, and to your honour and credit be it said, you never wronged me of the smallest article, and, moreover, I never heard a coarse word escape your lips. I have trusted many of you who have been long tried by want of food. I have given you money to get change for me, and you never yet took advantage of me. This shows that there is still a spark of good in each of you. That spark I wish Society to de- velope, that you may be made what all must really desire to see you. Some two or three Sundays ago I was at Pentonville prison during Divine service. Society believes you to be hardened in heart and unimpressionable. Well, I saw some four hundred prisoners there weeping like children at the melting tale which the clergyman told. He spoke of the burial of a girl by torchlight, at which he offi- ciated, explaining that the reason why the

TICKET-OF-LEAVE MEN.

[From a Photograph.]

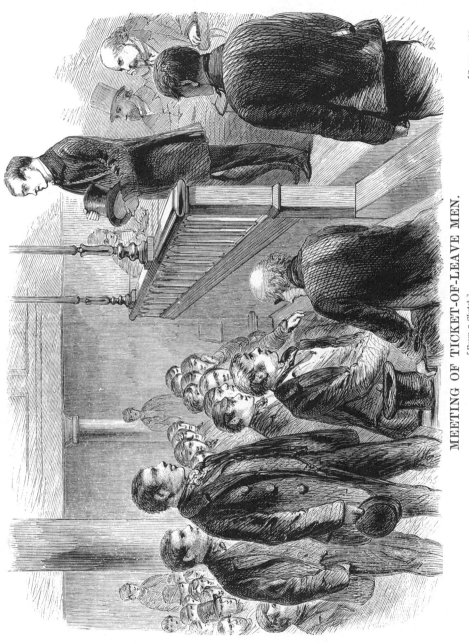

MEETING OF TICKET-OF-LEAVE MEN.

[*From a Sketch.*]

[*See page* 430.]

funeral took place so late was that the father of the deceased had to come about fifty miles to be present, and thence the delay. The old man's tears, he said, fell like rain on the coffin-lid; and yet, in his anguish, the bereaved parent exclaimed that he preferred to see his daughter a corpse than for her to live a life of infamy in the streets. (Sensation.) This sad story could not fail to touch a chord in each of your breasts. But to come to the ticket-of-leave system. The public generally believe that it is a most dangerous thing to set you free under that system. I know this is one of the most important experiments in connexion with the reformation of offenders that has ever been tried, and it has worked better than any other of which I have had experience. In 1853, the old mode of transportation was changed, and an Act passed directing that no person should be sentenced to transportation except for fourteen years or upwards, and that thenceforward sentence of penal servitude should be substituted for transportation for less than fourteen years. At the same time, a discretionary power was given to commute sentences of transportation into terms of penal servitude. Then, for the first time, was it ordained that it should be lawful for her Majesty, under the seal of her secretary of state, to grant any convict, now or hereafter sentenced to transportation, or to the punishment substituted for it, a license to be at large in the United Kingdom, or such part thereof as is expressed in the license, during a portion of his term of imprisonment. The holder of this license is not to be imprisoned by reason of his previous sentence; but if his license is revoked, he is to be apprehended and re-committed. Since the passing of that Act, and between September 1853 and December 31, 1855—a period of about two years and a quarter—the number of convicts released from public works and prisons has been 3880. To this number have to be added juveniles from Parkhurst prison, 297; and convicts from Bermuda and Gibraltar, 435: making a total of 4612. Of this aggregate, 140 have had their licenses revoked, and 118 have been sentenced to penal servitude and imprisonment; making together 258 who have had their licenses cancelled out of the entire 4612. Out of this 258, 27 were committed for breach of the vagrancy law, 20 for ordinary assaults, 8 for assaults on the police, 6 for breach of the game-laws, 2 for desertion from the militia, and 20 for misdemeanour; making together 84, and leaving 174 as the exact number who have relapsed into their former course of life. Thus it appears that only five and a-half per cent of the whole number of tickets-of-leave granted have been revoked. Now, considering that the number of re-committals to prison for England and Wales averages thirty-three in every hundred prisoners; this, I think, is a very favourable result of the ticket-of-leave experiment. Look-

ing at the extreme difficulty of a return to an honest life, it is almost astonishing that so low a per-centage as five and a half of the licenses in all England should have been revoked. You know that, during your imprisonment, there are four stages of probation. In certain prisons you have to do a prescribed amount of work, for which you receive a certain gratuity. The shoemakers, for instance, get 4*d.* every week if they make two and a-half pairs, 6*d.* for three pairs, and 8*d.* for four pairs. The tailors get 4*d.* if they make two suits of prison garments, 6*d.* for three suits, and 8*d.* for four. The matmakers get 4*d.* for thirty-six square feet of their work, 6*d.* for forty-five feet, and 8*d.* for fifty-four. The cotton-weavers get 4*d.* for twenty-four yards, 6*d.* for thirty, and 8*d.* for thirty-six. The cloth-weavers are paid in a similar manner. These sums are entered to your credit, and pass with you from prison to prison until they at last accumulate into an amount, which is handed over to you under certain restrictions on leaving. In the second stage of probation, you receive 6*d.* in addition to the ordinary weekly gratuity; in the third stage you receive an addition of 9*d.*; and in the fourth stage one of 1*s.* or 1*s.* 3*d.* This sum— large or small, according to the term of imprisonment—is placed to your credit on quitting the prison, and is thus distributed:—5*l.* to be paid immediately on discharge, or by post-office order on the convict's arrival at his native place. If the sum is over 5*l.* and under 8*l.* he receives 4*l.* on his discharge, and the balance at the end of two months; if over 8*l.* and under 12*l.*, half is paid on his discharge and the balance at the end of three months; if over 12*l.* and under 20*l.*, 5*l.* is paid on his discharge, half the balance in two months, and the remainder in three months. In order, however, to obtain this balance, it is necessary for you to be provided with certificates as to character, either from a clergyman, a magistrate, or the employer with whom the holder of the license is then at work. The applicants for these balances have been 1242 in number up to the 31st December last. Of these, 1225 have sent in certificates of a satisfactory nature, only 17 having been sent in of a contrary character—851 certificates were furnished by clergymen, 214 by magistrates, and 177 by employers under whom the persons liberated were engaged. In the 1225 cases above-mentioned, after the expiration of the prescribed number of months, the money was paid to the applicants. Considering the difficulty these persons must experience in obtaining the certificates required of them, the figures I have stated are highly satisfactory as to the working of the system; and I cannot, therefore, understand how society should have gone so far astray on this point as it has done. The public, however, believe ticket-of-leave men to be very dangerous characters—it does not know the training they undergo while in prison. A high authority tells me, that it is impossible for a gentleman's son to be trained with greater care at Eton or at any of the other public schools than each of you have been. When, however, Society sees two or three, or even some half-dozen of you relapse into your former practices, they jump to the conclusion that the same is the case with you all. They, in fact, think that relapses are the rule and amendment the exception, instead of the fact being quite the other way. This is like the self-delusion of the London apprentices, who fancy there are more wet Sundays in a year than rainy week-days, simply because they want to get out on Sundays, and are particularly vexed when the bad weather keeps them at home. (Laughter.) Now I have tried many experiments at the reformation of criminals, and one-half of them have failed. Yet I am not discouraged; for I know how difficult it is for men to lay aside their past habits. Every allowance ought, therefore, to be made, because they cannot be expected to become angels in a moment. The vice of the present system, in fact, is, that unless a criminal suddenly becomes a pattern man, and at once forgets all his old associates, Society will have none of you, and, as a certain gentleman has expressed it, 'you must all be shot down, and thrown into Society's dust-bin.' (Applause.) A well-known literary gentleman, who had moved in good society, had a daughter, with whom he lived at the east end of London. He was rather lax, perhaps, in the rearing of his child, allowing her to do pretty much as she liked. She once went to a concert, and got acquainted with a 'mobsman,' who accompanied her home, and at last introduced himself to her father as his daughter's suitor. Being a well-dressed, respectable-looking person, the father—good, easy man!—took a liking for him, and not being particular in his inquiries as to the lover's course of life, allowed them to marry. After their marriage, however, the daughter discovered what her husband's pursuits really were. She, of course, acquainted her father with the fact, who, in great distress of mind, called his son-in-law to him, and telling him that he had never had a stain upon his name or character, implored him by every argument he could urge to lead an honest life. The mobsman promised to comply. His father-in-law removed him from the neighbourhood in which he was staying, and placed him in the service of a large railway carrier. In this employ, having one day to take a parcel to a gentleman's house, up-stairs on the mantelpiece he saw a gold watch. This temptation was too much for him, and he seized the article and put it into his pocket. The theft was discovered before the offender had gone any distance; the man was soon arrested, but the father, by dint of great exertion, got him off, on returning the watch and communicating with its owner before the complaint was made at the police-office. The father again en-

treated his son-in-law to abandon his evil courses, but the latter said his old associations were too strong for him, and that he saw no other resource open for him than to leave London altogether. The old man accordingly took him with him to a residence on the banks of the Thames, where, at length, some of his old companions unfortunately met him, and told him of a 'crib' they were going to 'crack,' and of the heavy 'swag' they were likely to get. The prodigal's old habits were again too much for him. He accompanied his former associates in their criminal enterprise, was captured, and thrown again into prison—his father-in-law died in a mad-house, and his wife committed suicide. Thus fearful, then, are the effects of criminal associations, and therefore I am only surprised that so small a percentage of the ticket-of-leave men have yielded to a relapse. Successful, however, as the system has thus far proved, I yet see a considerable amount of evil in connexion with it; and this is the reason why I have called you together, hoping that some of the tales you have to relate will serve to rouse the public to a sense of your real position, and induce them to stretch forth a hand to save you from the ruin that on every hand threatens you. When you come out of prison, destitute as you are of character, there are only two or three kinds of employment open to you, and I therefore wish Society to institute some association to watch over you, to give you every possible advice, to lead you to good courses, and, moreover, to provide you with the means of getting some honest livelihood. (Applause.) I know that as a class you are distinguished mainly by your love of a roving life, and that at the bottom of all your criminal practices lies your indisposition to follow any settled occupation. Continuous employment of a monotonous nature is so irksome to you, that immediately you engage in it you long to break away from it. This, I believe, after long observation of your character, to be true of the majority of you; and you are able to judge if I am right in this conclusion. Society, however, expects, that if you wish to better yourselves, you will at once settle down as steadily as it does, and immediately conform to all its notions; but I am satisfied that if anything effectual is to be done in the way of reforming you, Society must work in consonance and not in antagonism with your nature. In this connexion it appears to me that the great outlet for you is street trading, where you are allowed to roam at will unchafed by restraints not congenial to your habits and feelings. In such pursuits a small fund for stock-money suffices, and besides, no character is required for those who engage in them. From the inquiries made by a gentleman who lately visited the places in which most of you live, I find that the great majority of you follow some form or other of street occupation. Still there is this difficulty in your way. The public requires its thoroughfares to be kept clear of obstruction, and I know that the police have been ordered to drive you away—to make you, as the phrase is, 'move on.' You may fancy that the police act thus of their own accord; but I learn from communication with the Commissioners, that the police have to receive requisitions from the shopkeepers and other inhabitants to enforce the Street Act, and are compelled to comply with them. In one instance a tradesman living in a street-market, where about five hundred poor persons were obtaining a livelihood, complained to the police of the obstruction thus occasioned to his business, which was of a 'fashionable' nature. The consequence was that the thoroughfare had to be cleared, and these five hundred persons were reduced almost to a state of starvation, and many of them were forced into the workhouse. Now I don't believe that this is right; and I am prepared to say to Society, that no one man in the kingdom should have the power to deprive so large a body of poor persons of all means of gaining an honest subsistence. (Loud applause.) At the same time, certain regulations must be respected; the streets even, you will allow, must not be blocked—(hear, hear)—there must be a free passage, and it is necessary to consider whether a plan may not be devised which will answer both ends. It strikes me that a certain number of poor men's markets might be established very advantageously; for the poor are so linked together that they would rather buy of the poor than the rich; and it is much to their credit that it is so. If spots of ground for markets of this kind were bought by benevolent individuals, and a small toll levied on admission to them, I am sure the speculation would be profitable to those who embarked in it, as well as beneficial to the interests—moral as well as pecuniary—of the street traders. Connected with these establishments there ought to be a school for the children of the traders, a bank for preserving your money, a cook-shop to prevent you from being obliged to take your meals at the public-house, together with many other useful adjuncts which might be grouped round the market. Such experiments have been tried before now. There is the old Rag-fair at Houndsditch, where formerly old clothes were sold in the streets. In that case a Jew bought a piece of land, to which poor traders were admitted on payment of a halfpenny per head, and the project succeeded so admirably that the owner of the ground soon became a rich man. At Paris similar markets have been instituted, and with success, by M. Delamarre; and in the same city there are also public kitchens, where cooked meat can be had at a cheap rate, so as to keep the poor people out of the public-houses. Lodging-houses for such of the men as choose to come to them would likewise be a valuable appendage to the suggested street-markets, but they must be free from the almost tyrannical supervision which prevails in the existing model lodging-houses in London. Whilst so much vexatious restriction is put upon men's liberties, they cannot be expected to frequent these places in the numbers they otherwise would. Lodging-houses for the reception of ticket-of-leave men on leaving prison might prevent them from being thrown loose upon the world until they have some prospect of a livelihood before them. I wish Society to take these men by the hand—to be lenient and considerate towards them, and not to be annoyed if one or two should recede from their good resolutions; for the experience of the reformatory institutions of London shows that there are often twenty-five per cent of relapses among their inmates. Therefore, if only five and a-half per cent of you fail in your laudable endeavours, as the returns I have quoted show, to be the whole proportion, then I say that you are a class who ought to be encouraged. By this means we shall be able to grapple effectually with this great trouble—viz. how to reform the great bulk of our criminals. Under these circumstances I have invited you here to-night, to give you an opportunity of telling Society what are your difficulties. There is a gentleman present who will publish your grievances all over the kingdom, and I charge you all to speak only the truth. You cannot benefit by any other course, and therefore be you a check the one upon the other; and if any one departs from the strict fact, do you pull him up. Thus you will show the world that you have met here with an earnest desire to better yourselves—thus you will present a spectacle that will go far to convince Society that it runs no risk in giving you your liberty —and prevail upon it to regard not wholly without compassion the few members of your class who, yielding in an evil hour to the trying temptations which beset them, sink unhappily into their former delinquencies." (Loud and prolonged applause.)

The men were then requested to ascend the platform, and relate their own experience, as well as to state their views of how their class could best be assisted. The first to respond to this invitation was a young man of neat and comparatively respectable appearance, who seemed to be known to the rest by the name of 'Peter,' and who, with great fluency and considerable propriety of expression, proceeded to narrate his own past career as follows:—

" Friends, I hope you will excuse any hesitation or stammering on my part while I stand in this unusual position. All the education I have received has been picked up in prison — understand that. As to the difficulties encountered by ticket-of-leave men I know nothing, save from my own personal experience. You cannot judge properly of the intentions of the convict, unless you begin with his career from the first time that he enters prison. Well, you must know, that I was transported for seven years. I was sent to Millbank, and there put to the tailoring business. From the outset I had a great partiality for books, and I then learnt to read and write better than I could do before. I also acquired a little grammar and arithmetic, simply to improve my mind; and if mental improvement is any part of moral improvement, I was, of course, morally improving also. I knew more arithmetic then than I do now, having lost my knowledge in consequence of excessive indulgence in intoxicating liquors. In fact, I got as far as the beginning of algebra—certainly a very abstruse science to tackle. After spending fourteen months in Millbank I went to Portland, where I had to wheel barrows from morning to night. I still persevered, however, with my books; and the great anxiety that constantly weighed on my mind was, what would become of me when I was liberated. I knew that the work I was doing would be well done; and I was far happier then than I am now, because I feel that there is no breakfast for me to-morrow morning till I go and thieve it; and that is the simple truth. (Applause.) I supposed that if I went to the Chaplain, who had delivered several charitable discourses, very much in accordance with my own feelings, he might assist me. I therefore stated my case to him, telling him that I really wished to become a better member of society. He listened to my tale, and wished me to see him once a-week, which I did. But the Chaplain at this time was the Rev. Mr. Moran (as we understood), and when I wanted books he would not encourage me, unless I consented to become a communicant. If I had done that I should have had more favour shown to me, and been provided with whatever I wished; but not feeling myself fit for such a thing, I therefore refused. I then waited till a change took place, and the Rev. Mr. Ubridge, (as we understood), a lover of science and literature, came — a clergyman whose system was altogether different, having none of these Roman Catholic restrictions. We were then allowed to think and do as we liked in regard to religion, and no man was forced to attend the communion-table unless he thought himself as fit for it as the Minister. I applied to the new Chaplain, and told him I considered my mind to have been much enlightened. I suppose everybody fancies the same, who knows a little, though not much. When my turn to be liberated approached they came to me in my separate cell, and I told them there was no chance of my bettering myself unless I could get an honest living. I said that I must go back to London, where I had first been transported, and that the only thing I expected was to

be transported again; for my bad character would be no recommendation to me—the police all knew me, and wherever they saw me they would point me out as a ticket-of-leave man. (Applause.) On my release I received 6l. 12s. I came to Southampton with one of the officers of the establishment, who was kind enough to ask me to take a drop of brandy. Not having had any spirits for four years previous, this little got into my head, and having drank another glass or two I was intoxicated, and I spent all my money that night—yes, and got locked up into the bargain. (Laughter.) If I did not quite spend all my money myself, somebody else helped me to spend it. I came to London without a farthing. I hadn't a friend in the world, and even at present, if I want a meal, I have no one to say 'Here it is for you.' What is a man in such a case, being without work, to do? Is he to starve? Well, I wore out two pairs of shoes, walking the streets for three months together, looking for a situation, but all in vain; and I became as emaciated as this post, (pointing to the pillar of the lamp on the platform,) having had nothing better than a bit of bread and a herring to eat, and not one ounce of animal food during all that period. I had a little pride, which kept me from begging. All the good feelings engendered in prison passed away. I returned to my old companions, with whom I went for about two months, when I was at length caught, and received another twelvemonth's imprisonment, which expired only last Monday fortnight. During the two months I was with my old companions I got a good living—I could always make my 5l. or 6l. a-week by practices which I did not like, but which I was driven to adopt, because the public would not let me earn 1l. honestly. Since, however, I received the card of admission to this meeting, I have not put my hand to a dishonest act, and if the promise it holds out is fulfilled I never will. I have little more to say. I attended here to-night in the hope of reaping some permanent benefit, and also to encourage those who, like myself, wish to become honest members of society. (Applause.) I trust the benevolent gentleman who has so humanely interested himself in this cause will be successful in his exertions on behalf of a body of unfortunate and persecuted beings, who, I should say, are more knocked about by the police, and more discouraged by the opinions of the public at large, than any other class in the United Kingdom. (Applause.) May God and right reason direct this movement, and bring it to a speedy and prosperous issue." (Loud cheers greeted "Peter," as he descended from the "tribune.")

The next spokesman was a thin-faced and diminutive, but shrewd-looking costermonger, of about twenty-five years of age, and tidier in appearance than many of his class, who said:—" Friends, I am only a little one, and you can't expect much from me; indeed, 'Peter' hasn't left me much to say. I will, however, begin at the beginning. At the age of ten I was left without father or mother, and others here could say the same. I was taught to get a living by selling oranges in the streets, and I kept at that for twelve months. I was afterwards induced to go along with a few Westminster boys, who went about thieving; and I had nobody to look after me. Having no friend, I nevertheless always got a good 'lift' from the police. I was soon arrested, and at Newgate received seven years' transportation. I spent three years and seven months at the Isle of Wight, and eleven months at Portsmouth. I would not have been kept so long at the Isle of Wight if I had been religious; but as I could not act the hypocrite I was obliged to give up this religion. During this time I never took the sacrament, as they wanted me to do. Well, I gets my liberty, and I had several pounds put into my hands when I left. I came to London-bridge station, and thought it was the Waterloo station, and fancying I was near Westminster, I looked about for the Victoria Theatre. A chap then said to me, 'You had better not be seen in those clothes.' I afterwards changed my dress and sold the other clothes. I soon found myself with only about three half-crowns in my pocket. My only friend was a cousin, who was engaged in buying hare-skins and rabbit-skins about the streets, and he recommended me to do the same. This was in the winter time, and I hardly knew one kind of skin from another. However, I did pretty well at this for two or three weeks; when, one day, as I was walking with a sack of skins upon my back through Tothill-street, Westminster, two policemen came up to me, and demanded to look into my bag. Rather than consent to this I went to the Police Court along with them. When I got there a policeman said to the inspector, that I was a 'ticket-of-leave,' and had something in my sack. I insisted on seeing the magistrate, and the inspector brought me to him, but instead of allowing me to speak to his worship, he spoke first, saying that I was very violent and saucy, and a 'ticket-of-leave.' Instead of hearing what I had to say under these circumstances, the magistrate, too, burst out, 'Oh, you are an insolent fellow, and a disgrace to society; if the Secretary of State knew of your doings, he would banish you.' And his worship, also muttering something about sending me to 'quod' for contempt of court, I thought it better to 'hook it.' During two years and a-half of my term at the Isle of Wight, having learnt something of shoe-making, I now travelled down to Northampton, but could get no work because I had no tools. Even what I did know of the trade was not enough to enable me to get a living by it. I then went on to Derby, and was near starving. I had no lodging. I was not quite so proud as 'Peter,' for I went up to a gentleman and told him the strength of it. I said, I am a 'ticket-of-leave.' He hardly understood me, but I tried to explain it to him, and he gave me a shilling. With this aid I got my shirt washed, put myself to rights, polished my boots, and up I goes to a magistrate to see what he would say about it. I told him I wanted to go to London, and could not walk all the way. This magistrate can tell whether I am now speaking the truth. I got an interview with him at Derby, and told him I was a ticket-of-leave man. He would scarcely believe me, and imagined rather that I was a returned convict. The police jeering me, said, 'How well polished his boots are! but we think him an impostor.' So, with no other help than the shilling I had obtained, I trudged along in my misery until, with the worms and maggots gnawing my belly, I reached London. Here my cousin got me into the 'market' again, and I married last Christmas twelvemonth, and have one child. I am now just managing to 'crack an honest crust;' and while I can do that I will never thieve more. (Applause.) I am not much of a talker, therefore I can only hope that the kind gentleman who has called us together will succeed in his praiseworthy endeavours to secure fair-play to our ill-used class. I have nothing more to say." (Loud cheers.)

The third speaker was a stonemason, of about thirty, and of a honest and industrious aspect, who said:—" My friends, I have but little to say regarding myself. I was sent away from Newgate to Wakefield in 1851, and put to work. As to gratuity money given to convicts, certainly none was allowed at Wakefield while I was there. As to our treatment there and at other places, I can say that I never had a bit of sweet meat all the time I was at Wakefield. I never had anything but mince-meat chopped up, always green, and others can testify to the same thing. One man got three days of bread and water for complaining of this. After staying thirteen months at Wakefield I went to Portsmouth, where I remained about three years and a half, during which time I certainly worked hard. There the treatment of the men differs greatly, according to their conduct. A man who behaves well is treated well; but those of a volatile spirit are treated badly. For myself I never had a report made against me all the time I was there, and I obtained my liberty under ticket-of-leave, although I was sentenced to ten years' imprisonment, at the end of four years and four months. A few others, who came later than I did, were fortunate enough to get their freedom about the same time. I was not jealous about that, but was glad to get away myself. I had a mother and sister to go to; and though my sister was in employment, I did not cost them anything. I got work at my own trade, and experienced few of the hardships which most of my class do when first liberated. I know one poor man who said this meeting was the last place that he would come to, as it would expose him. He has worked five weeks for a person in Gray's-Inn-lane. He had been in good circumstances, was a clerk, and under the eye of a minister. He had to sleep in a place where the vermin crawled over his bed, and he had to get up in the night and remove his clothes to keep them clean. For the five weeks he has been at work he has scarcely had the barest necessaries of subsistence. I have been to see this man every Sunday, and can safely say that he has not had sixpence in his pocket ever since he has been out of prison. He was engaged at fire-work making, but this trade becoming slack after the 5th of November, he was thrown upon the streets again. I will not say what became of the man afterwards, because that is not necessary. I will merely mention that he is now struggling on, depending entirely on the public for a meal of victuals. I have myself been to work in the city for two months, and have not been intoxicated once. I am not fond of drink. I am steady and mean to continue so, and I trust every one here will resolve to do the same, for you will find it much more to your comfort. I am fortunate enough to be able to earn a livelihood at my trade as a mason; but though I am not in want myself, I could not refrain from coming here to throw what light I could on this subject, and showing my readiness to help others who are in distress." (Applause.)

The next who mounted the platform was an elderly man, evidently much reduced in cirstances. He stated — "I am a dock-labourer, and in 1848 was convicted, though innocent, at the Old Bailey. I was within three miles of the place where the robbery of which I was accused was committed. I was certainly in company with the female who was robbed three hours before the theft occurred; but I had no hand in it, and yet I was sentenced to fourteen years' transportation. I passed my first eleven months at Millbank; then I went to Woolwich, and next to Gibraltar. At the latter place Mr. Armstrong is the overseer of the convicts, and he is the severest man ever known; not a worse being in the Australian or any penal settlements. Flogging went on there from before daylight till long after dark. I was six years and eight months under his system, and I received 4l. 14s. 6d. on leaving Gibraltar, 2l. 10s. of which was stopped to pay my passage to England. When I came home I strived as hard as any man to get an honest livelihood. I tried every experiment—I went all up and down Whitechapel, but no, the police would not allow me—they picked me out as a marked man. Then I worked fifteen or sixteen months at the Docks, but lately that employment has been very slack, and I have tried all the offices in vain for the last fortnight. I leave you to consider, therefore, what a man is to do when he strives to get a living and can't. No man in all London has seen more trouble than I have. In 1840 I got three years' imprisonment. When I came out a man borrowed my coat to walk through the City with, and next day, as I was going past Bow Church, I was taken up for a robbery which that man had committed, my coat being sworn to, as it had a stain on the collar. I was taken before Alderman Gibbs that morning, and fully committed for trial; and when I appeared at Newgate I got twelve months in the Compter gaol, though innocent. I had not been three months out of the Compter before I was taken up for beating a policeman, who said I threw a stone at him, but I never did. A fortnight afterwards the man who did it got fourteen days, and I gets two years for it, though I was not nigh the place. No man in London has suffered as I have done wrongfully, and none has been so 'worked up' as I am at this moment. For the last fortnight the winds have been such as to prevent a single ship from coming up the Channel, and morning after morning between five hundred and six hundred men regularly wait at the Docks for employment and cannot get it. When I am employed, it is at the West Quay; but the permanent labourers are served first. Such men as I have very little chance, as they bring persons from the other side of the Dock sooner than engage 'casualty' labourers. During the eighteen months that have elapsed since I came from Gibraltar, I have walked the streets of London whole days without breaking my fast; and since twelve o'clock yesterday up to this moment I have not done so. I really wish, sir, that something could be done for us all."

Mr. Mayhew asked the men whether they thought the formation of a society, and a system by which those who were in work could assist those who were out of it, would benefit them?

To this many voices answered, "Yes! yes!"

Mr. Mayhew continued: "I know that if your stock-money is once gone you are completely helpless. A man who had been tried for his life and sent to Australia came to me one day, when let out of prison, with a loaf under his arm, and said, 'This is all I have got to keep me, and if I ask for work there is a policeman at my heels to tell every one that I am a returned convict.' His case became desperate, when, about the time of the Great Exhibition, I offered to give him a little money if he would pledge me his word to do all that he could to lead an honest life. He shook hands with me, and promised to do so. He then had cards printed, and tried to make a living by selling gelatine sweets. After a little time he took a small huckster's shop, and subsequently married a lodging-house keeper, and has since been doing very well. I know that the period between the ages of twenty-five and fifty is the time when a roving life has its strongest attractions; but after that, when a man is hunted like a dog, he gets tired of it. I have seen frequent examples of this, and known whole families of poor people, with only sixpence at their command, to invest that small sum in sprats, and live a month upon it by turning it over and over.

"I once took a poor boy (a young thief) and got him a place at the *Daily News* office, when the printer and editor told me he was as good and as well-behaved as any boy on that establishment. The difficulty, however, was to separate him from his old 'pals.' He got among them on an Easter Monday, and was found picking pockets at a fair, and taken to prison; it was 'all up with him' till he had seen the misery of his course of life, but I am sure, if taken by the hand, he will ultimately become a good member of society. I mention this to show, that if a little leniency and kindness are evinced towards the men we may beat down the crime of the country to an enormous extent. But we must not fancy it possible that such persons can be made model-men in an instant. Indeed, I believe that the disposition shown to make converts to religion of you produces a large amount of hypocrisy. (Cries of Yes! yes!) If this leads you to become better men, in Heaven's name, say so; but if it engenders the worst form of evil, let it be exposed. That there are such things as miracles of instantaneous reformation, I don't deny; but the first thing wanted is some society to give men what will keep them from starving, clothe them, and find them in a lodging; and when they are thus placed in decent comfort, and made, as a necessary consequence, more kindly in their nature, other people may then come to them and try to make them religious. To attempt, however, to proselytise men who are famishing, appears to me a mockery and a delusion, and only the most depraved class of criminals would, I believe, yield to it." (Applause.)

The fifth ticket-of-leave man who addressed the assembly was a man of middle stature, slightly made, and between twenty-five and thirty. He said :—

"I was sentenced to seven years' transportation at the Old Bailey. I went to Wakefield and can confirm the statement of a previous speaker, that no gratuities are allowed there. I next went to Portsmouth, where I remained two years and two months, when I was discharged on ticket-of-leave. I returned to the neighbourhood from whence I was committed. A master who promised to give me constant employment had before this given me a certificate. I was discharged about eighteen months ago. Whilst I was at work for my master a female came up to me and asked me if I had seen two other women pass. I answered, 'No,' when she invited me to have something to drink ; and knowing the female,

I accepted her offer. While walking with her, only two doors from where I lived, a policeman came up and took us both into custody. This, I suppose, was because I was known to be a returned convict. The woman was charged with being concerned with others of her own sex with robbing a gentleman, and on being searched a portion of the money was found on her, but none on me. Moreover, the gentleman stating that there was no man engaged in the theft, I was discharged. I then resumed work, but was taken again upon a charge of burglary. Many of you may have heard of the case. I was in my shirt-sleeves when I was arrested. The case was tried before Mr. Brenham. I did not deny my name, and being a ticket-of-leave man I was remanded for a week. I was afterwards brought up and re-examined, and after a careful investigation I was discharged. If there had been the slightest suspicion attaching to me, from my character being known, I must have been either imprisoned for three months, or committed for trial. I again returned to my work, but in three weeks afterwards I was dragged out of my bed and locked up for three hours in the Bagnigge-wells station, whence I was taken to Bow-street. Three policemen had burst my bedroom-door open before six o'clock in the morning, and while it was yet dark. They said they wanted me, because I had been concerned with a female in the robbery which had occurred two nights previous, on Pentonville-hill. The inspector told me he had received an order from the Secretary of State to send me back to Portsmouth prison, my license being revoked. When I got to Bow-street I was placed before Mr. Hall, not in open court, but in a private room. That gentleman also told me that my license had been revoked, on the alleged grounds that I was living by dishonest means. I was sent back to prison accordingly; but through the intercession of my brother—a married man, who showed that I had been working for twelve months—I was again released. There was no just ground whatever for sending me back to prison. I have only been home a fortnight, and having no tools I don't know what to do. The master who employed me before has got another man."

MR. MAYHEW here remarked, that it would be a great encouragement to Society to help them, if those who were doing well assisted those who were doing badly; whereupon

PETER observed that "it was little help that the one could possibly give to the other. An Association (he said) was what was wanted, whereby the men's present urgent necessities could be relieved before they fell into mischief. A few days after a man's liberation he generally found that he had acted foolishly, and returned to his senses. If, therefore, a society took him by the hand, and gave him temporary shelter and counsel, it would be the best thing that could happen to him."

Those of the lads and men present who had been left without father or mother from an early age, were then requested to hold up their hands; when twenty out of the forty-eight did so.

A lame blacksmith and fitter, of about forty, whose garb and complexion were in strict keeping with his craft, and who spoke with not a few grains of stern bitterness in his tone, next mounted the rostrum. He said: " I have been transported, and am a ' spotted man,' with whom the police can do as they like. I was a long time at Dartmoor, one of the hardest convict stations a man can go to, and I did the prison work there. I went there in 1851, when an eminent doctor, Mr. McIntosh, belonged to the place, but having good health I did not need his assistance. While in the infirmary on several occasions, but not for ill-ness, I saw the medicine that was given to the patients. It was only a large bottle of salts. I have known a man to be cut out of his hammock, taken down-stairs, and buried, all in three hours; and I have heard the doctor say of a sick man, ' Let him drink out of a pail till he bursts.' (Some sensation.) I was a privileged man because I was handy, and fitted up almost the whole iron-work of the place. Once some books were pilfered; and at dinner-time there was a general turn over and search at parade. The ' searcher' was a very sedate man, at least in the eyes of the Governor, but he was the most malicious person that ever stripped. After feeling the pockets of the man next to me, this person called me out, and, contrary to the rule, took me into the yard and stripped me naked. I remonstrated, and wished him to choose a place not in the open air, but for this I was ordered to a cell, and while on my way there he borrowed a sword from an officer—the foreman of the smith's shop—and made a cut at me with the back edge of the weapon, in-flicting a wound of eighteen inches long. I went to my cell, and next morning I was, to my astonishment, charged with attempting to knock this very man down with a hammer! The Governor would not hear a word that I had to say. I was inspected by the doctor, and then put back, to appear afterwards before the directors. The charge against me was wholly false. The foreman of the smith's shop was a straightforward man, and when applied to about my character, he told the governor that a quieter man, and one more capable of doing his work than me, he could not wish to see. The accuser could not look me in the face; but if the foreman spoke the truth to the directors,—and he was a man who would speak nothing else,—he would have been sure to have his band removed from his cap. So, instead of my being taken before the directors, I was sent to my dinner; and I never received the least redress for the wrongs I endured.

" Before returning home I was classed as a permanent invalid, and yet I was kept at work on iron-work of three tons weight. After acting four years as a mechanic and a ' first-rater' at Dartmoor, I got invalided pay, and went home with about 7l. in my pocket. That is all the reward given to a good workman and well-conducted man at Dartmoor. I have heard much of Wakefield, and believe the sys-tem there will reform any man. It has a first-rate character; but as to Dartmoor, a man leaving it can have no reformation in him. At Dartmoor, when visitors wish to try the prisoners' soup, a basin of nice beef tea, standing smoking on the hob, and fit to show gentlemen, is offered them to taste. But this is not the soup which is really given to the convicts; that is merely a little rice and water. In fact, Dartmoor is one of the most villanous places a man can be put into. You have there to swab up two or three pails of water before you can rise in the morning. The brutality practised is terrible; and re-member, when a man is prejudiced against the treatment he receives, no permanent im-provement of his character is possible. Let any Dartmoor man here get up and deny what I say about the place, if he can. The aristocracy fancy that it is an excellent convict station, but it is not. I have seen clean and comfortable-looking men taken off parade, be-cause they would not do an officer's dirty work, and conducted to a covered passage, from which they have not come out again until they did so with faces cut about and bleeding, and with clothes all torn to pieces. I don't say that all the other convict establishments are like Dartmoor. I have seen bodies of seventy and eighty men come there from Wakefield—good-intentioned persons, and evidently having undergone religious impressions, to judge by their regularly kneeling down to prayers; but Dartmoor must contaminate them, and make them worse than ever before they leave it. I never had any particular religious feelings myself while at Dartmoor; but I am sure that a pious life is the most comfortable one under the canopy of heaven. I was very wrongfully sent away to that penal establishment. I had never been convicted before; and my only offence was being concerned in a tap-room drunken fight, for which I was charged with a misdemeanour. It was stated that I intended to do a man some grievous bodily harm, but it was proved that I had no weapon at the time larger than a penny-piece. I only left Dartmoor six or seven months ago. If I were in work, I should be most happy to give my mite towards the society that this gentleman (Mr. Mayhew) speaks of, for the benefit of the poor ticket-of-leave men; but the slackness of trade has thrown me out for the last month, and I have maintained myself and four others who are on my hands for half-a-year."

The concluding speaker was a young and cleanly-looking working man, of prepossessing address, who stated:—" I have experienced considerable oppression from the police, who, I think, want as much showing up as anybody. In January, 1852, I was sentenced to seven years' transportation. I stopped at the House of Correction for some time, and then went to Northampton borough gaol, where I lay eleven months. Thence I was sent to Woolwich, where I stayed about two years and five months, and was employed in dragging timber from one end of the yard to the other. However, I did very well there, and I find no fault with the place. When I got my liberty I returned home, where I had a father and mother and a sister; but as they were in humble circumstances, I did not like to throw myself on them for my support, and so I looked about for something to do. I am now keeping company with a young woman. One night as I was going home, at half-past twelve, after sitting some hours with her and her father, a policeman suddenly comes up to me, and tapping me on the shoulder, says: 'Holloa, George; so here you are! Mind I don't send you somewhere else for twelve months.' I answered: 'So you may, when I have given you occasion for it.' My landlord saw us, and said that I had done nothing. 'No,' said the policeman, 'or I would not allow him to go free;' and he then told me to move on. My young woman's father keeps a barber's shop; and this policeman goes up to him and acquaints him with my character, asking him whether he is aware that the young man his daughter keeps company with is a returned convict. The father tells her of it, at least she gives me broad hints that imply as much. This man then shows me up, and exposes me several times to the tradesmen in my neighbourhood. I then see what I can do. I cannot get a certificate of character, and I try to write one myself. Then I get several months' imprisonment, and now I have been out seven weeks. But I have not done anything dishonest. Still, if it goes on like this, I am sure I must be compelled to do that. A fortnight ago, as I was going home, the same policeman again interfered with me, and I was obliged to put up with his insults. Last week I wrote a letter to the captain of the hulks at Woolwich, telling him of the oppression I suffer. I received a letter from the chaplain, of course containing religious advice, but the answer I obtained from the captain of the hulks was, that the next time I am insulted I should write to him again, when he will acquaint the Secretary of State with it, and put it down, if possible. How can we hope to get employment from any tradesmen, if the policemen persist in telling who we are? I know that if I were an independent gentleman myself, I would not trust a man who had no reference of some kind."

Mr. Mayhew: "We will now break up this meeting. I will let you know when to meet again. When I can arrange the formation of a committee of gentlemen willing to connect themselves with the undertaking I have sketched out, we can hold another assemblage in public. (Cheers.) In the meantime, if I can assist any of you with the loan of a few shillings—but, mind you, come to me gently, and not thick and fast—I will do what I can to help you. (Hear, hear.) I am a person who work myself for all I get, and remember I call myself a 'shilling man,' and not one of your 'sovereign people' (Laughter); and when I say 'a loan,' I want you all to feel that by doing your best to repay me, you will enable me to extend the same assistance to a greater number of your class. (Hear, hear.) Colonel Jebb looks on you almost with the eye of a father, and it touches him to the quick to hear of any of you relapsing. I trust that we shall prove successful in our object; but let me in conclusion entreat you all to adhere faithfully to your good resolves; and I hope you will find far greater happiness in pursuing honest courses than dishonest ones." (Cheers.)

The meeting, which lasted from eight o'clock to half-past ten, and was most orderly throughout, then quietly dispersed.

THE END

INDEX.

3.